Contemporary Authors®

NEW REVISION SERIES

ISSN 0275-7176

Contemporary Authors®

**A Bio-Bibliographical Guide to
Current Writers in Fiction, General Nonfiction,
Poetry, Journalism, Drama, Motion Pictures,
Television, and Other Fields**

JAMES G. LESNIAK
Editor

NEW REVISION SERIES
volume 33

Gale Research Inc. · DETROIT · LONDON

STAFF

James G. Lesniak, *Editor, New Revision Series*

Marilyn K. Basel, Kevin S. Hile, Sharon Malinowski, Michael E. Mueller, Kenneth R. Shepherd, Diane Telgen, and Thomas Wiloch, *Associate Editors*

Michele Corbin, Elizabeth A. Des Chenes, Margaret Mazurkiewicz, Jani Prescott, Edward G. Scheff, and Michaela Swart Wilson, *Assistant Editors*

Jean W. Ross, *Interviewer*

Marian Gonsior, Anne Janette Johnson, Albert E. Kalson, Lauriat Lane, Jr., Edward Mullaly, Susan Salter, and Stephanie Tucker, *Contributing Editors*

Hal May, *Senior Editor, Contemporary Authors*

Victoria B. Cariappa, *Research Manager*

Mary Rose Bonk, *Research Supervisor*

Jane A. Cousins, Andrew Guy Malonis, and Norma Sawaya, *Editorial Associates*

Mike Avolio, Reginald A. Carlton, Clare Collins, Theodore J. Dumbrique, Shirley Gates, Sharon McGilvray, and Tracey Head Turbett, *Editorial Assistants*

Special acknowledgment is due to members of the
Contemporary Authors Original Volumes staff who assisted in the preparation of this volume.

The paper used in this publication meets the minimum requirements of American National Standard for Information Sciences—Permanence Paper for Printed Library Materials, ANS1 Z39.48-19B4. ∞™

Copyright © 1991
Gale Research Inc.
835 Penobscot Bldg.
Detroit, MI 48226-4094

Library of Congress Catalog Card Number 81-640179
ISBN 0-8103-1987-X
ISSN 0275-7176

Printed in the United States of America.

Published simultaneously in the United Kingdom
by Gale Research International Limited
(An affiliated company of Gale Research Inc.)

Contents

Indexing note: All *Contemporary Authors New Revision Series* entries are indexed in the *Contemporary Authors* cumulative index, which is published separately and distributed with even-numbered *Contemporary Authors* original volumes and odd-numbered revision volumes.

Authors and Media People
Featured in This Volume

Samuel Beckett (Irish-born playwright and poet from France who died in 1989)—Internationally esteemed as one of the premier playwrights of the "Theatre of the Absurd," Beckett crafted bleak and despairing dramas about the futility of human endeavor. *Waiting for Godot,* appraised by many to be his most important dramatic achievement, established his prominence in the United States.

Ingmar Bergman (Swedish filmmaker)—Bergman is widely regarded as an innovative screenwriter and director, earning numerous awards for his surrealistic and deeply personal films. Symbolically dense and frequently difficult to interpret, his work explores such themes as the artistic temperament, relationships between the sexes, and mankind's search for God.

Jorge Luis Borges (Argentine poet, short story writer and essayist who died in 1986)—An acclaimed figure whose influence upon world literature is immense, Borges will probably be best remembered as the author of short stories called *ficciones*. Thematically fond of the double, circular time, labyrinths, and the nature of man, he disregarded the constraints of the genres in which he worked and wrote poems that told little stories and stories that seemed more like lyrical essays.

Cleanth Brooks (American literary critic)—Advocating a formalist interpretation of poetry in which the structure of a work is paramount, Brooks became a leading figure in the school of New Criticism and, according to its founder, John Crowe Ransom, "the most forceful and influential critic of poetry that we have." He is also noted for his critical studies of William Faulkner.

Leonard Cyril Deighton (British spy novelist)—Master of the British espionage novel, Deighton writes with style and wit, distinguishing his work with painstaking accuracy and hypnotic realism. He has also authored mainstream fiction and material for the screen plus nonfiction about aviation and military history—fields in which he is considered an expert.

E. L. Doctorow (American novelist and playwright)—Doctorow is highly regarded for the serious, philosophical probing in his work and his unusual use of historical figures. Recognized primarily for fiction set in America during the first half of the twentieth century, he is especially praised for *The Book of Daniel, Ragtime, World's Fair,* and *Billy Bathgate.*

Anne Edwards (American biographer)—Focusing on celebrities who have coped with or surmounted difficult circumstances, Edwards has established her reputation by penning accounts of the lives of such famous women as Judy Garland, Katharine Hepburn, Margaret Mitchell, Countess Sonya Tolstoy, Shirley Temple, and Vivien Leigh. (Entry contains interview.)

William Faulkner (American novelist who died in 1962)—One of America's most eminent literary figures, Faulkner is extolled for his tragicomic vision, the vitality of his memorable characters, and the sustained eloquence of his engrossing prose. The novels set in his fictional Yoknapatawpha County comprise a saga that chronicles the passing of the Old South and documents his profound belief in the prevailing human spirit.

Federico Fellini (Italian filmmaker)—Fellini launched his career as a cartoon artist and tourist caricaturist in Rome but has become internationally acclaimed for his imaginative screenwork. Creator of such films as *La dolce vita, 8½, Fellini Satyricon,* and *Amarcord,* his name is synonymous with avant-garde imagery and the grotesque.

Robert Frost (American poet who died in 1963)—Aligned with no particular literary school, Frost bridged nineteenth-century poetry and modernism. A Pulitzer Prize winner noted for the grace of his vernacular idiom and avoidance of poetic diction, he was especially admired for his poetic rendering of the extraordinary within the ordinary.

Francine du Plessix Gray (Polish-born American journalist and novelist)—Columnist for the *New Yorker,* Gray has written novels appreciated for their wit and sensitivity. Her nonfiction works include the award-winning *Divine Disobedience: Profiles in Catholic Radicalism* and *Soviet Women: Walking the Tightrope.*

Lillian Hellman (American playwright and memoirist who died in 1984)—Hailed as one of the most influential playwrights of the twentieth century, Hellman imbued her work with intelligence and social conscience, and eluded labels. Successful on Broadway, she is best remembered for such plays as *The Children's Hour, The Little Foxes, Toys in the Attic,* and memoirs such as *An Unfinished Woman* and *Pentimento: A Book of Portraits.*

Henry A. Kissinger (American diplomat)—Winner of the 1973 Nobel Peace Prize for negotiations ending the Vietnam war and of the 1980 American Book Award for *White House Years,* former secretary of state Kissinger has devoted much of his time since leaving office to writing memoirs of his years with the Nixon administration. Critics commend his books for their lucid and detailed descriptions of internal politics before and during the Watergate years.

Stanley Kubrick (American filmmaker)—Celebrated for such films as *Lolita, Dr. Strangelove, 2001, A Clockwork Orange,* and *Full Metal Jacket,* Kubrick is a respected filmmaker who has turned out a small but widely praised body of work. Regularly writing the screenplays from which he works, he also oversees his projects from casting to final cut. A *Film Quarterly* contributor calls him "a critic of his age, one of its interpreters and one of its artists."

Lewis H. Lapham (American journalist)—Editor of *Harper's* magazine, Lapham infuses the journal with a distinctive point-of-view. As social critic and commentator, he has written two books exploring the premise that Americans hold money and material possessions as their main goal—*Fortune's Child* and *Money and Class in America.* (Entry contains interview.)

Doris Lessing (British novelist, playwright, and nonfiction writer)—Particularly lauded for her humanist vision, Lessing incisively portrayed a woman's search for social identity in *The Golden Notebook.* A prominent nominee for the Nobel Prize for literature on several occasions, she is considered by many to be one of the finest fiction writers of our time.

C. S. Lewis (Irish-born writer and literary critic from England who died in 1963)—Prolific writer of novels, children's fantasies, letters, critical literary studies and witty theological works that trace his own journey from atheism to Christianity, Lewis generated as much disapproval as praise during his lifetime; but his considerable popularity with readers of all ages continues.

Archibald MacLeish (American poet, playwright, essayist, and statesman who died in 1982)—One of the twentieth century's most renowned poets and recipient of three Pulitzer Prizes, MacLeish sought to reconcile the ideal with reality in his work. Drawing thematically upon both public and private concerns, he championed the dignity of the common man. He was dedicated to public service and was awarded the Presidential Medal of Freedom in 1977.

Thomas McGrath (American poet who died in 1990)—McGrath has been called "a major voice" in American poetry by many who believe that because of his radical-leftist political views, he has been neglected by the establishment critics and denied the recognition his achievement warrants. His most important work, *Letter to an Imaginary Friend,* is a long, ongoing, autobiographical poem that integrates personal experience with political concerns.

Henry Miller (American novelist, short story writer, and essayist who died in 1980)—Remembered for his best-selling autobiographical novels *Tropic of Cancer, Tropic of Capricorn,* and *Black Spring,* which detail his expatriate days in Paris, Miller made a significant contribution to American letters with his anti-artistic prose style and philosophy of personal hedonism and political anarchy.

Malcolm Muggeridge (British journalist who died in 1990)—A newspaper journalist and broadcaster for the BBC, Muggeridge is especially recognized for his *Winter in Moscow,* the first book to expose Joseph Stalin's policy of deliberate starvation of the Ukraine. He described his life in journalism in *Chronicles of Wasted Time.*

V. S. Naipaul (Trinidad-born British novelist)—A world-class writer whose novels are masterpieces of suspense, supple prose, personal vision, sharp wit, and serious concern with contemporary issues, Naipaul has won many major literary prizes for fiction. He is particularly praised for such works as *The Mystic Masseur, Mr. Stone and the Knight's Companion,* and *In a Free State.*

Harold Pinter (British playwright)—Pinter is one of the chief British writers for the modern stage, and his works are celebrated for originality, uniqueness of plot and character, inexplicable logic and inconclusive resolutions, and distinctive dialogue. He is also known for developing the now-famous theatrical device of the significant pause—a silence in the midst of conversation.

J. B. Priestley (English novelist, playwright, essayist, and journalist who died in 1984)—Considered a British institution, Priestley is frequently compared with Charles Dickens in matters of style and characterization in his fiction. An accomplished essayist, journalist, and social commentator, he was prolific in his output and was immensely popular.

Salman Rushdie (Indian novelist)—In fiction that blends history, myth, politics, and fantasy, Rushdie stunned the literary world with his second effort—the Booker McConnell Prize-winning *Midnight's Children,* which many critics called a tour de force. He became a household name when Shiite Muslim followers forced him into hiding to escape a death sentence following the furor over his *Satanic Verses* and claims that it insulted the Islamic religion.

Helen Hooven Santmyer (American novelist and short story writer who died in 1980)—Santmyer drew largely from personal experience in her fiction about small-town America between the end of the Civil War and the Great Depression. Best known for her *. . .And Ladies of the Club,* a mammoth novel spanning four generations of ordinary life in a rural Ohio town, she is admired for the atmosphere, historical authenticity, and vivid characterization in her work.

John Updike (American novelist, short story writer, and essayist)—Through the subtle complexity of his prose, Updike has earned a reputation as a masterful chronicler of the anxieties of middle-class America. He has won virtually every major American literary award, including the Pulitzer Prize, the American Book Award, and the National Book Critics Circle Award for his 1982 *Rabbit Is Rich.*

Theodore H. White (American political journalist who died in 1986)—White launched a new genre with his Pulitzer Prize-winning *The Making of the President: 1960* and earned praise for its brilliance and intelligence. Although his subsequent books on presidential elections were not as well received as their predecessor, he is considered to have, in the words of a *New York Times* contributor, "taught the American people more about politics than any writer of his generation."

Tom Wolfe (American writer, journalist, social commentator, and artist)—Wolfe is identified as one of the leaders of "New Journalism" writing. His American Book Award-winning study of the American space program, *The Right Stuff,* is considered by many to be his finest literary effort. *Bonfire of the Vanities,* his first attempt at writing a novel, proved successful as well, winning the National Book Critics Circle Award.

Herman Wouk (American novelist and playwright)—Best known for his Pulitzer Prize-winning *The Caine Mutiny,* Wouk is a popular writer whose novels are regularly featured by numerous book clubs. His more recent bestsellers, *The Winds of War* and *War and Remembrance,* have been adapted for television.

Preface

The *Contemporary Authors New Revision Series* provides completely updated information on authors listed in earlier volumes of *Contemporary Authors (CA)*. Entries for active individual authors from *any* volume of *CA* may be included in a volume of the *New Revision Series*. The sketches appearing in *New Revision Series* Volume 33, for example, were selected from more than twenty previously published *CA* volumes.

As always, the most recent *Contemporary Authors* cumulative index continues to be the user's guide to the location of an individual author's listing.

Compilation Methods

The editors make every effort to secure information directly from the authors. Copies of all sketches in selected *CA* volumes published several years ago are routinely sent to the listees at their last-known addresses. Authors mark material to be deleted or changed and insert any new personal data, new affiliations, new writings, new work in progress, new sidelights, and new biographical/critical sources. All returns are assessed, more comprehensive research is done, if necessary, and those sketches requiring significant change are completely updated and published in the *New Revision Series*.

If, however, authors fail to reply or are now deceased, biographical dictionaries are checked for new information (a task made easier through the use of Gale's *Biography and Genealogy Master Index* and other Gale biographical indexes), as are bibliographical sources such as *Cumulative Book Index* and *The National Union Catalog*. Using data from such sources, revision editors select and revise nonrespondents' entries that need substantial updating. Sketches not personally reviewed by the biographees are marked with an asterisk (*) to indicate that these listings have been revised from secondary sources believed to be reliable, but they have not been personally reviewed for this edition by the authors sketched.

In addition, reviews and articles in major periodicals, lists of prestigious awards, and, particularly, requests from *CA* users are monitored so that writers on whom new information is in demand can be identified and revised listings prepared promptly.

Format

CA entries provide biographical and bibliographical information in an easy-to-use format. For example, individual paragraphs featuring such rubrics as "Addresses," "Career," and "Awards, Honors" ensure that a reader seeking specific information can quickly focus on the pertinent portion of an entry. In sketch sections headed "Writings," the title of each book, play, and other published or unpublished work appears on a separate line, clearly distinguishing one title from another. This same convenient bibliographical presentation is also featured in the "Biographical/Critical Sources" sections of sketches where individual book and periodical titles are listed on separate lines. *CA* readers can therefore quickly scan these often lengthy bibliographies to find the titles they need.

Comprehensive Revision

All listings in this volume have been revised and/or augmented in various ways, though the amount and type of change vary with the author. In many instances, sketches are totally rewritten, and the resulting *New Revision Series* entries are often considerably longer than the authors' previous listings. Revised entries include additions of or changes in such information as degrees, mailing addresses, literary agents, career items, career-related and civic activities, memberships, awards, work in progress, and biographical/critical sources. They may also include extensive bibliographical additions and informative new sidelights.

Writers of Special Interest

CA's editors make every effort to include in each *New Revision Series* volume a substantial number of revised entries on active authors and media people of special interest to *CA*'s readers. Since the *New Revision Series* also includes sketches on noteworthy deceased writers, a significant amount of work on the part of *CA*'s editors goes into the revision of entries on important deceased authors. Some of the prominent writers, both living and deceased, whose sketches are contained in this volume are noted in the list on pages vii-viii headed Authors and Media People Featured in This Volume.

Exclusive Interviews

CA provides exclusive, primary information on certain authors in the form of interviews. Prepared specifically for *CA,* the never-before-published conversations presented in the section of the sketch headed "*CA* Interview" give users the opportunity to learn the authors' thoughts, in depth, about their craft. Subjects chosen for interviews are, the editors feel, authors who hold special interest for *CA*'s readers.

Authors and journalists in this volume whose sketches contain exclusive interviews are Anne Edwards, Howard Fast, Ken Follett, Thom Gunn, Lewis H. Lapham, and Myra Cohn Livingston.

Contemporary Authors Autobiography Series

Designed to complement the information in *CA* original and revision volumes, the *Contemporary Authors Autobiography Series* provides autobiographical essays written by important current authors. Each volume contains from twenty to thirty specially commissioned autobiographies and is illustrated with numerous personal photographs supplied by the authors. Common topics of discussion for these authors include their motivations for writing, the people and experiences that shaped their careers, the rewards they derive from their work, and their impressions of the current literary scene.

Autobiographies included in the series can be located through both the *CA* cumulative index and the *Contemporary Authors Autobiography Series* cumulative index, which lists not only personal names but also titles of works, geographical names, subjects, and schools of writing.

Contemporary Authors Bibliographical Series

The *Contemporary Authors Bibliographical Series* is a comprehensive survey of writings by and about the most important authors since World War II in the United States and abroad. Each volume concentrates on a specific genre and nationality and features approximately ten major writers. Series entries, which complement the information in other *CA* volumes, consist of three parts: a primary bibliography that lists works written by the author, a secondary bibliography that lists works about the author, and a bibliographical essay that thoroughly analyzes the merits and deficiencies of major critical and scholarly works.

These bibliographies can be located through both the *CA* cumulative index and the *Contemporary Authors Bibliographical Series* cumulative author index. A cumulative critic index, citing critics discussed in the bibliographical essays, also appears in each *Bibliographical Series* volume.

CA Numbering System

Occasionally questions arise about the *CA* numbering system. Despite numbers like "97-100" and "132," the entire *CA* series consists of only 108 physical volumes with the publication of *CA New Revision Series* Volume 33. The following information notes changes in the numbering system, as well as in cover design, to help users better understand the organization of the entire *CA* series.

CA **First Revisions**	• 1-4R through 41-44R (11 books) *Cover:* Brown with black and gold trim. There will be no further *First Revisions* because revised entries are now being handled exclusively through the more efficient *New Revision Series* mentioned below.
CA **Original Volumes**	• 45-48 through 97-100 (14 books) *Cover:* Brown with black and gold trim. • 101 through 132 (32 books) *Cover:* Blue and black with orange bands. The same as previous *CA* original volumes but with a simplified numbering system and updated cover design.
CA **New Revision Series**	• *CANR*-1 through *CANR*-33 (33 books) Cover: Blue and black with green bands. Includes only sketches requiring extensive change; **sketches are taken from any previously published *CA* volume.**

CA Permanent Series	• CAP-1 and CAP-2 (2 books) Cover: Brown with red and gold trim. There will be no further Permanent Series volumes because revised entries are now being handled exclusively through the more efficient New Revision Series mentioned above.
CA Autobiography Series	• CAAS-1 through CAAS-13 (13 books) Cover: Blue and black with pink and purple bands. Presents specially commissioned autobiographies by leading contemporary writers.
CA Bibliographical Series	• CABS-1 through CABS-3 (3 books) Cover: Blue and black with blue bands. Provides comprehensive bibliographical information on published works by and about major modern authors.

Retaining CA Volumes

As new volumes in the series are published, users often ask which CA volumes, if any, can be discarded. The Volume Update Chart on page xiii is designed to assist users in keeping their collections as complete as possible. All volumes in the left column of the chart should be retained to have the most complete, up-to-date coverage possible; volumes in the right column can be discarded if the appropriate replacements are held.

Cumulative Index Should Always Be Consulted

The key to locating an individual author's listing is the CA cumulative index, which is published separately and distributed with even-numbered original volumes and odd-numbered revision volumes. Since the CA cumulative index provides access to all entries in the CA series, the latest cumulative index should always be consulted to find the specific volume containing a listee's original or most recently revised sketch.

Those authors whose entries appear in the New Revision Series are listed in the CA cumulative index with the designation **CANR-** in front of the specific volume number. For the convenience of those who do not have New Revision Series volumes, the cumulative index also notes the specific earlier volumes of CA in which the sketch appeared. Below is a sample index citation for an author whose revised entry appears in a New Revision Series volume.

> Clavell, James (duMaresq) 1925-................CANR-26
> Earlier sketch in CA 25-28R
> See also CLC 6, 25
> See also MTCW

For the most recent CA information on Clavell, users should refer to Volume 26 of the New Revision Series, as designated by "CANR-26"; if that volume is unavailable, refer to CA 25-28 First Revision, as indicated by "Earlier sketch in CA 25-28R," for his 1977 listing. (And if CA 25-28 First Revision is unavailable, refer to CA 25-28, published in 1971, for Clavell's original listing.)

Sketches not eligible for inclusion in a New Revision Series volume because the biographee or a revision editor has verified that no significant change is required will, of course, be available in previously published CA volumes. Users should always consult the most recent CA cumulative index to determine the location of these authors' entries.

For the convenience of CA users, the CA cumulative index also includes references to all entries in these related Gale literary titles: Authors and Artists for Young Adults, Authors in the News, Bestsellers, Black Writers, Children's Literature Review, Concise Dictionary of American Literary Biography, Contemporary Literary Criticism, Dictionary of Literary Biography, Hispanic Writers, Major 20th-Century Writers, Short Story Criticism, Something About the Author, Something About the Author Autobiography Series, Twentieth-Century Literary Criticism, and Yesterday's Authors of Books For Children.

Acknowledgments

The editors wish to thank Judith S. Baughman for her assistance with copyediting.

Suggestions Are Welcome

The editors welcome comments and suggestions from users on any aspect of the *CA* series. If readers would like to suggest authors whose *CA* entries should appear in future volumes of the *New Revision Series,* they are cordially invited to write: The Editors, *Contemporary Authors New Revision Series,* 835 Penobscot Bldg., Detroit, MI 48226-4094; or, call toll-free at 1-800-347-GALE.

Volume Update Chart

IF YOU HAVE:	YOU MAY DISCARD:
1-4 First Revision (1967)	1 (1962) 2 (1963) 3 (1963) 4 (1963)
5-8 First Revision (1969)	5-6 (1963) 7-8 (1963)
Both 9-12 First Revision (1974) AND *Contemporary Authors Permanent Series,* Volume 1 (1975)	9-10 (1964) 11-12 (1965)
Both 13-16 First Revision (1975) AND *Contemporary Authors Permanent Series,* Volumes 1 and 2 (1975, 1978)	13-14 (1965) 15-16 (1966)
Both 17-20 First Revision (1976) AND *Contemporary Authors Permanent Series,* Volumes 1 and 2 (1975, 1978)	17-18 (1967) 19-20 (1968)
Both 21-24 First Revision (1977) AND *Contemporary Authors Permanent Series,* Volumes 1 and 2 (1975, 1978)	21-22 (1969) 23-24 (1970)
Both 25-28 First Revision (1977) AND *Contemporary Authors Permanent Series,* Volume 2 (1978)	25-28 (1971)
Both 29-32 First Revision (1978) AND *Contemporary Authors Permanent Series,* Volume 2 (1978)	29-32 (1972)
Both 33-36 First Revision (1978) AND *Contemporary Authors Permanent Series,* Volume 2 (1978)	33-36 (1973)
37-40 First Revision (1979)	37-40 (1973)
41-44 First Revision (1979)	41-44 (1974)
45-48 (1974) 49-52 (1975) ↓ ↓ 132 (1991)	NONE: These volumes will not be superseded by corresponding revised volumes. Individual entries from these and all other volumes appearing in the left column of this chart will be revised and included in the *New Revision Series.*
Volumes in the *Contemporary Authors New Revision Series*	NONE: The *New Revision Series* does not replace any single volume of *CA.* All volumes appearing in the left column of this chart must be retained to have information on all authors in the series.

Contemporary Authors®

NEW REVISION SERIES

**Indicates that a listing has been compiled from secondary sources believed to be reliable
but has not been personally verified for this edition by the author sketched.*

ABRAMS, M(eyer) H(oward)   1912-

PERSONAL: Born July 23, 1912, in Long Branch, NJ; son of Joseph (a merchant) and Sara (Shanes) Abrams; married Ruth Gaynes, September 1, 1937; children: Jane, Judith. *Education:* Harvard University, A.B., 1934, M.A., 1937, Ph.D., 1940; graduate study at Cambridge University, 1934-35. *Politics:* Independent.

ADDRESSES: Home—512 Highland Rd., Ithaca, NY 14850. *Office*—Department of English, 167 Goldwin Smith Hall, Cornell University, Ithaca, NY 14850.

CAREER: Harvard University, Cambridge, MA, instructor in English, 1938-42, research associate in Psycho-Acoustic Laboratory, 1942-45; Cornell University, Ithaca, NY, assistant professor, 1945-47, associate professor, 1947-53, professor of English, 1953-61, Frederic J. Whiton Professor, 1961-73, Class of 1916 Professor, 1973-83, Professor Emeritus, 1983—. Roache Lecturer at University of Indiana, 1963; Alexander Lecturer at University of Toronto; Ewing Lecturer at University of California at Los Angeles, 1975; Cecil Green Lecturer at University of British Columbia, 1980. Fellow of Center for Advanced Study in the Behavioral Sciences, 1967-68, and All Souls College, Oxford University, 1977; honorary senior fellow, School of Criticism and Theory, Dartmouth College.

MEMBER: Council of Scholars at the Library of Congress, National Humanities Center (member of Founders' Group), American Academy of Arts and Sciences (fellow), American Philosophical Society (fellow), British Academy (corresponding fellow), American Association of University Professors, Modern Language Association of America (member of executive council, 1961-64), English Institute, Cornell Club of New York, Phi Beta Kappa, Sigma Xi.

AWARDS, HONORS: Rockefeller Foundation fellowship, 1946-47; Ford Foundation fellowship, 1953; Fulbright scholar, University of Malta and Cambridge University, 1954; honorary member of faculty, Royal University of Malta, 1954—; Christian Gauss Prize, Phi Beta Kappa, 1954, for *The Mirror and the Lamp: Romantic Theory and the Critical Tradition;* citation, National Council of Teachers of English, 1958; Guggenheim fellowships, 1958, 1960-61; James Russell Lowell Prize, Modern Language Association of America, 1972, for *Natural Supernaturalism: Tradition and Revolution in Romantic Literature;* D.H.L., University of Rochester, 1978, Northwestern University, 1981,

and University of Chicago, 1982; Award in Humanistic Studies, American Academy of Arts and Sciences, 1984; Distinguished Scholar Award, Keats-Shelley Society, 1987; Award for Literature, American Academy and Institute of Arts and Letters, 1990.

WRITINGS:

The Milk of Paradise: The Effects of Opium Visions on the Works of De Quincey, Crabbe, Francis Thompson, and Coleridge, Harvard University Press, 1934, reprinted, Octagon, 1970.

The Mirror and the Lamp: Romantic Theory and the Critical Tradition, Oxford University Press, 1953.

A Glossary of Literary Terms, Rinehart, 1957, 5th edition, Holt, 1987.

Natural Supernaturalism: Tradition and Revolution in Romantic Literature, Norton, 1971.

The Correspondent Breeze: Essays in English Romanticism (includes previously published essays), Norton, 1984.

Doing Things with Texts: Essays in Criticism and Critical Theory (includes previously published essays), Norton, 1989.

EDITOR

The Poetry of Pope, Holt, 1954.

(And contributor) *Literature and Belief,* English Institute Essays, 1957, Columbia University Press, 1958.

(And contributor) *English Romantic Poets: Modern Essays in Criticism,* Oxford University Press, 1960, 2nd revised edition, 1975.

(General editor) *The Norton Anthology of English Literature,* Norton, 1962, 5th edition, two volumes, 1986.

(And contributor) *Wordsworth: A Collection of Critical Essays,* Prentice-Hall, 1972.

(Co-editor) William Wordsworth, *Prelude,* Norton Critical Editions, 1977.

CONTRIBUTOR

C. A. Patrides, editor, *Milton's Lycidas: Tradition and Form,* Holt, 1961.

Northrop Frye, editor, *Romanticism Reconsidered,* Columbia University Press, 1963.

Harold Bloom and Frederick W. Hilles, editors, *From Sensibility to Romanticism: Essays Presented to Frederick A. Pottle,* Oxford University Press, 1965.

Wolfgang Iser, editor, *Immanete Aesthetik, Aesthetische Reflexion: Lyrik als Paradigma der Moderne,* Wilhelm Fink (Munich), 1966.

Morton W. Bloomfield, editor, *In Search of Literary Theory,* Cornell University Press, 1972.

John Beer, editor, *Coleridge's Variety,* Macmillan, 1974.

English Literary History, [Baltimore], 1974.

Lawrence Lipking, editor, *High Romantic Argument: Essays for M. H. Abrams,* Cornell University Press, 1981.

Contributor to journals, including *ELH, Critical Inquiry, New York Review of Books, Partisan Review,* and *Notre Dame English Journal.*

WORK IN PROGRESS: The Philosophy and History of Literary Criticism and Aesthetic Theory.

SIDELIGHTS: M. H. Abrams is an American literary critic who has focused attention on the period of Wordsworth and Coleridge through his books *The Mirror and the Lamp* and *Natural Supernaturalism. Times Literary Supplement* contributor Geoffrey Galt Harpham calls Abrams "the most influential critic of Romantic literature of his generation." And Chris Baldick observes in another issue of the same periodical that "all attempts to focus or define the nature of Romanticism in English poetry have for the last thirty years been guided by the work of M. H. Abrams in his *The Mirror and the Lamp,* a great work of simplification in the best sense, which cut through the tangles of literary history by reassessing the Romantic movement." Harpham continues, "Abrams is not a theoretician, but a historian of criticism who recognizes that all discourse about art has both historical and theoretical extension."

The nineteenth-century Romantic period followed the Enlightenment, and primarily consisted of young artists rebelling against their elder's strict adherence to strict artistic ideals. According to Carl R. Woodring in *Prose of the Romantic Period,* the Romantic era broke from pervious traditions by asserting that "change and growth are the laws of life. . . . [Romantic writers] reacted passionately against the rationalistic, analytical, mechanistic, deterministic, hedonistic, and prudentially utilitarian doctrines of the Enlightenment." However, the very individuality and supposed spontaneity of Romantic artists had caused students of the age to focus on the writers' work and ignore any unifying critical theories. *The Mirror and the Lamp* solved this difficulty by contrasting the two periods through the use of metaphor. Abrams represents the eighteenth century by the mirror, which faithfully reflected the exterior, or scientific, world. The thought behind much nineteenth-century literature is shown as a lamp, which illuminates the soul of the artist and throws light upon life. As Abrams stated in *The Mirror and the Lamp:* "The title of the book identifies two common and antithetic metaphors of mind, one . . . to a reflector of external objects, the other to a radiant projector which makes a contribution to the objects it perceives. The first of these was characteristic of much of the thinking from Plato to the eighteenth century; the second typifies the prevailing romantic conception of the poetic mind." Charles Rosen notes in the *New York Review of Books* that *The Mirror and the Lamp* "is one of the most influential books on the early nineteenth century," and continues that Abrams "is a master of the themes of Romanticism. It is doubtful if anyone has surpassed, or that many have equaled, the range and depth of his reading."

Abrams's later work *Natural Supernaturalism* begins and ends with Wordsworth's unfinished poem "The Recluse"; it also moves into the twentieth century with perspectives on authors from Blake to James Joyce and D. H. Lawrence. In the *Dictio-*

nary of Literary Biography, William A. Ulmer comments that *Natural Supernaturalism* reaffirms but recasts "Shelley's claim that prevailing similarities in the philosophy and poetry of his age testify to a historically specific 'spirit of that age.' " The book also covers "religious" ground, in that Abrams ties the Romantics and their attempts to make man whole through unity with nature with the Christian concept of man's origins in the Garden of Eden and his eventual redemption and return to Paradise. Ulmer continues, "Abrams points out that Wordsworth and Coleridge's interest in reconciling man with himself and with nature rests on their sense of the 'fragmentation' of an original unity, and presupposes holistic criteria for human fulfillment."

Wayne C. Booth, in his work *Critical Understanding: The Powers and Limits of Pluralism,* raised questions about the method of *Naturalism and Supernaturalism*'s theses, and in response Abrams wrote in *Critical Inquiry* that his view of Romanticism is flexible and heuristic. "One source of confusion about what I tried to do [in *Natural Supernaturalism*] lies in my use of that pesky word 'Romantic' (and 'Romanticism'), which is one of those terms which historians can neither do with, nor make do without. . . . I don't believe that there exists an abstract entity, named 'Romanticism,' whose essential features are definable. . . . Instead, I use the word as an expository convenience to specify [parallels] . . . which are manifested in a great many important English and German writers . . . during those three or four decades after the outbreak of the French Revolution which, following common historical usage, I call the Romantic era."

Many of Abrams's independently published essays on Romanticism were gathered in *The Correspondent Breeze,* which was found to be practically "indispensable" by a *Washington Post Book World* contributor for "anyone wishing to understand the poetry of Wordsworth, Coleridge and Keats." Abrams's essays on critical theory are collected in *Doing Things with Texts,* where he argues with New Historicists and deconstructionists for the necessity of literary theory. "What puts Abrams out," explains Harpham, "is a representation of the text as 'uncanny' or 'unpredictable' in ways that necessarily exceed the conscious intentions of its author. For him, the critic's business is to work through shared linguistic and social conventions to produce an interpretation consonant with the author's intentions." Ulmer sees this as one of Abrams's chief aims, and concludes that through all the critic's work, "He has repeatedly avowed his faith in the human subject, determinable literary meaning, the possibility of valid historical understanding, and, finally, in a pluralism sensitive to literature's complexities and rich involvements in our moral, social, and intellectual experience."

BIOGRAPHICAL/CRITICAL SOURCES:

BOOKS

Abrams, M. H., *The Mirror and the Lamp,* Oxford University Press, 1953.

Booth, Wayne C., *Critical Understanding: The Powers and Limits of Pluralism,* University of Chicago Press, 1979.

Contemporary Literary Criticism, Gale, Volume 24, 1983.

Dictionary of Literary Biography, Gale, Volume 67: *Modern American Critics since 1955,* 1988.

Woodring, Carl R., *Prose of the Romantic Period,* Houghton, 1961.

PERIODICALS

America, November 13, 1971.

Critical Inquiry, spring, 1976

New York Review of Books, June 14, 1973.

Times Literary Supplement, December 27, 1985; August 17-23, 1990.

Washington Post Book World, October 19, 1986.

—*Sketch by Jani Prescott*

* * *

ADLER, Mortimer J(erome) 1902-

PERSONAL: Born December 28, 1902, in New York, N.Y.; son of Ignatz (a jewelry salesman) and Clarissa (a school teacher; maiden name, Manheim) Adler; married Helen Leavenworth Boynton, May 2, 1927 (divorced, 1961); married Caroline Sage Pring, February 22, 1963; children: (first marriage) Mark Arthur, Michael Boynton; (second marriage) Douglas Robert, Philip Pring. *Education:* Columbia University, Ph.D., 1928, B.A., 1983.

ADDRESSES: Office—Institute for Philosophical Research, 101 East Ontario St., Chicago, Ill. 60611.

CAREER: New York Sun, New York City, secretary to editor, 1915-17; Columbia University, New York City, instructor in psychology, 1923-30; University of Chicago, Chicago, Ill., associate professor, 1930-42, professor of philosophy of law, 1942-52; Institute for Philosophical Research, Chicago, president and director, 1952—; San Francisco Productions, Inc., Chicago, president, 1954—. Encyclopaedia Britannica, Inc., chairman of the board of editors, 1974—. Lecturer and assistant director of People's Institute (New York City), 1927-29; visiting lecturer, City College (now City College of the City University of New York), 1927, St. John's College (Annapolis, Md.), 1936, and University of Chicago, 1963-68; lecturer for U.S. Air Transport Command, 1943; University of North Carolina at Chapel Hill, university professor, 1988—, chairman of the national advisory board of the National Center for the Paideia Program, 1988—. Consultant to Ford Foundation, 1952-56. Honorary trustee, Aspen Institute, 1974—.

MEMBER: American Catholic Philosophical Association, American Philosophical Association, Phi Beta Kappa.

AWARDS, HONORS: Aquinas Medal, American Catholic Philosophical Association, 1976; Graduate Faculties Alumni Award for Excellence, Columbia University, 1977; Wilma and Roswell Messing Award, 1978; Distinguished Service Award, 1983; Distinguished Philosopher Award, 1984; The Golden Plato Award, 1985; John Jay Award, 1990; Laureate of the Lincoln Academy of Illinois, 1990.

WRITINGS:

Dialectic, Harcourt, 1927.

(With Maude Phelps Hutchins) *Diagrammatics,* Random House, 1932.

(With Jerome Michael) *Crime, Law and Social Science,* Harcourt, 1933, reprinted, Patterson Smith, 1971.

Art and Prudence: A Study in Practical Philosophy, Longmans, Green, 1937, reprinted, Arrio, 1978, revised edition published as *Poetry and Politics,* Duquesne University Press, 1965.

What Man Has Made of Man: A Study of the Consequences of Platonism and Positivism in Psychology, Longmans, Green, 1937, reprinted, Ungar, 1957.

Saint Thomas and the Gentiles, Marquette University Press, 1938.

Problems for Thomists: The Problem of Species, Sheed, 1940.

(Editor) *The Philosophy and Science of Man as a Foundation for Ethics and Politics,* University of Chicago, 1940.

(Editor of translation) *Jacques Maritain, Scholasticism and Politics,* Macmillan, 1940, 3rd edition, Bles, 1954.

How to Read a Book: The Art of Getting a Liberal Education, Simon & Schuster, 1940, revised and updated edition (with Charles Van Doren), 1972.

Hierarchy, College of St. Thomas (St. Paul, Minn.), 1940.

A Dialetic of Morals: Towards the Foundations of Political Philosophy, University of Notre Dame, 1941.

How to Think about War and Peace, Simon & Schuster, 1944.

(Associate editor) *The Great Ideas: A Syntopicon of Great Books of the Western World,* two volumes, Encyclopaedia Britannica, 1952, editor-in-chief, 2nd edition, 1990.

The Democratic Revolution, Industrial Indemnity, 1956.

The Capitalistic Revolution, Industrial Indemnity, 1957.

Liberal Education in an Industrial Democracy, Industrial Indemnity, 1957.

(With Louis O. Kelso) *The Capitalist Manifesto,* Random House, 1958, reprinted, Greenwood, 1975.

(With Milton Mayer) *The Revolution in Education,* University of Chicago Press, 1958.

The Idea of Freedom, Doubleday, Volume I: *A Dialectical Examination of the Conceptions of Freedom,* 1958, Volume II: *A Dialectical Examination of the Controversies About Freedom,* 1961.

Family Participation Plan for Reading and Discussing the Great Books of the Western World, with reading guides, Encyclopaedia Britannica, 1959.

(With Kelso) *The New Capitalists: A Proposal to Free Economic Growth from the Slavery of Savings,* Random House, 1961.

Great Ideas from the Great Books, Washington Square Press, 1961, revised and enlarged edition, 1963.

(Contributor) Arthur Allen Cohen, editor, *Humanistic Education and Western Civilization: Essays for Robert M. Hutchins,* Holt, 1964.

The Conditions of Philosophy: Its Checkered Past, Its Present Disorder, and Its Future Promise, Atheneum, 1965.

The Greeks, the West, and World Culture, New York Public Library, 1966.

The Difference of Man and the Difference It Makes, Holt, 1967.

Freedom: A Study of the Development of the Concept in the English and American Traditions of Philosophy, Magi Books, 1968.

(Editor with Van Doren) *The Negro in American History,* three volumes, Encyclopaedia Britannica Educational Corp., 1969.

The Time of Our Lives: The Ethics of Common Sense, Holt, 1970.

The Common Sense of Politics, Holt, 1971.

(With William Gorman) *The American Testament,* Praeger, 1975.

Some Questions about Language, Open Court, 1976.

Reforming Education: The Schooling of a People and Their Education Beyond Schooling, Westview, 1977.

Philosopher at Large: An Intellectual Autobiography, Macmillan, 1977.

(With Van Doren) *The Great Treasury of Western Thought: A Compendium of Important Statements and Comments on Man and His Institutions by the Great Thinkers in Western History,* Bowker, 1977.

Aristotle for Everybody: Difficult Thought Made Easy, Macmillan, 1978.

How to Think about God: A Guide for the 20th-Century Pagan, Macmillan, 1980.

Six Great Ideas, Macmillan, 1981.

The Angels and Us, Macmillan, 1982.

The Paideia Proposal: An Educational Manifesto, Macmillan, 1982.

How to Speak/How to Listen, Macmillan, 1983.

Paideia Problems and Possibilities, Macmillan, 1983.

The Paideia Program: An Educational Syllabus, Macmillan, 1984.

A Vision of the Future: Twelve Ideas for a Better Life and a Better Society, Macmillan, 1984.

Ten Philosophical Mistakes, Macmillan, 1985.

A Guidebook to Learning: For the Lifelong Pursuit of Wisdom, 1986.

We Hold These Truths: Understanding the Ideas and Ideals of the Constitution, Macmillan, 1987.

Reforming Education: The Opening of the American Mind (collected essays), Macmillan, 1989.

Intellect: Mind Over Matter, Macmillan, 1990.

Truth in Religion, Macmillan, 1990.

"THE GREAT IDEAS PROGRAM" SERIES, PUBLISHED BY ENCYCLOPAEDIA BRITANNICA

(With Peter Wolff) *A General Introduction to the Great Books and to a Liberal Education,* 1959.

(With Wolff) *The Development of Political Theory and Government,* 1959.

(With Wolff) *Foundations of Science and Mathematics,* 1960.

(With Seymour Cain) *Religion and Theology,* 1961.

(With Wolff) *Philosophy of Law and Jurisprudence,* 1961.

(With Cain) *Imaginative Literature,* Volume I: *From Homer to Shakespeare,* 1961, Volume II: *From Cervantes to Dostoevsky,* 1962.

(With Cain) *Ethics: The Study of Moral Values,* 1962.

(With V. J. McGill) *Biology, Psychology, and Medicine,* 1963.

(With Cain) *Philosophy,* 1963.

OTHER

"Great Books of the Western World" series, Encyclopaedia Britannica, associate editor, fifty-four volumes, 1952, editor-in-chief, (2nd edition) sixty volumes, 1990; editor-in-chief with Robert M. Hutchins, "The Great Ideas Today" series, Encyclopaedia Britannica, beginning 1961; editor with Hutchins, "Gateway to the Great Books" series, ten volumes, Encyclopaedia Britannica, 1963, revised edition, 1990; editor, "The Annals of America" series, twenty-three volumes, Encyclopaedia Britannica, 1968—. Contributor to professional journals and popular magazines, including *Commonweal, Social Frontier, New Scholasticism, Thomist, Saturday Review of Literature, Harper's,* and *Ladies' Home Journal.*

WORK IN PROGRESS: Several new books, including *Haves Without Havenots and Desires, Right and Wrong.*

SIDELIGHTS: America's John W. Donohue describes Mortimer Adler and John Dewey as "the two most widely known American practitioners of philosophy since the death of William James in 1910, although their scholarly reputations are unequal." A disciple of Aristotle and Aquinas, a believer in absolute and universal truths and values, Adler has fought against the pragmatism of Dewey—the dominant influence on twentieth-century American thought and education—for over fifty years. Best known as the progenitor of the Great Books Program, he has attempted to popularize reading of the classics and to persuade others of the universal truths they contain. The attempts have made him a popular philosopher at large but have alienated him from many members of the academic community.

A high school dropout who was nevertheless an omnivorous reader, Adler decided to become a philosopher at age fifteen

when he discovered Plato while reading John Stuart Mill's *Autobiography.* To this end, he attended Columbia University on a scholarship, finished the four-year program in three years, received a Phi Beta Kappa key, but failed to receive a B.A. degree because he refused to attend physical education classes and take the required swimming test. Nevertheless, he was appointed instructor in psychology at Columbia and after five years of teaching wrote his doctoral dissertation on the measurement of music appreciation. As John Murray Cuddihy wrote in the *New York Times Book Review,* Adler had become "the only Ph.D. in America with no B.A., no M.A., not even a high school diploma." (In 1983—sixty years late—Columbia relented, waived the physical education swimming requirements, and gave Adler his bachelor's degree and DeWitt-Clinton High School gave him his high school diploma. He was delighted to attend both his graduations.)

While an undergraduate at Columbia, Adler launched his philosophical attack on pragmatism—the position that truth is whatever is useful to a given society at a specific stage in its history—and its leading spokesman, John Dewey, who was also one of Adler's teachers. A *Time* writer says that Adler "became a bulldozer for truth. In class he bombarded John Dewey with long letters pointing out ambiguities and contradictions in his lectures." Influenced by the philosophy of Aristotle and St. Thomas Aquinas, Adler affirmed his belief in absolute and universal truths and values, charging that the failure to recognize their existence results from the application of the scientific method in areas where it is inappropriate. He argued that pragmatism, with its view of the scientific method as the preeminent model for all useful thought, creates moral and intellectual chaos, an effect that Adler considered apparent in progressive education.

After leaving Columbia for the University of Chicago at the invitation of Robert Maynard Hutchins, Adler expounded in numerous articles, books, and lectures his belief that a good education for all people everywhere (just because they are human) is to be found in the moral and intellectual disciplines that nurture the ability to think clearly and to exercise free will wisely. He asserted that progressive education, which emphasizes individual expression through a system of electives, is misguided and ultimately harmful: its subjectivity and relativity encourage aimlessness and superficiality. His ideas attracted attention, as evidenced by the success of his best-selling *How to Read a Book: The Art of Getting a Liberal Education.* Though some educators, according to the *Time* writer, "attacked him as a brash upstart who advocated a philosophical 'return to the Middle Ages,'" others supported him, particularly at Catholic colleges and universities where, John Donohue claims, "he was a legend" during the 1930s and 1940s.

At the University of Chicago, Adler put his educational theory to practice. He and Hutchins, the university's president and Adler's intellectual comrade-at-arms, managed to change academic requirements in favor of a broad training in the humanities, an education based primarily on close reading of the classics of Western civilization, the "Great Books." In 1946 they organized the Great Books Program, which brought together adults from all walks of life to discuss one of the classics every two weeks. To facilitate the project, 443 Great Books were reprinted in a 54-volume set by Encyclopaedia Britannica, Inc. Moreover, Adler directed production of the *Syntopicon* ("synthesis of topics"), an index to 102 "Great Ideas" in the Great Books. Donohue writes that "under Adler's generalship, a staff of thirty indexers [including the young Saul Bellow] and sixty clerical helpers took ten years to produce this remarkable tool at the cost of one million dollars. Ever since it appeared, it has refreshed the writers of term papers and has perhaps been surreptitiously consulted by their professors."

Since the Great Books Program, Adler has continued to promote public enlightenment, earning such nicknames as the "super-salesman of philosophy" and, according to John Murray Cuddihy, "the Charles Atlas of Western Intellection." "The underestimation of the human intelligence is the worst sin of our time," Adler told Michiko Kakutani of the *New York Times,* and he sees his task as the restoration of philosophy "to its proper place in our culture," to make it accessible to the person in the street. This goal is readily apparent in such works as *The Angels and Us* and *Aristotle for Everybody,* though in a *Washington Post* review of the latter, Carole Horn expresses surprise at one of Adler's statements: "Aristotle's books are much too difficult for beginners." In the *Chicago Tribune Book World,* Victor Power recommends *Six Great Ideas* "as a layman's tour of six philosophical concepts that hold within them the kernels of deeper thought. By examining the concepts of truth, goodness, beauty, justice, equality, and liberty, the layman may be tempted, as I was, to re-examine what Plato, Aristotle, Augustine, Aquinas, Hume, and others said about the assumption of their societies. . . . The object of this study is to remind us all of our common vocation to become thoughtful human beings." Partly because of his efforts to popularize philosophy, Adler has largely been ignored by the philosophical establishment, which Kakutani asserts "tends to regard any sort of popularization—as well as the attendant commercial success—with distrust, even disdain." He admits being "run out of the academy" to Kakutani, but says he is not bothered by it: "I thumbed my nose at them—so why should they pay any attention to me? They think you're spoonfeeding if you write something free of jargon and footnotes. But you're not spoon-feeding—you're simply avoiding putting obstacles in people's path."

But Adler's ostracism from the philosophical establishment is also due to his unfashionable Aristotelian-Thomistic line of thought. Adler, says the *Time* writer, "relishes dismissing most of philosophy since Thomas Aquinas as being snarled with pseudo problems. Modern philosophy, [he] claims . . . , got off to 'a very bad start' when Descartes and Locke committed the 'besetting sin of modern thought': they ignored Aristotle. Many contemporary philosophers would disagree." Theologian Robert Short, for example, does. Reviewing *How to Think about God* in the *Chicago Tribune Book World,* Short calls the book "an anachronism" and takes issue with Adler's lack of concern for modern philosophy: "Sixty years ago such a book might not have surprised us. But since that time the easy assumptions of classical Western philosophy have been questioned and shaken by one of the strongest anti-philosophical movements ever seen— existentialism. It is as though Adler is entirely unaware of the scathingly anti-philosophical attacks of such giants as Kierkegaard, Nietzsche, Dostoevsky, Heidegger, and Sartre. More probably, Adler hopes that by ignoring them they'll simply go away."

Despite such criticism, Adler remains true to the convictions formulated early in his life. Consistent with his belief that truth is absolute and not subject to change due to events in the world, he continues to attack the pervasive influence of pragmatism: "The twentieth century, for the most part, is an age in which relativism, skepticism, and subjectivism are rampant," he told Kakutani, "and that's what I'm mainly fighting against."

MEDIA ADAPTATIONS: Six Great Ideas was adapted for a television series of the same title, featuring Adler and Bill Moyers, Public Broadcasting Service, 1982.

BIOGRAPHICAL/CRITICAL SOURCES:

BOOKS

Adler, Mortimer J., *Philosopher at Large: An Intellectual Autobiography,* Macmillan, 1977.

PERIODICALS

America, April 29, 1978.
Aspen Institute Quarterly, Autumn 1989, Autumn 1990, Winter 1990.
Chicago Tribune, January 5, 1983, March 25, 1987, November 27, 1988, March 20, 1989, October 25, 1990.
Chicago Tribune Book World, March 9, 1980, May 3, 1981, April 11, 1982, September 26, 1982.
Commonweal, June 7, 1940, June 20, 1958.
Globe & Mail (Toronto), August 24, 1985.
Los Angeles Times, June 10, 1982, November 1, 1982.
Los Angeles Times Book Review, September 12, 1982.
New Statesman and Nation, January 4, 1941.
New Yorker, March 9, 1940.
New York Times, December 14, 1982.
New York Times Book Review, August 14, 1977, April 28, 1985.
Northwestern University Law Review, Spring/Summer 1990.
Saturday Review, May 24, 1958.
Saturday Review of Literature, March 9, 1940.
Time, March 18, 1940, March 17, 1952, April 6, 1959, July 25, 1977, May 30, 1983, May 4, 1987.
Times Literary Supplement, October 14, 1977.
Washington Post, May 25, 1978, April 3, 1980, May 8, 1982.
Washington Post Book World, November 14, 1982, June 26, 1983, September 18, 1983.
Yale Review, autumn, 1940.

*   *   *

ALVAREZ, A(lfred) 1929-

PERSONAL: Born August 5, 1929, in London, England; son of Bertie and Katie (Levy) Alvarez; married Ursula Graham Barr, 1956 (divorced, 1961); married Audrey Anne Adams, 1966; children: (first marriage) Adam Richard; (second marriage) Luke Lyon, Kate. *Education:* Corpus Christi College, Oxford, B.A., 1952, M.A., 1956. *Avocational interests:* Rock-climbing, poker, classical music.

ADDRESSES: Office—c/o New Yorker, 25 West 43rd St., New York, NY 10036. *Agent*—Wylie, Aitken & Stone, Ste. 2106, 250 West 57th St., New York, NY 10107.

CAREER: Oxford University, Corpus Christi College, Oxford, England, senior research scholar, 1952-55, and tutor in English, 1954-55; Princeton University, Princeton, NJ, Procter visiting fellow, 1953-54; Rockefeller Foundation, New York City, visiting fellow, 1955-56, 1958; *Observer,* London, England, poetry editor and critic, 1956-66; free-lance writer, 1956—. Gauss Seminarian and visiting lecturer, Princeton University, 1957-58; D. H. Lawrence fellow, University of New Mexico, 1958; drama critic, *New Statesman,* 1958-60; visiting professor at Brandeis University, Waltham, MA, 1960-61, and State University of New York at Buffalo, 1966.

MEMBER: Climbers' Club, Alpine Club.

AWARDS, HONORS: Vachel Lindsay Prize for Poetry (Chicago), 1961.

WRITINGS:

Stewards of Excellence, Scribner, 1958 (published in England as *The Shaping Spirit,* Chatto & Windus, 1958).

The End of It, privately printed, 1958.

The School of Donne, Chatto & Windus, 1961, Pantheon, 1962.

(Editor and author of introduction) *The New Poetry,* Penguin, 1962, revised edition, 1966.

(Contributor) Kenneth Allott, editor, *The Penguin Book of Contemporary Verse, 1918-1960,* Penguin, 1962.

Under Pressure: The Writer in Society, Eastern Europe and the U.S.A., Penguin, 1965.

Lost (poems), Turret Books, 1968.

Twelve Poems, The Review, 1968.

Beyond All This Fiddle: Essays, 1955-1967, Allen Lane, 1968, Random House, 1969.

(With Roy Fuller and Anthony Thwaite) *Penguin Modern Poets 18* (poems), Penguin, 1970.

Apparition (poems), University of Queensland Press, 1971.

The Savage God: A Study of Suicide, Weidenfeld & Nicolson, 1971, Random House, 1972.

Samuel Beckett, Viking, 1973 (published in England as *Beckett,* Fontana, 1973).

Hers, (novel), Weidenfeld & Nicolson, 1974, Random House, 1975.

Autumn to Autumn, and Selected Poems, 1953-1976, Macmillan (London), 1978.

(Editor with David Skilton) Thomas Hardy, *Tess of the D'Urbervilles,* Penguin, 1978.

Hunt (novel), Macmillan, 1978, Simon & Schuster, 1979.

Life after Marriage: Love in an Age of Divorce, Simon & Schuster, 1982 (published in England as *Life after Marriage: Scenes from Divorce,* Macmillan, 1982).

The Biggest Game in Town, Houghton, 1983.

Offshore: A North Sea Journey, Houghton, 1986.

Feeding the Rat, Atlantic Monthly Press, 1989.

Day of Atonement (novel), J. Cape, 1991.

Also author of screenplay, "The Anarchist," 1969. Contributor to *Observer, New Yorker, New York Review of Books,* and a number of other American and British periodicals. Advisory editor, "Penguin Modern European Poets" series, 1966-75.

SIDELIGHTS: As A. Alvarez summarized himself for *CA,* he "began as a literary critic, but by the end of the 1960s had grown weary of writing books about other people's books, so effectively gave up criticism in order to concentrate on his own creative work." Although his poetry and fiction have been getting a gradually warmer reception, it is as a critic that he has had his greatest success, because of his literary style as well as his conception of the critic's task. His style of criticism is refreshingly contemporary, characterized by a "brisk casualness" and absence of ponderous detail. Alvarez "accepts the full task of criticism. He not only defines and analyzes, but he also assesses and evaluates." Paul Delany writes, "Through his critical essays and *The Savage God* (a study of literature and suicide) Alvarez has become a leading advocate of what he has termed the 'Extremist' poets—Robert Lowell, Anne Sexton, John Berryman, Ted Hughes, Sylvia Plath—who have dared to explore in their art private obsessions with madness, suicide, political terror." The *New York Times*'s John Leonard describes his outlook as "a sensibility fashioned whole out of the bad dreams of the century, pressed upon by what Nabokov called 'the anonymous roller' that leaves a watermark [of paranoia] on every page."

Alvarez's first novel, *Hers,* was not well received. Russell Davies writes that as a critic Alvarez "would have been among the most merciless in pointing out the novel's thinness of texture." His poems in *Autumn to Autumn* fared somewhat better, though they were still accused of being "thin not trim, dull not austere" by one reviewer. Derek Stanford of *Books and Bookmen* calls *Au-*

tumn to Autumn "good, very good, strictly minor poetry, much of which poets with bigger names might justifiably be proud." Stuart Sutherland says of Alvarez's second novel: "*Hunt* is a very good novel, fast-moving and compulsive. . . . The prosaic is used to offset the sinister. The dialogue is accurate and witty." Even though Leonard points out that Alvarez borrows extensively from the works of other writers (Joseph Conrad, Graham Greene, and Ted Hughes, to name a few), he nevertheless finds *Hunt* to be relatively entertaining, mainly because Alvarez, "besides being well above the norm in intelligence, has a genuine talent for suspense." A *Contemporary Review* critic writes, "Taut, disturbing and expertly constructed, this is a novel not to be missed."

BIOGRAPHICAL/CRITICAL SOURCES:

BOOKS

Contemporary Literary Criticism, Gale, Volume 5, 1976, Volume 13, 1980.

Dictionary of Literary Biography, Gale, Volume 14: *British Novelists since 1960,* 1982, Volume 40: *Poets of Great Britain and Ireland since 1960,* 1985.

Fraser, G. S., *The Modern Writer and His World,* Deutsch, 1964.

Hamilton, Ian, *The Modern Poet,* Macdonald, 1968.

PERIODICALS

Books and Bookmen, April, 1968, June, 1978.

Book World, August 10, 1969, April 25, 1972.

Christian Science Monitor, January 4, 1962, August 2, 1969.

Contemporary Review, July, 1978.

Detroit News, February 14, 1982.

Guardian, February 24, 1961.

Listener, February 29, 1968.

Los Angeles Times, February 3, 1982.

Los Angeles Times Book Review, April 20, 1986, April 30, 1989.

New Review (London), March, 1978.

New Statesman, March 22, 1968, November 19, 1971, April 14, 1978, June 2, 1978.

Newsweek, February 1, 1982.

New Yorker, March 31, 1974.

New York Times, July 5, 1969, April 7, 1972, March 19, 1975, January 30, 1979, January 25, 1982, March 1, 1982, May 6, 1983.

New York Times Book Review, July 20, 1969, August 17, 1969, April 16, 1972, March 30, 1975, June 1, 1975, February 11, 1979, February 1, 1981, January 31, 1982, May 8, 1983, May 18, 1986.

Observer, March 3, 1968, December 20, 1970, May 7, 1978.

Poetry, November, 1959.

Saturday Review, August 2, 1969, April 5, 1975.

Spectator, December 18, 1971.

Time, February 8, 1982, May 30, 1983.

Times Literary Supplement, May 9, 1958, March 3, 1961, February 29, 1968, November 26, 1971, November 8, 1974, April 21, 1978, June 2, 1978, July 2, 1982, October 10, 1986, July 22, 1988.

Washington Post, July 5, 1986.

Washington Post Book World, February 14, 1982, May 29, 1983, June 25, 1989.

*   *   *

ANGUS, Fay   1929-

PERSONAL: Born May 25, 1929, in Brisbane, Australia; came to the United States, 1957, naturalized, 1967; daughter of Ernest

William and Amy Beatrice Westwood; married John S. Angus (a civil engineer), September 3, 1957; children: Anne, Ian. *Education:* Attended convent school in Shanghai, China. *Religion:* Christian.

ADDRESSES: Home—405 North Canon Dr., Sierra Madre, CA 91024.

CAREER: Writer, 1974—. Public speaker at Rotary, Kiwanis, Lions and other service clubs, and at international inspirational and writers' conferences.

MEMBER: International PEN, International Platform Association, National League of American Pen Women, Church Women United, California Federation of Chaparral Poets.

WRITINGS:

Between Your Status and Your Quo, Regal Books, 1975.
Up to Heaven and down to Earth, Regal Books, 1977.
The White Pagoda, Tyndale, 1978.
The Catalyst, Tyndale, 1979.
How to Do Everything Right and Live to Regret It!, Harper, 1983.
Running around in Spiritual Circles, Harper, 1985.
Heartstrings, C. R. Gibson, 1988.
Moments Light and Bright, C. R. Gibson, 1988.
Warm and Cozy Christmas Thoughts, C. R. Gibson, 1989.
The Nutcracker (pop-up edition), Simon & Schuster, 1989.
The Gentle Art of Being There, C. R. Gibson, 1990.

WORK IN PROGRESS: A novel set in China, with a movie treatment.

SIDELIGHTS: Fay Angus believes that "laughter may be the best medicine for everything—from minor daily crises to serious doubts about God's goodness." She comments on this theme in *How to Do Everything Right and Live to Regret It!:* "When we raise our children on a lap full of laughter, we program into them the merry heart that Solomon says is a 'continual feast.' It will nourish them all their lives." She also combines inspirational messages with her humor: "God is God of the impossible; he is hope of the hopeless. When we are powerless to help ourselves, or when no one is able to help us, God moves his miracles through our lives." "Humor," Angus told *CA,* "is the tilt of the soul that keeps us looking up, even though we may be feeling down." Angus's sense of humor and inspirational tone have led her to be called a kind of spiritual Erma Bombeck.

About her childhood years in China, Angus added: "One just can't grow up in China and be interned for two and a half years during the war without writing about it, so I knew that at some time I'd write my autobiography. I'm glad I waited and let the experience incubate and mature a bit, as it gave me a better perspective. *The White Pagoda* is the China story, the story of a young girl growing up in metropolitan Shanghai and the impressions of her teenage years in a prisoner-of-war camp in Yangchow. *The Catalyst* is a sequel, a romantic story of my quest for faith.

"With a background in China, naturally I'll return. I've done a lot of interviews on the China situation and the exciting potential of their Great Leap Outward. My novel in progress has a China base and I hope to spend several months over there."

With regard to her capacity as public speaker, Angus said she "sees our lives as a whole series of new beginnings and uses the word *determination* to move us onward with a forward thrust. Her life slogan is: *Never let a problem to be solved become more important than a person to be loved,*" and she added that she be-

lieves "the gift of encouragement is one of the most important we can give each other."

BIOGRAPHICAL/CRITICAL SOURCES:

BOOKS

Angus, Fay, *How to Do Everything Right and Live to Regret It!,* Harper, 1983.
Angus, Fay, *Running around in Spiritual Circles,* Harper, 1985.

*   *   *

ANTHONY, John
  See CIARDI, John (Anthony)

*   *   *

ANTSCHEL, Paul   1920-1970
  (Paul Celan)

PERSONAL: Born November 23, 1920, in Cernowitz, Rumania; committed suicide by drowning, sometime in April, 1970, in France; married Gisele de Lestrange (an artist), 1950; children: Eric. *Education:* Earned licence es lettres in Paris, 1950. *Religion:* Jewish.

CAREER: Poet and translator. Lecturer at L'Ecole Normale Superieure of University of Paris, 1959-70.

AWARDS, HONORS: Literary Prize of City of Bremen, 1958; Georg Buechner Prize, German Academy of Language and Literature, 1960.

WRITINGS:

POETRY; UNDER PSEUDONYM PAUL CELAN

Der Sand aus den Urnen, Sexl (Vienna), 1948.
Mohn und Gedaechtnis: Gedichte (title means "Poppy and Memory"), Deutsche Verlags-Anstalt (Stuttgart), 1952.
Von Schwelle zu Schwelle: Gedichte (title means "From Threshold to Threshold"), Deutsche Verlags-Anstalt, 1955.
Sprachgitter, S. Fischer, 1959, translation by Joachim Neugroschel published as *Speech-Grille and Selected Poems,* Dutton, 1971.
Gedichte: Eine Auswahl, edited by Klaus Wagenbach, S. Fischer, 1959.
Der Meridian: Rede anlaesslich der Verleihung des Georg-Buechner-Preises, Darmstadt, a, 22. Oktober 1960, S. Fischer, 1961.
Die Niemandsrose (title means "The No Man's Rose"), S. Fischer, 1963.
Atemkristall, Brunidor, 1965.
Gedichte (title means "Poetry"), Moderner Buch-Club, 1966.
Atemwende: Gedichte, Suhrkamp, 1967.
Fadensonnen, Suhrkamp, 1968.
Ausgewaehlte Gedichte: Zwei Reden, Suhrkamp, 1968.
Lichtzwang, Suhrkamp, 1970.
Schneepart, Suhrkamp, 1971.
Strette. Suivis du Meridien et d'Entretien dans la montagne, Mercure de France, 1971.
Nineteen Poems, translation by Michael Hamburger, Carcanet Press, 1972.
Selected Poems, translation by Hamburger and Christopher Middleton, Penguin, 1972.
Gedichte: In zwei Banden, Suhrkamp, 1975.
Zeitgehoeft: Spaete Gedichte aus dem Nachlass, Suhrkamp, 1976.
Poesie/Paul Celan; a cura di Moshe Kahne e Marcella Bagnasco, A. Mondadori (Italy), 1976.

Paul Celan: Poems, translation by Hamburger, Persea Books, 1980, published as *Poems of Paul Celan,* 1989.
Gesammelte Werke in fuenf Baenden, 5 volumes, Suhrkamp, 1983.
Todesfuge, Edition Gunnar A. Kaldewey, 1984.
65 Poems, Raven Arts Press (Dublin), 1985.
Last Poems, translation by Katherine Washburn and Margret Guillemin, North Point Press, 1986.

Also author of *Breath Crystal: Translations of Paul Celan,* translation by Walter Billeter, Ragman Productions (Australia), and of *Conversation in the Mountains,* translation by Rosmarie Waldrop.

OTHER; UNDER PSEUDONYM PAUL CELAN

Edgar Jene und der Traum vom Traume, Agathon (Vienna), 1948.
Paul Celan: Prose Writings and Selected Poems, translation by Walter Billeter, Paper Castle (Victoria, Austrlaia), 1977.
Collected Prose, translation by Rosemarie Waldrop, Carcanet Press, 1986.

Translator of numerous works into German. Also author of works represented in anthologies, including *Modern German Poetry, 1910-1960,* edited by Hamburger and C. Middleton, 1962, *Twentieth-Century German Verse,* edited by P. Bridgewater, 1963, and *Modern European Poetry,* edited by W. Barnstone, 1966.

SIDELIGHTS: Paul Antschel, best known under his pseudonym Paul Celan, was regarded as one of the most important poets to emerge from post-World War II Europe. According to one critic, he "made a more original and substantial contribution to modern poetry than any other German-language poet of his generation." His work bears the influence of both the French surrealists and Rilke in terms of poetic devices and linguistic stylization. His thematic obsession, however, is the extermination of the Jews during World War II. A writer for the *Times Literary Supplement* wrote that Celan "makes us aware of the horror of our age in a way that is the more powerful for being oblique. The humble and familiar images . . . combine with others that suggest blinding, mutilation and empaling, burning, whipping and shooting, hunting down and shutting in with walls and barbed wire—festering memories of Auschwitz which are relevant not only to Germany and not only to an era that ended in 1945."

Celan began writing poetry shortly after the war. His first book in 1947 caused little stir in the German literary community. His second collection, "Poppy and Memory," received much more critical attention, and Celan quickly became a reputable poet. Among his most popular poems is "Death Fugue," a stark recreation of activities at Auschwitz which was featured in both of the early collections. Paul Auster called it "literally a fugue composed of words, and the incessant, rhythmical repetitions and variations of phrases evoke a nightmare more devastating than any forthright description could." This description is exemplified in the stanza which includes the lines "death is a master from Germany / his eye is blue / he shoots you with bullets of lead / his aim is true / a man lives in the house your / golden hair Margarete / he sets his hounds on us he gives / us a grave in the air he plays with the serpent and / dreams death is a master from / Germany." Despite its high regard, "Death Fugue" was later refuted by Celan as, according to Auster, "too obvious and superficially realistic," and he disallowed its inclusion in collections.

As Celan progressed, his poetry became increasingly inaccessible. "The poems grow shorter," observed John Hollander,

"denser and less easily rewarding toward the end of the poet's career, and more starkly impressive." His poetry also became less depressing. One critic wrote, "The worst, we are made to feel, has been faced, and out of despair has come a new beauty which *is* truth. . . ." The same reviewer added that the collection *Atemwende* "shows a poet projecting his breath into emptiness and feeling it return . . . charged with a numinous power." Aside from its rather positive stance, *Atemwende* was also noted for its attention to the language itself. "The author of *Atemwende* is obsessed by words and obsessed by forms," contended a writer for the *Times Literary Supplement.* The critic attributed Celan's brighter outlook to his new interest in words. "And this new reality has been uniquely embodied in language," the critic claimed: "language, in fact, has helped not just to shape it, but to bring it life."

Celan pursued his interest in economy of form in *Lichtzwang,* a collection published the same year as his death. A reviewer for the *Times Literary Supplement* wrote that "his poems are very much word-sculptures." Jerry Glenn believed that Celan was moving towards a union of his early realist style with his later structure-conscious poems. He also noted in a review of *Lichtzwang,* "There are some fine poems here, poems which will justly become a part of the permanent legacy of German literature."

Celan committed suicide by drowning in 1970. In a eulogy, Auster called him "one of the truly great poets of our time." In the same article, he observed that by reading the collected works, one could perceive a developing sense of despair within Celan. Referring to the poems, Auster wrote, "One feels both a shrinking and an expansion in them, as if, by traveling to the inmost recesses of himself, Celan had somehow vanished, joining with the greater forces beyond him, and at the same time sinking more deeply into his terrifying sense of isolation." Celan once revealed, "I have tried to write poetry in order to acquire a perspective of reality for myself." Perhaps he forecast his own fate when he wrote, "You were my death: / you I could hold / when all fell away from me."

BIOGRAPHICAL/CRITICAL SOURCES:

BOOKS

Brierley, David, *"Der Meridian": Ein Versuch zur Poetik und Dichtung Paul Celans,* Lang, 1984.
Celan, Paul, *Speech-Grille and Selected Poems,* Dutton, 1971.
Celan, Paul, *Selected Poems,* Penguin, 1972.
Chalfen, Israel, *Paul Celan: Eine Biographie seiner Jugend,* Suhrkamp, 1979.
Contemporary Literary Criticism, Gale, Volume 10, 1979, Volume 19, 1981.
Dictionary of Literary Biography, Volume 69: *Contemporary German Fiction Writers,* first series, Gale, 1988.
Glenn, Jerry, *Paul Celan,* Twayne, 1973.
Meinecke, Dietlind, editor, *Uber Paul Celan,* Suhrkamp, 1973.
Neumann, Peter Horst, *Zur Lyrik Paul Celans,* Vandenhoeck & Ruprecht, 1968.

PERIODICALS

Books Abroad, spring, 1971.
Chicago Review, Volume 29, number 3, 1978.
Commentary, February, 1976.
New York Times Book Review, July 18, 1971.
Studies in Twentieth Century Literature, fall, 1983.
Times Literary Supplement, December 7, 1967, September 18, 1970, September 29, 1984.

ATWOOD, Margaret (Eleanor) 1939-

PERSONAL: Born November 18, 1939, in Ottawa, Ontario, Canada; daughter of Carl Edmund (an entomologist) and Margaret (Killam) Atwood; married Graeme Gibson (a writer); children: Jess. *Education:* University of Toronto, B.A., 1961; Radcliffe College, A.M., 1962; Harvard University, graduate study, 1962-63, and 1965-67. *Politics:* "William Morrisite." *Religion:* "Immanent Transcendentalist."

CAREER: Writer. University of British Columbia, Vancouver, lecturer in English literature, 1964-65; Sir George Williams University, Montreal, Quebec, lecturer in English literature, 1967-68; York University, Toronto, Ontario, assistant professor of English literature, 1971-72; House of Anansi Press, Toronto, editor and member of board of directors, 1971-73; University of Toronto, Toronto, writer-in-residence, 1972-73; University of Alabama, Tuscaloosa, writer-in-residence, 1985; New York University, New York, N.Y., Berg Visiting Professor of English, 1986; Macquarie University, North Ryde, Australia, writer-in-residence, 1987.

MEMBER: Amnesty International, Writers' Union of Canada (vice-chairman, 1980-81), Royal Society of Canada (fellow), Canadian Civil Liberties Association (member of board, 1973-75), PEN International, Canadian Centre, American Academy of Arts and Sciences (honorary member), Anglophone (president, 1984-85).

AWARDS, HONORS: E. J. Pratt Medal, 1961, for *Double Persephone;* President's Medal, University of Western Ontario, 1965; YWCA Women of Distinction Award, 1966; Governor General's Award, 1966, for *The Circle Game,* and 1986, for *The Handmaid's Tale;* first prize in Canadian Centennial Commission Poetry Competition, 1967; Union Prize, *Poetry,* 1969; Bess Hoskins Prize, *Poetry,* 1969 and 1974; D.Litt., Trent University, 1973, Concordia University, 1980, Smith College, 1982, University of Toronto, 1983, Mount Holyoke College, 1985, University of Waterloo, 1985, and University of Guelph, 1985; LL.D., Queen's University, 1974; City of Toronto Book Award, 1977; Canadian Booksellers' Association Award, 1977; Periodical Distributors of Canada Short Fiction Award, 1977; St. Lawrence Award for fiction, 1978; Radcliffe Medal, 1980; *Life before Man* named notable book of 1980 by the American Library Association; Molson Award, 1981; Guggenheim fellowship, 1981; named Companion of the Order of Canada, 1981; International Writer's Prize, Welsh Arts Council, 1982; Book of the Year Award, Periodical Distributors of Canada and the Foundation for the Advancement of Canadian Letters, 1983; Ida Nudel Humanitarian Award, 1986; Toronto Arts Award for writing and editing, 1986; *Los Angeles Times* Book Award, 1986, for *The Handmaid's Tale;* named Woman of the Year, *Ms.* magazine, 1986; Arthur C. Clarke Award, 1987; Commonwealth Literature Prize, 1987; Council for the Advancement and Support of Education silver medal, 1987; named *Chatelaine* magazine's Woman of the Year.

WRITINGS:

POEMS

Double Persephone, Hawkshead Press, 1961.
The Circle Game, Cranbrook Academy of Art (Bloomfield Hills, Mich.), 1964, revised edition, Contact Press, 1966.
Kaleidoscopes Baroque: A Poem, Cranbrook Academy of Art, 1965.
Talismans for Children, Cranbrook Academy of Art, 1965.
Speeches for Doctor Frankenstein, Cranbrook Academy of Art, 1966.

The Animals in That Country, Oxford University Press (Toronto), 1968, Atlantic-Little, Brown, 1969.
The Journals of Susanna Moodie, Oxford University Press, 1970.
Procedures for Underground, Atlantic-Little, Brown, 1970.
Power Politics, House of Anansi Press, 1971, Harper, 1973.
You Are Happy, Harper, 1974.
Selected Poems, 1965-1975, Oxford University Press, 1976, Simon & Schuster, 1978.
Marsh Hawk, Dreadnaught, 1977.
Two-Headed Poems, Oxford University Press, 1978, Simon & Schuster, 1981.
Notes Toward a Poem That Can Never Be Written, Salamander Press, 1981.
True Stories, Oxford University Press, 1981, Simon & Schuster, 1982.
Snake Poems, Salamander Press, 1983.
Interlunar, Oxford University Press, 1984.
Selected Poems II: Poems Selected and New, 1976-1986, Oxford University Press, 1986.

Also author of *Expeditions,* 1966, and *What Was in the Garden,* 1969.

NOVELS

The Edible Woman, McClelland & Stewart, 1969, Atlantic-Little, Brown, 1970.
Surfacing, McClelland & Stewart, 1972, Simon & Schuster 1973.
Lady Oracle, Simon & Schuster, 1976.
Life before Man, McClelland & Stewart, 1979, Simon & Schuster, 1980.
Bodily Harm, McClelland & Stewart, 1981, Simon & Schuster, 1982.
Encounters with the Element Man, Ewert, 1982.
Unearthing Suite, Grand Union Press, 1983.
The Handmaid's Tale, McClelland & Stewart, 1985, Houghton, 1986.
Cat's Eye, Doubleday, 1989.

STORY COLLECTIONS

Dancing Girls and Other Stories, McClelland & Stewart, 1977, Simon & Schuster, 1982.
Bluebeard's Egg and Other Stories, McClelland & Stewart, 1983, Fawcett, 1987.
Murder in the Dark: Short Fictions and Prose Poems, Coach House Press, 1983.

OTHER

The Trumpets of Summer (radio play), Canadian Broadcasting Corporation (CBC), 1964.
Survival: A Thematic Guide to Canadian Literature, House of Anansi Press, 1972.
The Servant Girl (teleplay), CBC-TV, 1974.
Days of the Rebels, 1815-1840, Natural Science Library, 1976.
The Poetry and Voice of Margaret Atwood (recording), Caedmon, 1977.
Up in the Tree (juvenile), McClelland & Stewart, 1978.
(Author of introduction) Catherine M. Young, *To See Our World,* GLC Publishers, 1979, Morrow, 1980.
(With Joyce Barkhouse) *Anna's Pet* (juvenile), James Lorimer, 1980.
Snowbird (teleplay), CBC-TV, 1981.
Second Words: Selected Critical Prose, House of Anansi Press, 1982.
(Editor) *The New Oxford Book of Canadian Verse in English,* Oxford University Press, 1982.

(Editor with Robert Weaver) *The Oxford Book of Canadian Short Stories in English,* Oxford University Press, 1986.

(With Peter Pearson) *Heaven on Earth* (teleplay), CBC-TV, 1986.

(Editor) *The Canlit Foodbook,* Totem, 1987.

(Editor with Shannon Ravenal) *The Best American Short Stories, 1989,* Houghton, 1989.

Contributor to anthologies, including *Five Modern Canadian Poets,* 1970, *The Canadian Imagination: Dimensions of a Literary Culture,* Harvard University Press, 1977, and *Women on Women,* 1978; contributor to periodicals, including *Atlantic, Poetry, Kayak, New Yorker, Harper's, New York Times Book Review, Saturday Night, Tamarack Review, Canadian Forum,* and other publications.

MEDIA ADAPTATIONS: The Handmaid's Tale was filmed by Cinecom Entertainment Group, 1990.

SIDELIGHTS: As a poet, novelist, story writer, and essayist, Margaret Atwood holds a unique position in contemporary Canadian literature. Her books have received critical acclaim in the United States, Europe, and her native Canada, and she has been the recipient of numerous literary awards. Ann Marie Lipinski, writing in the *Chicago Tribune,* describes Atwood as "one of the leading literary luminaries, a national heroine of the arts, the *rara avis* of Canadian letters." Atwood's critical popularity is matched by her popularity with readers. She is a frequent guest on Canadian television and radio, her books are best-sellers, and "people follow her on the streets and in stores," as Judy Klemesrud reports in the *New York Times.* Atwood, Roy MacGregor of *Maclean's* explains, "is to Canadian literature as Gordon Lightfoot is to Canadian music, more institution than individual." Atwood's popularity with both critics and the reading public has surprised her. "It's an accident that I'm a successful writer," she tells MacGregor. "I think I'm kind of an odd phenomenon in that I'm a serious writer and I never expected to become a popular one, and I never did anything in order to become a popular one."

Atwood first came to public attention as a poet in the 1960s with her collections *Double Persephone,* winner of the E. J. Pratt Medal, and *The Circle Game,* winner of a Governor General's Award. These two books marked out the terrain which all of Atwood's later poetry would explore. *Double Persephone* concerns "the contrast between the flux of life or nature and the fixity of man's artificial creations," as Linda Hutcheon explains in the *Dictionary of Literary Biography. The Circle Game* takes this opposition further, setting such human constructs as games, literature, and love against the instability of nature. Human constructs are presented as both traps and shelters, the fluidity of nature as both dangerous and liberating. Sherrill Grace, writing in her *Violent Duality: A Study of Margaret Atwood,* sees the central tension in all of Atwood's work as "the pull towards art on one hand and towards life on the other." This tension is expressed in a series of "violent dualities," as Grace terms it. Atwood "is constantly aware of opposites—self/other, subject/object, male/female, nature/man—and of the need to accept and work within them," Grace explains. "To create, Atwood chooses violent dualities, and her art re-works, probes, and dramatizes the ability to see double."

Linda W. Wagner, writing in *The Art of Margaret Atwood: Essays in Criticism,* believes that in Atwood's poetry "duality [is] presented as separation." This separation leads her characters to be isolated from one another and from the natural world, resulting in their inability to communicate, to break free of exploitative social relationships, or to understand their place in the natural

order. "In her early poetry," Gloria Onley writes in the *West Coast Review,* ". . . [Atwood] is acutely aware of the problem of alienation, the need for real human communication and the establishment of genuine human community—real as opposed to mechanical or manipulative; genuine as opposed to the counterfeit community of the body politic." Speaking of *The Circle Game,* Wagner writes that "the personae of those poems never did make contact, never did anything but lament the human condition. . . . Relationships in these poems are sterile if not destructive."

Atwood's sense of desolation, especially evident in her early poems, and her use of frequently violent images, moves Helen Vendler of the *New York Times Book Review* to claim that Atwood has a "sense of life as mostly wounds given and received." Speaking of *The Circle Game* and *Procedures for Underground,* Peter Stevens notes in *Canadian Literature* that both collections contain "images of drowning, buried life, still life, dreams, journeys and returns." In a review of *True Stories* for *Canadian Forum,* Chaviva Hosek states that the poems "range over such topics as murder, genocide, rape, dismemberment, instruments of torture, forms of torture, genital mutilation, abortion, and forcible hysterectomy," although Robert Sward of *Quill and Quire* explains that many reviewers of the book have exaggerated the violence and give "the false impression that all 38 poems . . . are about torture." Yet, Scott Lauder of *Canadian Forum* speaks of "the painful world we have come to expect from Atwood."

Suffering is common for the female characters in Atwood's poems, although they are never passive victims. In more recent works they take active measures to improve their situations. Atwood's poems, Onley states, concern "modern woman's anguish at finding herself isolated and exploited (although also exploiting) by the imposition of a sex role power structure." Speaking to Klemesrud, Atwood explains that her suffering characters come from real life: "My women suffer because most of the women I talk to seem to have suffered." By the early 1970s, this stance had made Atwood into "a cult author to faithful feminist readers," as Lipinski reports. Atwood's popularity in the feminist community was unsought. "I began as a profoundly apolitical writer," she tells Lindsy Van Gelder of *Ms.,* "but then I began to do what all novelists and some poets do: I began to describe the world around me."

Atwood's feminist concerns are evident in her novels as well, particularly in *The Edible Woman, Surfacing, Life before Man, Bodily Harm,* and *The Handmaid's Tale.* These novels feature female characters who are, Klemesrud reports, "intelligent, self-absorbed modern women searching for identity. . . . [They] hunt, split logs, make campfires and become successful in their careers, while men often cook and take care of their households." Like her poems, however, Atwood's novels "are populated by pained and confused people whose lives hold a mirror to both the front page fears—cancer, divorce, violence—and those that persist quietly, naggingly—solitude, loneliness, desperation," Lipinski writes.

The Edible Woman tells the story of Marian McAlpin, a young woman engaged to be married, who rebels against her upcoming marriage. Her fiance seems too stable, too ordinary, and the role of wife too fixed and limiting. Her rejection of marriage is accompanied by her body's rejection of food. Even a spare vegetarian diet cannot be eaten. Eventually Marian bakes a sponge cake in the shape of a woman and feeds it to her fiance because, she explains, "You've been trying to assimilate me." After the engagement is broken, she is able to eat some of the cake herself.

Reaction to *The Edible Woman* was divided, with some reviewers pointing to flaws commonly found in first novels. John Stedmond of *Canadian Forum,* for example, believes that "the characters, though cleverly sketched, do not quite jell, and the narrative techniques creak a little." Linda Rogers of *Canadian Literature* finds that "one of the reasons *The Edible Woman* fails as a novel is the awkwardness of the dialogue." But other critics note Atwood's at least partial success. Tom Marshall, writing in his *Harsh and Lovely Land: The Major Canadian Poets and the Making of a Canadian Tradition,* calls *The Edible Woman* "a largely successful comic novel, even if the mechanics are sometimes a little clumsy, the satirical accounts of consumerism a little drawn out." Millicent Bell of the *New York Times Book Review* calls it "a work of feminist black humor" and claims that Atwood's "comic distortion veers at times into surreal meaningfulness." And Hutcheon describes *The Edible Woman* as "very much a social novel about the possibilities for personal female identity in a capitalistic consumer society."

Surfacing, Atwood's second novel, is "a psychological ghost story," as Marshall explains it, in which a young woman confronts and accepts her past during a visit to her rural home. She comes to realize that she has repressed disturbing events from her memory, including an abortion and her father's death. While swimming in a local lake, she has a vision of her drowned father which "drives her to a healing madness," Marshall states. Hutcheon explains that "*Surfacing* tells of the coming to terms with the haunting, separated parts of the narrator's being . . . after surfacing from a dive, a symbolic as well as a real descent under water, where she has experienced a revealing and personally apocalyptic vision."

Many of the concerns found in Atwood's poetry reappear in *Surfacing.* The novel, Roberta Rubenstein writes in *Modern Fiction Studies,* "synthesizes a number of motifs that have dominated [Atwood's] consciousness since her earliest poems: the elusiveness and variety of 'language' in its several senses; the continuum between human and animal, human being and nature; the significance of one's heritage . . . ; the search for a location (in both time and place); the brutalizations and victimizations of love; drowning and surviving." Margaret Wimsatt of *Commonweal* agrees with this assessment. "The novel," Wimsatt writes, "picks up themes brooded over in the poetry, and knits them together coherently." Marshall believes that both *The Edible Woman* and *Surfacing* "are enlargements upon the themes of [Atwood's] poems. In each of them a young woman is driven to rebellion against what seems to be her fate in the modern technological 'Americanized' world and to psychic breakdown and breakthrough."

In *Life before Man,* Atwood dissects the relationships between three characters: Elizabeth, a married woman who mourns the recent suicide of her lover; Elizabeth's husband, Nate, who is unable to choose between his wife and his lover; and Lesje, Nate's lover, who works with Elizabeth at a museum of natural history. All three characters are isolated from one another and unable to experience their own emotions. The fossils and dinosaur bones on display at the museum are compared throughout the novel with the sterility of the characters' lives. As Laurie Stone notes in the *Village Voice, Life before Man* "is full of variations on the theme of extinction." Similarly, Rubenstein writes in the *Chicago Tribune* that the novel is a "superb living exhibit in which the artifacts are unique (but representative) lives in progress."

Although *Life before Man* is what Rosellen Brown of *Saturday Review* calls an "anatomy of melancholy," MacGregor sees a tempering humor in the novel as well. *Life before Man,* MacGre-

gor writes, "is not so much a story as it is the discarded negatives of a family album, the thoughts so dark they defy any flash short of Atwood's remarkable, and often very funny, insight." Comparing the novel's characters to museum pieces and commenting on the analytical examination to which Atwood subjects them, Peter S. Prescott of *Newsweek* finds that "with chilly compassion and an even colder wit, Atwood exposes the interior lives of her specimens." Writing in the *New York Times Book Review,* Marilyn French makes clear that in *Life before Man,* Atwood "combines several talents—powerful introspection, honesty, satire and a taut, limpid style—to create a splendid, fully integrated work."

The novel's title, French believes, relates to the characters' isolation from themselves, their history, and from one another. They have not yet achieved truly human stature. "This novel suggests," French writes, "that we are still living life before man, before the human—as we like to define it—has evolved." Prescott raises the same point. The novel's characters, he writes, "do not communicate; each, in the presence of another, is locked into his own thoughts and feelings. Is such isolation and indeterminacy what Atwood means when she calls her story 'Life before Man'?" This concern is also found in Atwood's previous novels, French argues, all of which depict "the search for identity . . . a search for a better way to be—for a way of life that both satisfies the passionate, needy self and yet is decent, humane and natural."

Atwood further explores this idea in *Bodily Harm.* In this novel Rennie Wilford is a Toronto journalist who specializes in light, trivial pieces for magazines. She is, Anne Tyler explains in the *Detroit News,* "a cataloguer of current fads and fancies." Isabel Raphael of the London *Times* calls Rennie someone who "deals only in surfaces; her journalism is of the most trivial and transitory kind, her relationship with a live-in lover limited to sex, and most of her friends 'really just contacts.'" Following a partial mastectomy, which causes her lover to abandon her, Rennie begins to feel dissatisfied with her life. She takes on an assignment to the Caribbean island of St. Antoine in an effort to get away from things for a while. Her planned magazine story focusing on the island's beaches, tennis courts, and restaurants is distinctly facile in comparison to the political violence she finds on St. Antoine. When Rennie is arrested and jailed, the experience brings her to a self-realization about her life. "Death," Nancy Ramsey remarks in the *San Francisco Review of Books,* "rather than the modern sense of ennui, threatens Rennie and the people around her, and ultimately gives her life a meaning she hadn't known before."

Bodily Harm, Frank Davey of the *Canadian Forum* believes, follows the same pattern set in Atwood's earlier novels: "Alienation from natural order . . . , followed by descent into a more primitive but healing reality . . . , and finally some reestablishment of order." Although Davey is "troubled" by the similarities between the novels and believes that "Atwood doesn't risk much with this book," he concludes that "these reservations aside, *Bodily Harm* is still a pleasure to read." Other critics have few such reservations about the book. Anatole Broyard of the *New York Times,* for example, claims that "the only way to describe my response to [*Bodily Harm*] is to say that it knocked me out. Atwood seems to be able to do just about everything: people, places, problems, a perfect ear, an exactly-right voice and she tosses off terrific scenes with a casualness that leaves you utterly unprepared for the way these scenes seize you." Tyler calls Atwood "an uncommonly skillful and perceptive writer," and goes on to state that, because of its subject matter, *Bodily Harm* "is not always easy to read. There are times when it's downright unpleasant, but it's also intelligent, provocative, and in the end—against all expectations—uplifting."

In *The Handmaid's Tale* Atwood turns to speculative fiction, creating the dystopia of Gilead, a future America in which Fundamentalist Christians have killed the president and members of Congress and imposed their own dictatorial rule. In this future world, polluted by toxic chemicals and nuclear radiation, few women can bear children; the birthrate has dropped alarmingly. Those women who can bear children are forced to become Handmaids, the official breeders for society. All other women have been reduced to chattel under a repressive religious hierarchy run by men.

The Handmaid's Tale is a radical departure from Atwood's previous novels. Her strong feminism was evident in earlier books, but *The Handmaid's Tale* is dominated by the theme. As Barbara Holliday writes in the *Detroit Free Press,* Atwood "has been concerned in her fiction with the painful psychic warfare between men and women. In 'The Handmaid's Tale,' a futuristic satire, she casts subtlety aside, exposing woman's primal fear of being used and helpless." Atwood's creation of an imaginary world is also new. As Mary Battiata notes in the *Washington Post, The Handmaid's Tale* is the first of Atwood's novels "not set in a worried corner of contemporary Canada."

Atwood was moved to write her story only after images and scenes from the book had been appearing to her for three years. She admits to Mervyn Rothstein of the *New York Times,* "I delayed writing it . . . because I felt it was too crazy." But she eventually became convinced that her vision of Gilead was not far from reality. Some of the anti-female measures she had imagined for the novel actually exist. "There is a sect now, a Catholic charismatic spinoff sect, which calls the women handmaids," Atwood tells Rothstein. "A law in Canada," Battiata reports, "[requires] a woman to have her husband's permission before obtaining an abortion." And Atwood, speaking to Battiata, points to repressive laws in effect as late as 1988 in the totalitarian state of Romania as well: "No abortion, no birth control, and compulsory pregnancy testing, once a month." *The Handmaid's Tale,* Elaine Kendall explains in the *Los Angeles Times Book Review,* depicts "a future firmly based upon actuality, beginning with events that have already taken place and extending them a bit beyond the inevitable conclusions. 'The Handmaid's Tale' does not depend upon hypothetical scenarios, omens, or straws in the wind, but upon documented occurrences and public pronouncements; all matters of record." Stephen McCabe of the *Humanist* calls the novel "a chilling vision of the future extrapolated from the present."

Yet, several critics voice a disbelief in the basic assumptions of *The Handmaid's Tale.* Mary McCarthy, in her review for the *New York Times Book Review,* complains that "I just can't see the intolerance of the far right . . . as leading to a super-biblical puritanism." And although agreeing that "the author has carefully drawn her projections from current trends," McCarthy believes that "perhaps that is the trouble: the projections are too neatly penciled in. The details . . . all raise their hands announcing themselves present. At the same time, the Republic of Gilead itself, whatever in it that is not a projection, is insufficiently imagined." Richard Grenier of *Insight* objects that the Fundamentalist-run Gilead does not seem Christian: "There seems to be no Father, no Son, no Holy Ghost, no apparent belief in redemption, resurrection, eternal life. No one in this excruciatingly hierarchized new clerical state . . . appears to believe in God." Grenier also finds it improbable that "while the United States has hurtled off into this morbid, feminist nightmare, the rest of

the democratic world has been blissfully unaffected." Writing in the Toronto *Globe and Mail,* William French states that Atwood's "reach exceeds her grasp" in *The Handmaid's Tale,* "and in the end we're not clear what we're being warned against." Atwood seems to warn of the dangers of religious fanaticism, of the effects of pollution on the birthrate, and of a possible backlash to militant feminist demands. The novel, French states, "is in fact a cautionary tale about *all* these things . . . but in her scenario, they interact in an implausible way."

Despite this flaw, French sees *The Handmaid's Tale* as being "in the honorable tradition of *Brave New World* and other warnings of dystopia. It's imaginative, even audacious, and conveys a chilling sense of fear and menace." Prescott also compares *The Handmaid's Tale* to other dystopian novels. It belongs, he writes, "to that breed of visionary fiction in which a metaphor is extended to elaborate a warning. . . . Wells, Huxley and Orwell popularized the tradition with books like 'The Time Machine,' 'Brave New World' and '1984'—yet Atwood is a better novelist than they." Christopher Lehmann-Haupt sees *The Handmaid's Tale* as a book that goes far beyond its feminist concerns. Writing in the *New York Times,* Lehmann-Haupt explains that the novel "is a political tract deploring nuclear energy, environmental waste, and antifeminist attitudes. But it [is] so much more than that—a taut thriller, a psychological study, a play on words." Van Gelder agrees. The novel, she writes, "ultimately succeeds on multiple levels: as a page-turning thriller, as a powerful political statement, and as an exquisite piece of writing." Lehmann-Haupt concludes that *The Handmaid's Tale* "is easily Margaret Atwood's best novel to date."

Just as *The Handmaid's Tale* is Atwood's most direct expression of her feminism, *Survival: A Thematic Guide to Canadian Literature* is the most direct presentation of her strong belief in Canadian nationalism. In the book Atwood discerns a uniquely Canadian literature, distinct from its American and British counterparts, and she discusses the dominant themes to be found in it. Canadian literature, she argues, is primarily concerned with victims and with the victim's ability to survive. Atwood, Onley explains, "perceives a strong sado-masochistic patterning in Canadian literature as a whole. She believes that there is a national fictional tendency to participate, usually at some level as Victim, in a Victor/Victim basic pattern." But "despite its stress on victimization," Hutcheon writes "this study is not a revelation of, or a reveling in, [masochism]." What Atwood argues, Onley believes, is that "every country or culture has a single unifying and informing symbol at its core: for America, the Frontier; for England, the Island; for Canada, Survival."

Several critics find that Atwood's own work exemplifies this primary theme of Canadian literature. Her examination of destructive sex roles and her nationalistic concern over the subordinate role Canada plays to the United States are variations on the victor/victim theme. As Marge Piercy explains in the *American Poetry Review,* Atwood believes that a writer must consciously work within his or her nation's literary tradition. Atwood argues in *Survival,* Piercy writes, "that discovery of a writer's tradition may be of use, in that it makes available a conscious choice of how to deal with that body of themes. She suggests that exploring a given tradition consciously can lead to writing in new and more interesting ways." Because Atwood's own work closely parallels the themes she sees as common to the Canadian literary tradition, *Survival* "has served as the context in which critics have subsequently discussed [Atwood's] works," Hutcheon states.

Atwood's prominent stature in Canadian letters rests as much on her published works as on her efforts to define and give value to her nation's literature. "Atwood," Susan Wood states in the *Washington Post Book World,* "has emerged as a champion of Canadian literature and of the peculiarly Canadian experience of isolation and survival." Hutcheon notes Atwood's "important impact on Canadian culture" and believes that her books, "internationally known through translations, stand as testimony to Atwood's significant position in a contemporary literature which must deal with defining its own identity and defending its value."

Although she has been labelled a Canadian nationalist, a feminist, and even a gothic writer, Atwood incorporates and transcends these categories. Writing in *Saturday Night* of Atwood's several perceived roles as a writer, Linda Sandler concludes that "Atwood is all things to all people . . . a nationalist . . . a feminist or a psychologist or a comedian . . . a maker and breaker of myths . . . a gothic writer. She's all these things, but finally she's unaccountably Other. Her writing has the discipline of a social purpose but it remains elusive, complex, passionate. It has all the intensity of an act of exorcism." Atwood's work finally succeeds because it speaks of universal concerns. As Piercy explains, "Atwood is a large and remarkable writer. Her concerns are nowhere petty. Her novels and poems move and engage me deeply, can matter to people who read them."

BIOGRAPHICAL/CRITICAL SOURCES:

BOOKS

Atwood, Margaret, *The Edible Woman,* McClelland & Stewart, 1969, Atlantic-Little, Brown, 1970.

Contemporary Literary Criticism, Gale, Volume 2, 1974, Volume 3, 1975, Volume 4, 1975, Volume 8, 1978, Volume 13, 1980, Volume 15, 1980, Volume 25, 1983, Volume 44, 1987.

Davidson, Arnold E. and Cathy N. Davidson, editors, *The Art of Margaret Atwood: Essays in Criticism,* House of Anansi Press, 1981.

Dictionary of Literary Biography, Volume 53: *Canadian Writers since 1960,* Gale, 1986.

Gibson, Graeme, *Eleven Canadian Novelists,* House of Anansi Press, 1973.

Grace, Sherrill, *Violent Duality: A Study of Margaret Atwood,* Vehicule Press, 1980.

Grace, Sherrill and Lorraine Weir, editors, *Margaret Atwood: Language, Text and System,* University of British Columbia Press, 1983.

Lecker, Robert and Jack David, editors, *The Annotated Bibliography of Canada's Major Authors,* ECW, 1980.

Marshall, Tom, *Harsh and Lovely Land: The Major Canadian Poets and the Making of a Canadian Tradition,* University of British Columbia Press, 1978.

Sandler, Linda, editor, *Margaret Atwood: A Symposium,* University of British Columbia, 1977.

Twigg, Alan, *For Openers: Conversations with 24 Canadian Writers,* Harbour, 1981.

Woodcock, George, *The Canadian Novel in the Twentieth Century,* McClelland & Stewart, 1975.

PERIODICALS

American Poetry Review, November/December, 1973, March/April, 1977, September/October, 1979.

Atlantic, April, 1973.

Book Forum, Volume 4, number 1, 1978.

Books in Canada, January, 1979, June/July, 1980, March, 1981.

Canadian Forum, February, 1970, January, 1973, November/December, 1974, December/January, 1977-78, June/July, 1981, December/January, 1981-82.

Canadian Literature, autumn, 1971, spring, 1972, winter, 1973, spring, 1974, spring, 1977.

Chicago Tribune, January 27, 1980, February 3, 1980, May 16, 1982, March 19, 1989.

Chicago Tribune Book World, January 26, 1986.

Christian Science Monitor, June 12, 1977.

Commonweal, July 9, 1973.

Communique, May, 1975.

Detroit Free Press, January 26, 1986.

Detroit News, April 4, 1982.

Essays on Canadian Writing, spring, 1977.

Globe and Mail (Toronto), July 7, 1984, October 5, 1985, October 19, 1985, February 15, 1986, November 15, 1986, November 29, 1986, November 14, 1987.

Hudson Review, autumn, 1973, spring, 1975.

Humanist, September/October, 1986.

Insight, March 24, 1986.

Journal of Canadian Fiction, Volume 1, number 4, 1972.

Los Angeles Times, March 2, 1982, April, 22, 1982, May 9, 1986, January 12, 1987.

Los Angeles Times Book Review, October 17, 1982, February 9, 1986, December 23, 1987.

Maclean's, January 15, 1979, October 15, 1979, March 30, 1981.

Malahat Review, January, 1977.

Manna, Number 2, 1972.

Meanjin, Volume 37, number 2, 1978.

Modern Fiction Studies, autumn, 1976.

Ms., January, 1987.

New Leader, September 3, 1973.

New Orleans Review, Volume 5, number 3, 1977.

Newsweek, February 18, 1980, February 17, 1986.

New York Times, December 23, 1976, January 10, 1980, February 8, 1980, March 6, 1982, March 28, 1982, September 15, 1982, January 27, 1986, February 17, 1986, November 5, 1986.

New York Times Book Review, October 18, 1970, March 4, 1973, April 6, 1975, September 26, 1976, May 21, 1978, February 3, 1980, October 11, 1981, February 9, 1986.

Observer, June 13, 1982.

Ontario Review, spring/summer, 1975.

Open Letter, summer, 1973.

Parnassus: Poetry in Review, spring/summer, 1974.

People, May 19, 1980.

Poetry, March, 1970, July, 1972, May, 1982.

Publishers Weekly, August 23, 1976.

Quill and Quire, April, 1981, September, 1984.

Room of One's Own, summer, 1975.

San Francisco Review of Books, January, 1982, summer, 1982.

Saturday Night, May, 1971, July/August, 1976, September, 1976, May, 1981.

Saturday Review, September 18, 1976, February 2, 1980.

Saturday Review of the Arts, April, 1973.

Shenandoah, Volume 37, number 2, 1987.

Studies in Canadian Literature, summer, 1977.

This Magazine Is about Schools, winter, 1973.

Time, October 11, 1976.

Times (London), March 13, 1986, June 4, 1987, June 10, 1987.

Times Literary Supplement, March 21, 1986, June 12, 1987.

University of Toronto Quarterly, summer, 1978.

Village Voice, January 7, 1980.

Vogue, January, 1986.

Washington Post, April 6, 1986.

Washington Post Book World, September 26, 1976, December 3,
    1978, January 27, 1980, March 14, 1982, February 2, 1986.
Waves, autumn, 1975.
West Coast Review, January, 1973.

B

BAILLEN, Claude
See DELAY(-TUBIANA), Claude

*   *   *

BARNES, Peter 1931-

PERSONAL: Born January 10, 1931, in London, England; son of Frederick and Martha (Miller) Barnes; married Charlotte Beck, 1960.

ADDRESSES: Home—7 Archery Close, Connaught St., London W2 2BE, England. Agent—Margaret Ramsay Ltd., 14-A Goodwin's Court, London WC2 4LL, England.

CAREER: Films and Filming magazine, London, England, critic, 1954; Warwick Film Productions Ltd., London, story editor, 1956; playwright, 1963—; stage director, 1970—.

AWARDS, HONORS: John Whiting Playwrights Award, 1968, for The Ruling Class; Evening Standard Annual Drama Award for most promising playwright, 1969; The London Observer named "Red Noses" best new play, 1985; Olivier Award, 1985.

WRITINGS:

PLAYS

"The Time of the Barracudas" (two-act), first produced in San Francisco at Curran Theatre, 1963.

"Sclerosis" (one-act), first produced in Edinburgh, Scotland, at Traverse Theatre, 1963.

The Ruling Class (two-act; first produced in Nottingham, England, at Playhouse Theatre, 1968; produced in Washington, D.C., at Kreeger Theatre, 1971), Grove, 1969.

Leonardo's Last Supper and Noonday Demons (two one-acts; both first produced in London at Open Space Theatre, 1969), Heinemann, 1970.

Lulu (adaptation and consolidation of two plays by Frank Wedekind; two-act; first produced in Nottingham at Playhouse Theatre, 1970), Heinemann, 1971.

"The Devil Is an Ass" (adaptation of play by Ben Jonson; two-act), first produced in Nottingham at Playhouse Theatre, 1973.

The Bewitched (two-act; first produced in London by Royal Shakespeare Company at Aldwych Theatre, 1974), Heinemann, 1974.

(And director) The Frontiers of Farce (adaptation of plays The Purging by Georges Feydeau and The Singer by Wedekind; first produced in London, 1976), Heinemann, 1977.

(And director) "For All Those Who Get Despondent" (cabaret; adaptation of works by Bertolt Brecht and Wedekind), produced in London, 1977.

Laughter! (produced in London at Royal Court Theatre, 1978), Heinemann, 1978.

(And director) "Antonio" (adaptation of John Marston's plays Antonio and Mellida and Antonio's Revenge), produced in Nottingham, 1979.

(And director) "The Devil Himself " (revue; adaptation of works by Wedekind), produced in London, 1980.

Barnes' People: Seven Monologues (broadcast, 1981), published in Collected Plays, Heinemann, 1981 (also see below).

Collected Plays, Heinemann, 1981.

(And director) "Somersaults" (revue), produced in Leicester, England, at Haymarket Theatre, 1981.

Barnes' People II: Seven Duologues (broadcast, 1984), Heinemann, 1984.

Red Noses (produced in London, 1985), Faber, 1986.

"Scenes from a Marriage" (adaptation of Feydeau's play), produced in London at the Barbican, 1986.

Real Long John Silver and Other Plays: Barnes' People III, Faber, 1986.

(And director) "Bartholomew Fair" (adaptation of Ben Jonson's play), produced in London, 1987.

Also author and adapter of plays for radio broadcasts.

SCREENPLAYS

"Violent Moment," Anglo Amalgamated, 1958.

"The White Trap," Anglo Amalgamated, 1959.

"Breakout," Anglo Amalgamated, 1959.

"The Professionals," Anglo Amalgamated, 1961.

"Off Beat," British Lion, 1961.

"Ring of Spies," British Lion, 1965.

"Not With My Wife, You Don't," Warner Bros., 1966.

"The Ruling Class" (adaptation of own play), United Artists, 1972.

Barnes's screenplays also include "Leonardo's Last Supper," 1977, and "Spaghetti House," 1983.

OTHER

"The Man with a Feather in His Hat" (television script), British ABC, 1960.

SIDELIGHTS: David William, director of the American premier of Barnes' award winning drama *The Ruling Class* wrote: "Just as *Streetcar [Named Desire]* is about America, although not only about America, so *The Ruling Class* is about England, although not only England. England provides the local habitation and the name. But beneath the vivid, specific narrative surface of the play swirl the dangerous currents of fantasy and the subconscious. One of the special triumphs of the play is the vision and the wit with which the dramatist has incarnated the life of the psyche: its tensions and paradox, hilarity and horror. For the play is both funny and frightening: a playful nightmare.

"The appalling injury that can be done by society and the individual (or both, acting in some dreadful collusion) to society and the individual in order to perpetuate a status quo regardless of the demands of humanity and truth—this is the material out of which Peter Barnes has shaped a swift and resonant play. The silhouette never shrinks to one of propaganda; the spell is the artist's, unique and surprising."

BIOGRAPHICAL/CRITICAL SOURCES:

BOOKS

Contemporary Literary Criticism, Gale, Volume 5, 1976, Volume 56, 1989.
Dictionary of Literary Biography, Volume 13: *British Dramatists Since World War II,* Gale, 1982.
Dukore, Bernard F., *The Theatre of Peter Barnes,* Heinemann, 1981.

PERIODICALS

Times (London), October 25, 1986, June 3, 1987.

* * *

BARON, David
See PINTER, Harold

* * *

BASSANI, Giorgio 1916-
(Giacomo Marchi)

PERSONAL: Born April 4, 1916, in Bologna, Italy. *Education:* Graduated from University of Bologna.

ADDRESSES: Home—Via G. B. DeRossi 33, Rome, Italy.

CAREER: Novelist and poet. Accademia Nazionale d'Arte Drammatica, Rome, Italy, instructor in history of theatre, 1957-68; Radio Televisione Italiana, Rome, vice-president, 1964-65.

AWARDS, HONORS: Charles Veillon prize in Italian literature, 1955, for *Gli ultimi anni di Clelia Trotti;* Strega prize, 1956, for *Cinque storie ferraresi;* Viareggio prize, 1962, for *Il giardino dei Finzi-Contini;* Campiello prize, 1969, for *L'airone;* Nelly Sachs prize, 1969; also recipient of Premi Roma.

WRITINGS:

(Under pseudonym Giacomo Marchi) *Una citta di rianura,* [Italy], 1940.
Storie dei poveri amanti e altri versi (poetry), Astrolabio (Rome), 1946.
Te lucis ante (poetry), [Italy], 1947.

Un altra liberta (poetry), [Italy], 1951.
(Author of introduction) *Giovanni Omiccioli,* De Luca (Rome), 1952.
Gli ultimi anni di Clelia Trotti (novella; also see below), Nistri-Lischi (Pisa), 1955.
Cinque storie ferraresi (short stories), Einaudi (Rome), 1956, published as *Dentro le mura,* Mondadori (Milan), 1973, translation by Isabel Quigly published as *A Prospect of Ferrara,* Faber, 1962, translation by William Weaver published as *Five Stories of Ferrara,* Harcourt, 1971.
Gli occhiali d'oro (novel), Einaudi, 1958, 2nd edition, 1962, translation by Quigly published as *The Gold-Rimmed Spectacles,* Atheneum, 1960.
Le storie ferraresi (novellas; includes *Gli ultimi anni di Clelia Trotti*), Einaudi, 1960.
Una notte del '43 (novella), Einaudi, 1960.
(Author of introduction) Mimi Quilici Buzzacchi, *Paesaggio di Spina,* De Luca, 1962.
Il giardino dei Finzi-Contini (novel), Einaudi, 1962, translation by Quigly published as *The Garden of the Finzi-Continis,* Atheneum, 1965.
L'alba ai vetri: Poesie 1942-1950, Einaudi, 1963.
Dietro la porta (novel), Einaudi, 1964, translation by Weaver published as *Behind the Door,* Harcourt, 1972.
Due novelle, Stamperia di Venezia (Venice), 1965.
Le parole preparate, e altri seritti di letteratura, Einaudi, 1966.
L'airone (novel), Mondadori, 1968, translation by Weaver published as *The Heron,* Harcourt, 1970.
Giorgio Bassani: Ansprachen und Dokumente zur Verleihung des Kulturpreises der Stadt Dortmund, Nelly-Sachs-Preis, am 7. Dezember 1969, Stadt- und Landesbibliothek (Dortmund), 1971.
L'odore del fieno (short stories), Mondadori, 1972, translation by Weaver published as *The Smell of Hay,* Harcourt, 1975.
Epitaffio (poetry; also see below), Mondadori, 1974.
Il romanzo di Ferrara, Mondadori, 1974.
In gran segreto (poetry; also see below), Mondadori, 1978.
In rima e senza (poetry), Mondadori, 1982.
Rolls Royce and Other Poems (contains selections from *Epitaffio* and *In gran segreto* in English and Italian), translation by Francesca Valente and others, Aya Press, 1982.
Di la dal cuore, Mondadori, 1984.
Italian Stories, Schocken, 1989.

Editor of journal *Botteghe Oscure* from its founding; editor of *Paragone,* 1953-71.

MEDIA ADAPTATIONS: The Garden of the Finzi-Continis was adapted for film by Vittorio De Sica, c. 1970.

BIOGRAPHICAL/CRITICAL SOURCES:

BOOKS

Contemporary Literary Criticism, Volume 9, Gale, 1978.

* * *

BECKETT, Samuel (Barclay) 1906-1989

PERSONAL: Born April 13, 1906, in Foxrock, Dublin, Ireland; died of respiratory failure, December 22, 1989, in Paris, France; son of William Frank (a quantity surveyor) and Mary (an interpreter for the Irish Red Cross; maiden name Roe) Beckett; married Suzanne Dechevaux-Dumesnil (a pianist). *Education:* Attended Portora Royal School, County Fermanagh, Ireland; Trinity College, Dublin, B.A. (French and Italian), 1927, M.A., 1931.

CAREER: Ecole Normale Superieure, Paris, France, lecturer in English, 1928-30; Trinity College, University of Dublin, Dublin, Ireland, lecturer in French, 1930-32 (resigned because "he could not bear the absurdity of teaching to others what he did not know himself"). During the early 1930s he, among others, helped James Joyce, who was then nearly blind, by taking dictation and by copying out parts of *Finnegans Wake.* (Beckett never served as secretary to Joyce as many believe. A. J. Leventhal, writing for Beckett, told *CA* that "there was never any question of a formal position. . . . It's very hard to kill this story.") From 1932 to 1936 Beckett traveled extensively in England and Europe, residing briefly in London and in several European cities. He settled permanently in Paris in 1937. From about 1940 to 1943, Beckett was involved with the French resistance movement and had to hide from the Germans. He spent these years working as a farm hand near Roussillon, an isolated region in southeast France. Since the early 1940s, Beckett has devoted most of his time to writing. *Wartime service:* Storekeeper and interpreter for Irish Red Cross Hospital, St. Lo, France, 1945-46; decorated.

AWARDS, HONORS: Hours Press (Paris) award for the best poem concerning time, 1930, for "Whoroscope"; Italia Prize, 1957, for "All that Fall," and 1959, for "Embers"; *Village Voice* Off-Broadway (Obie) awards for best new play, 1958, for "Endgame," and 1964, for "Play," for distinguished play, 1960, for "Krapp's Last Tape," and for best foreign play, 1962, for "Happy Days"; Litt.D., Trinity College, Dublin, 1959; International Publishers prize, 1961 (shared with Jorge Luis Borges), for all literary work, especially *Molloy, Malone meurt, L'Innommable,* and *Comment c'est.*

WRITINGS:

NOVELS

Murphy (written in English), Routledge & Kegan Paul, 1938, Grove, 1957, French translation by Beckett, Bordas (Paris), 1947.

Molloy (fragment of an earlier version published in *transition,* number 6, 1950, together with an early fragment of *Malone Dies* under collective title, "Two Fragments"; also see below), Editions de Minuit, 1951, English translation by Beckett and Patrick Bowles, Grove, 1955.

Malone meurt, Editions de Minuit, 1951, English translation by Beckett published as *Malone Dies,* Grove, 1956.

Watt (written in English), Olympia Press (Paris), 1953, Grove, 1959, rewritten, and translated into French by the author, Editions de Minuit, 1968.

L'Innommable, Editions de Minuit, 1953, English translation by Beckett published as *The Unnameable,* Grove, 1958.

Three Novels: Molloy, Malone Dies, [and] *The Unnameable,* Grove, 1959.

Comment c'est, Editions de Minuit, 1961, English translation by Beckett published as *How It Is,* Grove, 1964 (excerpts published in *X* [a London magazine], number 1, 1959, and, under title "From an Unabandoned Work," in *Evergreen Review,* September-October, 1960).

Imagination morte imaginez (although only 14 pages long, Beckett called this work a novel), Editions de Minuit, 1965, English translation by Beckett published as *Imagination Dead Imagine,* Calder & Boyars, 1965.

Mercier et Camier, Minuit, 1970, translation by Beckett published as *Mercier and Camier,* Calder & Boyars, 1974, Grove, 1975.

PLAYS

"Le Kid," produced in Dublin, 1931.

En Attendant Godot (first produced in Paris at Theatre de Babylone, January 5, 1953), Editions de Minuit, 1952, English translation by Beckett entitled *Waiting for Godot* (U.S. premiere in Miami Beach, Florida, at Coconut Grove Playhouse, January, 1956; Broadway production at John Golden Theatre, April, 1956), Grove, 1954.

All That Fall (radio play written in English; produced in London for BBC Third Programme, January 13, 1957), Grove, 1957, updated for American radio, 1968-69, French translation by Robert Pinget and Beckett published as *Tous ceux qui tombent,* Editions de Minuit, 1957.

Fin de partie [and] *Acte sans paroles* (both first produced in French on double bill in London at Royal Court Theatre, April 3, 1957), Editions de Minuit, 1957, English translation by Beckett published as *Endgame* [and] *Act Without Words* ("Endgame," a play in one act, produced in New York at Cherry Lane Theatre, 1958; "Act Without Words," a mime for one player, with music by John Beckett, produced in New York at Living Theatre, 1959), Grove, 1958.

From an Abandoned Work (written in English; produced in London for BBC Third Programme, 1957), first published in *Evergreen Review,* Volume 1, number 3, 1957, Faber & Faber, 1958.

Krapp's Last Tape [and] *Embers* (both written in English; "Krapp's Last Tape" first produced in London at Royal Court Theatre, October 28, 1958, then at Provincetown Playhouse, 1960; "Embers" first produced in London for BBC Third Programme, June 24, 1959), Faber & Faber, 1959, published as *Krapp's Last Tape and Other Dramatic Pieces* (also contains "All that Fall," "Act Without Words [I]," and "Act Without Words II" [written in English]), Grove, 1960.

Happy Days (written in English; first produced in New York at Cherry Lane Theatre, September 17, 1961), Grove, 1961, French translation by Beckett published as *Oh les beaux jours,* Editions de Minuit, 1963.

Dramatische Dichtungen (trilingual edition of dramatic works originally published in French; German translations by Elmar Tophoven), Suhrkamp Verlag, 1963-64.

Play and Two Short Pieces for Radio (written in English; contains "Play" [first produced in Ulm, Germany, 1963, then in New York at Cherry Lane Theatre, 1964], "Words and Music" [first published in *Evergreen Review,* November-December, 1962], and "Cascando" [first published in *Dublin Magazine,* October-December, 1936; also see below]), Faber & Faber, 1964.

"Film" (22-minute mime adaptation, by Mariu Karmitz, of "Play"), directed by Alan Schneider for Evergreen Theatres, and starring Buster Keaton, M. K. Productions, 1966.

Comedie et actes divers (contains "Comedie," "Va et vient," "Cascando" [French translation by Beckett of play included in *Play and Two Short Pieces for Radio*], "Paroles et musiques [French translation by Beckett of "Words and Music"], "Dis Joe" [French translation by Beckett of "Eh, Joe?"; also see below], and "Acte sans paroles II" [French translation by Beckett of "Act Without Words II"]; also see below), Editions de Minuit, 1966.

Eh, Joe? and Other Writings (written in English for television; first produced by New York Television Theatre, 1966; also see below), Faber & Faber, 1967.

Come and Go (121-word "dramaticule," first published in French as "Va et vient" in *Comedie et actes divers*), Calder & Boyars, 1967.

Cascando and Other Short Dramatic Pieces, Grove, 1968.

Breath and Other Shorts, Faber, 1971.

Not I, Faber, 1971.

That Time, Faber, 1976.

Footfalls, Faber, 1976.

Ends and Odds: Eight New Dramatic Pieces, Faber, 1977.

Rockaby and Other Short Pieces, Grove, 1981.

Catastrophe et autres dramaticules: Cette fois, Solo, Berceuse, Impromptu d'Ohio, Editions de Minuit, 1982.

Three Occasional Pieces, Faber, 1982.

Collected Shorter Plays, Grove, 1984.

Ohio Impromptu, Catastrophe, and What Where, Grove, 1984.

The Complete Dramatic Works, Faber, 1986.

"Rough for Radio II" (radio play), National Public Radio (NPR), 1989.

Also author of "Eleutheria" (French language play), c. 1947. Many of Beckett's works have been adapted for radio and television broadcast.

OTHER

(Contributor) *Our Exagmination round His Factification for Incamination of Work in Progress* (on James Joyce and *Finnegans Wake*), Shakespeare & Co. (Paris), 1929, New Directions, 1939, 2nd edition, 1962.

Whoroscope: Poem on Time (written in English), Hours Press (Paris), 1930.

Proust (criticism, written in English), Chatto & Windus, 1931, Grove, 1957.

More Pricks Than Kicks (ten short stories, written in English), Chatto & Windus, 1934, special edition, Calder & Boyars, 1966.

Echo's Bones and Other Precipitates (poems, written in English), Europa Press (Paris), 1935.

Nouvelles et textes pour rien (fiction; contains "L'Expulse," "Le Calmant," and "La Fin," and thirteen monologues), Editions de Minuit, 1955, translation by Beckett and others published in England as *No's Knife: Collected Shorter Prose, 1947-1965* (also includes "From an Abandoned Work," "Enough," "Imagination Dead Imagine," and "Ping"; also see below), Calder & Boyars, 1967, published as *Stories and Texts for Nothing,* Grove, 1967.

A Samuel Beckett Reader, edited by John Calder, Calder & Boyars, 1967.

(With Georges Duthuit and Jacques Putnam) *Bram van Velde* (criticism of the painter's work), Falaise (Paris), 1958, English translation by Olive Chase and Beckett, Grove, 1960.

Henri Hayden, Waddington Galleries, 1959.

Gedichte (in French and German; contains "Echo's Bones" and 18 poems written between 1937 and 1949; German translations by Eva Hesse), Limes Verlag (Wiesbaden), 1959.

Poems in English, Calder & Boyars, 1961, Grove, 1962.

(With Georges Duthuit) *Proust and Three Dialogues* (criticism), Calder & Boyars, 1965.

Assez, Editions de Minuit, 1966.

Ping, Editions de Minuit, 1966.

Tete-mortes (includes *Imagination morte imaginez, bing, Assez,* and a new novella, *Tete-mortes*), Editions de Minuit, 1967.

Poemes, Editions de Minuit, 1968.

L'Issue, Georges Visat, 1968.

Sans, Editions de Minuit, 1969, translation by Beckett published as *Lessness,* Calder & Boyars, 1971.

Sejour, Georges Richar, 1970.

Premier amour, Editions de Minuit, 1970, translation by Beckett published as *First Love,* Calder & Boyars, 1973.

Le Depeupleur, Editions de Minuit, translation by Beckett published as *The Lost Ones,* Grove, 1972.

The North, Enitharmon Press, 1972.

Abandonne, Georges Visat, 1972.

Au loin un oiseau, Double Elephant Press, 1973.

First Love and Other Shorts, Grove, 1974.

Fizzles, Grove, 1976.

For to End Yet Again and Other Fizzles, Calder, 1976.

I Can't Go On: A Selection from the Works of Samuel Beckett, edited by Richard Seaver, Grove Press, 1976.

All Strange Away, Gotham Book Mart, 1976.

Collected Poems in English and French, Grove, 1977, revised edition published as *Collected Poems 1930-1978,* Calder, 1984.

Four Novellas, Calder, 1977, published as *The Expelled and Other Novellas,* Penguin, 1980.

Six Residua, Calder, 1978.

Company, Grove, 1980.

Mal vu mal dit, Editions de Minuit, 1981, translation by Beckett published as *Ill Seen Ill Said,* Grove, 1982.

Worstward Ho, Grove, 1983.

Disjecta: Miscellaneous Writings and a Dramatic Fragment, edited by Ruby Cohn, Calder, 1983, Grove, 1984.

Collected Shorter Prose 1945-1980, Calder, 1984.

Happy Days: The Production Notebook, edited by James Knowlson, Faber, 1985, Grove, 1986.

Nohow On: Company; Ill Seen Ill Said (short fiction), J. Calder, 1989.

Stirrings Still, J. Calder/Blue Moon Books, 1989.

Also author of the short story "Premier amour" which was perhaps intended to complete a quartet begun with "L'Expulse," "Le Calmant," and "La Fin." Contributor to *transition, New Review, Evergreen Review, Contempo, Les Temps Modernes, Merlin, Spectrum,* and other periodicals.

SIDELIGHTS: "He wanders among misty bogs turned surreal, he talks to the wee folk of his own bad dreams, he files reports on introspected black visions with a kind of blarney eloquence. Like an actress cradling a doll for her stage baby, his language keens and croons about tales that are not quite there." Melvin Maddocks is talking about Samuel Beckett. "It is neither night nor morning. A man must find himself without the support of groups, or labels, or slogans," writes R. D. Smith. And Beckett, by removing his characters from nearly all recognizable contexts, Smith continues, is "engaged in finding or saving" himself. Martin Esslin writes: "What is the essence of the experience of being? asks Beckett. And so he begins to strip away the inessentials. What is the meaning of the phrase 'I am myself'? he asks . . . and is then compelled to try to distinguish between the merely accidental characteristics that make up an individual and the essence of his self." The *Time* reviewer noted: "Some chronicle men on their way up; others tackle men on their way down. Samuel Beckett stalks after men on their way out." Such is the tone of most discussions of Beckett's work. But no reviewer could communicate the unique power of Beckett's writing, his use of "a language in which the emptiness of conventional speech is charged with new emotion." "While [his] lesser colleagues work in rhetoric," writes Smith, Beckett produces poetry. "Well," says Harold Pinter, "I'll buy his goods, hook, line, and sinker, because he leaves no stone unturned and no maggot lonely. He brings forth a body of beauty. His work is beautiful." Leo Bersani, somewhat less politely, writes: "I know of no writer who has come closer than Beckett in his novels to translating the rhythms of defecation into sentence structure." And B. S. Johnson thinks Beckett is "the greatest prose stylist and the most original writer living."

Along with the work of Ionesco, Genet, and Pinter, Beckett's stark plays are said to compose the "Theatre of the Absurd." But to so label Beckett's work is to disqualify one of his own first premises—that, since no human activity has any intrinsic meaning, it is pointless to ascribe traditional or categorical significance to the existence of an object or the performance of a deed. George Wellwarth discusses Beckett's concept of a protean reality: "What all these things—the sameness of human beings and their actions, the vanity of human ambition, the uselessness of thought—amount to is a pessimism deeper than any that has ever been put into words before. Throughout Beckett's work we can find evidence of his conviction that everything is hopeless, meaningless, purposeless, and, above all, agonizing to endure. Beckett's people are leveled off and merged into each other by being all more or less physically disabled—as if this were really the common condition on earth. . . . Beckett is a prophet of negation and sterility. He holds out no hope to humanity, only a picture of unrelieved blackness; and those who profess to see in Beckett signs of a Christian approach or signs of compassion are simply refusing to see what is there." Perhaps Beckett himself states his dilemma most succinctly in *L'Innommable:* "Dans ma vie, puisqu'il faut l'appeler ainsi, il y eut trois choses, l'impossibilite de parler, l'impossibilite de me taire, et la solitude." One must speak; man cannot possibly communicate with his fellows, but the alternative—silence—is irreconcilable with human existence.

Smith and Esslin, however, insist that Beckett does not intend to express unqualified despair, but that, by stripping significance from the world, he is showing us the one way to achieve redemption (although any salvation, according to Beckett's essentially deterministic philosophy, is necessarily only a respite). Smith writes: "Beckett's characters remain at their darkest moments anguished human beings: Beckett, when intellectually at his most pitiless, feels and suffers with them." And Esslin states that Beckett's message "is anything but gloomy or despairing." He writes: "On the contrary: the starkness of [his] reminders of the evanescence of life and the certainty of death, [his] uncompromising rejection of any easy solution or cheap illusion of comfort ultimately has a liberating effect; such is the nature of man that in the very act of facing up to the reality of his condition his dignity is enhanced; we are only defeated by things by which we are taken unawares; what we know and have faced up to we can master." Alec Reid also believes that Beckett's message must be interpreted optimistically. "Beckett's world," he writes, "is one of darkness, of disembodied voices, of ignorance, impotence, and anguish. But even as he insists that he knows nothing, can know nothing, Beckett reminds us of an astronaut, a human surrounded by nothing, walking on nothing. Our spacemen are no cause for despair; no more are Mr. Beckett's explorations." But then, according to *Time* magazine, "Beckett's champions argue that his threnodies in dusky twilight represent the existential metaphor of the human condition, that the thin but unwavering voices of his forlorn characters speak the ultimate statement of affirmation, if only because the merest attempt at communication is itself affirmation."

But in case the reader of Beckett criticism should come to regard this question as the black and white one of "despair" versus "optimism," Richard N. Coe adds new terms to the argument: "To class Beckett himself as the simple incarnation of 'despair' is a drastic oversimplification. To begin with, the concept of 'despair' implies the existence of a related concept 'hope,' and 'hope' implies a certain predictable continuity in time—which continuity

Beckett would seriously question. 'Despair,' with all its inherent moral overtones, is a term which is wholly inadequate to describe Beckett's attitude towards the human condition; nor is this condition, in the most current sense of the definition, 'absurd.' It is literally and logically impossible. And in this central concept of 'impossibility,' his thought has most of its origins—as does also his art."

Although John Gassner was not happy with the scholarly complexity of the critical response to Beckett's work (he wrote: "To a parvenu intelligentsia, it would seem that a work of art exists not for its own sake but only for the possibilities of interpreting it"), some critics believe that Beckett's theater is most meaningful when considered within the context of a recognizable literary tradition. Kenneth Allsop writes: "His harsh, desolate, denuded style is entirely and unmistakably his own, but his literary 'form,' the stream-of-consciousness device which most young British writers wouldn't dream of using nowadays for fear of being thought quaint, derives from his years as secretary to James Joyce. That is only a partial explanation. He is in a monolithic way the last of the Left Bank Mohicans of the Twenties; the others of the *avant-garde* died or deserted or prospered, but Beckett was a loyal expatriate." Esslin, J. D. O'Hara, and John Fletcher prefer to align Beckett with the philosophers. "Although Beckett himself is not aware of any such influence," Esslin writes, "his writings might be described as a literary exposition of Sartre's Existentialism." O'Hara sees his work as exponential to the philosophy of Descartes: "In Beckett's world of post-Cartesian dualism, the mind has no connection to the body, its values worth nothing there, and so it cannot logically concern itself with the body's problems." Fletcher concludes that "whatever the truth of the matter, one thing is certain. Beckett has ranged freely among the writings of the philosophers, where he has found confirmation and justification of the metaphysical obsessions that haunt his work: the gulf set between body and mind, the epistemological incertitude. His genius has achieved the transmutation of such speculative problems into art." But, according to Coe, one must keep in mind that "Beckett has renounced his claim to erudition. The main theme of his work is impotence, of mind just as much as of body."

The problem of analyzing and interpreting Beckett's work, on the other hand, has been met with a somewhat surprising amount of scholarship and erudition. But David Hesla's criticism, in which the novels are considered as the expression of Beckett's personal enigma, is equally effective. Hesla notes that the dilemma which confronts the contemporary writer, according to Beckett, "is constituted . . . by the fact that the writer must take seriously two opposed and apparently irreconcilable claims to his allegiance. On the one hand, he must recognize that the principal fact about modern man's life is that it is a 'mess,' a 'confusion,' a 'chaos.' On the other hand, the writer, as artist, has an obligation to form. But to admit the 'mess' into art is to jeopardize the very nature of art; for the mess 'appears to be the very opposite of form and therefore destructive of the very thing that art holds itself to be.' " Hesla quotes Beckett as saying: "It only means that there will be a new form; and that this form will be of such a type that it admits the chaos and does not try to say that the chaos is really something else. The form and the chaos remain separate. The latter is not reduced to the former. That is why the form itself becomes a preoccupation, because it exists as a problem separate from the material it accommodates. To find a form that accommodates the mess, that is the task of the artist now." Hesla notes that with *Watt* "Beckett has begun a process of removing from his artificial world those tangibles by which the reader usually is able to orient himself in time and space, and those causal relationships amongst the incidents of the plot by which the reader is able to discern the conditions of necessity and probability which—be they never so strained or extraordinary—determine in part the structural coherence and the 'meaning' of the story. . . . In *Watt* he has found the form which permits 'the mess' to enter art without destroying it. He has developed a literary method—the negative way—which is capable of accommodating chaos without reducing it to form. Furthermore, in developing this method he has developed an instrument of greater precision for the explication of a world-view which was only roughly sketched out in *Murphy.* Beckett's work after *Watt* has, in a certain sense, consisted largely in refining and adapting both the manner and the matter of his new art."

Most critics agree that it was with the publication of *Waiting for Godot* that Beckett's prominence was established in the United States. Many, in fact, still consider this play to be his most important work. H. A. Smith calls it "the most comprehensively and profoundly evocative play of the last thirty years," and William R. Mueller and Josephine Jacobsen write: "*Waiting for Godot,* of all of Beckett's dramatic works, expresses most clearly and explicitly the fundamental tension—to wait or not to wait—which is found to a lesser degree in his other writings. The human predicament described in Beckett's first play is that of man living on the Saturday after the Friday of the crucifixion, and not really knowing if all hope is dead or if the next day will bring the new life which has been promised," Allsop found the play's message less ambiguous. He writes: "*Godot* is a hymn to extol the moment when the mind swings off its hinges. . . . Beckett is unconcerned with writing requiems for humanity, for he sees life as polluted and pointless: he merely scrawls its obituary, without bitterness or compassion because he cannot really believe it is worth the words he is wasting." Gassner also found the play to be a straightforward pronouncement, but he did not accept it as a prediction of certain doom. "To all this tohu and bohu about the profundity and difficulty of the play," he wrote, "my reply is simply that there is nothing painfully or exhilaratingly ambiguous about *Waiting for Godot* in the first place. It presents the view that man, the hapless wanderer in the universe, brings his quite wonderful humanity—his human capacity for hope, patience, resilience, and, yes, for love of one's kind, too, as well as his animal nature—to the weird journey of existence. He is lost in the universe and found in his own heart and in the hearts of his fellow men." Bert O. States adds parenthetically: "Convicts and children love it!"

Kenneth Tynan believes that the implications of *Waiting for Godot* are significant not only in themselves, but for all of contemporary theater. He writes: "A special virtue attaches to plays which remind the drama of how much it can do without and still exist. By all known criteria, Beckett's *Waiting for Godot* is a dramatic vacuum. Pity the critic who seeks a chink in its armour, for it is all chink. It has no plot, no climax, no *denouement;* no beginning, no middle, and no end. Unavoidably, it has a situation, and it might be accused of having suspense. . . . *Waiting for Godot* frankly jettisons everything by which we recognise theatre. It arrives at the custom-house, as it were, with no luggage, no passport, and nothing to declare; yet it gets through, as might a pilgrim from Mars. It does this, I believe, by appealing to a definition of drama much more fundamental than any in the books. A play, it asserts and proves, is basically a means of spending two hours in the dark without being bored. . . . It forced me to reexamine the rules which have hitherto governed the drama; and, having done so, to pronounce them not elastic enough."

Some critics found *Endgame* to be an even more powerful expression of Beckett's negativism. Gassner wrote: "Nothing happens in *Endgame* and that nothing is what matters. The author's feeling about nothing also matters, not because it is true or right but because it is a strongly formed attitude, a felt and expressed viewpoint. . . . The yardsticks of dialectical materialism and moralism are equally out in appraising the play. Dialectical materialism could only say that *Endgame* is decadent. Moralism and theology would say that the play is sinful, since nothing damns the soul so much as despair of salvation. Neither yardstick could tell us that this hauntingly powerful work of the imagination is art."

Although critics discuss his plays more frequently than his novels, Beckett himself considers his novels to be his major work. Alec Reid notes: "For Beckett each novel is a journey into the unknown, into an area of utter lawlessness." And the *Times Literary Supplement* reviewer, in his discussion of *Imagination Dead Imagine,* summarizes Beckett's work thus: "[This novel] certainly describes two people in an imaginary situation and it is equally certainly a work of large implications and a desolate, cruel beauty. It might not seem so, however, if it had not been apparent for some time that Mr. Beckett's prose narratives compose a single, long saga of exclusion and heroic relinquishment as well as of the desperate, perhaps unavailing, pursuit of finality." A. I. Leventhal writes: "When Beckett changes to writing his novels in French he leaves behind him much of the humour, grim as it was, in his previous work. He has less interest in making his characters indulge in games to pass the time as in *Waiting for Godot.* They are now concentrating on their *penible* task of dying." Frank Kermode offers this analysis of the novels: "In Beckett's plays the theatrical demand for communicable rhythms and relatively crude satisfactions has had a beneficent effect. But in the novels he yields progressively to the magnetic pull of the primitive, to the desire to achieve, by various forms of decadence and deformation, some Work that eludes the intellect, avoids the spread nets of habitual meaning. Beckett is often allegorical, but he is allegorical in fitful patches, providing illusive toeholds to any reader scrambling for sense." Bersani hasn't discovered the toeholds (and laughs behind his hand at those who have), nor does he think he will, if, as he says, he continues to take Beckett "seriously." Bersani writes: "The most interesting fact about Samuel Beckett's novels is that they are, at their best, almost completely unreadable." Bersani, citing Beckett's expressed desire to fail (to be an artist, for Beckett, is to fail), finds his "extreme attempt to render literature autonomous" to be not only "an ironic reminder of the ultimate dependence of literature on life," but also a generally suspicious undertaking. "The attempt to eliminate 'occasion' from art," he writes, "is in itself an occasion, and insofar as this attempt is a process of what [Ruby] Cohn has called progressive 'retrenchment,' the process rather than the achievement becomes the subject of Beckett's work."

The fact that most of Beckett's important work was originally written in French is far more than coincidentally significant to his stylistic achievement. Coe explains: "Beckett, in the final analysis, is trying to say what cannot be said; he must be constantly on his guard, therefore, never to yield to the temptation of saying what the words would make him say. Only when language is, as it were, defeated, bound hand and foot; only when it is so rigorously disciplined that each word describes exactly and quasiscientifically the precise concept to which it is related and no other, only then, by the progressive elimination of that which precisely is, is there a remote chance for the human mind to divine the ultimate reality which is not. And this relentless, almost masochistic discipline, which reaches its culmination in *Comment c'est,* Beckett achieves by writing in a language which is not his own—in French." John Barth explains, however, that Beckett's denuded French is yet only another step in his creative process and must not be construed as a total achievement. Barth writes: "Beckett has become virtually mute, musewise, having progressed from marvelously constructed English sentences through terser and terser French ones to the unsyntactical, unpunctuated prose of *Comment c'est* and 'ultimately' to wordless mimes. One might extrapolate a theoretical course for Beckett: language, after all, consists of silence as well as sound, and the mime is still communication, . . . but by the language of action. But the language of action consists of rest as well as movement, and so in the context of Beckett's progress immobile, silent figures still aren't altogether ultimate. . . . For Beckett, at this point in his career, to cease to create altogether would be fairly meaningful: his crowning work, his 'last word.' What a convenient corner to paint yourself into!"

Few critics have discussed Beckett's ideas (or the man himself) apart from their manifestation in his work. And Beckett would doubtless have it so. As Robert Wernick writes, "so striking is the personality that emerges from [his] gloomy plays and so striking is the occasionally glimpsed, gaunt pterodactylous face of the real-life Samuel Beckett that many people assume the two are identical. A whole folklore of anecdote has grown up around Beckett, in which he appears as a fanatic solitary, brooding eternally . . . on the black mystery of the human race. . . . It is true that he has built a wall around his country house, but he denies that he built it, as people contend, to shut out the view. It is true he avoids all the trappings of the celebrity life, gives no interviews, attends no cultural congresses. But then, why should he?" Alec Reid met Beckett in New York during the making of "Film" and described him as "a close- knit person, all of a piece." Reid says that Beckett "believes that physical movement conveys at least as much as the words. . . . Once the initial reserve has evaporated Beckett reveals a genius for companionship, a remarkable ability to make those around him feel the better for his presence."

In 1967 the Firehouse Theatre of Minneapolis, directed by Marlow Hotchkiss, performed *Act Without Words I* and *Act Without Words II* simultaneously. Also in 1967, Jack Emery composed and performed an hour-long, one-man program consisting of "a selection of the desperate reveries and furious tirades of half a dozen of Samuel Beckett's dying heroes," including Malone, Hamm, and the Unnameable. The *Punch* reviewer writes: "Many of the passages are fatiguing to follow in the original novels but so conversational are the rhythms of Beckett's language and so eloquently does Mr. Emery speak them (except when he essays a scream) that the effect in a dark, hushed theatre of this grim gallows humour is electrifying. There is more to life than talking of waiting for death, but Beckett has phrases—'Vent the pent!'—that resound in the mind with the urgency of great poetry." Emery's program, which premiered at Arts Theatre, London, was also produced in Glasgow, Edinburgh, and Exeter.

BIOGRAPHICAL/CRITICAL SOURCES:

BOOKS

Allsop, Kenneth, *The Angry Decade,* Copp, 1958.
Armstrong, William A., and others, editors, *Experimental Drama,* G. Bell, 1963.
Beckett at Sixty (a festschrift by twenty-four of his friends), Calder & Boyars, 1967.
Coe, Richard N., *Beckett,* Oliver & Boyd, 1964.
Cohn, Ruby, *Samuel Beckett: The Comic Gamut,* Rutgers University Press, 1962.

Contemporary Literary Criticism, Gale, Volume 1, 1973, Volume 2, 1974, Volume 3, 1975, Volume 4, 1975, Volume 6, 1976, Volume 9, 1978, Volume 10, 1979, Volume 11, 1979, Volume 14, 1980, Volume 18, 1981, Volume 29, 1984.
Dictionary of Literary Biography, Gale, Volume 13: *British Dramatists since World War II,* 1982, Volume 15: *British Novelists, 1930-1959,* 1983.
Esslin, Martin, *The Theatre of the Absurd,* Doubleday-Anchor, 1961.
Fletcher, John, *Samuel Beckett's Art,* Barnes & Noble, 1967.
Gassner, John, *Theatre at the Crossroads,* Holt, 1960.
Guicharnaud, Jacques, and June Beckelman, *Modern French Theatre from Giraudoux to Beckett,* Yale University Press, 1961.
Hoffman, Frederick J., *Samuel Beckett: The Language of Self,* Southern Illinois University Press, 1962.
Kenner, Hugh, *Samuel Beckett,* J. Calder, 1962.
Kermode, Frank, *Puzzles and Epiphanies,* Chilmark, 1962.
Kostelanetz, Richard, editor, *On Contemporary Literature,* Avon, 1954.
Lumley, Frederick, *New Trends in Twentieth-Century Drama,* Oxford University Press, 1967.
Simpson, Alan, *Beckett and Behan and a Theatre in Dublin,* Routledge & Kegan Paul, 1962.
Smith, H. A., and R. D. Smith, contributors, *Contemporary Theatre,* Stratford-upon-Avon Studies 4, edited by John Russell Brown and Bernard Harris, Edward Arnold, 1962.
Tindall, William York, *Samuel Beckett,* Columbia University Press, 1964.
Tynan, Kenneth, *Curtains,* Atheneum, 1961.
Wellwarth, George, *Theatre of Protest and Paradox,* New York University Press, 1964.

PERIODICALS

Atlantic, August, 1967.
Carleton Miscellany, winter, 1967.
Christian Science Monitor, July 27, 1967.
Comparative Literature, winter, 1965.
Critique, spring, 1963, winter, 1964-65.
Esquire, September, 1967.
Hudson Review, spring, 1967.
Kenyon Review, March, 1967.
Life, February 2, 1968.
Listener, August 3, 1967.
Livres de France, January, 1967.
London Magazine, August, 1967.
Manchester Guardian, April 21, 1966.
New Statesman, February 14, 1964, March 25, 1966, July 14, 1967.
New York Review of Books, March 19, 1964, December 7, 1967.
New York Times, July 21, 1964, February 27, 1966, April 19, 1966, July 20, 1967, September 14, 1967.
Observer, July 16, 1967.
Partisan Review, spring, 1966.
Punch, August 2, 1967.
Saturday Review, October 4, 1958.
Time, July 14, 1967.
Times Literary Supplement, December 21, 1962, January 30, 1964, June 30, 1966.
Tri-Quarterly, winter, 1967.
Tulane Drama Review, summer, 1967.
Village Voice, April 6, 1967, July 13, 1967.

PERIODICALS

Chicago Tribune, December 27, 1989.
Los Angeles Times, December 27, 1989.
New York Times, December 27, 1989.

*   *   *

BEHAN, Brendan   1923-1964

PERSONAL: Born February 9, 1923, in Dublin, Ireland; died of alcoholism, jaundice, and diabetes, March 20, 1964; son of Stephen (a house painter, labor leader, and soldier) and Kathleen (Kearney) Behan; married Beatrice ffrench-Salkeld (a painter); children: one daughter. *Education:* Attended Irish Catholic schools. *Religion:* Roman Catholic.

ADDRESSES: Home—London, England.

CAREER: Apprenticed as a house painter, 1937; arrested in Liverpool, England, 1939, convicted of possessing explosives and sent to Borstal (a reform school), 1939-42; arrested and convicted in Dublin, 1942, for revolutionary activities and sentenced to three years in an Irish prison, 1942-45; worked as house painter, seaman, free-lance journalist, and writer, 1945-64.

MEMBER: Fianna Eireann (youth organization), Irish Republican Army (IRA).

WRITINGS:

The Quare Fellow: A Comedy-Drama (three-act play; first produced in Dublin at Pike Theatre, 1954), Grove, 1956.
Borstal Boy, Hutchinson, 1958, Knopf, 1959.
The Hostage (three-act play; first produced in Dublin, 1958), Grove, 1958, third revised edition, Methuen, 1962.
Brendan Behan's Island: An Irish Sketch-Book, Geis, 1962.
Hold Your Hour and Have Another (collected articles), Little, Brown, 1963.
Brendan Behan's New York, Geis, 1964.
The Scarperer, Doubleday, 1964.
The Quare Fellow and The Hostage: Two Plays, Grove, 1964.
Confessions of an Irish Rebel, Hutchinson, 1965, Geis, 1966.
Richard's Cork Leg, edited by Alan Simpson, Grove, 1974.
The Complete Plays, introduction by Simpson, Grove, 1978.
Poems and a Play in Irish (includes "An Giall"), Gallery Books, 1981.
After the Wake, edited by Peter Fallon, O'Brien Press, 1981.

Behan's writings have been translated into Italian, French, and German.

MEDIA ADAPTATIONS: Frank McMahon adapted *Borstal Boy* for the stage; the play won an Antoinette Perry ("Tony") Award and a New York Drama Critics Circle Award as best play of the 1969-70 season. Shay Duffin adapted Behan's works for the play "Shay Duffin Is Brendan Behan: Confessions of an Irish Rebel" in the early 1970s. Both "The Quare Fellow" and "The Hostage" have been made into films.

SIDELIGHTS: Once characterized as "a professional young Irishman," Brendan Behan, in both his life and work, took the role to heart. Even before his early death in 1964 from alcoholism, jaundice, and diabetes, he had become a legend. Stories of his drunken antics and of his youthful "terrorist" activities for the IRA prevailed in the media over mention of his literary creations. His work was often dismissed as the careless outpouring of a sensation-hungry revolutionary without a revolution.

But serious connections have been drawn between the content of Behan's writing, particularly his major plays "The Quare Fellow" and "The Hostage," his politics, and his self-destructive drinking. In his work, as in his life, laughter and the despair of dying are commingled with intoxicating effect. Behan himself once said that he possessed "a sense of humor that would cause me to laugh at a funeral, providing it wasn't my own." About his comedies critic Alfred Kazin stated: "There is the constant suggestion in Behan's work that the laughter which supports despair does not always hide despair. But Behan's is the despair of an authentic predicament, of the actualities of life at the present time." Ted Boyle, in his book *Brendan Behan,* commented: "A good deal of the comedy in Behan's plays portrays the hysteria which overcomes the human being caught in a situation over which he has no control." The criminal about to be hanged in "The Quare Fellow" and the British soldier being held for exchange with a captured IRA member in "The Hostage" are both examples of this comedic circumstance.

Behan's work is also characterized by his talent for realistic dialogue, the gift of his "tape-recorder ear." His later works in fact were taken down on tape, transcribed, and then edited by others. But even in his earlier writing there is the same fidelity to common speech patterns. Kazin commented: "What Behan has done, coming in too late to participate in the Irish literary renaissance, is to identify himself not with the abstract cause of art but with the profane and explosive speech of the streets, the saloons, the prisons."

In 1970 Frank McMahon adapted *Borstal Boy* for the theater. The dramatization, like the book, portrays Behan's early prison years, incorporating the addition of a narrator, the older Behan, who relates the story from downstage. The play conveys, as critic Alan Bunce wrote, "a florid reflection of Behan's adult personality—mellow, tartly philosophical, a mixture of Hibernian ruefulness with lambent humor."

BIOGRAPHICAL/CRITICAL SOURCES:

BOOKS

Atkinson, Brooks, *Tuesdays and Fridays,* Random House, 1963.
Behan, Dominic, *My Brother Brendan,* Frewin, 1965, Simon & Schuster, 1966.
Boyle, Ted E., *Brendan Behan,* Twayne, 1969.
Contemporary Literary Criticism, Gale, Volume 1, 1973, Volume 8, 1978, Volume 11, 1979, Volume 15, 1980.
Dictionary of Literary Biography, Volume 13: *British Dramatists since World War II,* Gale, 1982.
Jeffs, Rae, *Brendan Behan: Man and Showman,* Hutchinson, 1966, World Publishing, 1968.
Kazin, Alfred, *Contemporaries,* Little, Brown, 1959.
Lumley, Frederick, *New Trends in Twentieth-Century Drama,* Oxford University Press, 1967.
McCann, Sean, *The World of Brendan Behan,* Frewin, 1966.
Simpson, Alan, *Beckett and Behan and a Theatre in Dublin,* Routledge & Kegan Paul, 1962.

PERIODICALS

Books Abroad, spring, 1967.
Chicago Tribune, March 12, 1982.
Christian Science Monitor, April 8, 1970.
New York Times, November 4, 1983.
Times (London), October 15, 1986.
Times Literary Supplement, April 22, 1983.
Washington Post Book World, July 4, 1982.

BELL, Marvin (Hartley) 1937-

PERSONAL: Born August 3, 1937, in New York, N.Y.; son of Saul and Belle (Spector) Bell; married Mary Mammosser, 1958 (marriage ended); married Dorothy Murphy; children: Nathan Saul, Jason Aaron. *Education:* Alfred University, B.A., 1958; attended Syracuse University, 1958; University of Chicago, M.A., 1961; University of Iowa, M.F.A., 1963.

ADDRESSES: Office—Writers' Workshop, University of Iowa, Iowa City, Iowa 52242.

CAREER: University of Iowa, Writers' Workshop, Iowa City, visiting lecturer, 1965, assistant professor, 1967-69, associate professor, 1969-75, professor of English, 1975—. Visiting lecturer, Oregon State University, 1969, Goddard College, 1972, University of Hawaii, 1981, and University of Washington, 1982; member of faculty, Bread Loaf Writers' Conference, 1973-78 and 1980-82. *Military service:* U.S. Army, 1964-65; first lieutenant.

AWARDS, HONORS: Lamont Award from the Academy of American Poets, 1969, for *A Probable Volume of Dreams;* Bess Hokin Award, *Poetry* (magazine), 1969; Emily Clark Balch Prize, *Virginia Quarterly Review,* 1970; Guggenheim fellowship, 1976; National Endowment for the Arts Fellowship, 1978; Prize, *American Poetry Review,* 1981.

WRITINGS:

POETRY

Poems for Nathan and Saul (pamphlet), Hillsdale Press, 1966.
Things We Dreamt We Died For, Stone Wall Press, 1966.
A Probable Volume of Dreams, Atheneum, 1969.
Woo Havoc (pamphlet), Barn Dream Press, 1971.
The Escape into You, Atheneum, 1971.
Residue of Song, Atheneum, 1974.
Stars Which See, Stars Which Do Not See, Atheneum, 1978.
These Green-Going-to-Yellow, Atheneum, 1981.
(With William Stafford) *Segues: A Correspondence in Poetry,* Godine, 1983.
Drawn by Stones, by Earth, by Things Which Have Been in the Fire, Atheneum, 1984.
New and Selected Poems, Atheneum, 1987.

CONTRIBUTOR TO ANTHOLOGIES

Major Young Poets, edited by Al Lee, World Publishing, 1971.
New Voices in American Poetry, edited by David Allan Evans, Winthrop Publishing, 1973.
Preferences, edited by Richard Howard, Viking, 1974.
American Poetry Anthology, edited by Daniel Halpern, Avon, 1975.
Fifty Poets, edited by Alberta Turner, McKay, 1977.
Contemporary American Poets, edited by Mark Strand, New American Library, 1969.
New Yorker Book of Poems, Viking, 1969.

OTHER

Old Snow Just Melting: Essays and Interviews, University of Michigan Press, 1983.

Writer of column, "Homage to the Runner," for *American Poetry Review,* 1975-78. Editor and publisher, *Statements,* 1959-64; poetry editor, *North American Review,* 1964-69, and *Iowa Review,* 1969-71.

SIDELIGHTS: American poet and critic Marvin Bell "is a poet of the family. He writes of his father, his wives, his sons, and himself in a dynamic interaction of love and loss, accomplish-

ment, and fear of alienation. These are subjects that demand maturity and constant evaluation. A complete reading of Bell's canon shows his ability to understand the durability of the human heart. Equally impressive is his accompanying technical sophistication," comments William M. Robins in the *Dictionary of Literary Biography.* The son of a Jew who immigrated from the Ukraine, Bell writes of distance and reconciliation between people, often touching on his complex relationship to his heritage.

For example, *A Probable Volume of Dreams* opens with a poem addressed to the poet's father, initiating a dialogue that continues throughout Bell's works. "Although Bell is never narrowly confessional, it is important to note just how much the death of the father—his profound absence and presence—helps shape Bell's poetry and create possible worlds. *The* father: Bell's own dead father, and his growing sense of himself as a father who has sons and who, like him, will someday die," writes Arthur Oberg in *The American Poetry Review.* In addition to this motif, the poems "tell how unlinear life and art are, how 'progress' is a deception of the nineteenth century, how increasingly distant the finishing line for the poet-runner proves to be," Oberg observes. *A Probable Volume of Dreams* won the Lamont Award from the Academy of American Poets in 1969.

Concern with the self and its relationships in the earlier poetry has given way to reflections on the self in relation to nature in later books, such as *Stars Which See, Stars Which Do Not See.* Speaking of this development to Wayne Dodd and Stanley Plumly in an *Ohio Review* interview, Bell said that attention to nature has always been an integral part of his life. He grew up among farmers, so the rural life that so fascinated other writers during the 1960s back-to-nature movement was not Bell's inspiration. His first work came from his interest "in what language could make all by itself. . . . And I was interested in relationships between people. I wrote one whole book of poems-in-series about the relationships between a couple of people, or among several people. But now, for whatever good reasons, I *am* interested in allowing nature to have the place in my poems that it always had in my life," he said.

Bell also said the change in subject matter signalled a change in attitude—personal and cultural. "That is," he said, "contemporary American poetry has been tiresome in its discovery of the individual self, over and over and over, and its discovery of emotions that, indeed, we all have: loneliness, fear, despair, ennui, etcetera. I think it can get tiresome when the discovery of such emotions is more or less all the content there is to a poem. We know these things. . . . So I sort of write poetry nowadays from some other attitudes, I think, that came upon me without my ever really thinking about them. I think, for example, that it's ultimately pleasanter and healthier and better for everyone if one thinks of the self as being very small and very unimportant. . . . And I think, as I may not always have thought, that the only way out of the self is to concentrate on others and on things outside the self."

Bell sometimes refers to this development as an achievement of poetic modesty. He told Dodd and Plumly, "There is a kind of physical reality that we all share a sense of. I mean, we might argue about what reality is, but we all know how to walk across a bridge—instead of walking across the water, for instance. And it seems to me that one definition of modesty in poetry would be a refusal to compromise the physical facts of what it is that is showing up in one's poems," Bell explained.

Speaking of his personal aesthetic, he told the interviewers, "I would like to write poetry which finds salvation in the physical world and the here and now and which defines the soul, if you will, in terms of emotional depth, and that emotional depth in terms of the physical world and the world of human relationships." Regarding style, he added, "I'd like to write a poetry which has little if any insistence about it, as little as possible. I would like to write a poetry which doesn't seem either to buttonhole the reader, or demand too much allegiance, or demand that too much of the world be given up for the special world of the poem."

Reviewers comment that Bell's later poems fulfill these aspirations. G. E. Murray, writing in the *Georgia Review,* declares, "I am impressed by this poet's increasing ability to perceive and praise small wonders. There is life and health in this book, and if sometimes Bell's expression is quiet and reserved, his talent is not. Altogether, *Stars Which See, Stars Which Do Not See* demonstrates an important transitional phase for the poet—a subdued, graceful vein that enables him to 'speak of eyes and seasons' with an intimacy and surehandedness that informs and gratifies. . . . I believe Marvin Bell is on a track of the future—a mature, accessible and personalized venture into the mainstream of contemporary American verse." Of the same book, David St. John writes in *Parnassus,* "Many poets have tried to appropriate into their poems a gritty, tough-talking American character, and to thereby earn for themselves some . . . 'authenticity.'. . . In *Stars Which See, Stars Which Do Not See,* Bell has found within his *own* voice that American voice, and with it the ability to write convincingly about the smallest details of a personal history."

BIOGRAPHICAL/CRITICAL SOURCES:

BOOKS

Contemporary Literary Criticism, Gale, Volume 8, 1978, Volume 31, 1985.
Dictionary of Literary Biography, Volume 5: *American Poets since World War II,* Gale, 1980.
Malkoff, Karl, *Crowell's Handbook of Contemporary American Poetry,* Crowell, 1973.

PERIODICALS

American Poetry Review, May-June, 1976.
Antaeus, spring/summer, 1982.
Antioch Review, spring, 1982.
Chicago Review, Volume 28, number 1, 1976.
Hudson Review, August, 1985.
Iowa Review, winter, 1981.
Missouri Review, summer, 1982.
Nation, February 2, 1970.
New Republic, March 29, 1975.
New York Times Book Review, April 8, 1984, November 11, 1984.
Ohio Review, Volume 17, number 3, 1976.
Parnassus, fall/winter, 1972.
Shenandoah, summer, 1971.
Stand, Volume 13, number 4, 1972.

—*Sketch by Marilyn K. Basel*

* * *

BENVENISTE, Asa 1925-1990

PERSONAL: Born August 25, 1925, in New York City; immigrated to England, 1950; naturalized British citizen, 1965; died April 13, 1990; son of Samaya and Alegre (Levy) Benveniste; married Penelope Walker (an artist), December 9, 1949; children: Jasper, Paul, Mark. *Education:* New School for Social Re-

search, B.A., 1948; studied French language and literature at the Sorbonne, Paris, France. *Politics:* "Anarchist, but benign." *Religion:* Jewish.

ADDRESSES: Home—68 Bridge Lanes, Hebden Bridge, West Yorkshire HX7 6AT, England.

CAREER: Poet. Jewish News Agency, New York City, researcher, 1947; *Zero Quarterly,* co-editor, 1948-56, worked in Paris, France, Tangier, Morocco, and London, England; *Nugget Magazine,* London, correspondent, 1957-58; Paul Hamlyn Ltd., London, senior art editor, 1959-61; Studio Vista Ltd., London, senior editor, 1961-63; Trigram Press, London, executive editor and publisher, beginning 1965. *Military service:* U.S. Army, 1943-46.

WRITINGS:

POETRY

Poems of the Mouth, Trigram Press, 1966.
(With Jack Hirschman) *A Word in Your Season: A Portfolio of Six Serigraphs,* Trigram Press, 1967.
Count Three, Maya, 1969.
The Atoz Formula, Trigram Press, 1969.
Free Semantic No. 2., Wallrich Books, 1970.
Umbrella, Wallrich Books, 1972.
(With Ray Di Palma and Tom Raworth) *Time Being,* Blue Chair, 1972.
Blockmakers Black, Steam Press, 1973.
Certainly Metaphysics, Blue Chair, 1973.
It's the Same Old Feeling Again, Trigram Press, 1973.
Edge, Joe DiMaggio Press, 1974.
(With Brian Marley) *Dense Lens,* Trigram Press, 1975.
(With Marc Vaux) *Colour Theory,* Trigram Press, 1977.
Loose Use, Pig Press, 1977.
Blocks from the Collection of Roger Tomlin, Arc Publications, 1979.
Language, Enemy, Pursuit, Poltroon Press, 1980.
5 x 5, Trigram Press, 1981.
Throw Out the Lifeline, Lay Out the Corse: Poems, 1965-1985, Anvil Press Poetry, 1983.
Pommes Poems, Arc Publications, 1988.

OTHER

Autotypography: A Book of Design Priorities (nonfiction), Latimer New Dimensions, 1974.
Invisible Ink (autobiography), Singing Horse Press, 1989.

Also author of books of poems, *Listen,* 1976, *A Part Apart,* 1976, and *Opium War,* published by Spot Press; author of radio plays, "Tangier for the Traveller," 1956, and "Piano Forte," 1957. Contributor to periodicals, including *Ambit, Transatlantic Review, New Departures, European Judaism, South West Review,* and *Atlantic Review.*

SIDELIGHTS: Asa Benveniste once told *CA:* "I am trying to find and work in the obscurest language possible, in order to find the final clarity. I did not speak English, or any other language, until I was five. The first word caused the most excruciating pleasure I have ever felt."

OBITUARIES:

PERIODICALS

Times (London), April 26, 1990.*

BERGMAN, (Ernst) Ingmar 1918-
(Ernest Riffe; Buntel Eriksson, a joint pseudonym)

PERSONAL: Born July 14, 1918, in Uppsala, Sweden; son of a chaplain to the Royal Court of Stockholm; married Else Fisher (a dancer), 1943; married Ellen Lundstroem (a dancer), 1945 (divorced, 1950); married Gun Grut (a journalist), 1950; married Kaebi Laretei (a pianist), 1959 (separated, 1965); married Ingrid von Rosen, 1971; children: (first marriage) Lena; (second marriage) Eva, Jan, Anna, Mats; (third marriage) Ingmar; (fourth marriage) Daniel; one other child. *Education:* Attended University of Stockholm.

ADDRESSES: Home—Titurelstrasse 2, D-8000 Munich 8, West Germany.

CAREER: Writer, director, and producer of motion pictures, teleplays, and stage productions. Director with Maaster Olofsgaarden, 1938-40, and Student Theater in Stockholm, 1941; Svensk Filmindustri, 1942-69, began as scriptwriter and editor, artistic adviser, 1961-69; director of Haelsingborg City Theater, 1944-46, Gothenburg City Theater, 1947-52, Malmoe City Theater, 1952-59, Royal Dramatic Theater in Stockholm, 1963-66, and Munich Residenzteater, 1977-82. Founder of the film production companies Cinematograph, Sweden, 1968, and Personafilm, Munich, West Germany, 1977.

AWARDS, HONORS: Grand Prix du Cinema, Cannes Film Festival, 1946, for "Hets"; Sao Paolo Film Festival prize, 1954, for "Gycklarnas afton"; comedy prize, Cannes Film Festival, 1956, for "Sommarnattens leende"; special award, Cannes Film Festival, 1957, and Joseph Bernstein Award for best foreign import, 1958, both for "Det sjunde inseglet"; Golden Bear award, International Berlin Film Festival, 1957, for "Smultronstaellet"; director's prize, Cannes Film Festival, 1958, for "Naera livet"; Gold Plaque, Swedish Film Academy, 1958; Academy Award for best foreign language film, Academy of Motion Picture Arts and Sciences, 1960, for "Jungfrukaellan," and 1961, for "Saasom i en spegel"; co-recipient (with Charles Chaplin) of Erasmus Prize, Netherlands, 1965; awards for best director and for best film, National Society of Film Critics, 1967, for "Persona"; National Society of Film Critics award, 1968, for "Skammen"; Irving G. Thalberg Memorial Award, Academy of Motion Picture Arts and Sciences, 1971; award for best director, National Society of Film Critics, 1971, for "En passion"; award for best screenwriter, National Society of Film Critics, and awards for best screenwriter, best director, and best film, New York Film Critics, all 1972, all for "Viskningar och rop"; D.Phil., Stockholm University, 1975; Goethe Prize, 1976; Great Gold Medal, Swedish Academy of Letters, 1977; best director award, New York Film Critics, 1983, and Academy Award for best foreign language film, 1984, both for "Fanny and Alexander"; decorated Commander of the Legion of Honor, 1985; numerous other film awards.

WRITINGS:

(With others) *Film and Dreams: An Approach to Bergman,* edited and introduced by Vlada Petric, Redgrave, 1981.

A Project for the Theatre, edited and introduced by Frederick J. Marker and Lise-Lone Marker, Ungar, 1983.

Laterna Magica, Norstedt, 1987, translation by Joan Tate published as *The Magic Lantern: An Autobiography,* Viking, 1988 (published in England as *The Magic Lantern: An Autobiography by Ingmar Bergman,* Hamish Hamilton, 1988).

SCREENPLAYS

(And assistant director) "Hets" (released in the United States as "Frenzy" and as "Torment"; also see below), Svensk Filmindustri, 1944.

(Adapter and director) "Kris" (released in the United States as "Crisis"; from the play by Leck Fisher, "Moderdyret"), Svensk Filmindustri, 1945.

(Adapter with Herbert Grevenius, and director) "Det regnar paa vaar kaerlek" (released in the United States as "It Rains Our Love"; from the play by Oskar Braathen, "Bra mennesker"), Sveriges Folkbiografer, 1946.

"Kvinna utan ansikte" (released in the United States as "Woman without a Face"), Svensk Filmindustri, 1947.

(Adapter and director) "Skepp till Indialand" (released in the United States as "A Ship to India" and as "Land of Desire"; from the play by Martin Soederhjelm), Sveriges Folkbiografer, 1947.

(Co-adapter and director) "Hamnstad" (released in the United States as "Port of Call"; from a story by Olle Laensberg), Svensk Filmindustri, 1948.

(Co-author) "Eva," Svensk Filmindustri, 1948.

(And director) "Faengelse" (released in the United States as "Prison" and as "The Devil's Wanton"), Terrafilm, 1949.

(And director) "Till glaedje" (released in the United States as "To Joy"), Svensk Filmindustri, 1949.

(With Grevenius, and director) "Sommarlek" (released in the United States as "Summer Interlude" and as "Illicit Interlude"), Svensk Filmindustri, 1950.

(With Grevenius) "Fraanskild" (released in the United States as "Divorced"), Svensk Filmindustri, 1951.

(And director) "Kninnors vantan" (released in the United States as "Waiting Women" and as "Secrets of Women"), Svensk Filmindustri, 1952.

(Adapter with P. A. Fogelstroem, and director) "Sommaren med Monika" (released in the United States as "Summer with Monika"; from the novel of the same title by Fogelstroem), Svensk Filmindustri, 1952.

(And director) "Gycklarnas afton" (title means "Sunset of the Clown"; released in the United States as "The Naked Night" and in England as "Sawdust and Tinsel"), Sandrews, 1953.

(And director) "En lektion i kaerlek" (released in the United States as "A Lesson in Love"), [Sweden], 1954.

(And director) "Kvinnodroem" (released in the United States as "Journey into Autumn" and as "Dreams"), Sandrews, 1955.

(And director) "Sommarnattens leende" (released in the United States as "Smiles of a Summer Night"; also see below), Svensk Filmindustri, 1955.

(With Alf Sjoeberg) "Sista paret ut" (released in the United States as "The Last Couple Out"), Svensk Filmindustri, 1956.

(Adapter and director) "Det sjunde inseglet" (released in the United States as "The Seventh Seal"; from the play by Bergman, "Traemalning"; also see below), Svensk Filmindustri, 1956, translation by Lars Malmstrom and David Kushner published as *The Seventh Seal,* Simon & Schuster, 1960, revised edition, Lorrimer (London), 1984.

(And director) "Smultronstaellet" (released in the United States as "Wild Strawberries"; also see below), Svensk Filmindustri, 1957, translation by Malmstrom and Kushner published as *Wild Strawberries,* Simon & Schuster, 1960.

(With Ulla Isaksson, and director) "Naera livet" (released in the United States as "The Magician" and as "The Face"; also see below), Svensk Filmindustri, 1958.

(Adapter and director) "Djaevunes oega" (released in the United States as "The Devil's Eye"; adapted from a Danish radio play), Svensk Filmindustri, 1960.

Four Screenplays of Ingmar Bergman, translation by Malmstrom and Kushner, Simon & Schuster, 1960, reprinted as *Four Screenplays of Ingmar Bergman: Smiles of a Summer Night, The Seventh Seal, The Magician, and Wild Strawberries,* 1989.

(And director) "Saasom i en spegel" (released in the United States as "Through a Glass Darkly"; also see below), Svensk Filmindustri, 1961.

(With Erland Josephson, under joint pseudonym Buntel Eriksson, and director) "Lustgaarden" (released in the United States as "The Pleasure Garden"), Svensk Filmindustri, 1961.

(And director) "Nattvardsgaesterna" (released in the United States as "Winter Light"; also see below), Svensk Filmindustri, 1962.

(And director) "Tystnaden" (released in the United States as "The Silence"; also see below), Svensk Filmindustri, 1963.

En filmtrilogi: Saasom i en spegel, Nattvardsgaesterna, Tystnaden, PAN/Norstedt, 1963, translation by Paul Britten Austin published as *A Film Trilogy: Through a Glass Darkly, Winter Light, The Silence,* Orion Press, 1967, published as *Three Films by Ingmar Bergman,* Grove, 1970, reprinted as *A Film Trilogy: Through a Glass Darkly, The Communicants (Winter Light), and The Silence,* Marion Boyars, 1988.

(With Josephson, under joint pseudonym Buntel Eriksson, and director) "Foer att inte tala om alla dessa kvinnor" (released in the United States as "Now about These Women" and as "All These Women"), Svensk Filmindustri, 1964.

(And director) "Persona" (also see below), Svensk Filmindustri, 1966.

(And director) "Vargtimmen" (released in the United States as "The Hour of the Wolf "; also see below), Svensk Filmindustri, 1966.

(And director) "Skammen" (released in the United States as "Shame"; also see below), Svensk Filmindustri, 1967.

(And director) "Riten" (released in the United States as "The Rite" and as "The Ritual"), Svensk Filmindustri/Cinematograph, 1969.

"En passion" (released in the United States as "A Passion" and as "A Passion of Anna"; also see below), Svensk Filmindustri/Cinematograph, 1969.

(And director) "Faaroedokument" (documentary; released in the United States as "Faro Document"), Cinematograph, 1969.

(And director) "The Touch" (also see below), Cinematography/ABC Pictures, 1970.

(Adapter and director) "The Lie" (television screenplay; from a play by Bergman), British Broadcasting Corp. (BBC-TV), 1972.

(And director) "Viskningar och rop" (released in the United States as "Cries and Whispers"; also see below), Cinematograph, 1972.

Bergman: Persona and Shame, translation by Keith Bradfield, Penguin, 1972 (published in England as *Persona; and Shame: The Screenplays of Ingmar Bergman,* Marion Boyars, 1972, reprinted as *Persona and Shame: Two Screenplays,* 1984).

Filmberaettelser, three volumes, PAN/Norstedt, 1973.

Scener ur ett iiktenshap (originally produced for Swedish television; also see below), Norstedt, 1973, translation by Alan Blair published as *Scenes from a Marriage,* Pantheon, 1974.

(And director) "Ansikte mot ansikte" (co-produced by Bergman for BBC-TV as "Face to Face"; also see below), Cinematograph, 1976, translation by Blair published as *Face to Face,* Pantheon, 1976.

Four Stories by Ingmar Bergman: The Touch, Cries and Whispers, The Hour of the Wolf, The Passion of Anna, translation by Blair, Doubleday, 1976.

Ormens aegg (originally released in West Germany as "Das Schlangenei"; U.S. production directed by Bergman released as "The Serpent's Egg," Paramount, 1977), Norstedt, 1977, translation by Blair published as *The Serpent's Egg,* Pantheon, 1977.

Hoestsonaten (originally released in West Germany as the film "Herbstsonate"; released in the United States as "Autumn Sonata"; also see below), PAN/Norstedt, 1978, translation by Blair published as *Autumn Sonata,* Pantheon, 1978.

The Marriage Scenarios (contains "Scenes from a Marriage," "Face to Face," and "Autumn Sonata"), translation by Blair, Pantheon, 1978.

(And director and narrator) "Faaroe-dokument 1979" (documentary; released in the United States as "Faro 1979"), Cinematograph, 1980.

(And director) "Aus dem Leben der Marionetten," [West Germany], 1980, translation by Blair published as *From the Life of the Marionettes,* Pantheon, 1980.

Fanny och Alexander (originally produced for Swedish television; Svensk Filminstitut, 1982; released in the United States as "Fanny and Alexander"), Norstedt, 1982, translation by Blair published as *Fanny and Alexander,* Pantheon, 1982.

(And director) "After the Rehearsal" (television screenplay), Cinematograph, 1984.

PLAYS

"Rakel och biografvaktmaestaren" (title means "Rachel and the Cinema Doorman"; also see below), first produced in Gothenburg, Sweden, at Gothenburg City Theater, 1945.

"Dagen slutar tidget" (title means "The Day Ends Early"; also see below), first produced at Gothenburg City Theater, 1947.

"Mig till skraeck" (title means "To My Terror"; also see below), first produced at Gothenburg City Theater, 1947.

Jack hos skadespelarna (title means "Jack among the Actors"), Albert Bonniers, 1948.

Moraliteter (title means "Morality Plays"; contains "Rakel och biografvadtmaestaren," "Dagen slutar tidget," and "Mig till skraeck"), Albert Bonniers, 1948.

"Hets" (title means "Torment"; adapted from the screenplay of the same title by Bergman), first produced in Oslo, Norway, 1948.

"Mordet i barjaerna" (title means "Murder at Barjaerna"), first produced in Malmoe, Sweden, at Malmoe City Theater, 1952.

"Traemalning" (title means "Wood Painting"), first produced in Stockholm, Sweden, at Royal Dramatic Theater, 1955.

(Adapter) August Strindberg, *A Dream Play,* translated by Michael Meyer, Secker & Warburg, 1972.

"Scenes from a Marriage" (adapted from his screenplay), produced in Munich, 1981, new adaptation (with Rita Russek) produced in London, 1990.

Also author of "Kaspers doed" (title means "Death of Punch"), first produced in 1942, and "Staden" (title means "The City"), first produced for radio in 1951. Author of unproduced plays, including "Resamrater" (title means "Travel Companions"), "Stationen" (title means "Station"), "De Ensamma" (title means "The Lonely Ones"), "Trivolet" (title means "The Fun Fair"), "Fullmanen" (title means "Full Moon"), "Dimman" (title means "The Fog"), and "Om en moerdare" (title means "About a Murder").

OTHER

Contributor of essays to numerous film journals and periodicals, including *Cinemathek, Svenska radiopjaeser, Biografbladet, Tulane Drama Review,* and, under pseudonym Ernest Riffe, *Chaplin.*

WORK IN PROGRESS: "Good Intentions," a six-hour television series to be adapted as a two-part movie, will be written by Bergman and directed by Bille August. It concerns the ten years of his parents' marriage before Bergman's birth.

SIDELIGHTS: Throughout his career as an internationally renowned filmmaker and screenwriter, Swedish director Ingmar Bergman has imbued his work with the concerns, fears, and hopes of his own life. "Films would seem to be the most personal part of Bergman's life," asserts John Osborne in the *New York Review of Books.* "Certainly his personal life is openly reflected in them." As in his movies, Bergman's 1988 autobiography, *The Magic Lantern,* reveals the importance of this link, while also employing a highly subjective writing technique that is similar to the style he uses in many of his screenplays. "*The Magic Lantern* is constructed much like a Bergman film," acknowledges London *Times* contributor David Thompson; "real memories [are] intermingled with fantasized encounters and flashes forward to the last few years [of his life]." This stylistic approach has led *Time* reviewer Richard Schickel to call *The Magic Lantern* "one of the finest self-portraits of an artist written in our time." But "what Bergman is [also] saying," adds Schickel, "is that however acutely his art reflected his sense of life, it was much more important to him as a refuge from life. It was the place where he could at least briefly impose order on life's terrible confusions, find for himself a sustaining moment of peace and grace."

Once an unhappy, sickly child, Bergman was the son of a strict Lutheran minister, who often locked Bergman in a closet or forced him to wear a dress as punishment for even the most insignificant transgression. The psychological effects of this abusive treatment left a strong impression on Bergman, and for this reason "Bergman never—presumably could not—shut the window to his childhood," notes Lloyd Rose in the *Voice Literary Supplement.* Becoming rebellious, Bergman adulated Adolf Hitler for a short time, until he was confronted with the shocking truth of the Nazi concentration camps. This realization led the young Bergman to feel "despair" and "self-contempt," he reveals in his autobiography. But as a student at the University of Stockholm, he finally found a certain release from his frustrations in the writings of Swedish playwright and novelist August Strindberg. In a quote taken by Charles Champlin in a *Los Angeles Times* article, Bergman said that "[Strindberg] expressed things I'd experienced and which I couldn't find words for." The expressionistic style of Strindberg's writing would thereafter have a profound influence on the director's work.

Although Bergman is best known for his films, he reveals in *The Magic Lantern* that, like Strindberg, his real love is for the stage. Indeed, he has worked for several playhouses in Sweden, including a position as chief director of Sweden's most prestigious theater, the Royal Dramatic Theatre. But "from a strictly professional point of view," admits Bergman in his autobiography, "my years as a theatre director were wasted." The plays that he has written for the stage have not achieved the acclaim his films

have, and are relatively unknown today. "Yet," Champlin asserts, "it's obvious that his writing for the theatre was an immensely useful preparation for the kind of intimate, intense drama of characters and relationships that Bergman was to write for the screen." Arlene Croce declares in *Commonweal* that the filmmaker "has in fact created a theater of the film."

Bergman began his film career in 1943, when he left college for a position with Svensk Filmindustri. According to Peter Harcourt in his *Six European Directors: Essays on the Meaning of Style,* "the problems of loneliness, humiliation, and of the essential isolation of the human spirit" have dominated the director's work since that time. *Film Quarterly* critic Eugene Archer writes that the filmmaker's "early films [are] strange, exceedingly personal, and deeply provocative, sometimes deriving from the Protestant environment of his own childhood." Works like "Torment" and "Summer with Monika" are "dramas of adolescent revolt," continues Archer. They also project Bergman's early pessimistic view of human nature, as well as a "preoccupation with youth and the vulnerability of innocence," remarks *Ingmar Bergman* author Robin Wood. For example, in "Torment," a student is abused by a sadistic teacher, who, it is later revealed, murdered the student's girlfriend. The film ends with the boy forsaking society to become an outcast. A similar ending occurs in "Summer with Monika," in which a young boy and girl become lovers and leave the city for the northern woods of Sweden. "Bergman's youthful pessimism is climaxed by *Faengelse* (Prison)," observes Archer, "which depicts modern life as a total hell from which there can be no salvation because man has lost the ability to believe in God."

However, the films of Bergman's early period are not all pessimistic. "Smile of a Summer Night," reports Archer, is "a delightful comedy of manners in the tradition of the French boudoir farce." But the critic also notes that, like most of the director's movies, it "is subject to a dual interpretation, and an underlying serious meaning is readily apparent." The comedic aspects of the film are balanced by themes concerning the loss of love, frustration, and humiliation. "The Naked Night," a much gloomier film about a couple's loss of dignity in their search for reconciliation, echoes the themes presented in "Smiles of a Summer Night." These two completely different films also share in common the "analysis of the human condition, of man's attitude toward the great abstract questions," according to Joern Donner in his *The Personal Vision of Ingmar Bergman.*

Several of these first films have been praised by critics, "Summer Interlude" being the point where Archer believes Bergman "attained complete maturity as a director." The movie is about a summer romance that is overshadowed by a sense of disaster. "His films since 1950 [the year 'Summer Interlude' was released]," says Archer, "are, without exception, masterful in their evocations of mood and movement, the principle ingredients of cinematic style." However, in his book *Cinema Eye, Cinema Ear: Some Key Film-Makers of the Sixties,* John Russell Taylor argues that "Prison" is really the director's first early significant work. "['Prison'] has all the marks of a key work in his career," Taylor opines, "wildly bundling together any number of themes which are to recur later. . . . Moreover, it is the first of Bergman's films which demonstrate any real desire . . . to experiment with the medium, to use it positively as a means of expression in itself, rather than recording with competence but no special aptitude." Taylor also feels that "Smiles of a Summer Night" is important in that "for the first time, and virtually for the last, all Bergman's diverse talents [are seen] together in a single film."

Despite the quality of these productions, Bergman did not receive significant international recognition until the release of the 1956 film "The Seventh Seal." By this time, the director had gathered about him a small troupe of actors, actresses, and behind-the-scenes people who would regularly work with him throughout his career, often filming at Bergman's favorite location, the Faeroe Islands north of Britain. Liv Ullmann, Max von Sydow, Gunnar Bjoernstrand, Bibi Andersson, Ingrid Thulin, and Harriet Andersson often appear as stars in Bergman's films; Bergman also relied on the talents of photography directors Sven Nykvist and Gunnar Fisher for thirty-two of his films. With this capable staff, and with the enthusiastic support of Svensk Filmindustri, Bergman began a new phase in his career with "The Seventh Seal" that is notable for its artistic freedom. "The Seventh Seal" and a number of the films that followed it also delineate a period that is dominated by one theme: mankind's search for God.

Bergman's preoccupation with this theme goes back to his childhood and the Protestant indoctrination he received from his father. Bergman "absorbed his [father's] chill upbringing into his marrow," attests Rose. "There's never been a director . . . more Protestant. Carried to its (theo)logical extreme, Protestantism is as absurd as something out of [Samuel] Beckett. It completely jettisons cause and effect. God may save you or He may damn you, but your actions have nothing to do with it . . . and if God—by an act of divine judgement totally beyond your comprehension—decides to let you burn, tough luck. As a director, Bergman is often accused of being mysterious and indecipherable. At least he comes by it honestly."

In "The Seventh Seal" Bergman's search for God comes to life in a medieval knight's quest for meaning after the Crusades. "The film," explains Birgitta Steene in a *Scandinavian Studies* article, "illustrates [the] gradual alienation of man from God by depicting in the crusader a human being at first engaged in a holy enterprise but at last willing to sell his soul to the Devil—could he only find him! For the Devil, he argues with insane logic, must know God since he only exists in opposition to God." But the knight's doubts are not the characteristic concerns of a medieval man, according to Steene, who notes that "he is closer to a modern skeptic whose burning need of faith cannot be fulfilled because he refuses to accept a god who does not give intellectual proof of his existence."

Some reviewers have criticized Bergman's presentation of modern concerns within a medieval motif. *Encounter* contributor Caroline Blackwood, for example, objects to the filmmaker's use of "all the old morbid medieval metaphors which formed the staple fare of silent German movies of the 'twenties." Blackwood also finds it difficult "to see anything very 'illuminating' in Bergman monotonously repeating that all knowledge and learning are instruments of the Devil." Many other reviewers, though, share the sentiment of Peter Cowie's *Sweden 2* assessment: "The Seventh Seal" is a "triumphant blend of literary antecedent and visual metaphor that makes [it] such a profound and ambitious film, unequaled in the Swedish cinema as an exercise in tempered expressionism."

Another accomplishment of "The Seventh Seal," says Steene, is that it "sets up a dichotomy, which is to remain a basic one in Bergman's production, between a god who is a silent monster and torturer of man, and a god who is a lover of life." Several of the Bergman films which followed express one side or the other of this dichotomy. "Wild Strawberries," for example, "represents the culmination and fulfillment of the Christian side of Bergman," according to Wood, for "the presence of a benevolent deity seems to permeate the film." Although "Wild Strawberries" is not as overtly religious as "The Seventh Seal," a positive message about God's presence is expressed when the protagonist, Isak Borg, is made to realize through a series of dreams that he has been a cold and heartless person. Seeing the error of his ways, Isak decides to return home and asks his parents to forgive him for neglecting them. "It is significant that the Bergman film embodying the Christian virtues of love, forgiveness, humility, should be centrally concerned with forgiveness between parents and children," notes Wood, who concludes that "Isak Borg's relationship to Bergman himself is obvious."

Another production with a positive affirmation of God is "Through a Glass Darkly." In this case, the director clearly presents God as a god of love. This "intensely personal work," as Cowie calls it in a *Films and Filming* article, concerns a self-involved father and the lack of communication he has with his children. By the end of the movie, there is a reconciliation between the father and his son when the father asserts that God is love. Symbolically, this conclusion is significant because, as Steene points out, "from the children's point of view the father has become connected, if not identified with their image of God." Although critics like Wood consider "Through a Glass Darkly" to be an "extremely important" film for the director, the reviewer also believes it to be "extremely unsatisfactory." The movie's conclusion, elaborates Wood, "is beyond question the worst ending in mature Bergman" because "the consistent undermining of the father throughout the film suggests Bergman's lack of confidence in his last words. They are indeed mere words." Nevertheless, this movie is significant since, as Harcourt suggests, it marks the beginning of a period in the director's career in which he attempts to bring his audience "closer to fewer and fewer people, perhaps with deliberate ambition to 'illuminate the human soul.' "

As in "Through a Glass Darkly," "Winter Light" involves a father-child relationship; but it also extrapolates the situation by involving characters outside the family. In this case, a minister, Tomas Ericsson, is unable to prevent the suicide of a fisherman because his parents' inability to show Tomas affection has left him incapable of showing love for others. Again, the parents in the film represent God; and Tomas's failure to communicate with God causes him to isolate himself from others. There is, however, some hope in "Winter Light" in Tomas's resolve to cling to his religious faith despite his tenuous belief in God. However, in Bergman's "The Silence" (originally entitled "God's Silence"), God's presence is completely abrogated. Unlike "Through a Glass Darkly" and "Winter Light," the father in "The Silence" is dead when the plot begins. Bergman examines the consequences of the father's (i.e. God's) total absence through the use of language, which is "related to Bergman's religious questioning and his portrayal of the father-child relationship," according to Steene in *Cinema Journal.* "When God dies away," Steene concludes, ". . .language looses its communicative and healing power." The film illustrates this theme by isolating its characters, two sisters and their nephew, in a country whose people speak a language they do not understand. The final scene underlines the theme when one of the character's efforts to read a list of translations is drowned out by the noise of a passing train.

With the completion of "The Silence," Bergman dropped his obsession with theology, considering his films on the subject "bogus," according to Roger Manvell in *The International Dictionary of Films and Filmmakers.* By this time, surmises Schickel in a *Life* review, "Bergman has . . . accepted [God's] death and, indeed, seems to find that event no longer worthy of comment.

His absence is now simply one of the terms of our existence." With the trilogy comprised of "Persona," "The Hour of the Wolf," and "Shame," the director focuses more on another of his favorite subjects: the artistic character. Compared to Bergman's films about God, Stanley Kauffman describes "Persona" in his *Figures of Light: Film Criticism and Comment* as "a successful work of art," the early trilogy being "masterfully made, but . . . introspectively remote rather than dramatized."

"Persona" is about an actress who suddenly, inexplicably refuses to speak. All attempts by her nurse to encourage the actress to speak fail; but the experience results in the nurse's realization that she, like the actress, has been wearing a mask that conceals her true self. Vernon Young, author of *Cinema Borealis: Ingmar Bergman and the Swedish Ethos,* is somewhat less enthusiastic about "Persona" than Kauffman, comparing its artistic value to "The Hour of the Wolf." "Any expectation that 'Persona' was more than a skirmish in [Bergman's] inconclusive battle with the duplicity of the artist was certainly frustrated by 'The Hour of the Wolf,' " Young remarks. "['The Hour of the Wolf'] is pure dementia . . . ; in it Bergman explores nothing; this is wholly a disintegration product, replying to no serious question." In "The Hour of the Wolf" an artist is plagued by demons. Whether the demons are real or not is never explained, nor is any reason given for the artist's torture. Because nothing is fully explained, reviewers like Young consider the movie too obscure, although others such as *Film Quarterly* contributor Ernest Callenbach praise Bergman as being "personally brave in the sense of being willing to work with dangerous psychic material."

Reviews of "Shame" have generally been much more positive than for "The Hour of the Wolf." This time, Bergman places two artists in the middle of a war and describes their futile efforts to remain neutral for the sake of their art. "Shame" stirred some controversy among Bergman's compatriots, who felt the movie was a sarcastic comment on Sweden's neutrality during both World Wars. But a number of critics have praised "Shame" for its unique view on war. " 'Shame' is in fact quite remarkable among war films," attests Callenbach, "and takes its place among a tiny honorable handful that may be considered genuinely antiwar." In Wood's book, the author offers even higher tribute: " 'Shame' is Bergman's masterpiece to date [1969] and one of the greatest films of the last decade."

An important element in Bergman's films has always been the role of his female characters, who, explains *Film Quarterly* contributor Joan Mellen, "sometimes serve Bergman to express his agony over our ultimate inability to derive meaning from life." Beginning with the director's "A Passion," women play an increasingly important part in his films. "It wasn't until 'A Passion' that I really got to grips with the man-woman relationship," Bergman is quoted as saying in Manvell's essay. In this essay Bergman also states that his later films illustrate his "ceaseless fascination with the whole race of women." Besides his use of expressionism, this is an aspect of Bergman's work that bears an affinity with Strindberg. But whereas Strindberg became bitter after his second divorce, Bergman's four divorces have not changed his views about women. Strindberg and Bergman "differ markedly in tone," observes Champlin: "Bergman usually compassionate, however candid in his depictions, Strindberg more often misogynistic."

Two films that explore this theme as it pertains to the institution of marriage are "A Passion" and "Scenes from a Marriage." One of Bergman's most experimental works in terms of photography, the use of color, and the manner in which he interrupts the film with interpretive narratives by the actors, "A Passion" delves into the relationships of two men and two women who are isolated on an island. When they become involved in one another's lives, their fears and insecurities are revealed. Harcourt believes that, up to this point in the filmmaker's career, "A Passion" is the most complete movie involving "the essential isolation of the human spirit." Several critics, such as Schickel, feel that in this film "the art of Ingmar Bergman reaches its pinnacle. Though it is one of his rare color films, it is in every important way his most austere and elliptical work, a thing of silences and enigmas that nevertheless makes very clear the tragic vision of life that possesses its author." "Scenes from a Marriage" also deals with man-woman relationships. Originally made for television, some reviewers have complained that it has a soap opera quality that, as *Esquire* contributor John Simon reports, makes it "too commonplace." Disagreeing with this opinion, Simon avers that the married couple in the film "are not platitudes; they are encyclopedias" meant to represent all of us. *Film Quarterly* contributor Marsha Kinder is also enthusiastic about "Scenes from a Marriage," calling it "emotional dynamite." The movie, she concludes, achieves "a depth of characterization previously thought possible only in the novel."

With "Cries and Whispers," a movie about the relationships between four women, Bergman examines the nature of women in the greatest depth yet. According to Julian C. Rice's *Massachusetts Review* article, "Bergman defines his principal theme [in 'Cries and Whispers'] as a concern with the 'wholeness inside every human being.' This 'wholeness' is the basis upon which relationships with other human beings are formed." But some critics, like Mellen, object to this film's portrayal of women, claiming that Bergman "provides one of the most retrograde portrayals of women on the contemporary screen." Other reviewers, however, believe this interpretation misses the point of the film. In *Salmagundi,* Robert Boyers remarks that the suffering of Bergman's female characters in "Cries and Whispers" is not indicative of any misogynistic feelings on the director's part. Bergman, writes Boyers, no more punishes women "than he punishes men who are cold and all but indifferent to their functions as integrated human beings." Robert E. Lauder similarly asserts in *Christian Century* that "the truth of the matter is that the filmmaker is involved in a love-hate relationship with women and men— and indeed with himself." In a quote taken by *Times Literary Supplement* critic S. S. Prawer, Bergman explains that "Cries and Whispers" is really "a first attempt at circumscribing the image I have of my mother. . . . Mama was the overwhelming experience of my childhood."

The conclusion of "Cries and Whispers" foreshadows the optimism of Bergman's later movie, "Face to Face." "Cries and Whispers," remarks Rice, "suggests that wholeness and communication are indeed possible, if only for fleeting redemptive moments." However, according to Lauder, in "Face to Face" there is a "clear presence of hope." But this increasing tone of optimism in Bergman's work was destroyed for a time when the director suffered the greatest humiliation of his life. Having entrusted his finances to dishonest advisers, in 1976 the filmmaker unwittingly found himself the subject of a tax scandal that led him to a nervous breakdown. Eventually cleared of the charges, Bergman nevertheless exiled himself to West Germany. It is here that the director filmed his nightmarishly violent and skeptical film about pre-Hitler Germany, "The Serpent's Egg." The film was an immense critical failure, however, largely due to its overly-grim nature and because the political statement it makes demonstrates, as *Film Quarterly* contributor Ronald S. Librach notes, that politics is not "Bergman's strongest intellectual suit."

After "The Serpent's Egg" Bergman got back on his feet with "Autumn Sonata" and "From the Life of the Marionettes," produced in Norway and West Germany respectively. These films return to the director's concern with interpersonal relationships, while focusing on "very few characters in an elementary situation," says Gilberto Perez in a *New York Arts Journal* article on "Autumn Sonata." "Bergman," Perez comments further, "feels he's getting down to the essential of the human condition," by limiting the scope of these later productions. With the completion of these movies, the filmmaker decided to return to his homeland, where he filmed what he vowed would be his last motion picture for the screen. The result was Bergman's longest movie yet, "Fanny and Alexander," a three-hour-long multigenerational work containing virtually all of the themes expressed in the director's previous films.

This major effort, says its creator in a London *Times* article by Michiko Kakutani, represents "the sum total of my life as a filmmaker." "Fanny and Alexander," observes Kakutani, "is at once a nostalgic reinvention of the director's own childhood and a mature summation of his work. All the familiar Bergman themes and motifs are here—the humiliation of the artist, the hell and paradise of marriage, the quest for love and faith—but they are infused, this time, with a new tenderness and compassion. . . . Bergman seems to have achieved a measure of distance from and acceptance of his own past." *New York Times* critic Vincent Canby also recognizes this new, uncharacteristic mood of Bergman's, calling it "something that, in Bergman, might pass for serenity." Among critics, "Fanny and Alexander" has been generally well received, although a few, like *Washington Post* reviewer Gary Arnold, feel that "the movie has a text that tends to ramble and gush . . . and the host's powers of invention frequently go on the fritz." *Los Angeles Times* contributor Sheila Benson, however, writes that the film is "so lavish, so detailed and so satisfying that we want it to go on forever."

Fears that Bergman's career had come to an end with the production of "Fanny and Alexander" were soon dispelled with the release of the short television drama, "After the Rehearsal." "After the Rehearsal," however, does not violate Bergman's promise to cease making movies for the theater, since the director never said anything about the television media. His next project, "Good Intentions," is also made for television. Although written by Bergman, it is directed by Bille August, a Danish director. The movie is about the ten years of the filmmaker's parents' marriage before he was born. With "Good Intentions" Bergman finally accepts his parents, portraying them with more sympathy than ever before. "Until I wrote this manuscript," says Bergman in Steve Lohr's *New York Times* article, "I never really knew how complicated their lives were. . . . We always regret that we did not ask our parents more, really get to know them while they were alive." "If [this] sounds like a belated reconciliation with his parents," remarks Lohr, "it may be. But Mr. Bergman is at pains to emphasize to anyone listening that he has perhaps mellowed with age, but that the inner turmoil that has been a hallmark of both the man and the artist is still intact. 'The anger and the creativity are so closely intertwined with me,' he said. 'And there's plenty of anger left.'"

BIOGRAPHICAL/CRITICAL SOURCES:

BOOKS

Bergman, Ingmar, *The Magic Lantern: An Autobiography,* Viking, 1988.
Bjoerkman, Stig, Torsten Manns, and Jonas Sima, editors, *Bergman on Bergman: Interviews with Ingmar Bergman,* Simon & Schuster, 1973.
Contemporary Literary Criticism, Volume 16, Gale, 1981.
Cowie, Peter, *Sweden 2,* A. S. Barnes, 1970.
Donner, Joern, *The Personal Vision of Ingmar Bergman,* Indiana University Press, 1964.
Donner, Joern, *The Films of Ingmar Bergman,* Dover, 1972.
Gibson, Arthur, *The Silence of God: Creative Response to the Films of Ingmar Bergman,* Harper, 1969.
Harcourt, Peter, *Six European Directors: Essays on the Meaning of Film Style,* Penguin Books, 1974.
Jones, G. William, editor, *Talking with Ingmar Bergman,* Southern Methodist University Press, 1983.
Kael, Pauline, *Reeling,* Little, Brown, 1976.
Kaminsky, Stuart M., and Joseph F. Hill, editors, *Ingmar Bergman: Essays in Criticism,* Oxford University Press, 1975.
Kauffman, Stanley, *Figures of Light: Film Criticism and Comment,* Harper, 1971.
Lyon, Christopher, editor, *The International Dictionary of Films and Filmmakers,* Volume 2, St. James Press, 1984.
Schickel, Richard, *Second Sight: Notes on Some Movies, 1965-1970,* Simon & Schuster, 1972.
Simon, John, *Ingmar Bergman Directs,* Harcourt, 1972.
Slayton, Ralph Emil, *Ingmar Bergman's "The Seventh Seal": A Criticism,* University Microfilms International, 1973.
Sontag, Susan, *Styles of Radical Will,* Farrar, Straus, 1969.
Steene, Birgitta, *Ingmar Bergman,* Twayne, 1968.
Taylor, John Russell, *Cinema Eye, Cinema Ear: Some Key Film-Makers of the Sixties,* St. Martin's, 1964.
Wood, Robin, *Ingmar Bergman,* Praeger, 1969.
Young, Vernon, *Cinema Borealis: Ingmar Bergman and the Swedish Ethos,* David Lewis, 1971.

PERIODICALS

America, January 24, 1976.
Chicago Tribune, February 20, 1981, July 5, 1983, September 11, 1988.
Christian Century, October 27, 1976.
Cinema Journal, fall, 1970.
Commonweal, March 11, 1960.
Cue, December 28, 1968.
Encounter, April, 1961.
Esquire, January, 1975.
Film Literature Quarterly, spring, 1980.
Film Quarterly, summer, 1959, summer, 1968, fall, 1969, fall, 1973, winter, 1974-75.
Films and Filming, January, 1963.
Film Society Review, January, 1972.
Globe and Mail (Toronto), August 23, 1986.
Life, April 26, 1968.
Listener, April 5, 1979.
Los Angeles Times, January 15, 1974, June 29, 1983, June 20, 1984, September 16, 1987, September 18, 1988.
Massachusetts Review, winter, 1975.
Newsweek, November 24, 1975, April 12, 1976, September 26, 1988.
New York, April 12, 1976.
New York Arts Journal, Number 13, 1979.
New York Review of Books, October 27, 1988.
New York Times, January 22, 1978, January 27, 1978, June 17, 1983, July 3, 1983, June 21, 1984, September 7, 1988, September 6, 1989.
New York Times Book Review, February 21, 1965, August 4, 1974, September 18, 1988.
New York Times Magazine, December 7, 1975.
Quarterly Review of Film Studies, February, 1977.
Salmagundi, winter, 1978.

Scandinavian Studies, February, 1965.
Sight and Sound, winter, 1962-63, summer, 1965, summer, 1978.
Spectator, June 4, 1988.
Take One, March-April, 1972.
Time, November 13, 1972, April 12, 1976, January 30, 1978, September 26, 1988.
Times (London), July 6, 1983, May 19, 1988, June 24, 1989.
Times Literary Supplement, September 26, 1968, February 28, 1975, June 24, 1977, June 17, 1988.
Tulane Drama Review, December, 1960.
Voice Literary Supplement, March, 1989.
Washington Post, June 30, 1983, July 1, 1983, August 22, 1984, August 24, 1984.
Washington Post Book World, September 25, 1988.*

—*Sketch by Kevin S. Hile*

* * *

BETJEMAN, John   1906-1984
(Epsilon, Richard M. Farren)

PERSONAL: Born August 28, 1906, in Highgate, London, England; died after a long battle with Parkinson's Disease, May 19, 1984, in Trebetherick, Cornwall, England; son of Ernest Edward (a merchant and manufacturer) and Mabel (Dawson) Betjeman; married Penelope Valentine Hester Chetwode, 1932; children: Paul, Candida. *Education:* Attended Marlborough College, Oxford, 1925-27, and Magdalen College, Oxford, 1925-28. *Religion:* Church of England.

ADDRESSES: Home—The Mead, Wantage, Berkshire, England.

CAREER: After leaving school taught cricket and English at a London school; worked as an insurance broker; United Kingdom press attache, Dublin, Ireland, 1941-42; held a post with the British Admiralty, London, 1944; served with British Council, 1944-46. In October, 1972, Queen Elizabeth II appointed him Poet Laureate of England succeeding C. Day Lewis. Member of Royal Fine Arts Commission; governor of Pusey House.

MEMBER: Royal Society of Literature (fellow; Companion of Literature, 1968), Royal Institute of British Architects (honorary associate), American Academy of Arts and Letters (honorary member, 1973), Victorian Society (founder); Athenaeum, Beefsteak Club, Kildare Street Club (Dublin).

AWARDS, HONORS: Heinemann Award, 1948, for *Selected Poems;* Foyle Poetry Prize, 1955, for *A Few Late Chrysanthemums,* and 1959, for *Collected Poems;* Russell Loins Memorial Fund award, 1956; Duff Cooper Prize for *Collected Poems;* Queen's gold medal for poetry, 1960, for *Collected Poems;* Commander, Order of British Empire, 1960; knighted, 1969; D.Litt., University of Reading, University of Birmingham; LL.D., Aberdeen University.

WRITINGS:

VERSE

Mount Zion; or, In Touch with the Infinite, James Press, 1931.
Continual Dew: A Little Book of Bourgeois Verse, J. Murray, 1937.
(Under pseudonym Epsilon) *Sir John Piers,* Westmeath Examiner (Mullingar, Ireland), 1938.
Old Lights for New Chancels: Verses Topographical and Amatory, J. Murray, 1940.
New Bats in Old Belfries: Poems by John Betjeman, J. Murray, 1945.

Slick but Not Streamlined: Poems and Short Pieces, selected and with an introduction by W. H. Auden, Doubleday, 1947.
Selected Poems, compiled with an introduction by John Sparrow, J. Murray, 1948.
St. Katherine's Church, Chiselhampton, Oxfordshire: Verses Turned in Aid of a Public Subscription Towards the Restoration of the Church of St. Katherine, Chiselhampton, [Chiselhampton], 1950.
A Few Late Chrysanthemums: New Poems, J. Murray, 1954, Transatlantic, 1954.
Poems in the Porch, S.P.C.K., 1954.
Collected Poems, compiled and with an introduction by the Earl of Birkenhead, J. Murray, 1958, Houghton, 1959, enlarged edition, J. Murray, 1962, 3rd enlarged edition published as *John Betjeman's Collected Poems,* 1970, Houghton, 1971, 4th edition, J. Murray, 1980.
John Betjeman (selected poems), E. Hulton, 1958.
Poems, Vista Books, 1960.
Summoned by Bells (autobiography in verse), Houghton, 1960, new edition, J. Murray, 1976.
A Ring of Bells, selected with an introduction by Irene Slade, J. Murray, 1962, Houghton, 1963.
High and Low, J. Murray, 1966, Houghton, 1967.
Six Betjeman Songs, music by Mervyn Horder, Duckworth, 1967.
A Nip in the Air, J. Murray, 1975, Norton, 1976.
Betjeman in Miniature: Selected Poems of Sir John Betjeman, Gleniffer Press, 1976.
Metro-land, Warren, 1977.
The Best of Betjeman, selected by John Guest, J. Murray, 1978.
Church Poems, J. Murray, 1981.
Uncollected Poems, J. Murray, 1982.

WORKS ON ARCHITECTURE

Ghastly Good Taste; or, A Depressing Story of the Rise and Fall of English Architecture, Chapman & Hall, 1933, St. Martin's, 1971, reprinted, David & Charles, 1986.
An Oxford University Chest, illustrated by L. Moholy-Nagy and others, J. Miles, 1938.
Antiquarian Prejudice, Hogarth Press, 1939.
Cities and Small Towns ("Britain in Pictures" series), Collins, 1943.
English Cities and Small Towns, Collins, 1943.
First and Last Loves, J. Murray, 1952, Soccer, 1962.
The English Town in the Last Hundred Years (Rede Lecture), Cambridge University Press, 1956.
(Under pseudonym Richard M. Farren) *Ground Plan to Skyline,* Newman Neame, 1960.
The City of London Churches, Pitkin Pictorials, 1965.
Ten Wren Churches, illustrated by R. Beer, Editions Electo, 1970.
A Pictorial History of English Architecture, Macmillan, 1972.
London's Historic Railway Stations, Transatlantic, 1972.
West Country Churches, Society of SS Peter and Paul, 1973.

EDITOR

Shell Guide to Cornwall, Architectural Press, 1934, published as *Cornwall Illustrated,* Architectural Press, 1935, revised edition published as *Cornwall: A Shell Guide,* Faber, 1964.
Cornwall Illustrated in a Series of Views, Architectural Press, 1934.
Devon Shell Guide, Architectural Press, 1936, revised edition, Faber, 1955.
(With Geoffrey Taylor) *English, Scottish, and Welsh Landscape, 1700-c. 1860,* Muller, 1944.

Watergate Children's Classics, Watergate Classics (London), 1947.

(With John Piper) *Murray's Buckinghamshire Architectural Guide,* J. Murray, 1948.

(With Piper) *Murray's Berkshire Architectural Guide,* J. Murray, 1949.

(With Piper) *Shropshire: A Shell Guide,* Faber, 1951.

(With Taylor, and contributor) *English Love Poems,* Faber, 1957.

An American's Guide to English Parish Churches, Including the Isle of Man, McDowell, Obolensky, 1958 (published in England as *Collins Guide to English Parish Churches,* Collins, 1958, revised edition, 1959, subsequent revised editions published as *Collins Pocket Guide to English Parish Churches,* Volume 1: *The North,* Volume 2: *The South,* 1968.

Altar and Pew: Church of England Verses, E. Hulton, 1959.

(With Winnifred Hindley) *A Wealth of Poetry,* Blackwell, 1963.

(And author of introduction) Charles Tennyson Turner, *A Hundred Sonnets,* Hart-Davis, 1960, Dufour, 1961.

(And author of introduction and commentaries) *Victorian and Edwardian London from Old Photographs,* Viking, 1969.

(With David Vaisey) *Victorian and Edwardian Oxford from Old Photographs,* Batsford, 1971.

(With J. S. Gay) *Victorian and Edwardian Brighton from Old Photographs,* Batsford, 1972.

General editor of "Shell Guides" series, Architectural Press, 1934-64.

OTHER

(Author of introduction) Henry J. Newbolt, *Selected Poems,* Nelson, 1940.

Vintage London, Collins, 1942.

John Piper, Penguin, 1944.

(Contributor) Walter James Turner, editor, *A Panorama of Rural England,* Chantecleer Press/Hastings House, 1944.

(Contributor) Turner, editor, *The Englishman's Country,* Collins, 1945.

(Contributor) *Studies in the History of Swindon,* [Swindon], 1950.

The English Scene: A Reader's Guide (includes reading list by L. Russell Muirhead), Cambridge University Press for the National Book League, 1951.

(Contributor) *Gala Day London,* Harvill, 1953.

(Author of introduction) William Purcell, *Onward Christian Soldier,* Longmans, 1957.

(Illustrator) Basil Fulford Lowther Clarke, *English Churches,* London House & Markwell, 1964.

(Contributor) *Moments of Truth* (poetry), privately printed, [London], 1965.

(Contributor) Greater London Council, Historic Buildings Board, *Do You Care About Historic Buildings?,* [London], 1970.

(Contributor) *The Twelfth Man* (in honor of Prince Philip's 50th birthday), Cassell, 1971.

(Contributor) Robin Maugham, *The Barrier,* W. H. Allen, 1973.

A Plea for Holy Trinity Church, Sloan Street, Church Union, 1974.

John Betjeman's Oxford, Oxford University Press, 1980.

Lord Mount Prospect, Tragara Press, 1981.

(Contributor) *Likes and Dislikes: A Private Anthology,* Tragara Press, 1981.

Betjeman's Cornwall, J. Murray, 1984.

Betjeman's London, edited by Pennie Denton, J. Murray, 1988.

Member of staff of *Architectural Review;* film critic for *London Evening Standard;* book reviewer, *Daily Herald* (London); book critic, *Daily Telegraph,* 1952; columnist, *Spectator,* 1954-58.

SIDELIGHTS: John Betjeman, Poet Laureate of England until his death in 1984, has been called a "poet of nostalgia." Jocelyn Brooke wrote in *Ronald Firbank and John Betjeman:* "Modern 'progress' is anathema to him, he loathes 'processed' food, plastics, vita-glass, the Welfare State and (one may infer) democracy, though fortunately for us is still able to laugh at them." His technique is not original, though his sensibility is highly so. He can be "lyrically funny." Brooke continued, "Perhaps he can best be described as a writer who uses the medium of light verse for a serious purpose: not merely as a vehicle for satire or social commentary, but as a means of expressing a peculiar and specialized form of aesthetic emotion, in which nostalgia and humour are about equally blended."

"As his commentators generally observe," Ralph J. Mills pointed out in *Descant,* "John Betjeman is a phenomenon in contemporary English literature, a truly popular poet. The sudden fame won by his *Collected Poems . . .* which sold about 100,000 copies, brought him a wide reputation and made him quickly into a public personality." Betjeman was also admired by such poets and critics as W. H. Auden and Edmund Wilson. Mills said: "Certainly it is very rare in our day to see much accord between distinguished critics and poets on the one hand and the general public on the other; but the very complexity of Betjeman's personality and feelings beneath the skillful though apparently simple surface of his verse probably unites, in whatever different kinds of levels of appreciation, the otherwise remote members of his audience."

Mills called Betjeman a "topographical poet," in the sense that his poems that describe some action or event take place in a particular location, which he describes in great detail. The critic declared that "there is further wide attraction in the fact that his poetry is literal and descriptive rather than symbolic; social rather than private; nostalgic-though balanced by humor and occasional irony, as well as a pervasive lightness of touch; beautifully and precisely evocative of place, period, and the moods they generate. And the manner of his poetry is musically graceful and various in form." Although Betjeman named Eliot, Aldous Huxley, and the Sitwells as influences on his poems, "the clearest and strongest line of descent in his writing," Mills stated, "leads back to 18th and 19th century poets such as Cowper, Crabbe, Tennyson, Dowson, Hardy; the Irish poets Tom Moore and William Allingham; and a host of lesser figures."

An architect as well as a poet, Betjeman was aptly praised by W. H. Auden, in the introduction to *Slick But Not Streamlined,* as a topophile, whose poetry is concerned with actual places, to whom "a branch railroad is as valuable as a Roman wall, a neo-Tudor teashop as interesting as a Gothic cathedral." Auden added: "Topophilia . . . cannot survive at velocities greater than that of a somewhat rusty bicycle. (Hence, Betjeman's obsession with that vehicle.)" Betjeman was passionately involved in projects to preserve buildings of architectural or historical interest. He told Willa Petschek that he was even more interested "in saving groups of buildings of towns that can be ruined by 'a single frightful store that looks like a drive-in movie. The only way to prevent more and more ugly buildings going up,' he has said, 'is to draw people's attention to what's good in all periods.' " Betjeman made numerous appearances on television to promote preservation of his various causes, and became, as Petschek said, "a cherished national cult."

Betjeman championed his causes in his poetry as well; he wrote lovingly of the places of his childhood, and buildings and monuments in danger of destruction. Petschek declared that "Betjeman's approach to architecture (which he values second only to poetry) enabled him to recognize the 'living force' of 19th-century buildings, especially the Victorian Gothic. Partly through his verse and topographical writings, his guidebooks, poetry readings and TV appearances, but also through his warmth and peculiar genius for imparting enthusiasm for everything from rood screens to ladies' legs, he has made the public accept a rapid reversal in taste."

"The detailed recreation of the past in *Summoned by Bells,* as well as in briefer poems," Mills wrote, "is evidence of an almost Proustian memory in Betjeman, who confirms this by saying in the poem that 'Childhood is measured out by sounds and smells/ And sights, before the dark of reason grows.' Indeed, his richest imaginative resources seem to lie in the lost worlds of his childhood and early youth, their emerging interests and passionate attachments; they are restored and transformed in his poems." "But the same past, of course," Mills continued, "harbors the origins of the poet's melancholy, guilt, sense of evil, fear of pain and death, and apparent need for a kind of overmastering love; his authentic religious convictions do not develop, however, until quite a bit later . . . the elements in life which hold profound significance and value for him—except his mature Anglican faith— that is to say, his love for poetry and will to be a poet; his sensitive awareness of landscape; his passion for churches, railways, towns, and architecture: all those materials on which his writing thrives initially appealed to him in his youth." Betjeman says in *Summoned by Bells:* "For myself/I knew as soon as I could read and write/That I must be a poet."

Collected Poems, which brought Betjeman into the limelight, was enthusiastically received by many critics, but not by all of them. T. J. Ross wrote: "Though his ear is as flawless as Tennyson's and his effects sometimes as remarkable, Betjeman creates a world which, unlike the Victorian's, is a miniature." Ross believed that when Betjeman involved the reader completely with his subject "the result [was] poor." Only when he kept the reader at a distance did he bring his work up to the level of "first-rate minor art." Thom Gunn called Betjeman's treatment of the middle class "entirely superficial." A *Times Literary Supplement* reviewer wrote: "Whether or not all Mr. Betjeman's verse is poetry, all his poetry is verse, and in this it is a pleasant change from the shapeless and unarticulated matter . . . offered us by so many of his contemporaries. For Mr. Betjeman is a born versifier, ingenious and endlessly original; his echoes of Tennyson and Crabb, Praed and Father Prout, are never mere *pastiche;* and he is always attentive to the sound of his words, the run of his lines, the shape of his stanzas." Louise Bogan had high praise for Betjeman's work: "Since the early thirties, [he] has been producing light verse in which very close to but not crossing the line of parody, he has revived a whole set of emotional attitudes that can only be called Victorian. . . . His verse forms, elaborately varied, reproduce an entire set of neglected Victorian techniques, which he manipulates with the utmost dexterity and taste. His diction and his observation are delightfully fresh and original. And it is a pleasure to let down our defenses and be swept along by his anapaestic lines, with their bouncing unstressed syllables, and to meet no imperfect or false rhymes in the process; to recognize sentiment so delicately shaded, so sincerely felt, that it becomes immediately acceptable even to our modern sensibilities, grown used to the harsh, the violent, and the horrifying. We often, however, come upon a poem that brings us up short, to experience a melancholy, an irony that is close to Hardy or pa-

thos that is timeless. . . . However light his means, his purpose is never trivial."

"John Betjeman has been described," Petschek wrote, "as looking like a highly intelligent muffin: a small, plump, rumpled man with luminous, soft eyes, a chubby face topped by wisps of white hair and imparting a distinct air of absent-mindedness. He has an eager manner, a kind of old-fashioned courtesy and a sudden, schoolboy laugh which crumples his face like a paper bag." Betjeman once owned a waistcoat which once belonged to Henry James. He told Petschek: "Of course, I only wear it for weddings and funerals." In 1957 Petschek wrote: "[Betjeman's] doll's house study is a jumble of books: old copies of verse, typography and ecclesiology and files of correspondence. The walls are covered with red William Morris wallpaper and pictures by Rossetti, John Piper and Sargent. In the corner a 17th-century clock chimes brassily every quarter hour and the telephone rings continually."

Norman wrote that "after a miserable and pestered home life [Betjeman] found Oxford 'too delightful'; he lounged about in a shantung tie and took lavender-perfumed baths, so much so that C. S. Lewis, his tutor, thought him 'a pretentious playboy.' . . . His great love was the revival of the Gothic style in Victorian architecture. Sometimes, driving a car, he would take both hands from the wheel and yell, 'Phew! Gothic.' " Peter Bull, writing in *The Teddy Bear Book,* told of an afternoon that he and his teddy bear, Theodore, were invited to lunch by Betjeman and Archibald Ormsby-Gore, his "Teddy Bear companion for nearly sixty years," of whom Betjeman spoke in *Summoned by Bells.* Bull discovered that Archibald "had Baptist leanings and disapproved strongly of drinking and smoking. This had led to a certain amount of disagreement with Mr. Betjeman. . . . But the two of them get along rather famously on the whole. . . . Baptist or Protestant, Mr. Ormsby-Gore has tremendous personality—not very surprisingly, I suppose—and he has to keep up with his friend Mr. Betjeman, who is one of the most beloved and revered wits in Britain. . . . In the 1968 Summer Academy Exhibition in London an extraordinary picture by Jann Haworth showed [Betjeman] in triplicate as a teddy bear, his face at different angles surrounded by fur. The work was called 'A Valentine to John Betjeman.' "

Betjeman confided to Norman that "All his life . . . he's felt ruin 'very close'; yet the occasional depressions in his poems must not be interpreted as a desperate man's thought. . . . Betjeman says: 'It's a tone of voice—good old English melancholy, like Hardy, Hood and Tennyson—solid village gloom.' "

MEDIA ADAPTATIONS: Recordings by the author of his own work include "The Poems of John Betjeman: The Golden Treasury of John Betjeman," Spoken Arts; "Poems," Argo; "Summoned by Bells," Argo. Donald Swann has set some of Betjeman's poems to music.

BIOGRAPHICAL/CRITICAL SOURCES:

BOOKS

A Garland for the Laureate: Poems Presented to Sir John Betjeman on His 75th Birthday, Celandine Press, 1981.
Betjeman, John, *Slick But Not Streamlined,* introduction by W. H. Auden, Doubleday, 1947.
Brooke, Jocelyn, *Ronald Firbank and John Betjeman,* Longmans, Green, 1962.
Bull, Peter, *The Teddy Bear Book,* Random House, 1970.
Contemporary Literary Criticism, Gale, Volume 2, 1974, Volume 6, 1976, Volume 10, 1979, Volume 34, 1985, Volume 43, 1987.

Delaney, Frank, *Betjeman Country,* J. Murray, 1983.
Dictionary of Literary Biography, Volume 20: *British Poets, 1914-1945,* Gale, 1983.
Dictionary of Literary Biography Yearbook 1984, Gale, 1985.
Stapleton, Margaret L., *Sir John Betjeman: A Bibliography of Writings by and about Him,* Scarecrow Press, 1974.
Stem, Gladys, *And Did He Stop and Speak to You,* Regnery, 1958.

PERIODICALS

Book World, September 15, 1968.
Books and Bookmen, May, 1967.
Christian Century, February 22, 1961, June 5, 1963.
Commonweal, March 3, 1961.
Descant, spring, 1969.
Listener, January 26, 1967.
London Magazine, March, 1967.
New Statesman, December 3, 1960, January 6, 1961, October 3, 1969.
Newsweek, November 28, 1960.
New Yorker, April 18, 1959, September 2, 1967, May 23, 1970.
New York Herald Tribune Lively Arts, December 4, 1960.
New York Review of Books, May 18, 1967.
New York Times Book Review, September 24, 1967, December 7, 1969.
New York Times Magazine, August 13, 1967.
Poetry Review, summer, 1967.
Punch, April 29, 1970.
Spectator, December 2, 1960, April 18, 1970.
Time, February 2, 1959, December 5, 1960, October 23, 1972, December 4, 1972.
Times (London), May 22, 1984.
Times Literary Supplement, December 12, 1958, November 10, 1966, May 21, 1970.

OBITUARIES:

PERIODICALS

Chicago Tribune, May 21, 1984.
Los Angeles Times, May 21, 1984.
New York Times, May 20, 1984.
Sunday Times (London), May 20, 1984.
Time, May 28, 1984.
Times (London), May 21, 1984.
Washington Post, May 20, 1984.

*   *   *

BLIGHT, Rose
   See GREER, Germaine

*   *   *

BLYTON, Enid (Mary) 1897-1968
(Mary Pollock)

PERSONAL: Born August 11, 1897, in East Dulwich, London, England; died November 28, 1968; daughter of Thomas Carey and Theresa Mary (Harrison) Blyton; married Major Hugh Alexander Pollock (an editor), 1924 (divorced December, 1942); married Kenneth F. Durrell Waters (a surgeon), 1943 (died, 1967); children: Gillian, Imogen. *Education:* Attended Guildhall School of Music, 1916, and National Froebel Union teaching school, Ipswich, 1918. *Avocational interests:* Gardening, reading, bridge, and golf.

CAREER: Teacher at boys' preparatory school in Kent, England, 1919; private tutor to a family in Surbiton, Surrey, En-

gland, 1920; formed Durrell Waters, Ltd., with her second husband, to handle business contracts with publishers, 1950; writer and editor of poems, stories, and educational articles. Shaftesbury Society Babies' Home, Beaconsfield, committee member, 1948, later chairperson, 1954-67; also sponsored children's clubs to support other charitable organizations for children and animals.

AWARDS, HONORS: The Island of Jersey, U.K., paid tribute to Blyton's "Noddy" characters by portraying them on a 1970 commemorative stamp.

WRITINGS:

Child Whispers (poems), J. Saville, 1922.
Real Fairies (poems), J. Saville, 1923.
Responsive Singing Games, J. Saville, 1923.
The Enid Blyton Book of Fairies, George Newnes, 1924, reprinted, 1964, new edition, 1967.
Songs of Gladness, music by Alec Rowley, J. Saville, 1924.
The Zoo Book, George Newnes, 1924.
The Enid Blyton Book of Bunnies, George Newnes, 1925.
Silver and Gold (poems), illustrated by Lewis Baumer, Thomas Nelson, 1925.
The Bird Book, illustrated by Ronald Green, George Newnes, 1926.
The Enid Blyton Book of Brownies, George Newnes, 1926, reprinted, Dean, 1967.
Tales Half Told, Thomas Nelson, 1926.
The Animal Book, George Newnes, 1927, reprinted, 1954.
Let's Pretend, illustrated by I. Bennington Angrave, Thomas Nelson, 1928.
Nature Lessons, Evans Brothers, 1929.
Tarrydiddle Town, Thomas Nelson, 1929.
Cheerio! A Book for Boys and Girls, Birn Brothers, 1933.
Five Minute Tales, Methuen, 1933.
Let's Read, Birn Brothers, 1933.
My First Reading Book, Birn Brothers, 1933.
Read to Us, Birn Brothers, 1933.
The Enid Blyton Poetry Book, Methuen, 1934.
The Old Thatch Series (eight volumes), Johnston, 1934-35; (a second series, eight volumes), 1938-39.
The Red Pixie Book, George Newnes, 1934.
Round the Year with Enid Blyton, Evans Brothers, 1934.
Ten Minute Tales, Methuen, 1934, new editon, Mayflower, 1976.
The Children's Garden, George Newnes, 1935.
The Green Goblin Book, George Newnes, 1935, abridged edition published as *Feefo, Tuppeny and Jinks,* Staples Press, 1951.
Hedgerow Tales, Methuen, 1935, new edition, Hutchinson, 1986.
Hop, Skip and Jump, J. Coker, 1935.
The Tale of Mr. Wumble, J. Coker, 1935.
The Famous Jimmy, illustrated by Benjamin Rabier, Muller, 1936, Dutton, 1937.
Fifteen Minute Tales, Methuen, 1936, new edition, Mayflower, 1976.
The Yellow Fairy Book, George Newnes, 1936.
Adventure of the Wishing Chair, illustrated by Hilda McGavin, George Newnes, 1937, new edition, Dean, 1982.
Enid Blyton's Sunny Stories, George Newnes, 1937-52.
The Adventures of Binkle and Flip, illustrated by Kathleen Nixon, George Newnes, 1938, new edition, Dean, 1967.
Billy-Bob Tales, illustrated by May Smith, Methuen, 1938, reprinted, Mayflower, 1977.
Mr. Galliano's Circus, George Newnes, 1938, reprinted, Dean, 1972.
Boys' and Girls' Circus Book, News Chronicle, 1939.

The Enchanted Wood, George Newnes, 1939, new edition, Dean, 1979.

Hurrah for the Circus!, illustrated by E. H. Davie, George Newnes, 1939, new edition, Beaver Books, 1985.

Naughty Amelia Jane, George Newnes, 1939, reprinted, Beaver Books, 1981.

Birds of Our Garden, illustrated by Green and Ernest Aris, George Newnes, 1940.

Boys' and Girls' Story Book, George Newnes, 1940.

The Children of Cherry Tree Farm, illustrated by Harry Rountree, Country Life, 1940, new edition, Hamlyn, 1979.

Mister Meddle's Mischief, illustrated by Joyce Mercer and Rosalind M. Turvey, George Newnes, 1940, new edition, Beaver Books, 1981.

The Naughtiest Girl in the School, George Newnes, 1940, new edition, beaver Books, 1986.

Tales of Betsy May, illustrated by F. Gale Thomas, Methuen, 1940, new edition, Mayflower, 1976.

The Treasure Hunters, illustrated by E. Wilson and Joyce Davies, George Newnes, 1940, new edition, Armada Books, 1983.

Twenty Minute Tales, Methuen, 1940, new edition, Mayflower, 1972.

The Adventures of Mr. Pink-Whistle, George Newnes, 1941, new edition, Beaver Books, 1981.

The Adventurous Four, George Newnes, 1941, new edition, Beaver Books, 1986.

A Calendar for Children, George Brothers, 1941, revised edition, 1950.

Five O'Clock Tales, Methuen, 1941.

The Children of Willow Farm, illustrated by Rountree, Country Life, 1942, new edition, Beaver Books, 1980.

Circus Days Again, George Newnes, 1942, new edition, Dean, 1973.

Enid Blyton Happy Story Book, Hodder & Stoughton, 1942.

Enid Blyton Readers, Macmillan, Books 1-3, 1942, Books 4-6, 1944, Book 7, 1948, Books 10-12, 1950.

Enid Blyton 5 Little Books (first of a series), Evans Brothers, 1942.

Hello, Mr. Twiddle!, illustrated by McGavin, George Newnes, 1942, new edition, Beaver Books, 1985.

I'll Tell You a Story, illustrated by Eileen A. Soper, Macmillan, 1942.

I'll Tell You Another Story, Macmillan, 1942.

John Jolly at Christmas Time, Evans Brothers, 1942.

Land of Far-Beyond, Methuen, 1942, new edition, Mayflower, 1977.

More Adventures of Willow Farm, Country Life, 1942, new edition, Dean, 1974.

Naughtiest Girl Again, George Newnes, 1942, new edition, Dean, 1972.

The O'Sullivan Twins, Methuen, 1942, reprinted, Mayflower, 1967, reprinted with new illustrations, Methuen, 1970.

Shadow, the Sheep Dog, George Newnes, 1942, new edition, Armada Books, 1984.

Six O'Clock Tales, illustrated by Dorothy M. Wheeler, Methuen, 1942.

Bimbo and Topsy, illustrated by Lucy Gee, George Newnes, 1943, new edition, Beaver Books, 1981.

Dame Slap and Her School, illustrated by Wheeler, George Newnes, 1943.

John Jolly by the Sea, Evans Brothers, 1943.

John Jolly on the Farm, Evans Brothers, 1943.

The Magic Faraway Tree, illustrated by Wheeler, George Newnes, 1943, reprinted, Dean, 1981.

Merry Story Book, illustrated by Soper, Hodder & Stoughton, 1943.

Polly Piglet, illustrated by Soper, Brockhampton Press, 1943.

Seven O'Clock Tales, Methuen, 1943.

The Toys Come to Life, illustrated by Soper, Brockhampton Press, 1943.

At Appletree Farm, Brockhampton Press, 1944.

Billy and Betty at the Seaside, Valentine & Sons, 1944.

A Book of Naughty Children, Methuen, 1944, new edition, Mayflower, 1976.

The Boy Next Door, illustrated by Bestall, George Newnes, 1944, new edition, Armada Books, 1984.

The Christmas Book, illustrated by Treyer Evans, Macmillan, 1944.

Come to the Circus, illustrated by Soper, Brockhampton Press, 1944, new edition, Beaver Books, 1985.

The Dog That Went to Fairyland, Brockhampton Press, 1944.

Eight O'Clock Tales, illustrated by Wheeler, Methuen, 1944.

Enid Blyton's Nature Lover's Books, illustrated by Donia Nachshen and Noel Hopking, Evans Brothers, 1944.

Jolly Little Jumbo, Brockhampton Press, 1944.

Jolly Story Book, illustrated by Soper, Hodder & Stoughton, 1944.

Rainy Day Stories, illustrated by Nora S. Unwin, Evans Brothers, 1944, new edition, Purnell, 1983.

Tales of Toyland, illustrated by McGavin, George Newnes, 1944.

The Three Golliwogs, George Newnes, 1944, reprinted, Dean, 1968.

The Blue Story Book, illustrated by Soper, Methuen, 1945, new edition, Mayflower.

The Brown Family, illustrated by E. Buhler and R. Buhler, News Chronicle, 1945.

The Conjuring Wizard and Other Stories, illustrated by Soper, Macmillan, 1945.

Enid Blyton Nature Readers, Macmillan, Numbers 1-20, 1945, Numbers 21-30, 1946.

The Family at Red Roofs, illustrated by W. Spence, Lutterworth, 1945.

Hollow Tree House, illustrated by Elizabeth Wall, Lutterworth, 1945.

John Jolly at the Circus, Evans Brothers, 1945.

The Naughtiest Girl Is a Monitor, George Newnes, 1945, new edition, Dean, 1973.

Round the Clock Stories, illustrated by Unwin, National Magazine, 1945.

The Runaway Kitten, illustrated by Soper, Brockhampton Press, 1945.

Sunny Story Book, Hodder & Stoughton, 1945.

The Teddy Bear's Party, illustrated by Soper, Brockhampton Press, 1945.

The Twins Go to Nursery Rhyme Land, illustrated by Soper, Brockhampton Press, 1945.

Amelia Jane Again, George Newnes, 1946, new edition, Beaver Books, 1981.

The Bad Little Monkey, illustrated by Soper, Brockhampton Press, 1946.

The Children at Happy House, illustrated by Kathleen Gell, Basil Blackwell, 1946.

Chimney Corner Stories, illustrated by Pat Harrison, National Magazine, 1946.

The Enid Blyton Holiday Book, twelve volumes, Low, 1946.

The Folk of the Faraway Tree, illustrated by Wheeler, George Newnes, 1946, de luxe edition, Deans International, 1983.

Gay Story Book, illustrated by Soper, Hodder & Stoughton, 1946.

Little White Duck and Other Stories, illustrated by Soper, Macmillan, 1946.

The Put-Em-Rights, illustrated by Wall, Lutterworth, 1946.

The Red Story Book, Methuen, 1946, new edition, Mayflower, 1966.

The Surprising Caravan, illustrated by Soper, Brockhampton Press, 1946.

Tales of Green Hedges, illustrated by Gwen White, National Magazine, 1946.

The Train That Lost Its Way, illustrated by Soper, Brockhampton Press, 1946.

The Adventurous Four Again, George Newnes, 1946, new edition, Beaver Books, 1986.

At Seaside Cottage, illustrated by Soper, Brockhampton Press, 1947.

Before I Go to Sleep: A Book of Bible Stories and Prayers for Children at Night, Latimer House, 1947.

Enid Blyton's Treasury, Evans Brothers, 1947.

The Green Story Book, illustrated by Soper, Methuen, 1947.

The Happy House Children Again, illustrated by Gell, Basil Blackwell, 1947.

House-at-the-Corner, illustrated by Elsie Walker, Lutterworth, 1947.

Jinky Nature Books, four parts, E. J. Arnold, 1947.

Little Green Duck and Other Stories, Brockhampton Press, 1947.

Lucky Story Book, illustrated by Soper, Hodder & Stoughton, 1947.

Rambles with Uncle Nat, illustrated by Unwin, National Magazine, 1947.

A Second Book of Naughty Children, illustrated by Gell, Methuen, 1947, new edition, Mayflower, 1976.

The Smith Family, three volumes, E. J. Arnold, 1947.

The Very Clever Rabbit, illustrated by Soper, Brockhampton Press, 1947.

The Adventures of Pip, Low, 1948.

Enid Blyton's Bedtime Series, two parts, Brockhampton Press, 1948.

Children of Other Lands, J. Coker, 1948.

Come to the Circus! (not the same as the 1944 book published under the same title), illustrated by Joyce M. Johnson, George Newnes, 1948.

Just Time for a Story, illustrated by Grace Lodge, Macmillan, 1948.

Jolly Tales, Johnston, 1948.

Let's Garden, illustrated by William McLaren, Latimer House, 1948.

Let's Have a Story, illustrated by George Bowe, Pitkin, 1948.

The Little Girl at Capernaum, illustrated by Walker, Lutterworth, 1948.

Mister Icy-Cold, Shakespeare Head Press, 1948.

More Adventures of Pip, Low, 1948.

Nature Tales, Johnston, 1948.

Now for a Story, illustrated by Frank Varty, Harold Hill, 1948.

The Red-Spotted Handkerchief and Other Stories, illustrated by Gell, Brockhampton Press, 1948.

The Little Boy Jesus, J. Coker, 1948.

The Secret of the Old Mill, illustrated by Soper, Brockhampton Press, 1948.

Six Cousins at Mistletoe Farm, illustrated by Peter Beigel, Evans Brothers, 1948, reprinted, Collins, 1967.

Tales After Tea, Laurie, 1948.

Tales of the Twins, illustrated by Soper, Brockhampton Press, 1948.

They Ran Away Together, illustrated by Jeanne Farrar, Brockhampton Press, 1948.

We Want a Story, illustrated by Bowe, Pitkin, 1948.

The Bluebell Story Book, Gifford, 1949.

Bumpy and His Bus, illustrated by Wheeler, George Newnes, 1949.

A Cat in Fairyland and Other Stories, Pitkin, 1949, reprinted, Hutchinson, 1986, published as *A Cat in Fairyland and Other Tales,* David & Charles, 1987.

Chuff the Chimney Sweep, Pitkin, 1949.

The Circus Book, Latimer House, 1949.

The Dear Old Snow Man, Brockhampton Press, 1949.

Don't Be Silly, Mr. Twiddle, George Newnes, 1949, new edition, Mayflower, 1973.

The Enchanted Sea, Pitkin, 1949, published as *The Enchanted Sea and Other Tales,* David & Charles, 1987.

Enid Blyton's Daffodil Story Book, Gifford, 1949.

Enid Blyton's Good Morning Book, illustrated by Don and Ann Goring, National Magazine, 1949.

Humpty Dumpty and Belinda, Collins, 1949.

Jinky's Joke and Other Stories, illustrated by Gell, Brockhampton Press, 1949.

Mr. Tumpy and His Caravan, illustrated by Wheeler, Sidgwick & Jackson, 1949.

My Enid Blyton Bedside Book, twelve volumes, Arthur Barker, beginning 1949.

Oh, What a Lovely Time, Brockhampton Press, 1949.

A Story Party at Green Hedges, illustrated by Lodge, Hodder & Stoughton, 1949.

The Strange Umbrella, Pitkin, 1949.

Tales After Supper, Laurie, 1949.

Those Dreadful Children, illustrated by Lodge, Lutterworth, 1949.

Tiny Tales, Littlebury, 1949.

The Astonishing Ladder and Other Stories, illustrated by Soper, Macmillan, 1950.

A Book of Magic, J. Coker, 1950.

The Enid Blyton Pennant Series, thirty parts, Macmillan, 1950.

The Magic Knitting Needles and Other Stories, Macmillan, 1950.

Mister Meddle's Muddles, illustrated by Turvey and Mercer, George Newnes, 1950, new edition, Beaver Books, 1981.

Mr. Pink-Whistle Interferes, illustrated by Wheeler, George Newnes, 1950, new edition, Beaver Books, 1981.

The Poppy Story Book, Gifford, 1950.

Round the Year Stories, J. Coker, 1950.

Rubbalong Tales, illustrated by Norman Meredith, Macmillan, 1950.

Six Cousins Again, illustrated by Maurice Tulloch, Evans Brothers, 1950, new edition, Collins, 1967.

Tales about Toys, Brockhampton Press, 1950.

The Three Naughty Children and Other Stories, illustrated by Soper, Macmillan, 1950, new edition, Mayflower, 1974.

Tricky the Goblin and Other Stories, illustrated by Soper, Macmillan, 1950, new edition, Mayflower, 1976.

What an Adventure, Brockhampton Press, 1950.

The Wishing Chair Again, George Newnes, 1950, de luxe edition, Deans International, 1983.

Yellow Story Book, illustrated by Gell, Methuen, 1950.

Benny and the Princess and Other Stories, Pitkin, 1951.

Buttercup Story Book, Gifford, 1951.

Down at the Farm, Low, 1951.

Father Christmas and Belinda, Collins, 1951.

The Flying Goat and Other Stories, Pitkin, 1951.

Gay Street Book, illustrated by Lodge, Latimer House, 1951.

Hello Twins, Brockhampton Press, 1951.

Let's Go to the Circus, Odhams, 1951.

The Little Spinning Mouse and Other Stories, Pitkin, 1951.

The Magic Snow-Bird and Other Stories, Pitkin, 1951.

A Picnic Party with Enid Blyton, illustrated by Lodge, Hodder & Stoughton, 1951.

Pippy and the Gnome and Other Stories, Pitkin, 1951.

The Proud Golliwog, Brockhampton Press, 1951.

The Runaway Teddy Bear and Other Stories, Pitkin, 1951.

The Six Bad Boys, illustrated by Mary Gernat, Lutterworth, 1951.

'Too-Wise' the Wonderful Wizard and Other Stories, Pitkin, 1951.

Up the Faraway Tree, illustrated by Wheeler, George Newnes, 1951.

Bright Story Book, illustrated by Soper, Brockhampton Press, 1952.

(With W. E. Johns and others) *The Children's Jolly Book,* Odhams, 1952.

Bible Pictures, New Testament, Macmillan, 1952.

Come Along Twins, Brockhampton Press, 1952.

Enid Blyton Tiny Strip Books (series), Low, 1952.

Enid Blyton's Animal Lover's Book, Evans Brothers, 1952.

Enid Blyton's Colour Strip Books, Low, 1952.

Enid Blyton's Omnibus, illustrated by Jessie Land, George Newnes, 1952.

The Mad Teapot, Brockhampton Press, 1952.

Mandy, Mops and Cubby Again, Low, 1952.

Mandy, Mops and Cubby Find a House, Low, 1952.

Mr. Tumpy Plays a Trick on Saucepan, Low, 1952.

My First Enid Blyton Book (followed by *My Second* to *My Eighth Enid Blyton Book*), Latimer House, 1952, reprinted in new editions, Granada, 1983-84.

My First Nature Book (followed by *My Second* and *My Third Nature Book*), illustrated by Soper, Macmillan, 1952.

The Queer Adventure, illustrated by Meredith, Staples Press, 1952.

Snowdrop Story Book, Gifford, 1952.

The Story of My Life (autobiography), Pitkin, 1952, new edition, Grafton Books, 1986.

The Very Big Secret, illustrated by R. Gervis, Lutterworth, 1952, new edition, Sparrow Books, 1980.

Clicky the Clockwork Clown, Brockhampton Press, 1953.

Enid Blyton's Christmas Story, illustrated by Fritz Wegner, Hamish Hamilton, 1953.

Gobo and Mr. Fierce, Low, 1953.

Here Come the Twins, Brockhampton Press, 1953.

(Translator) *Little Gift Books,* illustrated by Pierre Probst, Hackett, 1953.

Mandy Makes Cubby a Hat, Low, 1953.

Mr. Tumpy in the Land of Wishes, Low, 1953.

My Enid Blyton Story Book, illustrated by Willy Schermele, Juvenile Productions, 1953.

Snowball the Pony, illustrated by Iris Gillespie, Lutterworth, 1953, new edition, Sparrow Books, 1983.

The Story of Our Queen, illustrated by F. Stocks May, Muller, 1953.

Visitors in the Night, Brockhampton Press, 1953.

Well, Really, Mr. Twiddle!, illustrated by Mc Gavin, George Newnes, 1953, new edition, Beaver Books, 1982.

The Adventure of the Secret Necklace, illustrated by Isabel Veevers, Lutterworth, 1954, new edition, Sparrow Books, 1984.

The Castle Without a Door and Other Stories, Pitkin, 1954.

The Children at Green Meadows, illustrated by Lodge, Lutterworth, 1954, new edition, Collins, 1974.

Enid Blyton's Friendly Story Book, illustrated by Soper, Brockhampton Press, 1954.

Enid Blyton's Marigold Story Book, Gilford, 1954.

The Greatest Book in the World, illustrated by Mabel Peacock, British & Foreign Bible Society, 1954.

Little Strip Picture Books (series), Low, 1954.

The Little Toy Farm and Other Stories, Pitkin, 1954.

Merry Mister Meddle!, illustrated by Turvey and Mercer, George Newnes, 1954, new edition, Mayflower, 1976.

More About Amelia Jane, illustrated by Sylvia I. Venus, George Newnes, 1954, new edition, Dean, 1974.

Away Goes Sooty, illustrated by Probst, Collins, 1955.

Benjy and the Others, illustrated by Gell, Latimer House, 1955.

Bimbo and Blackie Go Camping, illustrated by Probst, Collins, 1955.

Bobs, illustrated by Probst, Collins, 1955.

Christmas with Scamp and Bimbo, Collins, 1955.

Enid Blyton's Little Bedtime Books, eight volumes, Low, 1955.

Neddy the Little Donkey, illustrated by Romain Simon, Collins, 1955.

Enid Blyton's Sooty, illustrated by Probst, Collins, 1955.

Enid Blyton's What Shall I Be?, illustrated by Probst, Collins, 1955.

Foxglove Story Book, Gilford, 1955.

Gobbo in the Land of Dreams, Low, 1955.

Golliwog Grumbled, Brockhampton Press, 1955.

Holiday House, illustrated by Lodge, Evans Brothers, 1955.

Laughing Kitten, photographs by Paul Kaye, Harvill, 1955.

Mandy, Mops and Cubby and the Whitewash, Low, 1955.

Mischief Again, photographs by Kaye, Harvill, 1955.

Mr. Pink-Whistle's Party, illustrated by Wheeler, George Newnes, 1955, new edition, Mayflower, 1973.

Mr. Tumpy in the Land of Boys and Girls, Low, 1955.

More Chimney Corner Stories, illustrated by P. Harrison, Latimer House, 1955.

Playing at Home, illustrated by Sabine Schweitzer, Methuen, 1955.

Run-About's Holiday, illustrated by Lilian Chivers, Lutterworth, 1955, new edition, Sparrow Books, 1981.

The Troublesome Three, illustrated by Leo, Sampson Low, 1955.

The Clever Little Donkey, illustrated by Simon, Collins, 1956.

Colin the Cow-Boy, illustrated by R. Caille, Collins, 1956.

Enid Blyton's Animal Tales, illustrated by Simon, Collins, 1956.

Four in a Family, illustrated by Tom Kerr, Lutterworth, 1956, new edition, Sparrow Books, 1974.

Let's Have a Party, photographs by Kaye, Harvill, 1956.

Scamp at School, illustrated by Probst, Collins, 1956.

(Contributor) *Children's Own Wonder Book,* Odhams, 1956.

New Testament Picture Books 1-2, Macmillan, 1957.

Birthday Kitten, illustrated by Lodge, Lutterworth, 1958, new edition, Saprrow Books, 1980.

Clicky Gets Into to Trouble, illustrated by Molly Brett, Brockhampton Press, 1958.

Mr. Pink-Whistle's Big Book, Evans Brothers, 1958.

My Big Ears Picture Book, Low, 1958.

Rumble and Chuff, illustrated by David Walsh, Juvenile Productions, 1958.

(With others) *The School Companion,* New Educational Press, 1958.

Adventure of the Strange Ruby, Brockhampton Press, 1960, new edition, Beaver Books, 1979.

Adventure Stories, Collins, 1960, new edition, Armada Books, 1982.

Clicky and Tiptoe, illustrated by Brett, Brockhampton Press, 1960.

Happy Day Stories, illustrated by Marcia Lane Foster, Evans Brothers, 1960.

Mystery Stories, Collins, 1960, new edition, Sparrow Books, 1981.

Old Testament Picture Books, Macmillan, 1960.

Tales at Bedtime, illustrated by McGavin, Collins, 1960.

Will the Fiddle, illustrated by Lodge, Instructive Arts, 1960.

The Big Enid Blyton Book (selections), Hamlyn, 1961.

Happy Holiday, Clicky, illustrated by Brett, Brockhampton Press, 1961.

The Four Cousins, illustrated by Joan Thompson, Lutterworth, 1962.

Stories for Monday, Oliphants, 1962.

Stories for Tuesday, Oliphants, 1962.

The Boy Who Wanted a Dog, illustrated by Sally Michel, Lutterworth, 1963, new edition, Sparrow Books, 1980.

Enid Blyton's Sunshine Picture Story Book (first of a series), World Distributors, 1964.

Happy Hours Story Book, Dean, 1964.

Story Book for Fives to Sevens, illustrated by Dorothy Hall and Grace Shelton, Parrish, 1964.

Storytime Book, Dean, 1964.

Tell-a-Story Books, World Distributors, 1964.

Trouble for the Twins, Brockhampton Press, 1965.

The Boy Who Came Back, illustrated by Walker, Lutterworth, 1965.

Easy Reader (first of a series), Collins, 1965.

Enid Blyton's Sunshine Book, Dean, 1965.

Enid Blyton's Treasure Box, Low, 1965.

The Man Who Stopped to Help, illustrated by Walker, Lutterworth, 1965.

Enid Blyton's Playbook (first of a series), Collins, 1966.

The Fairy Folk Story Book, Collins, 1966.

Enid Blyton's Fireside Tales, Collins, 1966, new edition, Purnell, 1972.

Gift Book, illustrated by Schermele, Purnell, 1966.

The Happy House Children, Collins, 1966.

John and Mary, series of nine books, illustrated by Fromont, Brockhampton Press, 1966-68.

Pixie Tales, Collins, 1966.

Pixieland Story Books, Collins, 1966.

Stories for Bedtime, Dean, 1966.

Stories for You, Dean, 1966.

Holiday Annual Stories, Low, 1967.

Holiday Magic Stories, Low, 1967.

Holiday Pixie Stories, Low, 1967.

Holiday Toy Stories, Low, 1967.

The Playtime Story Book, Numbers 1-4, World Distributors, 1967.

Adventures on Willow Farm, Collins, 1967.

Brownie Tales, Collins, 1968.

The Playtime Books, Numbers 9-12, World Distributors, 1968.

Once Upon a Time, Collins, 1968.

Bedtime Stories, Purnell, 1970.

Funtime Tales, Purnell, 1972.

The Boy Who Turned into an Engine, Mayflower, 1973.

Rag, Tag and Bobtail, Mayflower, 1975.

Enid Blyton's A Shock for Shelia, and Other Stories, Dean, 1976.

Enid Blyton's Julia Saves Up, and Other Stories, Dent, 1976.

Enid Blyton's The Story That Came True, and Other Stories, Dean, 1976.

Enid Blyton's Sunnyside Stories, Purnell, 1976.

Enid Blyton's The Train That Went to Fairyland, and Other Stories, Dent, 1976.

Enid Blyton's Twilight Tales, Purnell, 1976.

Gift Book of Bedtime Stories, Dean, 1978.

Girl Who Found Sixpence, Collins, 1982.

The Hidey-Hole, Sparrow Books, 1982.

Timothy's Tadpoles, Collins, 1982.

Billy's Bicycle, Collins, 1982.

Little Stray Cat, Collins, 1983.

Happy Time Stories, Purnell, 1983.

Clockwork Mouse in Trouble, Collins, 1983.

Big Bad Dog, Collins, 1983.

Good Gracious Me!, Collins, 1984.

Bedtime Story Book, Collins, 1984.

Fairy and the Cracker, Collins, 1984.

Bedtime Books (twelve volumes), Granada, 1984.

One New Laid Egg, Collins, 1984.

Shuffle the Shoemaker, Granada, 1985.

The Enchanted Sea and Other Stories, Hutchinson, 1986.

Bedtime Book, Deans International, 1986.

The Little Green Imp and Other Stories, Beaver Books, 1985.

Goodnight Stories, Treasure Press, 1986.

The Goblin Aeroplane and Other Stories, Hutchinson, 1986, published as *The Goblin Aeroplane and Other Tales,* David & Charles, 1987.

Puppy in Wonderland and Other Stories, Hutchinson, 1986, published as *Puppy in Wonderland and Other Tales,* David & Charles, 1987.

"SECRET" SERIES

The Secret Island, Basil Blackwell, 1938, reprinted, May Fair Books, 1965.

The Secret of Spiggy Holes, Basil Blackwell, 1940, reprinted, May Fair Books, 1965.

The Secret Mountain, Basil Blackwell, 1941, reprinted with new illustrations, Collins, 1969.

The Secret of Killimooin, Basil Blackwell, 1943, new edition, Collins, 1966.

The Secret of Moon Castle, Basil Blackwell, 1953, reprinted with new illustrations, 1981.

"JOSIE, CLICK AND BUN" SERIES; ALL ILLUSTRATED BY D.M. WHEELER

The Little Tree House: Being the Adventures of Josie, Click and Bun, George Newnes, 1940, reprinted as *Josie, Click and Bun and the Little Tree House,* 1951.

The Further Adventures of Josie, Click and Bun, George Newnes, 1941, new edition, Beaver Books, 1982.

Josie, Click and Bun Again, George Newnes, 1946.

More About Josie, Click and Bun, George Newnes, 1947.

Welcome Josie, Click and Bun, George Newnes, 1952, new edition, Beaver Books, 1982.

"ST. CLARE'S" SERIES

The Twins at St. Clare's, Methuen, 1941, new edition, 1981.

Summer Term at St. Clare's, Methuen, 1943, new edition, 1972.

Claudine at St. Clare's, Methuen, 1944, new edition, 1970.

The Second Form at St. Clare's, illustrated by W. Lindsay Cable, Methuen, 1944, new edition, 1973.

Fifth Formers at St. Clare's, illustrated by Cable, Methuen, 1945, new edition, 1970.

"FIVE" SERIES

Five on a Treasure Island (also see below), Hodder & Stoughton, 1942, new edition, Longman, 1977.

Five Go Adventuring Again (also see below), Hodder & Stoughton, 1943, published as *Five Find a Secret Way,* Atheneum, 1972.

Five Run Away Together, illustrated by Soper, Hodder & Stoughton, 1944, reprinted with new illustrations, 1968; published as *Five Run Away to Danger,* Atheneum, 1972.

Five Go to Smugglers' Top, Hodder & Stoughton, 1945, new edition, 1967.

Five Go Off in a Caravan, illustrated by Soper, Hodder & Stoughton, 1946, new edition, 1983.

Five on Kirrin Island Again, Hodder & Stoughton, 1947, new edition, 1983; published as *Five Guard a Hidden Discovery,* Atheneum, 1972.

Five Go Off to Camp, Hodder & Stoughton, 1948, new edition, 1983; published as *Five on the Track of a Spook Train,* Atheneum, 1972.

Five Get Into Trouble (also see below), illustrated by Soper, Hodder & Stoughton, 1949, new edition, 1983; new edition published as *Five Caught in a Treacherous Plot,* illustrated by Betty Maxey, Atheneum, 1972.

Five Fall Into Adventure (also see below), illustrated by Soper, Hodder & Stoughton, 1950, new edition, 1984; new edition illustrated by Maxey, Atheneum, 1972.

Five on a Hike Together (also see below), illustrated by Soper, Hodder & Stoughton, 1951, new edition, 1984.

Five Have a Wonderful Time, illustrated by Soper, Hodder & Stoughton, 1952, new edition, 1984.

Five Go Down to the Sea, illustrated by Soper, Hodder & Stoughton, 1953, new edition, 1984.

Five Go to Mystery Moor, Hodder & Stoughton, 1954, new edition, 1985.

Five Have Plenty of Fun, Hodder & Stoughton, 1955, new edition, 1985.

Five on a Secret Trail, illustrated by Soper, Hodder & Stoughton, 1956, new edition, 1985; reprinted with illustrations by Betty Maxey, Atheneum (New York), 1972.

Five Go to Billycock Hill, illustrated by Soper, Hodder & Stoughton, 1956, new edition, 1985.

Five Get Into a Fix, illustrated by Soper, Hodder & Stoughton, 1958, new edition, 1986.

Five on Finniston Farm, illustrated by Soper, Hodder & Stoughton, 1960, new edition, 1986.

Five Go to Demon's Rocks, illustrated by Soper, Hodder & Stoughton, 1961, new edition, 1986; reprinted with illustrations by Maxey, Atheneum, 1972.

Five Have a Mystery to Solve, illustrated by Soper, Hodder & Stoughton, 1962.

Five Are Together Again, illustrated by Soper, Hodder & Stoughton, 1963.

Fabulous Famous Five (contains *Five Get into Trouble, Five Fall into Adventure,* and *Five on a Hike Together*), illustrated by Maxey, Hodder & Stoughton, 1974.

The Famous Five, Edito-Service (Geneva), 1981.

Famous Five Bumper Double: Five on a Treasure Island and Five Go Adventuring Again, Hodder & Stoughton, 1986.

"FAMOUS FIVE ADVENTURE GAMES" SERIES

Wrecker's Tower Game, Hodder & Stoughton, 1984.
The Haunted Railway Game, Hodder & Stoughton, 1984.
Sinister Lake Game, Hodder & Stoughton, 1985.
Whispering Island Game, Hodder & Stoughton, 1985.
Secret Airfield Game, Hodder & Stoughton, 1986.

"MARY MOUSE" SERIES

Mary Mouse and the Doll's House, Brockhampton Press, 1942.

More Adventures of Mary Mouse, Brockhampton Press, 1943.
Little Mary Mouse Again, Brockhampton Press, 1944.
Hallo, Little Mary Mouse, illustrated by Olive F. Openshaw, Brockhampton Press, 1945.
Mary Mouse and Her Family, illustrated by Openshaw, Brockhampton Press, 1946.
Here Comes Mary Mouse Again, Brockhampton Press, 1947.
How Do You Do, Mary Mouse, Brockhampton Press, 1948.
We Do Love Mary Mouse, Brockhampton Press, 1950.
Welcome Mary Mouse, illustrated by Openshaw, Brockhampton Press, 1950.
Hurrah for Mary Mouse, Brockhampton Press, 1951.
A Prize for Mary Mouse, Brockhampton Press, 1951.
Mary Mouse and Her Bicycle, illustrated by Openshaw, Brockhampton Press, 1952.
Mary Mouse and the Noah's Ark, illustrated by Openshaw, Brockhampton Press, 1953.
Mary Mouse to the Rescue, Brockhampton Press, 1954.
Mary Mouse in Nursery Rhyme Land, Brockhampton Press, 1955.
A Day with Mary Mouse, illustrated by Frederick White, Brockhampton Press, 1956.
Mary Mouse and the Garden Party, illustrated by White, Brockhampton Press, 1957.
Mary Mouse Goes to the Fair, illustrated by White, Brockhampton Press, 1958.
Mary Mouse Has a Wonderful Idea, illustrated by White, Brockhampton Press, 1959.
Mary Mouse Goes to Sea, illustrated by White, Brockhampton Press, 1960.
Mary Mouse Goes Out for the Day, illustrated by White, Brockhampton Press, 1961.
Fun with Mary Mouse, illustrated by R. Paul-Hoeye, Brockhampton Press, 1962.
Mary Mouse and the Little Donkey, illustrated by Paul-Hoeye, Brockhampton Press, 1964.

METHUEN "MYSTERY" SERIES

The Mystery of the Burnt Cottage, illustrated by J. Abbey, Methuen, 1943, reprinted, British Book Center, 1973.
The Mystery of the Disappearing Cat, illustrated by Abbey, Methuen, 1944, reprinted, British Book Center, 1973.
Mystery of the Secret Room, Methuen, 1945, reprinted, British Book Center, 1975.
Mystery of the Spiteful Letters, illustrated by Abbey, Methuen, 1946, reprinted, British Book Center, 1976.
The Mystery of the Missing Necklace, Methuen, 1947, reprinted, British Book Center, 1975.
The Mystery of the Hidden House, illustrated by Abbey, Methuen, 1948, reprinted, British Book Center, 1973.
The Mystery of the Pantomime Cat, Methuen, 1949, reprinted with new illustrations, 1970.
The Mystery of the Invisible Thief, Methuen, 1950, new edition, 1972.
The Mystery of the Vanished Prince, illustrated by Evans, Methuen, 1951, new edition, 1973.
The Mystery of the Strange Bundle, illustrated by Evans, Methuen, 1952, new edition, 1973.
The Mystery of Holly Lane, illustrated by Evans, Methuen, 1953, reprinted with new illustraions, 1970.
The Mystery of Tally-Ho Cottage, illustrated by Evans, Methuen, 1954, reprinted with new illustrations, 1970.
Mystery of the Missing Man, illustrated by Lilian Buchanan, Methuen, 1956, new edition, 1973.

Mystery of the Strange Messages, illustrated by Buchanan, Methuen, 1957.

The Mystery of Banshee Towers: A Story about the Five-Find-Outers and Dog, illustrated by Buchanan, Methuen, 1961, new edition illustrated by Jenny Chapple, 1973.

The Mystery That Never Was, illustrated by Gilbert Dunlop, Methuen, 1961, new edition, Armada Books, 1982.

COLLINS "MYSTERY" SERIES

The Rockingdown Mystery, illustrated by Dunlop, Collins, 1949, reprinted with new illustrations, 1970.

The Rilloby Fair Mystery, illustrated by Dunlop, Collins, 1950, reprinted with new illustrations, 1973.

The Rubadub Mystery, illustrated by Dunlop, Collins, 1952, new edition, 1969.

Ring O'Bells Mystery, Collins, 1955, reprinted with new illustrations, 1972.

Rat-a-Tat Mystery, Collins, 1956, new edition, 1970.

Ragamuffin Mystery, Collins, 1959, new edition, 1972.

"ADVENTURE" SERIES

The Island of Adventure, illustrated by Stuart Tresilian, Macmillan, 1944, new edition, 1983; reprint published as *Mystery Island,* 1945.

The Castle of Adventure, illustrated by Tresilian, Macmillan, 1946, new edition, Macmillan (London), 1983.

The Valley of Adventure, illustrated by Tresilian, Macmillan, 1947, new edition, 1983.

The Sea Adventure, illustrated by Tresilian, Macmillan, 1948, new edition, 1983.

The Mountain of Adventure, Macmillan, 1949, new edition, 1983.

The Ship of Adventure, illustrated by Tresilian, Macmillan, 1950, new edition, 1983.

The Circus of Adventure, illustrated by Tresilian, Macmillan, 1952.

River of Adventure, illustrated by Tresilian, Macmillan, 1955, new edition, 1983.

"FAMILY" SERIES

The Caravan Family, illustrated by William Fyffe, 1945.

The Saucy Jane Family, illustrated by Ruth Gervis, Lutterworth, 1947, new edition, Sparrow Books, 1982.

The Pole Star Family, illustrated by Ruth Gervis, Lutterworth, 1950.

The Seaside Family, illustrated by Ruth Gervis, Lutterworth, 1950.

The Buttercup Farm Family, illustrated by Ruth Gervis, Lutterworth, 1951, new edition, Arrow Books, 1981.

The Queen Elizabeth Family, illustrated by Ruth Gervis, Lutterworth, 1951, new edition, Beaver Books, 1985.

"MALORY TOWERS" SERIES

First Term at Malory Towers, Methuen, 1946, new edition, 1972.

The Second Form at Malory Towers, Methuen, 1947, reprinted with new illustrations, 1970.

Third Year at Malory Towers, illustrated by Stanley Lloyd, Methuen, 1948, reprinted with new illustrations, 1970.

The Upper Fourth at Malory Towers, Methuen, 1949, reprinted with new illustrations, 1970.

In the Fifth at Malory Towers, illustrated by Lloyd, Methuen, 1950, new edition, Mayflower, 1967.

Last Term at Malory Towers, illustrated by Lloyd, Methuen, 1951, new edition, 1973.

"NODDY" SERIES

Little Noddy Goes to Toy Land, illustrated by Harmsen Van Der Beek, Low, 1949, reprinted as *Enid Blyton's Noddy Goes to Toyland,* Macdonald Purnell, 1986.

Hurrah for Little Noddy, Low, 1950, published as *Enid Blyton's Hurrah for Little Noddy,* Purnell, 1986.

The Big Noddy Book (series of eight books), illustrated by Van Der Beek, Low, 1951.

Here Comes Noddy Again, Low, 1951, reprinted as *Enid Blyton's Here Comes Noddy Again,* Purnell, 1986.

Noddy and Big Ears Have a Picnic, Low, 1951.

Noddy and His Car, Low, 1951, reprinted as *Enid Blyton's Noddy and His Car,* Purnell, 1986.

Noddy Goes to the Seaside, Low, 1951.

Noddy Has More Adventures, Low, 1951.

Noddy Has a Shock, Low, 1951.

Noddy Off to Rocking Horse Land, Low, 1951.

A Tale of Little Noddy, Low, 1951.

Enid Blyton's Noddy's Ark of Books, Low, 1952.

Noddy and Big Ears, Low, 1952.

Noddy and the Witch's Wand, Low, 1952.

Noddy's Car Gets a Squeak, Low, 1952.

Noddy Colour Strip Book, illustrated by Van Der Beek, Low, 1952.

Noddy Goes to School, Low, 1952.

Noddy's Penny Wheel Car, Low, 1952.

Well Done, Noddy, Low, 1952.

New Noddy Colour Strip Book, Low, 1953.

The New Big Noddy Book, Low, 1953, reprinted as *Enid Blyton's Big Noddy Book,* Purnell, 1976.

Noddy and the Cuckoo's Nest, Low, 1953.

Noddy at the Seaside, Low, 1953.

Noddy Cut-Out Model Book, Low, 1953.

Noddy Gets Captured, Low, 1953.

Noddy Is Very Silly, Low, 1953.

Noddy's Garage of Books (five books), illustrated by Van Der Beek, Low, 1953.

Enid Blyton's Noddy Giant Painting Book, Low, 1954.

Enid Blyton's Noddy Pop-Up Book, Low, 1954.

How Funny You Are, Noddy!, Low, 1954.

Noddy Gets into Trouble, Low, 1954.

Noddy and the Magic Rubber, Low, 1954.

Noddy's Castle of Books (five parts), illustrated by Van Der Beek, Low, 1954.

Noddy in Toyland, Low, 1955.

Noddy Meets Father Christmas, Low, 1955.

You Funny Little Noddy!, Low, 1955.

Be Brave Little Noddy!, Low, 1956.

A Day with Noddy, Low, 1956.

Enid Blyton's Noddy Playday Painting Book, Low, 1956.

Noddy and His Friends, Low, 1956.

Noddy and Tessie Bear, Low, 1956.

Noddy Nursery Rhymes, Low, 1956.

The Noddy Toy Station Books, Numbers 1-5, Low, 1956.

Do Look Out, Noddy!, Low, 1956.

Noddy and the Bumpy Dog, Low, 1957.

Noddy's New Big Book, Low, 1957.

My Noddy Picture Book, Low, 1958.

Noddy Has an Adventure, Low, 1958.

The Noddy Shop Book, Numbers 1-5, Low, 1958.

Noddy's Own Nursery Rhymes, Low, 1958.

You're a Good Friend, Noddy!, Low, 1958.

A.B.C. with Noddy, Low, 1959.

Noddy and Bunkey, Low, 1959.

Noddy Goes to Sea, Low, 1959.

Noddy's Car Picture Book, Low, 1959.
Cheer Up, Little Noddy!, Low, 1960.
Noddy Goes to the Fair, Low, 1960.
Noddy's One, Two, Three Book, Low, 1960.
Noddy's Tall Blue Book (also *Green, Orange, Pink, Red,* and *Yellow Books*), Low, 1960.
Mr. Plod and Little Noddy, Low, 1961.
Noddy's Toyland Train Picture Book, Low, 1961.
A Day at School with Noddy, Low, 1962.
Noddy and the Tootles, Low, 1962.
Noddy and the Aeroplane, Low, 1964.
Learn to Count with Noddy, Low, 1965.
Learn to Go Shopping with Noddy, Low, 1965.
Learn to Read About Animals with Noddy, Low, 1965.
Learn to Tell the Time with Noddy, Low, 1965.
Noddy and His Friends: A Nursery Picture Book, Low, 1965.
Noddy Treasure Box, Low, 1965.
Noddy and His Passengers, Low, 1967.
Noddy and the Magic Boots [and] *Noddy's Funny Kite,* Low, 1967.
Noddy and the Noah's Ark Adventure Picture Book, Low, 1967.
Noddy in Toyland Picture Book, Low, 1967.
Noddy Toyland ABC Picture Book, Low, 1967, reprinted as *Noddy's Toyland ABC,* Purnell.
Noddy's Aeroplane Picture Book, Low, 1967.
Noddy's Aeroplane, Purnell, 1983.
Noddy's rainy day Book, Purnell, 1983.
Noddy's Tea Party, Purnell, 1983.
Noddy's Treasury, Purnell, 1984.
Noddy and the Honey, Purnell, 1985.
Noddy and the Naughty Boys, Purnell, 1985.
Noddy Tricks Mr. Sly, Purnell, 1985.
Noddy and the Snowhouse, Purnell, 1985.
Noddy Bedside Book, Purnell, 1985.
Noddy's Balloon: Pop-Up Book, Purnell, 1985.
Noddy's Umbrella: Pop-Up Book, Purnell, 1985.
Noddy Clock Book, Purnell, 1986.
Noddy Goes to Toyland, Purnell, 1986.

"SECRET SEVEN" SERIES

The Secret Seven, illustrated by George Brook, Brockhampton Press, 1949, new edition published as *The Secret Seven and the Mystery of the Empty House* edited by M. Hughes Miller, illustrated by Tom Dunnington, Childrens Press, 1972.
The Secret Seven Adventure, illustrated by Brook, Brockhampton Press, 1950, new edition published as *The Secret Seven and the Circus Adventure* edited by Miller, illustrated by Dunnington, Childrens Press, 1972.
Well Done, Secret Seven, illustrated by Brook, Brockhampton Press, 1951, new edition published as *The Secret Seven and the Tree House Adventure* edited by Miller, illustrated by Dunnington, Childrens Press, 1972.
Secret Seven on the Trail, illustrated by Brook, Brockhampton Press, 1952, new edition published as *The Secret Seven and the Railroad Mystery,* edited by Miller, illustrated by Dunnington, Childrens Press, 1972.
Go Ahead Secret Seven, illustrated by Bruno Kay, Brockhampton Press, 1953, new edition published as *The Secret Seven Get Their Man,* edited by Miller, illustrated by Dunnington, Childrens Press, 1972.
Good Work, Secret Seven, illustrated by Kay, Brockhampton Press, 1954, new edition published as *The Secret Seven and the Case of the Stolen Car,* edited by Miller, illustrated by Dunnington, Childrens Press, 1972.

Secret Seven Win Through, illustrated by Kay, Brockhampton Press, 1955, new edition published as *The Secret Seven and the Hidden Cave Adventure,* edited by Miller, illustrated by Dunnington, Childrens Press, 1972.
Three Cheers Secret Seven, illustrated by Burgess Sharrocks, Brockhampton Press, 1956, new edition published as *The Secret Seven and the Grim Secret,* edited by Miller, illustrated by Dunnington, Childrens Press, 1972.
Secret Seven Mystery, illustrated by Sharrocks, Brockhampton Press, 1957, new edition published as *The Secret Seven and the Missing Girl Mystery,* edited by Miller, illustrated by Dunnington, Childrens Press, 1972.
Puzzle for the Secret Seven, illustrated by Sharrocks, Brockhampton Press, 1958, reprinted, Firecrest, 1986; new edition published as *The Secret Seven and the Case of the Music Lover,* edited by Miller, illustrated by Dunnington, Childrens Press, 1972.
Secret Seven Fireworks, illustrated by Sharrocks, Brockhampton Press, 1959, new edition published as *The Secret Seven and the Bonfire Adventure,* edited by Miller, illustrated by Dunnington, Childrens Press, 1972.
Good Old Secret Seven, illustrated by Sharrocks, Brockhampton Press, 1960, new edition published as *The Secret Seven and the Old Fort Adventure,* edited by Miller, illustrated by Dunnington, Childrens Press, 1972.
Shock for the Secret Seven, illustrated by Sharrocks, Brockhampton Press, 1961, new edition published as *The Secret Seven and the Case of the Dog Lover,* edited by Miller, illustrated by Dunnington, Childrens Press, 1972.
Look Out Secret Seven, illustrated by Sharrocks, Brockhampton Press, 1962, new edition published as *The Secret Seven and the Case of Missing Medals,* edited by Miller, illustrated by Dunnington, Childrens Press, 1972.
Fun forr the Secret Seven, illustrated by Sharrocks, Brockhampton Press, 1963, new edition published as *The Secret Seven and the Case of the Old Horse,* edited by Miller, illustrated by Dunnington, Childrens Press, 1972.

"BOM" SERIES

Bom and His Magic Drumstick, Brockhampton Press, 1956.
Bom the Little Toy Drummer, Brockhampton Press, 1956.
Enid Blyton's Bom Painting Book, Dean, 1956.
Bom Goes Adventuring, illustrated by Paul-Hoeye, Brockhampton Press, 1958.
Bom and the Clown, Brockhampton Press, 1959.
Bom and the Rainbow, Brockhampton Press, 1959.
Hullo Bom and Wuffy Dog, illustrated by Paul-Hoeye, Brockhampton Press, 1959.
Bom Goes to Magic Town, Brockhampton Press, 1960.
Here Comes Bom, illustrated by Paul-Hoeye, Brockhampton Press, 1960.
Bom at the Seaside, illustrated by Paul-Hoeye, Brockhampton Press, 1961.
Bom Goes to the Circus, illustrated by Paul-Hoeye, Brockhampton Press, 1961.

PLAYS

A Book of Little Plays, Thomas Nelson, 1927.
The Play's the Thing, music by A. Rowley, Home Library Book Co., 1927, reprinted in two volumes as *Plays for the Older Children* [and] *Plays for Younger Children,* George Newnes, 1940.
Six Enid Blyton Plays, Methuen, 1935.
The Blyton-Sharman Musical Plays for Juniors, six parts, A. Wheaton, 1939.

George H. Holroyd, editor, *Cameo Plays* (only Book 4 by Blyton), E. J. Arnold, 1939.

How the Flowers Grow, and Other Musical Plays, A. Wheaton, 1939.

School Plays: Six Plays for School, Basil Blackwell, 1939.

The Wishing Beam and Other Plays, Basil Blackwell, 1939.

Finding the Tickets, Evans Brothers, 1955.

Mr. Sly-One and Cats, Evans Brothers, 1955.

Mother's Meeting, Evans Brothers, 1955.

Who Will Hold the Giant?, Evans Brothers, 1955.

Enid Blyton's Book of the Famous Play Noddy in Toyland, Low, 1956.

RETELLER

Aesop's Fables, Thomas Nelson, 1928.

Old English Stories, Thomas Nelson, 1928.

Pinkity's Pranks and Other Nature Fairy Stories, Thomas Nelson, 1928.

Joel C. Harris, *Tales of Brer Rabbit,* Thomas Nelson, 1928.

The Knights of the Round Table, George Newnes, 1930.

Tales From the Arabian Nights, George Newnes, 1930.

Tales of Ancient Greece, George Newnes, 1930.

Tales of Robin Hood, George Newnes, 1930.

The Adventures of Odysseus: Stories From World History, Evans Brothers, 1934.

The Story of the Siege of Troy: Stories From World History, Evans Brothers, 1934.

Tales of the Ancient Greeks and Persians: Stores From World History, Evans Brothers, 1934.

Tales of the Romans: Stories From World History, Evans Brothers, 1934.

Harris, *Heyo, Brer Rabbit!,* George Newnes, 1938.

Harris, *The Further Adventures of Brer Rabbit,* George Newnes, 1942.

Harris, *Brer Rabbit and His Friends,* J. Coker, 1938.

Jean de Brunhoff, *The Babar Story Book,* Methuen, 1941 (excerpt published separately as *Tales of Babar,* Methuen, 1942).

The Children's Life of Christ, Methuen, 1943.

Tales from the Bible, illustrated by Soper, Methuen, 1944.

The First Christmas, photographs by Paul Henning, Methuen, 1945, new edition, Grafton Books, 1986.

The Boy With the Loaves and Fishes, illustrated by Walker, Lutterworth, 1948.

Brer Rabbit Book (series of eight books), Latimer House, 1948.

Enid Blyton Bible Pictures, Old Testament, illustrated by John Turner, Macmillan, 1949.

The Enid Blyton Bible Stories, Old Testament, Macmillan, 1949.

Robin Hood Book, Latimer House, 1949.

The Two Sillies and Other Stories, J. Coker, 1952.

Bible Stories From the Old Testament, illustrated by Lodge, Muller, 1955.

Bible Stories From the New Testament, illustrated by Lodge, Muller, 1955.

Harris, *Brer Rabbit Again,* Dean, 1963, new edition, Awards Publications, 1982.

Tales of Brave Adventure, Dean, 1963.

Harris, *Enid Blyton's Brer Rabbit's a Rascal,* Dean, 1965.

Tales of Long Ago (selections from *Tales of Ancient Greece* and *Tales from the Arabian Nights*), Dean, 1965.

Baby in the Bulrushes and the Kind Princess, Granada, 1985.

The Burning Bush and the Rescue of the Slaves, Granada, 1985.

Path through the Sea and Bread from the Sky, Granada, 1985.

Noah Builds His Ark and the Terrible Flood, Granada, 1985.

Samson the Strong Giant and Gideon the Brave Soldier, Granada, 1985.

Daniel in the Lion's Den [and] *The Little Slave Girl,* Granada, 1985.

David and Goliath, Granada, 1985.

Little Boy Jesus, Grafton Books, 1986.

The Good Samaritan, Grafton Books, 1986.

In the Beginning and Other Stories, Granada, 1985.

The Story of Easter, Grafton Books, 1986.

Three Wise Men, Grafton Books, 1986.

Three Wise Men and the Angel's Warning, Grafton Books, 1986.

Twelve Disciples, Grafton Books, 1986.

The Last Supper, Grafton Books, 1986.

Loaves and Fishes, Grafton Books, 1986.

EDITOR

The Teacher's Treasury, three volumes, George Newnes, 1926.

Sunny Stories for Little Folks, George Newnes, 1926-36.

Modern Teaching in the Infant School, four volumes, George Newnes, 1932.

Modern Teaching: Practical Suggestions for Junior and Senior Schools, six volumes, George Newnes, 1928.

(And contributor) *Pictorial Knowledge,* ten volumes, George Newnes, 1930.

Treasure Trove Readers (junior series), A. Wheaton, 1934.

Nature Observation Pictures, Warne, 1935.

Thomas A. Coward, *Birds of the Wayside and Woodland,* Warne, 1936.

The Enid Blyton Bible Stories, New Testament, fourteen volumes, Macmillan, 1953.

Enid Blyton's Favourite Book of Fables from the Tales of La Fontaine, Collins, 1955.

Story Book of Jesus, illustrated by Walker, Macmillan, 1956.

The Children's Book of Prayers, Muller, 1963.

UNDER NAME MARY POLLOCK

Children of Kidillin, George Newnes, 1940.

Three Boys and a Circus (also see below), George Newnes, 1940.

Adventures of Scamp (also see below), George Newnes, 1943, bound with *Three Boys and a Circus* and published under name Enid Blyton as *Dog Stories,* Collins, 1959.

The Secret of Chuff Castle, George Newnes, 1943.

Smuggler Ben, George Newnes, 1943.

Mischief at St. Rollo's, George Newnes, 1947.

OTHER

Author of *Enid Blyton's All about the Circus,* W. & A. K. Johnston & G. W. Bacon (Scotland). Also author and editor of several periodicals and annuals, including *Enid Blyton's Magazine,* (London), beginning 1953; *Playways Annual,* Lutterworth, 1953; *Enid Blyton Magazine Annual* (first of a series), Evans Brothers, 1954; *Sunny Stories Annual,* (London), 1954; *Enid Blyton's Annual,* (London), beginning 1957; *Enid Blyton's Bom Annual,* (London), 1957; *Enid Blyton's Bedtime Annual,* (Manchester), 1966; and *The Big Enid Blyton Story Annual,* Purnell, 1973-76.

SIDELIGHTS: Enid Blyton, who also wrote under the name Mary Pollock, originally planned to make music her career and was working towards her L.R.A.M. (Licentiate of the Royal Academy of Music) examination when she decided to become a school teacher instead. In addition to her work in the educational field, Blyton also took pleasure in writing fiction for children. As a child, Blyton was gifted with a vivid imagination and a sense for writing. At the age of fourteen, the budding author embarked on a literary career with the publication of her poem in a children's magazine edited by Arthur Mee. Since then, approximately six hundred books and countless articles have been written by Blyton. Translations of the author-educator's works can be found in ninety-three languages, including Russian, Hebrew, Indonesian, Tamil, Swahili, and Fijian.

At the peak of her writing career, Blyton usually produced six to ten thousand words a day, and still had time to play with her two daughters or read stories to them. Blyton wrote for children of all ages, with whom she was enormously popular. She deplored contemporary violence in comic books and movies, and believed that literature for young children should instill absolutely sound Christian morals. In spite of (perhaps because of) her tremendous popularity with child readers, Blyton has been attacked by some critics and librarians who claim that her work is trivial and unreal. Some British libraries refuse to stock her books. Against this, Blyton has been solidly backed by educators and ministers of all creeds.

BIOGRAPHICAL/CRITICAL SOURCES:

BOOKS

Blyton, Enid Mary, *Story of My Life* (autobiography), Pitkin, 1952.
Stoney, Barbara, *Enid Blyton: A Biography,* Hodder & Stoughton, 1974.

PERIODICALS

New York Times, September 15, 1946.
Saturday Review of Literature, September 28, 1946.
Springfield Republican, March 11, 1945.
Weekly Book Review, March 11, 1945.

OBITUARIES:

PERIODICALS

New York Times, November 29, 1968.
Publishers Weekly, December 30, 1968.
Time, December 6, 1968.*

*   *   *

BOBROWSKI, Johannes 1917-1965

PERSONAL: Born April 9, 1917 in Tilsit, East Prussia, Germany (now Sovetsk, Russia); died September 2, 1965, in East Berlin, East Germany; son of Gustav Bobrowski (a railroad official); married Johanna Puddrus; children: four. *Education:* Educated in Germany. *Religion:* Lutheran. *Politics:* East German Christian Democratic Union.

CAREER: Poet, novelist, short story writer. Verlag Lucie Groszer (publisher), East Berlin, East Germany, reader, 1952-59; Union Verlag (publisher), East Berlin, reader, 1959-65. *Military service:* German Army, 1939-49; prisoner of war in Russia, 1945-49, did forced labor as a miner in the Donets region.

AWARDS, HONORS: Gruppe 47 Prize, 1962; Alma Koenig Prize, 1962; Heinrich Mann prize, 1965; Charles Veillon prize, 1965; F. C. Weiskopf prize, 1967.

WRITINGS:

Sarmatische Zeit: Gedichte (title means "Sarmatian Times: Poems"; also see below), Deutsche Verlags-Anstalt, 1961.
Schattenland Stroeme: Gedichte (title means "Shadowland Streams: Poems"), Deutsche Verlags-Anstalt, 1962, 3rd edition, 1963, bound with *Sarmitische Zeit: Gedichte,* Wilhelm Heyne Verlag, 1962.

Levin's Muehle: 34 Saetze ueber meinen Grossvater (novel), 5. Fischer, 1964, translation by Janet Cropper published as *Levin's Mill,* Calder & Boyars, 1970, reprinted, 1988.
Boehlendorff und Andere Erzaehlungen (short stories; title means "Boehlendorff and Other Stories"; also see below), Deutsche Verlags-Anstalt, 1965, translation by Frances Golffing published as *Boehlendorff,* Typographeum, 1989.
Mauesefest, und andere Erzaehlungen (title means "Mouse Feast, and Other Stories"; also see below), K. Wagenbach, 1965.
Boehlendorff und Maeusefest: Erzaehlungen (title means "Boehlendorff and Mouse Feast: Stories"), Union Verlag, 1966.
Das Land Sarmatien: Gedichte (title means "The Sarmatian Country: Poems"), Deutscher Taschenbuch Verlag, 1966.
Wetterzeichen: Gedichte (title means "Storm Signals: Poems"), Union Verlag, 1966.
Johannes Bobrowski liest Lyrik und Prosa (with two phonograph records; title means "Johannes Bobrowski Reads Lyric Poetry and Prose"), Union Verlag, 1966, altered edition published as *Nachbarschaft,* K. Wagenbach, 1967.
Selbstzeugnisse und Beitraege ueber sein Werk, Union Verlag, 1967.
Der Mahner: Erzaehlungen (title means "The Dun: Stories"), Union Verlag, 1967, reissued as *Der Mahner: Erzaehlungen und andere Prosa aus dem Nachlass* (title means "The Dun: Stories and Other Posthumous Prose"), K. Wagenbach, 1968.
Das Tierhaeuschen (juvenile; adaptation of *Terem-teremok* by Samuil Marshak), Kinderbuchverlag, 1967, translation by Moya Gillespie published as *The House in the Meadow,* Harvey House, 1970.
Litauische Claviere (novel; title means "Lithuanian Pianos"), Union Verlag, 1967, reprinted, K. Wagenbach, 1983.
Im Windgestraeuch: Gedichte aus dem Nachlass (title means "Into the Windy Bushes: Posthumous Poems"), selection by Eberhard Haufe, Deutsche Verlags-Anstalt, 1970.
Johannes Bobrowski (poems), Verlag Neues Leben, 1972.
Lipmanns Leib: Erzaehlungen (title means "Lipmann's Body: Stories"), selection by Wilhelm Dehn, P. Reclam, 1973.
Gedichte: 1952-1965 (title means "Poems: 1952-1965"), Insel-Verlag, 1974.
Literarisches Klima; ganz neue Xenien, doppelte Ausfuehrung, with illustrations by Klaus Ensikat, Union-Verlag (Berlin), 1977.
Ja, ich sprech in den Wind: Lyrik und Prosa, edited by Juergen P. Wallmann, Guetersloher Verlagshaus Mohn, 1978.
Erzaehlungen (short stories), edited by Bernd Leistner, Reclam, 1978.
Maeusefest [and] *Der Mahner,* K. Wagenbach, 1981.
Meine Liebsten Gedichte, Deutsche Verlags-Anstalt, 1985.
Gesammelte Werke, Volume 1: *Die Gedichte,* Volume 3: *Die Romane,* Volume 4: *Die Erzaehlungen, Vermischte Prosa und Selbstzeugnisse,* edited by Eberhard Haufe, Deutsche Verlags-Anstalt, 1987-88.

EDITOR

Gustav Schwab, *Die schoensten Sagen des klassichen Altertums,* Altberiliner Verlag, 1954.
Schwab, *Die Sagen von troja und von der Irrfahrt und Heimkehr des Odysseus,* Altberliner Verlag, 1955.
Hans Clauert, der maerkische Eulenspiegel (juvenile), Altberliner Verlag, 1956.
Johann Paul Friedrich, *Leben Fibels,* Union Verlag, 1963.
(And compiler) *Wer mich und Ilse sieht im Grase: Deutsche Dichter des 18. Jahrhunderts ueper die Liebe und das Fr-*

auenzimme, (title means "Whoever Sees Me and Ilse Lying in the Grass: German Poems of the Eighteenth Century on Love and Women"), Euienspiegei Veriag, 1964.

TRANSLATOR

(With Guenther Deicke) Boris Pasternak, *Initialen der Leidenschaft,* Verlag Volk und Welt, 1969.

Translator of poems by Konstantin Biebl into German.

ENGLISH COLLECTIONS

Shadow Land: Selected Poems (contains poems from *Sarmatische Zeit* and *Schattenland Stroeme*), translated by Ruth Mead and Matthew Mead, Alan Swallow, 1966, 2nd edition, 1966, new edition published as *Shadow Lands,* Anvil Press Poetry, 1984.

I Taste Bitterness (contains stories from *Boehlendorff und Maeusefest*), translated by Marc Linder, Seven Seas Publishers, 1970.

(With Horst Bienek) *Selected Poems: Johannes Bobrowski and Horst Bienek* (contains poems from *Sarmatische Zeit* and *Schattenland Stroeme*), Penguin, 1971.

From the Rivers: Selected Poems, translated by R. Mead and M. Mead, Anvil Press, 1975.

Lithuanian Pianos, translations by Carl J. Hoffman, Adler, 1987.

Work represented in *Penguin Book of Twentieth Century German Verse,* edited by P. Bridgewater, 1963; *Contemporary German Poetry,* edited by G. C. Schwebell, 1964; *German Writing Today,* edited by C. Middleton, 1967; *Seventeen Modern German Poets,* edited by S. S. Prawer, 1971; *East German Poetry,* edited by M. Hamburger, 1972; and *Three German Stories,* edited by Elisabeth Langgaesser, translation by Michael Bullock, Oasis Books, 1984.

OTHER

Johannes Bobrowski liest die Erzaehlungen Der Mahner und Der Tanzer Malige (sound recording, two discs), Union-Verlag, 1980.

Work represented in *Deutsche Lyrik auf der anderen Seite* (title means "Poetry on the Other Side"), 1960. Contributor of poetry to journals and magazines, including *Das innere Reich* and *Sinn und Form.*

SIDELIGHTS: Johannes Bobrowski spent his childhood, he said, "on both sides of the River Memel," dividing his time between Tilsit, the East Prussian town where he was born, and his grandfather's farm in Lithuania. In 1928 the family moved to the nearby city of Koenigsberg (now Kaliningrad), which is renowned for its musical and literary associations. Bobrowski went to school there, studied the classics, and learned to play the organ and the clavichord, acquiring a taste for Baroque music. Above all he experienced the sharp contrast between what he called "the patriarchal closed-in-ness" of village life and the sophisticated worldly preoccupations of a trading port with a rich cultural history. Bobrowski was later to become a devoted student of the history, geography, and folklore of the region in which he grew up, and a collector of books and atlases of local interest. As Brian Keith-Smith wrote in his monograph on Bobrowski, "these interests . . . gave him a peculiarly balanced combination of close attachment to the significance of local life, where the quality of the individual character and his expression meant so much, and of the detachment of an observer with a developed taste for the strict form of some of the highest achievements of classical post-Renaissance and ancient classical culture."

In 1938 the family moved again, this time to Berlin. After studying art history there for a year, Bobrowski was inducted into the German army and sent first to Poland, then to Russia. He had already tried his hand as a painter and as a composer, but had been discouraged by the greater talent of some of his friends. It was in an attempt to record his impressions of Russia that he turned to poetry, as he later explained: "I began to write near Lake Ilmen in 1941 about the Russian landscape, but as a foreigner, a German. This became [my] theme . . . the Germans and the European East—because I grew up around the River Memel, where Poles, Lithuanians, Russians and Germans lived together, and among them all the Jews—a long history of unhappiness and guilt, for which my people is to blame, ever since the days of the Teutonic Knights. Not to be undone, perhaps, or expiated, but worthy of hope and honest endeavor in German poems."

Apart from a few poems published during the war in the magazine *Das innere Reich,* Bobrowski's work did not begin to appear until he had returned from his long captivity in Russia and settled into his career as a publisher's reader in East Berlin. A group of poems was published in the important East German magazine *Sinn und Form* in 1955, and some of these were included in the West German anthology *Deutsche Lyrik auf der anderen Seite* ("Poetry on the Other Side," 1960); thereafter all of Bobrowski's poetry appeared in both East and West Germany. The most important influence on his early work was the nature poet Friedrich Klopstock, but it was Peter Huchel, the editor of *Sinn und Form,* who showed him his true direction as a poet. Bobrowski told an interviewer in 1965 that he "first read a poem of [Huchel's] in Soviet prison camp, in a newspaper, and it impressed me immensely. That's where I came to see people in a landscape—to such an extent that to this day I do not care for an unpeopled natural setting. I am no longer charmed by the elemental forces of a landscape, but by nature only when seen in connection with, and as a field of, the effective activity of man."

Most of Bobrowski's poems are concerned with what the ancient geographers called Sarmatia, the steppe country between the Vistula and the Volga. In his verse this borderland becomes archetypal and mythical, a "shadowland" alive with "the traces of peoples lost"—the old Prussians, Lithuanians, Poles, Russians, gypsies, and Jews who had lived there, their gods and heroes, languages and legends, lingering on in artifacts and cave paintings, in old songs, and superstitions, and ancient place-names. For example, "Pruzzische Elegie" ("Prussian Elegy," 1952), the longest and one of the best known of his poems, conjures up the pagan world of the Old Prussians, celebrating the simplicity and naturalness of their way of life, lamenting their extermination in the name of Christianity by the Teutonic Knights, but suggesting that something of their essence survives in the landscape itself. "Gestorbene Sprache" ("Dead Language") implies a question: Is Old Prussian dead because only traces of it remain, or is the dead language of the title actually modern German, which is unable to express the deep connections between man and nature?

A *Times Literary Supplement* critic noted that Bobrowski's poetry "is beautifully lyrical, and yet impersonal, oracular in the manner of [Friedrich] Hoelderlin. The perceptions are enacted in language that is stark, dynamic, and almost invariably concrete, outstanding for its nervous strength and its total precision. Like his prose, it is dense in the sense of being radically condensed and richly allusive. By invoking a river or village he evokes a whole world and a whole tradition." Bobrowski favored free verse, marked by harsh German inversions, and typically began a poem with a few short and explosive substantives—what John Flores, writing in *Poetry in East Germany, 1945-1970,* has called a "stuttering" of nouns—leading on to a final cry for communication. Bobrowski himself believed that "the language of poetry has the triadic function of *remembrance* (the mytho-historic and immediate past), *communication* (bringing the past meaningfully into the present), and the causation of *effective change* (a vision of the future)." The change he most wanted was progress towards what he called "nachbarschaft"—a sense of community and neighborly companionship between different races, and between different members of the same race.

This was also the principal theme of Bobrowski's fiction, to which he turned increasingly in his later years. Keith-Smith observed that a Bobrowski short story most often begins with "a detailed building-up of the setting with usually an emphatic concentration on the forces within it that form a link with the past. . . . Then comes the intrusion into that setting of the character who belongs to the past yet lingers on in the present." There is always a threat behind these stories, Keith-Smith suggested—the threat of Nazi terror, of officialdom, sometimes only of thoughtless inhumanity. Most of Bobrowski's stories were set in the pastoral "Sarmatian" world of the poems, but the eleven stories and prose sketches in his posthumous third collection, *Der Mahner,* most of them written in the highly productive last few months of his life, were more contemporary in their concerns. However, as one reviewer wrote in the *Times Literary Supplement,* here as elsewhere Bobrowski's "constant concern was Man. In these new stories his deep moral and social concerns and the sinewy classical style in which they are expressed are unchanged."

Levin's Mill, considered to be the best of Bobrowski's two novels, is set in 1874 in a Prussian village. The narrator describes how his grandfather Johann, a prosperous old German miller, ruthlessly put his young Jewish competitor out of business, but then was driven from the village himself by public disapproval. Bobrowski uses this theme to illustrate the innate hostility between the various racial and religious elements in his "Sarmatian" village, but also the mutual respect and "nachbarschaft" that enable the community to survive. H. M. Waidson wrote that the novel's style combines "the lyrical evocation of nature . . . and of human emotion, with a darting humor. Interpolated in the main narrative are a series of visionary 'hauntings' that befall the grandfather when he is unconscious and recall episodes involving his ancestors in earlier centuries, while the twentieth-century grandson who tells the story provides a present-day perspective."

Bobrowski's other novel, *Litauische Claviere,* also reflects his interest in the history and folklore of his native region. In the novel, two writers conducting research for an opera they plan to write visit an expert on their subject. Two crowds have also convened in the village where he lives: Lithuanians and German Nationalists, each celebrating different holidays. In their confrontation, and the Germans kill a Lithuanian farmer. Critics recognized the two groups as symbols of a pastoral past in conflict with fascism. "The novel is also a comment on the writer's role in society," Robert Acker observed in *Dictionary of Literary Biography.* "J. P. Wieczorek argues convincingly that Bobrowski wanted to demonstrate that the author's function is to provide hope to a cynical world; he was trying to show that his refusal to employ socialist realism and his concentration on the past do not represent formalism or an esoteric retreat from practical affairs but rather provide a method for tackling contemporary problems. . . . He shows that the writer can make practical application of the ideas he has gleaned from his study of history. The artist can contribute to mutual understanding in a troubled world."

Bobrowski finished *Litauische Claviere* only a few weeks before his premature death from peritonitis. After his death, his works were praised by an official Marxist critic as "exemplary Christian contributions to the development of the socialist literature of the nation." Peter Demetz, a western critic, complained that Bobrowski "never said a word against inhuman Soviet policies in the Baltic states," but suggested that towards the end of his life "he was feeling more and more like a speechless stranger among his people. In his last poem, 'Das Wort Mensch'/ 'The Word Man,' published posthumously on June 8, 1966, he confessed to his disgust for a society that prided itself on repeating mechanically the empty vocabulary of humanitarianism without ever being truly humane: 'Where love is lacking, do not / utter the word.' " Siegfried Mandel, however, could not agree that this poem had "the force of direct accusation against specific contemporary persecutions," and concluded that Bobrowski had chosen "in a muted voice, to pit moral vision against political expediency."

Most critics were content to regard Bobrowski as a writer in whose work humanism "again assumed a vital meaning." Bobrowski was also the author of two books for children and of some outstanding translations, notably of the poetry of Boris Pasternak and the Czech poet Konstantin Biebl. He is universally regarded as one of the finest and most original German poets of his generation, and his poems have been translated into all the major European languages.

BIOGRAPHICAL/CRITICAL SOURCES:

BOOKS

Dehn, Mechthild and Wilhelm Dehn, *Johannes Bobrowski: Prosa; Interpretationen,* Oldenbourg, 1972.

Dictionary of Literary Biography, Volume 75: *Contemporary German Fiction Writers, Second Series,* Gale, 1988.

Flores, John, *Poetry in East Germany, 1945-1970,* Yale University Press, 1971.

Gajek, Bernhard and Eberhard Haufe, *Johannes Bobrowski: Chronik—Einfuehrung—Bibliographie,* Lang, 1977.

Gruetzmacher, Curt, *Das Werk Johannes Bobrowskis,* Fink, 1974.

Hoefert, Sigfrid, *West-Ostliches in der Lyrik Johannes Bobrowskis,* Verlag Uni-Druck, 1966.

Keith-Smith, Brian, editor, *Essays on Contemporary German Literature,* Volume 4: *German Men of Letters,* Oswald Wolff, 1966.

Keith-Smith, *Johannes Bobrowski,* Oswald Wolff, 1970.

Meckel, Christoph Meckel, *Erinnerung an Johannes Bobrowski,* Eremiten-Presse, 1978.

Prawer, Siegbert Salomon, editor, *Essays in German Language, Culture and Society,* University of London Press, 1969.

Rostin, Gerhard, editor, *Johannes Bobrowski: Selbstzeugnisse und neue Beitraege ueben sein Werk,* Union-Verlag, 1975.

Wolf, Gerhard and Gerhard Rostin, *Johannes Bobrowski: Selbstzeugnisse und Beitraege ueber sein werk,* Union Verlag, 1967, revised edition, 1975.

Wolf, *Johannes Bobrowski: Leben und Werk,* Volk und Wissen, 1984.

PERIODICALS

Forum for Modern Language Studies, Volume 2, number 4, 1966.

German Life and Letters, January, 1979; July, 1982.

Germanic Review, January, 1966.

London Magazine, November, 1967.

Times (London), September 4, 1965.

Times Literary Supplement, September 21, 1962; January 14, 1965; April 20, 1967; February 22, 1968; March 11, 1988.
Sinn und Form, Volume 18, 1966.*

* * *

BOGAN, Louise 1897-1970

PERSONAL: Born August 11, 1897, in Livermore Falls, Me.; died February 4, 1970, in New York, N.Y.; daughter of Daniel Joseph and Mary Helen (Shields) Bogan; married Curt Alexander, 1916 (died, 1920); married Raymond Holden (a poet), 1925 (divorced, 1937); children: (first marriage) Mathilde. *Education:* Attended Boston University 1915-16.

ADDRESSES: Home—New York, N.Y.

CAREER: Poet and critic. Free-lance writer in New York City, 1919-25; poetry editor, *New Yorker,* 1931-69. Visiting professor at University of Washington, Seattle, 1948, University of Chicago, 1949, University of Arkansas, 1952, Seminar in American Studies, Salzburg, Austria, 1952, and Brandeis University, Waltham, Massachusetts, 1964-65.

MEMBER: American Academy of Arts and Letters and Academy of American Poets.

AWARDS, HONORS: John Reed Memorial Prize, 1930, and Helen Haire Levinson Memorial Prize, 1937, both from *Poetry;* Guggenheim fellowship, 1933 and 1937; Library of Congress Fellowship in American Letters, 1944; Library of Congress Chair in Poetry, 1945-46; Harriet Monroe Poetry Award, 1948; National Institute of Arts and Letters grant, 1951; Bollingen Prize in Poetry, 1955, for *Collected Poems, 1923-1953;* L.H.D., Western College for Women, 1956; Academy of American Poets fellowship, 1958; Litt.D., Colby College, 1960; Brandeis University Creative Arts Award in Poetry, 1961; National Endowment for the Arts grant, 1967.

WRITINGS:

POETRY

Body of This Death, McBride, 1923.
Dark Summer, Scribner, 1929.
The Sleeping Fury, Scribner, 1937.
Poems and New Poems, Scribner, 1941.
Collected Poems, 1923-1953, Noonday Press, 1954.
The Blue Estuaries: Poems, 1923-1968, Farrar, Straus, 1968.

OTHER

Women, Ward Ritchie, 1929.
Achievement in American Poetry, 1900-1950 (criticism), H. Regnery, 1951.
(Translator) Yvan Goll, *Elegy of Ihpetonga* [and] *Masks of Ashes,* Noonday Press, 1954, reprinted, 1985.
Selected Criticism: Prose, Poetry, Noonday Press, 1955.
(With Archibald MacLeish and Richard Wilbur) *Emily Dickinson: Three Views,* Amherst College Press, 1960, reprinted Norwood Editions, 1977.
(Translator with Elizabeth Mayer) Ernest Juenger, *The Glass Bees,* Noonday Press, 1961.
(Translator) Goll, *The Myth of the Pierced Rock,* Allen Press, 1962.
(Translator with Mayer) Johann Wolfgang von Goethe, *Elective Affinities,* Regnery, 1963.
(Editor and translator with Elizabeth Roget) Jules Renard, *Journal,* Braziller, 1964.
(Editor with William Jay Smith) *The Golden Journey: Poems for Young People,* Reilly & Lee, 1965.

(Author of afterword) Virginia Woolf, *A Writer's Diary, Being Extracts From the Diary of Virginia Woolf,* New American Library, 1968.
A Poet's Alphabet: Reflections on the Literary Art and Vocation, edited by Robert Phelps and Ruth Limmer, McGraw-Hill, 1970.
(Translator with Mayer of verse) Goethe, *The Sorrows of Young Werther, and Novella,* Random House, 1971.
What the Woman Lived: Selected Letters of Louise Bogan, 1920-1970, edited by Ruth Limmer, Harcourt, 1973.
Journey Around My Room: The Autobiography of Bogan, a Mosaic, edited by Limmer, Viking, 1980.

Also author of *Works in the Humanities Published in Great Britain 1939-1946: A Selected List,* 1950. Contributor of verse to *New Republic;* contributor of literary criticism to *New Yorker, Nation, Poetry: A Magazine of Verse,* and *Atlantic Monthly.* Bogan's papers are collected at Amherst College.

SIDELIGHTS: Louise Bogan has been called by some critics the most accomplished woman poet of our time. Her subtle, restrained, intellectual style was greatly influenced by the English metaphysical poets. Many have placed her in the same category with George Herbert, John Donne, and Henry Vaughan. Bogan belonged to a group of brilliant minor poets described by some as the "reactionary generation." Aware of the success of Ezra Pound and T. S. Eliot, Bogan and others chose to follow the traditional English form of expression of the seventeenth century, which included the use of meters. Although she utilized traditional techniques, her poetry is modern, her language immediate and contemporary. Bogan's poetry contains a personal quality derived from personal experience, but it is not private. Her poems, most critics agree, are economical in words and masterpieces of crossed rhythms in which the meter opposes word groupings.

Sleeping Fury was one of the earlier published books of poems by Louise Bogan. The *Springfield Republican* noted that "Miss Bogan's poetry appeals to the comparative few who appreciate delicacy and artistry in verse." *Books* review said Bogan "has achieved a mastery of form rare in the realm of modern poetry. There is creative architecture in even the slightest of her lyrics. Miss Bogan works not as a landscape painter (while her visual imagery is exact, it does not depend on color alone), nor yet as a musician—although in many of her poems, the auditory imagery is superior to the visual: the ear listens, even as the eye sees. Her art is that of a sculpture." A *Nation* critic wrote, "Distinguished is the word one always thinks of in connection with Louise Bogan's poetry. Whatever form she tries, her art is sure, economical, and self-definitive. There is never in her poems a wasted adjective or phrase but always perfect clarity and a consistent mood precisely set down. She can write the completely artless lyric or the very subtle poem worked out through complex imagery."

Reviewing *Poems and New Poems* in *Saturday Review,* William Rose Benet noted, "Her poetry is, and always has been, intensely personal. She has inherited the Celtic magic of language, but has blended it somehow with the tartness of New England." Marianne Moore further observed in *Nation,* "Women are not noted for terseness, but Louise Bogan's art is compactness compacted. Emotion with her, as she has said of certain fiction is 'itself form, the kernel which builds outward form from inward intensity.' She uses a kind of forged rhetoric that nevertheless seems inevitable."

Collected Poems, 1923-1953 was reviewed in the *New York Times* by Richard Eberhart. "Louise Bogan's poems adhere to the center of English with a dark lyrical force," wrote Eberhart. "What she has to say is important. How she says it is pleasing. She is a compulsive poet first, a stylist second. When compulsion and style meet, we have a strong, inimitable Bogan poem." *Saturday Review* commented, "Louise Bogan is mistress of precise images and commands an extensive range of poetic accents and prosodic effects; she is also a musician, whose notes are as crystalline as those of Chopin's Preludes. More than this, one cannot read far in her pages without realizing that at the core of her poetry is mind-stuff which it is fashionable to call metaphysical." These poems are also important because they deal intelligently with the themes of sexual love and bodily decay.

The Blue Estuaries: Poems, 1923-1968 was the final collection of poems published before Louise Bogan's death. The *New York Times* reviewed the book: "Now that we can see the sweep of 45 years work in this collection of over a hundred poems, we can judge what a feat of character it has been. . . . [Her diction] stems from the severest lyrical tradition in English. . . . [Her language is] as supple as it is accurate, dealing with things in their own tones."

With the assistance of William Jay Smith, Louise Bogan compiled an anthology of poems for children. *The Golden Journey: Poems for Young People,* with poems ranging from Shakespeare to Dylan Thomas, was described by James Dickey as possibly "the best general anthology of poems for young people ever compiled. By the poems they present, by their arrangement and timing, the editors subtly hold out the possibility that a child—thought a child—is capable of rising to good poems, and so of becoming, through an encounter which also requires much of him, something more than he was. . . . [This book] could have been selected only by poets as distinguished as these two, and by human beings who realize that to make the wrong concessions to children is injurious to them."

Louise Bogan also wrote a great deal of criticism. *Achievement in American Poetry, 1900-1950* was a brief account of American poetry during the first half of this century. The *Chicago Tribune* described the book as "a delight. Like all Miss Bogan's criticism, this book is full of acute, spirited, and authoritative judgments of writers and works, expressed with grace and wit." The *New York Times* added, "Louise Bogan not only manages to compress a formidable amount of factual information into her small compass but also contrives to do a great deal of satisfactory talking about her facts." The *United States Quarterly Book Review* commented, "Miss Bogan's clarity of style, her ability to compress a great deal of information into a few lucid, interesting phrases, and her severely just appraisal form the chief attractions of this volume."

BIOGRAPHICAL/CRITICAL SOURCES:

BOOKS

Bogan, Louise, *What the Woman Lived: Selected Letters of Louise Bogan, 1920-1970,* edited by Ruth Limmer, Harcourt, 1973.
Contemporary Literary Criticism, Gale, Volume 2, 1974, Volume 39, 1986, Volume 46, 1988.
Dictionary of Literary Biography, Volume 45: *American Poets, 1880-1945,* Gale, 1986.
Frank, Elizabeth, *Louise Bogan: A Portrait,* Knopf, 1985.
Smith, William Jay, *Louise Bogan: A Woman's Words,* Library of Congress, 1971.

PERIODICALS

Books, May 30, 1937.

Chicago Tribune, November 4, 1951.
Nation, April 24, 1937, November 15, 1941.
New York Times, November 25, 1951, May 30, 1954.
New York Times Book Review, November 7, 1965, October 13, 1968.
Saturday Review, April 18, 1937, April 25, 1942, July 3, 1954, February 21, 1970.
United States Quarterly Book Review, March, 1952.

OBITUARIES:

PERIODICALS

Antiquarian Bookman, February 16, 1970.
Newsweek, February 16, 1970.
New Yorker, February 14, 1970.
New York Times, February 5, 1970.
Publishers Weekly, February 23, 1970.
Time, February 16, 1970.
Washington Post, February 6, 1970.*

*   *   *

BONNEFOY, Yves 1923-

PERSONAL: Born July 24, 1923, in Tours, France; son of Elie and Helene (Maury) Bonnefoy; married Lucille Vine, 1968; children: one daughter. *Education:* University of Paris, degree in philosophy.

ADDRESSES: Office—College de France, 11 Place Marcelin-Berthelor, 75005 Paris, France.

CAREER: Writer. College de France, Paris, France, professor, 1981—. Has taught literature at various universities, including Brandeis, 1962-64, Johns Hopkins, Princeton, Yale, and Geneva. Co-founder of *L'ephemere* (art and literature journal), 1967.

AWARDS, HONORS: Prix de I' Express, for *Hier regnant desert,* and *L'Improbable,* 1958; Cecil Hemly Award, 1967, for *On the Motion and Immobility of Douve;* Prix des Critiques, 1971; Prix Montaigne, 1978; named honorary fellow, Modern Language Association, 1981; Grand Prix de Loesie, Academie Francaise, 1981; Grand Prix Societe des bens de Lettres, 1987; Bennett Award, *Hudson Review,* 1988.

WRITINGS:

POEMS

Din mouvement et de l'immobilite de Douve, Mercure de France (Paris), 1953, translation by Galway Kinnell published as *On the Motion and Immobility of Douve,* Ohio University Press, 1968.
Hier regnant desert (title means "In Yesterday's Desert Realm") Mercure de France, 1958.
Anti-Platon (title means "Against Plato"), Maeght (Paris), 1962.
Pierre ecrite, Mercure de France, 1965, bilingual edition with translation by Susanna Lang published as *Pierre ecrite-Words in Stone,* University of Massachusetts Press, 1976.
Selected Poems, translation by Anthony Rudolf, J. Cape, 1968.
Dans le leurre din seuil (title means "In the Lure of the Threshold"), Mercure de France, 1975.
Poemes, Mercure de France, 1978, translation by Richard Pevear published as *Poems, 1959-1975,* Random House, 1985.
The Origin of Language, G. Nama (New York), 1980.
Things Dying, Things Newborn, translation by Anthony Rudolf, Menard Press, 1986.

CRITICISM

Peintures murales de la France gothique (title means "Mural Paintings of Gothic France"), P. Hartmann (Paris), 1954.

L'Improbable (title means "The Improbable"), Mercure de France, 1959.

La Seconde Simplicite (title means "The Second Simplicity"), Mercure de France, 1961.

Rimbaud par lui-meme, Seuil, 1961, translation by Paul Schmidt published as *Rimbaud,* Harper, 1973.

Miro, La Bibliotheque des arts (Paris), 1964, translation by Judith Landry published as *Miro,* Viking, 1967.

Un reve fait a Mantoue (title means "A Dream Dreamt in Mantoue"), Mercure de France, 1967.

La Poesie francaise et le principe d'identite (title means "French Poetry and the Principle of Identity"), Maeght, 1967.

Rome 1630: l'horizon din premier baroque (title means "Rome 1630: Early Baroque and Its Context"). Flammarion, 1970.

L'arrierepays (title means "The Hinterland"), Editions d'Art Albert Skira (Geneva), 1972.

(With Jacques Thuillier) *Garache,* Maeght, 1975.

L'Ordalie (title means "The Ordeal"), Maeght, 1975.

Terre seconde (title means "The Second World"), Association des Amis de Ratilly, 1976.

Rue traversiere (title means "The Cross Street"), Mercure de France, 1977.

Le Nuage rouge (title means "The Red Cloud"), Mercure de France, 1977.

Entretiens sur la poesie, La Baconniere, 1980.

La Presence et l'Image, Mercure de France, 1983.

The Act and the Place of Poetry: Selected Essays, University of Chicago Press, 1989.

TRANSLATOR

Leonora Carrington, *Une chemise de nuit de flanelle,* Les Pas perdus, 1951.

William Shakespeare, *Henri IV, Jules Cesar, Hamlet, Le Conte d'hiver, Venus et Adonis,* [and] *Le Viol de Lucrece* (also see below), Club Francais du Livre, 1957-60.

Shakespeare, *Jules Cesar,* Mercure de France, 1960.

Shakespeare, *Hamlet* (also see below), Mercure de France, 1962.

Shakespeare, *Le Roi Lear* (also see below), Mercure de France, 1965.

Shakespeare, *Romeo et Juliette,* Mercure de France, 1968.

Shakespeare, *Hamlet* [and] *Le Roi Lear,* Gallimard, 1978.

Shakespeare, *Macbeth,* Mercure de France, 1983.

SIDELIGHTS: In a review of Galway Kinnell's translation of *Din mouvement et de l'immobilite de Douve* in *Poetry,* Ralph J. Mills, Jr. pointed out that "by general critical consensus Yves Bonnefoy is one of the finest poets to emerge in France since World War II." Bonnefoy has been placed in the tradition of Baudelaire, Rimbaud, and Jouve, and has been associated as well with the post-war surrealists. A metaphysical poet, he is distinguished, according to critic Michael Hamburger, by the conviction that "poetry has to do with truth and with salvation."

Bonnefoy's first volume of poetry established his reputation. A sequence of short poems separated into several sections, *Douve* is a difficult work, described by Mills as "reminiscent in part of the hermetic qualities of Mallarme and Valery and others whose technique involves obliquity, spiritual plenitude and vacancy." "Douve" is a female principle, which Bonnefoy himself defined as the relationship between consciousness and nothingness, and she variously represents earth, woman, love, and poetry. The progress of the poem portrays changing moods and metaphysical transformations and sets up dialectics such as mind/spirit, hope/despair, and life/death.

The difficulty of Bonnefoy's poetry arises in part from its remoteness from modern English and American poetry. Hamburger explained: "Its language functions in a radically different way, its movement proceeds in a radically different direction; and above all it assumes an order of pure ideas, or of pure subjectivity, that can be evoked poetically with a minimum of sensuous substantiation." These distinctions are reinforced by what Bonnefoy calls the "semitransparency" of French words, as contrasted with the earthy opaqueness of English. It is his view that the very language in which he writes is fraught with dangers and deficiencies for the poet, against which he must constantly struggle to sustain a "passionate intensity."

Bonnefoy is a respected critic and scholar, as well as a poet, and has written essays on literature, art, and architecture. His translations of Shakespeare are considered to be among the best in French.

BIOGRAPHICAL/CRITICAL SOURCES:

BOOKS

Caws, Mary Anne, *Yves Bonnefoy,* Twayne, 1984.

Contemporary Literary Criticism, Gale, Volume 9, 1978, Volume 15, 1980.

Gavronsky, Serge, *Poems and Texts,* October House, 1969.

Hamburger, Michael, *The Truth of Poetry,* Harcourt, 1970.

Kostelanetz, Richard, editor, *Yale French Studies 21,* 1958.

Naughton, John T., *The Poetics of Yves Bonnefoy,* University of Chicago Press, 1984.

On Contemporary Literature, Avon, 1964.

Thelot, Jerome, *Poetique d'Yves Bonnefoy,* Droz (Geneva), 1983.

PERIODICALS

Poetry, January, 1969, June 1976.

World Literature Today, summer, 1979.

*   *   *

BONOMA, T(homas) V(incent) 1946-

PERSONAL: Born September 18, 1946, in Cleveland, OH; son of Emil A. (a businessman) and Marie (a homemaker; maiden name, Pucci) Bonoma; married Elaine Moelhattan (a consultant), January 15, 1977; children: Thomas, Matthew, Jonathan, Benjamin. *Education:* Ohio University, B.A. (cum laude), 1968; University of Miami, M.S., 1969; State University of New York at Albany, Ph.D., 1972.

ADDRESSES: Office—Benckiser North America, 10 Rogers St., Cambridge, MA 02142.

CAREER: State University of New York at Albany, instructor in psychology, 1971-72; Institute for Juvenile Research, Chicago, IL, senior research fellow, 1972-74, senior research scientist, 1974-75; University of Pittsburgh, Pittsburgh, PA, associate professor of business administration and psychology, 1975-79, research associate of Center for International Studies and research fellow at Center for Arms Control and International Security Studies, 1975-79, director of Bureau of Business Research, 1978-79; Harvard University, Boston, MA, associate professor, 1979-85, professor of business administration, 1985—, director of MBA program, 1986-88; Benckiser North America, Cambridge, MA, currently president, and executive vice-president of Benckiser Gmb H.

Lecturer at Roosevelt University, 1973-74, and Loyola University, 1974-75; visiting assistant professor at Northwestern University, 1974-75. Speaker at professional meetings, workshops, and conferences. Marketing and management consultant to American businesses.

MEMBER: American Institute for Decision Sciences, American Marketing Association, American Psychological Association, Association for Consumer Research, Society for the Psychological Study of Social Issues, Blue Key.

AWARDS, HONORS: Marketing Science Institute grants, 1975, 1977-78; senior Fulbright-Hays grant, 1978.

WRITINGS:

(With J. T. Tedeschi and B. R. Schlenker) *Conflict, Power, and Games: The Experimental Study of Interpersonal Relations,* Aldine, 1973.

Escalation and De-Escalation: A Social Psychological Perspective, Sage Publications, 1975.

(With Gerald Zaltman and W. J. Johnston) *Industrial Buying Behavior* (monograph), Marketing Science Institute, 1977.

(With D. P. Slevin) *Executive Survival Manual,* Wadsworth, 1978.

(Editor with Zaltman) *The 1978 Review of Marketing,* American Marketing Association, 1978.

(Editor with Zaltman) *Organizational Buying Behavior* (monograph), American Marketing Association, 1978.

(With Zaltman) *Psychology for Management,* Wadsworth, 1979.

Management Marketing: Text Cases and Reading, Free Press, 1983.

(With Benson Shapiro) *Segmenting the Industrial Market,* Lexington Books, 1983.

The Marketing Edge, Free Press, 1985.

(With T. Kosnik) *Marketing Management,* Irwin, 1990.

CONTRIBUTOR

Zaltman, Philip Kotler, and Ira Kaufman, editors, *Creating Social Change,* Holt, 1972.

Tedeschi, editor, *The Social Influence Processes,* Aldine, 1972.

Dennis Krebs, editor, *Readings in Social Psychology: Contemporary Perspectives,* Harper, 1976.

M. Kaplan and S. Schwartz, editors, *Human Judgment and Decision Processes in Applied Settings,* Academic Press, 1977.

Daniel Druckman, editor, *Negotiation: A Social Psychological Perspective,* Sage Publications, 1978.

Zaltman, editor, *Handbook of Nonprofit Management,* American Management Association, 1979.

Zaltman, editor, *Consumer Behavior,* Wiley, 1979.

R. Bagozzi, editor, *Sales Management,* Marketing Science Institute, 1979.

Marketing Survival Manual, CBI Publishing, 1980.

Industrial Marketing, Business Publications, 1980.

OTHER

Also author, with B. Clark, of *Marketing Performance Assessment,* 1987, and *Social Conflict.* Co-editor of *Annual Review of Marketing.* Contributor of more than one hundred articles and reviews to professional journals. Co-editor, *Journal of Social Issues,* 1977, and *American Behavioral Scientist,* 1978; member of editorial review board, *Behavioral Science* and *Journal of Marketing Research.*

SIDELIGHTS: T. V. Bonoma's professional interests include marketing management, marketing implementation, marketing performance assessment, industrial marketing, consumer influence processes, social power, social conflict and resolution, group dynamics, individual and social decision-making, social

evaluation, and application of scientific findings to practical and managerial concerns.

BIOGRAPHICAL/CRITICAL SOURCES:

PERIODICALS

New York Times Book Review, October 20, 1985.

*   *   *

BOONE, Gene   1962-

PERSONAL: Born December 26, 1962, in Darlington, SC; son of Vernon Lee and Macy Louise (Tyner) Boone.

ADDRESSES: Home—Route #2, P.O. Box 194, Society Hill, SC 29593. *Office*—R.S.V.P. Press, P.O. Box 394, Society Hill, SC 29593.

CAREER: Full-time writer, 1980—; R.S.V.P. Press, Society Hill, SC, editor, 1983—.

WRITINGS:

Waiting to Be Published, Exploits Ltd., 1984.
Crocodile Tears (poems), Cerred Books, 1984.
Markets for Writers, R.S.V.P. Press, 1985.
Black and Blue (poems), R.S.V.P. Press, 1988.

Also contributor to anthologies, including *Lyrical Treasures, Classic and Modern,* Arts Press, 1983, *Anti-Reagan Anthology,* Poetry Associates, 1984, and *Anti-War Poems,* Volumes 1 and 2, Vesta (Canada). Contributor to periodicals, including *Woman's Circle, Fate, Standard,* and *Poet.*

WORK IN PROGRESS: Name Your Pet, a guide for animal lovers, for Quik Ref Publishing.

SIDELIGHTS: Gene Boone told *CA:* "I feel strongly that in order to be secure and progressive as writers, we must concentrate on subjects and categories that interest us, both as writers and readers. I think that when we do what we enjoy, our writing is better received by our readers. It is much easier to be true and dedicated to a project that is a labor of love.

"I refer to my this in my first book, *Writing to Be Published.* I truly enjoy writing on subjects that pertain to writing because I am interested in helping beginning writers reach their goals. I hope that my personal experiences will suit this purpose to some extent.

"I try never to limit myself in my writing pursuits. For example, I work in several categories, including nonfiction, fiction, and poetry. I have learned that not limiting myself to one specific area of writing has enabled me to attain many of my goals. It has also helped me to feel more fulfilled and productive through my writing."

*   *   *

BORGES, Jorge Luis   1899-1986
(F[rancisco] Bustos; joint pseudonyms: H[onorio] Bustos Domecq, B. Lynch Davis, B. Suarez Lynch)

PERSONAL: Born August 24, 1899, in Buenos Aires, Argentina; died June 14, 1986, in Geneva, Switzerland, of liver cancer; buried in Plainpalais, Geneva, Switzerland; son of Jorge Guillermo Borges (a lawyer, teacher, and writer) and Leonor Acevedo Suarez (a translator); married Elsa Astete Millan, September 21, 1967 (divorced, 1970); married Maria Kodama, April 26,

1986. *Education:* Attended College Calvin, Geneva, Switzerland, 1914-18.

ADDRESSES: Home—Geneva, Switzerland.

CAREER: Writer. Miguel Cane branch library, Buenos Aires, Argentina, municipal librarian, 1937-46; teacher of English literature at several private institutions and lecturer in Argentina and Uruguay, 1946-55; National Library, Buenos Aires, director, 1955-73; University of Buenos Aires, Buenos Aires, professor of English and U.S. literature, beginning 1956. Visiting professor or guest lecturer at numerous universities in the United States and throughout the world, including University of Texas, 1961-62, University of Oklahoma, 1969, University of New Hampshire, 1972, and Dickinson College, 1983; Charles Eliot Norton Professor of Poetry, Harvard University, 1967-68.

MEMBER: Argentine Academy of Letters, Argentine Writers Society (president, 1950-53), Modern Language Association of America (honorary fellow, 1961-86), American Association of Teachers of Spanish and Portuguese (honorary fellow, 1965-86).

AWARDS, HONORS: Buenos Aires Municipal Literary Prize, 1928, for *El idioma de los argentinos;* Gran Premio de Honor from Argentine Writers Society, 1945, for *Ficciones, 1935-1944;* Gran Premio Nacional de la Literatura (Argentina), 1957, for *El Aleph;* Prix Formentor from International Congress of Publishers (shared with Samuel Beckett), 1961; Commandeur de l'Ordre des Lettres et des Arts (France), 1962; Ingram Merrill Foundation Award, 1966; Matarazzo Sobrinho Inter-American Literary Prize from Bienal Foundation, 1970; nominated for Neustadt International Prize for Literature, *World Literature Today* and University of Oklahoma, 1970, 1984, and 1986; Jerusalem Prize, 1971; Alfonso Reyes Prize (Mexico), 1973; Gran Cruz del Orden al merito Bernando O'Higgins from Government of Chile, 1976; Gold Medal from French Academy, Order of Merit from Federal Republic of Germany, and Icelandic Falcon Cross, all 1979; Miguel de Cervantes Award (Spain) and Balzan Prize (Italy), both 1980; Ollin Yoliztli Prize (Mexico), 1981; T. S. Eliot Award for Creative Writing from Ingersoll Foundation and Rockford Institute, 1983; Gold Medal of Menendez Pelayo University (Spain), La Gran Cruz de la Orden Alfonso X, el Sabio (Spain), and Legion d'Honneur (France), all 1983; Knight of the British Empire. Recipient of honorary degrees from numerous colleges and universities, including University of Cuyo (Argentina), 1956, University of the Andes (Colombia), 1963, Oxford University, 1970, University of Jerusalem, 1971, Columbia University, 1971, and Michigan State University, 1972.

WRITINGS:

POETRY

Fervor de Buenos Aires (title means "Passion for Buenos Aires"), Serantes (Buenos Aires), 1923, revised edition, Emece, 1969.

Luna de enfrente (title means "Moon across the Way"), Proa (Buenos Aires), 1925.

Cuaderno San Martin (title means "San Martin Copybook"), Proa, 1929.

Poemas, 1923-1943, Losada, 1943, 3rd enlarged edition published as *Obra poetica, 1923-1964,* Emece, 1964, translation published as *Selected Poems, 1923-1967* (bilingual edition; also includes prose), edited, with an introduction and notes, by Norman Thomas di Giovanni, Delacorte, 1972.

Seis poemas escandinavos (title means "Six Scandinavian Poems"), privately printed, 1966.

Siete poemas (title means "Seven Poems"), privately printed, 1967.

El otro, el mismo (title means "The Other, the Same"), Emece, 1969.

Elogio de la sombra, Emece, 1969, translation by di Giovanni published as *In Praise of Darkness* (bilingual edition), Dutton, 1974.

El oro de los tigres (also see below; title means "The Gold of Tigers"), Emece, 1972.

Siete poemas sajones/Seven Saxon Poems, Plain Wrapper Press, 1974.

La rosa profunda (also see below; title means "The Unending Rose"), Emece, 1975.

La moneda de hierro (title means "The Iron Coin"), Emece, 1976.

Historia de la noche (title means "History of Night"), Emece, 1977.

The Gold of Tigers: Selected Later Poems (contains translations of *El oro de los tigres* and *La rosa profunda*), translated by Alastair Reid, Dutton, 1977.

La cifra, Emece, 1981.

Also author of *Los conjurados* (title means "The Conspirators"), 1985.

ESSAYS

Inquisiciones (title means "Inquisitions"), Proa, 1925.

El tamano de mi esperanza (title means "The Measure of My Hope"), Proa, 1926.

El idioma de los argentinos (title means "The Language of the Argentines"), M. Gleizer (Buenos Aires), 1928, 3rd edition (includes three essays by Borges and three by Jose Edmundo Clemente), Emece, 1968.

Figari, privately printed, 1930.

Las Kennigar, Colombo (Buenos Aires), 1933.

Historia de la eternidad (title means "History of Eternity"), Viau y Zona (Buenos Aires), 1936, revised edition published as *Obras completas,* Volume 1, Emece, 1953, reprinted, 1978.

Nueva refutacion del tiempo (title means "New Refutation of Time"), Oportet y Haereses, 1947.

Aspectos de la literatura gauchesca, Numero (Montevideo), 1950.

(With Delia Ingenieros) *Antiguas literaturas germanicas,* Fondo de Cultura Economica (Mexico), 1951, revised edition with Maria Esther Vazquez published as *Literaturas germanicas medievales,* Falbo, 1966, reprinted, Emece, 1978.

Otras inquisiciones, Sur (Buenos Aires), 1952, published as *Obras completas,* Volume 8, Emece, 1960, translation by Ruth L. C. Simms published as *Other Inquisitions, 1937-1952,* University of Texas Press, 1964.

(With Margarita Guerrero) *El "Martin Fierro,"* Columba, 1953, reprinted, Emece, 1979.

(With Bettina Edelberg) *Leopoldo Lugones,* Troquel (Buenos Aires), 1955.

(With Guerrero) *Manual de zoologia fantastica,* Fondo de Cultura Economica, 1957, translation published as *The Imaginary Zoo,* University of California Press, 1969, revised Spanish edition with Guerrero published as *El libro de los seres imaginarios,* Kier (Buenos Aires), 1967, translation and revision by di Giovanni and Borges published as *The Book of Imaginary Beings,* Dutton, 1969.

La poesia gauchesca (title means "Gaucho Poetry"), Centro de Estudios Brasileiros, 1960.

(With Vazquez) *Introduccion a la literatura inglesa,* Columba, 1965, translation by L. Clark Keating and Robert O. Evans published as *An Introduction to English Literature,* University Press of Kentucky, 1974.

(With Esther Zemborain de Torres) *Introduccion a la literatura norteamericana,* Columba, 1967, translation by Keating and Evans published as *An Introduction to American Literature,* University Press of Kentucky, 1971.

(With Alicia Jurado) *Que es el budismo?* (title means, "What Is Buddhism?"), Columba, 1976.

Nuevos ensayos dantescos (title means "New Dante Essays,") Espasa-Calpe, 1982.

SHORT STORIES

Historia universal de la infamia, Tor (Buenos Aires), 1935, revised edition published as *Obras completas,* Volume 3, Emece, 1964, translation by di Giovanni published as *A Universal History of Infamy,* Dutton, 1972.

El jardin de senderos que se bifurcan (also see below; title means "Garden of the Forking Paths"), Sur, 1941.

(With Adolfo Bioy Casares, under joint pseudonym H. Bustos Domecq) *Seis problemas para Isidro Parodi,* Sur, 1942, translation by di Giovanni published under authors' real names as *Six Problems for Don Isidro Parodi,* Dutton, 1983.

Ficciones, 1935-1944 (includes *El jardin de senderos que se bifurcan*), Sur, 1944, revised edition published as *Obras completas,* Volume 5, Emece, 1956, reprinted, with English introduction and notes by Gordon Brotherson and Peter Hulme, Harrap, 1976, translation by Anthony Kerrigan and others published as *Ficciones,* edited and with an introduction by Kerrigan, Grove, 1962 (published in England as *Fictions,* John Calder, 1965), reprinted, Limited Editions Club (New York), 1984.

(With Bioy Casares, under joint pseudonym H. Bustos Domecq) *Dos fantasias memorables,* Oportet & Haereses, 1946, reprinted under authors' real names with notes and bibliography by Horacio Jorge Becco, Edicom (Buenos Aires), 1971.

El Aleph, Losada, 1949, revised edition, 1952, published as *Obras completas,* Volume 7, Emece, 1956, translation and revision by di Giovanni in collaboration with Borges published as *The Aleph and Other Stories, 1933-1969,* Dutton, 1970.

(With Luisa Mercedes Levinson) *La hermana de Eloisa* (title means "Eloisa's Sister"), Ene (Buenos Aires), 1955.

(With Bioy Casares) *Cronicas de Bustos Domecq,* Losada, 1967, translation by di Giovanni published as *Chronicles of Bustos Domecq,* Dutton, 1976.

El informe de Brodie, Emece, 1970, translation by di Giovanni in collaboration with Borges published as *Dr. Brodie's Report,* Dutton, 1971.

El matrero, Edicom, 1970.

El congreso, El Archibrazo, 1971, translation by di Giovanni in collaboration with Borges published as *The Congress* (also see below), Enitharmon Press, 1974, translation by Alberto Manguel published as *The Congress of the World,* F. M. Ricci (Milan), 1981.

El libro de arena, Emece, 1975, translation by di Giovanni published with "The Congress" as *The Book of Sand,* Dutton, 1977.

(With Bioy Casares) *Nuevos cuentos de Bustos Domecq,* Libreria de la Cuidad, 1977.

Rosa y azul (contains "La rosa de Paracelso" and "Tigres azules"), Sedmay (Madrid), 1977.

Veinticinco agosto 1983 y otros cuentos de Jorges Luis Borges (includes interview with Borges), Siruela, 1983.

OMNIBUS VOLUMES

La muerte y la brujula (stories; title means "Death and the Compass"), Emece, 1951.

Obras completas, ten volumes, Emece, 1953-67, published as one volume, 1974.

Cuentos (title means "Stories"), Monticello College Press, 1958.

Antologia personal (prose and poetry), Sur, 1961, translation published as *A Personal Anthology,* edited and with foreword by Kerrigan, Grove Press, 1967.

Labyrinths: Selected Stories and Other Writings, edited by Donald A. Yates and James E. Irby, preface by Andre Maurois, New Directions, 1962, augmented edition, 1964, reprinted, Modern Library, 1983.

Nueva antologia personal, Emece, 1968.

Prologos (title means "Prologues"), Torres Aguero (Buenos Aires), 1975.

(With others) *Obras completas en colaboracion* (title means "Complete Works in Collaboration"), Emece, 1979.

Narraciones (stories), edited by Marcos Ricardo Bamatan, Catedra, 1980.

Borges: A Reader (prose and poetry), edited by Emir Rodriguez Monegal and Reid, Dutton, 1981.

Ficcionario: Una antologia de sus textos, edited by Rodriguez Monegal, Fondo de Cultura Economica, 1985.

Textos cautivos: Ensayos y resenas en "El Hogar" (1936-1939) (title means "Captured Texts: Essays and Reviews in 'El Hogar' [1936-1939]"), edited by Rodriguez Monegal and Enrique Sacerio-Gari, Tusquets, 1986.

El aleph borgiano (chiefly book reviews which appeared in journals, 1922-84), edited by Juan Gustavo Cobo Borda and Martha Kovasics de Cubides, Biblioteca Luis-Angel Arango (Bogota), 1987.

Biblioteca personal: Prologos, Alianza, 1988.

OTHER

(Author of afterword) Ildefonso Pereda Valdes, *Antologia de la moderna poesia uruguaya,* El Ateneo (Buenos Aires), 1927.

Evaristo Carriego (biography), M. Gleizer, 1930, revised edition published as *Obras completas,* Volume 4, Emece (Buenos Aires), 1955, translation by di Giovanni published as *Evaristo Carriego: A Book about Old Time Buenos Aires,* Dutton, 1984.

(Translator) Virginia Woolf, *Orlando,* Sur, 1937.

(Editor with Pedro Henriquez Urena) *Antologia clasica de la literatura argentina* (title means "Anthology of Argentine Literature"), Kapelusz (Buenos Aires), 1937.

(Translator and author of prologue) Franz Kafka, *La metamorfosis,* [Buenos Aires], 1938, reprinted, Losada, 1976.

(Editor with Bioy Casares and Silvina Ocampo) *Antologia de la literatura fantastica* (title means "Anthology of Fantastic Literature"), with foreword by Bioy Casares, Sudamericana, 1940, enlarged edition with postscript by Bioy Casares, 1965, translation of revised version published as *The Book of Fantasy,* with introduction by Ursula K. Le Guin, Viking, 1988.

(Author of prologue) Bioy Casares, *La invencion de Morel,* Losada, 1940, reprinted, Alianza, 1981, translation by Simms published as *The Invention of Morel and Other Stories,* University of Texas Press, 1964, reprinted, 1985.

(Editor with Bioy Casares and Ocampo and author of prologue) *Antologia poetica argentina* (title means "Anthology of Argentine Poetry"), Sudamericana, 1941.

(Translator) Henri Michaux, *Un barbaro en Asia,* Sur, 1941.

(Compiler and translator with Bioy Casares) *Los mejores cuentos policiales* (title means "The Best Detective Stories"), Emece, 1943, reprinted, Alianza, 1972.

(Translator and author of prologue) Herman Melville, *Bartleby, el escribiente,* Emece, 1943, reprinted, Marymar (Buenos Aires), 1976.

(Editor with Silvina Bullrich) *El compadrito: Su destino, sus barrios, su musica* (title means "The Buenos Aires Hoodlum: His Destiny, His Neighborhoods, His Music"), Emece, 1945, 2nd edition, Fabril, 1968.

(With Bioy Casares, under joint pseudonym B. Suarez Lynch) *Un modelo para la muerte* (novel; title means "A Model for Death"), Oportet & Haereses, 1946.

(Compiler and translator with Bioy Casares) *Los mejores cuentos policiales: Segunda serie,* Emece, 1951.

(Editor and translator with Bioy Casares) *Cuentos breves y extraordinarios: Antologia,* Raigal (Buenos Aires), 1955, revised and enlarged edition, Losada, 1973, translation by Kerrigan published as *Extraordinary Tales,* Souvenir Press, 1973.

(With Bioy Casares) *Los orilleros* [and] *El paraiso de los creyentes* (screenplays; titles mean "The Hoodlums" and "The Believers' Paradise"; "Los orilleros" produced by Argentine director Ricardo Luna, 1975), Losada, 1955, reprinted, 1975.

(Editor and author of prologue, notes, and glossary with Bioy Casares) *Poesia gauchesca* (title means "Gaucho Poetry"), two volumes, Fondo de Cultura Economica, 1955.

(Translator) William Faulkner, *Las palmeras salvajes,* Sudamericana, 1956.

(Editor with Bioy Casares) *Libro del cielo y del infierno* (anthology; title means "Book of Heaven and Hell"), Sur, 1960, reprinted, 1975.

El hacedor (prose and poetry; Volume 9 of *Obras completas;* title means "The Maker"), Emece, 1960, translation by Mildred Boyer and Harold Morland published as *Dreamtigers,* University of Texas Press, 1964, reprinted, 1985.

(Editor and author of prologue) *Macedonio Fernandez,* Culturales Argentinas, Ministerio de Educacion y Justicia, 1961.

Para las seis cuerdas: Milongas (song lyrics; title means "For the Six Strings: Milongas"), Emece, 1965.

Dialogo con Borges, edited by Victoria Ocampo, Sur, 1969.

(Translator, editor, and author of prologue) Walt Whitman, *Hojas de hierba,* Juarez (Buenos Aires), 1969.

(Compiler and author of prologue) Evaristo Carriego, *Versos,* Universitaria de Buenos Aires, 1972.

Borges on Writing (lectures), edited by di Giovanni, Daniel Halpern, and Frank MacShane, Dutton, 1973.

(With Bioy Casares and Hugo Santiago) *Les Autres: Escenario original* (screenplay; produced in France and directed by Santiago, 1974), C. Bourgois (Paris), 1974.

(Author of prologue) Carlos Zubillaga, *Carlos Gardel,* Jucar (Madrid), 1976.

Cosmogonias (title means "Cosmogonies"), Libreria de la Ciudad, 1976.

Libro de suenos (transcripts of Borges's and others' dreams; title means "Book of Dreams"), Torres Aguero, 1976.

(Author of prologue) Santiago Dabove, *La muerte y su traje,* Calicanto, 1976.

Borges—Imagenes, memorias, dialogos, edited by Vazquez, Monte Avila, 1977.

Adrogue (prose and poetry), privately printed, 1977.

(Editor with Maria Kodama) *Breve antologia anglosajona,* Emece, 1979.

Borges oral (lectures), edited by Martin Mueller, Emece, 1979.

Siete noches (lectures), Fondo de Cultura Economica, 1980, translation by Weinberger published as *Seven Nights,* New Directions, 1984.

(Compiler) Paul Groussac, *Jorge Luis Borges selecciona lo mejor de Paul Groussac,* Fraterna (Buenos Aires), 1981.

(Compiler and author of prologue) Francisco de Quevedo, *Antologia poetica,* Alianza, 1982.

(Compiler and author of introduction) Leopoldo Lugones, *Antologia poetica,* Alianza, 1982.

(Compiler and author of prologue) Pedro Antonio de Alarcon, *El amigo de la muerte,* Siruela (Madrid), 1984.

(With Kodama) *Atlas* (prose and poetry), Sudamericana, 1984, translation by Kerrigan published as *Atlas,* Dutton, 1985.

En voz de Borges (interviews), Offset, 1986.

Libro de dialogos (interviews), edited by Osvaldo Ferrari, Sudamericana, 1986, published as *Dialogos ultimos,* 1987.

Editor with Bioy Casares of series of detective novels, "The Seventh Circle," for Emece, 1943-56. Contributor, under pseudonym F. Bustos, to *Critica* (Buenos Aires), 1933. Contributor, with Bioy Casares under joint pseudonym B. Lynch Davis, to *Los anales de Buenos Aires,* 1946-48. Founding editor of *Prisma* (mural magazine), 1921; founding editor of *Proa* (Buenos Aires literary revue), 1921 and, with Ricardo Guiraldes and Pablo Rojas Paz, 1924-26; literary editor of weekly arts supplement of *Critica,* beginning 1933; editor of biweekly "Foreign Books and Authors" section of *El Hogar* (magazine), 1936-39; co-editor with Bioy Casares of *Destiempo* (literary magazine), 1936; editor of *Los anales de Buenos Aires* (literary journal), 1946-48.

SIDELIGHTS: "Jorge Luis Borges [was] a great writer," noted French author Andre Maurois in his preface to the Argentine poet, essayist, and short story writer's *Labyrinths: Selected Stories and Other Writings,* "who . . . composed only little essays or short narratives. Yet they suffice for us to call him great because of their wonderful intelligence, their wealth of invention, and their tight, almost mathematical style. Argentine by birth and temperament, but nurtured on universal literature, Borges [had] no spiritual homeland."

Borges was nearly unknown in most of the world until 1961 when, in his early sixties, he was awarded the Prix Formentor—the International Publishers Prize—an honor he shared with Irish playwright Samuel Beckett. Before winning the award, according to Gene H. Bell-Villada in *Borges and His Fiction: A Guide to His Mind and Art,* "Borges had been writing in relative obscurity in Buenos Aires, his fiction and poetry read by his compatriots, who were slow in perceiving his worth or even knowing him." The award made Borges internationally famous: a collection of his short stories, *Ficciones,* was simultaneously published in six different countries, and he was invited by the University of Texas to come to the United States to lecture, the first of many international lecture tours.

Borges's international appeal was partly a result of his enormous erudition which is apparent in the multitude of literary allusions from cultures around the globe contained in his writing. "The work of Jorge Luis Borges," Anthony Kerrigan wrote in his introduction to the English translation of *Ficciones,* "is a species of international literary metaphor. He knowledgeably makes a transfer of inherited meanings from Spanish and English, French and German, and sums up a series of analogies, of confrontations, of appositions in other nations' literatures. His Argentinians act out Parisian dramas, his Central European Jews are wise in the ways of the Amazon, his Babylonians are fluent in the paradigms of Babel." In the *National Review* Peter Witonski commented: "Borges' grasp of world literature is one of the fundamental elements of his art."

The familiarity with world literature evident in Borges's work was initiated at an early age, nurtured by a love of reading. His paternal grandmother was English, and, consequently, since she lived with the Borgeses, English and Spanish were spoken in the family home. Jorge Guillermo Borges, Borges's father, had a large library of English and Spanish books in which his son, whose frail constitution made it impossible to participate in more strenuous activities, spent many hours. "If I were asked to name the chief event in my life," Borges stated in "An Autobiographical Essay" that originally appeared in the *New Yorker* and was later included in *The Aleph and Other Stories, 1933-1969,* "I should say my father's library."

Under his grandmother's tutelage, Borges learned to read English before he could read Spanish. Among the first books he read were works in English by Twain, Poe, Longfellow, Stevenson, and Wells. In Borges's autobiographical essay he recalled reading even the great Spanish masterpiece, Cervantes's *Don Quixote,* in English before reading it in Spanish. Borges's father encouraged writing as well as reading: Borges wrote his first story at age seven, and, at nine, saw his Spanish translation of Oscar Wilde's "The Happy Prince" published in a Buenos Aires newspaper. "From the time I was a boy . . .," Borges noted in his autobiographical essay, "it was tacitly understood that I had to fulfill the literary destiny that circumstances had denied my father. This was something that was taken for granted. . . . I was expected to be a writer."

Borges became a writer whose works were compared to those of many others, Franz Kafka and James Joyce in particular, but whose style was unique. Critics were forced to coin a new word—Borgesian—to capture the magical world invented by the Argentine master. As Jaime Alazraki noted in *Jorge Luis Borges,* "As with Joyce, Kafka, or Faulkner, the name of Borges has become an accepted concept; his creations have generated a dimension that we designate 'Borgesian.'" And, in *Atlantic,* Keith Botsford declared: "Borges is . . . an international phenomenon, . . . a man of letters whose mode of writing and turn of mind are so distinctively his, yet so much a revealed part of our world, that 'Borgesian' has become as commonplace a neologism as the adjectives 'Sartrean' or 'Kafkaesque.'"

Perhaps the most profound consequence of this Borgesian style was the dramatic change it engendered in Latin American literature. "As [Mexican novelist] Carlos Fuentes remarked," according to Bell-Villada in *Nation,* "without Borges the modern Latin American novel simply would not exist." In *Jorge Luis Borges* George R. McMurray explained that "prior to 1950, the vast majority of Latin American novelists relied on traditional realism to depict life in their native lands and convey messages of social protest. Borges not only liberated Latin American literature from documentation but also restored imagination as a major fictional ingredient." Borges's greatest accomplishment, James E. Irby notes in his introductory remarks to *Labyrinths,* was to rise above the regionalism favored by the writers of his time and "to transmute his circumstances into an art as universal as the finest in Europe."

U.S. writers did not escape Borges's influence. "The impact of Borges on the United States writing scene," commented Bell-Villada, "may be almost as great as was his earlier influence on Latin America. The Argentine reawakened for us the possibilities of farfetched fancy, of formal exploration, of parody, intellectuality, and wit." Bell-Villada specifically noted Borges's presence in works by Robert Coover, Donald Barthelme, and John Gardner. Another important novelist, John Barth, confessed Borges's influence in his own novels. The critic concluded that Borges's work paved "the way for numerous literary trends on both American continents, determining the shape of much

fiction to come. By rejecting realism and naturalism, he . . . opened up to our Northern writers a virgin field, led them to a wealth of new subjects and procedures."

The foundation of Borges's literary future was laid in 1914 when the Borgeses took an ill-timed trip to Europe. There, the outbreak of World War I stranded them temporarily in Switzerland, where Borges studied French and Latin in school, taught himself German, and began reading the works of German philosophers and expressionist poets. He was also introduced to the poetry of Walt Whitman in German translation and soon began writing poetry imitative of Whitman's style. "For some time," Rodriguez Monegal wrote in *Borges: A Reader,* "the young man believed Whitman was poetry itself."

After the war the Borgeses settled in Spain for a few years. During this extended stay Borges published reviews, articles, and poetry and became associated with a group of avant-garde poets called Ultraists (named after the magazine, *Ultra,* to which they contributed). Upon Borges's return to Argentina, in 1921, he introduced the tenets of the movement—they believed, for example, in the supremacy of the metaphor—to the Argentine literary scene. His first collection of poems, *Fervor de Buenos Aires,* was written under the spell of this new poetic movement. Although in his autobiographical essay he expressed regret for his "early Ultraist excesses" and in later editions of *Fervor de Buenos Aires* eliminated more than a dozen poems from the text and considerably altered many of the remaining poems, Borges still saw some value in the work. In his autobiographical essay he noted, "I think I have never strayed beyond that book. I feel that all my subsequent writing has only developed themes first taken up there; I feel that all during my lifetime I have been rewriting that one book."

One poem from the volume, "El truco" (a card game), for example, seems to testify to the truth of Borges's statement. In the piece he introduced two themes that appear over and over again in his later writing: circular time and the idea that all people are but one person. "The permutations of the cards," Rodriguez Monegal observed in *Jorge Luis Borges: A Literary Biography,* "although innumerable in limited human experience, are not infinite: given enough time, they will come back again and again. Thus the cardplayers not only are repeating hands that have already come up in the past. In a sense, they are repeating the former players as well: they are the former players."

The decade from 1920 to 1930 was a period of intense activity for Borges. Not only did he publish seven books—four collections of essays and three of poetry—but he also founded three magazines and contributed to nearly a dozen other publications. But although these early works met with some success, it was his work in fiction that would bring him worldwide fame. As McMurray noted, Borges's "highly original short stories—the most important written during the 1940s and early 1950s—. . . made him one of the most widely acclaimed writers of our time."

Illusion is an important part of Borges's fictional world. In *Borges: The Labyrinth Maker,* Ana Maria Barrenechea called it "his resplendent world of shadows." But illusion is present in his manner of writing as well the fictional world he describes. In *World Literature Today,* William Riggan quoted Icelandic author Sigurdur Magnusson's thoughts on this aspect of Borges's work. "With the possible exception of Kafka . . .," Magnusson stated, "no other writer that I know manages, with such relentless logic, to turn language upon itself to reverse himself time after time with a sentence or a paragraph, and effortlessly, so it seems, come upon surprising yet inevitable conclusions."

Because of Borges's choice of words and the way he used them, the reader is never sure about the possible outcome of the work until he has finished reading it. But, even then, subsequent readings often reveal subtle shades of meaning or entirely new conclusions. In "The South," for example, one cannot be certain if the protagonist, Juan Dahlmann, dies in his hospital bed or in a knife duel. In "The Shape of the Sword" the reader listens to the narrator tell the story of a despicable traitor and only in the last lines of the story does he learn that the narrator is actually talking about himself. The reader cannot even be certain that once he has finished a Borges story that what he read was actually a story. Borges's short narrative "The Approach to al-Mu'tasim," written as a book review of a non-existent book, was originally published in a collection of essays, *Historia de la eternidad.* Even the writer's friends were fooled by the story: Adolfo Bioy Casares, with whom Borges collaborated on many projects, tried to order the book under review from its alleged publisher in London (Borges had used the name of an actual publishing house in the text). Borges didn't acknowledge the hoax until five years later when the story was published in a fiction collection. But the apparent reality of "The Approach to al-Mu'tasim" is not unique to that story. As D. P. Gallagher noted in *Modern Latin American Literature:* "The stories often look real. Borges indeed always deploys illusionists' tricks to make them look so, before demolishing them as fictions. The stories are full of scholarly footnotes, references to real people, precise dates, all sorts of devices designed to give an appearance of reality to extraordinary things. Borges himself appears as a character in several stories and so do some of his friends."

Borges expertly blended the traditional boundaries between fact and fiction and between essay and short story and he was similarly adept at obliterating the border between other genres as well. In a tribute to Borges which appeared in the *New Yorker* after the Argentine's death in 1986, Mexican poet and essayist Octavio Paz wrote: "He cultivated three genres: the essay, the poem, and the short story. The division is arbitrary. His essays read like stories, his stories are poems; and his poems make us think, as though they were essays." In *Review,* Ambrose Gordon, Jr., similarly noted, "His essays are like poems in their almost musical development of themes, his stories are remarkably like his essays, and his poems are often little stories." Borges's "Conjectural Poem," for example, is very much like a short story in that it is an account of the death of one of his ancestors, Francisco Narciso de Laprida. Another poem, "The Golem," is a short narrative relating how Rabbi Low of Prague created an artificial man.

To deal with the problem of actually determining to which genre a prose piece by Borges might belong, Martin S. Stabb proposed in *Jorge Luis Borges* that the usual manner of grouping all of Borges's short fiction as short stories was invalid. Stabb instead divided the Argentine's prose fiction into three categories which took into account Borges's tendency to blur genres: " 'essayistic' fiction," "difficult-to-classify 'intermediate' fiction," and those pieces deemed "conventional short stories." Other reviewers saw a comparable division in Borges's fiction but chose to emphasize the chronological development of his work, noting that his first stories grew out of his essays, his "middle period" stories were more realistic, while his later stories were marked by a return to fantastic themes.

Others commentators on Borges's work chose to avoid classification by genre altogether and concentrated instead on thematic studies. This could be done quite easily for many of Borges's poetic themes, for example, are also found in his work in prose. In *Spanish American Literature: A History* Enrique Anderson-

Imbert lists some of the motifs commonly found in Borges's poetry as "time, the meaning of the universe, [and] the personality of man." These same major concerns are found in Borges's essays and fiction as well. When used to examine Borges's short stories, this method recalls Borges's own insistence on exploring fantastic literature based on four key elements. "Borges once claimed that the basic devices of all fantastic literature are only four in number: the work within the work, the contamination of reality by dream, the voyage in time, and the double," Irby explained. "These are both his essential themes—the problematical nature of the world, of knowledge, of time, of the self—and his essential techniques of construction."

When dealing with a body of work as rich and multifaceted as Borges's, a combination of both interpretive methods seems to impart the most accurate picture of Borges's fiction. Stabb began his study of Borges's "essayistic fiction" with this explanation: "These, and other pieces like them, are often based on readily identified philosophic notions, though many of the personalities used by Borges to make his points are fictional. In none of them is there any real narrative: several are based on invented literary notes describing fictitious authors and their works. It would not be difficult to imagine most of them cast in the form of a traditional essay." In *The Narrow Act: Borges' Art of Illusion,* Ronald J. Christ noted that these characteristics listed by Stamm are very common in Borges. He remarked, "The point of origin for most of Borges' fiction is neither character nor plot, considered in the traditional sense; but instead, a proposition, an idea, a metaphor." Stabb included in this type of fiction the stories "Funes the Memorious," "Pierre Mehard, Author of the *Quixote,*" and "Three Versions of Judas." These stories elaborate a multitude of ideas, including the uselessness of unordered knowledge, the impossibility of originality in literature, and the true nature of Jesus.

"Funes the Memorious," listed in Richard Burgin's *Conversations with Jorge Luis Borges* as one of the Argentine's favorite stories, is about Ireneo Funes, a young man who cannot forget anything. His memory is so keen that he is surprised by how different he looks each time he sees himself in a mirror because, unlike the rest of us, he can see the subtle changes that have taken place in his body since the last time he saw his reflection. The story is filled with characteristic Borgesian detail. Funes's memory, for instance, becomes excessive as a result of an accidental fall from a horse. In Borges an accident is a reminder that man is unable to order his existence because the world has a hidden order of its own. Alazraki saw this Borgesian theme as "the tragic contrast between a man who believes himself to be the master and maker of his fate and a text or divine plan in which his fortune has already been written." The deliberately vague quality of the adjectives Borges typically uses in his sparse descriptive passages is also apparent: Funes's features are never clearly distinguished because he lives in a darkened room, he was thrown from his horse on a dark "rainy afternoon," and the horse itself is described as "blue-gray"— neither one color or the other. "This dominant chiaroscuro imagery," commented Bell-Villada, "is further reinforced by Funes's name, a word strongly suggestive of certain Spanish words variously meaning 'funereal,' 'ill-fated,' and 'dark.' " The ambiguity of Borges's descriptions lends a subtle, otherworldly air to this and other examples of his fiction.

Bell-Villada noted another important aspect of the story. When the narrator visits Funes he finds the young man reciting from memory a portion of an actual book, an ancient Roman text entitled *Natural History* written by Pliny, which deals with memory. This is an example of what Bell-Villada called "a typical hall-of-mirrors effect: someone with a perfect memory reciting from memory a passage on memory." According to Bell-Villada "the hall-of-mirrors effect" is comparable to "the work within a work" device mentioned by Borges as essential to fantastic fiction. "Borges is especially renown," Bell-Villada continued, "for his use of . . . the work of art within a work of art. Some of his most celebrated tales ('Pierre Menard,' 'Tlon, Uqbar, Orbis Tertius') deal with nonexistent books and authors. Borges even has a special essay, 'Partial Magic in the *Quixote*,' which deals with a kind of derivative: those works in which a literary character finds himself depicted in a book or a play."

In "Partial Magic in the *Quixote*" (also translated as "Partial Enchantments of the *Quixote*") Borges describes several occasions in world literature when a character reads about himself or sees himself in a play, including episodes from Shakespeare's plays, an epic poem of India, Cervantes's *Don Quixote,* and *The One Thousand and One Nights.* "Why does it disquiet us to know," Borges asked in the essay, "that Don Quixote is a reader of the *Quixote,* and Hamlet is a spectator of *Hamlet?* I believe I have found the answer: those inversions suggest that if the characters in a story can be readers or spectators, then we, their readers, can be fictitious."

With his analysis of this literary device Borges offered his own interpretation of what John Barth referred to in the *Atlantic* as "one of Borges' cardinal themes." Barrenechea explained Borges's technique, noting: "To readers and spectators who consider themselves real beings, these works suggest their possible existence as imaginary entities. In that context lies the key to Borges' work. Relentlessly pursued by a world that is too real and at the same time lacking meaning, he tries to free himself from its obsessions by creating a world of such coherent phantasmagorias that the reader doubts the very reality on which he leans." For example, in one of Borges's variations on "the work within a work," Jaromir Hladik, the protagonist of Borges's story "The Secret Miracle," appears in a footnote to another of Borges's stories, "Three Versions of Judas." The note refers the reader to the *Vindication of Eternity,* a work said to be written by Hladik. In this instance, Borges used a fictional work written by one of his fictional characters to lend an air of erudition to another fictional work about the works of another fictional author.

Borges took "the work within a work" device one step further than any of the examples he spoke of in "Partial Magic in the *Quixote.*" One of his favorite literary allusions was to what he referred to as the six-hundred-and-second night of *A Thousand and One Nights.* On this night, Borges recalled, due to a copyist error, Scheherezade began to tell the Sultan the story of *A Thousand and One Nights* by mistake. Although Borges often referred to this episode, it is just another of his *ficciones,* never having been actually included in the original Arabic text. Thus, each time Borges talks about the episode, he is telling a tale about a fictional character telling a tale about telling a tale. As Barth pointed out, the episode is "a literary illustration of the *regressus in infinitum* [the infinite regression], as are almost all of Borges' principal images and motifs." It is as if two mirrors faced each other on the wall, each endlessly reflecting the reflection of the other.

The effect of referring to a work familiar to his readers in one of his stories and then making up a story about it lends an atmosphere of reality to Borges's fiction. A similar effect is created by the footnotes found in several of Borges's stories such as "Three Versions of Judas" and "Pierre Menard, Author of the *Quixote.*" The use of footnotes is an example of how Borges blended essay and fiction to create his "essayistic fiction." Both

stories, just like Borges's "Approach to al-Mu'tasim," were written as book reviews of works written by Borges's fictional authors and, thus, differ sharply in form and content from the traditional short story.

These intrusions of reality on the fictional world are characteristic of Borges's work. He also uses a device, which he calls "the contamination of reality by dream," to produce the same effect of uneasiness in the reader as "the work within the work" but through directly opposite means. Two examples of stories using this technique are "Tlon, Uqbar, Orbis Tertius" and "The Circular Ruins." The first, which Stabb included in his "difficult-to-classify 'intermediate' fiction," is one of Borges's most discussed works. It tells the story, according to Barrenechea, "of an attempt of a group of men to create a world of their own until, by the sheer weight of concentration, the fantastic creation acquires consistency and some of its objects—a compass, a metallic cone—which are composed of strange matter begin to appear on earth." By the end of the story, the world as we know it is slowly turning into the invented world of Tlon. Stabb called the work "difficult-to-classify" because, he commented, "the excruciating amount of documentary detail (half real, half fictitious) . . . make[s] the piece seem more like an essay" than a short story. There are, in addition, footnotes and a postscript to the story as well as an appearance by Borges himself and references to several other well-known Latin American literary figures, including Borges's friend, Bioy Casares.

"The Circular Ruins," which Stabb considered a "conventional short story," describes a very unconventional situation. (The story is conventional, however, in that there are no footnotes or real people intruding on the fictive nature of the piece.) In the story a man decides to dream about a son until the son becomes real. Later, after the man accomplishes his goal, much to his astonishment, he discovers that he in turn is being dreamt by someone else. "The Circular Ruins" includes several themes seen throughout Borges's work, including man's attempt to establish order in a chaotic universe, the infinite regression, the symbol of the labyrinth, and the idea of all men being one.

The futility of any attempt to order the universe, seen in "Funes the Memorious" and in "The Circular Ruins," is also found in "The Library of Babel" where, according to Alazraki, "Borges presents the world as a library of chaotic books which its librarians cannot read but which they interpret incessantly." The library was one of Borges's favorite images, often repeated in his fiction. In another work, Borges uses the image of a chessboard, however, to elaborate the same theme. In his poem "Chess," he speaks of the king, bishop, and queen who "seek out and begin their armed campaign." But, just as the dreamer dreams a man and causes him to act in a certain way, the campaign is actually being planned by someone other than the members of royalty. "They do not know it is the player's hand," the poem continues, "that dominates and guides their destiny." In the last stanza of the poem Borges uses the same images to suggest the infinite regression: "God moves the player, he in turn, the piece. / But what god beyond God begins the round / of dust and time and sleep and agonies?" Another poem, "The Golem," which tells the story of an artificial man created by a rabbi in Prague, ends in a similar fashion: "At the hour of anguish and vague light, / He would rest his eyes on his Golem. / Who can tell us what God felt, / As he gazed on His rabbi in Prague?" Just as there is a dreamer dreaming a man, and beyond that a dreamer dreaming the dreamer who dreamt the man, then, too, there must be another dreamer beyond that in an infinite succession of dreamers.

The infinite doubling effect inherent in the image of the dreamer who dreams a dreamer and the contrast between a chaotic universe and the order sought by man evoke an image that will be forever linked with Borges's name: the labyrinth. Like the mirror facing the mirror, "the labyrinth is born of duplication," John Sturrock observed in *Paper Tigers: The Ideal Fictions of Jorge Luis Borges*, "of the postulation of an alterative to a given reality, and founded on duplication thereafter." Alazraki concluded: "The labyrinth expresses both sides of the coin: it has an irreversible order if one knows the solution (the gods, God) and it can be at the same time a chaotic maze if the solution constitutes an unattainable secret (men). The labyrinth represents to a greater or less degree the vehicle through which Borges carries his world view to almost all his stories."

The title of the story "The Circular Ruins" suggests a labyrinth. In another story, "The Babylon Lottery," Stabb commented, "an ironically detached narrator depicts life as a labyrinth through which man wanders under the absurd illusion of having understood a chaotic, meaningless world." Labyrinths or references to labyrinths are found in nearly all of Borges's fiction. The labyrinthine form is often present in his poems, too, especially in Borges's early poetry filled with remembrances of wandering the labyrinth-like streets of old Buenos Aires.

In "The Circular Ruins" Borges's returns to another favorite theme: circular time. This theme embraces another device mentioned by Borges as typical of fantastic literature: time travel. Borges's characters, however, do not travel through time in machines; their travel is more on a metaphysical, mythical level. Circular time—a concept also favored by Nietzsche, one of the German philosophers Borges discovered as a boy—is apparent in many of Borges's stories, including "Three Versions of Judas," "The Garden of the Forking Paths," "Tlon, Uqbar, Orbis Tertius," "The Library of Babel," and "The Immortal." It is also found in another of Borges's favorite stories, "Death and the Compass," in which the reader encounters not only a labyrinth but a double as well. Stabb offered the story as a good example of Borges's "conventional short stories."

"Death and the Compass" is a detective story. Erik Lonnrot, the story's detective, commits the fatal error of believing there is an order in the universe that he can understand. When Marcel Yarmolinsky is murdered, Lonnrot refuses to believe it was just an accident; he looks for clues to the murderer's identity in Yarmolinsky's library. Red Scharlach, whose brother Lonnrot had sent to jail, reads about the detective's efforts to solve the murder in the local newspaper and contrives a plot to ambush him. The plan works because Lonnrot, overlooking numerous clues, blindly follows the false trail Scharlach leaves for him.

The final sentences—in which Lonnrot is murdered—change the whole meaning of the narrative, illustrate many of Borges's favorite themes, and crystalize for the reader Borges's thinking on the problem of time. Lonnrot says to Scharlach: " 'I know of one Greek labyrinth which is a single straight line. Along that line so many philosophers have lost themselves that a mere detective might well do so, too. Scharlach, when in some other incarnation you hunt me, pretend to commit (or do commit) a crime at A, then a second crime at B . . . , then a third crime at C. . . . Wait for me afterwards at D. . . . Kill me at D as you now are going to kill me at Triste-le-Roy.' 'The next time I kill you,' said Scharlach, 'I promise you that labyrinth, consisting of a single line which is invisible and unceasing.' He moved back a few steps. Then, very carefully, he fired."

"Death and the Compass" is in many ways a typical detective story, but this last paragraph takes the story far beyond that pop-

ular genre. Lonnrot and Scharlach are doubles (Borges gives us a clue in their names: *rot* means red and *scharlach* means scarlet in German) caught in an infinite cycle of pursuing and being pursued. "Their antithetical natures, or inverted mirror images," McMurray observed, "are demonstrated by their roles as detective/criminal and pursuer/pursued roles that become ironically reversed." Rodriguez Monegal concluded: "The concept of the eternal return . . . adds an extra dimension to the story. It changes Scharlach and Lonnrot into characters in a myth: Abel and Cain endlessly performing the killing."

Doubles, which Bell-Villada defined as "any blurring or any seeming multiplication of character identity," are found in many of Borges's works, including "The Waiting," "The Theologians," "The South," "The Shape of the Sword," "Three Versions of Judas," and "Story of the Warrior and the Captive." Borges's explanation of the story "The Theologians" (included in his collection, *The Aleph and Other Stories, 1933-1969*) reveals how a typical Borgesian plot involving doubles works: "In 'The Theologians' you have two enemies," Borges told Burgin in an interview, "and one of them sends the other to the stake. And then they find out somehow they're the same man." In a *Studies in Short Fiction* essay Robert Magliola noticed that "almost every story in *Dr. Brodie's Report* is about two people fixed in some sort of dramatic opposition to each other." In two pieces, "Borges and I" (also translated as "Borges and Myself ") and "The Other," Borges appears as a character along with his double. In the former, Borges, the retiring Argentine librarian, contemplates Borges, the world-famous writer. It concludes with one of Borges's most-analyzed sentences: "Which of us is writing this page, I don't know."

Some critics saw Borges's use of the double as an attempt to deal with the duality in his own personality: the struggle between his native Argentine roots and the strong European influence on his writing. They also pointed out what seemed to be an attempt by the author to reconcile through his fiction the reality of his sedentary life of an almost-blind scholar with the longed for adventurous life of his dreams based on that led by his famous ancestors who actively participated in Argentina's wars for independence. This latter tendency is especially evident in "The South," a largely autobiographical story about a library worker who, Bell-Villada noted, like Borges, "is painfully aware of the discordant strains in his ancestry."

The double is also based on what Alazraki called "the pantheistic notion that one man is all men." This suggests, Alazraki observed, "the negation of individual identity, or more exactly, the reduction of all individuals to a general and supreme identity which contains all." Borges developed this theme starting with his very first book. One of its earliest manifestations occurs in Borges's introduction to the 1923 edition of *Fervor de Buenos Aires*, which Norman Thomas di Giovanni quoted in *Selected Poems, 1923-1967*. Borges wrote: "If in the following pages there is some successful verse or other, may the reader forgive me the audacity of having written it before him. We are all one; our inconsequential minds are much alike, and circumstances so influence that it is something of an accident that you are the reader and I am the writer . . . of my verse." Other glimpses of the theme occur in the stories, "Tlon, Uqbar, Orbis Tertius" and "Everything and Nothing." In a footnote to "Tlon, Uqbar, Orbis Tertius" Borges noted: "All men are the same man. All men who repeat a line from Shakespeare *are* William Shakespeare." "Everything and Nothing," which considers the life of a British actor and playwright, also deals with the oneness of all men and recalls Borges's fondness for the image of the infinite number of dreamers from "The Circular Ruins." "Before or after dying" the playwright confronts God saying, "I who have been so many men in vain want to be one and myself." God replies, "Neither am I anyone; I have dreamt the world as you dreamt your work, my Shakespeare, and among the forms in my dream are you, who like myself are many and no one."

The idea that all men are one, which Anderson-Imbert observed calls for the "obliteration of the I," is perhaps Borges's farthest step towards a literature devoid of realism. In this theme we see, according to Christ, "the direction in Borges' stories away from individual psychology toward a universal mythology." This explains why so few of Borges's characters show any psychological development; instead of being interested in his characters as individuals, Borges typically uses them only to further his philosophical beliefs.

All of the characteristics of Borges's work, his blending of genres, confusion of the real and the fictive, his favorite themes and symbols, seem to come together in one of his most quoted passages, the final paragraph of his essay "A New Refutation of Time." While in *Borges: A Reader* Rodriguez Monegal called the essay Borges's "most elaborate attempt to organize a personal system of metaphysics in which he denies time, space, and the individual 'I,'" Alazraki noted that it contains a summation of Borges's belief in "the heroic and tragic condition of man as dream and dreamer."

"Our destiny . . . ," wrote Borges in the essay, "is not horrible because of its unreality; it is horrible because it is irreversible and ironbound. Time is the substance I am made of. Time is a river that carries me away, but I am the river; it is a tiger that mangles me, but I am the tiger; it is a fire that consumes me, but I am the fire. The world, alas, is real; I, alas, am Borges."

MEDIA ADAPTATIONS: "Emma Zunz," a short story, was made into a movie called "Dias de odio" ("Days of Wrath") by Argentine director Leopoldo Torre Nilsson, 1954, a French television movie directed by Alain Magrou, 1969, and a film called "Splits" by U.S. director Leonard Katz, 1978; "Hombre de la esquina rosada," a short story, was made into an Argentine movie of the same title directed by Rene Mugica, 1961; Bernardo Bertolucci based his "La strategia de la ragna" ("The Spider's Stratagem"), a movie made for Italian television, on Borges's short story "El tema del traidor y del heroe," 1970; Hector Olivera, in collaboration with Juan Carlos Onetti, adapted Borges's story "El muerto" for the Argentine movie of the same name, 1975; Borges's short story "La intrusa" was made into a Brazilian film directed by Carlos Hugo Christensen, 1978; three of the stories in *Six Problems for Don Isidro Parodi* were dramatized for radio broadcast by the British Broadcasting Corporation.

BIOGRAPHICAL/CRITICAL SOURCES:

BOOKS

Alazraki, Jaime, *Jorge Luis Borges,* Columbia University Press, 1971.

Anderson-Imbert, Enrique, *Spanish-American Literature: A History,* Volume 2: *1910-1963,* 2nd edition, Wayne State University Press, 1969.

Barrenechea, Ana Maria, *Borges: The Labyrinth Maker,* translated by Robert Lima, New York University Press, 1965.

Bell-Villada, Gene H., *Borges and His Fiction: A Guide to His Mind and Art,* University of North Carolina Press, 1981.

Borges, Jorge Luis, *Ficciones,* translated by Anthony Kerrigan and others, edited and with an introduction by Kerrigan, Grove Press, 1962.

Borges, Jorge Luis, *Labyrinths: Selected Stories and Other Writings,* edited by Donald A. Yates and James E. Irby, New Directions, 1964.

Borges, Jorge Luis, *The Aleph and Other Stories, 1933-1969,* translated and revised by Norman Thomas di Giovanni in collaboration with Borges, Dutton, 1970.

Borges, Jorge Luis, *Selected Poems, 1923-1967,* translated and edited, with an introduction and notes, by Norman Thomas di Giovanni, Delacorte Press, 1972.

Borges, Jorge Luis, *Borges: A Reader,* edited by Emir Rodriguez Monegal and Alastair Reid, Dutton, 1981.

Burgin, Richard, *Conversations with Jorge Luis Borges,* Holt, 1969.

Christ, Ronald J., *The Narrow Act: Borges' Art of Illusion,* New York University Press, 1969.

Contemporary Literary Criticism, Gale, Volume 1, 1973, Volume 2, 1974, Volume 3, 1975, Volume 4, 1975, Volume 6, 1976, Volume 8, 1978, Volume 9, 1978, Volume 10, 1979, Volume 13, 1980, Volume 19, 1981, Volume 44, 1987, Volume 48, 1988.

Dictionary of Literary Biography: Yearbook, 1986, Gale, 1987.

Gallagher, D. P., *Modern Latin American Literature,* Oxford University Press, 1973.

McMurray, George R., *Jorge Luis Borges,* Ungar, 1980.

Rodriguez Monegal, Emir, *Jorge Luis Borges: A Literary Biography,* Dutton, 1978.

Stabb, Martin S., *Jorge Luis Borges,* Twayne, 1970.

PERIODICALS

Atlantic, January, 1967, August, 1967, February, 1972, April, 1981.

Nation, December 29, 1969, August 3, 1970, March 1, 1971, February 21, 1972, October 16, 1972, February 21, 1976.

National Review, March 2, 1973.

Review, spring, 1972, spring, 1975, winter, 1976, January-April, 1981, September-December, 1981.

Studies in Short Fiction, spring, 1974, winter, 1978.

World Literature Today, autumn, 1977, winter, 1984.

Yale Review, October, 1969, autumn, 1974.

OBITUARIES:

PERIODICALS

Detroit News, June 15, 1986, June 22, 1986.

Los Angeles Times, June 15, 1986.

Nation, June 28, 1986.

New Republic, November 3, 1986.

New Yorker, July 7, 1986.

New York Review of Books, August 14, 1986.

New York Times, June 15, 1986.

Publishers Weekly, July 4, 1986.

Time, June 23, 1986.

USA Today, June 16, 1986.

Washington Post, June 15, 1986.*

　　　　　　　　　　　　　　　　—*Sketch by Marian Gonsior*

＊　　＊　　＊

BOWYER, (Raymond) Chaz 1926-

PERSONAL: Born September 29, 1926, in Weymouth, England; son of Reginald (a builder) and Dorothy (Northam) Bowyer; widowed; children: Katharin, Jeff, Lisa Janine. *Education:* Attended high school in Solihull and Nelson, England.

ADDRESSES: Home and office—77 Southern Reach, Mulbarton, Norwich NR14 8BU, England.

CAREER: Royal Air Force, 1943-69, retired as sergeant; served as armament technician, airman, and instructor in explosives and armaments; stationed in Egypt, Libya, Palestine, Singapore, and Aden; writer, 1958—.

MEMBER: Royal Air Force Association (life member).

WRITINGS:

The Flying Elephants, Macdonald & Co., 1972.
Mosquito at War, Ian Allan, 1973.
(Editor) *Bomber Pilot, 1916-18,* Ian Allan, 1974.
(Editor) *Fighter Pilot on the Western Front,* William Kimber, 1975.
Hurricane at War, Ian Allan, 1975.
Airmen of World War I, Arms & Armour Press, 1975.
Sunderland at War, Ian Allan, 1976.
(Editor) *Wings over the Somme,* William Kimber, 1976.
Beaufighter at War, Ian Allan, 1976.
Hampden Special, Ian Allan, 1977.
Path Finders at War, Ian Allan, 1977.
Albert Ball, V.C., William Kimber, 1977.
History of the R.A.F., Hamlyn, 1977.
Sopwith Camel: King of Combat, Glasney Press, 1978.
For Valour: The Air V.C.s, William Kimber, 1978.
Guns in the Sky: The Air Gunners, Dent, 1979.
Coastal Command at War, Ian Allan, 1979.
Fighter Command, 1936-38, Dent, 1980.
Spitfire: A Tribute, Arms & Armour Press, 1980.
Bomber Group at War, Ian Allan, 1980.
(Editor) *Fall of an Eagle: Ernst Udet,* William Kimber, 1980.
Eugene Esmonde, V.C., D.S.O., William Kimber, 1981.
Desert Air Force at War, Ian Allan, 1981.
Age of the Biplane, Bison Books, 1981.
Air War over Europe, 1939-45, William Kimber, 1981.
Encyclopedia of British Military Aircraft, Arms & Armour, 1982.
Wellington at War, Ian Allan, 1982.
Bomber Barons, William Kimber, 1983.
Images of Air War, 1939-45, Batsford, 1983.
R.A.F. Handbook, 1939-45, Ian Allan, 1984.
Bristol Blenheim, Ian Allan, 1984.
Fighter Pilots of the R.A.F., 1939-45, William Kimber, 1984.
Mosquito Squadrons of the R.A.F., Ian Allan, 1984.
Men of the Desert Air Force, William Kimber, 1984.
Gloster Meteor, Ian Allan, 1985.
Men of Coastal Command, William Kimber, 1985.
Bristol F2B: King of the Two-Seaters, Ian Allan, 1985.
Tales from the Bombers, William Kimber, 1985.
The Wellington Bomber, William Kimber, 1986.
Beaufighter, William Kimber, 1987.
RAF Operations, 1918-38, William Kimber, 1988.
The Short Sunderland, Aston Publications, 1989.
Handley Page Bombers of World War I, Aston Publications, 1990.
Flying Boats of the RNAS and RAF, Aston Publications, in press.

Author of booklets. Former editor, *Journal of the Cross and Cockade Society.*

SIDELIGHTS: Chaz Bowyer told *CA:* "My motivation? Primarily to place on permanent record *accurate* accounts of men, deeds, and events connected with Royal Air Force history. This is exemplified (perhaps) by *For Valour,* which is now accepted as the standard reference work on the subject. I am tired of reading historical drivel as perpetrated by 'well-known' authors, most of whom are simply novelists or journalists with no background knowledge of genuine aviation history. Too many 'mili-

tary historians' are simply writers jumping on the history bandwagon only for profit."

*   *   *

BRADBURY, Malcolm (Stanley) 1932-

PERSONAL: Born September 7, 1932, in Sheffield, England; son of Arthur and Doris (Marshall) Bradbury; married Elizabeth Salt, October, 1959; children: Matthew, Dominic. *Education:* University College, University of Leicester, B.A. (first class honors), 1953; University of London, M.A., 1955; attended University of Manchester, 1956-58, received Ph.D., 1964.

ADDRESSES: Office—School of English and American Studies, University of East Anglia, Norwich, Norfolk NR4 7TJ, England.

CAREER: University of Hull, Hull, England, staff tutor in literature and drama in department of adult education, 1959-61; University of Birmingham, Birmingham, England, lecturer in English language and literature, 1961-65; University of East Anglia, Norwich, England, lecturer, 1965-67, senior lecturer, 1967-69, reader in English, 1969-70, professor of American studies, 1970—. Teaching fellow, Indiana University, 1955-56; junior fellow, Yale University, 1958-59; fellow, Harvard University, 1965-66; visiting professor, University of California, Davis, 1966; visiting fellow, All Souls College, Oxford University, 1969; visiting professor, University of Zurich, 1972; Fanny Hurst Professor of Writing, Washington University, 1982; Davis Professor, University of Queensland, and visiting professor, Griffith University, 1983. Chairman of British Council English Studies Seminar, 1976-84; chairman of judges for Booker-McConnell Prize for Fiction, 1981; director of Radio Broadland (independent radio station).

MEMBER: British Association of American Studies, Society of Authors, P.E.N., Royal Society of Literature (fellow).

AWARDS, HONORS: British Association of American Studies junior fellow in United States, 1958-59; American Council of Learned Societies fellow, 1965-66; Heinemann Prize, Royal Society of Literature, 1975, for *The History Man;* named among twenty best British writers by Book Marketing Council, 1982; shortlisted for Booker-McConnell Prize for Fiction, 1983, for *Rates of Exchange;* International Emmy Award, 1987, for "Porterhouse Blue"; honorary fellow of Queen Mary College, University of London; Commander, British Empire.

WRITINGS:

Eating People Is Wrong (novel), Secker & Warburg, 1959, Knopf, 1960.
Phogey!; or, How to Have Class in a Classless Society (also see below), Parrish, 1960.
All Dressed Up and Nowhere to Go: The Poor Man's Guide to the Affluent Society (also see below), Parrish, 1962.
Evelyn Waugh (critical study), Oliver & Boyd, 1962.
Stepping Westward (novel), Secker & Warburg, 1965, Houghton, 1966.
(With Allan Rodway) *Two Poets* (verse), Byron Press, 1966.
What Is a Novel?, Edward Arnold, 1969.
The Social Context of Modern English Literature, Schocken, 1971.
Possibilities: Essays on the State of the Novel, Oxford University Press, 1972.
The History Man (novel), Secker & Warburg, 1975, Houghton, 1976.
Who Do You Think You Are?: Stories and Parodies, Secker & Warburg, 1976.

The Outland Dart: American Writers and European Modernism, Oxford University Press, 1978.

Saul Bellow (critical study), Methuen, 1982.

All Dressed Up and Nowhere to Go (contains revised versions of *Phogey!* and *All Dressed Up and Nowhere to Go*), Pavilion, 1982.

Rates of Exchange (novel), Knopf, 1983.

The Modern American Novel, Oxford University Press, 1983.

Why Come to Slaka?, Secker & Warburg, 1986.

Cuts: A Very Short Novel (novella), Harper, 1987.

My Strange Quest for Mensonge, Penguin, 1988.

No, Not Bloomsbury (collected essays), Columbia University Press, 1988.

Unsent Letters: Irreverent Notes from a Literary Life, Penguin, 1988.

The Modern World: Ten Great Writers, Penguin, 1989.

(With Richard Ruland) *From Puritanism to Postmodernism: A History of American Literature,* Routledge, 1991.

DRAMA

(With David Lodge and James Duckett) "Between These Four Walls" (stage revue), first produced in Birmingham, England, 1963.

(With Lodge, Duckett, and David Turner) "Slap in the Middle" (stage revue), first produced in Birmingham, England, 1965.

(With Chris Bigsby) "The After Dinner Game" (television play), British Broadcasting Corporation (BBC), 1975.

(With Bigsby) "Stones" (television play), BBC, 1976.

"Love on a Gunboat" (television play), BBC, 1977.

"The Enigma" (television play based on a story by John Fowles), BBC, 1980.

"Standing in for Henry" (television play), BBC, 1980.

"Congress" (radio play), BBC, 1981.

The After Dinner Game: Three Plays for Television, Arrow Books, 1982.

"Rates of Exchange" (television series based on own novel), BBC, 1985.

"Blott on the Landscape" (television series adapted from novel by Tom Sharpe), BBC, 1985.

Author, with wife, Elizabeth Bradbury, of radio play "This Sporting Life," 1974-75; "Porterhouse Blue," for television, adapted from work by Tom Sharpe, 1987.

EDITOR

E. M. Forster: A Collection of Critical Essays, Prentice-Hall, 1965.

Mark Twain, *"Pudd'nhead Wilson" and "Those Extraordinary Twins,"* Penguin, 1969.

E. M. Forster, *"A Passage to India": A Casebook,* Macmillan, 1970.

(With David Palmer) *Contemporary Criticism,* Edward Arnold, 1970, St. Martin's, 1971.

(With Eric Mottram and Jean Franco) *The Penguin Companion to American Literature,* McGraw, 1971 (published in England as *The Penguin Companion to Literature,* Volume III: *U.S.A.,* Allen Lane, 1971), published as *The Avenal Companion to English and American Literature,* Avenal Books, 1981.

(With Palmer) *Metaphysical Poetry,* Indiana University Press, 1971.

(With Palmer) *The American Novel and the Nineteen Twenties,* Edward Arnold, 1971.

(With Palmer) *Shakespearian Comedy,* Edward Arnold, 1972.

(With James McFarlane) *Modernism: 1890-1930,* Penguin, 1976.

The Novel Today: Contemporary Writers on Modern Fiction, Rowman & Littlefield, 1977.

(With Palmer) *Decadence and the 1890s,* Edward Arnold, 1979.

(With Palmer) *The Contemporary English Novel,* Edward Arnold, 1979.

(With Palmer) *Contemporary Theatre,* Holmes & Meier, 1979.

(With Howard Temperley) *An Introduction to American Studies,* Longman, 1980.

Stephen Crane, *The Red Badge of Courage* (critical edition), Dent, 1983.

(With Palmer) *Shakespearean Tragedy,* Holmes & Meier, 1984.

The Penguin Book of Modern British Short Stories, Penguin, 1988.

General editor, "Stratford-upon-Avon Studies," Edward Arnold, 1970-81, and "Contemporary Writers," Methuen.

MEDIA ADAPTATIONS: The History Man was adapted as a four-part television series by Christopher Hampton, BBC, 1979.

WORK IN PROGRESS: A novel; a television series.

SIDELIGHTS: Herbert Burke calls Malcolm Bradbury's first novel, *Eating People Is Wrong,* "a novel . . . about how weary academic life is in the English Midlands of the '50s—but this is not a weary novel. Often truly comic, its satire has many barbs and they often draw blood. . . . If seriousness of intent—a sociology of the British establishment of the times as seen through the microcosm of the academy—gets in the way of hearty satire, bawdiness is not lacking." According to Martin Tucker, the author "has written a first novel that is sloppy, structurally flabby, occasionally inane, frequently magnificent and ultimately successful. It is as if [Charles] Dickens and Evelyn Waugh sat down together and said 'Let's write a comic novel in the manner of Kingsley Amis about a man in search of his lost innocence who finds it.' The result is one of the most substantial and dazzling literary feasts this year." Not all reviewers have been so generous in their appraisal of the book, however. Patrick Dennis writes: "While Malcolm Bradbury's first novel is brilliant, witty, sensitive, adult, funny and a lot of other pleasant and desirable things, it is not a good novel. And I know why: Mr. Bradbury has been so busy entertaining himself with his brilliance, wit, etc., that he has quite forgotten about those less gifted people who are expected to buy, read and enjoy his book. . . . While his knaves and fools are elegantly written, his 'sympathetic' characters are so feckless or so grotesque that one has almost no feeling for them." And a *New Yorker* critic finds that "there are no funny situations, and the few comic episodes that occur are much too light, and perhaps also too tired, to stand up against the predominant, tragic predicament that is [the main character's] life . . . and even if this spectacle were more richly decorated than it is with jokes and puns and so on, it would not be good enough. Mr. Bradbury has created a serious and very human character, and has obscured him with jugglers."

Stepping Westward, Bradbury's second novel, also about university life, has been hailed by a *Times Literary Supplement* reviewer as "a *vade mecum* for every youthful or aspiring first visitor to the United States. Every situational joke, every classic encounter is exactly and wittily exploited. The dialogue is often marvellously acute, the tricks of American speech expertly 'bugged.' " On the other hand, however, Rita Estok says that "the school, faculty and students do not ring true; in fact, it is almost a travesty on university life. James Walker, the principal character, never becomes believable and remains unsympathetic throughout the story. *Stepping Westward,* be it a travesty or satire on university life, fails to hit the mark as either." And Bernard McCabe writes: "Within this very funny book Mr. Bradbury proposes a serious novel about freedom and community and friendship's inevitable failures. The result is interesting, but too schematic and analytical to be really successful. The comedy works, though, thanks to Bradbury's artful writing. I leave to some future scholar the precise significance of the recurrent buttocks-motif and ear-motif. . . . [The author's] exaggerated versions of [university life] work by lending a British ear and eye to the oddities of the American scene."

Robert Nye says that Bradbury, in his third novel, *The History Man,* "achieves some charming comic efforts—and not a few cruel ones. Bradbury has a baleful eye for human weakness. He describes with skill and obvious relish. The result is a clever, queer, witty, uncomfortable sort of book—a book whose prose possesses considerable surface brilliance but with a cutting edge concealed beneath." Margaret Drabble calls the book "a small narrative masterpiece," and she feels that "one of the reasons why this novel is so immensely readable is its evocation of physical reality; it may be a book about ideas, but the ideas are embodied in closely observed details. . . . A thoroughly civilized writer, [Bradbury] has written a novel that raises some very serious questions about the nature of civilization without for a moment appearing pretentious or didactic—a fine achievement."

Bradbury's fourth novel, *Rates of Exchange,* was published in 1983 to praise from critics such as *New York Times Book Review* contributor Rachel Billington, who labels it "an astonishing tour de force." The tale of a linguist traveling to a fictive Eastern bloc country, *Rates of Exchange* takes on the subject of language itself and "manages to be funny, gloomy, shrewd and silly all at once," according to Joel Conarroe in the *Washington Post Book World.* Bradbury's inventive use of language—both the locals' fractured English and their native Slakan, a hybrid of several European languages—is a highlight for many reviewers. Notes Anatole Broyard in the *New York Times,* "Bradbury is in such virtuoso form that he can even make you enjoy an entire book in which the majority of the characters speak various degrees of broken English." Although some critics take issue with the book's pacing, characterization, and sometimes uneasy mixture of humor and seriousness, many value its wit and pungent observations on travel. Writes *Los Angeles Times* reviewer Elaine Kendall, "Hilarious and accurate, deepened by the author's concern for subtle political and social factors, 'Rates of Exchange' turns tour de force into an unequivocal compliment, elevating the genre to a major literary category."

Bradbury told *CA:* "As a novelist, I achieved five novels (and a volume of short stories) in thirty years. It may seem a slow record, but then I have been a critic, reviewer, and professor of American studies too, as well as a regular writer for television. I believe the writer has a responsibility for literary study, and this belief has gone into my teaching of creative writing and my editorship of series like Methuen Contemporary Writers, where I and my fellow editor Chris Bigsby have sought to show that we live in a major period of literary creation very different from that of the earlier part of the century. I believe in fact we live in a remarkable international age of fiction, and this has affected my own writing. Though I started with provincial themes and in a relatively realistic mode I have grown vastly more international in preoccupation and far more experimental in method. Looking back over my books, they now seem to me to follow the curve of the development of British fiction from the 1950s: from the comic social realism of the postwar period through to a much harsher, more ironic vision which involves the use of fictiveness and fantasy—though always, in my case, with an edge of tragic commentary on the world we live in as this dark century moves

to its end. I think I have grown far more exact as a writer, more concerned to deal with major themes, to escape provincial limitations, and to follow the fate of liberal hopes through the many intellectual, moral, and historical challenges it has now to face. As I said in a previous entry for *CA:* 'Serious writing is not an innocent act; it is an act of connection with the major acts of writing achieved by others. It is also . . . a new set of grammars, forms, and styles for the age we live in.'

"My books have been widely translated and are set-texts in schools and universities, and *The History Man* was made into a British Broadcasting Corporation television series. This has done a good deal to free me of the unfortunate label of being a 'university novelist,' since my aims are wider. I have myself been considerably influenced by writing for television, and I think the imagery and grammar of film and television has brought home new concepts of presentation and perception to the novel. I have also been influenced by (and perhaps also have influenced) younger writers like Ian McEwan and Clive Sinclair who have been in my creative writing classes at the University of East Anglia. I have fought for a view of the novel in Britain as a serious and experimental form, and I believe it has increasingly become so. I believe in our great need for fiction; in *Rates of Exchange,* set in Eastern Europe before the fall of the Berlin Wall, I tried to relate our awareness of an oppressive modern reality forged by the fictions of politicians and the structures of ideology to our need for true fictions that can challenge them. My basic themes, though, remain the same: the conflict between liberal humanism and the harsh systems and behaviorisms of the modern world, and the tragic implications, which, however, I believe must be expressed in comic form. In an age when the big ideologies grow tired, we need the abrasive vision of the writer, and in some of our great contemporaries of the novel, from Saul Bellow to Milan Kundera, I think we find that. So the novel is what gives me hope, and lasting pleasure."

BIOGRAPHICAL/CRITICAL SOURCES:

BOOKS

Bigsby, Christopher, and Heide Ziegler, editors, *The Radical Imagination and the Liberal Tradition: Interviews with English and American Novelists,* Junction Books, 1982.
Contemporary Literary Criticism, Volume 32, Gale, 1985.
Dictionary of Literary Biography, Volume 14: *British Novelists since 1960,* Gale, 1983.

PERIODICALS

Booklist, April 15, 1960.
Books and Bookmen, April, 1983.
Christian Science Monitor, February 18, 1976.
Commonweal, April 22, 1960.
Globe and Mail (Toronto), September 12, 1987, August 20, 1988.
Library Journal, March 1, 1960, June 1, 1966.
Literary Review, October, 1983.
Los Angeles Times, October 21, 1983, December 9, 1988.
Los Angeles Times Book Review, October 18, 1987, September 25, 1988.
National Review, May 2, 1960.
New Statesman, October 31, 1959.
Newsweek, October 24, 1983.
New York Times, April 10, 1960, October 1, 1983, November 7, 1987, January 30, 1989.
New York Times Book Review, February 8, 1976, November 20, 1983, October 18, 1987, September 25, 1988.
New Yorker, July 16, 1960, May 3, 1976.
San Francisco Chronicle, April 26, 1960.

Saturday Review, April 9, 1960, May 21, 1966.

Time, June 3, 1966, November 14, 1983.

Times (London), April 7, 1983, January 14, 1988, May 12, 1988, June 4, 1988.

Times Literary Supplement, November 13, 1959, August 5, 1965, November 7, 1975, September 3, 1982, April 8, 1983, February 22, 1985, October 24, 1986, June 12, 1987, November 12, 1987, May 13, 1988.

Tribune Books (Chicago), August 28, 1988.

Washington Post, October 14, 1987.

Washington Post Book World, November 20, 1983, July 3, 1988.

*   *   *

BRAINE, John (Gerard) 1922-1986

PERSONAL: Born April 13, 1922, in Bradford, Yorkshire, England; died of a hemorrhaging ulcer, October 28, 1986, in London, England; son of Fred and Katherine (Henry) Braine; married Helen Patricia Wood, 1955; children: Anthony, Frances, Felicity. *Education:* Leeds School of Librarianship, A.L.A., 1949. *Politics:* Conservative. *Religion:* Roman Catholic.

CAREER: Bingley Public Library, Bingley, England, assistant, 1940-48, chief assistant librarian, 1948-51; librarian at Northumberland County Library, England, 1954-56, and West Riding County Library, England, 1956-57; writer, 1957-86. Member of North Regional Advisory Council, British Broadcasting Corp., 1960-64. *Military service:* Royal Navy, 1942-43.

MEMBER: Arts Theatre Club, Library Association, Authors' Club, Bingley Little Theatre, Bradford Civic Theatre.

WRITINGS:

"The Desert in the Mirror" (play), first produced in Bingley, England, 1951.

Room at the Top (also see below), Houghton, 1957, reprinted, Methuen, 1980.

The Vodi, Eyre & Spottiswoode, 1959, published as *From the Hand of the Hunter,* Houghton, 1960.

Life at the Top (also see below), Houghton, 1962, reprinted, Routledge, Chapman & Hall, 1980.

The Jealous God, Eyre & Spottiswoode, 1964, Houghton, 1965.

The Crying Game, Houghton, 1968.

Stay With Me Till Morning (also see below), Eyre & Spottiswoode, 1970, published as *The View From Tower Hill,* Coward, 1971.

The Queen of a Distant Country (also see below), Methuen, 1972, Coward, 1973.

Writing a Novel, Coward, 1974.

The Pious Agent, Eyre Methuen, 1975, Atheneum, 1976.

Waiting for Sheila (also see below), Eyre Methuen, 1976.

Finger of Fire, Eyre Methuen, 1977.

J. B. Priestley, Weidenfeld & Nicolson, 1978, Barnes & Noble, 1979.

One and Last Love, Eyre Methuen, 1981.

The Two of Us, Methuen, 1984.

These Golden Days, Methuen, 1985.

Contributor to numerous newspapers and periodicals in England and the United States.

FILMSCRIPTS

"Room at the Top," Remus, 1958.

"Life at the Top," Remus, 1965.

"Man at the Top" series, Thames Television, 1970 and 1972.

"Waiting for Sheila" (based on his novel of the same name), Yorkshire Television, 1977.

"Queen of a Distant Country" (based on his novel of the same title), Yorkshire Television, 1978.

"Stay With Me Till Morning" (based on his novel of the same title), Yorkshire Television, 1980.

SIDELIGHTS: With the publication of his first novel, *Room at the Top,* John Braine achieved almost instant literary recognition. The story of a young and ambitious working-class Englishman who eventually joins the urban upper-class that he pretends to disdain, the book drew an overwhelmingly favorable response from both readers and critics. Of the book's theme, Anthony Burgess wrote: "*Room at the Top* was taken by many to be a straight account of achieved ambition. Young man puts boss's daughter in family way and then has it made. But there was much more to the book than that—there was guilt, betrayal of love, the sense that the price of success can be too high and that this, alas, is usually only discovered when success is attained." James W. Lee believed that *Room at the Top* "is a novel which epitomizes its age. Like Ernest Hemingway's *The Sun Also Rises* and F. Scott Fitzgerald's *The Great Gatsby, Room at the Top* probes deeply and tellingly into a central problem of the times. Braine's Joe Lampton is a creation of the postwar British welfare state." Judy Simons, writing in the *Dictionary of Literary Biography,* included Braine with the Angry Young Men of Britain's 1950s, a group of writers who "asserted an ethic of individualism and of rebellious, amoral youth. . . . Braine was in the forefront of the wave of populist writers who, with a contempt for avant-garde fictional devices, rejected notions of artistic elitism and of the refined sensibilities and unique moral position of the writer."

Unfortunately, many of Braine's succeeding novels failed to evoke the same high critical praise as did *Room at the Top.* "Nearly a decade later," wrote John Lahr in his review of *The Crying Game,* "Braine is still scrutinizing English mores with a vicar's scowl, obsessed by evil but unable to fathom it, shocked by the inhumanity of permissiveness without the ability to create characters of human sinew." Felicia Lamport describes *The View From Tower Hill* as a "curiously tepid work" and adds: "Over another signature, *The View From Tower Hill* might have seemed less pallid, but Braine's name triggers expectations of the kind of vitality, power, and urgency that filled his *Room at the Top.* John Braine's bodies are no longer smoldering with life but serenely and prosperously middleaged." Pamela Marsh, in perhaps the harshest assessment of Braine's later work, stated that "John Braine is one of those who have become tagged as a 'one-novel man.'"

According to R. G. G. Price, however, this kind of criticism was unjust: "Early reviews of Mr. Braine took him as more of a highbrow novelist than he ever set out to be and later ones became disgruntled and even hinted at metropolitan corruption of standards. This was unfair. He's no Proust but on the level he aims at he is very good." Moreover, reviews of Braine's later novel, *The Queen of a Distant Country,* indicate a renewed understanding between the author and his critics. "After some dreadful potboiling," wrote a critic for the *Times Literary Supplement* about the book, "John Braine has produced a novel of real unforced style and feeling." Jan B. Gordon allowed that "Braine continues to speak to us with a certain urgency," and that *The Queen of a Distant Country* "talks directly to a civilization which must now cope with the apathy of a youth which has plugged itself into the system and finds its ideals either co-opted or commercialized."

Critical response was a matter of little importance to Braine. "The people who write the reviews of my books," Simons quoted Braine as saying, "are not the people whom I particularly want to read them, and therefore I'm not interested in what they think." Simons explained that Braine was "defiantly anti-intellectual" and he "consistently maintained his pose of artistic naivete in a literary world that he felt was becoming increasingly elitist and alienated from popular concerns." In similar terms, Alan Warren Friedman in an article for the *Dictionary of Literary Biography* pointed out that Braine was "intensely professional in his attitude toward writing, and contemptuous of the safe and overcivilized academic backgrounds of many of his literary contemporaries, whom he sees as removed from the pressures of modern life and, consequently, limited in the truth they can convey."

In an interview with Kenneth Allsop, Braine said that the novelist's responsibility is "to show his age as it really is. . . . But a writer must be a civilized and tolerant human being, possessing, above all, intellectual integrity. . . . The writer doesn't have to inhabit a rarified moral or intellectual plane, but he must always be, no matter how imperfectly, the conscience of society."

BIOGRAPHICAL/CRITICAL SOURCES:

BOOKS

Allsop, Kenneth, *The Angry Decade,* P. Owen, 1958.
Contemporary Literary Criticism, Gale, Volume 1, 1973, Volume 3, 1975, Volume 41, 1987.
Dictionary of Literary Biography, Volume 15: *British Novelists, 1930-1959,* Gale, 1983.
Dictionary of Literary Biography Yearbook, 1986, Gale, 1987.
Karl, Frederick R., *The Contemporary English Novel,* Farrar, Straus, 1962.
Lee, James W., *John Braine,* Twayne, 1968.

PERIODICALS

Books and Bookmen, April, 1968.
Christian Science Monitor, December 12, 1968.
Commonweal, April 23, 1965, December 14, 1973.
Harper's, April, 1965.
National Observer, November 25, 1968.
Newsweek, April 30, 1973.
New York Times Book Review, April 19, 1959, October 27, 1968, May 27, 1973, May 2, 1976.
Observer (London), February 18, 1979.
Punch, September 4, 1968.
Saturday Review, October 6, 1962, February 27, 1971.
Times Literary Supplement, October 27, 1972, June 20, 1975.
Writer, May, 1972.

OBITUARIES:

PERIODICALS

AB Bookman's Weekly, November 24, 1986.
Chicago Tribune, October 31, 1986.
Los Angeles Times, October 30, 1986.
New York Times, October 30, 1986.
Time, November 10, 1986.
Times (London), October 30, 1986.
Wall Street Journal, October 30, 1986.
Washington Post, October 30, 1986.*

*   *   *

BRANFIELD, John (Charles) 1931-

PERSONAL: Born January 19, 1931, in Burrow Bridge, Somerset, England; son of Allan Frederick (a civil servant) and Bessie (Storey) Branfield; married Kathleen Elizabeth Peplow, 1955;

children: Susan, Frances, Stephen, Peter. *Education:* Queens' College, Cambridge, M.A., 1956; University of Exeter, M.Ed., 1972. *Avocational interests:* Walking, sailing.

ADDRESSES: Home—Mingoose Villa, Mingoose, Mount Hawke, Truro, Cornwall TR4 8BX, England. *Agent*—A. P. Watt & Son, 20 John St., London WC1N 2DR, England.

CAREER: Writer. Camborne Grammar School, Cornwall, England, English teacher and head of department, 1961-76; affiliated with Camborne Comprehensive School, 1976-81.

AWARDS, HONORS: Walter Hines Page Scholar, 1974; Arts Council Writers' Award, 1978; Carnegie Gold Medal commendation, Library Association (Britain), 1980.

WRITINGS:

A Flag in the Map, Eyre & Spottiswoode, 1960.
Look the Other Way, Eyre & Spottiswoode, 1963.
In the Country, Eyre & Spottiswoode, 1966.
The Poison Factory (young adult novel), Harper, 1972 (published in England as *Nancekuke,* Gollancz, 1972).
Why Me? (juvenile), Harper, 1973 (published in England as *Sugar Mouse,* Gollancz, 1973).
The Scillies Trip, Gollancz, 1975.
The Day I Shot My Dad (teleplay), British Broadcasting Corp. (BBC-TV), 1975.
Castle Minalto, Gollancz, 1979, Atheneum, 1982.
The Fox in Winter (young adult novel), Gollancz, 1980.
Brown Cow, Gollancz, 1983.
Thin Ice (young adult novel), Gollancz, 1983.
The Falklands Summer (young adult novel), Gollancz, 1987.
The Day I Shot My Dad and Other Stories, Gollancz, 1989, David & Charles, 1990.

SIDELIGHTS: British writer John Branfield is noted for his young adult novels, several of which deal with social issues while presenting believable characters. *The Poison Factory,* for example, follows a teenager after her father's suspicious death from cancer inspires her to become an anti-poison gas activist. A *Times Literary Supplement* critic observes that "what gives [the novel] a special quality is the feeling of other lives going on around Helen and her obsession. The minor characters . . . are all credible and sometimes very funny," creating a "readable" book. Similarly, *The Fox in Winter* portrays "in a mature and sensitive manner, the blooming of an affectionate and respectful friendship" between a teenager and a ninety-year old, as Jennifer Moody summarizes in the *Times Literary Supplement.* Margery Fisher of *Growing Point* calls the novel "honest," praising it for "using humour, domestic verisimilitude and vividly drawn landscape to give credibility to the characters." Branfield "has proved triumphantly that the twentieth century's 'great unmentionable' *can* be spoken of in front of the children, and to their great advantage," Moody concludes. *The Fox in Winter* "is a worthwhile addition to teenage literature."

BIOGRAPHICAL/CRITICAL SOURCES:

PERIODICALS

Growing Point, March, 1981.
Times Literary Supplement, April 28, 1972; December 14, 1979; September 19, 1980; November 25, 1983; March 6, 1987.

*   *   *

BRENTON, Howard 1942-

PERSONAL: Born December 13, 1942, in Portsmouth, England; son of Donald Henry and Rose Lilian (Lewis) Brenton;

married Jane Margaret Fry, January 31, 1970; children: Samuel John. *Education:* St. Catherine's College, Cambridge, B.A. (honors), 1965.

ADDRESSES: Agent—Margaret Ramsey, 14A Goodwin's Court, St. Martin's Lane, London WC2, England.

CAREER: Has worked as stage manager for various repertory companies in England; performed as an actor with Brighton Combination, 1969; Royal Court Theatre, London, England, resident dramatist, 1972—.

AWARDS, HONORS: John Whiting Award, 1970; bursary awards from Arts Council of Great Britain, 1971, for "Christie in Love"; *Evening Standard* award, c. 1976, for "Weapons of Happiness"; London Standard Award, c. 1985, and *Plays and Players* award for best new play, 1985, both for "Pravda."

WRITINGS:

PUBLISHED PLAYS

Revenge (first produced on West End at Royal Court Theatre Upstairs, 1969), Eyre Methuen, 1969.
Christie in Love and Other Plays (includes the one-act plays "Christie in Love," "Heads," and "The Education of Skinny Spew"), Methuen, 1970.
(Co-author) *Lay By* (first produced in Edinburgh, Scotland, 1971), Calder & Boyars, 1972, Riverrun, 1988.
Plays for Public Places (includes the one-act plays "Gum and Goo," "Wesley," and "Scott of the Antarctic; or, What God Didn't See"), Eyre Methuen, 1972.
Hitler Dances (first produced in London at Traverse Theatre Workshop, 1972), Methuen, 1982.
Magnificence (first produced on West End at Royal Court Theatre, 1973), Methuen, 1973.
(With David Hare) *Brassneck* (first produced in Nottingham, England, at Nottingham Playhouse), Methuen, 1974.
The Churchill Play, Methuen, 1974.
Weapons of Happiness (first produced in London), Methuen, 1976.
Epsom Downs, Methuen, 1977.
Sore Throats and Sonnets of Love and Opposition (includes "Sore Throats"), Methuen, 1979.
Plays for the Poor Theatre, Methuen, 1980.
The Romans in Britain, Eyre Methuen, 1980.
Thirteenth Night [and] *A Short Sharp Shock!* (first by Brenton; second with Tony Howard), Eyre Methuen, 1981.
(Adapter) Georg Buechner, *Danton's Death: A New Version* (from a translation by Jane Fry), Methuen, 1982.
The Genius (produced in London, 1983), Methuen, 1983.
(With Tunde Ikoli) *Sleeping Policemen,* Heinemann Educational, 1984.
Bloody Poetry (produced in London, 1984), Methuen, 1985.
(With Hare) *Pravda* (produced in London, 1985), Methuen, 1985.
Brenton Plays: One, Heinemann Educational, 1987.

UNPUBLISHED PLAYS

"Ladder of Fools," first produced in Cambridge, England, 1965.
"Winter, Daddykins," first produced in Dublin, Ireland, 1965.
"It's My Criminal," first produced in London, 1966.
"A Sky-Blue Life" (adaptations of stories by Maksim Gorky), first produced in London, 1966; revised version produced in London at Open Space Theatre, 1971.
"Gargantua," first produced in Brighton, England, 1969.
"Fruit," first produced in London at Royal Court Theatre Upstairs, 1970.

"How Beautiful with Badges," first produced in London at Open Space Theatre, 1972.
"Measure for Measure" (adaptation from play of same title by William Shakespeare), first produced in Exeter, England, 1972.
(Co-author) "England's Ireland," first produced in Amsterdam, Netherlands, 1972.
(With David Edgar) "A Fart for Europe," first produced in London, 1972.
"The Screens" (adaptation from a play by Jean Genet), first produced in Bristol, England, 1973.
(Adapter) Bertolt Brecht, "Conversations in Exile" (from a translation by David Dollenmayer), produced in New York City, 1987.
"Greenland," produced in London, 1988.

Also author of "Government Property," 1975, "Deeds" (with Trevor Griffiths, Hare, and Ken Campbell), 1978, "The Thing" (for children), 1982, and "Iranian Nights" (with Tariq Ali), 1989.

OTHER

Notes from a Psychotic Journal and Other Poems, privately printed, 1969.
"Skin Flicker" (screenplay; based on a book by Tony Bicat), British Film Institute, 1973.
The Saliva Milkshake, (television play; broadcast 1975), TQ Publications, 1977.
Dead Head (television series; broadcast 1986), Heinemann Educational, 1987.
Diving for Pearls (novel), Walker, 1989.

Also author of television plays, including "Lushly," 1971, "The Paradise Run," 1976, and "Desert of Lies," 1984. Translator of Bertolt Brecht's "Life of Galileo," 1980.

BIOGRAPHICAL/CRITICAL SOURCES:

BOOKS

Contemporary Literary Criticism, Volume 31, Gale, 1985.
Dictionary of Literary Biography, Volume 13: *British Dramatists since World War II,* Gale, 1982.

PERIODICALS

Chicago Tribune, January 15, 1989.
Los Angeles Times, April 6, 1984.
New York Times, June 20, 1985, May 29, 1986, January 7, 1987, November 3, 1987.
Plays and Players, February, 1972, January, 1986.
Time, June 10, 1985.
Times (London), September 14, 1983, November 7, 1984, May 4, 1985, April 27, 1988, June 3, 1988.
Times Literary Supplement, June 23-29, 1989.

*   *   *

BRION, Guy
  See MADSEN, Axel

*   *   *

BROCK, Horace Rhea 1927-

PERSONAL: Born August 26, 1927, in Leggett, TX; son of Hobby B. and Winona (Epperson) Brock; married Frances Euline Williams (a professor), May 24, 1955; children: Alan Howard, Mary Ann, Charles. *Education:* Sam Houston State University, B.S., 1946, B.B.A. and M.A., both 1951; University of Texas, Ph.D., 1954.

ADDRESSES: Home—1900 Westridge St., Denton, TX 76201. *Office*—School of Business Administration, North Texas State University, Denton, TX 76203.

CAREER: University of Arkansas, Fayetteville, assistant professor of accounting, 1953-54; North Texas State University, Denton, assistant professor, 1954-55, associate professor of accounting, 1955-57; Ohio State University, Columbus, associate professor of accounting, 1957-58; North Texas State University, professor of accounting, 1958-67, chairman of department, 1966-67; Michigan State University, East Lansing, adviser to U.S. Agency for International Development project in Istanbul, Turkey, 1967-69; North Texas State University, distinguished professor of accounting and chairman of department, 1969-80, director of extractive industries accounting research, 1980—, dean of College of Business, 1983-84. *Military service:* U.S. Air Force, 1946-49.

MEMBER: American Institute of Certified Public Accountants, American Accounting Association, Texas Society of Certified Public Accountants, Beta Gamma Sigma.

WRITINGS:

(With C. Aubrey Smith) *Accounting for Oil and Gas Producers,* Prentice-Hall, 1960.
(With Charles E. Palmer and John E. Price) *College Accounting: Theory/Practice,* 2nd edition, McGraw, 1969, 3rd edition published as *Accounting: Principles and Applications* (also see below), 1974, 6th edition, 1990.
(With Palmer and Price) *Cost Accounting: Theory/Practice,* 2nd edition, McGraw, 5th edition, 1988.
(With Palmer) *College Accounting for Secretaries,* McGraw, 1971.
(With Palmer and Price) *Accounting: Basic Principles,* 3rd edition (abridgment of *Accounting: Principles and Applications*), McGraw, 1974, 6th edition, 1990.
Accounting Concepts, McGraw, 1974, 6th edition, 1990.
Accounting for Oil and Gas Producing Companies, Professional Development Institute, North Texas State University, Part 1, 1981, Part 2 (with John P. Klingstedt and Donald Jones): *Amortization, Conveyances, Full Costing and Disclosures,* 1982.
(With Palmer) *Sole Proprietorship Merchandising Business Practice Set: Schier Furniture Company,* 2nd edition, McGraw, 1981.
(With Palmer) *Sole Proprietorship Service Business Practice Set: Garden Real Estate,* McGraw, 1981.
(With Ray Sommerfeld, Hershel Anderson, and John Everett) *Harcourt Brace Tax Course,* Harcourt, 1984.
(With Klingstedt and Jones) *Petroleum Accounting,* 3rd edition, Professional Development Institute, North Texas State University, 1990.

Also author of *Intermediate and Advanced Accounting,* 1966. Editor with Anderson and Sommerfeld of "An Introduction to Taxation" series, Harcourt, 1969—, 17th edition, 1989. Editor, *Journal of Extractive Industries Accounting.*

*   *   *

BRODRIBB, (Arthur) Gerald (Norcott) 1915-

PERSONAL: Born May 21, 1915, in St. Leonards, Sussex, England; son of Arthur Williamson (a doctor) and Violet Brodribb; married Jessica Barr, April 3, 1954; children: Michael Bryan.

Education: Received Diploma in Education, 1939; Oxford University, M.A., 1950; Institute of Archaeology, London, Ph.D., 1983.

ADDRESSES: Home—Stubbles, Ewhurst Green, Robertsbridge, Sussex, England.

CAREER: Canford Boys' Public School, Wimborne, England, assistant master, 1944-54; Hydneye House, East Sussex, England, headmaster, 1954-72; Beaufort Park Roman Excavation, East Sussex, co-director, 1972—. Manager of Ewhurst United Football Club, 1975—.

MEMBER: Society of Antiquaries (fellow), Cricket Writers Club, Marylebone Cricket Club.

WRITINGS:

Next Man In: A Study of Cricket Law, Putnam, 1952, revised edition, Pelham Books, 1985.
The Bay and Other Poems, Mountjoy Press, 1953.
(Editor) *Book of Cricket Verse,* Rupert Hart-Davis, 1954.
(With Henry Sayen) *A Yankee Looks at Cricket,* Putnam, 1956.
Hit for Six, Heinemann, 1960.
The Croucher: A Biography of Gilbert Jessop, London Magazine Editions, 1974.
Maurice Tate: A Biography, London Magazine Editions, 1978, revised edition, Constable & Co., 1985.
Roman Brick and Tile, Alan Sutton Publishing, 1987.
Cricket at Hastings: The Story of a Ground, Spellmount, 1989.

Also author of *Hastings and Men of Letters,* 1954, revised edition, Old Hastings Preservation Society, 1971, *Felix on the Bat,* 1962, *Stamped Tiles of Classic Britannia,* 1969, revised edition, 1978, and *The Art of Nicholas Felix,* 1985. Contributor of more than two hundred articles to cricket and archaeology periodicals.

WORK IN PROGRESS: Further work on Gilbert Jessop and Nicholas Felix.

SIDELIGHTS: Gerald Brodribb told *CA:* "My first cricket note was published when I was only fourteen years old. Much later I became a classical scholar interested in Roman archaeology and discerned a notable Roman site at Beaufort Park. The discovered bathhouse is likely to become one of the most notable small sites in Britain."

BIOGRAPHICAL/CRITICAL SOURCES:

PERIODICALS

Times Literary Supplement, November 15, 1985.

*   *   *

BROOKE-HAVEN, P.
See WODEHOUSE, P(elham) G(renville)

*   *   *

BROOKS, Cleanth 1906-

PERSONAL: Born October 16, 1906, in Murray, KY; son of Cleanth (a minister) and Bessie Lee (Witherspoon) Brooks; married Edith Amy Blanchard, September 12, 1934 (died, October, 1986). *Education:* Vanderbilt University, B.A., 1928; Tulane University, M.A., 1929; Oxford University, Rhodes scholar, 1929-32, B.A. (with honors), 1931, B.Litt., 1932. *Politics:* Independent Democrat. *Religion:* Episcopalian.

ADDRESSES: Home—70 Ogden St., New Haven, CT 06511.

CAREER: Louisiana State University, Baton Rouge, 1932-47, began as lecturer, became professor of English, visiting professor, 1970 and 1974; Yale University, New Haven, CT, professor of English, 1947-60, Gray Professor of Rhetoric, 1960-75, professor emeritus, 1975—. Visiting professor of English at University of Texas, summer, 1941, University of Michigan, summer, 1942, University of Chicago, 1945-46, Kenyon School of English, summer, 1948 (fellow, 1948—), University of Southern California, 1953, Breadloaf School of English, 1963, University of South Carolina, 1975, Tulane University, 1976, University of North Carolina, 1977 and 1979, and University of Tennessee, 1978 and 1980; research professor with Bostick Foundation, 1975; Lamar Lecturer, 1984; Jefferson Lecturer, 1985. Member of advisory committee for Boswell Papers, 1950; Library of Congress, fellow, 1953-63, member of council of scholars, 1984-87; American Embassy, London, England, cultural attache, 1964-66; National Humanities Center, fellow, 1980-81.

MEMBER: Modern Language Association of America, American Academy of Arts and Sciences, National Institute of Arts and Letters, American Philosophical Society, American Association of University Professors, Royal Society of Literature, Phi Beta Kappa, Yale Club (New York), Athenaeum, Savile (both London).

AWARDS, HONORS: Guggenheim fellow, 1953 and 1960; senior fellow, National Endowment for the Humanities, 1975; Explicator Award, c. 1980, for *William Faulkner: Toward Yoknapatawpha and Beyond;* D.Litt. from Upsala College, 1963, University of Kentucky, 1963, University of Exeter, 1966, Washington and Lee University, 1968, Tulane University, 1969, University of the South, 1975, and Newberry College, 1979; L.H.D. from University of St. Louis, 1958, Centenary College, 1972, Oglethorpe University, 1976, St. Peter's College, 1978, Lehigh University, 1980, Millsaps College, 1983, University of New Haven, 1984, and University of South Carolina, 1984.

WRITINGS:

EDITOR

(With others) *An Approach to Literature,* Louisiana State University Press, 1936, 5th edition, Prentice-Hall, 1975.

(Editor with Robert Penn Warren, and coauthor) *Understanding Poetry,* Holt, 1938, 4th edition, 1975, transcript of tape recording to accompany 3rd edition entitled *Conversations on the Craft of Poetry: Cleanth Brooks and Robert Penn Warren, with Robert Frost, John Crowe Ransom, Robert Lowell, and Theodore Roethke,* Holt, 1961.

(With Warren) *Understanding Fiction,* F. S. Crofts, 1943, 3rd edition, Prentice-Hall, 1979, abridged edition published as *The Scope of Fiction,* 1960.

(General editor with A. F. Falconer and David Nichol Smith) *The Percy Letters,* 1944-88, volumes 1-6, Louisiana State University Press, volumes 7-9, Yale University Press; editor of Volume 2: *The Correspondence of Thomas Percy and Richard Farmer* and Volume 7: *The Correspondence of Thomas Percy and William Shenstone.*

(With Robert Heilman) *Understanding Drama,* Holt, 1945.

The Poems of John Milton (1645 edition), Harcourt, 1951.

(With Warren) *An Anthology of Stories from the "Southern Review,"* Louisiana State University Press, 1953.

Tragic Themes in Western Literature: Seven Essays by Bernard Knox [and Others], Yale University Press, 1956.

(With Warren and R. W. B. Lewis) *American Literature: The Makers and the Making,* two volumes, St. Martin's, 1973, paperbound edition published in four volumes, 1974.

Southern Review, managing editor with Robert Penn Warren, 1935-41, editor with Warren, 1941-42; member of advisory board, *Kenyon Review,* 1942-60.

OTHER

The Relation of the Alabama-Georgia Dialect to the Provincial Dialects of Great Britain, Louisiana State University Press, 1935.

Modern Poetry and the Tradition, University of North Carolina Press, 1939.

The Well Wrought Urn, Reynal & Hitchcock, 1947, Harcourt, 1956.

(With Warren) *Modern Rhetoric,* Harcourt, 1949, 4th edition, 1979, abridged edition, 1961.

(With Warren) *Fundamentals of Good Writing,* Harcourt, 1950.

(Contributor) *Humanities: An Appraisal,* University of Wisconsin Press, 1950.

(With William Wimsatt) *Literary Criticism: A Short History,* Knopf, 1957.

Metaphor and the Function of Criticism, Institute for Religious and Social Studies, c. 1957.

The Hidden God: Studies in Hemingway, Faulkner, Yeats, Eliot and Warren, Yale University Press, 1963.

William Faulkner: The Yoknapatawpha Country, Yale University Press, 1963.

A Shaping Joy: Studies in the Writer's Craft, Harcourt, 1972.

William Faulkner: Toward Yoknapatawpha and Beyond, Yale University Press, 1978.

(Contributor) Louis D. Dollarhide and Ann J. Abodie, editors, *Eudora Welty: A Form of Thanks,* University Press of Mississippi, 1979.

Cleanth Brooks at the United States Air Force Academy, April 11-12, 1978 (lectures), edited by James A. Grimshaw, Jr., Department of English, U.S. Air Force Academy, 1980.

William Faulkner: First Encounters, Yale University Press, 1983.

The Language of the American South, University of Georgia Press, 1985.

On the Prejudices, Predilections, and Firm Beliefs of William Faulkner, Louisiana State University Press, 1987.

Author of recorded lectures on works by William Faulkner. Contributor of articles and reviews to literary journals.

SIDELIGHTS: Maxwell Geismar introduces Cleanth Brooks as "a brilliant critic of literary technique and rhetoric, particularly in modern verse, and . . . a leading figure in the formalist school of New Critics." Considering Brooks's development as a critic, John Paul Pritchard noted that "Brooks sounded his first note for metaphor as the prime characteristic of poetry in 1935." Pritchard observed that Brooks and Robert Penn Warren, in *Understanding Poetry* (1938), asserted that "the poem . . . must be grasped as a literary object before it can be otherwise considered. . . . A poem proves itself by its effect, and its effect arises not out of the things used but from the poet's use of them. . . . Verse controls words and entices the reader's imagination by its recurrent rhythms to the willing temporary suspension of disbelief."

Central to Brooks's critical position is his contention that a poem cannot be paraphrased without essential loss. Pritchard writes: "In Brooks's eyes the basic critical ill is the tendency to confuse comment on the poem with its essential core. Critics are prone to restate the poem in a prose paraphrase as a step toward elucidating it. Such a procedure, he declares, presumes the paraphrasable part of the poem to be its essential part. But the act splits the poem, which is by nature a whole, into form and content. . . . It totally ignores the poetic function of metaphor and meter."

In a discussion of *The Well Wrought Urn* (1947), Rene Wellek wrote: "Brooks attacks [as] the 'heresy of paraphrase,' all attempts to reduce the poem to its prose content, and he has defended a well defined absolutism: the need of judgement against the flaccid surrender to relativism and historicism. But . . . Brooks has taken special pains to demonstrate that his absolutism of values is not incompatible with a proper regard for history." Speaking of Brooks's critical approach, Wellek notes: "Brooks analyzes poems as structures of opposites, tensions, paradoxes, and ironies with unparalleled skill. Paradox and irony are terms used by him very broadly. Irony is not the opposite of an overt statement, but [according to Brooks] 'a general term for the kind of qualification which the various elements in a context receive from the context.' " In a later discussion of Brooks's approach, Wellek explains: "Irony for Brooks indicates the recognition of incongruities, the ambiguity, the reconciliation of opposites which Brooks finds in all good, that is, complex poetry. Poetry must be ironic in the sense of being able to withstand ironic contemplation."

John Crowe Ransom, a poet and himself a critic, was generally conceded to have christened Brooks and others of similar critical opinion the "New Critics." In 1955 Ransom wrote: "It seems to me that Brooks just now is probably the most forceful and influential critic of poetry that we have. But this does not imply that his authority is universally accepted, for it has turned out even better than that. Where he does not gain assent, he arouses protest and countercriticism. His tone toward other critics is that of an independent, and his tone toward scholars who are occasional critics is cool. This is why a new book by Brooks is a public service."

Ransom goes on to say: "Of course there will be readers who will go all the way with Brooks as if under a spell. I believe the peculiar fascination of his view of poetry is due to its being a kind of modern version of the ancient doctrine of divine inspiration or frenzy. For Brooks, the poem exists in its metaphors. The rest of it he does not particularly remark. He goes straight to the metaphors, thinking it is they which work the miracle that is poetry; and naturally he elects for special notice the most unlikely ones. Hence paradox and irony, of which he is so fond."

In later years, Brooks's critical study extended from the examination of poetry to the study of the novels of William Faulkner. James B. Meriwether wrote of Brooks's *William Faulkner: The Yoknapatawpha Country* (1963): "Brooks's emphasis is literary, not sociological; but his fine synthesis of the major elements in the culture upon which most of Faulkner's best fiction draws is a valuable corrective to studies which have distorted that fiction through a misapprehension of its social and historical background." Meriwether goes on to say that Brooks's book on Faulkner "is one of the best critical studies of any American novelist, and perhaps the most important single critical study yet made of any American novelist of this century."

BIOGRAPHICAL/CRITICAL SOURCES:

BOOKS

Bryher, Jackson R., editor, *Sixteen Modern American Authors,* Norton, 1973.
Contemporary Literary Criticism, Volume 24, Gale, 1983.
Dictionary of Literary Biography, Volume 63: *Modern American Critics, 1920-1955,* Gale, 1988.
Krieger, Murray, *The New Apologists for Poetry,* University of Minnesota Press, 1956.

Poems and Essays, Vintage, 1955.
Pritchard, John Paul, *Criticism in America,* University of Oklahoma Press, 1956.
Simpson, Lewis P., editor, *The Possibilities of Order: Cleanth Brooks and His Work,* Louisiana State University Press, 1975.
Wellek, Rene, *Concepts of Criticism,* Yale University Press, 1963.
Wellek, Rene, *Discriminations,* Yale University Press, 1970.

PERIODICALS

Globe and Mail (Toronto), February 25, 1984.
Los Angeles Times, November 18, 1983.
New York Herald Tribune Books, July 28, 1963.
New York Review of Books, January 9, 1964, May 7, 1987.
New York Times Book Review, December 10, 1972, May 21, 1978, November 13, 1983.
Southern Review, winter, 1974.
Times Literary Supplement, March 30, 1984.
Washington Post, August 31, 1983.

*   *   *

BUSTOS, F(rancisco)
See BORGES, Jorge Luis

*   *   *

BUSTOS DOMECQ, H(onrio)
See BORGES, Jorge Luis

*   *   *

BUTOR, Michel (Marie Francois) 1926-

PERSONAL: Born September 14, 1926, in Mons-en-Baroeul, France; son of Emile (a railway inspector) and Anne (Brajeux) Butor; married Marie-Josephe Mas, August 22, 1958; children: Cecile, Agnes, Irene, Mathilde. *Education:* Sorbonne, University of Paris, license en philosophie, 1946, diplome d'etudes superieures de philosophie, 1947.

ADDRESSES: Home—Aux Antipodes, chemin de Terra Amata, 23 boulevard Carnot, 06300 Nice, France. *Office*—Faculte des Lettres, University of Geneva, 3 place de l'Universite, 1211 Geneva 4, Switzerland. *Agent*—Georges Borchardt, 136 East 57th St., New York, N.Y., 10022.

CAREER: Teacher of philosophy, Sens, France, 1950; teacher of French in Minya, Egypt, 1950-51, Manchester, England, 1951-53, Salonica, Greece, 1954-55, Geneva, Switzerland, 1956-57; Centre Universitaire de Vincennes, Vincennes, France, associate professor, 1969; University of Nice, Nice, France, associate professor, 1970-73; University of Geneva, Geneva, Switzerland, professor of modern French language and literature, 1975—; writer. Visiting professor of French at several universities in the United States. Advisory editor, Editions Gallimard, Paris, 1958—.

AWARDS, HONORS: Prix Felix Fenelon, 1957, for *L'Emploi du temps;* Prix Theophraste Renaudot, 1957, for *La Modification;* Grand Prix de la Critique Litteraire, Association de Critiques Litteraire, 1960, for *Repertoire;* Ford Foundation grant, 1964; Chevalier de l'Ordre National du Merite; Chevalier des Arts et des Lettres; Docteur es lettres, University of Paris.

WRITINGS:

NOVELS

Passage de Milan, Editions de Minuit, 1954.

L'Emploi du temps, Editions de Minuit, 1956, translation by Jean Stewart published as *Passing Time,* Simon & Schuster, 1960, recent edition, Riverrun, 1980.

La Modification, Editions de Minuit, 1957, translation by Stewart published in America as *Change of Heart,* Simon & Schuster, 1959, published in England as *Second Thoughts,* Faber, 1968, subsequent French edition published as *La Modification* [suivi de] *Le Realisme mythologique de Michel Butor,* the latter by Michel Leiris, Union Generale d'Editions, 1963, French language edition edited by J. Guicharnod published in America by Ginn, 1970.

Degres, Gallimard, 1960, translation by Richard Howard published as *Degrees,* Simon & Schuster, 1961.

6810000 litres d'eau par seconde: Etude stereophonique, Gallimard, 1965, translation by Elinor S. Miller published as *Niagara,* Regnery, 1969.

Portrait de l'artiste en jeune singe, capriccio, Gallimard, 1967.

Passing Time [and] *A Change of Heart: Two Novels,* translated by Stewart, Simon & Schuster, 1969.

Intervalle, Gallimard, 1973.

Matiere de reves, Editions de Minuit, Volume I, same title, 1975, Volume II: *Second sous-sol,* Gallimard, 1976, Volume III: *Troisieme dessous,* Gallimard, 1977, Volume IV: *Quadruple fond,* Gallimard, 1981, Volume V: *Mille et un plis,* Gallimard, 1985.

POEMS

Cycle sur neuf gouaches d'Alexandre Calder (edition consists of 500 copies signed by the artist and the author), La Hune (Paris), 1962.

Illustrations, Gallimard, 1964.

Litanie d'eau (contains ten original engravings by Gregory Masurovsky; edition consists of 105 copies), La Hune, 1964.

(Author of poems) Ruth Francken, *In den Flammen* (watercolors), epigram by Herbert Read, Belser (Stuttgart), 1965.

Comme Shirley (contains drawings by Masurovsky), La Hune, 1966.

Tourmente (contains drawings by Pierre Alechinsky, Bernard Dufour, and Jacques Herold; edition of 130 copies), Fata Morgana (Montpellier), 1968.

Illustrations II, Gallimard, 1969.

L'Oeil des sargasses, illustrated with an original frontispiece by Masurovsky, Editions "Lettera Amorosa," 1972.

Travaux d'approche: Eocene, Miocene, Pliocene, Gallimard, 1972.

L'Oreille de la lune: Voyage en compagnie de Jules Verne, illustrated with engravings by Robert Blanchet, R. Blanchet, 1973.

Illustrations III, Gallimard, 1973.

Illustrations IV, Gallimard, 1976.

Elseneur: Suite dramatique, La Thiele, 1979.

Sept a la demi-douzaine, Lettres de casse, 1982.

NONFICTION

Zanartu (brochure on Enrique Zanartu), Galerie Editions, 1958.

Le Genie de lieu (essays), Volume I: same title, Grasset, 1958, translation by Lydia Davis published as *The Spirit of Mediterranean Places,* Marlboro Press, 1986, Volume II: *Ou,* Gallimard, 1971, Volume III: *Boomerang* (also see below), Gallimard, 1978.

Herold (catalogue for exhibition, May 26-June 16, 1959), Galerie La Cour d'Ingres (Paris), 1959.

Repertoire: Etudes et conferences, 1948-1959 (essays), Editions de Minuit, 1960.

Une histoire extraordinaire: Essai sur un reve de Baudelaire, Gallimard, 1961, translation by Howard published as *Histoire extraordinaire: Essay on a Dream of Baudelaire's,* J. Cape, 1969.

Mobile: Etude pour un representation des Etats-Unis, Gallimard, 1962, translation by Howard published as *Mobile: Study for a Representation of the United States,* Simon & Schuster, 1963.

Description de San Marco, Gallimard, 1963, translation by Barbara Mason published as *Description of San Marco,* York Press, 1983.

Repertoire II: Etudes et conferences, 1959-1963 (essays, addresses, lectures), Editions de Minuit, 1964.

(Contributor) *Open to the World* (essays), Times Literary Supplement, 1964.

(Editor) Michael Eyquem de Montaigne, *Essays,* Union Generale d'Editions, 1964.

Les Oeuvres d'art imaginaires chez Proust (Casal Bequest lecture), Athlone Press (London), 1964.

Bernard Saby (conversation between Butor and Saby; published in conjunction with exhibition at L'Oeil, Galerie d'Art, Paris), Imprimerie Reunies (Lausanne), 1964.

Herold (conversation with Herold; not the same as earlier book), Musee de Poche, 1964.

Essais sur les modernes, Gallimard, 1964.

(Author of text) Bernard Larsson, *Die ganze Stadt Berlin* (photographs), Butor's French translated by Helmut Scheffel, Nannen (Hamburg), 1964.

(Author of text with Harold Rosenberg) Saul Steinberg, *Le Masque* (cartoons; photos by Inge Morath), Maeght, 1966.

(Author of text) *Dialogue des regnes [Cuivres originaux de] Jacques Herold* (original engravings by Herold; edition of 75 copies signed by author and artist), Fequet et Baudier (Paris), 1967.

Paysage de repons [suivi de] *Dialogues des regnes,* Albeuve (Castella), 1968.

La Banlieue de l'aube a l'aurore: Mouvement brownien (contains illustrations by Dufour), Fata Morgana, 1968.

Repertoire III (essays), Editions de Minuit, 1968.

Essais sur "Les Essais" (essays on the essays of Montaigne; contains extracts from *Essays*), Gallimard, 1968.

(With Henri Pousseur) *Votre Faust, fantaisie variable, genre opera* (includes a lecture given by Pousseur and an interview with Pousseur and Butor), Centre d'etudes et de recherches marxistes (Paris), 1968.

Inventory: Essays, edited with an introduction by Howard, Simon & Schuster, 1969.

Essais sur le roman, Gallimard, 1969.

Les Mots dans la peinture, Albert Skira (Geneva), 1969.

La Rose des vents: 32 rhumbs pour Charles Fourier, Gallimard, 1970.

Entretiens avec Georges Charbonnier, Gallimard, 1970.

Dialogue avec 33 variations de Ludwig van Beethoven sur une valse de Diabelli, Gallimard, 1971.

(With Denis Hollier) *Rabelais; ou, C'etait pour rire,* Larousse, 1972.

Les Sept Femmes de Gilbert le Mauvais (autre Heptaedre), Fata Morgana, 1972.

Repertoire IV (critical essays), Editions de Minuit, 1974.

(With Jean Clair and Suzanne Houbart-Wilkin) *Delvaux,* Cosmos (Brussells), 1975, translation published as *Delvaux's Paintings,* Wofsy Fine Arts, 1987.

Tapies, Fondation Marguerite et Aime Maeght (Saint-Paul, France), 1976.

Letters from the Antipodes (a selection from *Boomerang*), translated from the French by Michael Spencer, Ohio University Press, 1981.

Repertoire V, Editions de Minuit, 1982.

(Contributor) *Index des premiers ecrits pedagogiques de J.-J. Rousseau,* Slatkine, 1982.

(With Michel Sicard) *Problemes de l'art contemporain a partir des travaux d'Henri Maccheroni,* C. Bourgois, 1983.

(With Michel Launay) *Resistances: Conversations aux antipodes* (discussion), P.U.F., 1983.

Improvisations sur Flaubert (critical essays), Difference, 1984.

Alechinsky dans le texte, Galilee, 1984.

(With Christian Dotrement) *Cartes et lettres: Correspondance 1966-1979* (correspondance), Galilee, 1986.

Also author of introduction for: James Joyce, *Finnegans Wake,* Gallimard, 1962; William Styron, *La Proie des flammes* (*Set This House on Fire*), Gallimard, 1962; Fyodor Dostoievski, *Le Joueur* (*The Gambler*), Le Livre de Poche, 1963.

TRANSLATOR

(With Lucien Goldmann) Gyorgy Lukacs, *Breve Histoire de la litterature allemande (du XVIIIe siecle a nos jours),* Nagel, 1949.

Aron Gurwitsch, *Theorie du champ de la conscience (The Field of Conscience),* Desclee de Brouwer, 1957.

William Shakespeare, *Tout est bien fini qui finit bien* (translation of *All's Well That Ends Well*), published in *Oeuvres completes,* Volume V, Formes et Reflets, 1959.

Bernardino de Sahagun, *De l'origine des dieux,* Fata Morgana, 1981.

OTHER

Reseau aerien (radio script commissioned by French Broadcasting System; first performed June 16, 1962), Gallimard, 1962.

L'Art de Michel Butor, edited by Claude Book-Senninger and Jack Kolbert, Oxford University Press, 1970.

(With Pierre Barberis and Roland Barthes) *Ecrire, pour quoi? Pour qui?,* P.U.G., 1974.

(With Alechinsky) *La Reve de l'ammonite,* Fata Morgana, 1975.

Tout l'Oeuvre peint de Piet Mondrian, Flammarion, 1976.

(With Alechinsky and Jean-Yves Bosseur) *Materiel pour un Don Juan,* T. Bouchard, 1978.

Envois, Gallimard, 1980.

(With Michel Launay and Henri Maccheroni) *Vanite: Conversation dans les Alpes-Maritimes,* Balland, 1980.

Explorations, Editions de l'Aire, 1981.

(With Chris Marker) *Le Depays,* Herscher, 1982.

Brassee d'avril, Difference, 1982.

(With Pierre Berenger) *Naufrages de l'arche,* published with *Adieu a la galerie de zoologie* by Yves Laissus, Difference, 1982.

Vieira Da Silva: Peintures, Difference, 1983.

Expres, Gallimard, 1983.

Alechinsky: Frontieres et bordures, Galilee (Paris), 1984.

(With Masurovsky) *Dimanche matin,* Instant Perpetuel, 1984.

Loisirs et brouillons, 1964-1984, D. Bedou, 1984.

Herbier lunaire, Difference, 1984.

Avant-gout, Ubacs, 1984.

Improvisations sur Henri Michaux, Fata Morgana, 1985.

(With Stephane Bastin) *La Famille Grabouillage,* D. Bedou, 1985.

(With Herold) *Hors-d'oeuvre,* Instant Perpetuel, 1985.

Chantier, D. Bedou, 1985.

(With Axel Cassel) *Le Scribe,* Spuren, 1985.

L'oeil de Prague: Dialogue avec Charles Baudelaire autour des travaux de Jiri Kolar, suivi de reponses et de Le Prague de Kafka par Jiri Kolar, Difference, 1986.

Avant-gout II, Ubacs, 1987.

Le Retour de Boomerang, Presses Universitaires de France, 1988.

Contributor to numerous publications in France and elsewhere.

SIDELIGHTS: Along with Samuel Beckett, Nathalie Sarraute, and Alain Robbe-Grillet, Butor has been at the vanguard of twentieth-century French literature, engaged in writing what is sometimes referred to by Jean-Paul Sartre's phrase, the "anti-novel," or, the "new novel." The exponents of the new novel, according to Sartre, "make use of the novel in order to challenge the novel, to destroy it before our very eyes while seeming to construct it, to write the novel of a novel unwritten and unwritable." The new novel adds an objective exposition of setting and character, and concentrates on "existence as it is being formed rather than analyzing it after it has happened," Patricia J. Jaeger writes.

For Butor, the novel is an instrument of knowledge, a searching depth-study of personality. He avoids chronological time in favor of "human time" measured in the interior of each character's mind. Jaeger comments: "Butor seems to base most of his books . . . on an examination of the effect of the past, present and future on each other. He is especially aware of the propensity of the human mind to shift its perception of the past in light of new information available only in the present." In addition to juxtaposing several levels of time, he offers no solutions, preferring to focus on the transition of action not on its outcome.

Butor himself sees the novel form as the perfect instrument for combining the two principal interests of his youth, philosophy and poetry. Of Butor's stylistic qualities Laurent Le Sage writes: "Butor's books are like those European museums and galleries he is fond of visiting with his readers, full to the rafters of the most painstaking and minute word-painting, as if there were nothing he could leave out. His descriptions often have a lyrical, even rhapsodical quality." The formation of this style can perhaps be traced to Butor's first encounter with Shelley's poetry at the age of fourteen, when he discovered, he writes, "a lyricism of which the French classics gave me no idea, above all a new sonority, a new way of making words take fire from the rhythm."

Butor has been greatly influenced by Proust. He said once that he had read all of *Remembrance of Things Past* ten times. Henri Peyre writes: "Butor's is the finest mind among those who have undertaken to renovate the novel since 1950—the only one who at times recalls the density and the complex orchestration of the Proustian saga fiction or whose universal intellectual and artistic curiosity grants him a place in the literature of the last third of our century comparable to that of Sartre at mid-century. He received Sartre's blessing and he himself has been generous as well as clear-sighted in praising the avatars of Sartrian thought since 1960." Peyre maintains that until the publication of *Degres* Butor was the "favorite of critics and of philosophers."

Butor has also been influenced by Joyce, whom he greatly admired. The structure of *Passage de Milan*—the entire novel covers twelve hours of time and takes place within an apartment house in Paris, where the residents' lives are regulated by a series of rituals which tend to isolate them from each other rather than bring them closer together—is reminiscent of Joyce's structure in *Ulysses*. A similar structure is used in *L'Emploi du temps*. The novel is in five parts, corresponding to the five months during which the main character keeps a diary. The parts of the novel are each divided into five chapters, for each of the weeks, or portions of weeks in a month. Since Revel does not work on weekends each week has five days. Butor has thus created a schedule for the framework of the book, although he can with his title also be referring to the uses of passing of time. The structure can also be seen in Bleston, the city which Butor creates, and all the details which he carefully sets down. Leon Roudiez states that "Butor is concerned with Bleston not as a city contrasted to the country or the sea, but as a city among cities, as a microcosm of civilization, like Paris in *Passage de Milan*." The great scope of these first two novels, although they are contained in the framework Butor has provided for them, includes myriad details about the lives of the many people encountered in both books.

La Modification is unlike the first two novels since it "[focuses] on the single action of one individual," as Roudiez says, "clearly circumscribed in time and space, actually and symbolically." Butor uses the second person narrative here very successfully. Roudiez states that the second person "allows for an ambiguous author-reader-character relationship, with the reader oscillating between identification with the prosecuting author, or with the guilty character." The reader is then able to choose, "he is free to act either in good faith or in bad faith." Peyre comments that *La Modification* is "a paradox sustained through two hundred and thirty pages without artificiality or weariness. The stark simplicity of the theme and the unities of time and place, the stillness in the midst of motion, are arresting." Peyre recounts Butor's statement to a *Figaro Litteraire* interviewer: "The narrative absolutely had to be told from the point of view of a character . . . I needed an interior monologue beneath the level of the character himself, with a form between the first and third person. The *vous* allows me to describe the situation of the character and the manner in which language emerges in him."

Degres has elicited both favorable and unfavorable criticism. Peyre considers the novel a failure, "even as an exercise in the technique of fiction." Harry T. Moore describes the novel as "a microscopic investigation of the life processes themselves, more detailed even than the explorations of Sarraute and Robbe-Grillet, with fewer clues as to what is happening. It is therefore somewhat more difficult to read, but the book remains a fascinating experiment; it deals more thoroughly with space-time concepts than other novels of its school." Roudiez states that *Degres* "is a masterpiece. The initial impetus to the narrative lies in an attempt to recapture the meaning and consciousness of a given hour in the life of a contemporary French lycee, its teachers, and its students, at the beginning of the school year." Roudiez finds that the "architecture" of the novel "is one aspect . . . of which most readers are not aware, and this in itself is an indication of how successfully it has been integrated into the work as a whole." It is divided into three parts, and these are further divided. There are many triangular relationships among characters as well.

Since *Degres* Butor has used his methods of structure and categorization in even more unusual ways. *Mobile* is considered by some to be a novel, but most people would agree that it is not really a novel. Butor's subtitle, "study," in the sense of the French *etude,* is probably the best way to categorize the work. He has used the experience of a trip across the United States for the material of this work, although it is not an actual trip, and many of the facts are not completely accurate. Miller describes the book as "a tiresome montage of disconnected images relieved

by catalogues of names, advertising slogans, the prose of road signs." He says that *Mobile* is "a poor imitation of the expressionist techniques." Roudiez would disagree. He says that Butor's "is the phenomenological approach, whereby the book is examined in its attributes as a material object." He finds "a certain amount of virtuosity" in the book. Again, the architecture is not obvious, and Butor has been criticized for this, but a very definite structure is present. Most important for the reader, Roudiez states, "is the manner in which the components have been assembled in order to produce the picture, or 'representation.' Discontinuous accounts of the 1692 Salem trials and of writings by Franklin and Jefferson, newspaper extracts, advertisements, signs, brief statements, names of people, cities, counties, and states form a strange mosaic or, as the text suggests at one point, a patchwork quilt. Naturally, the juxtaposition is not haphazard; as with the states themselves, the basic order is alphabetical (almond through vanilla for ice cream, B.P. through Texaco for gasoline, among others), and a number of complicated modifications are subsequently introduced in order to achieve maximum effect from various confrontations: the procedure is . . . not unrelated to the surrealist image. . . . *Mobile* is a stunning display of colors. A profusion of contrasting tints is found in the flora, the fauna, the human artifacts, and the people themselves."

A resemblance can he seen between *Mobile* and *Description de San Marco,* although the latter is concerned strictly with San Marco, and does not go off in the directions that *Mobile* does. Both of these works have unusual typographical arrangements which help to clarify that which is place. Margins of different sizes are used to differentiate between different elements in the narratives, and in *Mobile* . . . use of italic as well as Roman type is significant. Both books led the way to *Reseau aerien,* which uses the same devices. The book departs from the printed page in the sense that it was written for radio broadcast, and involves not only dialogue but sound as well, which can only be described, and not actually heard, in print. Roudiez writes that "the total impression is one of a choral song of mankind in which unidentified individuals blend their common preoccupations about different things and countries into elemental melodies of love and hate. Trivial concerns, expressed in prosaic fashion, dominate in the early dialogues. Later, as distance, imagination, and dreams affect each traveler, the themes become more basically human; the language waxes lyrical, discursive logic makes way for instinctive association, and ordinary talk is metamorphosed into poetry."

6810000 litres d'eau par seconde is described by Miller as "a story in which Niagara Falls are thunderously dominant. The action, chiefly concerned with newly married couples and older ones nostalgically returning, covers a year, presenting events somewhat in the manner of *Mobile,* with different kinds of type and with speeches intended to be read at different pitches." Butor visited Niagara Falls at different seasons so that he would have more than one set of impressions to write about. He has even written himself in to the book as Quentin, a visiting professor of French. John Sturrock writes: "In its devious and sybilline way, [the book] embodies everything that Butor believes about the function and lofty moral virtues of literature. Making a book for him is an exemplary effort at anamnensis, the model of how we ought all of us to set about salvaging our own past."

Butor as an essayist should not be overlooked. Audrey Foote comments on the essays included in *Inventory:* "Both [Butor's] choice of subjects and his treatment of them reflect a mind of muscular intellectuality, a Huguenot or puritan taste for austerity and economy, and above all an intense need to impose discipline, almost geometric order and unity." Moore comments: "Butor is a critic of pronounced originality, discernment, versatility, wit, and force."

MEDIA ADAPTATIONS: La Modification was filmed by Rene Thevenet-Fono Roma, 1970.

BIOGRAPHICAL/CRITICAL SOURCES:

BOOKS

Albers, R. M., *Michel Butor*, Editions Universitaire, 1964.
Contemporary Literary Criticism, Gale, Volume I, 1973, Volume III, 1975, Volume VIII, 1978, Volume XI, 1979, Volume XV, 1980.
Dictionary of Literary Biography, Volume LXXXIII: *French Novelists Since 1960*, Gale, 1989.
Le Sage, Laurent, *The French New Novel*, Pennsylvania State University Press, 1962.
Lydon, Mary, *Perpetuum Mobile: A Study of the Novels and Aesthetics of Michel Butor*, University of Alberta Press, 1980.
McWilliams, Dean, *The Narrative of Butor: The Writer as Janus*, Ohio University Press, 1978.
Moore, Harry T., *French Literature Since World War II*, Southern Illinois University Press, 1966.
Peyre, Henri, *French Novelists of Today*, Oxford University Press, 1967.
Rahv, Betty T., *From Sartre to the New Novel*, Kennikat Press, 1974.
Roudiez, Leon S., *Michel Butor*, Columbia University Press, 1965.
Spencer, Michael, *Butor*, Twayne, 1974.
Sturrock, John, *The French New Novel: Claude Simon, Michel Butor, Alain Robbe-Grillet*, Oxford University Press, 1969.

PERIODICALS

Book World, February 9, 1969.
Books Abroad, spring, 1968, spring, 1969, spring, 1970, winter, 1971, spring, 1971.
Critique (Paris), February, 1958.
Critique: Studies in Modern Fiction, winter, 1963-64.
French Review, December, 1961, October, 1962.
Kentucky Romance Quarterly, Volume XXXVIII, Number I, 1985.
Les Temps Modernes, April, 1957.
Livres de France, June-July, 1963.
New Statesman, April 7, 1967.
New York Herald Tribune Book Review, August 4, 1963.
New York Review of Books, April 23, 1970.
New York Times Book Review, July 7, 1963, December 28, 1969, August 31, 1986.
Review of Contemporary Fiction, fall, 1985.
Saturday Review, December 18, 1965, August 5, 1967, May 3, 1969.
Times Literary Supplement, March 4, 1965, March 17, 1966, June 22, 1967, April 11, 1968, January 1, 1971, August 6, 1971, August 3, 1973, May 17, 1974, July 18, 1975, October 7, 1977.
Tri-Quarterly Review, winter, 1967.
World Literature Today, autumn, 1977, winter, 1977, winter, 1979, summer, 1981, spring, 1982, autumn, 1983, winter, 1983, spring, 1984, summer, 1984, spring, 1985.
Yale French Studies, summer, 1959.
Yale Review, June, 1959.

BYATT, A(ntonia) S(usan Drabble) 1936-

PERSONAL: Born August 24, 1936, in Sheffield, England; daughter of John Frederick (a judge) and Kathleen Marie (Bloor) Drabble; married Ian Charles Rayner Byatt (an economist), July 4, 1959 (divorced, 1969); married Peter John Duffy; children: (first marriage) Antonia, Charles (died, 1972); (second marriage) Isabel, Miranda. *Education:* Newnham College, Cambridge, B.A. (first class honors), 1957; graduate study at Bryn Mawr College, 1957-58, and Somerville College, Oxford, 1958-59. *Politics:* "Radical."

ADDRESSES: Home—37 Rusholme Rd., London SW15 3LF, England.

CAREER: University of London, London, England, staff member in extra-mural department, 1962-71, University College, lecturer, 1972-80, senior lecturer in English, 1981-83, admissions tutor in English, 1980-83; full-time writer, 1983—. Associate of Newnham College, Cambridge, 1977-87; fellow of University College, London, 1984—. Part-time lecturer in department of liberal studies, Central School of Art and Design, London, 1965-69; British Council Lecturer in Spain, 1978, India, 1981, and in Germany, Australia, Hong Kong, China, and Korea; George Eliot Centenary Lecturer, 1980. Has done several radio broadcasts and interviews. Member of panel of judges for Booker Prize, 1973, Hawthornden Prize, and David Higham Memorial Prize; member of British Broadcasting Corp. (BBC) Social Effects of Television Advisory Group, 1974-77, member of Communications and Cultural Studies Board of the Council for National Academic Awards, 1978; member of Kingman Committee on the Teaching of English, 1987-88.

MEMBER: Society of Authors (member of committee of management, 1984-88; chairman of committee, 1986-88).

AWARDS, HONORS: English Speaking Union fellowship, 1957-58; fellow of the Royal Society of Literature, 1983; Silver Pen Award for *Still Life;* D. Litt. from University of Bradford, 1987; Booker Prize, 1990, for *Possession.*

WRITINGS:

The Shadow of a Sun (novel), Harcourt, 1964.
Degrees of Freedom: The Novels of Iris Murdoch (literary criticism), Barnes & Noble, 1965.
The Game (novel), Chatto & Windus, 1967, Scribner, 1968.
(Contributor) Isobel Armstrong, editor, *The Major Victorian Poets Reconsidered*, Routledge & Kegan Paul, 1969.
Wordsworth and Coleridge in Their Time (literary criticism), Nelson, 1970, Crane, Russak, 1973, reissued as *Unruly Times*, Hogarth, 1989.
Iris Murdoch, Longman, 1976.
The Virgin in the Garden (first novel in tetralogy), Chatto & Windus, 1978, Knopf, 1979.
(Editor and author of introduction) George Eliot, *The Mill on the Floss*, Penguin, 1979.
Still Life (second novel in tetralogy), Chatto & Windus, 1986, Scribner, 1987.
Sugar and Other Stories, Scribner, 1987.
(Editor) George Eliot, *Selected Essays, Poems and Other Writings*, Penguin, 1989.
(Editor) Robert Browning, *Dramatic Monologues*, Folio Society, 1990.
Possession: A Romance (novel), Chatto & Windus, 1990.
Passions of the Mind (essays), Random House, 1990.

Author of prefaces to the following novels: Elizabeth Bowen, *The House in Paris,* 1976; Grace Paley, *Enormous Changes at the Last Minute,* 1979; Paley, *The Little Disturbances of Man,* 1980; Willa Cather, *My Antonia,* and *A Lost Lady,* 1980, and *My Mortal Enemy; Shadow on the Rock, Death Comes to the Archbishop, O Pioneers!, Lucy Gayheart,* and *The Professor's House.*

Also author of dramatized radio documentary on Leo Tolstoy, July, 1978; author of dramatized portraits of George Eliot and Samuel Taylor Coleridge, for the National Portrait Gallery. Regular reviewer for the London *Times* and the *New Statesman;* contributor of reviews to *Encounter, New Review,* and *American Studies.* Member of editorial board of *Encyclopaedia,* Longman-Penguin, 1989.

WORK IN PROGRESS: Babel Tower, the third novel of the tetralogy; a book of short stories.

SIDELIGHTS: Because of A. S. Byatt's wide experience as a critic, novelist, editor, and lecturer, she "offers in her work an intellectual kaleidoscope of our contemporary world," writes Caryn McTighe Musil in *Dictionary of Literary Biography.* "Her novels, like her life, are dominated by an absorbing, discriminating mind which finds intellectual passions as vibrant and consuming as emotional ones." Musil indicates that Byatt's first novel, *The Shadow of a Sun,* reflects the author's own struggle to combine the role of critic with that of novelist on the one hand and the role of mother with that of visionary on the other. *The Game,* "a piece of technical virtuosity," according to Musil, "is also a taut novel that explores with a courage and determined honesty greater than [D. H.] Lawrence's the deepest levels of antagonism that come with intimacy. Widely reviewed, especially in Great Britain, *The Game* established Byatt's reputation as an important contemporary novelist, though the book's readership was not extensive."

Byatt's novel *The Virgin in the Garden* is described by *Times Literary Supplement* reviewer Michael Irwin as a "careful, complex novel." The book's action is set in 1953, the year of the coronation of Queen Elizabeth II, and Irwin indicates that "its theme is growing up, coming of age, tasting knowledge." The book "is a highly intellectual operation," points out Iris Murdoch in *New Statesman.* "The characters do a great deal of thinking, and have extremely interesting thoughts which are developed at length." "The novel's central symbol," Musil relates, "is Queen Elizabeth I, a monarch Byatt sees as surviving because she used her mind and thought things out, unlike her rival, Mary, Queen of Scots, who was 'very female and got it wrong.' " In Musil's opinion, the work initiates "the middle phase of [Byatt's] career as a novelist. Much denser [than her previous novels] and dependent on her readers' erudition," *The Virgin in the Garden* "achieves a style that suits Byatt. It blends her acquisitive, intellectual bent with her imaginative compulsion to tell stories," Musil points out. With publication of *The Virgin in the Garden,* maintains Musil, "Byatt has come fully into her own as a fiction writer and has guaranteed her place in literary histories of the future."

Byatt told *CA:* "Perhaps the most important thing to say about my books is that they try to be about the life of the mind as well as of society and the relations between people. I admire—am excited by—intellectual curiosity of any kind (scientific, linguistic, psychological) and also by literature as a complicated, huge, interrelating pattern. I also like recording small observed facts and feelings. I see writing and thinking as a passionate activity, like any other.

"I hope I am a European writer as well as being a local English one. I am at the moment exercised by the problem of communicable detail—can an Italian or a Californian or an Indian take any interest in or appreciate the nuances of an English bus queue? How many readers will have read Milton's *Paradise Lost* or Homer's *The Aeneid?* How many who have not will be annoyed to find them in my books? (This is a reaction I still find puzzling).

"I held a full-time university reading post for eleven years and now feel entirely happy, for the first time in my life, at the prospect of writing full time, thinking things out from beginning to end, and reading for my own purposes. I enjoyed teaching John Donne, Robert Browning, George Eliot, Charles Dickens, Samuel Taylor Coleridge, John Keats, Wallace Stevens, Emily Dickinson, and Henry James. But now reading is even more exciting. The novelist I most love is Marcel Proust. After him Balzac, Dickens, Eliot, Thomas Mann and James, Iris Murdoch, Ford Maddox Ford, and Willa Cather. And Leo Tolstoy and Fyodor Dostoevsky.

"Of course I am a feminist. But I don't want to be required to write to a feminist programme, and I feel uneasy when this seems to be asked of me. I am a bit too old to be a naturally political animal."

BIOGRAPHICAL/CRITICAL SOURCES:

BOOKS

Contemporary Literary Criticism, Volume 19, Gale, 1981.
Dictionary of Literary Biography, Volume 14: *British Novelists Since 1960,* Gale, 1983.

PERIODICALS

Books and Bookmen, January 4, 1979.
Chicago Tribune Book World, January 12, 1986.
Encounter, July, 1968.
Globe and Mail (Toronto), October 13, 1990.
Los Angeles Times, November 18, 1985.
Ms., June, 1979.
New Leader, April 23, 1979.
New Statesman, November 3, 1978.
New York Times Book Review, July 26, 1964, March 17, 1968, April 1, 1979, November 24, 1985, July 19, 1987.
Times (London), June 6, 1981, April 9, 1987, March 1, 1990.
Times Literary Supplement, January 2, 1964, January 19, 1967, November 3, 1978, June 28, 1985, March 2, 1990.
Tribune Books (Chicago), November 18, 1990.
Washington Post, March 16, 1979, November 22, 1985.

C

CABLE, James (Eric) 1920-
(Grant Hugo)

PERSONAL: Born November 15, 1920, in London, England; son of Eric Grant (a consul-general) and Margaret (Skelton) Cable; married Viveca Hollmerus, 1954; children: Charles. *Education:* Corpus Christi College, Cambridge, Ph.D., 1973.

ADDRESSES: Office—8 Essex Close, Cambridge CB4 2DW, England.

CAREER: Diplomatic Service, London, England, served in H.M. Forces, 1941-46, joined H.M. Foreign Service, 1947, vice-consul in Batavia (now Djakarta), 1949, second secretary in Djakarta, 1950, charge d'affaires, 1951-52, second secretary in Helsinki, Finland, 1952, and in Foreign Office in London, 1953, became first secretary, 1953, member of British delegation to Geneva Conference on Indochina, 1954, first secretary in Budapest, Hungary, 1956, head of chancery and consul in Quito, Ecuador, 1959, charge d'affaires, 1959-60, in Foreign Office, 1961-63, head of Southeast Asia department, 1963-66, counselor in Beirut, Lebanon, 1966, charge d'affaires, 1967-69, head of western organizations department at Foreign and Commonwealth Office, 1970-71, counselor in contingency studies, 1971, head of planning staff, 1971-75, assistant under-secretary of state, 1972-75, ambassador to Finland in Helsinki, 1975-80; writer. Research associate at Institute for Strategic Studies, 1969-70.

MEMBER: International Institute for Strategic Studies, British International Studies Association.

AWARDS, HONORS: Companion of Order of St. Michael and St. George, 1967; knight commander of Royal Victorian Order, 1976; Grand Cross of Order of Finnish Lion, 1976.

WRITINGS:

(Under pseudonym Grant Hugo) *Britain in Tomorrow's World,* Columbia University Press, 1969.
(Under pseudonym Grant Hugo) *Appearance and Reality in International Relations,* Columbia University Press, 1970.
Gunboat Diplomacy, Praeger, 1971, revised edition published as *Gunboat Diplomacy, 1919-1979,* St. Martin's, 1981.
The Royal Navy and the Siege of Bilbao, Cambridge University Press, 1979.
Britain's Naval Future, Macmillan, 1983.
Diplomacy at Sea, Macmillan, 1985.

The Geneva Conference of 1954 on Indochina, Macmillan, 1986.
Political Institutions and Issues in Britain, Macmillan, 1987.
Navies in Violent Peace, Macmillan, 1989.

Contributor to various journals.

WORK IN PROGRESS: Plan Buccaneer: Intervention at Abadan.

SIDELIGHTS: James Cable's years of diplomatic service to Great Britain have resulted in several books examining political issues. One of these, *The Royal Navy and the Siege of Bilbao,* is "the story of how the British Government tried to cope at a stage in [the Spanish Civil War] which brought all these elements into play for the first time: the maintenance of trade and of food shipments and the evacuation of refugees in the face of a Nationalist blockade; the attempt to maintain the principles of Non-Intervention and, at the same time, to continue to act as a great power, with only minor interests at stake; all came together in a series of decisions and actions," as *Times Literary Supplement* critic Peter Nailor describes it. "It is, of necessity, a tangled story," Nailor continues. "The records are not well preserved, and many recollections are partial. But James Cable . . . weaves the story deftly together and unravels many of its tangles to show how puzzled and uncertain, and fearful, many of the ideas and the agents of British policy-making then were."

Similarly, the essays in *Diplomacy at Sea,* while "the majority have a naval flavour . . . draw more widely on [Cable's] diplomatic experience and views," Bryan Ranft observes in the *Times Literary Supplement.* Overall, the critic remarks, Cable's work "is marked by clarity and wit, and the subtlety of its conceptual differentiations, the aptness of its historical examples, and its telling references to his personal diplomatic experiences, show the author at his best." "As a retired ambassador, [Cable's] viewpoint is that of a professional observer and interpreter of politics who is neither a practitioner nor an academic," John Campbell notes in his *Times Literary Supplement* review of *Political Institutions and Issues in Britain.* "He is appropriately lucid, sceptical and, in the end, mildly elegiac." As a result, Campbell concludes, "in a discipline dominated by indigestible textbooks and arcane monographs his book . . . is a pleasure to read."

BIOGRAPHICAL/CRITICAL SOURCES:

PERIODICALS

Times (London), August 6, 1981.

Times Literary Supplement, February 15, 1980; May 27, 1983; November 8, 1985; November 13-19, 1987.

*　　*　　*

CALDWELL, Erskine (Preston) 1903-1987

PERSONAL: Born December 17, 1903, in White Oak (some sources say Moreland), GA; died of emphysema and lung cancer, April 11, 1987, in Paradise Valley, AZ; son of Ira Sylvester (a minister) and Caroline Preston (a schoolteacher; maiden name, Bell) Caldwell; married Helen Lannigan, March 3, 1925 (divorced); married Margaret Bourke-White (a photographer), February 27, 1939 (divorced, 1942); married June Johnson, December 21, 1942 (divorced, 1955); married Virginia Moffett Fletcher, January 1, 1957; children: (first marriage) Erskine Preston, Dabney Withers, Janet; (third marriage) Jay Erskine. *Education:* Attended Erskine College, 1920-21, University of Virginia, 1922-26, and University of Pennsylvania, 1924.

ADDRESSES: Agent—McIntosh & Otis, Inc., 475 Fifth Ave., New York, NY 10017.

CAREER: Held various jobs, including mill laborer, cotton picker, cook, waiter, taxicab driver, farmhand, cottonseed shoveler, stonemason's helper, soda jerk, professional football player, bodyguard, stagehand in a burlesque theater, and a hand on a boat running guns to a Central American country in revolt; *Journal,* Atlanta, GA, reporter, 1925; script writer in Hollywood, CA, 1933-34 and 1942-43; newspaper correspondent in Mexico, Spain, Czechoslovakia, Russia, and China, 1938-40; war correspondent in Russia for *Life* Magazine, PM, and Columbia Broadcasting System, Inc., 1941; writer.

MEMBER: American Academy and Institute of Arts and Letters (honorary member), Authors League of America, P.E.N., Phoenix Press Club (life member), San Francisco Press Club (life member).

AWARDS, HONORS: Yale Review Award for fiction, 1933, for short story "Country Full of Swedes."

WRITINGS:

The Bastard (novel; also see below), Heron Press, 1929.
Poor Fool (novel; also see below), Rariora Press, 1930.
American Earth (short story collection), Scribner, 1931, published as *A Swell-Looking Girl,* MacFadden-Bartell, 1965.
Mamma's Little Girl, privately printed, 1932.
Tobacco Road (novel; also see below), Scribner, 1932.
Message for Genevieve, privately printed, 1933.
God's Little Acre (novel), Viking, 1933.
We Are the Living (short story collection), Viking, 1933.
Some American People, R. M. McBride & Co., 1935.
Tenant Farmer, Phalanx Press, 1935.
Journeyman (novel), Viking, 1935.
Kneel to the Rising Sun and Other Stories by Erskine Caldwell, Viking, 1935.
The Sacrilege of Alan Kent (novel; also see below), Falmouth Book House, 1936, reprinted with illustrations by Alexander Calder, Galerie Maeght, 1975.
You Have Seen Their Faces (nonfiction), photographs by Margaret Bourke-White, Viking, 1937.
Southways (short story collection), Viking, 1938.
North of the Danube (nonfiction), photographs by Bourke-White, Viking, 1939.
Trouble in July (novel), Duell, 1940.
Jackpot: The Short Stories of Erskine Caldwell (also see below), Duell, 1940.

Say, Is This the U.S.A.? (nonfiction), photographs by Bourke-White, Duell, 1941.
All Night Long: A Novel of Guerrilla Warfare in Russia, Duell, 1942.
All-out on the Road to Smolensk (nonfiction), Duell, 1942 (published in England as *Moscow under Fire: A Wartime Diary, 1941,* Hutchinson, 1942).
Russia at War (nonfiction), photographs by Bourke-White, Hutchinson, 1942.
Georgia Boy (novel; also see below), Duell, 1943, published as *Georgia Boy and Other Stories,* Avon, 1946.
Twenty-two Great Modern Short Stories from Jackpot, Avon, 1944.
Stories by Erskine Caldwell, Duell, 1944.
Tragic Ground (novel), Duell, 1944.
A Day's Wooing and Other Stories, Grosset, 1944.
The Caldwell Caravan: Novels and Stories by Erskine Caldwell, World Publishing, 1946.
A House in the Uplands (novel), Duell, 1946.
The Sure Hand of God (novel; also see below), Duell, 1947.
Midsummer Passion and Other Stories from Jackpot, Avon, 1948.
This Very Earth (novel), Duell, 1948.
Where the Girls Were Different and Other Stories, Avon, 1948, published as *Where the Girls Were Different,* MacFadden-Bartell, 1965.
Place Called Estherville (novel), Duell, 1949.
Episode in Palmetto (novel), Duell, 1950.
(Editor) Albert Nathaniel Williams, *Rocky Mountain Country,* Duell, 1950.
The Humorous Side of Erskine Caldwell, edited by Robert Cantwell, Duell, 1951.
Call It Experience: The Years of Learning How to Write, Duell, 1951, published as *Call It Experience,* MacFadden-Bartell, 1966.
The Courting of Susie Brown (short story collection), Duell, 1952, (published in England as *The Courting of Susie Brown and Other Stories,* Pan Books, 1958).
A Lamp for Nightfall (novel), Duell, 1952.
Complete Stories, Duell, 1953, published as *The Complete Stories of Erskine Caldwell,* Little, Brown, 1953.
Love and Money (novel), Duell, 1954.
Gretta (novel), Little, Brown, 1955.
Gulf Coast Stories, Little, Brown, 1956.
The Pocket Book of Erskine Caldwell Stories: Thirty-one of the Most Famous Short Stories, Pocket Books, 1957.
Certain Women (short story collection), Little, Brown, 1957.
Molly Cottontail (juvenile), Little, Brown, 1958.
Claudelle Inglish (novel), Little, Brown, 1959 (published in England as *Claudelle,* Heinemann, 1959).
When You Think of Me (short story collection), Little, Brown, 1959.
Three by Caldwell—Tobacco Road, Georgia Boy, The Sure Hand of God: Three Great Novels of the South, Little, Brown, 1960.
Men and Women: Twenty-two Stories, Little, Brown, 1961, published as *Men and Women,* MacFadden-Bartell, 1965.
Jenny by Nature (novel), Farrar, Straus, 1961.
Close to Home (novel), Farrar, Straus, 1962.
The Bastard, Poor Fool [and] *The Sacrilege of Alan Kent,* Bodley Head, 1963.
The Last Night of Summer (novel), Farrar, Straus, 1963.
A Woman in the House, MacFadden-Bartell, 1964.
Around about America (nonfiction), illustrated by wife, Virginia M. Caldwell, Farrar, Straus, 1964.

In Search of Bisco, Farrar, Straus, 1965.

The Deer at Our House (juvenile), Collier, 1966.

In the Shadow of the Steeple (also see below), Heinemann, 1967.

Writing in America, Phaedra Publishers, 1967.

Miss Mamma Aimee (novel), New American Library, 1967.

Summertime Island (novel), World Publishing, 1968.

Deep South: Memory and Observation (nonfiction; Part 1 first published in England as *In the Shadow of the Steeple*), Weybright, 1968.

The Weather Shelter (novel), World Publishing, 1969.

The Earnshaw Neighborhood (novel), World Publishing, 1971.

Annette (novel), New American Library, 1973.

Afternoons in Mid-America: Observations and Impressions (nonfiction), illustrated by V. M. Caldwell, Dodd, 1976.

Stories of Life, North and South, Dodd, 1983.

The Black and White Stories of Erskine Caldwell, edited by Ray McIver, Peachtree Publications, 1984.

With All My Might: An Autobiography, Peachtree Publications, 1987.

Also author of screenplays "A Nation Dances" and "Volcano." Editor, "American Folkways," twenty-five volumes, 1940-55.

A collection of Caldwell's manuscripts is housed in the Baker Library of Dartmouth College, Hanover, NH.

MEDIA ADAPTATIONS: Several of Caldwell's novels have been made into films, including *Tobacco Road,* Twentieth Century-Fox Film Corp., 1941, *God's Little Acre,* United Artists Corp., 1958, and *Claudelle Inglish* (under the title "Claudelle"), Warner Brothers, Inc., 1961. *Tobacco Road* was also adapted for the stage by Jack Kirkland and ran on Broadway for more than seven years.

SIDELIGHTS: As one of America's most banned and censored writers, in addition to being one of its most financially successful, Erskine Caldwell was often "patronized or ignored by academic critics and serious readers," according to James Korges, author of a critical study of the man who has been called "the South's literary bad boy." Korges continued: "Many know of *Tobacco Road* and *God's Little Acre,* but tend to dismiss them as merely popular or salacious novels. Few seem to know the full range of the man's work: his text-picture documentaries, such as the remarkable *North of the Danube;* his charming books for children; his neglected *Georgia Boy,* a book that stands with [William] Faulkner's last work as one of the finest novels of boyhood in American literature; and his short stories, some of which rank with the best of our time. . . . Younger readers dismiss him as a writer of the old pornography, for how tame, demure, almost tidy seem the passages that were read aloud in courts as evidence of Caldwell's obscenity. . . . Younger critics seem unwilling to read Caldwell with care. . . . That much of [his] work 'grew towards trash' [in the words of Faulkner] does not alter the fact that Caldwell has produced an important body of work in both fiction and nonfiction."

In spite of the fact that, as Korges pointed out, Caldwell was more than just a novelist, his specialty through the years was the depiction of the seamier side of life in the American South—the bigotry, poverty, and misery among small-town "white trash." The son of a Presbyterian minister who made frequent moves from congregation to congregation throughout the South, Caldwell had ample opportunities as a boy to observe the various people and lifestyles of his native region. He often accompanied his father on visits to the homes of his parishioners, for example, and for a time he even drove a country doctor on his rounds. As he once explained to an interviewer: "You learned a lot living in

small towns those days before they became smaller versions of the big towns."

Ten of Caldwell's novels—*Tobacco Road, God's Little Acre, Journeyman, Trouble in July, Tragic Ground, A House in the Uplands, The Sure Hand of God, This Very Earth, Place Called Estherville,* and *Episode in Palmetto*—comprise what the author himself referred to as "a cyclorama of Southern life." Unlike Faulkner's mythical Yoknapatawpha County, however, Caldwell's "cyclorama" does not seek to link his characters and events in any kind of overall historical framework; his goal, according to Korges, was to discover "scenes and actions that [embody] themes and types in the present."

Very few, if any, of Caldwell's characters or themes inspire admiration or optimism. His point of view was essentially pessimistic—man is more or less doomed to a life of pain and hurt, subject to the whims of chance and the effects of the actions of others. Virtually everything that happens—whether the results are bad or good—is regarded by Caldwell's characters as a manifestation of the will of God. And though there is room for humor in Caldwell's work, it is of a very bitter variety that only serves to reinforce the author's dark vision of life. One reviewer, W. M. Frohock, saw this type of humor as Caldwell's greatest strength. In his book *The Novel of Violence in America,* Frohock wrote: "There is a special sort of humor in America, native to our earth and deep-rooted in our history. Its material is the man who has been left behind in the rush to develop our frontiers, the man who has stayed in one place, out of and away from the main current of our developing civilization, so largely untouched by what we think of as progress that his folkways and mores seem to us, at their best, quaint and a little exotic—and, at their worst, degenerate. . . . [This type of humor] has been the main source, as well as the great strength, of Erskine Caldwell's novels."

For the most part, Caldwell's characters exhibit the last quality— degeneracy—far more than the former qualities of quaintness and exoticism. This characteristic has inspired much of the negative reaction against his two best-known novels, *Tobacco Road* and *God's Little Acre.* Southerners in particular have found his graphic descriptions of incest, adultery, lynchings, prostitution, lechery, murder, and the excesses of that "old-time religion" to be extremely offensive. Joseph Wood Krutch observed in *The American Drama since 1918: An Informal History:* "[Of] Mr. Caldwell one may see that the rank flavor of his work is as nearly unique as anything in contemporary literature. . . . like [Faulkner] he loves to contemplate the crimes and perversions of degenerate rustics; like both [Ernest Hemingway and Faulkner], his peculiar effects are made possible only by the assumption of an exaggerated detachment from all the ordinary prejudices of either morality or taste and a consequent tendency to present the most violent and repulsive scenes with the elaborate casualness of a careful pseudo-naivete. . . . His starveling remnant of the Georgia poor-white trash is not only beyond all morality and all sense of dignity or shame, it is almost beyond all hope and fear as well. As ramshackle and as decayed as the moldy cabins in which it lives, it is scarcely more than a parody on humanity."

"That [his] material would fall most easily into a tragic or quasi-tragic pattern is obvious enough," continued Krutch. "Caldwell does violence to all our expectations when he treats it as comedy, but he succeeds because he manages to prevent us from feeling at any moment any real kinship with the nominally human creatures of the play. . . . The characters themselves are represented as creatures so nearly subhuman that their actions are almost without human meaning and that one does not feel with them because they themselves obviously feel so little. . . . [But] his race of curiously depraved and yet curiously juicy human grotesques are alive in his plays whether they, or things like them, were ever alive anywhere else or not . . . and no attempts at analysis can deprive them of their life."

Korges agreed that Caldwell's characters are "alive" and that they personify very real human needs and desires. *Tobacco Road,* he proposed, "is about tenacity in the spirits of men and women deserted by God and man. The book is not about tobacco or Georgia, about sexology, or sociology, but is instead a work of literary art about the animal tug toward life that sustains men even in times of deprivation. . . . Life's major vital signs are eating and sexual intercourse, the two motives wittily, grossly, and magnificently rendered [by the author]. . . . The book is also a study in relationships and desertions. Man in this symbolic landscape is frustrated in his relationship to the soil because fertility has deserted the land. The sterile relationship of man to land is paralleled in the sterile [relationships between the main characters]."

Korges also discovered this same theme of sterility in the novel he considered Caldwell's masterpiece, *God's Little Acre.* He questioned its reputation as an " 'expose' of southern mentality or habits," insisting that it is instead "a novel of rich sexuality, sexuality being in this symbolic landscape . . . the one impressive life-sign. Yet just as the farm produces neither cotton nor gold . . . , so no woman in the novel is pregnant, despite all the sexuality. . . . [But] *God's Little Acre* can be read more meaningfully as a novel about dream and reality, power and impotence, the force of life and the force of death. The characters are studies of how single-mindedness of purpose or desire shapes people and compels them to behave in certain ways as economic, sexual, political, or theological agents. Each character . . . is identified by and with his driving motive. . . . Part of the darkness in Caldwell's vision of life . . . is that [their] yearnings are defeated as they are acted out."

The theme of sterility also appears in a more general sense in Caldwell's work. Despite appearances to the contrary, the preservation of family values plays an important part in his novels. In a less "somber" manner than someone like John Steinbeck, for example, Caldwell emphasized the richness of rural family life as opposed to the sterility and brutality of life in the city. Thus, as Korges pointed out, "the emotional poverty of the city folks is set off against the richness of feeling of the impoverished country folk, free from the economic meanness of making good marriages or of charging for sex."

For the most part, critics of the 1930s did not recognize these subliminal shades of meaning in Caldwell's work. Those who were not disgusted by his stories were amused by what they called his "burlesque"-type humor. Commenting on *Tobacco Road,* for example, Horace Gregory of *Books* noted that "Caldwell's humor, like Mark Twain's, has at its source an imagination that stirs the emotions of the reader. The adolescent, almost idiotic gravity of [his] characters produces instantaneous laughter and their sexual adventures are treated with an irreverence that verges upon the robust ribaldry of a burlesque show." A *Forum* critic reported that "Caldwell recites the orgiastic litany calmly and with a serene detachment. Such detachment is not likely to be shared by most readers, who, if they take the book seriously, will probably finish it—if they do finish it—with disgust and a slight retching; but anyone who considers it as subtle burlesque is going to have a fine time."

The *Nation* reviewer, on the other hand, appeared to sense that there was something more to *Tobacco Road* than just entertainment. He wrote: "The notion has gone about that the deliquescent characters, their squalor, their utter placidity, make Caldwell's writing 'primitive'; his sentence structure has made possible the belief that his work is naive; and because the setting is rural and the humors supposedly exaggerated, he is said to resemble Mark Twain and Bret Harte. These false notions have completely obscured what is an original, mature approach to the incongruities existing in a people who ignore the civilization that contains them as completely as the civilization ignores them."

Though *God's Little Acre* also offended some critics, more seemed willing to identify and comment on its literary merits. The *Saturday Review of Literature* critic, after having admitted that it was a novel "that will lift the noses of the sensitive," concluded that it "is nevertheless a beautifully integrated story of the barren Southern farm and the shut Southern mill, and one of the finest studies of the Southern poor white which has ever come into our literature. . . . Mr. Caldwell has caught in poetic quality the debased and futile aspiration of men and women restless in a world of long hungers which must be satisfied quickly, if at all."

The *Forum* reviewer wrote: "There has been considerable genteel ballyhoo in behalf of Erskine Caldwell but this novel is the first thing he has done which seems to this reader to justify in any way the praise the critics have heaped upon him. Despite its faults . . . it is immensely superior to *Tobacco Road* and *American Earth.* This superiority results from the fact that the author has stressed that element in which he is at his best, poor-white rural comedy."

Horace Gregory, commenting once again in *Books,* also agreed that "as a novel *God's Little Acre* has its faults, and there are flaws that in the work of a less gifted writer would be fatal to his progress. . . . But even as it stands I believe the book is an important step in the development of an important young novelist."

After this 1930s "golden age" came a gradual decline in the quality of Caldwell's work, a decline from which many critics believed the author never really recovered. More and more frequently, noted Korges, Caldwell turned to "sensational plotting and trite characterization . . . mixed with a good deal of superficial psychological comment and superficial motivation." Edward Hoagland of the *New York Times Book Review* declared that Caldwell simply "vegetated." He wrote: "The trouble with Caldwell seems to have been that he was finally lackadaisical. The eye that could distill so narrowly, the decent heart that roamed *Tobacco Road,* . . . rather soon stopped looking for new insights. . . . [In his later works] there is no bite or discipline, no old-pro's vigor of craftsmanship. Even his way with dialogue . . . has fallen off to casual indifference."

Walton Beacham of *Nation* acknowledged the value of Caldwell's early contributions, but essentially agreed with Hoagland that the author failed to grow and change with the public's demands for new material: "Not until Caldwell came along as a portrait painter were there clear models of the Southerner, or one type of Southerner, and Caldwell's books became primers, if not prerequisites, for all the other Southern novels read in subsequent years. . . . For at least a decade [his] characters became synonymous with the Southerner, and readers outside the region believed he alone could instruct them in the Southerner's obscure psyche. . . . Sadly, it has been to Caldwell's detriment that he does his journalism so effectively, and so realistically that we believed he was making the sort of myths and metaphors Hemingway had with his journalistic fiction. . . . Having performed the vital service of unlocking fundamental mysteries of the South, Caldwell's photographs became not only unnecessary but annoying. Yes, yes, we said to Caldwell, you've shown us the ugliness and we know too well how it looks. Show us something else. Make the ugliness into something worthwhile which will alleviate our fears. But Caldwell refused, and he outgrew his usefulness, making a nuisance of himself by continuing to show us the obvious, and refusing to create myths which would help set things right again."

Korges, on the other hand, concluded his study of Caldwell on an optimistic note. He wrote: "Caldwell, now in such disrepute among academic critics, will one day be 'discovered,' and his reputation will rest on a few books. . . . Such a selection from the large and uneven body of Caldwell's writing will make clear the strength of his best work in fiction and nonfiction, and will reveal what is now obscured by the very bulk of his output: his is a solid achievement that supports the assertion that he is one of the important writers of our time."

BIOGRAPHICAL/CRITICAL SOURCES:

BOOKS

Allen, Walter, *The Modern Novel,* Dutton, 1965.
Authors in the News, Volume 1, Gale, 1976.
Beach, Joseph Warren, *American Fiction: 1920-1940,* Russell, 1960.
Caldwell, Erskine, *With All My Might: An Autobiography,* Peachtree Publications, 1987.
Contemporary Authors, Autobiography Series, Volume 1, 1984.
Contemporary Literary Criticism, Gale, Volume 1, 1973, Volume 8, 1978, Volume 14, 1980, Volume 50, 1988.
Dictionary of Literary Biography, Gale, Volume 9: *American Novelists, 1910-1945,* 1981, Volume 86: *American Short-Story Writers, 1910-1945, First Series,* 1989.
Frohock, W. M., *The Novel of Violence in America,* revised edition, Southern Methodist University Press, 1957.
Kazin, Alfred, *On Native Grounds,* Reynal, 1942.
Korges, James, *Erskine Caldwell,* University of Minnesota Press, 1969.
Krutch, Joseph Wood, *The American Drama since 1918: An Informal History,* Random House, 1939.
Newquist, Roy, *Counterpoint,* Rand McNally, 1964.

PERIODICALS

Atlantic, July, 1962, November, 1963, May, 1965, October, 1968.
Best Sellers, September 1, 1968, November 15, 1969.
Book Week, May 23, 1943.
Book World, March 24, 1967.
Books and Bookmen, June, 1968.
Books, February 21, 1932, February 5, 1933.
Chicago Daily Tribune, March 4, 1933.
Commonweal, August 21, 1964.
Forum, May, 1932, March, 1933.
Journal and Constitution (Atlanta), May 13, 1973.
Nation, July 6, 1932, October 18, 1933, June 11, 1977.
National Observer, March 25, 1968.
New Republic, March 23, 1932, February 8, 1933, November 6, 1944.
Newsday, October 11, 1969.
New Statesman, March 17, 1961, August 31, 1962.
Newsweek, April 5, 1965.
New Yorker, May 22, 1965.
New York Herald Tribune Book Review, March 30, 1958, April 5, 1959, June 10, 1962.
New York Times, February 5, 1933, April 25, 1943.

New York Times Book Review, February 23, 1958, March 19, 1961, June 17, 1962, April 4, 1965, January 4, 1970, November 14, 1976.
Playboy, May, 1968.
Punch, May 8, 1968.
Saturday Review, May 2, 1959, May 1, 1965.
Saturday Review of Literature, March 5, 1932, February 18, 1933.
Spectator, August 24, 1962.
Springfield Republican, February 15, 1933.
Time, August 25, 1961, June 19, 1964.
Times Literary Supplement, June 26, 1969.

OBITUARIES:

PERIODICALS

Chicago Tribune, April 13, 1987.
Dallas Times Herald, April 13, 1987.
Detroit Free Press, April 13, 1987.
Los Angeles Times, April 13, 1987.
New York Post, April 13, 1987.
New York Times, April 13, 1987.
Time, April 20, 1987.
Washington Post, April 13, 1987.*

*   *   *

CALLAGHAN, Morley Edward   1903-

PERSONAL: Born September 22, 1903, in Toronto, Ontario, Canada; son of Thomas and Mary (Dewan) Callaghan; married Loretto Florence Dee, April 16, 1927; children: Michael, Barry. *Education:* St. Michael's College, University of Toronto, B.A., 1925; Osgoode Hall Law School, LL.B., 1928.

ADDRESSES: Home—20 Dale Ave., Toronto, Ontario, Canada.

CAREER: Novelist and short story writer, 1926—. Worked as reporter on *Toronto Daily Star* while in college; stories written during this time found their way, via Ernest Herningway, into Paris literary magazines of that day, including Ezra Pound's *Exile,* and he gave up the idea of practicing law to become a professional writer. Spent a year in Paris, 1928-29, other periods in New York and Pennsylvania, before returning to Toronto, Ontario, to live. Worked during World War II with the Royal Canadian Navy on assignment for the National Film Board, and traveled across Canada as chairman of the radio program "Citizen's Forum."

AWARDS, HONORS: Governor General's Literary Award for fiction (Canada), 1952, for *The Loved and the Lost;* gold medal of Royal achievement of special significance in imaginative literature, 1960; medal of merit, City of Toronto, 1962; LL.D., University of Western Ontario, 1965; Canada Council Molson prize ($15,000), 1970; Royal Bank of Canada award ($50,000) for distinguished work, 1970.

WRITINGS:

NOVELS

Strange Fugitive, Scribner, 1928, Hurtig, 1970.
It's Never Over, Scribner, 1930, reprinted, Macmillan (Toronto), 1972.
No Man's Meat (also see below; novella), Edward W. Titus, At the Sign of the Black Manikin (Paris), 1931.
A Broken Journey, Scribner, 1932, reprinted, Macmillan (Toronto), 1976.

Such Is My Beloved, Scribner, 1934, reissued with an introduction by Malcolm Ross, McClelland & Stewart, 1957.

They Shall Inherit the Earth (also see below), Random House, 1935, reissued with an introduction by F. W. Watt, McClelland & Stewart, 1962.

More Joy in Heaven, Random House, 1937, reissued with an introduction by Hugo McPherson, McClelland & Stewart, 1960.

The Varsity Story, Macmillan, 1948.

Luke Baldwin's Vow (juvenile), Winston, 1948, reprinted, Scholastic Inc., 1974.

The Loved and the Lost, Macmillan, 1951.

The Many Colored Coat, Coward, 1960, original magazine version published as *The Man with the Coat,* Exile Editions, 1988.

A Passion in Rome, Coward, 1961.

A Fine and Private Place, Mason/Charter, 1975.

Close to the Sun Again, Macmillan, 1977.

No Man's Meat and The Enchanted Pimp, Macmillan (Toronto), 1978.

A Time for Judas, Macmillan (Toronto), 1983, St. Martin's, 1984.

Our Lady of the Snows, Macmillan (Toronto), 1985, St. Martin's, 1986.

OTHER

A Native Argosy (short stories), Scribner, 1929, Books for Libraries, 1970.

Now That April's Here, and Other Stories, Random House, 1937.

"Turn Again Home" (play; based on the novel *They Shall Inherit the Earth*), first produced in New York City, 1940, produced under title "Going Home" by the New Play Society, Toronto, 1950.

"To Tell the Truth" (play), first produced by the New Play Society, Toronto, 1949.

Morley Callaghan's Stories, Macmillan, 1959, 2 volume edition, MacGibbon & Kee, 1962.

That Summer in Paris: Memories of Tangled Friendships with Hemingway, Fitzgerald, and Some Others, Coward, 1963.

Stories, Macmillan (Toronto), 1967.

An Autumn Penitent, Macmillan (Toronto), 1973.

The Lost and Found Stories of Morley Callaghan, Lester & Orpen Dennys/Exile Editions, 1985.

Contributor of short stories to *Scribner's, New Yorker, Harper's Bazaar, Maclean's, Esquire, Cosmopolitan, Saturday Evening Post, Yale Review,* and numerous other magazines.

SIDELIGHTS: Edmund Wilson wrote in *0 Canada:* "The Canadian Morley Callaghan, at one time well known in the United States, is today perhaps the most unjustly neglected novelist in the English-speaking world." Wilson noted that "when I talked about Callaghan [in the late 1950s], such people as remembered his existence were likely to think he was dead." Wilson offers several explanations for the fact that Callaghan is virtually unknown outside his native country, the most "striking" reason being "the partial isolation of that country [Canada] from the rest of the cultural world. . . . My further reading of Callaghan's novels has suggested another reason . . . for their relative unpopularity. Almost all of them end in annihilating violence or, more often, in blank unfulfillment. . . . All these endings have their moral point: recognition of personal guilt, loyalty in personal relationships, the nobility of some reckless devotion to a Christian ideal of love which is bound to come to grief in the world. But they are probably too bleak for the ordinary reader. . . . Only a very sober, self-disciplined and 'self-directed' writer could have persisted, from decade to decade, in submitting these parables to the public. They are almost invariably tragic, but their tragedy avoids convulsions and it allows itself no outbreak in tirades."

In *That Summer in Paris* Callaghan documents his experiences as a *Toronto Daily Star* cub reporter and his 1929 trip to Paris, where he became acquainted with and formed opinions on various literary figures, most notably Ernest Hemingway and F. Scott Fitzgerald. William Saroyan said in a review: "Each of the three writers was waging a fight of some kind that the others did not know about, could scarcely guess about, and could not help with. Callaghan's fight seems to have been the easiest—simply to write well and to go on writing well, which he managed to do, which he is still doing, which he does in this book, slight and anecdotal as it is."

Wilson mentioned the universal appeal of Callaghan's work, a quality cited frequently in critical reviews: "The novels of Morley Callaghan do not deal with his native Canada in any editorial or informative way, nor are they aimed at any popular taste, Canadian, 'American' or British. They center on situations of primarily psychological interest that are treated from a moral point of view yet without making moral judgments of any conventional kind." A *Canadian Forum* columnist called *Morley Callaghan's Stories* "one of the few major achievements of Canadian prose, more powerful than any single Callaghan novel and more worthy of enduring than any single work of his better publicized peers: Anderson, Hemingway and Fitzgerald. Mr. Callaghan does have his limits: he plays no games with time and infinity. Literary innovations leave him cold, the corporational vulture which feeds us all never enters into his fiction. . . . There is one major unreality to which he returns time and time again: emotion. . . . But for his era, when the media, the false prophets, the corporations, did not place so much underbrush between the human being and life (underbrush which the modern writer must deal with), Callaghan created a method that worked extraordinarily well. Never has the urban low bourgeois been dealt with quite so humanely, quite so creatively."

MEDIA ADAPTATIONS: In 1958 Klenman-Davidson Productions filmed *Now That April's Here.*

AVOCATIONAL INTERESTS: Spectator sports.

BIOGRAPHICAL/CRITICAL SOURCES:

BOOKS

Cameron, Donald, *Conversations with Canadian Novelists, Part Two,* Macmillan (Toronto), 1973.

Conron, Brandon, *Morley Callaghan,* Twayne, 1966.

Contemporary Literary Criticism, Gale, Volume 3, 1975, Volume 14, 1980, Volume 41, 1987.

Dictionary of Literary Biography, Volume 68: *Canadian Writers, 1920-1959,* Gale, 1988.

Hoar, Victor, *Morley Callaghan,* Copp, 1969.

Lecker, Robert and Jack David, editors, *The Annotated Bibliography of Canada's Major Authors 5,* ECW Press, 1984.

Morley, Patricia, *Morley Callaghan,* McClelland & Stewart, 1978.

Wilson, Edmund, *O Canada,* Farrar, Straus, 1965.

PERIODICALS

Canadian Forum, March, 1960, February, 1968.

Canadian Literature, summer, 1964.

Dalhousie Review, autumn, 1959.

New Republic, February 9, 1963.

New Yorker, November 26, 1960.

Queen's Quarterly, autumn, 1957.
Tamarack Review, winter, 1962.

* * *

CARR, John Dickson 1906-1977
(Carr Dickson, Carter Dickson)

PERSONAL: Born November 30, 1906, in Uniontown, Pa.; died February 27, 1977, in Greenville, S.C.; son of Wood Nicholas (a U.S. Congressman and the postmaster of Uniontown) and Julia Carr; married Clarice Cleaves, 1931; children: Julia, Bonita, Mary. *Education:* Haverford College, graduate, 1928.

CAREER: Writer, 1930-77. British Broadcasting Corp., London, England, radio script writer during Second World War.

MEMBER: Mystery Writers of America (president, 1949), Baker Street Irregulars; Detection Club (honorary secretary), Savage Club, and Garrick Club (all London).

AWARDS, HONORS: Edgar Allan Poe Award, Mystery Writers of America, 1949, for *The Life of Sir Arthur Conan Doyle,* and 1969; Grand Master Award, Mystery Writers of America, 1962; received two prizes from *Ellery Queen's Mystery Magazine,* one for the story "The Gentleman from Paris."

WRITINGS:

Poison in Jest, Harper, 1932, reprinted, Macmillan, 1985.
(Under pseudonym Carr Dickson) *The Bowstring Murders,* Morrow, 1933.
The Burning Court, Harper, 1937, reprinted, International Polygonics, 1985.
(Under pseudonym Carter Dickson, with John Rhode) *Fatal Descent,* Dodd, Mead, 1939, (published in England as *Drop to His Death,* Heinemann, 1939).
The Emperor's Snuffbox, Harper, 1942, reprinted, Carroll & Graf, 1986.
The Bride of Newgate, Harper, 1950, reprinted, Carroll & Graf, 1986.
The Devil in Velvet, Harper, 1951, reprinted, Carroll & Graf, 1987.
The Nine Wrong Answers, Harper, 1952, reprinted, Carroll & Graf, 1986.
Captain Cut-Throat, Harper, 1955, reprinted, Carroll & Graf, 1988.
Patrick Butler for the Defense, Harper, 1956.
(Under pseudonym Carter Dickson) *Fear Is the Same,* Morrow, 1956.
Fire, Burn!, Harper, 1957, reprinted, Carroll & Graf, 1987.
Scandal at High Chimneys: A Victorian Melodrama, Harper, 1959, reprinted, Carroll & Graf, 1988.
The Witch of the Lowtide: An Edwardian Melodrama, Harper, 1961.
The Demoniacs, Harper, 1962.
Papa La-Bas, Harper, 1968, reprinted, Carroll & Graf, 1989.
The Ghosts' High Noon, Harper, 1969.
Deadly Hall, Harper, 1971, reprinted, Carroll & Graf, 1989.
The Hungry Goblin: A Victorian Detective Novel, Harper, 1972.

"HENRI BENCOLIN" MYSTERY NOVELS

It Walks by Night, Harper, 1930, reprinted, Zebra Books, 1986.
Castle Skull, Harper, 1931, reprinted, Zebra Books, 1987.
The Lost Gallows, Harper, 1931, reprinted, Carroll & Graf, 1986.
The Corpse in the Waxworks, Harper, 1932, reprinted, Macmillan, 1984, (published in England as *The Waxworks Murder,* Hamish Hamilton, 1932).

The Four False Weapons; Being the Return of Bencolin, Harper, 1937, reprinted, 1989.

"DR. GIDEON FELL" MYSTERY NOVELS

Hag's Nook, Harper, 1933, reprinted, International Polygonics, 1985.
The Mad Hatter Mystery, Harper, 1933, reprinted, 1989.
The Blind Barber, Harper, 1934, published as *The Case of the Blind Barber,* Macmillan, 1984.
The Eight of Swords, Harper, 1934, reprinted, Zebra Books, 1986.
Death-Watch, Harper, 1935.
The Three Coffins, Harper, 1935, reprinted, International Polygonics, 1986, (published in England as *The Hollow Man,* Hamish Hamilton, 1935).
The Arabian Nights Murder, Harper, 1936, reprinted, 1989.
To Wake the Dead, Harper, 1938, reprinted, 1989.
The Crooked Hinge, Harper, 1938, reprinted, 1989.
The Problem of the Green Capsule, Harper, 1939, reprinted, International Polygonics, 1986, (published in England as *The Black Spectacles,* Hamish Hamilton, 1939).
The Problem of the Wire Cage, Harper, 1939, reprinted, State Mutual Book, 1982.
The Man Who Could Not Shudder, Harper, 1940.
The Case of the Constant Suicides, Harper, 1941, reprinted, 1989.
Death Turns the Tables, Harper, 1941, reprinted, International Polygonics, 1985, (published in England as *The Seat of the Scornful,* Hamish Hamilton, 1942).
Till Death Do Us Part, Harper, 1944, reprinted, International Polygonics, 1989.
He Who Whispers, Harper, 1946, reprinted, International Polygonics, 1986.
The Sleeping Sphinx, Harper, 1947, reprinted, International Polygonics, 1985.
The Dead Man's Knock, Harper, 1948, reprinted, Zebra Books, 1987.
Below Suspicion, Harper, 1949, reprinted, International Polygonics, 1986.
In Spite of Thunder, Harper, 1960, reprinted, Carroll & Graf, 1987.
The House at Satan's Elbow, Harper, 1965, reprinted, International Polygonics, 1987.
Panic in Box C, Harper, 1966, reprinted, Carroll & Graf, 1987.
Dark of the Moon, Harper, 1967, reprinted, Carroll & Graf, 1987.

STORY COLLECTIONS

(Under pseudonym Carter Dickson) *The Department of Queer Complaints,* Morrow, 1940, published as *Scotland Yard: Department of Queer Complaints,* Dell, 1944.
Dr. Fell, Detective, and Other Stories, Spivak, 1947.
The Third Bullet and Other Stories, Harper, 1954.
(With Adrian Conan Doyle) *The Exploits of Sherlock Holmes,* Random House, 1954.
The Men Who Explained Miracles, Harper, 1963.
The Door to Doom and Other Detections, edited by Douglas C. Greene, Harper, 1980.

NONFICTION

The Murder of Sir Edmund Godfrey, Harper, 1936, reprinted, International Polygonics, 1989.
The Life of Sir Arthur Conan Doyle, Harper, 1949, reprinted, Carroll & Graf, 1987.
(Contributor) Francis M. Nevins, Jr., editor, *The Mystery Writer's Art,* Bowling Green University Popular Press, 1970.

EDITOR

Maiden Murders, Harper, 1952.

Arthur Conan Doyle, *Great Stories,* British Book Centre, 1959.

RADIO SCRIPTS

The Dead Sleep Lightly (collection of radio scripts), edited by Douglas C. Greene, Doubleday, 1983.

Also author of over 75 scripts for "Appointment with Fear," "Suspense," "Cabin B-13," "The Silent Battle," and other radio shows of the 1930s and 1940s.

UNDER PSEUDONYM CARTER DICKSON; "SIR HENRY MERRIVALE" MYSTERY NOVELS

The Plague Court Murders, Morrow, 1934.

The White Priory Murders, Morrow, 1934.

The Red Widow Murders, Morrow, 1935, reprinted, International Polygonics, 1988.

The Unicorn Murders, Morrow, 1935, reprinted, International Polygonics, 1989.

The Magic Lantern Murders, Heinemann, 1936, published as *The Punch and Judy Murders,* Morrow, 1937, reprinted, International Polygonics, 1988.

The Third Bullet, Hodder & Stoughton, 1937.

The Peacock Feather Murders, Morrow, 1937, reprinted, International Polygonics, 1987, (published in England as *The Ten Teacups,* Heinemann, 1937).

Death in Five Boxes, Morrow, 1938, reprinted, Dorchester Publishing, 1977.

The Judas Window, Morrow, 1938, reprinted, International Polygonics, 1987, published as *The Crossbow Murders,* Berkley Publishing, 1964, reprinted, Zebra Books, 1989.

The Reader Is Warned, Morrow, 1939.

And So to Murder, Morrow, 1940, reprinted, Zebra Books, 1988.

Nine—And Death Makes Ten, Morrow, 1940, reprinted, International Polygonics, 1987, published as *Murder in the Atlantic,* World Publishing, 1950, (published in England as *Murder in the Submarine Zone,* Heinemann, 1950).

Seeing Is Believing, Morrow, 1941, published as *Cross of Murder,* World Publishing, 1959.

The Gilded Man, Morrow, 1942, reprinted, International Polygonics, 1988, published as *Death and the Gilded Man,* Pocket Books, 1947.

She Died a Lady, Morrow, 1943, reprinted, Zebra Books, 1987.

He Wouldn't Kill Patience, Morrow, 1944, reprinted, International Polygonics, 1988.

The Curse of the Bronze Lamp, Morrow, 1945, reprinted, Carroll & Graf, 1984, (published in England as *Lord of the Sorcerers,* Heinemann, 1946).

My Late Wives, Morrow, 1946, reprinted, Zebra Books, 1988.

The Skeleton in the Clock, Morrow, 1948, reprinted, Dorchester Publishing, 1977.

A Graveyard to Let, Morrow, 1949, reprinted, Dorchester Publishing, 1978.

Night at the Mocking Widow, Morrow, 1950, reprinted, Zebra Books, 1988.

Behind the Crimson Blind, Morrow, 1952, reprinted, Zebra Books, 1989.

The Cavalier's Cup, Morrow, 1953, reprinted, Zebra Books, 1987.

SIDELIGHTS: As the author of seventy novels, the creator of the historical mystery, the writer of some of radio's finest mystery programs, and the official biographer of Sir Arthur Conan Doyle, John Dickson Carr was one of the mystery field's most esteemed figures. In a tribute to the author in the *Armchair De-*

tective, R. E. Briney described Carr as "a master of the classic detective story and an unparalleled exponent of the 'locked room' or 'impossible crime' story." In 1962 he was named a Grand Master by the Mystery Writers of America for his many contributions to the genre.

"If there's one thing I can't stand, it's a nice *healthy* murder," Carr once complained to Robert Lewis Taylor of the *New Yorker.* No such murders found their way into Carr's many novels. He specialized in a rather macabre, atmospheric brand of mystery fiction in which there was always a hint of the supernatural. His murders occurred in such exotic locales as opium dens, waxworks, and medieval castles. "His books," Julian Symons wrote in *Mortal Consequences: A History—From the Detective Story to the Crime Novel,* "are full of reference to macabre events and possibilities." Carr had "one of the murkiest imaginations in the entire field of letters," Taylor explained. The critic added that "It is Carr's Halloween mind that sets him apart." Commenting on *The Crooked Hinge,* a *New York Times* reviewer called Carr "an unexcelled master in this field of creepy erudition, swift-moving excitement, and suspense through atmosphere." Speaking of *The Arabian Nights Murders,* the *Manchester Guardian* critic noted that Carr "conveys admirably the atmosphere of mingled farce and terror, and one can always be sure that through the maze of marvels he constructs he will guide his readers by the thread of logic and sound reasoning."

Like other Golden Age mystery writers of the 1930s, Carr was adept at writing an intricate puzzler. The locked room mystery, or "impossible crime" story, was his particular forte. Donald A. Yates, writing in *Armchair Detective,* found that Carr specialized in "making the seemingly impossible possible. . . . His favorite and most entertaining pastime [was] creating and solving one locked room puzzle after another." In *It Walks by Night,* the victim is found beheaded in a room whose only two doors were constantly under observation by police officers. In *The Problem of the Wire Cage,* the victim is found strangled in the middle of a clay tennis court, and only his own footprints lead to the body. One of the finest examples of the locked room mystery, according to George N. Dove in *Clues: A Journal of Detection,* is Carr's *The Three Coffins* (published in England as *The Hollow Man*). Dove called the book "a real masterpiece of complexity." In that novel, Carr even included a "Locked Room Lecture" which Symons called "a splendidly lively and learned discussion of locked-room murders and their possible solutions."

Under his own name, Carr wrote mystery novels featuring Dr. Gideon Fell, a portly, flamboyant figure modeled after G. K. Chesterton. Under the pseudonym Carter Dickson he chronicled the cases of Sir Henry Merrivale, a "buffoon given to profanity, with a lordly sneer," as a writer for the *New York Times* described him. Both detectives are among the mystery genre's most popular characters. Carr's series detectives, according to Briney, "will last as long as the detective itself."

In addition to his mystery novels set in the present day, Carr also pioneered the historical mystery genre—puzzlers set in a meticulously-researched historical setting. The first of these books, *The Bride of Newgate,* was set in the England of the early nineteenth century and dealt with the murder of a leading lord. It was followed by *The Devil in Velvet,* in which a Cambridge professor solves a seventeenth century murder. That book proved to be one of Carr's most popular works, outselling all of his other novels. In *The Hungry Goblin* Carr enjoyed a little twist on his own formula, portraying 19th century British novelist Wilkie Collins as a detective.

During the Second World War, Carr worked for the British Broadcasting Corp. as a writer of propaganda broadcasts about the work of the Resistance movement in occupied Europe. At this time he also originated the popular "Suspense" and "Appointment with Fear" radio series for which he wrote some seventy-five scripts. These scripts were written, Carr once explained, "under the slight difficulty that during the blitz our house was twice demolished while we were inside it." Francis M. Nevins, Jr., in an article for *Armchair Detective*, claimed that Carr's "scripts for 'Suspense' . . . are among the finest mysteries ever written for radio and remain a superb listening experience almost thirty-five years later."

In 1949, Carr was approached by the family of Sir Arthur Conan Doyle to write the official biography of the creator of Sherlock Holmes. Working with family letters, Doyle's notebooks, and what the *New York Times* described as "whole rooms full of personal papers," Carr assembled a "vital and exciting portrait of Sir Arthur," as Elizabeth Johnson of *Commonweal* noted. Writing in the *San Francisco Chronicle*, J. H. Jackson called the biography "a beautiful piece of work. . . . Most will finish the book feeling that they have met an extraordinarily many-sided man, an individual who lived with gusto and vigor the kind of life he believed to be good. . . . Part of this is Doyle himself; part of it is Carr's skill. The combination makes a notable biography."

Carr explained his prolific output as the result of long, hard work. He typically wrote "all day every day, including Sunday, and often far into the night," as Taylor recounted. Carr was once quoted as saying, "I insisted on loafing 18 hours a day at the typewriter ever since I was old enough to know one letter from another." The owner of a vast reference library on such subjects as crime, witchcraft, poison, and murder, he was rarely stuck for an idea. "Plotting," Taylor related, "is easy for Carr—he habitually sees the entire network of human relations as a slough of intrigue—and the blocking out of the separate scenes is perhaps his favorite chore. He hates the actual writing, however, and does it in anguish, emerging from each long session hollow-eyed and spent."

Described by W. Murchison, Jr., of *National Review* as "an unapologetic Tory—an old-fashioned champion of gentility, taste, standards and romance," Carr possessed, according to John Boland of *Books and Bookmen*, an "impeccable style," while his books featured "the faultless construction that we have long come to accept as his trade mark." In his essay for *The Mystery Writer's Art*, Carr defined a mystery novel as "a hoodwinking contest, a duel between author and reader." His formula for a successful mystery? "Merely state your evidence," he advised, "and the reader will mislead himself."

MEDIA ADAPTATIONS: The short story "Death in the Dressing Room" was adapted as an episode in the "Murder Clinic" radio series and first broadcast by the British Broadcasting Corp., September 29, 1942; the short story "Man with a Cloak" was filmed in 1951, "Dangerous Crossing" in 1953, and "Colonel March of Scotland Yard" in 1954; *Fire, Burn!* was adapted for radio by John Keir Cross and first broadcast by the BBC, July 5, 1958; *The Hollow Man* was adapted for radio by Cross and first broadcast by the BBC, January 10, 1959; *The Emperor's Snuffbox* was filmed as "City after Midnight" in 1959; the film rights to the short story "The Gentleman from Paris" were sold.

BIOGRAPHICAL/CRITICAL SOURCES:

BOOKS

Contemporary Literary Criticism, Volume 3, Gale, 1975.

French, Larry L., editor, *Notes for the Curious: A John Dickson Carr Memorial Journal*, Carrian (Chesterfield, Mo.), 1978.
Haycraft, Howard, *Murder for Pleasure: The Life and Times of the Detective Story*, Appleton, 1941.
Hoyt, C. A., editor, *Minor American Novelists*, Southern Illinois University Press, 1970.
Nevins, Francis M., Jr., editor, *The Mystery Writer's Art*, Bowling Green University Popular Press, 1970.
Symons, Julian, *Mortal Consequences: A History—From the Detective Story to the Crime Novel*, Harper, 1972.

PERIODICALS

Armchair Detective, January, 1970, October, 1978, winter, 1979.
Books and Bookmen, December, 1971.
Clues: A Journal of Detection, fall/winter, 1986.
Life, December 29, 1953.
Manchester Guardian, March 6, 1936.
National Review, October 8, 1971.
New Yorker, January 20, 1945, September 8, 1951, September 15, 1951.
New York Times, January 9, 1938, October 16, 1938.
Publishers Weekly, June 27, 1960.

OBITUARIES:

PERIODICALS

Armchair Detective, April, 1977.
Newsweek, March 14, 1977.
New York Times, March 1, 1977.
Time, March 14, 1977.
Washington Post, March 2, 1977.*

—*Sketch by Thomas Wiloch*

*   *   *

CAULDWELL, Frank
See KING, Francis (Henry)

*   *   *

CAUTE, David 1936-
(John Salisbury)

PERSONAL: Born December 16, 1936, in Alexandria, Egypt; son of Edward (a colonel in the British Army Dental Corps) and Rebecca Caute; married Catherine Shuckburgh, 1961 (marriage dissolved, 1970); married Martha Bates (an editor), 1973; children: (first marriage) Daniel, Edward; (second marriage) Rebecca, Anna. *Education:* Wadham College, Oxford, B.A., 1959, M.A. and D.Phil., 1963. *Politics:* Labour Party. *Religion:* Atheist.

ADDRESSES: Home—41 Westcroft Sq., London W6 0TA, England.

CAREER: Writer. All Souls College, Oxford University, Oxford, England, fellow, 1959-65; Harvard University, Cambridge, MA, Henry fellow, 1960-61; Brunel University, Uxbridge, England, reader in social and political theory, 1967-70. Visiting professor, New York University, 1966-67, Columbia University, 1966-67, and University of Bristol, 1985; University of California, regents lecturer, 1974. *New Statesman*, London, England, literary editor, 1979-81. Writers Guild of Great Britain, co-chairman, 1981-82. *Military service:* British Army, 1955-56.

AWARDS, HONORS: London Authors' Club Award and John Llewelyn Rhys Prize, both 1960, both for *At Fever Pitch*.

WRITINGS:

At Fever Pitch (novel), Deutsch, 1959, Pantheon, 1960.

Comrade Jacob (novel), Deutsch, 1961, Pantheon, 1962.

Songs for an Autumn Rifle (play), first produced at the Edinburgh Festival by the Oxford Theatre Group, 1961.

Communism and the French Intellectuals, 1914-1960, Macmillan, 1964.

The Left in Europe since 1789, McGraw, 1966.

The Decline of the West (novel), Macmillan, 1966.

(Editor) *The Essential Writings of Karl Marx,* Macmillan, 1967.

The Demonstration (play; first produced at Nottingham Playhouse, 1969; also see below), Deutsch, 1970.

Frantz Fanon (monograph), Viking, 1970 (published in England as *Fanon,* Fontana, 1970).

The Occupation (novel; also see below), Deutsch, 1971, McGraw, 1972.

The Illusion: An Essay on Politics, Theatre and the Novel (also see below), Deutsch, 1971, Harper, 1972.

The Confrontation: A Trilogy (contains *The Demonstration, The Occupation,* and *The Illusion: An Essay on Politics, Theatre and the Novel*), Deutsch, 1971.

(With Ralph Miliband) *Nineteenth-Century European Socialism,* BFA Educational Media (Santa Monica, CA), 1972.

The Fellow-Travellers: A Postscript to the Enlightenment, Macmillan, 1973, revised and expanded edition published as *The Fellow-Travellers: Intellectual Friends of Communism,* Yale University Press, 1988.

Fallout (play), first broadcast on British Broadcasting Corp. (BBC Radio), 1973.

The Fourth World (play), first produced in London at the Royal Court Theatre, 1973.

Cuba, Yes?, McGraw, 1974.

Collisions: Essays and Reviews, Quartet Books, 1974.

The Great Fear: The Anti-Communist Purge under Truman and Eisenhower, Simon & Schuster, 1978.

(Under pseudonym John Salisbury) *The Baby-Sitters* (novel), Atheneum, 1978, published as *The Hour before Midnight,* Dell, 1980.

Brecht and Company (television screenplay), first produced on BBC-TV, 1979.

(Under pseudonym John Salisbury) *Moscow Gold* (novel), Futura, 1980.

Under the Skin: The Death of White Rhodesia, Northwestern University Press, 1983.

The Zimbabwe Tapes (radio play), first produced on BBC Radio, 1983.

The K-Factor (novel), M. Joseph, 1983.

The Espionage of the Saints: Two Essays on Silence and the State, Hamish Hamilton, 1986.

News from Nowhere (novel), Hamish Hamilton, 1986.

Henry and the Dogs (radio play), first produced on BBC Radio, 1986.

Sanctions (radio play), first produced on BBC Radio, 1988.

The Year of the Barricades: A Journey through 1968, Harper, 1988 (published in England as *'68: The Year of the Barricades,* Hamish Hamilton, 1988).

Veronica or The Two Nations (novel), Hamish Hamilton, 1989, Arcade/Little, Brown, 1990.

Contributor to periodicals, including *New Statesman, Partisan Review, Times Literary Supplement,* and *Spectator.*

MEDIA ADAPTATIONS: Comrade Jacob was adapted as the 1975 film, "Winstanley," directed by Kevin Brownlow.

SIDELIGHTS: David Caute, an English novelist, playwright, and historian, has consistently dealt with the subjects of socialism, communism, and the relationship between the West and Third World countries in his writings. His interest in these areas has lead him to write several novels dealing with important political events in Africa. But the author's forays into so many different genres—plays, novels, political theory, and history—"makes one cast about anxiously for some common thread, a unifying theme," says Alan Ryan in *Listener.* That thread is defined by the author in his *Collisions: Essays and Reviews* as "the inclination to walk to and fro across the bridges which join, or can be made to join, history, politics and literature." Thus, the author has striven to write fiction and nonfiction books that deal with themes that are pertinent to society as a whole. Caute, remarks *Dictionary of Literary Biography* contributor Gerald Steel, "is one of the most intellectually stimulating novelists of recent decades in England—a 'public' rather than a 'private' writer." In the United States, however, his work has not received as much attention as it has in England.

A number of Caute's books are drawn from his own personal experiences. *At Fever Pitch,* his first novel, is based on his adventures as an infantryman stationed in the Gold Coast just before it became independent Ghana. In this story, the author parallels soldier Michael Glyn's personal voyage towards sexual maturity with the confrontations between the British and Africans. Tying these two subjects together, Caute attempts what Steel calls an "exploration of the sexual psychology of militarism." Reviewers like *Spectator* writer Simon Raven have described the novelist's blending of sexual and military themes as "vigorous, intelligent and keen," but they have also complained that Caute tries to do too much. The "organization of the book suffers as a result," concludes one *Times Literary Supplement* reviewer. However, overall reception of *At Fever Pitch* has been positive, and it received the London Authors Club Award and John Llewelyn Rhys Memorial Prize.

Since *At Fever Pitch,* Caute has written several more novels set in Africa that address the issue of the exploitation of Africans by white colonists. The most ambitious of these books, *The Decline of the West,* has garnered a great deal of criticism. Set in the fictional African country of Coppernica, *The Decline of the West* describes the post-revolutionary turmoil of a newly-independent nation similar to that which existed in Zaire and Algeria during their formative years. Some critics have felt that this novel about how Europeans justified their violent acts in Africa by falling back on biased beliefs in white superiority relies too heavily upon history. One *Times Literary Supplement* reviewer, for example, writes that though the premise of *The Decline of the West* is "politically sound," the "characters are papier-mache versions of real public figures." In a *New York Times Book Review* article, Laurence LaFore comments that *The Decline of the West* "is perhaps better as fictional history than as a work of art, but it is still an important and imposing novel." There have also been critics—such as *New Leader* contributor Raymond Rosenthal—who believe that violence is overemphasized in the novel. There is, attests Rosenthal, a "hysterical wallowing in violence and torture . . . in almost every paragraph of Caute's book." However, Rosenthal does not doubt Caute's "sincere desire to help the Africans in their struggle for independence, or at least to illuminate their struggle." And LaFore concludes that "the author's task, an enormous one, has been impressively completed. . . . He has advanced an important thesis, conceived an important tragedy and composed a fascinating story."

Zimbabwe, formerly Rhodesia, is the subject of two more of Caute's novels and his nonfiction work, *Under the Skin—The*

Death of White Rhodesia, which concerns the author's first-hand reports and impressions of the last days of white rule in that country. *The K-Factor* is a fictional "re-working" of *Under the Skin* dealing with racial stratification in Rhodesia, according to Roger Owen in the *Times Literary Supplement.* As with Caute's other novels, a number of reviewers feel that the author gets mixed results by attempting to blend complicated personal situations with political events. London *Times* critic Isabel Raphael, for one, asserts that "Caute tells a good, tense story, and writes sharp, fast-moving dialogue. But he tries to keep too many balls in the air at once." In *News from Nowhere,* the story of an author and academician who travels to Rhodesia just as Caute had, similar remarks about the author's penchant for complicated plotting have been made by critics. Victoria Glendinning remarks in the London *Times* that the reporter's "adventures amid the faction-fighting and betrayals of emerging Zimbabwe are frankly confusing, as is some of the writing." But she likens Caute's intricate plotting techniques to those of John le Carre as providing a "pleasurable confusion. It never did le Carre any harm."

Like the character Richard Stern in *News from Nowhere,* the protagonist Steven Bright in Caute's trilogy, *The Confrontation,* is an academician. Bright resembles his creator in a number of ways: he is the author of a book entitled *The Rise of the East,* which many critics have noted is similar to Caute's *The Decline of the West,* has strong leanings toward leftist politics, resigned from All Souls College for political reasons, and has taught at New York University. *The Confrontation* consists of a play, *The Demonstration,* an essay ostensibly written by Bright, *The Illusion,* and a novel, *The Occupation.* "The trilogy indicates that Bright is Dr. Caute's alter ego," observes a *Times Literary Supplement* writer. "This is not a reader's deduction but an explicit suggestion by the author, repeated several times. These may not be autobiographical works but they are certainly confessional ones."

Alienation—the gap between people's public and private lives—and the factors that cause it, such as the difference between art and reality, the generation gap, and the political struggles between left and right, is a major theme of all three books in *The Confrontation. The Illusion* addresses this subject as it relates to literature, favoring a Marxist/Brechtian approach to writing. As Bernard Bergonzi explains in *The Contemporary English Novel,* "Bright-Caute argues for an alignment of revolutionary art and radical politics; for a literature and theatre that will be dialectical in the play between art and reality—*contra* the structuralists, who are scathingly treated in *The Illusion,* Caute believes in distinguishing between the two—and for an exposure of the essentially illusory nature of fictional and dramatic realism, and the necessity of alienation as Brecht understood it."

The Demonstration, explains John Russell Taylor in his *The Second Wave: British Drama for the Seventies,* "illuminat[es] many of the problems the dramatist faces if he tries to use contemporary reality as the basis of art." In this play, Steven Bright is a drama professor in England who tries to control his young, rebellious students by redirecting their energies against the establishment into a play called *Pentagon 37.* But Bright's plan backfires when illusion and reality change places and "he is brought to a realization of his own rejection and impotence." Bright's character is firmly against what he considers the decadence of capitalism, but at the same time he fears the extremist practices of his students. He wants to "keep conscience, comforts and status equally intact," observes Benedict Nightingale in *New Statesman,* but the irreconcilability of these aims ultimately results in his disillusionment.

The Occupation, which follows Bright's life as a visiting professor in New York several years before the events in *The Demonstration,* involves his personal struggle to understand his place in the world, a personal preoccupation that eventually leads to a breakdown. The plot, says *National Review* critic John R. Coyne, Jr., is surrealistic, centering on "scenes occurring either in [Bright's] office or in his mind or both in which he argues with sitting-in New Left students." Bergonzi notices that *The Occupation* represents Caute's "rejection of the Old Left" attitudes that are represented by the character Hamilton Snout, "an ageing socialist hack writer and editor." Furthermore, Bergonzi surmises that because Snout applauds Bright's *The Rise of the East* "Caute may here be . . . disowning *The Decline of the West.*"

During his career, Caute has written numerous fiction and nonfiction works centering on leftist politics. His second novel, *Comrade Jacob,* relates the story of Gerard Winstanley's attempt to establish a collective settlement during Oliver Cromwell's rule. It is an allegory about contemporary communism, and as such Bergonzi chides in a *Spectator* review that one "is constantly aware of the Marxist spectacles through which [Caute] regards his subject." Nevertheless, Bergonzi describes *Comrade Jacob* as a "well-written and highly intelligent book." Similarly, a *Times Literary Supplement* reviewer calls the novel "a remarkable, and moving, evocation of a stirring and significant experiment in English history."

Another fiction work, the play *Songs for an Autumn Rifle,* about the 1956 revolt in Hungary, is also directly concerned with socialism; but most of Caute's books that deal directly with socialism and communism have been nonfiction. Such works as *Communism and the French Intellectuals, 1914-1960, The Fellow-Travellers: Intellectual Friends of Communism,* and *The Great Fear: The Anti-Communist Purge under Truman and Eisenhower* have been applauded by critics for covering previously uncharted areas about how and why communism has appealed to some and appalled others. *The Fellow-Travellers,* which is about the travels of Andre Gide, George Bernard Shaw, Jean-Paul Sartre and other well-known figures to the Soviet Union and their impressions of communism, has been praised by *New Statesman* reviewer Neil McInnes and others for its "rich . . . fund of fascinating information." H. Stuart Hughes, writing in the *New York Review of Books,* also calls Caute's study of McCarthyism in *The Great Fear* a work "of first-rate importance." Some critics, however, have felt that the author's leftist sympathies in *The Great Fear* give it a slanted viewpoint. "The gravest deficiency in Caute's work," states Sidney Hook in *Encounter,* "is its failure to state fairly and come to grips with the arguments and evidence of those whom he denounces." A *New York Times Book Review* article by Arthur Schlesinger, Jr., pinpoints the problem as Caute's "accept[ance of] the fallacy that has disabled many latter-day commentators on that unhappy time: that there was no tenable middle ground; that to oppose Stalinism made McCarthyism inevitable."

Although Caute has been criticized for letting his leftist preferences show through in both his nonfiction and fiction, Steel reports that the author has become aware of this tendency in his writing. In 1976, Caute wrote: "Nowadays I'm more preoccupied by questions of literary form than I used to be." His more recent novel, *Veronica or The Two Nations,* "is more descriptive than prescriptive," remarks Nina King in the *Washington Post Book World,* "offering no simple solutions for the social ills it depicts." Combining a story of love and incest with social and political themes, Caute tells of the mutual love Michael Parsons and Bert Frame share for Michael's half-sister, Veronica, during their school days in England. Michael, who comes from an upper class background, later becomes a ruthless, self-serving Tory politician and a prime candidate to succeed Margaret Thatcher, while Bert becomes a tabloid writer. Bert, who originally came from London's poor East End, resents Michael personally, but he also opposes him politically. The novel concludes when Bert manages to ruin Michael's career by revealing that the politician favors the legalization of incest because he once committed the act with his half sister.

Sometimes referred to as a conceit of Benjamin Disraeli's *Sybil, or The Two Nations* in which Disraeli described England as two disparate nations, one rich and one poor, *Veronica or The Two Nations* has been praised by a number of critics for its dramatic presentation of England's social ills. *New Statesman* contributor Richard Deveson, for example, calls the novel a "defiantly intelligent and an instantly absorbing read [that] is partly on the state of the nation, self-consciously echoing *Sybil:* a confrontation of ruler and ruled." But unlike the author's earlier novels, *Veronica* does not clearly favor leftist politics. Caute, observes King, "seems more than a little ambivalent himself about the working-class leftists of the new era." Indeed, as Mark Wormald points out in the *Times Literary Supplement,* "Caute invites us to question the legitimacy of any extreme assertion, any self which claims to know itself utterly." King notes that although Caute's other novels have not been widely noticed in the United States this "should change with *Veronica,* which in addition to its engrossing plot and political insight, is beautifully constructed."

BIOGRAPHICAL/CRITICAL SOURCES:

BOOKS

Bradbury, Malcolm, and David John Palmer, general editors, *The Contemporary English Novel,* Arnold, 1979.
Contemporary Authors Autobiography Series, Volume 4, Gale, 1986.
Contemporary Literary Criticism, Volume 29, Gale, 1984.
Dictionary of Literary Biography, Volume 14: *British Novelists since 1960,* Gale, 1982.
Taylor, John Russell, *The Second Wave: British Drama for the Seventies,* Hill & Wang, 1971.

PERIODICALS

Annals of the American Academy of Political and Social Science, March, 1965.
Antioch Review, June, 1973.
Chicago Tribune Book World, July 31, 1983.
Commentary, March, 1965; June, 1973; June, 1978.
Commonweal, May 14, 1965.
Encounter, February, 1970; January, 1979.
Esquire, July, 1973.
Harper's, January, 1967; June, 1968.
Journal of American Studies, December, 1977.
Listener, September 8, 1966; September 17, 1970; July 22, 1971; January 25, 1972; January 25, 1973; May 9, 1974; March 6, 1975; September 28, 1978; February 24, 1983; February 6, 1986.
London Magazine, September, 1966; June, 1983.
London Review of Books, July 7, 1983; May 8, 1986; November 20, 1986.
Los Angeles Times Book Review, August 7, 1983; February 14, 1988.
Nation, June 27, 1966; January 16, 1967; April 22, 1978; May 5, 1984.
National Review, September 15, 1972; January 5, 1973; April 13, 1973.
New Leader, November 7, 1966; December 23, 1974.

New Statesman, May 12, 1961; September 15, 1961; July 10, 1964; March 4, 1966; November 18, 1969; July 23, 1971; January 9, 1973; March 1, 1974; September 15, 1978; February 25, 1983; May 25, 1983; September 19, 1986; June 30, 1989.
Newsweek, March 19, 1973.
New York Review of Books, April 20, 1978.
New York Times, April 27, 1962; July 28, 1970; May 9, 1978; September 5, 1978; March 4, 1988.
New York Times Book Review, October 9, 1966; May 14, 1971; April 8, 1973; March 19, 1978; May 20, 1979.
Observer, February 1, 1959; May 14, 1961; April 10, 1966; September 11, 1966; December 18, 1966; January 11, 1970; July 25, 1971; January 21, 1973; September 21, 1973; February 10, 1974; February 27, 1977; September 10, 1978; February 27, 1983; May 22, 1983; September 7, 1986; January 10, 1988; July 2, 1989.
Observer Review, January 11, 1970.
Progressive, February, 1971; August, 1978.
Saturday Review, October 8, 1966; June 6, 1970; March 18, 1978.
Spectator, February 6, 1959; May 12, 1961; March 11, 1966; September 9, 1966; January 12, 1968; January 27, 1973; March 9, 1974; September 23, 1978; February 26, 1983; June 11, 1983; February 8, 1986; October 18, 1986; January 16, 1988; August 12, 1989.
Time, June 2, 1961.
Times (London), February 5, 1959; September 8, 1966; November 20, 1969; January 17, 1970; July 22, 1971; January 22, 1973; March 14, 1973; September 14, 1978; May 26, 1983; September 4, 1986; January 14, 1988; June 29, 1989.
Times Literary Supplement, February 13, 1959; May 19, 1961; October 22, 1964; September 8, 1966; November 3, 1966; January 29, 1970; December 3, 1971; July 6, 1973; May 3, 1974; November 17, 1978; March 11, 1983; June 3, 1983; November 3, 1983; April 4, 1986; September 26, 1986; January 29, 1988; April 15, 1988; August 25, 1989.
Tribune Books (Chicago), March 27, 1988.
Village Quarterly Review, winter, 1967.
Washington Post Book World, July 22, 1979; August 7, 1983; August 26, 1990.

—*Sketch by Kevin S. Hile*

*   *   *

CELAN, Paul
See ANTSCHEL, Paul

*   *   *

CHAPMAN, James (Keith) 1919-
(Hamish Keith)

PERSONAL: Born April 24, 1919, in Gagetown, New Brunswick, Canada; son of Harry Keith (a barber) and Hazel E. (McGowan) Chapman; married Rhoda Ellen Wilson, October 15, 1941. *Education:* University of New Brunswick, B.A., 1950, M.A., 1952; University of London, Ph.D., 1954.

ADDRESSES: Home—509 Montgomery, Fredericton, New Brunswick, Canada.

CAREER: University of New Brunswick, Fredericton, instructor, 1951-54, assistant professor, 1954-58, associate professor, 1958-64, professor of history, 1964-84, chairman of department, 1970-74. *Military service:* Royal Canadian Air Force, navigator and instructor, 1940-46.

MEMBER: Atlantic Association of Historians (co-founder), New Brunswick Historical Society, York-Sunbury Historical Society, Queens County Historical Society.

AWARDS, HONORS: LL.D., Mount Allison University, 1984.

WRITINGS:

Dr. Edwin Jacob: A Biography, University of New Brunswick Press, 1963.
The Career of Arthur Hamilton Gordon, First Lord Stanmore: 1829- 1912, University of Toronto Press, 1964.
A Political Correspondence of the Gladstone Era: The Letters of Lady Sophia Palmer and Sir Arthur Gordon, 1884-1889, American Philosophical Society, 1971.
(Contributor) J. M. Bumstead, editor, *Canadian History before Confederation: Essays and Interpretations,* Dorsey, 1972.
(Editor) W. Austin Squires, *History of Fredericton: The Last 200 Years,* City of Fredericton, 1980.
River Boy: Life along the St. John, Brunswick Press, 1980.
Hair from a Stallion's Tail, Centennial Print and Litho, 1982.
River Boy Returns, Brunswick Press, 1983.
River Boy at War, Fiddlehead Poetry Books/Goose Lane Editions, 1985.
Gagetown: As We Were, A Short History with Illustrations, Queens County Historical Society and Museum, 1986.
(With H. O. Warwick) *The Mount House on Mount Ararat Farm,* Queens County Historical Society and Museum, 1989.

Contributor to *Canadian Forum, Canadian Historical Review, Acadiensis,* and *Historical Reflections;* contributor, under pseudonym Hamish Keith, to *Atlantic Advocate.*

WORK IN PROGRESS: A Skein of Yarns.

*   *   *

CHAPPELL, Fred (Davis) 1936-

PERSONAL: Surname rhymes with "apple"; born May 28, 1936, in Canton, NC; son of James Taylor (a furniture retailer) and Anne (Davis) Chappell; married Susan Nicholls, August 2, 1959; children: Heath (son). *Education:* Duke University, B.A., 1961, M.A., 1964. *Politics:* Democrat.

ADDRESSES: *Home—*305 Kensington Rd., Greensboro, NC. *Agent—* Rhoda Weyr, 216 Vance St., Chapel Hill, NC 27514.

CAREER: Brown Supply Co., Candler, NC, general manager, 1957-59; Candler Furniture Co., Candler, credit manager, 1959-60; Duke University Press, Durham, NC, proofreader, 1961; University of North Carolina at Greensboro, professor of English, 1964—.

AWARDS, HONORS: Woodrow Wilson fellow; National Defense Act fellow; Rockefeller Foundation grant, 1966; National Institute and American Academy awards in literature, 1968; Prix de Meilleur des Lettres Etrangers, French Academy, 1971, for *Dagon;* Roanoke-Chowan Poetry Cup, 1972, for *The World between the Eyes,* 1978, for *River: A Poem,* and 1979, for *Bloodfire: A Poem;* Sir Walter Raleigh Award, 1973, for *The Gaudy Place;* Bollingen Prize in Poetry, Yale University Library, 1985.

WRITINGS:

NOVELS

It Is Time, Lord, Atheneum, 1963.
The Inkling, Harcourt, 1965.
Dagon, Harcourt, 1968, reprinted, St. Martin's, 1986.
The Gaudy Place, Harcourt, 1973.

I Am One of You Forever, Louisiana State University Press, 1985.
Brighten the Corner Where You Are, St. Martin's, 1989.

POETRY

The World between the Eyes, Louisiana State University Press, 1971.
River: A Poem, Louisiana State University Press, 1975.
The Man Twice Married to Fire, Unicorn Press, 1977.
Bloodfire: A Poem, Louisiana State University Press, 1978.
Wind Mountain: A Poem, Louisiana State University Press, 1979.
Awakening to Music, Briarpatch Press, 1979.
Earthsleep: A Poem, Louisiana State University Press, 1980.
Driftlake: A Lieder Cycle, Iron Mountain Press, 1981.
Midquest: A Poem (contains *River: A Poem, Bloodfire: A Poem, Wind Mountain: A Poem,* and *Earthsleep: A Poem*), Louisiana State University Press, 1981.
Castle Tzingal, Louisiana State University Press, 1984.
Source, Louisiana State University Press, 1986.
First and Last Words, Louisiana State University Press, 1989.

OTHER

Moments of Light (story collection), New South Co., 1980.
The Fred Chappell Reader (contains excerpts from his poetry, novels, and short stories), St. Martin's, 1987.

Contributor to *Sewanee Review, Triquarterly, Saturday Evening Post, American Review,* and other periodicals. Contributing editor, *Skyhook, Red Clay Reader, Shenandoah,* and *Georgia Review;* advisory editor, *Greensboro Review, Appalachian Heritage, Brown Bag* and *Denver Quarterly;* editor, *Archive* and *Fly by Night.*

SIDELIGHTS: An acclaimed poet and novelist, Fred Chappell draws on his childhood memories to write of the Southern experience. His early novels focused on characters who, according to David Paul Ragan of the *Dictionary of Literary Biography,* "have been displaced by a new society which has usurped an older, more stable culture," while his more recent novels are full of humor and tall tales. Winner of the Bollingen Prize in Poetry, Chappell is best known for *Midquest: A Poem,* a long poetic work concerning the author's thirty-fifth birthday. Writing in the *Los Angeles Times Book Review,* Frank Levering states: "Not since James Agee and Robert Penn Warren has a Southern writer displayed such masterful versatility. Together with only a handful of his American contemporaries, Chappell reminds us of the almost forgotten phrase 'man of letters.' "

Employing the conventions of the Southern gothic novel, Chappell's early books explored a world of violence, illicit sex, and degradation, relating these social phenomena to the destruction of traditional Southern society. "As Chappell grew up," Ragan explains, "he observed a culture undergoing a transition from a primarily agrarian economy to a society in which one's ties with the land and the stability this connection instills became more and more distant. This upheaval underlies all of Chappell's work."

It Is Time, Lord, Chappell's first novel, concerns James Christopher, a weak and despondent man whose personality disintegrates as he drifts through a number of superficial relationships. The book's narrative structure combines chapters set in the present with the protagonist's unreliable journal entries about past events. Because of these conflicting narratives, the reality of the situation becomes unclear, echoing the protagonist's own mental state. R. A. Francoeur of *Best Sellers* finds that Chappell "skillfully interweaves memory and consciousness to produce an intriguing blend of fantasy and reality." He believes that "the main spirit of this book lies in the simplicity of its style and the sharpness of its descriptions. With clean verbal strokes Chappell brings his characters into focus." Nelson Aldrich of the *New York Herald Tribune Book Review* agrees with Francoeur. Aldrich judges "the descriptions of a farming childhood and the portraits of [Christopher's] grandparents and father [to be] done with a hard, sure talent."

In his second novel, *The Inkling,* Chappell again uses a complex narrative structure, this one cyclical, beginning and ending the novel with the same scene. Set in North Carolina and involving five characters in the same family, the story concerns the young boy Jan and his struggle to develop self-control in the face of his sister's growing insanity, his mother's death, and his own seduction by an aunt. It is another story of failure and personality disintegration. Kenneth Lamott of *Book Week* admits that "Chappell writes like a whiz" but states: "I cannot promise to keep the peace if I am exposed to another bright young Southern writer who is hooked on incest, barnyard sadism, imbecility, and domestic bloodletting." In similar terms, the reviewer for the *Times Literary Supplement* writes: "If Mr. Chappell's considerable powers are to be used satisfactorily he must break away from or perhaps redirect the, by now, stale Southern myth of Carson McCullers and Tennessee Williams." In contrast to these opinions, C. P. Collier of *Best Sellers* judges *The Inkling* to be "a short, complex novel with a fine sense of dramatic assurance, disarming simplicity, and disquieting perception." He calls it "a wondrous piece of fresh and vigorous writing. Mr. Chappell moves smoothly from passions and cruelties to the beautiful imagery of dreams and the musings of a deluded mind. . . . For those readers who like good writing, in spite of the subject or the incidents, this is a small masterpiece."

Dagon, Chappell's third novel and winner of the French Academy's Prix de Meilleur des Lettres Etrangers, borrows setting and themes from the Southern gothic but includes elements from surrealism, mysticism, and the horror fiction of H. P. Lovecraft, as well. It is the first of Chappell's novels to use a conventional narrative structure. Like the previous novels, *Dagon* deals with the destruction of personality. Its protagonist is Peter Leland, a minister who returns to his family estate in North Carolina to research pagan beliefs in America. He soon comes under the influence of Mina, a teenage girl who is both a sadist and nymphomaniac. She slowly destroys Leland's self-esteem, causes him to murder his wife, brutalizes and tortures him, and finally kills him in a sacrificial ritual to the pagan god Dagon. But Leland's personality survives even his physical death to metamorphose into a new form of life in a realm where, Ragan states, "metaphor and substance become one." Although advised by friends to omit the conclusion of the novel, Chappell believes his ending to be, according to Ragan, "a conscious effort 'to alleviate the agony of [the novel].' "

Writing in the *Contemporary Authors Autobiography Series,* Chappell explains his reasons for writing the novel: "*Dagon* was designed as a horror story, tenuously and ironically connected to that tradition of horror fiction initiated by H. P. Lovecraft, the Cthulhu mythos. I had all sorts of strange ideas about the book; it was to be pop art metaphysics, for one thing, in which the garish conventions of pulp horror stories accurately depicted the terrors of contemporary civilization; it was to be rooted in a posited secret American history, an underground religion operative since colonial times; and it was to retell the Biblical story of Samson in modern dress."

Critical response to *Dagon* often found the book well-written but lacking in motivation and believability. Robert B. Nordberg of *Best Sellers,* for example, calls the novel "absorbing" and Chappell's prose "skilled writing." "Nevertheless," Nordberg concludes, "it doesn't, somehow, make much sense." Peter Buitenhaus of the *New York Times Book Review* holds a similar opinion. Although he finds that "the style of the novel is of a very high order [and] its precise, dry elegance contrasts piquantly with its sleazy material," Buitenhaus believes "Chappell does not show adequately why Peter [Leland] suddenly nosedives from melancholy to mayhem and from scholarship to sadomasochism. Peter's lack of motivation makes him seem a mechanical figure, and it is hard to get excited by the systematic brutalization and torture that is meted out to him."

Other critics reacted more favorably to *Dagon.* David R. Slavitt, writing in the *Chicago Tribune,* calls it "a superb and terrifying work, closer in spirit to Nathaniel Hawthorne than to Stephen King and almost mystical in its rendering of a nihilism all too recognizable around us." The novel enjoys a high standing in the horror genre, where it is considered a classic among those works inspired by the writings of H. P. Lovecraft. Robert Hadji, writing in *The Penguin Encyclopedia of Horror and the Supernatural,* calls *Dagon* "the most literate work in the Lovecraftian canon." *Dagon*'s reception in Europe, particularly in France, was also highly favorable. "The warmth of [Chappell's] French reception," writes Ragan, "recalls that of William Faulkner, whose reputation as a novelist was very high in France while his work was being virtually ignored in this country."

With *The Gaudy Place,* Chappell decided to write a different kind of novel from what he had previously published. A novel in which, as Ragan quotes Chappell, "all the pieces fitted together, and that had a latitude of characterization in it." The result is a book that relies far more on plot than did Chappell's earlier works, and which depends on a carefully-developed sequence of events for its tragic ending.

The Gaudy Place is set in the seamy district of a North Carolina city where a prostitute, her pimp, and a teenage gambler briefly cross paths with a respectable professor and his family. Divided into five chapters, each told from a different character's perspective, the novel is, the reviewer for *New Republic* believes, "a series of character studies connected by an unpretentious plot." Writing in the *New York Times Book Review,* Jonathan Yardley argues that the novel's only fault is this use of character studies. "In shifting from one [character] to another Chappell does not maintain a consistent flow," Yardley argues. Despite the problem, the critic finds that "the novel has considerable strengths: sharp, precise prose; several fine comic scenes; good dialogue; and, most important, an accurate feel for the new urban South." The *Choice* critic judges it "an almost perfectly executed, modest novel."

After publishing *The Gaudy Place,* Chappell abandoned writing novels to turn his attention to poetry. "Now for the first time," Chappell writes in his entry for the *CA Autobiography Series,* "I could begin to think directly about the most important intellectual and artistic endeavor in the world: the composition of poetry." His most ambitious work is *Midquest,* "a four-volume poetic autobiography," as Chappell describes it in the *CA Autobiography Series.*

Telling of a single day—the poet's thirty-fifth birthday— *Midquest* is an examination of the midpoint in a life, a time of rumination and assessment. The poem exhibits a range of voices and styles. "Chappell," Christopher Benfey writes in the *Boston Review,* "uses a variety of meters, forms, and genres in *Midquest;*

there are verse letters, dramatic monologues, conversation poems, elemental odes." "Chappell's is a highly flexible, theatrical voice," Ellen Tucker explains in *Chicago Review.* "His mind is intensely engaged with what he calls 'moral ideas,' but these he tests less through their logical or analogical development than through the assumption of the posture appropriate to each. He relishes the music in language, and a fine ear enables him to invent meters suitable to each pose."

Because of the poem's length, Chappell is also able to incorporate an impressive array of references in *Midquest,* drawing from his childhood, his North Carolina home, and his wide reading. "*Midquest* is partly Chappell's *Prelude,* looking back to his childhood in the mountains of North Carolina, his extended family, and his poetic apprenticeship," Benfey writes. "Part of Chappell's power," writes Robert Morgan in the *American Poetry Review,* "is his willingness to put all of himself into this work. He gives to his poetry a great reservoir of learning, lyric hymning, alternating with science fiction and fantasy, country music. . . . That he is willing to invest so many facets of himself is our gain. For we come to feel the wholeness of a human being. There is the recognition that this is truly a man, in the gaudy landscape of our times, yes, and seen from more angles than we normally see, and with greater focus and knowledge, but nevertheless a man in touch at times with the absurd and corny, at times with the sublime." Slavitt believes that Chappell's poems "are not only technically accomplished but deeply moving, and perfectly accessible, if only attention is paid. Chappell should be our generation's Robert Frost, whom he in some degree resembles and in many ways surpasses."

After a lapse of twelve years, Chappell turned again to writing novels with *I Am One of You Forever,* a novel set in the North Carolina of the 1940s and focusing on a rural mountain family. As the family's son, Jess, looks back on the time from his perspective as an adult, he recounts the many visits they had from eccentric uncles and aunts. The novel, then, is structured as "a series of farfetched and winning stories," according to George Core of the *Washington Post Book World.* David Guy, writing in the *New York Times Book Review,* praises Chappell as "a fine technician of narrative prose who writes with marvelous economy, gives his characters letter-perfect dialogue and describes them with wonderful vividness." The reviewer for *Publishers Weekly* finds that *I Am One of You Forever,* "like the writings of Faulkner and Welty, invents its own mythic region."

In 1989, Chappell published *Brighten the Corner Where You Are,* a novel involving the same characters found in *I Am One of You Forever,* and presenting a single day in the life of Joe Roberts, a high school teacher in trouble with the school board for his teaching of evolution. As Sharon Oard Warner writes in the *New York Times Book Review,* "Chappell has concocted a tall tale that's part philosophy, part science lesson and part 'campfire powwow,' a story so ridiculous and endearing that excess becomes one of its chief virtues." Harry Middleton of the *Los Angeles Times Book Review* states: "In this deeply felt, warm, and funny novel, Fred Chappell, one of the South's and indeed the country's finest writers, introduces us to a character whose passion for life, for the hardness of truth, changes not only his life, but the lives of those around him. . . . Chappell, a master storyteller, weaves a wonderful tale, one full of wild humor and honest humanity, all of it surfacing in but a single day in a man's life."

The Fred Chappell Reader contains selections from the author's poetry, short stories, and novels, including the entire text of *Dagon.* The volume, several critics believe, presents Chappell as an uncommonly talented writer in several genres. Levering be-

lieves the collection "offers a panoramic view of Chappell's range and depth," while displaying the author's "own distinct voice, a blend of elegant erudition and a kind of earthy, Appalachian folk wisdom." Reviewing the book for the *Washington Post Book World,* Frederick Busch calls Chappell a "writer of breadth and distinction."

The *Reader* also highlights the similarities in Chappell's work, whatever the genre. Busch argues that "Chappell in his work as a whole examines dreams, fears and the particular beauties of his native North Carolina with a country kid's instinct for what's before him, and a metaphysician's squint at what lies far beyond such beautiful harshness." Morgan also speaks of this underlying concern: "There is a wholeness about the work of Chappell. Everything he does seems a piece of the same cloth, whether story, poem, novel or essay, and whatever he does fits with all the rest. It is the voice that dominates and is recognizable, no matter where you start any of his works, speaking with great richness of mind and language, deeply learned, acid at times, but always improvising, engaging whatever is at hand with all its attention, true overall to a wonderful good will and wit. Whether the subject be his parents or Linnaeus, he demonstrates the same gift for luminous phrase and detail. All his work has the tone of the gifted rememberer and tale teller delighting in his powers and flights of merrymaking memory."

BIOGRAPHICAL/CRITICAL SOURCES:

BOOKS

Contemporary Authors Autobiography Series, Gale, Volume 4, 1986.
Contemporary Literary Criticism, Gale, Volume 40, 1986.
Dictionary of Literary Biography, Volume 6: *American Novelists since World War II, Second Series,* Gale, 1980.
Garrett, George, editor, *Craft So Hard to Learn: Conversations with Poets and Novelists about the Teaching of Writing,* Morrow, 1972.
Sullivan, Jack, editor, *The Penguin Encyclopedia of Horror and the Supernatural,* Viking, 1986.

PERIODICALS

American Book Review, July-August, 1981.
American Poetry Review, July-August, 1982.
Best Sellers, August 15, 1963; August 15, 1965; September 1, 1968.
Book Week, August 15, 1965.
Boston Review, February, 1986.
Chicago Review, summer, 1981.
Chicago Tribune, April 9, 1987; October 24, 1989.
Choice, October, 1973.
Georgia Review, spring, 1973.
Hollins Critic, April, 1973.
Hudson Review, spring, 1976.
Library Journal, February 15, 1973.
Los Angeles Times Book Review, May 24, 1987; September 17, 1989.
Mississippi Quarterly, fall, 1978.
New Republic, June 2, 1973.
New York Herald Tribune Book Review,
New York Times, January 16, 1985.
New York Times Book Review, September 8, 1963; September 29, 1968; May 13, 1973; September 15, 1985; October 1, 1989.
Publishers Weekly, March 15, 1985.
Saturday Review, August 10, 1963.
Sewanee Review, April, 1970; July, 1976.
Southern Review, October, 1976.

Times Literary Supplement, November 10, 1966.
Virginia Quarterly Review, winter, 1969; summer, 1973.
Washington Post Book World, March 29, 1987; October 1, 1989.

—*Sketch by Thomas Wiloch*

* * *

CIARDI, John (Anthony) 1916-1986
(John Anthony)

PERSONAL: Surname pronounced *Char*-dee; born June 24, 1916, in Boston, Mass.; died of a heart attack, March 30, 1986, in Edison, N.J.; son of Carminantonia (an insurance agent) and Concetta (De Benedictus) Ciardi; married Myra Judith Hostetter, July 28, 1946; children: Myra Judith, John Lyle Pritchett, Benn Anthony. *Education:* Attended Bates College, 1934-36; Tufts College (now University), A.B. (magna cum laude), 1938; University of Michigan, M.A., 1939. *Politics:* Democrat.

ADDRESSES: Home—359 Middlesex Ave., Metuchen, N.J. 08840; and 725 Windsor Lane, Key West, Fla. 33040.

CAREER: Poet and critic. University of Kansas City, Kansas City, Mo., instructor in English, 1940-42, 1946; Harvard University, Cambridge, Mass., Briggs-Copeland Instructor in English, 1946-48, Briggs-Copeland Assistant Professor of English, 1948-53; Rutgers University, New Brunswick, N.J., lecturer, 1953-54, associate professor, 1954-56, professor of English, 1956-61; *Saturday Review,* New York, N.Y., poetry editor, 1956-72. Bread Loaf Writers' Conference, lecturer beginning 1947, director, 1955-72; lecturer in American poetry, Salzburg Seminar in American Studies, 1951. Editor with Twayne Publishers, 1949; served as a judge in Children's Literature Section of National Book Awards, 1969. Host of "Accent," a weekly educational program presented by Columbia Broadcasting System-Television, 1961-62. Has given public poetry readings. *Military service:* U.S. Army Air Forces, 1942- 45; served as gunner on B-29 in air offensive against Japan; became technical sergeant; received Air Medal with Oak Leaf Cluster.

MEMBER: American Academy of Arts and Sciences (fellow), National Institute of Arts and Letters (fellow), National College English Association (director, 1955-57; president, 1958-59), Northeast College English Association (past president), Phi Beta Kappa.

AWARDS, HONORS: Avery Hopwood Award for poetry, University of Michigan, 1939; Oscar Blumenthal Prize, 1943; Eunice Tietjens Award, 1945; Levinson Prize, 1946; Golden Rose trophy of New England Poetry Club, 1948; Fund for the Advancement of Education grant, 1952; Harriet Monroe Memorial Prize, 1955; Prix de Rome, American Academy of Arts and Letters, 1956-57; Litt.D., Tufts University, 1960; Junior Book Award, Boys' Clubs of America, 1962, for *The Man Who Sang the Sillies;* D.Hum., Wayne State University, 1963, and Keane College of New Jersey, 1976; LL.D., Ursinus College, 1964; L.H.D., Kalamazoo College, 1964, Bates College, 1970, Washington University, 1971, and Ohio Wesleyan University, 1971.

WRITINGS:

POETRY

Homeward to America, Holt, 1940.
Other Skies, Atlantic Monthly Press, 1947.
Live Another Day: Poems, Twayne, 1949.
As If: Poems New and Selected, Rutgers University Press, 1955.
I Marry You: A Sheaf of Love Poems, Rutgers University Press, 1958.
Thirty-Nine Poems, Rutgers University Press, 1959.

In the Stoneworks, Rutgers University Press, 1961.
In Fact, Rutgers University Press, 1962.
Person to Person, Rutgers University Press, 1964.
This Strangest Everything, Rutgers University Press, 1966.
An Alphabestiary, Lippincott, 1967.
A Genesis, Touchstone Publishers (New York), 1967.
The Achievement of John Ciardi: A Comprehensive Selection of his Poems with a Critical Introduction (poetry textbook), edited by Miller Williams, Scott, Foresman, 1969.
Lives of X (autobiographical poetry), Rutgers University Press, 1971.
The Little That Is All, Rutgers University Press, 1974.
For Instance, Norton, 1979.
Selected Poems, University of Arkansas Press, 1984.
The Birds of Pompeii, University of Arkansas Press, 1985.
Echoes: Poems Left Behind, University of Arkansas Press, 1989.
Poems of Love and Marriage, University of Arkansas Press, 1989.

JUVENILES

The Reason for the Pelican (poetry), Lippincott, 1959.
Scrappy the Pup (poetry), Lippincott, 1960.
The Man Who Sang the Sillies (poetry), Lippincott, 1961.
I Met a Man (poetry), Houghton, 1961.
You Read to Me, I'll Read to You (poetry), Lippincott, 1962.
The Wish-Tree (fiction), Crowell-Collier, 1962.
John J. Plenty and Fiddler Dan: A New Fable of the Grasshopper and the Ant (poetry), Lippincott, 1963.
You Know Who (poetry), Lippincott, 1964.
The King Who Saved Himself from Being Saved (poetry), Lippincott, 1965.
The Monster Den; or, Look What Happened at My House—and to It (poetry), Lippincott, 1966.
Someone Could Win a Polar Bear (poetry), Lippincott, 1970.
Fast and Slow: Poems for Advanced Children and Beginning Parents (poetry), Houghton, 1975.
Doodle Soup, Houghton, 1986.

TRANSLATOR

Dante Alighieri, *The Inferno* (poetry; also see below), Rutgers University Press, 1954.
Dante, *The Purgatorio* (poetry; also see below), New American Library, 1961.
Dante, *The Paradiso* (poetry; also see below), New American Library, 1970.
The Divine Comedy (includes *The Inferno, The Purgatorio,* and *The Paradiso*), Norton, 1977.

RECORDINGS

"About Eskimos and Other Poems" (cassette phonotape), Spoken Arts, 1974.
"What Do You Know about Poetry?: An Introduction to Poetry for Children" (cassette phonotape), Spoken Arts, 1974.
"What Is a Poem?: A Discussion of How Poems Are Made" (phonodisc), Spoken Arts, 1974.
"Why Noah Praised the Whale and Other Poems" (cassette phonotape), Spoken Arts, 1974.

OTHER

(Editor) *Mid-Century American Poets,* Twayne, 1950.
(Author of introduction) Fritz Leiber and others, *Witches Three* (prose), Twayne, 1952.
(Contributor) William White, *John Ciardi: A Bibliography,* Wayne State University Press, 1959.

(Editor and contributor) *How Does a Poem Mean?* (prose), Houghton, 1960, 2nd edition (with Miller Williams), 1975.

Dialogue with an Audience (collection of *Saturday Review* essays), Lippincott, 1963.

(Editor with James M. Reid and Laurence Perrine) *Poetry: A Closer Look* (prose), Harcourt, 1963.

(Contributor) A. L. Bader, editor, *To the Young Writer* (prose), University of Michigan Press, 1965.

(Contributor) *Dante Alighieri: Three Lectures* (prose), Library of Congress, 1965.

(Author of introduction) John A. Holmes, *The Selected Poems,* Beacon Press, 1965.

(With Joseph B. Roberts) *On Poetry and the Poetic Process* (prose), Troy State University Press, 1971.

Manner of Speaking (selected *Saturday Review* columns), Rutgers University Press, 1972.

(With Isaac Asimov) *Limericks, Too Gross,* Norton, 1978.

A Browser's Dictionary and Native's Guide to the Unknown American Language, Harper, 1980.

(With Laurence Urdang and Frederick Dickerson) *Plain English in a Complex Society,* Poynter Center, Indiana University, 1980.

(With Asimov) *A Grossery of Limericks,* Norton, 1981.

A Second Browser's Dictionary and Native's Guide to the Unknown American Language, Harper, 1983.

Good Words to You: An All-New Browser's Dictionary and Native's Guide to the Unknown American Language, Harper, 1987.

The Complete Browser's Dictionary: The Best of John Ciardi's Two Browser's Dictionaries in a Single Compendium of Curious Expressions and Intriguing Facts, Harper, 1988.

Saipan: The War Diary of John Ciardi, University of Arkansas Press, 1988.

The Hopeful Trout and Other Limericks, Houghton, 1989.

Also contributor of short story, under name John Anthony, to science fiction anthology *A Decade of Fantasy and Science Fiction: Out of This World Masterworks by Masterminds of the Near and the Far Out.* Contributor of articles and essays to periodicals. Contributing editor, *Saturday Review,* 1955—, and *World Magazine,* 1970-72.

WORK IN PROGRESS: Additional volumes of *A Browser's Dictionary;* a book of juvenile poems; a book of "senile" poems.

SIDELIGHTS: To millions of Americans, the late John Ciardi was "Mr. Poet, the one who has written, talked, taught, edited, translated, anthologized, criticized, and propelled poetry into a popular, lively art," according to Peter Comer of the *Chicago Tribune.* Although recognized primarily as a poet and critic, Ciardi's literary endeavors encompassed a vast range of material. From juvenile nonsense poetry to scholarly verse translations, Ciardi made an impact upon the general public. His poetry received popular approval while his academic research attracted critical kudos. Driven by his love of words and language, John Ciardi provided lively and frequently controversial offerings to the literary scene.

The son of Italian immigrants, Ciardi, at age three, lost his father in an automobile accident. Ciardi recalls a peaceful youth, enlivened by the addition of Irish and Italian families to the neighborhood. His tranquil life developed into a series of bruises and black eyes as the neighborhood children clashed frequently. Perhaps due to his heritage, Ciardi's interest in Italian literature has resulted in translations of Dante's *Inferno* that many authorities consider classics.

Once a denizen of the English faculties at Harvard and Rutgers, Ciardi, in 1961, broke with formalized education in favor of pursuing his own literary endeavors full-time. He remained a part of the academic community through countless lectures and poetry readings each year, in addition to numerous appearances on educational television. Influenced by his favorite teacher at Tufts University, poet John Holmes, Ciardi decided early in his college career to devote time to writing verse. He turned to composing juvenile poetry as a means of playing and reading with his own children. His juvenile selections have been enormously successful, especially *I Met a Man.* Ciardi's position as a poetry critic with *Saturday Review* developed from his own verse publications, but he told Comer that "it was a hobby job," adding, "I think at most it earned me $4,000 a year."

Ciardi was strongly in favor of exposing poetry to mass audiences. Aware of the linguistic and allusive complexities inherent in "good" verse and acknowledging the public's general aversion to poems, he consciously attempted to address the average reader through much of his work. While not sacrificing his message for popularity and renown, Ciardi nevertheless gained a large public following. While critics acclaimed the intellectual elements in his work, the reading public derived equal meaning and relevance from his poetry. In his preface to *Dialogue with an Audience,* Ciardi expressed the hope that some readers "can be brought to a more than merely general interest in poetry."

Ciardi's work has inspired both praise and criticism from reviewers. Edward Cifelli writes in the *CEA Critic:* "Ciardi's verse is intensely personal, introspective, and self-revealing. His poems reflect the quiet considerations of a thoughtful, sensitive man. They are not white-hot representations of emotion: Ciardi more often thinks about passion. His diction is less emotionally charged than it is intricately patterned. Frequently passion emerges in Ciardi 'imagery' only after it has been filtered through the poet's sense of the ironic or comic." Cifelli also believes that "[Ciardi] focuses with remarkable clarity on the elements upon which one builds a theme into a poem," adding, "The theme that exemplifies the great diversity of Ciardi's talent is poetry itself." In the *Dictionary of Literary Biography,* Alice Smith Haynes analyzes the totality of the poet's verse and its connected relativity: "Just as [Ciardi] maintains that Dante must be experienced as a whole, so his poetry, more than that of most poets, must be seen as an interrelated body of parts." In the *Chicago Tribune,* Reed Whittemore, also a poet and essayist, observes: "If [Ciardi's] poetry has any persistent theme, it is probably that human nonsense and folly are persistent. He is a cynic all right. . . . But he is not all cynic. The positive feelings do slop pleasantly through." Corner illustrates Ciardi's literary success: "John Ciardi long has been the rare American who could walk into a bank, declare his occupation as 'poet,' and emerge with a mortgage."

Ciardi's verse often breaks with contemporary poetic tendencies. Whittemore writes that current poetry "has gone off to make a kind of fin-de-siecle career of mental lapses, to put bright images in odd places on mostly empty pages, and to plow up acres and acres of private sensibility"; Whittemore states that since Ciardi has not "lapsed" into this new set of poetic criteria, his recent work has become somewhat "unfashionable." John W. Hughes of the *Saturday Review* also finds limitations in twentieth-century verse, but unlike Whittemore, feels Ciardi's reputation survives the shift in poetic direction: "Ciardi follows Wordsworth and Frost in molding the blank verse to the flowing immediacy of his remembrances, and in so doing explodes some of the mind-forged manacles that shackle modern poetry." Ciardi himself, in the *Writer,* alluded to changing poetry values and their effect on his appeal. He commented: "Too many poets today, especially the activist poets, think that the only prerequisite [to writing good poetry] is the excitation of their own ignorance. I become unpopular with them. . . . The very fact that I would suggest [that a poet needs training] makes me a reactionary, war-loving, establishment racist out to oppress the poor. I have no answer. Just goodbye."

As a critic, Ciardi frequently provoked controversy with his frank and often candidly honest reviews. Known for promoting poetry, he nonetheless never shied away from denigrating what he considers unworthy verse. The first major disturbance surrounding his assessment of poetry stemmed from his unfavorable *Saturday Review* article about Anne Morrow Lindbergh's *The Unicorn.* Such forthright criticism in 1957 shocked readers and prompted voluminous mail protest. Ciardi defended his position in later issues of the magazine, arguing that a critic's role is to examine the work itself, not the popularity of the artist. He also maintained that the primary responsibility of good poetry lies to itself, and that the publishing arena should not serve simply to enhance any particular individual's reputation. Ciardi's fresh approach to criticism set the mood for later evaluative standards not yet accepted in the late 1950s.

Ciardi held firm convictions regarding the process of self-evaluation of one's work. In the *Writer,* he asserted that unsuccessful poems reveal valuable information which may prove valuable to future achievement: "I learned that the rate at which one recognizes his own badness is the rate at which he grows as a writer." Ciardi did not deny the sentiment behind failed verse; he simply defined the writer's abortive attempt to identify and describe the experience: "When a bad writer thinks he has caught the miracle, or some piece of it, his wrong impression is invariably due to the fact that he *felt* a poem but did not manage to *write* one. The miracle stayed inside his head. . . . He has *lived* a poem; he has not *made* one." Further, Ciardi advocated "ruthless" examination of one's work, claiming: "The wastebasket is a prime resource. . . . It forces me to recognize what I have done badly."

About the creative process itself, Ciardi argued in the *Writer* that "it isn't easy to make a poem," adding: "It is better than easy: it is joyously, consumingly difficult. As it is difficult, too, though without joy, to face one's failures." Noting that the creation of successful verse requires definite skill, he wrote: "I insist that a poet needs at least as much training as does a concert pianist. More, I think, but that is already too much for the ignorantly excited." Believing that "the minimum requirement for a good poem is a miracle," he explained: "The poem must somehow turn out better than anyone—the poet included—had any right to expect. No matter how small the miracle, the hope of it is my one reason for writing." He also felt the poem's strength will lead the writer unerringly: "The poet cannot know where he is going: he must take his direction from the poem itself."

Despite his love of the humble literary life, Ciardi did not snub financial gain. In the *Writer,* he indicated that although his writing "has been a love affair, not a sales campaign," he cherished the "bonuses—grants, prizes, even a small, slow rain of checks," commenting: "How could I fail to rejoice in that overflow of good? I wish it to every writer, and wish him my sense of joy in it." Stating that "I have never known of anyone who turned to poetry in the expectation of becoming rich by it," he cited his own satisfaction as "total payment." Ciardi nevertheless "kept his fingers in . . . many literary pies," in Corner's words. Corner noted that the poet was fond of saying, "I am my broker's keeper."

Eschewing quick, financially-rewarding pieces in favor of a multitude of more demanding projects, Ciardi had no patience with glibly mawkish poets. In spite of, or perhaps because of, his popularity with the public, Ciardi ascertained that his work met his own rigorous approval before publishing even a stanza of verse. Describing Rod McKuen and Edgar Guest as "writers whose remouthing of sentiments catches some tawdry emotional impulse in commercial quantities," he thought that such poets "believe seriously in the inanities they write." Ciardi explained, "I doubt that they have sold out to the dollar sign: more tragically, they have sold out to themselves."

One of Ciardi's late passions emerged in his conversation with Corner: "I'm not a complicated man, and I don't have any gripping internal problems. But I get interested in things. Words have become a happy obsession." His linguistic research culminated in a multi-volume work, *The Browser's Dictionary.* In the first volume, Ciardi indulged his interest in etymology, word derivations, and linguistic development throughout the entries. Concentrating on precision, the tome reflected Ciardi's commitment to bringing the intricacies of language closer to the reading public.

Reassessing his writing career, John Ciardi told Corner that perhaps his first works exhibit indiscriminate editing: "Early on I was offered more chances to publish than was really good for me, and I lacked the character to say no. . . . I need to go back over everything and take only the ones that stay memorable for me, probably less than half I've published. And I'd like to signalize that the other ones are fakes. . . . I denounce them. . . . I did not write them." Despite his concern over quality, Ciardi remained immersed in literary pursuits. His opinion in the *Writer* that "what passes as our poetry has too largely been taken over by loud illiterates and by officiously important editors" belies his constant quest for self-improvement. He wrote "as an alcoholic drinks, compulsively." This "tough-guy poet, the art's Edward C. Robinson, with his feelings leaking out unexpectedly in the midst of flat, machine-gun commentary," in Whittemore's words, explained to Corner: "I find I like what I do . . . and enjoy working at the things I enjoy. To me that's a description of blessedness." Perhaps to ensure the perpetuation of his poetic dominion even in death, John Ciardi created his own epitaph: "Here, time concurring (and it does);/Lies Ciardi. If no kingdom come,/A kingdom was. Such as it was/This one beside it is a slum."

AVOCATIONAL INTERESTS: "Indifferent golf and neglected gardening."

BIOGRAPHICAL/CRITICAL SOURCES:

BOOKS

Ciardi, John, *Lives of X,* Rutgers University Press, 1971.
Contemporary Literary Criticism, Gale, Volume 10, 1979, Volume 40, 1986, Volume 44, 1987.
Dictionary of Literary Biography, Volume 5: *American Poets since World War II,* Gale, 1980.
Dictionary of Literary Biography Yearbook: 1986, Gale, 1987.
Hopkins, Lee Bennett, *Books Are by People,* Citation Press, 1969.
John Ciardi, Twayne, 1980.
White, William, *John Ciardi: A Bibliography,* Wayne State University Press, 1959.

PERIODICALS

America, July 27, 1957.
Book Week, September 29, 1963, November 1, 1964, November 8, 1970, September 24, 1972, September 28, 1980.

Booklist, December 1, 1972, February 1, 1975, October 15, 1979, July 15, 1980.
CEA Critic, November, 1973.
Chicago Review, autumn-winter, 1956, summer, 1957.
Chicago Tribune, December 16, 1979, September 8, 1980.
Choice, October, 1967, February, 1972, February, 1975, June, 1979.
Christian Science Monitor, December 24, 1964, May 7, 1975, October 23, 1978, January 2, 1980.
Contemporary Literature, winter, 1968.
Critic, December, 1963-January, 1964.
Detroit Free Press, February 28, 1964.
Explicator, December, 1968, May, 1970.
Nation, September 13, 1958.
National Observer, November 30, 1970.
New York Times Book Review, April 16, 1950, July 4, 1954, August 3, 1958, November 11, 1962, May 12, 1963, November 10, 1963, October 4, 1964, November 1, 1964, November 8, 1970, May 4, 1975, November 16, 1975, August 17, 1980.
New York Herald Tribune, November 11, 1962, August 11, 1963.
Poetry, September, 1940, May, 1948, July, 1956, October, 1958, December, 1962, July, 1963, December, 1967, July, 1975.
Prairie Schooner, winter, 1972-73.
Saturday Review, January 28, 1956, November 10, 1962, March 23, 1963, December 14, 1963, June 3, 1967, February 6, 1971, May 22, 1971, November 27, 1971. May 31, 1975.
Time, February 18, 1957, February 26, 1979.
University of Kansas City Review, autumn, 1949.
Virginia Quarterly Review, winter, 1964, spring, 1965.
Wall Street Journal, May 28, 1971.
Writer, March, 1964, August, 1976, June, 1980.
Yale Review, March, 1956.

OBITUARIES:

PERIODICALS

Chicago Tribune, April 3, 1986.
Detroit News, April 2, 1986.
Milwaukee Sentinel, April 1, 1986.
Newsweek, April 14, 1986.
New York Times, April 2, 1986.
Time, April 14, 1986.
Washington Post, April 2, 1986.
Woodbridge News Tribune (Woodbridge, N.J.), September 25, 1986.*

*   *   *

CLERK, N. W.
See LEWIS, C(live) S(taples)

*   *   *

COATES, Willson H(avelock) 1899-1976

PERSONAL: Born August 1, 1899, in Takayama (near Sendai), Japan; son of Canadian missionaries, Harper H. and Agnes (Wintemute) Coates; died September 23, 1976; married Hilda Altschule (an artist), September 17, 1928. *Education:* University of British Columbia, B.A., 1920; Oxford University, B.A. (honors), 1923, M.A., 1926; Cornell University, Ph.D., 1926.

ADDRESSES: Home—220 Highland Pkwy., Rochester, NY 14620. *Office—* Department of History, University of Rochester, Rochester, NY 14627.

CAREER: University of Rochester, Rochester, NY, instructor, 1925-28, assistant professor, 1928-35, associate professor,

1935-47, professor of history, 1947-65, professor emeritus, 1965-76. Visiting professor at Sarah Lawrence College, Bronxville, NY, 1947-48, and Trinity College, Hartford, CT, 1967. Public panel member, War Labor Board, 1944-45; U.S. Department of State consultant at Lucknow University, 1957. Rochester Police Advisory Board, member, 1963-70, chairman, 1965-70. *Military service:* Canadian Army, Field Artillery, 1918; became sergeant.

MEMBER: American Historical Association, Conference on British Studies, American Association of University Professors, Association of American Rhodes Scholars.

AWARDS, HONORS: Rhodes scholar, 1921-23; research grants, Social Science Research Council and American Council of Learned Societies, 1938, 1949, 1971; Folger Shakespeare Library fellowship, 1951; literary award, Friends of the Rochester Public Library, 1973.

WRITINGS:

(Editor and author of introduction and notes) *The Journal of Sir Simonds D'Ewes: From the First Recess of the Long Parliament to the Withdrawal of King Charles from London,* Yale University Press, 1942, reprinted, Shoe String Press, 1970.
An Analysis of Major Conflicts in Seventeenth-Century England, New York University Press, 1960.
(With Hayden V. White) *The Emergence of Liberal Humanism: An Intellectual History of Western Europe,* McGraw, Volume 1: *From the Italian Renaissance to the French Revolution,* 1966, Volume 2: *The Ordeal of Liberal Humanism: An Intellectual History of Western Europe since the French Revolution,* 1970.
(Editor with Esther S. Cope) *Proceedings of the Short Parliament of 1640,* Longwood, 1977.
(Editor with Anne Steele Young and Vernon F. Snow) *The Private Journals of the Long Parliament: January 3 to March 5, 1642,* Yale University Press, 1982.

Contributor of eight articles and seventy reviews to historical journals. Editor, *Journal of British Studies,* Volumes 1-9, 1961-70. Founder and editor, *The Comparative Study in Society and History.*

WORK IN PROGRESS: Cultural Interchange between East and West: The Case of Agnes Wintemute and Harper H. Coates in Japan.*

*   *   *

COLEMAN, Kenneth 1916-

PERSONAL: Born April 28, 1916, in Devereux, GA; son of John Amoss (a merchant) and Nolia (Lee) Coleman. *Education:* University of Georgia, A.B., 1938, M.A., 1940; University of Wisconsin, Ph.D., 1952. *Politics:* Democrat. *Religion:* Anglican. *Avocational interests:* Architecture and how it reflects life of the period in which a house was built.

ADDRESSES: Home—220 Dearing St., Athens, GA 30605.

CAREER: University of Georgia, began as instructor, 1949, became assistant professor at Atlanta Campus, assistant professor at Athens campus, 1955-61, associate professor, 1961-68, professor of history, 1968-76, professor emeritus, 1976—. Member of Athens-Clarke Heritage Foundation board of directors, and of Georgia Bicentennial Commission. *Military service:* U.S. Army Reserve, 1941-56; active duty, 1941-46; served in European theatre; became lieutenant colonel.

MEMBER: American Historical Association, Southern Historical Association, Georgia Historical Society, Athens Historical Society (past president).

WRITINGS:

Georgia History in Outline, University of Georgia Press, 1955, 3rd edition, 1978.

The American Revolution in Georgia, University of Georgia Press, 1958.

(Contributor) Horace Montgomery, editor, *Georgians in Profile: Historical Essays in Honor of Ellis Merton Coulter,* University of Georgia Press, 1958.

(With Sarah B. Gover Temple) *Georgia Journeys: Being an Account of the Lives of Georgia's Oroginal Settlers and Many Other Early Settlers from the Founding of the Colony in 1732 until the Institution of Royal Government in 1754,* University of Georgia Press, 1961.

Confederate Athens, University of Georgia Press, 1968.

Athens, 1861-1865: As Seen through Letters in the University of Georgia Libraries, University of Georgia Press, 1969.

Colonial Georgia, A History, Scribner, 1976.

(With Numan V. Bartley and others) *A History of Georgia,* University of Georgia Press, 1977.

(Editor with Milton Ready) *The Colonial Records of the State of Georgia* (Coleman not associated with previous volumes), University of Georgia Press, Volume 20, 1976; Volume 27: *Original Papers of Governor John Reynolds, 1754-1756,* 1976; Volume 28, Part 1: *Original Papers of Governors Reynolds, Ellis, Wright, President Habersham, and Others, 1764-1782,* 1979; Volume 28, Part 2: *Original Papers of Governor Wright, Prsedent Habersham, and Others, 1974-1782,* 1979; Volume 29: *Original Papers, Correspondence to the Trustees, James Ogelthorpe, and Others, 1732-1735,* 1982; Volume 30: *Trustees' Letter Book, 1738-1745,* 1985; Volume 31: *Trustees' Letter Book, 1745-1752,* 1986; Volume 32: *Entry Books of Commissions, Powers, Instructions, Leases, Grants of Land, etc. by the Trustees, 1732-1738,* 1989.

(Editor with Charles Stephen Gurr) *Dictionary of Georgia Biography,* two volumes, University of Georgia Press, 1983.

(Contributor) Harvey H. Jackson and Phinizy Spalding, editors, *Forty Years of Diversity: Essays on Colonial Georgia,* University of Georgia Press, 1984.

Contributor to *Agricultural History* and regional history journals.

* * *

COLLIER, Christopher 1930-

PERSONAL: Born January 29, 1930, in New York, NY; son of Edmund (a writer) and Katharine (Brown) Collier; married Virginia Wright (a teacher), August 21, 1954; married second wife, Bonnie Bromberger (a librarian), December 6, 1969; children: (first marriage) Edmund Quincy, Sally McQueen; (second marriage) Christopher Zwissler. *Education:* Clark University, Worcester, MA, B.A., 1951; Columbia University, M.A., 1955, Ph.D., 1964.

ADDRESSES: Home—876 Orange Center Rd., Orange, CT 06477. *Office*—Department of History, University of Connecticut, Storrs, CT 06269.

CAREER: Teacher in public schools in Greenwich, CT, 1955-58, and New Canaan, CT, 1959-61; Columbia University, Teachers College, New York, NY, instructor in history, 1958-59; University of Bridgeport, Bridgeport, CT, instructor,

1961-64, assistant professor, 1964-67, associate professor, 1967-7l, professor of history, 1971-78, David S. Day Professor of History, 1978-84, chairman of department, 1978-81; University of Connecticut, Storrs, professor of history, 1981—. Visiting professor, Humanities Institute of Fairfield University, summer, 1966, State University of New York College at Purchase, 1969-73, University of Connecticut, summers, 1970-75 and New York University, spring, 1974; visiting lecturer, Yale University, 1977; Columbia University Seminar on Early American History, chairman, 1978-79. Project editor, Instructional Materials, Films, Inc., 1975-76. Associate director, National Defense Education Act Institute in History for public school teachers, summers, 1967-68. Director, NEH Institute for College Teachers, 1989. Consultant to Connecticut Research Commission, museums and historical societies, text, trade, and scholarly publishers, law firms, public utilities, radio, and television. *Military service:* U.S. Army, 1952-54.

MEMBER: American Historical Association, Organization of American Historians, Connecticut-Historical Society, Association for the Study of Connecticut History (co-founder).

AWARDS, HONORS: Newbery Honor, Jane Addams Peace Prize, American Library Association notable book citation, and American Book Award nomination, all 1975, *My Brother Sam Is Dead;* Christopher Award, 1985, for *Decision in Philadelphia;* Wilbur Cross Award for service in the Humanities, 1986; many other awards for children's literature.

WRITINGS:

(Editor) *Public Records of the State of Connecticut, 1965-1967,* State Library of Connecticut, 1967.

Roger Sherman's Connecticut: Yankee Politics and the American Revolution, Wesleyan University Press, 1971.

Connecticut in the Continental Congress, Pequot Press, 1973.

Roger Sherman: Puritan Politician, New Haven Colony Historical Society, 1976.

(Contributor) George Willauer, editor, *Lyme Miscellany,* Wesleyan University Press, 1977.

(Contributor) *Long Island Sound: The People and the Environment,* Oceanic Society, 1978.

The Pride of Bridgeport: Men and Machines in the Nineteenth Century, Bridgeport Museum of Art, Science, and Industry, 1979.

The Literature of Connecticut History, Connecticut Humanities Council, 1983.

WITH BROTHER, JAMES L. COLLIER

My Brother Sam Is Dead (juvenile), Scholastic Book Services, 1974.

The Bloody Country (juvenile), Scholastic Book Services, 1976.

The Winter Hero (juvenile), Scholastic Book Services, 1978.

Jump Ship to Freedom (juvenile), Delacorte, 1981.

War Comes to Willy Freeman (juvenile), Delacorte, 1982.

Who Is Carrie? (juvenile), Delacorte, 1984.

Decision in Philadelphia: The Constitutional Convention of 1787, Random House/Reader's Digest Press, 1985.

OTHER

Editor, Monographs in British History and Culture, 1967-72, and *Connecticut History Newsletter,* 1967-73. Contributor to history journals.

WORK IN PROGRESS: Historical Geography of Connecticut; Beginnings of Political Parties in Connecticut; Prudence Crandall; juvenile fiction.

SIDELIGHTS: Christopher Collier wrote: "When I was about fourteen years old I read Irving Stone's *They Also Ran* (I still have the very same copy), a collection of short biographies of presidential candidates who lost. That is the first history I recall reading for fun, but ever since then I have made the study of history my principal concern. Having grown up during the Great Depression in what used to be called 'straightened circumstance,' the idea of doing something that brought a steady paycheck appealed to me. That meant teaching history, an objective I decided upon as a sophomore in high school.

"It was when I was teaching eighth-grade American history that I was inspired to write historical novels. Surely there must be a better—more interesting and memorable—way to teach such exciting stuff as history is made of than through the dull, dull textbooks we used. My brother had already written some novels for teenagers, and after about fifteen years of hounding him, he finally agreed to help me out. The result was *My Brother Sam Is Dead.*"

*   *   *

COLLIER, James L(incoln) 1928-
(Charles Williams)

PERSONAL: Born June 27, 1928, in New York, NY; son of Edmund and Katharine (Brown) Collier; married Carol Burrows, September 2, 1952 (divorced); married Ida Karen Potash; children: (first marriage) Geoffrey Lincoln, Andrew Kemp. *Education:* Hamilton College, A.B., 1950.

ADDRESSES: Home—South Quaker Hill Rd., Pawling, NY 12564.

CAREER: Free-lance writer.

AWARDS, HONORS: Child's Study Association Book Award, 1971, for *Rock Star;* Newberry Honor Book Award, American Book Award nomination, National Book Award nomination, and Jane Addams Peace Prize, all for *My Brother Sam Is Dead;* London Observer Book of the Year Award, and American Book Award nomination, both for *The Making of Jazz: A Comprehensive History;* Christopher Award for books that affirm the highest values of the human spirit, 1985, for *Decision in Philadelphia: The Constitutional Convention of 1787.*

WRITINGS:

Cheers, Avon, 1961.
Somebody Up There Hates Me, Macfadden, 1962.
The Hypocritical American: An Essay on Sex Attitudes in America, Bobbs-Merrill, 1964.
Battleground: The United States Army in World War II, Norton, 1965.
A Visit to the Firehouse, Norton, 1967.
The Teddy Bear Habit: Or, How I Became a Winner, Norton, 1967.
(With others) *Sex Education U.S.A.: A Community Approach,* Sex Information and Education Council of the United States, 1968.
Which Musical Instrument Shall I Play?, Norton, 1969.
Rock Star, Four Winds, 1970.
Danny Goes to the Hospital, Norton, 1970.
Practical Music Theory: How Music Is Put Together from Bach to Rock, Norton, 1970.
Why Does Everybody Think I'm Nutty?, Grosset, 1971.
The Hard Life of the Teenager, Four Winds, 1972.
It's Murder at St. Basket's, Grosset, 1972.
Inside Jazz, Four Winds, 1973.

Jug Bands and Hand Made Music, Grosset, 1973.
The Making of Man, Four Winds, 1974.
(With brother, Christopher Collier) *My Brother Sam Is Dead,* Four Winds, 1974.
Rich and Famous, Four Winds, 1975.
Give Dad My Best, Four Winds, 1976.
(With C. Collier) *The Bloody Country,* Four Winds, 1976.
Making Music for Money, F. Watts, 1976. *CB,* F. Watts, 1977.
The Great Jazz Artists, Four Winds, 1977.
(With C. Collier) *The Winter Hero,* Four Winds, 1978.
The Making of Jazz: A Comprehensive History, Four Winds, 1978.
(With C. Collier) *Jump Ship to Freedom,* Delacorte, 1981.
(With C. Collier) *War Comes to Willy Freeman,* Delacorte, 1983.
Planet Out of the Past, Macmillan, 1983.
Louis Armstrong: An American Genius, Oxford University Press, 1983, published as *Louis Armstrong: An American Success Story,* Macmillan, 1985.
(With C. Collier) *Who Is Carrie?,* Delacorte, 1984.
(With C. Collier) *Decision in Philadelphia: The Constitutional Convention of 1787,* Random House/Reader's Digest Press, 1986.
When the Stars Begin to Fall, Delacorte, 1986.
Outside Looking In, Macmillan, 1987.
Duke Ellington, Oxford University Press, 1987.
The Reception of Jazz in America, Institute for Studies in American Music, 1988.
The Winchesters (juvenile fiction), Macmillan, 1989.
Benny Goodman and the Swing Era, Oxford University Press, 1989.

UNDER PSEUDONYM CHARLES WILLIAMS

Author of *Fire of Youth,* Magnet Books.

OTHER

Contributor to *The Grove Dictionary of American Music* and *The Grove Dictionary of Jazz.* Contributor of 600 articles to magazines.

SIDELIGHTS: A critic reviewing *The Making of Jazz: A Comprehensive History* for *New Statesman* writes: "James Lincoln Collier's history is refreshingly old-fashioned—and correctly so—in setting [the creation of jazz] in New Orleans, just as it sticks to the theory of the Diaspora, with jazz not necessarily winding its way up the Mississippi but at least hurrying along the railroads." While this reviewer points out some ommissions and misstatements, he excuses them, holding that "the occasional goof, even a few patches of dull writing, cannot stop this being the best general history since Marshall Stearn's *The Story of Jazz.*"

John McDonough of *down beat* agrees, asserting that "the Collier book is quite simply the finest general survey of jazz history since Marshall Stearn's *Story of Jazz* nearly 20 years ago. And since Stearns is somewhat obsolete at this point, *The Making of Jazz* now must be considered *the* basic jazz history in current publication." According to McDonough, "A major strength of the book is the way Collier so clearly sorts out the musicological issues and makes them understandable, with a little effort, to the untrained reader. Points are made in terms of specific performance citations to which the reader can turn. Even the most seasoned fan will probably learn much from this work."

Critics give Collier's biographies of jazz music greats Louis Armstrong and Duke Ellington mixed reviews. Anatole Broyard of the *New York Times,* for example, comments, "Mr. Collier, who is himself a musician, is at his best in analyzing Armstrong's playing," describing his trademarks "as a sharp attack, a broad terminal vibrato, an intimate, highly individual voice and a revolutionary style of playing around, or away from, the beat." Jim Miller comments in *Newsweek* that "one virtue of Collier's book is its evocation of [the] gin-soaked, dance-crazed, utterly commercial world" in which Armstrong "cheerfully labored." Less interesting, says Broyard—and more debatable, say other critics—are Collier's "sociological observations." For instance, "The question as to whether jazz was or was not originally folk music struck me as muddled in [Collier's] account," Broyard maintains. "He seems correct, however, in trying to rescue jazz from the left-wing critics of the 1930s and 40s who insisted on calling it proletarian music."

Critics generally take issue with Collier's attempts to psychoanalyze his subjects, observing that Collier's portraits of Louis Armstrong, Duke Ellington, and Benny Goodman tend to diminish rather than enlighten the personalities behind the music that so significantly enriched American culture. At other times, comments Larry Kart of the *Chicago Tribune,* Collier "appeals to some never quite defined norm of psychological well-being in order to dismiss any human trait that doesn't appeal to him"—as when Collier finds it odd that Ellington autographed a photo for his own mother. "Such conclusions are bound to be controversial," Michiko Kakutani writes in the *New York Times,* "and Mr. Collier tries to ground his arguments carefully in close readings of individual compositions and detailed examinations of their evolution. The general reader may find some of these passages overly technical and may reasonably contest some of the author's assertions. . . . But whether or not one agrees with Mr. Collier, the volume remains interesting in the light it sheds on Ellington's work methods and the musical motifs and patterns of his compositions."

BIOGRAPHICAL/CRITICAL SOURCES:

BOOKS

Children's Literature Review, Volume 3, Gale, 1978.
Collier, James L., *Duke Ellington,* Oxford University Press, 1987.

PERIODICALS

Chicago Tribune, November 3, 1983; October 21, 1987.
down beat, November 2, 1978.
Globe and Mail, December 3, 1983; November 14, 1987.
Los Angeles Times, November 20, 1983; December 20, 1987.
Los Angeles Times Book Review, November 20, 1983; September 20, 1987; December 17, 1989.
New Statesman, January 26, 1979.
Newsweek, October 10, 1983; October 12, 1987.
New York Times, October 8, 1983; September 5, 1987; November 18, 1989.
New York Times Book Review, November 26, 1972; February 25, 1973; December 30, 1973; November 3, 1974; May 2, 1976; February 14, 1982; May 8, 1983; October 30, 1983; July 7, 1985; November 22, 1987; December 3, 1989.
Times Literary Supplement, May 4, 1984; July 29, 1988; August 4, 1988.
Tribune Books (Chicago), November 5, 1989.
Washington Post, April 15, 1986.
Washington Post Book World, January 17, 1982; May 8, 1983; October 27, 1985; October 1, 1989.

COMMONER, Barry 1917-

PERSONAL: Born May 28, 1917, in New York, N.Y.; son of Isidore (a tailor) and Goldie (Yarmolinsky) Commoner; married Gloria C. Gordon (a psychologist), December 1, 1946; children: Lucy Alison, Fredric Gordon. *Education:* Columbia University, A.B., 1937; Harvard University, M.A., 1938, Ph.D., 1941. *Religion:* Humanist.

ADDRESSES: Office—Queens College Center for the Biology of Natural Systems, Flushing, N.Y. 11367.

CAREER: Queens College (now of the City University of New York), Flushing, N.Y., instructor in biology, 1940-42; *Science Illustrated* magazine, New York, N.Y., associate editor, 1946-47; Washington University, St. Louis, Mo., associate professor, 1947-53, professor of plant physiology, 1953-76; chairman of department of botany, 1965-69, director of Center for the Biology of Natural Systems, 1965-81, professor of environmental science, 1976-81; Queens College, Flushing, director of Center for the Biology of Natural Systems, 1981—, professor of earth and environmental science, 1981-87, professor emeritus, 1987—. Visiting professor of community health at Albert Einstein College of Medicine, 1981-87. St. Louis Committee for Environmental Information (formerly St. Louis Committee for Nuclear Information), co-founder, member of board of directors, 1958—, vice-president, 1958-65, president, 1965-66; Scientists Institute for Public Information, member of board of directors, 1963—, chairman, 1969—; member of board of directors, Universities National Anti-War Fund; member of board of consulting experts, Rachel Carson Trust for Living Environment, 1967—; member of advisory board or council, University of Oklahoma Law Center Committee, 1967-70, U.S. Department of the Interior study group on sonic boom, 1967-68, Office of Education council on environmental education, 1971—, Coalition Health Communities, 1975, U.S. Department of Commerce secretary's advisory council, 1976, New York State Commission on Science and Technology, 1981—, Commission for Responsible Genetics, 1983—, and Vietnam Veterans of America Foundation council on dioxin, 1985—. Trustee of Institute for Environmental Education. Citizens Party candidate for president of United States, 1980. *Military service:* U.S. Naval Reserve, 1942-54; served in Naval Air Force and as liaison officer with Senate Committee on Military Affairs; became lieutenant.

MEMBER: American Association for the Advancement of Science (fellow; member of board of directors, 1967—), American Institute of Biological Sciences (member of governing board, 1965-67), Society of General Physiologists (member of council, 1961), American Society of Plant Physiologists, American Society of Biological Chemists, American Association of University Professors, National Parks Association (member of board of directors, 1968—), American Chemical Society, American School Health Association, Ecological Society of America, Federation of American Scientists, British Soil Association (honorary life vice-president, 1968—), Sigma Xi, Phi Beta Kappa.

AWARDS, HONORS: Newcomb Cleveland Prize from American Association for the Advancement of Science, 1953; LL.D. from University of California, 1967, and Grinnell College, 1981; First International Humanist Award from International Humanist and Ethical Union, 1970; Phi Beta Kappa Award, 1972, and International Prize for Safeguarding the Environment from the City of Cervia, Italy, 1973, both for *The Closing Circle;* commander in the Order of the Merit (Italy), 1977; Premio Iglesias (Sardinia, Italy), 1978, for *The Poverty of Power,* and 1982, for *The Politics of Energy;* American Institute of Architects Medal, 1979; D.Sc. from Hahnemann Medical College, 1963, Clark

University, 1967, Grinnell College, 1968, Lehigh University, 1969, Williams College, 1970, Ripon College, 1971, Colgate University, 1972, Cleveland State University, 1980, and St. Lawrence University, 1988.

WRITINGS:

Science and Survival, Viking, 1966.
(With others) *Balance and Biosphere: A Radio Symposium on the Environmental Crisis,* Canadian Broadcasting Corp., 1971.
The Closing Circle: Nature, Man, and Technology, Knopf, 1971 (published in England as *The Closing Circle: Confronting the Environmental Crisis,* Cape, 1972), 2nd edition, Bantam, 1974.
(Contributor) *Electric Power Consumption and Human Welfare: The Social Consequences of the Environmental Effects of Electric Power Use,* Washington University, 1972.
(Editor) Virginia Brodine, *Air Pollution,* Harcourt, 1973.
(With others) *The Effect of Recent Energy Price Increases on Field Crop Production Costs,* Center for the Biology of Natural Systems, Washington University, 1974.
(Editor) Julian McCaull and Janice Crossland, *Water Pollution,* Harcourt, 1974.
(Editor with Howard Boksenbaum and Michael Corr) *Energy and Human Welfare,* Volume 1: *The Social Costs of Power Production,* Volume 2: *Alternative Technologies for Power Production,* Volume 3: *Human Welfare: The End Use for Power,* Macmillan Information, 1976.
The Poverty of Power: Energy and the Economic Crisis, Random House, 1976.
Energy (essays from *New Yorker*), New Yorker, 1976.
Reliability of Bacterial Mutagenesis Techniques to Distinguish Carcinogenic and Noncarcinogenic Chemicals, Environmental Protection Agency, 1976.
The Politics of Energy, Knopf, 1979.
Making Peace With the Planet, Pantheon, 1990.

OTHER

Power to the Person (sound recording), Big Sur Recordings, 1971.
The Destruction of Our Environment (sound recording), Pacifica Tape Library, 1972.
The Human Meaning of the Environmental Crisis (sound recording), Big Sur Recordings, 1973.
The Environment and the Energy Crisis (sound recording), Encyclopedia Americana/CBS News Audio Resource Library, 1973.
Freedom and the Environment (sound recording), Pennsylvania State Library, 1976.

Contributor of more than two hundred articles to journals in his field. Member of editorial board, *International Review of Cytology,* 1957-65, *Problems of Virology,* 1956-60, *American Naturalist,* 1959-63, *Theoretical Biology,* 1960-64, *Science Year,* 1967-72, *World Book Encyclopedia,* 1968-73, *Environmental Pollution,* 1969-79, *National Wildlife,* 1970—, and *Environment Magazine,* 1977—; honorary member of editorial advisory board, *Chemosphere,* 1972—; member of board of sponsors, *In These Times,* 1976—.

WORK IN PROGRESS: Research on the origins and significance of the environmental and energy crises, and other technical studies.

SIDELIGHTS: In a review of Barry Commoner's *Closing Circle,* Christopher Lehmann-Haupt wrote: "Dr. Commoner's is not a Doomsday book at all. . . . Dr. Commoner presents as lucid a description of ecology and its laws as I have yet come across. In between, he illustrates how those laws have been broken with di-

sastrous consequences. . . . He weighs the impacts on the environment of our population explosion and in particular our shockingly high per capita consumption of natural resources."

Commoner explains, "Human beings have broken out of the circle of life, driven not by biological need, but by the social organization which they have devised to 'conquer' nature; means of gaining wealth that are governed by requirements conflicting with those which govern nature. The end result is the environmental crisis, a crisis of survival. Once more, to survive, we must close the circle. We must learn how to restore to nature the wealth that we borrow from it."

BIOGRAPHICAL/CRITICAL SOURCES:

BOOKS

Chisholm, Anne, *Philosophers of the Earth,* Dutton, 1972.
Contemporary Literary Criticism, Volume 1, Gale, 1982.

PERIODICALS

Los Angeles Times, May 2, 1990.
Nation, September 22, 1979.
New Republic, November 6, 1971, August 18, 1979.
Newsweek, November 1, 1971, December 27, 1971, May 31, 1976.
New York Review of Books, August 5, 1976.
New York Times, April 22, 1970, January 15, 1988.
New York Times Book Review, November 6, 1966, October 17, 1971, May 23, 1976, June 5, 1977, July 29, 1979, April 22, 1990.
Saturday Review, May 15, 1976, September 1, 1979.
Spectator, January 22, 1977.
Time, February 2, 1970, May 31, 1976.
Village Voice, May 3, 1976.
Washington Post Book World, October 10, 1971, May 9, 1976, December 12, 1976, June 24, 1979.*

* * *

CORNWELL, David (John Moore) 1931-
(John le Carre)

PERSONAL: Born October 19, 1931, in Poole, Dorsetshire, England; son of Ronald Thomas Archibald and Olive (Glassy) Cornwell; married Alison Ann Veronica Sharp, 1954 (divorced, 1971); married Valerie Jane Eustace, 1972; children: (first marriage) Simon, Stephen, Timothy; (second marriage) Nicholas. *Education:* Attended Bern University, 1948-49; Lincoln College, Oxford, B.A. (with honours), 1956.

ADDRESSES: Agent—Bruce Hunter, David Higham Ltd., 5-8 Lower John St., W1R 4HA, England.

CAREER: Writer. Eton College, Buckinghamshire, England, tutor, 1956-58; British Foreign Office, second secretary in Bonn, West Germany, 1960-63, consul in Hamburg, West Germany, 1963-64.

AWARDS, HONORS: British Crime Novel Award, 1963; Somerset Maugham Award, 1964; Edgar Allan Poe Award, Mystery Writers of America, 1965; Gold Dagger, Crime Writers Association, 1978; Black Memorial Award, 1978; Grand Master Award, Mystery Writers of America, 1986; Diamond Dagger, Crime Writers Association, 1988.

WRITINGS:

Call for the Dead, Gollancz, 1960, Walker, 1962, published as *The Deadly Affair,* Penguin, 1966.

A Murder of Quality, Gollancz, 1962, Walker, 1963.

The Spy Who Came In from the Cold, Coward, 1963.

The Incongruous Spy: Two Novels of Suspense (contains *Call for the Dead* and *A Murder of Quality*), Walker, 1964.

The Looking Glass War, Coward, 1965.

"Dare I Weep, Dare I Mourn" (screenplay), produced on "Stage 66" by American Broadcasting Corp., 1966.

A Small Town in Germany, Coward, 1968.

(Author of introduction) Bruce Page, Phillip Knightley, and David Leitch, *The Philby Conspiracy,* Doubleday, 1968.

The Naive and Sentimental Lover, Knopf, 1971.

Tinker, Tailor, Soldier, Spy, Knopf, 1977.

Smiley's People, Knopf, 1980.

The Quest for Karla (contains *Tinker, Tailor, Soldier, Spy, The Honourable Schoolboy,* and *Smiley's People*), Knopf, 1982.

The Little Drummer Girl, Knopf, 1983.

A Perfect Spy, Knopf, 1986.

The Russia House, Knopf, 1989.

The Secret Pilgrim, Knopf, 1991.

SIDELIGHTS: The novels of David Cornwell, written under the pseudonym John le Carre, depict the clandestine world of Cold War espionage as a morally ambiguous realm where treachery, deceit, fear, and betrayal are the norm. The atmosphere in a le Carre novel, writes a reviewer for the *Times Literary Supplement,* is one of "grubby realism and moral squalor, the frazzled, fatigued sensitivity of decent men obliged to betray or kill others no worse than themselves." Le Carre uses his fiction to dramatize what he sees as the moral bankruptcy of the Cold War. In an open letter published in *Encounter,* le Carre writes: "There is no victory and no virtue in the Cold War, only a condition of human illness and a political misery." Leonard Downie, Jr., quotes le Carre in a *Washington Post* article as saying, "We are in the process of doing things in defense of our society which may very well produce a society which is not worth defending." It is this paradox, and the moral ambiguity which accompanies it, that informs le Carre's espionage novels and makes them, many critics believe, among the finest works of their genre. Le Carre's novels are believed by some critics to have raised the entire espionage genre to a more respectable and serious level of literature. "The espionage novel," writes Joseph McClellan in the *Washington Post Book World,* for example, "has become a characteristic expression of our time . . . and John le Carre is one of the handful of writers who have made it so." "More than any other writer," George Grella states in the *New Republic,* "[le Carre] has established the spy as an appropriate figure and espionage as an appropriate activity for our time, providing both symbol and metaphor to explain contemporary history."

Le Carre began writing espionage fiction in the early 1960s while working as a diplomat with the British Foreign Office in London. He had earlier worked for an undisclosed length of time with the British Secret Service, and there is some speculation among reviewers that le Carre's work as a diplomat was also espionage-related, a speculation le Carre dismisses as untrue. Nevertheless, his novels reveal an intimate knowledge of the workings of the British government's espionage bureaucracy. "Le Carre's contribution to the fiction of espionage," writes Anthony Burgess in the *New York Times Book Review,* "has its roots in the truth of how a spy system works. . . . The people who run Intelligence totally lack glamour, their service is short of money, [and] they are up against the crassness of politicians. Their men in the field are frightened, make blunders, grow sick of a trade in which the opposed sides too often seem to interpenetrate and wear the same face." Geoffrey Stokes, writing in the *Village Voice,* goes so far as to claim that in le Carre's novels, "bureau-

cracy [is] transformed into poetry." Because of his diplomatic position when he first began writing, Cornwell was not permitted to publish anything under his real name, and so the pseudonym John le Carre was born. "Le Carre" is French for "the square." "I've told so many lies about where I got the name from," Downie quotes le Carre as explaining, "but I really don't remember. The one time I did the celebrity circuit in America, I was reduced to inventing the fiction that I'd been riding on a bus to the foreign office and abstracted the name from a shoeshop. But that was simply because I couldn't convince anybody it came from nowhere."

Although the source for his pseudonym is now forgotten, the initial inspiration for le Carre's fiction is easily found. It comes from the sensational disclosures in the 1950s that several high-ranking members of the British Secret Service and Foreign Office were actually Soviet agents. These deep-penetration agents, called "moles," had infiltrated the British espionage establishment during the Second World War and had, over a period of years, risen to extremely sensitive positions. Of the several spies discovered, the most highly placed was Kim Philby, a man generally acknowledged to be the greatest traitor in British history. Philby had been in charge of British counter intelligence against the Soviet Union while secretly working for the Soviets, and was responsible for betraying hundreds of British agents to their deaths. These real-life espionage revelations caught the interest of the British reading public and such books as Ian Fleming's "James Bond" spy series became best-sellers. Le Carre, too, because of his own intelligence work, was intrigued and disturbed by the discovery of traitors in the British Secret Service. Grella states that le Carre has an "obsession with the relationship between love and betrayal" and has consistently explored this theme in all of his fiction.

Le Carre wrote his first two novels, *Call for the Dead* and *A Murder of Quality,* while working for the Foreign Office, first in London and then in Bonn, West Germany. At that time, the German capital was a center for intelligence operations. "You couldn't have been [in Germany] at that period," le Carre tells Miriam Gross of the *Chicago Tribune Magazine,* "without being aware of the shadow of an enormous intelligence apparatus." Le Carre introduced George Smiley, an intelligence agent featured in many of his later novels, in *Call for the Dead.* Smiley is an "improbable spy master," writes Richard W. Noland in *Clues: A Journal of Detection.* "[He is] short, fat, quiet and wears 'really bad clothes, which hung about his squat frame like skin on a shrunken toad,' " Noland quotes from *Call for the Dead.* Though physically unimposing, Smiley is a brilliant espionage agent who has served in the British Secret Service for more than thirty years. In *Call for the Dead,* Smiley investigates the suicide of a Foreign Office clerk who had just been given a security clearance, while in *A Murder of Quality* he tracks down the murderer of a schoolmaster's wife.

It wasn't until the publication of *The Spy Who Came In from the Cold* in 1963 that le Carre's work attracted widespread critical and popular acclaim. An immediate world-wide best-seller (the book has sold over twenty million copies since it first appeared), *Spy* enabled le Carre to leave his position with the Foreign Office to write full time. He tells Nicholas Wapshott of the London *Times:* "I had said to my accountant, if my assets reach 20,000 pounds, would you let me know? . . . When he told me I had reached that amount, with *The Spy Who Came In from the Cold,* it was a great relief. . . . I gave in my resignation." The novel tells the story of Alec Leamas, a fifty-year old British intelligence agent who wishes to retire from active duty and "come in from the cold," as he describes it. He is persuaded to take on one last assignment before leaving the Secret Service: a pretended defection behind the Iron Curtain to give false information to the East Germans implicating one of their high-ranking intelligence officers as a British agent. It is thought that the officer will then be imprisoned, thereby removing him from effective espionage work against the British. Leamas's real mission, and the treachery of his superiors, only gradually becomes clear to him as the plot unfolds.

Le Carre's pessimism about East-West relations is clearly evident in *Spy,* where both sides in the Cold War conflict are depicted as amoral and murderous. "The bureaucracies of East and West," writes Noland, describing the situation as related in *Spy,* "wage the Cold War by one simple rule—operational convenience. . . . In the name of operational convenience and alliances of expediency, any and all human values—including love and life itself—are expendable." In *Spy,* writes a *Times Literary Supplement* critic, le Carre puts forth the ideas that "the spy is generally a weak man, the tool of bureaucrats who are neither scrupulous nor particularly efficient, and that there is nothing to choose between 'us' and 'them' in an ethical sense." This is underlined when Leamas and his girlfriend are pitted against the intelligence agencies of both Britain and East Germany, "the two apparently opposed organizations on one side and helpless human beings . . . on the other," as Julian Symons writes in *Mortal Consequences: A History from the Detective Story to the Crime Novel.* Symons believes that *Spy* is the best of le Carre's novels because in *Spy* "the story is most bitterly and clearly told, the lesson of human degradation involved in spying most faithfully read."

Many of the qualities in le Carre's writing that are most praised by critics were first displayed in *Spy.* One of these is an authenticity and realism not usually found in espionage fiction. "Here is a book," Anthony Boucher writes in the *New York Times Book Review,* "a light year removed from the sometimes entertaining trivia which have (in the guise of spy novels) cluttered the publishers' lists." A reviewer for the *Times Literary Supplement* believes that, in *Spy,* "the technicalities of [spy] network organization carry a stamp of authenticity seldom found in stories of this nature," although the critic decries the "basically sensational" subject matter.

To make his work seem as authentic as possible, le Carre introduces a number of slang terms peculiar to the espionage underworld. Words like "mole," borrowed from the Soviet KGB, and "circus," a nickname for the British Secret Service, are used throughout *Spy.* Some of these terms are actual espionage jargon, but many were invented by le Carre himself. "I thought it very important," le Carre tells Gross, "to give the reader the illusion of entering the secret world, and to that end I invented jargon that would be graphic and at the same time mysterious. Some people find it irritating. I rather like it." Le Carre, Downie reports, "borrowed 'mole' from the KGB and is pleased that it has quickly become part of the real spy language of the West."

Graham Greene sets the tone for most critical commentary about *The Spy Who Came In from the Cold* when he calls it, as K. G. Jackson of *Harper* quotes Greene, "the best spy novel I have ever read." D. B. Hughes of *Book Week* also praises *Spy* as "a beautifully written, understated and immensely perilous story. . . . Only rarely does a book of this quality appear—an inspired work and one in which the author's own inner excitement kindles the page." Several critics feel that with this novel le Carre transcends the espionage genre entirely, writing not category fiction but literature. Noland finds, for example, that with *The Spy Who Came In from the Cold* le Carre's "spy fiction became something more than most conventional spy fiction. It became, in fact, a political statement about the moral confusion and bankruptcy of the Cold War." Boucher also sees something more to le Carre's novel. "The author develops his story superbly," he writes, "both as a compelling and dazzlingly plotted thriller, and as a substantial and penetrating novel of our time. [Le Carre is one of] the small rank of [espionage] writers who can create a novel of significance, while losing none of the excitement of the tale of sheer adventure."

This high critical praise has continued with each succeeding espionage novel le Carre has published. *The Looking Glass War,* for example, is described by Hughes as "a superb spy story, unflawed, a bitter, cruel, dispassionate—yet passionate—study of an unimportant piece of espionage and the unimportant little men who are involved in it." A group of British agents mount an operation into East Germany that is doomed to failure under present political conditions, a fact which the agents refuse to see. Symons argues in *New Review* that in both *Spy* and *The Looking Glass War,* betrayal is the primary theme. In the first, an agent is betrayed to further the career of a more highly placed agent. In the second, an entire operation is abandoned and the people involved in it are left to die. It is possible, Symons writes, "to see espionage activities as brave and patriotic . . . , and yet to view them also as basically disgusting, outrages to the human personality. From such a point of view these two books seem to say an ultimate word about the nature of spying."

Le Carre draws heavily upon his time at the British Foreign Office in writing *A Small Town in Germany,* a novel set in Bonn, West Germany. The novel relates the story of a British diplomat who disappears with very sensitive documents which may damage Britain's chances of joining the Common Market. Speaking of the novel in a *Nation* review, John Gliedman states that le Carre "has long been a master of the essential machinery of the spy and detective novel. He has also shown himself to be a sensitive observer of character and manner, within the limits of the genre. But nothing which has come before quite prepares us for the literary distinction of this effort—the quality of its prose, the complexity of its construction, the cunning of some of its dialogue. . . . It represents something of a breakthrough in the use of the spy genre for serious purposes. *A Small Town in Germany* is that rarest of all things in contemporary fiction—good art which is also popular art." Robert Ostermann, writing in *National Observer,* agrees that *A Small Town in Germany* is better than le Carre's previous fiction. He calls it "broader in scope and more confidently crafted; tuned with exquisite fineness to the sliding nuances of its characters; shot through with the physical presence of Bonn, . . . and conveyed in a tough, precise prose that matches the novel's mordant tone down to the smallest metaphor."

Tinker, Tailor, Soldier, Spy, le Carre's next espionage novel, begins a loosely connected trilogy in which George Smiley is pitted against the Russian master spy "Karla." Writing in *Newsweek,* Alexis Gelber and Edward Behr report that "with *Tinker, Tailor* and Smiley, [le Carre] hit his stride." *Tinker, Tailor* is a fictionalized treatment of the Kim Philby spy case in which Smiley goes after a Soviet mole in British intelligence, a mole placed and directed by Karla. The novel's structure "derives from the action of Smiley's search," writes Noland. "[Smiley] must pursue his man through the maze of official documents." Knowing that the mole must be a highly placed agent, Smiley goes back through the records of intelligence operations, seeking a pattern of failure which might be attributed to the machinations of a particular agent. His investigation finally becomes, Noland believes, "a moral search . . . a quest for some kind of truth about England."

As in previous novels, le Carre examines the ramifications of betrayal, but this time in greater depth than he had previously attempted. The mole Smiley uncovers has not only betrayed his country and friends but has seduced Smiley's wife as well. The critic for the *Times Literary Supplement* sees a "moral dilemma" at the center of the book: "Smiley gets his man. In doing so he removes from another man his last illusions about friendship, loyalty and love, and he himself is left drained in much the same way. It is a sombre and tragic theme, memorably presented." Similarly, Richard Locke writes in the *New York Times Book Review* of the "interlocking themes of sexual and political betrayal" to be found in *Tinker, Tailor*. Writing in *Clues: A Journal of Detection,* Holly Beth King sees a deeper significance to the novel's title, which is derived from a children's nursery rhyme. King sees a "whole intricately woven set of relationships between adults and children, between innocence and disillusionment, between loyalty and betrayal that gives the novel's title a deeper resonance."

Although the complexity of *Tinker, Tailor* is praised by many critics, Pearl K. Bell writes in *New Leader* that "it is myopic and unjust to link le Carre with high art." Bell believes that a more correct evaluation of le Carre would see him as "a master craftsman of ingeniously plotted suspense, weaving astoundingly intricate fantasies of discovery, stealth, surprise, duplicity, and final exposure." Similarly, Locke finds that "le Carre belongs to the select company of such spy and detective story writers as Arthur Conan Doyle and Graham Greene in England and Dashiell Hammett, James M. Cain, Raymond Chandler, and Ross Macdonald in America. There are those who read crime and espionage books for the plot and those who read them for the atmosphere . . . le Carre's books . . . offer plenty for both kinds of readers." Bell concludes that le Carre is "unarguably the most brilliantly imaginative practitioner of the [espionage] genre today." Writing in *Newsweek,* Peter S. Prescott defines what sets le Carre's espionage fiction apart from many other works in the genre. "Le Carre's work is above all plausible," he writes, "rooted not in extravagant fantasies of the cold war but in the realities of the bureaucratic rivalry summoned up through vapors of nostalgia and bitterness, in understated pessimism, in images of attenuation and grinding down." In *Tinker, Tailor,* Stokes argues, "Smiley is merely the protagonist; bureaucracy itself is the hero. . . . Without the structure bureaucracy imposes on the random accumulation of facts that assail us on a daily basis, there is indeed only 'perpetual chaos.' "

Smiley's running battle with the Soviet spy master Karla continues in *The Honourable Schoolboy,* a novel set in Hong Kong, where British intelligence is investigating a prosperous businessman who seems to be working for the Soviets. Several critics point out a similarity between le Carre's novel and Joseph Conrad's novel *Lord Jim.* The character Jerry Westerby, a British intelligence officer and friend of Smiley, is very similar to Conrad's character Jim. "Le Carre," Noland states, "obviously has Conrad's romantic protagonist in mind in his portrait of Westerby and in many of the events of the story." This "huge and hugely engrossing new thriller . . . ," writes David Ansen in *Newsweek,* "keeps opening out, like a Conrad adventure, into ever-widening pools of moral and emotional complexity."

Again concerned with one of Karla's moles, this one working inside Communist China, *The Honourable Schoolboy* traces Smiley's diligent efforts to discover and capture the agent for the West. As in previous novels, *Schoolboy* depicts an agent, this time Westerby, who is at odds with the amorality of espionage work and who, because of his belief in human values, loses his life in the course of an espionage operation. "The point, surely," writes Noland, "is that such romantic heroism is not very useful in the world of Cold War espionage." "It is difficult not to overpraise [*The Honourable Schoolboy*]," Mollie Panter-Downes writes in her *New Yorker* review. Although believing the novel too long, the plot "essentially thin," and le Carre's "fondness for stylistic mocking" embarrassing, Panter-Downes nonetheless praises *The Honourable Schoolboy.* "It has a compelling pace," she states, "a depth beyond its genre, a feeling for even the least of its characters, a horrifying vision of the doomed and embattled Southeast Asian left in the wake of the Vietnam War, and a dozen set pieces—following, fleeing, interrogating—that are awesomely fine."

Not all critics are as impressed with the novel. Louis Finger, writing in the *New Statesman,* believes that "the things that are wrong with le Carre, at the level of seriousness he no doubt feels he's aimed for here, totally debilitate the book's appeal as a run-of-the-mill espionage yarn." Responding to critics who classify le Carre's work as literature, Clive James of the *New York Review of Books* states that "raising le Carre to the plane of literature has helped rob him of his more enviable role as a popular writer who could take you unawares."

Le Carre brings his trilogy to a close with *Smiley's People,* the last confrontation between George Smiley and the Soviet master spy Karla. No longer content to thwart Karla's agents, Smiley works in this novel to force Karla himself to defect to the West. This operation is done off the record because the British Secret Service, due to political pressure, cannot engage in an offensive intelligence operation. It becomes instead a personal mission involving the retired Smiley and the friends and espionage contacts he has gathered over the years. "Smiley and his people," Noland states, "carry it out by personal choice and commitment, not for the British (or American) establishment. The whole operation is a victory for personal human loyalty and skill."

Despite the success of the operation, there is an ambiguity about it which brings into question the morality of espionage. "Smiley and his people are fighting for decency," writes Michael Wood in the *New York Times Book Review,* "but there is more blood on their hands than they or anyone else care to contemplate." Julian Moynihan clarifies this in *New Republic.* "We know," Moynihan writes, "that Smiley has ruined many lives, some innocent, in his tenacious pursuit of Karla; . . . and we just don't believe that the dirty tricks of one side are OK because they were ordered up by a decent little English guy with a disarming name." "If this is the end of the Smiley stories . . . ," writes Joseph McClellan in the *Washington Post Book World,* "it is an appropriately ambiguous conclusion to a series that has dealt splendidly in ambiguities from the beginning."

"In *Smiley's People,*" Tom Buckley states in *Quest/80,* "le Carre has done what no sensible person would have thought possible. He has written a novel at least as good as, and in some respects better than, his masterpiece, *The Spy Who Came In from the Cold.*" Jonathan Yardley agrees in an article for the *Washington Post,* calling it "the best of the le Carre's novels." Yardley goes on to evaluate le Carre's achievement as a writer by stating that he "has produced a body of work that is notable for technical brilliance, depth, and consistency of themes, and absolute verisimilitude."

In *The Little Drummer Girl,* le Carre turns to a different world arena for his setting—the Middle East refugee camps of the Palestinians. "It is as if Mr. le Carre," writes Anatole Broyard of the *New York Times,* "has had enough of British politics, as if he feels that neither Britain nor the Soviet Union is at the hot center of things anymore." Le Carre had originally planned to write a Smiley story set in the Middle East but could not find a convincing plot for his character. Because the espionage activity in this novel is of an active and open variety, unusual for le Carre, there is a great deal more action in *Drummer Girl* than is usual for a le Carre novel. There is also a female protagonist, le Carre's first, who is recruited by the Israelis to infiltrate a Palestinian terrorist group and set up its leader for assassination. "The Israelis triumph in the novel," William F. Buckley, Jr., writes in *National Review,* "even as they do in life. But Mr. le Carre is careful to even up the moral odds. . . . He permits the Palestinian point to be made with rare and convincing eloquence." Writing in *Esquire,* Martin Cruz Smith gives the opinion that *The Little Drummer Girl* is "the most balanced novel about Jews and Arabs, outrage for outrage and tear for tear, I've read." "Without condoning terrorism," Gelber and Behr write, "the book makes the reasons for it understandable—perhaps the first popular novel to do so."

Because of this insistence upon looking at both sides in the Middle East conflict as having valid reasons for waging war, le Carre succeeds, many critics believe, in presenting the situation in its complexity. It is through the character of Charlie, an actress recruited by the Israelis for the mission, that le Carre presents the arguments of both the Arabs and Jews. Charlie is first converted to the Israeli position by Israeli Intelligence and then, in order to play the part of a Palestinian sympathizer convincingly, she is indoctrinated in the Palestinian position. "In the course of the story," Hope Hale Davis states in the *New Leader,* "we have a chance, with Charlie, to become passionately partisan on one side and then the other, and also—with less risk to the psyche than Charlie suffers—both sides at once." According to Mark Abley, writing in *Maclean's,* le Carre "is resigned to the fact that neither side will be pleased by his controversial new novel." This is because le Carre portrays both sides as amoral killers, much the way he portrays both sides in the Cold War. Le Carre tells *Newsweek:* "There was no way of telling the story attractively unless one accepted certain premises—that terrible things were being done to the Jews. I began with the traditional Jewish hero looking for a Palestinian 'baddie.' Once into the narrative, the reader, I believed, would be prepared to consider more ambiguous moral preoccupations."

Some reviewers, however, see le Carre as an apologist for the Palestine Liberation Organization (PLO) and *The Little Drummer Girl* as lacking the moral ambiguity that characterizes his earlier books. "Here, one might have thought, is an ideal subject for moral ambiguity," David Pryce-Jones writes in the *New Republic.* "Le Carre finds it clear-cut. To him, the Palestinians are good, the Israelis bad." In their review of the book for *Chronicles of Culture,* Rael Jean Isaac and Erich Isaac acknowledge that le Carre does introduce the kind of moral ambiguities and correspondences between adversaries that he uses in other novels, "but these suggestions of ambiguity and correspondence are deceptive, for le Carre sets Israel up as the villain of this novel. . . . Le Carre employs meretricious techniques to make Israel appear guilty of the vicious practices that the PLO has made famous."

Speaking of the relationship between his life and writings to Fred Hauptfuhrer of *People,* le Carre reveals: "If I write knowledgeably about gothic conspiracies, it's because I had knowledge of them from earliest childhood." In several published interviews, le Carre has spoken of his personal life and how the business dealings and political ambitions of his father colored his own views of the world. Because his father often found himself in legal or financial trouble due to his sometimes questionable business deals, the family found itself, le Carre tells Gross, "often liv-

ing in the style of millionaire paupers. . . . And so we arrived in educated, middle-class society feeling almost like spies, knowing that we had no social hinterland, that we had a great deal to conceal and a lot of pretending to do." In an interview with Melvyn Bragg in the *New York Times Book Review,* le Carre states: "From early on, I was extremely secretive and began to think that I was, so to speak, born into occupied territory." He tells *Newsweek* that "there is a correlation, I suppose, between the secret life of my father and the secret life I entered at a formative age." Le Carre fictionalized his relationship with his father in the 1986 novel, *A Perfect Spy.*

"As for my own writing," le Carre tells Gross, "the real fun is the fun of finding that you've enchanted people, enchanted them in the sense that you've admitted them to a world they didn't know about. And also that you've given them a great deal of relief, in a strange way, because they've discovered a bit of life interpreted for them in ways that, after all, they find they understand."

MEDIA ADAPTATIONS: The Spy Who Came In from the Cold was filmed by Paramount in 1965; *Call for the Dead* was filmed as "The Deadly Affair" by Columbia in 1967; *The Looking Glass War* was filmed by Columbia in 1970; *Tinker, Tailor, Soldier, Spy* was filmed for television by the British Broadcasting Corp. in 1980; *Smiley's People* was filmed for television by the British Broadcasting Corp. in 1982; *The Little Drummer Girl* was filmed by Warner Brothers; *A Perfect Spy* was a seven-hour BBC-TV series and was shown on public television's "Masterpiece Theatre" in the United States; a film version of *The Russia House,* written by Tom Stoppard, directed by Fred Schepisi, and starring Sean Connery and Michelle Pfeiffer, is scheduled for release in 1990.

BIOGRAPHICAL/CRITICAL SOURCES:

BOOKS

Bestsellers 89, Issue 4, Gale, 1989.
Contemporary Literary Criticism, Gale, Volume 3, 1975, Volume 5, 1976, Volume 9, 1978, Volume 15, 1980, Volume 28, 1984.
Dictionary of Literary Biography, Volume 87: *British Mystery and Thriller Writers since 1940, First Series,* Gale, 1989.
Harper, Ralph, *The World of the Thriller,* Press of Case Western University, 1969.
Palmer, Jerry, *Thrillers: Genesis and Structure of a Popular Genre,* St. Martin's, 1979.
Symons, Julian, *Mortal Consequences: A History from the Detective Story to the Crime Novel,* Harper, 1972.

PERIODICALS

Armchair Detective, spring, 1980.
Book Week, January 26, 1964.
Chicago Tribune, June 19, 1989.
Chicago Tribune Book World, March 6, 1983.
Chicago Tribune Magazine, March 23, 1980.
Christian Science Monitor, January 14, 1980.
Chronicles of Culture, August, 1983.
Clues: A Journal of Detection, fall/winter, 1980, fall/winter, 1982.
Commentary, June, 1983.
Detroit News, August 29, 1982.
Esquire, April, 1983.
Globe and Mail (Toronto), June 10, 1989.
Harper, January, 1964, November, 1965, December, 1968.
Life, February 28, 1964.
Listener, July 4, 1974.

Los Angeles Times, May 31, 1989, October 16, 1989.

Los Angeles Times Book Review, June 18, 1989.

Maclean's, March 7, 1983.

Nation, December 30, 1968.

National Observer, October 28, 1968.

National Review, March 13, 1983.

New Leader, June 24, 1974, March 7, 1983.

New Republic, July 31, 1976, January 19, 1980, April 18, 1983.

New Review, July, 1974.

New Statesman, July 12, 1974, September 23, 1977.

Newsweek, October 28, 1968, June 17, 1974, September 26, 1977, March 7, 1983, June 5, 1989.

New York, December 24, 1979, October 25, 1982.

New Yorker, October 3, 1977.

New York Review of Books, October 27, 1977, February 7, 1980, April 14, 1983.

New York Times, January 28, 1969, September 22, 1977, February 25, 1983.

New York Times Book Review, January 12, 1964, June 5, 1965, March 11, 1966, January 27, 1967, June 30, 1974, September 25, 1977, January 6, 1980, March 13, 1983, May 21, 1989.

New York Times Magazine, September 8, 1974.

People, August 19, 1974.

Publishers Weekly, September 19, 1977.

Quest/80, January, 1980.

Salmagundi, summer, 1970.

Saturday Review, July 24, 1965.

Spectator, July 6, 1974.

Time, January 17, 1964, May 29, 1964, September 29, 1980.

Times (London), September 6, 1982, June 24, 1989.

Times Literary Supplement, September 13, 1963, June 24, 1965, September 24, 1971, July 19, 1974, September 9, 1977, August 4, 1989.

Tribune Books (Chicago), May 21, 1989.

Village Voice, October 24, 1977, January 14, 1980.

Washington Post, September 29, 1980, November 29, 1982, May 25, 1989, October 14, 1989.

Washington Post Book World, December 8, 1974, December 23, 1979, June 4, 1989.

*   *   *

COUSINS, Norman 1915-1990

PERSONAL: Born June 24, 1915, in Union Hill, NJ; died November 31, 1990, in Westwood, CA; son of Samuel and Sara Barry (Miller) Cousins; married Ellen Kopf, June 23, 1939; children: Andrea, Amy Loveman, Candis Hitzig, Sara Kit. *Education:* Attended Teachers College, Columbia University.

ADDRESSES: Home—2644 Eden Pl., Beverly Hills, Calif. 90201. *Office*—Department of Psychiatry and Biobehavioral Sciences, 2859 Slichter Hall, University of California, Los Angeles, Calif. 90024.

CAREER: New York Evening Post, New York City, educational editor, 1934-35; *Current History,* New York City, 1935-40, began as book critic, became literary editor and managing editor; *Saturday Review of Literature* (now *Saturday Review*), New York City, executive editor, 1940-42, editor, 1942-71; *World,* New York City, editor, 1972-73; *Saturday Review/World,* New York City, editor, 1973-74; *Saturday Review,* New York City, editor, 1975-78; University of California, Los Angeles, currently professor of medical humanities and affiliated with Brain Research Institute. McCall's Corp., New York City, vice-president and director, beginning 1961.

Office of War Information, Overseas Bureau, member of editorial board, 1943-45; co-chairman of national campaign board of 1943 Victory Book Campaign. U. S. Government diplomat and lecturer in India, Pakistan, and Ceylon, 1951; Japan-America exchange lecturer, Japan, 1953. Chairman of board of directors of National Educational Television, 1969-70; member of Commission to Study Organized Peace; member of board of directors of Freedom House and Willkie Memorial Foundation; member of board of directors of Columbia University Conference on Science, Philosophy, and Religion. Chairman of Connecticut Fact Finding Commission on Education, 1948-52; founder and president of United World Federalists, 1952-54, honorary president, 1954-56; co-chairman of National Committee for a Sane Nuclear Policy, 1957-63.

MEMBER: American Council of Learned Societies (member-at-large), National Planning Association, National Academy of Sciences (member of committee on international relations), United Nations Association (director of U.S. Division), World Association of World Federalists, Council on Foreign Relations, National Press Club, Overseas Press Club (member of board of governors), P.E.N. (vice-president of American Center, 1952-55), Century Club, Coffee House (New York).

AWARDS, HONORS: Thomas Jefferson Award for the Advancement of Democracy in Journalism, 1948; Tuition Plan award for outstanding service to American education, 1951; Benjamin Franklin citation in magazine journalism, 1956; Wayne State University award for national service to education, 1958; New York State Citizens Education Commission award, 1959; John Dewey Award for Education, 1959; New York State Citizens Education Community award, 1959; Eleanor Roosevelt Peace award, 1963; Publius award, United World Federalists, 1964; Overseas Press Club award, 1965; Distinguished Citizen award, Connecticut Bar Association, 1965; New York Academy of Public Education award, 1966; Family of Man award, 1968; Annual award, Aquinas College, 1968; national magazine award, Association of Deans of Journalism Schools, 1969.

Peace medal, United Nations, 1971; Sarah Josepha Hale award, 1971; Carr Van Anda award for contributions to journalism, Ohio State University, 1971; Gold medal for literature, National Arts Club, 1972; Journalism Honor award, University of Missouri School of Journalism, 1972; Irita Van Doren book award, 1972; award for service to the environment, Government of Canada, 1972; Henry Johnson Fisher award as magazine publisher of the year, Magazine Publishers Association, 1971; Human Resources award, 1977; Convocation medal, American College of Cardiology, 1978; Author of the Year award, American Society of Journalists and Authors, 1981; American Book Award nomination in paperback nonfiction, 1982, for *Anatomy of an Illness as Perceived by the Patient.*

Also recipient of nearly fifty honorary doctorate degrees, including: Litt.D., American University, 1948, and Elmira College, Ripon College, Wilmington College, and University of Vermont, all 1957, and Western Michigan University; L.H.D., Boston University and Colby College, both 1953, Denison University, 1954, and Colgate University, 1958; L.L.D., Washington and Jefferson College, 1956, and Syracuse University and Albright College, both 1957; Ed.D., Rhode Island College of Education, 1958.

WRITINGS:

The Good Inheritance: The Democratic Chance, Coward, 1942.

(Editor) *A Treasury of Democracy,* Coward 1942.

Modern Man Is Obsolete, Viking, 1945.

(Editor with William Rose Benet) *An Anthology of the Poetry of Liberty,* Modern Library, 1945.

(Editor) *Writing for Love or Money: Thirty-Five Essays Reprinted from the Saturday Review of Literature,* Longmans, Green, 1949, reprinted, Books for Libraries Press, 1970.

(Contributor) John W. Chase, editor, *Years of the Modern,* Longmans, Green, 1949.

(With Jawaharlal Nehru) *Talks with Nehru,* Day, 1951.

Who Speaks for Man?, Macmillan, 1953.

Amy Loveman, 1881-1955, A Eulogy (pamphlet), Overbrook Press, 1956.

The Religious Beliefs of the Founding Fathers, 1958.

(Editor) *In God We Trust,* Harper, 1958.

(Editor) Francis March, *Thesaurus Dictionary,* Doubleday, 1958.

The Rejection of Nothingness (pamphlet), Pacific School of Religion, 1959.

Dr. Schweitzer of Lambarene, Harper, 1960, reprinted, Greenwood Press, 1973.

In Place of Folly, Harper, 1961, revised edition, Washington Square Press, 1962.

Can Cultures Co-Exist? (symposium), Ministry of Scientific Research & Cultural Affairs (New Delhi), 1963.

(With others) "*. . . Therefore Choose Life, That Thou Mayest Live, Thou and Thy Seed,*" Center for the Study of Democratic Institutions, 1965.

(Editor) *Profiles of Nehru: America Remembers a World Leader,* Indian Book Co., 1966.

(Editor) *Great American Essays,* Dell, 1967.

Present Tense: An American Editor's Odyssey, McGraw, 1967.

(With others) *Issues: 1968,* University Press of Kansas, 1968.

Profiles of Gandhi: America Remembers a World Leader, Indian Book Co., 1969.

The Improbable Triumvirate: John F. Kennedy, Pope Paul, Nikita Khruschev: An Asterisk to the History of a Hopeful Year, 1962-1963, Norton, 1972.

The Celebration of Life: A Dialogue on Immortality and Infinity, Harper, 1974.

The Quest for Immortality, Harper, 1974.

(Editor with Mary L. Dimond) *Memoirs of a Man: Grenville Clark,* Norton, 1975.

Anatomy of an Illness as Perceived by the Patient: Reflections on Healing and Regeneration, G. K. Hall, 1979, published as *Anatomy of an Illness as Perceived by the Patient,* Bantam, 1981.

Reflections on Healing and Regeneration, G. K. Hall, 1980.

Human Options: An Autobiographical Notebook, Norton, 1981.

The Physician in Literature, Saunders, 1981.

Healing and Belief, Mosaic Press, 1982.

The Healing Heart: Antidotes to Panic and Helplessness, Norton, 1983.

The Trial of Dr. Mesmer: A Play, Norton, 1984.

Albert Schweitzer's Mission: Healing and Peace, Norton, 1985.

The Human Adventure: A Camera Chronicle, Saybrook, 1986.

The Pathology of Power, Norton, 1987.

(Editor) *The Republic of Reason: The Personal Philosophies of the Founding Fathers,* Harper, 1988.

(Author of commentary) *Jason Sitwell's Book of Spoofs,* Dutton, 1989.

Head First: The Biology of Hope, Dutton, 1989.

Also author of *The Last Defense in a Nuclear Age,* 1960. Also featured in sound recording "Betting One's Life on the Future of Print," Development Digest, 1973. Editor *U. S. A.,* 1943-45; member of board of editors, *Encyclopaedia Britannica;* editorial supervisor, *March's Dictionary-Thesaurus,* 1980.

SIDELIGHTS: "I get a kick out of challenging the odds," Norman Cousins told *Publishers Weekly* interviewer Lisa See. His life and career gave him ample opportunity to do just that. As longtime editor of *Saturday Review,* Cousins bolstered that magazine's circulation to 650,000. He also served as a diplomat during three presidential administrations, became a professor of medical humanities, and produced numerous books on political and social issues. In the process, Cousins fended off a life-threatening disease and a massive coronary, both times using his own regimen of nutritional and emotional support systems as opposed to traditional methods of treatment (and he chronicles his experiences in two books, *Anatomy of an Illness as Perceived by the Patient: Reflections on Healing and Regeneration* and *The Healing Heart: Antidotes to Panic and Helplessness*). "Cousins has led a wonderful, if strangely related, series of overlapping lives," comments See. "He is a complex meshing of science and letters. He is serious and silly, intellectual and maniacal."

Cousins is often described as the man who laughed his way to health, a simplified explanation of the controversial healing method the author/editor employed when he was diagnosed in the mid-1960s as having ankylosing spondylitis. The degenerative disease causes the breakdown of collagen, the fiberous tissue that binds together the body's cells. Almost completely paralyzed, given only a few months to live, Cousins ordered himself checked out of the hospital where he had spent weeks undergoing tests. He moved into a hotel room and began taking extremely high doses of vitamin C, counting on the ascorbic acid to oxygenate his bloodstream, counteracting the effects of the illness. At the same time, intent on maintaining a positive mental outlook, Cousins exposed himself to equally high doses of humor—old "Candid Camera" tapes, Marx Brothers movies, and books by P. G. Wodehouse, Robert Benchley, and James Thurber. This unusual regimen started to work: "I made the joyous discovery that ten minutes of genuine belly laughter had an anesthetic effect and would give me at least two hours of pain-free sleep," writes Cousins in *Anatomy of an Illness.* Slowly, the patient regained use of his limbs. As his condition steadily improved over the following months, Cousins resumed his busy life, eventually returning to work full-time at the *Saturday Review.*

As Cousins notes in his book, "the will to live is not a theoretical abstraction, but a physiologic reality with therapeutic characteristics." While not denying that the right attitude can certainly help a patient through his illness, some of his critics have questioned the nature of Cousins's ailment and the healing methods he now swears by. In a *Commentary* article Florence A. Ruderman takes exception to the author's case history as related in *Anatomy of an Illness.* Ruderman emphasizes that she does believe the " 'positive emotions' play a role in health. But the 'positive emotions' that are a force in maintaining life, well-being, resistance to disease, or recuperative or regenerative capacity, are those that stem from deep, relatively constant levels of one's psychological nature, one's inner being. They are affected by long-term circumstances of life and by major life events."

The critic also asks if Cousins's treatment can be adapted by the general public—and if it should be at all. "Should *all* patients have the same rights and freedom that Cousins had?," she writes. "If not, why is it inspiring that such rights and deference were accorded to Cousins? Under what circumstances should doctors allow patients to choose their own drugs, invent their own routines and regimens—in effect, direct their doctors? . . . How was it possible for so many doctors to greet [the author's] account with enthusiasm, and ignore every substantive and ethical issue in it?" Responding to Ruderman's charge, Cousins says in the *Publishers Weekly* article that "she didn't see the medical reports and didn't interview the doctors." Another criticism, he adds, "in the *Mt. Sinai Journal of Medicine, . . .* said that I might have had a nominal remission. That may be right, but the doctors didn't think so at the time."

Others find more to recommend in *Anatomy of an Illness.* Daphne Abeel suggests in *New Republic* that Cousins's story "is a tribute to what may be achieved by the individual. It is not a brief for self-cure in any and all circumstances, as he is quick to point out. And it must be said that not every patient will possess Cousins's unusual curiosity and knowledge about medicine. Still, his example of gumption and faith will offer hope to many." And *Washington Post* critic Richard Restak calls the book "an entertaining and instructive example of an inspired participation on the part of a patient in his own treatment."

In December, 1980, some fifteen years after winning his bout with ankylosing spondylitis, Cousins suffered a near-fatal heart attack while on a teaching assignment in California. Again faced with the challenge of restoring his health, Cousins responded by telling his doctors at the UCLA Intensive Care unit that they were "looking at what is probably the darndest healing machine that has ever been wheeled into the hospital," according to Joel Elkes's *Saturday Review* article on *The Healing Heart.* "As before," Elkes continues, "Cousins makes his body a personal laboratory and befriends the society within his skin. He refuses morphine; he asks for a change in the visiting routine to ensure rest. Gradually he improves."

One major obstacle Cousins faced in his recovery was the treadmill test, designed to chart the progress of his heart rate. The patient was "scared stiff at *being* exercised, at an accelerating pace, on a moving band over which he had no control," explains Elkes. "He tries to suppress his fear, but fails and has to stop. He tries again and cannot manage." Realizing his fear was the factor in slowing his progress, Cousins adopted a more relaxed life style, changing his diet and avoiding stressful situations. "As his health improves, Cousins repeats the treadmill examination," Fred Rosenfelt reports in the *Los Angeles Times.* "This time, he controls the machine while listening to classical music and comedy tapes. His test is better."

In publishing these findings in *The Healing Heart,* Cousins again met with mixed reaction. Rosenfelt, for instance, while acknowledging that the author's "opinion of the salutary effects of positive emotion is widely accepted," nevertheless wonders "how many patients have the fortitude to disagree with their physicians and follow an alternative recovery program after a major heart attack? Furthermore, if a large number of individuals do so, how many will improve or worsen?" Elkes, on the other hand, argues that *The Healing Heart* is not a medical textbook, but a study of "awareness, listening, trust, choice, and intention, and about the intelligent use of a benevolent, centering will. It is about communication and partnership between the healer and the healed. It addresses as complementary the art of medicine and the science of medicine, the person and the institution, and freedom of choice and professional responsibility. [The book] affirms hope and belief as biologically constructive forces: not as blind faith, but as belief guided by knowledge and tempered by reason. It asserts that the quality of a person's life is the sum of the quality of his days."

Despite his bouts with near-fatal ailments, Cousins remained an active literary force. His most popular book of the late 1980s was almost certainly *Head First,* a further elucidation of his beliefs and concerns regarding medicine and doctor-patient relations. Another key work, 1987's *The Pathology of Power,* addresses the issue of world peace. Wray Herbert, writing in the *Washington Post Book World,* hailed this volume as "an important and disturbing document."

Cousins's books have been translated into several languages.

MEDIA ADAPTATIONS: Anatomy of an Illness as Perceived by the Patient: Reflections on Healing and Regeneration was adapted into a television movie for Columbia Broadcasting System. Titled "Anatomy of an Illness," the film starred Ed Asner as Cousins and was broadcast on May 15, 1984.

BIOGRAPHICAL/CRITICAL SOURCES:

BOOKS

Cousins, Norman, *Present Tense: An American Editor's Odyssey,* McGraw, 1967.

Cousins, Norman, *Anatomy of an Illness as Perceived by the Patient: Reflections on Healing and Regeneration,* G. K. Hall, 1979, published as *Anatomy of an Illness as Perceived by the Patient,* Bantam, 1981.

Cousins, Norman, *Human Options: An Autobiographical Notebook,* Norton, 1981.

Cousins, Norman, *The Healing Heart: Antidotes to Panic and Helplessness,* Norton, 1983.

PERIODICALS

Chicago Tribune, December 26, 1979.
Commentary, May, 1980.
Detroit News, June 22, 1980.
Esquire, February, 1980.
Los Angeles Times, September 29, 1983.
Los Angeles Times Book Review, December 13, 1981, October 24, 1982, December 3, 1989.
National Review, April 30, 1982, December 9, 1983.
New Republic, September 29, 1979.
New Statesman, October 3, 1980.
New York Times, June 22, 1972, September 15, 1979, May 8, 1984, May 15, 1984.
New York Times Book Review, January 1, 1984.
People, June 1, 1979.
Publishers Weekly, September 23, 1983.
Saturday Review, September-October, 1983.
Time, August 30, 1982.
Times Literary Supplement, March 30, 1984.
Washington Post, October 9, 1979, November 9, 1981.
Washington Post Book World, April 12, 1987, November 5, 1989.*

* * *

CUNNINGHAM, E. V.
    See FAST, Howard (Melvin)

D

DALE, Robert D(ennis) 1940-

PERSONAL: Born August 23, 1940, in Neosho, MO; son of Ivan A. and Jewel M. (Kingry) Dale; married Carrie Lou Kondy, August 25, 1962; children: Cassidy Steele, Amy Dawn. *Education:* Southwest Baptist College (now University), A.A., 1960; Oklahoma Baptist University, B.A., 1962; Southwestern Baptist Theological Seminary, B.D., 1966, Ph.D., 1970; postdoctoral study at Southern Methodist University, Kansas University, and North Carolina Central University.

ADDRESSES: Home—2006 Raintree Ave., Richmond, VA 23233. *Office*—Virginia Baptist General Board, 2828 Emerywood Dr., P.O. Box 8568, Richmond, VA 23226.

CAREER: Ordained Baptist minister, 1960; pastor of Baptist church in Pierce City, MO, 1959-60; Young Men's Christian Association (YMCA), Shawnee, OK, counselor, 1960-62; youth minister at Baptist church in Fort Worth, TX, 1963-65; pastor of Baptist church in Wynnewood, OK, 1965-68; associate pastor of Baptist church in Dallas, TX, 1968-70; pastor of Baptist church in Lawrence, KA, 1970-72; Baptist Sunday School Board, Nashville, TN, consultant and supervisor in church administration department, 1973-77; Southeastern Baptist Theological Seminary, Wake Forest, IL, professor of pastoral leadership and church ministries, 1977-88, director of doctoral studies, 1977-88, acting dean, 1988; Virginia Baptist General Board, Richmond, director of Division of Church and Minister Support, 1989—. Adjunct professor of field education, Vanderbilt University Divinity School, 1974-77.

WRITINGS:

Growing a Loving church, Convention Press, 1974.
A Pastor's Guide to Marriage Counseling, Material Services, 1976.
(With wife, Carrie Kondy Dale) *Making Good Marriages Better,* Broadman, 1978.
To Dream Again, Broadman, 1981.
(With Bill Bruster) *How to Encourage Others,* Broadman, 1983.
(With C. K. Dale) *Marriage: Partnership of the Committed,* Sunday School Board of the Southern Baptist Convention, 1983.
Surviving Difficult Church Members, Abingdon, 1984.
(With Delos Miles) *Evangelizing the Hard-to-Reach,* Broadman, 1986.

Sharing Ministry with Volunteer Leaders, Convention Press, 1986.
Pastoral Leadership, Abingdon, 1986.
(With Truman Brown) *Reviving the Plateaued Church,* Broadman, in press.

Also author of scripts and audiotapes. Also contributor to books. Columnist for *Mature Living.* Contributor to periodicals.

WORK IN PROGRESS: A theology of religious leadership.

SIDELIGHTS: Robert D. Dale told *CA:* "I am a 'people detective'—especially people in families and congregations. I listen to the questions I hear repeatedly in these group settings and try to answer them. The 'along the way' discoveries I've made in researching these issues have led to some of my best writing and most enjoyable teaching. My Christian values keep me curious and (I hope) realistic about human nature."

*   *   *

DAVIS, Melodie M(iller) 1951-

PERSONAL: Born December 2, 1951, in Sarasota, FL; daughter of Vernon U. (a farmer) and Bertha (a homemaker; maiden name, Stauffer) Miller; married Stuart Davis (a factory laborer), May 29, 1976; children: Michelle, Tanya, Doreen. *Education:* Attended University of Barcelona, 1973-74; Eastern Mennonite College, B.A., 1975. *Religion:* "Mennonite- Presbyterian."

ADDRESSES: Home—Route 2, Box 494, Harrisonburg, VA 22801. *Office*—Media Ministries Department, Mennonite Board of Missions, 1251 Virginia Ave., Harrisonburg, VA 22801.

CAREER: Nursery school teacher and day camp leader in Hazard, KY, 1970- 71; WVPT-TV, Harrisonburg, VA, production assistant, 1974-75; Mennonite Board of Missions, Harrisonburg, writer and producer of media programs, 1975—. Writing teacher at Eastern Mennonite College. Leader of retreats and television awareness training workshops. Elder in the Presbyterian Church.

MEMBER: Virginia Press Women (district director).

AWARDS, HONORS: Has received numerous writing awards from National Federation of Press Women and Virginia Press Women.

WRITINGS:

On Troublesome Creek, Herald Press, 1983.
For the Next Nine Months: Meditations for Expectant Mothers, Zondervan, 1984.
Working, Mothering, and Other Minor Dilemmas, Word, Inc., 1984.
You Know You're a Mother When . . . , Zondervan, 1986.
Facing Tough Times, Choice Books, 1987.
Becoming a Better Friend, Bethany House, 1988.
Following God's Call (video curriculum), Herald Press, 1989.
(Contributor) *The Marriage Collection,* Zondervan, 1989.

Also author of video script for "All God's People" and other videos. Author of syndicated column "Another Way" in twenty newspapers. Contributor to periodicals, including *Christian Living, With, Presbyterian Survey, Purpose, Voice,* and *Builder.*

WORK IN PROGRESS: Departure, an autobiographical book based on her year in Spain; a book arising from her syndicated columns.

SIDELIGHTS: Melodie M. Davis told *CA:* "I suppose before someone gets their first book published it is natural to dream about how famous and rich this is going to make you, whereas all published writers know that most—the vast majority of writers—are known only to a small group of readers. Therefore the writer gets to the point where the motivation is not riches or fame but simply being faithful to a calling, of continuing to write simply because it is the way a writer deals with life. Writing is not any more noble than plumbing or building roads or nursing to make a living; in its most elemental form, it is simply putting one word after another in sentences!

"I keep saying I'm going to stop writing and do something that makes more money. Then I find myself writing again because something in me does not feel complete or whole if life is not spilling out on a printed page."

*   *   *

DEIGHTON, Len
See DEIGHTON, Leonard Cyril

*   *   *

DEIGHTON, Leonard Cyril 1929-
(Len Deighton)

PERSONAL: Born February 18, 1929, in Marylebone, London, England; married Shirley Thompson (an illustrator), 1960. *Education:* Attended St. Martin's School of Art, London, three years; Royal College of Art, graduate.

ADDRESSES: Office—25 Newman St., London W.1, England.

CAREER: Author. Worked as a railway lengthman, an assistant pastry cook at the Royal Festival Hall, 1951, a manager of a gown factory in Aldgate, England, a waiter in Piccadilly, an advertising man in London and New York City, a teacher in Brittany, a co-proprietor of a glossy magazine, and as a magazine artist and news photographer; steward, British Overseas Airways Corporation (BOAC), 1956-57; producer of films, including "Only When I Larf," based on his novel of the same title, 1969.

WRITINGS:

UNDER NAME LEN DEIGHTON

Only When I Larf (novel), M. Joseph, 1968, published as *Only When I Laugh,* Mysterious Press, 1987.

"Oh, What a Lovely War!" (screenplay), Paramount, 1969.
Bomber: Events Relating to the Last Flight of an R.A.F. Bomber Over Germany on the Night of June 31, 1943 (novel), Harper, 1970.
Declarations of War (story collection), J. Cape, 1971, published as *Eleven Declarations of War,* Harcourt, 1975.
Close-Up (novel), Atheneum, 1972.
SS-GB: Nazi-Occupied Britain, 1941 (novel), J. Cape, 1978, Knopf, 1979.
Goodbye, Mickey Mouse (novel; Book-of-the-Month Club selection), Knopf, 1982.
Winter: A Novel of a Berlin Family (Book-of-the-Month Club alternate selection), Knopf, 1988.

Also author of television scripts "Long Past Glory," 1963, and "It Must Have Been Two Other Fellows," 1977. Also author of weekly comic strip on cooking, *Observer,* 1962—.

ESPIONAGE NOVELS; UNDER NAME LEN DEIGHTON

The Ipcress File, Fawcett, 1962, reprinted, Ballantine, 1982.
Horse Under Water (Literary Guild selection), J. Cape, 1963, Putnam, 1967.
Funeral in Berlin, J. Cape, 1964, Putnam, 1965.
The Billion Dollar Brain, Putnam, 1966.
An Expensive Place to Die, Putnam, 1967.
Spy Story, Harcourt, 1974.
Yesterday's Spy, Harcourt, 1975.
Twinkle, Twinkle, Little Spy, J. Cape, 1976, published as *Catch a Falling Spy,* Harcourt, 1976.
XPD, Knopf, 1981.
Berlin Game, Knopf, 1983.
Mexico Set (Literary Guild selection), Knopf, 1985.
London Match, Knopf, 1985.
Spy Hook (Book-of-the-Month Club selection), Knopf, 1988.
Spy Line, Knopf, 1989.
Spy Sinker, Harper, 1990.

NONFICTION; UNDER NAME LEN DEIGHTON

(Editor) *Drinks-man-ship: Town's Album of Fine Wines and High Spirits,* Haymarket Press, 1964.
Ou est le garlic; or, Len Deighton's French Cookbook, Penguin, 1965, revised edition published as *Basic French Cooking,* J. Cape, 1979.
Action Cookbook: Len Deighton's Guide to Eating, J. Cape, 1965.
Len Deighton's Cookstrip Cook Book, Bernard Geis Associates, 1966.
(Editor with Michael Rand and Howard Loxton) *The Assassination of President Kennedy,* J. Cape, 1967.
(Editor and contributor) *Len Deighton's London Dossier,* J. Cape, 1967.
Len Deighton's Continental Dossier: A Collection of Cultural, Culinary, Historical, Spooky, Grim and Preposterous Fact, compiled by Victor and Margaret Pettitt, M. Joseph, 1968.
Fighter: The True Story of the Battle of Britain, J. Cape, 1977, Knopf, 1978.
(With Peter Mayle) *How to Be a Pregnant Father,* Lyle Stuart, 1977.
(With Arnold Schwartzman) *Airshipwreck,* J. Cape, 1978, Holt, 1979.
(With Simon Goodenough) *Tactical Genius in Battle,* Phaidon Press, 1979.
Blitzkrieg: From the Rise of Hitler to the Fall of Dunkirk, Coward, 1980.
Battle of Britain, Coward, 1980.

WORK IN PROGRESS: Spy Sinker, the third and final novel in Deighton's second trilogy about the adventures of British intelligence agent Bernard Samson.

SIDELIGHTS: With his early novels, especially *The Ipcress File* and *Funeral in Berlin,* Len Deighton established himself as one of the mainstays of modern espionage fiction. He is often ranked—along with Graham Greene, John le Carre, and Ian Fleming—among the foremost writers in the field. Deighton shows a painstaking attention to accuracy in depicting espionage activities, and in his early novels this realism was combined with a light ironic touch that set his work apart. Deighton, David Quammen remarks in the *New York Times Book Review,* is "a talented, droll and original spy novelist."

Deighton's early novels are written in an elliptical style that emphasizes the mysterious nature of the espionage activities portrayed. They feature a nameless British intelligence officer who is quite different from the usual fictional spy. This officer is a reluctant spy, cynical, and full of wisecracks. Unlike many other British agents, he is also, Julian Symons states in *Mortal Consequences: A History—From the Detective Story to the Crime Novel,* "a working-class boy from Brunley, opposed to all authority, who dislikes or distrusts anybody outside his own class. He is set down in a world of terrifying complexity, in which nobody is ever what he seems." "The creation of this slightly anarchic, wise-cracking, working-class hero," T. J. Binyon writes in the *Times Literary Supplement,* "was Deighton's most original contribution to the spy thriller. And this, taken together with his characteristic highly elliptical expositional manner, with his fascination with the technical nuts and bolts of espionage, and with a gift for vivid, startling description, make the first seven [of Deighton's spy] stories classics of the genre." Peter S. Prescott of *Newsweek,* speaking of the early novels featuring Deighton's nameless hero, finds that the style, marked by "oblique narration, nervous laughter and ironic detachment, . . . effectively transformed [Deighton's] spy stories into comedies of manners."

Deighton's elliptical style in these early books is clipped and episodic, deliberately omitting vital explanations of what his characters are discussing or thinking. This style, Robin W. Winks writes in the *New Republic,* makes Deighton's "plots seem more complex than they are. . . . Because very little is stated explicitly, sequences appear to begin in mid-passage, and only through observation of the action does one come to understand either the motives of the villains, or the thought processes of the heroes." In these novels, Winks concludes, "Deighton had patented a style in which every third paragraph appeared to have been left out." Although this style confuses some readers—Prescott claims that Deighton's "specialty has always been a nearly incoherent plot"—Pearl K. Bell finds it well suited to the subject matter of Deighton's novels. Writing in *New Leader,* Bell states that Deighton's "obsessive reliance on the blurred and intangible, on loaded pauses and mysteriously disjointed dialogue, did convey the shadowy meanness of the spy's world, with its elusive loyalties, camouflaged identities and weary brutality."

Deighton was an immediate success with his first novel, *The Ipcress File,* a book that the late Anthony Boucher of the *New York Times Book Review* admits "caused quite a stir among both critics and customers in England." Introducing Deighton's nameless protagonist in an adventure that takes him to a nuclear testing site on a Pacific atoll, to the Middle East, and behind the Iron Curtain, the book continues to be popular for its combination of a serious espionage plot with a parody of the genre. As Richard Locke observes in the *New York Times Book Review, The Ipcress*

File possesses "a Kennedy-cool amorality . . . , a cross of Hammett and cold war lingo."

Critics praise the book's gritty evocation of intelligence work, ironic narrative, and comic touches. Boucher calls it "a sharply written, ironic and realistic tale of modern spy activities." Deighton's humor attracts the most attention from John B. Cullen of *Best Sellers,* who claims that in *The Ipcress File* "Deighton writes with a tongue-in-cheek attitude. . . . No one is spared the needle of subtle ridicule, but the author still tells a plausible story which holds your attention throughout." However, for Robert Donald Spectar of the *New York Herald Tribune Book Review* Deighton's humor ruins the espionage story. "Deighton," Spectar writes, "has combined picaresque satire, parody, and suspense and produced a hybrid more humorous than thrilling." But this opinion is disputed by G. W. Stonier in the *New Statesman.* Comparing Deighton with James Bond creator Ian Fleming, Stonier finds Deighton to be "a good deal more expert and twice the writer" and believes "there has been no brighter arrival on the shady scene since Graham Greene." Even in 1979, some seventeen years after the book's initial publication, Julian Symons of the *New York Times Book Review* was moved to call *The Ipcress File* "a dazzling performance. The verve and energy, the rattle of wit in the dialogue, the side-of-the-mouth comments, the evident pleasure taken in cocking a snook at the British spy story's upper-middle-class tradition—all these, together with the teasing convolutions of the plot, made it clear that a writer of remarkable talent in this field had appeared."

Deighton's reputation as an espionage writer was enhanced by *Funeral in Berlin,* a story revolving around an attempt to smuggle a defecting East German biologist out of Berlin. With the assistance of a high-ranking Russian agent, former Nazi intelligence officers, and a free-lance operator of doubtful allegiance, Deighton's unnamed hero arranges the details of the defection. The many plot twists, and Deighton's enigmatic presentation of his story, prompt Stephen Hugh-Jones of *New Statesman* to admit, "I spent most of the book wondering what the devil was going on." Boucher finds the mysterious goings-on to be handled well. "The double and triple crosses involved," Boucher writes, "are beautifully worked out." Published at the same time as John le Carre's classic espionage tale *The Spy Who Came in From the Cold,* a novel also set in Germany's divided city, *Funeral in Berlin* compares favorably with its competitor. Boucher calls its plot "very nearly as complex and nicely calculated," while Charles Poore of the *New York Times* maintains it is "even better" than le Carre's book. It is, Poore concludes, "a ferociously cool fable of the current struggle between East and West." Andy East of *Armchair Detective* claims that *Funeral in Berlin* "has endured as Deighton's most celebrated novel."

Since these early novels, Deighton's style has evolved, becoming more expansive and less oblique. His "approach has grown more sophisticated," Mark Schorr relates in the *Los Angeles Times Book Review.* "His more recent writings offer a deft balance of fact, scene-setting and the who-can-we-trust paranoia that makes spy novels engrossing." Peter Elstob of *Books and Bookmen* elaborates on the change. Deighton "develops with each new book," Elstob believes. "He could have gone on repeating the formula of *The Ipcress File* with undoubted success, but instead he tried for more subtlety, for more convincing, more substantial characters."

Of his later espionage novels, perhaps his most important work has been the trilogy comprised of *Berlin Game, Mexico Set,* and *London Match.* Here, Deighton spins a long story of moles (agents working within an enemy intelligence organization), defection, and betrayal that also comments on his own writing career, the espionage genre, and the cold war between East and West that has inspired such fiction. Derrick Murdoch of the Toronto *Globe and Mail* calls the trilogy "Deighton's most ambitious project; the conventional spy-story turned inside-out."

The first novel of the trilogy, *Berlin Game,* opens with two agents waiting near the Berlin Wall for a defector to cross over from East Berlin. "How long have we been sitting here?" asks Bernie Samson, British agent and the protagonist of the trilogy. "Nearly a quarter of a century," his companion replies. With that exchange Deighton underlines the familiarity of this scene in espionage fiction, in his own early work and in the work of others, while commenting on the continuing relevance of the Berlin Wall as a symbol of East-West conflict, notes Anthony Olcott in the *Washington Post Book World.* Deighton, Olcott argues, "is not only aware of this familiarity, it is his subject. . . . Berlin and the Wall remain as much the embodiment of East-West rivalry as ever. . . . To read *Berlin Game* is to shrug off 25 years of acclimatization to the Cold War, and to recall what espionage fiction is about in the first place."

In *Berlin Game,* Samson works to uncover a Soviet agent secretly working at the highest levels of British intelligence. This, too, is a standard plot in spy fiction, inspired by the real-life case of Soviet spy Kim Philby. But, as the *New Yorker* critic points out, "Deighton, as always, makes the familiar twists and turns of spy errantry new again, partly by his grip of narrative, partly by his grasp of character, and partly by his easy, sardonic tone." Prescott claims that the novel does not display the wit of Deighton's earlier works, but the book overcomes its faults because of Deighton's overall skill as a storyteller. "Each scene in this story," Prescott writes, "is so adroitly realized that it creates its own suspense. Samson, the people who work for him, his wife, even the twits who have some reason to be working for Moscow, are interesting characters; what they say to each other is convincing. Besides, the book is full of Berlin lore: we can easily believe that Samson did grow up there and thinks of it as home." In like terms, Christopher Lehmann-Haupt of the *New York Times* holds that in *Berlin Game* "the immediate scene is always brilliantly clear, thanks mostly to Mr. Deighton's intimate familiarity with the Berlin landscape. Every building and street seems to have resonance for him, which he imparts to the reader." Olcott judges *Berlin Game* to be "among Deighton's best books" because "his Berlin, his characters, the smallest details of his narrative are so sharp." Olcott concludes that it is "a book to strip away the age-withered, custom-staled betrayals of all that quarter century of novels, perhaps even of history, and once again make painful, real, alive, the meaning of treason."

Mexico Set continues the story begun in *Berlin Game.* In the first book, Samson uncovers the spy in British intelligence---his own wife---and she defects to East Germany. To redeem himself in the eyes of his superiors, who now harbor understandable doubts about his own loyalty, Samson works in *Mexico Set* to convince a Russian KGB agent to defect. But the agent may only be a plant meant to further discredit Samson and destroy his credibility. If Samson cannot convince him to defect, his superiors may assume that he is secretly working for the Russians himself. But the Russian may defect only to provide British intelligence with "proof" of Samson's treason. As in *Berlin Game,* Deighton relates this novel back to the origins of the cold war and, "just when you've forgotten what the Cold War was all about, Len Deighton takes you right back to the [Berlin] Wall and rubs your nose on it," as Chuck Moss writes in the *Detroit News.*

Samson's efforts to persuade the Russian agent to defect take him from London to Mexico, Paris, and Berlin. "Every mile along the way," Noel Behn writes in the *Chicago Tribune,* "objectives seem to alter, friends and enemies become indistinguishable, perils increase, people disappear, people die." Behn finds it is Deighton's characters that make the story believable: "They strut forward one after the other—amusing, beguiling, arousing, deceiving, threatening—making us look in the wrong direction when it most behooves the prestidigitator's purpose." Ross Thomas also sees Deighton's characters as an essential ingredient in the novel's success. Writing in the *Washington Post Book World,* Thomas reports that Deighton "serves up fascinating glimpses of such types as the nearly senile head of British intelligence; a KGB major with a passion for Sherlock Holmes; and Samson's boyhood friend and Jewish orphan, Werner Volkmann," all of whom Thomas finds to be "convincing characters." Thomas concludes that *Mexico Set* is "one of [Deighton's] better efforts," while Behn calls the novel "a pure tale, told by an author at the height of his power."

In the final novel of the trilogy, *London Match,* the Russian agent has defected to the British. But Samson must now decide whether the defector is telling the truth when he insists that a high-ranking member of British intelligence is a Russian mole. The situation grows more complicated when the suspected mole, one of Samson's superiors, comes to Samson for help in clearing his name. *London Match* "is the most complex novel of the trilogy," Julius Lester writes in the *New York Times Book Review.*

But Lester finds *London Match*'s complexity to be a liability. He thinks "the feeling it conveys of being trapped in a maze of distorting mirrors is almost a cliche in spy novels now." Similarly, Gene Lyons of *Newsweek* calls *London Match* "not the most original spy story ever told." In his review of the book for the *Washington Post Book World,* J. I. M. Stewart criticizes Deighton's characterization. He states that "the characters, although liable to bore a little during their frequently over-extended verbal fencings, are tenaciously true to themselves even if not quite to human nature."

But even critics with reservations about some of the novel's qualities find aspects of the book to praise. Stewart lauds Deighton's ability to recreate the settings of his story. "The places, whether urban or rural, can be described only as triumphs alike of painstaking observation and striking descriptive power," Stewart writes. Lester finds this strength, too, calling "the best character" in the book "the city of Berlin. It is a living presence, and in some of the descriptions one can almost hear the stones breathing."

More favorable critics point to Deighton's handling of characters as one of the book's best features. Schorr, for example, believes that "Deighton gives a skilled and believable portrait of Samson. . . . Samson maintains his professional cool, but there is a sense that emotions are repressed, and not nonexistent, as with too many other spy heroes." Margaret Cannon of the Toronto *Globe and Mail* has nothing but praise for *London Match.* She calls the trilogy "some of [Deighton's] best work," and *London Match* "a brilliant climax to the story."

Deighton continues Samson's adventures in 1988's *Spy Hook,* the first story in a second trilogy about the British intelligence agent. In this thriller, Samson is charged with accounting for the disappearance of millions in Secret Service funds. At first, he suspects his ex-wife—who defected in the earlier *Berlin Game*—as the thief, but later Samson learns that his superiors have begun to suspect him for the crime. *Spy Hook* was chosen as a Book-of-the-Month Club selection and became a best-seller. Critical reception of the work was generally favorable, with reviewers praising the book's carefully developed and intricate plot, detailed settings, and suspenseful atmosphere. A number of reviewers, however, reacted negatively to the book's ending, which they feel is too ambiguous. "Deighton's craftsmanship—his taut action and his insightful study of complex characters under pressure—is very much in place here, but many . . . unanswered questions raised in *Spy Hook* remain just that at the novel's conclusion," states Don G. Campbell, for example, in the *Los Angeles Times Book Review*. Several critics, though, share Margaret Cannon's Toronto *Globe and Mail* assessment of *Spy Hook* as matching Deighton's previous achievements in the espionage genre. The novel, she writes, "promises to be even better than its terrific predecessors and proves that Deighton, the old spymaster, is still in top form." In 1989, Deighton followed *Spy Hook* with the trilogy's second installment, *Spy Line,* with the third and concluding book, *Spy Sinker,* to follow.

Although Deighton is best known for his espionage fiction, he has also written best-selling novels outside the espionage field, as well as books of military history. These other novels and books of history are usually concerned with the events and figures of the World War II. Among the most successful of his novels have been *SS-GB: Nazi-Occupied Britain, 1941* and *Goodbye, Mickey Mouse. Fighter: The True Story of the Battle of Britain* has earned Deighton praise as a writer of military history. Deighton's writing in other fields has shown him, Symons writes, to be "determined not to stay within the conventional pattern of the spy story or thriller."

SS-GB takes place in an alternative history of World War II, a history in which England lost the crucial Battle of Britain and Nazi Germany conquered the country. The story takes place after the conquest when Scotland Yard superintendent Douglas Archer investigates a murder and finds that the trail leads to the upper echelons of the Nazi party. An underground plot to rescue the king of England, who is being held prisoner in the Tower of London, and the ongoing efforts of the Nazis to develop the atom bomb also complicate Archer's problems. "As is usual with Mr. Deighton," John Leonard writes in *Books of the Times,* "there are as many twists as there are betrayals."

Deighton's ability to fully render what a Nazi-occupied Britain would be like is the most widely-noted strength of the book. "The atmosphere of occupied England," Michael Demarest writes in his review of *SS-GB* for *Newsweek,* "is limned in eerie detail. . . . In fact, Deighton's ungreened isle frequently seems even more realistic than the authentic backgrounds of his previous novels." "What especially distinguishes 'SS-GB,' " Leonard believes, "is its gritty atmosphere, the shadows of defeat on every page. Yes, we think, this is what martial law would feel like; this is the way the Germans would have behaved; this is how rationing and the black market and curfews and detention camps would work; this is the contempt for ourselves that we would experience."

Although Michael Howard of the *Times Literary Supplement* agrees that "there can be little doubt that this is much the way things would have turned out if the Germans had won the war in 1940," he nonetheless concludes that "on this level of imaginative creation Mr. Deighton is so good that the second level, the plot itself, seems by comparison unnecessarily silly and confused." This criticism of the novel's plot is shared by Paul Ableman of the *Spectator,* who complains: "From about Page 100, the subversive thought kept surfacing: what is the point of this kind of historical 'might have been'? . . . I fear [the novel] ultimately lost its hold on me. We could have been given the same yarn set in occupied France."

But Symons and many other reviewers judge *SS-GB* a successful and imaginative novel. It is, Symons writes, "a triumphant success. It is Mr. Deighton's best book, one that blends his expertise in the spy field with his interest in military and political history to produce an absorbingly exciting spy story that is also a fascinating exercise in might-have-been speculation." And Demarest concludes his review by predicting that *SS-GB* "is on its way to becoming a worldwide classic of the 'What If?' genre."

Goodbye, Mickey Mouse, another Deighton novel about World War II, concerns a group of American pilots in England who run fighter protection for the bombers making daylight runs over Germany. It is described by Thomas Gifford of the *Washington Post Book World* as "satisfying on every imaginable level, but truly astonishing in its recreation of a time and place through minute detail." Equally high praise comes from Peter Andrews, who writes in his review for the *New York Times Book Review:* "Deighton's latest World War II adventure novel is such a plain, old-fashioned, good book about combat pilots who make war and fall in love that it defies a complicated examination. . . . 'Goodbye, Mickey Mouse' is high adventure of the best sort but always solidly true to life."

Not all reviewers were so enthusiastic, but even those with reservations about the novel's ultimate quality were impressed with the way Deighton presented the scenes of aerial combat. "As long as he keeps his propellers turning," Prescott allows in his *Newsweek* review, "Deighton's book lives. He understands the camaraderie of pilots and to a lesser degree the politics of combat. . . . It's a pity that his people, like his prose, are built from plywood." Similarly, the reviewer for *Harper's* reports that "the book is oddly anemic—except on the subject of fighter planes. Deighton's obsession with planes makes the combat sequences lurid and exciting. If only the rest of the book were too."

While sharing the belief that Deighton writes extremely well about aerial combat, Lehmann-Haupt sees a more serious side to the novel which, for him, raises it "above the merely entertaining." Deighton, Lehmann-Haupt writes, "has an almost uncanny ability to make war action in the air come visually alive. . . . But what is most intriguing about 'Goodbye, Mickey Mouse' is that it explores a profound but little noticed aspect of war—namely, the necessity it creates for parents to send their children off to death." The book's title, the last words of a dying pilot to his friend, Lieutenant Morse, nicknamed Mickey Mouse, are "also an expression of farewell to childhood and its trivialities, as well as what a father or mother might say to a departing son," Lehmann-Haupt concludes. Gifford, too, interprets the novel on a more serious level. Speaking of the generation who fought in the Second World War, many of whom are "approaching the time when they will one by one pass into our history," Gifford finds Deighton's novel a tribute to that generation and its monumental fight. "Some of them," Gifford writes, "are fittingly memorialized in Deighton's hugely assured novel."

The crucial Battle of Britain, which figures prominently in *SS-GB,* and the air battles of that period, which appear in *Goodbye, Mickey Mouse,* are further explored in the nonfiction *Fighter,* a history of the Royal Air Force defense of England during the Battle of Britain. A highly acclaimed popular account of what Noble Frankland of the *Times Literary Supplement* calls "among the handful of decisive battles in British history," *Fighter* "is the best, most dispassionate story of the battle I have read," Drew Middleton states in the *New York Times Book Review,* "and I say that even though the book destroyed many of my illusions and, indeed, attacks the validity of some of what I wrote as an eyewitness of the air battle 38 years ago."

The Battle of Britain took place over several months of 1940. After overrunning France, the Nazi leadership focused their attention on softening up England for an invasion. They launched extensive bombing raids against the British Isles, attacking the city of London, air bases, factories, and seaports. The Royal Air Force, vastly outnumbered by their opponents, bravely fought the Germans to a standstill which resulted in the proposed invasion being delayed and ultimately canceled. Or so most historians relate the story.

Deighton dispels some of the myths about the Battle of Britain still widely believed by most historians. He shows, for example, that a major reason for the failure of the German offensive was the decision to shift the main attack from British airfields to the city of London. The Nazis hoped that bombing the civilian population would cause Britain to sue for peace. But leaving the airfields alone only allowed the Royal Air Force to launch their fighter planes against the German bombers. And when bomber losses rose too high, the Nazi invasion plans were called off.

Other insights into the Battle of Britain include the facts "that British anti-aircraft fire was ineffective, that some R.A.F. ground personnel fled under fire, that the Admiralty provoked costly skirmishes. . . . The book resounds with exploded myths," Leonard Bushkoff writes in the *Washington Post Book World.* Deighton also shows that British estimates of German losses were far higher than they actually were, while British losses were reported to be less serious than was actually the case. But Bushkoff sees the importance of these revelations to be inconsequential. "Is debunking sufficient to carry a book that essentially is a rehash of earlier works?" he asks. Frankland admits that Deighton is sometimes "prone to get his technicalities wrong," but finds that "the Battle of Britain after all is a very difficult subject. No two people seem quite to agree about when it began, when it ended, what were its turning points or why they occurred. . . . Len Deighton cuts through this fog incisively and utterly correctly." In his article for the *Saturday Review,* George H. Reeves reports that "there is a profusion of detail in *Fighter* . . . that will delight the military history specialist, and Deighton's well-paced narrative and techniques of deft characterization will also hold the attention of the general reader." He believes that Deighton "has turned his hand with commendable results to the writing of military history."

In all of his writing, whether fiction or nonfiction, Deighton shows a concern for an accurate and detailed presentation of the facts. He has included appendices in several novels to explain to his readers such espionage esoterica as the structure of foreign intelligence organizations and the effects of various poisons. Howard claims that Deighton "takes enormous, almost obsessional care to get the background to his books exactly right."

Part of Deighton's research involves extensive travel throughout the world; he is reported to have contacts in cities as far-flung as Anchorage and Casablanca. These research trips have sometimes proven dangerous. Hugh Moffett notes that Deighton was once "hauled into police barracks in Czechoslovakia when he neglected to renew his visa." And Russian soldiers once took him into custody in East Berlin. For *Bomber: Events Relating to the Last Flight of an R.A.F. Bomber Over Germany on the Night of June 31, 1943,* Deighton made three trips to Germany and spent several years in research, gathering some half million words in notes. Research for the books *Fighter* and *Blitzkreig: From the Rise of Hitler to the Fall of Dunkirk* took nearly nine years. But these efforts have paid off. MacLeish believes that in a Deighton

novel, "the atmospherics ring forever true. Deighton seems to know the places he writes about." Speaking of *XPD,* Les Whitten of the *Washington Post Book World* finds that "the research on exotic guns, cars, poisons, trains, wall safes, foliage is shining and satisfying evidence of the hard work Deighton has done to make his background genuine and informative."

Deighton turns to historical fiction in his 1987 book *Winter: A Novel of a Berlin Family.* The story of a well-to-do German family led by a banker and war financier, *Winter* depicts how cultural and historical factors influence the attitudes of his two sons, one of whom joins the murderous Nazi party, while the other moves to the United States and marries a Jewish woman. The mixed criticism for *Winter* revolves around Deighton's sympathetic portrayals of his Nazi characters and around the novel's wide historical scope, which some reviewers feel is inadequately represented, mainly through dialogue rather than plot.

Deighton's position as one of the most prominent of contemporary espionage writers is secure. Cannon describes him as "one of the finest living writers of espionage novels." Schorr relates that it was Rudyard Kipling who "first called espionage the 'Great Game,' and no one is more adept at providing a fictional play-by-play than Len Deighton." Writing in *Whodunit?: A Guide to Crime, Suspense and Spy Fiction* about his life as a writer, Deighton reveals: "I have no formal training and have evolved a muddled sort of system by trial and error. . . . My own writing is characterized by an agonizing reappraisal of everything I write so that I have to work seven days a week. . . . The most difficult lesson to learn is that thousands and thousands of words must go into the waste paper basket." Summing up his feelings about being a best-selling author, Deighton concludes, "It's not such a bad job after all; except for sitting here at this damned typewriter."

MEDIA ADAPTATIONS: The Ipcress File was filmed by Universal in 1965, *Funeral in Berlin* by Paramount in 1966, *The Billion Dollar Brain* by United Artists in 1967, and *Only When I Larf* by Paramount in 1969; *Spy Story* was filmed in 1976; film rights to *An Expensive Place to Die* have been sold. Deighton's nameless British spy hero was given the name Harry Palmer in the film adaptations of his adventures.

BIOGRAPHICAL/CRITICAL SOURCES:

BOOKS

Bestsellers 89, Issue 2, Gale, 1989.
Contemporary Literary Criticism, Gale, Volume 4, 1975, Volume 7, 1977, Volume 22, 1982, Volume 46, 1988.
Keating, H. R. F., editor, *Whodunit?: A Guide to Crime, Suspense and Spy Fiction,* Van Nostrand, 1982.
Symons, Julian, *Mortal Consequences: A History—From the Detective Story to the Crime Novel,* Harper, 1972.

PERIODICALS

Armchair Detective, winter, 1986.
Best Sellers, November 15, 1963, January 1, 1968.
Books and Bookmen, September, 1967, December, 1971.
Books of the Times, February, 1979, August, 1981.
British Book News, December, 1980.
Chicago Tribune, February 24, 1985, December 27, 1987.
Chicago Tribune Book World, March 18, 1979, January 19, 1986.
Detroit News, February 3, 1985, February 9, 1986.
Globe and Mail (Toronto), December 1, 1984, December 14, 1985.
Harper's, November, 1982.
Life, March 25, 1966.

London Review of Books, March 19-April 1, 1981.
Los Angeles Times, November 26, 1982, March 23, 1987.
Los Angeles Times Book Review, March 17, 1985, February 16, 1986, November 22, 1987.
New Leader, January 19, 1976.
New Republic, December 13, 1975.
New Statesman, December 7, 1962, September 8, 1964, May 12, 1967, June 18, 1976, August 25, 1978.
Newsweek, January 18, 1965, January 31, 1966, June 26, 1972, October 14, 1974, February 19, 1979, December 27, 1982, December 19, 1983, February 11, 1985, January 13, 1986.
New Yorker, February 3, 1968, May 7, 1979, February 6, 1984.
New York Herald Tribune Book Review, November 17, 1963.
New York Times, January 12, 1965, October 17, 1970, October 16, 1976, September 20, 1977, May 13, 1981, June 21, 1981, December 7, 1982, December 12, 1983, December 21, 1987.
New York Times Book Review, November 10, 1963, January 17, 1965, May 21, 1967, January 14, 1968, October 4, 1970, April 13, 1975, July 9, 1978, February 25, 1979, May 3, 1981, November 14, 1982, January 8, 1984, March 10, 1985, December 1, 1985, January 10, 1988, December 25, 1988.
Playboy, May, 1966.
Saturday Review, January 30, 1965, June 10, 1978.
Spectator, September 24, 1977, September 2, 1978, April 18, 1981.
Time, March 12, 1979, April 27, 1981, January 13, 1986, December 28, 1987, December 5, 1988.
Times Literary Supplement, February 8, 1963, June 1, 1967, June 22, 1967, September 25, 1970, June 16, 1972, May 3, 1974, October 28, 1977, September 15, 1978, March 13, 1981, October 21, 1983.
Tribune Books (Chicago), January 1, 1989, January 8, 1989.
Village Voice, February 19, 1979.
Wall Street Journal, May 21, 1980.
Washington Post, October 9, 1970, December 13, 1988, December 12, 1989.
Washington Post Book World, September 29, 1974, June 4, 1978, March 20, 1979, April 14, 1981, November 7, 1982, January 8, 1984, January 27, 1985, December 15, 1985, December 20, 1987.

*   *   *

DELAPORTE, Theophile
See GREEN, Julian (Hartridge)

*   *   *

DELAY(-TUBIANA), Claude   1944-
(Claude Baillen)

PERSONAL: Born December 22, 1944, in Paris, France; daughter of Jean (a psychiatrist, professor, writer, and member of the French Academy) and Marie-Madeleine (Carrez) Delay; married Norbert Baillen (divorced); married Raoul Tubiana (a professor and surgeon); children: (first marriage) Isabelle, Maria. *Education:* Received Diploma in Political Science and Ph.D. (psychology and psycho-pathology); studied at Institute of Political Science of Paris, Sorbonne, and Societe Psychanalytique de Paris.

ADDRESSES: Home—45 Rue des Archives, 75003 Paris, France.

CAREER: Psychoanalyst and writer.

WRITINGS:

(Under name Claude Baillen) *Chanel Solitaire* (biography), Gallimard, 1971, (under name Claude Delay), new edition, 1983, translation by Barbara Bray published under same title, Quadrangle, 1974.
Paradis Noir (novel), Gallimard, 1976.
Roger La Grenouille (biography), Pauvert, 1978.
Le Hammam (novel), Gallimard, 1985.
Les ouragans sont lents (novel), Des Femmes, 1988.

MEDIA ADAPTATIONS: Chanel Solitaire was produced as a film by Larry Spangler in 1981.

BIOGRAPHICAL/CRITICAL SOURCES:

PERIODICALS

Times Literary Supplement, October 4, 1985.
World Literature Today, autumn, 1977.

*   *   *

DESAI, Anita   1937-

PERSONAL: Born June 24, 1937, in Mussoorie, India; daughter of D. N. (a businessman) and Toni (Nime) Mazumdar; married Ashvin Desai (an executive), December 13, 1958; children: Rahul, Tani, Arjun, Kiran. *Education:* Delhi University, B.A., 1957.

*ADDRESSES:*c/o Heinemann Ltd., 10 Upper Grosvenor St., London W1X 9PA, England.

CAREER: Writer. Member of Advisory Board for English, Sahitya Akademi, New Delhi, India, 1972—.

MEMBER: Royal Society of Literature (fellow).

AWARDS, HONORS: Winifred Holtby Prize, Royal Society of Literature, 1978; Sahitya Academy award, 1979; *Guardian* award for children's book, 1982.

WRITINGS:

Cry, the Peacock (novel), P. Owen, 1963.
Voices in the City (novel), P. Owen, 1965.
Bye-Bye, Blackbird (novel), Hind Pocket Books, 1968.
The Peacock Garden (juvenile), India Book House, 1974.
Where Shall We Go This Summer? (novel), Vikas Publishing House, 1975.
Cat on a Houseboat (juvenile), Orient Longmans, 1976.
Fire on the Mountain (novel), Harper, 1977.
Games at Twilight and Other Stories, Heinemann, 1978, Harper, 1980.
Clear Light of Day (novel), Harper, 1980.
The Village by the Sea (juvenile), Heinemann, 1982.
In Custody (novel), Heinemann, 1984, Harper, 1985.
Baumgartner's Bombay (novel), Knopf, 1989.

Contributor of short stories to periodicals, including *Thought, Envoy, Writers Workshop, Quest, Indian Literature, Illustrated Weekly of India, Fesmina,* and *Harper's Bazaar.*

WORK IN PROGRESS: An untitled novel.

SIDELIGHTS: Indian writer Anita Desai focuses her novels upon the personal struggles of her Indian characters to cope with the problems of contemporary life. In this way, she manages to portray the cultural and social changes that her native country has undergone since the departure of the British. One of Desai's major themes is the relationships between family members, and especially the emotional tribulations of women whose independence is suppressed by Indian society. For example, her first novel, *Cry, the Peacock,* concerns a woman who has found it impossible to assert her individuality; the theme of the despairing woman is also explored in Desai's *Where Shall We Go This Summer?* Other novels explore life in urban India (*Voices in the City*), the clash between eastern and western cultures (*Bye-Bye, Blackbird*), and the differences between the generations (*Fire on the Mountain*).

Desai is frequently praised by critics for her ability to capture the local color of her country and the ways in which eastern and western cultures have blended together there, a skill that has become more developed with each successive novel. A large part of this skill is due to her use of imagery, one of the most important devices in Desai's novels. Because of this emphasis on imagery, Desai is referred to by such reviewers as *World Literature Today* contributor Madhusudan Prasad as an "imagist-novelist. . . . [Her use of imagery is] a remarkable quality of her craft that she has carefully maintained in all her later fiction" since *Cry, the Peacock.* Employing this imagery to suggest rather than overtly explain her themes, Desai's plots sometimes appear deceptively simple; but, as Anthony Thwaite points out in *New Republic,* "she is such a consummate artist that she [is able to suggest], beyond the confines of the plot and the machinations of her characters, the immensities that lie beyond them—the immensities of India."

BIOGRAPHICAL/CRITICAL SOURCES:

BOOKS

Bellioppa, Meena, *The Fiction of Anita Desai,* Writers Workshop, 1971.
Contemporary Literary Criticism, Gale, Volume 19, 1981, Volume 37, 1986.
Mukheijee, Meenakshi, *The Twice-Born Fiction,* Arnold Heinemann, 1972.
Srinivasa Iyengar, K. R., *Indian Writing in English,* Asia Publishing House, 1962.
Verghese, Paul, *Indian Writing in English,* Asia Publishing House, 1970.

PERIODICALS

Chicago Tribune, September 1, 1985.
Chicago Tribune Book World, August 23, 1981.
Globe and Mail (Toronto), August 20, 1988.
Los Angeles Times, July 31, 1980.
Los Angeles Times Book Review, March 3, 1985. April 9, 1989.
New Republic, March 18, 1985.
New York Times, November 24, 1980, February 22, 1985, March 14, 1989.
New York Times Book Review, November 20 1977, June 22, 1980, November 23, 1980, April 9, 1989.
Time, July 1, 1985.
Times (London), September 4, 1980.
Times Literary Supplement, September 5, 1980, September 7, 1984, October 19, 1984, July 15, 1988.
Tribune Books (Chicago), March 5, 1989.
Washington Post Book World, January 11, 1981, October 7, 1984, March 31, 1985, February 26, 1989.
World Literature Today, summer, 1984.*

*   *   *

DIAMOND, Jay   1934-

PERSONAL: Born January 25, 1934, in New York; son of Charles (a retailer) and Helen (a retailer; maiden name, Klar)

Diamond; married Ellen Clements (an artist), June 1, 1958; children: Sheri, Caryn, David. *Education:* City College (now Baruch College of the City University of New York), B.B.A., 1955; New York University, M.A., 1965. *Avocational interests:* Golf, travel, theater, opera.

ADDRESSES: Home—3780 Greentree Dr., Oceanside, NY 11572. *Office*—Department of Marketing-Retailing-Fashion, Nassau Community College, Stewart Ave., Garden City, NY 11530.

CAREER: Helen Diamond (retail chain), Brooklyn, NY, partner and buyer, 1955-64; New York Community College, Brooklyn, instructor in retailing and marketing, 1964-65; Nassau Community College, Garden City, NY, assistant professor, 1965-67, associate professor, 1967-70, professor of marketing and retailing, 1970—, department chairman, 1969-80, dean of business, 1980-82. Adjunct instructor, City College of the City University of New York and Pratt Institute, 1955-64.

MEMBER: National Retail Merchants Association (associate member).

WRITINGS:

(With Gerald Pintel) *The Mathematics of Business* (includes workbook), Prentice-Hall, 1970, 4th edition, 1990.
(With Pintel) *Retailing,* Prentice-Hall, 1971, 4th edition, 1987.
(With Pintel) *Principles of Marketing* (includes study guide), Prentice-Hall, 1972, 4th edition, 1990.
(With Pintel) *Basic Business Mathematics,* Prentice-Hall, 1972, 4th edition, 1990.
(With Pintel) *Introduction to Contemporary Business* (includes study guide), Prentice-Hall, 1975.
(With Pintel) *Retail Buying,* Prentice-Hall, 1976, 3rd edition, 1989.
(With Pintel) *Successful Selling,* Reston, 1980.
(With wife, Ellen Diamond) *Contemporary Visual Merchandising,* Glencoe/McGraw-Hill, 1989.
(With E. Diamond) *The World of Fashion,* Harcourt, 1990.

Contributor to *World Book Encyclopedia,* 1989.

WORK IN PROGRESS: With Ellen Diamond, *Fashion Advertising and Promotion,* 1992, and *Fashion Apparel and Accessories,* 1993, both for Delmar Publications.

SIDELIGHTS: Jay Diamond told *CA:* "What started out as a 'dare' to write a business mathematics textbook has resulted in my becoming 'the most published Community College author in the United States on marketing, retailing, fashion, business and business mathematics.' "

Although most of his books have been written with Gerald Pintel, Diamond's most recent works are with his wife, Ellen, "who has significantly contributed to the writings. . . . Our ability to produce well-received textbooks stems from the fact that we enjoy working together and have abilities that complement each other."

*   *   *

DICKSON, Carr
See CARR, John Dickson

*   *   *

DICKSON, Carter
See CARR, John Dickson

DOCTOROW, E(dgar) L(aurence) 1931-

PERSONAL: Born January 6, 1931, in New York, NY; son of David R. (a music store proprietor) and Rose (a pianist; maiden name, Levine) Doctorow; married Helen Esther Setzer (a writer), August 20, 1954; children: Jenny, Caroline, Richard. *Education:* Kenyon College, A.B. (with honors), 1952; Columbia University, graduate study, 1952-53.

ADDRESSES: c/o Random House Publishers, 201 East 50th St., New York, NY 10022.

CAREER: Script reader, Columbia Pictures Industries, Inc., New York City; New American Library, New York City, senior editor, 1959-64; Dial Press, New York City, editor-in-chief, 1964-69, vice president, publisher, 1968-69; University of California, Irvine, writer in residence, 1969-70; Sarah Lawrence College, Bronxville, NY, member of faculty, 1971-78; New York University, New York City, Glucksman Professor of English and American Letters, 1982—. Creative writing fellow, Yale School of Drama, 1974-75; visiting professor, University of Utah, 1975; visiting senior fellow, Princeton University, 1980-81. *Military service:* U.S. Army, Signal Corps, 1953-55.

MEMBER: American Academy and Institute of Arts and Letters, Authors Guild (director), PEN (director), Writers Guild of America, East, Century Association.

AWARDS, HONORS: National Book Award nomination, 1972, for *The Book of Daniel;* Guggenheim fellowship, 1973; Creative Artists Service fellow, 1973-74; National Book Critics Circle Award and Arts and Letters award, 1976, both for *Ragtime;* L.H.D., Kenyon College, 1976; Litt.D., Hobart and William Smith Colleges, 1979; National Book Award nomination, 1980, for *Loon Lake;* National Book Award, 1986, for *World's Fair;* National Book Award nomination, 1989, and PEN/Faulkner Award for Fiction, National Book Critics Circle Award, and William Dean Howells Medal, all 1990, all for *Billy Bathgate.*

WRITINGS:

NOVELS

Welcome to Hard Times, Simon & Schuster, 1960, reprinted, Fawcett, 1988 (published in England as *Bad Man from Bodie,* Deutsch, 1961).
Big as Life, Simon & Schuster, 1966.
The Book of Daniel (also see below), Random House, 1971, reprinted, Fawcett, 1987.
Ragtime, Random House, 1975.
Loon Lake, Random House, 1980.
World's Fair, Random House, 1985.
Billy Bathgate, Random House, 1989.

OTHER

(Contributor) Theodore Solotaroff, editor, *New American Review 2,* New American Library, 1968.
Drinks before Dinner (play; first produced Off-Broadway at Public Theater, November 22, 1978), Random House, 1979.
American Anthem, photographs by Jean-Claude Suares, Stewart, Tabori, 1982.
Daniel (screenplay; based on author's *The Book of Daniel*), Paramount Pictures, 1983.
Lives of the Poets: Six Stories and a Novella, Random House, 1984.

MEDIA ADAPTATIONS: In 1967, Metro-Goldwyn-Mayer produced a movie version of *Welcome to Hard Times,* which starred Henry Fonda. Doctorow, who had nothing to do with the film adaptation, has referred to it as the second worst movie ever made. Unlike with *Welcome to Hard Times,* he was involved, at least for a time, with the film version of *Ragtime,* which was released in 1981. Dino De Laurentiis hired Robert Altman to direct the film, and after scrapping someone else's screenplay, Altman convinced Doctorow to write one. De Laurentiis eventually fired Altman, and then Doctorow's script was rejected for being too long. Milos Forman eventually took over the directing, and offered Doctorow the chance to rewrite the screenplay; he declined. Forman and playwright Michael Weller wrote the screenplay; it starred James Cagney in his last screen performance.

SIDELIGHTS: E. L. Doctorow is a highly regarded novelist and playwright known for his serious philosophical probings, the subtlety and variety of his prose style, and his unusual use of historical figures in fictional works. Doctorow's first novel, *Welcome to Hard Times,* was inspired, he told Jonathan Yardley of the *Miami Herald,* by his job as a reader for Columbia Pictures, where he "was accursed to read things that were submitted to this company and write synopses of them." "I had to suffer one lousy Western after another," continued Doctorow, "and it occurred to me that I could lie about the West in a much more interesting way than any of these people were lying. I wrote a short story, and it subsequently became the first chapter of that novel." The resulting book, unlike many Westerns, is concerned with grave issues. As Wirt Williams notes in the *New York Times Book Review,* the novel addresses "one of the favorite problems of philosophers: the relationship of man and evil. . . . Perhaps the primary theme of the novel is that evil can only be resisted psychically: when the rational controls that order man's existence slacken, destruction comes. [Joseph] Conrad said it best in *Heart of Darkness,* but Mr. Doctorow has said it impressively. His book is taut and dramatic, exciting and successfully symbolic." Similarly, Kevin Stan, writing in the *New Republic,* remarks: "*Welcome to Hard Times . . .* is a superb piece of fiction: lean and mean, and thematically significant. . . . He takes the thin, somewhat sordid and incipiently depressing materials of the Great Plains experience and fashions them into a myth of good and evil. . . . He does it marvelously, with economy and with great narrative power."

After writing a Western of sorts, Doctorow turned to another form not usually heralded by critics: science-fiction. In *Big as Life,* two naked human giants materialize in New York harbor. The novel examines the ways in which its characters deal with a seemingly impending catastrophe. Like *Hard Times, Big as Life* enjoyed much critical approval. A *Choice* reviewer, for example, comments that "Doctorow's dead pan manner . . . turns from satire to tenderness and human concern. A performance closer to James Purdy than to [George] Orwell or [Aldous] Huxley, but in a minor key." In spite of reviewers' praise, however, *Big as Life,* like *Welcome to Hard Times,* was not a large commercial success.

The Book of Daniel, Doctorow's third book, involves yet another traditional form, the historical novel. It is a fictional rendering of the 1950s trial and execution of Julius and Ethel Rosenberg. The Rosenbergs were Communists who were convicted of and executed for conspiracy to commit espionage. Many feel that they were victims of the sometimes hysterical anti-communist fever of the 1950s. As with *Welcome to Hard Times* and *Big as Life,* Doctorow has modified the traditional form to suit his purposes. The work is not an examination of the guilt or innocence of his characters, the Isaacsons, but as David Emblidge observes in *Southwest Review,* a look at the events from the point of view of the couple's children, particularly their son Daniel. Thus many critics argue that the book, unlike typical historical novels, is largely independent of historical fact. Jane Richmond, writing in *Partisan Review,* believes that "if Julius and Ethel Rosenberg had never existed, the book would be just as good as it is." In like manner, Stanley Kauffmann, in the *New Republic,* remarks: "I haven't looked up the facts of the Rosenberg case; it would be offensive to the quality of this novel to check it against those facts."

Many critics were very impressed with the achievement of *The Book of Daniel.* Kauffmann terms it "the political novel of our age, the best American work of its kind that I know since Lionel Trilling's *The Middle of the Journey.*" P. S. Prescott of *Newsweek* adds that *The Book of Daniel* "is a purgative book, angry and more deeply felt than all but a few contemporary American novels, a novel about defeat, impotent rage, the passing of the burden of suffering through generations. . . . There is no question here of our suspending disbelief, but rather how when we have finished, we may regain stability." And Richmond calls it "a brilliant achievement and the best contemporary novel I've read since reading Frederick Exley's *A Fan's Notes.* . . . It is a book of infinite detail and tender attention to the edges of life as well as to its dead center."

In *Ragtime,* Doctorow forays deeper into historical territory. The novel interweaves the lives of an upper-middle-class WASP family, a poor immigrant family, and the family of a black ragtime musician with historical figures such as I. P. Morgan, Harry Houdini, Henry Ford, and Emma Goldman. Particularly intriguing to readers is that Doctorow shows famous people involved in unusual, sometimes ludicrous, situations. In the *Washington Post Book World,* Raymond Sokolov notes that "Doctorow turns history into myth and myth into history. . . . [He] continually teases our suspicion of literary artifice with apparently true historical description. . . . On the one hand, the 'fact' tugs one toward taking the episode as history. On the other, the doubt that lingers makes one want to take the narrative as an invention." Sokolov argues that Doctorow "teases" the reader in order to make him try "to sort out what the author is doing. That is, we find ourselves paying Doctorow the most important tribute. We watch to see what he is doing."

Newsweek's Walter Clemons also finds himself teased by *Ragtime*'s historical episodes: "The very fact that the book stirs one to parlor-game research is amusing evidence that Doctorow has already won the game: I found myself looking up details because I wanted them to be true." In addition, George Stade, in the *New York Times Book Review,* expresses a belief similar to Sokolov's. "In this excellent novel," Stade writes, "silhouettes and rags not only make fiction out of history but also reveal the fictions out of which history is made. It incorporates the fictions and realities of the era of ragtime while it rags our fictions about it. It is an anti-nostalgic novel that incorporates our nostalgia about its subject."

David Emblidge, however, provides a more somber view of Doctorow's use of history. He contends that there is a motif common to *Welcome to Hard Times, The Book of Daniel,* and *Ragtime:* "This motif is the idea of history as a repetitive process, almost a cyclical one, in which man is an unwilling, unknowing pawn, easily seduced into a belief in 'progress.'" Doctorow intertwines historical figures and fictional characters to mock a romantic theory of history. "Again the point of view," Emblidge continues, "in political terms, is that history . . . is far from progressive evolution toward peace among men. *Ragtime* is an indictment of the recurrent malignancies of spirit beneath the period's chimerical technological progress and social harmony." Emblidge even finds that ragtime music, which superimposes me-

lodic improvisation on "fundamental repetition," "becomes symbolic of the historical process: endless recurrence under a distracting facade of individualistic variation."

Not all critics admire Doctorow's manipulation of history. In *Books and Bookmen,* Paul Levy maintains that *Ragtime* "falsifies history. Freud, Jung, Emma Goldman, Henry Ford, Pierpont Morgan, Stanford White and Harry Houdini simply did not perpetrate the grotesqueries they are made to commit in its pages. That is all. There is no problem. The characters in *Ragtime* that bear those famous names are not historical personages; they are merely pawns in Doctorow's particularly dotty and tasteless game of chess." On the other hand, Doctorow denies the need for historical accuracy. In a *Publishers Weekly* interview he suggests that the figures represent "images of that time" and are used "because they carried for me the right overtones of the time." And when asked if some of the incidents actually occurred, Doctorow declined to answer directly: "What's real and what isn't? I used to know but I've forgotten. Let's just say that *Ragtime* is a mingling of fact and invention—a novelist's revenge on an age that celebrates nonfiction."

Ragtime's political content also generates debate. Several reviewers believe that *Ragtime* presents a simplistic leftist viewpoint. Hilton Kramer of *Commentary,* for instance, contends that "the villains in *Ragtime,* drawn with all the subtlety of a William Gropper cartoon, are all representatives of money, the middle class, and white ethnic prejudice. . . . *Ragtime* is a political romance. . . . The major fictional characters . . . are all ideological inventions, designed to serve the purposes of a political fable." Similarly, Jeffrey Hart, writing in the *National Review,* objects that Doctorow judges his revolutionary and minority characters much less harshly than the middle and upper-class WASP figures, which results in "what can be called left-wing pastoral," a form of sentimentality.

In spite of some protest on political and historical grounds, *Ragtime* garnered copious praise. "*Ragtime,*" Eliot Fremont-Smith of the *Village Voice* comments, "is simply splendid. . . . It's a bag of riches, totally lucid and accessible, full of surprises, epiphanies, little time-bombs that alter one's view of things, and enormous fun to read." Walter Clemons finds that "*Ragtime* is as exhilarating as a deep breath of pure oxygen." In the *New Republic,* Doris Grumbach remarks that "*Ragtime* is a model of a novel: compact because it is perfectly controlled, spare, because a loose end would have detracted from the shape it has, completely absorbing, because once in, there is no possible way out except through the last page." Kauffmann, in a *Saturday Review* critique, adds that "*Ragtime* is a unique and beautiful work of art about American destiny, built of fact and logical fantasy, governed by music heard and sensed, responsive to cinema both as method and historical datum, shaken by a continental pulse."

The prose style of *Ragtime* is especially hailed. Yet at least a few readers denigrate *Ragtime*'s writing. In the *Village Voice,* Greil Marcus calls it "all surface." And Jonathan Raban, writing in *Encounter,* feels that *Ragtime* "is chock-a-block with glittering, unexamined conceits . . . , little firecrackers that glow with suggestive, but finally fraudulent brilliance, because they can be pursued no further than the sentences which encapsulate them." In contrast, Grumbach notes: "My enthusiasm for [*Ragtime*] is based primarily on the quality of the prose, an ingenious representation in words and sentences of Scott Joplin's rag rhythms." "Like ragtime," remarks R. Z. Sheppard of *Time,* "Doctorow's book is a native American fugue, rhythmic, melodic and stately. . . . Its lyric tone, fluid structure and vigorous rhythms give it a musical quality that explanation mutes." Moreover, Kauffmann, in *Saturday Review,* finds that the book is written "exquisitely. . . . The 'ragtime' effect is fundamentally to capture a change in the rhythm of American life, a change to the impelling beat of a new century."

That many reviewers focus on the power of *Ragtime*'s prose, that some describe it as "completely absorbing" and "totally lucid and accessible" would be no surprise to Doctorow. For as he explains to John F. Baker in the *Publishers Weekly* interview, in writing *Ragtime* he "was very deliberately concentrating on the narrative element. I wanted a really relentless narrative, full of ongoing energy. I wanted to recover that really marvelous tool for a novelist, the sense of motion." Furthermore, Doctorow told Jonathan Yardley: "I don't think a writer can ignore seventy years of optical technology. . . . You can't ignore the fact that children grow up now and see a commercial which in thirty seconds or a minute has five or eight scenes and tells a whole story. . . . People understand things very rapidly today, and I really want to keep one step ahead of them." Doctorow also remarks to Yardley that "in a certain sense [*Ragtime*] was an act of exploration, to find out what it itself was about. I did that with *Daniel,* too. [In] the first two books I was very calculating, and I think that was a mistake. I learned to trust the act of writing and not to impose the degree of control that could kill whatever might happen."

In *Loon Lake,* Doctorow continues to experiment with prose style and to evoke yet another period in American history, the Depression. The novel's plot revolves around the various relationships between an industrial tycoon, his famous aviatrix-wife, gangsters and their entourage, an alcoholic poet, and Joe, a young drifter who stumbles onto the tycoon's opulent residence in the Adirondacks. The novel works on several levels with "concentrically expanding ripples of implication," according to Robert Towers in the *New York Times Book Review.* For the most part, however, it is Doctorow's portrait of the American dream versus the American reality which forms the novel's core. As Christopher Lehmann-Haupt of the *New York Times* explains, "[*Loon Lake*] is a complex and haunting meditation on modern American history."

Time's Paul Gray believes that "Doctorow is . . . playing a variation on an old theme: The American dream, set to the music of an American nightmare, the Depression." Lehmann-Haupt infers a similar correlation and elaborates: "This novel could easily have been subtitled *An American Tragedy Revisited.* . . . *Loon Lake* contains [several] parallels to, as well as ironic comments on, the themes of [Theodore] Dreiser's story. . . . Had Dreiser lived to witness the disruptions of post-World War II American society—and had he possessed Mr. Doctorow's narrative dexterity—he might have written something like *Loon Lake.*"

Doctorow's extraordinary narrative style has generated much critical comment. "The written surface of *Loon Lake* is ruffled and choppy," Gray remarks. "Swatches of poetry are jumbled together with passages of computerese and snippets of mysteriously disembodied conversation. Narration switches suddenly from first to third person, or vice versa, and it is not always clear just who is telling what." A reviewer for the *Chicago Tribune* finds such "stylistic tricks" annoyingly distractive. "We balk at the frequent overwriting, and the clumsy run-on sentences," he reports. "We can see that Doctorow is trying to convey rootlessness and social unrest through an insouciant free play of language and syntax . . . ; the problem is that these eccentricities

draw disproportionate attention to themselves, away from the characters and their concerns."

Doctorow, seemingly in anticipation of such criticism, defends his unconventional narrative approach in a *New York Times Book Review* interview with Victor S. Navasky: "[In *Loon Lake*] you don't know who's talking so that's one more convention out the window. That gives me pleasure, and I think it might give pleasure to readers, too. Don't underestimate them. People are smart, and they are not strangers to discontinuity. There's an immense amount of energy attached to breaking up your narrative and leaping into different voices, times, skins, and making the book happen and then letting the reader take care of himself."

While reviewers note certain structural flaws in *Loon Lake,* they praise the novel's overall literary significance and indicate that it is something of a milestone in Doctorow's career. "*Loon Lake* is not as elegantly formed as *Ragtime,*" Stade comments in *Nation,* ". . . but it is even more ambitious particularly in its mixture of styles and in its reach for significance." Gray echoes this assessment when he writes: "Doctorow may try to do too much in *Loon Lake.* . . . But the author's skill at historical reconstruction, so evident in *Ragtime,* remains impressive here; the novel's fragments and edgy, nervous rhythms call up an age of clashing anxiety. *Loon Lake* tantalizes long after it is ended." Moreover, Stade finds that *Loon Lake* contains "a tone, a mood, an atmosphere, a texture, a poetry, a felt and meditated vision of how things go with us" that is only hinted at in Doctorow's four previous novels. And the *Chicago Tribune* reviewer, despite his earlier criticism, concludes: "*Loon Lake* is highly interesting—for its relationship among the other novels . . . in Doctorow's developing portrayal of modern America; for its echoes of and associations with other fiction . . . ; for its maverick theorizing about capitalism vs. socialism vs. individuality; and its intrinsic picturesqueness and dramatic power. At its best, this straining, challenging book becomes an unpleasantly accurate synthesis of the American experience; a fractious, swaggering song of ourselves."

Doctorow's play, *Drinks before Dinner,* seems to have been created through an analogous act of exploration. In *Nation,* he states that the play "originated not in an idea or a character or a story but in a sense of heightened language, a way of talking. It was not until I had the sound of it in my ear that I thought about saying something. The language preceded the intention. . . . The process of making something up is best experienced as fortuitous, unplanned, exploratory. You write to find out what it is you're writing." In composing *Drinks before Dinner,* Doctorow worked from sound to words to characters. Does this "flawed" method of composition show a "defective understanding of what theater is supposed to do?" wonders Doctorow. His answer: "I suspect so. Especially if we are talking of the American theater, in which the presentation of the psychologized ego is so central as to be an article of faith. And that is the point. The idea of character as we normally celebrate it on the American stage is what this play seems to question."

Doctorow's experiment garners a mixed response from drama critics. In *Village Voice,* Michael Feingold observes that in *Drinks before Dinner* Doctorow "has tried to do something incomparably more ambitious than any new American play has done in years—he has tried to put the whole case against civilization in a nutshell." According to Feingold, the intent is defeated by a "schizoid" plot and "flat, prosy, and empty" writing. "I salute his desire to say something gigantic," Feingold concludes; "how I wish he had found a way to say it fully, genuinely, and dramatically." Richard Eder of the *New York Times* responds more positively: "Mr. Doctorow's turns of thought can be odd, witty and occasionally quite remarkable. His theme—that the world is blindly destroying itself and not worrying about it—is hardly original, but certainly worth saying. And he finds thoughtful and striking ways of saying it, even though eventually the play becomes an endless epigram, a butterfly that turns into a centipede." "Still, a play of ideas is rare enough nowadays," Eder observes, "and Mr. Doctorow's are sharp enough to supplement intellectual suspense when the dramatic suspense bogs down."

Doctorow's more recent books, *World's Fair* and *Billy Bathgate,* are both set in 1930s-era New York and have received wide critical acclaim. *World's Fair,* considered by many reviewers to be autobiographical in nature, relates a boy's experiences in New York City during the depression and ends with his visit to the 1939 World's Fair. Although *World's Fair* received an American Book Award, many critics view the author's next novel, *Billy Bathgate,* to be an even greater achievement. The story of 15-year-old Billy Behan's initiation into the world of organized crime is a "grand entertainment that is also a triumphant work of art," according to *Washington Post Book World* contributor Pete Hamill. A number of reviewers especially appreciated Doctorow's ability to avoid cliched characters: "Even the various gangsters [in *Billy Bathgate*] are multidimensional," Anne Tyler remarked with pleasure in the *New York Times Book Review.* The completion of *Billy Bathgate* was also a milestone for its author. Discussing *Billy Bathgate* in the *Washington Post,* Doctorow revealed that he felt he had been "liberated by it to a certain extent. . . . Certain themes and preoccupations, that leitmotif that I've been working with for several years. I think now I can write anything. The possibilities are limitless. I've somehow been set free by this book."

BIOGRAPHICAL/CRITICAL SOURCES:

BOOKS

Authors in the News, Volume 2, Gale, 1976.
Bestsellers 89, Issue 3, Gale, 1989.
Concise Dictionary of American Literary Biography: Broadening Views, 1968-1988, Gale, 1989.
Contemporary Literary Criticism, Gale, Volume 6, 1976, Volume 11, 1979, Volume 15, 1980, Volume 18, 1981, Volume 37, 1986, Volume 44, 1987.
Dictionary of Literary Biography, Gale, Volume 2: *American Novelists since World War II,* 1978, Volume 28: *Twentieth-Century American-Jewish Fiction Writers,* 1984.
Dictionary of Literary Biography Yearbook: 1980, Gale, 1981.
Johnson, Diane, *Terrorists and Novelists,* Knopf, 1982.
Levine, Paul, *E. L. Doctorow,* Methuen, 1985.
Trenner, Richard, editor, *E. L. Doctorow: Essays and Conversations,* Ontario Review Press, 1983.

PERIODICALS

American Literature, March, 1978.
American Scholar, winter, 1975/1976.
Atlantic Monthly, September, 1980.
Best Sellers, June 1, 1966, August 15, 1971.
Books and Bookmen, June, 1976.
Chicago Tribune, September 28, 1980.
Choice, November, 1966.
Commentary, October, 1975, March, 1986.
Detroit Free Press, February 19, 1989.
Detroit News, November 10, 1985.
Drama, January, 1980.
Encounter, February, 1976.

Globe and Mail (Toronto), March 11, 1989.
Hudson Review, summer, 1986.
Journal of Popular Culture, fall, 1979.
London Magazine, February, 1986.
Los Angeles Times Book Review, November 24, 1985, March 5, 1989.
Manchester Guardian, February 23, 1986.
Miami Herald, December 21, 1975.
Midstream, December, 1975.
Midwest Quarterly, autumn, 1983.
Modern Fiction Studies, summer, 1976.
Nation, June 2, 1979, September 27, 1980, November 17, 1984, November 30, 1985.
National Review, August 15, 1975, March 14, 1986.
New Leader, December 16-30, 1985.
New Republic, June 5, 1971, July 5, 1975, September 6, 1975, September 20, 1980, December 3, 1984.
Newsweek, June 7, 1971, July 14, 1975, November 4, 1985.
New York, September 29, 1980, November 25, 1985.
New Yorker, December 9, 1985.
New York Herald Tribune, January 22, 1961.
New York Review of Books, August 7, 1975, December 19, 1985.
New York Times, August 4, 1978, November 24, 1978, September 12, 1980, November 6, 1984, October 31, 1985, February 9, 1989, November 30, 1989.
New York Times Book Review, September 25, 1960, July 4, 1971, July 6, 1975, September 28, 1980, December 6, 1984, November 10, 1985, February 26, 1989.
Partisan Review, fall, 1972.
People, March 20, 1989.
Progressive, March, 1986.
Publishers Weekly, June 30, 1975.
Saturday Review, July 17, 1971, July 26, 1975, September, 1980.
South Atlantic Quarterly, winter, 1982.
Southwest Review, autumn, 1977.
Springfield Republican, September 18, 1960.
Time, July 14, 1975, September 22, 1980, December 18, 1985.
Times Literary Supplement, February 14, 1986.
Tribune (Chicago), May 14, 1990.
Village Voice, July 7, 1975, August 4, 1975, December 4, 1978, November 26, 1985.
Wall Street Journal, February 7, 1986.
Washington Post, April 6, 1990.
Washington Post Book World, July 13, 1975, September 28, 1980, November 11, 1984, November 17, 1985, February 19, 1989.

*   *   *

DuBRIN, Andrew J(ohn) 1935-

PERSONAL: Born March 3, 1935, in New York City; son of Albert E. (A salesman) and Louise (Walsh) DuBrin; single (divorced 1984); children: Drew, Douglas, Melanie. *Education:* Hunter College (now Hunter College of the City University of New York), A.B., 1956; Purdue University, M.S., 1957; Michigan State University, Ph.D., 1960. *Politics:* "No party affiliation." *Religion:* "No preference."

ADDRESSES: Home—2100 Clover, Rochester, NY 14618. *Office*—College of Business, Rochester Institute of Technology, Rochester, NY 14623.

CAREER: Certified psychologist in state of New York; International Business Machines Corp. (IBM), Kingston, NY, personnel research psychologist in Data Services Division, 1962-63; Clark, Cooper, Field & Wohl, New York City, psychological consultant, 1963-64; Rohrer, Hibler & Replogle, New York City, psychological consultant, 1964-70, partner in charge of Rochester, NY office, 1967-70; Rochester Institute of Technology, Rochester, NY, associate professor 1970-72, professor of behavioral science, 1972—, chairman of department of management, 1981-84; president, Andrew J. DuBrin Group, 1984—. Diplomate in industrial psychology, American Board of Professional Psychology. *Military service:* U.S. Army, chief clinical psychology officer, 1960-62; became captain.

MEMBER: American Psychological Association, Phi Beta Kappa.

WRITINGS:

The Practice of Managerial Psychology: Concepts and Methods for Manager and Organization Development, with instructor's manual, Pergamon, 1972.
Women in Transition, C. C. Thomas, 1972.
The Singles Game, Books for Better Living, 1973.
Survival in the Sexist Jungle, Books for Better Living, 1974.
Fundamentals of Organizational Behavior: An Applied Perspective, Pergamon, 1974, 2nd edition, 1978.
Managerial Deviance: How to Handle Problem People in Key Jobs, Van Nostrand, 1976.
The New Husbands and How to Become One, Nelson-Hall, 1976.
Casebook of Organizational Behavior, Pergamon, 1977.
Survival in the Office: How to Move Ahead or Hang On, Van Nostrand, 1977.
Human Relations: A Job-Oriented Approach, Reston, 1978, 3rd edition, 1984.
Winning at Office Politics, Van Nostrand, 1978.
Effective Business Psychology, Reston, 1980, 3rd edition, 1989.
The Practice of Supervision: Achieving Results Through People, Business Publications, 1980.
Personnel and Human Resource Management, Kent Publishing, 1981.
Contemporary Applied Management, Business Publications, 1982, 3rd edition, 1989.
Bouncing Back: How to Handle Setbacks in Your Work and Personal Life, Prentice-Hall, 1982.
Human Relations for Career and Personal Success, Reston, 1983.
Foundations of Organizational Behavior, Prentice-Hall, 1984.
(With Henry Sisk and J. Clifton Williams) *Management and Organization,* 5th edition (DuBrin not associated with previous editions), Southwestern, 1985.
The Last Straw: How to Benefit from Trigger Events in Your Life, Charles M. Thomas, 1987.
Winning Office Politics: DuBrin's Guide for the 1990's, Prentice-Hall, 1990.

SIDELIGHTS: Andrew J. DuBrin told *CA:* "People often say to me, 'Are you working on another book?' I respond, 'Definitely. Writing has become my primary occupation, not an occasional hobby.'"

*   *   *

DUERRENMATT, Friedrich 1921-1990

PERSONAL: Born January 5, 1921, in Konolfingen, Bern, Switzerland; son of Rienhold (a Protestant minister) and Hulda (Zimmermann) Duerrenmatt; married Lotti Geissler (an actress), 1946, (died, 1983); married Charlotte Kerr (a journalist), 1984; children: (first marriage) Peter, Barbara, Ruth. *Education:* Attended University of Bern, 1941, and University of Zurich, 1942-43. *Avocational interests:* Painting, astronomy.

ADDRESSES: Home—Pertuis-du-Sault 74-76, Neuchatel, Switzerland.

CAREER: Playwright, novelist, short story writer, essayist, critic, dramatist, and painter.

MEMBER: Modern Language Association of America (honorary fellow).

AWARDS, HONORS: Welti-Stiftung fuer das Drama, City of Bern, 1948, for *Es steht geschrieben;* Literaturpreis, City of Bern, 1954, for *Ein Engel kommt nach Babylon;* Hoerspielpreis der Kriegsblinden (Berlin), 1957, for *Die Panne;* Prix Italia, RAI (Venice), 1958, for *Abendstunde im Spaetherbst;* Preis zur Foerderung des Bernischen Schrifttums, 1959, for *Das Versprechen;* Schiller-Preis, City of Mannheim, 1959, for *Grieche sucht Griechin;* New York Drama Critics Circle Awards for best foreign play, 1959, for *The Visit;* Grillparzer-Preis, Oesterreichische Akademie der Wissenschaften, 1968, for *Der Besuch der alten Dame;* Grosser Schiller-Preis, Schweizer Stiftung, 1969, for *Die Physiker;* Grosser Literaturpreis, Canton of Bern, 1969; doctor honoris causa, Temple University, 1969, Hebrew University, 1977, University of Nice, 1977, and University of Neuchatel, 1981; International Writers Prize, Welsh Arts Council, University of Wales, 1976; Buber-Rosenzweig-Medaille (Frankfort), 1977; Grosser Literaturpreis, City of Bern, 1979.

WRITINGS:

STAGE PLAYS

Es steht geschrieben: Ein Drama; mit zwei Zeichnungen vom Autor (title means "It Is Written"; first produced in Zurich, Switzerland, at Schauspielhaus, April 19, 1947), Schwabe (Basel), 1947, new version published as *Die Wiedertaeufer: Ein Komoedie in zwei Teilen* (title means "The Annabaptists"; first produced in Zurich at Schauspielhaus, March 16, 1967), Arche (Zurich), 1967.
Der Blinde: Ein Drama (title means "The Blind Man"; first produced in Basel, Switzerland, at Stadttheater, January 10, 1948), Buehnenverlag Bloch Erben (Berlin), 1947, revised edition, Arche, 1965.
Romulus der Grosse: Eine ungeschichtliche historische Komoedie in vier Akten (first produced in Basel at Stadttheater, April 25, 1949, new version produced in Zurich at Schauspielhaus, October 24, 1957), Arche, 1958, revised version, 1964, 2nd edition, 1968.
Die Ehe des Herrn Mississippi: Eine Komoedie (first produced in Munich, West Germany, at Kammerspiele, March 26, 1952, translation by E. Peters and R. Schnorr produced in London, England, at Arts Theatre, September 30, 1959, as *The Marriage of Mr. Mississippi*), Oprecht (Zurich), 1952, revised edition published as *Die Ehe des Herrn Mississippi: Buehnenfassung und Drehbuch,* Arche, 1966.
Ein Engel kommt nach Babylon: Eine Komoedie in drei Akten (first produced in Munich at Kammerspiele, December 22, 1953, new version produced in Zurich at Schauspielhaus, October 24, 1957), Arche, 1954, revised edition published as *Ein Engel kommt nach Babylon: Eine fragmentarishe Komoedie in drei Akten,* 1958, translation by George White (produced at University of California, 1962), published as *An Angel Comes to Babylon,* K. Hellmer, c. 1962.
Der Besuch der alten Dame: Ein tragische Komoedie; mit einem Nachwort (first produced in Zurich at Schauspielhaus, January 29, 1956, produced in New York City, May 5, 1958), Arche, 1956, translation by Maurice Valency published as *The Visit: A Play in Three Acts,* Random House, 1958,

translation by Patrick Bowles published as *The Visit: A Tragi-Comedy,* Grove, 1962.

(With Paul Burkhard) *Frank der Fuenfte: Oper einer Privatbank* (satirical opera; title means "Frank the Fifth: Opera of a Private Bank"; first produced in Zurich at Schauspielhaus, March 19, 1959), music by Burkhard, Arche, 1960, published as *Frank der Fuenfte: Eine Komoedie,* Bochumer Fassung (Zurich), 1960, revised edition, Arche, 1964.

Die Physiker: Eine Komoedie in zwei Akten (first produced in Zurich at Schauspielhaus, February 20, 1962, produced in New York City at Martin Beck Theatre, October 13, 1964), Arche, 1962, translation by James Kirkup published as *The Physicists: A Play in Two Acts,* Samuel French, 1963, published as *The Physicists,* Grove, 1964.

Herkules und der Stall des Augias: Eine Komoedie (expanded version of radio play; first produced in Zurich at Schauspielhaus, March 20, 1963), Arche, 1963, translation by Agnes Hamilton published as *Hercules and the Augean Stables,* Dramatic Publishing, 1963.

An Angel Comes to Babylon [and] *Romulus the Great: Two Plays* (latter a translation of *Romulus der Grosse*), translated by William McElwee and Gerhard Nellhaus, respectively, Grove, 1964.

Four Plays, 1957-62 (contains *Romulus the Great, The Marriage of Mr. Mississippi, An Angel Comes to Babylon,* and *The Physicists;* bound with essay, "Problems of the Theatre"), translated by Gerhard Nellhaus and others, J. Cape, 1964, published as *Four Plays,* Grove, 1965.

Der Meteor: Eine Komoedie in zwei Akten (first produced in Zurich at Schauspielhaus, January 20, 1966), Arche, 1966, translation by James Kirkup published as *The Meteor,* Dramatic Publishing, 1966, published as *The Meteor: A Comedy in Two Acts,* J. Cape, 1973, Grove, 1974.

(Adaptor) *Koenig Johann: Nach Shakespeare* (first produced in Basel at Basles Theatres, September 18, 1968), Arche, 1968.

Play Strindberg: Totentanz nach August Strindberg (first produced in Basel at Basles Theatres, February 8, 1969), Arche, 1969, translation by James Kirkup (produced in New York City at Forum Theatre of Lincoln Center, June 3, 1971), published as *Play Strindberg: Choreographed by Friedrich Duerrenmatt,* Dramatic Publishing, 1970, published as *Play Strindberg: The Dance of Death Choreographed,* Grove, 1973.

(Adaptor) *Goethes Urfaust: Ergaenzt durch das Buch von Doktor Faustus aus dem Jahre 1589* (first produced in Zurich at Schauspielhaus, October 20, 1970), Diogenes, 1980.

Portraet eines Planeten (first produced in Dusseldorf, West Germany, at Kleines Haus, November 27, 1970), Arche, 1971.

(Adaptor) *Titus Andronicus: Eine Komoedie nach Shakespeare* (first produced in Dusseldorf at Schauspielhaus, December 12, 1970), Arche, 1970.

Der Mitmacher, ein Komplex: Text der Komoedie, Dramaturgie, Erfahrungen, Berichte, Erzaehlungen (includes play and commentary by Duerrenmatt), Arche, 1976, play published singularly as *Der Mitmacher: Eine Komoedie,* 1978.

Die Frist: Eine Komoedie (first produced in Zurich at Schauspielhaus, October 6, 1977), Arche, 1977.

Die Panne: Komoedie (adaptation of novella), Diogenes, 1980.

Koenig Johann [and] *Titus Andronicus: Shakespeare-Umarbeitungen,* Diogenes, 1980.

Der Meteor [and] *Dichterdaemmerung: Nobelpreistraegerstuecke,* Diogenes, 1980.

Achterloo: Eine Komoedie in zwei Akten (first produced in Zurich, 1983), Diogenes, 1983.

RADIO PLAYS

Herkules und der Stall des Augias: Mit Randnotizen eines Kugelschreibers, Arche, 1954.

Das Unternehmen der Wega: Ein Hoerspiel (title means "The Vega Enterprise"; broadcast in 1954), Arche, 1958, reprinted, 1974.

Naechtliches gespraech mit einem verachteten Menschen: Ein Kurs fuer Zeitgenossen, Arche, 1957, translation by Robert David Macdonald published as *Conversation at Night with a Despised Character: A Curriculum for Our Times,* Dramatic Publishing, 1957.

Der Prozess um des Esels Schatten: Ein Hoerspiel (nach Wieland—aber nicht sehr) (title means "The Trial of the Ass's Shadow"), Arche, 1958.

Stranitzky und der Nationalheld: Ein Hoerspiel (title means "Stranitzky and the National Hero"), Arche, 1959.

Abendstunde im Spaetherbst: Ein Hoerspiel (produced by British Broadcasting Corp., September 24, 1959), Arche, 1959 translation by Gabriel Karminski published as *Episode on an Autumn Evening,* Dramatic Publishing, 1959, different translation published as "Incident at Twilight" in *Postwar German Theatre,* edited by M. Benedikt and G. E. Wellwarth, Macmillan, 1968.

Der Doppelgaenger: Ein Spiel, Arche, 1960.

Die Panne: Ein Hoerspiel (first published as novel), Arche, 1961, published as *Die Panne: Ein Hoerspiel und eine Komoedie,* Diogenes, 1980.

Drei Hoerspiele, edited by Henry Regensteiner, Holt, 1965.

Vier Hoerspiele, Volk & Welt (Berlin), 1967.

Naechtliches Gespraech mit einem verachteten Menschen [and] *Stranitzky und der Nationalheld* [and] *Das Unternehmen der Wega: Hoerspiele und Kabarett,* Diogenes, 1980.

Also author of "Sammelband," 1960.

FICTION

Pilatus (story), Vereinigung Oltner Buecherfreunde (Olten), 1949.

Der Nihilist (story), Holunderpresse (Horgen), 1950, reprinted as *Die Falle,* Arche, 1952.

Der Tunnel (story), Arche, 1952.

Das Bild des Sisyphos (story), Arche, 1952.

Die Stadt: Prosa I-IV (title means "The City"; story collection), Arche, 1952.

Der Richter und sein Henker (novel; originally serialized in *Der Beobachter,* 1950), Benziger (Einsiedeln), 1952, translation by Cyrus Brooks published as *The Judge and His Hangman,* Jenkins, 1954, translation by Theresa Pol under same title, Harper, 1955.

Der Verdacht (novel; originally serialized in *Der Beobachter*), Benziger, 1953, translation by Eva H. Morreale published as *The Quarry,* Grove, 1961.

Grieche sucht Griechin: Eine Prosakomoedie (novel), Arche, 1955, new edition, 1957, translation by Richard Winston and Clara Winston published as *Once a Greek . . . ,* Knopf, 1965.

Die Panne: Eine noch moegliche Geschichte (title means "The Breakdown"; novel), Arche, 1956, new edition, 1960, translation by R. Winston and C. Winston published as *Traps,* Knopf, 1960 (published in England as *A Dangerous Game,* J. Cape, 1960).

Das Versprechen: Requiem auf den Kriminalroman (novel; originally written as screenplay), Arche, 1958, translation by R. Winston and C. Winston published as *The Pledge,* Knopf, 1959.

Die Panne [and] *Der Tunnel,* edited by F. J. Alexander, Oxford University Press, 1967.

Der Richter und sein Henker [and] *Die Panne,* Volk & Welt, 1969.

Der Sturz (story), Arche, 1971.

Der Hund [and] *Der Tunnel* [and] *Die Panne: Erzaehlungen* (stories), Diogenes, 1980.

Grieche sucht Griechin [and] *Mister X macht Ferien* [and] *Nachrichten ueber den Stand des Zeitungswesens in der Steinzeit: Grotesken,* Diogenes, 1980.

The Judge and His Hangman [and] *The Quarry: Two Hans Barlach Mysteries,* afterword by George Stade, David Godine, 1983.

Justiz: Roman (novel), Diogenes, 1985.

Minotaurus: Eine Ballade (story), drawings by Duerrenmatt, Diogenes, 1985.

Der Auftraug; oder, Vom Beobachten des Beobachters der Beobachter: Novelle in vierundzwanzig Saetzen (novel), Diogenes, 1986, translation by Joel Agee published as *The Assignment: or, On the Observing of the Observer of the Observers,* Random House, 1988.

The Execution of Justice (novel), translated by John E. Wood, Random House, 1989.

NONFICTION

Theaterprobleme (essay), Arche, 1955, reprinted, 1973.

Friedrich Schiller: Eine Rede (speech), Arche, 1960.

(With Werner Weber) *Der Rest ist Dank* (speeches), Arche, 1961.

Theater-Schriften und Reden (essays and speeches), edited by Elisabeth Brock Sulzer, Arche, Volume 1: *Theater-Schriften und Reden,* 1966, Volume 2: *Dramaturgisches und Kritisches,* 1972, translation by H. M. Waidson published as *Writings on Theatre and Drama,* J. Cape, 1976.

Monstervortrag ueber Gerechtigkeit und Recht nebst einem helvetischen Zwischenspiel: Eine kleine Dramaturgie der Politik (lecture), Arche, 1969.

Saetze aus Amerika, Arche, 1970.

Zusammenhaenge: Essay ueber Israel; eine Konzeption, Arche, 1976.

Albert Einstein: Ein Vortrag (lecture), Diogenes, 1979.

Literatur und Kunst: Essays, Gedichte und Reden, Diogenes, 1980.

Philosophie und Naturwissenschaft: Essays, Gedichte und Reden, Diogenes, 1980.

Politik: Essays, Gedichte und Reden, Diogenes, 1980.

Kritik: Kritiken und Zeichnungen, Diogenes, 1980.

Also author of *Israel: Eine Rede,* 1975.

EXHIBITION CATALOGS

(Author of introduction) Willy Guggenheim, *Varlin: Kunsthalle Basel, 28. Oktober-25. November 1967,* [Basel], 1967.

(With Giovanni Testor) *Varlin: Peintures; 12 fevrier-27 mars 1982,* Galerie Claude Bernard/Galerie Albert Loeb, 1982.

(With Andre Kamber) *"Hommage a Hans Liechti": 28. June bis 13. August, 1983,* Medici (Solothurn), 1983.

(With Peter Selz) *Varlin, 1900-1977: Paintings; April 9-May 17, 1986,* Claude Bernard Gallery, 1986.

INTERVIEWS

Gertrun Simmerling and Christof Schmind, editors, *Literarische Werkstatt: Interview mit Friedrich Duerrenmatt,* R. Oldenbourg (Munich), 1972.

Gespraech mit Heinz Ludwig Arnold, Arche, 1976.

(With Dieter Fringeli) *Nachdenken mit und ueber Friedrich Duerrenmatt: Ein Gespraech,* Jeger-Moll (Breitenbach), 1977.

Die Welt als Labyrinth: Die Unsicherheit unserer Wirklichket; Franz Kreuzer, im Gespraech mit Friedrich Duerrenmatt und Paul Watzlawick, Dueticke (Vienna), 1982.

OMNIBUS EDITIONS

Komoedien (also see below), Arche, Volume 1: *Komoedien I,* 1957, 7th edition, 1965, Volume 2: *Komoedien II und fruehe Stuecke,* 1963, Volume 3: *Komoedien III,* 1970.

Gesammelte Hoerspiele (radio plays), Arche, 1961.

Komoedien, Deutsche Buch-Gemeinschaft (Berlin), 1968.

Werkausgabe in dreissig Baenden: Das dramatische Werk, thirty volumes, Diogenes, 1981.

Friedrich Duerrenmatt: Plays and Essays, edited by Volkmar Sander, Continuum, 1982.

Friedrich Duerrenmatt: His Five Novels, Pan Books, 1985.

OTHER

Friedrich Duerrenmatt liest: "Herkules und der Stall des Augias" [and] *"Eine Kurzfassung der Komoedie"* (recording), Deutsche Grammophon Gesellschaft, 1957.

It Happened in Broad Daylight (screenplay version of *The Pledge*), Continental, 1960.

Die Ehe des Herrn Mississippi: Ein Drehbuch mit Szenenbildern (filmscript adaptation of stage play), Sanssouci (Zurich), 1961.

Naechtliches Gespraech (recording), Schallplatten Club, 1963.

Die Heimat im Plakat: Ein Buch fuer Schweizer Kinder (satirical drawings), Diogenes, 1963.

Problems of the Theatre: An Essay Translated from the German by Gerhard Nellhaus (translation of *Theaterprobleme*) [and] *The Marriage of Mr. Mississippi: A Play Translated from the German by Michael Bullock,* Grove, 1964.

(With Gore Vidal) *Romulus: The Broadway Adaptation, by Gore Vidal* [and] *The Original Romulus the Great, by Friedrich Duerrenmatt,* translated by G. Nellhaus, preface by Vidal, Grove, 1966.

Zeichnungen gerechtfertigt durch Friedrich Duerrenmatt, Diogenes, 1972.

(Author of introduction) Hans Falk, *Hans Falk,* ABC (Zurich), 1975.

Duerrenmatt: Bilder und Zeichnungen (paintings and drawings), edited by Christian Strich, Diogenes, 1978.

Lesebuch: Friedrich Duerrenmatt, Arche, 1978.

(Author of foreword) Tomi Ungerer, *Babylon,* Diogenes, 1979.

Herkules und der Stall des Augias [and] *Der Prozess um des Esels Schatten* [and] *Griechische Stuecke,* Diogenes, 1980.

Play Strindberg [and] *Portrait eines Planeten: Uebungsstucke fuer Schauspieler* (exercises for actors), Diogenes, 1980.

Stoffe I-III, Diogenes, 1981.

(With Dorothea Christ) *Hildi Hess: Mit Texten von Dorothea Christ und Friedrich Duerrenmatt,* edited by Daniel Keel, Diogenes, 1981.

Denken mit Duerrenmatt: Denkanstosse; ausgewahlt und zusammengestellt von Daniel Keel; mit sieben Zeichnungen des Dichters, drawings by Duerrenmatt, Diogenes, 1982.

Die Erde ist zu schoen. . . .: Die Physiker [and] *Der Tunnel* [and] *Das Unternehmen der Wega,* Arche, 1983.

(With wife, Charlotte Kerr) *Rollenspiele: Protokoll einer fiktiven Inszenierung und Achterloo III* (includes play, *Achterloo III*), Diogenes, 1986.

Also author of television adaptation of *The Judge and His Hangman,* 1957. Work appears in numerous anthologies, including

The Modern Theatre, edited by R. W. Corrigan, Macmillan, 1946; *The Best Plays of 1964-65,* edited by O. L. Guernsey, Jr., Dodd, 1965; *Postwar German Theatre,* edited by M. Benedikt and G. E. Wellwarth, Macmillan, 1968; and *Die Besten klassischen und modernene Hundegeschichten,* Diogenes, 1973. Drama critic for *Die Weltwoche,* 1951-52.

MEDIA ADAPTATIONS: The Visit: A Drama in Three Acts was adapted by Maurice Valency from *Der Besuch der Alten Dame* and published by Samuel French, 1956; Valency's adaptation was later published as *The Visit: A Play in Three Acts,* Random House, 1958, and produced in New York City in 1958. *Fools Are Passing Through* was adapted by Maximilian Slater from *Die Ehe des Herrn Mississippi* and produced in New York City at Jan Hus Auditorium, April 2, 1958. *The Deadly Game* was adapted by James Yaffe from *Traps* and produced in New York City at Longacre Theatre, February 2, 1960; Yaffe's *The Deadly Game: A Play in Two Acts; Adapted from the Novel "Traps" by Friedrich Duerrenmatt* was published by Dramatists Play Service, 1966. *The Jackass* was adapted by George White from *Der Prozess um des Esels Schatten* and produced in New York City at Barbizon Plaza Theatre, March 23, 1960. *Romulus: A New Comedy* was adapted by Gore Vidal from *Romulus the Great* and produced in New York City, 1962; Vidal's *Romulus: A New Comedy; Adapted from a Play of Friedrich Duerrenmatt* was published by Dramatists Play Service, 1962. *The Visit of the Old Lady: Opera in Three Acts by Gottfried von Einem* was adapted from *Der Besuch der Alten Dame* (English version by Norman Tucker) and published by Boosey & Hawkes, 1972. *Chicago Radio Theatre Production of Friedrich Duerrenmatt's Play Strindberg* was released as a cassette recording, Allmedia Dramatic Workshop, 1977.

A dramatization of *The Judge and His Hangman* was televised in the United States in 1956, and an adaptation of *The Deadly Game* in 1957. Duerrenmatt's works have also been adapted as motion pictures, including an adaptation of *The Visit* by Twentieth Century-Fox Film Corp., 1964, *Fools Are Passing Through* (an adaptation of *The Marriage of Mr. Mississippi*), 1961, and an adaptation of one of Duerrenmatt's short stories by Sergeo Amidei for an Italian film, 1972.

SIDELIGHTS: Acclaimed Swiss playwright and critic Friedrich Duerrenmatt is considered to be one of the most important German-language dramatists of the twentieth century. His most famous works include *Der Besuch der alten Dame* (*The Visit*), regarded by many to be his finest play, and *Der Physiker* (*The Physicists*), one of the most frequently performed plays of the German stage. *The Visit,* a huge success on Broadway in addition to Germany, is the story of a wealthy old woman who returns to her impoverished hometown with the intent of financially rewarding the townspeople if they enact revenge on an old suitor of the woman's. According to Frederick Lumley in *New Trends in Twentieth Century Drama, The Visit* "raises Duerrenmatt to the level of the leading playwright of our times. Not only is it a good play in itself, it is one of the most forceful statements ever made on the corruption of the power of money, a radical indictment of the values of our society and the hypocrisy on which it is built." The grotesque comedy *The Physicists* depicts three insane nuclear physicists in an asylum who believe they are Albert Einstein, Sir Isaac Newton, and August Ferdinand Moebius. Possessing the knowledge of how to destroy the world, each physicist goes as far as murdering others to prevent others from discovering what they know; the play raises questions regarding definitions of madness, in addition to the limits of scientific responsibility. A reviewer for the *Times Literary Supplement* comments that in both plays "drama is generated by the pursuit of

a ruthless, absolute logic in the teeth of anarchy," while "success rests in part on the way in which a tragi-comic ambivalence of plot is carried through into the language and the stage-realization."

Duerrenmatt once summarized his approach to the theatre: "I would ask you not to look upon me as the spokesman of some specific movement in the theatre or of a certain dramatic technique, nor to believe that I knock at your door as the traveling salesman of one of the philosophies current on our stages today, whether as existentialist, nihilist, expressionist, or satirist, or any other label put on the compote dished up by literary criticism. For me, the stage is not a battlefield for theories, philosophies, and manifestos, but rather an instrument whose possibilities I seek to know by playing with it. . . . My plays are not for what people have to say: what is said is there because my plays deal with people, and thinking and believing and philosophizing are all, to some extent at least, a part of human behavior."

For Duerrenmatt, the playwright's task is to present a new, fantastic, even grotesque and bizarre world upon a stage by using everything at his command: language, irony, ideas, and what Adolf D. Klarmann calls "theatrical pyro-technics." Klarmann cites a few of these from Duerrenmatt's work: "Figures appear out of trap doors, enter through windows and clocks, scenery flies up and down in full view, torture wheels are outlines against the sky, moon dances are performed on roofs, angels alight on chandeliers, chickens run across the stage, in short, every conceivable trick of the trade of the theatre, of the cabaret, the burlesque, and the movies is applied with a lusty abandon."

Believing that true tragedy is impossible to create in a world, he calls his dramatic pieces comedies, though the comedy to be found therein is no more merry than gallows humor. Duerrenmatt writes: "The task of art, insofar as art can have a task at all, and hence also the task of drama today, is to create something concrete, something that has form. This can be accomplished best by comedy. . . . [But] we can achieve the tragic out of comedy. We can bring it forth as a frightening moment, as an abyss that opens suddenly. . . . [The conceit employed by comedy] easily transforms the crowd of theatregoers into a mass which can be attacked, deceived, outsmarted into listening to things it would otherwise not so readily listen to. Comedy is a mousetrap in which the public is easily caught and in which it will get caught over and over again. Tragedy on the other hand, predicates a true community, a kind of community whose existence in our day is but an embarrassing fiction."

Although he is primarily known as a dramatist, Duerrenmatt has also written acclaimed fiction and is best known for his mystery and detective novels, including *Der Richter und sein Henker* (*The Judge and His Hangman*) *Der Verdacht* (*The Quarry*), and *Das Versprechen* (*The Pledge*). *The Judge and His Hangman* was a German best-seller when it appeared in 1950 and, according to Saad Elkhadem in *International Fiction Review,* "is undoubtedly one of the most exciting and entertaining novels in German literature." Elkhadem contends that the novel's popularity is due mainly to "its gripping incidents and breath-taking plot," while "from a narrative point of view, [the] pure event-novel testifies to the remarkable talent of Duerrenmatt as an imaginative fabulist and beguiling storyteller." *Dictionary of Literary Biography* contributor Roger A. Crockett notes "there is a distinctly dramatic quality to Duerrenmatt's prose," adding that "the same pessimistic view of history, the same distrust of absolutes, and the same dominance of coincidence over rational planning which characterize his dramas also pervade his prose."

"Duerrenmatt is a disillusioned analyst of the human character," writes George Wellwarth in *The Theater of Protest and Paradox.* "Even the plays with political themes are ultimately about the human beings rather than issues. Like Ionesco, like Beckett, like all the writers of the dramatic avant-garde in fact, Duerrenmatt feels deep down in himself that the problems of humanity are insoluble. And so he takes refuge from this knowledge in a mordantly sardonic portrayal of life." Duerrenmatt's recurring themes, according to Wellwarth, are "the effect of the possession of power on the human souls," and the senselessness of death, which "renders human acts trivial." But, Wellwarth contends, "Duerrenmatt always implies that events must be resisted. Nothing is inevitable and determined in Duerrenmatt. The fact that things are insignificant from a cosmic viewpoint does not alter the fact that they are significant in the immediate present: it merely argues that they are finally insoluble and will always repeat themselves." Duerrenmatt once commented: "The universal escapes my grasp. I refuse to find the universal in a doctrine. The universal for me is chaos. The world (hence the stage which represents this world) is for me something monstrous, a riddle of misfortunes which must be accepted but before which one must not capitulate."

BIOGRAPHICAL/CRITICAL SOURCES:

BOOKS

Arnold, Armin, *Friedrich Duerrenmatt,* translated by Arnold with Sheila Johnson, Ungar, 1972.

Bauland, Peter, *The Hooded Eagle: Modern German Drama on the New York Stage,* Syracuse University Press, 1968.

Block, H. M., and H. Salinger, editors, *Creative Vision,* Evergreen, 1960.

Bogard, Travis, and William I. Oliver, editors, *Modern Drama,* Oxford University Press, 1965.

Cole, Toby, editor, *Playwrights on Playwriting,* Hill & Wang, 1961.

Contemporary Literary Criticism, Gale, Volume 1, 1973, Volume 4, 1975, Volume 8, 1978, Volume 11, 1979, Volume 15, 1980, Volume 43, 1987.

Corrigan, Robert W., *The Theatre in Search of a Fix,* Delacorte Press, 1973.

Daemmrich, Horst S., and Diether H. Haenicke, editors, *The Challenge of German Literature,* Wayne State University Press, 1971.

Dictionary of Literary Biography, Volume 69: *Contemporary German Fiction Writers, First Series,* Gale, 1988.

Esslin, Martin, *Reflections: Essays on Modern Theatre,* Doubleday, 1969.

Fickert, J. K., *To Heaven and Back,* University Press of Kentucky, 1972.

Hansel, J., *Friedrich Duerrenmatt: Bibliographie,* Gehlen, 1968.

Hayman, Ronald, editor, *The German Theatre: A Symposium,* Barnes & Noble, 1975.

Jenny, U., *Duerrenmatt: A Study of His Play,* Methuen, 1971.

Knapp, Gerhard P., *Friedrich Duerrenmatt: Studien zu seinem Werk,* Lother Stiehm, 1976.

Knapp, Gerhard P., and Gerd Labroisse, editors, *Facetten: Studien zum 60. Geburtstag Friedrich Duerrenmatt,* Peter Lang, 1981.

Lumley, Frederick, *New Trends in Twentieth Century Drama,* Oxford University Press, 1967.

Mayer, Hans, *Steppenwolf and Everyman,* translated and introduced by Jack D. Zipes, Crowell, 1971.

Peppard, Murray, *Friedrich Duerrenmatt,* Twayne, 1969.

Symons, Julian, *Mortal Consequences: A History; from the Detective Story to the Crime Novel,* Harper, 1972.

Tynan, Kenneth, *Curtains,* Atheneum, 1961.

Wager, Walter, editor, *The Playwrights Speak,* Delacorte Press, 1967.

Wellwarth, George, *The Theater of Protest and Paradox: Developments in the Avant-garde Drama,* New York University Press, 1964.

Whitton, Kenneth S., *The Theatre of Friedrich Duerrenmatt: A Study in the Possibility of Freedom,* Oswald Wolff, 1980.

Wilbert-Collins, E., *Bibliography of Four Contemporary Swiss-German Authors: Friedrich Duerrenmatt, Max Frisch, Robert Walser, Albin Zollinger,* Francke, 1967.

PERIODICALS

Books Abroad, autumn, 1967.
Christian Century, October 28, 1964.
Christian Science Monitor, July 22, 1965; August 7, 1965.
Comparative Drama, spring, 1982.
Contemporary Literature, autumn, 1966; summer, 1970.
Esquire, May, 1961.
Forum for Modern Language Studies, January, 1976.
Genre, December, 1975.
German Life and Letters, January, 1974.
German Quarterly, January, 1962.
International Fiction Review, July, 1977.
Maske und Kothurn, Volume 2, 1977.
Modern Drama, June, 1977.
Modern Fiction Studies, winter, 1971-72.
Monatshefte, spring, 1971.
Mosaic, spring, 1972.
Nation, January 9, 1960; May 4, 1963.
New York Times, October 18, 1964; July 10, 1965; June 4, 1971; February 5, 1989.
New York Times Book Review, June 13, 1965; August 6, 1989.
Renascence, winter, 1985.
Saturday Review, July 17, 1965.
Stage, January 20, 1972.
Time, December 10, 1973.
Times (London), June 29, 1989.
Times Literary Supplement, January 11, 1964; July 14, 1966; October 27, 1972; October 16, 1981; October 29, 1982; May 16, 1986.
Tribune Books (Chicago), March 6, 1988.
Voice Literary Supplement, February, 1984.
World Literature Today, winter, 1978; autumn, 1981; summer, 1982; summer, 1984; spring, 1986; summer, 1986; autumn, 1987.

*   *   *

DUFFY, Maureen 1933-

PERSONAL: Born October 21, 1933, in Worthing, Sussex, England; daughter of Cahia Patrick Duffy and Grace Rose Wright. *Education:* King's College, London, B.A. (with honors), 1956. *Politics:* Socialist. *Religion:* None.

ADDRESSES: Home—8 Roland Gardens, London SW7, England. *Agent*—Jonathan Clowes, 22 Prince Albert Rd., London NW1, England.

CAREER: Novelist. Teacher of creative writing in England in state schools and to adults 1951-53, 1956-60; has also taught adult classes more recently in Amherst and London.

MEMBER: Writers Guild of Great Britain (deputy chairman; joint chairman, 1978-79), British Copyright Council (vice chairman, 1980—), Authors Lending and Copyright Society (chairman, 1981—).

AWARDS, HONORS: City of London Festival Playwright's Award, 1961, for "The Lay-Off"; Arts Council of Great Britain scholarships, 1963, for drama, 1966, for literature.

WRITINGS:

"The Lay-Off " (play), produced at the City of London Festival, 1961.
That's How It Was, Hutchinson, 1962.
(Translator) Domenico Rea, *A Blush of Shame,* Barrie & Rockliff, 1963.
The Single Eye, Hutchinson, 1964.
The Microcosm, Simon & Schuster, 1966.
"The Silk Room" (play), produced in England at Watford Civic Theatre, 1966.
The Paradox Players, Hutchinson, 1967, Simon & Schuster, 1968.
Lyrics for the Dog Hour (poems), Hutchinson, 1968.
Wounds, Knopf, 1969.
Rites (play; produced by the National Theatre Repertory Co. in London at Jeannetta Cochrane Theatre, spring, 1969), Methuen, 1969.
"Solo, Olde Thyme" (play), produced in Cambridge, 1970.
Love Child, Knopf, 1971.
The Venus Touch (poems), Weidenfeld & Nicolson, 1971.
The Erotic World of Faery, Hodder & Stoughton, 1972.
All Heaven in a Rage, Knopf, 1973 (published in England as *I Want to Go to Moscow,* Hodder & Stoughton, 1973).
"A Nightingale in Bloomsbury Square" (play), produced at the Hampstead Theatre, 1974.
Capital, Braziller 1976.
The Passionate Shepherdess: Aphra Behn (biography), J. Cape, 1977.
(Editor with Alan Brownjohn) *New Poetry* (anthology), Arts Council of Great Britain, 1977.
Housespy (novel), Hamish Hamilton, 1978.
Memorials of the Quick and the Dead (poems), Hamish Hamilton, 1979.
Inherit the Earth (social history), Hamish Hamilton, 1980.
Gor Saga (novel), Viking, 1982.
Londoners (novel), Methuen, 1983.
Men and Beasts: An Animal Rights Handbook, Paladin, 1984.
Collected Poems, Hamish Hamilton, 1985.
(Editor) Aphra Behn, *Oroonoko and Other Stories,* Methuen, 1986.
Change, Methuen, 1987.
A Thousand Capricious Chances: A History of the Methuen List 1889-1989, Methuen, 1989.

Also author of *Evesong* (poems), published by Sappho Publications.

SIDELIGHTS: "British critics have compared [Maureen Duffy] to Virginia Woolf," writes a reviewer for *Time,* "noting that both have the knack of tuning the physical world precisely to the pitch of the characters' emotions. Miss Duffy has a special talent for describing landscape, seascape and weather." Duffy's ability to handle description and develop characters is perhaps most apparent in her fourth novel, *The Paradox Players.* David Lawson notes: "Miss Duffy's sparse, restrained style captures the brooding emptiness of river living, but the reader is ever aware of the pulse and flow of the life there." A critic for the *New Yorker* writes that "no one character in [*The Paradox Players*] is outstanding, although each human being and each animal is impeccably drawn and treated with thorough understanding. As a

study in gray, animated and given sad meaning by the slow movement of gray figures, gray weather, and fateful gray light, her book is a work of art."

Some reviewers are disturbed, however, by what Frank Littler calls an "obstinate lack of focus" in Duffy's work. M. K. Margoshes suggests that "perhaps it was the author's intention to write in a disjointed and disorganized manner to convey the feeling of confusion that exists in the subjects' lives." The critic for the *Times Literary Supplement* regrets the uncertainty he finds in the "larger implications" of her work because, as he writes, she "handles detail so beautifully and can suggest what her characters see, imagine and remember with such precision and life." According to Piers Brendon, "Maureen Duffy has a muted voice, but its attenuated tones subtly invade the consciousness and linger echoing in the memory."

Valentine Cunningham comments on a more recent novel: "Duffy is as much interested in language as in story. . . . And *Capital*'s celebration of London doesn't just recollect the past but tries to recreate it in the styles of the past—one of the braver methods of Joyce—even if 222 pages isn't quite up to *Ulysses*'s scope. . . . The room Maureen Duffy's proceedings allows her for irony is immense, and opportunities for sly humour rarely go unexploited."

BIOGRAPHICAL/CRITICAL SOURCES:

BOOKS

Contemporary Literary Criticism, Volume 37, Gale, 1986.
Dictionary of Literary Biography, Volume 14: *British Novelists since 1960,* Gale, 1983.

PERIODICALS

Books and Bookmen, October, 1967, November, 1967.
Bookseller, March 27, 1971.
New Statesman, September 9, 1975.
New Yorker, October 5, 1968.
New York Times, August 17, 1969, March 19, 1976.
New York Times Book Review, August 17, 1969, May 27, 1973.
Observer, September 17, 1967.
Spectator, October 13, 1967, May 1, 1971, October 29, 1983.
Time, September 13, 1968.
Times Literary Supplement, May 26, 1966, September 28, 1967, July 3, 1969, July 5, 1971, November 10, 1972, June 8, 1973, September 19, 1975, April 7, 1978, November 6, 1981, October 7, 1983, May 15, 1987, August 11, 1989.
Washington Post Book World, April 11, 1971.

*   *   *

DUNN, Douglas (Eaglesham)   1942-

PERSONAL: Born October 23, 1942, in Inchinnan, Renfrewshire, Scotland; son of William Douglas (a factory worker) and Margaret (McGowan) Dunn; married Lesley Balfour Wallace (senior keeper of an art gallery), November 26, 1964 (died March 13, 1981); married Lesley Jane Bathgate (a graphic designer and artist), August 10, 1985; children: one son. *Education:* Scottish School of Librarianship, A.L.A., 1962; University of Hull, B.A. (English; first class honors), 1969.

ADDRESSES: Home—Braeknowe, Grey St., Tayport, Fife DD6 8HU, Scotland. *Agent*—Pat Kavanagh, A. D. Peters & Co. Ltd., 10 Buckingham St., London WC2N 6BU, England.

CAREER: Renfrew County Library, Renfrewshire, Scotland, junior library assistant, 1959-62; University of Strathclyde, Andersonian Library, Glasgow, Scotland, library assistant, 1962-64; Akron Public Library, Akron, OH, assistant librarian, 1964-66; University of Glasgow, Chemistry Department Library, Glasgow, librarian, 1966; University of Hull, Brynmor Jones Library, Hull, England, assistant librarian, 1969-71, writer in residence, 1974-75; poet and free-lance writer. Writer in residence at University of New England (Australia), 1984, and Duncan of Jordanstone College of Art, Dundee District Library, 1986-88; University of Dundee, writer in residence, 1981-82, honorary visiting professor, 1987-89.

MEMBER: Royal Society of Literature (fellow), Scottish P.E.N., Society of Authors.

AWARDS, HONORS: Eric Gregory Award, Society of Authors, 1968, for manuscript collection; Scottish Arts Council Publication Award, 1970, and Somerset Maugham Award, Society of Authors, 1972, both for *Terry Street;* Scottish Arts Council Publication Award, 1975, and Geoffrey Faber Memorial Prize, 1976, both for *Love or Nothing;* Hawthornden Prize, 1982, for *St. Kilda's Parliament;* Whitbread Literary Awards for poetry and for book of the year, 1985, both for *Elegies;* honorary LL.D., University of Dundee, 1987.

WRITINGS:

POEMS

Terry Street, Faber, 1969, Chilmark, 1973.
Backwaters, The Review, 1971.
The Happier Life, Faber, 1972, Chilmark, 1973.
Love or Nothing, Faber, 1974.
Barbarians, Faber, 1979.
Europa's Lover, Bloodaxe Books, 1982.
St. Kilda's Parliament, Faber, 1982.
Elegies, Faber, 1985.
Selected Poems: 1964-1983, Faber, 1986.
Northlight, Faber, 1988.
New and Selected Poems, Nineteen Sixty-six to Nineteen Eighty-eight, Ecco Press, 1989.

EDITOR

New Poems, 1972-73: The P.E.N. Anthology, Hutchinson, 1973.
A Choice of Lord Byron's Verse, Faber, 1974.
Two Decades of Irish Writing, Carcanet Press, 1975.
What Is to Be Given: Selected Poems of Delmore Schwartz, Carcanet Press, 1976.
The Poetry of Scotland, Batsford, 1979.
Poetry Book Society Supplement, Poetry Book Society, 1979.
A Rumoured City: New Poets from Hull, Bloodaxe Books, 1982.

To Build a Bridge, Lincolnshire and Humberside Arts Association, 1982.

FOR RADIO AND TELEVISION

Scotsmen by Moonlight (play), BBC-Radio, 1977.
(Author of verse commentary) *Running,* BBC-TV, 1977.
Ploughman's Share (play), BBC-TV, 1979.
Wedderburn's Slave, BBC-Radio Scotland, 1980.
(Author of verse commentary) *Anon's People,* BBC-TV Scotland, 1984.
The Telescope Garden, BBC-Radio, c. 1985.

OTHER

Secret Villages (short stories), Dodd, Mead, 1985.

Contributor to *New Statesman, Poetry Nation, Times Literary Supplement, New Yorker, Punch, London Magazine, New Review,* and *Listener.* Poetry reviewer, *Encounter,* beginning 1971; special editor, "British Poetry Issue," *Antaeus 12,* 1973.

WORK IN PROGRESS: A book of short stories; a novel; editing *Faber Book of Twentieth-Century Scottish Poetry.*

BIOGRAPHICAL/CRITICAL SOURCES:

BOOKS

Contemporary Literary Criticism, Gale, Volume 6, 1976, Volume 40, 1986.
Dictionary of Literary Biography, Volume 40: *Poets of Great Britain and Ireland since 1960,* Gale, 1985.
Haffenden, John, *Viewpoints: Poets in Conversation with John Haffenden,* Faber, 1981.

PERIODICALS

Listener, August 9, 1973.
Los Angeles Times Book Review, July 28, 1985.
New Statesman, June 16, 1972, December 6, 1974.
Observer (London), July 2, 1972, October 20, 1974.
Oxford Poetry, Volume 2, number 2, 1985.
Spectator, July 22, 1972, January 4, 1975.
Times Literary Supplement, June 9, 1972, January 31, 1975, October 2, 1981, January 7, 1983, August 19, 1983, May 31, 1985, April 5, 1985, October 21-27, 1988.
Virginia Quarterly Review, spring, 1975.

*   *   *

DURRENMATT, Friedrich
  See DUERRENMATT, Friedrich

E

ECO, Umberto 1932-

PERSONAL: Born January 5, 1932, in Alessandria, Italy; son of Giulio and Giovanna (Bisio) Eco; married Renate Ramge (a teacher) September 24, 1962; children: Stefano, Carlotta. *Education:* University of Turin, Ph.D., 1954.

ADDRESSES: Home—Via Melzi d'Eril 23, 20154 Milano, Italy. *Office*—Universita di Bologna, Via Toffano 2, Bologna, Italy.

CAREER: RAI (Italian Radio-Television), Milan, Italy, editor for cultural programs, 1954-59; University of Turin, Turin, Italy, assistant lecturer, 1956-63, lecturer in aesthetics, 1963-64; University of Milan, Milan, lecturer on faculty of architecture, 1964-65; University of Florence, Florence, Italy, professor of visual communications, 1966-69; Milan Polytechnic, Milan, professor of semiotics, 1969-71; University of Bologna, Bologna, Italy, associate professor, 1971-75, professor of semiotics, 1975—. Visiting professor, New York University, 1969, 1976, Northwestern University, 1972, University of California, San Diego, 1975, Yale University, 1977, 1980, 1981, and Columbia University, 1978. Lecturer on semiotics at various institutions throughout the world, including University of Antwerp, Ecole Pratique des Hautes Etudes, University of London, Nobel Foundation, University of Warsaw, University of Budapest, University of Toronto, Murdoch University—Perth, and Amherst College. Member of the Council for the United States and Italy. *Military service:* Italian Army, 1958-59.

MEMBER: International Association for Semiotic Studies (secretary-general, 1972-79, vice-president, 1979—), James Joyce Foundation (honorary trustee).

AWARDS, HONORS: Premio Strega and Premio Anghiari, both 1981, both for *Il nome della rosa;* named honorary citizen of Monte Cerignone, Italy, 1982; Prix Medicis for best foreign novel, 1982, for French version of *Il nome della rosa; Los Angeles Times* fiction prize nomination, 1983, and best fiction book award from Association of Logos Bookstores, both for *The Name of the Rose;* McLuhan Teleglobe Canada Award from UNESCO's Canadian Commission, 1985, for achievement in communications; honorary degrees from Catholic University, Leuven, 1985, Odense University, 1986, Loyola University, Chicago, 1987, State University of New York at Stony Brook, 1987, Royal College of Arts, London, 1987, and Brown University, 1988.

WRITINGS:

IN ITALIAN

Filosofi in liberta, Taylor (Turin), 1958, 2nd edition, 1959.

(Contributor) *Momenti e problema di storia dell'estetica,* Marzorati, 1959.

Opera aperta: Forma e indeterminazione nelle poetiche contemporanee (includes *Le poetiche di Joyce;* also see below), Bompiani, 1962, revised edition, 1972, translation by Anna Cancogni published as *The Open Work,* Harvard University Press, 1989.

Diario minimo, Mondadori, 1963, 2nd revised edition, 1976.

Apocalittici e integrati: Comunicazioni di massa e teoria della cultura di massa, Bompiani, 1964, revised edition, 1977.

Le poetiche di Joyce, Bompiani, 1965, 2nd edition published as *Le poetiche di Joyce dalla "Summa" al "Finnegans Wake,"* 1966.

Appunti per una semiologia delle comunicazioni visive (also see below), Bompiani, 1967.

(Author of introduction) Mimmo Castellano, *Noi vivi,* Dedalo Libri, 1967.

La struttura assente (includes *Appunti per una semiologia delle comunicazioni visive*), Bompiani, 1968, revised edition, 1983.

La definizione dell'arte (title means "The Definition of Art"), U. Mursia, 1968.

(Editor) *L'uomo e l'arte,* Volume 1: *L'arte come mestiere,* Bompiani, 1969.

(Editor with Remo Faccani) *I sistemi di segni e lo strutturalismo sovietico,* Bompiani, 1969, 2nd edition published as *Semiotica della letteratura in URSS,* 1974.

(Editor) *Socialismo y consolacion: Reflexiones en torno a "Los misterios de Paris" de Eugene Sue,* Tusquets, 1970, 2nd edition, 1974.

Le forme del contenuto, Bompiani, 1971.

(Editor with Cesare Sughi) *Cent'anni dopo: Il ritorno dell'intreccio,* Bompiani, 1971.

Il segno, Isedi, 1971, 2nd edition, Mondadori.

(Editor with M. Bonazzi) *I pampini bugiardi,* Guaraldi, 1972.

(Editor) *Estetica e teoria dell'informazione,* Bompiani, 1972.

(Contributor) *Documenti su il nuovo medioevo,* Bompiani, 1973.

(Editor) *Eugenio Carmi: Una pittura de paesaggio?,* G. Prearo, 1973.

Il costume di casa: Evidenze e misteri dell'ideologia italiano, Bompiani, 1973.

Beato di Liebana: Miniature del Beato de Fernando I y Sancha, F. M. Ricci, 1973.

Il superuomo di massa: Studi sul romanzo popolare, Cooperativa Scrittori, 1976, revised edition, Bompiani, 1978.

(Co-editor) *Storia di una rivoluzione mai esistita l'esperimento Vaduz,* Servizio Opinioni, RAI, 1976.

Dalla periferia dell'Impero, Bompiani, 1976.

Come si fa una tesi di laurea, Bompiani, 1977.

Lector in fabula: La cooperazione interpretative nei testi narrativa (also see below), Bompiani, 1979.

(Contributor) *Carolina Invernizio, Matilde Serao, Liala,* La Nuova Italia, 1979.

(Contributor) *Convegno su realta e ideologie dell'informazione,* Milan, 1978, Il Saggiatore, 1979.

(With others) *Perche continuiamo a fare e a insegnare arte?,* Cappelli, 1979.

Sette anni di desiderio, Bompiani, 1983.

Sugli specchi e altri saggi, Bompiani, 1985.

IN ENGLISH TRANSLATION

Il problema estetico in San Tommaso, Edizioni di Filosofia, 1956, 2nd edition published as *Il problema estetico in Tommaso d'Aquino,* Bompiani, 1970, translation by Hugh Bredin published as *The Aesthetics of Thomas Aquinas,* Harvard University Press, 1988.

(Editor with G. Zorzoli) *Storia figurata delle invenzioni: Dalla selce scheggiata al volo spaziali,* Bompiani, 1961, translation by Anthony Lawrence published as *The Picture History of Inventions From Plough to Polaris,* Macmillan, 1963, 2nd Italian edition, Bompiani, 1968.

(Editor with Oreste del Buono) *Il caso Bond,* Bompiani, 1965, translation by R. Downie published as *The Bond Affair,* Macdonald, 1966.

(Editor with Jean Chesneaux and Gino Nebiolo) *I fumetti di Mao,* Laterza, 1971, translation by Frances Frenaye published as *The People's Comic Book: Red Women's Detachment, Hot on the Trail, and Other Chinese Comics,* Anchor Press, 1973.

Il nome della rosa, Bompiani, 1980, translation by William Weaver published as *The Name of the Rose,* Harcourt, 1983.

Postscript to "The Name of the Rose" (originally published in Italian), translation by Weaver, Harcourt, 1984.

Art and Beauty in the Middle Ages (originally published in Italian), translation by Bredin, Yale University Press, 1986.

Travels in Hyper Reality (originally published in Italian), edited by Helen Wolff and Kurt Wolff, translation by Weaver, Harcourt, 1986.

Il pendolo di Foucault (novel), Bompiani, 1988, translation by Weaver published as *Foucault's Pendulum,* Harcourt, 1989.

The Aesthetics of Chaosmos: The Middle Ages of James Joyce (originally published in Italian), translation by Ellen Esrock, Harvard University Press, 1989.

The Bomb and the General (juvenile; originally published in Italian), translation by Weaver, illustrations by Eugenio Carmi, Harcourt, 1989.

IN ENGLISH

A Theory of Semiotics, Indiana University Press, 1976, translation from original English manuscript published as *Trattato di semiotica generale,* Bompiani, 1975.

The Role of the Reader: Explorations in the Semiotics of Texts, Indiana University Press, 1979, revised Italian edition published as *Lector in fabula: La cooperazione interpretative nei testi narrativa,* Bompiani, 1979.

Semiotics and the Philosophy of Language, Indiana University Press, 1984.

(Editor with Thomas A. Sebeok) *Sign of the Three: Dupin, Holmes, Peirce,* Indiana University Press, 1984.

(Editor with others) *Meaning and Mental Representations,* Indiana University Press, 1988.

The Three Astronauts (for children), Harcourt, 1989.

(Editor with Costantino Marmo) *On the Medieval Theory of Signs,* John Benjamins, 1989.

The Limits of Interpretation, Indiana University Press, 1991.

OTHER

Many of Eco's books have been translated into foreign languages. Contributor to numerous encyclopedias, including *Enciclopedia Filosofica* and *Encyclopedic Dictionary of Semiotics.* Also contributor to proceedings of the First Congress of the International Association for Semiotic Studies. Columnist for *Il giorno, La stampa, Corriere della Sera,* and other newspapers and magazines. Contributor of essays and reviews to numerous periodicals, including *Times Literary Supplement.* Member of editorial board, *Semiotica, Poetics Today, Degres, Structuralist Review, Text, Communication, Problemi dell'informazione,* and *Alfabeta;* nonfiction senior editor, Casa Editrice Bompiani, Milan, 1959-75; editor, *VS-Semiotic Studies.*

SIDELIGHTS: No one expected *The Name of the Rose* to become an internationally acclaimed best-seller, least of all Umberto Eco, the man who wrote the book. A respected Italian scholar, Eco had built his literary reputation on specialized academic writing about semiotics—the study of how cultures communicate through signs. Not only was *The Name of the Rose* his first novel, it was also a complex creation, long on philosophy and short on sex—definitely not blockbuster material, especially not in Italy where the market for books is small. Eco himself considered the initial press run of 15,000 copies excessive, according to the London *Times.* That was in 1980. By 1983 *The Name of the Rose* had been translated into more than twenty languages, won several of Europe's most prestigious literary prizes, and sold millions of hardback copies worldwide. Today the novel is considered a publishing phenomenon, and people in the book business are still asking themselves why.

Some experts attribute its success to the current interest in fantasy literature. "For all its historical accuracy, *The Name of the Rose* has the charm of an invented world," Drenka Willen, Eco's editor at Harcourt Brace Jovanovich, told *Newsweek.* Others chalk it up to snob appeal. "Every year there is one great *unread* best-seller. A lot of people who will buy the book will never read it," Howard Kaminsky, president of Warner Books, suggests in that same *Newsweek* article.

But perhaps the most plausible explanation is the one offered by Franco Ferrucci in the *New York Times Book Review:* "The answer may lie in the fact that Mr. Eco is the unacknowledged leader of contemporary Italian culture, a man whose academic and ideological prestige has grown steadily through years of dazzling and solid work." In addition to semiotics—a field that he almost singlehandedly legitimatized—Eco is an expert on logic, literature, aesthetics, and history. In fact, in Eco's opinion, the science of semiotics embraces not only these, but all aspects of culture. Academics have been reading Eco's hypotheses for years in specialized texts such as *A Theory of Semiotics* and *The Role of the Reader: Explorations in the Semiotics of Texts.* While these works are unintelligible to the public at large, some of Eco's concepts have begun to filter down. "Only a specialist or a panicky grad student would read a book called *A Theory of Semiotics*," Walter Kendrick observes, "but a general reader might well pick up a semiotic novel if it promised to give the gist of the matter without bogging down in jargon. For most readers," Kendrick continues in the *Village Voice Literary Supplement*, "*The Name of the Rose* is worth reading as a sugarcoated version of that otherwise unpalatable subject."

On one level *The Name of the Rose* is a murder mystery in which a number Catholic monks are inexplicably killed. The setting is an ancient monastery in northern Italy, the year is 1327, and the air is rife with evil. Dissention among rival factions of the Franciscan order threatens to tear the church apart, and each side is preparing for a showdown. On one side stand the Spiritualists and the emperor Louis IV who endorse evangelical poverty; on the other, the corrupt Pope John XXII and the monks who believe that the vow of poverty will rob the church of earthly wealth and power. In an effort to avoid a confrontation, both sides agree to meet at the monastery—a Benedictine abbey that is considered neutral ground. To this meeting come William of Baskerville, an English Franciscan empowered to represent the emperor, and Adso, William's disciple and scribe. Before the council can convene, however, the body of a young monk is discovered at the bottom of a cliff, and William, a master logician in the tradition of Sherlock Holmes, is recruited to solve the crime, assisted by Adso, in Watson's role. As the murders proliferate in seeming fulfillment of an apocalyptic prophecy, the sleuths engage in passionate debates about the meaning of scriptures. These theological digressions, which are grounded in fact and frequently studded with Latin quotations, lend a historical dimension to the book. What's more, the evidence that William and Adso pursue involves secret symbols and coded manuscripts—in other words, semiotics.

Nowhere is the importance of decoding symbols more apparent than in the library—an intricate labyrinth that houses all types of books, including volumes on pagan rituals and black magic. The secret of the maze is known to only a few, among them the master librarian whose job it is to safeguard the collection and supervise the circulation of appropriate volumes. William suspects that the murders relate to a forbidden book—a rare work with "the power of a thousand scorpions"—that some of the more curious monks have been trying to obtain. "What the temptation of adultery is for laymen and the yearning for riches is for secular ecclesiastics, the seduction of knowledge is for monks," William explains to Adso. "Why should they not have risked death to satisfy a curiosity of their minds, or have killed to prevent someone from appropriating a jealously guarded secret of their own?"

After being put off the track by a number of red herrings, William finally locates the prohibited book and the "Anti-Christ" who has committed the murders. To reveal the culprit would spoil the story, but it can be reported that the volume in question turns out to be the "lost" second volume of Aristotle's *Poetics,* which extols comedy as a force for good. This the murderer could not stand. As Gerard Reedy explains in his *America* review, the killer "fears that this authoritative explication of comic genres will undermine the seriousness of truth." Believing that Christ never laughed, the murderer cannot abide the laughter of others. He "did a diabolical thing because he loved his truth so lewdly that he dared anything in order to destroy falsehood," William explains to Adso, adding: "Perhaps the mission of those who love mankind is to make people laugh at the truth, *to make truth laugh,* because the only truth lies in learning to free ourselves from insane passion for the truth."

This statement appears to reflect Eco's attitude as well as William's. "It is almost too obvious that William is Mr. Eco himself," Franco Ferrucci points out in the *New York Times Book Review.* Writing in the *Village Voice Literary Supplement* Walter Kendrick explains the connection between William's philosophy and modern semiotics: "Throughout the book, the naive realism of Adso, the narrator, bumps heads with the nominalism of William, his mentor. Realism and nominalism were schools of medieval philosophy. . . . But the two positions correspond rather well to the common sense of a modern reader and the apparent nihilism of a semiotician. . . . Baldly stated, realism maintains that the names of things are directly attached to the essence of what they denote, that universals are 'realer' than particulars. Nominalism attributes no reality to names; they are merely human ways of organizing a world that would otherwise be unmanageable."

Some medievalists have suggested that this is a distinctly modern point of view, out of place in William's world. His comment upon finally solving the case is revealing. "I behaved stubbornly," he tells Adso, "pursuing a semblance of order, when I should have known well there is no order in the universe." Kendrick points out that "such an idea goes far beyond all the heresies for which fourteenth-century people were burned at the stake; not only shouldn't William have known it, he wouldn't have thought it for another 600 years." While acknowledging the inaccuracy, Walter Goodman excuses it in the name of poetic license. "In this novel," he writes in the *New York Times,* "imagination carries the day. William of Baskerville may be an anachronism, but Mr. Eco wants us to know that his rationality, tolerance and compassion would have added light to what used to be known as the Dark Ages." In a letter to *CA,* Eco contests these criticisms. "Many medievalists say that I am correctly mirroring the most advanced ideas of the fourteenth century," he writes, adding that the novel has prompted several articles in academic journals as well as a symposium at the University of Louvain.

If William speaks for reason, Adso—the young novice who, in his old age, will relate the story—represents the voice of faith. Ferrucci believes that Adso reflects the author's second side: "The Eco who writes *The Name of the Rose* is Adso: a voice young and old at the same time, speaking from nostalgia for love and passion. William shapes the story with his insight; Adso gives it his own pathos. He will never think, as William does, that 'books are not made to be believed but to be subjected to inquiry'; Adso writes to be believed."

Another way Eco's novel can be interpreted is as a parable of modern life. The vehement struggle between church and state mirrors much of recent Italian history with its "debates over the role of the left and the accompanying explosion of terrorist violence," writes Sari Gilbert in the *Washington Post.* Eco acknowledges the influence that former Italian premier Aldo Moro's 1978 kidnapping and death had on his story, telling Gilbert that it "gave us all a sense of impotence," but he also warned that the book was not simply a *roman a clef.* "Instead," he told Herbert Mitgang in a *New York Times Book Review* article, "I hope readers see the roots, that everything that existed then—from banks and the inflationary spiral to the burning of libraries—exists today. We are always approaching the time of the anti-Christ. In the nuclear age, we are never far from the Dark Ages."

As with his first novel, Eco's second novel was an international best-seller. Published in 1989 in English as *Foucault's Pendulum,* the book is similar to *The Name of the Rose* in that it is a semiotic murder mystery wrapped in several layers of meaning. The plot revolves around Casaubon the narrator and two Milan editors who break up the monotony of reviewing manuscripts on the occult by combining information from all of them into one computer program called the Plan. Initially conceived as a joke, the Plan connects the Knights Templar—a medieval papal order who fought in the Crusades—with other occult groups throughout history. The program produces a map indicating the geographical point at which the powers of the earth can be controlled. That point is in Paris, France, at Foucault's Pendulum. When occult groups including Satanists get wind of the Plan, they go so far as to kill one of the editors in their quest to gain control of the earth. While this is the basic plot, readers who move through it will also encounter William Shakespeare, Rene Descartes, Tom and Jerry, Karl Marx, Rhett Butler and Scarlett O'hara, Sam Spade, Frederick the Great of Prussia, Nazis, Rosicrucians, and Jesuits. Eco orchestrates all of these and other diverse characters and groups into his multilayered semiotic story.

Some of the interpretations of the book critics have suggested include reading it as nothing more than an elaborate joke, as an exploration of the ambiguity between text as reality and reality as text, and as a warning that harm comes to those who seek knowledge through bad logic and faulty reasoning. Given this range of interpretation and Eco's interest in semiotics, *Foucault's Pendulum* is probably best described as a book about many things, including the act of interpretation itself.

Foucault's Pendulum generated a broad range of commentary. Some critics faulted the book for digressing too often into scholarly minutia, and others felt Eco had only mixed success in relating the different levels of his tale. Several reviewers, however, praised *Foucault's Pendulum.* Comparing the work to his first novel, Herbert Mitgang, for example, said in the *New York Times* that the book "is a quest novel that is deeper and richer than 'The Name of the Rose.' It's a brilliant piece of research and writing—experimental and funny, literary and philosophical—that bravely ignores the conventional expectations of the reader." Eco offered his own opinion of his novel in *Time:* "This was a book conceived to irritate the reader. I knew it would provoke ambiguous, nonhomogeneous responses because it was a book conceived to point up some contradictions."

In 1979—before the publication of his two best-selling novels—Eco told *CA:* "I think the duty of a scholar is not only to do scientific research but also to communicate with people through various media about the most important issues of social life from the point of view of his own discipline."

MEDIA ADAPTATIONS: Jean-Jacques Annaud directed a 1986 film adaptation of Eco's novel, *The Name of the Rose;* the movie starred Sean Connery as William of Baskerville.

BIOGRAPHICAL/CRITICAL SOURCES:

BOOKS

Bestsellers 90, Issue 2, Gale, 1990.
Contemporary Literary Criticism, Volume 28, Gale, 1984.
Eco, Umberto, *The Name of the Rose,* translation by William Weaver, Harcourt, 1983.

PERIODICALS

America, August 3, 1983.
American Anthropologist, September, 1978.
Art Journal, winter, 1976-77.
Atlantic, November, 1989.
Corriere della Sera, June 1, 1981.
Harper's, August, 1983.
International Philosophical Quarterly, June, 1980.
Journal of Communication, autumn, 1976.

Language, Volume 53, number 3, 1977.
Language in Society, April, 1977.
Los Angeles Times, November 9, 1989.
Maclean's, July 18, 1983.
Merkur, Volume 37, number 1, 1983.
New Republic, September 5, 1983.
Newsweek, July 4, 1983, September 26, 1983, September 29, 1986, November 13, 1989.
New York Review of Books, July 21, 1983.
New York Times, June 4, 1983, December 13, 1988, October 11, 1989.
New York Times Book Review, June 5, 1983, July 17, 1983, October 15, 1989.
People, August 29, 1983.
Quaderni Medievali, June 1, 1981.
Time, June 13, 1983, March 6, 1989.
Times (London), September 29, 1983, November 3, 1983.
Times Literary Supplement, July 8, 1977, March 3, 1989.
Village Voice Literary Supplement, October, 1983, November, 1989.
Wall Street Journal, June 20, 1983, November 14, 1989.
Washington Post, October 9, 1983, November 26, 1989.
Washington Post Book World, October 29, 1989.*

*   *   *

EDWARDS, Anne   1927-

PERSONAL: Born August 20, 1927, in Portchester, N.Y.; daughter of Milton and Marian (Fish) Josephson; married Stephen Citron (an author, composer and lyricist), 1980; children: Michael Dean Edwards, Catherine Edwards Sadler. *Education:* Attended University of California, Los Angeles, 1943-46, and Southern Methodist University, 1947-48.

ADDRESSES: Home—Blandings Way, 240 Indian Trail, New Milford, CT 06776. *Agent*—International Creative Management, 40 West 57th St., New York, NY 10019; and A. P. Watt, 20 John St., London WC1R 4HL, England.

CAREER: Child performer on the stage; junior writer, Metro-Goldwyn-Mayer, 1944; free-lance film writer in Hollywood, 1950-54; free-lance film and television writer in England and Europe, 1954-72. Writer and lecturer.

AWARDS, HONORS: Books-Across-the-Sea Ambassador Book Award, English-Speaking Union of the United States, for *The Road to Tara: The Life of Margaret Mitchell.*

MEMBER: Authors Guild (president, 1981-85), Authors League of America (member of council, 1978-90).

WRITINGS:

(Author of original story and co-author of screenplay) *Quantez,* Universal Pictures, 1957.
(Author of original story and screenplay) *A Question of Adultery,* NTA Pictures, 1959.
(Adaptor with Sidney Buchman and Isobel Lennart) *Funny Girl* (screenplay), Columbia, 1967.
(Adaptor) *A Child's Bible,* illustrations by Charles Front and David Christian, Golden Books, 1967, reprinted, Paulist Press, 1986.
The Survivors (fiction), Holt, 1968.
Miklos Alexandrovitch Is Missing (fiction), Coward, 1970 (published in England as *Alexandrovitch Is Missing!,* Hodder, 1970).
Shadow of a Lion (fiction), Coward, 1971.
Haunted Summer (fiction), Coward, 1972.
The Hesitant Heart (fiction), Random House, 1973.

Child of Night (fiction), Random House, 1975 (published in England as *Raven Wings,* Futura, 1979).

Judy Garland: A Biography, Simon & Schuster, 1975.

(With husband, Stephen Citron) *The Inn and Us* (reminiscences), Random House, 1976.

Vivien Leigh: A Biography, Simon & Schuster, 1976.

The Great Houdini (juvenile), Putnam, 1976.

P. T. Barnum (juvenile), illustrations by Marylin Hafner, Putnam, 1976.

Sonya: The Life of Countess Tolstoy, Simon & Schuster, 1981.

The Road to Tara: The Life of Margaret Mitchell, Ticknor & Fields, 1983.

Matriarch: Queen Mary and the House of Windsor, Morrow, 1984.

A Remarkable Woman: A Biography of Katharine Hepburn, Morrow, 1985, published as *Katharine Hepburn: A Biography,* Hodder, 1987.

Early Reagan: The Rise to Power, Morrow, 1987 (published as *Early Reagan: An American Hero,* Hodder, 1987).

The De Milles: An American Family, Abrams, 1988.

Shirley Temple: American Princess, Morrow, 1988.

Royal Sisters: Queen Elizabeth and Princess Margaret, Morrow, 1990.

Wallis: The Novel, Morrow, 1991.

Author of scripts for television and of screenplays; adaptor of screenplay, *The Steps,* 1965. Contributor of stories and articles to *Harper's, McCalls, Cosmopolitan, Dial, Architectural Digest,* the *Daily Mail* (London), and the *Washington Post.*

WORK IN PROGRESS: One More Song, with music and lyrics by Citron, based on *Judy Garland: A Biography; Laura,* with music and lyrics by Citron based on Vera Caspary's novel, *Laura; The Grimaldis and Monaco.*

SIDELIGHTS: While also a writer of juvenile biographies, novels and screenplays, Anne Edwards has founded her reputation on her personal accounts of famous people. Her subjects have included Judy Garland, Vivien Leigh, Ronald Reagan, Cecil B. DeMille, Katharine Hepburn, Countess Sonya Tolstoy (wife of novelist Leo Tolstoy), and Margaret Mitchell. Edwards explained to *Publishers Weekly* interviewer Genevieve Stuttaford that her books "are always conceived around a theme. An idea hits me, then I develop the story or, in the case of a biography, think of a person who exemplifies that theme. Vivien, Judy and Sonya were vastly interesting people and symbolic of certain things: Judy, the exploitation of a woman; Vivien, somebody who suffered from manic-depression; Sonya, an intelligent woman subjugated to a man who used her, drained her, made a villain of her."

The research involved in producing *Sonya: The Life of Countess Tolstoy* took Edwards from France, where she met one of the Tolstoy grandchildren, to Valley Cottage, N.Y., the home of Sasha Tolstoy, who in 1978 was the last living member of Leo and Sonya's family of thirteen children. Finally, Edwards visited the Soviet Union where the authorities, as Stuttaford writes, "held up her visa for a year because [Edwards] candidly acknowledged the purpose of her trip. The Countess is . . . persona non grata at home, and although her biographer, like any other tourist, was allowed to visit the Tolstoy home in Moscow she otherwise found the Soviets decidedly unhelpful. Through Sergei Tolstoy in Paris she privately established contacts with Muscovites who were able to make available to her material from the Tolstoy archives."

The picture of Sonya Tolstoy that Edwards presents in her biography is one of a talented, but repressed woman who struggled against the restraints of nineteenth-century Russian society. As Betty Lukas puts it in her *Los Angeles Times* review of the book, Sonya was "the most liberated woman of her time and place; she was also, quite possibly, the most enslaved." Edwards's account describes Sonya's attempts to establish her own identity in a world framed by her older husband's moodiness and Russia's changing social and political goals. "There are many different and equally valid methods of approaching a biography," notes Barbara Mertz in her *Washington Post* article about *Sonya.* "This one does not pretend to be a significant addition to serious Tolstoy scholarship; it avoids pretentious psychological analyses and extensive social commentary. It tells a straightforward story of one woman's tribulations and triumphs, and does it with charm."

Another large-scale project for Edwards involved both the author of the classic *Gone with the Wind* and the novel itself. With *Road to Tara: The Life of Margaret Mitchell,* the biographer again examines a woman's rebellion against her society. As Diane McWhorter sees it in her *New York Times Book Review* article, Margaret Mitchell "seems to have gone through life in a state of self-destructive ambivalence. After the death in 1918 of her mother, a militant suffragette, [Mitchell] dropped out of Smith College and abandoned her ambition to study with Freud in Vienna. Back in the socially striving household of her father, a lawyer, Mitchell acted out the 'conflicting emotions of inferiority and contempt' stirred up by Atlanta society. Understandably, the Junior League refused membership to a hard-drinking debutante who made crude jokes and smoked in public, but [Mitchell] never expected or got over the rejection."

The men in her life also influenced young "Peggy" Mitchell. Her first fiance, Clifford Henry, was a World War I casualty. He had "homosexual tendencies" and is said to have been the character model for *Gone with the Wind*'s Ashley Wilkes. Mitchell then married Red Upshaw—described by McWhorter as "a rakehell Annapolis dropout and rumrunner, brilliant but feckless—the model for you know who." Mitchell completed the lengthy saga of one Pansy O'Hara's Civil War-era romances at a Georgia plantation called Fontenoy Hall and submitted the manuscript to Macmillan. Harold Latham, editor in chief of the publishing house, sent the young author a $500 advance with a telegram reading, "We undertake publication with tremendous enthusiasm and large hopes." Following a few name changes, *Gone with the Wind* was released on June 30, 1936. "Macmillan thought [the work] would sell about 27,500 copies," writes Jonathan Yardley in the *Washington Post Book World.* "Macmillan was wrong."

Word-of-mouth publicity had swept the country just prior to the novel's publication—"the word spread, and spread still further that a book was coming that you must not miss. Bookstores doubled and redoubled their orders," writes Yardley. The impact of *Gone with the Wind* was dramatic and lasting. And it is Edwards's view, says Yardley, "that the fame enjoyed by Margaret Mitchell in the months following this 'tremor of excitement' was comparable to that which befell Charles A. Lindbergh a decade before: the bestowal of 'immediate national adulation' upon a person who had emerged from utter obscurity with an accomplishment that seized the popular imagination. It is her further contention that . . . Mitchell found precious little pleasure in her sudden wealth and celebrity—that the person who 'should have been the happiest woman in America' was miserable because 'drastic changes had taken place in [her] life and she was incapable of accepting them,' because 'what she wished for was a return to the way things had been and that wish could never be granted.' "

"The most serious fault of [*Road to Tara*]," writes McWhorter, "is the lack of a point of view. Mitchell's paralyzing ambivalence is never subjected to coherent analysis. . . . And although [the novelist's] racial views are reported here, they merit more critical attention, given their significance for her work." On the other hand, *Los Angeles Times Book Review* critic June Schwarzmann finds that Edwards treats her subject "gently, avoiding a prescient tone that can mar biography. In episodic narrative as compelling as fiction, [*Road to Tara*] spotlights the stumbling blocks in Mitchell's passage from tomboy to Southern belle to celebrated author." The book, Schwarzmann concludes, "reminds us of the novel's klieg power in illuminating experience, and of the darker side of success."

Another rendering of a strong and charismatic woman is *A Remarkable Woman: A Biography of Katharine Hepburn*. Edwards calls Hepburn "the theater and film's grand dame, a staunch survivor of indomitable strength whose very presence inspired courage." The author's unauthorized biography follows Hepburn's career from employment by David O. Selznick for $1500 per week through her appearances in 1930s and 1940s screwball comedies, to her pivotal role in the "African Queen" in 1951, which "replaced forever" her former image as "the Bryn Mawr society-girl" with "one of a more mature woman, a person who had the strength to endure the worst hardships and survive as ably as any man."

A Remarkable Woman also covers Hepburn's relationship with the already-married Spencer Tracy, and records that while "Around 1960 stories began appearing in the press coupling their names. . . . People simply preferred to believe that Tracy and Hepburn were really and truly longtime friends, devoted, faithful to each other and yet faithful to the tenets of Tracy's religion and marriage vows. And perhaps that is the truth." Yardley, however, in a *Washington Post* article, contends that the relationship "gets inconsistent treatment from Edwards, who repeatedly refers to it as an 'affair' yet at one point coyly notes that 'no one but them will ever know' whether it was anything except platonic." Edwards also details activities indulged in by the actress that might surprise those who accepted her cool, sophisticated Hollywood image. Julia Cameron writes in the *Chicago Tribune Book World* that Edwards "makes us privy to a Hepburn we might prefer not to know. . . . We meet a Katharine Hepburn whose idea of girlish sport is breaking and entering into stranger's houses" and who "rather routinely has affairs with the producers and directors who advance her career—regardless of their marital status." Cameron continues, "Once you glimpse the Hepburn in [Edwards's] pages, you wonder how Hepburn got away with the myth she herself has so successfully created." But *Detroit News* contributor Christian Kassel finds it "refreshing to encounter a glittery personality who did not force her offspring to eat coat hangers or threaten co-stars with incurable diseases." He continues that *A Remarkable Woman* "is critically encompassing, safely tedious, and ultimately, the work a Hepburn fan can accept verbatim."

Early Reagan "is quite unlike any Hollywood biography ever done before," declares Bruce Cook in the *Washington Post Book World*. The book records the ex-president's life from his Illinois childhood as the son of an alcoholic shoe salesman up to his successful California gubernatorial campaign. *Chicago Tribune Books* contributor Jon Wiener sees *Early Reagan* as a prime source of "Hollywood gossip, the inside dope." And according to *New York Times Book Review* contributor Robert Sklar, *Early Reagan* "is rich in detail about the social milieu of [Reagan's] early years in Illinois and in the portraits of his family and his marriages. [*Early Reagan*] adds considerably to our knowledge

of the Reagan era's foundation." The biography includes information on Reagan's activities as an informer for the F.B.I. while serving as president of the Screen Actor's Guild. This position conflicted with Reagan's early support of Roosevelt and the Democratic party; *New York Times* contributor Walter Goodman approves Edwards's attitude toward her subject, and states that "while making plain that Mr. Reagan's politics, especially in his cooperation with the Communist-hunters in Hollywood, is not to her taste, Ms. Edwards does not let her opinions obtrude on her reporting."

"From time to time, the book does seem over-researched and a bit overwritten," Cook admits. But overall, the reviewer feels "All that this amounts to, however, is a half-hearted complaint that a good book—one written with sympathy, understanding, yet a healthy critical spirit—could have been a little bit better." And Goodman concludes, "Critics and admirers of the President are likely to come away from [*Early Reagan*] mulling what the state of the nation might be had Ronald Reagan been a more successful actor."

CA INTERVIEW

CA interviewed Anne Edwards by telephone on July 18, 1989, at her home in New Milford, Connecticut.

CA: Though you're probably best known for your celebrity biographies, you've written about literary figures too, in both biography and fiction, and you were for many years a screenwriter. Somehow all these interests coincided nicely. To begin with, how did you happen to go to Hollywood and get involved in screenwriting?

EDWARDS: First, I don't consider myself a celebrity biographer; I really consider myself a historian. I believe that most of my biographies of film personalities have incorporated the history of the film industry. I was interested, of course, in the people I thought were exciting film personalities and needed books written about them, but at the same time I felt that all these pieces put together gave a very full picture of the film industry and its impact on our society. Second, over half of the biographies I have written are not about film stars. Politics and literature have entered into my writing consistently, and it happened in Mr. Reagan's case that he crossed both paths.

As to the question of Hollywood, I was brought up in Beverly Hills, so films were part of my background. Hollywood found me when I was very young. I had written a musical which was presented locally when I was in high school. Of course young people around the world contributed to amateur theater; the difference was that I lived where talent scouts could come and see my work, which indeed they did, and they signed me to a contract as a junior writer at Metro-Goldwyn-Mayer when I was only seventeen. That's how that happened. In those days—we're talking about the forties—they were scouting for writers and composers just as they were for actors.

CA: Did you really grow up wanting to write?

EDWARDS: I think I always wanted to write. I did perform when I was very young; I wrote music and lyrics for myself and sang. I won some kind of Tommy Dorsey songwriting contest for lyrics when I was fifteen. I thought the lyric was a fine way of expressing myself, which it was. But when I realized I wasn't going to be a Dorothy Fields, that I wasn't truly gifted as a lyricist, I turned to the idea of writing stories. I consider myself first and foremost a storyteller.

CA: I've read that you majored in Russian literature in college.

EDWARDS: I was a theater arts major at UCLA for the first two years of college, and also took some courses in film. These were not easy times, but since I had earned enough money in six months as a junior writer at Metro to finance my education, I quit films and went back to school. After two years life and circumstance took me to Dallas, Texas, where I went to SMU. I had always adored Russian literature and Russian music and so I switched my major—although there was a fabulous theater teacher at Southern Methodist University at the time, Margot Jones, who was one of the first people to produce theater in the round, and I was involved in her group for a time.

CA: What do you find to be the pros and cons of writing about still living subjects, like Katharine Hepburn and Ronald Reagan, compared with writing about subjects who are dead, like Margaret Mitchell and Sonya Tolstoy?

EDWARDS: You never can have a finished story if you're writing about someone who's alive, because you don't have the perspective of time. With the Reagan book, I decided that the only way to do a proper biography was to do it in two volumes, and I do hope someday to finish the second one. The first volume, *Early Reagan,* which ended with his election as governor of California, had the benefit of distance. I found that very difficult in the Hepburn book; I don't really know how we'll feel about Katharine Hepburn in twenty-five years.

There's an advantage to writing a book about someone who is living, or who has not been dead too long, in that there may be direct witnesses you can interview. I consider myself a revisionist biographer; I won't write a book unless I feel I can add something new and revelatory. I often call myself a literary detective; interviews are an important part of uncovering the truth. Of course writing a biography about someone who is deceased has the advantage of eliminating the problem of libel—that is, if you tell the truth!

CA: Do you try to gather most of your material before you begin to write, or do the research and writing overlap widely?

EDWARDS: They overlap. I know authors who do all the research first, but I'm afraid my computer doesn't have enough bytes for that or something—I don't seem to be able to do it. I always like to get my general research done first so that I know the waves of someone's life and what happened historically in the background. All of my books put people into their proper perspective. If you don't understand the times people are living in, you really haven't understood their lives and you can't interpret them correctly. So I first have to do that and find out what were the important influences upon their lives, and who might be alive that I can speak to, who might have left letters, diaries, or other documents that I can seek out.

Once I've done that first step, I make every effort to interview the early people in the subject's life first. I like to work in continuity. That is a kind of utopian view of research; it doesn't always happen, because, first of all, people's time schedules don't always permit it, and, second, sometimes you're dealing with very elderly people and you know that if you don't get to them first, you may not get to them at all. So, after the early research, the general research, I do the first interviews and the first deep research. Then I start the writing, and then I go back and repeat the process three or four times during the book. Working in continuity gives me a sense of living the person's life with them.

CA: Do you ever start out with feelings about a subject that are later drastically altered by something you find in your research, or just by your closeness to the subject over a long period of time?

EDWARDS: Yes, everyone does. But whatever has drawn you to a subject is usually something that will remain with you to the very end. Your opinion about the person or how they lived their life or the kind of person they are may change drastically. The subject who comes to mind as the most dramatic change for me is Margaret Mitchell. Half-way through *Road to Tara* I decided I really didn't want to complete the book, I had felt so strongly about her in various ways. I felt I should put it aside. I spoke to my editor about it, and she suggested I take some time off from it and do something else. I did that, and I have to say that when I came back I saw the complete person. I also saw all these terrible blemishes that I hadn't seen before, and they made me angry, but I was able to deal with it this time and I think it made a much better book.

CA: You told Genevieve Stuttaford for Publishers Weekly *about some of the problems you ran into researching* Sonya: The Life of Countess Tolstoy. *Was she your most difficult biographical subject?*

EDWARDS: Certainly there were problems that existed with *Sonya* that had nothing to do with the actual writing, which was itself difficult. I wanted to go to Russia for research. But this was in the late seventies and it was difficult for me to get a visa to do the work I wanted to do; and it took a long time. Technicalities made writing the book complicated.

But I had an incredible bit of good fortune. I managed to get a very lengthy series of interviews with Alexandra (Sasha), Sonya's youngest daughter. That was a breakthrough, and it happened by pure chance. I think the greatest things that happen to a biographer usually do happen that way. Sasha had an emotional love-hate relationship with her mother and a great passion for her father. She had felt that Sonya had placed obstacles in her relationship with her father, and she had a lot of resentment. She had written two books about her parents and their relationship, and the books were not truthful. But because they were written by Alexandra Tolstoy, she had been quoted copiously by Tolstoy's biographers, who repeated statements and scenes that Sasha had either fabricated or slanted. She had great guilt about this.

I managed somehow through a woman who was Sasha's companion at the time to get her to at least see me. She was ninety-three years old, very ill, but still alert. She spoke English, but with her infirmity fell back often into Russian. I don't speak Russian but my daughter does, so I came to the first meeting, which was at the Tolstoy Foundation in Valley Cottage, New York, with my daughter. Somehow, seeing the two of us, mother and daughter together, broke down the barrier. Sasha started crying. She said, "You have a relationship with your daughter that I wish my mother had had with me." With that it turned around, and she said, "I must correct these things I have written."

I don't know that *Sonya* was my hardest book, but there were many things that were difficult about it: certainly all the Russian names; all the children that Sonya had; all the years that could have been very dull; the fact that Tolstoy was such an overbearing person; the sexism that made the story, I was afraid, a little too heavy-handed. There were many problems involved, but strangely enough, it was one of my favorite books.

CA: Are there things in biographical practice that you consider absolutely taboo, and, conversely, things you feel obliged to do in writing someone's life?

EDWARDS: I don't feel books should be written just for exploitation and no other reason. I don't believe in including a story or anecdote simply to sell books. That kind of thing strikes me as unnecessary and usually is uninformative as well. But I find that even people writing their own memoirs are aware of the selling value of sexy tidbits. I deliberately left out things in Shirley Temple's life that I thought were pretty boring, and I was amused to find that those were the highlights of her own book. Someone dropped his pants in front of her. Well, many young women have had a man expose himself. I don't really think it belongs in a book unless the incident affected you so strongly you couldn't look at a man's penis for the rest of your life.

I also feel very strongly about notes and about backing up every bit of material I have. I never speculate unless I've had the viewpoints of several people who were close to the subject. I think we can rewrite history by employing the truth and by taking advantage of new material. But a lot of authors rewrite it to sell books.

CA: The Hesitant Heart was based on the life of Emily Dickinson, Child of Night *was inspired by the life of Edgar Allan Poe, and* Haunted Summer *was about Byron and the Shelleys. How did you decide to use those stories for fiction rather than do something biographical about the writers?*

EDWARDS: Perhaps because of the romantic times in which they lived. All three of those books share a kind of lyrical romanticism. I felt I could evoke the atmosphere better and give the reader a sense of the period and the subjects' views in a novel. I loved writing those three books, particularly *Haunted Summer.* It's one of my favorite books, and I think it's one of my best and it is straight-on factually. It was written first-person in the voice of Mary Shelley and was a great challenge. I threw myself back into the period (1816) and enjoyed the process very much. First-person narrative is fun for a writer to do, and I hope to do it again.

CA: Your work on Vivien Leigh, whose story you published in 1976, led you to Margaret Mitchell as the subject of the 1983 book Road to Tara. *Did that in turn lead you to the contract for the* Gone with the Wind *sequel?*

EDWARDS: No, it had nothing to do with it. David Brown and Dick Zanuck were the ones who originally had the rights and were going to produce a sequel adapted from my book, which was called *Tara: The Continuation of "Gone with the Wind."* In 1968 they had purchased my novel *The Survivors* for a film and liked my work and so engaged me to write the sequel. They weren't even aware that I was writing the life of Vivien Leigh. It was a coincidence. They came to me because they liked my style of writing and they knew I had spent some years of my life in the South and that I had family there. I believe I was one of nine or ten authors that they spoke to.

CA: What happened to the movie project?

EDWARDS: I finished the book, Zanuck and Brown loved it, Metro loved it, Stephens Mitchell, Margaret's brother, had approved it, everything was go-ahead, and then Stephens died and his estate filed suit stating that they still owned the rights. After something like seven years and several appeals they got the rights back, but as Metro-Goldwyn-Mayer and Zanuck-Brown had paid me to do the book, they did not get my work, and hired someone else to write a new one.

CA: You did a family story in The DeMilles, *published in 1988. Would you like to do more family or group biographies?*

EDWARDS: I think all my books are group biographies now; I seem to be going with that. The book I'm currently working on

is called *Sisters.* It's a study of Queen Elizabeth and Princess Margaret and their impact on each other's lives. The DeMilles had a strong family relationship. That doesn't always happen in families, but you could not tell Cecil B. DeMille's story or anyone else's in that talented family without telling all of them.

CA: Did Sisters *grow out of* Matriarch, *your earlier book on Queen Mary?*

EDWARDS: Yes, it did.

CA: You've repeatedly credited your husband, musician and composer Stephen Citron, for his help in your work. How does he lend support and aid?

EDWARDS: It isn't just support and aid; he does a great deal more than that. I like to do all my own research, all my own interviews, unlike a lot of writers—not that I'm faulting them on it; everyone works differently. But I've never been able to send anyone else into a library or to an interview for me and say, "Come back with what I want." I'm always afraid they're going to miss something. Steve is very talented and has a major career of his own, but he always takes that time with me when I am doing the in-depth interviewing and the work in libraries. He goes through the papers with me, because he knows a great deal of what I need. He's wonderfully supportive and intuitive, and very, very good. I tape all of my interviews, and he helps me do that. I feel we are a team; I help him when I can and he works with me.

CA: Do you have a dream book, a biography you'd love to write or an idea for a novel, that you haven't gotten to yet?

EDWARDS: In actual truth, I am so contracted that it's almost beyond my ken to even think of it. I am signed for four books, three more biographies and a novel, which I've been working on for a long time and which I will finish next year. I pick it up between other projects. These four books take me into something like 1997.

CA: I hope you get at least a small rest between books.

EDWARDS: Well, I'm a workaholic. I complain a lot, but I love writing, and I find that I get panicked when I have time on my hands.

BIOGRAPHICAL/CRITICAL SOURCES:

BOOKS

Edwards, Anne, *A Remarkable Woman: A Biography of Katharine Hepburn,* Morrow, 1985.
Edwards, Anne, *The Road to Tara: The Life of Margaret Mitchell,* Ticknor & Fields, 1983.

PERIODICALS

Chicago Tribune, February 9, 1981, May 23, 1983.
Chicago Tribune Book World, October 6, 1985.
Detroit News, October 20, 1985.
Los Angeles Times, May 14, 1981, July 7, 1983.
Los Angeles Times Book Review, August 21, 1983.
New York Times, July 17, 1987.
New York Times Book Review, April 19, 1981, August 28, 1983, July 26, 1987.
Publishers Weekly, March 6, 1981.
Tribune Books (Chicago), July 5, 1987.
Washington Post, April 6, 1981, October 9, 1985.
Washington Post Book World, May 8, 1983, July 19, 1987.

—Interview by Jean W. Ross

EPSILON
See BETJEMAN, John

*   *   *

ERICSON, Walter
See FAST, Howard (Melvin)

*   *   *

ERIKSON, Erik H(omburger) 1902-

PERSONAL: Born June 15, 1902, in Frankfurt-am-Main, Germany; came to U.S., 1933, naturalized citizen, 1939; son of Danish parents; after mother's second marriage used stepfather's surname Homburger until his naturalization; married Joan Mowat Serson, April 1, 1930; children: Kai T., Jon M., Sue (Mrs. Harland G. Bloland). *Education:* Graduated from the Vienna Psychoanalytic Institute in 1933; received certificate from the Maria Montessori School; studied under Anna Freud; also studied at Harvard University Psychological Clinic.

CAREER: Practicing psychoanalyst, beginning in 1933. Training psychoanalyst, 1942. Teacher and researcher at Harvard University, School of Medicine, Department of Neuropsychiatry, Cambridge, Mass., 1934-35, Yale University, School of Medicine, New Haven, Conn., 1936-39, University of California, Berkeley, and San Francisco, 1939-51, San Francisco Psychoanalytic Institute, San Francisco, Calif., and Menninger Foundation, Topeka, Kan., 1944-50; Austen Riggs Center, Stockbridge, Mass., senior staff member, 1951-60; visiting professor, 1951-60, Western Psychiatric Institute, Pittsburgh, Pa., Massachusetts Institute of Technology, Boston, Mass., and University of Pittsburgh, School of Medicine, Pittsburgh; Harvard University, professor of human development and lecturer on psychiatry, 1969-70, professor emeritus, 1970—. Trustee of Radcliffe College, Cambridge.

MEMBER: American Psychological Association (fellow), American Psychoanalytic Association (life member), American Academy of Arts and Science, National Academy of Education, Cambridge Scientific Club, Signet Society, Phi Beta Kappa.

AWARDS, HONORS: Harvard University, M.S., 1960, LL.D., 1978; University of California, LL.D., 1968; Loyola University, Sc.D., 1970; National Book Award for philosophy and religion, and Pulitzer Prize, both 1970, both for *Gandhi's Truth;* Yale University, Soc.Sc.D., 1971; Brown University, LL.D., 1972; National Association for Mental Health research award, and Aldrich Award from American Academy of Pediatrics, both 1974; Golden Bagel award from Mt. Zion Hospital, San Francisco, Calif., 1976; Lund University, Fil.Dr.H.C., 1980.

WRITINGS:

Observations on the Yurok: Childhood and World Image, University of California Press, 1943.
Childhood and Society, Norton, 1950, revised edition, 1963.
Young Man Luther: A Study in Psychoanalysis and History, Norton, 1958.
Identity and the Life Cycle, International Universities Press, 1959. (Editor) *Youth: Change and Challenge,* Basic Books, 1963, published as *The Challenge of Youth,* Doubleday, 1963.
Insight and Responsibility: Lectures on the Ethical Implications of Psychoanalytic Insight, Norton, 1964.
Identity: Youth and Crisis, Norton, 1968.
Gandhi's Truth: On the Origins of Militant Nonviolence, Norton, 1969.

(With Huey P. Newton) *In Search of Common Ground,* edited by Kai T. Erikson, Norton, 1973.
Dimensions of a New Identity: The 1973 Jefferson Lectures, Norton, 1974. *Life History and the Historical Moment,* Norton, 1975.
Toys and Reasons: Stages in the Ritualizations of Experience, Norton, 1976.
Identity and the Life Cycle: A Reissue, Norton, 1980.
The Life Cycle Completed: A Review, Norton, 1982.
(With Joan M. Erikson and Helen Q. Kivnick) *Vital Involvement in Old Age: The Experience of Old Age in Our Time,* Norton, 1986.
A Way of Looking at Things: Selected Papers From 1930 to 1980, edited by Stephen Schlein, Norton, 1987.

CONTRIBUTOR

P. G. Davis, editor, *The Cyclopedia of Medicine,* Volume XII, Davis, 1940.
R. C. Barker and others, *Child Behavior and Development,* McGraw, 1943.
O. Fenichel and others, editors, *The Psychoanalytic Study of the Child,* Volume I, International Universities Press, 1945.
Phyllis Greenacre and others, editors, *The Psychoanalytic Study of the Child,* Volume II, International Universities Press, 1946.
M. J. E. Seen, editor, *Symposium on the Healthy Personality,* Josiah Macy, Jr. Foundation, 1950.
C. J. Friedrich, editor, *Totalitarianism,* Harvard University Press, 1954. Clara Thompson, *An Outline of Psychoanalysis,* Random House, 1955.
Helen Witmer and Ruth Kotinsky, editors, *New Perspectives for Research in Juvenile Delinquency,* U.S. Department of Health, Education, and Welfare, 1956.
B. Schaffner, editor, *Group Processes,* Josiah Macy, Jr. Foundation, 1956. J. M. Tanner and B. Inhelder, editors, *Discussions on Child Development,* International Universities Press, Volume III, 1958, Volume IV, 1960.
Daniel H. Funkenstein, editor, *The Student and Mental Health,* World Federation of Mental Health and International Association of Universities, 1959.
Psychological Issues, Volume I, International Universities Press, 1959. (Author of introduction) Blaine and McArthur, *Emotional Problems of the Student,* Crofts, 1961.
Sir Julian Huxley, editor, *The Humanist Frame,* Harper, 1961.
(And editor) *Adulthood: Essays,* Norton, 1978.

SIDELIGHTS: David Elkind calls Erik H. Erikson "the most widely known and read psychoanalyst in America today." He adds: "like the other giants of psychology, Freud and Piaget, Erikson is not an experimentalist but rather a gifted and sensitive observer and classifier of human behavior and experience. Like Freud, Erikson knows how to use his own psyche as a delicate register of what is universal in man and of what is particular to himself. And, like Piaget, Erikson has been concerned with epigenesis, with the emergent phenomena in human growth. In Erikson's case, this has amounted to a concern with how new feelings, attitudes, and orientations arise in the course of personality development, and how these new features fit within the continuous pattern that is the human life cycle."

Reviewing Erikson's Pulitzer Prize-winning biography, *Gandhi's Truth,* Christopher Lasch writes that this book "even more brilliantly than its predecessor, *Young Man Luther,* shows that psychoanalytic theory, in the hands of an interpreter both resourceful and wise, can immeasurably enrich the study of 'great lives' and of much else besides. With these books Erikson has single-handedly rescued psychoanalytic biography from neglect and disrepute." Elizabeth Hardwick states that "*Gandhi's Truth* opens up for our enlightenment so many thoughts about Gandhi that one almost loses sight of the peculiar, tranquil contribution of Erikson's own temperament upon that of his subject. There is a sort of hidden fullness and richness in this work—hidden in the discreet, rather genteel style, in the mood always courteous and forever wondering. Erikson's mind is free of the temptation to dramatize in a journalistic way and to schematize in the way of his profession, psychoanalysis." Geoffrey Gorer agrees: "In his earlier writings Erik Erikson showed himself to be one of the most insightful and innovative writers on psychoanalytical themes, above all in his work with young children and adolescents. More recently he has shown his awareness of the relevance of cultural differences in the interpretation of the behaviour of members of different societies and in *Young Man Luther,* of the importance of historical context." However, he then adds that "these critical and analytical faculties are almost entirely replaced by a pious uncritical acceptance of the whole myth about Gandhi as a modern saint who, with his unparalleled insight and skills, single-handedly mobilised the whole Indian population and enabled them to throw out the wicked British Empire."

BIOGRAPHICAL/CRITICAL SOURCES:

BOOKS

Maier, Henry W., *Three Theories of Child Development,* Harper, 1965.

PERIODICALS

American Scholar, summer, 1965.
American Sociological Review, December, 1960.
Antioch Review, winter, 1969-70.
Canadian Forum, February, 1970.
Chicago Tribune, December 17, 1986, June 29, 1987.
Christian Century, April 17, 1968, April 8, 1970.
Commonweal, March 13, 1970.
Los Angeles Times Book Review, February 1, 1987.
Nation, June 3, 1968, November 22, 1969.
New Leader, April 8, 1968.
New Republic, October 18, 1969.
New Statesman, January 17, 1969.
Newsweek, August 10, 1964, August 18, 1969, December 21, 1970.
New York Herald Tribune Book Review, November 16, 1958.
New York Times, June 14, 1988.
New York Times Book Review, November 19, 1950, March 31, 1968, September 14, 1969, April 5, 1987.
Observer Review, January 4, 1970.
Saturday Review, January 16, 1971.
Time, November 30, 1970.
Times Literary Supplement, September 9, 1983, February 26, 1988.
Village Voice, November 20, 1969.
Vogue, December, 1969.
Washington Post, June 29, 1968.
Washington Post Book World, November 9, 1986, June 14, 1987.*

*   *   *

ERIKSSON, Buntel
  See BERGMAN, (Ernst) Ingmar

ESCANDON, Ralph 1928-

PERSONAL: Born May 21, 1928, in Barranquilla, Colombia; son of Antonio J. (a businessman) and Leonor (Hernandez) Escandon; married Lena Hilda Moore (an elementary school teacher), June 6, 1955; children: Willie Rafael. *Education:* Union College, Lincoln, NE, B.A., 1957; University of Nebraska, M.A., 1959; University of Omaha, additional study, 1966-67; Interamerican University, Saltillo, Mexico, Ph.D., 1968. *Religion:* Seventh-day Adventist. *Avocational interests:* traveling, photography, numismatics, water skiing, snow skiing, jogging, and tennis.

ADDRESSES: Home—280 Washburn, Angwin, CA 94508. *Office*—Department of Modern Languages, Pacific Union College, Angwin, CA 94508.

CAREER: University of Nebraska, Lincoln, instructor, 1958-60; Creighton University, Omaha, NE, instructor in Spanish, 1960-62; Cali Junior Academy, Cali, Colombia, principal, 1962-66; University of Omaha (now University of Nebraska at Omaha), assistant professor of Spanish literature, 1966-67; Pacific Union College, Angwin, CA, associate professor of Latin American literature and history, 1968, currently professor of Spanish, chairman of department of modern languages, 1977-1982.

AWARDS, HONORS: Plaque, Exchange Club (Cuaynabo, PR), 1978; first prize, Hispanic Cultural Festival of Las Vegas, 1987, for *Destination without Departure.*

MEMBER: Phi Sigma Iota.

WRITINGS:

Curiosidades matematicas, Editorial Novaro, 1965, reprinted, 1980.
Excentricidades y rarezas, Editorial Novaro, 1967.
Tesoro de anecdotas favoritas, Editorial Novaro, 1972.
Humo y Ceniza (novel), Editorial Iztaecittuatl, 1972.
Have Fun Being a Christian, Review and Herald, 1973.
Adelante, entusiasta juventud (young adult), Editorial Novaro, 1973.
El origen de muchas cosas, Editorial Novaro, 1973.
Smoke and Ashes (novel), Dorrance, 1973.
Curiosidades Biblicas al alcance de todos, Editorial Novaro, 1975.
Senderos de Victoria, prologue by Sergio V. Collins, Pacific Press, 1977, 2nd edition, Ediciones Interamericans (Mountain View, CA), 1977.
Para usted que quierre ser escritor, Interamerican, 1977.
Intermediate Spanish, Home Study Institute, 1978.
Proteja a sus hijos, Pacific Press, 1979.
Vers la victoire, Pacific Press, 1980.
Ingles para doctores y enfermeras, Editores Mexicanos Unidos, 1981.
Ingles para secretarias, Editores Mexicanos Unidos, 1981.
Pensamientos inolvidables, Editorial Diana (Mexico), 1982.
Como Llegar a Ser Vencedor, Casa Bautista, 1982.
Bilingual Vocabulary for the Medical Profession — Vocabulario bilingue para le profesion medica, South-Western, 1982.
Frases celebres para toda ocasion, Editorial Diana, 1982.
Para ti, joven, que quieres triunfar (proverbs), Editorial Diana, 1983.
Relaciones publicas al alcance de todos, Editorial Universo, 1983.
Destino sin partida, Masterbook, 1983.
Como superar los problemas juveniles, Masterbook, 1983.
Curiosidades e Testes Biblicos, Publicadora Brasileira, 1985.
El Libro Completo de las Relaciones Humanas, Universo, 1985.

Destination without Departure, Mundo Graf, 1986.
Una Vida Saturada de Milagros, Riverside Quickprint, 1987.

Also author of *Como mantener la aromonia en el hogar, Caprichos del idioma, Al borde del abismo,* and *Spanish for Secretaries.* Contributor of articles to periodicals, including *Review and Herald, Jeventud, Spanish for Today, Message, El Vocero,* and *El Gato.*

F

FALLON, Martin
See PATTERSON, Harry

*   *   *

FARREN, Richard M.
See BETJEMAN, John

*   *   *

FAST, Howard (Melvin) 1914-
(E. V. Cunningham, Walter Ericson)

PERSONAL: Born November 11, 1914, in New York, NY; son of Barney and Ida (Miller) Fast; married Bette Cohen (an artist), June 6, 1937; children: Rachel, Jonathan. *Education:* Attended National Academy of Design. *Avocational interests:* "My home, my family, the theater, the film, and the proper study of ancient history. And the follies of mankind."

ADDRESSES: Home—Greenwich, CT 06830. *Agent*—Sterling Lord Agency, 660 Madison Ave., New York, NY 10021.

CAREER: Worked at several odd jobs and as a page in the New York Public Library prior to 1932; writer, 1932—. Affiliated with U.S. Office of War Information, 1942-44; correspondent with special Signal Corps unit and war correspondent in China-India-Burma theater, 1944-45; foreign correspondent for *Esquire* and *Coronet,* 1945. Member of World Peace Council, 1950-55; American Labor Party candidate for U.S. Congress, 23rd New York District, 1952. Has given numerous lectures and made numerous appearances on radio and television programs.

AWARDS, HONORS: Breadloaf Literary Award, 1937; Schomburg Award for Race Relations, 1944; Newspaper Guild award and Jewish Book Council of America annual award, both 1947; International Peace Prize from the Soviet Union, 1954; Screenwriters annual award, 1960; Secondary Education Board annual book award, 1962; American Library Association "notable book" citation, 1972, for *The Hessian;* Emmy Award, Television Academy, 1976.

WRITINGS:

Two Valleys, Dial, 1933.
Strange Yesterday, Dodd, 1934.
Place in the City, Harcourt, 1937.
Conceived in Liberty: A Novel of Valley Forge (also see below), Simon & Schuster, 1939.

The Last Frontier, Duell, Sloan & Pearce, 1941.
The Romance of a People, Hebrew Publishing, 1941.
Lord Baden-Powell of the Boy Scouts, Messner, 1941.
Haym Salomon, Son of Liberty, Messner, 1941.
The Unvanquished (also see below), Duell, Sloan & Pearce, 1942.
The Tall Hunter, Harper, 1942.
(With wife, Bette Fast) *The Picture-Book History of the Jews,* Hebrew Publishing, 1942.
Goethals and the Panama Canal, Messner, 1942.
Citizen Tom Paine (also see below), Duell, Sloan & Pearce, 1943, Grove Press, 1983.
The Incredible Tito, Magazine House, 1944.
Freedom Road, Duell, Sloan & Pearce, 1944, reprinted, Amsco School Publications, 1970.
Patrick Henry and the Frigate's Keel and Other Stories of a Young Nation, Duell, Sloan & Pearce, 1945.
The American: A Middle Western Legend (Literary Guild selection), Duell, Sloan & Pearce, 1946.
(With William Gropper) *Never Forget: The Story of the Warsaw Ghetto,* Book League of the Jewish Fraternal Order, 1946.
(Editor) *The Selected Works of Tom Paine,* Modern Library, 1946.
The Children, Duell, Sloan & Pearce, 1947.
(Editor) *Best Short Stories of Theodore Dreiser,* World Publishing, 1947.
Clarkton, Duell, Sloan & Pearce, 1947.
Tito and His People, Contemporary Publishers, 1948.
My Glorious Brothers, Little, Brown, 1948, new edition, Hebrew Publications, 1977.
Departure and Other Stories, Little, Brown, 1949.
Intellectuals in the Fight for Peace, Masses & the Mainstream, 1949.
The Proud and the Free (also see below), Little, Brown, 1950.
Literature and Reality, International Publishers, 1950.
Spartacus (also see below), Blue Heron, 1951, Citadel, 1952, reprinted, Buccaneer Books, 1982.
Peekskill, U.S.A.: A Personal Experience, Civil Rights Congress, 1951.
Tony and the Wonderful Door, Blue Heron, 1952, reprinted, Knopf, 1968.
The Passion of Sacco and Vanzetti: A New England Legend, Blue Heron, 1953.
Silas Timberman, Blue Heron, 1954.
The Last Supper, and Other Stories, Blue Heron, 1955.

The Story of Lola Gregg, Blue Heron, 1956.
The Naked God: The Writer and the Communist Party, Praeger, 1957.
Moses, Prince of Egypt, Crown, 1958.
The Winston Affair, Crown, 1959.
The Howard Fast Reader, Crown, 1960.
April Morning, Crown, 1961, reprinted, Bantam, 1976.
The Edge of Tomorrow (stories), Bantam, 1961.
Power, Doubleday, 1962.
Agrippa's Daughter, Doubleday, 1964.
Torquemada, Doubleday, 1966.
The Hunter and the Trap, Dial, 1967.
The Jews: Story of a People, Dial, 1968.
The General Zapped an Angel, Morrow, 1970.
The Crossing (based on his screenplay of the same title; also see below), Morrow, 1971, New Jersey Historical Society, 1985.
The Hessian (based on his screenplay of the same title; also see below), Morrow, 1972.
A Touch of Infinity: Thirteen Stories of Fantasy and Science Fiction, Morrow, 1973.
The Immigrants, Houghton, 1977.
The Art of Zen Meditation, Peace Press, 1977.
The Second Generation, Houghton, 1978.
The Establishment, Houghton, 1979.
The Legacy, Houghton, 1980.
The Magic Door (juvenile), Avon, 1980.
Time & the Riddle: Thirty-One Zen Stories, Houghton, 1981.
Max, Houghton, 1982.
The Outsider, Houghton, 1984.
The Immigrant's Daughter, Houghton, 1985.
The Dinner Party, Houghton, 1987.
The Call of Fife and Drum: Three Novels of the Revolution (contains *The Unvanquished, Conceived in Liberty,* and *The Proud and the Free*), Citadel, 1987.
The Pledge, Houghton, 1988.
The Confession of Joe Cullen, Houghton, 1989.
Being Red (biography), Houghton, 1990.

Author of weekly column, *New York Observer,* 1989—.

PLAYS

The Hammer, produced in New York, 1950.
Thirty Pieces of Silver (produced in Melbourne, 1951), Blue Heron, 1954.
George Washington and the Water Witch, Bodley Head, 1956.
(With Dalton Trumbo) *Spartacus* (screenplay; based on novel of the same title), produced in 1960.
The Crossing, produced in Dallas, TX, 1962.
The Hill (screenplay), Doubleday, 1964.
David and Paula, produced in New York City at American Jewish Theater, November 20, 1982.
Citizen Tom Paine: A Play in Two Acts (produced in Washington, DC at the John F. Kennedy Center for the Performing Arts, 1987), Houghton, 1986.

Also author of *The Hessian,* 1971, and television script, *What's a Nice Girl Like You . . . !,* based on his novel *Shirley.*

UNDER PSEUDONYM E. V. CUNNINGHAM; NOVELS

Sylvia, Doubleday, 1960.
Phyllis, Doubleday, 1962.
Alice, Doubleday, 1963.
Shirley, Doubleday, 1963.
Lydia, Doubleday, 1964.
Penelope, Doubleday, 1965.
Helen, Doubleday, 1966.

Margie, Morrow, 1966.
Sally, Morrow, 1967.
Samantha, Morrow, 1967.
Cynthia, Morrow, 1968.
The Assassin Who Gave Up His Gun, Morrow, 1969.
Millie, Morrow, 1973.
The Case of the One-Penny Orange, Holt, 1977.
The Case of the Russian Diplomat, Holt, 1978.
The Case of the Poisoned Eclairs, Holt, 1979.
The Case of the Sliding Pool, Delacorte, 1981.
The Case of the Kidnapped Angel, Delacorte, 1982.
The Case of the Angry Actress, Delacorte, 1984.
The Case of the Murdered Mackenzie, Delacorte, 1984.
The Wabash Factor, Doubleday, 1986.

UNDER PSEUDONYM WALTER ERICSON

Fallen Angel, Little, Brown, 1951.

MEDIA ADAPTATIONS: More than ten of Fast's novels and stories have been adapted for production as motion pictures, including "Man in the Middle," based on his novel *The Winston Affair,* 1964, "Mirage," based on a story he wrote under the pseudonym Walter Ericson, 1965, "Penelope," based on his novel of the same title, 1966, "Jigsaw," based on his novel *Fallen Angel,* 1968, and "Freedom Road," based on his novel of the same title, 1980. "The Immigrants" was broadcast as a television miniseries in 1979.

SIDELIGHTS: Howard Fast has published novels, plays, screenplays, stories, historical fiction, and biographies in a career that dates from the early days of the Great Depression. Fast's works have been translated into some eighty-two languages and have sold millions and millions of copies worldwide; some observers feel that he may be the most widely read writer of the twentieth century.

Although best known for his highly successful San Francisco family saga (*The Immigrants, The Second Generation, The Establishment, The Legacy,* and *The Immigrant's Daughter*), Fast has also authored numerous well-received historical novels, many of them about the American Revolution. *Los Angeles Times* contributor Elaine Kendall writes: "For half a century, Fast's novels, histories and biographies have appeared at frequent intervals, a moveable feast with a distinct political flavor." *Washington Post* correspondent Joseph McLellan finds Fast's work "easy to read and relatively nourishing," adding that the author "demands little of the reader, beyond a willingness to keep turning the pages, and he supplies enough activity and suspense to make this exercise worthwhile."

In the *Dictionary of Literary Biography,* Anthony Manousos suggests that Fast's long and prolific career may be divided into three periods, reflecting crucial shifts in his political alignment. During his first decade as a novelist, Fast explored America's heritage of freedom, primarily from a liberal viewpoint. Toward the end of the Second World War, Fast became a member of the Communist party, and his fiction through the mid-1950s dramatized mankind's struggle for a classless society. Eventually Fast renounced communism and began to create works with a more ambivalent political and religious view. Each period in Fast's career has yielded bestsellers—historical novels such as *Freedom Road* and *Citizen Tom Paine* are still in print, as is his Cold War era novel *Spartacus.* "I've had a good long run," Fast told *Publishers Weekly.* "I've survived, and there were times I never thought I would. And now, when I'm a bestseller again [with the 'Immigrants' series], my kids tell me: 'Dad, you've been recycled.' "

The grandson of Ukrainian immigrants, Fast grew up in New York City. His family always struggled to make ends meet, so he went to work as a teen and found time to indulge his passion—writing—in his spare moments. His first novel, *Two Valleys*, was published in 1933 when he was only eighteen. Thereafter he began writing full time, and within a decade he had earned considerable reputation as a historical novelist with his realistic tales of American frontier life.

Fast found himself drawn to the downtrodden peoples in America's history—the Cheyenne Indians and their tragic attempt to regain their homeland (*The Last Frontier*), the starving soldiers at Valley Forge (*Conceived in Liberty: A Novel of Valley Forge*), and black Americans trying to survive the Reconstruction era in the South (*Freedom Road*). In *Publishers Weekly*, John F. Baker calls these works "books on which a whole generation of radicals was brought up." A *Christian Science Monitor* contributor likewise notes: "Human nature rather than history is Howard Fast's field. In presenting these harassed human beings without any heroics he makes us all the more respectful of the price paid for American liberty." *Freedom Road* in particular was praised by the nation's black leaders for its depiction of one race's struggle for liberation; the book became a bestseller and won the Schomberg Award for Race Relations in 1944.

During the Second World War Fast worked as a correspondent for several periodicals and the Office of War Information. After the conflict ended he found himself at odds with the Cold War mentality developing in the United States. At the time Fast was a member of the Communist party and a contributor of time and money to a number of anti-fascist causes. His writing during the period addressed such issues as the abuse of power, the suppression of labor unions, and communism as the basis for a utopian future. Works such as *Clarkton*, *My Glorious Brothers*, and *The Proud and the Free* were widely translated behind the Iron Curtain and earned Fast the International Peace Prize in 1954.

Baker notes that Fast's political views "made him for a time in the 1950s a pariah of the publishing world." The author was jailed for three months on a contempt of Congress charge for refusing to testify about his political activities. Worse, he found himself blacklisted to such an extent that no publishing house would accept his manuscripts. A less successful writer might have been forced out of the business, but Fast could support his family on royalties he received from previous books. He founded his own publishing house, Blue Heron Press, and printed his work himself.

Fast released *Spartacus* under the Blue Heron imprint in 1951 (the novel was subsequently picked up by Citadel Press). A fictional account of a slave revolt in ancient Rome, *Spartacus* became a bestseller after it was made into a feature film in 1960. By that time Fast had grown disenchanted with the Communist party and had formally renounced his ties to it. In a discussion of Fast's fiction from 1944 through 1960, *Nation* correspondent Stanley Meisler contends that the "older writings must not be ignored. They document a unique political record, a depressing American waste. They describe a man who distorted his vision of America to fit a vision of communism, and then lost both."

Fast still writes historical fiction—even the "Immigrants" series chronicles modern-day international issues—but his more recent works explore religion, culture, and politics from a wide-ranging perspective. Manousos writes: "The crises that Fast's protagonists undergo in his latest novels tend to be personal and religious as well as political, thus reflecting Fast's own attempt to find a more compassionate and comprehensive social philosophy than that offered by communism or partisan liberalism." Today the author sees himself primarily as an old-fashioned storyteller, crafting tales of action, passion, and adventure. Manousos claims that it is as a storyteller that Fast has his greatest appeal. The critic concludes: "[Fast's] knack for sketching lifelike characters and creating brisk, action-packed narratives has always insured him a wide readership."

Fast has also published a number of detective novels under the pseudonym E. V. Cunningham. Many of these feature a fictional Japanese-American detective named Masao Masuto who works with the Beverly Hills Police Department. Fast told *Publishers Weekly:* "Critics can't stand my mainline books, maybe because they sell so well, [but] they love Cunningham. Even the *New Yorker* has reviewed him, and they've never reviewed me." In the *New York Times Book Review*, Newgate Callendar calls detective Masuto "a well-conceived character whose further exploits should gain him a wide audience." *Globe and Mail* contributor Derrick Murdoch also finds Masuto "a welcome addition to the lighter side of crime fiction."

In addition to his novels and short stories, Fast has written plays, screenplays, and even juvenile literature. A number of his works have also been adapted for the screen by other writers, most notably *The Immigrants* for a television miniseries. "Functional and efficient, Fast's prose is a machine in which plot and ideals mesh, turn and clash," Kendall concludes. "The reader is constantly being instructed, but the manner is so disarming and the hectic activity so absorbing that the didacticism seldom intrudes upon the entertainment."

CA INTERVIEW

CA interviewed Howard Fast on September 11, 1989, at his home in New York City.

CA: You've described in The Naked God *how, as a very young boy, you read your way through the fiction shelves and a great deal of nonfiction at the public library as a sort of antidote to the "work, poverty and hunger" of life. What gave you the courage and inspiration to try writing yourself?*

FAST: That's impossible to answer. All I can say is that it was something I had to do, so I did it. When I look back from this point of view, at age seventy-five, I can ask myself the same question and I have no answer.

CA: You were certainly writing very early. Your first novel, Two Valleys, *was published when you were eighteen, and a second,* Strange Yesterday, *by the time you were twenty. Was there some good luck involved in your getting the attention of publishers at such a young age?*

FAST: No. Rather than luck, it was sheer perseverance. I wrote eleven unpublished books; I had great energy. I guess in that way I learned to write. Of course, this is so far back, so long ago, that I almost look upon it as you would, as an outsider.

CA: "Great energy" seems an understatement. You were working from the age of eleven to help support the family, along with all the reading and writing.

FAST: When I think of it now, having just gotten over a bout of sciatica, I say to myself, Where on God's earth does such energy come from? But the truth is, if you're young and healthy and strong, you have a great flood of energy. And I was very keenly aware that there was no one to help me; I had to do it on my own. In that sense I was not the only one working this way. There are endless stories of people who have accomplished the same thing. We're survivors; whatever the circumstances are, we survive and we go on.

CA: Did your early period of reading in the New York Public Library also engender the love of history that permeates your writing?

FAST: Yes. You must remember that this was at a time, as incredible as it may sound, before radio, though radio was beginning to come in. It was certainly before television. Movies were still an occasional thing and a very rare treat. One turned to books, and the stories that would be most fascinating to a slum child were the stories of the wonderful adventures and events that existed only in history. In that way you entered first into history as romance and mythology. It intrigued me to a point where I felt I had to enter into history as a reality. This has been a process throughout my life, because the unveiling of history is endless. It's rewritten, reconstructed, reinterpreted by every age.

CA: And the young generation in this age seems to be largely lacking in any sense of it.

FAST: Yes. That's a great tragedy in our education today.

CA: What do you consider both the license and the limits in writing historical fiction and fictional biography?

FAST: There again is a question that no one can answer, simply because we have decided in our country—and I think very correctly—that we will put no limits on what a person can write. This gives people the freedom to falsify history, to distort history, to do all sorts of things to history. The only thing that moderates and controls this freedom is the consensus of the handful of very fine historians that we have in this country. So we cannot put a limit on anything.

CA: Are there both obligations and limits, though, that you impose upon yourself in writing historical fiction?

FAST: I try to understand it. Historical fiction is a curious thing. When I wrote the five books about California that began with *The Immigrants,* with the action starting in my own lifetime, all the young people considered them to be historical fiction. So yesterday is historical fiction. You read the *New York Times;* you read another newspaper; you balance what you read; you try it out in your own mind; you look under the covers, so to speak; and you try desperately to put together the reality and the truth. For example, in the wonderful Australian film *Gallipoli* there is an uncovering of one of the great lies in history that resulted in the deaths of thousands of young men. It's a sort of detective work, and very interesting detective work.

CA: You told John Baker for Publishers Weekly *that* April Morning *and* The Hessian *are two of your favorites among your books, and in* The Naked God *you named* The Proud and the Free *as a book you were especially pleased with. Does your particular fondness for these books have something to do with the fact that they're set in the Revolutionary period of America's history?*

FAST: Possibly. Most of my life has been spent in Connecticut, and the scene is there, though *April Morning* is set in Massachusetts, not far away. When I finished *The Hessian,* I felt that in terms of construction and in terms of its content, it was the one nearly perfect book I had ever written, and certainly the best

book I had ever written. I'm very egotistical about *The Hessian.* I think it's one of the best novels written in this country in the whole post-war period. But I try to be objective when I say that. Other books have been far more successful, but this one, to me, makes a very important statement about the human condition.

CA: In connection with your comments on The Proud and the Free, *you also mentioned your concern with recreating the speech of the time. How did you approach that challenge?*

FAST: I remember my father's speech. I remember that grandfather's speech was not that different. When I read Mark Twain, I find the speech to be no different. Of course I can't hear it; I can only read it. I have a good ear for speech. When I was a kid, I wandered all over the South, and wherever I was there, I picked up the accent and found I could reproduce it. It's almost like having an ear for music. I think there are certain places in the South where the speech has been frozen—very interesting places. In South Carolina, where you're calling from, that's true particularly around the Peedee Swamp. I tried to be reasonable about the speech, to look at the writers of the time. Of course the one great guide we have to the speech of young America is Mark Twain; unfortunately we don't have many others.

CA: To research The Last Frontier, *your fifth published book, you and your wife went to live on an Indian reservation in Oklahoma, and you've just now mentioned traveling in the South. Does your research often take you far from home, and to unusual sources?*

FAST: It used to. When we were young, we wandered all over the United States. The excitement of discovering the United States when there were very few roads was a wonderful thing. Today that still goes on, but perhaps less so. The wonder is gone. That's what you lose when you get old.

CA: Do you like to do all the research first, as much as that's possible, and then start writing, or do you prefer to interweave those two main parts of the process?

FAST: I used to do most of the research first. I have not written any real historical novels for many years—the last one I wrote was *The Hessian,* which was published in 1972. But when I was doing them, I would do the research first. And today I still do the research for my books myself, and I try to get at least the sources in hand before I start.

CA: Freedom Road, *your 1944 book on Reconstruction, has been published in more than eighty languages. Does it continue to have a life, to bring you responses from readers?*

FAST: I must say that in the past two or three years it has tapered off. Until about three years ago, though, I would get at least two or three requests each year for reprinting. The book was published in 1944, so it's forty-five years old now. But it is kept in print in the United States, in paperback.

CA: Do your more recent books attract new readers who then go back and read some of the earlier books?

FAST: I don't know. I've wondered about that. Most of the new readers think I've just arrived on the scene. For instance, since I began to write the California books about Barbara Lavette, and all I did after that, I would say that the reprint company for my books, Dell, has sold twelve million copies of the books. Most of those are the newer books; some of them are the old books. *Spartacus* always gets reprinted. That remains in print. *April*

Morning is a school book, so every kid in America has read it, more or less. It's steady fare in the secondary schools, in the seventh or eighth grade. So that stays in print, and it's gone through endless editions.

CA: The characters for that series you began with The Immigrants *have gone a long way indeed. Did you envision five or more books when you started?*

FAST: I always said to myself that I wanted to write a book someday about a woman, a wonderful woman who would combine qualities of women I had known. So I began with Barbara Lavette. To get her born, I had to deal with her origins. My intention was to write a single book, but it got so massive that, when I finished the first six hundred pages, the publisher said, This becomes impossible. You'll have to break it up. So I broke it up. I left Barbara finally at age sixty-eight, in *The Immigrant's Daughter,* uncertain as to whether I would ever go on.

CA: Some reviewers have noted that Barbara Lavette is like her creator in rather important ways. Do you feel she's somewhat autobiographical?

FAST: Yes. I had her born when I was born simply to have the chronology clear, and I immersed her in a lot of events that happened to me: the Spanish Civil War, the events of World War II, and so forth. So either through her or through her family the books are more or less a history of the sixty-eight years from 1914 to 1982.

CA: Your last two books, The Dinner Party *and* The Confession of Joe Cullen, *are shorter and more tightly structured that the big novels you've mostly written. Does this change have some significance you'd like to comment on?*

FAST: They're a sort of revolt against the very big book that becomes a bestseller. Books like *Joe Cullen* and *The Dinner Party* do not become massive bestsellers, because they're books that hit you between the eyes and make you think and make you wonder and make you uncomfortable. This is not a quality of the big bestsellers. But they're good for me to write. I think they're good books. And I think they deal with subjects that must be handled, but on which nobody is writing. So I'm very delighted that I wrote them.

CA: The Confession of Joe Cullen *is having a lively circulation in the public library here.*

FAST: My books do circulate wonderfully in the libraries. Books today are very expensive, and most people who love books can't afford to buy them.

CA: What's your writing pattern now? Has it changed much over the years?

FAST: It hasn't. There's nothing mechanical about it. I write in the morning, in the evening, whenever the mood takes me.

CA: As E. V. Cunningham you've done a series of books with women's names for titles and a series of mysteries featuring the Nisei detective Masao Masuto. How different a readership and reception do you have as Cunningham from your following as Howard Fast?

FAST: It is different. The detective books have become enormously popular. The Europeans are absolutely mad about them.

Right now they are preparing in Grenoble, France, for a world conference of mystery writers. They've been on the phone pleading with me to get over there and join it! Also, Cunningham won the Prix de la Policia in France. He's very popular there. I write these books for fun. They're almost a relaxation from the other books.

CA: They're so different from the others.

FAST: They're different, but I think there's a connection underneath.

CA: Like Masuto in the detective series, you're a practitioner of Zen Buddhism. What attracted you to Zen, and how do you find it useful in your life?

FAST: Buddhism is the gentlest of all religions. It's a religion that asks nothing but decent human behavior. Zen simply means sitting meditation. The word zen is the Japanese word from the Chinese word *ch'an,* which means to sit. So Zen Buddhism is a form of Buddhism which is chiefly marked by meditation. It's good for the human soul, it's good for the body, it's good for the mind, it's good for your equanimity. The only thing it's not good for is your hip muscles!

CA: With all of your writing, do you have time to do much reading?

FAST: Very little fiction. I read a great deal of nonfiction. I read politics, I read history. But I find that most novels I pick up are written in a vacuum, as if there were no atom bombs in the world, no misery, no hunger. So I've lost patience with fiction.

CA: "Big" books may be coming back, though.

FAST: I think that's true; everything's changing. I think the rate of change is incredible. Whereas twenty years ago I wouldn't have given many odds for the survival of man, I think now we may make it, we may survive. I'm much more hopeful.

CA: Both The Dinner Party *and* The Confession of Joe Cullen *were concerned with current politics, specifically our involvement in Central America. Besides expressing your concern through your writing, are you still active politically?*

FAST: Other than giving money to various causes, and I do a weekly column in the *New York Observer,* in which I can vent my outrage. Otherwise I have no political activity at all. I figure writing is the most and the best I can do.

CA: You said in The Naked God *that "as man finally, in his own good time, puts aside all tyrannies, so will there be an end of the Communist movement as we know it." Do you think that's beginning to happen with the changes taking place now in Russia and the Communist bloc?*

FAST: Yes. I have always felt it was inevitable. This doesn't mean that Russia will ever cease to be a socialist country; I think it will always be a socialist country. But I think the Communist Party structure must disintegrate, because it's a destructive structure.

CA: The Naked God detailed a very painful period of your life, your involvement with the Communist Party and finally your break with it. How do you look back now on that bitter decade of the 1950s, when you were jailed and blacklisted?

FAST: I look back upon it with objectivity. It was a long time ago, and I try to write about it now with great objectivity. It's something that I never regretted. There is no way to imagine war or to imagine jail or to imagine being a father or a mother. These things can only be understood if you live through them. Maybe that's a price that a writer should pay.

CA: Have you thought of doing a full autobiography, in which those years would be put into the perspective of your lifetime?

FAST: Yes. My next book is a book of memoirs. It's almost complete; it should be out in just a year from now. This is the first half. It goes on from my birth until 1956. The second part will not be done for a couple of years yet.

CA: Beyond the memoirs, are there ideas for more books, big or little?

FAST: Oh, yes! Of course, this is a question of age too. One of the men I've loved most in my life was Louis Untermeyer, who not only continued to write and work until he was ninety-two, but his mind was clear as a bell. But that's a very rare thing. Here I am at age seventy-five, and I say, Well, today is all right, but I don't know about tomorrow! But I'm pretty much with it, and I have high hopes for other books.

BIOGRAPHICAL/CRITICAL SOURCES:

BOOKS

Contemporary Literary Criticism, Volume 23, Gale, 1983.
Dictionary of Literary Biography, Volume 9: *American Novelists, 1910-1945,* Gale, 1981.
Meyer, Hershel D., *History and Conscience: The Case of Howard Fast,* Anvil-Atlas, 1958.
Newquist, Roy, *Counterpoint,* Rand McNally, 1964.
Rideout, Walter B., *The Radical Novel in the United States: Some Interrelations of Literature and Society,* Harvard University Press, 1956.

PERIODICALS

Atlantic, September, 1944; June, 1970.
Best Sellers, February 1, 1971; September 1, 1973; January, 1979; November, 1979.
Books, September 23, 1934; June 25, 1939.
Book Week, May 9, 1943.
Catholic World, September, 1953.
Chicago Tribune, April 21, 1987.
Christian Science Monitor, July 8, 1939; August 23, 1972; November 7, 1977.
Detroit News, October 31, 1982.
Globe & Mail (Toronto), September 15, 1984; March 1, 1986.
Library Journal, November 15, 1978.
Los Angeles Times, November 11, 1982; November 11, 1985; November 21, 1988.
Masses & Mainstream, December, 1950.
Nation, April 5, 1952; May 30, 1959.
New Republic, August 17, 1942; August 14, 1944; November 4, 1978.
New Statesman, August 8, 1959.
New Yorker, July 1, 1939; May 1, 1943.
New York Herald Tribune Book Review, July 21, 1963.
New York Herald Tribune Books, July 27, 1941.
New York Times, October 15, 1933; June 25, 1939; April 25, 1943; February 3, 1952; September 24, 1984; February 9, 1987; March 10, 1987.

New York Times Book Review, October 13, 1933; April 25, 1943; February 3, 1952; March 4, 1962; July 14, 1963; February 6, 1966; October 2, 1977; October 30, 1977; May 14, 1978; June 10, 1979; August 20, 1989.
Publishers Weekly, August 6, 1979; April 1, 1983.
Saturday Review, March 8, 1952; January 22, 1966; September 17, 1977.
Saturday Review of Literature, July 1, 1939; July 26, 1941; May 1, 1943; December 24, 1949.
Spectator, August 15, 1958; April 3, 1959; May 30, 1959.
Springfield Republican, November 5, 1933.
Time, November 6, 1977.
Times Literary Supplement, November 11, 1939.
Washington Post, October 4, 1979; September 26, 1981; September 25, 1982; September 3, 1985; February 9, 1987; March 3, 1987.
Washington Post Book World, October 23, 1988.
Weekly Book Review, April 25, 1943.
Yale Review, September, 1941.

—*Sketch by Anne Janette Johnson*

—*Interview by Jean W. Ross*

*   *   *

FAULKNER, William (Cuthbert) 1897-1962

PERSONAL: Surname originally Falkner, later changed to Faulkner; born September 25, 1897, in New Albany, Miss.; died July 6, 1962, in Byhalia, Miss.; son of Murry Cuthbert (a railroad worker, owner of a cottonseed oil and ice plant, livery stable operator, hardware store employee, secretary and business manager at University of Mississippi) and Maud (Butler) Falkner; married Lida Estelle Oldham Franklin, June 20, 1929; children: Alabama (died, 1931), Jill (Mrs. Paul Dilwyn Summers, Jr.); (step-children) Victoria, Malcolm Argyle. *Education:* Attended University of Mississippi, 1919-20.

ADDRESSES: Home—Rowan Oak, Oxford, Miss.

CAREER: First National Bank, Oxford, Miss., clerk, 1916; Winchester Repeating Arms Co., New Haven, Conn., ledger clerk, 1918; Lord & Taylor, New York, N.Y., bookstore clerk, 1921; University of Mississippi, Oxford, postmaster, 1921-24; worked as roof painter, carpenter, and paper hanger, New Orleans, La., 1925; deckhand on Genoa-bound freighter, 1925; full-time writer, 1925-62. Coal shoveler at Oxford Power Plant, 1929. Screenwriter for Metro-Goldwyn-Mayer, 1932-33, and for Warner Bros., 1942-45, 1951, 1953, and 1954. Chairman of Writer's Group People-to-People Program, 1956-57. Writer in residence, University of Virginia, 1957-62. *Military service:* British Royal Air Force, cadet pilot, 1918; became honorary second lieutenant.

MEMBER: American Academy of Arts and Letters, Sigma Alpha Epsilon.

AWARDS, HONORS: Elected to National Institute of Arts and Letters, 1939; O. Henry Memorial Short Story Awards, 1939, 1940, and 1949; elected to American Academy of Arts and Letters, 1948; Nobel Prize for Literature, 1949; William Dean Howells Medal, American Academy of Arts and Letters, 1950; National Book Award, 1951, for *Collected Stories;* Legion of Honor of Republic of France, 1951; National Book Award and Pulitzer Prize, both 1955, both for *A Fable;* Silver Medal of the Greek Academy, 1957; gold medal for fiction, National Institute of Arts and Letters, 1962.

WRITINGS:

POETRY

Vision in Spring, privately printed [Mississippi], 1921.

The Marble Faun (also see below), Four Seas (Boston), 1924.

This Earth, a Poem, drawings by Albert Heckman, Equinox, 1932.

A Green Bough (contains *The Marble Faun*), H. Smith and R. Haas, 1933, published as *The Marble Faun* [and] *A Green Bough,* Random House, 1965.

Mississippi Poems (also see below), limited edition with introduction by Joseph Blotner and afterword by Luis Daniel Brodsky, Yoknapatawpha Press (Oxford, Mississippi), 1979.

Helen, a Courtship [and] *Mississippi Poems,* introductory essays by Carvel Collins and Joseph Blotner, Tulane University and Yoknapatawpha Press, 1981.

NOVELS

Soldiers' Pay, Boni & Liveright, 1926, published with author's speech of acceptance of Nobel Prize, New American Library of World Literature, 1959.

Mosquitoes, Boni and Liveright, 1927.

Sartoris (abridged version of *Flags in the Dust;* also see below), Harcourt, 1929.

The Sound and the Fury, J. Cape & H. Smith, 1929.

As I Lay Dying, J. Cape & H. Smith, 1930, new and corrected edition, Random House, 1964.

Sanctuary, J. Cape & H. Smith, 1931, published as *Sanctuary: The Original Text,* edited with afterword and notes by Noel Polk, Random House, 1981.

Light in August, H. Smith and R. Haas, 1932.

Pylon, H. Smith and R. Haas, 1935.

Absalom, Absalom!, Random House, 1936, casebook edition edited by Elisabeth Muhlenfeld published as *William Faulkner's Absalom, Absalom!,* Garland Publishing, 1984.

The Unvanquished, drawings by Edward Shenton, Random House, 1938.

The Wild Palms, Random House, 1939.

The Hamlet (first book in the "Snopes Trilogy"; also see below), Random House, 1940.

Intruder in the Dust, Random House, 1948.

Requiem for a Nun, Random House, 1951.

A Fable, Random House, 1954.

The Town (second book of the "Snopes Trilogy"; also see below), Random House, 1957.

The Long Hot Summer: A Dramatic Book from the Four-Book Novel; The Hamlet, New American Library, 1958.

The Mansion (third book in the "Snopes Trilogy"; also see below), Random House, 1959.

The Reivers, a Reminiscence, Random House, 1962 (condensation published as *Hell Creek Crossing,* illustrations by Noel Sickles, Reader's Digest Association, 1963), New American Library, 1969.

Snopes: A Trilogy, Volume 1: *The Hamlet,* Volume 2: *The Town,* Volume 3: *The Mansion,* Random House, 1965.

Flags in the Dust (unabridged version of *Sartoris*), edited with an introduction by Douglas Day, Random House, 1973.

Mayday, University of Notre Dame Press, 1976.

SHORT FICTION

These Thirteen (also see below; contains "Victory," "Ad Astra," "All the Dead Pilots," "Crevasse," "Red Leaves", "A Rose for Emily," "A Justice," "Hair," "That Evening Sun," "Dry September," "Mistral," "Divorce in Naples," and "Carcassonne"), J. Cape & H. Smith, 1931.

Doctor Martino, and Other Stories (also see below), H. Smith and R. Haas, 1934.

Go Down, Moses, and Other Stories (also see below), Random House, 1942 (also published in a limited edition), published as *Go Down, Moses,* Vintage, 1973.

Three Famous Short Novels (contains "Spotted Horses," "Old Man," and "The Bear"), Random House, 1942, published as *Three Famous Short Novels: Spotted Horses; Old Man; The Bear,* Vintage, 1978.

Knight's Gambit, Random House, 1949 (published in England as *Knight's Gambit: Six Stories,* Chatto & Windus, 1960).

Collected Stories, Random House, 1950, published as *Collected Stories of William Faulkner,* Vintage, 1977 (published in England as *Collected Short Stories,* Volume 1: *Uncle Willy and Other Stories,* Volume 2: *These Thirteen,* Volume 3: *Dr. Martino and Other Stories,* Chatto & Windus, 1958, reprinted, 1978).

Mirrors of Chartres Streets (includes sketches), introduction by William Van O'Connor, illustrations by Mary Demopoulous, Faulkner Studies (Minneapolis), 1953.

Big Woods (contains "The Bear," "The Old People," "A Bear Hunt," and "Race at Morning"), drawings by Edward Shenton, Random House, 1955.

Jealousy, and Episode (originally published in New Orleans *Times-Picayune,* 1925), limited edition, Faulkner Studies (Minneapolis), 1955.

Uncle Willy, and Other Stories, Chatto & Windus, 1958.

Selected Short Stories, Modern Library, 1961.

Bear, Man, and God: Seven Approaches to William Faulkner's "The Bear" (contains "The Bear," "Delta Autumn," and selections from other works), edited by Francis Lee Utley, Lynn Z. Bloom, and Arthur F. Kinney, Random House, 1964.

The Wishing Tree (children's fiction), with illustrations by Don Bolognese, Random House, 1964.

The Tall Men, and Other Stories, edited with notes by K. Sakai, Apollonsha (Kyoto), 1965.

A Rose for Emily, edited by M. Thomas Inge, Merrill, 1970.

Fairchild's Story, limited edition, Warren Editions (London), 1976.

Uncollected Stories of William Faulkner, edited by Joseph Blotner, Random House, 1979.

Short fiction anthologized in *Post Stories, 1957* ("The Waifs"), Random House, 1980.

SCREENPLAYS

"Today We Live," Metro-Goldwyn-Mayer, 1933.

(With Joel Sayre) *The Road to Glory* (Twentieth Century-Fox, 1936), with afterword by George Garrett, Southern Illinois University Press, 1981.

(With Nunnally Johnson) "Banjo on My Knee," Twentieth Century-Fox, 1936.

(With Sam Hellman, Lamar Trotti, and Gladys Lehman) "Slave Ship," Twentieth Century-Fox, 1937.

(With Sayre, Fred Guiol, and Ben Hecht) "Gunga Din," 1939.

(With Jean Renoir) "The Southerner," Universal, 1945.

(With Jules Furthman) *To Have and Have Not* (Warner Bros., 1945), based on novel by Ernest Hemingway, edited with introduction by Bruce F. Kawin, University of Wisconsin Press, 1980.

(With Leigh Brackett and Jules Furthman) "The Big Sleep," Warner Bros., 1946.

(With Harry Kurnitz and Harold Jack Bloom) "Land of the Pharoahs," Warner Bros., 1955.

Faulkner's MGM Screenplays, University of Tennessee Press, 1982.

OTHER

"Marionettes" (one-act play) first produced at University of Mississippi, March 4, 1921; published as *The Marionettes,* limited edition, Bibliographical Society, University of Virginia, 1975, published as *The Marionettes: A Play in One Act,* Yoknapatawpha Press (Oxford, Miss.), 1978.

Sherwood Anderson and Other Famous Creoles: A Gallery of Contemporary New Orleans, drawings by William Spratling, Pelican Bookshop Press, 1926.

Idyll in the Desert, limited edition, Random House, 1931.

Miss Zilphia Gant, limited edition, Book Club of Texas, 1932.

Salmagundi (contains poem by Ernest M. Hemingway), limited edition, Casanova Press (Milwaukee), 1932.

The Portable Faulkner, edited by Malcolm Cowley, Viking, 1946, revised and expanded edition, 1967 (published in England as *The Essential Faulkner,* Chatto & Windus, 1967).

Notes on a Horsethief, illustrations by Elizabeth Calvert, Levee Press (Greenville, Miss.), 1950.

William Faulkner's Speech of Acceptance upon the Award of the Nobel Prize for Literature, Delivered in Stockholm on the Tenth of December, 1950, [New York], 1951.

(And author of foreword) *The Faulkner Reader: Selections from the Works of William Faulkner,* Random House, 1954.

Faulkner's County: Tales of Yoknapatawpha County, Chatto & Windus, 1955.

Faulkner on Truth and Freedom: Excerpts from Tape Recordings of Remarks Made by William Faulkner during His Recent Manila Visit, Philippine Writer's Association (Manila), 1956, reprinted, 1978.

Faulkner at Nagano, edited by Robert A. Jelliffe, Kenkyusha (Tokyo), 1956.

New Orleans Sketches, introduction by Carvel Collins, Rutgers University Press, 1958.

Faulkner in the University: Class Conferences at the University of Virginia, 1957-1958 (interviews and conversations), edited by Frederick L. Gwynn and Joseph Blotner, University Press of Virginia, 1959.

William Faulkner: Early Prose and Poetry, compiled and introduced by Carvel Collins, Little, Brown, 1962.

Faulkner's University of Mississippi Pieces, compiled and introduced by Carvel Collins, Kenkyusha (Tokyo), 1962.

William Faulkner's Library: A Catalogue, compiled with an introduction by Joseph Blotner, University Press of Virginia, 1964.

Faulkner at West Point (interviews), edited by Joseph L. Fant III and Robert Ashley, Random House, 1964.

The Faulkner-Cowley File: Letters and Memories, 1944-1962, edited by Cowley, Viking, 1966.

Essays, Speeches and Public Letters, edited by James B. Merriwether, Random House, 1966.

The Best of Faulkner, Chosen by the Author, special edition, World Books Society, 1967.

Man, introduction by Bernard H. Porter, limited edition, [Rockland, Me.], 1969.

Faulkner's University Pieces, compiled with an introduction by Carvel Collins, Folcroft Press, 1970.

Selected Letters of William Faulkner, edited by Joseph Blotner, limited edition, Franklin Library, 1976, Random House, 1977.

Also author of *Faulkner on Love: A Letter to Marjorie Lyons,* limited edition edited by Richard Lyons, Merrykit Press (Fargo, N.D.), 1974; and *Faulkner's Ode to the Louver, Speech at Teatro Municipal, Caracas, 1961,* edited by James B. Merriwether, State College of Mississippi, 1979. Featured on sound recordings: *William Faulkner Reads Selections from His Novel: The Sound and the Fury—Dilsey,* Listening Library, 1976; *William Faulkner Reads a Selection from His Novel: Light in August,* Listening Library, 1979. Also contributor of poems, short stories, and articles to magazines and newspapers, including *New Orleans Times-Picayune, New Republic, Saturday Evening Post, Scribner's,* and *Sports Illustrated.*

SIDELIGHTS: William Faulkner is considered one of America's greatest twentieth-century novelists. He spent most of his literary career in the South, which both inspired and informed his fiction. Many critics have expressed amazement that Faulkner, in many ways such an isolated and provincial artist, was able to produce such impressive, universal work. Perhaps John W. Aldridge put it best when he wrote, "Working alone down there in that seemingly impenetrable cultural wilderness of the sovereignly backward state of Mississippi, he managed to make a clearing for his mind and a garden for his art, one which he cultivated so lovingly and well that it has come in our day to feed the imagination of literate men throughout the civilized world."

Most of the biographical facts about Faulkner have been thoroughly documented. He was born into a genteel Southern family that had played a significant part in the history of Mississippi. His great-grandfather, William Clark Falkner, was a colorful figure who had built railroads, served in the Confederate Army, and written a popular novel, *The White Rose of Memphis.* An indifferent student, Faulkner dropped out of Oxford High School in 1915 and then worked for a time as a clerk in his grandfather's bank. During this period he wrote bad imitative verse and contributed drawings to the University of Mississippi's yearbook, *Ole Miss.* When the United States declared war on Germany, Faulkner tried to enlist but was rejected because of his small stature.

Instead of going to war, Faulkner went to New Haven, Connecticut, to visit his friend Phil Stone, then a student at Yale. Stone had recognized Faulkner's talent early on and had encouraged his literary bent. The two men read and discussed Balzac and the French Symbolist poets. Although some critics have pointed to Stone as the determining factor in Faulkner's success, Michael Millgate theorized that the "apparent passivity of the younger man [Faulkner], his willingness to accept the position of listener, learner, recipient, and protege, undoubtedly led Stone to exaggerate in his own mind, and in public and private statements, the real extent of his influence. . . . Inevitably, Faulkner grew beyond Stone." At this time, however, Stone and Faulkner were still close friends. With Stone's help, Faulkner hatched a scheme to get admitted into the Royal Canadian Air Force. By affecting a British accent and forging letters of recommendation from nonexistent Englishmen, Faulkner was accepted into the RAF.

The war ended before Faulkner saw combat duty. He returned to his hometown, where he intermittently attended Ole Miss as a special student. His dandified appearance and lack of a stable job led townspeople to dub him "Count No' Count." On August 6, 1919, he surprised them when his first poem, "L'Apres-midi d'un faune," was published in *New Republic;* later in the same year the *Mississippian* published one of his short stories, "Landing in Luck." After Faulkner dropped out of Ole Miss, he went to New York City at the invitation of Stark Young, a Mississippi novelist and drama critic. While he was there, Faulkner worked for Elizabeth Prall as a bookstore clerk.

Back at Oxford, Faulkner was hired as university postmaster, but his mind was rarely on his duties. Before putting magazines into the proper subscriber's post office box, he read through the issues. He brought his writing to the post office with him and became so immersed in what he was doing that he ignored patrons. Eventually his laxness came to the attention of the postal inspector, and he resigned rather than be fired. Faulkner remarked that he quit the job because he "didn't want to be at the beck and call of every son-of-a-bitch with the price of a two-cent stamp."

His career in the postal service over, Faulkner called on Elizabeth Prall in New Orleans. She was now married to novelist Sherwood Anderson, and the two men struck up a friendship. The association with Anderson helped Faulkner realize that his true metier was not poetry but the novel. Faulkner's first book, *The Marble Faun,* a collection of verse, was published after he arrived in New Orleans in 1924. Sales were so poor that most of the five hundred copies were sold to a bookstore for a mere ten cents a volume. Acting upon Anderson's advice, Faulkner wrote a novel and set it in the South. Anderson told Faulkner he would recommend the book, entitled *Soldiers' Pay,* to a publisher as long as he didn't have to read it. Although the two men were very close for several months, a rift developed between them. Millgate postulated that "Faulkner's early realisation that Anderson's way was not to be his way must always have been a source of strain in their relationship." During this period in New Orleans, Faulkner also contributed short stories and sketches to the *Times-Picayune.*

In 1925, Faulkner joined the American literary expatriates and went to Europe. He did not remain there long, however, and after a brief stay in New Orleans, he returned to Oxford, where he finally settled down. While he had been in Europe, *Soldiers' Pay* had appeared on the bookstands. It attracted some favorable notices but was not a commercial success. Years later, Robert Penn Warren, also a Southern writer, remembered his own reactions when he first read *Soldiers' Pay* in the spring of 1929: "As a novel, *Soldiers' Pay* is no better than it should be, but it made a profound and undefinable impression on me." *Mosquitoes,* a mildly satirical novel on literary life in New Orleans, came out in 1927. Faulkner then penned *Flags in the Dust,* the first of his novels to be set in Yoknapatawpha County.

Early in 1928 *Flags in the Dust* was being shuffled from one publisher to another without success, and Faulkner had grown disgusted with the entire publication process. Abruptly, he decided to stop worrying about whether or not others liked his manuscripts. "One day I seemed to shut a door," he recalled, "between me and all publishers' addresses and book lists. I said to myself, Now I can write. Now I can make myself a vase like that which the old Roman kept at his bedside and wore the rim slowly away with kissing it. So I, who never had a sister and was fated to lose my daughter in infancy, set out to make myself a beautiful and tragic little girl." The story that Faulkner sat down to write was, of course, *The Sound and the Fury,* and "the beautiful and tragic little girl" was Caddy Compson. It was *The Sound and the Fury* that helped Faulkner establish a solid reputation among critics. Stirred by Faulkner's novel, Lyle Saxon wrote, "I believe simply and sincerely this is a great book." A reviewer for the Boston Evening Transcript called *The Sound and the Fury* a novel "worthy of the attention of a Euripides."

When writing his next novel, *As I Lay Dying,* Faulkner did not experience the same rapture he had felt when he was working on *The Sound and the Fury. As I Lay Dying* was written in a six-week period while Faulkner was working the night shift at a powerhouse. The constant humming noise of a dynamo serenaded him while he wrote his famous tour de force on the nature of being. By the time *As I Lay Dying* came out in 1930, John Bas-

sett observed that "Faulkner's name, if not a household word, was at least known to many critics and reviewers, who spoke of him no longer as a neophyte, or a new voice in fiction, but as one either continuing his development in fruitful ways or floundering after several attempts, in either case as a writer known to the literary world."

Faulkner was not recognized by the general public until *Sanctuary,* one of his most violent and shocking novels, appeared in 1931. When he wrote *Sanctuary,* Faulkner later admitted, he had one purpose in mind: to make money. By this time he had a family to support, and out of desperation he concocted a book he thought would sell to the masses. Faulkner was ashamed when he saw the printer's galleys of the book and extensively rewrote his potboiler so that it would have a more serious intent. The scandalous subject matter of *Sanctuary* appealed to the reading public, and it sold well. For a brief time Faulkner became a minor celebrity, but the rest of the decade did not go as well. Many reviewers had favorable comments to make about *Sanctuary*—Andre Malraux declared it "marks the intrusion of Greek tragedy into the detective story"—but in the view of others, the novel proved that Faulkner was merely a purveyor of the monstrous, the gory, and the obscene, and they judged his subsequent books in the same light. Faulkner was also a victim of the times. The Depression caused book sales in general to plummet, but his novels were particularly unpopular because they were not in keeping with the nation's mood. Warren speculated that critics and the public became disenchanted with Faulkner because his books offered no practical solutions to the pressing problems of the day—feeding the hungry and providing jobs for the millions of unemployed. Some readers were offended by Faulkner's novels because they were not written in the optimistic spirit of the New Deal, while still others discerned fascist tendencies in his work.

During the 1930s and 1940s Faulkner wrote many of his finest books, including *Light in August, Absalom, Absalom!, The Wild Palms, The Hamlet,* and *Go Down, Moses.* They brought in very little revenue, however, and he was forced to work in Hollywood as a screenwriter. Faulkner worked on and off in Hollywood for a number of years, but he was never happy there. He fled from the movie capital as soon as he had amassed enough money to pay his bills.

It should not be assumed that Faulkner was completely unappreciated during this time period. Bassett pointed out that the majority of reviews were positive, and that between 1939 and 1942 several important examinations of Faulkner appeared in literary journals and in literary histories. Although hardly noticed by the public, Faulkner was esteemed by many of his fellow writers. His work had also attracted a substantial following in France. Maurice Coindreau translated several of Faulkner's novels and short stories into French, and his fiction received perceptive treatment from such critics as Andre Malraux, Maurice LeBreton, Jean Pouillon, and Jean-Paul Sartre.

Despite Faulkner's stature in literary circles at home and abroad, in the 1940s his books gradually began dropping out of print, partly because of lack of popular interest, partly because of the war effort. By 1945 all seventeen of his books were out of print. In 1946 the publication of *The Portable Faulkner,* edited by Malcolm Cowley, created a resurgence of interest in Faulkner. Cowley's introduction to the volume, with its emphasis on the Southern legend that Faulkner had created in his works, served as a springboard for future critics. "Faulkner performed a labor of imagination that has not been equaled in our time, and a double labor," Cowley asserted. "First, to invent a Mississippi county that was like a mythical kingdom, but was complete and living in all its details; second, to make his story of Yoknapatawpha County stand as a parable or legend of all the Deep South."

Fifteen of Faulkner's novels and many of his short stories are set in Yoknapatawpha County, which bears a close resemblance to the region in northern Mississippi where Faulkner spent most of his life. Faulkner defined Yoknapatawpha as an "Indian word meaning water runs slow through flat land." The county is bounded by the Tallahatchie River on the north and by the Yoknapatawpha River on the south. Jefferson, the county seat, is modeled after Oxford. Up the road a piece is Frenchman's Bend, a poverty-stricken village. Scattered throughout the countryside are ramshackle plantation houses, farmhouses, and the hovels of tenant farmers. Depicted in both the past and the present, Yoknapatawpha is populated with a vast spectrum of people—the Indians who originally inhabited the land, the aristocrats, those ambitious men who fought their way into the landed gentry, yeoman farmers, poor whites, blacks, carpetbaggers, and bushwhackers. Faulkner was proud of the kingdom he had erected in his imagination. On a map of Yoknapatawpha County he prepared for the first edition of *Absalom, Absalom!,* he wrote, "William Faulkner, Sole Owner & Proprietor."

Although there are some inconsistencies in the Yoknapatawpha novels and although the books are certainly not arranged in a neat chronological order, the saga does have unity. Millgate called this unity "a unity of inspiration, of a single irradiating tragi-comic vision." In order to appreciate Faulkner's vision fully, one must read the entire saga, which Yardley described as "a tapestry of incomparable intricacy, past and present woven together in a design that can be comprehended through one book but that gains astonishing richness when seen as a whole." The greatness of Faulkner's design led critics to recognize that he was not just a provincial writer. Like the works of such famous regional authors as Robert Frost, Thomas Hardy, and William Butler Yeats, Faulkner's novels have a universal appeal. Faulkner created, Arthur Edelstein remarked, a "hallucinated version of the Deep South which has escaped its local origins to become a region of the modern consciousness."

Those who investigated the Yoknapatawpha legend began exploring other aspects of Faulkner's fiction. Warren Beck observed that Faulkner's reiteration of certain words and his habit of piling one adjective upon another sometimes help to create a mood or to accentuate a particular character trait. For examples, Beck turned to *Absalom, Absalom!* In that novel, Miss Rosa's persistent use of the word "demon" indicates her crazed obsession, while the description of the "long still hot weary dead September afternoon" when Quentin hears Miss Rosa's story emphasizes not only the muggy weather but also the spiritual malaise of the characters. Joseph Blotner noted that sometimes Faulkner followed James Joyce's lead and "would omit all punctuation to denote the flowing stream of consciousness." This technique was used in Benjy's and Quentin's sections in *The Sound and the Fury.* As for Faulkner's vague pronoun references, Helen Swink surmised that he used them because he wanted to adapt the art of the oral storyteller to the written page. In attempting to sound like he was spinning yarns aloud, Faulkner used vague pronoun references because this is a characteristic of oral speech.

Most often, Faulkner's style is keyed to his themes. One of Faulkner's chief thematic preoccupations is the past, and this theme is also reflected in his form. In a famous analogy, Jean-Paul Sartre compared the Faulknerian character's point of view to that "of a passenger looking backward from a speeding car,

who sees, flowing away from him, the landscape he is traversing. For him the future is not in view, the present is too blurred to make out, and he can see clearly only the past as it streams away before his obsessed and backward-looking gaze." Faulkner's pages are filled with characters who are fettered to the past. Millgate pointed out that in *The Sound and the Fury* the suicidal Quentin Compson searches "for a means of arresting time at a moment of achieved perfection, a moment when he and Caddy could be eternally together in the simplicity of their childhood relationship." The Reverend Gail Hightower in *Light in August* is also locked in the past, endlessly reliving the glory of his grandfather's cavalry charge. Robert Hemenway believed that in *As I Lay Dying* Faulkner is showing "that the South, like the Bundrens, must bury the past; that it cannot remain true—without courting tragedy or absurdity—to the promises given to dead ancestors or to the illusions of former glory." In "A Rose for Emily," Emily Grierson's embracing of her dead lover becomes a gruesome symbol of what happens when one clings to the past.

The stylistic methods most closely associated with Faulkner's treatment of the past are his use of long sentences, flashbacks, and multiple viewpoints. Aiken suggested that Faulkner utilizes complicated sentence structures because he wants "a medium without stops or pauses, a medium which is always *of the moment,* and of which the passage from moment to moment is as fluid and undetectable as in the life itself which he is purporting to give." Swink posited that the confusing sentences that withhold meaning from the reader "intensify the emotional experience," while Millgate claimed that these sentences enable Faulkner "to hold a single moment in suspension while its full complexity is explored." The flashbacks are even more clearly related to Faulkner's interest in the past. Edward Murray pointed out that in *Light in August* the minds of Joe Christmas, Gail Hightower, Joanna Burden, and Lena Grove frequently revert back to the past, but "the flashbacks are not there merely to supply expository material for the actions in the present that need further explanation. Since the past is Faulkner's subject—or a large part of it—the flashbacks are not simply 'functional': they are thematically necessary."

By telling a story from several points of view, Faulkner adds a further dimension to his concept of time. The past is part of the present; thus, it is subject to re-evaluation and re-interpretation. Faulkner's view of time as a continuum has certain moral implications, Millgate explained: "The all important point consisted in the idea that there could be no such thing as 'was': since time constituted a continuum the chain of cause and effect could never be broken, and every human action must continue to reverberate, however faintly, into infinity. Hence the all-importance of conduct, of personal responsibility for all one's actions." This belief partially accounts for Faulkner's frequent allusions to the Bible. "Faulkner's true domain is that of the eternal myths, particularly those popularized by the Bible," Maurice Coindreau observed. "The themes that he prefers, his favorite images and metaphors, are those which ornament the fabric of the Old Testament." Like the writers of the Old Testament, Faulkner believes that the sins of the fathers are visited upon their children. Many of his characters are plagued by guilt, precipitated by their own sins as well as by the actions of their forefathers, who had callously shoved aside the Indians, enslaved the blacks, and laid waste the land.

Perhaps the greatest moral burden borne by Southerners was slavery. Much of Faulkner's fiction shows the evil that results from the failure to recognize the humanity of black people. Certainly many of the slave owners he depicts are cruel to their human property. In *Go Down, Moses,* Carothers McCaslin seduces Eunice, one of his Negroes. Years later he seduces the daughter who resulted from that union, thus driving Eunice to suicide. One of the reasons that Thomas Sutpen's grand design fails in *Absalom, Absalom!* is his acceptance of racism. When Sutpen leaves Haiti to found a dynasty in Mississippi, he abandons his black wife and infant son because their color would not be acceptable to Southerners. That deed comes back to haunt Sutpen and the children from his second marriage, Judith and Henry. Sutpen's mulatto son shows up and wants to marry Judith. As horrified by the thought of miscegenation as he is by the possibility of incest, Henry guns down his half brother. This is only one incident in *Absalom, Absalom!* that demonstrates, as John V. Hagopian pointed out, how "the novel as a whole clearly repudiates Southern racism."

Men do not only exploit one another, Faulkner points out; they also exploit the earth. Cleanth Brooks noted that "Faulkner seems to accept the Christian doctrine of original sin. Men are condemned to prey upon nature. The only question is whether in doing so they will exercise some kind of restraint and love the nature that they are forced to use, or whether they will exploit nature methodically and ruthlessly, in a kind of rape."

Another important aspect of Faulkner's fiction is love between family members. Cowley observed that Faulkner's books "have what is rare in the novels of our time, a warmth of family affection, brother for brother and sister, the father for his children—a love so warm and proud that it tries to shut out the rest of the world." But family life has eroded in Faulkner's fiction, at least partially because society is debilitated. "Faulkner's recurrent dramatization of the decay of families," Philip Momberger reflected, "e.g., the deterioration of the Compson, Sutpen, and Sartoris lines—is an expression in the domestic sphere of a more general, public disintegration: the collapse of the ideal of 'human family' in the modern world and the resulting deracination of the individual." Momberger went on to say that the social ideal that underpins Faulkner's work is "a state of communal wholeness within which, as within a coherent and loving family, the individual's identity would be defined, recognized, and sustained."

Although a person's ties to the community are important, Faulkner suggests that men must never let the community become the sole arbiter of their values. Brooks stated that the "community is at once the field for man's action and the norm by which his action is judged and regulated" and further indicated that Faulkner's "fiction also reveals keen awareness of the perils risked by the individual who attempts to run counter to the community. The divergent individual may invite martyrdom; he certainly risks fanaticism and madness." For examples of divergent individuals, Brooks turned to *Light in August.* In that novel, many of the characters are social outcasts—Joe Christmas because of his suspected Negro blood, Joanna Burden because of her abolitionist background, Gail Hightower because he does not conform to the conventional behavior of a minister, Percy Grimm because he did not serve in World War I.

Established religion also comes under close scrutiny in Faulkner's fiction, and his characters are often deeply disturbed by the rigid attitudes of the church-going populace. In *Sanctuary,* Horace Benbow is taken aback when the Christian community refuses to help a man who is falsely accused of murder. Waggoner declared that in that novel "Southern fundamentalist Protestantism is pictured as selfrighteous moralism." Calvinist righteousness is also attacked in *Light in August,* where Hightower comes to realize that rigid religious attitudes encourage people to crucify themselves and others. One of the people they feel compelled to crucify is Joe Christmas, who is clearly an outcast in the community. The major significance in Christmas's name, O'Connor noted, "is the irony of Joe Christmas' being pursued and harassed throughout his life by voices of Christian righteousness."

Allied with the theme of the individual running counter to the community and its values is the theme of a young boy's initiation into manhood. This initiation process usually involves some ritualistic gesture or task that a youth must perform in order to achieve knowledge and manhood, and a choice, as Brooks observed, "between a boy's ties with his community—his almost fierce identification with it—and his revulsion from what the community seems committed to do." After he kills his first deer, Ike McCaslin is initiated into manhood by Sam Fathers, who anoints his forehead with the deer's blood. This initiation process is the first step in Ike's decision to eschew the values of society. *The Unvanquished* consists of a series of short stories recounting the growth of Bayard Sartoris. In the final story, Bayard refuses to avenge the death of his father. By so doing, he defies the community, for the townspeople think vengeance is honorable. Chick Mallison in *Intruder in the Dust* is another sensitive adolescent who is forced to choose between the community's standards and what his heart tells him is right. Faulkner's last novel, *The Reivers, a Reminiscence,* also deals with a young boy's initiation into manhood. When he runs away to Memphis with Boon Hogganbeck and Ned McCaslin, Lucius Priest is forced to grow up.

M.E. Bradford pointed out that the thematic corollary to Faulkner's consideration of a young man's coming into his majority is the question of pride, "or pride's proper role in the formation of good character and of its necessary limitation in contingency. The gentleman, the exemplar of ordinate pride and enactor of a providentially assigned place, sums up in his person the possibility of a civil and religiously grounded social order. In him either presumption or passivity is communal and spiritual disaster." Closely linked to pride is the Faulknerian concept of honor, the need for a man to prove himself. In Faulkner's novels, exaggerated notions of honor lead to trouble. Quentin Compson's fanatic defense of his sister's honor is narcissistic; his "insistence upon honor and dignity have become extreme, forms of self love," O'Connor noted. In *As I Lay Dying,* the Bundren family's attempt to honor Addie's dying wish is ludicrous, yet Brooks pointed out that Cash and Jewel "exhibit true heroism—Cash in his suffering, Jewel in his brave actions." The scruple of honor is also of great significance in *The Hamlet.* After Eula Varner becomes pregnant, her honor is ironically preserved when her father pays Flem Snopes to marry her. Even Mink Snopes has a warped sense of honor that compels him to kill Zack Houston. But Mink discovers that his cousin Flem is so devoid of honor that he won't even help Mink when he is arrested. Mink evens this score in a later novel, *The Mansion.* When he is released from prison, Mink kills Flem for the sake of honor.

When Faulkner's characters are initiated into manhood, they lose their innocence and are forced to face reality. The world they discover is one in which good and evil are intermingled. The "Snopes Trilogy," Stanley Edgar Hyman claimed, that is "Faulkner's fullest exploration of natural evil." In *The Hamlet,* the heartless Flem Snopes is pitted against V. K. Ratliff, an itinerant sewing machine salesman. Flem is almost the perfect embodiment of evil, whereas Ratliff, John Lewis Longley demonstrated, is a man "who is willing to actively commit himself against evil, but more important, to form actions of positive good." Although Flem is depicted as the incarnation of evil in *The Hamlet,* commentators have noted that he is portrayed more sympathetically in the succeeding two books in the trilogy. This treatment is in keeping with Faulkner's view of the nature of man. "I think that you really can't say that any man is good or bad. I grant you there are some exceptions, but man is the victim of himself or his fellows, or his own nature, or his environment, but no man is good or bad either. He tries to do the best he can within his rights," the novelist once said.

From today's perspective, it is difficult to understand the outcry that arose when Faulkner was awarded the Nobel Prize in 1949. The preponderance of criticism has shown that his concerns are ultimately moral, but at that time many readers still considered Faulkner a naturalistic monster. Reflecting the views of many other small-town newspapers, the editor of the *North Mississippi Herald* declared that Faulkner was a member of the "privy school of literature." Even the *New York Times* expressed the fear that the rest of the world might consider Yoknapatawpha County an accurate depiction of life in America. Faulkner's reply to those who accused him of promoting immorality was contained in his acceptance speech. He explained that it is the writer's duty and privilege "to help man endure by lifting his heart, by reminding him of the courage and honor and hope and pride and compassion and pity and sacrifice which have been the glory of his past. The poet's voice need not merely be the record of man, it can be one of the props, the pillars, to help him endure and prevail."

Faulkner's stirring acceptance speech caused many to change their opinion of him overnight. Suddenly he became a moral hero. As Herman Spivey pointed out, the truth is that Faulkner's outlook had undergone no dramatic change; from the beginning of his writing career he had concerned himself with "the old verities and truths of the heart, the old universal truths lacking which any story is ephemeral and doomed." Faulkner's later books became didactic, however, often seeming to be mere echoes of his Nobel Prize acceptance speech. Spivey contended that in Faulkner's later novels "there is a major and regrettable shift from mythic and symbolic and implicit communication to allegorical and explicit communication." In *A Fable,* which Faulkner hoped would be his masterpiece, allegory is used to convey a moral message. Few critics were happy with the book's general and abstract statements. Brendan Gill called *A Fable* "a calamity," while Charles Rolo termed it "a heroically ambitious failure."

Though Faulkner occasionally failed greatly, he usually succeeded mightily. Whatever the faults of his later books, few would dispute the general excellence of his canon. Even Faulkner seemed overwhelmed by his achievement. Toward the end of his life, he wrote to a friend: "And now I realize for the first time what an amazing gift I had: uneducated in every formal sense, without even very literate, let alone literary, companions, yet to have made the things I made. I don't know where it came from. I don't know why God or gods or whoever it was, elected me to be the vessel. Believe me, this is not humility, false modesty: it is simply amazement."

Each of Faulkner's novels has been translated into at least one other language, and several have been translated into as many as thirteen languages.

AVOCATIONAL INTERESTS: Aviation, raising and training horses, hunting, sailing.

MEDIA ADAPTATIONS: The following novels by Faulkner have been adapted for movies: "Intruder in the Dust," Metro-Goldwyn-Mayer, 1949; "Tarnished Angels" (based on *Pylon*), Universal, 1957; "The Long Hot Summer" (based on *The Hamlet*), Twentieth Century-Fox, 1958; "The Sound and the Fury," Twentieth Century-Fox, 1959; "Sanctuary" (also includes parts of *Requiem for a Nun*), Twentieth Century-Fox, 1961; "The Reivers," Cinema Center Films, 1969. *The Sound and the Fury* was adapted for television in 1955, and several of Faulkner's short stories have been adapted for television, including "An Error in Chemistry" and "The Brooch."

BIOGRAPHICAL/CRITICAL SOURCES:

BOOKS

Aldridge, John W., *The Devil in the Fire,* Harper's Magazine Press, 1972.

Backman, Melvin, *Faulkner, The Major Years: A Critical Study,* Indiana University Press, 1966.

Beck, Warren, *Man in Motion: Faulkner's Trilogy,* University of Wisconsin Press, 1961.

Beck, *Faulkner,* University of Wisconsin Press, 1976.

Blotner, Joseph L., *Faulkner: A Biography,* two volumes, Random House, 1974.

Blotner, editor, *Selected Letters of William Faulkner,* Random House, 1977.

Brooks, Cleanth, *The Yoknapatawpha Country,* Yale University Press, 1963.

Brooks, *Toward Yoknapatawpha and Beyond,* Yale University Press, 1978.

Campbell, Harry M., and Reuel M. Foster, *William Faulkner: A Critical Appraisal,* University of Oklahoma Press, 1951, reprinted, Cooper Square, 1971.

Concise Dictionary of Literary Biography: The Age of Maturity, 1929-1941, Gale, 1989.

Contemporary Literary Criticism, Gale, Volume 1, 1973, Volume 3, 1975, Volume 6, 1976, Volume 8, 1978, Volume 9, 1978, Volume 11, 1979, Volume 14, 1980, Volume 18, 1981, Volume 28, 1984, Volume 52, 1989.

Cowley, Malcolm, editor, *The Faulkner-Cowley File: Letters and Memories,* Viking, 1966.

Cowley, *The Second Flowering: Works and Days of the Lost Generation,* Viking, 1973.

Dictionary of Literary Biography, Gale, Volume 9: *American Novelists, 1910-1945,* 1981, Volume 11: *American Humorists, 1800-1950,* 1982, Volume 44: *American Screenwriters, Second Series,* 1986.

Dictionary of Literary Biography Documentary Series, Volume 2, Gale, 1982.

Dictionary of Literary Biography Yearbook 1986, Gale, 1987.

Faulkner, John, *My Brother Bill: An Affectionate Reminiscence,* Trident, 1963.

Faulkner, William, *Faulkner at West Point,* edited by Joseph L. Fant and Robert Ashley, Random House, 1964.

Gold, Joseph, *William Faulkner: A Study in Humanism from Metaphor to Discourse,* University of Oklahoma Press, 1966.

Hoffman, Frederick J., and Olga W. Vickery, editors, *William Faulkner: Two Decades of Criticism,* Michigan State University Press, 1951.

Hoffman and Vickery, editors, *William Faulkner: Three Decades of Criticism,* Michigan State University Press, 1960.

Hoffman, *William Faulkner,* Twayne, 1961.

Howe, Irving, *William Faulkner: A Critical Study,* Random House, 1952.

Hyman, Stanley Edgar, *Standards: A Chronicle of Books for Our Time,* Horizon Press, 1966.

Merriwether, James B., *The Literary Career of William Faulkner: A Bibliographical Study,* Princeton University Press, 1961.

Merriwether, and Michael Millgate, *Lion in the Garden: Interviews with William Faulkner,* Random House, 1968.

Millgate, *The Achievement of William Faulkner,* Random House, 1966.

Miner, Ward L., *The World of William Faulkner,* Duke University Press, 1952.

Slatoff, Walter J., *Quest for Failure: A Study of William Faulkner,* Cornell University Press, 1960.

Vickery, *The Novels of William Faulkner: A Critical Interpretation,* Louisiana State University Press, 1959, revised edition, 1964.

Vogel, Dan, *The Three Masks of American Tragedy,* Louisiana State University Press, 1974.

Volpe, Edmond, *Reader's Guide to William Faulkner,* Farrar, Straus, 1964.

Wagner, Linda Welshimer, *William Faulkner: Four Decades of Criticism,* Michigan State University Press, 1973.

Warren, Robert Penn, editor, *Faulkner: A Collection of Critical Essays,* Prentice-Hall, 1967.

PERIODICALS

American Literature, May, 1973.
Georgia Review, summer, 1972.
Journal of Popular Culture, summer, 1973.
Modern Fiction Studies, summer, 1973, winter, 1973-74, summer, 1975.
New Republic, September 8, 1973.
Sewanee Review, winter, 1970, autumn, 1971.
Southern Review, summer, 1968, autumn, 1972.
Studies in Short Fiction, summer, 1974.
Twentieth Century Literature, July, 1973.*

*   *   *

FELLINI, Federico   1920-

PERSONAL: Born January 20, 1920, in Rimini, Italy; son of Urbano (a businessman) and Ida (Barbiani) Fellini; married Giulietta Masina (an actress), October 30, 1943. *Education:* Attended the University of Rome. *Religion:* Roman Catholic.

ADDRESSES: Home—Corso d'Italia 356, Rome, Italy. *Office*—141a Via Marguatta 110, Rome, Italy.

CAREER: Contributor of cartoons to periodicals and tourist caricaturist in Rome, Italy, 1936-37; *Marc' Aurelio* (weekly magazine), Rome, story editor, 1937; scriptwriter for radio and writer of skits and dialogue for Macario and other traveling comedians, 1938-39; became interested in writing screenplays and began working in various production capacities for the Italian director Mario Mattoli in 1939; radio sketchwriter, 1939-42; collaborated on screenplays and continued production work with Roberto Rossellini and Alberto Lattuada, 1940-50; founder with Alberto Lattuada, Capitoleum Production Company, 1950; founder with Angelo Rizzoli, Federiz Production Company, 1961; also comic with the Fabrizzi vaudeville troupe and circus performer. Principal film appearances include: the part of the Stranger in "Il miracolo" in "L'Amore," 1948, member of Fellini's troupe in "I Clowns," 1970, "C'eravamo tanto amati," 1974, and "We All Loved Each Other So Much," 1977; appeared as himself in "Alex in Wonderland," 1970, "Ciao, Federico!" (documentary; also known as "So Long, Federico!"), 1970, "Roma" 1972, "Il tassinaro" (also known as "The Cabbie"), 1983, and "Federico Fellini's Intervista," 1987.

AWARDS, HONORS: First prizes in Rome, Venice, Zurich, and Cannes Film Festivals, awards for best foreign film from New York Film Critics and National Board of Review of Motion Pictures (United States), all 1946, all for "Roma citta aperta"; grand

prize from World Film Festival, 1947, and awards for best foreign film from New York Film Critics and National Board of Review of Motion Pictures, 1948, for "Paisa"; Nastro d'Argento (Italy's highest film award), 1948, for "Senza pieta," 1950, for "Luci del varieta," and 1951, for "Europa '51"; New York Film Critics Award, 1950, for "L'Amore"; grand prize from Venice Film Festival, 1954, New York Film Critics award, 1956, Screen Directors Guild award for best direction of foreign film, 1956, and Academy Award (Oscar) for best foreign film, American Academy of Motion Picture Arts and Sciences, 1956, all for "La strada"; Academy Award, 1957, for "Le notti di Cabiria"; first prize at Cannes Film Festival, 1960, and New York Film Critics Award, 1961, both for "La dolce vita"; Academy Award, 1963, for "8 1/2"; Golden Globe Award, Hollywood Foreign Press Association, 1965, for "Giulietta degli spiriti"; Academy Award and New York Film Critics award, both 1974, both for "Amarcord"; honored by Film Society of Lincoln Center, 1985; Prix du 40th Anniversaire from Cannes Film Festival, 1987; Moscow Film Festival Award; and many other film awards. D.H.L., Columbia University, 1970.

WRITINGS:

(With Dominique Delouche) *Entretiens avec Federico Fellini* (excerpts of interview appearing on Belgian television), Radiodiffusion Television Belge, 1962.

(Author of text with Francoise Sagan) *Mirror of Venus,* photographs by Wingate Paine, Random House, 1966.

(Contributor) Renzo Renzi, editor, *La mia Rimini* (memoirs and descriptions of Rimini), Cappelli, 1967.

(Contributor with Louis Malle and Roger Vadim) *Tre passi nel delirio* (filmscript anthology; all scripts based on short stories by Edgar Allan Poe), edited by Liliana Betti, Ornella Valta, and Bernadino Zapponi, Cappelli, 1968.

Fellini, L'Arc (Aix-en-Provence), 1971.

Fellini on Fellini, translated by Isabel Quigley, Delacorte/S. Lawrence, 1976.

Fellinis Filme, edited by Christian Strich, Diogenes Verlag, 1976, translation with foreword by Georges Simenon published as *Fellini's Films: The Four Hundred Most Memorable Stills from Federico Fellini's Fifteen and a Half Films,* Putnam, 1977.

(Author of text) *Balthus, Paintings and Drawings 1934 to 1977,* Pierre Matisse Gallery (New York), 1977.

Fare un film, Einaudi (Turin), 1980.

(Contributor of drawings) Pier Marco de Santi, *I disegni di Fellini,* Laterza (Rome), 1982.

(Author of introduction) *Fellini's Faces: 418 Pictures from the Photo-Archives of Federico Fellini,* edited by Strich, translated by Chantal d'Aulnis, Holt, 1982.

Moraldo in the City [and] *A Journey with Anita* (unproduced plays), edited and translated by John C. Stubbs, University of Illinois Press, 1983.

Comments on Film, edited by Giovanni Grazzini, California State University Press (Fresno), 1988.

SCREENPLAYS

(With Sergio Amidei and Rossellini; and assistant director) "Roma, citta aperta" (released in the United States as "Open City"; also known as "Rome, Open City"), Mayer-Burstyn, 1945.

(With Amidei, Rossellini, and Annalena Limentani; and assistant director) "Paisa" (also known as "Paisan"), Mayer-Burstyn, 1946.

(Contributor) "L'Amore" (film trilogy; contains Fellini's "Il miracolo" ["The Miracle"]), first released in Italy, 1948; released in the United States as "Ways of Love," Joseph Burstyn, 1950.

(With Tullio Pinelli) "Senza pieta" (released in the United States as "Without Pity"), Lux, 1948.

(With Ennio Flaiano, Alberto Lattuada, and Pinelli; director with Lattuada; and producer) "Luci del varieta" (released in the United States as "Variety Lights" and "Lights of Variety," Pathe; also see below), 1950.

(With Pinelli and Flaiano; and director) "Lo sceicco bianco" (released in the United States as "The White Sheik," Janus/API, 1956; also see below), [Italy], 1951.

(With Flaiano and Pinelli; and director) "I vitelloni" (also known as "Vitelloni, The Young and the Passionate," and "Spivs"; released in the United States as "The Young and the Passionate," Janus, 1956; also see below), [Italy], 1953.

(With Pinelli; and director) La Strada (also known as "The Road"; released in 1954; released in the United States by Trans-Lux, 1956; also see below), Bianco e Nero (Rome), 1955.

(With Flaiano and Pinelli; and director) Il bidone (also known as "The Swindler"; film released in 1955; released in the United States by Astor, 1962; also see below), translation from the Italian into French by Dominique Delouche, published under same title, Flammarion (Paris), 1956.

(With Flaiano, Pinelli, and Pier Paolo Pasolini; and director) Le notti di Cabiria (also known as "Nights of Cabiria" and "Cabiria"; film released by Lopert, 1956), edited by Lino del Fra, Cappelli (Bologna), 1957.

(With Flaiano, Pinelli, and Brunello Rondi; and director) La dolce vita (title means "The Sweet Life"; film released in 1959; released in the United States by Astor-American International, 1961; also see below), edited by Tullio Kezich, Cappelli, 1961.

(With Flaiano and Pinelli; and director of second act) "Boccaccio '70" (contains "Le tentazioni del dottor Antonio"; also known as "The Temptation of Dr. Antonio"; also see below), Gray, 1961.

(With Flaiano, Pinelli, and Rondi; and director) 8 1/2 (also known as "Otte e mezzo" and "Federico Fellini's 8 1/2"; film released by Embassy, 1963), Cappelli, 1963.

(With Flaiano, Pinelli, and Rondi; and director) Giulietta degli spiriti (also known as "Juliet of the Spirits," "Juliette des esprits," and "Julia und die Geister"; film released in 1965), edited by Kezich, Cappelli, 1965, translation by Howard Greenfield published as Juliet of the Spirits, Orion Press, 1965, new edition with transcription of final screenplay by John Cohen, translation by Cecilia Perrault, Ballantine, 1966.

(With Zapponi and Clement Biddle Wood; and producer) "Never Bet the Devil Your Head, or Toby Dammit" (also known as "Il ne faut jamais parier sa tete contre le diable"), in "Spirits of the Dead" (also known as "Histoires extraordinaires" and "Tre passi nel delirio"; film released in 1968; released in the United States by American International, 1969; also see below), published as Tre passi nel delirio, Cappelli, 1968.

(And director and narrator) "Fellini: A Director's Notebook" (television film; also known as "Block-notes di un Regista") first broadcast by National Broadcasting Corp. (NBC-TV), April 11, 1969.

(With Zapponi and Rondi; and producer and author of book's preface) Fellini Satyricon (includes critical essays and conversations; also known as "Satyricon"; film released in the United States by United Artists, 1969), edited by Dario Zaponelli, translation by Eugene Walter and John Matthews, Cappelli, 1969, Ballantine, 1970.

(With Zapponi; and director) I Clowns (also known as "The Clowns"; film released by Levitt-Pickman, 1970), edited by Renzi, Cappelli, 1970, published with block notes as Fellini TV, 1972.

(With Zapponi; and director) Roma (also known as "Fellini Roma"; film released in the United States, United Artists, 1972), edited by Zapponi, Cappelli, 1972.

(With Tonino Guerra; and director) Amarcord (film released in 1973; released with subtitle I Remember in the United States by Warner Brothers/New World, 1974), Rizzoli (Milan), 1973.

(With Zapponi; and director and production designer) "Il Casanova di Federico Fellini" (also known as "Fellini's Casanova" and "Casanova"; film released by Universal, 1976), published as Casanova sceneggiature originale, Einaudi, 1981.

(And director) "Prova d'orchestra" (also known as "Orchestra Rehearsal"), New Yorker, 1978.

(With Zapponi and Rondi; and director) La citta della donne (also known as "City of Women"; film released by Gaumont, 1980), Garzanti (Milano), 1980.

(With Guerra; and director) E la nave va (also known as "And the Ship Sails On"; film released by Vides, 1983), Diogenes Verlag, 1983.

(With Guerra and Pinelli; and director) "Ginger et Fred" (also known as "Ginger and Fred"), Metro-Goldwyn-Mayer/United Artists, 1986.

(With Gianfranco Angelucci; and director) "Federico Fellini's Intervista" (also known as "Intervista" and "The Interview"), Aljosha-RAI-TV/Cinecitta/Fernlyn, 1987.

Also author of films "Chi l'ha vistro?," 1942, "Quarta pagina," 1942, "Campo del fiori" (also known as "The Path of Hope"), 1943, "Tutta la citta canta," 1943, and "L'ultima carrozzella," 1943. Co-author of films "Il delitto di Giovanni Episcopo," 1947, "Il passatore," 1947, "La fumeria d'oppio" (also known as "Ritorna Za-la-mort"), 1947, L'ebreo errante, 1947, "Il mulino del po," 1948, "In nome della legge" (also known as "Mafia"), 1948, "La citta dolente," 1948, "Francesco giullare di dio," 1949, "Il cammino della speranza," 1950, "Persiane chiuse," 1950, "La citta si difende," 1951, "Cameriera bella presenza offresi," 1951, "Il brigante di Tacca del Lupa," 1952, "Un 'agenzia matrimoniale" (also known as "The Matrimonial Agency") in "Amore in citta" (also known as "Love in the City"), 1953, and "Fortunella," 1958. Uncredited screenwork includes "Documento Z-3," 1941, "Avanti, c'e posto," 1942, "Apparizione," 1943, and "Europa '51," 1952.

OMNIBUS EDITIONS

8 1/2 (includes "Le tentazioni del dottor Antonio"), edited by Camilla Cederna, Cappelli, 1965.

Il Primo Fellini (includes "Lo sceicco bianco," "I vitelloni," "La strada," and "Il bidone"), edited by Betti and Eschilo Tarquini, Cappelli, 1969.

Three Screenplays (includes "The Young and the Passionate," "The Swindler," and "The Temptation of Doctor Antonio"), translation by Judith Green, Orion Press, 1970.

Quattro Film (includes "I vetelloni," "La dolce vita," "8 1/2," and "Giuliletta degli spiriti"), Einaudi, 1974.

OTHER

Also gag writer for Mario Mattoli in "Lo vedi come soi . . . lo vedi come sei?!," 1939, "Non me lo dire!," 1940, and "Il pirata sono io!," 1940.

WORK IN PROGRESS: A film to be titled either "Voice of the Moon" or "Voices of the Moon."

SIDELIGHTS: In 1956 a small item appeared in the *New York Times,* a film review of "The White Sheik." Referring to its young writer-director, critic Bosley Crowther noted, "In fairness to [Federico] Fellini, we will not speculate on his talents until we see a few more of his films." Time has borne out the Italian *auteur,* and now the Fellini name is virtually synonymous with avant-garde imagery and lively flights of fancy. Indeed, the term "Felliniesque" now describes any unusual, even grotesque, sight. The description most often applied to the artist is "neorealist," a word denoting a re-examination of reality. Many scholars and filmgoers like to compare a Fellini production with a circus; circus themes pervade almost all his works. A "typical" Fellini film contains elements of the mythic, the religious, the sensual, and the symbolic. In the director's first big movie, "La Strada," for example, "the whole of Fellini can be found in [the first sequence]," according to Peter Harcourt in his book *Six European Directors: Essays on the Meaning of Film Style.* In this gentle tale of a waif who joins a circus troupe, the director's "thematic center is here," writes Harcourt. "To begin with, reinforced by the title itself ['La Strada' translates as 'The Street'], there is the sense of life as a journey, as a constant tearing away from things known and a plunging into the unfamiliar." In Fellini, the author continues, "there is seldom any sense of direction or eventual goal. The form of his films tends to be circular, the characters usually ending where they begin."

The early Fellini canon boasts several important titles—"Juliet of the Spirits," "Nights of Cabiria," and especially the notorious "La Dolce Vita." In this latter production the writer-director's vision of "the sweet life"—a modern exploration of hedonism—includes a scathing sendup of Rome's upper classes, and a kind of matriarchal society in which "men become mere consorts, lover-kings, ridiculous, impotent," as *Hudson Review* critic Norman Holland puts it. "As with any important work," says Holland, "*La Dolce Vita* defines its own art. Fellini's concern about turning people into images finds its expression in what might be called the rotogravure style of the film. [The director] had both sets and costumes of *La Dolce Vita* designed to photograph in exaggerated blacks and whites, so that everything in the film would have the hard, contrasty look of a flash photo. . . . Fellini's sense of the new, the unexpected, his theme of improvisation, finds its expression in the episodic structure."

Many critics and audiences saw "La Dolce Vita" as an attack on all modern society, with its shallow, self-centered characters and materialistic themes. In John Russell Taylor's opinion, the movie has in it "the making of a summary of Fellini so far, a complete statement of his mature views on all the recurrent themes in his work." In his book *Cinema Eye, Cinema Ear: Some Key Film Makers of the Sixties,* Taylor goes on to say that those who see "La Dolce Vita" as a permanent "gesture of despair" are wrong. Taylor thinks it is "highly doubtful if Fellini ever sets out to make a film of ideas, putting forward a certain interpretation of society and human personality: these may emerge, though invariably defined exclusively in terms of the single, special case (his films are more like novels or fairy-tales than allegories), but embodying them never seems to be the first impulse toward creation."

Another movie closely associated with its director is "8 1/2." Its autobiographical tone alone caused critics to take special notice: "8 1/2" concerns the rocky career and tempestuous romances of a famous film director. In this work, as in "La Dolce Vita" and another Fellini film, "Satyricon," the extras get almost as much attention as the stars. That's because the former cartoonist in the writer-director compels him to find "grotesque," exaggerated faces to people his scenes (often Fellini will sketch the type of face he wants and a production assistant will scan the Italian streets to find a person who matches the sketch). "People coming out of 'La Dolce Vita' and '8 1/2' could be heard asking, 'Where do you suppose he found them?'—as if he were a magician or a zookeeper who had turned up some fabulous specimens," notes Pauline Kael in a *New Yorker* article. "This increasingly strange human zoo into which he thrusts us is what people refer to when they say that there is a Fellini world."

In some ways, the 1974 release "Amarcord" was another breakthrough for the director—a Fellini film for those who don't like Fellini films. The most mainstream of his major movies, "Amarcord" is "simple and classic to the point of self-denial," according to Taylor, this time in a *Sight and Sound* review. "It resolves itself into a succession of scenes from provincial life, strung loosely round the experiences of Bobo, the representative of Fellini in the film, during the summer of 1935, aged about 15-16." Some critics felt Fellini had betrayed his own style in "Amarcord." Foster Hirsch, in a *Film Quarterly* review, for example, while calling the work "the director's warmest, most subdued film," adds, "it is also his safest. I miss the grand flourishes, the master showmanship, the epic heightening, that I've come to expect from Fellini. *Amarcord* lacks the vigor and drive, the joyous high spirits and sense of release that have been for me the chief pleasures of [the filmmaker's] work." "Who really wants a tasteful, restrained Fellini?" asks Taylor. "Inevitably, the bits of ['Amarcord'] one remembers are those which come closest to the old reprobate Fellini we love or loathe according to taste."

Vincent Canby, on the other hand, sees "Amarcord" as a "haunting, funny, beautiful work that makes most other recent movies . . . look as drab as winter fields without snow." In his *New York Times* column, Canby praises the film's "[circus] pace, drive, good spirits, fascination with costume and masquerade." The characters "tumble onto the screen one after another, as if there weren't going to be enough time to get through all the acts." "Like many of Fellini's films, *Amarcord* is dialectic, and contrasts boisterous public events with poignant private dreams," as *Western Humanities Review* writer Louis D. Giannetti believes. "A prominent motif in the film deals with community rituals, where the loneliness and isolation of individuals are temporarily assuaged: the opening bonfire to banish winter and welcome the spring, the Fascist rally. . . . [The private dreams] are generally associated with romantic fantasies, usually in some sexual form."

Every major artist suffers a big setback at one time or another, and for Fellini the time came in 1977, with "Casanova." A most untraditional retelling of the life of the eighteenth century's greatest lover, this movie so thoroughly put off critics and audiences that it was almost left unreleased. Typical critical reaction comes from *Village Voice*'s Andrew Sarris, who suggests that, in years to come, "Casanova" "may seem even more inexplicable than it does now. The continuity is so ragged and so gratuitous that the present film seems to have been hacked out of a much longer version with all the vital thematic connections severed."

By 1979 the director was back in production with "City of Women" and "Orchestra Rehearsal," each a parable of class consciousness. "City of Women" deals with the "fantastic journey," as Canby describes it in his *New York Times* review, of a man called Snaporaz (played by Fellini regular Marcello Mastroianni) who finds himself attracted to a mystery woman on a train. When Snaporaz follows her off the train, he finds himself "heading into a Forest of Arden as only Mr. Fellini could imagine it," Canby says. Snaporaz has happened into the City of Women, where men are the docile underclass, and most women are totalitarian in nature. "Snaporaz is ignored, ridiculed, tolerated, threatened, frightened, flirted with and, eventually, abducted by a muscular, motor bike-riding farm woman who agrees to drive Snaporaz back to his station but, instead, attempts to rape him in a lonely peapatch," Canby notes. He goes on to call "City of Women" "overlong, even for a Fellini aficionado, [but] spellbinding, a dazzling visual display that is part burlesque, part Folies-Bergeres and all cinema."

"Orchestra Rehearsal" starts out on a gentle note—a group of Italian musicians gathers in an empty chapel. They seem moody as they tune up, but when they prepare to play, "an offscreen interviewer begins to question them about themselves and their instruments," explains Melton Davis in a *New York Times* piece. "Rivalries flare, along with vanity, childish disputes, scurrilous remarks." Things don't get much better when their conductor, a German, shows up. "If the string section plays, the brass players smoke and cackle," states Davis. "One musician plays his four notes, then glues his ear to a transistor radio. Furious, the conductor shouts. Two trade union representatives stop their card game to proclaim a break. When the conductor protests, the union representatives call a double break." "Orchestra Rehearsal," a satire on Italy's political elite, raised almost as big a furor in 1979 as "La Dolce Vita" did fifteen years earlier. As Davis elaborates: "Controversy arose over the film's artistic validity, its esthetic qualities, its political content and, of course, the director's intent. Variously labeled a metaphor, a warning, an indictment, it is, according to some critics, the director's first 'political' film, one depicting a chaotic Italy headed inevitably for dictatorship."

A relatively low-keyed Fellini film, "And the Ship Sails On," came out in 1984. In this story, set on a cruise ship in wartime 1914, the writer-director "does to a number of favored opera scores what he does to the reality of conventional movies," suggests Canby in his *New York Times* column. The cruise has been organized to honor the great diva of the day, Edmea Tetua, whose recent death has not canceled the party plans. The passengers and crew break periodically into arias, with the plot, "if one can call it that, also [involving] a homesick rhinoceros being shipped to an Amsterdam zoo, and an Austro-Hungarian battleship, whose captain demands the return of [a group of] Serbian refugees," writes Canby. All this leads to an allegory of the conflicts that led to World War I. To *Washington Post* critic Gary Arnold, "the allegory is allegorical to a fault—so schematic that it doesn't allow the characters a life-sustaining format. . . . It's difficult to believe Fellini felt powerfully drawn to the period or any of the characters." But Canby, while admitting that "the movie has its share of lost moments," ultimately praises "And the Ship Sails On" as a film "constantly being brought up to new peaks of pleasure in ways that only Mr. Fellini can carry off."

For his 1986 extravaganza, "Ginger & Fred," Fellini took on mass media in the form of a garish television production that showcases "special" talent like "a troupe of dancing dwarfs, an ancient monk who performs miracles, a transvestite who comforts convicts, and a woman who was paid for not watching TV for a month, reducing her to a weeping, hysterical wreck," as *Newsweek*'s Jack Kroll describes it. Into this whirlpool comes an aging dance team, nicknamed after Ginger Rogers and Fred Astaire, who used to entertain in Italy during World War II. Summoned to Rome to appear on the television show for its extra-glitzy Christmas special, the dancers, who have not seen each other in thirty years, face a bittersweet reunion. "Ginger,"

now a no-nonsense businesswoman, is still in fine fettle, while "Fred," a boozy old rebel, can barely dip. That "Fred" is played by longtime leading-man Mastroianni, and "Ginger" by Fellini's wife, Giullietta Massina (who appeared periodically throughout her husband's films, most notably as the young waif in "La Strada"), adds a poignant note to the proceedings, many critics suggest. "Yes, we do get to see this 'Ginger and Fred' eventually dance—but Fellini milks the big moment for all it's worth by delaying it with a power-failure blackout on the TV studio's gaudy neon-and-mirror set," notes *Los Angeles Times* critic Kevin Thomas.

Though television is the target in "Ginger & Fred," "anyone expecting an Italian 'Network' will be disappointed," offers Tom Shales in a *Washington Post* review. "Fellini sees television merely as a symptom of cultural pollution. It's everywhere, like the uncollected garbage piled up on Roman streets." Still, while "Ginger & Fred" is "no laugh riot," says Shales, "it might be considered a smile riot, if there can be such a thing. It's a hard movie to love, but Fellini retains enough of the old irreverent bravado so that it would be a much harder one to hate." Kroll takes a more enthusiastic view of "Ginger & Fred," writing: "Amid all the extravagant characters the most chilling . . . is the deadpan young woman who shepherds the show's guests, a cute bitch who shows no human feeling whatsoever. For Fellini emotional coldness has always been the supreme sin." In this work, the critic concludes, Fellini has produced a "scathing but sweet elegy for elegance and grace."

"If one were to single out one quality that distinguishes Fellini's career-long imaginative evolution," writes Frank Burke in *Southwest Review*, "it would be the drive for individuation, the search for ever more authentic ways of rendering growth in his world. Even his early movies—films of increasing alienation—reveal growing pressure for individuation within his imagination and his characters. . . . And as Fellini's imagination refines its capacity to create unique and singular creatures, it also evolves beyond stories of individuation-through-alienation to stories of individuation-through-integration."

MEDIA ADAPTATIONS: "Nights of Cabiria" was adapted into the stage and movie musical "Sweet Charity"; "8 1/2" was adapted into the stage musical "Nine."

BIOGRAPHICAL/CRITICAL SOURCES:

BOOKS

Alpert, Hollis, *Fellini, a Life,* Atheneum, 1986.
Benderson, Albert, *Critical Approaches to Federico Fellini's "8 1/2,"* Arno, 1974.
Betti, Liliana, *Fellini,* Little, Brown, 1979.
Contemporary Literary Criticism, Volume 16, Gale, 1980.
Fellini, Federico, *Fare un film,* Einaud, 1980.
Fellini, Federico, *Fellini,* L'Arc, 1971.
Fellini, Federico, *Fellini on Fellini,* Delacorte/S. Lawrence, 1976.
Harcourt, Peter, *Six European Directors: Essays on the Meaning of Film Style,* Penguin, 1974.
Hughes, Eileen L., *On the Set of Fellini Satyricon: A Behind-the-Scenes Diary,* Morrow, 1970.
Ketchan, Charles B., *Federico Fellini,* Paulist Press, 1976.
Murray, Edward, *Fellini, the Artist,* Ungar, 1977.
Rosenthal, Stuart, *The Cinema of Federico Fellini,* A. S. Barnes, 1974.
Salachas, Gilbert, *Federico Fellini,* Crown, 1969.
Solmi, Angelo, *Fellini,* Humanities, 1968.

Taylor, John Russell, *Cinema Eye, Cinema Ear: Some Key Film Makers of the Sixties,* Hill & Wang, 1964.

PERIODICALS

American Film, May, 1979.
Chicago Tribune, February 19, 1980.
Commonweal, March 15, 1963.
Film Culture, November 1, 1956, January, 1958.
Film Quarterly, fall, 1975.
Hudson Review, autumn, 1961.
Los Angeles Times, February 15, 1984, April 11, 1986.
Nation, September 15, 1979.
Newsweek, March 31, 1986.
New York, February 21, 1977.
New Yorker, March 14, 1970.
New York Review of Books, December 23, 1965.
New York Times, April 26, 1956, September 20, 1974, February 18, 1979, August 17, 1979, November 12, 1979, April 8, 1981, January 22, 1984, January 26, 1984, June 18, 1989.
Sight and Sound, autumn, 1970.
Southwest Review, winter, 1979.
Time, January 23, 1984, March 31, 1986.
Times (London), November 6, 1986, November 7, 1986.
Times Literary Supplement, November 18, 1983.
Village Voice, February 28, 1977.
Washington Post, May 11, 1982, February 10, 1984, April 16, 1986.
Western Humanities Review, spring, 1976.*

—*Sketch by Susan Salter*

* * *

FERGUSON, William (Rotch) 1943-

PERSONAL: Born February 14, 1943, in Fall River, MA; son of William III (in insurance) and Helen (Rotch) Ferguson; married Lucy Emerson Collins, July 8, 1962 (divorced, 1968); married Raquel Halty, June 22, 1968 (divorced, 1980); married Nancy King, November 26, 1983. *Education:* Harvard University, B.A., 1965, M.A., 1970, Ph.D., 1975.

ADDRESSES: Home—1 Tahanto Rd., Worcester, MA 01602. *Office*—Estabrook 302, Clark University, Worcester, MA 01610.

CAREER: Ferguson Press, Cambridge, MA, owner, 1964-80; Halty Ferguson Publishing Co. (publishers of modern poetry), Cambridge, owner, 1970-80; Boston University, Boston, MA, instructor, 1971-77; Clark University, Worcester, MA, assistant professor, 1977-84, associate professor, 1984—, chairman of foreign languages department, 1990—; Metacom Press, Worcester, owner, 1980—.

WRITINGS:

Revolution Dream (poetry), Pym-Randall, 1970.
Light of Paradise (poetry), Penmaen Press, 1973.
Dream Reader (poetry), Halty Ferguson, 1973.
Freedom and Other Fictions, Knopf, 1984.

WORK IN PROGRESS: A novel; "short stories of a Magical Realist character."

* * *

FISHER, Philip 1941-

PERSONAL: Born October 11, 1941, in Pittsburgh, PA; son of Leo (a federal government employee) and Anna (a nurse; maiden name, Walker) Fisher; children: Mark. *Education:* University of Pittsburgh, B.A. (magna cum laude), 1963; Harvard University, M.A., 1966, Ph.D., 1970.

ADDRESSES: Home—82 Irving St., Cambridge, MA 02138. *Office*—Department of English, Warren House, Harvard University, Cambridge, MA 02138.

CAREER: University of Virginia, Charlottesville, assistant professor of English, 1970-72; Brandeis University, Waltham, MA, assistant professor, 1972-79, associate professor, 1979-84, professor of English, beginning 1984; currently professor of English, Harvard University, Cambridge, MA. Visiting Andrew Mellon Assistant Professor, Harvard University, 1976-77; visiting professor, Free University of Berlin, 1981, University of Konstanz, 1986, and Yale University, 1986. Fellow, Wissenschafts-Kulleg (Institute for Advanced Study), Berlin, 1987-88.

MEMBER: Phi Beta Kappa.

AWARDS, HONORS: Nomination for National Book Critics Circle Award in Criticism, 1985, for *Hard Facts: Setting and Form in the American Novel.*

WRITINGS:

Making up Society: The Novels of George Eliot, University of Pittsburgh Press, 1981.
Hard Facts: Setting and Form in the American Novel, Oxford University Press, 1984.
Making and Effacing Art, Oxford University Press, 1990.

WORK IN PROGRESS: A study of the passions in literature and philosophy, *Vehemence and Wonder; New Cambridge History of American Literature.*

BIOGRAPHICAL/CRITICAL SOURCES:

PERIODICALS

Times Literary Supplement, November 22, 1985.

* * *

FLETCHER, Leon 1921-

PERSONAL: Born August 28, 1921, in San Francisco, CA; married: wife's name, Vivian; children: Nancy, Lorie. *Education:* College of San Mateo, A.A., 1941; San Jose State College (now California State University), B.A., 1943; Columbia University and University of California, Berkeley, graduate study; University of Southern California, M.S., 1958; University of California, Los Angeles, further graduate study, 1965. *Avocational interests:* Sailing and boating.

CAREER: High school speech and English teacher in Monterey, CA, 1947-50; Taft College and High School, Taft, CA, director of public information, 1954-59, instructor in speech, radio, television, and English at college, 1959-62, director of instructional improvement at college, 1962-63; University of California, Los Angeles, research assistant in teacher education, 1963-64, communications media specialist for Nigeria project, 1964-65; Monterey Peninsula College, Monterey, CA, coordinator of instructional services, 1965-70, instructor in speech, beginning 1971. Columbia Broadcasting System, producer and director of educational television series, 1958-59; consultant to more than twenty educational agencies and institutions. *Military service:* U.S. Naval Reserve, 1942-57, active duty, 1943-45, 1950-54; became lieutenant commander; received seventeen combat awards and five personal commendations.

MEMBER: Speech Association of America, National News Registry, Western Speech Association, California Teachers Association.

WRITINGS:

Education through Television, Educational Television Research Association, 1956.
Showmanship and Scholarship, Fearon, 1958.
On the Rostrum (booklet), Standard Oil Co., 1960.
Educational Television Review (booklet), Pacific Coast Publishers, 1961.
Guidelines for Teacher-Training in Educational Television, California Council on Teacher-Training, 1963.
Basic Public Speaking, Data-Guide, 1964.
(Editor) *Cases in Junior College Administration* (study book), University Council of the University of California at Los Angeles, 1964.
Spotlight on Science (booklet), California Department of Education, 1964.
Self-Enhancing Education (training booklet), Sanford Press, 1966.
How to Design and Deliver a Speech, Chandler Publishing, 1973, 3rd edition, Harper, 1985.
Public Speaking, United Telephone Co. of Ohio, 1974.
How to Speak Like a Pro, Ballantine, 1983.
Speaking to Succeed in Business Industry Professions, Harper, 1988.

FILMSTRIPS

Public Speaking, Bailey Films, 1964.
Nigeria, Bailey Films, 1966.
Russia, Bailey Films, 1967.
Korea, Encore Visual Education, 1974.

OTHER

Also author of educational manuals. Contributor of about a 170 articles to popular magazines and to journals, including *Sail, America, TV Guide, School Executive, Junior College Journal, Audio-Visual Instruction,* and *Nigerian Television News.*

BIOGRAPHICAL/CRITICAL SOURCES:

PERIODICALS

Washington Post Book World, June 26, 1983.*

* * *

FOLLETT, Ken(neth Martin) 1949-
(Martin Martinsen, Symon Myles, Bernard L. Ross, Zachary Stone)

PERSONAL: Born June 5, 1949, in Cardiff, Wales; son of Martin D. (a tax inspector) and Lavinia C. (Evans) Follett; married Mary Emma Ruth Elson, January 5, 1968 (divorced, September 20, 1985); married Barbara Broer, November 8, 1985; children: (first marriage) Emanuele, Marie-Claire. *Education:* University College, London, B.A., 1970. *Avocational interests:* Music.

ADDRESSES: Home—London, England. *Agent*—Writers House, Inc., 21 West 26th St., New York, NY 10010.

CAREER: Trainee journalist at *South Wales Echo,* 1970-73; *Evening News,* London, England, reporter, 1973-74; Everest Books Ltd., London, editorial director, 1974-76, deputy managing director, 1976-77; writer, 1977—.

AWARDS, HONORS: Edgar Award from Mystery Writers of America, 1978, for *Eye of the Needle.*

WRITINGS:

NOVELS

The Shakeout, Harwood-Smart, 1975.
The Bear Raid, Harwood-Smart, 1976.
The Secret of Kellerman's Studio, Abelard, 1976.
Eye of the Needle (Literary Guild selection), Arbor House, 1978 (published in England as *Storm Island,* Macdonald & Jane's, 1978).
Triple, Arbor House, 1979.
The Key to Rebecca, Morrow, 1980.
The Man from St. Petersburg, Morrow, 1982.
Lie Down with Lions, Hamilton, 1985, Morrow, 1986.
The Pillars of the Earth (Literary Guild selection), Morrow, 1989.

NONFICTION

(With Rene Louis Maurice) *The Heist of the Century,* Fontana Books (London), 1978, published as *The Gentlemen of 16 July,* Arbor House, 1980, revised edition published as *Under the Streets of Nice: The Bank Heist of the Century,* National Press, 1986.
On Wings of Eagles, Morrow, 1983.

UNDER PSEUDONYM MARTIN MARTINSEN

The Power Twins and the Worm Puzzle: A Science Fantasy for Young People, Abelard, 1976.

UNDER PSEUDONYM SYMON MYLES

The Big Needle, Everest Books, 1974, published as *The Big Apple,* Kensington, 1975.
The Big Black, Everest Books, 1974.
The Big Hit, Everest Books, 1975.

UNDER PSEUDONYM BERNARD L. ROSS

Amok: King of Legend, Futura, 1976.
Capricorn One, Futura, 1978.

UNDER PSEUDONYM ZACHARY STONE

The Modigliani Scandal, Collins (London), 1976, reprinted under name Ken Follett, Morrow, 1985.
Paper Money, Collins, 1977, reprinted under name Ken Follett, Morrow, 1987.

OTHER

Also author of film scripts, "Fringe Banking," for British Broadcasting Corp., 1978, "A Football Star," with John Sealey, 1979, and "Lie Down with Lions," for Scott Reeve Enterprises, 1988. Contributor to periodicals, including *New Statesman* and *Writer.*

MEDIA ADAPTATIONS: Eye of the Needle was adapted for the screen by Stanley Mann for United Artists, 1981. *The Key to Rebecca* was filmed as an Operation Prime Time television miniseries in April, 1985; *On Wings of Eagles* was filmed by Edgar Schenick Productions as television miniseries, 1985.

WORK IN PROGRESS: Night Over Water, a novel, to be published in 1991.

SIDELIGHTS: Ken Follett has blended historical event and action-adventure fiction in a series of bestselling novels, including *Eye of the Needle, Triple, Lie Down with Lions,* and *The Pillars of the Earth.* Follett's work has proven immensely successful in the United States, making the native of Wales one of the world's youngest millionaire authors. Follett penned his first bestseller before he turned thirty, and each of his subsequent novels has made a debut with a massive first printing and vast publicity. *Washington Post* correspondent Paul Hendrickson claims that Follett has earned a reputation as an "international thriller writer with a genius for threading the eye of the literary needle."

"I was a great liver in fantasy worlds from an early age," Follett told the *Washington Post.* The son of an internal revenue clerk, Follett grew up in Cardiff, Wales and attended the University of London. After graduating with a degree in philosophy in 1970, he worked as a newspaper reporter, first in Cardiff and then in London. He began writing fiction on the side when he needed extra money for car repairs. "It was a hobby for me," he told the *Chicago Tribune.* "You know, some men go home and grow vegetables. I used to go home and write novels. A lucrative hobby. I sold them for far more than you could sell vegetables for."

Follett's early works were published under various pseudonyms. Most of these novels are murder mysteries or crime fiction, based loosely on cases he covered as a reporter for the London *Evening News.* The author admitted in the *Los Angeles Times* that he learned how to write good books "by writing mediocre ones and wondering what was wrong with them." In order to further his knowledge of the book business, Follett joined the staff of Everest Books in 1974. Remembering his decision to move to the publishing house, Follett told the *Chicago Tribune:* "A good deal of it was curiosity to know what made books sell. Some books sell and others don't. All the books I had written up to that point fell into the category of those that did not."

Follett began to use his own name on his work in 1975, when he turned to spy fiction. Within three years his dream of writing a bestseller had been fulfilled with the publication of *Eye of the Needle,* a World War II thriller about a ruthless Nazi spy and a crippled pilot's wife. In the *Washington Post Book World,* Roderick MacLeish calls *Eye of the Needle* "quite simply the best spy novel to come out of England in years," and *Newsweek* correspondent Peter Prescott describes the work as "rubbish of the very best sort . . . a triumph of invention over convention." *Eye of the Needle,* which won the Edgar Allan Poe Award from the Mystery Writers of America, has since sold more than ten million copies worldwide.

With *Eye of the Needle* Follett established himself as a new sort of thriller writer—one who found a compromise between the serious and the popular. Follett's works have been cited for their special sensitivity to female characters as well as for an overall psychological complexity not often found in adventure stories. As Andrew F. Macdonald and Gina Macdonald note in the *Dictionary of Literary Biography,* a positive feature of Follett's novels "is his humanizing of his villains. All are well rounded and complete, with credible motives and understandable passions—if anything, they are sometimes so sympathetic that they jeopardize the reader's relationship with the hero." In another *Dictionary of Literary Biography* entry, Michael Adams contends that the author's heroines "are realistically portrayed women who have led fairly ordinary lives but who are capable of heroics when needed." By creating such sympathetic heroines, Follett has been able to lure female readers to novels that traditionally appeal primarily to men.

Follett's forte—in fiction and nonfiction—is the variation upon history. Every human relationship is somehow blighted or molded by the complexities of world politics, and all the emotional and sexual entanglements are played out against a backdrop of historical events. Andrew and Gina Macdonald write: "Each of [Follett's] best works grows out of news stories and historical events. Cinematic in conception, they follow a hunter-hunted pattern that leads to exciting chase scenes and games of

wit and brinkmanship." Several of Follett's books confront the complex issues of Middle Eastern politics, and his novel *Lie Down with Lions* offers an ambiguous portrait of the factional strife in Afghanistan. *Time* contributor Michael Demarest claims that the author's strength remains "an acute sense of geographical place, and the age-old knowledge that character is action. . . . He brilliantly reproduces a distant terrain, complete with sounds and smells and tribal rites."

The danger in this sort of writing is that it can be anticlimactic, since the reader already knows how the historical conflict was resolved. In *Newsweek,* Allan J. Mayer explains that Follett manages to keep his adventures exciting even though the outcome may be evident. "Good thrillers are like elegant geometrical proofs," the critic writes. "Their drama lies not in their ultimate outcome but in their method. Though we know that the good guys will eventually triumph, we don't know how; a good thriller should keep us guessing until the last page. Ken Follett [does] just that." *New Republic* contributor Lisa Derman likewise notes that Follett "has taken one convention of the spy novel—spy accomplishes dangerous mission, barely avoiding treacherous counter-agents—and turned it inside out. . . . So the tension in the well-constructed thriller stems solely from [the hero] keeping one step ahead of his opponents. His mission . . . is complicated enough to keep one wondering how it ever could be concluded successfully."

The Pillars of the Earth, published in 1989, represents a thematic departure for Follett. A massive historical novel set in twelfth century England, *The Pillars of the Earth* concerns the construction of a vast cathedral and its creators' efforts to keep the building from falling into rival hands. *Booklist* reviewer Margaret Flanagan writes: "Follett has skillfully crafted an extraordinary epic buttressed by a succession of suspenseful subplots." Flanagan adds that *The Pillars of the Earth* is "a towering triumph of romance, rivalry, and spectacle from a major talent."

Unlike many of his contemporaries, Follett positively relishes the label "popular writer." He told the *Dictionary of Literary Biography:* "I'm not under the illusion that the world is waiting for my thoughts to appear in print. People want to be told a story, and that's what I'm up to. I think of myself as a craftsman more than an artist." Although he likes to read such noted English writers as Thomas Hardy, Jane Austen, and George Eliot, Follett remains satisfied with his own aims and accomplishments. "What I enjoy," he told the *Chicago Tribune,* "is writing a book and then having *millions* of people read it and love it. I wouldn't want to write something that ten people loved; so I'm constrained by what I think are the preferences of my readers. If I'm careful, I'll take them along with me."

CA INTERVIEW

CA interviewed Ken Follett by telephone on October 16, 1989, at his home in London, England.

CA: Though you made your reputation as a writer of thrillers, your latest novel, The Pillars of the Earth, *is set in the twelfth century and grew out of your fascination with cathedrals, which you said in a publicity release began in the early 1970s. In fact you submitted an outline for a cathedral book in 1976 that was rejected, and then went on to write* Eye of the Needle. *How did you know when the time was finally right for what became* The Pillars of the Earth?

FOLLETT: It's difficult to say. I just felt ready to do it. I felt I could cope with it, and I suppose I also felt that I had written enough thrillers. I felt the need of a break from that, or maybe the need to stop doing thrillers altogether.

CA: So the fascination with cathedrals came first, and that led you to study the Middle Ages generally?

FOLLETT: Exactly. First of all I was interested in the architecture, then I became interested in how the cathedrals were built, and then I became interested in that period of history generally.

CA: There's a lot of very nice detail in your book about everyday matters in twelfth-century England. For instance, there was a whole set of laws, sometimes contradicted by accepted common practice, governing the license to towns to hold markets. Were such details easily turned up in your research?

FOLLETT: I suppose what happens is that I use intriguing details that I come across. If you set out to discover some particular detail, that can be very difficult. But if you're just, as it were, trawling for intriguing details, they come aplenty and it's only a question of using them. For example, the fact that markets were not considered in competition if they were two-thirds of a day's journey apart was an odd detail that intrigued me, and I knew I would make use of it one way or another. When I wanted to find out actually how much stonemasons were paid in this period, it was very, very difficult. In fact, I eventually realized that the information just isn't available.

CA: I imagine there were plenty of facts to base a good guess on.

FOLLETT: Yes. About 1215, not long after the period of my book, there begins to be some information available about people's wages. So I only had to go back less than a hundred years. Of course nobody knows what would have happened to inflation, or deflation, in that period. But I'm comfortable that my money figures are not very far out.

CA: How did you find the people of the twelfth century to be fundamentally different from us, and how like us?

FOLLETT: I think you can only write a novel about another historical period on the assumption that the people in that period are basically the same as people of today. Otherwise the readers wouldn't identify with the characters in the story. So my presumption is that people are different only in superficial ways, and that their fundamental passions are the same. I think the most striking differences in the way people lived must have been twofold. One, the insecurity of life in the Middle Ages must have made life then very difficult. There was a great deal more crime—many more murders and robberies. Many more people died before living out their natural life- span. That's why the figures for life-expectancy in the Middle Ages tend to be very low. It's not because people died of old age when they were forty; it's because so many people never reached old age. They died of injury, died in battle, died of disease. The other thing, which I made a little of but not much of in the book, is that the concept of privacy as we know it now had not been invented. People slept communally and didn't feel invaded, as it were, by the presence of other people all around them when they were in bed and making love and all that sort of thing.

CA: How is the book doing in both our countries at this point, and what translations will it be going into?

FOLLETT: It's been number two on the *New York Times* bestseller list for five weeks. I haven't yet been able to knock Tom Clancy off the number-one spot. There are 450,000 copies in print. I'm very, very pleased. It's just been published in this country, and it's a little early yet to say how well it's doing here. The principal translations will appear around September, 1990. It will be translated into all the languages that have a publishing industry, which comes to about twenty.

CA: According to all accounts, your first book was prompted by a car repair bill. That book, The Big Needle, *was a mystery. Were you attracted to that genre by your own preferences as a reader?*

FOLLETT: I suppose at that time I wasn't aware, really, of the difference between a mystery and a suspense novel, and those early books of mine had elements of both, though they were predominantly mysteries. The reason I emphasize the distinction in interviews is that the first successful book I wrote was a pure suspense novel, with no mystery element.

CA: That was Eye of the Needle, *published in England as* Storm Island.

FOLLETT: Yes. So in a sense I started to do well when I cut the mystery element out of my work. Why it was there in the first place, I think, was because I did not have as clear a sense of direction as I later came to have.

CA: Does Eye of the Needle *continue to draw new readers and attract them to your other books?*

FOLLETT: It's selling about 50,000 copies a year, so it certainly is continuing to attract new readers. Whether they are people who then go on to read my other books, or are people who've read the latest book that's being advertised and then have gone back to the earlier ones, I don't know.

CA: I imagine too that the movie made from Eye of the Needle *helps the book too.*

FOLLETT: Yes. The year that the movie came out in the United States, 1981, my publisher printed an extra million copies and sold 750,000.

CA: In Twentieth-Century Crime and Mystery Writers, *Jane S. Bakerman nicely describes your approach in* Eye of the Needle, The Key to Rebecca, Triple, *and* The Man from St. Petersburg. *She says, "Follett chooses a moment of international crisis, suggests what forces might have conspired to alter the outcome of that crisis, and spins a tale which sets his fictional history back upon its factual course." How have you generally gone about choosing the moments and crises you've set your stories in?*

FOLLETT: In the case of the six books that begin with *Eye of the Needle* and finish with *Lie Down with Lions,* I have looked for that rather rare situation in which an individual spy or secret agent could have done something which might have changed the course of history. That was always my formula for finding the right sort of situation. Generally speaking, I don't think that spies and secret agents make any real difference to the course of battles and wars and history. But perhaps occasionally they do, and I've looked for situations in which they might have.

CA: Have you always been interested in history and politics?

FOLLETT: I suppose that's true—all my adult life, anyway.

CA: On Wings of Eagles *was a true adventure story, about the rescue of H. Ross Perot's men from Iran, where they were being held hostage. What did you find to be the pros and cons of writing from fact rather than being able to invent your plot?*

FOLLETT: The advantage is that you don't have to do any of that hard imaginative work of thinking up the story. The disadvantage is that real life—in its raw form, at any rate—is never quite the right shape for a good book. Things in real life don't happen with the kind of timing and other elements that are required to create suspense. So the skill of creating suspense in a nonfiction book lies in the arrangement of the material, such things as choosing from whose point of view to tell a particular scene, finding ways to make the kind of tedious, everyday situations that go into a real-life story more gripping to the reader of the story than they were to the people who lived through them.

CA: When you have a lot of research to do for a book, as you did for On Wings of Eagles *and certainly for* The Pillars of the Earth, *how do you handle the material while you're in the gathering and planning stages of your work?*

FOLLETT: There are two things I do, which I mentioned earlier. There's the general fishing expedition, looking for pertinent details and striking facts and vivid ideas, which consists of reading or skimming through books about the period, looking at magazines and pictures and so on, and sometimes reading novels set in that period of time. Then there's the searching after the particular, which is where I have a lot of help from my researchers. Some of that stuff I do myself just from my own library or going to libraries here in London, and sometimes I call my researcher in New York and tell him what I want and he gets it for me. *On Wings of Eagles* was different because most of the research for that consisted of interviewing participants in the drama, so I talked to them with a tape recorder and had the interviews transcribed. Then I would go over the interview when writing a draft, then show the draft to the interviewee, and next time we met we would talk over his comments on my draft and talk about things I realized I'd forgotten to ask him in the first interview.

CA: Do you use a computer for keeping such material stored and finding it later?

FOLLETT: I have only just invested in a full-scale word processor, since I finished *Pillars of the Earth.* But maybe that would be a good way to deal with the research material.

CA: How methodically do you plot out your books in advance?

FOLLETT: Very fully; I spend a long time writing the outline. The outline for *Pillars of the Earth* took me a year and three months to write. When an outline is finished, the story is very clearly mapped out, so the process of writing the manuscript is almost a process of filling in the details.

CA: When you sit down to write every day, then, you have a very good idea where you're going and what you're going to be doing?

FOLLETT: Yes, a very clear idea.

CA: Reviewers and critics often remark on what interesting female characters you create. Is that worth a comment?

FOLLETT: I do think it distinguishes me from most other thriller writers. It's rare to find credible women in thrillers; thrillers do tend to be a rather macho genre. I think people who say the female characters are distinctive in my work are probably right. I certainly try to keep that up. It partly comes just out of my own inclinations. I actually find it far more interesting to write women than men, particularly in a dangerous situation, because men's reactions in a dangerous situation tend to be a choice of cliches, whereas a woman's reaction could be anything. So it's partly my interest. But it's partly because, now that I've established that reputation, it's commercially quite important for me to have strong women characters in my stories. That's obviously what a lot of my readers are enjoying.

CA: And I imagine you hear from a lot of female readers.

FOLLETT: Yes, I get a lot of mail from women readers—more, I think, from women than from men.

CA: What do you enjoy reading for pleasure?

FOLLETT: I've lately been reading all of Larry McMurtry—since *Lonesome Dove,* which is the best novel by a living writer that I've read for many years. I also like Pat Conroy. I don't read many living English writers. I read the Latin American writers: Gabriel Garcia Marquez, Jorge Amado, Isabel Allende. Finally, I read quite a lot of Victorian novels. I'm reading Trollope at the moment.

CA: I was interested to read recently that you play bass guitar in a blues band. That would seem to be a perfect activity for breaks from writing.

FOLLETT: That's just what it is. Writing, particularly writing books that feature intrigue very heavily, is a process of calculating and plotting and twists and turns. It's very cerebral. Playing the guitar in a blues bank is totally sensory. And because it's so loud, it excludes all other thought anyway. I do it whenever I can. It depends somewhat on my kids; it's a family thing that we do, and now they're getting so much better than me that it's kind of condescending of them to let me play bass with them. We did in fact play several hours yesterday, and I have blisters on my fingers today to prove it.

CA: You lived in France for a while and at one time kept an apartment in New York City. Is London pretty much home for you now?

FOLLETT: Yes. I have only one house now, this one in London.

CA: You still do a lot of traveling, though, it would seem.

FOLLETT: This year I've been traveling a lot. I went to New York several times for discussions with the publishers about the marketing of *The Pillars of the Earth,* and then of course I did a tour. I'm now about to go on a tour of the Far East to promote the book there, and next year I imagine I'll do a European tour and a Scandinavian tour for the translations. In between publicity tours, nowadays I try to minimize my traveling. It takes too much time, and it's time away from the novel that I'm working on. It's not just the few days that you spend in New York or wherever it is, it's the preparation time before you go—the packing and unpacking—and also recovering from the trans-Atlantic flight, which takes more time as you get older. It really is much better to stick at the writing for long, long periods of time—months and months—without taking any more than a weekend off. And since that's the way most people in the world work, why should we complain?

CA: You indicated earlier that The Pillars of the Earth *may have marked the end of the thrillers and the beginning of a new direction in your work. Can you say more about that?*

FOLLETT: I'm working on an idea that has a suspense element in the story but is not actually a full-blooded suspense story. I have been working since I finished *The Pillars of the Earth*, which was in March, on a kind of sequel. But I think that idea is not going to make it. After working on it for six months, I've dropped it to work on another story, which I will work on very seriously for several months. At some point I may look again at the idea I've dropped, but the likelihood is that I will not do that story now. So I'm working on a story that is set in 1939, just at the outbreak of World War II. But it will be a mainstream, middlebrow novel like *The Pillars of the Earth*, not a thriller like *Eye of the Needle*.

CA: *Do you worry, with this change, about possibly losing some of the following you've had for the thrillers?*

FOLLETT: I don't think that's happening to any great extent. It's very hard to tell, of course. But because my thrillers have always been a little bit different in that they always placed less emphasis on the machinery—the weapons, the airplanes, and so on—and more emphasis on the emotions of the characters, and because they had the strong female element so that they weren't so macho, I suspect that my big fans are probably the kind of readers who would anyway quite enjoy a mainstream novel. I suspect that my readers are not the hard-core masculine-thriller readers.

CA: *Genres and labels aside, do you have long-term plans and dreams as a writer?*

FOLLETT: Pillars is the achievement of a long-term plan, so at the moment I don't have any clear dream of the future.

BIOGRAPHICAL/CRITICAL SOURCES:

BOOKS

Bestsellers 1989, issue 4, Gale, 1990.
Contemporary Literary Criticism, Volume 18, Gale, 1981.
Dictionary of Literary Biography, Volume 87: *British Mystery and Thriller Writers since 1940,* first series, Gale, 1989.
Dictionary of Literary Biography Yearbook: 1981, Gale, 1982.
Reilly, John M., editor, *Twentieth Century Crime and Mystery Writers,* St. Martin's, 1985.

PERIODICALS

Booklist, June 15, 1989.
Chicago Tribune, October 14, 1983; October 25, 1987; September 10, 1989.
Chicago Tribune Book World, October 5, 1980.
Detroit Free Press, September 10, 1989.
Globe and Mail (Toronto), September 2, 1989.
Library Journal, July, 1989.
Los Angeles Times, October 1, 1980; June 3, 1990.
Los Angeles Times Book Review, October 7, 1979; September 28, 1980; May 30, 1982; September 11, 1983; February 16, 1986.
New Statesman, April 10, 1987.
Newsweek, August 7, 1978; September 29, 1980.
New Yorker, August 21, 1978; August 16, 1982.
New York Times, May 12, 1978; October 3, 1979.
New York Times Book Review, July 16, 1978; September 21, 1980; May 9, 1982; June 30, 1985; January 26, 1986; September 10, 1989.
People, September 25, 1978.
Publishers Weekly, January 17, 1986; June 30, 1989; July 21, 1989; June 30, 1989.
Saturday Review, August, 1978.

Time, October 30, 1978; November 5, 1979; September 29, 1980; May 3, 1982.
Times Literary Supplement, December 26, 1980; June 4, 1982.
Washington Post, October 11, 1979; September 15, 1980; September 7, 1983; September 21, 1983; June 1, 1985.
Washington Post Book World, April 25, 1982; February 2, 1986; November 1, 1987; August 20, 1989.
Writer, June, 1979.

—*Sketch by Anne Janette Johnson*

—*Interview by Jean W. Ross*

*　　*　　*

FRIEL, Brian 1929-

PERSONAL: Birth-given name, Bernard Patrick Friel; born January 9, 1929, in Omagh, Tyrone, Northern Ireland; son of Patrick (a teacher) and Christina (MacLoone) Friel; married Anne Morrison, December 27, 1955; children: Paddy (daughter), Mary, Judy, Sally, David. *Education:* Attended St. Columb's College, 1941-46; St. Patrick's College, Maynooth, Ireland, B.A., 1948; St. Joseph's Teachers Training College (now St. Joseph's College of Education), graduate study, 1949-50. *Avocational interests:* Reading, trout fishing, slow tennis.

ADDRESSES: Home—Drumaweir House, Greencastle, Donegal, Ireland. *Agent*—International Creative Management, 40 West 57th St., New York, NY 10019; Curtis Brown, 162-168 Regent St., London W1R 5TB, England.

CAREER: Teacher at primary and post-primary schools in and around Derry City, Northern Ireland, 1950-60; writer, 1960—. Tyrone Guthrie Theater, observer, 1963; co-founder of Field Day Theatre Company, 1980. Member of Irish Senate.

MEMBER: Irish Academy of Letters, Aosdana.

AWARDS, HONORS: Macauley fellowship from Irish Arts Council, 1963; Christopher Ewart-Biggs Memorial Prize, British Theatre Association Award, and *Plays and Players* Award for best new play, all 1981, for *Translations; Evening Standard* award for best play of the season, 1988, for *Aristocrats.* D.Litt., Rosary College (Chicago), 1974, National University of Ireland, 1983, New University of Ulster, 1986.

WRITINGS:

PLAYS

The Francophile, produced in Belfast, 1960; produced as *The Doubtful Paradise,* Belfast, 1960.
The Enemy Within (three-act; produced in Dublin, 1962), Proscenium Press, 1975.
The Blind Mice, produced in Dublin, 1963.
Philadelphia, Here I Come! (first produced in Dublin at Gaiety Theatre, September 28, 1964; produced on Broadway at Helen Hayes Theatre, February 16, 1966), Faber, 1965, Farrar, Straus, 1966.
The Loves of Cass McGuire (first produced on Broadway at Helen Hayes Theatre, October 6, 1966), Farrar, Straus, 1967.
Lovers (two one-acts, *Winners* and *Losers;* first produced in Dublin at Gate Theatre, summer, 1967; produced on Broadway at Vivian Beaumont Theatre, June 25, 1968), Farrar, Straus, 1968.
Crystal and Fox [and] *The Mundy Scheme* (*Crystal and Fox* first produced in Dublin, 1968; produced in Los Angeles at Mark Taper Forum, February, 1969; produced in New

York, March, 1972; *The Mundy Scheme* first produced in Dublin at Olympia Theatre, June 11, 1969; produced on Broadway at Royale Theatre, December 11, 1969), Farrar, Straus, 1970.

The Gentle Island (two-act; first produced in Dublin at Olympia Theatre, 1971), Davis-Poynter, 1973.

The Freedom of the City (two-act; first produced in Dublin at Abbey Theatre, 1972; produced in Chicago at Goodman Theatre, 1974; produced on Broadway, 1974), S. French, 1974.

Volunteers (first produced in Dublin at Abbey Theatre, 1975), Faber, 1979.

Living Quarters (first produced in Dublin at Abbey Theatre, 1977), Faber, 1978.

The Faith Healer (produced in New York City, 1979), Faber, 1980.

Aristocrats (three-act; produced in Dublin, 1979), Gallery Press, 1980.

Translations (produced in Derry, 1980), Faber, 1981.

American Welcome (produced in New York City, 1980), published in *The Best Short Plays 1981*, Chilton, 1981.

(Translator) *Anton Chekhov's "Three Sisters"* (produced in Derry, 1981), Gallery Books, 1981.

The Communication Cord (produced in Derry, 1982), Faber, 1983.

Selected Plays of Brian Friel, Faber, 1984, Catholic University Press, 1986.

(Adapter) *Fathers and Sons* (based on a novel by Ivan Turgenev), first produced in London, 1987; produced in New Haven, CT, 1988.

Making History, produced in London, 1988.

Dancing at Lughnasa, produced in London, 1990.

OTHER

A Saucer of Larks (stories), Doubleday, 1962.

The Gold in the Sea (stories), Doubleday, 1966.

Selected Stories, Gallery Books, 1979.

The Diviner: Brian Friel's Best Short Stories, Devin, 1983.

(Editor) Charles McGlinchey, *The Last of the Name*, Blackstaff Press, 1986.

Author of screen adaptation of his play *Philadelphia, Here I Come!*, c. 1970; also has written for British and Irish radio and television. Contributor of stories to periodicals, including *New Yorker*.

MEDIA ADAPTATIONS: The Loves of Cass McGuire was produced on television in Dublin.

SIDELIGHTS: Brian Friel is noted for his deft use of language and his interest in Irish life and history; among his best-known plays are *Philadelphia, Here I Come!*, from 1964, and the more recent *Translations*, first produced in 1980. The story of a hopeful but heretofore luckless Irishman who immigrates to the United States, *Philadelphia* was Friel's first major success, remarkable for its adept use of a dual role: the lead actor plays both the private and public sides of the character as individual entities. The play was a long-running success in New York City and was eventually filmed as well. *Translations* was a widely welcomed, "vibrant, deeply moving work of art in which everything seems to have come together for its author," according to *Chicago Tribune* critic Richard Christiansen. Set in 1833, when British authorities mapped and renamed Ireland's old Gaelic towns, the play shows the beginning of the end of traditions and cultural identity and the roots of the modern divided Ireland. Christiansen deemed it "glorious," writing that in this work Friel "found the theme, the period of history, the language and the passion

to create a work that resonates with poetic metaphor, taking a specific incident and turning it into a profound and moving drama of universal meaning."

BIOGRAPHICAL/CRITICAL SOURCES:

BOOKS

Contemporary Literary Criticism, Gale, Volume 5, 1976, Volume 42, 1987.

Dantanus, Ulf, *Brian Friel: The Growth of an Irish Dramatist*, Faber, 1987.

Dictionary of Literary Biography, Volume 13: *British Dramatists since World War II*, Gale, 1982.

Maxwell, D. E. S., *Brian Friel*, Bucknell University Press, 1973.

PERIODICALS

Chicago Tribune, September 24, 1982.

Los Angeles Times, February 3, 1984, September 19, 1989.

New York Times, April 7, 1979, December 11, 1979, April 15, 1981, February 24, 1983, November 12, 1983, April 26, 1989, April 30, 1989.

Times (London), May 9, 1983, July 11, 1987, June 4, 1988, December 7, 1988, October 17, 1990.

Times Literary Supplement, October 15, 1982, June 3, 1983.

*   *   *

FROST, Robert (Lee) 1874-1963

PERSONAL: Born March 26, 1874, in San Francisco, Calif.; died January 29, 1963, in Boston, Mass.; son of William Prescott (a newspaper reporter and editor) and Isabel (a teacher; maiden name, Moodie) Frost; married Elinor Miriam White, December 19, 1895 (died, 1938); children: Elliott (deceased), Lesley (daughter), Carol (son; deceased), Irma, Marjorie (deceased), Elinor Bettina (deceased). *Education:* Attended Dartmouth College, 1892, and Harvard University 1897-99.

CAREER: Poet. Held various jobs between college studies, including bobbin boy in a Massachusetts mill, cobbler, editor of a country newspaper, schoolteacher, and farmer. Lived in England, 1912-15. Tufts College, Medford, Mass., Phi Beta Kappa poet, 1915 and 1940; Amherst College, Amherst, Mass., professor of English and poet-in-residence, 1916-20, 1923-25, and 1926-28; Harvard University, Cambridge, Mass., Phi Beta Kappa poet, 1916 and 1941; Middlebury College, Middlebury, Vt., co-founder of the Bread-Loaf School and Conference of English, 1920, annual lecturer, beginning 1920; University of Michigan, Ann Arbor, professor and poet-in-residence, 1921-23, fellow in letters, 1925-26; Columbia University, New York City, Phi Beta Kappa poet, 1932; Yale University, New Haven, Conn., associate fellow, beginning 1933; Harvard University, Charles Eliot Norton Professor of Poetry, 1936, board overseer, 1938-39, Ralph Waldo Emerson Fellow, 1939-41, honorary fellow, 1942-43; associate of Adams House; fellow in American civilization, 1941-42; Dartmouth College, Hanover, N.H., George Ticknor Fellow in Humanities, 1943-49, visiting lecturer.

MEMBER: International PEN, National Institute of Arts and Letters, American Academy of Arts and Letters, American Philosophical Society.

AWARDS, HONORS: Levinson Prize, *Poetry* magazine, 1922; Pulitzer Prize for poetry, 1924, for *New Hampshire*, 1931, for *Collected Poems*, 1937, for *A Further Range*, and, 1943, for *A Witness Tree;* Golden Rose Trophy, New England Poetry Club, 1928; Russell Loines Prize for poetry, National Institute of Arts and Letters, 1931; Mark Twain medal, 1937; Gold Medal of the

National Institute of Arts and Letters, 1939; Gold Medal of the Poetry Society of America, 1941 and 1958; Gold Medal, Limited Editions Club, 1949; unanimous resolution in his honor and gold medal from the U.S. Senate, March 24, 1950; American Academy of Poets Award, 1953; Medal of Honor, New York University, 1956; Huntington Hartford Foundation Award, 1958; Emerson-Thoreau Medal, American Academy of Arts and Sciences, 1958; participated in President John F. Kennedy's inauguration ceremonies, 1961, by reading his poems "Dedication" and "The Gift Outright"; Congressional Gold Medal, 1962; Edward MacDowell Medal, 1962; Bollingen Prize in Poetry, 1963; inducted into American Poet's Corner at Cathedral of St. John the Divine, 1986. Chosen poet laureate of Vermont by the State League of Women's Clubs; more than forty honorary degrees from colleges and universities, including Oxford and Cambridge Universities, Amherst College, and the University of Michigan.

WRITINGS:

POETRY

Twilight, [Lawrence, Mass.], 1894, reprinted, University of Virginia, 1966.
A Boy's Will, D. Nutt, 1913, Holt, 1915.
North of Boston, D. Nutt, 1914, Holt, 1915, reprinted, Dodd, 1977.
Mountain Interval, Holt, 1916.
New Hampshire, Holt, 1923, reprinted, New Dresden Press, 1955.
Selected Poems, Holt, 1923.
Several Short Poems, Holt, 1924.
West-Running Brook, Holt, 1928.
Selected Poems, Holt, 1928.
The Lovely Shall Be Choosers, Random House, 1929.
The Lone Striker, Knopf, 1933.
Two Tramps in Mud-Time, Holt, 1934.
The Gold Hesperidee, Bibliophile Press, 1935.
Three Poems, Baker Library Press, 1935.
A Further Range, Holt, 1936.
From Snow to Snow, Holt, 1936.
A Witness Tree, Holt, 1942.
A Masque of Reason (verse drama), Holt, 1942.
Steeple Bush, Holt, 1947.
A Masque of Mercy (verse drama), Holt, 1947.
Greece, Black Rose Press, 1948.
Hard Not to Be King, House of Books, 1951.
Aforesaid, Holt, 1954.
The Gift Outright, Holt, 1961.
"Dedication" and "The Gift Outright" (poems read at the presidential inaugural, 1961; published with the inaugural address of J. F. Kennedy), Spiral Press, 1961.
In the Clearing, Holt, 1962.
Stopping by Woods on a Snowy Evening, Dutton, 1978.
Early Poems, Crown, 1981.
A Swinger of Birches: Poems of Robert Frost for Young People (with audio cassette), Stemmer House, 1982.
Spring Pools, Lime Rock Press, 1983.
Birches, illustrated by Ed Young, Holt, 1988.

Also author of *And All We Call American,* 1958.

POEMS ISSUED AS CHRISTMAS GREETINGS

Christmas Trees, Spiral Press, 1929.
Neither Out Far Nor In Deep, Holt, 1935.
Everybody's Sanity, [Los Angeles], 1936.
To a Young Wretch, Spiral Press, 1937.
Triple Plate, Spiral Press, 1939.

Our Hold on the Planet, Holt, 1940.
An Unstamped Letter in Our Rural Letter Box, Spiral Press, 1944.
On Making Certain Anything Has Happened, Spiral Press, 1945.
One Step Backward Taken, Spiral Press, 1947.
Closed for Good, Spiral Press, 1948.
On a Tree Fallen Across the Road to Hear Us Talk, Spiral Press, 1949.
Doom to Bloom, Holt, 1950.
A Cabin in the Clearing, Spiral Press, 1951.
Does No One but Me at All Ever Feel This Way in the Least, Spiral Press, 1952.
One More Brevity, Holt, 1953.
From a Milkweed Pod, Holt, 1954.
Some Science Fiction, Spiral Press, 1955.
Kitty Hawk, 1894, Holt, 1956.
My Objection to Being Stepped On, Holt, 1957.
Away, Spiral Press, 1958.
A-Wishing Well, Spiral Press, 1959.
Accidentally on Purpose, Holt, 1960.
The Woodpile, Spiral Press, 1961.
The Prophets Really Prophesy as Mystics, the Commentators Merely by Statistics, Spiral Press, 1962.
The Constant Symbol, [New York], 1962.

COLLECTIONS

Collected Poems of Robert Frost, Holt, 1930, new edition, 1939, reprinted, Buccaneer Books, 1983.
Selected Poems, Holt, 1934, reprinted, 1963.
Come In, and Other Poems, edited by Louis Untermeyer, Holt, 1943, reprinted, F. Watts, 1967, enlarged edition published as *The Road Not Taken: An Introduction to Robert Frost,* reprinted as *The Pocket Book of Robert Frost's Poems,* Pocket Books, 1956.
The Poems of Robert Frost, Modern Library, 1946.
You Come Too: Favorite Poems for Young Readers, Holt, 1959, reprinted, 1967.
A Remembrance Collection of New Poems by Robert Frost, Holt, 1959.
Poems, Washington Square Press, 1961.
Longer Poems: The Death of the Hired Man, Holt, 1966.
Selected Prose, edited by Hyde Cox and Edward Connery Lathem, Holt, 1966, reprinted, Collier Books, 1968.
Complete Poems of Robert Frost, Holt, 1968.
The Poetry of Robert Frost, edited by Lathem, Holt, 1969.
Robert Frost: Poetry and Prose, edited by Lawrence Thompson and Lathem, Holt, 1972.
Selected Poems, edited by Ian Hamilton, Penguin, 1973.

LETTERS

The Letters of Robert Frost to Louis Untermeyer, Holt, 1963.
Selected Letters, edited by Thompson, Holt, 1964.

OTHER

A Way Out: A One-Act Play, Harbor Press, 1929.
The Cow's in the Corn: A One-Act Irish Play in Rhyme, Slide Mountain Press, 1929.
(Contributor) John Holmes, editor, *Writing Poetry,* Writer, Inc., 1960.
(Contributor) Milton R. Konvitz and Stephen E. Whicher, editors, *Emerson,* Prentice-Hall, 1962.
Robert Frost on "Extravagance" (the text of Frost's last college lecture, Dartmouth College, November 27, 1962), [Hanover, N.H.], 1963.

Robert Frost: A Living Voice (contains speeches by Frost), edited by Reginald Cook, University of Massachusetts Press, 1974.

(With Caroline Ford) *The Less Travelled Road,* Bern Porter, 1982.

Stories for Lesley, edited by Roger D. Sell, University Press of Virginia, 1984.

Frost's papers are collected at the libraries of the University of Virginia, Amherst College, and Dartmouth College, and the Huntington Library in San Marino, California.

SIDELIGHTS: Robert Frost holds a unique and almost isolated position in American letters. "Though his career fully spans the modern period and though it is impossible to speak of him as anything other than a modern poet," writes James M. Cox, "it is difficult to place him in the main tradition of modern poetry." In a sense, Frost stands at the crossroads of nineteenth-century American poetry and modernism, for in his verse may be found the culmination of many nineteenth-century tendencies and traditions as well as parallels to the works of his twentieth-century contemporaries. Taking his symbols from the public domain, Frost developed, as many critics note, an original, modern idiom and a sense of directness and economy that reflect the imagism of Ezra Pound and Amy Lowell. On the other hand, as Leonard Unger and William Van O'Connor point out in *Poems for Study,* "Frost's poetry, unlike that of such contemporaries as Eliot, Stevens, and the later Yeats, shows no marked departure from the poetic practices of the nineteenth century." Although he avoids traditional verse forms and only uses rhyme erratically, Frost is not an innovator and his technique is never experimental.

Frost's theory of poetic composition ties him to both centuries. Like the nineteenth-century Romantics, he maintained that a poem is "never a put-up job. . . . It begins as a lump in the throat, a sense of wrong, a homesickness, a loneliness. It is never a thought to begin with. It is at its best when it is a tantalizing vagueness." Yet, "working out his own version of the 'impersonal' view of art," as Hyatt H. Waggoner observed, Frost also upheld T. S. Eliot's idea that the man who suffers and the artist who creates are totally separate. In a 1932 letter to Sydney Cox, Frost explained his conception of poetry: "The objective idea is all I ever cared about. Most of my ideas occur in verse. . . . To be too subjective with what an artist has managed to make objective is to come on him presumptuously and render ungraceful what he in pain of his life had faith he had made graceful."

To accomplish such objectivity and grace, Frost took up nineteenth-century tools and made them new. Lawrence Thompson has explained that, according to Frost, "the self-imposed restrictions of meter in form and of coherence in content" work to a poet's advantage; they liberate him from the experimentalist's burden—the perpetual search for new forms and alternative structures. Thus Frost, as he himself put it in "The Constant Symbol," wrote his verse regular; he never completely abandoned conventional metrical forms for free verse, as so many of his contemporaries were doing. At the same time, his adherence to meter, line length, and rhyme scheme was not an arbitrary choice. He maintained that "the freshness of a poem belongs absolutely to its not having been thought out and then set to verse as the verse in turn might be set to music." He believed, rather, that the poem's particular mood dictated or determined the poet's "first commitment to metre and length of line."

Critics frequently point out that Frost complicated his problem and enriched his style by setting traditional meters against the natural rhythms of speech. Drawing his language primarily from the vernacular, he avoided artificial poetic diction by employing the accent of a soft-spoken New Englander. In *The Function of*

Criticism, Yvor Winters faulted Frost for his "endeavor to make his style approximate as closely as possible the style of conversation." But what Frost achieved in his poetry was much more complex than a mere imitation of the New England farmer idiom. He wanted to restore to literature the "sentence sounds that underlie the words," the "vocal gesture" that enhances meaning. That is, he felt the poet's ear must be sensitive to the voice in order to capture with the written word the significance of sound in the spoken word. "The Death of the Hired Man," for instance, consists almost entirely of dialogue between Mary and Warren, her farmer-husband, but critics have observed that in this poem Frost takes the prosaic patterns of their speech and makes them lyrical. To Ezra Pound "The Death of the Hired Man" represented Frost at his best—when he "dared to write . . . in the natural speech of New England; in natural spoken speech, which is very different from the 'natural' speech of the newspapers, and of many professors."

Frost's use of New England dialect is only one aspect of his often discussed regionalism. Within New England, his particular focus was on New Hampshire, which he called "one of the two best states in the Union," the other being Vermont. In an essay entitled "Robert Frost and New England: A Revaluation," W. G. O'Donnell noted how from the start, in *A Boy's Will,* "Frost had already decided to give his writing a local habitation and a New England name, to root his art in the soil that he had worked with his own hands." Reviewing *North of Boston* in the *New Republic,* Amy Lowell wrote, "Not only is his work New England in subject, it is so in technique. . . . Mr. Frost has reproduced both people and scenery with a vividness which is extraordinary." Many other critics have lauded Frost's ability to realistically evoke the New England landscape; they point out that one can visualize an orchard in "After Apple-Picking" or imagine spring in a farmyard in "Two Tramps in Mud Time." In this "ability to portray the local truth in nature," O'Donnell claims, Frost has no peer. The same ability prompted Pound to declare, "I know more of farm life than I did before I had read his poems. That means I know more of 'Life.' "

Frost's regionalism, critics remark, is in his realism, not in politics; he creates no picture of regional unity or sense of community. In *The Continuity of American Poetry,* Roy Harvey Pearce describes Frost's protagonists as individuals who are constantly forced to confront their individualism as such and to reject the modern world in order to retain their identity. Frost's use of nature is not only similar but closely tied to this regionalism. He stays as clear of religion and mysticism as he does of politics. What he finds in nature is sensuous pleasure; he is also sensitive to the earth's fertility and to man's relationship to the soil. To critic M. L. Rosenthal, Frost's pastoral quality, his "lyrical and realistic repossession of the rural and 'natural,' " is the staple of his reputation.

Yet, just as Frost is aware of the distances between one man and another, so he is also always aware of the distinction, the ultimate separateness, of nature and man. Marion Montgomery has explained, "His attitude toward nature is one of armed and amicable truce and mutual respect interspersed with crossings of the boundaries" between individual man and natural forces. Below the surface of Frost's poems are dreadful implications, what Rosenthal calls his "shocked sense of the helpless cruelty of things." This natural cruelty is at work in "Design" and in "Once by the Pacific." The ominous tone of these two poems prompted Rosenthal's further comment: "At his most powerful Frost is as staggered by 'the horror' as Eliot and approaches the hysterical edge of sensibility in a comparable way. . . . His is still the modern mind in search of its own meaning."

The austere and tragic view of life that emerges in so many of Frost's poems is modulated by his metaphysical use of detail. As Frost portrays him, man might be alone in an ultimately indifferent universe, but he may nevertheless look to the natural world for metaphors of his own condition. Thus, in his search for meaning in the modern world, Frost focuses on those moments when the seen and the unseen, the tangible and the spiritual intersect. John T. Napier calls this Frost's ability "to find the ordinary a matrix for the extraordinary." In this respect, he is often compared with Emily Dickinson and Ralph Waldo Emerson, in whose poetry, too, a simple fact, object, person, or event will be transfigured and take on greater mystery or significance. The poem "Birches" is an example: it contains the image of slender trees bent to the ground-temporarily by a boy's swinging on them or permanently by an ice-storm. But as the poem unfolds, it becomes clear that the speaker is concerned not only with child's play and natural phenomena, but also with the point at which physical and spiritual reality merge.

Such symbolic import of mundane facts informs many of Frost's poems, and in "Education by Poetry" he explained: "Poetry begins in trivial metaphors, pretty metaphors, 'grace' metaphors, and goes on to the profoundest thinking that we have. Poetry provides the one permissible way of saying one thing and meaning another. . . . Unless you are at home in the metaphor, unless you have had your proper poetical education in the metaphor, you are not safe anywhere."

Frost's own poetical education began in San Francisco where he was born in 1874, but he found his place of safety in New England when his family moved to Lawrence, Massachusetts, in 1884 following his father's death. The move was actually a return, for Frost's ancestors were originally New Englanders. The region must have been particularly conducive to the writing of poetry because within the next five years Frost had made up his mind to be a poet. In fact, he graduated from Lawrence High School, in 1892, as class poet (he also shared the honor of co-valedictorian with his wife-to-be Elinor White); and two years later, the *New York Independent* accepted his poem entitled "My Butterfly," launching his status as a professional poet with a check for $15.00.

To celebrate his first publication, Frost had a book of six poems privately printed; two copies of *Twilight* were made—one for himself and one for his fiancee. Over the next eight years, however, he succeeded in having only thirteen more poems published. During this time, Frost sporadically attended Dartmouth and Harvard and earned a living teaching school and, later, working a farm in Derby, New Hampshire. But in 1912, discouraged by American magazines' constant rejection of his work, he took his family to England, where he could "write and be poor without further scandal in the family." In England, Frost found the professional esteem denied him in his native country. Continuing to write about New England, he had two books published, *A Boy's Will* and *North of Boston,* which established his reputation so that his return to the United States in 1915 was as a celebrated literary figure. Holt put out an American edition of *North of Boston,* and periodicals that had once scorned his work now sought it.

Since 1915 Frost's position in American letters has been firmly rooted; in the years before his death he came to be considered the unofficial poet laureate of the United States. On his seventy-fifth birthday, the U.S. Senate passed a resolution in his honor which said, "His poems have helped to guide American thought and humor and wisdom, setting forth to our minds a reliable representation of ourselves and of all men." In 1955, the State of Vermont named a mountain after him in Ripton, the town of his legal residence; and at the presidential inauguration of John F. Kennedy in 1961, Frost was given the unprecedented honor of being asked to read a poem, "The Gift Outright," which he wrote for the occasion.

Though Frost allied himself with no literary school or movement, the imagists helped at the start to promote his American reputation. *Poetry: A Magazine of Verse* published his work before others began to clamor for it. It also published a review by Ezra Pound of the British edition of *A Boy's Will,* which Pound said "has the tang of the New Hampshire woods, and it has just this utter sincerity. It is not post-Miltonic or post-Swinburnian or post Kiplonian. This man has the good sense to speak naturally and to paint the thing, the thing as he sees it." Amy Lowell reviewed *North of Boston* in the *New Republic,* and she, too, sang Frost's praises: "He writes in classic metres in a way to set the teeth of all the poets of the older schools on edge; and he writes in classic metres, and uses inversions and cliches whenever he pleases, those devices so abhorred by the newest generation. He goes his own way, regardless of anyone else's rules, and the result is a book of unusual power and sincerity." In these first two volumes, Frost introduced not only his affection for New England themes and his unique blend of traditional meters and colloquialism, but also his use of dramatic monologues and dialogues. "Mending Wall," the leading poem in *North of Boston,* describes the friendly argument between the speaker and his neighbor as they walk along their common wall replacing fallen stones; their differing attitudes toward "boundaries" offer symbolic significance typical of the poems in these early collections.

Mountain Interval marked Frost's turn to another kind of poem, a brief meditation sparked by an object, person or event. Like the monologues and dialogues, these short pieces have a dramatic quality. "Birches," discussed above, is an example, as is "The Road Not Taken," in which a fork in a woodland path transcends the specific. The distinction of this volume, the *Boston Transcript* said, "is that Mr. Frost takes the lyricism of 'A Boy's Will' and plays a deeper music and gives a more intricate variety of experience."

Several new qualities emerged in Frost's work with the appearance of *New Hampshire,* particularly a new self-consciousness and willingness to speak of himself and his art. The volume, for which Frost won his first Pulitzer Prize, "pretends to be nothing but a long poem with notes and grace notes," as Louis Untermeyer described it. The title poem, approximately fourteen pages long, is a "rambling tribute" to Frost's favorite state and "is starred and dotted with scientific numerals in the manner of the most profound treatise." Thus, a footnote at the end of a line of poetry will refer the reader to another poem seemingly inserted to merely reinforce the text of "New Hampshire." Some of these poems are in the form of epigrams, which appear for the first time in Frost's work. "Fire and Ice," for example, one of the better known epigrams, speculates on the means by which the world will end. Frost's most famous and, according to J. McBride Dabbs, most perfect lyric, "Stopping by Woods on a Snowy Evening," is also included in this collection; conveying "the insistent whisper of death at the heart of life," the poem portrays a speaker who stops his sleigh in the midst of a snowy woods only to be called from the inviting gloom by the recollection of practical duties. Frost himself said of this poem that it is the kind he'd like to print on one page followed with "forty pages of footnotes."

West-Running Brook, Frost's fifth book of poems, is divided into six sections, one of which is taken up entirely by the title poem.

This poem refers to a brook which perversely flows west instead of east to the Atlantic like all other brooks. A comparison is set up between the brook and the poem's speaker who trusts himself to go by "contraries"; further rebellious elements exemplified by the brook give expression to an eccentric individualism, Frost's stoic theme of resistance and self-realization. Reviewing the collection in the *New York Herald Tribune*, Babette Deutsch wrote: "The courage that is bred by a dark sense of Fate, the tenderness that broods over mankind in all its blindness and absurdity, the vision that comes to rest as fully on kitchen smoke and lapsing snow as on mountains and stars—these are his, and in his seemingly casual poetry, he quietly makes them ours."

A Further Range, which earned Frost another Pulitzer Prize and was a Book-of-the-Month Club selection, contains two groups of poems subtitled "Taken Doubly" and "Taken Singly." In the first, and more interesting, of these groups, the poems are somewhat didactic, though there are humorous and satiric pieces as well. Included here is "Two Tramps in Mud Time," which opens with the story of two itinerant lumbermen who offer to cut the speaker's wood for pay; the poem then develops into a sermon on the relationship between work and play, vocation and avocation, preaching the necessity to unite them. Of the entire volume, William Rose Benet wrote, "It is better worth reading than nine-tenths of the books that will come your way this year. In a time when all kinds of insanity are assailing the nations it is good to listen to this quiet humor, even about a hen, a hornet, or Square Matthew. . . . And if anybody should ask me why I still believe in my land, I have only to put this book in his hand and answer, 'Well-here is a man of my country.'"

Most critics acknowledge that Frost's poetry in the forties and fifties grew more and more abstract, cryptic, and even sententious, so it is generally on the basis of his earlier work that he is judged. His political conservatism and religious faith, hitherto informed by skepticism and local color, became more and more the guiding principles of his work. He had been, as Randall Jarrell points out, "a very odd and very radical radical when young" yet became "sometimes callously and unimaginatively conservative" in his old age. He had become a public figure, and in the years before his death, much of his poetry was written from this stance.

Reviewing A Witness Tree in *Books,* Wilbert Snow noted a few poems "which have a right to stand with the best things he has written": "Come In," "The Silken Tent," and "Carpe Diem" especially. Yet Snow went on: "Some of the poems here are little more than rhymed fancies; others lack the bullet-like unity of structure to be found in 'North of Boston.'" On the other hand, Stephen Vincent Benet felt that Frost had "never written any better poems than some of those in this book." Similarly, critics were let down by *In the Clearing.* One wrote, "Although this reviewer considers Robert Frost to be the foremost contemporary U.S. poet, he regretfully must state that most of the poems in this new volume are disappointing. . . . [They] often are closer to jingles than to the memorable poetry we associate with his name." Another maintained that "the bulk of the book consists of poems of 'philosophic talk.' Whether you like them or not depends mostly on whether you share the 'philosophy.'"

Indeed, many readers do share Frost's philosophy, and still others who do not nevertheless continue to find delight and significance in his large body of poetry. In October, 1963, President John F. Kennedy delivered a speech at the dedication of the Robert Frost Library in Amherst, Massachusetts. "In honoring Robert Frost," the President said, "we therefore can pay honor to the deepest source of our national strength. That strength takes many forms and the most obvious forms are not always the most significant. . . . Our national strength matters; but the spirit which informs and controls our strength matters just as much. This was the special significance of Robert Frost." The poet would probably have been pleased by such recognition, for he had said once, in an interview with Harvey Breit: "One thing I care about, and wish young people could care about, is taking poetry as the first form of understanding. If poetry isn't understanding all, the whole world, then it isn't worth anything."

BIOGRAPHICAL/CRITICAL SOURCES:

BOOKS

Anderson, Margaret, *Robert Frost and John Bartlett: The Record of a Friendship,* Holt, 1963.

Barry, Elaine, compiler, *Robert Frost on Writing,* Rutgers University Press, 1973.

Barry, Elaine, *Robert Frost,* Ungar, 1973.

Breit, Harvey, *The Writer Observed,* World PublishIng, 1956.

Concise Dictionary of American Literary Biography: The Twenties, 1917-1929, Gale, 1989.

Contemporary Literary Criticism, Gale, Volume 1, 1973, Volume 3, 1975, Volume 4, 1975, Volume 9, 1978, Volume 10, 1979, Volume 13, 1980, Volume 15, 1980, Volume 26, 1983, Volume 34, 1985, Volume 44, 1987.

Cook, Reginald L., *The Dimensions of Robert Frost,* Rinehart, 1958.

Cook, Reginald L., *Robert Frost: A Living Voice,* University of Massachusetts Press, 1974.

Cox, James M., *Robert Frost: A Collection of Critical Essays,* Prentice-Hall, 1962.

Cox, Sidney, *Swinger of Birches: A Portrait of Robert Frost,* New York University Press, 1957.

Dictionary of Literary Biography, Volume 54: *American Poets, 1880-1945, Third Series,* Gale, 1987.

Dodd, Loring Holmes, *Celebrities at Our Hearthside,* Dresser, 1959.

Doyle, John R., Jr., *Poetry of Robert Frost: An Analysis,* Hallier, 1965.

Evans, William R., editor, *Robert Frost and Sidney Cox: Forty Years of Friendship,* University Press of New England, 1981.

Francis, Robert, recorder, *A Time to Talk: Conversations and Indiscretions,* University of Massachusetts Press, 1972.

Frost, Lesley, *New Hampshire's Child: Derry Journals of Lesley Frost,* State University of New York Press, 1969.

Gerber, Philip L., *Robert Frost,* Twayne, 1966.

Gould, Jean, *Robert Frost: The Aim Was Song,* Dodd, 1964.

Grade, Arnold, editor, *Family Letters of Robert and Elinor Frost,* State University of New York Press, 1972.

Greiner, Donald J., *Checklist of Robert Frost,* Charles E. Merrill, 1969.

Greiner, Donald J. and Charles Sanders, *Robert Frost: The Poet and His Critics,* American Library Association, 1974.

Hall, Donald, *Remembering Poets,* Hater, 1977.

Isaacs, Emily Elizabeth, *Introduction to Robert Frost,* A. Swallow, 1962, reprinted, Haskell House, 1972.

Jarrell, Randall, *Poetry and the Age,* Vintage, 1955.

Jennings, Elizabeth, *Frost,* Barnes & Noble, 1966.

Lathem, Edward C. and Lawrance Thompson, editors, *Robert Frost: Farm Poultryman; The Story of Robert Frost's Career As a Breeder and Fancier of Hens,* Dartmouth Publishers, 1963.

Lathem, Edward C., editor, *Interviews with Robert Frost,* Rinehart, 1966.

Lathem, Edward C., editor, *A Concordance to the Poetry of Robert Frost,* Holt Information Systems, 1971.

Lentriccia, Frank, *Robert Frost: Modern Poetics and the Landscapes of Self,* Duke University Press, 1975.

Lowell, Amy, *Tendencies in Modern American Poetry,* Macmillan, 1917.

Mertins, Marshall Louis and Esther Mertins, *Intervals of Robert Frost: A Critical Bibliography,* University of California Press, 1947, reprinted, Russell, 1975.

Mertins, Marshall Louis, *Robert Frost: Life and Talks—Walking,* University of Oklahoma Press, 1965.

Munson, Gorham B., *Robert Frost: A Study in Sensibility and Good Sense,* G. H. Doran, 1927, reprinted, Haskell House, 1969.

Newdick, Robert Spangler, *Newdick's Season of Frost: An Interrupted Biography of Robert Frost,* edited by William A. Sutton, State University of New York Press, 1976.

Orton, Vrest, *Vermont Afternoons with Robert Frost,* Tuttle, 1971.

Pearce, Roy Harvey, *The Continuity of American Poetry,* Princeton, 1961.

Poirier, Richard, *Robert Frost,* Oxford University Press, 1977.

Pound, Ezra, *The Literary Essays of Ezra Pound,* New Directions, 1954.

Pritchard, William H., *Frost: A Literary Life Reconsidered,* Oxford University Press, 1984.

Reeve, Franklin D., *Robert Frost in Russia,* Little, Brown, 1964.

Rosenthal, M. L., *The Modern Poets,* Oxford University Press, 1965.

Shepley, Elizabeth, *Robert Frost: The Trial by Existence,* Holt, 1960.

Sohn, David A. and Richard Tyre, *Frost: The Poet and His Poetry,* Holt, 1967.

Spiller, Robert E. and others, *Literary History of the United States,* 4th revised edition, Macmillan, 1974.

Squires, Radcliffe, *Major Themes of Robert Frost,* University of Michigan Press, 1969.

Tharpe, Jac, editor, *Frost: Centennial Essays II,* University Press of Mississippi, 1976.

Thompson, Lawrence, *Fire and Ice: The Art and Thought of Robert Frost,* Holt, 1942, reprinted, Russell, 1975.

Thompson, Lawrence, *Robert Frost,* University of Minnesota Press, 1959.

Thompson, Lawrence, editor, *Selected Letters of Robert Frost,* Holt, 1964.

Thompson, Lawrence, *Robert Frost: The Early Years, 1874-1915,* Holt, 1966.

Thompson, Lawrence, *Robert Frost: The Years of Triumph, 1915-1938,* Holt, 1970.

Thompson, Lawrence and R. H. Winnick, *Robert Frost: The Later Years, 1938-1963,* Holt, 1976.

Unger, Leonard and William Van O'Connor, *Poems for Study,* Holt, 1953.

Untermeyer, Louis, *Makers of the Modern World,* Simon & Schuster, 1955.

Untermeyer, Louis, *Lives of the Poets,* Simon & Schuster, 1959.

Untermeyer, Louis, *Robert Frost: A Backward Look,* U.S. Government Printing Office, 1964.

Van Egmond, Peter, *The Critical Reception of Robert Frost,* G. K. Hall, 1974.

Waggoner, Hyatt H., *American Poetry from the Puritans to the Present,* Houghton, 1968.

Wagner, Linda Welshimer, editor, *Robert Frost: The Critical Reception,* B. Franklin, 1977.

West, Herbert Faulkner, *Mind on the Wing,* Coward, 1947.

Winters, Yvor, *The Function of Criticism,* A. Swallow, 1957.

PERIODICALS

America, December 24, 1977.
American Literature, January, 1948.
Atlantic, February, 1964, November, 1966.
Bookman, January, 1924.
Books, May 10, 1942.
Boston Transcript, December 2, 1916.
Commonweal, May 4, 1962, April 1, 1977.
New Republic, February 20, 1915.
New York Herald Tribune, November 18, 1928.
New York Times, October 19, 1986.
New York Times Book Review, July 17, 1988.
New York Times Magazine, June 11, 1972, August 18, 1974.
Poetry, May, 1913.
Saturday Review of Literature, May 30, 1936, April 25, 1942.
South Atlantic Quarterly, summer, 1958.
Times Literary Supplement, December 14, 1967.
Virginia Quarterly Review, summer, 1957.
Wisconsin Library Bulletin, July, 1962.
Yale Review, spring, 1934, summer, 1948.

OBITUARIES:

PERIODICALS

Current Biography, March, 1963.
Illustrated London News, February 9, 1963.
Newsweek, February 11, 1963.
New York Times, January 30, 1963.
Publishers Weekly, February 11, 1963.*

*   *   *

FULLER, Elizabeth 1946-

PERSONAL: Born September 22, 1946, in Cleveland, OH; daughter of Lewis Frank (in insurance) and Isabelle (Rooney) Brancae; married John Grant Fuller (a writer), November 18, 1976; children: Christopher. *Education:* Attended Ohio State University, 1965-66. *Politics:* Democrat. *Religion:* Unitarian.

ADDRESSES: Home and office—72 River Rd., Weston, CT 06883. *Agent*—Roberta Pryor Literary Agents, Inc., 24 West 55th, New York, NY 10017.

CAREER: Northwest Orient Airlines, Minneapolis, MN, flight attendant, 1968-75; researcher, 1975-78; writer, 1978—. Inventer of board game, "Fleece the Flock: The TV Evangelist Game," Regent Continental Games, 1989.

MEMBER: Nuclear Freeze Movement.

WRITINGS:

My Search for the Ghost of Flight 401 (nonfiction), Berkley Publishing, 1978.

Poor Elizabeth's Almanac (nonfiction), Berkley Publishing, 1980.

Not Just a Love Story (play), first produced in Bridgeport, CT, at University of Bridgeport, November 5, 1981.

Having Your First Baby after Thirty: A Personal Journey from Infertility to Childbirth (nonfiction), Dodd, 1983.

Nima: A Sherpa in Connecticut (nonfiction), Dodd, 1984.

The Touch of Grace, Dodd, 1986.

Everyone Is Psychic: The Edgar Cayce Way to Unlock Your Own Hidden Psychic Ability for a Richer, More Rewarding Life (nonfiction), Crown, 1989.

Me and Jezebel, Berkley Publishing, 1991.

WORK IN PROGRESS: Christopher and the Magic Monster Trap, children's book.

SIDELIGHTS: Elizabeth Fuller told *CA:* "*Nima: A Sherpa in Connecticut* tells the story of our young Sherpa guide on our trek to the base of Mt. Everest. Nima was suffering from tuberculosis, and we brought him back to the United States for special treatment. Under good medical attention Nima completely recovered and also became completely Americanized. Never having seen television, he became addicted. One morning he came to breakfast and announced he was going to buy an American Express card because Sir Edmund Hilary had said: 'No leave home without one.' (Hilary, of course, is almost a Sherpa god.) I found Nima using three kinds of toothpaste: 'This one,' he said, 'no holes. This one make breath good. This one make teeth white.' When he first greeted us in America he bowed and said, '*Nameste.*' When he left after six months he said, 'Take it easy, ya hear?' He had saved the money he earned here, and now back in the high Himals, he has built his dream tea house on the yak caravan route to Tibet.

"*Poor Elizabeth's Almanac* tells of our long, no-bath trek in the Himalayas and an incident when I started automatic writing to spill out more than one hundred proverbs one night. Critics found them unusual and not at all soupy: 'If you heard it through the grapevine, the wine is probably sour.' 'Men of few words—should be.' 'He who worries about the future has every reason to.' 'If your dreams never come true, stop dreaming.' 'There are only two people who should ponder the past—historians and bores.' The proverbs went on and on like that, and I know I could never write anything like that consciously. Must have been the 14,000-foot altitude!

"*My Search for the Ghost of Flight 401* is a sequel to my husband's *The Ghost of Flight 401,* in which I helped him research the strange happenings following the crash of an Eastern Airlines jet in the Everglades in 1972. As part of my research I interviewed scores of flight attendants, pilots, and other airline personnel who claim to have seen the dead pilot reappear aboard other Eastern ships to warn if anything dangerous was to happen. During this time I became a serious student of the paranormal. My book tells of my sudden psychic developments in conjunction with researching this story.

"From both my work with Northwest Orient as a flight attendant and from helping my husband research his books, I've touched down in most of the major areas of the world. Most interesting were the high altitude monasteries in the Himalayas, the Spice Islands of Indonesia, and the Asmat head hunters in West Irian. I also enjoyed observing helicopter rescues in the Alps, probing the dioxin tragedy in four towns north of Milan, exploring the Komodo dragons of that island, spotting humpback whales in the Banda Sea, and investigating the strange powers of the Dutch mystic Croiset in Holland.

"I have discovered, however, that I don't need a visa to continue writing. I have settled into the semi-comfortable life of a full-time mother and full-time writer. *Having Your First Baby after Thirty* was started during my sixth month of pregnancy, after I had gone through several years of unsuccessful attempts to conceive. Now I am no longer trying to populate the world, nor am I traveling to remote, exotic lands."

G

GARDAM, Jane 1928-

PERSONAL: Born July 11, 1928, in Coatham, Yorkshire, England; daughter of William (a schoolmaster) and Kathleen (Helm) Pearson; married David Gardam (a Queen's counsel), April 20, 1954; children: Timothy, Mary, Thomas. *Education:* Bedford College, London, B.A. (with honors), 1949, graduate study, 1949-52. *Politics:* Liberal Democrat. *Religion:* Church of England. *Avocational interests:* Trying to grow roses.

ADDRESSES: Home—Haven House, Sandwich, Kent, England.

CAREER: Post Graduate Research Center, London University, London, England, staff member, 1949-52; *Weldons Ladies Journal,* London, England, sub-editor, 1952-53; *Time and Tide,* London, assistant literary editor, 1953-55; writer. Organizer of hospital libraries for Red Cross, 1950.

MEMBER: Royal Society of Literature (fellow).

AWARDS, HONORS: David Higham Prize for fiction and W. Holtby Award, both 1977, both for *Black Faces, White Faces;* runner-up citation, Booker Prize, 1978, for *God on the Rocks;* Whitbread Award, 1983, for *The Hollow Land;* Katherine Mansfield Award, 1984, for *The Pangs of Love.*

WRITINGS:

JUVENILE FICTION

A Few Fair Days (short stories), Macmillan, 1971.
Bridget and William, illustrated by Janet Rawlings, Julia MacRae, 1981.
The Hollow Land, illustrated by Rawlings, Julia MacRae, 1981.
Horse, illustrated by Rawlings, Julia MacRae, 1982.
Kit, illustrated by William Geldart, Julia MacRae, 1984.
Kit in Boots, Julia MacRae, 1986.
Swan, Julia MacRae, 1986.
Through the Doll's House Door (novel), Julia MacRae, 1987.

ADULT FICTION

A Long Way from Verona (novel), Macmillan, 1971, reprinted, Hamish Hamilton, 1986.
Black Faces, White Faces (short stories), Hamish Hamilton, 1975, published as *The Pineapple Bay Hotel,* Morrow, 1976.
The Summer after the Funeral (novel), Macmillan, 1973.
Bilgewater (novel), Hamish Hamilton, 1976.

God on the Rocks (novel), Morrow, 1979.
The Sidmouth Letters (short stories), Morrow, 1980.
The Pangs of Love (short stories; also see below), Hamish Hamilton, 1983.
Crusoe's Daughter (novel), Atheneum, 1986.
Showing the Flag (short stories), Penguin, 1989.

Also author of *The Queen of the Tambourine,* 1990.

OTHER

Also author of scripts for television films, including "The Easter Lilies," based on the author's book *The Pangs of Love.* Author of essays on Lady Mary Wortley Montagu, 1983, and Gertrude Bell, 1988. Contributor of short stories to magazines.

SIDELIGHTS: Hailed in Great Britain as a writer of talent and originality, Jane Gardam has enjoyed success with children's fiction as well as with short stories and novels expressly for adults. In fact, in an essay for the *Dictionary of Literary Biography,* critic Patricia Craig expresses the opinion that categorizing Gardam's fiction strictly as "juvenile" or "adult" does the writer's work a disservice. The appeal of Gardam's fiction, writes Craig, "should not be restricted by any factor of age in the reader. . . . All of Gardam's work is marked by certain admirable characteristics: economy of style, exuberance and humor, a special relish for the startling and the unexpected."

Proof of Gardam's ability to touch readers of various ages can be found in the awards she has won: the David Higham Prize for *Black Faces, White Faces,* short stories for adults, and the prestigious Whitbread Award for *The Hollow Land,* a work ostensibly for juveniles. Jane Miller outlines Gardam's strengths in a *Times Literary Supplement* review: "[She] has a spectacular gift for detail, of the local and period kind, and for details which make characters so subtly unpredictable that they ring true, and her humor is tough as well as delicate."

Young teens on the brink of adult discovery are often the central characters in Gardam's juvenile fiction. Craig feels that Gardam's works "recreate directly the sensations and impressions of childhood." Craig also notes a slightly autobiographical cast in a number of the juvenile novels: "Although to an extent transformed in the course of writing, certain elements of Gardam's early life seem to have made a fairly consistent pattern in her books: the girl with a much younger brother; the schoolmaster or clergyman father; the Yorkshire or Cumbria locations. Each book, however, has a distinctive feeling, a mood and atmosphere all its own. Gardam repeats her motifs but not her effects. . . . [She] makes high comedy of the fidgets and fancies of adolescence, with her heroine constantly on the brink of some contretemps or social disaster; but the narrative is charged as well with a kind of muted fairy-tale glamour."

Gardam received critical acclaim for her first three children's books, but she was still virtually unknown as an author when she published her first work for adults, *Black Faces, White Faces*. The short story collection, which appeared in the United States as *The Pineapple Bay Hotel*, won Britain's David Higham for best first novel, even though it was Gardam's fourth book and not a novel at all. Craig explains that the stories in Gardam's story collections are interrelated within each volume, but "what is important is not the classification [as novel or collection] but the degree of acuity brought to bear on a theme." Indeed, publication of *Black Faces, White Faces* expanded Gardam's critical audience considerably and accorded her highly favorable reviews that have continued with subsequent story collections and novels.

Victoria Glendinning describes Gardam in the *Times Literary Supplement,* with emphasis on her adult themes: "She is a very English writer, in that her observation is at its sharpest on matters of class and status, and her most poisonous darts reserved for the upper middle classes, or rather for the female residue who no longer have servants to exploit and are ending their days in seedy stinginess." "Her manifold traps are hidden away under glass and satin," notes Raymond Sokolov in the *Washington Post Book World.* "The voice you hear is an odd combination of girl and grande dame, a voice that trills out the most sinister truths as if they were part of the court circular." In a London *Times* review of *The Pangs of Love,* Elaine Feinstein suggests that Gardam "is a spare and elegant master of her art, which is neither genteel nor gentle, and she spares the well-bred less than the vulgar, and the predictably English abroad least of all."

Throughout Gardam's fiction, juvenile and adult alike, the author explores eccentric behavior in central characters as well as supporting ones. In Craig's words, "she is interested in the discrepancy between the face one presents to the world and one's actual feelings, and the comedy which results from lack of face." A *Times Literary Supplement* reviewer also notes that Gardam's characters, "young and old, are observed with unwavering directness, their emotional hang-ups and outlets quietly understated so that the adolescent reader can take or leave the undertones." According to Craig, however, "the fanciful and highly colored in Gardam's work are always disciplined by a northern toughness and plainness of expression. . . . One of [her] greatest strengths as a writer is the ability to confine her observations to the most telling; every detail is there for a purpose."

Perhaps the most incisive comment on Gardam's talent comes from a *Times Literary Supplement* review of *A Long Way from Verona:* "Jane Gardam is a writer of such humorous intensity— glorious dialogue, hilarious set-pieces—that when one reads her for the first time one laughs aloud and when rereading her, the acid test for funny books, one's admiration increases a hundredfold." In the years since Gardam began publishing fiction, Craig concludes, she "has shown herself to be a novelist of rare inventiveness and power."

BIOGRAPHICAL/CRITICAL SOURCES:

BOOKS

Blishen, Edward, editor, *The Thorny Paradise: Writers on Writing for Children,* Kestrel, 1975.

Children's Literature Review, Volume 12, Gale, 1987.
Contemporary Literary Criticism, Volume 43, Gale, 1987.
Dictionary of Literary Biography, Volume 14: *British Novelists since 1960,* Gale, 1983.

PERIODICALS

Horn Book, October, 1978, December, 1978.
Los Angeles Times Book Review, December 21, 1980.
New Statesman, November 12, 1971, October 13, 1978, April 11, 1980.
New York Times, December 19, 1980.
New York Times Book Review, May 7, 1972, February 17, 1974, August 11, 1974, May 2, 1976, April 27, 1986.
Observer, February 13, 1983.
Spectator, November 13, 1971, December 22, 1973, November 29, 1975, December 11, 1976, November 25, 1978, May 3, 1980, February 19, 1983.
Times (London), February 10, 1983, February 9, 1985.
Times Educational Supplement, November 20, 1981.
Times Literary Supplement, November 22, 1971, December 3, 1971, November 23, 1973, September 19, 1975, December 10, 1976, October 13, 1978, April 18, 1980, March 27, 1981, September 18, 1981, February 10, 1984, May 31, 1985, July 10, 1987, July 7, 1989.
Washington Post, April 21, 1986.
Washington Post Book World, May 2, 1976, January 8, 1978.

*   *   *

GARDNER, John (Champlin), Jr. 1933-1982

PERSONAL: Born July 21, 1933, in Batavia, N.Y.; died in a motorcycle accident, September 14, 1982, in Susquehanna, Pa.; son of John Champlin (a dairy farmer) and Priscilla (a high school literature teacher; maiden name, Jones) Gardner; married Joan Louise Patterson, June 6, 1953 (divorced, 1976); married Liz Rosenberg, 1980 (divorced); children: Joel, Lucy. *Education:* De Pauw University, student, 1951-53; Washington University, St. Louis, A.B., 1955; State University of Iowa, M.A., 1956, Ph.D., 1958.

ADDRESSES: Office—c/o Boskydell Artists Ltd., 72 Monument Ave., Bennington, Vt. 05201.

CAREER: Oberlin College, Oberlin, Ohio, instructor, 1958-59; Chico State College (now California State University), Chico, Calif., instructor, 1959-62; San Francisco State College (now San Francisco State University), San Francisco, Calif., assistant professor of English, 1962-65; Southern Illinois University, Carbondale, professor of English, 1965-74; Bennington College, Vt., instructor, 1974-76; Williams College, Williamstown, Mass., and Skidmore College, Saratoga Springs, N.Y., instructor, 1976-77; George Mason University, Fairfax, Va., instructor, 1977-78; founder and director of writing program, University of New York at Binghamton, 1978-82; author, 1976-82. Distinguished visiting professor, University of Detroit, 1970-71; visiting professor, Northwestern University, Evanston, Ill., 1973.

MEMBER: Modern Language Association of America, American Association of University Professors.

AWARDS, HONORS: Woodrow Wilson fellowship, 1955-56; Danforth fellowship, 1972-73; Guggenheim fellowship, 1973-74; National Education Association award, 1972; *Grendel* named one of 1971's best fiction books by *Time* and *Newsweek; October Light* named one of the ten best books of 1976 by *Time* and *New York Times;* National Book Critics Circle award for fiction, 1976, for *October Light;* Armstrong Prize, 1980, for *The Temptation Game.*

WRITINGS:

NOVELS

The Resurrection, New American Library, 1966, reprinted, Random House, 1987.

The Wreckage of Agathon, Harper, 1970.

Grendel, Knopf, 1971, reprinted, Random House, 1989.

The Sunlight Dialogues, Knopf, 1972.

Jason and Medeia (novel in verse), Knopf, 1973, reprinted, Random House, 1986.

Nickel Mountain: A Pastoral Novel, Knopf, 1973, reprinted, Random House, 1989.

October Light, Knopf, 1976, reprinted, Random House, 1989.

Freddy's Book, Knopf, 1980.

Mickelsson's Ghost, Knopf, 1982.

JUVENILES

Dragon, Dragon and Other Timeless Tales, Knopf, 1975.

Gudgekin the Thistle Girl and Other Tales (Junior Literary Guild selection), Knopf, 1976.

In the Suicide Mountains, Knopf, 1977.

A Child's Bestiary (light verse), Knopf, 1977.

King of the Hummingbirds, and Other Tales, Knopf, 1977.

Vlemk, the Box Painter, Lord John Press, 1979.

CRITICISM

(Editor with Lennis Dunlap) *The Forms of Fiction,* Random House, 1961.

(Editor and author of introduction) *The Complete Works of the Gawain-Poet in a Modern English Version with a Critical Introduction,* University of Chicago Press, 1965.

(Editor with Nicholas Joost) *Papers on the Art and Age of Geoffrey Chaucer,* Southern Illinois University Press, 1967.

(Editor and author of notes) *The Gawain-Poet: Notes on Pearl and Sir Gawain and the Green Knight, with Brief Commentary on Purity and Patience,* Cliffs Notes, 1967.

Morte D'Arthur Notes, Cliffs Notes, 1967.

Sir Gawain and the Green Knight Notes, Cliffs Notes, 1967.

(Editor and author of notes) *The Alliterative Morte Arthure, The Owl and the Nightingale and Five Other Middle English Poems* (modern English version), Southern Illinois University Press, 1971.

The Construction of the Wakefield Cycle, Southern Illinois University Press, 1974.

The Construction of Christian Poetry in Old English, Southern Illinois University Press, 1975.

The Life and Times of Chaucer, Knopf, 1977.

The Poetry of Chaucer, Southern Illinois University Press, 1978.

On Moral Fiction, Basic Books, 1978.

On Becoming a Novelist, Harper, 1983.

The Art of Fiction: Notes on Craft for Young Writers, Knopf, 1984.

OTHER

The King's Indian and Other Fireside Tales (novellas), Knopf, 1974, reprinted, McKay, 1989 (published in England as *The King's Servant,* J. Cape, 1975).

(Contributor) Matthew Bruccoli and C. E. Frazer Clark, Jr., editors, *Pages,* Volume 1, Gale, 1976.

William Wilson (libretto; also see below), New London Press, 1978.

Poems, Lord John Press, 1978.

Three Libretti (includes *William Wilson, Frankenstein,* and *Rumpelstiltskin*), New London Press, 1979.

MSS: A Retrospective, New London Press, 1980.

The Art of Living and Other Stories, Knopf, 1981.

(Editor with Shannon Ravenel) *The Best American Short Stories of 1982,* Houghton, 1982.

(Translator with Nobuko Tsukui) Kikuo Itaya, *Tengu Child,* Southern Illinois University Press, 1983.

(Translator with John R. Maier) *Gilgamesh: A Translation,* Knopf, 1984.

Stillness and Shadows, edited by Nicholas Delbanco, Knopf, 1986.

Also author of *The Temptation Game* (radio play), 1980. Contributor of short stories to *Southern Review, Quarterly Review of Literature,* and *Perspective;* of poetry to *Kenyon Review, Hudson Review,* and other literary quarterlies; and of articles to *Esquire, Saturday Evening Post,* and other magazines. Founder and editor, *MSS* (a literary magazine).

SIDELIGHTS: John Champlin Gardner—not to be confused with the John Edmund Gardner who writes satiric mystery novels or John L. Gardner who was once the head of the Department of Health, Education and Welfare—was a philosophical novelist, a medievalist well versed in the classics, an educator, and an opinionated critic. Described by *Village Voice* contributor Elizabeth Stone as "Evel Knievel at the typewriter," Gardner stood for conservation of values from the past yet maintained a lifelong love-hate relationship with "the rules." Though he championed the moral function of literature, his long hair, leather jacket, and motorcycle classed him with nonconformists. The typical conflict in his work pits individual freedom against institutions that dominate by means of cultural "myths." In novels and stories, Paul Gray of *Time* summarizes, "Gardner sets conflicting metaphysics whirling, then records the patterns thrown out by their lines of force. One situation consistently recurs, . . . an inherited past must defend itself against a plotless future."

Gardner's novels provoked a wide range of critical responses, and, unlike many "academic" fictions, were appreciated by a large audience. Three of his novels were bestsellers. "Very few writers, of any age, are alchemist enough to capture the respect of the intellectual community *and* the imagination of others who lately prefer [Jacqueline] Susann and [Judith] Krantz. Based on critical acclaim, and sales volume, it would seem that this man accomplished both," Craig Riley wrote in *Best Sellers.* Carol A. MacCurdy reported in *Dictionary of Literary Biography Yearbook, 1982,* "Many critics consider *Grendel* (1971) a modern classic, *The Sunlight Dialogues* an epic of the 1970s, and *October Light* [which won the National Book Critics Circle Award for fiction in 1976] a dazzling piece of Americana."

Gardner spent his apprenticeship in literature as a medievalist, devoting himself to the writings of Chaucer and Dante, stories about King Arthur and Sir Gawain, and other classics. His studies were largely well received. Walter Clemons of *Newsweek* called *The Life and Times of Chaucer* "a very appealing investigative biography." Adding to the reader's interest, he said, was the fact that "Gardner's scholarship is solid and thorough, but he wears his mortarboard in a rakish tilt." Of *The Poetry of Chaucer* Clemons declared, "the energy, enthusiasm and complexity of Gardner's argument stirs one to read Chaucer afresh."

Gardner's notes on *Morte D'Arthur, Sir Gawain and the Green Knight,* and the Gawain poet have helped younger readers to appreciate these classics. His books for children also draw from his knowledge of medieval literature. They are fairy tales retold with original twists, "hip" tales in which familiar characters speak in today's cliches, or where unlikely contemporary characters are revived by the magic of the past. For example, in *Dragon, Dragon and Other Tales,* losers win and heroes lose. "Kings prove powerless, young girls mighty. The miller wins the princess, but she proves to be a witch. Tables are turned this way and that, with consequences that are hilarious and wonderful," Jonathan Yardley related in the *New York Times Book Review.* Like most of Gardner's fairy tales, *In the Suicide Mountains*—the story of three outcasts who find happiness after hearing some old folktales—is for adults as well.

Gardner always worked on several book projects at a time and did not publish his novels in the order that they were finished. Gardner's first published novel, *The Resurrection,* traces a philosophy professor's thoughts after he learns his life will be shortened by leukemia. David Cowart observed in *Dictionary of Literary Biography,* "The book asks the question Gardner would ask in every succeeding novel: how can existential man—under sentence of death—live in such a way as to foster life-affirming values, regardless of how ultimately provisional they may prove?" *The Resurrection* introduces features that recur in later books: an embedded second narrative, usually a "borrowed" text; a facility with fictional techniques; and an emotional impact Cowart describes as "harrowing."

Gardner's second published novel, *The Wreckage of Agathon,* proved his skill as an antiquarian, as a writer who could bring forward materials from ancient history and weave them into "a novel transcending history and effectively embracing all of it, a philosophical drama that accurately describes the wreckage of the 20th century as well as of Agathon, and a highly original work of imagination," wrote Christopher Lehmann-Haupt of the *New York Times.* Built of mostly dialogue, it exposed Gardner's "manic glee in disputation," or "delight in forensic and rhetorical flashiness for its own sake," Cowart observed. Its themes include the relation between individuals and the social orders they encounter. *The Wreckage of Agathon* "delineates the mental motion of the individual as sacred, whether he's a seer or not . . . and it exuberantly calls into question society's categorical insistances—the things brought into being at our own expense to protect us against ourselves, other people, and, putatively, other societies," Paul West wrote in the *New York Times Book Review.*

The Sunlight Dialogues also grapples with this theme. In a *Washington Post Book World* review, Geoffrey Wolff called *The Sunlight Dialogues* "an extended meditation on the trench warfare between freedom and order." The Sunlight Man—a policeman-turned-outlaw embittered by the loss of his family—and Police Chief Fred Clumly, obsessed with law and order, duel to the death in this novel. Emerging in the conflict between them is Gardner's examination of how these two forces impinge on art. Wolff commented, "While all men wish for both—freedom and order—the conflict between them is dramatized by every decision that an artist makes. The artist will do what he will. . . . No: the artist does what he must, recognizes the limits, agrees to our rules so that we can play too. No; . . . it's *his* cosmos. And so it goes."

Grendel retells the *Beowulf* tale from the monster's point of view. This new tack on the sea of the familiar hero myth allowed Gardner to fathom new insights into the conflict between order and chaos. In the *New York Times,* Richard Locke explained how the uncivil behavior of "civilized" man contributed to Grendel's murderous career: "Though twice he attempts to shed his monsterhood, become human, join these other verbal creatures, . . . he's misunderstood on both occasions, and the rat-like humans attack him in fear. So, racked with resentment, pride and vengeful nihilism, outraged by mankind's perversity (for the noble values of the poet's songs are betrayed in a trice by the beery warlords), Grendel commences his cynical war." Though confirmed in cynicism, the monster remains haunted by the words of The Shaper, the poet who revives inspiration and hope in the hearts of his listeners. In this way, Gardner demonstrated the power of art and its role in Western culture.

Gardner employed symbolism on many levels in *Grendel.* By breaking the novel into twelve sections corresponding to the signs of the zodiac, Gardner constructed a "cosmic" novel, since twelve is a symbol of the cosmos. By setting his story into this construction, the progression of the twelve signs became at the same time the twelve years of Grendel's conflict with civilization. "In numerology a number multiplied by itself represents an intensification of the original symbolism," Cowart pointed out; and this structure intensifies the ending, in which "Grendel learns that he too—death itself, symbolically—is mortal." The monster's last words—"Poor Grendel's had an accident. . . . *so may you all*"—hint at the complexity of moral questions, since it implies both the momentary monstrosity of the executioner Beowulf and the monster's relief at his release from a life of despair and violence. Other critics also recognize that by placing the monster's reign on a cyclical form, Gardner meant to affirm the regenerative power of life that puts death—and all that is monstrous—into perspective. Thus, "In this short novel," Cowart wrote, "Gardner burnishes the classic at the same time that he creates a new masterpiece."

Nickel Mountain: A Pastoral Novel explored again the complex relationship between order and chaos, particularly as they relate to human responsibility for events in a world that seems to give random accident free play. Narrator Henry Soames, proprietor of an all-night diner, has a ringside seat to the "horror of the random," to cite Cowart, in the lives of his patrons. Slow-moving and dominated by routine, the pastoral life around the diner is interrupted by a series of fatal accidents, including auto wrecks and house fires. Touching Henry more closely is the man who fell to his death on the stairs while recoiling from Henry's shout. Debates ensue about limits to the assignment of blame. Some of Gardner's characters feel that the assignment of guilt, though painful, is preferable to seeing themselves as victims of mere chance. As *London Magazine* contributor Herbert Lomas put it, recognitions of personal failure or weakness are "what lead you to love, brotherhood and God. It's through weakness and failure that you find warmth, . . . see your need for mercy and forgiveness, and thus everyone's, and feel the beginnings of sacramental consciousness." "Here, as in his other fiction," wrote Michael Wood in the *New York Review of Books,* "Gardner shows a marvelous gift for making *stories* ask balanced, intricate questions, for getting his complex questions into tight stories."

Henry's bout with guilt in *Nickel Mountain* stemmed from a personal tragedy Gardner suffered early in his life. The eleven-year-old Gardner was at the wheel of a tractor that ran over and killed his seven-year-old brother David. Though it was an accident, he believed he could have prevented it. Daily flashbacks to the accident troubled him until he had written the story "Redemption" in 1979, a story based on his memory of the accident. Because writing the story demanded concentration on the scene in order to take narrative control of it, his terror was diffused. But the question of human responsibility versus chance continued to surface in many of Gardner's novels and stories, suggesting that this question had become, for him, a habit of mind.

What was an internal conflict in *Nickel Mountain* became open debate in Gardner's next bestseller. *October Light* pits American conservativism against liberalism embodied in a seventy-year-old

Vermont farmer and his eighty-year-old feminist sister. In a characteristic rage about declining morals, James shoots Sally's television set and locks her into an upstairs room. They shout their arguments through the closed door. Sally finds a store of apples in the attic and parts of a "trashy" book about marijuana smugglers, *The Smugglers of Lost Soul's Rock,* and refuses to come out, even after her niece unlocks the door. She sees correspondences between the book's plot and her conflict with James. More vulnerable to his intimidating anger is James's son Richard, who commits suicide. Gardner exposed the regrettable stubbornness of both sides of their conflict and at the same time implied the paucity of absurdist literature in the "trashy" parody of postmodern literature Sally reads.

By the novel's end, James revises his opinions to accommodate a wider range of sensibility. "In *October Light,* then," reasoned Cowart, "we have a rustic world where the same horrors obtain as in the black-comic, nihilistic, 'smart-mouth satirical' novels typified by *Smugglers,* but Gardner convinces us that James Page can, at the age of seventy-two, come to self-knowledge—and that the thawing of this man's frozen heart holds much promise for all people who, bound in spiritual winter, have ever despaired of the spring."

"Using one obsession to attack another, [Gardner's] novels move with a pacing and complexity that are remarkable in current fiction," Josephine Hendin remarked in the *New Republic.* However, the novelist does not take sides. "Gardner's irresolution takes the form of an irony so pervasive it seems to stem from that well of American bitterness that made Herman Melville and Mark Twain, creators of distinctive American heroes, finally black about America's possibilities. Gardner presses his ambivalences into *October Light,* forcing his chauvinism and his nihilism against each other like monuments to two American civilizations. He achieves a disturbing, utterly original novel that gets as close as any book can to that acid cartoon, Grant Wood's 'American Gothic.' " Other critics suggested that Gardner was motivated to promote the exercise of moral sense more than to side with any particular philosophical stance.

Freddy's Book is a frame tale, a long story set into the "frame" of another narrative. A professor introduces a guest to his "monster" son, an eight-foot-tall recluse who has written a book. The shy giant's tome is the retelling of Sweden's liberation from Danish rule in the sixteenth century, glossed with the Devil's role as instigator of conflict on both sides who is eventually murdered by the knight Lars-Goren Bergkvist. "The final scene, in which the Devil is scaled like a mountain, is a marvelously virtuosic piece of narrative, with juxtapositions and counterpoints smacking as much of the screenwriter's art as the novelist's. Gardner is a masterful storyteller, even when, as in 'Freddy's Book,' he is curiously lacking in tone," John Romano wrote in the *New York Times Book Review.*

Lars-Goren, though flatly drawn in comparison to other Gardner characters, does his share of philosophical introspection. He ponders over his sudden fear of the Devil, and over the question, if evil can be destroyed, should it? The argument that evil is a foil against which good defines and proves itself is not a simple resolution, Lehmann-Haupt points out in *Books of the Times,* since Gardner let the Devil make this suggestion. Lars-Goren understands that since the Devil "is inherent in us or in our situation," evil may not be easily destroyed, Romano explained. However, added Romano, "Lars-Goren . . . acts *in spite of* what he knows, because, one gathers, the gesture itself is worth something, is perhaps worth everything."

In a *Chicago Tribune Book World* review, William Logan charged Gardner with plagiarism for using passages from a history of Sweden by Michael Roberts nearly verbatim in sections of *Freddy's Book.* Gardner rebutted that his attribution at the beginning of the book ("Numerous passages here are drawn, slightly altered, from other sources") should have been sufficient. His letter to the *Chicago Tribune* explained, "I used hundreds of sources. . . . To have acknowledged my hundreds of quotations and allusions would have been lunacy." He went on to explain that allusiveness is a trait of all medievalist literature: "The first step in literary composition, according to medieval rhetorical theory, is *inventio,* which is sometimes defined as 'the collection of old materials to be used in a new way.' Collage technique, the technique I practice, has nothing to do with plagiarism." Rather, he claimed, it was his homage paid to the vast store of literature that came before—his way of acknowledging the "dependency" of contemporary novelists on the accomplishments of earlier writers.

While writing *Mickelsson's Ghost,* Gardner deliberately tried to make the novel radically different from his prior works. The result, by comparison, said Curt Suplee of the *Washington Post,* "is a highbrow potboiler. . . . And it takes a wide-bodied and fast-moving narrative to carry all Gardner's themes, aiming them at the totalitarian threats in modern culture (metaphorically embedded in the Mormons and tax men) and a grand theological synthesis." Gardner explained to Suplee, "The two sort of big ghosts in the thing are Nietzsche and Luther: Luther's saying none of your works mean anything; and Nietzsche's saying works are everything. And if you get those two things together, you have courtly love. The lover does the most that he can possibly do, and then the grace of the lady saves him."

The title character, a philosophy professor, is troubled with a proliferation of "ghosts." The farm on which he has taken refuge from the world is haunted by apparitions of its previous owners, including the founder of Mormonism, Joseph Smith, and the still-living Hell's Angel who sold him the farm. Harassed by the Internal Revenue Service and the Sons of Dan (a fictional group of fanatic assassins), Mickelsson is haunted by his own crimes. After a teen he sleeps with gets pregnant, he robs an elderly man, hoping to pay the girl not to have an abortion. During the robbery, the man dies of a heart attack. Should Mickelsson, or should he not, think of himself as the murderer of the elderly miser? This and other questions of ethics—including how to assess the worth of individual human lives, Jack Miles noted in the *Los Angeles Times Book Review*—are the center of "this huge and ambitious book," Woiwode suggested, "and its grappling hook at your heart . . . is its questioning of our premises of what is real, or what 'reality' is; and in its brave examination of this, and of borderline states of supposed health, it becomes the kind of book that can alter one's way of looking at life."

Henry is also haunted by "hundreds of literary and philosophical and socio-historical echoes, most of them knit seamlessly into the story's unfurling," Woiwode related in the *Chicago Tribune Book World.* The ruling principle of the novel is excess as suggested in the title, *mickel* being the medieval word for "much." *New York Review of Books* contributor Robert Towers called it "an immense, baggy novel, loosely packed with four or five plots, several competing genres, a small army of characters, and enough thematic material to fuel a dozen all-night bull-sessions." Some readers found the excesses tedious while others found them delightful.

In addition to these novels, Gardner wrote a number of thought-provoking works on the purpose and craft of fiction. His criticism was hailed, as were his novels, as "disturbing." *On Moral Fiction,* written in part before his novels were published, contained many blunt statements that negatively assessed the works of other major novelists. Some of his statements contradicted others, such that his position was at times overstated, understated, or unclear. Some took these judgments as insults; and some critics, picking up the gauntlet, evaluated Gardner's subsequent works from a fighting stance. Yet others forgave the book's faults because they agreed with Gardner about the essentially humane quality of great literature.

Convinced that fiction exerts an important influence on our daily lives, Gardner claimed that novelists "should think always, of what harm they might inadvertently do, and not do it. If there is good to be said, the writer should remember to say it. If there is bad to be said, he should say it in a way that reflects the truth that, though we see the evil, we choose to continue among the living." For Gardner, "true" and "moral" art was art that "clarifies life, establishes models of human action, casts nets toward the future, carefully judges our right and wrong directions, celebrates and mourns. . . . It does not sneer or giggle in the face of death, it invents prayers and weapons. It designs visions worth trying to make fact." His comment that "real art creates myths a society can live instead of die by" has been cited often. He said in an interview with Joe David Bellamy in *The New Fiction* that fiction was furthermore a weapon against evil, which is overcome, as William Blake said, "by acts of imagination." His preface explaining his selections for *The Best American Short Stories of 1982* would later assert that the best fiction communicates its author's sincere and "serious personal concern" for others. Literary ambition alone is not enough to produce great literature, he claimed. "Eight million people died while we were thinking about how to become 'great writers,' " he told writers at a Bread Loaf conference, according to the *Washington Post*'s Chuck Cascio. Gardner declared, "You cannot be a great writer unless you feel greatly."

Having stated his standard so boldly, Gardner was judged by it himself. For instance, Romano maintained that while *Freddy's Book* was philosophical fiction, it wasn't moral, since it appeared to encourage the kind of exuberant destruction of evil that was "moved by vagrant, unexamined feelings" and is therefore prone to "slip over into immorality at any turn." Furthermore, Romano claimed, Gardner was "a better modernist than he [knew]." The complex structures and labyrinthine plots belonging to postmodernist literature such as that of John Barth and Jorge Luis Borges also flourish in Gardner's books. *National Review* critic Don Crinklaw observed that Gardner's work shares with that of Barth and William Gass a dependence on earlier literature, characters identified by their philosophical positions, and independence from the literary tastes of critics and casual readers. On a deeper level, Romano observed that the novelist's moral aesthetic fought with his love for "the fabulous, the enchanted," which was his "by training and inclination" as a medievalist. About this elemental contradiction, Romano stated, "It is fascinating and a little droll to see him struggling against his own gifts."

On Becoming a Novelist expressed Gardner's many thoughts about his vocation and outlined what it takes to be a professional novelist. Most important, he claimed, are "drive"—an unyielding persistence to write and publish; and faith—confidence in one's own abilities, belief in one's eventual success. The book restated his moral aesthetic. *Los Angeles Times Book Review* contributor Richard Rodriguez was struck by Gardner's passionate rejection of fictions that substitute "inconclusiveness," "pointlessly subtle games," or obsessive "puzzle-making" for essential storytelling. *The Art of Fiction: Notes on Craft for Young Writers* "originated as the so-called 'Black Book,' an underground text passed from hand to hand in university creative-writing departments," Stuart Schoffman noted in the *Los Angeles Times Book Review,* citing Gardner's comment from its preface that "it is the most helpful book of its kind." John L'Heureux remarked in the *New York Times Book Review* that "Gardner was famous for his generosity to young writers, and 'The Art of Fiction' is his posthumous gift to them."

Gardner's gift to literature, Charles Johnson noted in *Dictionary of Literary Biography Yearbook, 1982,* was "the literary strategy that fused theory and technique in his tales and novels. . . . Classical forms as vehicles infused with dignity, an affirmative worldview, and a timeless sense of value. . . . [He] offered us the achievements of the past—artistic and metaphysical—as models for the future."

MEDIA ADAPTATIONS: An animated film version of *Grendel* called *Grendel, Grendel, Grendel* was produced by Victorian Film Corporation in Australia in 1981.

BIOGRAPHICAL/CRITICAL SOURCES:

BOOKS

Bellamy, Joe David, editor, *The New Fiction: Interviews with Innovative American Writers,* University of Illinois Press, 1974.
Contemporary Literary Criticism, Gale, Volume 2, 1974, Volume 3, 1975, Volume 5, 1976, Volume 7, 1977, Volume 8, 1978, Volume 10, 1979, Volume 18, 1981, Volume 28, 1984, Volume 34, 1985.
Cowart, David, *Arches and Light: The Fiction of John Gardner,* Southern Illinois University Press, 1983.
Dictionary of Literary Biography, Volume 2: *American Novelists since World War II,* 1978.
Dictionary of Literary Biography Yearbook, 1982, Gale, 1983.
Gardner, John, *Grendel,* Knopf, 1971.
Gardner, *On Moral Fiction,* Basic Books, 1978.
Gardner, *Freddy's Book,* Knopf, 1980.
Gardner, *On Becoming a Novelist,* Harper, 1983.
Gardner, *The Art of Fiction: Notes on Craft for Young Writers,* Knopf, 1984.
Plimpton, George, editor, *Writers at Work: The Paris Review Interviews,* Viking, 1981.

PERIODICALS

Atlantic, January, 1984.
Books of the Times, May, 1980.
Chicago Tribune, March 16, 1980, April 13, 1980.
Chicago Tribune Book World, May 24, 1981, April 13, 1980, June 13, 1982, April 1, 1984.
Esquire, January, 1971, June, 1982.
Best Sellers, April, 1984.
Los Angeles Times Book Review, May 30, 1982, December 5, 1982, June 12, 1983, May 30, 1982, February 12, 1984.
National Review, November 23, 1973.
New Republic, February 5, 1977.
Newsweek, December 24, 1973, April 11, 1977.
New York Review of Books, March 21, 1974, June 24, 1982.
New York Times, September 4, 1970, November 14, 1976, December 26, 1976, January 2, 1977.
New York Times Book Review, November 16, 1975, March 23, 1980, May 17, 1981, May 31, 1981, June 20, 1982, February 26, 1984, July 20, 1986.
Time, January 1, 1973, December 30, 1974, December 20, 1976.

Times Literary Supplement, October 23, 1981, October 22, 1982, July 29, 1983.
Village Voice, December 27, 1976.
Washington Post, July 25, 1982, March 1, 1983.
Washington Post Book World, December 24, 1972, March 23, 1980, May 3, 1981, May 14, 1982.

OBITUARIES:

PERIODICALS

Chicago Tribune, September 16, 1982.
Publishers Weekly, October 1, 1982.
Newsweek, September 27, 1982.
New York Times, September 15, 1982.
School Library Journal, November, 1982.
Time, September 27, 1982.
Times (London), September 18, 1982.*

*   *   *

GEISMAR, Maxwell (David) 1909-1979

PERSONAL: Born August 1, 1909, in New York, N.Y.; died of a heart attack July 24, 1979, in Harrison, N.Y.; son of Leon and Mary (Feinberg) Geismar; married Anne Rosenberg, September 11, 1932; children: Katherine Geismar Seiden, Peter, Elizabeth Geismar Kentfield. *Education:* Columbia University, B.A., 1931, M.A., 1932.

ADDRESSES: Home and office—Winfield Ave., Harrison, N.Y. 10528.

CAREER: Sarah Lawrence College for Women (now Sarah Lawrence College), Bronxville, N.Y., member of department of English, 1933-45; free-lance writer, lecturer, historian, and critic, 1945-79. Boston University Libraries fellow, 1970.

AWARDS, HONORS: Guggenheim fellowship, 1943-44; National Institute of Arts and Letters grant in literature, 1952.

WRITINGS:

Writers in Crisis: The American Novel, 1925-1940, Houghton, 1942, reprinted, Dutton, 1971.
The Last of the Provincials: The American Novel, 1915-1925, Houghton, 1947.
Rebels and Ancestors: The American Novel, 1890-1915, Houghton, 1953.
American Moderns: From Rebellion to Conformity, Hill & Wang, 1960.
Henry James and the Jacobites, Houghton, 1963 (published in England as *Henry James and His Cult,* Chatto & Windus, 1965).
(Author of introduction) Eldridge Cleaver, *Soul on Ice,* McGraw, 1968.
(Author of introduction) Joseph North, editor, *New Masses: An Anthology of the Rebel Thirties,* International Publishers, 1969.
Mark Twain: An American Prophet, Houghton, 1970, abridged edition, McGraw, 1973.
Ring Larder and the Portrait of Folly, Crowell, 1972.

EDITOR

Portable Thomas Wolfe, Viking, 1946.
Theodore Dreiser, *Sister Carrie,* Pocket Books, 1949.
Herman Melville, *Moby Dick,* Washington Square Press, 1949.
Whitman Reader, Pocket Books, 1955.
Jack London, *Short Stories,* Hill & Wang, 1960.
Sherwood Anderson, *Short Stories,* Hill & Wang, 1962.
The Ring Larder Reader, Scribner, 1963.

(And author of introduction) *Emile Zola: The Naturalist Novel,* Harvest House (Montreal), 1964.
Melville, *Billy Budd,* Limited Editions, 1965.
Melville, *Benito Cereno,* Limited Editions, 1965.
Unfinished Business: James N. Rosenberg Papers, Marasia Press, 1967.
Mark Twain and the Three R's: Race, Religion, Revolution and Related Matters, Bobbs-Merrill, 1973.
The Higher Animals: A Mark Twain Bestiary, Crowell, 1976.

OTHER

Contributor to *Encyclopaedia Britannica* and *Compton's Encyclopedia.* Contributor to *New York Times, New York Herald Tribune, Nation, Yale Review, Virginia Quarterly Review, Atlantic, American Scholar,* and other periodicals. Contributing editor, *Nation,* 1945-50; senior editor, *Ramparts,* 1966; founding editor, *Scanlan's Monthly,* 1970; advisory editor, *Chicago Review,* 1973-79.

SIDELIGHTS: Maxwell Geismar was a prolific literary critic who contributed stimulating essays to nearly a dozen periodicals in the 1950s and 1960s. His reputation was established in the early 1940s with publication of *Writers in Crisis: The American Novel, 1925-1940,* a study of American fiction which Geismar continued in two later volumes covering the period from 1915 to where the first one began. Among his most widely reviewed works were contentious analyses of two American writers found in *Henry James and the Jacobites* and *Mark Twain: An American Prophet.*

According to *New York Times* contributor C. Gerald Fraser, Geismar "considered himself a historian who viewed American life through its writers" and, seeming to bear out the author's self-assessment, in these studies of James and Twain he weaves social commentary on the contemporary American scene with literary interpretation. Both books sought to undermine the prevailing critical consensus on the writer whose works were under review and both were highly controversial. As an example of the strong emotions the two volumes provoked, Fraser quoted one critic who called Geismar's book on James "one of the most furiously belligerent works of criticism written in modern times."

In *Henry James and the Jacobites* Geismar set out to disprove the commonly held contention that James was a great writer. K. T. Willis notes in *Library Journal* that Geismar preferred to think of James as a "major entertainer" rather than a "major writer." However, the *Atlantic*'s Phoebe Adams seemed to be one of the few critics who wholeheartedly praised the volume. She called it "stimulating and frequently surprising" and congratulated Geismar on his courage to speculate on the motivation behind the adulation some critics reserved for James.

Other reviewers were not as generous with their approval: both R. C. Le Clair and W. C. Jumper saw the book as insightful, but flawed. In Le Clair's *Christian Science Monitor* review, for example, the critic noted, "As a broadside attack on Henry James and the Jamesian cult of the past two decades, this is an important book" but lamented Geismar's "lapses into cheapness, poor taste, and occasional downright nastiness." In a similarly divided commentary, *Saturday Review* contributor Jumper claimed that Geismar was "completely wrong when he champions literature as the spontaneous outpouring of the 'unconscious' and when he condemns James for being 'too conscious' rather than 'unconscious.'. . . But [he] is more than partially right when he says that the Jamesian canon has become an object of adoration instead of an object of study with too many critics and teachers of writing."

When *Mark Twain: An American Prophet* appeared in 1970, many reviewers compared it to the author's study of James because both works stirred up similar controversy. As in his book on James, Geismar again attempted to discredit a commonly held critical belief. In Twain's case, Geismar felt that the majority of critics missed the most important part of the Missourian's canon: his social criticism. Geismar felt that the reason for this lapse was because of self-censorship by the so-called "Cold War critics" who refused to admit that a great American writer could have held doubts about the nature of our society.

Geismar's book was received with mixed reviews. In a supportive review of Geismar's thesis *Best Sellers* contributor Paul T. Majkut claimed that "by disregarding the claptrap of the '50's Cold War critics, the methods and terminology of both Freudianism and Formalism, Geismar has managed a new kind of biography that might best be described as *phenomenological*. That is, he refuses to deal with anything outside of the 'given' of Twain's life. Geismar, an ideal biographer, uses Twain to uncover Twain." A *Newsday* reviewer felt that Geismar rightly presented Twain as a prophetic writer and called the historian's look at Twain "a book that cries to be read." *Time*'s John Skow found Geismar's prose rather muddled but agreed with the premise "that Twain is too little known and understood as a critic of U.S. society."

Those critics who disapproved of Geismar's book seemed to especially object to the author's derogatory statements concerning previous Twain commentators. They also disagreed with Geismar's contention that Twain's best writing could be found in his later production and not, as most critics believe, in *The Adventures of Huckleberry Finn* and other early works. "Geismar calls 'nonsense' the view that *Huckleberry Finn* was Mark Twain's one masterpiece," Peter Shaw wrote in *Commentary*, "since 'his whole career was a classic.' Most readers would agree that there are brilliant passages throughout Twain's writings, but they would nevertheless have to notice much that is unfortunate." *Saturday Review* contributor Brom Weber observed that the book, "though opening as literary criticism and presenting a few genuinely valuable insights, declines rapidly into an obsessive political tirade against American culture and intellectuals of the past four decades."

A collection of Geismar's manuscripts, papers, and correspondence is housed at Boston University, Boston, Mass.

AVOCATIONAL INTERESTS: Reading, tennis.

BIOGRAPHICAL/CRITICAL SOURCES:

PERIODICALS

Atlantic, October, 1963.
Best Sellers, December 15, 1970.
Christian Science Monitor, October 10, 1963.
Commentary, March, 1971.
Library Journal, September 15, 1963.
Newsday, November 7, 1970.
Newsweek, November 9, 1970.
Saturday Review, May 3, 1958, October 5, 1963, February 27, 1971.
Time, November 30, 1970.

OBITUARIES:

PERIODICALS

AB Bookman's Weekly, August 20, 1979.
Newsweek, August 6, 1979.
New York Times, July 25, 1979.

Publishers Weekly, August 6, 1979.*

—*Sketch by Marian Gonsior*

* * *

GEROULD, Daniel C(harles) 1928-

PERSONAL: Surname is pronounced *Ger*-ald; born March 28, 1928, in Cambridge, MA; son of Russell (a newspaper editor) and Virginia (Vaughan) Gerould; married Eleanor A. Southwick (a teacher of music and collaborator with her husband on some translations), August 16, 1955; children: Alexander L. *Education:* University of Chicago, A.B., 1946, M.A., 1949, Ph.D., 1959; additional study at Harvard University, 1953; University of Paris, Diplome, 1955.

ADDRESSES: Home—33 West 42nd St., New York, NY 10036. *Office*—City University of New York, Graduate School and University Center, New York, NY 10036.

CAREER: University of Arkansas, Fayetteville, instructor in English and humanities, 1949-51; University of Chicago, Chicago, IL, instructor in humanities, 1955-59; San Francisco State College (now University), San Francisco, CA, assistant professor, 1959-61, associate professor, 1963-67, professor of English and world literature, 1967-71, chairman of department of world literature, 1961-71; City University of New York, Graduate Center, New York City, professor of theater and comparative literature, 1971—. Fulbright lecturer in American literature, University of Warsaw, 1968-70. Lecturer at Moscow State University, 1967, Charles University, Prague, 1969, and Poznan University, Poland, 1970. *Military service:* U.S. Army, 1951-53; instructor in English language and American literature on Okinawa, 1951-52.

MEMBER: Phi Beta Kappa.

AWARDS, HONORS: French Government scholarship to University of Paris, 1953-54; first prize in San Francisco Poetry Center national poetic drama competition, 1963, for "The Games of Narcissus"; Marian Kister Memorial Award of Roy Publishers, for best Polish-to-English translation, 1969, for *The Madman and the Nun and Other Plays* by Stanislaw Ignacy Witkiewicz.

WRITINGS:

Candaules, Commissioner (play; published in *First Stage,* fall, 1965), first performed on radio by Actors Workshop of San Francisco, 1966; performed Off-Broadway, 1970.
(Editor and translator with C. S. Durer) *The Madman and the Nun and Other Plays* by Stanislaw Ignacy Witkiewicz, University of Washington Press, 1968, published with *The Crazy Locomotive,* Applause Theatre Book Publishers, 1987.
(Editor and author of introduction with Bernard F. Dukore and contributor of translations) *Avant-Garde Drama between World Wars* (includes two plays and four essays translated by Gerould and others), Bantam, 1969.
(Contributor of translation with wife, Eleanor S. Gerould) John Gassner, editor, *Treasury of the Theatre,* 4th edition, Holt, 1970.
(With Dukore) *Avant-Garde Drama: A Casebook,* Crowell, 1976.
(Translator) Stanislaw Witkiewicz, *The Beelzebub Sonata: Plays, Essays and Documents,* PAJ Publications, 1980.
Witkacy: Stanislaw Ignacy Witkiewicz as an Imaginative Writer, University of Washington Press, 1981.
American Melodrama, PAJ Publications, 1983.
Polish Plays in Translation, CASTA, Graduate School and University Center of the City University of New York, 1983.

(Translator with Durer and adapter with Wlodzimierz Herman) Witkiewicz, *The Shoemakers,* produced Off-Broadway, 1987.

(Editor and translator) *Stanislaw Ignacy Witkiewicz: A Reader,* PAJ Publications, 1988.

(With Jadwiga Kosicka) *A Life of Solitude—Stanislawa Przybyszewska: A Biographical Study with Letters,* Northwestern University Press, 1989.

Also author of play in verse, *The Games of Narcissus,* 1963, and of plays *Explosion* (published in *BREAKOUT! In Search of New Theatrical Environments,* Swallow Press, 1971), 1969, *Tripstych,* 1970, and *The Travels of Perseus,* 1970. Contributor of translation with E. Gerould to special English-language edition of *Dialog,* 1971. Translator of plays and articles for theater journals.

WORK IN PROGRESS: A critical study on Stanislaw Ignacy Witkiewicz, for Twayne; *The Metaphysics of a Two-Headed Calf: Five Plays by Witkiewicz;* an original play, *Eva von Buttlar.*

BIOGRAPHICAL/CRITICAL SOURCES:

PERIODICALS

New York Times, April 29, 1970.
New York Times Book Review, October 8, 1989.
Times Literary Supplement, September 19, 1986.
Village Voice, February 12, 1970; June 4, 1970.*

* * *

GILBERT, Sandra M(ortola) 1936-

PERSONAL: Born December 27, 1936, in New York, NY; daughter of Alexis Joseph (a civil engineer) and Angela (Carvso) Mortola; married Elliot Lewis Gilbert (a professor of English), December 1, 1957; children: Roger, Katherine, Susanna. *Education:* Cornell University, B.A., 1957; New York University, M.A., 1961; Columbia University, Ph.D., 1968.

ADDRESSES: Office—Department of English, University of California, Davis, CA 95616.

CAREER: Queens College of the City University of New York, Flushing, lecturer in English, 1963-64, 1965-66; Sacramento State College (now California State University, Sacramento), lecturer in English, 1967-68; California State College (now California State University), Hayward, assistant professor of English, 1968-71; St. Mary's College, Moraga, CA, lecturer in English, 1972; Indiana University at Bloomington, associate professor of English, 1973-75; University of California, Davis, 1975-85, began as associate professor, became professor of English; Princeton University, Princeton, NJ, professor of English, 1985-89; University of California, Davis, professor of English, 1989—.

MEMBER: Modern Language Association of America.

AWARDS, HONORS: National Endowment for the Humanities fellowship, 1980-81; Rockefeller Foundation fellowship, 1982; Guggenheim fellowship, 1983.

WRITINGS:

Shakespeare's "Twelfth Night," Thor Publishing, 1964.
Two Novels by E. M. Forster, Thor Publishing, 1965.
D. H. Lawrence's "Sons and Lovers," Thor Publishing, 1965.
The Poetry of W. B. Yeats, Thor Publishing, 1965.
Two Novels by Virginia Woolf, Thor Publishing, 1966.
Acts of Attention: The Poems of D. H. Lawrence, Cornell University Press, 1973.
In the Fourth World: Poems, University of Alabama Press, 1978.

(With Susan Gubar) *The Madwoman in the Attic: The Woman Writer and the Nineteenth-Century Literary Imagination,* Yale University Press, 1979.

(Editor with Gubar) *Shakespeare's Sisters: Feminist Essays on Women Poets,* Indiana University Press, 1979.

The Summer Kitchen: Poems, Heyeck, 1983.

Emily's Bread: Poems, Norton, 1984.

(Editor with Gubar) *The Norton Anthology of Literature by Women: The Tradition in English,* Norton, 1985.

Blood Pressure: Poems, Norton, 1988.

(With Gubar) *No Man's Land: The Place of the Woman Writer in the Twentieth Century,* Yale University Press, Volume 1: *The War of the Words,* 1988, Volume 2: *Sexchanges,* 1989.

Also editor of Kate Chopin's *The Awakening and Other Stories,* Peter Smith. Contributor to anthologies, including *Best Little Magazine Fiction,* 1971, *Bicentennial Poetry Anthology,* 1976, *Contemporary Women Poets,* 1978, and *The Poetry Anthology,* 1978. Contributor of fiction and poetry to *Mademoiselle, Poetry, Epoch, Nation, New Yorker,* and other magazines.

WORK IN PROGRESS: The Tidal Wave: Poems; Mother Rights: Studies in Maternity and Creativity; (with Gubar) *No Man's Land: The Place of the Woman Writer in the Twentieth Century,* Volume 3: *Letters from the Front.*

SIDELIGHTS: In *The Madwoman in the Attic: The Woman Writer and the Nineteenth-Century Literary Imagination,* "Sandra Gilbert and Susan Gubar offer a bold new interpretation of the great 19th-century woman novelists, and in doing so they present the first pervasive case for the existence of a distinctly female imagination," writes Le Anne Schreiber in the *New York Times Book Review.* As Carolyn See notes in the *Los Angeles Times Book Review,* the authors examine how attitudes toward women and woman writers held by men and women alike shaped the literature of Jane Austen, Charlotte and Emily Bronte, Emily Dickinson, George Eliot, and Mary Shelley. According to See, Gilbert and Gubar reveal how these woman novelists used the "essentially destructive myth [that a woman writer was an aberration, 'the Devil Herself']—and their own fears about it to create their own myths, their own world views."

Rosemary Ashton describes *The Madwoman in the Attic* in the *Times Literary Supplement* as a "purposefully written book essentially without a thesis," whose "authors exhaust the reader with . . . formidable but unconvincing rhetoric." She adds, "It is hard not to suspect that they found just what they were looking for, and equally hard to give acceptance to their 'findings.' " Yet, in a *Washington Post Book World* review, Carolyn G. Heilbrun writes, "At last, feminist criticism, no longer capable of being called a fad, is clearly and coherently mapped out." Heilbrun concludes, "*The Madwoman in the Attic,* by revealing the past, will profoundly alter the present, making it possible, at last, for women writers to create their own texts."

More recently, Gilbert and Gubar have been working on a three volume book of feminist criticism entitled *No Man's Land: The Place of the Woman Writer in the Twentieth Century.* In a *Globe and Mail* review of the first volume, *The War of the Words,* Janice Kulyk Keefer calls the study a "thoroughly provocative (and provocatively thorough) revisioning of the genesis of modernism." Noting that *No Man's Land* was written to be a sequel to *The Madwoman in the Attic, New York Times Book Review* contributor Walter Kendrick remarks that if this latest work "achieves its complementary goal, it will set the direction of feminist criticism for the next generation of students and scholars."

Gilbert, who is also the author of a number of poetry collections, told *CA:* "I see myself as a poet, a critic, and a feminist, hoping that each 'self' enriches the others. As a poet, however, I'm superstitious about becoming too self-conscious; as a critic, I want to stay close to the sources of poetry; and as a feminist, I try to keep my priorities clear without sermonizing. Those *caveats* mean that a statement like this one necessarily has to be short—at least for now."

BIOGRAPHICAL/CRITICAL SOURCES:

PERIODICALS

Globe and Mail (Toronto), February 13, 1988.
Los Angeles Times Book Review, March 2, 1980, May 12, 1985.
Newsweek, July 15, 1985.
New York Times Book Review, December 9, 1979, April 28, 1985, February 19, 1989, March 12, 1989.
Times Literary Supplement, August 8, 1980, April 18, 1986, June 3, 1988.
Washington Post Book World, November 25, 1979, June 2, 1985, January 17, 1988.

*   *   *

GINZBURG, Natalia 1916-
(Alessandra Tournimparte)

PERSONAL: Born July 14, 1916, in Palermo, Italy; daughter of Carlo (a novelist and professor of biology) and Lidia (Tanzi) Levi; married Leone Ginzburg (an editor and political activist), 1938 (died, 1944); married Gabriele Baldini, 1950.

ADDRESSES: Home—Piazza Camp Marzio 3, Rome, Italy.

CAREER: Novelist, short story writer, dramatist, and essayist. Worked for Einaudi (publisher), Turin, Italy. Member of Italian parliament.

AWARDS, HONORS: Strega Prize, 1964, for *Lessico famigliare;* Marzotto Prize for European Drama, 1968, for *The Advertisement.*

WRITINGS:

(Under pseudonym Alessandra Tournimparte) *La strada che va in citta* (two short novels), Einaudi (Turin, Italy), 1942, reprinted under own name, 1975, translation by Frances Frenaye published under own name as *The Road to the City* (contains "The Road to the City" and "The Dry Heart"), Doubleday, 1949.
E stato cosi, Einaudi, 1947, reprinted, 1974.
Valentino (novella; also see below), Einaudi, 1951.
Tutti i nostri ieri (novel), Einaudi, 1952, translation by Angus Davidson published as *A Light for Fools,* Dutton, 1956, translation published as *Dead Yesterdays,* Secker & Warburg, 1956.
(With Giansiro Ferrata) *Romanzi del 900,* Ediziono Radio Italiana (Turin), 1957.
Sagittario (novella; also see below), Einaudi, 1957, translation published as *Sagittarius,* 1975.
Le voci della sera, Einaudi, 1961, new edition edited by Sergio Pacilici, Random House, 1971, translation by D. M. Low published as *Voices in the Evening,* Dutton, 1963.
Le piccole virtu (essays), Einaudi, 1962, translation by Dick Davis published as *The Little Virtues,* Seaver Books, 1986.
Lessico famigliare (novel), Einaudi, 1963, translation by Low published as *Family Sayings,* Dutton, 1967.
Cinque romanzi brevi (short novels and short stories), Einaudi, 1964.

Ti ho sposato per allegria (plays), Einaudi, 1966.
The Advertisement (play; translation by Henry Reed first produced in London at Old Vic Theatre, September 24, 1968), Faber, 1969.
Teresa (play), [Paris], 1970.
Mai devi domandarmi (essays), Garzanti (Milan) 1970, translation by Isabel Quigly published as *Never Must You Ask Me,* M. Joseph, 1973.
Caro Michele (novel), Mondadori (Milan), 1973, translation by Sheila Cudahy published as *No Way,* Harcourt, 1974, published as *Dear Michael,* Owen, 1975.
Paese di mare e altre commedie, Garzanti, 1973.
Vita immaginaria (essays), Mondadori, 1974.
Famiglia (contains novellas "Borghesia" and "Famiglia"), 1977, translation by Beryl Stockman published as *Family,* Holt, 1988.
La citte e la casa, 1984, translation by Davis published as *The City and the House,* Seaver Books, 1987.
All Our Yesterdays, translation by Davidson, Carcanet, 1985.
The Manzoni Family, translation by Marie Evans, Seaver Books, 1987.
Valentino and Sagittarius, translation by Avril Bardoni, Holt, 1988.

Also author of *Fragola e panna,* 1966, *La segretaria,* 1967, and "I Married You for the Fun of It," 1972.

SIDELIGHTS: Natalia Ginzburg is one of the best-known postwar Italian writers. Her cool, controlled, simple style of writing has impressed critics, while her intimate explorations of domestic life are praised for their authenticity and concern for traditional values. Annapaola Concogni of the *New York Times Book Review* explains that Ginzburg possesses an "ear tuned in to the subtlest frequencies of domestic life, its accents, its gestures, its ups and downs and constant contradictions." Isabel Quigly compares Ginzburg to Chekhov, finding that, when reading Ginzburg's fiction, "Inevitably, Chekhov comes to mind: not only because the long summer days, the endless agreeable but unrewarding chat, the whole provincial-intellectual set-up, recall him, but because the Italian charm, and volatility, and loquacity, and unselfconscious egocentricity, and inability to move out of grooves, and so on, that Miss Ginzburg so brilliantly captures, are all Chekhovian qualities."

"Natalia Ginzburg is at her best when dealing with detail," Marc Slonim writes of *A Light for Fools,* "and her descriptions of children and adolescents have a definite poetic flavor. Most of the incidents and characters are seen through the eyes of an adolescent, and the book has much of the naivete and charm of a child's vision. This 'point of view' in the Jamesian sense gives a unity of diction to the whole narrative." Similarly, Quigly comments, "She has an extraordinary gift for what you might call cumulative characterization-a method that dispenses almost entirely with description and builds up solid and memorable people by the gradual mounting up of small actions, oblique glances, other people's opinions."

Other reviewers are critical of Ginzburg's method of characterization. Thomas G. Bergin writes that the characters in *Voices in the Evening* "are, for the most part, like excellent line drawings, quite real but somehow not 'filled in.' Their bone structure is magnificent, but there is no flesh." And although Otis K. Burger finds the same novel to be "crisp, brittle, entertaining, and informative," he also remarks that "the very coolness of the style tends to defeat the subtle theme of the death of a family (and a love) through sheer lack of gumption. The brevity of the book and its semicomic treatment of a muted tragedy come to seem, not a strength but part of the general, fatal weariness. The 'voices in the evening' tend to cancel each other out—succeeding only too well in presenting people who, pallid to begin with, end as mere phantoms."

Although *Family Sayings* is on the surface a simple family tale, what is beneath and between the lines reveals the weight and worth of the novel. Raymond Rosenthal writes that "what started as a simple family chronicle takes on the timeless, magnificent aspect of an ancient tale, a Homeric saga. It is magical, exhilarating. In the last pages, after all is accomplished and the deaths, the bereavements, the terrible losses of war and social struggle have been counted up, so to speak, the mere fact that Natalia's mother is still telling the same old stories, and that her father—the counter-muse, the rationalistic ogre—is still there to provide the antiphonic accompaniment of grumbles and complaints, becomes mythical in the truest sense. The surface of this book is also its depths."

Gavin Ewart also praises *Family Sayings*. The book exhibits, Ewart notes, "a simple, distilled style, a reliance on the virtues of repetition, an awareness of the ridiculousness of human beings; a great love (reading between the lines) for both her father and her mother; the shadow of Proust. All these are in it. Dealing with more 'tragic' material, it has the control and the only slightly edited reality that one finds in *My Life and Hard Times* (remember Thurber?). Though this is verbal comedy and not farce, it still seems, like that masterpiece, to imply that life can be terrible, but also terribly funny."

No Way concerns Michael, a young revolutionary living in a basement apartment. Ginzburg develops the relationships between Michael and his friends through letters (most of which are written to Michael, few of which he answers). "While Michael is expending what turn out to be his last days," Martin Levin comments, "his father dies, his girlfriend Mara runs through a half dozen patrons, and his mother is jilted by her lover Philip. All of these relationships are assembled by epistolary connections that have the intricacy and the fragility of an ant city. The wit is mordant and comes directly out of paradox." Lynne Sharon Schwartz notes, "The contours of [Ginzburg's] sentences linger in the ear like phrases from great music, familiar, basic truths. Her characters, sad, thwarted, often drab types, are memorable in the manner of people one knew very long ago."

"What makes this book so wonderful," L. E. Sissman declares, "magical even—is that we are never bored by the imprisoned pacings and abortive flights of its people. They all become real and individual and fascinating through the technical gifts of the author. . . . *No Way* is a novel of the curdling of aspirations and the enfeebling of powers among those who heretofore held sway. Its quality lies in its reportorial accuracy, in its fine, warm, rueful equanimity, in its balance in the face of toppling worlds. It is a most remarkable book."

Writing in the *Los Angeles Times Book Review*, Peter Brunette calls Ginzburg "the undisputed doyenne of contemporary Italian letters. Both a successful playwright and essayist, she has also become, through a steady outpouring of quietly memorable fiction over the last four decades, a world-class novelist."

BIOGRAPHICAL/CRITICAL SOURCES:

BOOKS

Contemporary Literary Criticism, Gale, Volume 5, 1976, Volume 11, 1979, Volume 54, 1989.

PERIODICALS

London Magazine, May, 1967.
Los Angeles Times Book Review, December 27, 1987.
New Leader, March 13, 1967.
New Republic, September 14, 1974.
New Yorker, October 21, 1974.
New York Review of Books, January 23, 1975.
New York Times, January 5, 1957, October 6, 1963.
New York Times Book Review, September 1, 1974, June 26, 1988.
Saturday Review, September 21, 1963.
Spectator, August 24, 1956.
Times Literary Supplement, February 5, 1971, April 13, 1973, June 15, 1973, February 21, 1975, March 28, 1975, June 2, 1978.

* * *

GLEASNER, Diana (Cottle) 1936-

PERSONAL: Born April 26, 1936, in New Jersey; daughter of Delmer Leroy (a research chemist) and Elizabeth (Stanton) Cottle; married G. William Gleasner (a free-lance photographer), July 12, 1958; children: Stephen William, Suzanne Lynn. *Education:* Ohio Wesleyan University, B.A. (cum laude), 1958; University of Buffalo, M.A., 1964.

ADDRESSES: Home and office—132 Holly Ct., Denver, NC 28037.

CAREER: High school teacher of English and physical education in Kenmore, NY, 1958-64; free-lance writer, 1964—. Instructor at State University of New York at Buffalo, 1973-76.

MEMBER: American Society of Journalists and Authors, Travel Journalists Guild, Society of American Travel Writers.

WRITINGS:

ILLUSTRATED WITH PHOTOGRAPHS BY HUSBAND, BILL GLEASNER

Hawaiian Gardens, Oriental, 1977.
Kauai Travelers Guide, Oriental, 1977.
Oahu Traveler's Guide, Oriental, 1977.
Big Island Traveler's Guide, Oriental, 1978.
Maui Traveler's Guide, Oriental, 1978.
Breakthrough: Women in Writing, Walker & Co., 1980.
Sea Islands of the South, East Woods Press, 1980.
Rock Climbing, McKay, 1980.
Callaway Gardens, Peninsula Press, 1981.
Dynamite, Walker & Co., 1983.
Breakthrough: Women in Science, Walker & Co., 1983.
Charlotte: Touch of Gold, East Woods Press, 1983.
The Movies, Walker & Co., 1983.
Woodloch Pines—An American Dream, Peninsula Press, 1984.
Windsurfing, ICS Books, 1985.
Lake Norman—Our Inland Sea, Peninsula Press, 1986.
Florida: Off the Beaten Path, Globe Pequot Press, 1986.
Governor's Island—From the Beginning, Peninsula Press, 1988.
RVing America's Backroads—Florida, TL Enterprises, 1989.
Touring by Bus at Home and Abroad, Scott, Foresman/AARP Books, 1989.

OTHER

The Plaid Mouse, Daughters of St. Paul, 1966.
Pete Polar Bear's Trip down the Erie Canal, University of Buffalo Press, 1969.
Women in Swimming, Harvey House, 1976.
Women in Track and Field, Harvey House, 1977.

Illustrated Dictionary of Surfing, Swimming and Diving, Harvey House, 1980.

Contributor of more than one thousand articles to newspapers and magazines, including *Baltimore Sun, Better Homes and Gardens, Boston Herald, Bride's, Chicago Sun-Times, Cleveland Plain Dealer, Field and Stream, Good Housekeeping, Newsday, San Francisco Examiner, Science Digest,* and *Travel.*

SIDELIGHTS: Diana Gleasner once wrote *CA:* "My husband and I are a full-time freelance team. He handles the photography and I do the writing. I can't imagine a better life. Our career allows us to express our creative urges while pursuing our enthusiasm for travel, sports, people and outdoors recreation."

* * *

GOLDING, William (Gerald)   1911-

PERSONAL: Born September 19, 1911, in St. Columb, Cornwall, England; son of Alex A. (a schoolmaster) and Mildred A. Golding; married Ann Brookfield, 1939; children: David, Judith. *Education:* Brasenose College, Oxford, B.A., 1935, M.A., 1960.

ADDRESSES: Home—Cornwall, England.

CAREER: Writer. Was a settlement house worker after graduating from Oxford University; taught English and philosophy at Bishop Wordsworth's School, Salisbury, Wiltshire, England, 1939-40, 1945-61; wrote, produced, and acted for London equivalent of "very, very far-off-Broadway theatre," 1934-40, 1945-54. Writer in residence, Hollins College, 1961-62; honorary fellow, Brasenose College, Oxford University, 1966. *Military service:* Royal Navy, 1940-45; became rocket ship commander.

MEMBER: Royal Society of Literature (fellow), Savile Club.

AWARDS, HONORS: Commander, Order of the British Empire, 1965; D.Litt., University of Sussex, 1970, University of Kent, 1974, University of Warwick, 1981, Oxford University, 1983, and University of Sorbonne, 1983; James Tait Black Memorial Prize, 1980, for *Darkness Visible;* Booker McConnell Prize, 1981, for *Rites of Passage;* Nobel Prize for Literature, 1983, for body of work; LL.D., University of Bristol, 1984; knighted, 1988.

WRITINGS:

FICTION

Lord of the Flies, Faber, 1954, published with an introduction by E. M. Forster, Coward, 1955, casebook edition with notes and criticism, edited by James R. Baker and Arthur P. Ziegler, Jr., Putnam, 1964.
The Inheritors, Faber, 1955, Harcourt, 1962.
Pincher Martin, Faber, 1955, new edition, 1972, published as *The Two Deaths of Christopher Martin,* Harcourt, 1957.
Free Fall, Harcourt, 1960.
The Spire, Harcourt, 1964.
The Pyramid (novellas), Harcourt, 1967.
The Scorpion God: Three Short Novels (includes "Clonk Clonk," "Envoy Extraordinary" [also see below], and "The Scorpion God"), Harcourt, 1971.
Darkness Visible, Farrar, Straus, 1979.
Rites of Passage (first novel in trilogy), Farrar, Straus, 1980.
The Paper Men, Farrar, Straus, 1984.
Close Quarters (second novel in trilogy), Farrar, Straus, 1987.
Fire Down Below (third novel in trilogy), Farrar, Straus, 1989.

OTHER

Poems, Macmillan, 1934.
(Contributor) *Sometimes, Never* (anthology), Ballantine, 1956.
The Brass Butterfly: A Play in Three Acts (based on "Envoy Extraordinary"; first produced in Oxford, England at New Theatre, 1958; produced in London, England at Strand Theatre, April, 1958; produced in New York at Lincoln Square Theatre, 1965), Faber, 1958.
"Break My Heart" (play), BBC Radio, 1962.
The Hot Gates, and Other Occasional Pieces (nonfiction), Harcourt, 1965.
A Moving Target (essays and lectures), Farrar, Straus, 1982.
An Egyptian Journal (travel), Faber, 1985.

Contributor to periodicals.

SIDELIGHTS: William Golding has been described as pessimistic, mythical, spiritual—an allegorist who uses his novels as a canvas to paint portraits of man's constant struggle between his civilized self and his hidden, darker nature. With the appearance of *Lord of the Flies,* Golding's first published novel, the author began his career as both a campus cult favorite and one of the late twentieth-century's most distinctive—and debated—literary talents. Golding's appeal is summarized by the Nobel Prize committee, who issued this statement when awarding the author their literature prize in 1983: "[His] books are very entertaining and exciting. They can be read with pleasure and profit without the need to make much effort with learning or acumen. But they have also aroused an unusually great interest in professional literary critics [who find] deep strata of ambiguity and complication in Golding's work, . . . in which odd people are tempted to reach beyond their limits, thereby being bared to the very marrow."

Golding was born in England's west country in 1911. His father, Alex, was a follower in the family tradition of schoolmasters; his mother, Mildred, was a suffragette. The family home in Marlborough is characterized by Stephen Medcalf in *William Golding* as "darkness and terror made objective in the flint-walled cellars of their fourteenth-century house . . . and in the graveyard by which it stood." By the time Golding was seven years old, Medcalf continues, "he had begun to connect the darkness . . . with the ancient Egyptians. From them he learnt, or on them he projected, mystery and symbolism, a habit of mingling life and death, and an attitude of mind sceptical of the scientific method that descends from the Greeks."

When he was twelve, Golding "tried his hand at writing a novel," reports Bernard Oldsey in his *Dictionary of Literary Biography* article. "It was to be in twelve volumes and, unlike the kinds of works he had been reading [adventure stories of the Edgar Rice Burroughs and Jules Verne ilk], was to incorporate a history of the trade-union movement. He never forgot the opening sentence of this magnificent opus: 'I was born in the Duchy of Cornwall on the eleventh of October, 1792, of rich but honest parents.' That sentence set a standard he could not maintain, he playfully admitted, and nothing much came of the cycle."

Despite this setback the young man remained an enthusiastic writer and, on entering Brasenose College of Oxford University, abandoned his plans to study science, preferring to read English literature. At twenty-two, a year before taking his B.A. in English, Golding saw his first literary work published—a poetry collection simply titled *Poems.* In hindsight, the author called the pieces "poor, thin things," according to Medcalf. But, in fact, Medcalf remarks, "They are not bad. They deal with emotions—as they come out in the poems, rather easy emotions—of loss and grief, reflected in nature and the seasons."

After graduating from Oxford, Golding perpetuated family tradition by becoming a schoolmaster in Salisbury, Wiltshire. His teaching career was interrupted in 1940, however, when World War II found "Schoolie," as he was called, serving five years in the Royal Navy. Lieutenant Golding saw active duty in the North Atlantic, commanding a rocket launching craft. "What did I do?," he responds in Oldsey's article about his wartime experiences. "I survived." Present at the sinking of the *Bismarck,* and participating in the D-Day invasion, Golding later told Joseph Wershba of the *New York Post:* "World War Two was the turning point for me. I began to see what people were capable of doing."

On returning to his post at Bishop Wordsworth's School in 1945, Golding, who had enhanced his knowledge of Greek history and mythology by reading while at sea, attempted to further his writing career. He produced three novel manuscripts that remained unpublished. "All that [the author] has divulged about these [works] is that they were attempts to please publishers and that eventually they convinced him that he should write something to please himself," notes Oldsey. That ambition was realized in 1954, when Golding created *Lord of the Flies.*

The novel which established Golding's reputation, *Lord of the Flies* was rejected by twenty-one publishers before Faber & Faber accepted the forty-three-year-old schoolmaster's book. While the story has been compared to such previous works as *Robinson Crusoe* and *High Wind in Jamaica,* Golding's novel is actually the author's "answer" to nineteenth-century writer R. M. Ballantyne's children's classic *The Coral Island: A Tale of the Pacific Ocean.* These two books share the same basic plot line and even some of the same character names (two of the lead characters are named Ralph and Jack in both books). The similarity, however, ends there. Ballantyne's story, about a trio of boys stranded on an otherwise uninhabited island, shows how, by pluck and resourcefulness, the young castaways survive with their morals strengthened and their wits sharpened. *Lord of the Flies,* on the other hand, is "an allegory on human society today, the novel's primary implication being that what we have come to call civilization is, at best, not more than skin-deep," as James Stern explains in a *New York Times Book Review* article.

Initially, the tale of a group of schoolboys stranded on an island during their escape from atomic war received mixed reviews and sold only modestly in its hardcover edition. But when the paperback edition was published in 1959, thus making the book more accessible to students, the novel began to sell briskly. Teachers, aware of the student interest and impressed by the strong theme and stark symbolism of the work, assigned *Lord of the Flies* to their literature classes. And as the novel's reputation grew, critics reacted by drawing scholarly theses out of what was previously dismissed as just another adventure story.

Golding provides in *Time* a simple exegis of his book. "The theme," he says, "is an attempt to trace the defects of society back to the defects of human nature." Indeed, the book begins with a company of highly-bred young men ("We've got to have rules and obey them. After all, we're not savages. We're English, and the English are best at everything," one of them states) and in just a few weeks strips them of nearly every aspect of "civilization," revealing what Golding describes as man's "true" nature underneath. In *Lord of the Flies,* religion becomes pagan ritual— the boys worship an unknowable, pervading power that they call The Beast; even a group of choirboys becomes a chanting warrior troupe. Democratic society crumbles under barbarism. "Like

any orthodox moralist Golding insists that Man is a fallen creature, but he refuses to hypostatize Evil or to locate it in a dimension of its own. On the contrary Beelzebub, Lord of the Flies, is Roger and Jack and you and I, ready to declare himself as soon as we permit him to," John Peter points out in *Kenyon Review.* "One sees what Golding is doing," says Walter Allen in his book *The Modern Novel.* "He is showing us stripped man, man naked of all the sanctions of custom and civilization, man as he is alone and in his essence, or at any rate, as he can be conceived to be in such a condition."

In his study *The Tragic Past,* David Anderson, like many critics, sees Biblical implications in Golding's novel. "*Lord of the Flies,*" writes Anderson, "is a complex version of the story of Cain—the man whose smoke-signal failed and who murdered his brother. Above all, it is a refutation of optimistic theologies which believed that God had created a world in which man's moral development had advanced *pari passu* with his biological evolution and would continue so to advance until the all-justifying End was reached. What we have in [the book] is not moral achievement but moral regression. And there is no all-justifying End: the rescue-party which takes the boys off their island comes from a world in which regression has occurred on a gigantic scale— the scale of atomic war. The human plight is presented in terms which are unqualified and unrelieved. Cain is not merely our remote ancestor: he is contemporary man, and his murderous impulses are equipped with unlimited destructive power."

The work has also been called Golding's response to the popular artistic notion of the 1950s, that youth was a basically innocent collective, victims of adult society (as in J. D. Salinger's *Catcher in the Rye,* a novel that rivals *Lord of the Flies* in student popularity). In 1960, C. B. Cox deemed *Lord of the Flies* as "probably the most important novel to be published . . . in the 1950s." Cox, writing in *Critical Quarterly,* continued: "[To] succeed, a good story needs more than sudden deaths, a terrifying chase and an unexpected conclusion. *Lord of the Flies* includes all these ingredients, but their exceptional force derives from Golding's faith that every detail of human life has a religious significance. This is one reason why he is unique among new writers in the '50s. . . . Golding's intense conviction [is] that every particular of human life has a profound importance. His children are not juvenile delinquents, but human beings realising for themselves the beauty and horror of life."

Not every critic responded with admiration to *Lord of the Flies,* however. One of Golding's more vocal detractors is Kenneth Rexroth, who had this to say in *Atlantic:* "Golding's novels are rigged. All thesis novels are rigged. In the great ones the drama escapes from the cage of the rigging or is acted out on it as on a skeleton stage set. Golding's thesis requires more rigging than most and it must by definition be escape-proof and collapsing." Rexroth elaborates: "[The novel] functions in a minimal ecology, but even so, and indefinite as it is, it is wrong. It's the wrong rock for such an island and the wrong vegetation. The boys never come alive as real boys. They are simply the projected annoyances of a disgruntled English schoolmaster."

Jean E. Kennard voiced a different view in her study *Number and Nightmare: Forms of Fantasy in Contemporary Fiction:* "Golding's ability to create characters which function both realistically and allegorically is illustrated particularly well in *Lord of the Flies.* It is necessary for Golding to establish the boys as 'real' children early in the novel—something he achieves through such small touches as Piggy's attitude to his asthma and the boys' joy in discovering Piggy's nickname—because his major thesis is, after all, about human psychology and the whole force of the fable would be lost if the characters were not first credible to us as human beings."

The wide variety of critical reaction to Golding's first novel is assessed by Bernard Oldsey. In his article, Oldsey cites such writers as E. L. Epstein and Claire Rosenfield, who "analyzed the work as a fictionalized version of primitive psychology and anthropology. Frederick Karl," Oldsey goes on, "oversimplifying the political allegory, declared that 'When the boys on the island struggle for supremacy, they re-enact a ritual of the adult world, as much as the Fellows in [C. P.] Snow's *The Masters* work out the ritual power in the larger world.' The temptation to force the novel into an allegorical box was strong, since the story is evocative and the characters seem to beg for placement within handy categories of meaning. But Golding is a simply complicated writer; and . . . none of the boxes fits precisely. [Critics Ian Gregor and Mark Kinkead-Weekes] wisely concluded that 'Golding's fiction has been too complex and many sided to be reducible to a thesis and a conclusion. *Lord of the Flies* is imagined with a flexibility and depth which seem evidence of finer art than the polish and clarity of its surface.' "

Golding took his theme of tracing the defects of society back to the defects of human nature a step further with his second novel, *The Inheritors.* This tale is set at the beginning of human existence itself, during the prehistoric age. A tribe of Neanderthals, as seen through the characters of Lok and Fa, live a peaceful primitive life. Their happy world, however, is doomed: evolution brings in its wake the new race, *Homo sapiens,* who demonstrate their acquired skills with weapons by killing the Neanderthals. The book, which Golding has called his favorite, is also a favorite with several critics. And, inevitably, comparisons were made between *The Inheritors* and *Lord of the Flies.*

To Peter Green, in *A Review of English Literature,* for example, "it is clear that there is a close thematic connection between [the two novels]: Mr. Golding has simply set up a different working model to illustrate the eternal human verities from a new angle. Again it is humanity, and humanity alone, that generates evil; and when the new men triumph, Lok, the Neanderthaler, weeps as Ralph wept for the corruption and end of innocence [in *Lord of the Flies*]." Oldsey sees the comparison in religious terms: "[The *Homo sapiens*] represent the Descent of Man, not simply in the Darwinian sense, but in the Biblical sense of the Fall. Peculiarly enough, the boys [in *Lord of the Flies*] slide backward, through their own bedevilment, toward perdition; and Lok's Neanderthal tribe hunches forward, given a push by their *Homo sapiens* antagonists, toward the same perdition. In Golding's view, there is precious little room for evolutionary slippage: progression in *The Inheritors* and retrogression in *Lord of the Flies* have the same results. The Descent of Man and Man's Fall (that is to say, rationalism versus religion, the scientific view versus spiritual vision) constitute the crux of Golding's constant thematic structuring. This is true for all of his literary endeavors, but nowhere is it more apparent than in *The Inheritors.*"

Just as *Lord of the Flies* is Golding's rewriting, in his own terms, of *The Coral Island,* the author "said that he wrote *The Inheritors* to refute [H. G. Wells's controversial sociological study] *Outline of History,* and one can see that between the two writers there is a certain filial relation, though strained, as such relations often are," comments a *Times Literary Supplement* critic. "They share the same fascination with past and future, the extraordinary capacity to move imaginatively to remote points in time, the fabulizing impulse, the need to moralize. There are even similarities in style. And surely now, when Wells's reputation as a great writer is beginning to take form, it will be understood as high praise of Golding if one says that he is our Wells, as good in his own individual way as Wells was in his." Taken together, the author's first two novels are, according to Lawrence R. Ries, "studies in human nature, exposing the kinds of violence that man uses against his fellow man. It is understandable why these first novels have been said to comprise [Golding's] 'primitive period,' " as Ries states in his book *Wolf Masks: Violence in Contemporary Fiction.*

Golding's "primitive period" ended with the publication of his third novel, *Pincher Martin* (published in America as *The Two Deaths of Christopher Martin,* out of the publishers' concern for American readers who would not know that "pincher" is British slang for "petty thief "). Stylistically similar to Ambrose Bierce's famous short story "An Occurrence at Owl Creek Bridge," *Pincher Martin* is about a naval officer who, after his ship is torpedoed in the Atlantic, drifts aimlessly before latching on to a barren rock. Here he clings for days, eating sea anemones and trying his best to retain consciousness. Delirium overtakes Pincher Martin, though, and through his rambling thoughts he relives his past. The discovery of the sailor's corpse at the end of the story in part constitutes what has been called a "gimmick" ending, and gives the book a metaphysical turn—the reader learns that Pincher Martin has been dead from the beginning of the narrative.

The author's use of flashbacks throughout the narrative of *Pincher Martin* is discussed by Avril Henry in *Southern Review:* "On the merely narrative level [the device] is the natural result of Martin's isolation and illness, and is the process by which he is gradually brought to his ghastly self-knowledge." In fact, says Henry, the flashbacks "function in several ways. First the flashbacks relate to each other and to the varied forms in which they themselves are repeated throughout the book; second, they relate also to the details of Martin's 'survival' on [the rock]. . . . Third, they relate to the six-day structure of the whole experience: the structure which is superficially a temporal check for us and Martin in the otherwise timeless and distorted events on the rock and in the mind, and at a deeper level is a horrible parody of the six days of Creation. What we watch is an unmaking process, in which man attempts to create himself his own God, and the process accelerates daily."

And, while acknowledging the influences present in the themes of *Pincher Martin*—from Homer's *Odysseus* to *Robinson Crusoe* again—Medcalf further suggests that the novel is Golding's most autobiographical work to date. The author, says Medcalf, "gave Martin more of the external conditions of his own life than to any other of his characters, from [his education at] Oxford . . . through a period of acting and theatre life to a commission in the wartime Navy." Golding, too, has added another dimension from his own past, notes Medcalf: "His childhood fear of the darkness of the cellar and the coffin ends crushed in the walls from the graveyard outside [his childhood home]. The darkness universalizes him. It becomes increasingly but always properly laden with symbolism: the darkness of the thing that cannot examine itself, the observing ego: the darkness of the unconscious, the darkness of sleep, of death and, beyond death, heaven."

Each of Golding's first three novels, according to James Gindin in his *Postwar British Fiction: New Accents and Attitudes,* "demonstrates the use of unusual and striking literary devices. Each is governed by a massive metaphorical structure—a man clinging for survival to a rock in the Atlantic ocean or an excursion into the mind of man's evolutionary antecedent—designed to assert something permanent and significant about human nature. The metaphors are intensive, far-reaching; they permeate all the details and events of the novels. Yet at the end of each novel the metaphors, unique and striking as they are, turn into 'gimmicks' [Golding's own term for the device], into clever tricks that shift the focus or the emphasis of the novel as a whole." In Gindin's further criticism of Golding's "gimmicks," the critic states that such endings fail "to define or to articulate fully just how [the author's] metaphors are to be qualified, directed, shaped in contemporary and meaningful terms."

Gimmick endings notwithstanding, V. S. Pritchett sums up Golding's early books as romantic "in the austere sense of the term. They take the leap from the probable to the possible." Pritchett elaborates in a *New Statesman* review: "All romance breaks with the realistic novelist's certainties and exposes the characters to transcendent and testing dangers. But Golding does more than break; he bashes, by the power of his overwhelming sense of the detail of the physical world. He is the most original of our contemporaries."

To follow *Pincher Martin,* the author "said that he next wanted to show the patternlessness of life before we impose our patterns on it," according to Green. However, the resulting book, *Free Fall,* Green continues, "avoids the amoebic paradox suggested by his own prophecy, and falls into a more normal pattern of development: normal, that is, for Golding." Not unlike *Pincher Martin, Free Fall* depicts through flashbacks the life of its protagonist, artist Sammy Mountjoy. Imprisoned in a darkened cell in a Nazi prisoner-of-war camp, Mountjoy, who has been told that his execution is imminent, has only time to reflect on his past.

Despite the similarity in circumstance to *Pincher Martin,* Oldsey finds one important difference between that novel and *Free Fall.* In *Free Fall,* a scene showing Sammy Mountjoy's tortured reaction on (symbolically) reliving his own downfall indicates a move toward atonement. "It is at this point in Golding's tangled tale that the reader begins to understand the difference between Sammy Mountjoy and Pincher Martin," Oldsey says. "Sammy escapes the machinations of the camp psychiatrist, Dr. Halde, by making use of man's last resource, prayer. It is all concentrated in his cry of 'Help me! Help me!'—a cry which Pincher Martin refuses to utter. In this moment of desperate prayer, Sammy spiritually bursts open the door of his own selfishness."

Medcalf sees the story as Dantesque in nature (Mountjoy's romantic interest is even named Beatrice) and remarks: "Dante, like Sammy, came to himself in the middle of his life, in a dark wood [the cell, in Sammy's case], unable to remember how he came there. . . . His only way out is to see the whole world, and himself in its light. Hell, purgatory and heaven are revealed to him directly, himself and this world of sense in glimpses from the standpoint of divine justice and eternity." In *Free Fall* the author's intent "is to show this world directly, in other hints and guesses. He is involved therefore in shewing directly the moment of fall at which Dante only hints. He has a hero without reference points, who lives in the vertigo of free fall, therefore, reproachful of an age in which those who have a morality or a system softly refuse to insist on them: a hero for whom no system he has will do, but who is looking for his own unity in the world—and that, the real world, is 'like nothing, because it is everything.' Golding, however, has the advantage of being able to bring Dante's world in by allusion: and he does so with a Paradise hill on which Beatrice is met."

Several critics have taken special notice of Golding's use of names in *Free Fall*—and his selection of the novel's title itself. Peter M. Axthelm, in his book *The Modern Confessional Novel,* finds that "almost every proper name . . . implies something

about the character it identifies." The name Sammy Mountjoy, with its hedonistic ring, for example, contrasts sharply with that of his childhood guardian, Father Watts-Watt. The most crucial name in the book, though, states Axthelm, is that of the woman whom Sammy loves and abuses, Beatrice Ifor. Sammy reads her surname as "I-for," an extension of his own sexual passion. But her name can also be read as "If-or," indicating a spiritual choice—"in other words, she is the potential bridge between Sammy's two worlds," as Axthelm notes. Unable to reconcile the two sides of her character, Sammy "ignores the spiritual side of the girl and grasps only the 'I-for,' the self-centered, exploitative lust. He upsets the balance and destroys the bridge," says the critic.

"Many critics have commented that the title [*Free Fall*] has both a theological and a scientific significance," declares Kennard, "but Golding himself has, as usual, expressed it best: 'Everybody has translated this in terms of theology; well, okay, you can do it that way, which is why it's not a bad title, but it is in fact a scientific term. It is where your gravity has *gone;* it is a man in a space ship who has no gravity; things don't fall or lift, they float about; he is completely divorced from the other idea of a thing up *there* and centered on *there* in which he lives.' Sammy Mountjoy, narrator of *Free Fall,* has more insight and perhaps more conscience than Pincher Martin, but basically his is Pincher's problem. He is islanded, trapped in himself, 'completely divorced from the other idea of a thing up there.' " "Sammy is the character through whom Mr. Golding, one suspects, is beginning to be reconciled to the loss of his primal Eden," offers Green.

In Golding's fifth novel, *The Spire,* "the interest is all in the opacity of the man and in a further exploration of man's all-sacrificing will," writes Medcalf. Fourteenth-century clergyman Dean Jocelin "is obsessed with the belief that it is his divine mission to raise a 400-foot tower and spire above his church," as Oldsey describes. "His colleagues protest vainly that the project is too expensive and the edifice unsuited for such a shaft. His master builder (obviously named Roger Mason) calculates that the foundation and pillars of the church are inadequate to support the added weight, and fruitlessly suggests compromises to limit the shaft to a lesser height. The townspeople—amoral, skeptical, and often literally pagan—are derisive about 'Jocelin's Folly.' " Dean Jocelin, nonetheless, strives on. The churchman, in fact, "neglects all his spiritual duties to be up in the tower overseeing the workmen himself, all the while choosing not to see within and without himself what might interrupt the spire's dizzying climb," Oldsey continues. The weight of the tower causes the church's foundations to shudder; the townspeople increasingly come to see Jocelin as a man dangerously driven.

Finally, despite setbacks caused by both the workers (they "drink, fornicate, murder, and brawl away their leisure hours," according to Oldsey) and by the elements of nature (storms ravage the tower in its building stage), the spire nears completion. Dean Jocelin himself drives the final nail into the top of the edifice—and as he does, succumbs to a disease and falls from the tower to his death. "Whether he has been urged by Satan, God, or his own pride (much like that of Pincher Martin) is a moot question," stresses Oldsey, who also notes that "again Golding returns to the most obsessive subject in his fiction—The Fall."

The Spire "is a book about vision and its cost," observes *New York Review of Books* critic Frank Kermode. "It has to do with the motives of art and prayer, the phallus turned spire; with the deceit, as painful to man as to God, involved in structures which are human but have to be divine, such as churches and spires.

But because the whole work is a dance of figurative language such an account of it can only be misleading." Characteristic of all Golding's work, *The Spire* can be read on two levels, that of an engrossing story and of a biting analysis of human nature. As Nigel Dennis finds in the *New York Times Book Review,* Golding "has always written on these two levels. But 'The Spire' will be of particular interest to his admirers because it can also be read as an exact description of his own artistic method. This consists basically of trying to rise to the heights while keeping himself glued to the ground. Mr. Golding's aspirations climb by clinging to solid objects and working up them like a vine. This is particularly pronounced in [*The Spire*], where every piece of building stone, every stage of scaffolding, every joint and ledge, are used by the author to draw himself up into the blue."

With this book Golding completed his first decade in the literary eye. The author's prolific output—five novels in ten years—and the high quality of his work established him as one of the late twentieth-century's most distinguished writers. This view of Golding was cemented in 1965, when the author was named a Commander of the British Empire.

Thus, by 1965, Golding was evidently on his way to continuing acclaim and popular acceptance—but "then matters changed abruptly," as Oldsey relates. The writer's output dropped dramatically: for the next fifteen years he produced no novels and only a handful of novellas, short stories, and occasional pieces. Of this period—what Boyd refers to as the "hiatus in the Golding oeuvre"—*The Pyramid,* a collection of three related novellas (and considered a novel proper by some critics), is generally regarded as one of the writer's weaker efforts. The episodic story of a man's existence in the suspiciously-named English town of Stilbourne, *The Pyramid* proved a shock to "even Golding's most faithful adherents [who] wondered if the book was indeed a novel or if it contributed anything to the author's reputation. To some it seemed merely three weak stories jammed together to produce a salable book," says Oldsey. *The Pyramid,* however, does have its admirers, among them John Wakeman of the *New York Times Book Review,* who feels the work is Golding's "first sociological novel. It is certainly more humane, exploratory, and life-size than its predecessors, less Old Testament, more New Testament." And to a *Times Literary Supplement* critic the book "will astonish by what it is not. It is not a fable, it does not contain evident allegory, it is not set in a simplified or remote world. It belongs to another, more commonplace tradition of English fiction; it is a low-keyed, realistic novel of growing up in a small town—the sort of book H. G. Wells might have written if he had been more attentive to his style."

The Scorpion God, another collection of novellas, was somewhat better received. One *Times Literary Supplement* reviewer, while calling the work "not major Golding," nevertheless finds the book "a pure example of Golding's gift. . . . The title story is from Golding's Egyptological side and is set in ancient Egypt. . . . By treating the unfamiliar with familiarity, explaining nothing, he teases the reader into the strange world of the story. It is as brilliant a *tour de force* as *The Inheritors,* if on a smaller scale."

Golding's reintroduction to the literary world was acknowledged in 1979 with the publication of *Darkness Visible.* Despite some fifteen years absence from the novel, the author "returns unchanged," Samuel Hynes observes in a *Washington Post Book World* article. "[He is] still a moralist, still a maker of parables. To be a moralist you must believe in good and evil, and Golding does; indeed, you might say that the nature of good and evil is his only theme. To be a parable-maker you must believe that

moral meaning can be expressed in the very fabric of the story itself, and perhaps that some meanings can only be expressed in this way; and this, too, has always been Golding's way."

The title *Darkness Visible* derives from Milton's description of Hell in *Paradise Lost,* and from the first scenes of the book Golding confronts the reader with images of fire, mutilation, and pain—which he presents in Biblical terms. For instance, notes *Commonweal* reviewer Bernard McCabe, the novel's opening describes a small child, "horribly burned, horribly disfigured, [who walks] out of the flames at the height of the London blitz. . . . The shattered building he emerges from . . . is called 'a burning bush,' the firemen stare into 'two pillars of lighted smoke,' the child walks with a 'ritual gait,' and he appears to have been 'born from the sheer agony of a burning city.' " The rescued youth, dubbed Matty, the left side of whose face has been left permanently mutilated, grows up to be a religious visionary.

"If Matty is a force for light, he is opposed by a pair of beautiful twins, Toni and Sophy Stanhope," continues Susan Fromberg Schaeffer in her *Chicago Tribune Book World* review. "These girls, once symbols of innocence in their town, discover the seductive attractions of darkness. Once, say the spirits who visit Matty, the girls were called before them, but they refused to come. Instead, obsessed by the darkness loose in the world, they abandon morality, choosing instead a demonic hedonism that allows them to justify anything, even mass murder." "Inevitably, the two girls will . . . [embark on a] spectacular crime, and just as inevitably, Matty, driven by his spirit guides, must oppose them," sums up *Time*'s Peter S. Prescott. "The confrontation, as you may imagine, ends happily for no one."

Darkness Visible received mixed reviews overall, with much of the negative reaction focusing on the author's "embarrassing fictional stereotypes . . . and his heavy-handedly ironic attempt to create a visionary-moron in [Matty]," as Joyce Carol Oates relates in *New Republic.* And McCabe finds that although the novel "has its undeniable fascinations . . . [nevertheless] what I end up with is an impression of a very earnest writer, blessed with remarkable skills and up to all sorts of ingenuities, struggling with a dark vision of man, trying to express it through a complex art, making another attempt at another *tour de force,* and getting nowhere."

On the other hand, Hynes, who concedes that *Darkness Visible* is a "difficult novel," adds that "unlike many other contemporary novels, it is difficult because its meaning is difficult: it is not a complicated word game, or a labyrinth with a vacuum at the center. Golding, the religious man, has once more set himself the task of finding the signs and revelations, the parable, that will express his sense of the human situation. Difficult, yes—isn't morality difficult?—but worth the effort."

While *Darkness Visible* "could not by itself restore Golding to prominence," as Robert Towers points out in the *New York Review of Books,* the wave of renewed interest the book generated in its author paved the way for Golding's following novel, *Rites of Passage.* A tale of high-seas adventure, *Rites of Passage,* according to Towers, is "a first-rate historical novel that is also a novel of ideas—a taut, beautifully controlled short book with none of the windiness or costumed pageantry so often associated with fictional attempts to reanimate the past."

Some of the ideas explored in this book trace back to *Lord of the Flies* "and to the view [the author] held then of man as a fallen being capable of a 'vileness beyond words,' " as *New Statesman* writer Blake Morrison sees it. Set in the early nineteenth-century, *Rites of Passage* tells of a voyage from England to Australia as recounted through the shipboard diary of young aristocrat Edmund Talbot. "He sets down a vivid record of the ship and its characters," explains Morrison. They include "the irascible Captain Anderson . . . , the 'wind-machine Mr Brockleband,' the whorish 'painted Magdalene' called Zenobia, and the meek and ridiculous 'parson,' Mr Colley, who is satirised as mercilessly as the clerics in [Henry] Fielding's *Joseph Andrews.*" This latter character is the one through which much of the dramatic action in *Rites of Passage* takes place. For Colley, this "country curate . . . this hedge priest," as Golding's Talbot describes him, "is the perfect victim—self-deluding, unworldly, sentimentally devout, priggish, and terrified. Above all he is ignorant of the powerful homosexual streak in his nature that impels him toward the crew and especially toward one stalwart sailor, Billy Rogers," says Towers. Driven by his passion yet torn by doubt, ridiculed and shunned by the other passengers on the ship, Colley literally dies of shame during the voyage.

"It should be clear . . . that the ship is a microcosm of sorts, encapsulating an entire society or nation," Towers notes. "It may even have occurred to some that the concealed name of this obsolete old ship of the line, with its female figurehead obscenely nicknamed by the crew, might well be *Britannia.* At this hint of allegorizing I can imagine a shudder passing through certain prospective readers. But they need not fear. Though there is indeed a schoolmasterish streak in Golding, inclining him toward the didactic, tempting him to embellish his work with literary references . . . , he has in *Rites of Passage* constructed a narrative vessel sturdy enough to support his ideas. And because his ideas—about the role of class, about the nature of authority and its abuses, about cruelty (both casual and deliberate) and its consequences—because these themes and others are adequately dramatized, adequately incorporated, they become agents within the novel, actively and interestingly, at work within the fictional setting."

The author faced his harshest criticism to date with the publication of his 1984 novel *The Paper Men.* A farce-drama about an aging, successful novelist's conflicts with his pushy, overbearing biographer, *The Paper Men* "tells us that biography is the trade of the con man, a fatuous accomplishment, and the height of impertinence in both meanings of the word," according to London *Times* critic Michael Ratcliff. Unfortunately for Golding, most critics find *The Paper Men* to be sorely lacking in the qualities that distinguish the author's best work. Typical of their commentary is this observation from Michiko Kakutani of the *New York Times:* "Judging from the tired, petulant tone of [the novel], Mr. Golding would seem to have more in common with his creation than mere appearance—a 'scraggy yellow-white beard, yellow-white thatch and broken-toothed grin.' He, too, seems to have allowed his pessimistic vision of man to curdle his view of the world and to sour his enjoyment of craft."

Some reviewers call *The Paper Men* a work unworthy of a Nobel Prize winner (Golding had received the award just months prior to the book's publication); reacting to the outpouring of negative criticism, Blake Morrison says in the *Times Literary Supplement* that "all that can be said with confidence is that Golding's previous novels, even those that were coolly received on publication, have stood up well to subsequent re-readings, and that *The Paper Men* is certain to get a more patient treatment from future explicators than it has had from its reviewers. As for the author, he will have to console himself with [his lead character's] rather specious piece of reasoning on the poor reception of [his own novel]: 'You have to write the bad books if you're going to write the good ones.' "

Departing briefly from fiction, Golding has produced two books of "occasional pieces," works containing essays, reviews, and lectures. *The Hot Gates, and Other Occasional Pieces* was published in 1965; *A Moving Target* appeared in 1982, one year prior to the author's receipt of the Nobel Prize. Literary observations pervade *A Moving Target.* Golding speaks not only of the works of such authors as Samuel Richardson, Alexander Pope, and Jane Austen, he offers "advice" to aspiring writers and, "with pristine clarity, he answers critics, academics and 'dangerous' postgraduate students who have subjected his 'Lord of the Flies' to 'Freudian analysis, neo-Freudian analysis, Jungian analysis, Roman Catholic approval, . . . Protestant apprisal, nonconformist surmise, and Scientific Humanist misinterpretation,'" as *Los Angeles Times Book Review* contributor John Rechy observes.

But the most moving passage in the book, according to Gabriel Josipovici, writing in the *Times Literary Supplement,* is a pair of mood pieces that find Golding reliving his youthful infatuation with Egyptology, and a travel essay that finds the boy, a lifetime later, finally exploring Egypt in person. The critic opined: "This volume is fascinating . . . because it gives us a glimpse of two Goldings. The pieces about place, about Homer, about fairytales, convey the power of his imagination, his extraordinary ability to enter into and convey to us the strangeness and incomprehensibility of the world we live in. The lectures, on the other hand, give us a glimpse of the writer turning into a monument, not graciously but uneasily."

While he has faced extensive criticism and categorization in his writing career, the author is able to provide a brief, simple description of himself in Jack I. Biles's *Talk: Conversations with William Golding:* "I'm against the picture of the artist as the starry-eyed visionary not really in control or knowing what he does. I think I'd almost prefer the word 'craftsman.' He's like one of the old-fashioned shipbuilders, who conceived the boat in their mind and then, after that, touched every single piece that went into the boat. They were in complete control; they knew it inch by inch, and I think the novelist is very much like that."

MEDIA ADAPTATIONS: Pincher Martin was produced as a radio play for the British Broadcasting Corp. in 1958; *Lord of the Flies* was filmed by Continental in 1963, and by Castle Rock Entertainment in 1990.

AVOCATIONAL INTERESTS: Sailing, archaeology, and playing the piano, violin, viola, cello, and oboe.

BIOGRAPHICAL/CRITICAL SOURCES:

BOOKS

Allen, Walter, *The Modern Novel,* Dutton, 1964.
Anderson, David, *The Tragic Past,* John Knox Press, 1969.
Axthelm, Peter M., *The Modern Confessional Novel,* Yale University Press, 1967.
Babb, Howard S., *The Novels of William Golding,* Ohio State University Press, 1970.
Baker, James R., *William Golding: A Critical Study,* St. Martin's, 1965.
Biles, Jack I., *Talk: Conversations with William Golding,* Harcourt, 1971.
Biles, Jack I. and Robert O. Evans, editors, *William Golding: Some Critical Considerations,* University Press of Kentucky, 1979.
Burgess, Anthony, *The Novel Now: A Guide to Contemporary Fiction,* Norton, 1967.

Contemporary Literary Criticism, Gale, Volume 1, 1973, Volume 2, 1974, Volume 3, 1975, Volume 8, 1978, Volume 10, 1979, Volume 18, 1981, Volume 27, 1984.

Dick, Bernard F., *William Golding,* Twayne, 1967.

Dictionary of Literary Biography, Volume 15: *British Novelists, 1930-1959,* Gale, 1983.

Dictionary of Literary Biography Yearbook: 1983, Gale, 1984.

Gindin, James, *Postwar British Fiction: New Accents and Attitudes,* University of California Press, 1962.

Gindin, James, *Harvest of a Quiet Eve: The Novel of Compassion,* Indiana University Press, 1971.

Golding, William, *Lord of the Flies,* Faber, 1954, published with an introduction by E. M. Forster, Coward, 1955, reprinted, 1978.

Golding, William, *The Spire,* Harcourt, 1964.

Golding, William, *The Hot Gates, and Other Occasional Pieces,* Harcourt, 1965.

Golding, William, *Darkness Visible,* Farrar, Straus, 1979.

Golding, William, *Rites of Passage,* Farrar, Straus, 1980.

Golding, William, *A Moving Target,* Farrar, Straus, 1982.

Green, Peter, *A Review of English Literature,* Longmans, Green, 1960.

Hynes, Samuel, *William Golding,* Columbia University Press, 1964.

Johnson, Arnold, *Of Earth and Darkness: The Novels of William Golding,* University of Missouri Press, 1980.

Kennard, Jean E., *Number and Nightmare: Forms of Fantasy in Contemporary Fiction,* Archon Books, 1975.

Kinkead-Weekes, Mark and Ian Gregor, *William Golding: A Critical Study,* Faber, 1967.

Medcalf, Stephen, *William Golding,* Longman, 1975.

Oldsey, Bernard S. and Stanley Weintraub, *The Art of William Golding,* Harcourt, 1965.

Ries, Lawrence R., *Wolf Masks: Violence in Contemporary Fiction,* Kennikat Press, 1975.

Tiger, Virginia, *William Golding: The Dark Fields of Discovery,* Calder & Boyars, 1974.

PERIODICALS

Atlantic, May, 1965, April, 1984.

Chicago Tribune, October 7, 1983.

Chicago Tribune Book World, December 30, 1979, October 26, 1980, April 8, 1984.

Commentary, January, 1968.

Commonweal, October 25, 1968, September 26, 1980.

Critical Quarterly, summer, 1960, autumn, 1962, spring, 1967.

Critique: Studies in Modern Fiction, Volume 14, number 2, 1972.

Detroit News, December 16, 1979, January 4, 1981, April 29, 1984.

Kenyon Review, autumn, 1957.

Life, November 17, 1967.

Listener, October 4, 1979, October 23, 1980, January 5, 1984.

London Magazine, February-March, 1981.

London Review of Books, June 17, 1982.

Los Angeles Times Book Review, November 9, 1980, June 20, 1982, June 3, 1984.

New Republic, December 8, 1979, September 13, 1982.

New Statesman, August 2, 1958, April 10, 1964, November 5, 1965, October 12, 1979, October 17, 1980, June 11, 1982.

Newsweek, November 5, 1979, October 27, 1980, April 30, 1984.

New Yorker, September 21, 1957.

New York Post, December 17, 1963.

New York Review of Books, April 30, 1964, December 7, 1967, February 24, 1972, December 6, 1979, December 18, 1980.

New York Times, September 1, 1957, November 9, 1979, October 15, 1980, October 7, 1983, March 26, 1984, June 22, 1987.

New York Times Book Review, October 23, 1955, April 19, 1964, November 18, 1979, November 2, 1980, July 11, 1982.

Saturday Review, March 19, 1960.

South Atlantic Quarterly, autumn, 1970.

Southern Review, March, 1976.

Spectator, October 13, 1979.

Time, September 9, 1957, October 13, 1967, October 17, 1983, April 9, 1984, June 8, 1987.

Times (London), February 9, 1984, June 11, 1987.

Times Literary Supplement, October 21, 1955, October 23, 1959, June 1, 1967, November 5, 1971, November 23, 1979, October 17, 1980, July 23, 1982, March 2, 1984.

Twentieth Century Literature, summer, 1982.

Village Voice, November 5, 1979.

Washington Post, July 12, 1982, October 7, 1983, January 12, 1986.

Washington Post Book World, November 4, 1979, November 2, 1980, April 15, 1984.

Yale Review, spring, 1960.

*   *   *

GOLDSEN, Rose Kohn   1918-

PERSONAL: Born May 19, 1918, in Newark, NJ; daughter of Jacob Joseph and Ida (Mendel) Kohn; divorced. *Education:* New York University, B.A., 1943; Yale University, M.A., 1944, Ph.D., 1953.

ADDRESSES: Home—770 Elm St. Ext., Ithaca, NY 14850. *Office*—Department of Sociology, Cornell University, Ithaca, NY 14853.

CAREER: Columbia University, Bureau of Applied Social Research, New York City, research associate, 1938-42, 1946-48; Yale University, Institute of Human Relations, New Haven, CT, research associate, 1943-45; Cornell University, Ithaca, NY, 1949—, associate professor of sociology, beginning 1958. Fulbright lecturer in France, 1957-58. Syndicated radio and newspaper columnist.

MEMBER: Interamerican Psychological Association, American Sociological Association, American Association for Public Opinion Research.

WRITINGS:

(Co-author) *Puerto Rican Journey,* Harper, 1950.

What College Students Think, Van Nostrand, 1960.

Clearing the Air; or, How Fares the First Amendment: Is It Alive and Well?, Media Ithaca, Department of Sociology, Cornell University, c. 1970.

The Show and Tell Machine: How Television Works and Works You Over, Dial, 1976.

Also author of "Blowing the Whistle on Broadcasting," a series of radio programs. Contributor to professional journals.

SIDELIGHTS: Atlantic reviewer Phoebe Adams summarizes Rose Kohn Goldsen's theory about television and television viewing in one sentence taken from the author's widely-reviewed book on the subject, *The Show and Tell Machine: How Television Works and Works You Over:* "Although the broadcasting business likes to kid audiences into thinking they are the customers of television, they are in fact the product television offers for sale." Told from a highly critical viewpoint, the book wins initial approval from Jeff Greenfield in his *New York Times Book Re-*

view commentary on the work because he, too, believes there is much that should be changed about television; nevertheless, Greenfield finds Goldsen's critique of the industry too general. "So sweeping is her condemnation," Greenfield writes, "and so overstated the premise of television's power over all of us, that [this work] winds up undermining its own argument."

BIOGRAPHICAL/CRITICAL SOURCES:

PERIODICALS

Atlantic, November, 1977.
National Review, May 12, 1978.
New York Times Book Review, November 20, 1977.*

* * *

GOLDSMITH, Peter
　See PRIESTLEY, J(ohn) B(oynton)

* * *

GOLDTHORPE, J(ohn) E(rnest) 1921-

PERSONAL: Born June 10, 1921, in Cleethorpes, England; son of Samuel Leonard (a businessman) and Dorothy Elizabeth (a teacher; maiden name, Cooke) Goldthorpe; married Lois Muriel Anne Slater (a college lecturer in education), March 30, 1950; children: Timothy Peter, Susan Dorothy, Joy Barbara, Jonathan Christopher. *Education:* Christ's College, Cambridge, B.A., 1942, M.A., 1946; London School of Economics and Political Science, University of London, B.Sc. (economics), 1949, Ph.D., 1961. *Avocational interests:* Walking in northern England.

ADDRESSES: Home—218 Kirkstall Ln., Leeds LS6 3DS, England. *Office*—Department of Sociology, University of Leeds, Leeds LS2 9JT, England.

CAREER: Makerere University College, Kampala, Uganda, 1951-52, began as lecturer, became senior lecturer in sociology; University of Leeds, Leeds, England, beginning 1962, began as lecturer, became senior lecturer in sociology. *Military service:* Royal Navy, 1941-46. Royal Naval Volunteer Reserve; became lieutenant.

MEMBER: International African Institute, British Sociological Association, African Studies Association of the United Kingdom (past member of council), Society of Authors, Ramblers Association.

WRITINGS:

Outlines of East African Society, Makerere University College, 1958, revised edition, 1962.
(With F. B. Wilson) *Tribal Maps of East Africa and Zanzibar,* East African Institute of Social Research (Kampala, Uganda), 1960.
(Contributor) A. W. Southall, editor, *Social Change in Modern Africa,* International African Institute, 1961.
An African Elite, Oxford University Press (East Africa), 1965.
An Introduction to Sociology, Cambridge University Press, 1968, 3rd edition, 1985.
The Sociology of the Third World: Disparity and Development, Cambridge University Press, 1975, 2nd edition, 1984.
Family Life in Western Societies: A Historical Sociology of Family Relationships in Britain and North America, Cambridge University Press, 1987.

Also author of "Peoples of Kenya Resource Packet" for teaching about Africa south of the Sahara. Contributor of articles and re-

views to journals, including *Journal of Glaciology, Zaire, Universities Quarterly, British Journal of Sociology, Population Studies,* and *Sociological Review,* and to newspapers.

SIDELIGHTS: J. E. Goldthorpe once told *CA:* "Writing for me is very much a nine-to-five job, and I find I cannot write anything serious until I can confidently look ahead to large blocks of time—weeks, months—with nothing to think about except what I am writing about. Nothing, that is, at the intellectual, hopefully creative level. Of course, one can think about what's for supper or remember to pay the gas bill, but what is quite incompatible with writing is teaching, switching one's intellectual attention from day to day and hour to hour to different topics and areas of knowledge. Filling in the odd hour, or even day, is not possible. All my writing hitherto has been done, either in vacations, or sabbatical time. *Sociology of the Third World* was written during a 'semi-sabbatical' year when I was able to limit my teaching to what I was writing about, and my appearances in the University department to two days a week. Now I am looking forward eagerly to early retirement this time next year, when I shall be able to concentrate on writing, undistracted at last."

* * *

GOLSON, G(eorge) Barry 1944-

PERSONAL: Born December 12, 1944, in Lynn, MA; son of George Albert and Beverly Margaret (Barry) Golson; married Cynthia MacKenzie (a hospital employee), August 24, 1968. *Education:* Yale University, B.A., 1967; Stanford University, graduate study, 1967-68.

ADDRESSES: Office—*Playboy Magazine,* 747 Third Ave., New York, NY 10017.

CAREER: Atlas: World Press Review, New York City, managing editor and columnist, 1969-71; free-lance writer in Connecticut, 1971-72; *Playboy,* New York City, assistant articles editor, 1972-74, senior editor, 1974-76, executive editor, 1976—.

AWARDS, HONORS: Ford fellowship, 1968; first prize for satire in *Playboy* Writers' Awards competition, 1972.

WRITINGS:

(Contributor) *Is Nothing Sacred?,* Playboy Press, 1973.
(Editor) *The Playboy Interview,* Playboy Press, 1981.
(Editor) *The Playboy Interviews with John Lennon and Yoko Ono,* Playboy Press, 1981.
(Editor) *The Playboy Interview II,* Perigee, 1983.

SIDELIGHTS: G. Barry Golson has been in charge of the interview feature of *Playboy* magazine since 1972, and has conducted many of the interviews himself over the years. His *The Playboy Interview* and *The Playboy Interview II* contain an assortment of interviews from the magazine accompanied by his background notes concerning each dialogue. Commenting on *The Playboy Interview,* Charles Champlin of the *Los Angeles Times* observes, "However one reacts to anything else in [*Playboy*], there is no arguing that the exhaustive and often abrasive interviews (sometimes abrasively persistent in the asking, sometimes abrasively angry in the answering) are the best of their kind and are by now irreplaceable source documents on figures in recent history."

BIOGRAPHICAL/CRITICAL SOURCES:

PERIODICALS

Los Angeles Times, May 8, 1981.
New York Times, July 2, 1981.*

GRAHAM, James
 See PATTERSON, Harry

* * *

GRAY, Francine du Plessix 1930-

PERSONAL: Born September 25, 1930, in Warsaw, Poland (some sources say France); came to United States in 1941; naturalized citizen, 1952; daughter of Bertrand Jochaud (a diplomat and pilot for the Resistance) and Tatiana (Iacovleff) du Plessix; married Cleve Gray (a painter), April 23, 1957; children: Thaddeus Ives, Luke Alexander. *Education:* Attended Bryn Mawr College, 1948-50, and Black Mountain College, summers, 1951-52; Barnard College, B.A., 1952. *Politics:* Democrat. *Religion:* Roman Catholic.

ADDRESSES: Home—Greystones, Cornwall Bridge, CT 06754. *Agent*—Georges Borchardt, Inc., 136 East 57th St., New York, NY 10022.

CAREER: United Press International, New York City, reporter at night desk, 1952-54; *Realities* (magazine), Paris, France, editorial assistant for French edition, 1954-55; free-lance writer, 1955—; *Art in America,* New York City, book editor, 1964-66; *New Yorker,* New York City, staff writer, 1968—. Distinguished visiting professor at City College of the City University of New York, spring, 1975; visiting lecturer at Saybrook College, Yale University, 1981; adjunct professor, School of Fine Arts, Columbia University, 1983—. Judge of 1974 National Book Award in philosophy and religion. Attended Soviet-American Writers' Workshop in Batumin, U.S.S.R., 1979.

MEMBER: International PEN, Authors Guild, Authors League of America, National Book Critics Circle.

AWARDS, HONORS: Putnam Creative Writing Award from Barnard College, 1952; National Catholic Book Award from Catholic Press Association, 1971, for *Divine Disobedience: Profiles in Catholic Radicalism;* Front Page Award from Newswomen's Club of New York, 1972, for *Hawaii: The Sugar-Coated Fortress;* LL.D. from City University of New York, 1981, Oberlin College, 1985, University of Santa Clara, 1985.

WRITINGS:

Divine Disobedience: Profiles in Catholic Radicalism, Knopf, 1970.
Hawaii: The Sugar-Coated Fortress, Random House, 1972.
Lovers and Tyrants (novel), Simon & Schuster, 1976.
World Without End (novel), Simon & Schuster, 1981.
October Blood (novel), Simon & Schuster, 1985.
Adam and Eve and the City: Selected Nonfiction, Simon & Schuster, 1987.
Soviet Women: Walking the Tightrope, Doubleday, 1990.

Contributor of articles, stories, and reviews to periodicals, including *Vogue, New Yorker, Saturday Review, New York Review of Books, New York Times Book Review,* and *New Republic.*

WORK IN PROGRESS: A novel.

SIDELIGHTS: In 1976 *New Yorker* columnist Francine du Plessix Gray published *Lovers and Tyrants,* a book Caryl Rivers describes in *Ms.* as being "as rich in its texture as the lace tablecloths women of my grandmother's generation used to crochet." The novel, a startling and often touching autobiographical *bildungsroman,* gained the attention of many critics. "Every woman's first novel about her own break-through into adulthood is significant—liberation of any kind is significant—but Francine

du Plessix Gray has created, in hers, something memorable," comments Kathleen Cushman in the *National Observer.* "To the cathartic throes of autobiography she has added a good dose each of humor, irony, and skill; *Lovers and Tyrants* transcends its limited possibilities as a book about *Woman Oppressed* and crosses into the realm of art."

The eight parts of this novel of "ascent and liberation," as Joan Peters calls it in the *Nation,* describe various periods in the life of Stephanie, the heroine. It begins with her childhood in Paris as the daughter of a Russian mother and an aristocratic French father who wanted her to be a boy. She is raised by a hypochondriac governess and her childhood, she writes in the opening lines of the book, was "muted, opaque, and drab, the color of gruel and of woolen gaiters, its noises muted and monotonous as a sleeper's pulse. . . . My temperature was taken twice a day, my head was perpetually wrapped in some woolen muffler or gauze veiling. I was scrubbed, spruced, buffed, combed, polished, year round, like a first communicant." After her father's death in the Resistance, Stephanie and her mother move to New York where Stephanie attends a fancy boarding school. Later, a young adult, she returns to France to visit her relatives and has an affair with a French prince who describes himself as "style incarnate." Nearing thirty, she marries an architect, bears two sons, and continues her career as a journalist. She feels confined and dissatisfied in her marriage and leaves to tour the Southwest, writing about bizarre religious cults and taking up with a twenty-five-year-old homosexual who longs to be both a bisexual and a photographer and who continuously begs Stephanie to feed him. The theme of the novel, as Stephanie points out, is the tyranny of love: "Every woman's life is a series of exorcisms from the spells of different oppressors: nurses, lovers, husbands, gurus, parents, children, myths of the good life. The most tyrannical despots can be the ones who love us the most."

That theme, Gray acknowledges, came from experiences in her own life. In an essay for the *New York Times Book Review,* Gray writes that her late start in writing fiction was partially due to fear of disapproval from her father—even though he had died when she was eleven. *Lovers and Tyrants* grew out of her frustration as a young wife and mother. "I was married and had two children," Gray stated in the *New York Times Book Review* "The Making of an Author" column, "and since I live deep in the country and in relative solitude, encompassed by domestic duties, the journal [that I kept] became increasingly voluminous, angry, introspective. The nomad, denied flight and forced to turn inward, was beginning to explode. One day when I was 33, after I'd cooked and smiled for a bevy of weekend guests whom I never wished to see again, I felt an immense void, a great powerlessness, the deepest loneliness I'd ever known. I wept for some hours, took out a notebook, started rewriting one of the three stories that had won me my Barnard prize. It was the one about my governess. . . . It was to become, 12 years and two books of nonfiction later, the first chapter for *Lovers and Tyrants.* The process of finishing that book was as complex and lengthy as it was painful."

"There is something very French—Cartesian—in the orderly, rigid pattern that Francine's novel imposes on the random richness of Stephanie's life," remarks Audrey Foote in *Washington Post Book World.* "It is convenient, too; Gray herself has compared it to stringing beads. Once the themes are established, Stephanie-Francine is absolved of all problems of plot construction, free to proceed methodically yet meaningfully through the heroine's life, devoting every stage, every chapter to the unmasking of another 'jailer.' *Lovers and Tyrants* is an apt and total title; the book is a litany of oppressors, a rosary of named identities."

It is that process of naming her oppressors that is central to Stephanie's story, for, to her, that is the way to liberation. "We must name the identities of each jailer before we can crawl on toward the next stage of freedom," Stephanie writes in her journal. "To herself, and to me," says Peters, "Stephanie is simply a person trying to acknowledge and accommodate the forces that have acted on her and which remain a part of her."

The process of naming her oppressors and liberating herself from them (and from the strangling memories of past 'jailers') forms the crux of *Lovers and Tyrants.* But it is not only a personal liberation that Stephanie seeks. She views her situation as part of the historical oppression of women. When she leaves her husband and takes to the road, she says that she rebels "for all women, because we are killing each other in our doll's houses." Her ultimate desire, she tells the reader, is "to be free, to be a boy, to be God." Comments Rivers in *Ms.*: "[Stephanie] sees dropping out as the prelude to rebirth. She will be Kerouac, Dean; she will infringe on male territory. . . . *Lovers and Tyrants* may be a classic in a new genre of literature—the woman as wanderer, seeker of truth. . . . To take this journey with her is to confront not only the questions of love and freedom, but those of death and immortality and existence as well." Sara Sanborn considers the novel to be a feminist fable. "The theme of this novel," Sanborn writes in *Saturday Review,* "[is] the perpetual seduction of women by those who will offer tenderness and authority, the feminine materials of feminine transcendence."

The first three-fourths of the novel—the first-person sections describing her childhood, her return to France, and her marriage—is widely praised for its wit, fine writing, and evocative detail. "The author has no trouble persuading the reader that there was once a small girl in Paris named Stephanie," says *Time*'s Timothy Foote, as he notes the similarities between Stephanie's life and that of her creator's (the French and Russian parentage, the immigration to New York, the private schools, the fling in Paris, the career as a journalist, an artistic husband two sons, even, notes Foote, the same high cheekbones and large eyes). "Stephanie's remembrance of things past flashes with literary style and wit. Remarkable siblings, and sexual suitors are summoned up, often in hilarious detail, though they are mostly kept frozen at the edge of caricature by Stephanie's satiric perceptions." These early sections of the novel, writes Julian Moynahan in the *New York Times Book Review,* "are crammed with unforgettably drawn characters, rich emotion and complex social portraiture. In counterpoint they bring out contrasted aspects of French life that are both immemorial and contemporary, and that perhaps only a cultural 'amphibian' like Mrs. du Plessix Gray would clearly see." Joan Peters in *Nation* deems "the depiction of Stephanie's relationship with Paul . . . as complex a portrait of love and marriage as I have seen in recent novels."

While critical opinion of the beginning sections of *Lovers and Tyrants* is overwhelmingly favorable, reviews of the last chapters tend to be negative. Michael Wood, for example, in his *New York Review of Books* article calls the final chapters of *Lovers and Tyrants* "truly lamentable," citing sloppy writing and a final section that "has expanded too far into fantasy" as his reasons for such harsh criticism. "There is a great deal that goes on in the eighth, last, longest, and presumably climactic chapter of *Lovers and Tyrants,*" Christopher Lehmann-Haupt comments in the *New York Times.* "There is abundant activity. . . . There is sex. . . . But nowhere in that concluding chapter is it possible to find anything to rouse the reader from his intensifying somnolence. Nowhere is there an interesting unanswered question about the plot or the heroine's development. Nowhere is there activity or thought that one hasn't long since been able to pre-

dict. Nowhere is there articulation of Stephanie's problem that we haven't heard uttered before. ('God, I hate puritanism, wasp puritanism, all kinds. Do you realize it's puritanism got us into Vietnam?') Nowhere is there surprise. And that is why *Lovers and Tyrants,* for all the wit and thrust of its prose, is finally so exasperating. The drone of its intelligence ultimately bores."

Village Voice book editor Eliot Fremont-Smith also finds *Lovers and Tyrants* intelligent but at the same time lacking because of that intelligence. "I think something more basic is wrong," he remarks, referring to the abrupt change in the book's tone in the last sections, "and it has to do with intelligence and class. And tone. And tonyness. *Lovers and Tyrants* is nothing if not wonderfully intelligent. For much of the novel, the intelligence is presumed and shared; the reader is in really interesting company, and feels there by right of respectful invitation, and is so honored. But toward the end, the intelligence—not so much of Stephanie or her witty companion, but of the *book*—turns into something else, a sort of shrill IQ-mongering. Intellectual references from the very best places are tossed around like Frisbees; it becomes a contest, and a rather exclusionary one, with the reader on the sidelines. This subverts, first, credibility. (Such *constant* smartness, such unflagging articulation of sensibility, such memories! Don't they ever say Stekel when they mean Ferenczi? Don't they ever get tired?) It subverts, second, a sense of caring. A defensive reaction but that's what happens when one feels snubbed, or made the fool. In the end, *Lovers and Tyrants* seems more crass than Class; there is an unpleasant aftertaste of having been unexpectedly and for no deserving reason, insulted. This is inelegant."

Credibility is also seen as a problem by other reviewers of *Lover and Tyrants.* A major criticism of the novel is that, in the end, the story is not believable. "There is so much in this book to admire that I wish I could believe Stephanie's story. I don't," says Sara Sanborn in *Saturday Review.* "Stephanie seems twice-born, her sensibility as narrator formed more by other writers, from Henry James to Kate Millet, than by the events recounted, which also have their haunting familiarity. I don't believe for one minute that Stephanie really has two children: in twenty years the chief effect they have on her is to supply her with wise-child sayings. Finally, I don't believe in Stephanie's unvarying superiority. Even in her bad moments, she is more thoughtful, sensitive, and self-perceptive, more humorous, open, and finally free than anyone she encounters. The other characters seem to have their existence only to further her self-exploration." *Newsweek* reviewer Peter S. Prescott also agrees: "For three-quarters of its route, *Lovers and Tyrants* is a remarkably convincing, even exhilarating performance. [However,] toward the end, in a long section in the third person, I sensed the author striking poses, lecturing us a bit to emphasize points already amply developed, introducing two characters—a radical Jesuit and a homosexual youth—who are not as engaging as I suspect the author means them to be."

Time's Timothy Foote questions Stephanie's credibility as a character and narrator because, he says, "Stephanie's cries rise to heaven like those of De Sade's Justine, a girl one recollects, with far more justification for complaint." At the point Stephanie leaves her husband (who, Foote mentions, is a "fine husband, a kind man, a devoted father") and goes on the road, "Mrs. Gray abruptly switches from the first-person 'I' narrative form that has preserved whatever degree of credibility the story maintains. Stephanie in the third-person, Stephanie as 'she,' makes fairly ludicrous fiction. . . . This is an age that has learned any grievance must be accepted as both genuine and significant if the public weeping and wailing are long and loud enough. It would therefore be wise to take seriously Mrs. Gray's passionate meditation on the tyranny of love. Not as a novel, though." In the end, Michael Wood in *New York Review of Books* finds that "this hitherto solid and patient novel has expanded too far into fantasy, and has lost even the truth of seriously entertained wishes."

Concomitant to the lack of credibility that Stephanie suffers is what is perceived by some critics as her inability to reconcile her feminist beliefs with her actions. Writing in the *Nation*, Joan Peters observes that "one of the problems with *Lovers and Tyrants* is that not all the contradictions are accounted for or, it seems, planned for. Among the most perplexing of these is the tension between Stephanie's feminist analysis of her life and her persistent identification with men. On the one hand, she is quite strong in her analysis of how confining it is to be a woman, how discrimination operates, how few models women have, etc. . . . On the other hand, the actual record of Stephanie's life is a Freudian's delight and a feminist's nightmare. Again and again Stephanie realizes that she wants to be a boy." Peters then points out contradictions that belie Stephanie's words: "[her] need to be with men, her desire to be a boy, the absence of female friends, the Henry Milleresque sexual descriptions, her assumption that it is because Mishka couldn't love men that she was so cruel." Moynahan calls Stephanie "the unsatisfactory representation or symbol of modern woman in the throes of an unprecedented process of liberation." Earlier in his article, Moynahan had questioned the value of Stephanie's liberation, noting that despite her access to almost every pleasure desired and freedom from most worries, Stephanie slips "into madness out of a conviction that her freedom is obstructed."

Audrey Foote in *Washington Post Book World* says, "Gray writes with such passion, grace and wit, and her themes are so fashionable, that the reader is swept along in sympathetic credulity until he begins to scrutinize these tyrants." Stephanie's tyrants—governess, family, husband, lovers, friends—Foote points out, are hardly that, loving and indulging Stephanie in any way they can. Continues Foote: "Surely none of these 'lovers' in the wide sense she intends, can seriously be classified as 'tyrants.'. . . *En fin,* there is only one clue that her obsession with tyranny is not pure paranoia: the sex scenes. . . . They are significant in showing that Stephanie, so heroic if quixotic in defiance of imagined oppression, is, alas, a sexual masochist. 'He ordered,' 'she asked permission,' 'he commanded'—she *chooses* these dominating lovers, and her compliance, her collaboration explains her conviction: 'Our enslavers segregate us into zoos, with our full consent.' Speak for yourself, Stephanie! Thus finally the provocative title and grand design of this novel turn out to be based on little more than a retrogressive sexual taste, a dreary and dubious cliche. . . . She is in search of freedom—to do what? What does she want? What do women want? Francine never quite tells us about Stephanie (does *she* know?)"

Despite reservations about *Lovers and Tyrants,* most critics have, in the end, judged it favorably. Peters concludes that in spite of the book's limitations, "what *Lovers and Tyrants* does do, and does beautifully, is exploit the limited strength of the autobiographical genre. Gray presents a fascinating, intelligent woman whose personal contradictions concerning tradition, freedom, sex, culture, and religion shed light on the larger society in a way that is sometimes inadvertant, more often artistically controlled." Michael Wood concedes that *Lovers and Tyrants* "is an absorbing and intelligent book, if a little too icy to be really likeable." Finally, the *Village Voice*'s Fremont-Smith observes: "*Lovers and Tyrants* has all sorts of problems and gets tiresomely narcissistic and irritating; still, it is one of the very truly interesting and stimulating—one wants to argue with it and about it—

books I've read all year. . . . If Gray's book burns a bit, and it does, that should suggest fire as well as ice at its core."

World Without End, Gray's second novel, is also noted for its sensitivity and intelligence. The story of three lifelong friends who reunite in middle age to tour Russia and, hopefully, to "learn how to live the last third of our lives," *World Without End* is "an ambitious novel about love and friendship, faith and doubt, liberty and license," comments Judith Gies in *Saturday Review*. D. M. Thomas, writing in the *Washington Post Book World,* considers *World Without End* to be "clearly the work of a richly talented writer. . . . The book is struggling with an important subject: the conflict within each of us between the psychological hungers symbolized by America and Russia—individualism and brotherhood, anarchy and order. It is no small achievement to have explored interestingly one of the most crucial dilemmas of our age."

Doris Grumbach in *Commonweal* calls *World Without End* "a prime entry in the novel of intelligence. It is just that: the lives [Gray] tells about ring with authenticity for their times and their place." It is the novel's "intelligence"—its lengthy discourses on a variety of subjects and the articulate growing self-awareness of its characters—that holds the attention of many of its reviewers. The *New York Times*'s John Leonard notes the "lyric excess" of the characters's musings, but believes that Gray "has chosen to satirize the art, the religion and the politics of the last 35 years" through characters Sophie, Claire, and Edmund. "[Gray] has also chosen to forgive the creatures of her satire," says Leonard. "They are more disappointed in themselves than readers will be in them as characters."

For other critics, the intellectual discussions in *World Without End* are a hindrance to an appreciation of the novel. "Anyone not conversant with the intellectual and esthetic upheavals in American art and politics over the last 30 years ought not attempt to read this novel," suggests Henrietta Epstein in the *Detroit News,* "for these concerns, along with those of friendship and love, are at the heart of Francine du Plessix Gray's work." *Newsweek* reviewer Annalyn Swan concurs with Leonard that "some of this is obviously satire" and says that "when Gray is not trying to be wry, or brilliant, she can be wonderful." Swan concludes that Gray, "like many social critics who cross the line into fiction, . . . has not yet mastered the difference between show and tell, between writing fiction that lives and using fiction as a forum for ideas. What she aspires to here is a highbrow critique of art and society in the last twenty years. What she has written is a novel that strives too hard to impress. The prose is full of bad breathiness, the characters suffer from terminal solipsism, and the social criticism is often as cliched as the attitudes it attacks."

Esquire columnist James Wolcott also comments on Gray's satiric designs: "Tripping through *World Without End,* I kept telling myself that the book might be a spoofy lark—a Harlequin romance for art majors—but I have a lurking suspicion that Gray is serious. After all, the novel's theme—the pull and persistence of friendship—is butressed by quotations from Catullus and from Roland Barthes, and floating through the text are the sort of flowery phrases only a tremulously sincere epicurean would use." *Commentary*'s Pearl K. Bell is also highly critical of Gray's second novel. "Francine Gray's sententious dialogue about love and death and self-fulfillment does not blind us to the poverty of thought in what seems to have been conceived as a novel of ideas," the critic contends. "*World Without End* is not a novel of ideas, it is an adolescent daydream, an orgy of pseudo-intellectual posturing, a midnight bull session in a college dorm."

Grumbach finds that a distance is placed between the reader and the characters because of the intense intellectualism of the novel. She asserts that "despite the impressive and always accurate documentation of place (Edmund's visit to the Hermitage and the art he looks at there consumes five dense pages) and the character, social movements, parental backgrounds, lovers, husbands, visits with each other, letters and postcards [the three friends] exchange for all those years, do we ever feel close to these people? Curiously, not really. They are so detailed and cerebral, their talk is so elevated and informed, we know so many facts about their milieus that, somehow, passion is smothered." But, other critics disagree. Reynolds Price in the *New York Times Book Review,* for instance, finds that in *World Without End,* Gray "displays the one indispensable gift in a novelist—she generates slowly and authoritatively a mixed set of entirely credible human beings who shunt back and forth through credible time and are altered by the trip. Ample, generous and mature, the book is stocked with the goods a novel best provides."

Leonard also finds the book—and the characters in it—touching. "The reader chooses sides," he writes. "In this novel about Renaissance art and Puritanism, about Anglican convents and academic departments of art about friendship and that televised soap opera General Hospital—about lust and literature and missing fathers and saints full of greed and pride and envy—in this popcorn-popper of ideas, in which Edmund is the tourist of art, Claire the tourist of suffering and Sophie the tourist of everything, we are blessed with real people in the middle of an important argument about art and religion and sexuality. We are persuaded. . . . I chose Sophie to root for. It's been a long time in novels since I was a fan. Mrs. Gray tells us that 'Orpheus dismembered will continue to sing, his head floating down our rivers.' A real friend will either scoop up the head or hit it with a stick. Mrs. Gray scoops and sings."

Gray's second father was artist Alexander Liberman, art director of *Vogue* magazine. Her mother once worked at Saks Fifth Avenue, New York City, in the fashion industry. Drawing from this heritage, *October Blood* satirizes "the peculiar world of high fashion" and "sets out to tell a serious, even painful, story about three generations of remarkable women," Judith Viorst remarks in the *New York Times Book World Review.* Though *October Blood* received mixed reviews, Joanne Kaufman of *Book World* notes that "Gray is successful at showing that the concerns of the fashion world are as lightweight as a Chanel chemise."

Gray's next bestselling nonfiction book looks at another facet of her heritage, the Soviet ancestry of her mother and the other emigres who raised her in Paris. *Soviet Women: Walking the Tightrope* records Gray's observations of contemporary Soviet life and women's concerns she gathered on a visit to her mother's homeland. "The distinguished American journalist and novelist Francine du Plessix Gray has now brought us a rich and contradictory selection of Soviet women's opinions," Mary F. Zirin comments in the *Los Angeles Times Book Review.* Reading it, says Zirin, "is like turning a kaleidoscope—a new pattern emerges with every chapter. . . . Gray uses her novelistic skills to record talks with some women in which psychological pressure and suppressed rage can be sensed under a facade of stoic cheer." The government encourages women to hold jobs and to raise large families; abortion is the most well-known method of birth control, Gray reports. Each woman expects to have between seven and fourteen abortions before menopause; there are between five and eight abortions for every live birth, and one out of five babies is born with a defect. Women form deep commitments to each other but tend to see men as crude liabilities.

Carroll Bogert of *Newsweek* relates that *Soviet Women* offers some surprises: "Gray turns a predictable tale of oppression upside down. . . . Traditions have ensured a peculiar female dominance in a society where tremendous male chauvinism persists. . . . Ninety-two percent of Soviet women work, and they do nearly all domestic chores. One woman admits many women have 'a need to control that verges on the tyrannical, the sadistic.'" Furthermore, though the reforms of *glasnost* are viewed by outsiders as a move toward greater personal liberty for Soviet citizens, "the Bolshevik ideal of sexual equality is being trampled in the retreat from socialism," Bogert points out. Bogert concludes, "For Westerners who think Gorbachev's reforms will make Them more like Us, this fine writer has a valuable lesson to teach."

AVOCATIONAL INTERESTS: Tennis, gardening, cooking Provencal food.

BIOGRAPHICAL/CRITICAL SOURCES:

BOOKS

Contemporary Authors Autobiography Series, Volume 2, Gale, 1985.
Contemporary Literary Criticism, Volume 22, Gale, 1982.
Gray, Francine du Plessix, *Lovers and Tyrants,* Simon & Schuster, 1976.
Gray, *World Without End,* Simon & Schuster, 1981.

PERIODICALS

Book World, October 13, 1985.
Books and Bookmen, March, 1971.
Chicago Tribune Book World, May 31, 1981, August 15, 1982, March 25, 1990.
Commentary, August, 1981.
Commonweal, May 22, 1981.
Detroit News, December 16, 1981.
Esquire, June, 1981.
Harpers, November, 1976.
Listener, February 25, 1971, June 2, 1977.
Los Angeles Times Book Review, March 25, 1990.
Ms., November, 1976, July, 1981.
Nation, February 1, 1971, November 20, 1976.
National Observer, December 18, 1976.
National Review, November 12, 1976.
New Republic, June 27, 1970.
Newsweek, October 11, 1976, June 22, 1981, March 26, 1990.
New York Review of Books, November 11, 1976.
New York Times, October 8, 1976, September 15, 1979, May 19, 1981, August 20, 1981.
New York Times Book Review, May 31, 1970, October 17, 1976, May 24, 1981, September 12, 1982, October 6, 1985, March 11, 1990.
Progressive, November, 1981.
Saturday Review, June 13, 1970, October 30, 1976, May, 1981.
Time, November 1, 1976.
Times Literary Supplement, May 20, 1977.
Village Voice, November 22, 1976.
Wall Street Journal, October 25, 1976, June 1, 1981.
Washington Post Book World, August 29, 1976, October 24, 1976, May 24, 1981, March 11, 1990.

GREEN, Julian (Hartridge) 1900-
(Julien Green; pseudonyms: Theophile Delaporte,
David Irland)

PERSONAL: Also known under French version of name, Julien
Green; born September 6, 1900, in Paris, France; son of U.S. citi-
zens, Edward Moon (a special agent for the Southern Cotton Oil
Company) and Mary Adelaide (Hartridge) Green; children: Eric
Jourdan (adopted). *Education:* Attended Lycee Janson-de-
Sailly, Paris; attended University of Virginia, 1919-22; studied
drawing at La Grande Chaumiere, Paris, 1922-23. *Religion:*
Roman Catholic.

ADDRESSES: c/o Le Seuil, 27 rue Jacob, Paris 6e France.

CAREER: Writer, 1920—. Stayed several times in the United
States, including a visit to Virginia, 1933-34; went to America
in 1940 after France fell to Germany; lectured on French writers
at Princeton University, Goucher College, Mills College, and
Harvard University, 1940-1942; returned to Paris, 1945. *Wartime service:* World War I—Volunteered for the American Field
Service, 1917; served on the French front at Verdun; later
worked for six months with the Norton-Harjes Service (now the
Red Cross) in Italy until May, 1918; joined the French Army as
an American, training at the artillery school, Fontainebleau;
served in the region of Metz, and, after the armistice, went with
his regiment to the Saar on occupation duty; demobilized, 1919.
World War II—Joined U.S. Army, 1942; later held post in the
U.S. Office of War Information; made radio broadcasts to
France, 1943.

MEMBER: Academie de Baviere, Academie Royale de Bel-
gique, Academie Francaise, Academy of Arts and Letters, Academie of Mainz, Conseil litteraire de Monaco, Phi Beta Kappa.

AWARDS, HONORS: Prix Paul Flat, Academie Francaise, and
Femina-Bookman Prize, both 1928, both for *Adrienne Mesurat;*
Harper Prize, 1929-30, for *Leviathan;* Harper 125th Anniversary
Award, 1942, for *Memory of Happy Days;* Commandeur de la
Legion d'Honneur; Grand Prix Litteraire de Monaco, 1951, for
the whole of his work; Grand Prix National des Lettres, 1966;
Prix Ibico Reggino, 1968; Grand Prix, Academie Francaise,
1970; James Biddle Eustace Franco-American Award, 1972;
Grand Prix Litterature de Pologne, 1985; Prix des Universites
Alemaniques; Grand Prix Arts, Sciences et Lettres de Paris.

WRITINGS:

FICTION

Mont-Cinere (novel), Plon, 1926, translation of complete version
by Marshall A. Best published as *Avarice House,* Harper,
1927, complete French edition, Plon, 1928, new English
edition published as *Monte-Cinere,* edited by C. T. Stewart,
Harper, 1937.
Adrienne Mesurat (novel), Plon, 1927, translation by Henry
Longan Stuart published as *The Closed Garden,* Harper,
1928, new French edition (containing some manuscript
pages), Club des Libraires de France, 1957, revised edition,
Holmes & Meier, 1991.
Le Voyageur sur la terre (story; illustrated with a portrait of the
author by Jean Cocteau), Gallimard, 1927, translation by
Courtney Bruerton published as *The Pilgrim on the Earth,*
Harper, 1929.
Christine (story), Les Amis d'Edouard, 1927.
La Traversee inutile (story), Plon, 1927, published as "Levia-
than" in *Christine, suivi de Leviathan,* Editions des Cahiers
Libres, 1928.

Les Clefs de la mort (story; title means "The Keys of Death"),
J. Schiffrin (Paris), 1928.
Leviathan (novel; not the same work as the story, "Leviathan"),
Plon, 1929, translation by Vyvyan Holland published as
The Dark Journey, Harper, 1929.
Le Voyageur sur la terre (collection; contains "Leviathan,"
"Christine," "The Keys of Death," and "The Pilgrim on the
Earth"), Plon, 1930, translation by Bruerton published as
Christine, and Other Stories, Harper, 1930.
L'Autre Sommeil (novel), Gallimard, 1931, Plon, 1949.
Epaves (novel), Plon, 1932, translation by Holland published as
The Strange River, Harper, 1932.
Le Visionnaire (novel), Plon, 1934, translation by Holland pub-
lished as *The Dreamer,* Harper, 1934.
Minuit (novel), Plon, 1936, translation by Holland published as
Midnight, Harper, 1936.
Varouna (novel), Plon, 1940, translation by James Whitall pub-
lished as *Then Shall the Dust Return,* Harper, 1941.
Si j'etais vous (novel), Plon, 1947, revised edition, 1970, transla-
tion by J. H. F. McEwen published as *If I Were You,* Har-
per, 1949.
Moira (novel), Plon, 1950, translation by Denise Folliot pub-
lished under same title, Macmillan, 1951, new edition,
Quartet Books, 1988.
Le Malfaiteur (novel), Plon, 1955, general edition, 1956, aug-
mented edition, 1974, translation by sister, Anne Green,
published as *The Transgressor,* Pantheon 1957.
Chaque homme dans sa nuit (novel), Plon, 1960, translation by
A. Green published as *Each in His Darkness,* Pantheon,
1961.
L'Autre (novel), Plon, 1971, translation by Bernard Wall pub-
lished as *The Other One,* Harcourt, 1973.
La Nuit des fantomes (children's book; title means "Hallow-
een"), Plon, 1976.
Le Mauvais Lieu (novel), Plon, 1977.
L'apprenti psychiatre (story; first published in English as *The Ap-
prentice Psychiatrist* in *Quarterly Review,* 1920), translation
by son, Eric Jourdan, Le Livre de Poche, 1977.
Histoires de vertige (stories), Le Seuil, 1984.
Les Pays lointains (novel), Le Seuil, 1987.
Les Etoiles du Sud (novel), Le Seuil, 1989.

Les Pays lointains and *Les Etoiles du Sud* published as "Dixie"
in *La Pleiade.*

AUTOBIOGRAPHY

Journal, Volume 1: *Les Annees faciles, 1928-34,* Plon, 1938, revised edition published as *Les Annees faciles, 1926-34,* 1970;
Volume 2: *Derniers beaux jours, 1935-39,* Plon, 1939; Volume 3: *Devant la porte sombre, 1940-43,* Plon, 1946; Volume
4: *L'Oeil de l'ouragan, 1943-46,* Plon, 1949; Volume 5: *Le
Revenant, 1946-50,* Plon, 1951; Volume 6: *Le Miroir inte-
rieur, 1950-54,* Plon, 1955; Volume 7: *Le Bel aujourd'hui,
1955-58,* Plon, 1958; Volume 8: *Vers l'invisible, 1959-66,*
Plon, 1967; Volume 9: *Ce qui reste de jour, 1966-72,* Plon,
1972; Volume 10: *La bouteille a la Mer, 1972-76,* Plon,
1976; Volume 11: *La terre est si belle, 1976-78,* Le Seuil,
1982; Volume 12: *La lumiere du monde, 1978-81,* Le Seuil,
1982, Volume 13: *L'arc-en-ciel, 1981-84,* Le Seuil, 1988,
Volume 14: *L'expatrie, 1984-90,* Le Seuil, 1990.
Personal Record, 1928-39 (contains *Journal,* Volumes 1 and 2),
translation by Jocelyn Godefroi, Harper, 1939.
Memories of Happy Days (memoir), Harper, 1942.
(Contributor) *Les Oeuvres nouvelles* (includes "Quand nous ha-
bitions tous ensemble," reminiscences), Editions de la Maison Francaise (New York), 1943.

Journal: 1928-1958 (omnibus edition; contains Volumes 1-7), Plon, 1961, translation by A. Green published in abridged edition as *Diary, 1928-57,* edited by Kurt Wolff, Harcourt, 1964, new omnibus edition published as *Journal, 1928-66* (contains Volumes 1-8), two volumes, Plon, 1969.

Jeunes Annees (autobiography), Volume 1: *Partir avant le jour,* Grasset, 1963, translation by A. Green published as *To Leave before Dawn,* Harcourt, 1967; Volume 2: *Mille chemins ouverts,* Grasset, 1964; Volume 3: *Terre Lointaine,* Grasset, 1966; *Jeunesse,* Plon, 1974; published in two volumes with *Fin de Jeunesse* and additional unpublished material, Le Seuil, 1984.

Qui sommes-nous?, Plon, 1972.

Memories of Evil Days, edited by Jean-Pierre J. Piriou, University Press of Virginia, 1976.

Dans la gueule du Temps (journal), illustrated with 500 photographs, Plon, 1978.

Ce qu'il faut d'amour a l'homme, Plon, 1978.

Journal du Voyageur (traveler's diary), illustrated with 95 photos by the author, Le Seuil, 1990.

PLAYS

Sud (three-act; produced in Paris, 1953), Plon, 1953, translation by the author produced as "South," London, 1955, published in *Plays of the Year,* Volume 12, Elek, 1955, operatic version, with music by Kenton Coe, produced at Opera de Paris, 1973.

L'Ennemi (three-act; produced in Paris, 1954), Plon, 1954.

L'Ombre (three-act; produced at Theatre Antoine, 1956), Plon, 1956.

Demain n'exite pas; L'Automate (three- and four-act; produced in Germany, 1989), Le Seuil, 1985.

NONFICTION

(Under pseudonym Theophile Delaporte) *Pamphlet contre les Catholiques de France* (essay), Editions de la Revue des Pamphletaires (Paris), 1924, new edition, preface by Jacques Maritain, Plon, 1963.

Suite anglaise (essays), Cahiers de Paris, 1927.

Un Puritain homme de lettres: Nathaniel Hawthorne, Editions des Cahiers Libres, 1928.

Liberte cherie (essay), Plon, 1974, complete edition, Le Seuil, 1989.

Paris (essay), Editions du Champ Vallon, 1983.

Frere Francois, Le Seuil, 1983, translation by Peter Heinegg published as *God's Fool: The Life and Times of Francis of Assisi,* Harper, 1985.

Le Langage et son double/The Language and Its Shadow (essays; bilingual edition with translations by the author), Le Seuil, 1986.

L'homme et son ombre/ Man and His Ghost (essays; bilingual edition with translations by the author), Le Seuil, 1991.

OTHER

(Translator with A. Green) Charles Peguy, *Basic Verities: Prose and Poetry,* Pantheon, 1943.

(Translator with A. Green) Peguy, *Men and Saints,* Pantheon, 1944.

(Translator) Peguy, *God Speaks: Religious Poetry,* Pantheon, 1945.

(Translator) Peguy, *The Mystery of the Charity of Joan of Arc,* Pantheon, 1949.

Oeuvres Completes (collected works), ten volumes, Plon, 1954-65.

Bibliotheque de la Pleiade (collected works), six volumes, Gallimard, 1970-90.

Un grande amitie: Correspondance avec Jacques Maritain, 1926-1972, edited by Piriou, Plon, 1979, complete edition, edited by Jourdan, Gallimard, 1982, English translation by Bernard Doering published as *The Story of Two Souls: The Correspondence of Jacques Maritain and Julien Green,* edited by Henry Bars and Jourdan, Fordham University Press, 1988.

Pamphlet contre les catholiques de France, suivi de Ce qu'il faut d'amour a l'homme; L'Appel du desert; La Folie de Dieu, Gallimard, 1982.

(Translator) Lord Dunsany, *Merveilles et demons,* Le Seuil, 1991.

Also author of filmscripts *Leviathan,* 1962, and, with Jourdan, *La Dame de pique,* 1965; author, with Jourdan, of television and radio scripts *Je est un autre,* 1954, and *La Mort de Ivan llytch,* 1955. Contributor to *Revue Hebdomadaire, Revue Europeenne, Nouvelle Revue Francaise, Revue Universelle, La Parisienne, Revue des Deux Mondes, University of Virginia Magazine, American Scholar,* and other periodicals.

WORK IN PROGRESS: Volume 15 of the *Journal;* Volume 6 of *Bibliotheque de la Pleiade;* a play; a book on poets, with Eric Jourdan; *Pour faire peur,* a children' book.

MEDIA ADAPTATIONS: Extracts from Green's work, including a reading by Green himself, have been recorded in the series "Auteurs du 20e Siecle," Philips; a VHS videocassette, *Special Julien Green,* has been edited by Le Seuil, 1983-90.

SIDELIGHTS: In 1930 Courtney Bruerton wrote: "As Julien Green is the first American novelist to choose French as his medium of expression, so he is the first American to be ranked by competent critics as a great French writer." L. Clark Keating comments on the "irresistible appeal" which Green's work has held for critics, "many of whom have tried to find American sources and models for his characters and situations." Among his works which have American settings is *Avarice House;* this story, notes Keating, "is laid in a Virginia farmhouse, modeled on an uncle's manor house near Warrenton [where] Green spent several weeks during his first American sojourn." Discussing the similarities between Green and novelist Nathaniel Hawthorne, the critic suggests that "Green's sombre and fantastic imagination, and his preoccupation with violence and death, are often reminiscent of the nineteenth-century New Englander." He concludes that Hawthorne, "if not a model, has been an inspiration."

Andre Maurois, on the other hand, does not recognize a predominant English or American influence on Green's work: "For my part," writes Maurois, "I see very well wherein Green resembles the Brontes, but I see also wherein he resembles Balzac." According to I. W. Brock, Green is "unmistakably French" and "may be called American only because of his parentage. His ideas, language and philosophy are primarily French." Recognized for this, in 1971 Green became the first foreign member of the Academie Francaise.

The unusual nature of Green's background, however, tends to elude classification. Marilyn Gaddis points out: "By temperament and training Green was perhaps as much as ten years behind most boys of his generation. To begin with, he was the most confirmed French-speaking member of a household that was a miniature bilingual community. . . . Teased about his Confederate sympathies and Protestantism by his French schoolmates, Green withdrew into his own creative fantasy world." Samuel

Stokes writes that Green's parents "brought to Europe all sorts of furniture which caused considerable consternation among their French friends, but," he continues, "its appearance created an atmosphere." James Lord similarly affirms: "The emotional stress of this formative duality had a decisive effect upon the young author" which is "starkly reflected" in his works. For instance, Peter Hall, the London producer of *South,* has said that it is a play about "extremes: North versus South, white man against coloured man, the old world of Europe in contrast with the new world of America, the difficulty that the sexually normal have in understanding the sexually abnormal."

For Brock, the main strength of Green's work lies in its "psychological naturalism." Robert Kanters, emphasizing a different aspect, feels that the use of dreams in Green's work "is a natural way less between reality and the fantastic than between two different levels of reality."

L. Clark Keating says of Green as a man, that he is "solitary and takes pains to avoid a crowd. Although a traveler he has few of the earmarks of the tourist. Even in his diary he does not choose to write of the issues of the day." Defending this position, Marilyn Gaddis states: "It would be incorrect—and basically unfair—to call either his solitude or his lack of social commitment an escape. On the contrary he has faced and transcended the alienation which most of his readers bury or ignore." After a period of doubt and religious crisis, Green became "reconverted" to the Roman Catholic faith in 1939, and James Lord writes: "His personal, intellectual and moral adherence to the tenets of Roman Catholicism appears to be complete."

Although he is bilingual in English and French, Green found that when he tried to write in English, it was like "wearing clothes that were not made for me." His only imaginative story in English is "The Apprentice Psychiatrist," published in 1920. He has mastered a number of other languages; Robert de Saint-Jean reports: "During a voyage in Italy, I had the surprise of hearing Julien Green express himself easily in Italian: I knew he was reading Dante in the original text, but thought that he understood the language without being able to speak it, and especially to make himself understood. In Germany, the same experience." The critic also reports that Green has studied Greek and Latin assiduously. In 1935, he took lessons in Hebrew from a rabbi in Paris "after much time spent in floundering among contradictory versions of the Bible."

BIOGRAPHICAL/CRITICAL SOURCES:

BOOKS

Brisville, Jean-Claude, *A la reucoutie de Julien Green,* Bruxelles, 1947.

Burne, Glenn S., *Julian Green,* Twayne, 1972.

Contemporary Literary Criticism, Gale, Volume 3, 1975, Volume 11, 1979.

Cooke, M. G., *Hallucination and Death as Motifs of Escape in the Novels of Julien Green,* Catholic University of America Press, 1960.

Davin, Antonia, *Julien Green et le mal d'exister,* Louvain, 1973.

Davin, Antonia, *The Incomplete Julian Green,* Universite de Tasmanie (New Zealand), 1979.

Dunaway, John M., *The Metamorphoses of the Self: The Mystic, the Sensualist, and the Artist in the Works of Julien Green,* University Press of Kentucky, 1978.

Dictionary of Literary Biography, Gale, Volume 4: *American Writers in Paris, 1920-1939,* 1980, Volume 72: *French Novelists, 1930-1960,* 1988.

Gaddis, Marilyn, *The Critical Reaction to Julien Green (1926-56),* unpublished thesis, University of Missouri, 1958.

Green, Anne, *With Much Love,* Harper, 1948.

Green, Julien, *Journal* Volumes 1-10, Plon, 1938-76, Volumes 11-14, Le Seuil, 1982, translation of Volumes 1-7 by Anne Green published in an abridged edition as *Diary, 1928-57,* edited by Kurt Wolff, Harcourt, 1964.

Green, Julien, *Memories of Happy Days,* Harper, 1942, reprinted, Greenwood Press, 1969.

Green, Julien, *Jeunes Annees* (autobiography), Volume 1: *Partir avant le jour,* Grasset, 1963, translation by A. Green published as *To Leave before Dawn,* Harcourt, 1967; Volumes 2-3, Grasset, 1964-66, Volume 4, Plon, 1974.

Pozner, David, *Julian Green, His Life and Works,* Oxford University Press, 1956.

Saint Jean, Robert de, *Julien Green,* Editions du Seuil, 1967, enlarged and revised edition by Giovanni Lucera and Luc Estang, 1990.

Stokes, Samuel, *Julian Green and the Thorn of Puritanism,* King's Crown Press, Columbia University, 1955.

PERIODICALS

Biblio, December, 1949.

Bookman, August, 1932.

Emory University Quarterly, March, December, 1945.

French Review, March, 1950, May, 1955.

L'Express, February 15-21, 1971.

Livres de France, February, 1967.

London Magazine, January, 1967.

New Yorker, September 1, 1951.

New York Times Book Review, May 11, 1941, October 1, 1967.

PMLA, June, 1939.

Saturday Review of Literature, November, 1939.

Sewanee Review, April, 1932.

*   *   *

GREEN, Julien
See GREEN, Julian (Hartridge)

*   *   *

GREENBAUM, Sidney   1929-

PERSONAL: Born December 31, 1929, in London, England; son of Lewis and Nellie (Goldfinger) Greenbaum. *Education:* University of London, B.A. (Hebrew and Aramaic; with honors), 1951, M.A., 1953, Postgraduate Certificate in Education, 1954, B.A. (English; with honors), 1957, Ph.D., 1967. *Religion:* Jewish.

ADDRESSES: Office—Department of English, University College, University of London, Gower St., London WC1E 6BT, England.

CAREER: Primary school teacher in London, England, 1954-57; head of high school English department in London, 1957-64; University of London, London, tutor in adult evening courses at Goldsmith's College, 1963-66, instructor in English at University College, 1967-68; University of Oregon, Eugene, visiting assistant professor of English, 1968-69; University of Wisconsin—Milwaukee, visiting professor, 1969-70, associate professor, 1970-72, professor of English, 1972-83; University of London, Quain Professor of English Language and Literature at University College, 1983—. Visiting professor, Hebrew University of Jerusalem, 1972-73.

MEMBER: International Association of University Professors, Linguistic Association of Great Britain, Linguistic Society of America.

WRITINGS:

Studies in English Adverbial Usage, Longmans, Green, 1969, University of Miami Linguistics Series, 1970.

Verb-Intensifier Collocations in English: An Experimental Approach, Mouton, 1970.

(With Randolph Quirk) *Elicitation Experiments in English: Linguistic Studies in Use and Attitude,* University of Miami Linguistic Series, 1970.

(With Quirk, Geoffrey Leech, and Jan Svartvik) *A Grammar of Contemporary English,* Longman, 1972.

(With Quirk) *A Concise Grammar of Contemporary English,* Harcourt 1973 (published in England as *A University Grammar of English,* Longman, 1973).

Acceptability in Language, Mouton, 1977.

(With Leech and Svartvik) *Studies in English Linguistics: For Randolph Quirk,* Longman, 1980.

The English Language Today, Pergamon, 1984.

(With Quirk, Leech, and Svartvik) *A Comprehensive Grammar of the English Language,* Longman, 1985.

(With Charles Cooper) *Studying Writing: Linguistic Approaches,* Sage, 1986.

(Editor with Janet Whitcut) Ernest Gowers, *The Complete Plain Words,* 3rd edition, HMSO, 1986.

(With Whitcut) *Guide to English Usage,* Longman, 1988.

Good English and the Grammarian, Longman, 1988.

A College Grammar of English, Longman, 1989.

(With Quirk) *A Student's Grammar of the English Language,* Longman, 1990.

An Introduction to English Grammar, Longman, 1991.

Contributor to linguistic journals.

Author's works have been translated into Chinese, Japanese, and Russian.

WORK IN PROGRESS: The Oxford English Grammar, for Oxford University Press.

BIOGRAPHICAL/CRITICAL SOURCES:

PERIODICALS

The Times (London), May 23, 1985.
Times Literary Supplement, September 3, 1971, January 30, 1981.

*   *   *

GREER, Germaine 1939-
(Rose Blight)

PERSONAL: Born January 29, 1939, near Melbourne, Australia; daughter of Eric Reginal (a newspaper advertising manager) and Margaret May Mary (Lanfrancan) Greer; married Paul de Feu (a journalist), 1968 (divorced, 1973). *Education:* University of Melbourne, B.A., 1959; University of Sydney, M.A., 1961; Newnham College, Cambridge, Ph.D., 1967. *Politics:* Anarchist. *Religion:* Atheist.

ADDRESSES: Home—Tuscany, Italy. *Agent*—Curtis Brown Ltd., 162-68 Regent St., London W1R 5TA, England.

CAREER: Taught at a girls' school in Australia; University of Warwick, Coventry, England, lecturer in English, 1967-73; founder and director of Tulsa Centre for the Study of Women's Literature, 1979-82; writer. Has been an actress on a television comedy show in Manchester, England. Founder, director, Stump Cross Books. Lecturer, Newnham College.

WRITINGS:

The Female Eunuch, MacGibbon & Kee, 1970, McGraw, 1971.
The Obstacle Race: The Fortunes of Women Painters and Their Work, Farrar, Straus, 1979.
Sex and Destiny: The Politics of Human Fertility, Harper, 1984.
Shakespeare (literary criticism), Oxford University Press, 1986.
The Madwoman's Underclothes: Essays and Occasional Writings, Picador, 1986, Atlantic Monthly Press, 1987.
(Editor with Jeslyn Medoff, Melinda Sansone, and Susan Hastings) *Kissing the Rod: An Anthology of Seventeenth-Century Women's Verse,* Farrar, Straus, 1989.
Daddy, We Hardly Knew You, Viking Penguin, 1989.

Contributor to *River Journeys,* Hippocrene Books, c. 1985. Contributor to periodicals, including *Esquire, Listener, Oz, Spectator,* and, under pseudonym Rose Blight, *Private Eye.* Columnist, *London Sunday Times,* 1971-73. Co-founder of *Suck.*

WORK IN PROGRESS: A collected edition of the works of Aphra Behn for Stump Cross Books; a book on gardening; *The Change,* a book about the changes of middle age.

SIDELIGHTS: Germaine Greer's writings, which include *The Female Eunuch, The Obstacle Race: The Fortunes of Women Painters and Their Work, Sex and Destiny: The Politics of Human Fertility,* a literary study titled *Shakespeare,* and the essay collection *The Madwoman's Underclothes,* have earned her both praise and disparagement from mainstream, academic, and feminist critics. The praise has typically been offered for her scholarly insight—which is perhaps most notable in *Shakespeare* and her study of great but unrecognized women artists, *The Obstacle Race*—and the criticism for her refusal to routinely espouse whatever literary or feminist ideas are most popular at a given time. In 1989 she published a more personal book than her previous volumes, *Daddy, We Hardly Knew You,* which records the investigations into her father's life and personality that she began after her father's death in 1983.

Greer had become a media success upon the American publication of *The Female Eunuch* in 1971. Such celebrity was consistent with her roles as a television performer and as a self-avowed London "groupie" (her enthusiasm for jazz and popular music had brought her into contact with musicians and other members of Britain's underground culture); but critics seized upon her slick and frankly sexual image as counterproductive to the feminist cause she espoused. While her book climbed the best-seller charts in both the United States and England and *Vogue* magazine hailed her as "a super heroine," many members of the women's liberation movement questioned her authority. While *Newsweek* described her as "a dazzling combination of erudition, eccentricity and eroticism," some feminist writers wondered whether an indisputably attractive Shakespearean scholar could speak with understanding about the plight of women in general.

Nevertheless, *The Female Eunuch* sold. It was made a Book-of-the-Month Club alternate and a Book Find Club selection and was ultimately translated into twelve languages. During a United States promotional tour in the spring of 1971, Greer furthered her message on television and radio talk shows, in *Life* magazine, and in a well-publicized debate with Norman Mailer, a novelist and self-confirmed "male chauvinist."

Greer's basic argument, as explained in the book's introduction, is that women's "sexuality is both denied and misrepresented by being identified as passivity." She explains that women, urged from childhood to live up to an "Eternal Feminine" stereotype, are valued for characteristics associated with the castrate— "timidity, plumpness, languor, delicacy and preciosity"—hence the book's title. From the viewpoint of this primary assumption, Greer examines not only the problems of women's sexuality, but their psychological development, their relationships with men, their social position, and their cultural history. What most struck early critics of the book was that she considered "the castration of our true female personality . . . not the fault of men, but our own, and history's." Thus *Newsweek* considered Greer's work "women's liberation's most realistic and least anti-male manifesto"; and Christopher Lehmann-Haupt called it "a book that combines the best of masculinity *and* femininity."

BIOGRAPHICAL/CRITICAL SOURCES:

PERIODICALS

Detroit News, May 9, 1971.
Globe and Mail (Toronto), February 25, 1984, October 17, 1987, April 29, 1989, August 5, 1989.
Life, May 7, 1971.
Listener, October 22, 1970.
Los Angeles Times, March 7, 1984, November 26, 1987.
Los Angeles Times Book Review, September 6, 1987.
Newsweek, March 22, 1971.
New York Times, April 20, 1971, November 1, 1979, March 5, 1984, April 23, 1984.
New York Times Book Review, October 11, 1987, January 28, 1990.
Observer (London), October 11, 1970.
Publishers Weekly, May 25, 1984.
Time, April 16, 1984.
Times (London), March 20, 1986, October 23, 1986, March 20, 1989, March 25, 1989.
Times Literary Supplement, June 17, 1988, March 17, 1989, March 20, 1989.
Tribune Books (Chicago), January 21, 1990.
Washington Post, November 22, 1979, January 24, 1990.

*   *   *

GRENVILLE, Pelham
  See WODEHOUSE, P(elham) G(renville)

*   *   *

GRIEVE, C(hristopher) M(urray) 1892-1978
  (Hugh MacDiarmid; other pseudonyms: Isobel
  Guthrie, A. K. Laidlaw, James MacLaren, Pteleon)

PERSONAL: Born August 11, 1892, in Langholm, Dumfries-shire, Scotland; died of cancer, September 9, 1978, in Edinburgh, Scotland; son of James (a postman) and Elizabeth (Graham) Grieve; married Margaret Skinner, June, 1918 (divorced, January, 1932); married Valda Trevlyn, September 12, 1934; children: (first marriage) Christine, Walter; (second marriage) James Michael Trevlyn. *Education:* Attended Langholm Academy, Broughton Junior Student Centre (Edinburgh) and University of Edinburgh. *Politics:* Communist (formally, from 1934 to 1938 when he was expelled; rejoined Party, 1957).

ADDRESSES: Home—The Cottage, Brownsbank, Candymill, Biggar, Lanarkshire, Scotland.

CAREER: Joined Independent Labour Party at 16; became a journalist, 1912, working for a number of papers in Scotland and near the Welsh-English border; worked as a chief reporter and general factotum for *Montrose Review,* Montrose, Scotland, 1920-29; worked on *Vox,* London, England, 1929; lived in Liverpool, England, 1930, working as a public relations officer with the Organization for Advancing the Interests of Merseyside; returned to London to work for Unicorn Press; moved to Whalsay, Shetland Islands, 1933, and stayed until 1941; worked as manual laborer on a war job, Clydeside, 1941-43; worked on ships engaged in estuarial duties, British Merchant Service, 1943-45; moved to Glasgow, Scotland, 1945, then to Strathhaven, moved to Biggar, 1951. Labour member of town council of Montrose, 1923-28; justice of the peace, Angus, with life appointment, 1923-78; one of the founders of the National Party of Scotland, 1928; was a defeated candidate in the 1964 General Election, opposing Sir Alec Douglas-Home. Regular lecturer for Scottish University extramural departments, Workers' Educational Association, and Rationalist Press Association. Vice-president, British Peace Committee; founder-member, Committee of 100; director of theater workshop for Pioneer Theatres Ltd. *Military service:* Royal Army Medical Corps, 1915-20; served in Salonika, Italy, and France.

MEMBER: PEN (one of the founders of the Scottish Centre, 1927), World Burns Federation (life member), Saltire Society (life member).

AWARDS, HONORS: Civil List pension for services to literature, 1951; LL.D., University of Edinburgh, 1957.

WRITINGS:

Annals of the Five Senses (poetry and prose), C. M. Grieve, 1923, Faber, 1930.
Contemporary Scottish Studies (prose), L. Parsons (London), 1926, enlarged edition, Scottish Educational Journal, 1976.
Albyn; or, Scotland and the Future (prose), Dutton, 1927.
The Present Position of Scottish Music (prose), C. M. Grieve, (Montrose), 1927.

POETRY; UNDER PSEUDONYM HUGH MacDIARMID

Sangschaw, Blackwood (Edinburgh), 1925, 2nd edition, 1937.
Penny Wheep, Blackwood, 1926, 2nd edition, 1937.
A Drunk Man Looks at the Thistle, Blackwood, 1926, new edition, edited by John C. Weston, University of Massachusetts Press, 1971.
The Lucky Bag, Porpoise Press (Edinburgh), 1927.
To Circumjack Cencrastus; or, The Curly Snake, Blackwood, 1930.
First Hymn to Lenin and Other Poems, introduction by AE (George William Russell), Unicorn Press, 1931.
Second Hymn to Lenin, Valda Trevlyn (Thakeham), 1932, published in *Second Hymn to Lenin and Other Poems,* Nott, 1935.
Scots Unbound and Other Poems (also see below), E. Mackay (Stirling), 1932.
Tarras, [Edinburgh], 1932.
Stony Limits and Other Poems (also see below), Gollancz, 1934.
Selected Poems, Macmillan (London), 1934, enlarged edition published as *Speaking for Scotland: Selected Poems of Hugh MacDiarmid,* Contemporary Poetry (Baltimore), 1946.
Direadh, [Dunfermline], 1938, limited edition published as *Direadh I, II, and III,* K. Duvan and C. H. Hamilton, 1974.
Cornish Heroic Song for Valda Trevlyn, Caledonian Press (Glasgow), 1943.
Selected Poems of Hugh MacDiarmid, edited by R. Crombie Saunders, Maclellan (Glasgow), 1945.
Poems of the East-West Synthesis, Caledonian Press, 1946.

A Kist of Whistles: New Poems by Hugh MacDiarmid, Maclellan, 1947.

Selected Poems, edited by Oliver Brown, Maclellan, 1954.

In Memoriam James Joyce: From a Vision of World Language (also see below), Maclellan, 1955.

Stony Limits and Scots Unbound and Other Poems (composite volume), Castle Wynd (Edinburgh), 1956.

The Battle Continues, Castle Wynd, 1957.

Three Hymns to Lenin, Castle Wynd, 1957.

The Kind of Poetry I Want, K. D. Duval (Edinburgh), 1961.

Collected Poems of Hugh MacDiarmid, Macmillan (New York), 1962, revised edition, prepared by John C. Weston, 1967.

Bracken Hills in Autumn, C. H. Hamilton (Edinburgh), 1962.

Poetry like the Hawthorn (from *In Memoriam James Joyce*), [Hemel Hempstead, Hertfordshire], 1962.

Poems to Paintings by William Johnstone, 1933, K. D. Duval, 1963.

An Apprentice Angel, New Poetry Press, 1963.

The Ministry of Water, D. Glen (Glasgow), 1964.

Six Vituperative Verses, Satire Press, 1964.

The Terrible Crystal [and] *A Vision of Scotland,* D. Glen (Ayrshire), 1964.

The Fire of the Spirit, D. Glen (Glasgow), 1965.

Whuchulls, Akros (Preston, Lancashire), 1966.

(With Norman MacCaig) *Poems by Hugh MacDiarmid and Norman MacCaig,* University of Massachusetts, 1967.

Early Lyrics by Hugh MacDiarmid, edited by J. K. Annand, Akros, 1968, 2nd edition, 1969.

A Lap of Honour, MacGibbon & Kee, 1967, Swallow Press, 1969.

On a Raised Beach, Harris Press, 1967.

A Clyack-Sheaf, MacGibbon & Kee, 1969.

More Collected Poems, Swallow Press, 1970.

Selected Poems, edited by David Craig and John Manson, Penguin, 1970.

The Hugh MacDiarmid Anthology: Poems in Scots and English, edited by Michael Grieve and Alexander Scott, Routledge & Kegan Paul, 1972.

Poems, edited by Alistair Keith Campsie, Famedram, 1972.

Song of the Seraphion, Covent Garden Press, 1973.

Selected Lyrics, edited by Kulgin D. Duval and Colin H. Hamilton, Officina Bodoni (Verona), 1977.

The Socialist Poems of Hugh MacDiarmid, edited by T. S. Law and Thurso Berwick, Routledge & Kegan Paul, 1978.

Complete Poems, 2 volumes, edited by Michael Grieve and W. R. Aitken, Brian & O'Keeffe, 1978.

PROSE; UNDER PSEUDONYM HUGH MacDIARMID

The Present Condition of Scottish Arts and Affairs, PEN Club, 1927.

The Scottish National Association of April Fools, The University Press, Aberdeen, 1928.

Fidelity in Small Things, 1929.

Five Bits of Miller, privately printed (London), 1934.

At the Sign of the Thistle: A Collection of Essays, Nott, 1934.

Scotland in 1980, privately printed (Montrose), 1935.

Charles Doughty and the Need for Heroic Poetry, [St. Andrews], 1936.

Scottish Eccentrics, Routledge & Kegan Paul, 1936.

Scotland and the Question of a Popular Front against Fascism and War, Hugh MacDiarmid Book Club, 1938.

The Islands of Scotland: Hebrides, Orkneys, and Shetlands, Scribner, 1939.

Lucky Poet: A Self-Study in Literature and Political Ideas, Being the Autobiography of Hugh MacDiarmid, Methuen, 1943, enlarged edition, J. Cape, 1972.

Cunninghame Graham: A Centenary Study, Caledonian Press, 1952.

Francis George Scott: An Essay on the Occasion of His Seventy-Fifth Birthday, 25th January 1955, M. Macdonald (Edinburgh), 1955.

Burns Today and Tomorrow, Castle Wynd, 1959.

David Hume, Scotland's Greatest Son, Paperback Booksellers (Edinburgh), 1962.

The Man of (Almost) Independent Mind (on David Hume), Gordon (Edinburgh), 1962.

The Ugly Birds without Wings, Allan Donaldson (Edinburgh), 1962.

Sydney Goodsir Smith, C. H. Hamilton, 1963.

Tribute to Harry Miller, [Edinburgh], 1963.

The Company I've Kept, Hutchinson, 1966, University of California Press, 1967.

(With Owen Dudley Edwards, Gwynfor Evans, and Joan Rhys) *Celtic Nationalism,* Routledge & Kegan Paul, 1968.

The Uncanny Scot: A Selection of Prose, edited by Kenneth Buthlay, MacGibbon & Kee, 1968.

Selected Essays, edited by Duncan Glen, J. Cape, 1969, University of California Press, 1970.

John Knox, Ramsey Head, 1976.

Aesthetics in Scotland, edited by Alan Bold, B & N Imports, 1985.

EDITOR; UNDER PSEUDONYM HUGH MacDIARMID

Northern Numbers, three series, T. N. Foulis (Edinburgh), 1920 and 1921, third series privately printed (Montrose), 1922.

Robert Burns, 1759-1796, Benn, 1926.

Living Scottish Poets, Benn, 1931.

(And author of introduction) *The Golden Treasury of Scottish Poetry,* Macmillan (London), 1940.

Douglas Young, *Auntran Blads: An Outwale o Verses,* Maclellan, 1943.

(And author of introduction) William Soutar, *Collected Poems,* A. Dakers (London), 1948.

(With Maurice Lindsay) *Poetry Scotland,* number 4, Serif, 1949.

(And author of introduction) William Dunbar, *Selected Poems,* Maclellan, 1955.

(Author of foreword) *Sculpture & Drawings by Benno Schotz,* [Edinburgh], 1961.

Robert Burns, Love Songs, Vista Books (London), 1962.

Editor of *Scottish Chapbook* (monthly), 1922-23. Former editor of *Scottish Nation* and *Northern Review.*

OTHER; UNDER PSEUDONYM HUGH MacDIARMID

(Contributor of research) *The Rural Problem,* Constable, for Fabian Research Department, 1913.

(Translator from the Spanish) Ramon Maria de Tenreiro, *The Handmaid of the Lord,* Secker & Warburg, 1930.

(Contributor) *New Tales of Horror,* Hutchinson, 1934.

(With Lewis Grassic Gibbon) *Scottish Scene; or, The Intelligent Man's Guide to Albyn* (poetry and prose), Jarrolds, 1934.

(Translator from the Gaelic) Alexander MacDonald, *The Berlinn of Claranald,* Abbey Bookshop (St. Andrews), 1935.

(Contributor) John Rowland, editor, *Path and Pavement,* [London], 1937.

(Translator from the Swedish and editor, with Elspeth Harley Schubert) Harry Martinson, *Aniara: A Review of Man in Time and Space* (epic poem), Knopf, 1963.

(Translator from the German) Bertolt Brecht, *The Threepenny Opera,* Eyre Methuen, 1973.
Metaphysics and Poetry, Lothlorien, 1975.

Short plays include "Some Day," 1923, "The Purple Patch," 1924, "Jenny Spells," 1924, "The Candidate," 1924, "The Morning Post," 1924. Writer of scripts for radio and television. Contributor to *New Age, Glasgow Herald,* and other publications.

SIDELIGHTS: C. M. Grieve, best known under his pseudonym Hugh MacDiarmid, is credited with effecting a Scottish literary revolution which restored an indigenous Scots literature, and has been acknowledged as the greatest poet that his country has produced since Robert Burns. As a writer, political theorist, revolutionary, prophet, and multifarious personality, he was a man to be reckoned with, even by those who did not agree that he was one of Great Britain's greatest poets. Ian Hamilton wrote that MacDiarmid made enemies largely because "he makes his own rules, contemns categories, cracks open water-tight compartments, bestraddles disciplines, scorns social, cultural, and academic cliques and claques, and affirms . . . that it is not failure but low aim that is criminal."

MacDiarmid's opinions, Hamilton continued, "display in bewildering profusion the contradictions inherent in the Scottish character; but his poetry holds them all in the tension of Gregory Smith's 'Caledonian antisyzygy'. . . . He stands wherever extremes meet and clash, to absorb the turmoil. 'And damn consistency!' He has dedicated himself to the enlargement of human consciousness, and that is no neat and tidy business." Hamilton further stated that "Goethe is the only writer with whom Hugh MacDiarmid can be compared in intellectual audacity and imaginative voracity. It is impossible for a Scotsman . . . to see MacDiarmid simply as a poet. He is, also, more judiciously appreciated abroad than at home—except in England, where he is accorded the indifferent indulgence due to outstanding eccentrics. Politer and more considered noises have been made lately, but only, I suspect, to mark his graduation to Grand Old Man status. MacDiarmid, however, is no Grand Old Man. He is still as Douglas Young saw him: 'at bay on his native heath, sprouting fresh tines at every angle and bellowing to quell the pack'—an indomitable, irreconcilable, unpredictable, paradoxical, and unpuffable genius."

MacDiarmid's poetry is like he was—lyrical, argumentative, polemical, and contradictory. Unable to believe, as W. H. Auden does, that poetry makes nothing happen, MacDiarmid in 1926 stated that "the function of art is the extension of human consciousness." When he published *Direadh* he noted: "I turn from the poetry of beauty to the poetry of wisdom—of 'wisdom,' that is to say, the poetry of moral and intellectual problems, and the emotions they generate." Kenneth Buthlay, writing in *Hugh MacDiarmid (C. M. Grieve),* calls this later poetry, such as that contained in *In Memoriam James Joyce,* the "poetry of information." The early MacDiarmid, according to Iain Crichton Smith in *Hugh MacDiarmid: A Critical Survey,* began like Blake, with lyrics which contain "a fusion of the intellect and feeling which is highly unusual and at times hallucinatory. [Then both went on] to write long poems based rather insecurely on systems which are fairly private (even MacDiarmid's communism doesn't seem to be all that orthodox)." The change in MacDiarmid's poetry occurred about 1930. MacDiarmid explained: "I, like Heine after the success of his lyrics found . . . I could no longer go on with that sort of thing but required to break up the unity of the lyric and introduce new material of various kinds on different levels of significance. It took Heine years of agonized effort to find the new form he needed, and his later work, in

which he did find it, never won a measure of esteem like that secured by his early work. So in my case."

Much of the strength of MacDiarmid's reputation still rests on his early lyrics. Crichton Smith notes that the lyrical fusion of the masculine and feminine sensibility was later replaced by an attitude that was entirely masculine, dour, and willful, and, he believes, weaker as a result. An early volume, *A Drunk Man Looks at the Thistle,* was hailed by Oliver St. John Gogarty as "the most virile and vivid poetry written in English or any dialect thereof for many a long day." *A Drunk Man* is still considered to be one of the finest contemporary poems. According to Buthlay, the poem, "without quite bursting at the seams, is able to hold all or almost all of MacDiarmid—which is to say that it is crammed full of fine lyrics, satire, flyting, parody, burlesque, occasional verse, Rabelaisian jokes, metaphysical conceits, translations and adaptations, sustained meditations and speculations on philosophical and religious problems, elemental symbols, and allusions recondite and otherwise. . . . The ultimate subject of the work is the creative process itself. . . . When not deeply imaginative, . . . he has astonishing resources of metaphysical wit and satirical, fantastic, or grotesque humour at his command. Wit in the sense that Donne had wit, a mental and emotional and verbal agility in juggling with the mutations of possibility, permeates the whole poem."

Buthlay has also pointed out that MacDiarmid was, in a special sense, an eclectic poet. "One cannot derive his style from particular sources because the sources are so many and so fantastically varied. This has obvious dangers, and [MacDiarmid] speaks of his fear of having 'paralysed his creative faculties by over-reading.' What saved him from this in the end was the intense activity of a 'tiny specialist cell in his brain' which constantly experimented with an 'obscure ray . . . emanating from his subtle realisation that beyond the individual mind of each man was a collective mind'---that is, the 'collective unconscious' of Jung."

In his later poems MacDiarmid turned from imaginative to intellectual verse. He no longer said, as he had in 1923, that he was "quite certain that the imagination had some way of dealing with the truth which the reason had not, and that commandments delivered when the body is still and the reason silent are the most binding that the souls of men can ever know." Many critics were disappointed with MacDiarmid's intellectualism. Crichton Smith bemoaned the fact that MacDiarmid should think that "a poetry of ideas must necessarily be a more 'serious' poetry. These long poems may be intellectually exciting but they are not serious. They do not confront us with serious things. They do not, I think, react on us as whole human beings. . . . Now it is true that the movement of MacDiarmid's verse recognizes the difficulty of arriving at the truth. . . . There are times however, when MacDiarmid gives the idea that he himself knows the truth and that his ideas are essentially right."

"The weakness of MacDiarmid's use of facts," writes Buthlay, "is that he is oftener content to catalogue them with Whitman than to follow Thoreau's hint of the need to transmute them imaginatively into 'the substance of the human mind.' " Ian Gordon lamented the change to "a style that is inconsequent always, incoherent very often, and is all too seldom poetry." His admirers, according to Hamilton, "claim that MacDiarmid has triumphantly fashioned a loose, discursive, open-ended kind of meditative vehicle which is hospitable to ideas, facts and arguments, that he has marvellously broken free of fiddling post-symbolist constraints. The unconvinced, [however,] complain that he has merely granted himself a licence to be boringly opinionated, that he has ditched rhythm, metaphor and formal discipline in order to make room for muddled, self-admiring chat."

Then there are those who admit, as Louis Simpson does, that "in spite of everything, he is a superb poet." Even though, as Buthlay says, MacDiarmid wrote too much and discriminated too little, "he is a major poet, and there is no book he has written that does not, however partially or intermittently, testify to that fact." Late in life he turned to what the *Times Literary Supplement* called "infinitely expansible poetry on an epic scale." In Hamilton's opinion, the range of poetry to be found in *Collected Poems* "is breathtaking; and the faults, flaws, and fissures serve not to diminish but (as always with genius) to enhance its superhuman scale."

MacDiarmid's abiding interest was language, particularly its aural qualities. He originally wrote in English even though he disliked what he felt to be the English domination of Scottish literature and hoped that his countrymen would look to Europe for literary inspiration. He later decided that his own country's language should be revived, and became the leading figure in the Scottish Renaissance of the twenties, encouraging others to write in the eclectic Scots that he himself had chosen as a means of expression. During the early thirties he moved from this synthetic Scots, or "Lallans," to what Buthlay calls "synthetic English," a combination of English scientific terminology and "recondite elements of the English vocabulary." This experiment was short-lived, for by 1935, when *Second Hymn to Lenin and Other Poems* appeared, he no longer employed "synthetic English," and only the title poem was written (three years previously) in Scots. From about 1935 until shortly before his death he wrote almost entirely in English, although he did compose several longer poems in Scots, principally because he felt that, to quote T. S. Eliot, "many things can be expressed in Scots which cannot be expressed in English at all."

MacDiarmid turned to Scots not merely because he was a Scottish nationalist. To write in Scots was an act of faith, what MacDiarmid called "an experience akin to religious conversion." Moreover, he used Scots, as David Daiches explains, not as an alternative to English; he used it "for effects which are unobtainable in English." This un-Englishness in his writings led to comparisons with James Joyce. Edwin Muir in 1923 noted that "except Mr. Joyce, nobody at present is writing more resourceful English prose." Muir called *Sangschaw* "the product of a realistic, or more exactly a materialistic, imagination, which seizing upon everyday reality shows not the strange beauty which that sometimes takes on, but rather the beauty which it possesses normally and in use." MacDiarmid said about the aesthetic values of Scots: "One of the most distinctive characteristics of the Vernacular, part of its very essence, is its insistent recognition of the body, the senses. . . . This explains the unique blend of the lyrical and the ludicrous in primitive Scots sentiment. . . . The essence of the genius of our race is, in our opinion, the reconciliation it effects between the base and the beautiful, recognising that they are complementary and indispensable to each other." Buthlay notes, however, that by 1934, some former admirers were no longer enthusiastic about Vernacular poetry, and were, in fact, "expressing grave doubts about the possibilities of Scots as a literary medium." In 1936 Muir wrote: "[MacDiarmid] has written some remarkable poetry; but he has left Scottish verse very much where it was before."

The English never understood why a man capable of writing in English would choose to employ another language. (Buthlay reports that not one important English critic had anything favorable to say about *A Drunk Man Looks at the Thistle* until it ap-

peared in *Collected Poems* 36 years later.) Yet it is undeniable that MacDiarmid made Scots a reputable medium for poetry. M. L. Rosenthal still believes that MacDiarmid's best work was executed in Scots. Other critics say that he surpasses Burns. "Certainly he has a range of reference that has not been in Scottish poetry since Dunbar," writes Simpson. "He has written fine lyrics and discursive poems, in English as well as Scots."

Alan Denson notes that MacDiarmid was no mere theorist. "Like all true artists his concern and his language have been directed to the betterment of economic and educational conditions." He is not a humanitarian, however, and refuses to be called a humanist. He has been called everything from a Scottish nationalist and a Marxist internationalist to a Nietzschean communist. (The *Times Literary Supplement* once conjectured that "the years on Whalsay were perhaps a Zarathustran self-conquering.") His communism was, in any event, highly individualistic, "a stage on the way to Anarchism." He wrote in his autobiography: "I am . . . interested only in a very subordinate way in the politics of Socialism as a political theory; my real concern with Socialism is as an artist's organised approach to the interdependencies of life." Buthlay notes that MacDiarmid was "especially preoccupied with the source of 'inspiration' and the mysterious factors that go to produce 'genius,' because he believed the hope of mankind to lie in the possibility of evolving a race of men to whom what is now called 'genius' would be the norm. The tremendous significance of Lenin's revolution (*and Douglas's economics*) was that it promised to clear 'bread-and-butter problems' out of the way and establish much more favourable conditions for this all-important evolutionary process." As might be expected, these opinions were not universally well received. As Simpson says, MacDiarmid "was driven out of the market place; for years he lived in actual poverty on an island off the coast of Scotland. . . . In the thirties when the university Marxists—W. H. Auden, Spender and their friends—became fashionable, MacDiarmid remained obscure. He came from the working class; he meant what he said; he was embarrassing."

"You cannot read MacDiarmid 'just for the poetry'," writes Simpson; "he doesn't want to be read that way; he flings his opinions in your teeth." The *Times Literary Supplement* reviewer adds: "From his very beginnings Mr. MacDiarmid has never been interested in mere literature or even, whatever his gifts for it, in mere poetry; writing for him has been an aspect, an instrument, of political and cultural struggle, and his poems have increasingly tended towards the condition of the manifesto or the prophecy. Mere art he now sees as a temptation." In his instructional essays, for example, "he demonstrates the intrinsic interest in ideas and principles which has been the hidden descant to all his writings," writes Denson. "Warm in sentiment, genial in manner, every stratum in [his] essays is deeper, richer, and stronger than queasy appetites could stomach."

His principal pseudonym, Hugh MacDiarmid (he used others early in his career in order to review his own works), "is more of a *nom de guerre* than a *nom de plume*," writes Buthlay. "Hugh MacDiarmid is the scourge of the Philistines, the ruthless intellectual tough looking for a rumble." A *Times Literary Supplement* writer noted that, roughly, "C. M. Grieve was the professional journalist, the editor, the critic and publicist, the man who expressed hopes but also realistic doubts; Hugh MacDiarmid was the bard, the prophet, the enemy of compromise. The two identities, and the possibility of disagreement and discussion between them, saved their owner also from getting tied too sharply down to one narrow position."

"My story," MacDiarmid once said, ". . . is the story of an absolutist whose absolutes came to grief in his private life." In his last years he led "a quiet, rustic, ascetic life," according to Buthlay. In Scotland he became a legendary figure. Denson writes: "The spirit is everything, the letter a mere translation of the man. Is there elsewhere an emblem more apt to describe Hugh MacDiarmid's quality, as a man, than his own words? Perhaps only Mozart's music could depict such a poet."

BIOGRAPHICAL/CRITICAL SOURCES:

BOOKS

Aitken, William R., and others, *Hugh MacDiarmid: A Festschrift,* Dufour, 1963.
Buthlay, Kenneth, *Hugh MacDiarmid (C. M. Grieve),* Oliver & Boyd, 1964, revised edition, Scottish Academic Press, 1982.
Contemporary Literary Criticism, Gale, Volume 2, 1974, Volume 4, 1975, Volume 11, 1979, Volume 19, 1981.
Dictionary of Literary Biography, Volume 20: *British Poets, 1914-1945,* Gale, 1983.
Glen, Duncan, *Hugh MacDiarmid (Christopher Murray Grieve) and the Scottish Renaissance,* Chambers (Edinburgh), 1964.
Glen, Duncan, editor, *Hugh MacDiarmid: A Critical Survey,* Scottish Academic Press, 1972.
Poems Addressed to Hugh MacDiarmid (festschrift), edited by Duncan Glen, Akros, 1967.
Scott, P. C., and A. C. Davis, editors, *The Age of MacDiarmid: Essays on Hugh MacDiarmid and His Influence on Contemporary Scotland,* Mainstream, 1980.

PERIODICALS

Agenda (special MacDiarmid double number), autumn-winter, 1967-68.
Books Abroad, summer, 1967.
Harper's, August, 1967.
Irish Statesman, January 8, 1927.
Listener, August 10, 1967.
Nation, June 5, 1967.
New York Times Book Review, June 25, 1967.
Observer, August 13, 1967.
Poetry, July, 1948.
Punch, July 19, 1967.
Scottish Field, August, 1962.
Times Literary Supplement, December 31, 1964, August 24, 1967.*

*   *   *

GRIGSON, Geoffrey (Edward Harvey) 1905-1985

PERSONAL: Born March 2, 1905, in Pelynt, Cornwall, England; died November 28, 1985; son of William Shuckforth (a canon) and Mary (Boldero) Grigson; married Frances Galt, 1929 (died, 1937); married Burta Kunert, 1938 (marriage dissolved); married Jane McIntire (a writer); children: (first marriage) one daughter; (second marriage) one son, one daughter; (third marriage) one son. *Education:* St. Edmund Hall, Oxford, graduated. *Politics:* Labour. *Religion:* None.

ADDRESSES: Home—Broad Town Farm, Broad Town, Swinton, Wiltshire, England. *Agent*—David Higham Associates, 5-8 Lower John St., London W1R 4HA, England.

CAREER: Poet and professional writer. After college became member of London staff of *Yorkshire Post;* in 1929 began working on *Morning Post,* London, became literary editor; founded and edited *New Verse,* 1933-39, an avant-garde poetry magazine

which published early poems of Auden, MacNeice, Dylan Thomas, and others; had worked in publishing formerly in Talks Department of British Broadcasting Corp. and member of BBC Literary Advisory Committee.

AWARDS, HONORS: Duff Cooper Memorial Prize, 1971; Oscar Blumenthal Prize, 1971.

WRITINGS:

POETRY

Several Observations: Thirty-Five Poems, Cresset Press (London), 1939.
Under the Cliff and Other Poems, Routledge, 1943.
The Isles of Scilly and Other Poems, Routledge, 1946.
Legenda Suecana, privately printed, 1953.
The Collected Poems of Geoffrey Grigson: 1924-1962, Phoenix House (London), 1963.
A Skull in Salop and Other Poems, Dufour, 1967.
Ingestion of Ice-Cream and Other Poems, Macmillan, 1969.
Discoveries of Bones and Stones, and Other Poems, Macmillan, 1971.
Sad Grave of an Imperial Mongoose, Macmillan, 1973.
Angles and Circles and Other Poems, Gollancz, 1974.
The Fiesta and Other Poems, Secker & Warburg, 1978.
History of Him, Secker & Warburg, 1980.
Collected Poems, 1963-1980, Allison & Busby, 1982.
The Cornish Dancer and Other Poems, Secker & Warburg, 1983.
Montaigne's Tower and Other Poems, Secker & Warburg, 1984.
Persephone's Flowers and Other Poems, Secker & Warburg, 1986.

NONFICTION

Henry Moore, Penguin, 1943.
Wild Flowers in Britain, Hastings House, 1944.
Samuel Palmer: The Visionary Years, Kegan Paul, 1947.
English Romantic Art (catalogue prepared for an Arts Council of Great Britain Exhibition), [London], 1947.
An English Farmhouse and Its Neighbourhood, Parrish, 1948.
The Scilly Isles, with drawings and watercolors by Fred Uhlman, Elek, 1948, revised edition, Duckworth, 1977.
The Harp of Aeolus, and Other Essays on Art, Literature, and Nature, Routledge, 1948.
Places of the Mind (essays, some originally appeared in periodicals), Routledge & Kegan Paul, 1949.
Flowers of the Meadow, with illustrations by Robin Tanner, Penguin, 1950.
The Crest on the Silver: An Autobiography, Cresset, 1950.
Wessex, Collins, 1951.
A Master of Our Time: A Study of Wyndham Lewis, Methuen, 1951, reprinted, Gordon Press, 1989.
Essays from the Air (radio talks), Routledge & Kegan Paul, 1951.
West Country, Collins, 1951.
Gardenage; or, The Plants of Ninhursaga, Routledge & Kegan Paul, 1952.
(With Jean Cassou) *The Female Form in Painting,* Harcourt, 1953.
Freedom of the Parish, Phoenix House, 1954, reprinted, The Cornish Library, 1982.
Gerard Manley Hopkins, Longmans, for the British Council, 1955, revised edition, 1968.
The Englishman's Flora, Phoenix House, 1955, revised edition, 1975.
English Drawing from Samuel Cooper to Gwen John, Thames & Hudson, 1955.
The Shell Guide to Flowers of the Countryside (also see below), Phoenix House, 1955.

Jean Baptiste Camille Corot (Book-of-the-Month Club selection), Metropolitan Museum, 1956.

England, photographs by Edwin Smith, Thames & Hudson, 1957, Studio Publications, 1958.

(Author of commentary) Stevan Celebonovic, *Old Stone Age,* Philosophical Library, 1957.

(Author of commentary) Celebonovic, *The Living Rocks,* preface by Andre Maurois, translation by Joyce Emerson and Stanley Pococks, Philosophical Library, 1957.

Fossils, Insects, and Reptiles (also see below), Phoenix House, 1957.

The Painted Caves, Phoenix House, 1957.

Art Treasures of the British Museum, preface by Sir Thomas Kendrick, Abrams, 1957.

The Wiltshire Book, Thames & Hudson, 1957.

(Author of commentary) Henry Moore, *Heads, Figures and Ideas,* New York Graphic Society, 1958.

Looking and Finding and Reading and Investigating and Much Else (juvenile), drawings by Christopher Chamberlin, Phoenix House, 1958, reprinted, J. Baker, 1970.

Shell Guide to Trees and Shrubs (also see below), Phoenix House, 1958.

English Villages in Colour, Batsford, 1958.

A Herbal of All Sorts, Macmillan, 1959.

Shell Guide to Wild Life (also see below), Phoenix House, 1959.

English Excursions, Macmillan, 1959.

Samuel Palmer's Valley of Vision, Phoenix House, 1960.

Christopher Smart, Longmans, for the British Council, 1961.

The Shell Country Book, Phoenix House, 1962, Dent, 1973.

Poets in Their Pride, Phoenix House, 1962, Basic Books, 1964.

(With others) *The Shell Nature Book* (contains *The Shell Guide to Flowers of the Countryside, Fossils, Insects, and Reptiles, Shell Guide to Trees and Shrubs,* and *Shell Guide to Wild Life*), Basic Books, 1964.

The Shell Book of Roads, illustrated by David Gentleman, Ebury Press, 1964.

(With wife, Jane Grigson) *Shapes and Stories: A Book about Pictures* (juvenile), J. Baker, 1964, Vanguard, 1965.

The Shell Country Alphabet, M. Joseph, in association with George Rainbird, 1966.

(With J. Grigson) *Shapes and Adventures,* Marshbank, 1967, published as *More Shapes and Stories: A Book about Pictures,* Vanguard, 1967.

Ben Nicholson: Twelve New Works (brochure for exhibition), Marlborough Fine Art Ltd. and Marlborough New London Gallery, 1967.

Poems and Poets, Dufour, 1969.

Shapes and People: A Book about Pictures (juvenile), Vanguard, 1969.

Notes from an Odd Country, Macmillan, 1970.

Shapes and Creatures: A Book about Pictures (juvenile), Black, 1973.

The Contrary View: Glimpses of Fudge and Gold, Rowman & Littlefield, 1974.

A Dictionary of English Plant Names (and Some Products of Plants), Allen Lane, 1974.

Britain Observed: The Landscape through Artists' Eyes, Phaidon, 1975.

The Englishman's Flora, Hart-Davis MacGibbon, 1975.

The Goddess of Love: The Birth, Triumph, Death, and Return of Aphrodite, Constable, 1976, Stein & Day, 1977.

Twists of the Way, Mandeville, 1981.

Blessings, Kicks and Curses, Allison & Busby, 1982.

The Private Art: A Poetry Notebook, Allison & Busby, 1982.

Recollections: Mainly of Artists and Writers (memoir), Chatto & Windus, 1984.

(With J. Grigson) *Shapes, Animals and Special Creatures,* Vanguard, in press.

EDITOR

(With Denys Kilham Roberts, Gerald Gould, and John Lehmann) *The Year's Poetry,* John Lane, 1934.

(And author of introduction) *The Arts Today,* John Lane, 1935, reprinted, Kennikat, 1970.

(With Roberts) *The Year's Poetry, 1937-38,* John Lane, 1938.

New Verse: An Anthology (originally appeared in the first six years of the periodical *New Verse*), Faber, 1939.

(And author of introduction) *The Journals of George Sturt,* Cresset, 1941.

The Romantics: An Anthology, Routledge, 1942, Granger, 1978.

Visionary Poems and Passages; or, The Poet's Eye, with original lithographs by John Craxton, F. Muller (London), 1944.

The Mint: A Miscellany of Literature, two volumes, Routledge, 1946-48.

Before the Romantics: An Anthology of the Enlightenment, Routledge, 1946, reprinted, Salamander, 1984.

Poetry of the Present: An Anthology of the Thirties and After, Phoenix House, 1949.

Poems of John Clare's Madness, Routledge & Kegan Paul, 1949, Harvard University Press, 1951.

(And author of introduction) William Barnes, *Selected Poems,* Harvard University Press, 1950 (published in England as *Selected Poems of William Barnes,* Routledge & Kegan Paul, 1950).

(And author of introduction) *Selected Poems of John Dryden,* Grey Walls Press (London), 1950.

(And author of introduction) George Crabbe, *Poems,* Grey Walls Press, 1950.

(And author of introduction) John Clare, *Selected Poems,* Routledge & Kegan Paul, 1950.

The Victorians: An Anthology, Routledge & Kegan Paul, 1950.

(And author of commentary) Robert John Thomton, *Temple of Flora,* Collins, 1951.

About Britain, thirteen volumes, Collins, 1951.

(And author of introduction) Samuel Taylor Coleridge, *Poems,* Grey Walls Press, 1951.

(With Charles Harvard Gibbs-Smith) *People, Places, and Things,* four volumes, Grosvenor Press, 1954, published as *People, Places, and Things,* Hawthorn, Volume I: *People,* 1954, 2nd edition, 1957, Volume II: *Places,* 1954, 2nd edition, 1957, Volume III: *Things,* 1954, 2nd edition, 1957, Volume IV: *Ideas,* 1954, 2nd edition, 1957.

The Three Kings: A Christmas Book of Carols, Poems, and Pieces, G. Fraser (Bedford), 1958.

The Cherry Tree: A Collection of Poems (juvenile), Vanguard, 1959.

Country Poems, Hutton, 1959.

The Concise Encyclopedia of Modern World Literature, Hawthorn, 1963, revised 2nd edition, 1970.

O Rare Mankind!: A Short Collection of Great Prose, Phoenix House, 1963.

Watter Savage Landor, *Poems,* Centaur Press, 1964, Southern Illinois University Press, 1965.

The English Year from Diaries and Letters, Oxford University Press, 1967, reprinted, 1984.

A Choice of William Morris's Verse, Faber, 1969.

A Choice of Thomas Hardy's Poems, Macmillan (London), 1969.

A Choice of Robert Southey's Verse, Faber, 1970.

Pennethorne Hughes, *Thirty-Eight Poems,* Baker, 1970.

(And author of introduction) *Faber Book of Popular Verse*, Faber, 1971, published as *Gambit Book of Popular Verse*, Gambit, 1971.

Rainbows, Fleas, and Flowers: A Nature Anthology Chosen by Geoffrey Grigson (juvenile), Baker, 1971, Vanguard, 1974.

Unrespectable Verse, Allen Lane, 1971.

The Faber Book of Love Poems: Love Expected, Love Begun, The Plagues of Loving, Love Continued, Absences, Doubts, Division, Love Renounced, and Love in Death, Faber, 1973, reprinted, 1983.

Poet to Poet: Charles Cotton, Penguin, 1975.

The Penguin Book of Ballads, Penguin, 1975.

The Faber Book of Epigrams and Epitaphs, Faber, 1977.

The Faber Book of Nonsense Verse, Faber, 1979.

The Oxford Book of Satirical Verse: Chosen by Geoffrey Grigson, Oxford University Press, 1980.

The Faber Book of Poems and Places, Faber, 1980.

The Faber Book of Reflective Verse, Faber, 1984.

AUTHOR OF INTRODUCTION

Francis Bacon, *Essays*, Oxford University Press, 1937.

Horse and Rider: Eight Centuries of Equestrian Paintings, Thames & Hudson, 1950.

R. B. Beckett, *John Constable and the Fishers*, Routledge Kegan Paul, 1952.

English Country: A Series of Illustrations, Batsford, 1952.

William Allingham's Diary, Centaur, 1967.

Faber Book of Poems and Places, Faber, 1980.

Thomas Tusset, *Five Hundred Points of Good Husbandry*, Oxford University Press, 1983.

Henry James, *A Little Tour in France*, Oxford University Press, 1984.

OTHER

Contributor to *New Statesman, Listener, Encounter, Times Literary Supplement, Guardian, Observer, Sunday Times, New York Review of Books*, and other periodicals.

SIDELIGHTS: The poet Geoffrey Grigson remained in Britain's literary forefront for half a century, though his poetry often received less recognition than his critical essays and numerous anthologies of others' works. As a critic Grigson established a considerable reputation in the 1930s, when he simultaneously edited his prestigious periodical *New Verse* and served as the literary editor of the conservative newspaper *Morning Post*. In both of these publications, and subsequently in the pages of the *Times Literary Supplement, New Statesman*, the *New York Review of Books* and other journals, Grigson reviewed with "a ferocity and personal animus foreign to the general, indulgent tone of modern criticism," according to a London *Times* reporter. In a *Times Literary Supplement* article, Samuel Hynes wrote of Grigson: "Every review is . . . a headlong charge with beaver down and lance at the ready, against the slackness, the wrong-headedness, the vulgarity, the un-Grigsonness of the rest of the world." In his later years, however, Grigson increased his output of published poetry, and Hynes noted: "If posterity, that shadowy reader, returns to Grigson, it will probably not be for his prose. The poetry has a better chance. . . . For Grigson belongs to the class of habitual poets, the kind who write poetry all the time, as other people write journals or diaries or letters, as a means of self-definition and self-sustenance, a way of arresting the daily losses that time exacts."

Grigson was born in Pelynt, Cornwall in 1905, when his father, a canon, was fifty-nine years old. Perceiving a distance between himself and his natural parents, the young Grigson adopted a surrogate mother named Bessie from amongst the Pelynt villagers, and she nurtured within him a delight for the Cornish landscape and for gardening. *Dictionary of Literary Biography* contributor Douglas Loney suggested that Grigson's love for the vicarage garden of his childhood became "the deepest foundation stone of his eclectic, observing, curious poetry. . . . The young Grigson had discovered that the nature which he so loved could be ordered by a careful and patient art and so could achieve a significance reaching beyond its own borders." At every opportunity throughout the years of schooling he called "long purgatory," Grigson escaped to favorite rural areas to observe wildlife and indulge in amateur archaeology. He then brought with him to Oxford University, Loney wrote, "an intense appreciation of the poetry of Herbert, Coleridge, and Hopkins, for the vigor of their poetic language and their stylistic discipline, for their romantic questing, for their insistence . . . on the immediate and the particular, on nature, and on nature's reflection of something rather more elusive, something of the spirit."

After graduating from Oxford, Grigson briefly held a position with the *Yorkshire Post*, writing short articles and book reviews. In 1929 he moved to the *Morning Post*, where he eventually became literary editor. Using the proceeds from the sales of review copies sent to the *Morning Post*, he founded *New Verse* in 1933. The avant-garde periodical, published for six years and never boasting a circulation greater than one thousand, achieved a prestige that far outstripped its modest dimensions. According to Loney, *New Verse* "made in its brief life an important contribution to letters, more perhaps in providing a forum for the works of some of England's finest young poets between the wars than for Grigson's attacks upon critics and authors who dared to disagree with him." Hynes conversely claimed: "In his early *New Verse* days, Grigson marred his achievement as an editor by abusing writers whose only offense was not to please him; *New Verse* was an extraordinarily good journal, and the editing of it was a heroic act, but what one remembers most clearly about it now is likely to be not the high quality of its verse, but the violence of its attacks." In retrospect, Grigson castigated himself for the venomous reviews he penned for *New Verse*. Loney has quoted the author as saying, "I had not grown up enough . . . to realize that the neck of a beheaded fool grows three more foolish heads. The fun and slaughter now make me, if I recall them, rather sick."

Even after he discontinued *New Verse* in 1939 and began to publish his own poetry in books, Grigson maintained his reputation as an assessor of literary works. Other critics welcomed his forthright approach. In the *Spectator*, Peter Levi wrote: "Grigson fulfills perfectly the most important function of a critic even if he muffs some of the others. That is, he extends the reader's range and understanding, he shows one new things, he points to what is alive." P. J. Kavanagh stated in the *Spectator*: "Geoffrey Grigson has been a figure of such general cultural utility, . . . for so long . . . that it is odd to realize that anyone who praises him acquires a large number of unseen enemies. . . . This is because, in his detestation of the false, the merely fashionable, he has never been able to resist putting the boot in or, if that metaphor is too inelegant, planting a poisoned dart in the tenderest place, and then twisting." In 1974 a *Times Literary Supplement* reviewer claimed: "It would he hard to point to any critic who has so successfully combined an educated traditional taste with an acute awareness of what is going on around him. He has never succumbed either to the ineptitudes of academic criticism or to the standards of the flea-market by which most contemporary verse is judged."

Though a London *Times* writer suggests that the bitter tone of Grigson's criticism "may have sprung partly from the comparative non-recognition of his poetry," Grigson's verse was widely, and generally favorably, reviewed. Hynes described the work as springing from a tradition of "quotidian poetry . . . the poetry of the small, the homely, the contingent, the low-voiced, the ordinary. . . . It is a private record, a self alone in the world: there is rarely another person present, not many poems are direct address, almost none are third person narratives. The observations are exact but reticent, visual but not descriptive, and though they are full of natural details, they are painterly rather than nature poems." A *Times Literary Supplement* reviewer likewise noted Grigson's "interest in small, compact, isolated objects" in poems where "the density is pared down by his finely-wrought verse to a set of clean, separate perceptions, half-lights and ambiguities dispelled by a fastening on silhouetted shapes." "Quirky Mr. Grigson certainly is," wrote another *Times Literary Supplement* critic, who explained: "he enjoys oddments and oddities, and he seems to feel and think in short, sharp bursts, so that his poems are moments of delight and of irritation, little scraps and brief petulances. His touch is surer with objects and creatures than it is with people, even in the love poems." Loney concluded of Grigson's verse: "Although he may find it impossible to affirm any lasting reality beyond that which his senses reveal, he continues to celebrate the fleeting graces which he observes in the objects and events surrounding him." Roger Garfitt offered a similar assessment in *London Magazine:* "Grigson is particularly good at catching moments of subjective illumination and relating them to precise backgrounds, so that they form a kind of critique and history of present times. . . . The result is a poetry, of positive humanism, a redoubt of humane sensibility."

Unimpressed by the British academic community, Grigson never sought to align himself with a university. He worked instead at preparing anthologies, writing nature books, editing art books and museum catalogues, and even publishing an occasional book for children. The author of a *Times Literary Supplement* profile wrote of Grigson's eclectic oeuvre: "Under the often considerable pressures of earning a living he has never given way to the temptations of middlebrow literary good fellowship." Hynes noted that although "it is the criticism that has made his reputation," the best of Grigson's work "has been written in celebration of pictures, of places, of artists, of moments of vision, of the star that the black seeds make in a halved pear." More than one critic commented on a "Grigson paradox," as Valentine Cunningham termed it in the *Times Literary Supplement.* Cunningham cited the "mix of literary naturalist and nature-watching poet-critic," while another *Times Literary Supplement* contributor, after listing the natural history topics common to Grigson's essays, commented: "It seems strange that this Geoffrey Grigson should live in the same skin with the writer of sharp reviews and often sharper letters to periodicals." Hynes expressed the hope that readers in the future would award more attention to the positive side of Grigson's work. "It is a sad irony," Hynes concluded, "that because he has been so quick to attack and condemn others, he should not be recognized in his essential role, as one of the true celebrators of what is."

BIOGRAPHICAL/CRITICAL SOURCES:

BOOKS

Contemporary Literary Criticism, Gale, Volume 7, 1977, Volume 39, 1986.
Dictionary of Literary Biography, Volume 27: *Poets of Great Britain and Ireland, 1945-1960,* Gale, 1984.
Grigson, Geoffrey, *The Crest on the Silver: An Autobiography,* Cresset, 1950.
Grigson, *Recollections: Mainly of Artists and Writers,* Chatto & Windus, 1984.
Scarfe, Francis, *Auden and After,* Routledge, 1942.
Thwaite, Anthony, *Poetry Today, 1960-1973,* British Council, 1973.

PERIODICALS

Books Abroad, winter, 1967.
Book Week, December 19, 1965.
Book World, March 17, 1968.
Christian Science Monitor, November 30, 1967.
Economist, February 8, 1969.
Encounter, May, 1975.
Harper's, July, 1963.
Listener, November 16, 1967.
London Magazine, June, 1967, February/March, 1975.
New Review, February, 1975.
New Statesman, July 21, 1967, February 2, 1969, May 15, 1970, March 14, 1975.
New York Times Book Review, January 7, 1968.
Observer, June 18, 1967.
Poetry, April, 1970.
Review, September 3, 1970.
Saturday Review, November 13, 1965.
Spectator, June 14, 1968, August 2, 1975, December 18, 1976, December 1, 1982, September 22, 1984.
Times (London), October 23, 1980, November 4, 1982, December 16, 1982, October 27, 1983, January 24, 1985.
Times Literary Supplement, December 7, 1962, December 12, 1963, August 10, 1967, October 10, 1967, November 30, 1967, December 21, 1967, March 13, 1969, July 31, 1969, December 4, 1969, September 4, 1970, November 30, 1970, February 4, 1972, June 1, 1973, April 19, 1974, July 25, 1975, November 10, 1978, September 12, 1980, January 16, 1981, May 28, 1982, October 22, 1982, February 11, 1983, December 14, 1984.

OBITUARIES:

PERIODICALS

Observer, December 1, 1985.
Times (London), November 30, 1985.
Times Literary Supplement, January 17, 1986.

[Sketch verified by wife, Jane Grigson]

*   *   *

GUNN, Thom(son William) 1929-

PERSONAL: Born August 29, 1929, in Gravesend, England; son of Herbert Smith (a journalist) and Ann Charlotte (Thomson; a journalist) Gunn; unmarried. *Education:* Trinity College, Cambridge, B.A., 1953, M.A., 1958; attended Stanford University, 1954-55, 1956-58. *Religion:* Atheist. *Avocational interests:* Reading, films.

ADDRESSES: Home—1216 Cole St., San Francisco, CA 94117.

CAREER: Lived in Paris, 1950, and Rome, 1953-54; resident of California since 1954, except for one year in San Antonio, TX; visited Berlin, 1960. University of California, Berkeley, 1958-66, began as lecturer, became associate professor of English, visiting lecturer, 1973—, senior lecturer, 1989—. Freelance writer, 1966—. *Military service:* British Army, National Service, 1948-50.

AWARDS, HONORS: Levinson Prize, 1955; Somerset Maugham Award, 1959; American Institute of Arts and Letters grant, 1964; National Institute and American Academy Awards in Literature, 1964; Rockefeller award, 1966; Guggenheim fellowship, 1971; W. H. Smith Award 1980; PEN/Los Angeles Prize for poetry, 1983, for *Passages of Joy;* Robert Kirsch Award, 1988, for body of work focused on the American West; Shelley Memorial award, 1990.

WRITINGS:

(Editor) *Poetry from Cambridge,* Fortune Press, 1953.
Thom Gunn (poetry), Fantasy Press, 1953.
Fighting Terms: A Selection, Fantasy Press, 1954, revised edition, Faber, 1962, original edition reprinted, Bancroft Library, 1983.
The Sense of Movement, Faber, 1957, University of Chicago Press, 1959.
My Sad Captains, and Other Poems (also see below), University of Chicago Press, 1961.
(With Ted Hughes) *Selected Poems,* Faber, 1962.
(Editor with Hughes) *Five American Poets,* Faber, 1963.
A Geography, Stone Wall Press, 1966.
(With Ander Gunn) *Positives* (photographs by Ander Gunn; verse captions by Thom Gunn), Faber, 1966, University of Chicago Press, 1967.
Touch, Faber, 1967, University of Chicago Press, 1968.
The Garden of the Gods, Pym-Randall Press, 1968.
(Editor and author of introduction) Fulke Greville Brooke, *Selected Poems of Fulke Greville,* University of Chicago Press, 1968.
Poems, 1950-1966: A Selection, Faber, 1969.
The Explorers, R. Gilbertson, 1969.
The Fair in the Woods, Sycamore Press, 1969.
Sunlight, Albondocani Press, 1969.
Moly (also see below), Faber, 1971.
Moly [and] *My Sad Captains,* Farrar, Straus, 1973.
To the Air, David R. Godine, 1974.
(Editor) *Ben Jonson: Poems,* Penguin, 1974.
Jack Straw's Castle and Other Poems, Farrar, Straus, 1976.
Selected Poems 1950-1975, Farrar, Straus, 1979.
Talbot Road, Helikon Press, 1981.
The Passages of Joy, Farrar, Straus, 1982.
Games of Chance, Abattoir Press, 1982.
The Occasions of Poetry: Essays in Criticism and Autobiography, edited by Clive Wilmer, Farrar, Straus, 1982, expanded edition, North Point Press, 1985.
Lament, Doe Press, 1985.
Sidewalks, Albondocani Press, 1985.
The Hurtless Trees, Jordan Davies, 1986.
Night Sweats, R. Barth, 1987.
Undesirables, Pig Press, 1988.
Death's Door, Red Hydra Press, 1989.
At the Barriers, Nadja, 1989.
The Man with Night Sweats, Farrar, Straus, 1992.

Contributor of memoir to *My Cambridge,* 1977. Work represented in many anthologies, including: *Springtime,* edited by G. S. Fraser and I. Fletcher, Peter Owen, 1953, and *Mark in Time,* edited by R. Johnson and N. Harvey, Glide Publications, 1971. Poetry reviewer, *Yale Review,* 1958-64, and *London Magazine.* Contributor to *Encounter, Threepenny Review, Times Literary Supplement,* and other publications.

SIDELIGHTS: An English poet long resident in California, Thom Gunn combines a respect for traditional poetic forms with an interest in sensational topics, such as the Hell's Angels, LSD, and homosexuality. While Gunn wrote most of his early verse in iambic pentameter—a phase when his ambition was "to be the John Donne of the twentieth century"—his more recent poems assume a variety of forms, including syllabic stanzas and free verse. The course of his development is recorded in *Selected Poems 1950-1975,* in which "the language begins as English and progresses toward American," according to a *Nation* review by Donald Hall. "If [Gunn] belongs to a nation it is San Francisco; or perhaps homosexuality is his country—but I do not find him pledging allegiance to anything except his own alert, unforgiving, skeptical independence," Hall observes in the *Los Angeles Times Book Review.*

Gunn told *CA* that students of his work should read Paul Giles's article "Landscapes of Repetition" in *Critical Quarterly.* He explained, "I find it valuable because he reads me as I would want to be read, i.e. taking my later books for themselves rather than in light of the earlier books." Of his personal life, he wrote in 1983, "I am a completely anonymous person—my life contains no events, and I lack any visible personality. My books are so commonplace that I was once mistaken for an antique hat-stand (and I was wearing no hat). I lack motivation, circumstances, viewpoints on vital subjects, and illuminating personal data." As this comment reveals, Gunn is known for his reticence—and irony. Gunn's characteristic understatement about his life resurfaces in *The Occasions of Poetry: Essays in Criticism and Autobiography,* Ian Hamilton reports in the *Times Literary Supplement:* "The book's effort is to present the author as reflective and benign. We see him as fond and skilful explicator of Hardy and Fulke Greville, and as awed apprentice to Robert Duncan and William Carlos Williams."

Gunn's personal life—that of the radical nonconformist—is more interesting than he claims. Gunn's father was a journalist and his mother was a writer with socialist sympathies. Gunn attended a number of different schools as a result of his father's changing assignments and the attempt to evade German bombing raids. After graduating, he served in the British Army for two years, then lived in Paris where he read Proust and wrote fiction. Back at Cambridge's Trinity College, he concentrated on writing poetry and published the collection Fighting Terms in 1954. His early poetry—with its unembarrassed presentations of love as interpersonal combat—was considered violent against the tradition of gentility maintained in the 1940s. The young Gunn felt more at home in California, where he studied poetry with Yvor Winters and lived with his American lover.

Gunn's masterful fusion of "modern" and "traditional" elements has brought him critical acclaim. Writing in the *New York Times Book Review,* M. L. Rosenthal praises *Selected Poems 1950-1975,* noting that "Gunn has developed his craft so that by now even his freest compositions have a disciplined music." And, echoing this sentiment, *New York Review of Books* critic Stephen Spender suggests that the contradiction between the "conventional form" of Gunn's poems and their "often Californian 'with it' subject matter" is what distinguishes his work. Frank representations of violence, deviance, and the life of the counterculture based in San Francisco connect with "yesterday and tomorrow" in Gunn's art, remarks Charles Champlin of the *Los Angeles Times.* "It is," Spender elaborates, "as though A. E. Housman were dealing with the subject matter of *Howl,* or Tennyson were on the side of the Lotus Eaters."

In a *Poetry* article, Robert B. Shaw speculates that Gunn's fluctuation between metrical poems and free verse reflects an internal struggle: "On the one hand, the poet feels the attraction of a life ruled by traditional, even elitist values, and by purely individual preferences a private life in the classic sense, the pursuit of happiness. On the other hand, he feels a visionary impulse to shed his isolated individuality and merge with a larger whole." Commenting on the same tension in Gunn's work, Jay Parini notes in the *Massachusetts Review* that "Rule and Energy," "potentially counterdestructive principles, exist everywhere in [Gunn's] work, not sapping the poems of their strength but creating a tensed climate of balanced opposition. Any poet worth thinking twice about possesses *at least* an energetic mind; but it is the harnessing of this energy which makes for excellence. In Gunn's work an apparently unlimited energy of vision finds, variously, the natural boundaries which make expression—and clarity—possible."

Selected Poems 1950-1975 features examples of both metrical and free verse styles, prompting Rosenthal to conclude that it is "fortunate that American readers now have a single volume of Thom Gunn's selected poems. With their undemonstrative virtuosity, their slightly corrupt openness, their atmosphere of unfathomable secrets and their intimacy, so like that of a reticent friend who has something crucial to confess, these poems strike a chord at once insinuatingly familiar and infinitely alien."

Neither British nor American, Gunn resolutely evades easy classification, Hall observes in the *Los Angeles Times Book Review*. "The point is not legalities of citizenship (Gunn remains a resident alien, fitting a poet both domestic and estranged) but that he may not be labeled by nationality or anything else. His identity is his resistance to the limitations of identity. He belongs to uncertainty, exploration, movement and ongoingness. . . . Here is the man without conventional supports who refuses title and easychair, political party and national identity. For Gunn,"—who told *CA* "I join nothing,"—"affiliation seems a lie; change alone endures."

CA INTERVIEW

CA interviewed Thom Gunn by telephone on April 24, 1990, at his home in San Francisco, California.

CA: Your 1982 collection The Passages of Joy *takes its name from Samuel Johnson's work. Paul Giles said in his essay "Landscapes of Repetition" (*Critical Quarterly, *Summer 1987) that for Johnson, the passage of time "tended destructively to annihilate joy; but for Gunn, the flow of time positively contributes to it." Does that seem a valid and useful comment on the body of your work so far?*

GUNN: I suppose I agree with both statements, his statement about Johnson and his statement about me. I was using the phrase in Johnson's original sense, as a matter of fact—I was saying that we lose everything—and I was thinking specifically of the passages in the body.

CA: Your poetry does seem to have gotten more joyful as you've gone on.

GUNN: Young men are melancholy, and a lot of us get happier as we get older, as we know a little more and we're less sorry for ourselves. I teach a course in modern poetry at Berkeley, and the great hit is always [T. S. Eliot's] *The Waste Land,* because young people like poems of self-pity and they like self-dramatization.

CA: You tried to write novels before you settled in to concentrate on poetry, though you'd been writing poetry all along too. Were the attempts at novels a kind of apprenticeship or trial you needed to go through before you turned decisively to poems?

GUNN: I wanted to be a novelist all my teens. You want to be everything in your teens, but one of the things I most wanted was to be a novelist. I also would have liked to be a poet, and I would have liked to be a dramatist. But I didn't have the staying power to be a novelist, and I didn't have very much sense of being able to write dialogue, which you need to be a dramatist. So I got stuck with poetry. It amazes me that I had to go through those others before I decided to be a poet. I suppose it was more glamorous to be a novelist, or something like that.

CA: You told John Haffenden [in] Viewpoints: Poets in Conversation *that "the thing you want to write about gestates . . . and the process of writing becomes an exploration." Has that process of gestation and exploration changed for you over the years you've been writing?*

GUNN: No, not really. Every time you write a poem, it happens differently. There's no invariable pattern. My longest poem, for example, "Lament" (which will be in my next book, coming out in 1992), was written immediately after the death of a friend from AIDS. So there isn't always a long period of gestation, but there often is.

CA: The second part of My Sad Captains *marked a turning point in your work from the more philosophical, metrical verse to a gentler, more contemplative, syllabic verse. It was also the beginning of a concern with nature. How did nature come more to your attention as a subject for your poetry?*

GUNN: Nature's such a big thing; I don't think of it with a capital N in that sense. I don't know how it came about. When you write in a new form, you get a new subject matter. You didn't know you were going to, but you do. My form was a more accepting one; it was not imposing a form on my subject matter so much as accepting a form for my subject matter. And so the subject matter itself became wider, more inclusive. Every writer, I think, seeks to be more inclusive as he gets older. When I first started writing, I remember, a critic who was otherwise very complimentary toward me said that I had no sense of humor. Well, I had a sense of humor, but I couldn't get funny things into my poetry then. I had to learn how to get new things into my poetry. When I started to write, I could only write about the heroic. Bit my bit I've been able to write about more and more things. Most of the things have been there all along, but I haven't been able to write about them. The reason somebody like Whitman is so enviable is that he decided to write about everything, and he did.

CA: Can you tell when you start to write a poem whether it will be metrical or not?

GUNN: I may plan it that way as I start writing, but I don't just write it through, first line, then second line, and so on. I will usually start from rough notes that I've either made immediately before or made on some other occasion. And I write my notes very deliberately so that they're not too organized on the page, so that they do not dictate a form: they're just a collection of phrases, maybe outlining a possible argument for the poem, a possible structure, in terms of where it goes from one idea or feeling to another, but not in metrical form.

CA: So the subject matter doesn't necessarily dictate the form of the poem?

GUNN: No. It's a somewhat unknown moment, that moment of choice. Everybody's very curious about it, for obvious reasons—because they'd like to be able to learn how they too could write a poem. But it's not easy to say, and I keep it as fluid and undefined as I can, because I don't want to be self-imitative, for one thing, and because I don't know where it comes from.

CA: Taking LSD not only inspired the writing of Moly but also opened your work up generally, you've said. Could you say more about how the hallucinogen did that, exactly?

GUNN: It increased the subject matter, I guess, and it gave me more of an accepting attitude toward the world. I've written about this a good deal, and I don't know that I have a lot more to add.

CA: I have to ask another question you've already been asked many times: How do you feel you've been affected artistically and critically by being both English and American, as it were?

GUNN: That is a big question, and I never really know the answer to it. People often ask me if I think of myself of being an English poet or an American poet. Years ago I came across some reference to myself as an Anglo-American poet, and I thought, yes, that's what I am, an Anglo-American poet. That sums it up nicely. I don't get outside of myself enough to be able to answer this question very clearly. Some of these question are for critics [to] answer, not for the poet himself. Obviously, being English is very important to me since I spent my first twenty-five years in England. On the other hand, obviously, living in America is very important to me too, since I have spent more than half my life in this country. It's my life; I can't get outside of it enough to be able to say why it's important. The glib way of saying it is that I write in meter on American subjects. But that's a little too easy, to ready a formula; I'm not sure it says very much.

CA: It's not a question that concerns you critically or artistically, then?

GUNN: How can it? I don't think of such things. I think of my subject matter when I'm writing. I don't know what it means to be English; I don't know what it means to be American. There are so many ways of being American, so many ways of being English.

CA: You've referred in "My Life up to Now" (collected in The Occasions of Poetry*) to being lumped with the Movement as "categorizing foolishness," and some years ago you largely quit doing quick reviews of poetry, though you've continued to do some very fine critical essays. What do you feel poetry criticism should do to justify itself, and how well do you think it currently does whatever that is?*

GUNN: I view poetry criticism as something very practical. I write quite a bit nowadays—I've been writing a lot for the *Times Literary Supplement* the last few years and for other places. I see it as an extension of my role as teacher. I'm trying to show people how to read some poets they don't know about. I'm pointing to things, showing them a way into a new poet.

I'd like to say more about the Movement. I was not a member of the Movement, and I don't think the Movement was a movement; I think it was simply a period style that extended way beyond the people who were supposed to be involved in it. I never met most of the people in the Movement anyway that I was supposed to be part of.

CA: There was an earlier connection of that kind made between you and Ted Hughes too.

GUNN: Yes, but of course Ted Hughes wasn't called part of the Movement. I admire Ted enormously. We were put together as a publishing convenience; we had a *Selected Poems* out together when we were too young and had too little written for a full-scale *Selected Poems* each.

CA: I like your poem "Yoko," in which the voice is that of the dog rather than a human voice speaking for or about a dog. What can you say about the poem's genesis and development?

GUNN: It was inspired by the Newfoundland dog of a friend of mine whom I used to stay with in New York. She was a very lovable and noticeable dog, and I wanted to write a doggy poem. I didn't want it to be a human being saying amusing things about a dog, a kind of dog version of "Garfield," for example. A lot of good animal poems have done that. Look at Marianne Moore's "Peter," which is a wonderful poem. It's about a cat as a kind of human. But I was looking for a dog voice, and I had trouble with this. Then, in no way connected with writing the poem, I started to read Gertrude Stein's *Three Lives.* I borrowed the voice of her rather naive, trusting servant girls for Yoko's voice.

CA: There was a poem in Sierra *called "Meat," in which you lament the treatment of animals in the kind of factories they're raised in now rather than allowed free range. Are you concerned, as many people are, with animal rights?*

GUNN: Not really, but I dislike battery farms. I'm not really concerned with animal rights at all, because I'm much more concerned about human health, and it does seem to me that a certain amount of animal experimentation is necessary for trying out new drugs to cure things like AIDS.

CA: Your poetry is generous in its references and tributes to the work of other poets. Do you find familiarity with earlier poets largely missing among your students?

GUNN: If it is, I teach them those earlier poets. This is the terrible thing about many creative writing schools, that they're so divorced from literature. I think it's great that people should be able to learn creative writing, but they should only be able to take creative writing in connection with literature courses. All those places that give MFAs without requiring literature courses are not doing anybody a favor, least of all the students themselves. Keats decided to work his way through the English poets when he knew he was going to be a poet. And I think a poet should work his or her way through all the English and American poets and all the Modernist poets and as many foreign poets as possible.

CA: You said a while back that your friends tend to be plumbers and carpenters rather than writers. Do you see much of other poets now?

GUNN: I have poets among my friends. One of my neighbors is August Kleinzahler, a young poet who's very good and just had his second book out. I know one or two poets here and there.

CA: Are you doing many readings now?

GUNN: I do eight to ten a year. That's not so many as Diane Wakoski does, but it's quite enough for me. I'm getting better paid now by the University, so I don't need readings so much, which is nice for me. I don't enjoy readings that much in themselves, though I suppose I'd always want to do one or two a year.

But at one time, when I wrote "My Life up to Now," it was a necessity; I needed that extra couple of thousand dollars from doing readings wherever I could.

CA: Are you still teaching just one semester a year? That seems a good arrangement.

GUNN: Yes. It's a very good arrangement; I like it a lot.

CA: Do you get something back from the students?

GUNN: Always. Ezra Pound once said that he'd never taught a poem without learning more about it, and it's absolutely true.

CA: San Francisco has in the past been a place of great poetic ferment. Is there much of that now?

GUNN: I expect so, but I don't move that much in poetic circles. Robert Duncan, who was here, meant an awful lot to me when he was still alive. And I know some other poets here and there, as I said. It's like New York, like a capital city: it's always been receptive to the arts in general.

CA: What do you enjoy reading these days, in poetry or any other form?

GUNN: Everything. I like reading history and novels; I read quite widely. I don't read an awful lot of literary criticism, though every now and then I do, particularly if it's connected with my teaching.

CA: How do you feel about the poetry that's being written now in this country and in English generally?

GUNN: I find a great deal to enjoy and to learn from. I don't find the English poetry nowadays very interesting or bold. I think Philip Larkin has been a terrible deadening influence on English poetry because he's so scared of being pretentious. What is needed in England right now is a little more pretension, perhaps, a little more daring. There is one great English poet who has written in the last forty years or so, and that's Basil Bunting. But the English don't value him as they ought to. And I would exempt Ted Hughes from what I've just said. His recent book Wolfwatching is very fine. He's not part of the depressing timidity I find in English poetry. Otherwise I find most English poetry terribly timid. American poetry is much more interesting. I'm just reading Frank Bidart's poetry right now. He has a new book out called *In the Western Night*—it's very impressive; wild, amazing stuff. He's the poet that our parents warned us against. He does all the things you're not supposed to do—a terrific poet.

CA: You're not pessimistic about poetry in this country, then?

GUNN: Indeed not. In fact, my neighbor, August Kleinzahler, is very good. And there is a poet called Jim Powell who published his first book last year who I think is something else again. He's a sensational poet. There are a lot of really interesting poets around.

CA: What can you say about the book that's coming up?

GUNN: I've sent it off to the publisher. It consists of my poems from 1982, when my last book was published, to 1988. I stopped there and put it in the drawer. I find increasingly that it's very difficult for me to write poetry after the publication of a new book. This has been my way of cheating it. I finished the book,

I put it in a drawer, and I decided I wasn't going to publish it until ten years from the date of the previous book. I've just gone on writing, which is what I planned to do, so I guess my little game has worked. (On the other hand, when it gets published, maybe I'll dry up then. But meantime I've gotten a certain amount of the book after next written.) The book that's coming out in 1992 will have the title *The Man With Night Sweats,* which is the name of one of the poems in it.

CA: Are there new directions that you see in that book or the work you've done since completing it?

GUNN: Again, I don't know what my new directions are. I'm the poet. That's for critics to speak about. I'm not being coy; it's just that I don't think the writer is usually the best person to speak about such directions. They're much easier for somebody outside them to perceive.

BIOGRAPHICAL/CRITICAL SOURCES:

BOOKS

Bixby, George and Jack W. C. Hagstrom, *Thom Gunn: A Bibliography, 1940-78,* Rota (London), 1979.
Bold, Alan, *Thom Gunn and Ted Hughes,* Oliver & Boyd (Edinburgh), 1976.
Contemporary Literary Criticism, Gale, Volume 3, 1975; Volume 6, 1976; Volume 18, 1981; Volume 32, 1985.
Davie, Donald, *Under Briggflats,* [Chicago], 1990.
Dictionary of Literary Biography, Volume 27: *Poets of Great Britain and Ireland, 1945-1960,* Gale, 1984.
Haffenden, John, editor, *Viewpoints: Poets in Conversation,* Faber, 1981.
Jones, Peter, and Michael Schmidt, editors, *British Poetry since 1970,* Carcanet, 1980.
King, P. R., *Nine Contemporary Poets: A Critical Introduction,* Methuen, 1979.
Woods, Gregory, *Articulate Flesh,* Yale University Press, 1987.

PERIODICALS

Book World, September 16, 1973.
British Book News, April, 1987.
Critical Quarterly, summer, 1987.
Encounter, January, 1983.
Guardian, September 1, 1961.
Listener, August 12, 1982.
London Review of Books, July 15, 1982.
Los Angeles Times, November 7, 1988.
Los Angeles Times Book Review, November 6, 1988.
Massachusetts Review, spring, 1982.
Nation, November 10, 1979.
New Statesman, October 6, 1961; August 13, 1982.
New York Review of Books, September 20, 1973.
New York Times Book Review, June 16, 1974; January 20, 1980.
Observer, July 10, 1988.
PN Review, fall, 1989.
Poetry, August, 1958; May, 1974; September, 1975.
Saturday Review, June 1, 1961.
Sewanee Review, January, 1985.
Sierra, May/June, 1988.
Spectator, September 1, 1961.
Stand, spring, 1989.
Times Literary Supplement, September 29, 1961; January 1, 1967; October 5, 1967; April 24, 1969; April 16, 1971; August 30, 1974; July 23, 1982.
Village Voice, October 26, 1982.

World Literature Today, summer, 1986.

—*Interview by Jean W. Ross*

*   *   *

GUTHRIE, Isobel
  See GRIEVE, C(hristopher) M(urray)

H

HALL, Gimone 1940-

PERSONAL: Given name pronounced Ja-*mone;* born April 30, 1940, in Highland Park, IL; daughter of Timothy L. and Gladys (Gimon) McNamara; married Lawrence C. Hall (a journalist), July 13, 1963; children: Shannon Michelle, Colin Lawrence. *Education:* University of Texas, B.A., 1962.

ADDRESSES: Home—Million Wishes Farm, P.O. Box 485, Ottsville, PA 18942. *Agent*—Donald MacCampbell, Inc., 12 East 41st St., New York, NY 10017.

CAREER: Writer. *Corpus-Christi Caller-Times,* Corpus, Christi TX, news reporter, 1962.

WRITINGS:

The Blue Taper, Macfadden, 1970.
Witch's Suckling, Macfadden, 1970.
Devil's Walk, Macfadden, 1971.
The Silver Strand, Dell, 1974.
The Juliet Room, Manor Publishing, 1974.
Hide My Savage Heart, Pyramid Publications, 1977.
Rapture's Mistress, New American Library, 1978.
Fury's Sun, Passion's Moon, New American Library, 1979.
Ecstasy's Empire, New American Library, 1980.
The Jasmine Veil, New American Library, 1982.
Rules of the Heart, New American Library, 1984.
The Kiss Flower, New American Library, 1985.

Contributor of short stories to magazines.

WORK IN PROGRESS: Short stories.

SIDELIGHTS: Gimone Hall told *CA:* "What I enjoy most about writing is the adventure and friendship I experience from good characters. Like real people, good characters reveal themselves more and more the longer the writer lives with them. Capable of tumbling plots, they are also the ones to come to a writer's aid in time of trouble. The best solution to a problem in a book is usually provided by a good character."

*   *   *

HAMILTON, Clive
See LEWIS, C(live) S(taples)

HANDKE, Peter 1942-

PERSONAL: Born December 6, 1942, in Griffen, Carinthia, Austria; married Libgart Schwarz, 1966 (separated, 1972); children: one daughter. *Education:* Attended a Jesuit seminary, and University of Graz, 1961-65.

ADDRESSES: Home—53 rue Cecille-Dinant, F-92140 Clamart, France. *Office*—c/o Suhrkamp Verlag, Postfach 4229, 6000 Frankfurt am Main, Federal Republic of Germany.

CAREER: Dramatist, novelist, poet, essayist, and screenwriter, 1966—.

AWARDS, HONORS: Gerhart Hauptmann Prize, 1967; Schiller Prize, 1972; Buechner Prize, 1973; Kafka Prize, 1979 (refused).

WRITINGS:

FICTION

Die Hornissen (novel; title means "The Hornets"), Suhrkamp, 1966.
Der Hausierer (novel; title means "The Peddler"), Suhrkamp, 1967. *Begruessung des Aufsichtsrats* (experimental prose pieces; title means, "Welcoming the Board of Directors"), Residenz Verlag, 1967, also published in *Peter Handke* (see below).
Die Angst des Tormanns beim Elfmeter (novel), Suhrkamp, 1970, translation by Michael Roloff published as *The Goalie's Anxiety at the Penalty Kick,* Farrar, Straus, 1972 (also see below).
Der kurze Brief zum langen Abschied (novel), Suhrkamp, 1972, translation by Ralph Manheim published as *Short Letter, Long Farewell,* Farrar, Straus, 1974.
Die Stunde der wahren Empfindung (novel), Suhrkamp, 1975, translation by Manheim published as *A Moment of True Feeling,* Farrar, Straus, 1977.
Die linkshaendige Frau: Erzaehlung (novel), Suhrkamp, 1976, translation published as *The Left-Handed Woman,* Farrar, Straus, 1978 (also see below).
Langsame Heimkehr (title means "The Long Way Round"), Suhrkamp, 1979, translation by Manheim published in *Slow Homecoming* (also see below), Farrar, Straus, 1983.
Die Lehre der Sainte-Victoire (title means "The Lesson of Mont Saint-Victoire"), Suhrkamp, 1980, translation by Manheim published in *Slow Homecoming* (also see below), Farrar, Straus, 1983.

Kindergeschichte (title means "Children's Stories"), Suhrkamp, 1981, translation by Manheim published in *Slow Homecoming* (also see below), Farrar, Straus, 1983.

Slow Homecoming, translated by Manheim, Farrar, Straus, 1983.

Across (novella), translated by Manheim, Farrar, Straus, 1986.

Repetition (novel), translated by Manheim, Farrar, Straus, 1988.

The Afternoon of a Writer (novel), translated by Manheim, Farrar, Straus, 1989.

PLAYS

"Publikumsbeschimpfung" (first produced in Frankfurt at Theater am Turm, June 8, 1966), published in *Publikumsbeschimpfung und Andere Sprechstuecke* (see below), translation by Roloff published as "Offending the Audience" in *Kaspar and Other Plays* (see below).

"Selbstbezichtigung" (first produced in Oberhausen at Staedtische Buehnen, October 22, 1966), published in *Publikumsbeschimpfung und Andere Sprechstuecke* (see below), translation by Roloff published as "Self-Accusation" in *Kaspar and Other Plays* (see below).

"Weissagung" (first produced in Oberhausen at Staedtische Buehnen, October 22, 1966), published in *Publikumsbeschimpfung und Andere Sprechstuecke* (see below), translation by Roloff published as "Prophecy" in *The Ride Across Lake Constance and Other Plays* (see below).

"Hilferufe" (first produced in Stockholm, September 12, 1967), published in *Deutsches Theater der Gegenwart 2*, 1967, translation by Roloff published as "Calling for Help" in *Drama Review*, fall, 1970, and in *The Ride Across Lake Constance and Other Plays* (see below).

Kaspar (produced simultaneously in Frankfurt at Theater am Turm and in Oberhausen at Staedtische Buehnen, May 11, 1968), Suhrkamp, 1968, translation by Roloff under same title (produced in New York at the Brooklyn Academy of Music, February, 1973) published in *Kaspar and Other Plays* (see below), also published separately, Methuen, 1972.

"Das Mundel will Vormund sein" (first produced in Frankfurt at Theater am Turm, January 31, 1969), published in *Theatre Heute*, February, 1969, and in *Peter Handke* (see below), translation by Roloff published as "My Foot My Tutor" in *Drama Review*, fall, 1970, and in *The Ride Across Lake Constance and Other Plays* (see below).

Quodlibet (first produced in Basle at Basler Theater, January 24, 1970), published in *Theater Heute*, March, 1970, also privately printed, 1970, translation by Roloff published under same title in *The Ride Across Lake Constance and Other Plays* (see below).

Wind und Meer: 4 Hoerspiele (title means "Wind and Sea: Four Radio Plays"), Suhrkamp, 1970.

Der Ritt ueber den Bodensee (first produced in Berlin at Schaubuehne am Halleschen Ufer, January 23, 1971), Suhrkamp, 1971, translation by Roloff as *The Ride Across Lake Constance* (produced in New York at the Forum, Lincoln Center, January, 1972) published in *The Contemporary German Drama*, edited by Roloff, Equinox Books, 1972, published separately, Methuen, 1973 (also see below).

Die Unvernuenftigen sterben aus (first produced in Zurich, April, 1974), Suhrkamp, 1973, translation by Roloff and Karl Weber published as *They Are Dying Out*, Methuen, 1975 (also see below).

"A Sorrow Beyond Dreams," produced in New York City at Marymount Manhattan Playhouse, June, 1977.

Ueber die Doerfer: Dramatisches (dramatic poem; first produced in Salzburg, 1982), Suhrkamp, 1981.

(With Wim Wenders) "Wings of Desire" (screenplay), Orion, 1988.

GERMAN COLLECTIONS

Publikumsbeschimpfung und Andere Sprechstuecke (includes "Publikumsbeschimpfung," "Selbstbezichtigung," and "Weissagung"), Suhrkamp, 1966.

Peter Handke: Prosa, Gedichte, Theaterstuecke, Hoerspiel, Aufsaetze (includes "Begruessung des Aufsichtsrats," "Publikumsbeschimpfung," and "Das Mundel will Vormund sein"), Suhrkamp, 1969.

Stuecke (title means "Plays"), Suhrkamp, 1972.

Stuecke 2, Suhrkamp, 1973.

ENGLISH COLLECTIONS

Kaspar and Other Plays (includes "Kaspar," "Offending the Audience," and "Self-Accusation"), translated by Roloff, Farrar, Straus, 1969.

Offending the Audience (includes "Offending the Audience" and "Self-Accusation"), translated by Roloff, Methuen, 1971.

The Ride Across Lake Constance and Other Plays (includes "Prophecy," "Calling for Help," "My Foot My Tutor," "Quodlibet," and "They Are Dying Out"), translated by Roloff and Karl Weber, Farrar, Straus, 1976.

OTHER

Die Innenwelt der Aussenwelt der Innenwelt (poems), Suhrkamp, 1969, abridged translation by Roloff published as *The Innerworld of the Outerworld of the Innerworld*, Seabury, 1974.

(Compiler) *Der gewoehnliche Schrecken* (title means "The Ordinary Terror"), Residenz Verlag, 1969.

Deutsche Gedichte (title means "German Poems"), Euphorion-Verlag, 1969.

Chronik der laufenden Ereignisse (film scenario; title means "Chronicle of Current Events"), Suhrkamp, 1971.

Ich bin ein Bewohner des Elfenbeinturms (essays; title means "I Live in an Ivory Tower"), Suhrkamp, 1972.

Wunschloses Ungluock (biography), Residenz Verlag, 1972, translation by Manheim published as *A Sorrow Beyond Dreams*, Farrar, Straus, 1975.

Als das Wuenschen noch geholfen hat (poems), Suhrkamp, 1974, translation by Roloff published as *Nonsense and Happiness*, Urizen Books, 1976.

Falsche Bewegung (film scenario; title means "False Move"), Suhrkamp, 1975.

Three by Peter Handke (contains *A Sorrow Beyond Dreams, Short Letter Long Farewell, The Goalie's Anxiety at the Penalty Kick*), Avon, 1977.

(And director) "The Left-Handed Woman" (screenplay; adaptation of Handke's novel), 1978.

The Weight of the World (diary), translated by Manheim, Farrar, Straus, 1984.

WORK IN PROGRESS: A journal; also a novel—"a personal odyssey"—set in the Rocky Mountains and in Austria.

SIDELIGHTS: Nicholas Hern is one of a number of critics who have suggested that Peter Handke's legal training may have been an important influence on his prose style, pointing out that "most of his plays and novels consist of a series of affirmative propositions each contained within one sentence. . . . The effect . . . is not unlike the series of clauses in a contract or will or statute-book, shorn of linking conjunctions. It is as if a state of affairs or a particular situation were being defined and constantly redefined until the final total definition permits of no mite of ambiguity." Handke's prose has reminded other readers of the propositions making up Ludwig Wittgenstein's *Tractatus Logico-Philosophicus,* and the inquiries into language of Wittgenstein and the French structuralists touch on themes that are central to Handke's work. Discussing his more strictly literary masters, Handke said in 1977 that American novelist William Faulkner remains the most important of all writers to him.

Handke's remarkable style was first displayed in the experimental prose pieces he wrote and published in magazines while still at the university, and in *Die Hornissen,* which reminded reviewers of the French "new novel." This first novel appeared in the spring of 1966 and was generally well received, but it was not this alone that made him overnight a figure to be reckoned with on the German literary scene. In April, 1966, Handke went to the United States to participate in the twenty-eighth convention of Group 47, the famous association of German writers, which that year met in Princeton, New Jersey. On the last day of the conference Handke, then aged twenty-four, made the first move in a deliberate campaign of what came to be called "Handke-Publicity." In his book on Group 47 Siegfried Mandel wrote: "Shaking his Beatle-mane, Handke . . . railed against what he had been listening to: impotent narrative; empty stretches of descriptive (instead of analytical) writing pleasing to the ears of the older critics; monotonous verbal litanies, regional and nature idyllicism, which lacked spirit and creativeness. The audience warmed up to the invective with cheers, and later even those whose work had been called idiotic, tasteless, and childish came over to congratulate the Group 47 debutant and to patch things up in brotherly fashion. . . . As he stood among a circle of interviewers—a thin, energetic figure with thick, dark sunglasses—it became clear that he had arrived as a spokesman for the young and hitherto silent clique and reestablished confidence in the rejuvenating capacity of the group."

This assessment was fully confirmed a few months later, when Handke's first play was the major hit in a week of experimental new drama in Frankfurt. *Offending the Audience,* in which all the comfortable assumptions of bourgeois theatre are called in question and the audience is systematically mocked and insulted, was and has remained highly popular in German theatres. To a lesser extent, the same is true of Handke's other early "sprechstuecke"—plays which all in various ways investigate the role of language in defining the individual's social identity.

The power of language is the theme also of *Kaspar,* Handke's first full-length play. It is a matter of record that in 1828 in Nuremberg a sixteen-year-old boy was discovered who had apparently been confined all his life in a closet, and who was physically full-grown but mentally a baby. This was Kaspar Hauser, whose story has intrigued a number of writers, and who in Handke's play is indoctrinated with conventional moral precepts in the process of being taught to speak. As Nicholas Hern put it, "the play is an abstract demonstration of the way an individual's individuality is stripped from him by society, specifically by limiting the expressive power of the language it teaches him." Robert Brustein rejected the play's thesis, but found it all the same "sometimes penetrating, sometimes brilliant, always permeated by a fierce, if rather cold, intensity." In Germany *Kaspar* was voted play of the year, and it is regarded as one of the most important postwar German plays.

A number of other plays have followed, for radio, television, and the stage. The most discussed of these was Handke's second full-length play, *The Ride Across Lake Constance,* which, most critics thought, also dealt with the problems of communication, though in a baroque and bewildering fashion that fascinated even some reviewers, like Clive Barnes, who could make no sense of it at all. Hern wrote that in this play "Handke has moved from a Wittgensteinian distrust of language to a Foucaultian distrust of what our society calls reason. His play is by no means surrealist in externals only: it parallels the surrealists' cardinal desire—the liberation of men's minds from the constraints of reason. Thus Handke continues to demonstrate that the consistently *anti*-theatrical stance which he has maintained throughout his dramatic writing can none the less lend concrete theatrical expression to abstract, philosophical ideas, thereby generating a new and valid form of theatre."

Meanwhile, Handke had been establishing a second reputation as one of the most important of the young German novelists. His first success in this form was *The Goalie's Anxiety at the Penalty Kick,* which reflects the same preoccupations as his plays. As Russell Davies wrote, when Handke's alienated hero Bloch commits an apparently pointless murder, "it is the problem of language itself which upsets his mind and stomach. . . . One comes to realise that Handke is demonstrating how similar to the toils of madness are the inner wranglings of the writer as he fights to order his world." Frank Conroy called the book "an ambitious tour de force in which Handke deals with the interrelationships of man, external reality and time."

The partly autobiographical novel *Short Letter, Long Farewell,* about a young Austrian writer's haphazard journey across the United States to a dangerous meeting with his estranged wife, had a mixed but generally favorable reception. And there was little but praise for *A Sorrow Beyond Dreams,* Handke's profoundly sensitive account of his mother's life, which ended in suicide. Michael Wood wrote of it that "Handke's objective tone is a defense against the potential flood of his feelings, of course, but it is also a act of piety, an expression of respect: this woman's bleak life is not to be made into 'literature'. . . . Handke's mother is important not because she is an especially vivid case but because she is not, because she is one of many." Dramatized as a monologue by Daniel Freudenberger, it was staged by the Phoenix Theatre at the Marymount Manhattan Theatre early in 1977, and greatly praised.

Some reviewers were disappointed by *A Moment of True Feeling,* another fictional study in alienation, but Stanley Kauffmann was deeply impressed. He suggested that Handke was moving toward "the novel as poem" and concluded that "this new book proves further that, in power and vision and range, he is the most important new writer on the international scene since Beckett."

Handke has written: "I myself would support Marxism every time as the only possibility of solution but not its pronouncement in play, in the theatre." His refusal to use his plays and novels as vehicles for political propaganda has been much criticized by the New Left in Germany, but Handke maintains that literature and political commitment are incompatible. "It would be repugnant to me to twist my criticism of a social order into a story or to aestheticize it into a poem," he says in one of his essays. "I find that the most atrocious mendacity: to manipulate one's commitment into a poem or to make literature out of it, instead of just saying it loud."

BIOGRAPHICAL/CRITICAL SOURCES:

BOOKS

Boa, Elizabeth and J. H. Reid, *Critical Strategies: German Fiction in the Twentieth Century,* McGill-Queens University Press, 1972.

Contemporary Literary Criticism, Gale, Volume 5, 1976, Volume 8, 1978, Volume 10, 1979, Volume 15, 1980, Volume 38, 1986.

Falkenstein, Henning, *Peter Handke,* Colloquium Verlag, 1974.

Gilman, Richard, *The Making of Modern Drama,* Farrar, Straus, 1974.

Heintz, Guenter, *Peter Handke,* Klett, 1971.

Hern, Nicholas, *Peter Handke: Theatre and Anti-Theatre,* Wolff, 1971.

Mandel, Siegfried, *Group 47,* Southern Illinois University Press, 1973.

Rischbieter, Henning, *Peter Handke,* Friedrich, 1972.

Scharang, Michael, editor, *Uber Peter Handko,* Suhrkamp, 1973.

Schultz, Uwe, *Peter Handke,* Friedrich, 1973.

Ungar, Frederick, editor, *Handbook of Austrian Literature,* F. Ungar, 1973.

PERIODICALS

Chicago Tribune, December 1, 1989, December 15, 1989.

Drama Review, fall, 1970.

Globe and Mail (Toronto), March 10, 1990.

London Times, May 15, 1972, November 13, 1973, December 9, 1973.

Los Angeles Times, May 22, 1985, June 25, 1986, May 20, 1988.

Los Angeles Times Book Review, July 16, 1989.

New Republic, February 28, 1970, September 28, 1974.

Newsweek, July 3, 1978.

New York Review of Books, May 1, 1975, June 23, 1977.

New York Times, January 30, 1977, March 22, 1971, June 17, 1978, January 25, 1980, April 2, 1980, July 12, 1984, June 25, 1986, April 29, 1988, August 28, 1989.

New York Times Book Review, May 21, 1972, September 15, 1974, April 27, 1975, July 31, 1977, June 18, 1978, July 22, 1984, August 4, 1985, July 17, 1986, August 7, 1988, September 3, 1989.

Performance, September-October 1972.

Publishers Weekly, September 12, 1977.

Text und Kritik, Number 24, 1969 (Handke issue).

Times (London), April 3, 1980, July 25, 1985, August 4, 1988, July 8, 1989.

Times Literary Supplement, April 21, 1972, December 1, 1972, April 18, 1980, July 17, 1981, November 15, 1985, October 3, 1986.

Tribune Books (Chicago), July 3, 1988.

Universitas, February 25, 1970.

Washington Post Book World, July 28, 1985.

*   *   *

HARTLEY, L(eslie) P(oles) 1895-1972

PERSONAL: Born December 30, 1895, in Whittesley, Cambridgeshire, England; died December 13, 1972; son of Harry Bark (a justice of the peace) and Mary Elizabeth (Thompson) Hartley. *Education:* Balliol College, Oxford, B.A., 1922.

ADDRESSES: Home—Avondale, Bathford, Somerset SW7, England.

CAREER: Literary critic, novelist, and short story writer, 1923-72. Tutor in preparatory school in Northdown, England, during the early 1920s; Clark Lecturer, Trinity College, Cambridge, 1964. *Military service:* Served in World War II, 1916-18.

MEMBER: Athenaeum Club and Beefsteak Club (both London), Bath and County Club (Bath).

AWARDS, HONORS: James Tait Black Memorial Prize, 1947, for *Eustace and Hilda;* Catholic Book of the Year Award, 1951, for *My Fellow Devils;* W. H. Heinemann Foundation Award and *Daily Mail*'s Book of the Year Award, both 1953, both for *The Go-Between;* Commander of Order of the British Empire, 1956; Companion of Literature Award from Royal Society of Literature, 1972.

WRITINGS:

Night Fears, and Other Stories (short stories), Putnam, 1924.

Simonetta Perkins (novel), Putnam, 1925.

The Killing Bottle, Putnam, 1932.

The Shrimp and the Anemone (first novel in trilogy; also see below), Putnam (London), 1944, published in America as *West Window,* Doubleday, 1945, new edition with commentary and notes by Patricia D'Arcy, Bodley Head, 1967.

The Sixth Heaven (second novel in trilogy; also see below), Putnam (London), 1946, Doubleday, 1947, reprinted, Faber, 1964.

Eustace and Hilda (third novel in trilogy; also see below), Putnam (London), 1947.

The Travelling Grave, and Other Stories (short stories), Arkham House, 1948.

The Boat (novel), Putnam (London), 1949, Doubleday, 1950.

My Fellow Devils (novel), James Barrie, 1951, British Book Centre, 1959.

The Go-Between (novel), Hamish Hamilton, 1953, Knopf, 1954, revised edition with introduction by Hartley, Heinemann, 1963, reprinted, Scarbrough House, 1980.

The White Wand, and Other Stories (short stories), Hamish Hamilton, 1954.

A Perfect Woman (novel), Hamish Hamilton, 1955, Knopf, 1956.

The Hireling (novel), Hamish Hamilton, 1957, Rinehart, 1958.

Eustace and Hilda: A Trilogy (includes *The Shrimp and the Anenione, The Sixth Heaven, Hilda's Letter,* and *Eustace and Hilda*), introduction by David Cecil, Putnam, 1958, Dufour, 1961.

Facial Justice (science fiction novel), Hamish Hamilton, 1960, Doubleday, 1961.

Two for the River, Hamish Hamilton, 1961.

The Brickfield (novel; also see below), Hamish Hamilton, 1964.

The Betrayal (novel; also see below), Hamish Hamilton, 1966.

The Novelist's Responsibility: Lectures and Essays, Hamish Hamilton, 1967, Hillary House, 1968.

The Collected Short Stories of L. P. ley, introduction by David Cecil, Hamish Hamilton, 1968, published as *The Complete Short Stories of L. P. Hartley,* 1973, Beaufort Books, 1986.

Poor Clare (novel), Hamish Hamilton, 1968.

(Author of foreword) Cynthia Asquith, *Diaries 1915-1918,* Hutchinson, 1968, Knopf, 1969.

The Love-Adept: A Variation on a Theme (novel), Hamish Hamilton, 1969.

My Sister's Keeper, Hamish Hamilton, 1970.

The Harness Room (novel), Hamish Hamilton, 1971.

Mrs. Carteret Receives, and Other Stories (short stories), Hamish Hamilton, 1971.

The Collections, Hamish Hamilton, 1972.

The Will and the Way (novel), Hamish Hamilton, 1973.

The Brickfield [and] *The Betrayal,* Hamish Hamilton, 1973.

(Contributor of screenplay) Harold Pinter, editor, *Five Screenplays,* Grove, 1989.

Fiction reviewer for *Spectator, Observer, Week-End Review, Sketch,* and *Time and Tide.*

SIDELIGHTS: L. P. Hartley has been recognized as one of the major English authors of this century. A prolific writer, Hartley is author of novels, short stories, and literary criticism that have been praised for their intelligence, realism, and sensitivity.

"L. P. Hartley has a high reputation in England and deservedly so," stated Frederick R. Karl in *A Reader's Guide to the Contemporary English Novel*. What he starts out to do he accomplishes admirably; his novels are models of intelligent writing, good sense, sharp feeling for proportion, and clean design. His world of upper middle-class gentility unfolds without fuss or affection. Hartley is that rare novelist who knows what he whats to do and goes about it with a minimum of waste."

Walter Allen described Hartley in his book, *The Modern Novel: In Britain and the United States,* in this manner: "Hartley is one of a number of contemporary novelists who strike one as being very much at the centre of the English tradition of the novel. They are concerned with the behaviour of men and women in society, with the making of choices; and they are also scholarly novelists in the way that some painters and musicians are called scholarly. They approach the writing of fiction with a full knowledge of what has been done in the art before. They are conscious of the great exemplars. They are not the less original for this, but it means that generally they know precisely what it is they are doing, and what they are doing may very well be ambitious indeed."

Richard Jones once wrote that L. P. Hartley was "one of the last gentleman-writers with a sensibility schooled at a time when a limited number of people could spend a good deal of time being complex about very little."

MEDIA ADAPTATIONS: The Go-Between was produced as a motion picture starring Julie Christie and Alan Bates, by Columbia Pictures in 1971.

AVOCATIONAL INTERESTS: Rowing, swimming, walking.

BIOGRAPHICAL/CRITICAL SOURCES:

BOOKS

Allen, Walter, *The Modern Novel: In Britain and the United States,* Dutton, 1964.
Bien, Peter Adolph, *L. P. Hartley,* Pennsylvania State University Press, 1962.
Bloomfield, Paul, *L. P. Hartley,* Longman, 1962, revised edition, 1970.
Contemporary Literary Criticism, Gale, Volume 2, 1974, Volume 22, 1982.
Dictionary of Literary Biography, Volume 15: *British Novists, 1930-1959,* Gale, 1983.
Karl, Frederick R., *A Readers Guide to the Contemporary English Novel,* Farrar, Straus, 1962.

PERIODICALS

Books and Bookmen, July 1969.
Listener, November, 7, 1968.
London Magazine, February, 1969.
New York Times, July 25, 1954.
Observer, October 27, 1968.
Spectator, November 3, 1944.
Yale Review, autumn, 1954.

OBITUARIES:

PERIODICALS

AB Bookman, March 19, 1973.
Time, December 25, 1973.
Variety, January 17, 1973.*

HARVEY, Gina Cantoni   1922-

PERSONAL: Born March 30, 1922, in Gorizia, Italy; naturalized U.S. citizen, 1950; daughter of Alberto and Annette (Schuler) Cantoni; married Hugh E. Harvey, August 16, 1947; children: Katherine (Mrs. B. G. Burr), Hugh E., Jr. *Education:* Attended Liceo Torquato Tasso, Rome, 1937-39; University of Rome, D.Litt. (summa cum laude), 1943.

ADDRESSES: Office—Department of English, Northern Arizona University, Flagstaff, Ariz. 86001; and Southwest Educational Association, Box 181, Flagstaff, Ariz. 86002.

CAREER: Fort Lewis College, Durango, Colo., assistant professor of French and English, 1965-70; University of New Mexico, Albuquerque, associate professor of education, 1970-74; Northern Arizona University, Flagstaff, associate professor, 1974-80, professor of English, 1980—. Chairman of board of directors, Center for In-Service Education, Southwest Educational Association, 1972—.

MEMBER: International Reading Association, National Council of Teachers of English, American Association of University Professors, National Bilingual Education Association, Native American Bilingual Education Association, Teachers of English to Speakers of Other Languages.

AWARDS, HONORS: Named "Educator of the Year," Arizona Bilingual Council, 1977.

WRITINGS:

English as a Second Language on the Navajo Reservation, privately printed, 1961.
(With others) *The Italian Verb and Review of Expression Patterns,* John McKay, 1966.
Innovations and Progress in Navajo, Bureau of Indian Affairs, 1970.
Helpful Hints for New BIA Teachers: Navajo Area, Bureau of Indian Affairs, 1970.
Navajo Area In-Service Language Training, privately printed, 1971.
(Editor with M. F. Heiser) *Southwest Language and Linguistics Workshop,* School of Education, San Diego State University, 1975.

Contributor of articles on Indian English to periodicals, including *Southwest Studies in Indian English* and *Southwest Areal Linguistics.* Editor, *Arizona Bilingual Council Newsletter,* 1975—.

WORK IN PROGRESS: Indian Conceptual Development Model; Going to the Well: Ways of English Language Learning; a set of readers written by and for Indian children.*

*   *   *

HEATH, Roy A(ubrey) K(elvin)   1926-

PERSONAL: Born August 13, 1926, in Georgetown, British Guiana (now Guyana); son of Melrose A. (a teacher) and Jessie R. (a teacher) Heath; married Aemilia Oberli; children: three. *Education:* University of London, B.A., 1956.

ADDRESSES: Agent—Bill Hamilton, A. M. Heath & Co. Ltd., 40-42 William IV St., London WC2N 4DD, England.

CAREER: Worked in civil service in Guyana, 1942-50; held various clerical jobs in London, England, 1951-58; teacher of French and German in London, 1959—. Called to the Bar, Lincoln's Inn, 1964.

AWARDS, HONORS: Drama Award from Theatre Guild of Guyana, 1971, for *Inez Combray;* fiction prize from London *Guardian,* 1978, for *The Murderer;* Guyana Award for Literature, 1989, for *The Shadow Bride.*

WRITINGS:

Inez Combray (play), produced in Georgetown, Guyana, 1972.
A Man Come Home (novel), Longman, 1974.
The Murderer (novel), Allison & Busby, 1978.
From the Heat of the Day (novel), Allison & Busby, 1979.
One Generation (novel), Allison & Busby, 1980.
Genetha (novel), Allison & Busby, 1981.
Kwaku; or, The Man Who Could Not Keep His Mouth Shut (novel), Allison & Busby, 1982.
Orealla (novel), Allison & Busby, 1984.
Art and History (lectures), Ministry of Education (Georgetown, Guyana), 1983.
The Shadow Bride (novel), Collins, 1988.
Shadows round the Moon (memoir), Collins, 1990.

WORK IN PROGRESS: A novel.

SIDELIGHTS: Roy A. K. Heath told *CA:* "My work is intended to be a dramatic chronicle of twentieth-century Guyana."

BIOGRAPHICAL/CRITICAL SOURCES:

PERIODICALS

New York Times Book Review, January 15, 1984.
Times Literary Supplement, November 12, 1982, July 27, 1984.

*   *   *

HELLMAN, Lillian (Florence) 1906-1984

PERSONAL: Born June 20, 1906, in New Orleans, La.; died of cardiac arrest June 30, 1984, in Martha's Vineyard, Mass.; daughter of Max Bernard (a businessman) and Julia (Newhouse) Hellman; married Arthur Kober (a writer), December 30, 1925 (divorced, 1932). *Education:* Attended New York University, 1922-24, and Columbia University, 1924.

ADDRESSES: Home—630 Park Avenue, New York, N.Y. 10021; and Vineyard Haven, Mass. 02568. *Agent*—Harold Matson, 22 East 40th St., New York, N.Y. 10016.

CAREER: Playwright and author. Horace Liveright, Inc. (publisher), New York City, manuscript reader, 1924-25; theatrical playreader in New York City, 1927-30; Metro-Goldwyn-Mayer, Hollywood, Calif., scenario reader, 1930-31; returned to New York City, 1932, working as part-time playreader for producer Harold Shulman. Taught or conducted seminars in literature and writing at Yale University, 1966, and at Massachusetts Institute of Technology and Harvard University. Director of plays in New York City, including "Another Part of the Forest," 1946, and "Montserrat," 1949. Narrator, Marc Blitzstein Memorial Concert, New York City, 1964.

MEMBER: American Academy of Arts and Letters, American Academy of Arts and Sciences (fellow), Dramatists Guild (member of council), American Federation of Television and Radio Artists.

AWARDS, HONORS: New York Drama Critics Circle Award, 1941, for "Watch on the Rhine," and 1960, for "Toys in the Attic"; Academy Award nominations for screenplays "The Little Foxes," 1941, and "The North Star," 1943; M.A. from Tufts University, 1950; Brandeis University Creative Arts Medal in Theater, 1960-61; LL.D. from Wheaton College, 1961, Douglass

College of Rutgers University, Smith College, and New York University, all 1974, Franklin and Marshall College, 1975, and Columbia University, 1976; Gold Medal for drama from National Institute of Arts and Letters, 1964; National Book Award in Arts and Letters, 1969, for *An Unfinished Woman,* and nomination, 1974, for *Pentimento: A Book of Portraits;* elected to Theatre Hall of Fame, 1973; MacDowell Medal, 1976.

WRITINGS:

(Editor and author of introduction) Anton Chekhov, *Selected Letters,* Farrar, Straus, 1955, reprinted, 1984.
(Editor and author of introduction) Dashiell Hammett, *The Big Knockover* (selected stories and short novels), Random House, 1966 (published in England as *The Dashiell Hammett Story Omnibus,* Cassell, 1966).
An Unfinished Woman (memoirs; also see below), Little, Brown, 1969, reprinted, Macmillan (London), 1987.
Pentimento: A Book of Portraits (memoirs; also see below), Little, Brown, 1973.
Scoundrel Time (memoirs; also see below), introduction by Garry Wills, Little, Brown, 1976.
Three (contains *An Unfinished Woman, Pentimento: A Book of Portraits, Scoundrel Time,* and new commentaries by author), Little, Brown, 1979.
Maybe (memoirs), Little, Brown, 1980.
(With Peter S. Feibleman) *Eating Together: Recollections and Recipes,* Little, Brown, 1984.

PLAYS

The Children's Hour (first produced in New York City at Maxine Elliott's Theatre, November 20, 1934; also see below), Knopf, 1934, acting edition, Dramatists Play Service, 1953, reprinted, 1988.
Days to Come (first produced in New York City at Vanderbilt Theatre, December 15, 1936; also see below), Knopf, 1936.
The Little Foxes (three-act; first produced in New York City at National Theatre, February 15, 1939; also see below), Random House, 1939, acting edition, Dramatists Play Service, 1942, reprinted, 1986.
Watch on the Rhine (three-act; first produced on Broadway at Martin Beck Theatre, April 1, 1941; also see below), Random House, 1941, limited edition with foreword by Dorothy Parker, privately printed, 1942, acting edition, Dramatists Play Service, 1944, reprinted, 1986.
Four Plays (contains *The Children's Hour, Days to Come, The Little Foxes,* and *Watch on the Rhine*), Random House, 1942.
The Searching Wind (two-act; first produced in New York City at Fulton Theatre, April 12, 1944; also see below), Viking, 1944.
Another Part of the Forest (three-act; first produced at Fulton Theatre, November 20, 1946; also see below), Viking, 1947.
Montserrat (two-act; adapted from Emmanuel Robles's play; first produced at Fulton Theatre, October 29, 1949; also see below), Dramatists Play Service, 1950.
The Autumn Garden (three-act; first produced in New York City at Coronet Theatre, March 7, 1951; also see below), Little, Brown, 1951, revised acting edition, Dramatists Play Service, 1952.
The Lark (adapted from Jean Anouilh's play *L'Alouette;* first produced on Broadway at Longacre Theatre, November 17, 1955; also see below), Random House, 1956, acting edition, Dramatists Play Service, 1957.
(Author of book) Leonard Bernstein, *Candide: A Comic Opera Based on Voltaire's Satire* (first produced on Broadway at

Martin Beck Theatre, December 1, 1956; also see below), Random House, 1957.

Toys in the Attic (three-act; first produced Off-Broadway at Hudson Theatre, February 25, 1960; also see below), Random House, 1960, acting edition, Samuel French, 1960.

Six Plays (contains *Another Part of the Forest, The Autumn Garden, The Children's Hour, Days to Come, The Little Foxes,* and *Watch on the Rhine*), Modern Library, 1960, limited edition with illustrations by Mark Bellerose, Franklin Library, 1978.

My Mother, My Father and Me (adapted from Burt Blechman's novel *How Much?;* first produced on Broadway at Plymouth Theatre, April 6, 1963; also see below), Random House, 1963.

Collected Plays (contains *The Children's Hour, Days to Come, The Little Foxes, Watch on the Rhine, The Searching Wind, Another Part of the Forest, Montserrat, The Autumn Garden, The Lark, Candide, Toys in the Attic,* and *My Mother, My Father and Me*), Little, Brown, 1972.

The Little Foxes [and] *Another Part of the Forest,* Viking, 1973.

Also author of unpublished and unproduced play, "Dear Queen."

SCREENPLAYS

(With Mordaunt Shairp) "Dark Angel," United Artists, 1935.
"These Three" (based on "The Children's Hour"), United Artists, 1936.
"Dead End," United Artists, 1937.
"The Little Foxes" (based on her play), RKO, 1941.
The North Star, a Motion Picture about Some Russian People (released by RKO, 1943; later released for television broadcast as "Armored Attack"), introduction by Louis Kronenberger, Viking, 1943.
"The Searching Wind," Paramount, 1946.
"The Chase," Columbia, 1966.

CONTRIBUTOR OF PLAYS TO ANTHOLOGIES

Four Contemporary American Plays, Random House, 1961.
Six Modern American Plays, Random House, 1966.
A Treasury of the Theatre: Modern Drama from Oscar Wilde to Eugene Ionesco, Simon & Schuster, 1967.

OTHER

Pentimento: Memory as Distilled by Time (sound recording), Center for Cassette Studies, c. 1973.
Lillian Hellman: The Great Playwright Candidly Reflects on a Long Rich Life (sound recording), Center for Cassette Studies, c. 1977.
Conversations with Lillian Hellman, edited by Jackson R. Bryer, University Press of Mississippi, 1986.

Contributor of sketches to "Broadway Revue," produced in New York City, 1968; contributor of articles to *Collier's, New York Times, Travel and Leisure,* and other publications. Hellman's manuscripts are collected at the University of Texas at Austin.

SIDELIGHTS: She has been called one of the most influential female playwrights of the twentieth century; the voice of social consciousness in American letters; the theatre's intellectual standard-bearer—and yet Lillian Hellman always prided herself on avoiding easy labels. At the time of her death in 1984, the author/playwright could claim more long-running Broadway dramas—five—than could other renowned American writers like Tennessee Williams, Edward Albee, and Thornton Wilder. Ironically, though, Hellman was perhaps best remembered by a later generation of Americans for posing in a mink coat in an advertisement titled "What Becomes a Legend Most?"

Born in turn-of-the-century New Orleans to a struggling shoe merchant and his upper-middle-class wife, Hellman had the advantages of a solid education and a well-traveled childhood. Her ties to her mother had Hellman pondering well into adulthood. "So far apart were the temperaments of mother and daughter—for Hellman was always a spirited, independent child—that only after her mother had been dead for five years did [Hellman] realize how much she had loved her," according to Carol MacNicholas in a *Dictionary of Literary Biography* article on the playwright.

By the early 1920s Hellman had left college to work as a manuscript reader for a New York City publishing firm—her first professional foray into the world of writing that she would later dominate. For the ambitious Hellman, the benefits of working in publishing ran beyond five o'clock. "After working hours, [the publishers'] parties gave Hellman her firsthand acquaintance with the adventurous, often reckless life of the literary world of the 1920s," said MacNicholas. "The bohemian life appealed to the young woman who was just advancing into her own twenties; she enjoyed the glamour of the writer's world and nurtured the impulse to find excitement in whatever she did."

For Hellman, that impulse led her into an early marriage to press agent Arthur Kober, and career jumps into playreading and book reviewing. Following her husband to Paris, Hellman made side trips to 1929 Germany, where the embryonic Nazi movement gave the woman her first exposure to anti-Semitism, a theme that would later emerge in her plays "Watch on the Rhine" and "The Searching Wind." By 1930 the Kobers had moved to Hollywood, where Hellman read scripts for Metro-Goldwyn-Mayer. It was there, too, that she met the mystery novelist/screenwriter Dashiell Hammett.

Sensing that her marriage to Kober was failing, Hellman turned to Hammett, best known for the stylish suspense novel *The Thin Man* (some critics believe that Hammett based his suave detectives Nick and Nora Charles on himself and Hellman), and he became her lover and mentor. Hammett encouraged Hellman's first produced play, "The Children's Hour," in 1933 (an earlier play, "Dear Queen," was neither published nor produced). "A play about the way scandalmongering can ruin people's lives, ['The Children's Hour'] focuses on two young women, Karen Wright and Martha Dobie, who have set up a private boarding school," explained MacNicholas. "Their prospects for a happy and secure future are shattered when one of their pupils, Mary Tilford, a spoiled and vicious problem child, tells her grandmother, . . . a pillar of local society, about an abnormal sexual relationship between Karen and Martha." "The Children's Hour" caused a sensation in its time, not merely for its controversial subject matter (for a movie remake in 1936, a "safe" heterosexual triangle was substituted for the play's original theme), but also for its writer's obvious talent. "So far as sheer power and originality are concerned, [Hellman's] play is not merely the best of the year but the best of many years past," wrote J. W. Krutch in a 1935 *Nation* review.

With that success behind her, Hellman ushered in an era, from the late 1930s through the late 1940s, of classic dramas that helped shape a golden age of American theatre. Chief among them is "The Little Foxes," perhaps the playwright's best known work. An excoriating look at the rivalries and disloyalty among a turn-of-the-century Southern family, the play explores how the wealthy Hubbard clan of New Orleans schemes to keep itself rich and powerful, at the expense of both outsiders and each other. In this tale, "William Marshall, a visiting Chicago businessman, has displayed a willingness to establish a local cotton mill to be controlled by the Hubbards if they can raise enough money to buy fifty-one percent of the new company," as Mac-Nicholas explained. "An intense power struggle ensues, dividing the family into two camps: the powerful and cruel Hubbard siblings (Regina and her two brothers, Ben and Oscar), and those brought into the family by marriage (Horace, Regina's husband; Alexandra, their fair-minded daughter; and Birdie, Oscar's wife)." By the second act, added MacNicholas, every Hubbard is out for him- or herself.

"The Little Foxes," both in its stage and film incarnations, was a great popular and critical success. Some critics took its theme of greed as a parable for the rise of the industrial South; others saw the play as Hellman's look back at the turmoil within her own family. In 1946, seven years after "The Little Foxes" had premiered, Hellman produced what today is known as a "prequel": "Another Part of the Forest," which takes a look at the Hubbard clan twenty years earlier than when audiences had first met them. "Twenty years does not transport them to the age of innocence; their evil natures are already well cultivated," noted Richard Moody in his book *Lillian Hellman: Playwright.*

The mixed reviews of "Another Part of the Forest" focused on critics' speculation that Hellman had packed too much melodrama into the play. Moody found that the follow-up work did "not match the earlier play in concentrated power. [Hellman] has followed too many paths. If fewer crises had been packed into the two days [in which the story takes place], if the voices had been less strident, . . . [then the characters] might have become more fully realized, and our hearts might have become more committed." For all its structural faults, though, Moody called "Another Part of the Forest" "a strong and exciting play."

In between "The Little Foxes" and "Another Part of the Forest," Hellman premiered the political drama "Watch on the Rhine." This 1941 production focused on a Washington family and the war refugees they harbor. Among the boarders are a Rumanian count and his American wife, and an anti-Nazi German. Fear and prejudice follow the characters, resulting in tragedy. Except "for those who suffered through the Hitler years," remarked Moody, "the fierce impact of the play in 1941 cannot be fully sensed. If it appears melodramatic now, it appeared melodramatic then, but with a difference: the world was boiling with melodrama. Cruelty and villainy were not figments of the playwright's imagination, and it was almost impossible for a writer to tell us anything we didn't already know or to dramatize atrocities more effectively than events had already dramatized them." Hellman "knew that her fiction must do more than demonstrate the strange and awful truth that screamed from the front pages of every daily paper," he added. A critic of the day, Rosamond Gilder of *Theatre Arts,* called "Watch on the Rhine" "more faulty in structure" than "The Children's Hour" and "The Little Foxes," and also noted that Hellman, "whose hallmark has been an almost brutal cynicism, who has excelled in delineating mean, ruthless and predatory types, [here indulges] in a tenderness, an emotionalism that borders on the sentimental."

The 1950s saw Hellman writing three play adaptations— "Montserrat," "The Lark," and "Candide," the latter a musical—plus an original work, "The Autumn Garden." It wasn't until 1960, however, that the playwright had her next important original drama produced. "Toys in the Attic" examines the psychological effects of sudden wealth an a poor family. One of Hellman's best plays, according to Moody, "Toys in the Attic" "achieves the magnitude and human revelation that have always been the mark of serious drama." The plot revolves around two sisters, Carrie and Anna Berniers, who have devoted their lives to their ne'er-do-well younger brother, Julian. They find that he has married a wealthy but neurotic woman, and when Julian returns home to visit, he brings his bride and virtual fistfuls of cash, which he distributes indiscriminately. "The sudden reversal of fortune is too shocking to accept, and Carrie is convinced that her brother has gone crazy," noted MacNicholas.

With "Toys in the Attic," Hellman "picked up the sword of judgment many playwrights of the period [had] laid aside and [wielded] it with renewed vigor," said John Gassner in his book *Dramatic Soundings: Evaluations and Retractions Culled from 30 Years of Dramatic Criticism.* Gassner also found that it is "the special merit of Lillian Hellman's work that dreadful things are done by the onstage characters out of affectionate possessiveness, rather than out of ingrained villainy. Although the author's corresponding view of life is ironic and is trenchantly expressed, there is no gloating over human misery, no horror-mongering, no traffic with sensationalism in *Toys in the Attic.*"

"Toys in the Attic" was Hellman's last major play (she produced one more drama, "My Mother, My Father and Me," an adaptation of Burt Blechman's novel *How Much?,* but it ran only briefly in 1963). From 1969 on, Hellman became well regarded for a quartet of books recounting events in her life. From the beginning of her public life, the writer's politics had been intertwined with her career. As MacNicholas pointed out, "The origins of [Hellman's] liberalism are traced to her childhood: on the one hand, she witnessed her mother's family increase their fortunes at the expense of Negroes; on the other, she admired the dignity and tough-mindedness of her black nurse Sophronia. Dashiell Hammett, of course, was a radical who shared and influenced much of her life in the 1930s and 1940s."

With Hellman's first book of memoirs, *An Unfinished Woman,* the author took an unconventional approach to traditional autobiography, as Moody described it. "Only in the first third of the book does she allow chronology to govern her narrative. After that she swings freely among her remembrances of places, times, and people—all intimately observed, all colored with some special personal involvement."

The word "pentimento" describes a phenomenon in art wherein a painting fades to the point that one can see the rough sketches and previous drafts through the surface of the finished work. The word also serves as the title of Hellman's second book of memoirs, a look at the friends and relations that fueled Hellman's adult years. This book garnered much critical notice, most notably for its sophisticated writing style. "It is now apparent that *An Unfinished Woman* was the beginning—a try-out, if you will, and more hesitant than arrogant—of a new career for Lillian Hellman," declared *New York* critic Eliot Fremont-Smith. "*Pentimento: A Book of Portraits . . . ,* is its realization." Fremont-Smith also called the work one of "extraordinary richness and candor and self-perception, and triumph considering the courage such a book requires, a courage that lies, [the author] shows by example, far deeper than one is usually inclined to accept."

Muriel Haynes, in a *Ms.* review, called *Pentimento* "a triumphant vindication of the stories the author threw away in her twenties because they were 'no good.' These complex, controlled narratives profit from the dramatist's instinct for climax and immediate, sharp characterization; but they have an emotional purity her plays have generally lacked." Less impressed was *London Magazine* reviewer Julian Symons, who said that the memoir "is not, as American reviewers have unwisely said, a marvel and a masterpiece and a book full of perceptions about human character. It is, rather, a collection of sketches of a fairly familiar kind, which blend real people known to history and Lillian Hellman . . . with people known only by their Christian names in the book, who may be real or partly fictionalized." By far the best known section of the book is "Julia," the story of Hellman's friendship during the 1930s with a rich young American woman working in the European underground against the Nazis. The story was adapted into the popular film "Julia" in 1977.

In *Pentimento*, as in her other books, Hellman was occasionally criticized by the press for presenting her facts unreliably, "bending" the truth to support her views. Paul Johnson, a writer for the British journal *Spectator*, cited an article casting doubt whether "Julia" actually existed. "What [Boston University's Samuel McCracken] demonstrates, by dint of checking Thirties railway timetables, steamship passenger lists, and many other obscure sources, is that most of the facts Hellman provides about 'Julia's' movement and actions, and indeed her own, are not true." Johnson further suggested that what Hellman had been presenting all along is a left-wing apologia for World War II and the McCarthy era that followed.

Hellman, though no Stalinist, had in fact rebelled against the Cold War communism investigations during the postwar era—in one of her most memorable lines, she informed the House Un-American Activities Committee that she had no intention of cutting her conscience to fit that year's fashion. *Scoundrel Time* is based on the story of "the 67 minutes that [the author] spent before the [HUAC] in Washington in 1952, of what preceded the hearings, and what its consequences were," according to *Listener* critic David Hunt. Even though Hellman was "scrupulously specific in what she [said] in *Scoundrel Time*, carefully limiting her text to what she herself experienced, thought, said, and did, this memoir nevertheless applies directly to the essential experience of her time—in other words, to history," noted Bruce Cook in a *Saturday Review* article. "There are a couple of good reasons for this. First, and probably most important, is that this is a work of *literary* quality. As with . . . *An Unfinished Woman* and *Pentimento, Scoundrel Time* is a triumph of tone. No writer I know can match the eloquence of her ah-what-the-hell as she looks back over the whole sorry spectacle and tells with restraint and precision just what she sees." *Scoundrel Time*, in Maureen Howard's view, "is not a confessional book. Hellman has seldom told more than her work required. [HUAC figureheads] are sketched in, and she gives us the details of her own bewildering sadness during those hard times. . . . Her stories are guarded and spare by design," as Howard wrote in *New York Times Book Review*. *Ms.* critic Vivian Gornick shared this view, calling *Scoundrel Time* "a valuable piece of work. The kind of work that stands alone, untouched, in the midst of foolish criticism and foolish praise alike."

Among the Hellman memoirs, her last work, *Maybe: A Story*, represents the most obvious tie between fact and fiction. *New Republic* critic Maggie Scarf, who couldn't decide if the book were a novelized autobiography or an autobiographical novella, called "monumental despair" the "true subject of *Maybe*. For Lillian Hellman has gone swimming in the waters of time and memory and found herself adrift in a vast sea of unreliability—the shore of solid information . . . seems to recede each time she believes she has the true details in sight." The narrative covers the life of Sarah Cameron, "a woman whom Hellman knew very slightly but over a long period of time," according to Scarf. "Sarah may or may not have taken Lillian Hellman's first lover away from her; this malicious young man, Alex . . . , had devastated [the author] on their fourth and final session in bed by recommending that she take a bath," offered Robert Towers in a *New York*

Times Book Review piece. "But absorbing as this autobiographical material is, it does not compensate, in my opinion, for the emptiness at the heart of the book. Miss Hellman fails to bring Sarah Cameron into existence as even a remotely comprehensible woman. The evidence is so scattered, so inconsistent, so blurred by time and alcohol, that we are left with a wraith to insubstantial to evoke even a sense of mystery, much less to support a valid point about the ultimate unknowability of figures in our past."

To Gornick, this time in a *Village Voice* review, Hellman's digressions into her past seem unworthy of the author's talent. "The association between Hellman and Sarah herself has no substance whatever; it's all fragments and fancy speculations and peripheral incidents and mysterious allusions that seem only to provide the writer with an excuse to call up once again Hammett and the drinking years, the aunts in New Orleans, making movies for Sam Goldwyn. The effort to surround Sarah with metaphoric meaning is strained and painfully obvious." Walter Clemons, in a *Newsweek* review, saw the inconsistencies in *Maybe* in another way: "Her nonstory, for that is what her tale of Sarah turns out to be, is a tricky, nervy meditation on the fallibility of memory, the failure of attention, the casual aplomb of practiced liars, the shivery unpredictability of malice." Clemons also praised Hellman's sharp voice, given her advanced years and alcoholic history.

Even as she moved into her seventies, Hellman remained a vibrant force in the public eye. She fueled this reputation in 1980 when she sued her contemporary, Mary McCarthy (author of *The Group*), after McCarthy told Dick Cavett on his talk show that she found Hellman an overrated and dishonest writer. Hellman sought damages in excess of $1.7 million for "mental pain and anguish"; the suit, however, "died when she did," as Frank Rich put it in *New York Times Book Review*.

Maybe was Hellman's last major published work; a cookbook, co-written with longtime friend Peter Feibleman, came out shortly after her June, 1984, death. The news of Hellman's passing brought out a string of testimonials from notable writers, including these words by *Newsweek*'s David Ansen: "In her 60s, looking back on her life in her memoirs, Hellman found her indelible voice. The gallery of portraits in *Pentimento*—especially 'Julia'—are unforgettable: whether they prove to be as much fiction as fact, as some have accused, cannot diminish their power and glamour. She may have called herself 'unfinished,' but a more appropriate title would have been 'An Unmellowed Woman'. . . . The Hellman anger arose from her clear-eyed view of social injustice and strong moral convictions, and she remained true to her passion throughout her rich and tumultuous life. Not for her the modernist halftones of alienation and equivocation. The fire within her lit up the cultural landscape; its heat will be deeply missed."

MEDIA ADAPTATIONS: Marc Blitzstein adapted "The Little Foxes" as an opera, "Regina," in 1949. "Another Part of the Forest" was filmed by Universal in 1948, and "Toys in the Attic" was adapted for film by United Artists, 1963. Television adaptations include "Montserrat," 1971, and "The Lark." A section of Hellman's memoir *Pentimento* was adapted into the film "Julia" and released in 1977. In 1986, William Luce wrote a one-woman play, "Lillian," based on Hellman's life; the production ran briefly in New York City.

BIOGRAPHICAL/CRITICAL SOURCES:

BOOKS

Adler, Jacob H., *Lillian Hellman*, Vaughn, 1969.

Authors in the News, Gale, Volume 1, 1976, Volume 2, 1976.
Contemporary Literary Criticism, Gale, Volume 2, 1974, Volume 4, 1975, Volume 8, 1978, Volume 14, 1980, Volume 18, 1981, Volume 33, 1985, Volume 44, 1987, Volume 52, 1989.
Dictionary of Literary Biography, Gale, Volume 7: *Twentieth-Century American Dramatists,* 1981.
Dictionary of Literary Biography Yearbook: 1984, Gale, 1985.
Falk, Doris V., *Lillian Hellman,* Ungar, 1978.
Gassner, John, *Dramatic Soundings: Evaluations and Retractions Culled from 30 Years of Dramatic Criticism,* Crown, 1968.
Lederer, Katherine, *Lillian Hellman,* Twayne, 1979.
Moody, Richard, *Lillian Hellman: Playwright,* Bobbs-Merrill, 1972.
Wright, William, *Lillian Hellman: The Image, the Woman,* Simon & Schuster, 1986.

PERIODICALS

Chicago Tribune, March 30, 1980.
Listener, November 18, 1986.
London Magazine, August/September, 1974.
Ms., January, 1974, August, 1976.
Nation, May 22, 1935.
New Republic, August 2, 1980, August 13, 1984.
Newsweek, June 2, 1980.
New York, September 17, 1973.
New York Review of Books, June 10, 1976.
New York Times, November 13, 1980, August 26, 1984.
New York Times Book Review, September 23, 1973, April 25, 1976, June 1, 1980.
Saturday Review, April 17, 1976.
Spectator, July 14, 1984.
Theatre Arts, June, 1941.
Time, May 19, 1980.
Village Voice, May 19, 1980.
Washington Post, May 19, 1980.

OBITUARIES:

PERIODICALS

Chicago Tribune, July 1, 1984.
Los Angeles Times, July 1, 1984.
Newsweek, July 9, 1984.
New York Times, July 1, 1984.
Washington Post, July 1, 1984.*

—*Sketch by Susan Salter*

*   *   *

HERMAN, Walter
See WAGER, Walter H(erman)

*   *   *

HERSEY, John (Richard) 1914-

PERSONAL: Born June 17, 1914, in Tientsin, China; son of Roscoe Monroe (a Y.M.C.A. secretary in China) and Grace (a missionary; maiden name Baird) Hersey; married Frances Ann Cannon, April 27, 1940 (divorced, February, 1958); married Barbara Day Addams Kaufman, June 2, 1958; children: (first marriage) Martin, John, Ann, Baird; (second marriage) Brook (daughter). *Education:* Yale University, B.A., 1936; attended Clare College, Cambridge, 1936-37. *Politics:* Democrat.

ADDRESSES: Home—420 Humphrey St., New Haven, Conn. 06511.

CAREER: Private secretary, driver, and factotum for Sinclair Lewis, summer, 1937; writer, editor, and correspondent, *Time* magazine, 1937-44, correspondent in China and Japan, 1939, covered South Pacific warfare, 1942, correspondent in Mediterranean theater, including Sicilian campaign, 1943, and in Moscow, 1944-45; editor and correspondent for *Life* magazine, 1944-45; writer for *New Yorker* and other magazines, 1945—; made trip to China and Japan for *Life* and *New Yorker,* 1945-46; fellow, Berkeley College, Yale University, 1950-65; master, Pierson College, Yale University, 1965-70, fellow, 1965—; writer-in-residence, American Academy in Rome, 1970-71; lecturer, Yale University, 1971-75, professor, 1975—. Chairman, Connecticut Volunteers for Stevenson, 1952; member of Adlai Stevenson's campaign staff, 1956. Editor and director of writers' co-operative magazine, '47. Member of Westport (Conn.) School Study Council, 1945-50, of Westport Board of Education, l950-52, of Yale University Council Committee on the Humanities, 1951-56, of Fairfield (Conn.) Citizens School Study Council, 1952-56, of National Citizens' Commission for the Public Schools, 1954-56; consultant, Fund for the Advancement of Education, 1954-56; chairman, Connecticut Committee for the Gifted, 1954-57; member of Board of Trustees, Putney School, 1953-56; delegate to White House Conference on Education, 1955; trustee, National Citizens' Council for the Public Schools, 1956-58; member, visiting committee, Harvard Graduate School of Education, 1960-65; member, Loeb Theater Center, 1980—; Yale University Council Committee on Yale College, member, 1959-61, chairman, 1964-69; trustee, National Committee for Support of the Public Schools, 1962-68.

MEMBER: National Institute of Arts and Letters, American Academy of Arts and Letters (secretary, 1961-78, chancellor, 1981—), American Academy of Arts and Sciences, Authors League of America (member of council, 1946-70, vice-president, 1949-55, president, 1975-80), Authors Guild (member of council, 1946—), PEN.

AWARDS, HONORS: Pulitzer Prize, 1945, for *A Bell for Adano;* Anisfield-Wolf Award, 1950, for *The Wall;* Daroff Memorial Fiction Award, Jewish Book Council of America, 1950, for *The Wall;* Sidney Hillman Foundation Award, 1951, for *The Wall;* Howland Medal, Yale University, 1952; National Association of Independent Schools Award, 1957, for *A Single Pebble;* Tuition Plan Award, 1961; Sarah Josepha Hale Award, 1963; named honorary fellow of Clare College, Cambridge University, 1967. Honorary degrees: M.A., Yale University, 1947; L.H.D., New School for Social Research, 1950, Syracuse University, 1983; LL.D., Washington and Jefferson College, 1950; D.H.L., Dropsie College, 1950; Litt.D., Wesleyan University, 1954, Bridgeport University, 1959, Clarkson College of Technology, 1972, University of New Haven, 1975, Yale University, 1984, Monmouth College, 1985, William and Mary College, 1987.

WRITINGS:

Men on Bataan, Knopf, 1942.
Into the Valley: A Skirmish of the Marines, Knopf, 1943.
Hiroshima (first published in *New Yorker,* August 31, 1946), Knopf, 1946, school edition, Oxford Book Co., 1948.
Here to Stay: Studies on Human Tenacity, Hamish Hamilton, 1962, Knopf, 1963.
The Algiers Motel Incident, Knopf, 1968.
(With others) *Robert Capa,* Paragraphic, 1969.
Letter to the Alumni, Knopf, 1970.
(Editor) *Ralph Ellison: A Collection of Critical Essays,* Prentice-Hall, 1973.
(Editor) *The Writer's Craft,* Knopf, 1974.

The President, Knopf, 1975.
Aspects of the Presidency: Truman and Ford in Office, Ticknor & Fields, 1980.
Blues, Knopf, 1987.
(Author of commentary) John Armour and Peter Wright, *Manzanar,* Times, 1988.
Life Sketches, Knopf, 1989.

NOVELS

A Bell for Adano, Knopf, 1944, with new foreword by Hersey, Modern Library, 1946.
The Wall, Knopf, 1950.
The Marmot Drive, Knopf, 1953.
A Single Pebble, Knopf, 1956.
The War Lover, Knopf, 1959.
The Child Buyer, Knopf, 1960.
White Lotus, Knopf, 1965.
Too Far to Walk, Knopf, 1966.
Under the Eye of the Storm, Knopf, 1967.
The Conspiracy, Knopf, 1972.
My Petition for More Space, Knopf, 1974.
The Walnut Door, Knopf, 1977.
The Call: An American Missionary in China, Knopf, 1985.

SIDELIGHTS: In his article "The Novel of Contemporary History" for the *Atlantic Monthly* in 1949, John Hersey states: "Fiction is a clarifying agent. It makes truth plausible. Who had even a tenable theory about the Soviet purge trials until he had read Koestler's *Darkness at Noon?* Who understood the impact of Italian Fascism upon peasants, on the one hand, and upon thinking men, on the other, until he had read Silone's *Fontamara* and *Bread and Wine?* What is argued here is only this much: among all the means of communication now available, imaginative literature comes closer than any other to being able to give an impression of the truth."

This use of imaginative literature to present historical truth has been one of Hersey's major concerns. His Pulitzer Prize-winning *A Bell for Adano* is set in an Italian village occupied by American troops during World War II; *The Wall* is set in the Jewish ghetto in Warsaw at the close of that war; and Hersey's nonfiction work *Hiroshima* uses fictional techniques to present its story of Japanese atom bomb survivors. "Hersey [has] dedicated himself to the goal of chronicling the events and issues of his time," Sam B. Girgus notes in the *Dictionary of Literary Biography.*

"Hersey is an impressive figure in contemporary American letters," writes Nancy L. Huse in her study *The Survival Tales of John Hersey.* Huse finds in Hersey's work "a mind rebelling at the age's acceptance of nuclear weapons, the Holocaust, racism, and the annihilation of the individual in a technological society." This attitude "places Hersey as an intellectual contemporary of Bellow, Wright, Mailer and Agee," Huse argues. Similarly, Eva Hoffman, writing in the *New York Times,* notes that "it has been John Hersey's virtue as teacher and public figure . . . that, against all odds and the grain of the times, he has sustained the idea of writing as a moral mission." Jonathan Yardley of the *Washington Post Book World* finds that "Hersey's decency is both transparent and transcendent. He cares about matters that deserve to be cared about, and he writes about them with palpable passion."

MEDIA ADAPTATIONS: A Bell for Adano was adapted as a stage play by Paul Osborn and was first produced at the Cort Theater in New York in December, 1944, and was filmed by Twentieth Century-Fox in 1945; *The Wall* was dramatized by Millard Lampell and was first produced at the Billy Rose The-

ater in New York in December, 1960, and was filmed for television by Columbia Broadcasting System in 1982; *The War Lover* was filmed by Columbia Pictures in 1962; *The Child Buyer* was adapted as a stage play by Paul Shyre and was first produced at the University of Michigan Professional Theater Program in Ann Arbor in 1964.

AVOCATIONAL INTERESTS: Sailing, gardening, fishing, reading.

BIOGRAPHICAL/CRITICAL SOURCES:

BOOKS

Contemporary Literary Criticism, Gale, Volume 1, 1973, Volume 2, 1974, Volume 7, 1977, Volume 9, 1978, Volume 40, 1986.
Dictionary of Literary Biography, Volume 6: *American Novelists since World War II,* Gale, 1980.
Huse, Nancy Lyman, *John Hersey and James Agee: A Reference Guide,* G. K. Hall, 1978.
Huse, Nancy Lyman, *The Survival Tales of John Hersey,* Whitston, 1983.
Sanders, David, *John Hersey,* Twayne, 1967.

PERIODICALS

Atlantic Monthly, November, 1949, April, 1966.
Book Week, September 26, 1965.
Commonweal, March 5, 1965.
Life, March 18, 1966.
National Observer, February 8, 1965.
Newsweek, January 25, 1965, June 7, 1965.
New York Herald Tribune Book Review, August 29, 1946, March 5, 1950, August 20, 1950, June 3, 1956, September 25, 1960.
New York Times, April 22, 1985.
New York Times Book Review, February 6, 1944, February 26, 1950, June 10, 1956, September 25, 1960, January 19, 1965, February 28, 1966, May 10, 1987.
Publishers Weekly, May 10, 1985.
Saturday Review, November 2, 1946, March 4, 1950, June 2, 1956, January 23, 1965.
Time, June 4, 1956, January 29, 1965, March 25, 1966.
Times Literary Supplement, December 7, 1946.
Washington Post Book World, October 16, 1977.
Yale Review, winter, 1987.

*   *   *

HIGGINS, Jack
  See PATTERSON, Harry

*   *   *

HOCHHUTH, Rolf 1931-

PERSONAL: Born April 1, 1931, in Eschwege, Germany (now West Germany); son of Walter (a shoe-factory owner and accountant) and Ilse (Holzapfel) Hochhuth; married Marianne Heinemann, June 29, 1957 (divorced, 1972); children: Martin, Friedrich. *Education:* Studied bookkeeping at a vocational school; attended universities of Marburg, Munich, and Heidelberg, 1952-55. *Religion:* German Evangelical Church.

ADDRESSES: P.O. Box 661, 4002 Basel, Switzerland.

CAREER: Acted as city-hall runner for first postwar mayor (his uncle) of Eschwege, Germany; Verlag C. Bertelsmann (publisher), Guetersloh, Westphalia, Germany, reader and editor, beginning in 1955; Municipal Theatre, Basel, Switzerland, assistant director and playwright, 1963.

MEMBER: P.E.N. of Federal Republic of Germany.

AWARDS, HONORS: Gerhart Hauptmann Prize and Berliner Kunstpreis for *Der Stellvertreter;* Basel Art Prize, 1976.

WRITINGS:

Der Stellvertreter: Schauspiel (play; first produced in West Berlin at Volksbuehne Theatre, February 20, 1963; produced as "The Representative" by Royal Shakespeare Company, 1963; produced as "The Deputy" at Brooks Atkinson Theatre, New York City, February 26, 1964), foreword by Erwin Piscator, Rowohlt Taschenbuch, 1963, translation by Robert David MacDonald published as *The Representative*, Methuen, 1963, translation by Richard Winston and Clara Winston published as *The Deputy*, foreword by Albert Schweitzer, Grove, 1964.

Soldaten: Nekrolog auf Genf (play; first produced in West Berlin at Volksbuehne Theatre, October 9, 1967; translation produced as "Soldiers" at Royal Alexandra Theater, Toronto, Ontario, February 28, 1968; produced in New York at Billy Rose Theatre, May 1, 1968), Rowohlt Taschenbuch, 1967, translation by MacDonald published as *Soldiers: An Obituary for Geneva*, Grove, 1968.

Guerillas: Tragoedie in fuenf Akten (five-act play; first produced in Stuttgart, West Germany, May 15, 1970), Rowohlt Taschenbuch, 1970.

Krieg und Klassenkrieg (essays; title means "War and Class War"), foreword by Fritz J. Raddatz, Rowohlt Taschenbuch, 1971.

Die Hebamme: Komoedie (play; title means "The Midwife"; first produced in May, 1972), Rowohlt Taschenbuch, 1971.

Lysistrate und die NATO (play; title means "Lysistrata and NATO"; first produced February 22, 1974), Rowohlt Taschenbuch, 1973.

Zwischenspiel in Baden-Baden, Rowohlt Taschenbuch, 1974.

Die Berliner Antigone: Prosa und Verse (novella; title means "The Berlin Antigone"), Rowohlt Taschenbuch, 1975.

Tod eines Jaegers (play; title means "Death of a Hunter"), Rowohlt Taschenbuch, 1976.

Eine Liebe in Deutschland (novel), Rowohlt Taschenbuch, 1978.

Juristen: Drei Akte fuer sieben Spieler (play), Rowohlt Taschenbuch, 1979.

Tell '38, Rowohlt Taschenbuch, 1979, translated from the German, Little, Brown, 1984.

A German Love Story (novel), translated by John Brownjohn, Little, Brown, 1980.

"Judith" (play), first produced in Glasgow, Scotland, at Citizens' Theatre, November 9, 1984.

EDITOR

Wilhelm Busch, *Saemtliche Werke, und eine Auswahl der Skizzen und Gemaelde*, Volume I, S. Mohn, 1959, Volume II, C. Bertelsmann, 1960.

Wilhelm Busch, *Lustige Streiche in Versen und Farben*, Ruetten & Loening, 1960.

Wilhelm Busch, *Saemtliche Bildergeschichten mit 3380 Zichnungen und Fachsimilies*, Ruetten & Leoning, 1961.

Liebe in unserer Zeit: Sechzehn Erzaehlungen (short story anthology), two volumes, Bertelsmann Lesering, 1961.

Theodor Storm, *Am grauen Meer*, Mosaik-Verlag, 1962.

Die grossen Meister: Deutsche Erzaehler des 20. Jahrhunderts (short story anthology), two volumes, Bertelsmann Lesering, 1964.

Des Lebens Uberfluss, R. Mohn, c. 1969.

Ruhm und Ehre, Bertelsmann, 1970.

Oscar Tellgmann, *Kaisers Zeiten: Bilder einer Epoche*, Herbig, 1973.

Also editor of Otto Flake's *Die Deutschen*, 1962, and Thomas Mann's *Dichter und Herrscher*, 1963.

OTHER

Author of plays "The Employer," 1965, and "Anatomy of Revolution," 1969.

SIDELIGHTS: Critics almost universally agreed that no previous post-World War II dramatic work shook the conscience of Europe as did Rolf Hochhuth's "Deputy." The impact was equated with that, in their times, of Emile Zola's letter "J'Accuse" and Erich Maria Remarque's novel *All Quiet on the Western Front*. It was propitious in timing, arriving on the scene shortly after Adolf Eichmann's war crimes trial and between sessions of the Second Vatican Council.

The thesis of the play is that Pope Pius XII should have spoken out more strongly and firmly than he did against the mass executions of the Jews during the Nazi period in Germany, especially against *die Endloesung* (the Final Solution). The dramatis personae are not for the most part, at least according to Hochhuth, actual historical people. The main protagonist, Jesuit Father Riccardo Fontana, is considered the most fictional, although the writer was inspired in creating the role by the martyred Father Maximilian Kolbe (Prisoner Number 16670 in Auschwitz) and Bernhard Lichtenberg, prelate of St. Heldwig's Cathedral in Berlin; the work is dedicated to them.

Hochhuth has said that he became interested in the subject on which he has written because, as a member of the young generation in Germany, he shared a great feeling of guilt about the past which he couldn't explain, but about which he felt he must seek to become informed. One of the books that stimulated him to begin work on the play was *The Final Solution*, by Gerald Reitlinger, and, after the death of Pope Pius XII, he spent three years in research preparation, three months in Rome (although secret Vatican archives were open only to the year 1846). He also studied the Nuremburg Trial and Wehrmacht archives. A "Sidelights on History," composed of documentation and stage directions, was appended to the end of the published version of the play.

Performance of this published version would take six to eight hours; most actual performances last from two to three hours, and adaptations vary in different cities and languages. Hochhuth said in New York that "the most comprehensive version was shown in Vienna, the shortest in Berlin, the most modern in Paris."

Demonstrations accompanied many performances of the play. Especially intense was the one at the Theatre Athenee in Paris, where protesting persons showered pamphlets on the audience, threw stench bombs, and even clambered onto the stage. On the Broadway premiere, about 150 persons demonstrated outside the Brooks Atkinson Theater, including members of the American Nazi party who carried placards reading "Ban the Hate Show"; the doors of the theater were locked during intermission as a protective measure.

Producer and director Herman Shumlin reported that efforts were made to prevent presentation of "The Deputy" in the United States. Billy Rose withdrew his cooperation from the production. An interfaith group, however, headed by Edward Keating, editor of *Ramparts*, then a Roman Catholic paper for laymen, asked the public to regard the play with an open mind; Catholic reaction generally was more restrained than might have been expected, and, in some cases, contrite.

The play itself (its dramaturgy, blank verse and free rhythms), was not considered by critics as exceptional. It was described as old-fashioned, using late nineteenth-century techniques in weak German classical tradition. Hochhuth was, however, credited with recreating the flavor of Nazi jargon. A coincidental relationship between it and Johann von Schiller's *Don Carlos* was noted. It was also compared to Bertolt Brecht's *Heilige Johanne der Schlachthofe.*

Although critics tended to feel that "The Deputy" left a good bit to be desired artistically, most also saw other meaningful aspects to the work. David Boroff wrote in the *National Observer:* "Though it is both flawed and arguable, it has restored seriousness to the Broadway theater. Not since 'Death of a Salesman' or 'The Diary of Anne Frank' have audiences been so profoundly shaken." Walter Kerr, drama critic for the *New York Herald Tribune,* concurred in the opinion that the play is deficient as a play. But he, too, commented: "We are also left with the aftermath of 'The Deputy,' making a clamor in the world which may, hopefully, become the equivalent of a call to prayer. Any virtues the work possesses are extra-theatrical. They may indeed become virtues."

Hochhuth pointed out that the subject of his play has been discussed ever since 1946 by such men as Albert Camus in France and the Catholic thinkers Friedrich Heer and Reinhold Schneider in the German-speaking nations. In regard to his personal feelings about Catholicism he has stated: "My best school friend is a Catholic. In fact, so strict a Catholic that his parents were very much afraid that he would enter the priesthood. He is now in the Federal Department of Justice at Bonn. He is also my son's sponsor." Hochhuth was shocked to see the American Nazis demonstrating at the New York opening and asked: "Why is this permitted in a city that has so many survivors? However, I do understand that democracy permits such things."

The controversy that ensued over the production of his second play, "The Soldiers," was even greater. On April 24, 1967, against the protests of literary manager Kenneth Tynan and artistic director Laurence Olivier, who wanted the play performed, London's National Theatre decided that the play was unsuitable for production because it allegedly maligned certain notable Englishmen, principally Sir Winston Churchill. In the play, Hochhuth suggests that the death of General Wladyslaw Sikorski, the Polish exile leader during World War II, was not accidental but rather the result of the machinations of the British secret service and was, furthermore, the result of a plot about which Churchill had full knowledge. The Lord Chamberlain, Britain's theatrical censor at the time, suggested that he would allow the play to be publicly performed only if the relatives of the characters in the play gave their consent.

Hochhuth maintained that the play is "against the immorality of air warfare. . . . I cannot blame Churchill. I blame the rules. That is exactly my point in the play. That a great and very human man like Churchill should yet be ready, according to the rules, to blast a city like Hamburg." Hochhuth, in fact, had great admiration for Churchill and kept his portrait in his study in Basel. D. A. N. Jones believed that the play "does not disparage Churchill but concerns itself with the choices men have to make in times of national crisis." Frank Marcus maintained that it "strives for the unvarnished truth and finishes up as a tribute. The method is Schillerian: free verse and constructed in a series of confrontations. Abstract concepts like Honour, Truth, and

Fame volley across the net: it's like a Wimbledon of the spirit. The domination of Churchill is made absolute by surrounding him with an entourage of cardboard figures." Marcus added, "With almost Quixotic courage [Hochhuth] has dared to tackle the great moral issues of our time. For this he deserves our unqualified respect, if not our unqualified approval."

When asked whether he specializes in attacking prominent figures Hochhuth replied: "Not at all. When you are writing of great issues and dramas of history, great figures are necessary." Yet primarily because of these attacks his controversial plays received mixed reviews while at the same time succeeding at the box office. He claimed he always has documentary evidence to back his theories and he contended that an author of historical plays has no right to invent incidents or to suppress facts. He said, however, that he does not believe in the "Theater of Documentation" as such. He told Martin Esslin: "I became the champion of 'documentary theater' quite unintentionally. I only noticed what had happened when Piscator wrote a program note in which he used the term 'documentary theater.' I am very unhappy about this catchphrase, for I believe it means very little. Pure documentation can never be more than a bunch of documents. Something must always be *added* to make a play."

MEDIA ADAPTATIONS: Eine Liebe in Deutschland was adapted as the film "A Love in Germany," starring Hanna Schygulla, directed by Andrzei Wajda, Triumph Films, 1984.

BIOGRAPHICAL/CRITICAL SOURCES:

BOOKS

Contemporary Literary Criticism, Gale, Volume 4, 1975, Volume 11, 1979, Volume 18, 1981.
Der Streit un Hochhuths "Stellvertreter," Basilius Presse, 1963.
Summa Inuria; oder, Durfte der Papst schweigen? Hochhuths "Stellvertreter" in der oeffentlichen Kritik, Rowohlt Taschenbuch, 1963.
Ward, M. E., *Rolf Hochhuth,* G. K. Hall, 1977.

PERIODICALS

After Dark, August, 1970.
America, October 12, 1963, November 2, 1963, November 9, 1963, January 4, 1964, January 11, 1964, January 18, 1964, March 7, 1964, March 14, 1964.
Chicago Tribune, January 30, 1985.
Chicago Tribune Book World, June 15, 1980.
Christian Century, September 18, 1963, October 16, 1963.
Christian Science Monitor, May 6, 1968, July 1, 1972.
Commentary, March, 1964.
Commonweal, February 28, 1964, March 20, 1964, May 31, 1968.
Der Spiegel, February 27, 1963.
Detroit Free Press, March 29, 1964, September 24, 1967.
Drama, spring, 1968.
Globe and Mail (Toronto), February 26, 1968.
L'Express, October 3, 1963, December 19, 1963.
Life, March 13, 1964, June 7, 1968.
Listener, October 12, 1967.
London Magazine, January, 1968.
Los Angeles Times, November 15, 1984.
Los Angeles Times Book Review, June 22, 1980.
Nation, March 16, 1964, May 20, 1968, August 25, 1969, August 17, 1970.
National Observer, March 2, 1964, March 4, 1968.
New Leader, March 16, 1964.
New Republic, March 14, 1964.
New Statesman, October 4, 1963.

Newsweek, March 2, 1964, March 11, 1968, January 20, 1969, June 1, 1970.
New York Daily News, February 27, 1964.
New Yorker, December 28, 1963, March 7, 1964, May 11, 1968.
New York Herald Tribune, February 27, 1964.
New York Journal-American, February 27, 1964.
New York Post, February 27, 1964.
New York Review of Books, March 19, 1964.
New York Times, February 27, 1964, February 28, 1964, February 12, 1967, April 26, 1967, September 11, 1967, December 14, 1968, November 9, 1984.
New York Times Book Review, March 1, 1964.
New York Times Magazine, November 19, 1967.
New York World-Telegram, February 27, 1964.
Observer Review, October 15, 1967, May 12, 1968, October 27, 1968, December 15, 1968.
Reporter, January 30, 1964.
Saturday Night, March, 1968.
Saturday Review, March 14, 1964.
Spectator, October 4, 1963, December 20, 1968.
The Saturday Evening Post, February 29, 1964.
Time, November 1, 1963, March 6, 1964, May 10, 1968.
Times (London), April 10, 1980, November 9, 1984, November 12, 1984, May 10, 1985, October 7, 1986.
Times Literary Supplement, May 28, 1970, May 2, 1980.
Transatlantic Review, autumn, 1968.
Variety, August 5, 1970.
Village Voice, March 12, 1964.
Washington Post, January 19, 1969, May 3, 1972.
Zuericher Woche, September 27, 1963.

*   *   *

HOOD, Hugh (John Blagdon) 1928-

PERSONAL: Born April 30, 1928, in Toronto, Ontario, Canada; son of Alexander (a banker) and Marguerite (Blagdon) Hood; married Ruth Noreen Mallory (a painter and printmaker), April 22, 1957; children: Sarah Barbara, Dwight Alexander, John Arthur, Alexandra Mary. *Education:* Attended De La Salle College; University of Toronto, B.A., 1950, M.A., 1952, Ph.D., 1955. *Politics:* Radical socialist. *Religion:* Christian.

ADDRESSES: Home and office—4242 Hampton Ave., Montreal, Quebec, Canada H4A 2K9.

CAREER: St. Joseph College, West Hartford, Conn., associate professor, 1955-61; University of Montreal, Montreal, Quebec, professor of English, 1961—; novelist.

AWARDS, HONORS: President's Medals from University of Western Ontario, 1963, for story, and 1968, for article; Beta Sigma Phi prize, 1965; Canada Council, grants, 1968 and 1977, awards, 1971 and 1974; award from Province of Ontario, 1974; award from City of Toronto, 1976; Queen's Jubilee Medal, 1977; QSPELL Prize for best novel, Quebec Society for the the Promotion of English Language and Literature, 1988; Officer of the Order of Canada, 1988.

WRITINGS:

Flying a Red Kite (short stories), Ryerson, 1962, reprinted, Porcupine's Quill, 1987.
White Figure, White Ground (novel), Ryerson, 1964.
Around the Mountain: Scenes From Montreal Life (short stories), Peter Martin, 1967.
The Camera Always Lies (novel), Harcourt, 1967.
Strength Down Centre: The Jean Beliveau Story, Prentice-Hall, 1970.

A Game of Touch (novel), Longmans, Green, 1970.
The Fruit Man, the Meat Man and the Manager (short stories), Oberon Press, 1971.
You Can't Get There From Here (novel), Oberon Press, 1972.
The Governor's Bridge Is Closed: Twelve Essays on the Canadian Scene, Oberon Press, 1973.
The New Age/Le Nouveau Siecle (serial novel), Volume 1: *The Swing in the Garden,* Oberon Press, 1975, Volume 2: *A New Athens,* Oberon Press, 1977, Volume 3: *Reservoir Ravine,* Oberon Press, 1979, Volume 4: *Black and White Keys,* ECW Press, 1982, Volume 5: *The Scenic Art,* Stoddart, 1984, Volume 6: *The Motor Boys in Ottawa,* Stoddart, 1986, Volume 7: *Tony's Book,* Stoddart, 1988, Volume 8: *Property and Value,* Stoddart, 1990.
Dark Glasses (short stories), Oberon Press, 1976.
"Friends and Relations" (play), in *The Play's the Thing: Four Original Television Dramas,* edited by Tony Gifford, Macmillan, 1976.
Selected Stories, Oberon Press, 1978.
(With Seymour Segal) *Scoring: The Art of Hockey* (art book), Oberon Press, 1979.
None Genuine Without This Signature (short stories), ECW Press, 1980.
Trusting the Tale (essays), ECW Press, 1983.
August Nights (stories), Stoddart, 1985.
Five New Facts About Giorgione, Black Moss, 1987.
A Short Walk in the Rain: The Collected Stories II, Porcupine's Quill, 1989.
The Isolation Booth: The Collected Stories III, Porcupine's Quill, 1991.
Unsupported Assertions: Essays, Stoddart, 1991.

Contributor of short stories to periodicals, including *Canadian Forum, Exchange, Journal of Canadian Fiction, Tamarack Review, Queen's Quarterly,* and *Story.*

WORK IN PROGRESS: A collection of short stories, publication expected in 1992; more volumes of *The New Age/Le Nouveau Siecle,* including Volumes 9, Be Sure to Close Your Eyes, 10 and 11; *Watercourses,* an art book, with wife, Noreen Mallory; an essay collection.

SIDELIGHTS: Hugh Hood told *CA:* "I consider my *roman-fleuve, The New Age/Le Nouveau Siecle,* to be the great, major work of my life. It should occupy me for a generation, with the final volume appearing around the year 2000. Hence the title." Since writing those words, Hood has completed the three-quarters of his saga, which follows a Canadian family throughout the twentieth century. He added: "I have a very much clearer idea now than I did in the early 1970s of where I'm going with this work. I have the complete and perfected schema for the last volumes quite clearly defined in my imagination, including the closing lines of the work."

BIOGRAPHICAL/CRITICAL SOURCES:

BOOKS

Contemporary Literary Criticism, Gale, Volume 15, 1980, Volume 28, 1984.
Dictionary of Literary Biography, Volume 53: *Canadian Writers since 1960, First Series,* Gale, 1986.
Garebian, Keith, *Hugh Hood,* Twayne, 1983.
Morley, Patricia A., *The Comedians: Hugh Hood and Rudy Wiebe,* Clarke Irwin, 1977.
Struthers, J. R., *Before the Flood: Hugh Hood's Work in Progress,* ECW Press, 1979.

PERIODICALS

Globe and Mail, August 11, 1984, November 16, 1985, October 21, 1989.
Maclean's, October 22, 1979.
Saturday Night, October, 1982.

* * *

HOPE, A(lec) D(erwent)   1907-

PERSONAL: Born July 21, 1907, in Cooma, New South Wales, Australia; son of Percival (a clergyman) and Florence Ellen (Scotford) Hope; married Penelope Robinson, May 27, 1937 (some sources say May 21, 1938); children: Emily, Andrew, Geoffrey. *Education:* Sydney University, B.A., 1928; Oxford University, B.A., c. 1930. *Politics:* None.

ADDRESSES: Home—66 Arthur Circle, Forrest, Canberra, Australian Capital Territory 2603, Australia. *Office*—Australian National University, Canberra, G.P.O. Box 4, Canberra 2601, Australia. *Agent*— Curtis Brown Ltd., 27 Union St., Paddington, Sydney, New South Wales 2021, Australia.

CAREER: New South Wales Department of Education, New South Wales, Australia, teacher of English, c. 1933-36; New South Wales Department of Labor and Industry, administrator of vocational tests and guidance counselor for Youth Employment Bureau, two years during the period, 1933-36; Sydney Teachers' College, Sydney, New South Wales, lecturer in English and education, c. 1937-45; University of Melbourne, Melbourne, New South Wales, senior lecturer in English, c. 1945-50; Canberra University College, Canberra, Australian Capital Territory, professor of English, c. 1950-60; Australian National University, Canberra, professor of English, c. 1960-68; library fellow, 1967-72, visiting fellow, beginning in 1973; Sweet Briar College, Sweet Briar, Va., Sue Read Slaughter Professor of Poetry, 1970-71.

MEMBER: Australian Academy of Humanities, Australian Society of Authors (president, 1966), American Academy and Institute of Arts and Letters (honorary member).

AWARDS, HONORS: Grace Levin Prize for Poetry, 1956; Arts Council of Great Britain award for poetry, 1965; Britannica Australian Award for Literature, 1966 (some sources say 1965); Volkswagen Award for Literature, 1966; Myer Award for Australian Literature, 1967; Levinson Prize for Poetry, 1969; Ingram Merrill Award for Literature, 1969; Officer of the Order of the British Empire, 1972; Litt.D., Australian National University, 1972, University of New England, 1973, Monish University, Melbourne, 1976, University of Melbourne, 1976; Companion of the Order of Australia, 1981.

WRITINGS:

The Wandering Islands (poems), Edwards Shaw (Sydney), 1956.
(Compiler) *Australian Poetry, 1960,* Angus & Robertson (Sydney), 1960.
Poems, Hamish Hamilton, 1960, Viking, 1961.
(And author of introduction) *Selected Poems,* Angus & Robertson (Sydney), 1963.
Australian Literature, 1950-1962, Melbourne University Press, 1963.
The Cave and the Spring (essays), Rigby (Adelaide), 1965, University of Chicago Press, 1970, 2nd edition, Sydney University Press, 1974.
Collected Poems, 1930-1965, Viking, 1966.
New Poems: 1965-1969, Angus & Robertson, 1969, Viking, 1970.

Dunciad Minor: An Heroick Poem, Melbourne University Press, 1970.
Midsummer Eve's Dream: Variations on a Theme by William Dunbar (essays), Viking, 1970.
Collected Poems: 1930-1970, Angus & Robertson, 1972.
Selected Poems, Angus & Robertson, 1973.
Native Companions: Essays and Comments on Australian Literature, 1936-1966, Angus & Robertson, 1974.
A Late Picking: Poems, 1965-1974, Angus & Robertson, 1975.
A Book of Answers (poems), Angus & Robertson, 1978.
The Pack of Autolycus (essays), Australian National University Press, 1978.
The New Cratylus: Notes on the Craft of Poetry, Oxford University Press, 1979.
The Drifting Continent, and Other Poems, illustrations by Arthur Boyd, Brindalbella Press (Canberra), c. 1979.
Antechinus: Poems, 1975-1980, Angus & Robertson, 1981.
The Tragical History of Doctor Faustus, Australian National University Press, 1982.
The Age of Reason (poems), Melbourne University Press, 1985.
Selected Poems, edited by Ruth Morse, Carcanet, 1986.
Ladies From the Sea (play), Melbourne University Press, 1987.

SIDELIGHTS: A. D. Hope, Australia's foremost poet, has been called "one of the two or three best poets writing in English." David Kalstone notes that "his poise and sophistication remind one often of Auden," and Samuel French Morse claims that "of the books to own from 1966, Hope's [*Collected Poems, 1930-1965*] is certainly the one."

Jean Garrigue has said that, "in a sense, Hope is literary the way many poets have ceased to be. He is not breaking down form and inviting chaos." Morse explains: "The powerful satiric thrust, the extraordinary sense of self-possession, the sensuality of his imagination, and the all but arrogant clarity of his poems are apparent from the beginning; and these qualities and characteristics are the more surprising in a time when the significant rhetorical gesture has grown increasingly flabby." Garrigue adds: "Syntax is never ambiguous [in Hope's poems]; he favors coherence and logical connections. . . . He rhymes, he works in stanzaic forms. He seems grandly at home in his orderly arrangements. The right word is usually in the right place, but since the poems move in terms of the line, not in terms of the word, the emphasis is on the large unit."

Hope himself, according to Garrigue, has said that "poetry is principally concerned to 'express' its subject and in doing so to create an emotion which is the feeling of the poem and not the feeling of the poet." His success in creating such a poetry might be confirmed by Kalstone, who writes: "It is rare to find—as one does with Hope—poems that depend so successfully on a shared sense of community. His audience is fixed in position, ready to follow the action within the proscenium his poems assume."

Kalstone believes that Hope's skill is "partly one of reinterpretation. The literary scene is one we know, but the characters have been assigned new positions on stage." Kalstone continues: "We are led through a very familiar gallery of mythological, historical and Biblical subjects, and we are asked to see the flash of energy behind the traditional pose. . . . To put it another way, modern settings draw forward Hope the satirist, jaunty but rather uniformly critical of mechanized, overcivilized lives. But he rises to the challenge of the fable. His real gift is for narrative—not so much telling a story, as retelling it with an air of wisdom and experience. The story is a *tableau vivant,* action halted at a moment of high feeling, nuances revealed by the measured order in which we are directed to gestures and landscapes. It is an index of the success of recent American poetry, introspective, often jagged, that declarative sentences, direct syntax, firmly rhymed stanzas should sound now a little strange. These last are precisely Hope's resources, his assured way of drawing us from detail to detail, finishing a picture which stands powerful and separate."

Marius Bewley, on the other hand, adds qualification to his praise of Hope, although he agrees that the poet is "an accomplished and attractive writer." Bewley writes: "Hope is usually, but not always, intelligent in his poetry. One of the hesitations one feels about him is that he often seems to arrive at his intelligent ideas and clever arguments first, and wraps them up in skillful metrics later." And "only very rarely does his language and thought seem organically fused, to share one bloodstream, one flesh, one life." But, Bewley adds, "at his best—and [Hope] is often at his best—his poems achieve a sustained, assured, and musical rhetorical mode of speech."

Both Kalstone and Garrigue believe that Hope's love poems are his best; "they are sensual, sumptuous, dazzling," writes Garrigue. "Without bizarreries or mad touches, they are 'square,' if you will, dedicated to the myth of beauty and joy."

Hope told *CA* that he is interested in philosophy, biology, and history, and that he has no interest in hobbies or sports. He has "some knowledge" of Latin, French, German, Italian, and Spanish. He adds that he has "no very fixed convictions on anything" and adjures us to "see Keats on negative capability."

BIOGRAPHICAL/CRITICAL SOURCES:

BOOKS

A. D. Hope: A Bibliography, Libraries Board of South Australia, 1968.
Contemporary Literary Criticism, Gale, Volume 3, 1975, Volume 51, 1989.

PERIODICALS

Contemporary Literature, winter, 1968.
New Leader, March 27, 1967.
New York Review of Books, May 18, 1967.
Partisan Review, fall, 1967.
Times Literary Supplement, April 7, 1978, February 22, 1980, August 22, 1986.
Village Voice, June 15, 1967.*

* * *

HOPE, Margaret
See KNIGHT, Alanna

* * *

HUGHES, Ted 1930-

PERSONAL: Full name, Edward James Hughes; born August 17, 1930, in Mytholmroyd, West Yorkshire, England; son of William Henry (a carpenter) and Edith (Farrar) Hughes; married Sylvia Plath (a poet), 1956 (died, 1963); married Carol Orchard, 1970; children: (first marriage) Frieda Rebecca, Nicholas Farrar. *Education:* Pembroke College, Cambridge, B.A., 1954, M.A., 1959.

ADDRESSES: Office—c/o Faber & Faber Ltd., 3 Queen's Square, London WC1N 3AU, England.

CAREER: Writer. Instructor, University of Massachusetts—Amherst, Amherst, 1957-59. *Military service:* Royal Air Force, 1948-50.

AWARDS, HONORS: First prize, Young Men's and Young Women's Hebrew Association Poetry Center contest, 1957, and first prize, Guinness Poetry Awards, 1958, both for *The Hawk in the Rain;* Guggenheim fellowship, 1959-60; Somerset Maugham Award, 1960, Hawthornden Prize, 1961, and Abraham Wonsell Foundation awards, 1964-69, all for *Lupercal;* City of Florence International Poetry Prize, 1969, for *Wodwo;* Premio Internazionale Taormina, 1972; Queen's Medal for Poetry, 1974; *Season Songs* was a Children's Book Showcase Title, 1976; Officer, Order of the British Empire, 1977; voted Britain's best poet in 1979 poll by *New Poetry* magazine; Signal Poetry awards, 1979, for *Moon-Bells and Other Poems,* 1981, for *Under the North Star,* and 1983, for *The Rattle Bag: An Anthology of Poetry;* Royal Society of Literature Heinemann Award, 1980, for *Moortown;* runner-up for 1981 Neustadt International Prize for Literature; honorary doctorate degrees from Exeter College, 1982, Open University, 1983, Bradford College, 1984, and Pembroke College, 1986; named Poet Laureate of England, 1984; Kurt Maschler/Emil Award, National Book League (Great Britain), 1985, for *The Iron Man;* Guardian Award for children's fiction, 1985, for *What Is the Truth?: A Farmyard Fable for the Young.*

WRITINGS:

POETRY

The Hawk in the Rain, Harper, 1957.
Pike, Gehenna Press (Northampton, Mass.), 1959.
Lupercal, Harper, 1960.
(With Thom Gunn) *Selected Poems,* Faber, 1962.
Animal Poems, Gilbertson, 1967.
Gravestones, Exeter College of Art, 1967, published as *Poems,* 1968.
I Said Goodbye to the Earth, Exeter College of Art, 1969.
The Martyrdom of Bishop Farrer, Gilbertson, 1970.
Crow: From the Life and Songs of the Crow, Faber, 1970, Harper, 1971, revised edition, Faber, 1972, Harper, 1981.
Fighting for Jerusalem, Mid-NAG, 1970.
Selected Poems, 1957-1967, Faber, 1972, Harper, 1973.
Cave Birds (limited edition), Scolar Press, 1975, enlarged edition published as *Cave Birds: An Alchemical Drama,* Faber, 1978, Viking, 1979.
The Interrogator: A Titled Vulturess, Scolar Press, 1975.
Guadete, Harper, 1977.
Remains of Elmet: A Pennine Sequence, Rainbow Press, 1979, revised edition, Faber, 1979.
(Contributor) Michael Morpurgo, *All Around the Year,* J. Murray, 1979.
Moortown (also see below), Faber, 1979, Harper, 1980.
Selected Poems: 1957-1981, Faber, 1982, enlarged edition published as *New Selected Poems,* Harper, 1982.
Primer of Birds: Poems, Phaedon Press, 1982.
River, Faber, 1983, Harper, 1984.
Flowers and Insects: Some Birds and a Pair of Spiders, Knopf, 1986.
Tales of the Early World, Faber, 1988.
Wolfwatching, Faber, 1989.
Moortown Diary (originally published in *Moortown*), Faber, 1989.

POETRY; LIMITED EDITIONS

The Burning of the Brothel, Turret Books, 1966.
Recklings, Turret Books, 1966.
Scapegoats and Rabies: A Poem in Five Parts, Poet & Printer, 1967.

Poems: Ted Hughes, Fainlight, and Sillitoe, Rainbow Press, 1967.

A Crow Hymn, Sceptre Press, 1970.

A Few Crows, Rougemont Press (Exeter, Devon), 1970.

Amulet, privately printed, 1970.

Four Crow Poems, privately printed, 1970.

Autumn Song, privately printed, 1971.

Crow Wakes: Poems, Poet & Printer, 1971.

(With Ruth Fainlight and Alan Sillitoe) *Poems,* Rainbow Press, 1971.

In The Little Girl's Angel Gaze, Steam Press, 1972.

Prometheus on His Crag: 21 Poems, Rainbow Press, 1973.

Eclipse, Sceptre Press, 1976.

Sunstruck, Sceptre Press, 1977.

Chiasmadon, C. Seluzicki (Baltimore), 1977.

Orts, Rainbow Press, 1978.

Moortown Elegies, Rainbow Press, 1978.

A Solstice, Sceptre Press, 1978.

Calder Valley Poems, Rainbow Press, 1978.

Adam and the Sacred Nine, Rainbow Press, 1979.

Henry Williamson: A Tribute, Rainbow Press, 1979.

Four Tales Told by an Idiot, Sceptre Press, 1979.

PLAYS

"The Calm," first produced in Boston, Mass., 1961.

"The Wound," (also see below; radio play) produced, 1962, revised version produced on stage in London, 1972.

"Epithalamium," first produced in London, 1963.

"The House of Donkeys," first broadcast in 1965.

"The Price of a Bride" (juvenile), first broadcast in 1966.

(Adapter) *Seneca's Oedipus* (first produced in London at National Theatre, 1968), Faber, 1969, Doubleday, 1972.

The Coming of the Kings and Other Plays (juvenile; contains "Beauty and the Beast" [first broadcast, 1965; produced in London, 1971], "Sean, the Fool" [first broadcast in 1968; first produced in London, 1971], "The Devil and the Cats" [first broadcast, 1968; first produced in London, 1971], "The Coming of the Kings" [first televised, 1967; first produced in London, 1972; also see below], and "The Tiger's Bones" [first broadcast November 26, 1965]), Faber, 1970, enlarged edition (also contains "Orpheus" [first broadcast, 1971; also see below]) published as *The Tiger's Bones and Other Plays for Children,* Viking, 1975.

"Orghast," first produced in Persepolis, Iran, 1971.

Eat Crow, Rainbow Press, 1971.

The Coming of the Kings: A Christmas Play in One Act, Dramatic Publishing, 1972.

The Iron Man (based on his juvenile book; also see below; televised, 1972), Faber, 1973.

Orpheus, Dramatic Publishing, 1973.

Also author of radio plays, "The House of Aries," 1960, "A Houseful of Women," 1961, "Difficulties of a Bridegroom," 1963, "Dogs," 1964, and "The Head of Gold," 1967.

JUVENILE

Meet My Folks! (verse), Puffin, 1961, Bobbs-Merrill, 1973, enlarged edition, Faber, 1987.

The Earth-Owl and Other Moon-People (verse), Faber, 1963, Antheneum, 1964, published as *Moon-Whales and Other Moon Poems,* Viking, 1976, revised edition published as *Moon Whales,* Faber, 1988.

How the Whale Became and Other Stories, Faber, 1963, with new illustrations, Atheneum, 1964.

Nessie, The Mannerless Monster (verse), Chilmark, 1964, published with new illustrations as *Nessie the Monster,* Bobbs-Merrill, 1974.

The Iron Giant: A Story in Five Nights, Harper, 1968 (published in England as *The Iron Man: A Story in Five Nights,* with different illustrations, Faber, 1968), published with new illustrations, 1984.

Five Autumn Songs for Children's Voices, Gilbertson, 1968.

The Demon of Adachigahara (libretto), Oxford University Press, 1969.

Spring, Summer, Autumn, Winter (verse; limited edition), Rainbow Press, 1974, revised and enlarged edition published as *Season Songs,* Viking, 1975.

Earth-Moon (limited edition), with illustrations by the author, Rainbow Press, 1976.

Moon-Bells and Other Poems, Chatto & Windus, 1978.

"The Pig Organ; or, Pork with Perfect Pitch" (opera), first performed by English Opera Company at the Round House in London, January, 1980.

Under the North Star (verse), Faber, 1981.

(Editor with Seamus Heaney) *The Rattle Bag: An Anthology of Poetry,* Faber, 1982.

What Is Truth?: A Farmyard Fable for the Young (verse), Harper, 1984.

Ffangs the Vampire Bat and the Kiss of Truth, Faber, 1986.

EDITOR

(With Patricia Beer and Vernon Scannell) *New Poems 1962,* Hutchinson, 1962.

(With T. Gunn) *Five American Poets,* Faber, 1963.

Here Today, Hutchinson, 1963.

(With Alwyn Hughes) Sylvia Plath, *Ariel,* Faber, 1965, Harper, 1966.

(And author of introduction) Keith Douglas, *Selected Poems,* Chilmark, 1965.

Poetry in the Making: An Anthology of Poems and Programmes from "Listening and Writing," Faber, 1967, abridged edition published as *Poetry Is,* Doubleday, 1970.

(And author of introduction) Emily Dickinson, *A Choice of Emily Dickinson's Verse,* Faber, 1968.

(And translator with Assia Gutmann) Yehuda Amichai, *Selected Poems,* Cape Goliard Press, 1968, expanded edition published as *Poems,* Harper, 1969.

(And author of introduction; also see below) William Shakespeare, *With Fairest Flowers While Summer Lasts: Poems from Shakespeare,* Doubleday, 1971 (published in England as *A Choice of Shakespeare's Verse,* Faber, 1971).

Plath, *Crossing the Waters: Transitional Poems,* Harper, 1971 (published in England with differing contents as *Crossing the Waters,* Faber, 1971).

Plath, *Winter Trees,* Faber, 1971, Harper, 1972.

(And author of introduction) Plath, *Johnny Panic and the Bible of Dreams, and Other Prose Writings,* Faber, 1977, 2nd edition, Harper, 1979.

(With Janos Csokits and translator) Janos Pilinszky, *Selected Poems,* Persea Books, 1977.

(And translator) Amichai, *Amen,* Harper, 1977.

New Poetry 6, Hutchison, 1980.

(And author of introduction) Plath, *The Collected Poems,* Harper, 1981.

(With Seamus Heaney) *Arvon Foundation Poetry Competition: 1980 Anthology,* Kilnhurst, 1982.

Plath, *Sylvia Plath's Selected Poems,* Faber, 1985.

OTHER

(Contributor) *Writers on Themselves,* BBC Publications, 1964.

Wodwo (miscellany; includes play, "The Wound"), Harper, 1967.

Shakespeare's Poem (originally published as introduction to *With Fairest Flowers While Summer Lasts: Poems from Shakespeare),* Lexham Press, 1971.

(Adapter) *The Story of Vasco* (libretto; adaptation of a play by Georges Schehade; first produced in London, 1974), Oxford University Press, 1974.

(Translator) Charles Simic and Mark Strand, editors, *Another Republic,* Ecco Press, 1977.

(Translator with Amichai) Amichai, *Time,* Harper, 1979.

The Threshold (short story; limited edition), Steam Press, 1979.

(Consulting editor and author of foreword) Frances McCullough, editor, *The Journals of Sylvia Plath,* Dial, 1982.

(Translator with Csokits) Pilinszky, *The Desert of Love,* Anvil Press Poetry, 1988.

Contributor to numerous anthologies. Contributor to periodicals, including *New Yorker, New York Review of Books,* and *Spectator.* Founding editor, with Daniel Weissbrot, *Modern Poetry in Translation* (journal), 1964-71.

SIDELIGHTS: Ted Hughes's reputation as a poet of international stature was secured in the late 1950s with the publication of his first poetry collection, *The Hawk in the Rain.* According to *Dictionary of Literary Biography* contributor Robert B. Shaw: "Hughes's poetry signalled a dramatic departure from the prevailing modes of the period. The stereotypical poem of the time was determined not to risk too much: politely domestic in its subject matter, understated and mildly ironic in style. By contrast, Hughes marshalled a language of nearly Shakespearean resonance to explore themes which were mythic and elemental." Since that time, Hughes's poetry has fallen in and out of fashion with literary critics—he was excluded, for example, from an important anthology of British poetry published in the early 1980s—but he has continued to make his presence known. Many critics point to his poetic works of the last two decades, *Moortown* and *River,* in particular, as marking a returning to his former brilliance. His 1984 appointment as Poet Laureate of England assures his status as an important British poet for years to come.

Usually written contrary to the prevailing style, Hughes's work has always been controversial. "Critics rarely harbor neutral feelings toward Hughes's poetry," observes Carol Bere in *Literary Review.* "He has been dismissed as a connoisseur of the habits of animals, his disgust with humanity barely disguised; labeled a 'voyeur of violence,' attacked for his generous choreographing of gore; and virtually written off as a cult poet. . . . Others consider him to be the best poet writing today—admired for the originality and command of his approach; the scope and complexity of his mythic enterprise; and the apparent ease and freshness with which he can vitalize a landscape, free of any mitigating sentimentality."

To read Hughes's poetry is to enter a world dominated by nature, especially by animals. This holds true for nearly all of his books from *The Hawk in the Rain* and the bird of the title to *Moortown,* an examination of life on a farm. Apparently, Hughes love of animals was one of the catalysts in his decision to become a poet. According to London *Times* contributor Thomas Nye, Hughes once confessed "that he began writing poems in adolescence, when it dawned upon him that his earlier passion for hunting animals in his native Yorkshire ended either in the possession of a dead animal, or at best a trapped one. He wanted to capture not just live animals, but the aliveness of animals in their natural state: their wildness, their quiddity, the fox-ness of the fox and the crow-ness of the crow."

Hughes's apparent obsession with animals and nature in his poetry has brought the wrath of more than one critic down upon him. In *The Modern Poet: Essays from "The Review,"* Colin Falck, for instance, writes that the "real limitation of Hughes's animal poems is precisely that they conjure emotions without bringing us any nearer to understanding them. They borrow their impact from a complex of emotions that they do nothing to define, an in the end tell us nothing about the urban civilised human world that we read the poems in." Other commentators see Hughes concentration on animals as the poet's attempt to clarify his feelings on the human condition. "Stated in the broadest possible terms," notes Shaw, "Hughes's enterprise is to examine the isolated and precarious position of man in nature and man's chances of overcoming his alienation from the world around him. In pursuit of these interests Hughes focuses frequently (and often brilliantly) upon animals."

According to P. R. King, Hughes's emphasis on wild creatures is not so much evidence of his concern for them as it is a clue to the importance the poet reserves for what animals symbolize in his work. Through animal imagery, Hughes exalts the instinctive power of nature that he finds lacking in human society. "He sees in them," King writes in *Nine Contemporary Poets: A Critical Introduction,* "the most clear manifestation of a life-force that is distinctly non-human or, rather, is non-rational in its source of power. Hughes observes in modern man a reluctance to acknowledge the deepest, instinctual sources of energy in his own being, an energy that is related to the elemental power circuit of the universe and to which animals are closer than man." King believes that in Hughes's poetry written since *Crow* the poet "has moved on to express a sense of sterility and nihilism in modern man's response to life, a response which he connects with the dominance of man's rational, objective intellect at the expense of the life of emotions and imagination."

Hughes's best-known and most intriguing creations is an animal named Crow, who began appearing in his work in 1967 and eventually came to be the main character in several volumes of poetry, including *A Crow Hymn, Crow: From the Life and Songs of the Crow,* and *Crow Wakes.* In a *Time* review, Christopher Porterfield observes: "Crow is a sort of cosmic Kilroy. Alternately a witness, a demon and a victim, he is in on everything from the creation to the ultimate nuclear holocaust. At various times he is minced, dismembered, rendered cataleptic, but always he bobs back. In his graceless, ignoble way, he is the lowest common denominator of the universal forces that obsess Hughes. He is a symbol of the essential survivor, of whatever endures, however battered." In *Ted Hughes* Keith Sagar comments that in Crow he finds an "Everyman who will not acknowledge that everything he most hates and fears—the Black Beast—is within himself. Crow's world is unredeemable." *Newsweek*'s Jack Kroll calls *Crow* "one of those rare books of poetry that have the public impact of a major novel or a piece of superjournalism," and summarizes the effect of the character, noting: "In Crow, Ted Hughes has created one of the most powerful mythic presences in contemporary poetry."

Although critics applauded the mythic quality of Hughes's Crow sagas, many feel that in later works the poet's use of myth often met with disastrous results. *New Republic* contributor J. D. McClatchy, for instance, observed, "When 'The Thought-Fox' first fluttered the henhouse of English poetry in 1957, Hughes seemed a force of nature. . . . But from *Crow* on, the lines seemed to come unstitched, the mythic gestures sounded hollow." Reviewers, such as Richard Murphy and Sandra McPherson find Hughes at his best when he adheres to describing the natural world around him. In his *New York Review of Books* essay on the author, Murphy notes approvingly that in the progression of Hughes's career "demons and mythical birds rightly give way to the real creatures of his imagination." In like fashion, in *American Poetry Review* McPherson finds "when Hughes leaves for the country and helps a halfborn calf in delivery and gets his boots muddy, he gives us rich energized poetry. But few are likely to write anything but a satirical poem at the indoor beach. Similarly, when Hughes writes of mythical animals and heavenly landscapes, the writing is most of the time unpalatable, unattractive, even slightly ridiculous."

Both McPherson and *New Statesman* contributor Blake Morrison lament the appearance of the myth-inspired "Prometheus on His Crag" sequence in Hughes's *Moortown*. According to McPherson, in this series of poems Hughes strains "to get the point across of a violent, ugly territory of the universe, where understatement has been run out of town." In his *Los Angeles Times Book Review* critique of the volume Peter Clothier notes, "The strength of the book is in the first group of raw poems, the 'Moortown' of the title; its weakness is in flights to myth that dominate later sequences." But despite various objections raised to portions of the book, critics universally acclaim the poems signaled out by Clothier. "The weight and power of the book come in the title sequence," observes *Times Literary Supplement* contributor Peter Scupham, while Christopher Ricks similarly states in the *New York Times Book Review*, "The title sequence, 'Moortown' strikes me as one of [Hughes's] truest achievements in a very long time."

"Moortown" is a group of thirty-four poems which record Hughes's experiences working his Devonshire farm, culminating in a set of six pieces dedicated to the memory of his late father-in-law, Jack Orchard, who helped him run the farm. Filled with images of sheep and births of lambs and calves, the poems reveal Hughes as a tender observer of nature. The gentle, loving quality noted by critics, gives way at times to brutal descriptions of the harsh realities of farm life. In one poem, for instance, Hughes describes a newborn lamb and its mother lying on the ground "face to face like two mortally wounded duelists." While Joseph Parisi notes in the *Chicago Tribune Book World* that these poems show Hughes "at the height of his powers," McPherson explains that their strength comes from Hughes's respect for and intimate knowledge of his subject matter. "Hughes has to write out of love to make the most of his gifts. . . .," she maintains. "His poems which grow from close contact with their subject have the real healing effect and are as healthy a poetry as being written today."

Observing that four volumes of Hughes's poetry and three critical studies of his work had been published in the first few years of the eighties, Murphy began a review of several of Hughes's poetical offerings with the proclamation, "Ted Hughes is surviving." Hughes's survival as a poet seems to rest on what McClatchy calls his "capacity to change." Critics see his recent works as turning points in his career, marking the author with a new sensibility as more that just an "animal poet" but rather a poet who uses animals to express his insight into the enduring spirituality of nature. "Hughes's reputation rests on his very individual vision of the natural world. . . .," writes *Listener* contributor Dick Davis. "He is popular for this very reason—he brings back to our suburban, centrally- heated and, above all, *safe* lives reports from an authentic frontier of reality and the

imagination. His poems speak to us of a world that is constantly true in a way that we know our temporary comforts cannot be."

BIOGRAPHICAL/CRITICAL SOURCES:

BOOKS

Children's Literature Review, Volume 3, Gale, 1978.
Contemporary Literary Criticism, Gale, Volume 2, 1974, Volume 4, 1975, Volume 9, 1978, Volume 14, 1980, Volume 37, 1986.
Dictionary of Literary Biography, Volume 40: *Poets of Great Britain and Ireland since 1960, Part 1,* Gale, 1985.
Faas, Ekbert, *Ted Hughes: The Unaccommodated Universe,* Black Sparrow Press, 1980.
Gifford, Terry and Neil Roberts, *Ted Hughes: A Critical Study,* Faber, 1981.
Hamilton, Ian, editor, *The Modern Poet: Essays from "The Review,"* MacDonald, 1968.
King, P. R., *Nine Contemporary Poets: A Critical Introduction,* Methuen, 1979.
Sagar, Keith, *Ted Hughes,* Longman, 1972.
Sagar, Keith, *The Art of Ted Hughes,* enlarged edition, Cambridge University Press, 1978.
Sagar, Keith, *The Achievement of Ted Hughes,* Manchester University Press, 1983.

PERIODICALS

American Poetry Review, January-February, 1982.
Chicago Tribune Book World, February 22, 1981.
Listener, January 12, 1984.
Literary Review, spring, 1981.
Los Angeles Times Book Review, August 10, 1980.
New Republic, September 3, 1984.
New Statesman, January 4, 1980.
Newsweek, April 12, 1971.
New York Review of Books, June 10, 1982.
New York Times Book Review, July 20, 1980.
Time, April 5, 1971.
Times (London), January 8, 1987.
Times Literary Supplement, January 4, 1980.

*   *   *

HUGO, Grant
See CABLE, James (Eric)

*   *   *

HUNTER, Robert E(dwards) 1940-

PERSONAL: Born May 1, 1940, in Cambridge, MA; son of Robert, Jr. (a businessman) and Inez (Evans) Hunter; married Shireen Tahmasseb, 1980. *Education:* Wesleyan University, Middletown, CT, B.A. (with honors), 1962; London School of Economics and Political Science, London, Ph.D., 1969. *Politics:* Democrat. *Religion:* Protestant.

ADDRESSES: Home—613 Maryland Ave. N.E., Washington, D.C. 20002. *Office*—Center for Strategic and International Studies, Georgetown University, 1800 K St. N.W., Washington, D.C. 20006.

CAREER: U.S. Department of the Navy, Polaris Project, Washington, D.C. and London, England, administrative management intern, summers, 1961-63; assistant to Douglass Cater (special assistant to President Lyndon B. Johnson), Washington, D.C., 1964-65; University of London, London School of Economics and Political Science, London, England, lecturer in international relations, 1967-69; writer for 1968 presidential candidate Hubert H. Humphrey, 1968, 1969-70; Johns Hopkins University, School of Advanced International Studies, Washington, D.C., professional lecturer in international studies, 1972-73; foreign policy advisor to Senator Edward Kennedy, 1973-77; National Security Council, Washington, D.C., director of West European Affairs, 1977-79, director of Middle East Affairs, 1979-81; Georgetown University, Washington, D.C., senior fellow in Middle East studies of Center for Strategic and International Studies, 1981-89, professorial lecturer, 1983, director of European studies, 1983—, vice-president of regional programs, 1989—. Research associate, International Institute for Strategic Studies (London), 1967, 1968-69; fellow, Overseas Development Council, 1970-72, senior fellow, 1972-73. Associate executive director of platform committee, Democratic National Convention, 1972. Special advisor on Lebanon to the Speaker of the U.S. House of Representatives, 1983-84; head consultant to the National Bipartisan Commission on Central America, 1983-84.

MEMBER: International Institute for Strategic Studies, Council on Foreign Relations, American Political Science Association, Arms Control Association, Chicago Council on Foreign Relations, Phi Beta Kappa.

AWARDS, HONORS: Fulbright scholarship, London, England, 1962-63; Sustained Superior Performance Award from the National Security Council, 1979.

WRITINGS:

(With Michael Howard) *Israel and the Arab World: The Crisis of 1967* (monograph), Institute for Strategic Studies, 1967.

The Soviet Dilemma in the Middle East (monograph), Institute for Strategic Studies, 1969.

Security in Europe, Elek, 1969, 2nd edition, Indiana University Press, 1972.

(Editor and contributor) *The United States and the Developing World: Agenda for Action,* Overseas Development Council, 1973.

(Editor with John E. Reilly) *Development Today: A New Look at U.S. Relations with the Poor Countries,* Praeger, 1972.

President Control of Foreign Policy, Center for Strategic and International Studies, 1982.

(Editor) *Grand Strategy for the Western Alliance,* Westview, 1984.

(Editor) *NATO: The Next Generation,* Westview, 1984.

(Editor with Walter Laqueur) *European Peace Movements and the Future of the Western Alliance,* Transaction Books, 1984.

(Editor with Wayne Bernan and John Kennedy) *Making Government Work: From White House to Congress,* Westview, 1986.

(Editor with Dan Quayle and C. Elliott Farmer) *Strategic Defense and the Western Alliance,* Center for Strategic and International Studies, 1986.

(Editor) *Restructuring Alliance Commitments,* Center for Strategic and International Studies, 1988.

Organizing for National Security, Center for Strategic and International Studies, 1988.

Contributor to professional journals and to Washington, Baltimore, and New York newspapers; regular contributor to the *Los Angeles Times.* Contributing editor, *Washington Quarterly,* 1982-87.

HUSTON, James A(lvin) 1918-

PERSONAL: Born March 24, 1918, in Fairmount, IN; son of Alva Merrill and Nettie (Caskey) Huston; married Florence Webb, December 29, 1946 (died, 1982); married Anne Clark Marshall, June 5, 1983; children: (first marriage) Nita Diane, James Webb. *Education:* Indiana University, A.B. (with honors), 1939, A.M., 1940; New York University, Ph.D., 1947; additional study at St. John's College, Oxford, 1945, and University of Fribourg, summer, 1951. *Religion:* Christian (Disciples of Christ).

ADDRESSES: Home—300 Langhorne Lane, Lynchburg, VA 24501.

CAREER: Purdue University, Lafayette, IN, instructor, 1946-48, assistant professor, 1948-53, associate professor, 1953-60, professor of history, 1960-72; Lynchburg College, Lynchburg, VA, dean, 1972-84. Historian, Department of the Army, Office of Chief of Military History, 1951-53; E. J. King Professor of Maritime History, Naval War College, 1959-60; professor of international affairs and director of European studies, National War College, 1966-67, 1971-72. *Military service:* U.S. Army, infantry, 1942-46, 1951-53; became major; received Bronze Star with oak leaf cluster. U.S. Army Reserve, 1939-72; became colonel.

MEMBER: Southern Historical Association, Acacia, Phi Beta Kappa, Phi Delta Kappa.

WRITINGS:

Combat History of 134th Infantry, Army & Navy Publishing, 1948.

Biography of a Battalion, Courier Press, 1950.

Across the Face of France: Liberation and Recovery, 1944-1963, Purdue University, 1963.

Sinews of War, Office of Chief of Military History, 1966.

Out of the Blue: U.S. Army Airborne Operations in World War II, Purdue University, 1972.

(Editor) *Classical Selections on Great Issues,* ten volumes, University Press of America, 1982.

One for All: The United States and International Logistics through the Formative Period of NATO (1949-1969), University of Delaware Press, 1984.

Counterpoint: Tecumseh vs. William Henry Harrison (novel), Brunswick Publishing, 1987.

Outposts and Allies: U.S. Army Logistics in the Cold War, 1945-1953, Susquehana University Press, 1988.

Guns and Butter, Powder and Rice: U.S. Army Logistics in the Korean War, Susquehana University Press, 1989.

(With wife, Anne Marshall Huston) *Under the Double Cross* (novel), International University, 1989.

Logistics of Liberty, University of Delaware Press, 1990.

Contributor to books, including *An Introduction to American Government,* 1954, *D-Day: The Normandy Invasion in Retrospect,* 1971, and *Dictionary of American History,* 1976. Contributor of articles to history and military journals.

WORK IN PROGRESS: The Big Push: U.S. Army Logistics in World War I; School Days, with wife, Anne Marshall Huston, a critique of education.

SIDELIGHTS: James A. Huston told *CA:* "Writing is an extension of personality and a sharing of ideas and experience with others, and in this sharing the writer as well as the reader has an opportunity for growth. History is an extension of experience by which we gain perspective toward understanding situations and problems of our own day and from which we gain the basis for imagination in meeting current situations and problems. In the novel one is able, in a way, to deal with truth in an even greater dimension than in history. And in this larger sense the writer is no less concerned with truth and with themes which have continuing meaning than in writing history."

BIOGRAPHICAL/CRITICAL SOURCES:

PERIODICALS

Choice, May, 1973.
Indiana Magazine of History, September, 1967.
Journal of Southern History, August, 1967.

I

IFKOVIC, Edward 1943-

PERSONAL: Born June 16, 1943, in North Branford, CT; son of Anthony J. (a pattern maker) and Anna (Farkash) Ifkovic. *Education:* Southern Connecticut State University, B.S. (magna cum laude), 1965; University of North Carolina, M.A., 1966; University of Massachusetts, Ph.D., 1972.

ADDRESSES: Home—462 Broadview Terrace, Hartford, CT 06106. *Office*—Department of English, Tunxis Community College, Farmington, CT 06032.

CAREER: High school English teacher in Branford, CT, 1966-69; University of Massachusetts, Amherst, part-time lecturer in English, 1969-72; Tunxis Community College, Farmington, CT, assistant professor, 1972-74, professor of English, 1974—, chairman of department, 1974-77.

MEMBER: Modern Language Association of America, Popular Culture Association, Multi-Ethnic Literature in the United States.

WRITINGS:

(Editor) *American Letter: Immigrant and Ethnic Writing,* Prentice-Hall, 1975.
The Yugoslavs in America, Lerner, 1977.
For Love of Country: The Development of an American Identity in the Popular Novel, 1893-1913, Revisionist Press, 1976.
Anna Marinkovich (novel), Manyland Books, 1980.
Dream Street: The American Movies and the Popular Imagination (two volumes), Revisionist Press, 1980.
Mr. Dooley and Mr. Dunne: A Study of Finley Peter Dunne and His Mr. Dooley, Revisionist Press, 1982.
(Editor with Robert Di Pietro) *Ethnic Perspectives in American Literature: The European Contribution,* Modern Language Association of America, 1983.

Contributor to literary magazines, including *America, Review of Comparative Literature, American Notes and Queries, Journal of Popular Culture, Whitman Review, Crescent Review, Matica,* and *Zajednicar.*

WORK IN PROGRESS: Suppertime, a novel.

SIDELIGHTS: Edward Ifkovic wrote: "While I was a graduate student I met a woman from Zagreb, Croatia, in Yugoslavia, and she brought me back to my own Croatian roots. Not only did I explore the history of my family in America—dating from grandparents who arrived at Ellis Island around 1907—but I explored the history, literature, and language of the Old Country. In the process I came home to myself as an American with a particular ethnic history. . . . I saw ethnicity not as a divisive chauvinistic force but, instead, a force that leads out of diversity into unity. . . . I have been especially excited by the rise of the 'unmelted' white ethnics—the Polish, the Italian, the Jews, etc.— following after the new Black and Red consciousness."

BIOGRAPHICAL/CRITICAL SOURCES:

PERIODICALS

Library Journal, June 15, 1981.

* * *

IGGERS, Georg G(erson) 1926-

PERSONAL: Born December 7, 1926, in Hamburg, Germany; naturalized U.S. citizen; son of Alfred G. (a salesman) and Lizzie (Minden) Iggers; married Wilma Abeles (a college professor), December 23, 1948; children: Jeremy, Daniel, Karl Jonathan. *Education:* University of Richmond, B.A., 1944; University of Chicago, A.M., 1945, Ph.D., 1951; New School for Social Research, graduate study, 1945-46.

ADDRESSES: Home—100 Ivyhurst Rd., Buffalo, NY 14226. *Office*—Department of History, State University of New York at Buffalo, Buffalo, NY 14261.

CAREER: University of Akron, Akron, OH, instructor in German and Humanities, 1948-49; Philander Smith College, Little Rock, AR, associate professor of history, 1950-57; Dillard University, New Orleans, LA, associate professor, 1957-59, professor of history, 1959-63; Roosevelt University, Chicago, IL, associate professor of history, 1963-65; State University of New York at Buffalo, professor of history, 1965—, distinguished professor, 1978—, chair of department, 1981—. Visiting professor, University of Arkansas, 1956-57; visiting associate professor, Tulane University, 1958-60, and 1963; visiting professor, University of Rochester, 1970-71. Chairperson, Military and Draft Counseling Center of Buffalo.

MEMBER: International Commission on Historiography (vice-president, 1980 and 1990—), American Historical Association, French Historical Society, National Association for the Advancement of Colored People (chairperson of education committee of branches in Little Rock, New Orleans, and Buffalo), Peace Center of Western New York.

AWARDS, HONORS: American Philosophical Society grant, 1960; Guggenheim Foundation fellow, 1960-61; Rockefeller Foundation fellow, 1961-62; National Endowment for the Humanities senior fellow, 1971-72, 1978-79, and 1985-86; Fulbright Commission honorary fellow, 1978-79 and 1985-86, fellow, 1987; Erasmus Kittler Medal of the Technische Hochschule Darmstadt (West Germany), 1988; elected foreign member of the Academy of Science of the German Democratic Republic, 1990.

WRITINGS:

The Cult of Authority, Nijhoff, 1958.
(Editor and translator) *The Doctrine of Saint-Simon,* Beacon Press, 1958, reprinted, Schocken Books, 1972.
The German Conception of History: The National Tradition of Historical Thought from Herder to the Present, Wesleyan University Press, 1968, reprinted, 1983.
(Co-editor) Leopold von Ranke, *The Theory and Practice of History,* Bobbs-Merrill, 1973.
New Directions in European Historiography, Wesleyan University Press, 1975, revised edition, 1984.
(Co-editor) *International Handbook of Historical Studies: Contemporary Research and Theory,* Greenwood Press, 1979.
(Editor) *The Social History of Politics: Critical Perspectives in West German Historical Writing since 1945,* St. Martin, 1985.
(Editor with James M. Powell) *Leopold von Ranke and the Shaping of the Historical Discipline,* Syracuse University Press, 1989.
(Editor) *Marxist Historiography in Transformation: Historical Writings in East Germany in the 1980s,* Berg Publishers, 1991.

Contributor to professional journals.

WORK IN PROGRESS: A history of modern historiography.

＊　　＊　　＊

IGO, John N., Jr. 1927-

PERSONAL: Born May 29, 1927, in San Antonio, TX; son of John N. and Anna (Woller) Igo. *Education:* Trinity University, B.A., 1948, M.A., 1952. *Politics:* Democrat. *Religion:* Catholic. *Avocational interests:* Spanish survivals in the Southwest; Mexican literature; pre-Columbian literature; the 1890s; commedia dell'arte; myth.

ADDRESSES: Home—12505 Woller Rd., San Antonio, TX 78249. *Office*—Department of English, San Antonio College, San Antonio, TX 78284.

CAREER: Trinity University, San Antonio, TX, instructor in English and acquisitions librarian, 1952-53; San Antonio College, San Antonio, TX, 1953—, began as associate professor, now professor of English. Former chairman of parish board, Our Lady of Guadalupe Church, Helotes, TX.

MEMBER: Conference of College Teachers of English, Southwest American Literature Association, Texas Folklore Society, San Antonio Theatre Council (former chairman), National Poetry Foundation.

AWARDS, HONORS: National Society of Arts and Letters, National Literature Award, 1954, for poem, "The Third Temptation of St. John"; Southwest Writer's Conference, Chapbook Publication Award, 1962; Piper Foundation, Piper Professor of 1974; Nortex Publication Award for book of poems, 1977, for *Alien;* archbishop's outstanding service medal, 1976; Grothaus distinguished library service medal, Bexar Library Association, 1986.

WRITINGS:

God of Gardens (poems), American Weave Press, 1962.
(Editor) *Yanaguana,* privately printed by Flotsam Press, 1963.
A Chamber Faust (poems), Wake-Brook House, 1964.
Igo on Poetry (lectures), privately printed by Grace Philippi, 1965.
The Tempted Monk (poems), Hors Commerce Press, 1967.
Los Pastores, San Antonio College Library, 1967.
No Harbor, Else (poems), Et Cetera Press, 1972.
Golgotha (poem), Et Cetera Press, 1973.
Day of Elegies (poems), Et Cetera Press, 1975.
Alien (poems), Nortex Press, 1977.
San Antonio Remembers Will Rogers on the Centenary of His Birth, November 4th, 1879-1979, [San Antonio, TX], 1979.
Tropic of Gemini, Mullenix, 1981.
A Companion to 'Los Pastores', privately printed, 1987.
The Mitotes (poems), National Poetry Foundation, 1989.

Staff reviewer for *Choice* magazine, 1964—; theatre critic, *North San Antonio Times,* 1979-80 and 1983—, and *San Antonio Light,* 1981—. Contributor to *Poet Lore, Quixote,* and *Southwest Review.*

WORK IN PROGRESS: The J.V. Sonnets, a sonnet cycle; a one-man play about Aubrey Beardsley, *Aubrey, A Soiree; Huero, By Juan Yovoy,* a novel.

＊　　＊　　＊

IRLAND, David
See GREEN, Julian (Hartridge)

J

JACOBS, Ruth Harriet 1924-
(Ruth Miller)

PERSONAL: Born November 15, 1924, in Boston, MA; daughter of Samuel J. and Jane (Gordon) Miller; married Neal Jacobs, July 18, 1948 (divorced); children: Eliha, Edith Jane, Aaron Joel (deceased). *Education:* Boston University, B.S., 1964, postdoctoral study, 1977-78; Brandeis University, M.A., 1966, Ph.D., 1969. *Religion:* Quaker.

ADDRESSES: Home—75 Highledge Ave., Wellesley, MA 02181. *Office*—Wellesley College Center for Research on Women, Wellesley, MA 01610.

CAREER: Boston Herald-Traveler, Boston, MA, reporter, 1943-49; Boston University, Boston, MA, assistant professor, 1969-74, professor of sociology, 1974-82; Clark University, Worcester, MA, professor of sociology and department chairperson, 1982-89. Visiting professor, College of William and Mary, Williamsburg, VA, 1990; senior lecturer, Regis College, Weston, MA, 1990-91. Elderhostel teacher at the Rowe Conference Center, Rowe, MA, Regis College, Weston, MA, and Cook Theological School, Tempe, AZ. Affiliated with Wellesley College Center for Research on Women and Boston University Gerontology Center. Consultant in gerontology.

MEMBER: American Sociological Association, Society for the Study of Social Problems, American Aging Society, Clinical Sociology Association, Sociologists for Women in Society, Eastern Sociological Society, Massachusetts Sociological Association (vice-president, 1977-78), Boston Society for Gerontological Psychiatry, Center for Understanding Aging.

AWARDS, HONORS: American Association of University Women fellowship, 1972; grants from National Institute of Mental Health, 1972, 1975, National Science Foundation, 1977, and U.S. Department of Education, 1979-81; creative writing fellowships from Edna St. Vincent Millay Colony, Ossabaw, Alfred University, and Alden Dow Creativity Center; grants from Massachusetts Foundation for the Humanities, Public Policy, Wellesley and Weston arts foundations to teach creative writing to senior citizens; grant from Wellesley College to study depression in women.

WRITINGS:

Life After Youth: Female, Forty, What Next?, Beacon, 1979.

(With Barbara Vinick) *Re-Engagement in Later Life: Re-Employment and Re-Marriage,* Greylock, 1979.

Button, Button, Who Has the Button (poetic drama), Clark, University, 1983. *Older Women Surviving and Thriving,* Family Service America, 1988.

Out of Their Mouths, American Studies Press, 1988.

Contributor of about thirty articles to journals in sociology, anthropology, philosophy, psychology, history, and education, and of several poems to periodicals. Also contributor of articles and poems under name Ruth Miller to *Broomstick* and other periodicals.

WORK IN PROGRESS: Creative Living; an autobiography; a book of poetry; a book on depression in women.

SIDELIGHTS: Ruth Jacobs wrote: "Besides being a sociologist and poet, I am interested in a variety of other things. In 1977-78 I attended medical school to add to my gerontological expertise. I am especially interested in what happens to women when they age, and in *Life After Youth* I present a typology of role available for today's older women. In *Older Women Surviving and Thriving,* I present a twelve-session workshop model with handouts for self-help and leader-led groups. In *Button, Button, Who Has the Button,* I have written a full-length poetic drama, for reading or performing about twenty-one American women of all ages and types. This has been used at many conferences, churches, colleges, [and] woman's organizations.

"What I think I am dealing with in all my work is the concept of expendability—that at various points in history or in various places, certain people are considered unneeded and allowed to be expendable in the name of the economic or national good, or just through inadvertence or callousness. I have been more fortunate than many women in re-engaging life after my childrearing days were over. But I have a great deal of empathy and sympathy for women who are without meaningful roles in later life. *Life After Youth* is an attempt to help such women and the men in their lives, just as my writing on war or adolescence is aimed at helping other kinds of people. My writing stems from my social concern."

"Now at sixty-five I have given up a tenured university professorship for the second time and am teaching only now and then full time as a visiting professor. This allows me more time for writing and teaching poetry writing to senior citizens and for doing speaking and leading workshops on aging."

BIOGRAPHICAL/CRITICAL SOURCES:

PERIODICALS

Change, July, 1977.
New Directions for Women, summer, 1979.

* * *

JANIK, Carolyn 1940-

PERSONAL: Born August 29, 1940, in New Britain, CT; daughter of Leon V. (a grocer) and Genevieve (a bookkeeper; maiden name, Pustelnik) Lech; married Joseph J. Janik (an electrical engineer), August 4, 1962; children: David, Laura, William. *Education:* Mount Holyoke College, A.B., 1962; Southern Connecticut State College, M.S., 1972. *Religion:* Roman Catholic. *Avocational interests:* Music, reading, white water rafting, travel.

ADDRESSES: Home and office—29 Old Coach Rd., Basking Ridge, NJ 07920. *Agent*—Ellen Levine, 432 Park Ave. S., New York, NY 10016.

CAREER: High school English teacher in Glastonbury, CT, 1962-63; Allied Brokers, Branford, CT, real estate agent, 1968-70; John P. Hurley, Realtor, Morris Plains, NJ, real estate agent, beginning 1973.

MEMBER: American Society of Journalists and Authors.

WRITINGS:

The House Hunt Game, Macmillan, 1979.
Selling Your Home, Macmillan, 1980.
The Woman's Guide to Selling Residential Real Estate Successfully, Everest House, 1981.
The Complete Guide to Condos and Co-ops, New American Library, 1983.
All America's Real Estate Book, Viking, 1985.
Money-Making Real Estate, Viking, 1988.
Positive Moves, Weidenfield & Nicolson, 1988.
The Barn Book, W. H. Smith, 1990.
. . .And A Time to Sell, Penguin Books, 1991.
How You Can Profit from the S & L Bailout, Bantam, 1991.

SIDELIGHTS: "Although still licensed as a real estate agent, I am no longer working actively in the field," Carolyn Janik told *CA.* With regard to her writing, she added: "I try always to write in a conversational, readable style, for I feel every book is a conversation with the author (and always autobiographical)."

* * *

JOHNS, Janetta
See QUIN-HARKIN, Janet

* * *

JONES, Rodney W(illiam) 1943-

PERSONAL: Born July 16, 1943, in Landour, India; U.S. citizen born abroad; son of E. Keith (an Episcopalian minister) and Ruth (Vanleer) Jones; married Dawn Elaine Sestina (a musician), 1965; children: Alexander Keith, Gregory Millington. *Education:* Juniata College, A.B. (magna cum laude), 1964; Columbia University, M.A., 1965, Ph.D. (with distinction), 1970.

ADDRESSES: Home—11632 Sourwood Lane, Reston, VA 22091. *Office*—Washington Council on Non-Proliferation,

Johns Hopkins Foreign Policy Institute, 1619 Massachusetts Ave., N.W., Washington, DC 20036.

CAREER: Juniata College, Huntingdon, PA, instructor, 1966; Kansas State University, Manhattan, assistant professor of political science, 1969-70; Pomona College and Claremont Graduate School, Claremont, CA, assistant professor, 1970-76; University of Texas, Austin, visiting assistant professor of government, 1976-77; U.S. Department of State, Washington, DC, international affairs fellow of Council on Foreign Relations, 1977-78; Columbia University, New York, NY, associate professor of political science and member of Institute of War and Peace Studies, 1978-80; Georgetown University, Washington, DC, senior fellow and director of nuclear policy studies at Center for Strategic and International Studies, 1980-86. Consultant to federal government agencies. President, Policy Architects International, 1985—; executive director, Non-Proliferation Initiatives, 1986-89, and Washington Council on Non-Proliferation, 1989—.

MEMBER: International Institute of Strategic Studies, American Political Science Association, Middle East Institute, Association for Asian Studies, Asia Society, Society for Values in Higher Education, Arms Control Association.

AWARDS, HONORS: Fulbright fellow in Pakistan, 1974; senior fellow, American Institute for Indian Studies, 1974-75; Wattamull Prize nomination, 1976, for *Urban Politics in India: Area, Power, and Policy in a Penetrated System;* fellow, Council on Foreign Relations international affairs, 1977-78.

WRITINGS:

Urban Politics in India: Area, Power, and Policy in a Penetrated System, University of California Press, 1974.
Nuclear Proliferation: Islam, the Bomb, and South Asia, Sage Publications, 1981.
(With Steven A. Hildreth) *Modern Weapons and Third World Powers,* Westview, 1984.
(Editor) *Small Nuclear Forces and U.S. Security Policy: Threats and Potential Conflict in the Middle East and South Asia,* Lexington, 1984.
The Nuclear Suppliers and Non-Proliferation, Lexington, 1985.
Emerging Powers: Defense and Security in the Third World, Praeger, 1986.

CONTRIBUTOR

Donald B. Rosenthal, editor, *The City in Indian Politics,* Thomson Press (Delhi), 1976.
Manzuruddin Ahmed, editor, *Contemporary Pakistan: Politics, Economy, Society,* Carolina Academic, 1980.
Mahesh J. Mehta, editor, *Upadhyaya's Integral Humanism,* Deendayal Upadhyaya Committee of America (Edison, NJ), 1980.
William J. Taylor and Steven A. Maaranen, editors, *The Future of Conflict in the 1980s,* Lexington Books, 1982.
John J. Stremlau, editor, *The Foreign Policy Priorities of Developing Countries,* Westview, 1982.
Taylor and Robert Kupperman, editors, *Strategic Requirements for the Army to the Year 2000,* Lexington Books, 1984.
Jozef Goldblat, editor, *Non-Proliferation: The Why and Wherefore,* Stockholm International Peace Research Institute, 1985.
Neil Joeck, editor, *Strategic Consequences of Nuclear Proliferation,* Frank Cass, 1986.
William C. Potter, editor, *International Nuclear Trade and Non-Proliferation,* Lexington, 1990.

Contributor to political science and Asian studies journals and *Washington Quarterly.*

WORK IN PROGRESS: Research on third world security issues, military uses of space, and nuclear arms control.

SIDELIGHTS: Rodney W. Jones once told *CA:* "My interests are in shaping public policy and contributing to public education in national security and nuclear arms control. I am broadly concerned about issues of war and peace. I have had special experience with the Middle East and South Asia. Extensive work on India and Pakistan has led to foreign language competence in Hindi and Urdu. My recent work focuses on the proliferation of nuclear weapons as a threat to peace, and on policies that can help reduce the dangers of nuclear war resulting from proliferation.

"The two volumes on 'small nuclear forces' speculate about what the Middle East and South Asia will look like at the turn of the century, in the event nuclear powers emerge in those troubled regions. Both explore the problems of managing conflicts and crises after further proliferation has occurred. They conclude that the difficulties we then would face justify redoubled efforts to prevent or inhibit nuclear weapons spread while this remains possible. These studies put special emphasis on the defense policy dilemmas that additional proliferation will entail, opening up an area of study where little prior work has been done."

K

KARAGEORGHIS, Vassos 1929-

PERSONAL: Born April 29, 1929, in Trikomo, Cyprus; son of George Georghiou (a mason) and Panayiota (Georghiou) Karageorghis; married Jacqueline Girard (a teacher), March 21, 1953; children: Clio, Andreas. *Education:* University of London, B.A. (honors), 1952, certificate in archaeology, 1952, Ph.D., 1957. *Religion:* Greek Orthodox.

ADDRESSES: Home—16 Kastorias St., Nicosia 133, Cyprus. *Office*—Leventis Foundation, 28 Sofoulis St., Chanteclair Blvd., Office 114, Nicosia, Cyprus.

CAREER: Cyprus Museum, Nicosia, Cyprus, assistant curator, 1952-60, curator, 1960-63; Republic of Cyprus, Department of Antiquities, Nicosia, acting director, 1963-64, director of antiquities, 1964-89; advisor on cultural heritage to the President of the Republic of Cyprus, 1989—. Visiting professor or lecturer at universities and institutions in the United States and Europe, including University of California, Berkeley, 1967, State University of New York at Albany, 1973—, University of Aberdeen, 1975, and Institute for Advanced Study, Princeton, 1989-90; Oxford University, visiting fellow, Merton College, 1979, 1988, and All Souls College, 1982, senior research fellow, Merton College, 1980. Member of governing body of Cyprus Research Centre; chairman, National Committees for International Council of Museums and Monuments and Sites, 1964-89; council chairman, Pierides Foundation, 1990—; council member, A. G. Leventis Foundation, and Cultural Foundation of Bank of Cyprus, both 1990—. Director of excavations at Salamis, 1952-73, the Necropolis at Akhera and Pendayia, 1960, the Necropolis at Salamis, 1962-67, Kition, 1962-81, and Maa-Palaeokastro, Pyla-Kokkinokremos, 1979-87.

MEMBER: Greek Archaeological Society (honorary member of council), British Academy (corresponding fellow), Royal Society of Arts (fellow), German Archaeological Institute, Academie des Inscriptions et Belles Lettres, Royal Society for Humanistic Studies (Lund; fellow), Accademia dei Lincei, Royal Swedish Academy (foreign member), Austrian Academy of Sciences (corresponding member), Society of Antiquaries of London (honorary fellow), Academy of Athens (corresponding member).

AWARDS, HONORS: Prize from Societe des Etudes Grecques, Sorbonne, University of Paris, 1966; chevalier de l'Ordre National de la Legion d'Honneur, 1971; honorary doctorates from University of Lyon and University of Goeteborg, 1972, University of Athens, 1973, University of Birmingham, 1974, University of Toulouse, 1980, Brock University, 1987, Free University (Brussels), 1990, and Oxford University, 1990; fellow of University of London, 1975; R. B. Bennett Commonwealth Prize, 1978; Order of Merit, first class, Federal Republic of Germany, 1980.

WRITINGS:

Treasures in the Cyprus Museum, Department of Antiquities, Ministry of Communications and Works, Republic of Cyprus, 1962.

Corpus Vasorum Antiquorum, Department of Antiquities, Ministry of Communications and Works, Republic of Cyprus, Volume 1: *Cyprus Museum (Nicosia), Larnaca District Museum,* 1963, Volume 2: *Private Collections,* 1965.

Sculptures from Salamis, Department of Antiquities, Ministry of Communications and Works, Republic of Cyprus, Volume 1, 1964, Volume 2 (with Cornelius C. Vermeule), 1966.

Salamis, Department of Antiquities, Ministry of Communications and Works, Republic of Cyprus, 1964.

Nouveaux Documents pour l'Etude du Bronze Recent a Chypre, recueil critique et commente, Edition de Boccard, 1965.

Anaskaphai Salaminos, 1964-66, Department of Antiquities, Ministry of Communications and Works, Republic of Cyprus, 1966.

Excavations in the Necropolis of Salamis, Department of Antiquities, Ministry of Communications and Works, Republic of Cyprus, Volume 1, 1967, Volume 2, 1970, Volume 3, 1973, Volume 4, 1978.

Mycenaean Art from Cyprus, Department of Antiquities, Ministry of Communications and Works, Republic of Cyprus, 1968.

Cyprus, Hippocrene, 1968.

Salamis: Recent Discoveries in Cyprus, McGraw, 1969 (published in England as *Salamis in Cyprus: Homeric, Hellenistic, and Roman,* Thames & Hudson, 1969).

The Ancient Civilization of Cyprus, Cowles Education Corp., 1969.

(With Hans-Guenter Buchholz) *Altaegaeis und Altkypros,* E. Wasmuth, 1971, translation by Francisca Garvie published as *Prehistoric Greece and Cyprus: An Archaeological Handbook,* Phaidon, 1973.

Cypriote Antiquities in the Pierides Collection, Larnaca, Cyprus, privately printed, 1973.

(With Jean Des Gagniers) *La ceramique Chypriote de style figure: Age du fer, 1050-500 av. J. C.,* two volumes, Consiglio nazionale della ricerche, Istituto per gli studi micenei ed egeo-anatolici, 1974.

(With Darrell A. Amyx and others) *Cypriote Antiquities in San Francisco Bay Area Collections,* Soedra Vaegen, 1974.

(With Manolis Andronikos and Manolis Chatzidakis) *Ta hellenika mouseia,* [Athens], 1974, translation by Kay Cicellis published as *The Greek Museums,* Barrie & Jenkins, 1975.

Excavations at Kition, [Nicosia], Volume 1: *The Tombs,* 1974, Volume 4: *The Non-Cypriote Pottery,* 1981, Volume 5: *The Pre-Phoenician Levels,* 1985.

Cyprus Museum and Archaeological Sites of Cyprus, translated by Cicellis, new edition, Caratzas Brothers, 1975.

Alaas: A Protogeometric Necropolis in Cyprus, [Nicosia], 1975.

View from the Bronze Age: Mycenaean and Phoenician Discoveries at Kition, Dutton, 1976 (published in England as *Kition: Mycenaean and Phoenician Discoveries in Cyprus,* Thames & Hudson, 1976).

(With G. Clerc, E. Lagarce, and J. Leclant) *Fouilles de Kition,* Volume 2: *Objets egyptiens et egyptisants,* [Nicosia], 1976.

Ho politismos tes prolstorikes Kyprou, Ekdotike Athenon, 1976, translation published as *The Civilization of Prehistoric Cyprus,* 1976, Alpine Fine Arts Collection, 1983.

(With Des Gagniers) *Vases et figurines de l'age du bronze ancien et du bronze moyen a Chypre,* International Scholastic Book Service, 1976.

(With Paul Astrom and D. M. Bailey) *Hala Sultan Tekke: Excavations 1897-1971,* Paul Astroms Forlag, 1976.

The Goddess with Uplifted Arms in Cyprus, LiberLaeromedel/Gleerlup, 1977.

Recent Archeological Discoveries in Cyprus, Accademia nazionale dei Lincei, 1977.

Two Cypriote Sanctuaries of the End of the Cypro-Archaic Period, Consiglio nazionale delle ricerche, 1977.

(With C. G. Styrenius and M. G. Winbladh) *Cypriote Antiquities in the Medelhavsmuseet, Stockholm,* Volume 2: *Memoirs,* Medelhavsmuseet, 1977.

(With M. G. Guzzo Amadasi) *Fouilles de Kition,* Volume 3: *Inscriptions Pheniciennes,* [Nicosia], 1977.

(With Annie Caubet and Marguerite Yon) *Les Antiquites de Chypre: Age du Bronze,* Ministere de la culture, Editions de la Reunion des musees nationaux, 1981.

Ancient Cyprus: 7000 Years of Art and Archaeology, Louisiana State University Press, 1981.

Archaeology of Cyprus, Louisiana State University Press, 1982.

(With Emily Vermeule) *Mycenaean Pictorial Vase Painting,* Harvard University Press, 1982.

Cyprus: From the Stone Age to the Romans, Thames & Hudson, 1982.

(Editor with James D. Muhly and Robert Maddin) *International Archeological Symposium "Early Metallurgy in Cyprus, 4000-500 B.C.,"* Pierides Foundation/Department of Antiquities, Republic of Cyprus, 1982.

Palaepaphos-Skales: An Iron Age Cemetery in Cyprus, two volumes, Universitaetsverlag Konstanz, 1983.

(With M. Demas) *Pyla-Kokkinokremos: A Late 13th Century B.C. Fortified Settlement in Cyprus,* Department of Antiquities, Republic of Cyprus, 1984.

(Editor with Muhly) *Cyprus at the Close of the Late Bronze Age,* [Nicosia], 1984.

(With F. G. Maier) *Paphos, Archaeology, and History,* A. G. Leventis Foundation, 1984.

(With others) *Ancient Cypriote Art in the Pierides Foundation* (bilingual edition), Pierides Foundation, 1985.

(Editor) *Archaeology in Cyprus, 1960-1985,* A. G. Leventis Foundation, 1985.

(Editor) *La necropole d'Amathonte, Tombes 113-367,* Volume 2 (with O. Picard and C. Tytgat): *Ceramiques non chypriotes,* Volume 3 (with A. Hermary): *1: The Terracottas; 2: Statuettes, Sarcophages et steles decorees,* A. G. Leventis Foundation/Ecole Francaise d'Athenes, Service des Antiquites de Chypre, 1987.

The Archeology of Cyprus: The Ninety Years after Myres, [Oxford], 1987.

(With Demas) *Excavations at Maa-Palaeokastro 1979-1986,* [Nicosia], 1988.

Blacks in Ancient Cypriot Art, Menil Foundation, 1988.

The End of the Late Bronze Age in Cyprus, [Nicosia], 1990.

The A. G. Leventis Foundation and the Cultural Heritage of Cyprus, [Athens], 1990.

Tombs at Palaepaphos, [Nicosia], 1990.

Contributor to English, French, Greek, and German periodicals.

SIDELIGHTS: Vassos Karageorghis told *CA:* "I have been excavating and researching the archeology of Cyprus since 1952. My principle has been to publish the results of all my excavations in a definitive form, being conscious of the fact that an unpublished excavation is a negative contribution to scholarship. I have tried to be honest in my reporting knowing that perfection can never be achieved in a 'science' like archaeology, which demands continuous adaptation according to new evidence which constantly comes up from the ground as a result of new excavations. I have given ample 'food' and 'raw material' for students of Cypriote archaeology for many years to come. If some of my interpretations survive the test of time I shall be very happy.

"I have also written a number of popular books on Cypriote archaeology because I feel the need to share the enjoyments of discovery not only with my own colleagues but also with the wider public."

*   *   *

KEITH, Hamish
See CHAPMAN, James (Keith)

*   *   *

KEOHANE, Robert O(wen) 1941-

PERSONAL: Surname is pronounced Ko-han; born October 3, 1941, in Chicago, IL; son of Robert Emmet and Mary (Pieters) Keohane; married Sarah Ann Wright, June 16, 1962 (divorced, 1970); married Nannerl Overholser (president of Wellesley College), December 18, 1970; children: (first marriage) Sarah Elizabeth, Jonathan Wilmore; (second marriage) Nathaniel Owen, Stephan. *Education:* Shimer College, B.A., 1961; Harvard University, M.A., 1964, Ph.D., 1966.

ADDRESSES: Home—735 Washington St., Wellesley, MA 02181. *Office*—Center for International Affairs, Harvard University, Cambridge, MA 02138.

CAREER: Swarthmore College, Swarthmore, PA, instructor, 1965-67, assistant professor, 1967-71, associate professor of political science, 1971-73; Stanford University, Stanford, CA, associate professor, 1973-77, professor of political science, 1977-81, chairman of department, 1980-81; Brandeis University, Waltham, MA, professor of politics, 1981-85; Harvard University, Cambridge, MA, professor of government, 1985—, Stanfield Professor of International Peace, 1989—.

MEMBER: American Political Science Association (member of council, 1971-73), American Academy of Arts and Sciences, American Economic Association, Council on Foreign Relations, International Studies Association (president, 1988-89).

AWARDS, HONORS: Sumner prize, Harvard University, 1966; international affairs fellowship, Council on Foreign Relations, 1968-69, Grawemeyer Award for ideas improving world order, 1989.

WRITINGS:

(Editor with Joseph S. Nye) *Transnational Relations and World Politics,* Harvard University Press, 1972.
(With Nye) *Power and Independence: World Politics in Transition,* Little, Brown, 1977, 2nd edition, Scott, Foresman, 1989.
After Hegemony: Cooperation and Discord in the World Political Economy, Princeton University Press, 1984.
(Editor) *Neorealism and Its Critics,* Columbia University Press, 1986.
International Institutions and State Power: Essays in International Relations Theory, Westview, 1989.

Editor, *International Organization,* 1974-80. Contributor of articles to professional journals.

BIOGRAPHICAL/CRITICAL SOURCES:

PERIODICALS

Saturday Review, May 20, 1972.

* * *

KERNAN, Alvin B(ernard) 1923-

PERSONAL: Surname legally changed in 1943; born June 13, 1923, in Manchester, GA; son of Alvin Berbanks and Jimmie Katherine (Fletcher) Peters; married Suzanne Scoble, December 13, 1949; children: Geoffrey, Katherine, Marjorie, Alvin. *Education:* Williams College, B.A., 1949; Oxford University, B.A., 1951; Yale University, Ph.D., 1954.

ADDRESSES: Home—76 Battle Rd. Princeton, NJ 08540. *Office*—22 McCosh, Princeton University, Princeton, NJ 08540.

CAREER: Rensselaer Polytechnic Institute, Troy, NY, instructor in English, 1953-54; Yale University, New Haven, CT, instructor, 1954-59, assistant professor, 1959-63, associate professor, 1963-66, professor of English, 1966-73, associate provost, 1965-68, acting provost, 1970, director of Division of Humanities, 1970-72; Princeton University, Princeton, NJ, dean of Graduate School, 1973-77, Andrew Mellon and Avalon Professor of Humanities, 1977-88, professor emeritus, 1988—. *Military service:* U.S. Navy, 1941-45; served in Pacific theatre; became aviation chief petty officer; received Navy Cross, Distinguished Flying Cross, Air Medal.

MEMBER: Phi Beta Kappa.

AWARDS, HONORS: Morse fellowship, 1957-58; American Council of Learned Societies fellowship, 1961-62; National Endowment for the Humanities senior fellowships, 1968-69, 1981-82; William Clyde DeVane Medal for distinguished teaching from Yale chapter of Phi Beta Kappa, 1972; Berman Award in Humanities, Princeton University, 1984.

WRITINGS:

The Cankered Muse: Satire of the English Renaissance, Yale University Press, 1959.
Modern Satire, Harcourt, 1962.

The Plot of Satire, Yale University Press, 1965.
The Revels History of the Drama in English, Volume III: 1576-1613, Methuen, 1974.
The Playwright as Magician: Shakespeare's Image of the Poet in the English Public Theater, Yale University Press, 1979.
The Imaginary Library: An Essay on Literature and Society, Princeton University Press, 1982.
Printing Technology, Letters and Samuel Johnson, Princeton University Press, 1987.
Samuel Johnson and the Impact of Print, Princeton University Press, 1989.
The Death of Literature, Yale University Press, 1990.

EDITOR

William Shakespeare, *Julius Caesar,* Yale University Press, 1957.
Ben Jonson, *Volpone,* Yale University Press, 1962.
Character and Conflict: An Introduction to Drama, Harcourt, 1963, 2nd edition, 1969.
Shakespeare, *Othello,* New American Library, 1964.
Classics of the Modern Theater: Realism and After, Harcourt, 1965.
The Modern American Theater: A Collection of Critical Essays, Prentice-Hall, 1967.
(With J. Dennis Huston) *Classics of the Renaissance Theater,* Harcourt, 1969.
Modern Shakespearean Criticism: Essays on Style, Dramaturgy, and Major Plays, Harcourt, 1970.
(With Peter Brooks and Michael Holquist) *Man and His Fictions,* Harcourt, 1973.
Jonson, *The Alchemist,* Yale University Press, 1974.
(And author of foreword) *Two Renaissance Mythmakers, Christopher Marlowe and Ben Jonson,* Johns Hopkins University Press, 1977.

OTHER

General editor of Yale University Press series on Ben Jonson. Contributor to scholarly journals.

BIOGRAPHICAL/CRITICAL SOURCES:

PERIODICALS

Times Literary Supplement, June 20, 1980; September 3, 1982; December 18, 1987.

* * *

KING, Francis (Henry) 1923-
(Frank Cauldwell)

PERSONAL: Born March 4, 1923, in Adelboden, Switzerland; son of Eustace Arthur Cecil and Faith (Read) King. *Education:* Balliol College, Oxford, B.A., 1949, M.A., 1951.

ADDRESSES: Home—19 Gordon Place, London W8 4JE, England. *Agent*—A. M. Heath & Co., 40-42 William IV St., London WC2N 4DD, England.

CAREER: British Council lecturer in Florence, Italy, 1949-50, Salonica, Greece, 1950-52, and Athens, Greece, 1953-57, assistant representative in Helsinki, Finland, 1957-58, and regional director in Kyoto, Japan, 1959-63; *Sunday Telegraph,* London, England, literary critic, 1964—, drama critic, 1978—.

MEMBER: Royal Society of Literature (fellow), Society of Authors (England; chairman, 1975-77), PEN (president of English center, 1978—).

AWARDS, HONORS: Somerset Maugham Award, 1952, for *The Dividing Stream;* Katherine Mansfield Short Story Prize, 1965, for "The Japanese Umbrella"; Order of the British Empire, 1979; Yorkshire Post Prize, 1983.

WRITINGS:

To the Dark Tower (novel), Home & Van Thal, 1946.
Never Again (novel), Home & Van Thal, 1947.
An Air That Kills (novel), Home & Van Thal, 1948.
The Dividing Stream (novel), Longmans, Green, 1951.
Rod of Incantation (poems), Longmans, Green, 1952.
The Dark Glasses, Longmans, Green, 1954.
(Under pseudonym Frank Cauldwell) *The Firewalkers: A Memoir,* John Murray, 1955, reprinted under name Francis King, GMP, 1985.
(Editor) *Introducing Greece,* Methuen, 1956, revised edition, 1968.
The Widow (novel), Longmans, Green, 1957.
The Man on the Rock (novel), Pantheon, 1957.
So Hurt and Humiliated (short stories), Longmans, Green, 1959.
The Custom House (novel), Longmans, Green, 1961, Doubleday, 1962.
The Japanese Umbrella, and Other Stories, Longmans, Green, 1964.
The Last of the Pleasure Gardens (novel), Longmans, Green, 1965.
The Waves behind the Boat (novel), Longmans, Green, 1967.
The Brighton Belle, and Other Stories, Longmans, 1968.
A Domestic Animal (novel), Longmans, 1970.
(With Martin Huerlimann) *Japan,* translated from the German by D. J. S. Thomson, Thames & Hudson, 1970.
Flights (two short novels; contains "The Infection" and "The Cure"), Hutchinson, 1973.
A Game of Patience (novel), Hutchinson, 1974.
The Needle (novel), Hutchinson, 1975.
Hard Feelings, and Other Stories, Hutchinson, 1976.
Danny Hill: Memoirs of a Prominent Gentleman (farce), Hutchinson, 1977.
The Action (novel), Hutchinson, 1978.
E. M. Forster and His World, Scribner, 1978.
(Editor with Ronald Harwood) *New Stories,* Hutchinson, 1978.
Indirect Method, and Other Stories, Hutchinson, 1980.
(Editor and author of introduction) *My Sister and Myself: The Diaries of J. R. Ackerley,* Hutchinson, 1982.
Florence, Newsweek, 1982.
Act of Darkness (novel), Hutchinson, 1982, Little, Brown, 1983.
Voices in an Empty Room (novel), Little, Brown, 1984.
(Editor and author of introduction) Lafcadio Hearn, *Writings from Japan: An Anthology,* Penguin, 1984.
(Editor) *Twenty Stories: A South East Asia Collection,* Secker & Warburg, 1985.
One Is a Wanderer (selected stories), Little, Brown, 1985.
Frozen Music (novel), Hutchinson, 1987.
The Woman Who Was God (novel), Hutchinson, 1988.
Visiting Cards (novel), Constable, 1991.

Contributor to *Penguin Modern Stories, 12,* 1982.

SIDELIGHTS: A *New York Times* reviewer once referred to Francis King as a writer "with intensity of purpose skillfully concealed behind a facile style, swift-paced dialogue and a spoofing surface-irony." Others have used words such as "cold," "comfortless," and even "bloodless" to describe King's fiction, in which he grimly explores the "mad oddities of the human condition" in a very carefully composed and rather detached, yet completely gripping style. As a *Spectator* critic observes: "There has always been a dark side to Mr. King's novels, somewhat contradicting the conventional view of him as one of our more placid writers; although he is no Poe, and would not want to be, he is adept at casting various forms of terror and unease within his apparently calm, collected prose. . . . [He] never dabbles in overstatement. He is also too fastidious to bother with the throughly modern under-statement; he is, rather, a master of the precise statement—going very well with his constant effort to keep up appearances: the appearance of his characters, of his prose, and of the neatly but tightly formed shape of his narrative. But beneath this surface, some dark fantasies swoop and glitter. . . . [King's] darting imagination is only barely kept in check by the iron discipline he imposes upon his own writing."

A commentator in *Punch,* calling King "a master of the *frisson*" (literally, a shiver or shudder), notes that he has a "sure touch" in matters concerning "decadence and decay," or, as an *Observer Review* critic states, "murder, brutality and 'perversion' constantly appear in [King's stories in] the most surprising—and natural—way." A *Books and Bookmen* reviewer claims that readers "are at the mercy of whatever Mr. King chooses as his weapon: humour, wit, irony or compassion. His style is pared down to its lovely bones. His sentences lie in wait and blip you on the head, just as you were thinking how frank and nice they were. . . . His eye is wickedly sharp on detail, the eye of a painter, of a comedian. . . . [He] is fascinated by bizarre relationships. . . . [King writes] in gruesome but never tasteless detail. He is a fastidious, an elegant, a knowing writer."

King once told *CA:* "I see myself as being like a house-builder, patiently, persistently and laboriously placing brick on brick, to create the edifice that, however ramshackle, is my *oeuvre.* Some passers-by look up at that edifice and say 'That looks all right.' Others look up and say 'Shouldn't those windows be bigger? That roof looks as though it might leak.' I try not to be influenced by such comments, favourable or unfavourable. I merely want to carry out the invisible blue-print that is within me.

"When I once refused to accept the suggestions of an American editor as to how to improve one of my books, he wrote back resignedly: 'What a pity . . . We might have had a best-seller there.' Because of this mulishness (if that is how one must regard it), it is only in the last half-dozen years that my novels have started to make me an adequate income. In consequence I have always been obliged to do other jobs. . . . I do not regret the hours spent on these treadmills, since they have brought me into contact with people whom, otherwise, I might have never met. My years living abroad have been particularly valuable, freeing me from the English obsession with class. The profoundest experience of my life was my four- and-a-half years in Japan, where I developed self-discipline, a sense of duty and a love of hard work from the example of the Japanese.

"Critics often describe my view of the world as 'dark.' But it is a darkness illuminated (I hope) by acts of decency, generosity and valour. These acts are often performed in my novels (as in life) by seemingly insignificant people—the very old, the very young, the uneducated, the poor. Significantly, the woman whom I portray as a lay saint in *Act of Darkness* is, to most people in that novel, a figure of fun, to be mocked and patronised."

BIOGRAPHICAL/CRITICAL SOURCES:

BOOKS

Contemporary Literary Criticism, Gale, Volume 8, 1978, Volume 53, 1989.
Dictionary of Literary Biography, Volume 15: *British Novelists, 1930-1959,* Gale, 1983.

PERIODICALS

Books and Bookmen, June, 1968, December, 1975, November, 1978.

Book World, November 27, 1988.

Listener, April 27, 1967, September 12, 1974, October 2, 1975, December 16, 1976, October 19, 1978.

London Magazine, June, 1968.

Los Angeles Times, October 16, 1983.

New Statesman, June 23, 1967, September 5, 1975.

Newsweek, January 9, 1983.

New York Times, January 19, 1958, October 10, 1983, January 29, 1986.

New York Times Book Review, December 25, 1983, December 9, 1984, February 28, 1988, January 15, 1989.

Observer Review, April 28, 1968.

Punch, April 24, 1968.

Spectator, September 6, 1975, October 2, 1976, October 8, 1983.

Times (London), August 29, 1985, August 27, 1987, April 21, 1988.

Times Literary Supplement, May 11, 1967, September 13, 1974, April 29, 1978, November 14, 1980, April 30, 1982, October 23, 1983, September 13, 1985, April 29-May 5, 1988.

Washington Post Book World, December 7, 1984, March 27, 1988.

* * *

KIPLING, (Joseph) Rudyard 1865-1936

PERSONAL: Born December 30, 1865, in Bombay, India; died of intestinal hemorrhage, January 8, 1936, in London, England; buried in the Poets' Corner of Westminster Abbey in London; son of John Lockwood (an architect, teacher, and minister) and Alice (MacDonald) Kipling; married Caroline Starr Balestier, January 18, 1892; children: Josephine (died, 1899), John (killed in action, World War I), Elsie Bambridge. *Education:* Attended schools in England through the secondary level.

ADDRESSES: Home—Bateman's, Burwash, Sussex, England.

CAREER: Poet, essayist, novelist, journalist, and writer of short stories. Worked as a journalist for *Civil and Military Gazette,* Lahore, India, 1882-89; assistant editor and overseas correspondent for the Allahabad *Pioneer,* Allahabad, India, 1887-89; associate editor and correspondent for *The Friend,* Bloemfontein, South Africa, 1900, covering the Boer War. Rector of University of St. Andrews, 1922-25.

MEMBER: Academie des Sciences et Politiques (France; foreign associate member), Magdalene College, Cambridge (honorary fellow, 1932-36), Athenaeum Club (literary), Carlton Club (political).

AWARDS, HONORS: Poet laureate, 1895, and Order of Merit award (both refused); Nobel Prize for Literature, 1907; Gold Medal of Royal Society of Literature, 1926; LL.D. from McGill University, 1899; D.Litt. from Durham and Oxford universities, 1907, Cambridge University, 1908, Edinburgh University, 1920, Paris and Strasbourg universities, 1921; honorary Ph.D., Athens University, 1924.

WRITINGS:

POETRY

Schoolboy Lyrics, privately printed, 1881.

(With sister, Beatrice Kipling) *Echoes: By Two Writers,* Civil and Military Gazette Press (Lahore), 1884.

Departmental Ditties and Other Verses, Civil and Military Gazette Press, 1886, 2nd edition, enlarged, Thacker, Spink (Calcutta), 1886, 3rd edition, further enlarged, 1888, 4th edition, still further enlarged, W. Thacker (London), 1890, deluxe edition, 1898.

Departmental Ditties, Barrack-Room Ballads and Other Verses (contains the fifty poems of the fourth edition of *Departmental Ditties and Other Verses* and seventeen new poems later published as *Ballads and Barrack-Room Ballads*), United States Book Co., 1890, revised edition published as *Departmental Ditties and Ballads and Barrack-Room Ballads,* Doubleday & McClure, 1899.

Ballads and Barrack-Room Ballads, Macmillan, 1892, new edition, with additional poems, 1893, published as *The Complete Barrack-Room Ballads of Rudyard Kipling,* edited by Charles Carrington, Methuen, 1973, reprint published as *Barrack Room Ballads and Other Verses,* White Rose Press, 1987.

The Rhyme of True Thomas, D. Appleton, 1894.

The Seven Seas, D. Appleton, 1896, reprinted, Longwood Publishing Group, 1978.

Recessional (Victorian ode in commemoration of queen's jubilee), M. F. Mansfield, 1897.

Mandalay, drawings by Blanche McManus, M. F. Mansfield, 1898, reprinted, Doubleday, Page, 1921.

The Betrothed, drawings by McManus, M. F. Mansfield and A. Wessells, 1899.

Poems, Ballads, and Other Verses, illustrations by V. Searles, H. M. Caldwell, 1899.

Belts, A. Grosset, 1899.

Cruisers, Doubleday & McClure, 1899.

The Reformer, Doubleday, Page, 1901.

The Lesson, Doubleday, Page, 1901.

The Five Nations, Doubleday, Page, 1903.

The Muse Among the Motors, Doubleday, Page, 1904.

The Sons of Martha, Doubleday, Page, 1907.

The City of Brass, Doubleday, Page, 1909.

Cuckoo Song, Doubleday, Page, 1909.

A Patrol Song, Doubleday, Page, 1909.

A Song of the English, illustrations by W. Heath Robinson, Doubleday, Page, 1909.

If, Doubleday, Page, 1910, reprinted, Doubleday, 1959.

The Declaration of London, Doubleday, Page, 1911.

The Spies' March, Doubleday, Page, 1911.

Three Poems (contains "The River's Tale," "The Roman Centurion Speaks," "The Pirates in England"), Doubleday, Page, 1911.

Songs From Books, Doubleday, Page, 1912.

An Unrecorded Trial, Doubleday, Page, 1913.

For All We Have and Are, Methuen, 1914.

The Children's Song, Macmillan, 1914.

A Nativity, Doubleday, Page, 1917.

A Pilgrim's Way, Doubleday, Page, 1918.

The Supports, Doubleday, Page, 1919.

The Years Between, Doubleday, Page, 1919.

The Gods of the Copybook Headings, Doubleday, Page, 1919, reprinted, 1921.

The Scholars, Doubleday, Page, 1919.

Great-Heart, Doubleday, Page, 1919.

Danny Deever, Doubleday, Page, 1921.

The King's Pilgrimage, Doubleday, Page, 1922.

Chartres Windows, Doubleday, Page, 1925.

A Choice of Songs, Doubleday, Page, 1925.

Sea and Sussex, with an introductory poem by the author and illustrations by Donald Maxwell, Doubleday, Page, 1926.

A Rector's Memory, Doubleday, Page, 1926.

Supplication of the Black Aberdeen, illustrations by G. L. Stampa, Doubleday, Doran, 1929.

The Church That Was at Antioch, Doubleday, Doran, 1929.

The Tender Achilles, Doubleday, Doran, 1929.

Unprofessional, Doubleday, Page, 1930.

The Day of the Dead, Doubleday, Doran, 1930.

Neighbours, Doubleday, Doran, 1932.

The Storm Cone, Doubleday, Doran, 1932.

His Apologies, illustrations by Cecil Aldin, Doubleday, Doran, 1932.

The Fox Meditates, Doubleday, Doran, 1933.

To the Companions, Doubleday, Doran, 1933.

Bonfires on the Ice, Doubleday, Doran, 1933.

Our Lady of the Sackcloth, Doubleday, Doran, 1935.

Hymn of the Breaking Strain, Doubleday, Doran, 1935.

Doctors, The Waster, The Flight, Cain and Abel, The Appeal, Doubleday, Doran, 1939.

B.E.L., Doubleday, Doran, 1944.

SHORT STORIES

In Black and White, A. H. Wheeler (Allahabad), 1888, lst American edition, Lovell, 1890.

Plain Tales From the Hills, Thacker, Spink, 1888, 2nd edition, revised, 1889, lst English edition, revised, Macmillan, 1890, lst American edition, revised, Doubleday & McClure, 1899, reprint edited by H. R. Woudhuysen, Penguin, 1987.

The Phantom 'Rickshaw and Other Tales, A. H. Wheeler, 1888, revised edition, 1890, reprinted, Hurst, 1901.

The Story of the Gadsbys: A Tale With No Plot, A. H. Wheeler, 1888, 1st American edition, Lovell, 1890.

Soldiers Three: A Collection of Stories Setting Forth Certain Passages in the Lives and Adventures of Privates Terence Mulvaney, Stanley Ortheris, and John Learoyd, A. H. Wheeler, 1888, 1st American edition, revised, Lovell, 1890, reprinted, Belmont, 1962.

Under the Deodars, A. H. Wheeler, 1888, 1st American edition, enlarged, Lovell, 1890.

The Courting of Dinah Shadd and Other Stories, with a biographical and critical sketch by Andrew Lang, Harper, 1890, reprinted, Books for Libraries, 1971.

His Private Honour, Macmillan, 1891.

The Smith Administration, A. H. Wheeler, 1891.

Mine Own People, introduction by Henry James, United States Book Co., 1891.

Many Inventions, D. Appleton, 1893, reprinted, Macmillan, 1982.

Mulvaney Stories, 1897, reprinted, Books for Libraries, 1971.

The Day's Work, Doubleday & McClure, 1898, reprinted, Books for Libraries, 1971, reprinted with introduction by Constantine Phipps, Penguin, 1988.

The Drums of the Fore and Aft, illustrations by L. J. Bridgman, Brentano's, 1898.

The Man Who Would Be King, Brentano's, 1898.

Black Jack, F. T. Neely, 1899.

Without Benefit of Clergy, Doubleday & McClure, 1899.

The Brushwood Boy, illustrations by Orson Lowell, Doubleday & McClure, 1899, reprinted, with illustrations by F. H. Townsend, Doubleday, Page, 1907.

Railway Reform in Great Britain, Doubleday, Page, 1901.

Traffics and Discoveries, Doubleday, Page, 1904, reprinted, Penguin, 1987.

They, Scribner, 1904.

Abaft the Funnel, Doubleday, Page, 1909.

Actions and Reactions, Doubleday, Page, 1909.

Cold Iron, Macmillan, 1909.

A Doctor of Medicine, Macmillan, 1909.

The Wrong Thing, Macmillan, 1909.

Gloriana, Macmillan, 1909.

The Conversion of St. Wilfrid, Macmillan, 1909.

The Tree of Justice, Macmillan, 1909.

Brother Square-Toes, Macmillan, 1910.

Simple Simon, Macmillan, 1910.

A Priest in Spite of Himself, Macmillan, 1910.

A Diversity of Creatures, Doubleday, Page, 1917, reprinted, Macmillan, 1966.

"The Finest Story in the World" and Other Stories, Little Leather Library, 1918.

Debits and Credits, Doubleday, Page, 1926, reprinted, Macmillan, 1965.

Thy Servant a Dog, Told by Boots, illustrations by Marguerite Kirmse, Doubleday, Doran, 1930.

Beauty Spots, Doubleday, Doran, 1931.

Limits and Renewals, Doubleday, Doran, 1932.

The Pleasure Cruise, Doubleday, Doran, 1933.

Collected Dog Stories, illustrations by Kirmse, Doubleday, Doran, 1934.

Ham and the Porcupine, Doubleday, Doran, 1935.

Teem: A Treasure-Hunter, Doubleday, Doran, 1935.

The Maltese Cat: A Polo Game of the 'Nineties, illustrations by Lionel Edwards, Doubleday, Doran, 1936.

"Thy Servant a Dog" and Other Dog Stories, illustrations by G. L. Stampa, Macmillan, 1938, reprinted, 1982.

Their Lawful Occasions, White Rose Press, 1987.

NOVELS

The Light That Failed, J. B. Lippincott, 1891, revised edition, Macmillan, 1891, reprinted, Penguin, 1988.

(With Wolcott Balestier) *The Naulahka: A Story of West and East,* Macmillan, 1892, reprinted, Doubleday, Page, 1925.

Kim, illustrations by father, J. Lockwood Kipling, Doubleday, Page, 1901, new edition, with illustrations by Stuart Tresilian, Macmillan, 1958, reprinted, with introduction by Alan Sandison, Oxford University Press, 1987.

CHILDREN'S BOOKS

"Wee Willie Winkie" and Other Child Stories, A. H. Wheeler, 1888, 1st American edition, Lovell, 1890, reprinted, Penguin, 1988.

The Jungle Book (short stories and poems; also see below), illustrations by J. L. Kipling, W. H. Drake, and P. Frenzeny, Macmillan, 1894, adapted and abridged by Anne L. Nelan, with illustrations by Earl Thollander, Fearon, 1967, reprinted, with illustrations by J. L. Kipling and Drake, Macmillan, 1982.

The Second Jungle Book (short stories and poems), illustrations by J. L. Kipling, Century Co., 1895, reprinted, Macmillan, 1982.

"Captains Courageous": A Story of the Grand Banks, Century Co., 1897, abridged edition, illustrated by Rafaello Busoni, Hart Publishing, 1960, reprinted, with an afterword by C. A. Bodelsen, New American Library, 1981.

Stalky and Co. (short stories), Doubleday & McClure, 1899, reprinted, Bantam, 1985, new and abridged edition, Pendulum Press, 1977.

Just So Stories for Little Children (short stories and poems), illustrations by the author, Doubleday, Page, 1902, reprinted, Silver Burdett, 1986.

Rewards and Fairies (short stories and poems), illustrations by Frank Craig, Doubleday, Page, 1910, revised edition, with illustrations by Charles E. Brock, Macmillan, 1926, reprinted, Penguin, 1988.

Toomai of the Elephants, Macmillan, 1937.

How the Rhinoceros Got His Skin, illustrations by Feodor Rojankovsky, Garden City Publishing, 1942, reprinted, with illustrations by Leonard Weisgard, Walker, 1974, published as *How the Rhino Got His Skin,* Putnam, 1988, published with audiocassette, Picture Book Studio, 1988.

How the Leopard Got His Spots, illustrations by Rojankovsky, Garden City Publishing, 1942, reprinted, P. Bedrick, 1986, published with audiocassette, Picture Book Studio, 1989.

How the Camel Got His Hump, illustrations by Rojankovsky, Garden City Publishing, 1942, reprinted, with illustrations by Erica Weihs, Rand McNally, 1955, reprinted with new illustrations, Warne, 1988, published with audiocassette, Picture Book Studio, 1989.

The Elephant's Child, illustrations by Rojankovsky, Garden City Publishing, 1942, reprinted, with illustrations by Lorinda Bryan Cauley, Harcourt, 1988, published with audiocassette, Knopf, 1986.

Puck of Pook's Hill (short stories and poems), Doubleday, 1946, reprinted, New American Library, 1988.

The Cat That Walked by Himself, illustrations by Rojankovsky, Garden City Publishing, 1947, reprinted, with illustrations by William Stobbs, P. Bedrick, 1983.

Mowgli, the Jungle Boy, illustrations by William Bartlett, Grosset, 1951.

How the Whale Got His Throat, illustrations by Don Madden, Addison-Wesley, 1971, published as *How the Whale Got His Throat: Just So Stories,* Putnam, 1988.

Disney Read-Aloud Film Classics: The Jungle Book, Crown, 1981.

The Butterfly That Stamped: A Just So Story, illustrations by Alan Baker, P. Bedrick, 1982.

The Beginning of the Armadillos: A Just So Story, illustrations by Charles Keeping, P. Bedrick, 1983.

The Crab That Played With the Sea: A Just So Story, illustrations by Michael Freeman, P. Bedrick, 1983.

Cinderella and How the Elephant Got His Trunk, EDC, 1985.

Tales From the Jungle Book, adapted by Robin McKinley, Random House, 1985.

The Miracle of Purun Bhagat, Creative Education, 1985.

Rikki-Tikki-Tavi, Ideals, 1985.

The Sing-Song of Old Man Kangaroo, P. Bedrick, 1986.

Gunga Din, Harcourt, 1987.

How the Alphabet Was Made, P. Bedrick, 1987.

How the First Letter Was Written, P. Bedrick, 1987.

TRAVEL WRITINGS

Letters of Marque, A. H. Wheeler, 1891.

American Notes, M. J. Ivers, 1891, reprinted, Ayer Co., 1974, revised edition published as *American Notes: Rudyard Kipling's West,* University of Oklahoma Press, 1981.

From Sea to Sea and Other Sketches, two volumes, Doubleday & McClure, 1899, published as one volume, Doubleday, Page, 1909, reprinted, 1925.

Letters to the Family: Notes on a Recent Trip to Canada, Macmillan of Canada, 1908.

Letters of Travel, 1892-1913, Doubleday, Page, 1920.

Land and Sea Tales, Doubleday, Page, 1923.

Souvenirs of France, Macmillan, 1933.

Brazilian Sketches, Doubleday, Doran, 1940.

Letters From Japan, edited with an introduction and notes by Donald Richie and Yoshimori Harashima, Kenkyusha, 1962.

NAVAL AND MILITARY WRITINGS

A Fleet in Being: Notes of Two Trips With the Channel Squadron, Macmillan, 1899.

The Army of a Dream, Doubleday, Page, 1904, reprinted, White Rose Press, 1987.

The New Army, Doubleday, Page, 1914.

The Fringes of the Fleet, Doubleday, Page, 1915.

France at War: On the Frontier of Civilization, Doubleday, Page, 1915.

Sea Warfare, Macmillan, 1916, Doubleday, Page, 1917.

Tales of "The Trade," Doubleday, Page, 1916.

The Eyes of Asia, Doubleday, Page, 1918.

The Irish Guards, Doubleday, Page, 1918.

The Graves of the Fallen, Imperial War Graves Commission, 1919.

The Feet of the Young Men, photographs by Lewis R. Freeman, Doubleday, Page, 1920.

The Irish Guards in the Great War: Edited and Compiled From Their Diaries and Papers, two volumes, Doubleday, Page, 1923, Volume I: *The First Battalion,* Volume II: *The Second Battalion and Appendices.*

OTHER

The City of Dreadful Night and Other Places (articles), A. H. Wheeler, 1891.

(With Charles R. L. Fletcher) *A History of England,* Doubleday, Page, 1911, published as *Kipling's Pocket History of England,* with illustrations by Henry Ford, Greenwich, 1983.

"The Harbor Watch" (one-act play; unpublished), 1913.

"The Return of Imray" (play; unpublished), 1914.

How Shakespeare Came to Write "The Tempest," introduction by Ashley H. Thorndike, Dramatic Museum of Columbia University, 1916.

London Town: November 11, 1918-1923, Doubleday, Page, 1923.

The Art of Fiction, J. A. Allen, 1926.

Mary Kingsley, Doubleday, Doran, 1932.

Proofs of Holy Writ, Doubleday, Doran, 1934.

Something of Myself for My Friends Known and Unknown (autobiography), Doubleday, Doran, 1937, reprinted, Penguin Classics, 1989.

Rudyard Kipling to Rider Haggard: The Record of a Friendship, edited by Morton Cohen, Hutchinson, 1965.

"O Beloved Kids": Rudyard Kipling's Letters to His Children, selected and edited by Elliot L. Gilbert, Harcourt, 1984.

Many of Kipling's works first appeared in periodicals, including four Anglo-Indian newspapers, the *Civil and Military Gazette,* the *Pioneer, Pioneer News, Week's News;* the *Scots Observer* and its successor, the *National Observer; London Morning Post,* the London *Times,* the *English Illustrated Magazine, Macmillan's Magazine, McClure's Magazine, Pearson's Magazine, Spectator, Atlantic, Ladies' Home Journal,* and *Harper's Weekly.*

Works collected in more than one hundred omnibus volumes.

SIDELIGHTS: As quoted in Andrew Rutherford's *Kipling's Mind and Art,* the literary critic Edmund Wilson correctly observed in 1941, five years after Rudyard Kipling's death, that he had "in a sense been dropped out of modern literature." This fact of literary history is remarkable because during his lifetime Kipling published a vast amount of writing that was tremendously popular and critically acclaimed. Living in India, where he was born and raised—although he was educated in England—Kipling by age twenty-three had published a book of poems, *Departmental Ditties* (1886), a series of thirty-nine short stories collected under the title *Plain Tales From the Hills* (1888), and six briefer collections of short stories. Importantly, Kipling's work was read not only in colonial India; his fame quickly spread to the literary as well as commercial capital of the British empire, London.

During his life he was repeatedly offered—and repeatedly he refused—knighthood and membership in distinguished learned and political societies. Moreover, he was lionized by many of the most powerful contemporary men of letters, including Edmund Gosse, Thomas Hardy, Rider Haggard, W. E. Henley, Henry and William James, Andrew Lang, Charles Eliot Norton, and George Saintsbury. Kipling also shared the company of British royalty, ministers of states, and U.S. presidents Grover Cleveland, Theodore Roosevelt, and Woodrow Wilson. In 1907 Kipling was awarded the Nobel Prize for Literature, the first English writer to receive it. In 1927 a Kipling Society was formed in his honor, although he did not encourage it. In January, 1936, the daily changes in his declining health as he suffered from a fatal hemorrhage were reported by the major newspapers around the world. His ashes were set beside the memorial to Charles Dickens in England's most hallowed place for its great writers, Poets' Corner in Westminster Abbey. His collected stories—roughly 250 of them—had sold 15 million volumes, and he had published 5 novels, more than 500 poems, several books of history, speeches, travel writings, essays, and an autobiography. In his writing he may not have achieved the ideal he ascribes to St. Paul in a poem called "At His Execution"—to be "all things to all men." But through the quantity as well as the quality of his work and its popularity, Kipling seemed to come as close as a writer can to this criterion.

With such a record of achievement, why was Kipling "dropped out of modern literature"? The answer, in short, is that both the style and content of Kipling's work quickly went out of fashion when literary modernism gained acceptance. Kipling's writing was widely rejected as imperialist, paternalist, reactionary, jingoistic, simple-minded, militarist, and vulgar. Ironically, however, the great modernist poet T. S. Eliot was among the first to argue for Kipling's rehabilitation and revival. His not merely fashionable but timeless literary skill had already been recognized by another great modernist writer, James Joyce, who, as quoted in Norman Page's *Kipling Companion,* wrote to his brother in 1907 that "if I knew Ireland as well as R. K. seems to know India, I fancy I could write something good."

A subject of study by major writers and critics like T. S. Eliot and Edmund Wilson in 1941, George Orwell in 1942, and Lionel Trilling in 1943, Kipling's writings began in the 1940s to come out of the shadows of twentieth-century modernism. He was, and still is, as Shamsul Islam wrote in *Kipling's "Law,"* "perhaps the most controversial figure in English literature," yet his strengths as a writer remain. First, Kipling possessed strong ability as a storyteller. As Kingsley Amis noted in *Rudyard Kipling and His World,* Kipling's "range is wide: the tragic, the comic, the satiric, the macabre, anecdote, fantasy, history, science fiction, children's tales." As J. M. S. Tompkins suggested in *The Art of Rudyard Kipling,* the sheer "variety" and "the resource and depth of Kipling's art" are most impressive in both his prose and verse, for they are, as T. S. Eliot observed in his introduction to *A Choice of Kipling's Verse,* "inseparable." Storytelling was Kipling's strongest desire in prose and verse. Also, in the course of his work Kipling became the last great English writer to address frequently and directly issues of contemporary politics. He was, in addition, the last great English writer to make explicit and extensive allusions to Scripture. And, as Orwell noted, Kipling more than any "English writer of our times . . . added phrases to the language. He coined 'East is East, and West is

West,' 'And what should they know of England who only England know,' 'the light that failed,' 'The female of the species is more deadly than the male,' and 'East of Suez.' "

As Eliot—like Kipling's earliest readers—recognized, Kipling demonstrated "perfect competence" in his writing. Wilson, as quoted in *Kipling's Mind and Art,* thought that Kipling owed "his superiority as a craftsman" to his knowledge of "the ablest writers" of nineteenth-century fiction. Confirming Wilson's view, Kipling himself recalled in his autobiography that when he first arrived in London from India to pursue his literary ambitions he "was struck by the slenderness of some of the writers' equipment." He "could not see how they got along with so casual a knowledge of French work, and, apparently of much English grounding that I had supposed indispensable." On another occasion Kipling in part specified what he meant by the "English grounding" that he thought aspiring writers should have. He recommended reading William Hazlitt and, before the nineteenth century, Richard Crashaw "for words and emotions" and Jonathan Swift "purely for style." Kipling's style might be aptly characterized as a strange hybrid of Crashaw's extreme emotionalism, Swift's insistent literalness and lucidity, and Hazlitt's unpretentious yet sharp journalistic elegance.

Whatever his models for style, Kipling early in his life realized his literary predilections. He was "The Man Who Could Write," as the title of a poem of 1886 suggested. Moreover, Kipling worked seven years for an Anglo-Indian newspaper, the *Civil and Military Gazette.* He may have known the English literary greats but he also had to produce copy, realizing that as a writer he was essentially "a hireling, paid to do what [he] was paid to do." However negligibly Kipling regarded his early journalistic work, it gave him what every young writer needs most: the opportunity to practice basic writing skills. In addition, when the paper was short on news or advertising, Kipling was able to supply his earliest ballads as filler.

Schooled in the English classics but also in the necessary practicalities of journalistic prose, Kipling's style seemed to aspire to the virtues of both kinds of writing. He cultivated clear, easily understood, matter-of-fact statements but also claimed in the 1886 poem "A General Summary," "The artless songs I sing / Do not deal with anything / New or never said before." Kipling's profound sense of the timeless truths of great literature as opposed to the merely timely notions of good journalism was apparent in his appreciating that "if you go no further back than the [Bible's] Book of Job you will find that letters . . . were born perfect." Kipling practiced journalism as well as literature yet he believed in neither social nor literary progress. Rather, he seemed intent on perfecting a style of writing that would communicate as much and as well as possible with as many as possible. In his time he was successful in achieving this literary ideal. Not only his wide audience but also his literary peers attested to his success in appealing to many different levels of readers.

Approval of Kipling was not unanimous; Robert Buchanan, in an article from *Kipling: The Critical Heritage,* pronounced Kipling's writing vulgar, brutal, inflammatory, illiberal, irreligious, and sexually indecent—abuse that, as Orwell noted, Kipling's work might still draw. His egalitarian aesthetic ideal was and is challengeable. However, most interesting is Kipling's articulation of this ideal throughout his writing. As Kipling wrote in "The Last Rhyme of True Thomas," he wanted "To sing wi' the priests at the market-cross, / Or run wi' the dogs in the naked street." He knew the dangers if a writer tried to appeal too broadly, advising "never play down to your public—not because some of them do not deserve it, but because it is bad for your hand."

Nevertheless, Kipling also knew first hand the danger of writing to appeal to no one except the dead classics. At the outset of his career many writers and critics proclaimed that art should be created solely for its own sake. It need not have a social function or any function at all. Kipling's aim in writing was different. His art appealed not only to art but to society as well; he counted himself part of society: "I have eaten your bread and salt. / I have drunk your water and wine. / The deaths ye have died I have watched beside, / And the lives ye led were mine." Thus, according to Bonamy Dobree in *Rudyard Kipling: Realist and Fabulist,* Kipling revivified "the poetic diction of his day . . . and [came] back to poetry written 'in a language such as men doe use' as Ben Jonson put it." Regarding his own place and time and role as a writer, in the "Prelude to 'Barrack Room Ballads,'" Kipling professed to "Thomas Atkins," a representative name for every British soldier, "I have made for you a song, / . . . have tried for to explain / Both your pleasure and your pain."

The study of the style of Kipling's prolific work leads, as Bernard Bergonzi wrote in an essay for *The Age of Kipling,* to a recognition of "the strange complexity of his art, and . . . how completely it resists any neat and limiting formula." To consider only the poetry, his body of work encompasses a wide variety of poetic kinds, tone, diction, imagery, and prosodic technique. He was, in Dobree's words, a "master of versification," thriving within the traditional boundaries of rhyme and meter in English. Consequently, he had no need for modernist free verse, which he compared to "fishing with barbless hooks."

C. H. Sisson, writing in *English Poetry: 1900-1950,* considered Kipling's "real contribution to the verse of the twentieth century" to be "his plainness." To make such a quality a virtue in writing was a main tenet of much modernist poetry, too. However, in the nineteenth century also there was a beautiful plainness to be found in the verse of Christina Rossetti and Thomas Hardy, both of whom Kipling knew. He frequently matched their bleak yet stirring notes in works such as "The Widower": "For a season there must be pain— / For a little, little space shall lose sight of her face, / Take back the old life again / While She is at rest in her place." Kipling's poetry is admirably plain also because, as G. K. Chesterton recorded in *Heretics,* "he . . . perceived the significance and philosophy of steam and of slang." Chesterton was alluding in particular to Kipling's "McAndrew's Hymn," in which a steamship engineer pits his Scots Calvinist code of life, which he finds symbolized in the powerful workings of his steam engines, against contemporary materialism. Although the verse was composed in highly musical fourteen-syllable couplets, Kipling managed a slangy tone throughout. Furthermore, like many of Kipling's poems, "McAndrew's Hymn" is replete with allusions to the Bible's Old and New Testaments. To his credit as a poetic craftsman, Kipling let neither prosodic formality nor an almost evangelistic fervor vitiate his conversational diction, as is seen, too, in his making the very artificial and difficult sestina form accommodate plain speech in the "Sestina of the Tramp-Royal." "McAndrew's Hymn" also exemplifies Kipling's expertise in the dramatic monologue. Many of his best poems—such as "The Explorer," "Mulholland's Contract," and "The Mary Gloster"—are in this form, and interestingly Kipling extended it to include inanimate things. Poems like "The Deep Sea-Cables," "The Bell-Buoy," and "Song of the Dynamo" portray these things speaking their own special wisdom. Yet they are also plain objects in which Kipling identified near vatic significance.

Masterfully practicing his plain style in a wide variety of poetic kinds and genres, Kipling nevertheless managed to avoid sending a merely plain or banal message through his writing. His plain writing was frequently in the service of an actively philosophical and didactic mind. In his writing he spoke plainly but what his language signified was not necessarily easy to understand or accept. The opening lines of "Cities and Thrones and Powers" are plainly lyrical but their message is impossibly difficult: "Cities and Thrones and Powers / Stand in Time's eye / Almost as long as flowers, / Which daily die." In comparing the life span of civilizations and humankind to "This season's Daffodil" that "never hears / What change, what chance, what chill, / Cut down last year's," Kipling's imagery, like the evocation of the seasons in the Old Testament book of Ecclesiastes or Christ's exhortation in the New Testament to "consider the lilies of the field," sweetens the most bitter of historical truths. The simple stanza's placement of the word *almost* is particularly cutting.

Chesterton observed of Kipling that "above all, he . . . had something to say, a definite view of things to utter." In his autobiography Kipling recalled that as a young journalist he had to learn "that . . . statements of . . . facts are not well seen by responsible official authorities." His sister remembered him once writing a poem and wondering aloud, "What am I trying to say?" In his verse as well as his fiction Kipling frequently had a strong didactic purpose. English poet John Keats said, "We hate poetry that has a palpable design upon us," but Kipling had little sympathy with this sentiment. His verse especially had a "palpable design" on readers and consequently it often either enraged or pleased them immensely. Nevertheless, Kipling was fully aware of the dangers for a poet as well as for a young journalist with a "palpable design." Therefore, to mollify his strong views he frequently resorted to allegory. He admitted his predicament and stated its solution in a poem called "The Fabulists": "When all the world would keep a matter hid, / Since truth is seldom friend to any crowd, / Men write in fable, as old Aesop did, / Jest at that which none will name aloud. / And thus they needs must do, or it will fall / Unless they please they are not heard at all."

Notwithstanding Kipling's frequent and skillful use of allegory, his didacticism and its attendant clarity of verbal expression are among his writing's greatest strengths. As Eliot wrote, "We expect to have to defend a poet against the charge of obscurity; we have to defend Kipling against the charge of excessive lucidity." Each piece of his work can be considered as an illustration of a philosophical, ethical, or social dilemma, although it can be public or personal, grave or lighthearted. As quoted in *Aspects of Kipling's Art,* Graham Hough noted that Kipling "addresses his readers in confidence that he will be understood." For him this required more than verbal undertones and overtones, subtlety, implicitness, and suggestive evocation. His writing bears such qualities but in addition, in Sisson's words, "He seems to be after the irrefutable prose statement, whether the subject is important or not." For example his short stories, as in *Puck of Pook's Hill,* are laced with aphorisms, and his verse has been called poetry of statement or, in Robert Conquest's phrase from an essay in *The Age of Kipling,* "poetry of clarification." As C. S. Lewis said of Renaissance poet Philip Sidney's *Arcadia,* so can be said of Kipling's work in general: it is forensic on every page.

One more of the greatest strengths of Kipling's writing—and it is one through which he also hoped that "people would not only read but remember" him—is the oral quality of his work. It was written to be spoken. And it was spoken by him. As he recalled in his autobiography, "I made my own experiments in the weights, colours, perfumes, and attributes of words as read aloud so that they may hold the ear. . . . There is no line of my verse or prose which has not been mouthed till the tongue has made all smooth, and memory, after many recitals, has mechanically skipped the grosser superfluities." Attesting to Kipling's vocal enactment of his work in the midst of its composition, his cousin Florence Macdonald remembered how "when composing verse he would often set it to a tune, usually to a hymn tune, and I have heard him walking up and down the room singing a verse over and over again to get the lilt and swing of it." Another cousin, Angela Thirkell, reminisced how Kipling "used to try out" his work "on a nursery audience." If Kipling wrote some of the most notable children's stories in English then it is because he realized that children especially appreciate the greatness of literature by hearing it. According to Thirkell, *Kipling's Just So Stories* were "a poor thing in print compared with the fun of hearing them told in Cousin Ruddy's deep unhesitating voice. There was a ritual about them, each phrase having its special intonation which had to be exactly the same each time and without which the stories are dried husks. There was an inimitable cadence, an emphasis on certain words, an exaggeration of certain phrases, a kind of intoning here and there which made his telling unforgettable." Since Kipling devoted so much attention to the oral as well as aural quality of literature, particularly unfortunate and poignant is his being the last great English writer who was not recorded reading his own work.

Kipling's emphasis on "the weights, colours, perfumes . . . of words . . . mouthed till the tongue has made all smooth" in his "verse or prose" suggests, as James Harrison wrote in *Rudyard Kipling,* a kind of "love affair with the spoken word." Harrison further observes that "speech is Kipling's principal method of characterization . . . since [his] ear was attuned to a wide range of voices and accents, and he clearly enjoyed exercising his virtuoso skill at reproducing them on paper." He could give a text the tone of a music hall, as in "Tommy" or "The Widow at Windsor," or of a Westminster Abbey, as in the hymn of "Recessional." The American sailors of *Captains Courageous,* the lonely soldiers of *Barrack Room Ballads,* the British Viceroy of India ("One Viceroy Resigns"), the lowly Indian *bhisti* water carrier of the British Army during battle ("Gunga Din"), the animals of *The Jungle Book,* the incarnate Indian gods of "The Bridge Builders": Kipling gives these characters distinctive voices. Revealing his characters primarily through their manners of speaking, Kipling naturally was led to write many dramatic monologues and ballads, the two poetic forms that rely most on conversational tone. Moreover, throughout his works Kipling frequently imitated or parodied the ways that people actually speak—for instance, in his heavy use of dialect and slang—particularly revealing the influence of Dickens's writing.

Many themes recur in Kipling's work, among which are politics and the imperialism of the West in the East, soldiers and war, work and machines, art itself, and history. He spent most of his life until he was twenty-three in India. Predictably, therefore, it and the East in general were the setting and subject of much of his early writing. During Kipling's entire lifetime England ruled India. For that matter, British imperialism—or the British empire—also reached into South Africa, the Middle East, and Southeast Asia. As Eliot noted: "We must accustom ourselves to recognizing that for Kipling the Empire was not merely an idea, a good idea or a bad one; it was something the reality of which he felt. And in his expression of his feeling he was certainly not aiming at flattery of national, racial or imperial vanity, or attempting to propagate a political programme: he was aiming to communicate the awareness of something in existence of which he felt that most people were very imperfectly aware." In

his belief that England had a right and responsibility to rule foreign lands, Kipling differed from no major English writer before him. He avidly supported British imperialism while he bitterly criticized its administration. Nevertheless, in Andrew Rutherford's words, Kipling's "pride in imperial achievement" went along with his "awareness of the human cost to the Empire builders." Eric Stokes observed in an essay from *The Age of Kipling* that "Kipling's most ardent literary admirers have found [his] overt imperialism an embarrassment and try to shuffle it off." While Kipling's imperialism cannot be ignored or justified, his viewpoint was unique and neither politic nor patronizing. He repeatedly emphasized that the "human cost" for the building and maintaining of an empire was hardly suffered or even realized by the English who enjoyed its fruits at home or administered it from Whitehall.

Kipling's strong yet unique brand of imperialism was not the only distinguishing feature of his politics as reflected in his writing. Generally he was, in Dobree's words, attracted to "public themes." Usually taking the form of verse, Kipling's political observations had a wide circulation. They were highly respected too; so much so that between 1890 and World War I he was dubbed the people's laureate, although his frequently controversial, original, inflammatory, and unpredictable political sympathies probably prevented his appointment as the official poet laureate. He was the last in a tradition of great English poets—including Alfred Tennyson and William Wordsworth, Alexander Pope and Jonathan Swift, John Dryden, John Milton and Andrew Marvell—who directly, publicly, and polemically addressed the important political issues of their time. Orwell considered Kipling a "gutter patriot," and he earned this designation with ranting verses like "For All We Have and Are," written in 1914 to raise the British war fever by warning "The Hun is at the Gate." What George Shepperson in an essay for *The Age of Kipling* calls Kipling's "unadulterated patriotism," however, was not always positive. As Orwell also observed about Kipling's patriotic prose and poetry, "Few people who have criticized England from the inside have said bitterer things about her." For instance, his epitaph for "A Dead Statesman" could hardly comfort the political establishment: "I could not dig: I dared not rob: / Therefore I lied to please the mob. / Now all my lies are proved untrue / And I must face the men I slew. / What tale shall serve me here among / Mine angry and defrauded young?"

Such political writing is not merely timely. Like the great political yet literary English writers before him, Kipling in his best work can be appreciated without much knowledge of the detailed background of the issues and parties he was praising or blaming. The greatest political writing makes artful yet astute observations about the politics of all countries and all times, as does Kipling's "The Peace of Dives," which implies, in Ralph Durand's words, "that those who control the world's money decide between themselves how, and when, and for how long king should draw sword against king, and people rise up against people." Great political writing can also have a prophetic dimension—Orwell's *1984,* for instance. Kipling's poem "The Press," written in 1907, foretold how newspapers would achieve political power comparable to that of the biblical beast Leviathan: "That King over all the children of pride / Is the Press—the Press—the Press!"

Closely related to Kipling's imperialism and politics was his writing about soldiers and war. The lives of British soldiers in India, the far East, the Boer War, and World War I and the lives of veterans inspired many of his short stories and poems. C. E. Carrington claims that Kipling's literary "treatment of the British soldier" was the greatest since Shakespeare's in his history plays. Kipling portrayed soldiers at war and peace, in triumph and defeat, in hope and despair, ridiculous and serious, callous and sentimental, happy-go-lucky and self-determined, as heroes and cowards, saviors and murderers. According to Eliot, Kipling's "concern was to make the soldier known, not to idealize him." Furthermore, Kipling's writing about soldiers expressed anxiety and rage at civilian society's apathetic or mean and unjust treatment of them. Orwell contended "that Kipling's 'message' was one that the big public did not want, and, indeed has never accepted. The mass of the people, in the 'nineties as now, were anti-militarist, bored by the Empire, and only unconsciously patriotic." In his fiction Kipling tried to combat this tendency by writing detailed yet diverting accounts of the ups and downs of life in the military. In his poems he frequently adopted the persona or point of view of a British regular.

As a writer who had repeatedly portrayed military life Kipling was prepared to confront the unprecedented realities of World War I, although Paul Fussell has argued in *The Great War and Modern Memory* that no contemporary writer and not even the English language itself was able to adequately describe such horrors. Kipling wrote about the war in an impressive variety of ways. He edited a two-volume history entitled *The Irish Guards in the Great War,* about his son's battalion. He wrote poems about some of the new weaponry of "Mine Sweepers" and "Sea Warfare" and, in a poem called "Gethsemane," about a poison gas attack which he compares to a New Testament story about Christ's agony in the garden: "The men lay on the grass, . . . / I prayed my cup might pass. / It didn't pass—it didn't pass— / It didn't pass from me. / I drank it when we met the gas / Beyond Gethsemane." Kipling was also concerned with the plight of veterans after the war, writing poems about their prolonged battle fatigue such as "The Mother's Son," about their inability to control during peacetime their violent tendencies that the war encouraged as in "The Expert," about their transformation from experienced soldiers into scholars as portrayed in "The Scholars," and about their eventual recognition as possible heroes as related in "The Verdicts."

Kipling sought not to criticize or analyze the war but to memorialize its casualties. He did this most successfully in his "Epitaphs of the War." Appointed as the "Honorary Literary Advisor" for the Imperial War Graves Commission, he was the author of the general epitaph for all the veterans' cemeteries: "Their name liveth forevermore." However, Kipling's unofficial "Epitaphs of the War" were far more particular, emotional, and disturbing. Bergonzi judges them his "most moving and authentic poetry." They were about the fate of green recruits—and, critics say, Kipling's own son—as in "The Beginner": "On the first hour of my first day / In the front trench I fell / (Children in boxes at a play / Stand up to watch it well.)" They also treated the leveling ironies of social class on the battlefield, as in "A Servant": "We were together since the War began. / He was my servant—and the better man." They dealt with the inscrutable personal tragedy of "The Coward": "I could not look on Death, which being known, / Men led me to him, blindfolded and alone." And they portrayed the suffering and casualties among the parents who lost their children in war, as in "An Only Son": "I have slain my Mother. She / (Blessing her slayer) died of grief for me." Sharply reflecting the casualties of war among many different types of people both on the battlefield and at home, Kipling's "Epitaphs" are among the greatest poetic sequences of the twentieth century. They are the climax of his thirty years of writing on military topics.

Chesterton thought that Kipling's writing about soldiers and war was indicative of his interest in a larger topic: "He is a poet rather of all disciplines and skills." Moreover, C. S. Lewis in an essay from *The Age of Kipling* wrote that Kipling was "first and foremost the poet of work." Again Chesterton thought that "Kipling's subject is not that valour which properly belongs to war, but that interdependence of efficiency which belongs quite as much to engineers, or sailors, or mules, or railway engines. And thus it is that when he writes of engineers, or sailors, or mules, or steam engines, he writes at his best. The real poetry, the 'true romance'. . . is the romance of the divisions of labour and the discipline of all the trades. He sings the arts of peace much more accurately than the arts of war. . . . Everything is military in the sense that everything depends upon obedience. . . . Everywhere men have made the way for us with sweat and submission." There is plenty in Kipling's prose and verse to support Chesterton's point of view and "work" certainly is one of Kipling's major themes.

Kipling had a philosophy about work, and his writing manifested his work ethic. Often he would reduce or simplify a complex issue by determining the work it involved. For example, in "McAndrew's Hymn" the tough Calvinist McAndrew claims in his engine room that "From coupler-flange to spindle-guide I see Thy Hand, O God— / Predestination in the stride o' yon connectin'-rod. / John Calvin might ha' forged the same— enormous, certain, slow— / Ay, wrought it in the furnace-flame—my 'Institutio.' " Theology and religious commitment are understood through the technical terms of "crosshead-gibs" and "follower-bolts." When "McAndrew's Hymn" was first published, Kipling prefaced it with his recommendation that "to appreciate the poem thoroughly, it should be read in a ship's engine room when the engines are doing their work." In "The Wage Slaves" Kipling suggested that while idealism, the sublime, truth, and beauty may be "glorious" in "the guarded heights / Where the guardian souls abide," he nevertheless must live on a lower, more worldly and practical plane with "the bondslaves of our day, / Whom dirt and danger press— / Co-heirs of insolence, delay, / And leagued unfaithfulness." Similarly in "The Sons of Martha," verses that Carrington thinks "best summarize [Kipling's] social philosophy," he defended Martha's working while Mary meditated, although in the New Testament story Christ tells Martha that she should not criticize Mary because she, in the words of Luke's Gospel, "hath chosen that good part." Kipling disagreed, and in a like vein he suggested in "Cain and Abel," about an Old Testament story of fratricide, that Cain was treated unjustly because he worked harder than Abel.

It should be recalled that in his poem about Shakespeare Kipling called him "The Craftsman," that is, not the artist or poet or writer. Moreover, as he was interested in many kinds of work and workers so did Kipling regard writing itself to be work or craft as opposed to something more special called "art." Looking at "work," poet W. H. Auden distinguished the word from "labor" and "play." According to Auden, to play was a pleasure and to labor was not. To work, however, was a human ideal, and Auden considered writing to be work. Kipling wrote that for him, "mercifully, the mere act of writing was a physical pleasure." Nonetheless, Kipling repeatedly in his writing elevated various kinds of work as pleasure, indeed "physical pleasure." Since his father was an architect, and his uncle was the Victorian painter and illustrator Edmund Burne-Jones, Kipling when young would have had much direct experience of artists at work and performing like craftsmen. Such contact might have initially caused him to reject what W. L. Renwick in *Kipling's Mind and Art* called "romantic aestheticism that fails—or refuses—to understand that the fine work of art is also a good job of work."

Another recurrent theme in Kipling's writings, and one that appeared most frequently in the latter half of his literary career, was history. However, it was a history for the most part apolitical and ancient. It was rooted in the land, particularly the English countryside of Sussex, where Kipling had bought a large seventeenth-century house called Bateman's. In his autobiography Kipling recalled about the move "how patiently the cards were stacked and dealt into my hands. . . . The Old Things of our Valley glided into every aspect of our outdoor works. Earth, Air, Water, and People had been—I saw it at last—in full conspiracy to give me ten times as much as I could compass, even if I wrote a complete history of England, as that might have touched or reached our Valley." Kipling's at times feverish commitment to British imperialism and politics was cooled and soothed by the local "clay," "wiseturf," "white cliff-edge," "sunlight," "sea fogs," "sheep bells . . . ship bells," "dewpond," "close-bit thyme," "rolled scarp," "deep ghylls," and "huge oaks" of Sussex. Their "Memory, Use, and Love" were "deeper than . . . speech and thought, / Beyond . . . reasons's sway."

Published in 1906, Kipling's *Puck of Pook's Hill,* and its 1910 sequel, *Rewards and Fairies,* grew out of his living among Sussex's "ferny ride," "dympled track," "secret Weald," "little mill," "stilly woods," "windy levels," and "pastures wide and lone," as "Puck's Song" records. *Puck of Pook's Hill* presents the fairy Puck who, upon meeting two children, tells them a series of stories about the successive generations—from Roman times to the French Revolution—that have inhabited the land where these children now blithely play. Actually, Kipling himself while living in Sussex discovered an ancestral vision of history that prevailed regardless of the gloominess of the political present, which he bleakly characterized, in "The Storm Cone," as nothing less than history's apocalyptic midnight with "dawn . . . very far" and "the tempest long foretold" slowly approaching "but sure to hold." As Norman Page remarks, "Kipling's imagination was powerfully stimulated by the sense of the past evoked by the Sussex countryside and by archaeological and historical sites in the immediate vicinity" of his home. His theme became "the presence of the past in English rural life."

In his autobiography Kipling jauntily recalled that as a young newspaperman in India, when he was sent out on an assignment, "the dead of all times were about [him] in the vast forgotten Moslem cemeteries round the Station, where one's hoof of a morning might break through to the corpse below; skulls and bones tumbled out of our mud garden walls, and were turned up among the flowers by the Rains; and at every point were tombs of the dead. Our chief picnic rendezvous and some of our public offices had been memorials to desired dead women; and Fort Lahore . . . was a mausoleum of ghosts." Living and writing in Sussex, Kipling found a more pastoral historical setting than India, but still he delighted in the realization that "the dead of all times were" around him. As an extraordinarily popular writer in his time, he also suffused his writing with images of the living, entertaining readers with a vast and varied literary output.

MEDIA ADAPTATIONS: Kipling's writings adapted for film, stage, radio, or television include *The Light That Failed, The Naulahka, The Vampire, The Jungle Books, Captains Courageous, Kim, The Just So Stories, Gunga Din, Without Benefit of Clergy, The Man Who Would Be King,* "Mowgli and Kaa," "Mowgli Among the Wolves," "Wee Willie Winkie," "Soldiers Three," and "How the Animals Came to Live With Man."

BIOGRAPHICAL/CRITICAL SOURCES:

BOOKS

Amis, Kingsley, *Rudyard Kipling and His World,* Thames & Hudson, 1975, Scribner, 1975.

Barkenhead, Lord, *Rudyard Kipling,* Weidenfeld & Nicolson, 1978, Random House, 1978.

Bodelsen, C. A., *Aspects of Kipling's Art,* Barnes & Noble, 1964.

Carrington, Charles Edmund, *The Life of Rudyard Kipling,* Doubleday, 1955, published as *Rudyard Kipling,* Penguin, 1989.

Chandler, Lloyd H., *A Summary of the Work of Rudyard Kipling,* Grolier Club, 1930.

Chesterton, G. K., *Heretics,* John Lane, 1905.

Cornell, Louis L., *Kipling in India,* St. Martin's, 1966.

Durand, Ralph, *A Handbook to the Poetry of Rudyard Kipling,* Hodder & Stoughton, 1914.

Dictionary of Literary Biography, Gale, Volume 19: *British Poets, 1840-1914,* 1983, Volume 34: *British Novelists, 1890-1929: Traditionalists,* 1985.

Dobree, Bonamy, *Rudyard Kipling: Realist and Fabulist,* Oxford University Press, 1967.

Faber, Richard, *The Vision and the Need,* Faber, 1966.

Fido, Martin, *Rudyard Kipling,* Viking, 1974.

Flint, R. W., *Marinetti: Selected Writings,* Farrar, Straus, 1971.

Fussell, Paul, *The Great War and Modern Memory,* Oxford University Press, 1975.

Gilbert, Elliot L., editor, *"O Beloved Kids": Rudyard Kipling's Letters to His Children,* Harcourt, 1984.

Gilbert, *The Good Kipling: Studies in the Short Story,* Ohio University Press, 1970.

Gilbert, editor, *Kipling and His Critics,* P. Owen, 1965.

Green, Roger Lancelyn, editor, *Kipling: The Critical Heritage,* Barnes & Noble, 1971.

Gross, John, editor, *The Age of Kipling,* Simon & Schuster, 1972.

Gross, editor, *Rudyard Kipling: The Man, His Work, and His World,* Weidenfeld & Nicolson, 1972.

Harrison, James, *Rudyard Kipling,* Twayne, 1982.

Henn, T. R., *Kipling,* Oliver & Boyd, 1967.

Howe, Irving, editor, *The Portable Kipling,* Viking, 1982.

Islam, Shamsul, *Kipling's "Law": A Study of His Philosophy of Life,* foreword by J. M. S. Tompkins, Macmillan (London), 1975.

Kamen, Gloria, *Kipling: Storyteller of East and West,* Atheneum, 1985.

Kipling, Rudyard, *A Book of Words: Selections From Speeches and Addresses Delivered Between 1906 and 1927,* Doubleday, Doran, 1928.

Kipling, *A Choice of Kipling's Verse,* selected and introduced by T. S. Eliot, Faber, 1941, Scribner, 1943.

Kipling, *Rudyard Kipling: Illustrated,* Avenel Books, 1982.

Kipling, *Rudyard Kipling's Verse: Definitive Edition,* Doubleday, Doran, 1940.

Kipling, *Something of Myself for My Friends Known and Unknown,* Doubleday, Doran, 1937.

Orel, Harold, editor, *Kipling: Interviews and Recollections,* two volumes, Barnes & Noble, 1983.

Orwell, George, *The Collected Essays, Journalism, and Letters of George Orwell,* Volume 2: *My Country Right or Left, 1940-1943,* edited by Sonia Orwell and Ian Angus, Harcourt, 1968.

Page, Norman, *A Kipling Companion,* Macmillan, (London), 1984.

Rutherford, Andrew, editor, *Kipling's Mind and Art: Selected Critical Essays,* Stanford University Press, 1964.

Stewart, J. I. M., *Rudyard Kipling*, Dodd, 1966.

Stewart, J. I. M., *Eight Modern Writers*, Oxford University Press, 1963.

Stewart, James McG., *Rudyard Kipling: A Bibliographical Catalogue*, edited by A. W. Yeats, Dalhousie University Press and University of Toronto Press, 1959.

Sisson, C. H., *English Poetry: 1900-1950*, St. Martin's, 1971.

Tompkins, Joyce Marjorie Sanxter, *The Art of Rudyard Kipling*, Methuen, 1959.

Trilling, Lionel, *The Selected Letters of John Keats*, Doubleday, 1951.

Twentieth-Century Literary Criticism, Gale, Volume 8, 1982, Volume 17, 1985.

Wilson, Angus, *The Strange Ride of Rudyard Kipling: His Life and Works*, Secker & Warburg, 1977, Viking, 1978.

PERIODICALS

Dalhousie Review, fall, 1960.

Detroit Free Press, July 7, 1986.

Los Angeles Times Book Review, August 5, 1984.

Modern Fiction Studies, summer, 1961, summer, 1984.

Proceedings of the British Academy, Volume 51, 1965.

Sewanee Review, winter, 1944.

Times (London), December 6, 1984.

Times Literary Supplement, January 15, 1960, September 2, 1960.

*   *   *

KISSINGER, Henry A(lfred) 1923-

PERSONAL: Born May 27, 1923, in Fuerth, Germany; came to United States in 1938; naturalized in 1943; son of Louis and Paula (Stern) Kissinger; married Ann Fleischer, February 6, 1949 (divorced, July, 1964); married Nancy Sharon Maginnes, March 30, 1974; children: (first marriage) Elizabeth, David. *Education:* Harvard University, A.B. (summa cum laude), 1950, M.A., 1952, Ph.D., 1954.

ADDRESSES: Office—Suite 400, 1800 K Street N.W., Washington, D.C. 20006.

CAREER: Harvard University, Cambridge, Mass., instructor, 1954-55, lecturer, 1957-59, associate professor, 1959-62, professor of government, 1962-71, executive director of International Studies Seminar, 1951-71, member of faculty of Center for International Affairs, 1957-71, director of Defense Studies Program, 1958-71; United States Government, Washington, D.C., director of National Security Council and special assistant to President Nixon, 1969-74, secretary of state, 1973-77; Georgetown University, Washington, D.C., professor of diplomacy in School of Foreign Service and counselor to Center for Strategic and International Studies, 1977—; Kissinger Associates, Inc., Washington, D.C., chairman, 1977—.

Consultant, U.S. Operations Research Office, 1950-61, Psychological Strategy Board, 1952, Operations Coordinating Board, 1955, Weapons Systems Evaluation Group of Joint Chiefs of Staff, 1956-60, National Security Council, 1961-62, RAND Corporation, 1961—, Arms Control and Disarmament Agency, 1961-68, U.S. Department of State, 1965-69, and President's Foreign Intelligence Advisory Board, 1980—. Director of special studies project, Rockefeller Brothers Fund, Inc., 1956-58. Senior fellow, Aspen Institute, 1977—. Counselor to Chase Manhattan Bank, 1978—. Trustee of Rockefeller Brothers Fund, Inc., and Metropolitan Museum of Modern Art, 1978—. Lecturer at numerous universities in America and abroad. Con-

tributing analyst, ABC News, 1980—. *Military service:* U.S. Army, Counter-Intelligence Corps, 1943-46, received Bronze Star; U.S. Army Reserve, 1946-59, became captain.

MEMBER: American Political Science Association, American Academy of Arts and Sciences (member of special committee on international relations, 1961-62), Council on Foreign Relations (director of study group on nuclear weapons and foreign policy, 1955-56), Phi Beta Kappa, Century Club, River Club (both New York), Federal City Club, Metropolitan Club (both Washington, D.C.).

AWARDS, HONORS: Harvard University national scholarship; Harvard non-stipendiary fellowship; Harvard Detur; Rockefeller Foundation fellowship; Woodrow Wilson Prize for best book in fields of government, politics, and international affairs and Overseas Press Club citation, both 1958, both for *Nuclear Weapons and Foreign Policy;* Guggenheim fellowship, 1965-66; honorary doctorate, Brown University, 1969; "Man of the Year" citation from *Time* magazine, 1972; American Institute for Public Service Award for distinguished public service, and Nobel Peace Prize, both 1973; American Legion Distinguished Service Medal and Wateler Peace Prize, both 1974; Presidential Medal of Freedom, 1977; American Book Award, 1980, for *White House Years;* Books-across-the-Sea Ambassador of Honor Award from English-Speaking Union, 1984, for *Years of Upheaval.*

WRITINGS:

A World Restored: Castlereagh, Metternich and the Restoration of Peace, 1812-1822, Houghton, 1957, reprinted, 1973.

Nuclear Weapons and Foreign Policy, Harper, 1957, abridged edition, Norton, 1969.

The Necessity for Choice: Prospects of American Foreign Policy, Harper, 1961, reprinted, Greenwood Press, 1984.

The Troubled Partnership: A Reappraisal of the Atlantic Alliance, McGraw, 1965, reprinted, Greenwood Press, 1982.

(Editor) *Problems of National Strategy: A Book of Readings*, Praeger, 1966.

American Foreign Policy: Three Essays, Norton, 1969, 3rd edition, 1977.

White House Years (memoirs; first published serially in *Time*, October 1, 1979-October 15, 1979), Little, Brown, 1979.

For the Record: Selected Statements 1977-1980, Little, Brown, 1981.

Years of Upheaval (memoirs), Little, Brown, 1982.

American Foreign Policy: A Global View, Gower, 1982.

Report of the National Bipartisan Commission on Central America, U.S. Government Printing Office, 1984.

Observations: Selected Speeches and Essays, 1982-1984, Little, Brown, 1985.

(With McGeorge Bundy) *The Dimensions of Diplomacy*, University Microfilms International, 1989.

SIDELIGHTS: As director of the National Security Council and then secretary of state during the Nixon presidency, Henry A. Kissinger wielded enormous diplomatic authority, especially in foreign relations. In fact, writes Max Frankel in the *New York Times Book Review*, between the summers of 1973 and 1974, "the refugee from Nazi Germany became the most glamorous and probably most powerful man in America." Kissinger won the Nobel Prize for his efforts toward ending the Vietnam War; he also dealt with tense situations in the Middle East and the always sensitive arena of U.S.-Soviet relations. In the *New Republic*, John Osborne called Kissinger "the one indispensable man on Nixon's staff," a Harvard-trained academic who never seemed to fit into easy political categories. *Washington Post Book World* contributor Townsend Hoopes has similarly stated that as Nixon's closest advisor, Kissinger "became the one oasis of distinction in the desert of that mediocre and squalid administration."

Since "retiring" from public service in 1977, Kissinger has devoted most of his time to writing and to serving as a political analyst on television. He remains the most readily recognizable ex-cabinet member of any modern administration, "one of our most enduring elder statesmen," to quote a *Parade* magazine correspondent. Kissinger's best-known books include two detailed chronicles of his years in the Nixon administration, *White House Years* and *Years of Upheaval*. A work well over one thousand pages long, *White House Years* won the American Book Award in 1980; Hoopes finds the work "a pleasure to read," with "clean, sure narrative reporting, . . . gemlike definitions of complicated diplomatic situations and philosophic observations that occasionally rise to the level of majesty."

Heinz Alfred Kissinger—who changed his name to Henry when he came to the United States—was born in Fuerth, Germany in 1923. Kissinger's father was a school teacher who lost his job due to discrimination against Jews. In 1938 the Kissinger family fled Germany, settling in New York City. Henry attended school at George Washington High, earning straight A grades; he later went to night school to study accounting while working days in a factory. A wartime stint in the army offered Kissinger his first opportunities for advancement. Drafted in 1943, he first served in the 84th Infantry Division, then transferred to the Counter-Intelligence Corps. While still in his early twenties, Kissinger was placed in charge of reorganizing municipal governments in occupied Germany; he remained with the Military Intelligence Reserve until 1959.

After the Second World War, Kissinger decided to return to college. He won a New York state scholarship to Harvard University, where he earned his bachelor's, master's, and doctorate degrees in government. He then remained at Harvard as an instructor, eventually working his way to full professor. Concurrently he began to serve as a consultant to several government bureaus, including the army's Operations Research Office and the Psychological Strategy Board of the Joint Chiefs of Staff. In one capacity or another, Kissinger served the Eisenhower, Kennedy, and Johnson administrations, all while he carried a heavy load of responsibility at Harvard. He also authored several books during the period, especially *Nuclear Weapons and Foreign Policy* (1957) and *The Troubled Partnership: A Reappraisal of the Atlantic Alliance* (1965). Hoopes observes that these and other Kissinger works offer "the premise that the key to global balance in the modern world is the U.S.-Soviet relationship; . . . that there are really no other relationships of consequence. In his view, U.S.-Soviet interactions pervade every issue on the globe; there are no local isolable crises; 'linkage' is universal, and 'credibility' the only goal." *Nuclear Weapons and Foreign Policy* won the Woodrow Wilson Prize in 1958 and established Kissinger's reputation as an expert on global diplomacy.

In 1968 Kissinger offered his services as advisor and speechwriter to presidential candidate Nelson Rockefeller. Rockefeller did not win the Republican nomination, but the candidate who did—Richard Nixon—invited Kissinger to become his principal foreign policy advisor. Kissinger accepted the position of director of the National Security Council, and he quickly became more influential than several of Nixon's cabinet members. On trips abroad as well as in the most significant policy planning meetings, Kissinger often dominated; he is credited with the initiation of the first Strategic Arms Limitation Talks with the Soviet Union, with initiation of normal relations with Communist

China, and most importantly, with negotiations to end the Vietnam War. Hoopes writes: "Kissinger's rise to undoubted power and prominence . . . owed a great deal to Nixon's peculiar *modus operandi* in foreign and defense affairs. In a more open and discursive administration, he would have been only one of several competing advisers with his influence correspondingly diluted. Under Nixon, he became the principal keeper of the keys—*the* adviser, spokesman and negotiator on all major foreign policies."

As the Nixon administration became mired in the Watergate scandal, Kissinger was made Secretary of State. He served both Nixon and his successor Gerald Ford in this capacity until 1977. The last year of Nixon's presidency is chronicled in *Years of Upheaval*, a book that also explores Kissinger's role in the peace talks between Egypt and Israel. In the *Washington Post Book World*, McGeorge Bundy calls *Years of Upheaval* "a remarkable achievement," adding: "It has hundreds of pages that should be of deep interest to more general readers, and . . . it can be sampled to great advantage and indeed does not seem intended for complete study by every buyer." *New York Times* correspondent Christoper Lehmann-Haupt finds the work "brilliantly argued, skillfully paced, sensitively proportioned, consistently charming, altogether masterly and by far the most consequential memoir to come out of the Nixon administration." Frankel concludes: "[Kissinger] manages to present some ugly truths without burning too many bridges. That has been his craft, in life and in office, and so it is in print."

Kissinger has served more recent administrations as a member of the Foreign Intelligence Advisory Board. In that capacity he has made fact-finding missions to Latin America and elsewhere, strictly on a nonpartisan basis. Never one to avoid the limelight, Kissinger has also kept up a busy schedule of television appearances and public lectures—Hoopes notes that the statesman "understands better than most that this is the Age of Celebrity and that a popular image is an important reinforcement of power." Still, writes Hoopes, "the luster of Kissinger's image as statesman is more reliably maintained through his written works than through his television appearances." *Spectator* contributor Colin Welch claims that Kissinger's books offer "an insight into the workings of a mind at once fair and broad, lucid, powerful, benign and prodigiously well stocked. . . . This mind addresses itself successively to ever-changing circumstances and problems new or newly perceived, tirelessly exploring and reflecting, reaching conclusions *pro tem*, only to modify, reject or replace them later." Welch concludes: "We are confronted not with reasoning completed but with reasoning in progress, and, God willing, more to come."

WORK IN PROGRESS: A book "about the meaning of diplomacy," for Simon & Schuster.

BIOGRAPHICAL/CRITICAL SOURCES:

BOOKS

Allen, Gary, *Kissinger*, Devin-Adair, 1976.

Bell, Coral, *The Diplomacy of Detente: The Kissinger Era*, St. Martin's, 1977.

Blumenfeld, Ralph, and others, *Henry Kissinger: The Private and Public Story*, New American Library, 1974.

Brandon, Henry, *The Retreat of American Power: The Inside Story of How Nixon and Kissinger Changed American Policy for Years to Come*, Doubleday, 1973.

Brown, Seyom, *The Crises of Power: Foreign Policy in the Kissinger Years*, Columbia University Press, 1979.

Dickson, Peter, *Kissinger and the Meaning of History,* Cambridge University Press, 1978.

Kalb, Marvin and Bernard Kalb, *Kissinger,* Little, Brown, 1974.

Landau, David, *Kissinger: The Uses of Power,* Houghton, 1972.

Mazlish, Bruce, *Kissinger: The European Mind in American Policy,* Basic Books, 1976.

Morris, Roger, *Uncertain Greatness: Henry Kissinger and American Foreign Policy,* Harper, 1977.

Shawcross, William, *Sideshow: Kissinger, Nixon, and the Destruction of Cambodia,* Simon & Schuster, 1979.

Sobel, Lester A., editor, *Kissinger and Detente,* Facts on File, 1975.

Stoessinger, John G., *Henry Kissinger: The Anguish of Power,* Norton, 1976.

Szulc, Tad, *The Illusion of Peace: A Diplomatic History of the Nixon Years,* Viking, 1978.

PERIODICALS

Atlantic, December, 1969, May, 1979, February, 1980.

Books and Arts, December 21, 1979.

Chicago Tribune Book World, March 28, 1982.

Christian Century, September 3, 1969.

Detroit Free Press, January 12, 1979, November 14, 1979.

Detroit News, June 10, 1979.

Detroit News Magazine, November 11, 1979.

Harper's, January, 1971.

Los Angeles Times Book Review, February 1, 1981, April 18, 1982.

National Review, April 6, 1971.

New Republic, January 31, 1981.

Newsweek, December 16, 1968, October 26, 1970, November 2, 1970, September 3, 1973, March 1, 1976, April 30, 1979, October 29, 1979.

New Yorker, July 12, 1969, May 14, 1979.

New York Review of Books, June 28, 1979.

New York Times, December 3, 1968, February 19, 1970, October 17, 1973, October 16, 1979, October 23, 1979, March 24, 1982, April 13, 1987.

New York Times Book Review, June 29, 1969, April 22, 1979, November 11, 1979, February 1, 1981, April 4, 1982.

New York Times Magazine, June 1, 1969, November 14, 1971, October 28, 1973, December 16, 1979.

Parade, January 11, 1987.

Saturday Review, June 9, 1979.

Spectator, September 14, 1985.

Time, September 3, 1973, April 4, 1974, October 21, 1974, November 17, 1975, December 27, 1976, January 24, 1977, February 28, 1977, October 1, 1979, October 8, 1979, October 15, 1979.

Times (London), April 1, 1982.

Times Literary Supplement, October 15, 1982, December 13, 1985.

Village Voice, October 22, 1979.

Washington Post, October 14, 1979.

Washington Post Book World, April 27, 1969, April 29, 1979, November 25, 1979, March 28, 1982, August 11, 1985.

—*Sketch by Anne Janette Johnson*

*   *   *

KNIGHT, Alanna
(Margaret Hope)

PERSONAL: Born in County Durham, England; daughter of Herbert William Farrar (a businessman) and Gladys Lyall (Allan) Cleet; married Alexander Harrow Knight (a scientist), August 6, 1951; children: Christopher, Kevin. *Education:* Educated privately. *Religion:* Christian. *Avocational interests:* Travel in Europe, the Middle East, and the United States, creative knitting, classical music, walking, exploring old castles.

ADDRESSES: Home—24 March Hall Crescent, Edinburgh EH16 5HL, Scotland. *Agent*—Giles Gordon, Anthony Sheil Associates Ltd., 43 Doughty St., London WC1N 2LF, England; and Sanford J. Greenburger Associates Inc., 55 Fifth Ave., New York, NY 10003.

CAREER: Secretary, 1949-51; writer, 1964—.

MEMBER: Society of Antiquaries (Scotland; fellow), Society of Authors (Scotland), Scottish PEN, Crime Writers' Association, Romantic Novelists Association, Radiowriters Association.

AWARDS, HONORS: First novel award, Romantic Novelists Association, 1968, for *Legend of the Loch.*

WRITINGS:

NOVELS

Legend of the Loch, Lancer Books, 1970.

The October Witch, Lancer Books, 1971.

Castle Clodha, Avon, 1972.

Lament for Lost Lovers, Avon, 1973.

The White Rose, Avon, 1974.

A Stranger Came By, Avon, 1975.

The Passionate Kindness (also see below), Milton House, 1975.

A Drink for the Bridge, Macmillan (England), 1976, Corgi, 1977.

The Wicked Wynsleys, Leisure Books, 1977.

(Under pseudonym Margaret Hope) *Queen's Captain,* Mills & Boon, 1978.

The Black Duchess, Doubleday, 1980.

(Under pseudonym Margaret Hope) *Hostage Most Royal,* Mills & Boon, 1980.

(Under pseudonym Margaret Hope) *The Shadow Queen,* Mills & Boon, 1980.

Castle of Foxes, Doubleday, 1981.

Colla's Children, Macdonald, 1982.

(Under pseudonym Margaret Hope) *Perilous Voyage,* Mills & Boon, 1984.

The Clan, Macdonald, 1985.

Estella, St. Martin's, 1986.

Enter Second Murderer, St. Martin's, 1989.

Blood Line, St. Martin's, 1989.

Deadly Beloved, St. Martin's, 1990.

Killing Cousins, Macmillan, 1990.

A Quiet Death, Macmillan, 1991.

OTHER

The Private Life of Robert Louis Stevenson (two-act play; based on her novel *The Passionate Kindness;* first produced at Edinburgh Festival of Arts, 1974), Molendinar Press, 1980.

Girl on an Empty Swing (one-act play), New Playwrights Network, 1978.

(Author of introduction) *Reincarnation: The Best Short Stories of R. B. Cunninghame Graham,* Ticknor & Fields, 1980.

(Editor) *The Robert Louis Stevenson Treasury,* St. Martin's, 1986.

(Editor) *Robert Louis Stevenson in the South Seas: An Intimate Photographic Record,* Paragon House, 1987.

Also author of radio documentaries and plays. Contributor to anthologies, including *Scottish Short Stories* annual, 1978 and

1984, and *Winter's Crimes 21,* 1989. Contributor of articles and short stories to magazines and newspapers worldwide.

WORK IN PROGRESS: Completing second trilogy of "Inspector Faro" crime novels set in Victorian Edinburgh.

SIDELIGHTS: Alanna Knight told *CA* that she "began as a historical novelist. My research and writings on the life of Robert Louis Stevenson gave me a very clear insight into Victorian Edinburgh and paved the way for an historical crime series featuring my currently popular Victorian detective Inspector Faro."

*   *   *

KOESTLER, Arthur   1905-1983

PERSONAL: Born September 5, 1905, in Budapest, Hungary; committed suicide March 3, 1983, in London, England; became a British subject after World War II; son of Hendrik (a promoter) and Adela (Jeiteles) Koestler; married Dorothy Asher, 1935 (divorced, 1950); married Mamaine Paget, 1950 (divorced, 1952); married Cynthia Jefferies, 1965. *Education:* Attended University of Vienna, 1922-26.

CAREER: Writer. Worked as a farmer in Palestine, an assistant to an Arabian architect, and an editor of a Cairo weekly, 1926-29; became foreign correspondent for Ullstein Publications, Germany, serving as Middle East correspondent, 1927-29, and as Paris correspondent, 1929-30; became science editor of *Vossische Zeitung* and foreign editor of *B.Z.am Mittag,* 1930; became member of the Communist Party, 1931; was the only journalist taking part in the "Graf Zeppelin" Arctic expedition, 1931; in the thirties he traveled through Central Asia and spent one year in the U.S.S.R.; war correspondent in Spain for *News Chronicle,* 1936, captured by Fascists, 1937, sentenced to death, and released through the intervention of the British government; left Communist Party in 1938, at the time of the Moscow Trials; editor of *Zukunft,* 1938; in 1939, he was imprisoned in France after war was declared, released in 1940, and escaped to England; worked for the Ministry of Information, the British Broadcasting Corp., and as a night ambulance driver. *Military service:* French Foreign Legion, 1940; British Pioneer Corps, 1941-42.

AWARDS, HONORS: Chubb fellow, Yale University, 1950; Royal Society of Literature fellow, 1958, named Companion of Literature, 1974; fellow, Center for Advanced Study in the Behavioral Sciences, 1964-65; Sonning Prize, University of Copenhagen, 1968; LL.D., Queen's University, 1968; Commander of the Order of the British Empire, 1972; fellow, Royal Astronomical Society, 1976; D.Litt., Leeds University, 1977.

WRITINGS:

Von Weissen Naechten und Roten Tagen, Ukrainian State Publishers for National Minorities (Kharkov), 1933.
Menschenopfer Unerhoert, Carrefour (Paris), 1937.
Spanish Testament (autobiography), Gollancz, 1937, abridged edition published as *Dialogue with Death,* Macmillan, 1942, reprinted, Hutchinson, 1966.
Scum of the Earth (autobiography), Macmillan, 1941, reprinted, 1968.
The Yogi and the Commissar and Other Essays, Macmillan, 1945.
(Contributor) *The Challenge of Our Time,* P. Marshall, 1948.
Insight and Outlook: An Inquiry Into the Common Foundations of Science, Art, and Social Ethics, Macmillan, 1949.
Promise and Fulfillment: Palestine, 1917-1949 (history), Macmillan, 1949.

(Contributor) Richard Howard Stafford Crossman, editor, *The God That Failed: Six Studies in Communism,* Harper, 1950, reprinted, Arno, 1975.
Arrow in the Blue (first part of autobiography), Macmillan, 1952.
The Invisible Writing (second part of autobiography), Macmillan, 1954.
The Trail of the Dinosaur and Other Essays, Macmillan, 1955.
Reflections on Hanging, Gollancz, 1956, Macmillan, 1957.
The Sleepwalkers: A History of Man's Changing Vision of the Universe, Macmillan, 1959, excerpt published as *The Watershed: A Biography of Johannes Kepler,* Anchor Books, 1960.
The Lotus and the Robot (nonfiction), Hutchinson, 1960, Macmillan, 1961.
(With others) *Control of the Mind,* McGraw, 1961.
(With C. H. Rolph) *Hanged by the Neck: An Exposure of Capital Punishment in England,* Penguin, 1961.
(Editor) *Suicide of a Nation?: An Enquiry into the State of Britain Today,* Hutchinson, 1963, Macmillan, 1964.
The Act of Creation (nonfiction), Macmillan, 1964, new edition, Hutchinson, 1976.
(With others) *Studies in Psychology,* University of London Press, 1965.
(With others) *Celebration of the Bicentenary of John Smithson,* Smithsonian Institution Press, 1966.
The Ghost in the Machine (nonfiction), Hutchinson, 1967, Macmillan, 1968.
Drinkers of Infinity: Essays, 1955-1967, Hutchinson, 1968, Macmillan, 1969.
(Editor with J. R. Smythies) *Beyond Reductionism: New Perspectives in the Life Sciences,* Hutchinson, 1969, Macmillan, 1970, new edition, Hutchinson, 1972.
(Contributor) *The Ethics of Change,* Canadian Broadcasting Corp., 1969.
The Case of the Midwife Toad (nonfiction), Hutchinson, 1971, Random House, 1972.
The Roots of Coincidence (nonfiction), Random House, 1972.
The Lion and the Ostrich (lecture), Oxford University Press, 1973.
(With Alister Hardy and Robert Harvie) *The Challenge of Chance: Experiments and Speculations,* Hutchinson, 1973, published as *The Challenge of Chance: A Mass Experiment in Telepathy and Its Unexpected Outcome,* Random House, 1974.
The Heel of Achilles: Essays, 1968-1973, Hutchinson, 1974, Random House, 1975.
The Thirteenth Tribe: The Khazar Empire and Its Heritage, Random House, 1976.
(With Arnold Joseph Toynbee and others) *Life After Death,* McGraw, 1976.
Janus: A Summing Up, Random House, 1978.
Bricks to Babel: A Selection From 50 Years of His Writings, Chosen with New Commentary by the Author, Random House, 1981.
(With wife, Cynthia Koestler) *Stranger on the Square,* edited by Harold Harris, Random House, 1984.

NOVELS

The Gladiators, Macmillan, 1939, 2nd edition, Graphic Books, 1956.
Darkness at Noon (Book-of-the-Month Club selection), J. Cape, 1940, Macmillan, 1941, reprinted, Franklin Library, 1979.
Arrival and Departure, Macmillan, 1943, revised edition, Hutchinson, 1966, Macmillan, 1967.

Thieves in the Night: Chronicle of an Experiment, Macmillan, 1946, reprinted, 1967.

The Age of Longing, Macmillan, 1951, reprinted, Hutchinson, 1970.

The Call Girls, Hutchinson, 1972, Random House, 1973.

Also author of screenplay "Lift Your Head, Comrade," 1944. Contributor to *Encyclopaedia Britannica, Encyclopaedia of Philosophy,* and *Encyclopaedia of Sexual Knowledge.* Contributor to periodicals.

SIDELIGHTS: Arthur Koestler gained international recognition with the publication of his novel *Darkness at Noon,* a fictionalized account of the Moscow Trials of 1938 in which many Bolshevik revolutionaries were put to death by the Soviet Government. "Koestler's object," a reviewer for *Encounter* noted, "was to expose the reality which lay behind the facade of the great Russian state trials of the 1930s, and he did it so effectively that to thousands, even millions, of people, Communism and the Communist party . . . have never looked the same again." Peter Medawar observed that Koestler's novel "changed the direction of the flow of thought on political matters, and it is as such that he will live and continue to be read."

Darkness at Noon grew out of Koestler' own disillusionment with the Soviet Union and Communism after seven years of membership in the German Communist Party. He saw the Moscow Trials as both an abandonment of the Soviet Union's Communist ideals and as dangerously totalitarian in nature. "All the big shots, our heroes . . . were denounced, unmasked as British or American agents," Koestler said about the trials. "When most of my friends had been liquidated in the U.S.S.R., I sent my farewell letter to the German Communist Party." "I went to Communism as one goes to a spring of fresh water," Koestler once explained, "and I left Communism as one clambers out of a poisoned river strewn with the wreckage of flooded cities and the corpses of the drowned." As Jenni Calder observed, through his political writing Koestler presented "his life as an example that could teach and help the understanding of a certain period of history. He had made mistakes. These mistakes could be partially justified if they could be used to illustrate and interpret history."

Koestler's subsequent writings continued to examine the problems of political idealism and power. In such books as *The Yogi and the Commissar, Thieves in the Night,* and *Arrival and Departure,* he explored the problems involved in transforming one's ideals into political action. *The Yogi and the Commissar* contrasts the differences between religious and political ideals and methods of change. *Thieves in the Night* concerns the settlement of Israel by Jews who have long been victims and must now become rulers. *Arrival and Departure* is about a young revolutionary who suffers a nervous breakdown.

By the 1950s, Koestler concentrated less on his political writing and eventually gave it up entirely. "There was a danger," Philip Toynbee wrote, "that Koestler would remain in the constricting armour of his anti-Communism, but Koestler saw the danger clearly enough [and] shed that armour." Speaking of his abandonment of political writing, Koestler stated, "I have said all I have to say on these subjects which had occupied me for the best part of a quarter century; now the errors are atoned, the bitter passion has burnt itself out, Cassandra has gone hoarse—let others carry on."

Leaving politics behind him, Koestler devoted his energies to writing about scientific and philosophical matters. He became, as Robert Boyers wrote, "a learned and witty man who seems to enjoy writing about almost everything." Koestler examined such topics as evolution, psychology, the history of science, capital punishment, and the nature of artistic creation. "Koestler's ideas," Lothar Kahn stated, "probably range over a wider terrain than those of any other writer of our time. Few contemporaries have treated ideologies more analytically and in more original fashion." Medawar, admitting that Koestler "is not a scientist, though he has had some good ideas, . . . and he is not nearly critical or tough-minded enough to be a creative philosopher," believed that he is "an enormously intelligent man with a truly amazing power to apprehend knowledge and grasp the gist of quite difficult theories." P. Witonski disagreed. "Arthur Koestler's forays into the history of science," he wrote, "have done little to enhance his reputation, save among those uneducated in science."

Koestler's most widely-known non-political work was *The Act of Creation,* a study of the creative process in many aspects of human behavior. The book received a mixed critical reaction. E. R. Hilgard believed that "reading the book is a rich experience, for the author wanders widely through science, art, and literature, uses charming and varied analogies, and says countless quotable things. If his book is not the last word on creativity, that is not much of a weakness. It is a serious work, immensely learned, and thoughtful." Anthony Lejeune, however, calls *The Act of Creation* "an unsatisfactory book," claiming that "Mr. Koestler had a worthwhile idea" that "would have made an admirable short essay." Elizabeth Janeway notes that "though I can't help but point out [Koestler's] short-comings [in writing about] the field I know most about, there is something here." She praises Koestler as a "master of the very difficult trade of synthesizing a mass of material [and] of serving up to the general reader facts that he would otherwise never know, and—most important—of explaining why they matter and how they relate to each other."

Koestler holds a distinctive place in contemporary thought and letters. "Koestler," a writer for *Time* stated, "is a rare protean figure in modern intellectual life—a successful journalist, novelist, and popular philosopher. His concern for ultimate issues and his idealistic involvement lend weight to his fiction. His wit, clarity, and brilliance of exposition make his . . . volumes of political, scientific, and philosophical theory highly enjoyable as well as provocative." "To be the author," Alasdair MacIntyre stated, "of one great novel and several good ones, to have written imaginatively on the history of science and polemically on the nature of the human mind, to have involved oneself continually in argument on politics and religion—each of these alone would make up an exceptional intellectual life. But Koestler's life embraces them all."

MEDIA ADAPTATIONS: Darkness at Noon was made into a stage play by Sidney Kingsley and produced on Broadway in 1951. The book has also been translated into over thirty languages.

AVOCATIONAL INTERESTS: Chess, canoeing.

BIOGRAPHICAL/CRITICAL SOURCES:

BOOKS

Arthur Koestler, Cahiers de l'Herne (Paris), 1975.

Atkins, John, *Arthur Koestler,* Neville Spearman, 1956, reprinted, Norwood, 1977.

Baker, Denys Val, editor, *Writers of Today,* Sidgwick & Jackson, 1946.

Books in General, Chatto & Windus, 1953.

Breit, Harvey, *The Writer Observed,* World Publishing, 1956.

Burgess, Anthony, *The Novel Now: A Guide to Contemporary Fiction,* Norton, 1967.

Burgess, Anthony, *Urgent Copy: Literary Studies,* Norton, 1968.

Calder, Jenni, *Chronicles of Conscience: A Study of George Orwell and Arthur Koestler,* University of Pittsburgh Press, 1969.

Contemporary Literary Criticism, Gale, Volume 1, 1973, Volume 3, 1975, Volume 6, 1976, Volume 8, 1978, Volume 15, 1980, Volume 33, 1985.

The Crisis of the Human Person: Some Personalist Interpretations, Longmans, Green, 1949.

Harris, Harold, editor, *Astride the Two Cultures: Arthur Koestler at Seventy,* Random House, 1976.

Huber, Peter Alfred, *Arthur Koestler: Das Literarische Werk,* Fretz & Wasmuth Verlag, 1962.

Kahan, Lothar, *Mirrors of the Jewish Mind: A Gallery of Portraits of European Jewish Writers of Our Time,* A. S. Barnes, 1968.

Koestler, Arthur, *Spanish Testament,* Gollancz, 1937, abridged edition published as *Dialogue with Death,* Macmillan, 1942.

Koestler, Arthur, *Scum of the Earth,* Macmillan, 1941.

Koestler, Arthur, *Arrow in the Blue,* Macmillan, 1952.

Koestler, Arthur, *The Invisible Writing,* Macmillan, 1954.

Lewis, John and Reginald Bishop, *Philosophy of Betrayal,* Russia Today Society, 1945.

Mays, Wolfe, *Arthur Koestler,* Judson, 1973.

Merrill, Reed B. and Thomas Frazier, editors, *Arthur Koestler: An International Bibliography,* Ardis, 1978.

Mikes, George, *Arthur Koestler: The Story of a Friendship,* Deutsch, 1984.

Nevada, J., *Arthur Koestler,* Robert Anscombe & Co., 1948.

Orwell, George, *George Orwell: Critical Essays,* Secker & Warburg, 1954.

Pearson, Sidney A., Jr., *Arthur Koestler,* Twayne, 1978.

Sperber, Murray, *Arthur Koestler: A Collection of Critical Essays,* Prentice-Hall, 1978.

Woodcock, George, *The Writer and Politics,* Porcupine Press, 1948.

PERIODICALS

America, November 13, 1976.
Atlantic, December, 1968, May, 1973.
Books & Bookmen, December, 1972, May, 1976.
Book World, June 30, 1974.
Christian Century, February 26, 1975.
Christian Science Monitor, October 23, 1969, May 4, 1972.
Commentary, November, 1964.
Commonweal, March 4, 1977.
Contemporary Review, June, 1974.
Cornhill, autumn, 1946.
Critic, August, 1978.
Detroit News, April 2, 1972.
Economist, April 24, 1976.
Encounter, July, 1964, February, 1968, January, 1970.
Esquire, March, 1972.
Guardian Weekly, October 28, 1972.
Harper's, January, 1965.
Hudson Review, summer, 1968.
Life, December 29, 1972.
Listener, September 12, 1968, April 8, 1976.
Midstream, February, 1977.
Ms., October, 1975.
Nation, July 3, 1954, November 20, 1976.
National Review, November 17, 1964, June 30, 1970, November 12, 1976.

Natural History, June, 1972.
New Leader, May 14, 1973.
New Republic, February 1, 1975, May 13, 1978.
New Statesman, July 3, 1954, October 1, 1971.
Newsweek, August 30, 1976.
New Yorker, April 21, 1973.
New York Review of Books, December 17, 1964, October 28, 1976.
New York Times, June 23, 1970.
New York Times Magazine, August 30, 1970.
Observer, October 15, 1967, September 8, 1968, October 5, 1969.
Psychology Today, October, 1973, January, 1977.
Saturday Review, October 17, 1964, March 6, 1976.
Science, January 1, 1965, May 12, 1972.
Sewanee Review, autumn, 1965.
Spectator, October 1, 1965, April 27, 1974.
Time, March 1, 1968, August 23, 1976.
Times Literary Supplement, July 2, 1964, November 2, 1967, October 27, 1972, June 11, 1976.
Virginia Quarterly Review, autumn, 1978.
Wall Street Journal, July 26, 1973.
Washington Post, March 13, 1983.

OBITUARIES:

BOOKS

Dictionary of Literary Biography Yearbook: 1983, Gale, 1984.

PERIODICALS

Chicago Tribune, March 4, 1983.
Los Angeles Times, March 4, 1983.
Newsweek, March 14, 1983.
New York Times, March 4, 1983.
Publishers Weekly, March 18, 1983.
Time, March 14, 1983.
Times (London), March 4, 1983.
Washington Post, March 4, 1983.*

* * *

KOPPER, Edward A(nthony), Jr. 1937-

PERSONAL: Born May 8, 1937, in Philadelphia, PA; son of Edward Anthony (a teacher and politician) and Margaret Mary (a family counselor; maiden name, McBride) Kopper; married Margaret Mary Gorman (a hospital co-ordinator), June 18, 1966; children: Edward, Kevin. *Education:* St. Joseph's College (now St. Joseph's University), Philadelphia, PA, B.S., 1958; Temple University, M.A., 1961, Ph.D., 1963. *Politics:* Democrat. *Religion:* Roman Catholic.

ADDRESSES: Home—P.O. Box 59, Lyndora, PA 16045. *Office*—Department of English, Slippery Rock University, Slippery Rock, PA 16057.

CAREER: High school English teacher in Philadelphia, PA, 1959-61; Temple University, Philadelphia, instructor in English, 1961-63; Villanova University, Villanova, PA, assistant professor, 1963-66, associate professor of English, 1966-67; Indiana University at South Bend, assistant professor, 1967-68, associate professor of English, 1968-69; Slippery Rock University, Slippery Rock, PA, professor of English, 1969—, head of department, 1970-71, director of graduate studies in English, 1976—. Has appeared on local television programs.

MEMBER: Modern Language Association of America, College English Association, Association of Pennsylvania State College and University Faculty, American Committee for Irish Studies,

EAPSCU, James Joyce Foundation, Virginia Woolf Society, Northeast Modern Language Association (chairman of Early Twentieth Century British and American Literature Section, 1972; chairman of James Joyce Section, 1973; chairman of Modern and Contemporary Poetry Section, 1975), Phi Eta Sigma (honorary member).

AWARDS, HONORS: Named distinguished professor by State of Pennsylvania, 1975; First Interantional Development Award, 1986.

WRITINGS:

(Contributor) Michael H. Begnal and Fritz Senn, editors, *A Conceptual Guide to Finnegans Wake,* Pennsylvania State University Press, 1974.
Lady Isabella Persse Gregory, Twayne, 1976.
James Joyce's A Portrait of the Artist as a Young Man: A Critical Analysis, Simon & Schuster, 1976.
John Millington Synge: A Reference Guide, G. K. Hall, 1979.
James Joyce: New Glances (monograph), Modern British Literature Monograph Series, 1980.
Ulysses: Notes, Cliff's Notes, 1980, revised edition, 1981.
Graham Greene's The Power and the Glory, Cliff's Notes, 1986.
A J. M. Synge Literary Companion, Greenwood Press, 1988.
(Contributor) *Anglo-Irish Literature: A Guide to Finnegans Wake,* Pennsylvania State University Press, 1990.

Editor-in-chief and publisher, "Modern British Literature Monograph" series, 1976—. Contributor to *Proceedings of the Third Annual Conference of EAPSCU,* 1983. Contributor of over fifty articles and reviews to scholarly journals, including *James Joyce Quarterly, Journal of Modern Literature, Explicator, Modern Language Studies, Notes on Modern American Literature,* and *Studies in the Twentieth Century.* Founder and editor, *Modern British Literature,* 1976-81; member of editorial board, *Studies in the Humanities.* Editor and publisher, *Notes on Modern Irish Literature,* 1989—.

SIDELIGHTS: Edward A. Kopper, Jr., told *CA:* "As a literary critic and scholar, I try to examine an author's work in a new light, i.e., I try to provide for my audience some insight, however small, into an author's intent and scope. I eschew the philosophical and focus on what seems natural, the commonplace—although it is the everyday world heightened.

"In recent years, I have tended to weigh the author's intent more heavily than his work's 'unconscious' reverberations. Once a New Critic, I tend now to be an older one."

* * *

KRANTZ, Judith 1927-

PERSONAL: Born January 9, 1927, in New York, N.Y.; daughter of Jack D. (an advertising executive) and Mary (an attorney; maiden name, Braeger) Tarcher; married Stephen Krantz (an independent film producer and author); children: Nicholas, Anthony. *Education:* Wellesley College, B.A., 1948.

ADDRESSES: Home—Beverly Hills, Calif. *Agent*—Morton Janklow, 598 Madison Ave., New York, N.Y. 10022. *Office*—c/o Stephen Krantz Productions, Inc., 9601 Wilshire Blvd., Suite 343 Beverly Hills, Calif. 90210.

CAREER: Novelist. Fashion publicist in Paris, France, 1948-49; *Good Housekeeping,* New York City, fashion editor, 1949-56; contributing writer, *McCall's,* 1956-59, and *Ladies Home Journal,* 1959-71; contributing West Coast editor, *Cosmopolitan,* 1971-79.

WRITINGS:

NOVELS

Scruples, Crown, 1978.
Princess Daisy, Crown, 1980.
Mistral's Daughter (Doubleday Book Club selection; Literary Guild dual selection), Crown, 1982.
I'll Take Manhattan, Crown, 1986.
Till We Meet Again, Crown, 1988.
Dazzle, Crown, 1991.

SIDELIGHTS: "I'm living proof that you can never do anything until you try," Judith Krantz has maintained on numerous occasions since the publication of her first novel, *Scruples.* Before she achieved such phenomenal success as an author, Krantz worked as a fashion editor for *Good Housekeeping,* then became a freelance journalist after the birth of her eldest son. It wasn't until a number of years later, at the age of fifty-one, that she published *Scruples,* her first work of fiction since her college days. Cynthia Gorney notes in an interview with Krantz published in the *Washington Post:* "There had been one short-story writing class, in her sophomore year at Wellesley, but the professor gave her a B, so she dumped fiction writing." According to Gorney, Krantz "understood herself to be a journalist" during her years as a freelancer. "Journalists have notebooks," Krantz explains. "Journalists have tape recorders. I thought if I tried to do something from my imagination, there wasn't anything there. I didn't realize I had an imagination until I wrote *Scruples.*"

Krantz was encouraged to try writing fiction by her husband, independent film producer and author Stephen Krantz, who for years remarked that his wife had such an exceptional talent for description and a real eye for detail that she had to be a natural-born novelist. Krantz agrees with his assessment, stating in the *Washington Post:* "I'm a stickler for detail. I don't know if anybody doing the so-called commercial fiction researches as thoroughly as I do. I try to create characters who are a little bit larger than life."

After her youngest son graduated from high school, Krantz began working on a novel, writing six-and-a-half hours a day, five days a week. After nine months *Scruples* was completed. "I truly enjoy writing," the author revealed to Jill Gerston of the *Philadelphia Inquirer.* "If I didn't, I could never close myself in my room for almost a year." Krantz then asked family friend and lawyer Morton L. Janklow to read the manuscript. Janklow says he knew immediately that *Scruples* was destined to be a bestseller, and he agreed to serve as Krantz's literary agent. Although *Scruples* was at first rejected by an editor at Simon & Schuster, Crown Publishers eventually purchased the hardcover rights and released it in March of 1978. Four months later the novel became the number one bestseller, according to the *New York Times,* and remained on its bestseller list for almost one year.

Because *Scruples* sold more than 220,000 copies in hardcover and more than three million in paperback, there was much interest in Krantz's second novel, *Princess Daisy.* In September, 1979, six months before the hardcover edition was scheduled to appear in bookstores, Bantam Books purchased the paperback rights to *Princess Daisy* for an advance of $3,208,875, which was then the highest price ever paid for the reprint rights to a work of fiction. The sale ended what the *New York Times* describes as "a fourteen and a half hour auction that involved eight of the nine leading paperback [publishing] houses."

The purchase of reprint rights to *Princess Daisy* for such a huge sum triggered discussions concerning the high fees paid to successful authors for their work. According to Tony Chiu in the *New York Times,* "the sale [of Princess Daisy] renewed criticism among some publishing executives of the growing practice of investing in 'blockbuster' properties to the possible detriment of less commercial authors." Chiu goes on to state that one publishing executive "estimated the sum Bantam paid for the Krantz book could have obtained the reprint rights to sixty books not in the blockbuster category."

Replying to these objections, Marc Jaffe, then president and publisher of Bantam Books, stated according to *Publishers Weekly* that this point of view is "an accountant's, not an editor's way of looking at publishing. Bantam is in the business of publishing all across the spectrum of reader interest—books for young readers, reference works, translations, general nonfiction, novels of all kinds. We are also in the blockbuster business. We hope to continue to acquire blockbusters we're excited about at whatever the cost. We will also continue to acquire all the other kinds of books we publish."

Furthermore, Jaffe explains to Tom Zito of the *Washington Post, Princess Daisy* is the type of book that can really help publishing instead of injuring it: "This is a book that will pull people into the bookstores. There's nothing like a big best seller to pull the industry along." And Krantz's former editor at Crown, Larry Freundlich, states in the *New York Times* that "it's intellectual purblindness to think that if you give one author three million, you're taking it from someone else. That amount of money should not be considered anything other than investment capital—no publisher will pay it unless he is more than reasonably certain that it can be earned back. Judy Krantz writes subtly about love, and pointedly about merchandising. She's a remarkably good novelist speaking to the center of America's venal interest."

Krantz's ability to "pull people into the bookstores" amazes people in the publishing industry and disturbs many of her outspoken critics. Her "ability to tap a readership" (in the words of a *New York Times* writer) has led many to compare her to the late Jacqueline Susann, author of such books as *Valley of the Dolls, Once Is Not Enough,* and *The Love Machine.* Grace Glueck writes in the *New York Times Book Review* that "philosophically, Mrs. Krantz is an absolutist of the Susann persuasion. A painting is a masterpiece, or nothing; a woman is a beauty, or nobody; sex has to be the sun and the moon and the stars."

Krantz's interest in and talent for promoting her books has also been compared to Susann's. "She's very wise in the ways of publicity, just as Jacqueline Susann was," observes Kay Sexton, a vice-president of B. Dalton Bookseller, in *New York Times Magazine.* And in the same article, Howard Kaminsky, editor-in-chief of Warner Books (the paperback publisher of *Scruples*), remarks, "Both as promoters and novelists, Jackie and Judy are in the same tradition."

In order to publicize her first novel, Krantz spearheaded an extensive, $50,000 promotional campaign that included touring the country from coast-to-coast autographing copies of her novel at bookstores and appearing on television and radio talk shows. "It turned out that I was a natural on television," Krantz says in an interview with Claudia Dreyfus for *Newsday's LI* magazine. "I discovered that I had a quality that communicates itself on camera. Eventually, there came a time with *Scruples* when, instead of [our] running after publicity, it came to us." Krantz has given the promotion of her other novels the same dedication.

After the publication of *Mistral's Daughter,* Krantz told Penny Perrick of the *London Times* that she realizes her novels are not Pulitzer Prize material. "If [they] were, I'd think something terrible had happened. I know perfectly well that I'm not a literary writer, I just write the way it comes naturally. For lack of another word it is storytelling." On this same theme Krantz explains to Pat Nation of the *Los Angeles Times:* "I'm a storyteller. . . . If I can't be a Doris Lessing or Iris Murdoch, it doesn't depress me. What I do is entertainment and I do it as well as I can." Larry Freundlich, Krantz's former editor, remarks in the *New York Times Magazine:* "Judy's writing has the same attraction as *People* magazine. You learn about the lives of men and women. She answers all the burning questions you never dared ask. . . . It would make Judy's work grotesque to burden it with attempts at profundity and truth. She doesn't vulgarize her story by trying to make subtle points that don't exist." Krantz explains further in the *Chicago Tribune:* "If you deal in the world of glamour, and that's my turf . . . then you're not taken seriously as a writer, and everyone focuses on how much money you make. But I want to make something very plain—I'm not complaining. Because I chose my turf, and you can't complain when you get a little flack and you knew to expect it. It may hurt a little . . . but you can't complain. You can't have it both ways." As Helen Gurley Brown, a long-time friend of Krantz's and editor of *Cosmopolitan* magazine, observes in the *New York Times Magazine:* "So many people act as if it's easy to write like Judy; as if they could do it, too, if only they would denigrate themselves. They're insane with jealousy! The most difficult thing in the world is to make things simple enough, and enticing enough, to cause readers to turn the page."

MEDIA ADAPTATIONS: Scruples was produced as a three-part, six-hour television miniseries on CBS-TV in February, 1980; *Princess Daisy* was produced as a two-part, four-hour television miniseries on NBC-TV in November, 1983; *Mistral's Daughter* aired on CBS-TV in September, 1984.

BIOGRAPHICAL/CRITICAL SOURCES:

PERIODICALS

Booklist, April 1, 1980.
Chicago Sun Times, February 25, 1980.
Chicago Tribune, March 9, 1980.
Detroit Free Press, November 6, 1983.
Detroit News, September 30, 1979, February 10, 1980, November 6, 1983.
LI, July 6, 1980.
Library Journal, March 1, 1978, February 15, 1980, November 15, 1982.
London Times, May 13, 1983.
Los Angeles Times, May 19, 1978, September 25, 1979, November 26, 1982, July 13, 1988, August 11, 1988.
Newsweek, February 18, 1980.
New Yorker, October 13, 1980.
New York Post, March 3, 1978.
New York Times, September 14, 1979, January 30, 1980, March 2, 1980, December 8, 1982, September 24, 1984, May 1, 1986, May 2, 1986.
New York Times Book Review, March 19, 1978, March 2, 1980, January 2, 1983.
New York Times Magazine, March 2, 1980.
People, June 26, 1978, October 1, 1979, October 18, 1982, December 13, 1982.
Philadelphia Inquirer, May 19, 1980.
Publishers Weekly, January 16, 1978, September 24, 1979, January 11, 1980, July 17, 1981, October 15, 1982, May 16, 1986.
Time, February 18, 1980.

Village Voice, February 18, 1980.
Washington Post, March 3, 1978, September 14, 1979, February 26, 1980, August 3, 1988.
Washington Post Book World, January 27, 1980.*

* * *

KRAUS, C(lyde) Norman 1924-

PERSONAL: Born February 20, 1924, in Denbigh, VA; son of Clyde Henry and Phebe (Shenk) Kraus; married Ruth Elizabeth Smith, May, 1945; children: Yvonne, Jo Anne, John, Bonnie and Robert (twins). *Education:* Goshen College, B.A., 1946, B.D., 1951; Princeton University, Th.M., 1954; Duke University, Ph.D., 1961. *Politics:* Independent.

ADDRESSES: Home—1210 A Harmony Dr., Harrisonburg, VA 22801.

CAREER: Ordained minister of Mennonite church. High school social science teacher in Harrisonburg, VA, 1946-49; Maple Grove Church, Topeka, IN, pastor, 1950-54; Goshen College, Goshen, IN, instructor, 1951-53, assistant professor, 1954-58, associate professor, 1961-62, professor of religion, 1962-80, adjunct professor, 1980-89, director of Center for Discipleship, 1973-80. Mennonite Board of Missions, member of Health and Welfare Committee, 1967-74, member of Overseas Committee, 1976-80, member of staff on assignment in Japan, 1980-87. Visiting professor, Serampore Theological College, Bengal, India, 1966-67; teacher on special mission to Africa and Asia, 1974-75.

MEMBER: American Academy of Religion, American Society of Church History, Mennonite Historical Society, Phi Beta Kappa.

WRITINGS:

(Editor and contributor) *Bible Survey Course,* five volumes, Herald Press, 1956.
Integration: Who's Prejudiced, Herald Press, 1958, revised edition, 1964.
Dispensationalism in America: Its Rise and Development, John Knox, 1958.
The Healing Christ: Social Services and the Evangelical Mission, Herald Press, 1972.
The Community of the Spirit, Eerdmans, 1974.
The Authentic Witness, Eerdmans, 1979.
(Editor and contributor) *Evangelicalism and Anabaptism,* Herald Press, 1979.
(Editor and contributor) *Missions, Evangelism, and Church Growth,* Herald Press, 1980.
Jesus Our Lord: Christology from a Disciple's Perspective, Herald Press, 1987.
God Our Saviour: Theology in a Christological Mode, Herald Press, 1991.

Contributor to books, including *Peacemakers in a Broken World,* 1969, *The Compassionate Community,* 1970, *Kingdom, Cross, and Community,* 1976, *Essays on Biblical Interpretation,* 1984, and *The Variety of American Evangelicalism,* 1990. Contributor of articles to *Mennonite Quarterly Review.*

SIDELIGHTS: C. Norman Kraus told *CA:* "I accepted the Japan assignment after so many years of teaching in an American setting in part so that I could ask the theological questions in a radically different cultural context. How one asks the questions in large part conditions the answers, and the theological discussion in the West seems in many ways to have become ingrown. In Japan even the old questions demand new approaches."

KRIMSKY, Sheldon 1941-

PERSONAL: Born June 26, 1941, in New York, NY; son of Alex (a housepainter) and Rose (Skolnick) Krimsky; married Carolyn Boriss (an artist), June 28, 1970; children: Alyssa, Eliot. *Education:* Brooklyn College of the City University of New York, B.S., 1963; Purdue University, M.S., 1965; Boston University, Ph.D., 1970.

ADDRESSES: Office—Department of Urban and Environmental Policy, Tufts University, Medford, MA 02155.

CAREER: University of South Florida, Tampa, assistant professor of philosophy, 1970-73; Tufts University, Medford, MA, research associate in program for urban social and environmental policy, 1974—, associate director, 1975-78, acting director of urban and environmental studies, 1978-80, assistant professor, 1980-83, associate professor of urban and environmental policy, 1983—. Research associate in philosophy and history of science at Boston University, 1973—. Founder of International Network on the Social Impacts of Biotechnology.

MEMBER: American Association for the Advancement of Science, Council for Responsible Genetics.

WRITINGS:

Regulating Recombinant DNA Research in Controversy: Politics of Technical Decisions, Sage Publications, 1978.
Genetic Alchemy: The Social History of the Recombinant DNA Debate, M.I.T. Press, 1982.
(Contributor) W. C. Swap, editor, *Group Decisionmaking: Interdisciplinary Perspectives,* Sage Publications, 1982.
(Contributor) Gene F. Summers, editor, *Technology and Social Change,* Westview, 1983.
(Contributor) James C. Paterson, editor, *Citizen Participation in Science Policy,* University of Massachusetts Press, 1984.
(Contributor) R. Zilinskas and B. K. Zimmerman, editors, *The Gene-Splicing Wars: Reflections on the Recombinant DNA Controversy,* Macmillan, 1986.
(Contributor) Malcolm L. Goggin, editor, *Science and Technology in a Democracy: Who Should Govern,* University of Tennessee Press, 1986.
(Contributor) John R. Fowle, editor, *Application of Biotechnology: Environmental and Policy Issues,* Westview, 1987.
(With Alonzo Plough) *Environmental Hazards,* Auburn House, 1988.
(Contributor with R. Hubbard and C. Gracey) C. Byk, editor, *Artificial Procreation: The Present State of Ethics and Law,* Masson (Paris), 1989.

Contributor to science journals.

WORK IN PROGRESS: Biotechnology and Society.

* * *

KRUEGER, John R(ichard) 1927-

PERSONAL: Born March 14, 1927, in Fremont, NB; son of Edward Walter (a merchant) and Winifred Ada (Munger) Krueger; married Constance Orrice Peek, March 22, 1957 (divorced August 22, 1980); married Christine A. Kemery, December 22, 1980 (divorced October 26, 1984); children: (first marriage) Curtis E., Catherine A. *Education:* George Washington University, B.A. (with distinction), 1948, graduate study, 1948-51; University of Washington, Seattle, Ph.D., 1960. *Religion:* "Nonbeliever." *Avocational interests:* Music (violin and "amateur gospel pianist"), "oldest active member of Bloomington High-Flyers Trapeze Club-cum-Circus."

ADDRESSES: Home—1215 East Hunter Ave., Bloomington, IN 47401-5037. *Office*—Uralic-Altaic Studies, Goodbody 326, Indiana University, Bloomington, IN 47405-2401.

CAREER: U.S. Department of the Army, Arlington, VA, research analyst for Soviet and Eastern European affairs, 1948-52; University of Washington, Seattle, instructor in German, 1956-57; Reed College, Portland, OR, instructor in German and linguistics, 1958-60; University of California, Berkeley, lecturer in Oriental languages, 1961; Indiana University at Bloomington, 1961-84, began as assistant professor, became professor of Uralic-Altaic studies. Taught at Australian National University in department of Far Eastern history, 1987.

MEMBER: American Oriental Society, Finno-Ugric Society, Societas Uralo-Altaica, Mongolia Society, Tibet Society, Phi Beta Kappa.

AWARDS, HONORS: Fulbright grants, 1952-54, 1968.

WRITINGS:

(With K. Gronbech) *Introduction to Classical Mongolian,* Harrasowitz (Germany), 1955.
Poetical Passages in the Erdeni-yin Tobci, Mouton, 1961.
Chuvash Manual, Indiana University Press, 1961.
Yakut Manual, Indiana University Press, 1962.
Mongolian Epigraphical Dictionary, Indiana University Press, 1967.
(Editor) J. G. Hangin, *Basic Mongolian,* Indiana University Press, 1967.
(Editor) *Mongolian Folktales and Proverbs,* Mongolia Society, 1967.
Cheremis-Chuvash Lexical Relationships, Research Center for Language and Semiotic Studies, 1968.
The Kalmyk-Mongolian Vocabulary in Stralenberg's Geography of 1730, [Stockholm, Sweden], 1975.
Tuvan Manual, Indiana University Press, 1977.
Materials for an Oirat-Mongolian to English Citation Dictionary, 3 volumes (Part 3 published as *Materials for an Oirat-Mongolian to English Dictation Dictionary*), Mongolia Society, 1978-84.
Kazakh Introduction, Indiana University Press, 1980.

Also author of a Kazakh-English dictionary. Also contributor to *Encyclopaedia Britannica.* American co-editor of "Central Asiatic Studies," a monograph series; former editor of "Uralic and Altaic" series, Indiana University; co-editor of "Kalmyk Monograph" series. Contributor to professional journals.

WORK IN PROGRESS: Preparing a biography of the "Mad Baron of Mongolia," R. von Ungern-Sternberg; preparing a general study of language and dialect.

SIDELIGHTS: John R. Krueger told *CA* that he "has spent over thirty days at sea, lived over two years on an island, once collected nearly 10,000 different beer and soda cans, and since 1968 has travelled well over 100,000 airmiles." He also notes that in addition to his knowledge of European and Asian languages, he lived on a Flathead Indian reservation in the summer of 1957 to study the Salishan language.

*   *   *

KUBRICK, Stanley 1928-

PERSONAL: Born July 26, 1928, in Bronx, N.Y.; son of Jacques L. (a doctor) and Gertrude (Perveler) Kubrick; married Toba Metz (divorced, 1952); married Ruth Sobotka (a dancer; divorced); married Suzanne Christiane Harlan (a painter), April, 1958; children: three daughters. *Education:* Attended City College (now the City University of New York).

ADDRESSES: Home—P.O. Box 123, Boreham Wood, Hertfordshire, England. *Office*—c/o Louis C. Blau, 10100 Santa Monica Blvd., Los Angeles, Calif. 90067.

CAREER: Look magazine, New York, N.Y., staff photographer, 1946-50; screenwriter, producer, and director of motion pictures, 1951—.

AWARDS, HONORS: Best director award from New York Film Critics, 1964, for "Dr. Strangelove; or How I Learned to Stop Worrying and Love the Bomb"; nomination for best screenplay from Academy of Motion Picture Arts and Sciences, 1968, for "2001: A Space Odyssey"; best director award and best film award from New York Film Critics, and nominations for best director and best film from Academy of Motion Picture Arts and Sciences, all 1971, all for "A Clockwork Orange"; best director award and best English language film award from National Board of Review of Motion Pictures, and nominations for best director and best film from Academy of Motion Picture Arts and Sciences, all 1975, all for "Barry Lyndon."

WRITINGS:

SCREENPLAYS

"Day of the Fight" (one-reel short), RKO, 1951.
"Flying Padre," RKO, 1952.
"Killer's Kiss," United Artists, 1955.
"The Killing" (adapted from the novel *Clean Break,* by Lionel White), Harris-Kubrick, 1956.
(With Calder Willingham) "Paths of Glory" (adapted from the novel by Humphrey Cobb), United Artists, 1957.
(With James Harris and Vladimir Nabokov) "Lolita" (based on the novel by Nabokov), Metro-Goldwyn-Mayer, 1962.
(With Peter George and Terry Southern) "Dr. Strangelove; or, How I Learned to Stop Worrying and Love the Bomb" (adapted from the novel *Red Alert,* by George), Columbia, 1964.
(With Arthur C. Clarke) "2001: A Space Odyssey" (based on the short story "The Sentinel," by Clarke), Metro-Goldwyn-Mayer, 1968.
A Clockwork Orange (adapted from the novel by Anthony Burgess; produced by Warner Brothers, 1971), Abelard, 1972.
"Barry Lyndon" (adapted from the novel by William Makepeace Thackeray), Warner Brothers, 1975.
(With Diane Johnson) "The Shining" (based on the novel by Stephen King), Warner Brothers, 1980.
(With Gustav Hasford and Michael Herr) "Full Metal Jacket" (based on novel *The Short-Timers,* by Hasford), Warner Brothers, 1987.

OTHER

Contributor of articles to periodicals, including *Sight and Sound, London Observer, Films and Filming, Action,* and *New York Times.*

WORK IN PROGRESS: Two more films for Warner Brothers.

SIDELIGHTS: Filmmaker Stanley Kubrick has been writing, directing, and producing unorthodox movies for more than three decades. In an industry dominated by the corporate committee, Kubrick has managed to forge an independent career that is the envy of many of his peers. He oversees his projects from screenplay to premier, working in near autonomy from studios in London, England. The resulting films "are entertaining, aesthetically pleasing, and provoking, all at the same time," to quote Daniel

De Vries in *The Films of Stanley Kubrick.* Since his earliest forays into movie making, Kubrick has been loathe to repeat himself. He has produced a black comedy, a science fiction film, a costume drama, a horror movie, and a war drama, all of which have provoked enthusiastic debate among critics and the viewing public. As Vincent Canby notes in the *New York Times,* the iconoclastic Kubrick "keeps to his own ways, paying little attention to the fashions of the moment, creating fantastic visions that, in one way and another, are dislocated extensions of the world we know but would prefer not to recognize." Canby continues: "The best Kubrick films . . . are always somewhat off-putting when first seen. They're never what one has expected. No Kubrick film ever immediately evokes the one that preceded it. Yet it's so distinctive that it can't be confused with the work of any other director. . . . As movie follows movie, the Kubrick terrain never becomes familiar. You drive at your own risk, confident only that the director has been there before you."

Kubrick begins the long process of filmmaking by scouting for a story that provides the proper emotional pitch. He then fashions a screenplay based on the story and casts and directs the film himself. *New York Times* contributor Janet Maslin observes that Kubrick's movies "are never slavishly faithful to their sources. What finally matters, in his films, is less their identifiable ideas than their vast and genuine staying power." In the *Los Angeles Times,* Michael Wilmington suggests that one subject unites all of Kubrick's work. "No matter what his apparent background or theme," writes Wilmington, "Kubrick has become a master cinematic orchestrator of dread. Over and over again, in his films, in a style of shocking precision and strange beauty, he confronts us with horror and pain: the evils of warfare, murder, rape, oppression and, at the farthest pitch, nuclear annihilation. Kubrick's films have always seemed consumed by social injustice, and the inevitability of entropy, decay or death." De Vries calls Kubrick "a true screen poet" who "knows how to use visual images to communicate." In *Newsweek,* Jack Kroll concludes that no living film director "matches Kubrick in his ability to create a physical world that transmits a film's emotional frequency."

Like so many of his fellow film directors, Kubrick grew up fascinated by movies and photography. He was born in the Bronx, New York in 1928, the son of a prosperous doctor. Never a particularly distinguished student, Kubrick preferred to spend his time watching silent films, playing chess, and experimenting with his cameras. Kubrick told the *Washington Post:* "My sort of fantasy image of movies was created in the Museum of Modern Art, when I looked at [the films of] Stroheim and D. W. Griffith and Eisenstein. I was star struck by these fantastic movies. I was never star struck in the sense of saying, 'Gee, I'm going to go to Hollywood and make $5,000 a week and live in a great place and have a sports car.' I really was in love with movies." That distinction between art and commercialism would shape Kubrick's career. Almost immediately after graduating from high school he was able to land a job as staff photographer for *Look* magazine. He made his first motion picture, a one-reel short about a boxer called "Day of the Fight," when he was twenty-two years old.

By 1952 Kubrick was finding regular employment as a writer-director of informational short subjects for RKO and other companies. He was therefore able to finance several feature-length films that he wrote, directed, and edited himself. His first was "Killer's Kiss," a grim story about a boxer who tries to save a young woman from involvement with a ruthless gangster. United Artists bought "Killer's Kiss" in 1955 and ran it, with much success, as a second feature on double bills. The following year—after turning down a United Artists contract in favor of independent work—Kubrick released "The Killing," another *film noir* about small-time thieves. The movie earned international recognition for its young director and was "hailed as the sleeper of the year," according to Joseph Adamson III in the *Dictionary of Literary Biography.* Addressing himself to Kubrick's earliest motion picture efforts, *New York Times* contributor David Rabe writes: "There was a spirit at work, as distinct as the most developed novelistic voice. [Kubrick] seemed a man thinking rigorously and originally about the most crucial issues. What was more, he had control of a film technique flexible enough to render this theme with wit, intelligence and passion."

Having established himself as an independent filmmaker, Kubrick continued to develop the dark themes that he found so compelling. "Paths of Glory," released in 1957, concerns the court martial and execution of three privates in the French army. Kubrick wrote the screenplay, based on a novel by Humphrey Cobb, and he insisted on retaining the tragic ending. "Paths of Glory," writes Adamson, "was a great critical success, and its reputation has continued to grow." According to Jonathan Baumbach in *Film Culture,* the work "shows war in its naked ugliness, stripped of glory, heroics, and high-sounding causes." Following "Paths of Glory" Kubrick directed the costume drama "Spartacus," but he remained dissatisfied with the finished film because he did not enjoy his usual amount of control over it. He reasserted his autonomy with the 1962 film "Lolita," based on the best-selling novel by Vladimir Nabokov. Even though he had to bear in mind the standards of the Hollywood censors, Kubrick was able to bring to the screen the story of an erudite European and his passion for a very young girl. The film received mixed reviews; *Partisan Review* contributor Pauline Kael, for one, called it "black slapstick . . . so far out that you gasp as you laugh."

After completing "Lolita," Kubrick moved to England. He made the move for pragmatic, not political reasons—London provided excellent production facilities and a more congenial working atmosphere. In London Kubrick began work on a film about a central concern of his: the nuclear arms race. He based an original script on a novel, *Red Alert,* that dealt with a worldwide holocaust. Eventually Kubrick turned to farce to make his point, transforming a nuclear nightmare into "Dr. Strangelove; or, How I Learned To Stop Worrying and Love the Bomb." A black comedy starring Peter Sellers and George C. Scott, "Dr. Strangelove" revolves on the notion that one lunatic American general might precipitate a nuclear catastrophe while presidents and heads of state look on helplessly.

Its grim premise notwithstanding, "Dr. Strangelove" became an immensely popular comedy. As Adamson notes, the viewer "is shocked into laughing *at* the horror of the threat of nuclear destruction rather than in spite of it." Adamson adds that with "Dr. Strangelove," Kubrick achieved "that rarity of film history, the critical success that is also a box-office winner. . . . *Dr. Strangelove's* reputation has solidified over the years, as time has revealed it to be a landmark film, one of the most important of its decade." In the *New York Review of Books,* Robert Brustein calls the film "a work of comic anarchy, fashioned by a totally disaffected and disaffiliated imagination: it is thus the first American movie to speak truly for our generation." The critic concludes that "Dr. Strangelove" possesses "a great many distinctions as a work of the imagination. . . . [It] is a plague experienced in the nerves and the funny bone—a delirium, a conflagration, a social disaster. . . . *Dr. Strangelove* invests the film medium with a new exuberance, expansiveness, and broadness of vision. . . . Moreover, Kubrick's film is fun—this is its one debt to Hollywood."

Kubrick's next project, "2001: A Space Odyssey" consumed a then-unprecedented amount of time and money—more than six years and ten million dollars. Brought to the screen in 1968, the film follows the adventures of two astronauts and a computer who are searching for the origins of a mysterious lunar monolith. "2001" was a ground-breaking film in terms of special effects; Kubrick took great care to make space travel and life in orbit look as realistic as possible. Judith Shatnoff observes in *Film Quarterly* that the director "has succeeded in showing the romance of technology. His models of the lunar landscape are extraordinary. His attention to the details of space travel is accurate down to the toilet, or the Pan Am space hostess walking on the ceiling for the fun of it, a pen floating weightless in air, but especially he glorifies those pure white spacecraft waltzing in the ice-blue ether." Adamson notes that "2001" met with many hostile reviews from critics accustomed to more theatrically-oriented movies. "Although the completed film dismayed M-G-M executives as surely as it baffled New York critics," writes Adamson, "it turned out to be one of M-G-M's most profitable pictures of the period, saving the studio from bankruptcy. And in spite of the predictions of the critics, the 'boring' film immediately made an impact, attracting a large coterie of followers who came back for repeated viewings." Indeed, some critics have found much to praise in "2001." Shatnoff calls it "one of the visual masterpieces of modern cinema," and *Film Comment* contributor Elie Flatto concludes that in its artistic recreation of a future dominated by science, the work is "one of the most entertaining as well as insightful films ever to have appeared on screen."

If "2001" suggests that mankind might someday transcend earthly flaws, "A Clockwork Orange," released in 1971, explores those same flaws as expressions of free will. Set in the near future, "A Clockwork Orange" deals with the subjects of violence, mind control, and personality. Alex, the central character, is an anti-social lad who is brainwashed into submission, only to reassert himself in the end. According to Paul D. Zimmerman in *Newsweek,* Alex "embodies all of man's anarchic impulses. Shorn of his individuality in the penitentiary and of his fantasy life in the conditioning program, he ceases to be a human being in any real sense. His resurrection at the end, as he regains his ability to act out his lusts and aggressions, represents an ironic triumph of the human psyche over the forces that seek to control or diminish it." Adamson contends that "A Clockwork Orange" aroused a storm of debate as it explored "not only the usual sources of controversy—sex and violence—but also political domination, technological manipulation, religious sanctimony, and ideological hysteria." At any rate, the film was a critical and commercial success, earning Kubrick more Academy Award nominations than had any of his previous projects.

Kubrick's films bear little resemblance to one another, but critics are nevertheless able to detect certain recurring themes. Throughout most of his career, the filmmaker has been called a cynic with a black view of society. De Vries writes: "The Kubrick world is not exactly a pleasant place. It is marked by belief in the badness of human nature, and the suggestion that there is at work in the universe some malevolent force, whose chief aim is to destroy human beings and their expectations." According to Tom Milne in *Sight and Sound,* Kubrick's films begin with "a dilemma in which people are trapped by the mechanics of expediency—their own, other people's, or society's. The trap is set . . . and as we watch the mouse making his pitiful, obstinate attempts to steal the cheese before the steel closes in on him, we know that by the end the trap *will* be sprung." In *The Cinema of Stanley Kubrick,* Norman Kagan too suggests that every Kubrick work "is a prolonged contest conducted under duress in which characters' beliefs are often mocked, exploded, or prove lethal." Michael Wilmington likewise describes Kubrick as "one of our most brilliant nay-sayers," but adds that his work is not "inhuman or contemptuous," but rather "an overly sensitive antennae for the worst tendencies of our time: infernal killing machines and mad tyrannies, deadly snares and traps."

Kubrick's films of the 1980s tend to fit the "man in a trap" scenario. His 1980 work "The Shining," based on a Stephen King novel, explores a writer's descent into madness and murder. The 1987 film "Full Metal Jacket" shows the Vietnam War from the claustrophobic point of view of soldiers in an occupied city. Wilmington characterizes "Full Metal Jacket" as "a unique catalogue of terror . . . a series of near-monomaniacal, dead-ahead moves into darkness or despair." Kroll similarly notes that the movie "scorches you with the absolute chill of its depiction of the war as a plague of corruption and dehumanization." *Chicago Tribune* reviewer Gene Siskel concludes: "The humor in 'Full Metal Jacket' is so raw, its horror so unflinching, that seeing it reminds one that Kubrick's near-best work is more adult, more complex, and more audacious than the movies of virtually any other filmmaker today."

"Stanley Kubrick's unique contribution to contemporary film— what makes him loom larger than other directors who may make more 'perfect' films—is [his] capacity to tackle essential and awesome questions that intimidate filmmakers of lesser nerve and intellect," writes Zimmerman. "From a young man fascinated by the power and technique of filmmaking, he has grown into an artist with a deep concern for the fate of a species increasingly caught between the sweet orange of humanity and the cold clockwork of technology. It is a tribute to his artistry that this concern produced, not an arid cinema of ideas, but an ironic, galvanizing vision of those aspects of modern life that frighten us all." Adamson praises Kubrick for his "idea films that are structured on narrative frameworks," adding: "The triumph of Kubrick's ironic, sardonic sensibility has been to reconcile seemingly irreconcilable conflicts and embody in a single concept elements that have always been considered diametrically opposed. At his best, he arrives at the radical through the traditional and at emotional involvement through a sense of impersonal detachment." *Film Quarterly* contributor Hans Feldman concludes that Kubrick "is one of America's top film directors. He is more than that. Stanley Kubrick is a critic of his age, one of its interpreters and one of its artists."

AVOCATIONAL INTERESTS: Reading, listening to classical music, chess.

BIOGRAPHICAL/CRITICAL SOURCES:

BOOKS

Agel, Jerome, *The Making of Kubrick's 2001,* New American Library, 1970.
Clarke, Arthur C., *The Lost Worlds of 2001,* New American Library, 1972.
Contemporary Literary Criticism, Volume 16, Gale, 1981.
De Vries, Daniel, *The Films of Stanley Kubrick,* Eerdmans, 1973.
Dictionary of Literary Biography, Volume 26: *American Screenwriters,* Gale, 1984.
Geduld, Carolyn, *Filmguide to 2001: A Space Odyssey,* Indiana University Press, 1973.

Gelmis, Joseph, *The Film Director as Superstar,* Doubleday, 1970.

Kagan, Norman, *The Cinema of Stanley Kubrick,* Holt, 1972.

Kauffmann, Stanley, *Living Images: Film Comment and Criticism,* Harper, 1975.

Philips, Gene D., *Stanley Kubrick: A Film Odyssey,* Popular Library, 1975, revised edition, 1977.

Taylor, John Russell, *Directors and Directions: Cinema for the Seventies,* Hill & Wang, 1975.

Walker, Alexander, *Stanley Kubrick Directs,* Harcourt, 1971.

PERIODICALS

American Scholar, summer, 1972.

Artforum, February, 1969.

Chicago Tribune, June 21, 1987, July 26, 1987.

Christian Science Monitor, May 10, 1968.

Cinema, winter, 1972-73.

Esquire, July, 1958.

Eye, August, 1968.

Film Comment, summer, 1965, winter, 1969.

Film Culture, Volume 2, number 3, 1956, winter, 1957-58, February, 1958, spring, 1970.

Film Heritage, summer, 1968.

Film Quarterly, fall, 1964, fall, 1968, fall, 1976.

Holiday, February, 1964.

Hudson Review, autumn, 1962.

Journal of Popular Film, Volume 3, number 3, 1974.

Life, March 13, 1964.

Los Angeles Times, June 26, 1987, July 7, 1987, July 26, 1987, January 28, 1988, June 21, 1989.

Nation, June 3, 1968.

New Republic, May 4, 1968, January 1-8, 1972, January 3-10, 1976.

Newsweek, January 3, 1972, December 22, 1975, June 29, 1987.

New York, December 29-January 5, 1975-76.

New Yorker, November 12, 1966, June 9, 1980.

New York Review of Books, February 6, 1964.

New York Times, April 4, 1968, April 14, 1968, December 20, 1971, January 4, 1972, December 31, 1972, February 29, 1976, May 23, 1980, June 21, 1987, June 26, 1987.

New York Times Magazine, October 12, 1958, January 6, 1966.

Partisan Review, fall, 1962.

Playboy, September, 1968.

Salmagundi, summer-fall, 1977.

Saturday Review, April 20, 1968, December 25, 1971.

Sight and Sound, spring, 1956, spring, 1964, summer, 1968.

Take One, January, 1977.

Time, December 20, 1971, December 15, 1975, June 29, 1987.

Village Voice, February 13, 1964.

Washington Post, June 26, 1987, June 28, 1987, July 12, 1987.

—*Sketch by Anne Janette Johnson*

L

LAIDLAW, A. K.
See GRIEVE, C(hristopher) M(urray)

*   *   *

LAIRD, Betty A(nn) 1925-

*PERSONAL:*Born December 19, 1925, in Grand Island, NE; daughter of Myron E. (a railroad engineer) and Anna L. (a businesswoman, maiden name Youtsey) Olson; married Roy D. Laird (a professor of political science), September 3, 1946; children: Claude Myron, David Alan, Heather Lea. *Education:* Hastings College, B.A. (cum laude), 1948; graduate study at University of Nebraska, 1947-48, University of Washington, Seattle, 1955-56, and University of Kansas, 1960, 1967-68. *Politics:* Republican. *Religion:* Unaffiliated.

ADDRESSES: Home—Route 5, Box 102A, Lawrence, KS 66047.

CAREER: Teacher of English in junior high school, Grand Island, NE 1949-50; University of Washington, School of Business, Seattle, curriculum adviser, 1955-56; University of Kansas, Lawrence, assistant instructor in English, 1958-62, research assistant in political science, 1969-70, Slavic and Soviet Area Studies, Polish program administrator, 1972-73; independent research analyst, 1970—. Centron Corp. (film producers), Lawrence, actress in educational and commercial films since 1958. Co-owner and manager, Parker-Laird Enterprises, Overbrook, KS, 1976—. Director, Clinton Lake Museum, Clinton, KS, 1983-87.

MEMBER: American Association for the Advancement of Slavic Studies.

AWARDS, HONORS: Hastings College Alumni Citation, 1977; Clinton Lake Historical Society Recognition award, 1983.

WRITINGS:

(With husband, Roy D. Laird) *Soviet Communism and Agrarian Revolution,* Pelican, 1970.
(With R. D. Laird) *To Live Long Enough: The Memoirs of Naum Jasny, Scientific Analyst,* University Press of Kansas, 1976.
(With Martha Parker) *Soil of Our Souls,* Coronado Press, 1976.
(Editor with R. D. Laird and Joseph Hajda) *The Future of Agriculture in the Soviet Union and Eastern Europe: The 1976-80 Five Year Plans,* Westview, 1977.

(Editor with R. D. Laird and Ronald A. Francisco) *The Political Economy of Collectivized Agriculture: A Comparative Study of Communist and Non-Communist Systems,* Pergamon, 1979.
(Editor with R. D. Laird and Francisco) *Agricultural Policies in the U.S.S.R. and Eastern Europe,* Westview, 1980.
(Contributor with R. D. Laird) Fred Carstensen and Gregory Guroff, editors, *Entrepreneurship in Imperial Russia and the Soviet Union,* Princeton University Press, 1983.
(Contributor with R. D. Laird) Josef C. Brada and Karl-Eugen Waedekin, editors, *Socialist Agriculture in Transition,* Westview, 1987.
(With R. D. Laird) *A Soviet Lexicon: Important terms, Concepts, and Phrases,* Lexington Books, 1988.
(Contributor with R. D. Laird) Waedekin, editor, *Communist Agriculture,* Routledge, 1990.
Jasmine and the Sixth Age (a play in two acts), produced in Lawrence, KS, 1990.

Author of museum exhibit texts, *The Clinton Lake Communities: The First Twenty Years,* 1980; *Religion in the Clinton Lake Area,* 1983; *The J. C. Steele House,* 1983; *Readin', Writin', and 'Rithmetic,* 1984; *Living on the Land,* 1986; *Weatherworks,* 1988. Also author of several one-act plays produced in the Lawrence, KS area. Contributor to newspapers and academic journals.

WORK IN PROGRESS: Roses for Carey, a play in two acts and several short plays; (with Martha Parker) *The Study of War,* a new exhibit for the Clinton Lake Museum, 1991.

SIDELIGHTS: Betty A. Laird told *CA:* "Having tasted the sweet joys of writing fiction (two unpublished novels as well as my plays), I may never again be satisfied with a diet restricted to fact. However, perhaps unfettered imagination, like too much plum pudding, would lie heavy on the stomach."

*   *   *

LAIRD, Roy D(ean) 1925-

PERSONAL: Born July 15, 1925, in Blue Hill, NE; son of Claud Ross (a psychiatrist) and Amelia Frances (Krula) Laird; married Betty Ann Olson (a writer and editor), September 3, 1946; children: Claude Myron, David Alan, Heather Lea. *Education:* Hastings College, B.A., 1947; University of Nebraska, M.A., 1952; University of Glasgow, graduate study, 1952-53; University of

Washington, Seattle, Ph.D., 1956. *Religion:* Unitarian Universalist.

ADDRESSES: Home—Route 5, Box 102A, Lawrence, KS 66047. *Office*—Department of Political Science, University of Kansas, Lawrence, KS 66045.

CAREER: U.S. Government, Washington, DC, research analyst, 1956-57; University of Kansas, Lawrence, assistant professor, 1957-62, associate professor, 1962-66, professor of political science, 1968-90, graduate director of department, 1975—, acting chairman of Slavic and Soviet Area Center, 1967-68, 1969. Visiting lecturer at London School of Economics and Political Science, University of London, Oxford University, Warsaw University, University of Glasgow, University of Marburg, University of Munich, Pittsburg State University, Pennsylvania State University, Arizona State University Yale University, and numerous other colleges and universities; consultant to the Special Operations Research Office, Washington, 1960.

MEMBER: American Association for the Advancement of Slavic Studies, American Political Science Association, American Academy of Political and Social Sciences, Conference on Soviet Agricultural and Peasant Affairs (founder; member of executive board, 1962), Conference on Soviet and Communist Studies, International Symposium on Soviet Agriculture (founder), American Association of University Professors, Midwest Association for the Advancement of Slavic Studies (member of executive board, 1968-69), Central Slavic Association, Midwest Conference of Slavic Studies, Midwest Political Science Association, Western Social Science Association, Western Slavic Studies Association, Western Slavic Conference (vice-president, 1975-76), Kansas Political Science Association, Pi Sigma Alpha.

AWARDS, HONORS: Elizabeth Watkins Faculty Research fellowship, 1960; Rockefeller Foundation grant to do research in Europe, 1963-64; National Science Foundation grants to do research in Mexico, 1966, 1967-68; Fulbright grant to do research in Eastern Europe, 1967; National Aeronautics and Space Administration grant, 1971-72; Hesston Foundation grant, 1976-79; Lilly Foundation grant, 1976; Alumni citation, Hastings College, 1979; Volkswagon Foundation grant, 1981; Andersons Foundation grants, 1982-83, 1983-84; Ford Foundation and IREX conference grants, 1986-87.

WRITINGS:

Collective Farming in Russia: A Political Study of the Soviet Kolkhozy, University of Kansas, 1958.
The Rise and Fall of the M.T.S. as an Instrument of Soviet Rule, Government Research Center, University of Kansas, 1960.
(Editor) *Soviet Agricultural and Peasant Affairs,* University of Kansas Press, 1963, reprinted, Greenwood Press, 1982.
(Editor with Edward L. Crowley) *Soviet Agriculture: The Permanent Crisis,* Praeger, 1965.
Government of the U.S.S.R., Extramural Independent Study Center, University of Kansas, 1970.
(With wife, Betty A. Laird) *Soviet Communism and Agrarian Revolution,* Pelican, 1970.
The Soviet Paradigm: An Experiment in Creating a Monohierarchical Policy, Free Press, 1970.
(With B. A. Laird) *To Live Long Enough: The Memoirs of Naum Jasny, Scientific Analyst,* University Press of Kansas, 1976.
(Author of introduction) Martha Parker and B. A. Laird, *Soil of Our Souls,* House of Usher, 1976.
(Editor with B. A. Laird and Joseph Hajda) *The Future of Agriculture in the Soviet Union and Eastern Europe: The 1976-80 Five Year Plans,* Westview, 1977.

(Editor with B. A. Laird and Ronald A. Francisco) *The Political Economy of Collectivized Agriculture: A Comparative Study of Communist and Non-Communist Systems,* Pergamon, 1979.
(Editor with B. A. Laird and Francisco) *Agricultural Policies in the U.S.S.R. and Eastern Europe,* Westview, 1980.
(With Thomas Armstrong and others) *Grain Yields, Nitrates, Solar Cycles, and Public Policies,* University of Kansas Space Technology Center, 1981.
The Politburo: Demographic Trends, Gorbachev and the Future, Westview, 1986.
(With B. A. Laird) *A Soviet Lexicon: Important Terms, Concepts, and Phrases,* Lexington Books, 1988.

CONTRIBUTOR

Franklyn D. Holzman, editor, *Readings on the Soviet Economy,* Rand McNally, 1962.
Harry G. Shaffer, editor, *The Soviet Economy,* Appleton, 1963.
Claude E. Hawley and Ruth G. Weintraub, editors, *Administrative Questions and Political Answers,* Van Nostrand, 1966.
Jan S. Prybyla, editor, *The Triangle of Power, Conflict, and Accommodation: The United States, the Soviet Union, Communist China,* Pennsylvania State University Press, 1966.
Vladimir G. Treml and Robert Farrell, editors, *The Development of the Soviet Economy: Plan and Performance,* Praeger, 1968.
Shaffer and Prybyla, editors, *From Underdevelopment to Affluence: Western, Soviet, and Chinese Views,* Appleton, 1968.
Shaffer, editor, *The Soviet Economy: A Collection of Western and Soviet Views,* 2nd edition, Appleton, 1969.
Richard Cornell, editor, *The Soviet Political System: A Book of Readings,* Prentice-Hall, 1970.
Bernard W. Eissenstat, editor, *Lenin and Leninism,* Lexington Books, 1971. Joseph L. Nagie, editor, *Man, State and Society in the Soviet Union,* Praeger, 1972.
Ellen Mickiewicz, editor, *Handbook of Soviet Social Science Data,* Free Press, 1973.
Eissenstat, editor, *The Soviet Union in the Seventies and Beyond,* Lexington Books, 1975.
Zbigniew M. Fallenbuchl, editor, *Economic Development in the Soviet Union and Eastern Europe,* Volume 2, Praeger, 1976.
(With B. A. Laird) Fred Carstensen and Gregory Guroff, editors, *Entrepreneurship in Imperial Russia and the Soviet Union,* Princeton University Press, 1983.
Nish Jamgotch, Jr., editor, *Sectors of Mutual Benefits in U.S.-Soviet Relations,* Duke University Press, 1985.
(With B. A. Laird) Josef C. Brada and Karl-Eugen Waedekin, editors, *Socialist Agriculture in Transition,* Westview, 1987.
(Author of introduction) Stefan Hedlund, *Private Agriculture in the Soviet Union,* Routledge, 1989.
(With B. A. Laird) Waedekin, editor, *Communist Agriculture,* Routledge, 1990.
Grossman and Waedekin, editors, *Agriculture in the U.S.S.R. and Eastern Europe,* Routledge, 1990.

Contributor to *Modern Encyclopedia of Russia and the Soviet Union,* Academic International Press, 1990.

OTHER

Editor of "Slavic Series," University of Kansas, 1970. Contributor of about sixty articles and reviews to *New Republic, Kansas City Times, Christian Science Monitor, Osteuropa, Review of Socialist Law,* and social science journals in the United States and elsewhere.

WORK IN PROGRESS: Writing on trends in Soviet agriculture, on political trends in the Soviet system, and on world food problems.

SIDELIGHTS: R. D. Laird told *CA:* "When I was a child I loved books, and my earliest recollection of my intellectual awakening is of a conviction that to have something one had written published would be the most wonderful accomplishment of all. To feel that one's ideas and discoveries might influence others' thoughts and actions would be the great reward. Of course it was not until many years later that I dicovered I wanted to be a university professor and that my major teaching, research and writing interest would be Soviet affairs, particularly the economy of Soviet agriculture. Why that specialty? Simply put, my rural Nebraska background convinced me that collectivized agriculture had to be impossibly inefficient and wasteful. I am proud to say that every criticism of Soviet agriculture I have made over the last four decades has been echoed by Gorbachev and/or his followers in their attempt to revolutionize the Soviet rural scene."

*   *   *

LAPHAM, Lewis H(enry) 1935-

PERSONAL: Born January 8, 1935, in San Francisco, CA; son of Lewis Abbot (a banker) and Jane (Foster) Lapham; married Joan Brooke Reeves, August 10, 1972; children: Lewis Anthony Polk, Elizabeth Sophia, Winston Peale. *Education:* Yale University, B.A., 1956; additional study at Cambridge University, 1956-57.

ADDRESSES: Home—988 Fifth Ave., New York, NY 10021. *Office*—*Harper's,* 666 Broadway, New York, NY 10012.

CAREER: San Francisco Examiner, San Francisco, CA, reporter, 1957-60; *New York Herald Tribune,* New York City, reporter, 1960-62; *Saturday Evening Post,* New York City, writer, 1963-67; *Life,* New York City, writer, 1968-70; *Harper's,* New York City, managing cditor, 1971-75, editor, 1975—. Host and moderator of weekly public television program focusing on current books, "Bookmark," 1988—. Trustee of New School for Social Research and Louis B. Mayer Foundation.

MEMBER: Council on Foreign Relations, Yale Club, Century Club (New York City), Coffee House Club, National Golf Links.

WRITINGS:

Fortune's Child: A Portrait of the United States as Spendthrift Heir, Doubleday, 1980.
(Editor) *High Technology and Human Freedom,* Smithsonian, 1986.
Money and Class in America: Notes and Observations on Our Civil Religion, Weidenfeld & Nicolson, 1988.
(Compiler with Michael Pollan and Eric Etheridge; and author of introduction) *The Harper's Index Book,* Holt, 1987.
Imperial Masquerade, Grove-Weidenfeld, 1990.

SIDELIGHTS: Lewis H. Lapham is considered by many readers and peers to be one of this country's most gifted, insightful, and respected journalist writing today. From the beginning of his career as reporter for the *San Francisco Examiner* to his current post as editor of *Harper's* magazine, Lapham has thoroughly investigated and uniquely interpreted many elements of contemporary American life. Dedicated to his profession, Lapham has earned the reputation of a serious social critic, attempting to uncover dishonesty and corruption on all levels in order to reveal the truth and hopefully provoke thought and action in his readers.

Over the years, Lapham's articles and columns have provided readers with comprehensive and timely commentary written in a compelling and readable style. "[Lapham] is an author of style, with deliberations expressed in gracefully conceived prose," writes Robert Dahlin in *Publishers Weekly.* "Lapham brings formidable weapons to social criticism: wit, learning, a wide association with the people of privilege who are his chief subjects—and a journalist's nose for corruption," states a reviewer for *Atlantic.*

The list of issues Lapham has tackled is extensive and range from environmentalism, conservation of energy, federal aid to the arts, quality higher education, to politics and politicians, the spoiled upper class, and a discussion of Black leaders and role models. "Everyone and anything becomes fodder for Lapham's brilliant mind," remarks David Kaufman in *Inside Books.* "He makes connections that are simultaneously elusive, suggestive, and controversial."

Describing Lapham "as one of this country's most incisive and literate voices of conscience," Seymour Krim praises Lapham's "cool strength and courage" in expressing his opinions. Krim explains further in the *Chicago Tribune Book World* that Lapham "is a moralist who doesn't crowd us, but in his own smooth, Ivy League-way, just simply scares the hell out of us. He is like a C.I.A. agent working against the government that trained him, and his unflappable competence coupled with a mordant vision will give you the deserved shakes for weeks—or until, somehow, we turn this society around."

Lapham's first book, *Fortune's Child: A Portrait of the United States as Spendthrift Heir,* is a collection of thirty-one of previously published articles and columns. The theme behind this assortment of essays is that modern American life is in societal disrepair as a result of our nations's obsession with money, power, and material possessions. Walter Goodman writes in a *New York Times Review* that in his book Lapham provides numerous examples that reflect on "his displeasure with the national condition" and his fear what the future might bring if American's values and priorities are not corrected.

In apparent agreement with Goodman's assessment of the theme of *Fortune Child,* James Sloan Allen notes that Lapham credits "the hegemony of money" as the cause of America's state of "societal disrepair." Allen explains in the *Saturday Review* that Lapham's writings mirror his feeling that as "the inheritors of Western civilization's economic and cultural capital, Americans have felt no need to contribute substantively to it and have instead indulged themselves in the revelries of aimless affluence, cultural frivolity, and selfish competition for pieces of the patrimony. In consequence, Americans of all types have lost respect for both past and future and have banished from their lives the energies of will and imagination that nourish culture."

Discussing *Fortune's Child* a *Publishers Weekly* reviewer compliments Lapham's ability to present serious and important issues effecting our nation in such a readable and entertaining manner. The reviewer states that Lapham "examines aspects of the American scene—politics, energy, the cities, literature, movies, the news media—and offers examples of the American penchant for an innocent Eden. . . . This collection offers one man's coherent view of America and does it in a most entertaining, thought-provoking fashion." "Taken one at a time, as they were originally intended to be, these essays are entertaining, sometimes witty, often insightful," Philip Geyelin remarks in the *Washington Post Book World.*

In 1988 Lapham published *Money and Class in America: Notes and Observations on a Civil Religion,* a book many reviewers feel explore similar themes found in his first book. "It is the idolization of the dollar and the incumbent pathologies of wealth that account for the moral afflictions at every level of American civilization," Barbara Mahany believes is the thesis of *Money and Class in America*. Writing in the *Chicago Tribune*, Mahany continues: "Expounding upon this theme as [Lapham] examines the effects of the vacuous money dream on American class structure, culture, celebrity, crime and politics, Lapham peppers his observations with priceless anecdotes of the absurdities of the rich and the only-wishing-to-be-so."

In the *Los Angeles Times*, Garry Abrams states that *Money and Class in America* "is a long essay on American's obsession with money—how they get it, how they spend it for maximum status, how they protect it from the clutches of the undeserving and how the country seems to be mired in an era of gluttonous, grasping greediness." Abrams goes on to remark that while Lapham "offers no cures for what he sees as a spendthrift society . . . he does warn that in previous times of wretched excess the next step often has been recession—or war." "Technically speaking, Lapham is neither a prophet nor a historian nor a philosopher, yet he emerges as all three in *Money and Class in America*," notes writer for *Inside Books*. "Unlike the legion of books predicting imminent catastrophe for the American economy, Lapham's analysis is more concerned with dissecting the problem than forecasting it consequences."

Lapham explained his thoughts about writing *Money and Class in America* in a *Publishers Weekly* interview in this manner: "We need to realize that money is not the ultimate power of the world. It is not money itself, but the *love* of money that is the root of all evil. If you let this love blot out courage, work, art, romance—then you are closing yourself into a narrower and narrower cage. . . . I am not a prophet, but I do believe we need to get out from under this fear, to reconnect with ideas and spiritual values—that will be our saving grace."

CA INTERVIEW

CA interviewed Lewis Lapham by telephone on March 14, 1989, at his office in New York, New York.

CA: Money and Class in America: Notes and Observations on a Civil Religion, *first published in 1988 and now out in paperback, is closely related in theme to your 1980 book,* Fortune's Child, *a collection of essays you wrote for* Harper's *and other periodicals. For people who haven't read your introduction to the earlier book, would you say something about how your concern with America's money hunger began?*

LAPHAM: The two books could go together; they're two variations in a theme. The undertitle of the first book was *A Portrait of the United States as Spendthrift Heir,* and *Money and Class in America* is a development of that theme. Both books take the same premise, which is that, in 1945, at the end of the Second World War, the United States came into an immense fortune. We inherited essentially the treasuries of Western civilization. Europe had tried to commit suicide twice in the twentieth century, and the United States found itself the most powerful economic force as well as the most powerful military force in the world. It was the American century, the American supremacy, and it came very suddenly. People who in 1939 had joined the State Department with no other idea in mind than to make sure their mothers got through foreign customs without having to have their luggage inspected became proconsuls of the American empire in Japan, the Baltic, and Latin America.

This immense wealth accruing to the American account, the prosperity of the economic machinery that we had invented during the war, gave to the United States a feeling of amplitude and entitlement. To be American was, by definition, to be young, rich, and omnipotent. This was an attitude that really bloomed with the election of Jack Kennedy in 1960. Eisenhower was seen as a kind of avuncular regent; suddenly the Young Prince came to inherit the throne. There was a feeling that we could pay any price; no burden was too heavy, no war too obscure—we could do anything. That was essentially the drift of Kennedy's rhetoric, and we embarked on a period of new thought and expansionism of which he was the beau ideal. Prior to that we'd had the Marshall Plan; we'd undertaken to be the world's policemen, to sponsor the United Nations, to sponsor farm machinery, roads, and morality with what we believed to be unlimited resources both of cash and moral virtue.

Meanwhile, within the United States came rising lines of debt. We had installment buying, credit, and entitlement—the idea was that everybody was entitled to everything. Those attitudes were buffeted around toward the end of the sixties, when it became clear that we couldn't afford both guns and butter, as Lyndon Johnson said, both the Great Society and the war in Vietnam. The war bills began to come due in the seventies, and we proclaimed the age of scarcity. President Carter symbolized that, wearing his sweater, turning down the heat and turning out the lights at the White House.

Then there was Ronald Reagan. Reagan to me is very much like Kennedy, and his coming in is a kind of replay, the melodrama of the sixties replayed as farce. The sixties and the eighties are very similar in that they both subscribe to the manifesto of Peter Pan. In the sixties it was the troupe led by Peter Fonda on the open road to a spiritual kingdom. In the 1980s it was the Arcadian Californians, headed by John Wayne, on the way to Palm Springs. Both of them were saying, in essence, We live outside of time. The sixties generation's manifesto was, We will never grow up. In the eighties, with Reagan, it was, We will never grow old. The trouble is that in the eighties we had to borrow a lot of money to maintain the illusion. So the story of the eighties to me is the story of an imperial masquerade, of empire in the manner of Napoleon III's Second Empire in the middle of the nineteenth-century in France, which was marked by speculation, by hectic spending, by fashion, but drawing down heavily on, and in fact exhausting, the capital that had been accumulated. The sixties and seventies exhausted the capital—financial, intellectual, and moral—that had been accumulated in the Second World War.

So we were bankrupt in 1980; the interest rate was around twenty percent. Carter was saying it was the end of the world and was retiring to Camp David to brood upon the loss. The way to revive the prostrate elephant, or the spendthrift heir, of course, was to borrow. So we started borrowing. We started doing in the eighties what the profligate heir does when he finds himself short of cash; he starts selling the family silver, the furniture, Grandmother's paintings. That's what we've been doing for eight years. We've sold all of Hawaii to the Japanese. We've sold our steel business to the Japanese and the automobile business to the Japanese and Koreans and the textile business to the Taiwanese. We're now in a position where our major exports are rice, corn, wheat, scrap metal, and scrap paper. We are very much, as a nation, like the Confederate South prior to the Civil War. Just as the South was dependent on England and New England for its manufactures, we in the United States are increasingly dependent on Japan and Europe for our manufactures. It's a story of extravagance and profligacy, and both of my books go together in that sense. As I see it, this is a phenomenon that has been playing out over a long time, since 1945.

CA: You don't expect any quick fixes in George Bush's administration, then?

LAPHAM: No, I don't. Mr. Bush is up against it, because he's got not only the debt and the deficit to deal with, but now the problems of the savings and loans institutions. And if he's around in '92, there's going to be the problem of the European bloc. For the moment the United States is still awash in money. On the other hand, we're seeing a division between the rich and the poor of a fairly extreme kind, at least here in New York, where the gulf between the haves and the have-nots is becoming increasingly apparent. The whole question of who's up and who's down is always a topic of conversation at any point in history, but in the last eight years it's become more desperate than I can remember it.

CA: You started your writing career as a newspaper reporter in San Francisco, then went to the New York Herald Tribune *for two years before you began to work for magazines, including the* Saturday Evening Post, Life, *and finally* Harper's—*with writing for other publications mixed in. What was the lure of journalism?*

LAPHAM: I thought I was both a novelist manque and a historian manque. Journalism allowed me to write as I would like to do; it was the third best.

CA: As editor of Harper's, *what specific aims do you have for the magazine? What do you want to do and to publish in* Harper's *that's unique?*

LAPHAM: I think *Harper's* has got a niche, and I want to publish pieces that aren't apt to be published in most other magazines. I want to hear the singular voice of the writer. In the big magazines like *Time* and *Newsweek,* the voices all sound the same after a while. I find that increasingly true, I'm sorry to say, of magazines like the *New Yorker* and the *Atlantic.* In *Harper's* I like the first-person singular. The magazine is much more geared toward the humanities and toward history than it is toward political science or the social sciences. I'd rather hear somebody explain something to me in terms of the history of literature than in terms of psychology or sociology or political science. And I try to deal with the specific and the concrete rather than the general and the abstract. Also I want the writers to have very clear opinions of their own. As far as I'm concerned, I don't have to agree with what the author says; I just have to think the argument is made intelligently and honestly.

CA: You left your editorial position at the magazine in 1981, then went back two years later. What have you done at Harper's *that you're especially happy about?*

LAPHAM: I'm very happy about redesigning the magazine, in 1984. I was asked to go back in 1983 by Rick MacArthur, the publisher, who's a marvelous fellow and without whom I could have done nothing. I said I'd go back only on the condition that I could completely redesign the magazine, because I think that its older form, which was similar to the form of the *Atlantic* at present, was essentially a dead moon. I didn't think it could continue to exist in that form. People's reading habits have changed and I wanted to mix up the combinations in the magazine; I wanted to have some things that were short, to have a variety.

We live in a world in which we must compete with television and all of the other possible uses of time that are available to people.

It's not like the nineteenth century. *Harper's* started in 1850. I've read a lot of the magazines from that period, and they had a great deal of space; writers could go on forever and ever describing the interiors of rooms or the view from a flatboat going down the Ohio River. The reader had no other way of knowing what those scenes looked like—no photographs, no television, and probably they'd never been out of their hometowns. *Harper's* was the first magazine that was read on both sides of the Mason-Dixon Line. Prior to the Civil War, almost none of the people in the South had ever been in the North, and they had no idea what it was like. If you were in Richmond, Virginia, in 1855, your idea of Boston was probably about like our idea of Uzbekistan. All they had to go on were the very exaggerated and polemical accounts in their own papers. *Harper's* was the very first magazine that was in any sense of the word a national magazine, that was read on both sides of the Potomac River. In the nineteenth century, people looked to magazines of this sort as well as to newspapers and novels for descriptions of the world. That's not true in 1989; they look for descriptions of the world to film or television or their own travels. So you have to figure out a design for a magazine that will appeal to everybody who you know has got an eclectic sensibility and a short attention span.

CA: And I suspect we all have a short attention span, of necessity.

LAPHAM: Yes. I don't say it's a good or bad thing; I just think it happens to be part of the condition in which we live. You can regret it; you can wish it weren't true and that you lived in a world where people still wrote heroic couplets and read Dickens. But that's not the kind of world we live in. On the other hand, writing, to my mind, is still the finest form of expression. If you're faced with a readership that doesn't have very much time, you have to be sure that what you get into their hands is worth their trouble. The way the magazine is now designed gives me a lot more freedom. I no longer have to come up with twelve or thirteen fairly lengthy manuscripts a month, which is the problem now faced by the *Atlantic.* There probably aren't twelve or thirteen really first-rate manuscripts a month published in all the magazines. To get twelve or thirteen good pieces a month, I found myself reading something like a hundred and fifty manuscripts a month, most of them atrocious. If I only have to get one article or one essay a month, I can really work at it. I can find something that's worth not only my time but also the time of the reader.

CA: You spend a considerable amount of time yourself writing pieces for Harper's, *and obviously a great deal of time editing. What's a working day, week, month like for you as editor of the magazine?*

LAPHAM: I write a column once a month, and that takes me about a week, in the mornings. So there's one week in the month in which I'll come in the office and spend the mornings either thinking about or writing drafts of that column. This is always the last week in the month's cycle, since I wait to write the column until I know what's going on in the rest of the magazine. Other than setting aside that time, I do everything as it comes up—read, talk on the telephone, write letters, edit pieces. Now I have the television show I'm doing, too, "Bookmark," and that takes time.

CA: Yes. Tell me more about the show, and what you're trying to do so that it will succeed where other televised book shows have failed.

LAPHAM: Instead of just having critics sitting around talking about books, I'm putting on the author. The preferred forum is myself and the author of the book and then one or two other people, either authors or critics, who would offer a perspective, an angle of appreciation or argument with the text in hand. The point is, of course, is to get people interested enough to read the book.

CA: Maybe even buy the book.

LAPHAM: Maybe even buy the book! I take great pleasure in writers and in ideas and in talking about what people have to say. The challenge is to convey some of that enthusiasm on the television screen. And it seems to be doing quite well. Only eight shows have been aired out of the twenty-six I've been commissioned to do, and it's already on 235 stations around the country. It's got an audience now of a million and a half, which for PBS television is pretty good. I keep experimenting with the camera angles and the size and make-up of the panel; I'm trying to figure out how to get the best conversation.

CA: You must get immediate response to individual segments so that you have some idea how the changes are working.

LAPHAM: Absolutely not! The TV world is crazy. It's a very odd country. People watch but they don't write. We have two hundred thousand subscribers to *Harper's,* which for a magazine of this sort is a lot. But it's the same circulation that *Harper's* had in 1850. I do think that reading and writing are becoming rather special interests. I'm a member of the last generation brought up without television. We had to read, and we liked to read. I have children ages sixteen, twelve, and seven, and they do not read the way I did, despite the fact that the house is filled with books and their father is always going around mumbling about writers. It doesn't translate. They look at television; that's what their friends do, and it's their reference point. It's a different world that people live in now, and I assume that the business of reading and writing, on the level at which I'm interested in it, will be increasingly like the monks in the Middle Ages. I don't expect it to die out, but I expect it to be a more recherche enterprise that it was when I was younger. If you read the letters that were written during the Civil War, for example, you find that, although people couldn't spell, their expression was extraordinarily good and vivid. They were used to reading and writing, and there were no phones. Even people who were barely literate could write. We live in a world now in which there's a great deal of knowledge and information and communication, but we're not at home with the literary forms.

CA: You've hinted elsewhere that you'd like for your next book to be a novel. Is that a real possibility?

LAPHAM: I'd love to try that, but my next book is going to be another collection of essays, in the fall of 1989. It will include some of the ones I've written for *Harper's* and other journals between 1980 and 1988 that were not part of an earlier book. These are mostly about politics and foreign policy and the media and the literary world. When I get finished with the television show, which will be in June, depending on whether it's renewed or not I will sit down and think about what to write next. I would love to be able to write a novel. I'm finally getting old enough that I don't care whether it's what we think of as a conventional novel or not. A novel, I'm prepared to believe, is anything that you can get into between sixty and five hundred pages; I don't think there are any rules for it anyway. I don't think there's any real canon of critical standards now that means very much. The literary world is in a state of anarchy as far as I can tell.

BIOGRAPHICAL/CRITICAL SOURCES:

PERIODICALS

Atlantic, April 16, 1980.
Chicago Tribune, February 11, 1988.
Chicago Tribune Book World, March 16, 1980.
Inside Books, February, 1989.
Los Angeles Times, February 25, 1988.
New York Times Book Review, February 10, 1980.
Publishers Weekly, December 24, 1979; January 11, 1980; February 5, 1988.
Saturday Review, March 15, 1980.*

—*Interview by Jean W. Ross*

*   *   *

LAUERSEN, Niels H(elth)   1939-

PERSONAL: Born September 10, 1939, in Copenhagen, Denmark; immigrated to the United States in 1967, naturalized in 1972; son of Hans B. and Maria (Helth) Lauersen. *Education:* University of Copenhagen, B.S., 1962, M.D., 1967.

ADDRESSES: Home—750 Park Ave., New York, NY 10021. *Office*—784 Park Ave., New York, NY 10021. *Agent*—Diana Price, 185 East 85th St., New York, NY 10028.

CAREER: New York Hospital, New York City, associate professor of obstetrics and gynecology, 1972-79; Cornell University, Medical Center, New York City, researcher, 1972-79, associate professor of obstetrics and gynecology, 1979-84; Mount Sinai Medical Center, New York Medical College, New York City, professor of obstetrics and gynecology, 1985—. *Military service:* Danish Air Force, 1956-59.

MEMBER: Society of Gynecologic Investigation, American Fertility Society, American College of Obstetricians and Gynecologists (fellow), New York Obstetrical Society, American Federation of Television and Radio Artists.

WRITINGS:

(With Steven Whitney) *It's Your Body: A Woman's Guide to Gynecology,* Grosset, 1978.
(With Eileen Stukane) *Listen to Your Body: A Gynecologist Answers Women's Most Intimate Questions,* Simon & Schuster, 1981.
(With Howard Hochberg) *Clinical Perinatal Biochemical Monitoring,* Williams & Wilkins, 1981.
(Editor with Victor J. Reyniak) *Principles of Microsurgical Techniques in Infertility,* Plenum, 1982.
(With Stukane) *PMS: Premenstrual Syndrome and You—Next Month Can Be Different,* Simon & Schuster, 1983.
(Editor) *Modern Management of High-Risk Pregnancy,* Plenum, 1983.
Childbirth with Love: A Complete Guide to Fertility, Pregnancy, and Childbirth for Caring Couples, Putnam, 1984.
(With Judy Hendra) *It's Your Pregnancy: Questions You Ask Yourself and Are Afraid to Ask Your Obstetrician,* Simon & Schuster, 1986.
(With Constance DeSwaan) *The Endometriosis Answer Book: New Hope, New Help. Including the Endometriosis Diet That Promotes Healing,* Wade Rawson, 1987.
(With Whitney) *A Woman's Body: The New Guide to Gynecology,* Putnam, 1989.

WORK IN PROGRESS: Getting Pregnant: What Couples Need to Know Right Now, for Macmillan.

LAURENCE, (Jean) Margaret (Wemyss) 1926-1987

PERSONAL: Born July 18, 1926, in Neepawa, Manitoba, Canada; died of cancer, January 5 (some sources say January 6), 1987, in Lakefield, Ontario, Canada; buried in Lakefield, Ontario, Canada; daughter of Robert Harrison (a lawyer) and Verna Jean (Simpson) Wemyss; married John Fergus Laurence (a civil engineer), 1947 (divorced, 1969); children: Jocelyn, David. *Education:* University of Manitoba, B.A., 1947.

ADDRESSES: Home—Lakefield, Ontario, Canada. *Agent*—John Cushman Associates, 24 East 38th St., New York, N.Y. 10016.

CAREER: Writer. Worked as a reporter with the *Winnipeg Citizen;* writer in residence at University of Toronto, 1969-70, and University of Western Ontario, 1973; Trent University, Peterborough, Ontario, writer in residence, 1974, chancellor, 1981-83.

MEMBER: Royal Society of Canada (fellow).

AWARDS, HONORS: First Novel Award, Beta Sigma Phi, 1961; President's Medal, University of Western Ontario, 1961, 1962, and 1964, for best Canadian short stories; Governor General's Literary Award in fiction ($2,500), 1967, for *A Jest of God,* and 1975; senior fellowships from Canada Council, 1967 and 1971; honorary fellow of United College, University of Winnipeg, 1967; Companion of Order of Canada, 1971; Molson Prize, 1975; B'nai B'rith award, 1976; Periodical Distributors award, 1977; City of Toronto award, 1978; writer of the year award from Canadian Booksellers Association, 1981; Banff Centre award, 1983; numerous honorary degrees from institutions including Trent, Carleton, Brandon, Mount Allison, Simon Fraser, Queen's, McMaster, and Dalhousie universities and universities of Winnipeg, Toronto, and Western Ontario.

WRITINGS:

(Editor) *A Tree for Poverty* (Somali poetry and prose), Eagle Press (Nairobi), 1954.
This Side Jordan (novel), St. Martin's, 1960.
The Prophet's Camel Bell, Macmillan (London), 1963, published as *New Wind in a Dry Land,* Knopf, 1964.
The Tomorrow-Tamer, and Other Stories (short stories), Knopf, 1964.
The Stone Angel (novel), Knopf, 1964.
A Jest of God (novel), Knopf, 1966, published as *Rachel, Rachel,* Popular Library, 1968, published as *Now I Lay Me Down,* Panther, 1968.
Long Drums and Cannons: Nigerian Dramatists and Novelists 1952-1966, Macmillan, 1968.
The Fire-Dwellers (novel), Knopf, 1969.
A Bird in the House (short stories), Knopf, 1970.
Jason's Quest (for children), Knopf, 1970.
The Diviners (novel), Knopf, 1974.
Heart of a Stranger (essays), McClelland & Stewart, 1976, Lippincott, 1977.
Six Darn Cows (for children), Lorimer, 1979.
The Olden Days Coat (for children), McClelland & Stewart, 1979.
The Christmas Birthday Story (for children), Knopf, 1980.
Dance on the Earth: A Memoir, McClelland & Stewart, 1989.

Contributor of short stories to *Story, Prism, Queen's Quarterly, Saturday Evening Post,* and *Post Stories: 1962.*

SIDELIGHTS: Though she was not prolific, Margaret Laurence's fiction made her "more profoundly admired than any other Canadian novelist of her generation," according to Toronto *Globe and Mail* critic William French. Often set in the fictional Canadian small town of Manawaka, her novels and short stories earned praise for their compassion and realism and the skill with which they were told. They also aroused controversy—religious fundamentalists attempted to have one novel, *The Diviners,* banned from schools because it contained explicit descriptions of an abortion and a sexual affair. Laurence frequently explored the predicaments of women in society, and some of her characters are recognized as early feminists. Reviewers judge her work a powerful influence on Canadian writing; in an *Atlantic* review of *The Fire-Dwellers* one writer deemed her "the best fiction writer in the Dominion and one of the best in the hemisphere."

Non-Canadian subjects also appeared in Laurence's works. *The Prophet's Camel Bell* is an account of her experiences while living for two years in the Haud desert of Somaliland (now Somalia), with her husband, sharing the hardships and privations of desert life with their Somali workers. West Africa serves as the setting for the stories in *The Tomorrow-Tamer* and the source of the literature Laurence discussed in *Long Drums and Cannons: Nigerian Novelists and Dramatists 1952-1966.*

MEDIA ADAPTATIONS: The Jest of God was adapted as the film "Rachel, Rachel," starring Joanne Woodward and directed by Paul Newman, Warner Bros., 1968.

BIOGRAPHICAL/CRITICAL SOURCES:

BOOKS

Contemporary Literary Criticism, Gale, Volume 3, 1975, Volume 6, 1976, Volume 13, 1980, Volume 50, 1988.
Dictionary of Literary Biography, Volume 53: *Canadian Writers since 1960, First Series,* Gale, 1986.
Hind-Smith, Joan, *Three Voices: The Lives of Margaret Laurence, Gabrielle Roy, and Frederick Philip Grove,* Clarke Irwin, 1975.
Laurence, Margaret, *Dance on the Earth: A Memoir,* McClelland & Stewart, 1989.
Morley, Patricia, *Margaret Laurence,* Twayne, 1981.
New, W. H., editor, *Margaret Laurence: The Writer and Her Critics,* McGraw Hill Ryerson, 1977.
Thomas, Clara, *Margaret Laurence,* McClelland & Stewart, 1969.
Thomas, *The Manawaka World of Margaret Laurence,* McClelland & Stewart, 1975.
Verduyn, Christi, editor, *Margaret Laurence: An Appreciation,* Broadview Press, 1988.
Woodcock, George, editor, *A Place to Stand On: Essays by and About Margaret Laurence,* NeWest Press, 1983.

PERIODICALS

Atlantic, June, 1969, March, 1970.
Canadian Forum, February, 1969, September, 1970.
Chicago Tribune Book World, December 7, 1980.
Christian Science Monitor, June 12, 1969, March 26, 1970.
Fiddlehead, Number 80, 1969.
Globe and Mail (Toronto), December 14, 1985, January 10, 1987, March 5, 1988, November 4, 1989.
Maclean's, May 14, 1979.
New York Times Book Review, April 19, 1970.
Saturday Night, May, 1969.
World Literature Today, winter, 1982.

OBITUARIES:

PERIODICALS

Globe and Mail (Toronto), January 10, 1987.

Los Angeles Times, January 17, 1987.
Maclean's, January 19, 1987.
New York Times, January 7, 1987.
Publishers Weekly, February 20, 1987.
Times (London), January 7, 1987.
Washington Post, January 7, 1987.

* * *

LAURIE, Rona

PERSONAL: Born in Derby, England; daughter of Alan Rupert (a physician) and Alexandrina (Ross) Laurie; married Edward Lewis Neilson (a commander in the Royal Navy), August 28, 1961 (died, 1979). *Education:* University of Birmingham, B.A. (with honors); attended Royal Academy of Dramatic Art.

ADDRESSES: Home—21 New Quebec St., London W1H 7DD, England. *Office*—Department of Speech and Drama, Guildhall School of Music and Drama, Barbican, London EC2Y 8DT, England.

CAREER: Professional actress in London, England, 1939-58; Guildhall School of Music and Drama, London, examiner and lecturer in drama, 1958—, head of department of drama in education, 1970—. Drama coach at Royal College of Music, 1985-90; drama tutor for Studio 68 and Academy of Live and Recorded Arts.

MEMBER: Guild of Drama Adjudicators (chairperson, 1969-72), Society of Teachers of Speech and Drama (chairperson, 1977-79), British Federation of Music Festivals (adjudicator, 1958—), Poetry Society.

AWARDS, HONORS: Fellowship from Guildhall School of Music and Drama, 1967; Principal's Medal, Royal Academy of Dramatic Art.

WRITINGS:

(Editor with Edita Maisie Cobby) *Speaking Together,* Books 1 and 2, Pitman, 1964.
(Editor with Daniel Roberts) *The Eighth Anthology,* Guildhall School of Music and Drama, 1964.
(Editor) *A Hundred Speeches from the Theatre,* Evans Brothers, 1966, revised edition published as *One Hundred Speeches from the Theatre,* Crowell-Collier Press, 1973.
(With Cobby) *Adventures in Group-Speaking,* Pitman, 1967.
(Editor) *Scenes and Ideas,* Pitman, 1967.
(Editor with John Holgate) *The Eleventh Anthology,* Guildhall School of Music and Drama, 1969.
(Editor with Holgate) *The Thirteenth Anthology,* Guildhall School of Music and Drama, 1973.
Festivals and Adjudication, Pitman, 1975.
Children's Plays from Beatrix Potter, Warne, 1980.
(Co-editor) *The Seventeenth Anthology,* Guildhall School of Music and Drama, 1981.
Auditioning, J. Garnet Miller, 1985.
Mrs. Tiggy-Winkle and Friends, Puffin Books, 1986.
The Actor's Art and Craft, J. Garnet Miller, in press.

Contributor to *Speech and Drama* and *Onstage.*

SIDELIGHTS: Rona Laurie told *CA:* "I regard all my work, whether it be writing, acting, verse-speaking, directing, adjudicating, or teaching, as a seamless garment. My interest is in language, written or spoken, and its power of communicating ideas, stirring the imagination and heart, and stimulating thought in an increasingly materialistic age."

LAVE, Lester B(ernard) 1939-

PERSONAL: Born August 5, 1939; son of Israel and Esther (Axelrod) Lave; married Judith Rice (a professor), June 21, 1965; children: Tamara Rice, Jonathan Melville. *Education:* Reed College, B.A., 1960; Harvard University, Ph.D., 1963.

ADDRESSES: Home—1008 Devonshire Rd., Pittsburgh, PA 15213. *Office*—Department of Economics, Carnegie-Mellon University, Pittsburgh, PA 15213.

CAREER: Carnegie-Mellon University, Pittsburgh, PA, assistant professor, 1963-68, associate professor, 1968-70, professor of economics, 1970—, James H. Higgins Professor, 1984—, head of department, 1971—. Northwestern University, visiting assistant professor, 1965-66; Brookings Institution, senior fellow, 1978-82. Consultant to U.S. Department of Health, Education, and Welfare, Department of Defense, Department of Transportation, RAND Corp., Center for Naval Analysis, and General Motors Corp. Member of Pennsylvania Governor's Health Task Force, Pennsylvania Department of Health Data Task Force, and West Pennsylvania Regional Medical Program Advisory Committee.

MEMBER: American Economic Association, American Association for the Advancement of Science, Institute of Medicine, American Statistical Association, Society for Risk Analysis (past president), Association of Environmental and Resource Economists.

AWARDS, HONORS: Research grants from National Institute of Mental Health, 1963, Resources for the Future, Inc., 1966, 1970, and 1972, National Center for Health Services, 1967 and 1970, National Safety Council, 1967, National Science Foundation, 1982, 1985, 1987, 1988, 1990, and Environmental Protection Agency, 1987.

WRITINGS:

Technological Change: Its Conception and Measurement, Prentice-Hall, 1967.
(With Eugene P. Seskin) *Air Pollution and Health,* Johns Hopkins Press, 1977.
(With Lester Breslow and Jonathan Fielding) *Annual Review of Public Health,* Annual Reviews, 1980.
The Strategy of Social Regulation, Brookings Institution, 1981.
(With Robert Crandall) *The Scientific Basis of Health and Safety Regulation,* Brookings Institution, 1981.
(With Gilbert Owenn) *Clearing the Air,* Brookings Institution, 1981.
Quantitative Risk Assessment for Regulation, Brookings Institution, 1982.
(With Crandall, Howard Gruenspecht, and Theodore Keeler) *Regulating the Automobile,* Brookings Institution, 1986.
(With Arthur Upton) *Toxic Chemicals, Health, and the Environment,* Johns Hopkins Press, 1987.

Contributor to numerous journals, including *American Economic Review, Econometrica, Science, American Scientist, Nature, Journal of Political Economy, Quarterly Journal of Economics, Behavioral Science.*

WORK IN PROGRESS: Research on the environment, on risk management, and on improving regulation.

* * *

LAVIN, Mary 1912-

PERSONAL: Born June 11, 1912, in East Walpole, Mass.; immigrated to Ireland; daughter of Thomas and Nora (Mahon)

Lavin; married William Walsh (a lawyer), September 29, 1942 (died, 1954); married Michael MacDonald Scott, 1969; children: (first marriage) Valentine (daughter), Elizabeth, Caroline. *Education:* Early schooling in East Walpole, Mass.; attended Loreto Convent, Dublin, Ireland; University College, Dublin, B.A. (honors), 1934; National University of Ireland, M.A. (first class honors), 1938. *Religion:* Roman Catholic.

ADDRESSES: Home—Abbey Farm, Bective, Navan, County Meath, Eire; Apt. 5, Gilford Pines, Gilford Rd., Sandymount, Dublin 4, Eire.

CAREER: Short story writer, farmer. Taught French at Loreto Convent school.

MEMBER: Irish Academy of Letters (president, 1971-73), Irish P.E.N. (president, 1964-65).

AWARDS, HONORS: James Tait Black Memorial Prize for best book of fiction published in United Kingdom, 1944, for *Tales From Bective Bridge;* Guggenheim fellowships for fiction, 1959, 1961, and 1962; Katherine Mansfield-Menton Prize, 1962, for *The Great Wave, and Other Stories;* D.Litt. from National University of Ireland, 1968; Ella Lyman Cabot fellowship, 1969; Gold Medal from Eire Society (Boston), 1974; Gregory Medal, 1974; award from American Irish Foundation, 1979; Allied Irish Bank award, 1981.

WRITINGS:

Tales From Bective Bridge (short stories), Little, Brown, 1942, revised edition, Poolbeg, 1978.
The Long Ago, and Other Stories, M. Joseph, 1944.
The House in Clewe Street (novel; first published serially in *Atlantic Monthly* as "Gabriel Galloway," 1944-45), Little, Brown, 1945, reprinted, Penguin Books, 1988.
The Becker Wives, and Other Stories, M. Joseph, 1946, published as *At Sallygap, and Other Stories,* Little, Brown, 1947.
Mary O'Grady (novel), Little, Brown, 1950, reprinted, Penguin Books, 1986.
A Single Lady, and Other Stories, M. Joseph, 1951.
The Patriot Son, and Other Stories, M. Joseph, 1956.
A Likely Story (for children), Macmillan, 1957.
Selected Stories, Macmillan, 1959.
The Great Wave, and Other Stories (contains seven stories first published in *New Yorker*), Macmillan, 1961.
The Stories of Mary Lavin, Constable, Volume I, 1964, Volume II, 1973, Volume III, 1985.
In the Middle of the Fields, and Other Stories, Constable, 1967, Macmillan, 1969.
Happiness, and Other Stories, Constable, 1969, Houghton, 1970.
Collected Stories, introduction by V. S. Pritchett, Houghton, 1971.
A Memory, and Other Stories, Constable, 1972, Houghton, 1973.
The Second Best Children in the World (for children), Houghton, 1972.
The Shrine and Other Stories, Houghton, 1977.
Mary Lavin: Selected Stories, Penguin Books, 1981.
A Family Likeness (short stories), Constable, 1985.

Short stories anthologized in numerous collections.

WORK IN PROGRESS: A collection of ten short stories.

SIDELIGHTS: Born in the United States and transplanted to Ireland at an early age, Mary Lavin is "Irish in thought and feeling, and the short story is her most natural form of expression," Edward Weeks writes. He quotes her as saying: "It is in the short story that a writer distills the essence of his thought. I believe this because the short story, shape as well as matter, is determined by the writer's own character. Both are one. Short-story writing—for me—is only looking closer than normal into the human heart." Jean Stubbs of *Books* believes "Miss Lavin possesses the strength of gentleness. A serene radiance illuminates all her writing: the radiance of one who observes, accepts and meditates on the human condition. She has, thank God, eschewed mere cleverness in favour of wisdom, so we hear no strident trumpets, no shattering drums. She invites us to contemplate with her the infinite sadness and beauty of the world, the divine inconsequence of life. . . . She will not allow us to stand by and marvel, she insists that we become participants."

In a review of *In the Middle of the Fields,* Roger Baker of *Books and Bookmen* notes: "There is a curiously dated atmosphere about . . . [these] stories; it is as though the world came to a halt in 1939. Ironically, this may be some kind of tribute to her ability to isolate characters in their own rigidly bounded worlds. She approaches her people and their emotional conflicts with rich, lyrical poeticism that transcends the business of mere topicality. But this failure to pinpoint a specific space in time is somehow detracting to the total effect." Her *Collected Stories* has drawn admiration from reviewers and prompted comparisons with "her most noticeable mentors in the genre, Chekhov and Mansfield, and James and Joyce. From them, presumably, she gets the soul, the brittle beauty, the social intricacy, and the technical virtuosity which are the trademarks of her work," according to R. J. Thompson of Canisius College. "In sum," he concludes, "these stories make apparent her position as one of the most artful and perceptive masters of the story form in our day, a fact well recognized by her Irish countrymen who regard her as the only living equivalent of O'Faolain and O'Flaherty."

MEDIA ADAPTATIONS: One short story was used as the libretto of an opera by South African Eric Chisholm and performed at the South African Festival of Music in London.

BIOGRAPHICAL/CRITICAL SOURCES:

BOOKS

Bowen, Zack, *Mary Lavin,* Bucknell University Press, 1975.
Contemporary Literary Criticism, Gale, Volume 4, 1975, Volume 18, 1981.
Dictionary of Literary Biography, Volume 15: *British Novelists, 1930-1959,* Gale, 1983.
Kelly, Angeline A., *Mary Lavin, Quiet Rebel: A Study of Her Short Stories,* Barnes & Noble, 1980.
Peterson, Richard F., *Mary Lavin,* Twayne, 1978.

PERIODICALS

Best Sellers, July 15, 1971.
Books, January, 1970.
Books and Bookmen, May, 1967.
Library Journal, July, 1970.
Nation, November 8, 1971.
New York Times, July 2, 1971.
New York Times Book Review, March 24, 1970, August 8, 1971, November 25, 1973, October 30, 1977.
Saturday Review, August 7, 1971.
Times Literary Supplement, February 16, 1967, June 3, 1977, November 29, 1985.
Washington Post Book World, January 8, 1978.

*   *   *

LAYTON, Irving (Peter) 1912-

PERSONAL: Original surname, Lazarovitch; name legally changed; born March 12, 1912, in Neamtz, Rumania; immigrated to Canada, 1913; son of Moses and Keine (Moscovitch) Lazarovitch; married Faye Lynch, September 13, 1938; married Frances Sutherland, September 13, 1946; married Aviva Cantor (a writer of children's stories), September 13, 1961; married Harriet Bernstein (a publicist; divorced, March 19, 1984); children: (second marriage) Max Rubin, Naomi Parker; (third marriage) David Herschel; (fourth marriage) Samantha Clara. *Education:* Macdonald College, B.Sc., 1939; McGill University, M.A., 1946.

ADDRESSES: Home—6879 Monkland Ave., Montreal, Quebec, Canada H4B 1J5.

CAREER: Jewish Public Library, Montreal, Quebec, lecturer, 1943-58; high school teacher in Montreal, 1945-60; Sir George Williams University (now Sir George Williams Campus of Concordia University), Montreal, lecturer, 1949- 65, poet in residence, 1965-69; University of Guelph, Guelph, Ontario, poet in residence, 1969-70; York University, Toronto, Ontario, professor of English literature, 1970-78; Concordia University, Sir George Williams Campus, Montreal poet in residence 1978—. *Military service:* Canadian Army, Artillery, 1942-43; became lieutenant.

MEMBER: PEN.

AWARDS, HONORS: Canada Foundation fellow, 1957; Canada Council award, 1959; Governor-General's Medal for *A Red Carpet for the Sun;* President's Medal, University of Western Ontario, 1961, for poem "Keine Lazarovitch 1870-1959"; Prix Litteraire de Quebec, 1963, for *Balls for a One-Armed Juggler;* Canada Council Special Arts Award, 1967; D.C.L., Bishops University, 1972, and Concordia University, 1975.

WRITINGS:

Here and Now, First Statement, 1945.
Now Is the Place (poems and stories), First Statement, 1948.
The Black Huntsmen, privately printed, 1951.
Love the Conqueror Worm, Contact, 1951.
(With Louis Dudek and Raymond Souster) *Cerberus,* Contact, 1952.
In the Midst of My Fever, Divers, 1954.
The Long Peashooter, Laocoon, 1954.
The Cold Green Element, Contact, 1955.
The Blue Propeller, Contact, 1955.
The Blue Calf, Contact, 1956.
Music on a Kazoo, Contact, 1956.
The Improved Binoculars (selected poems), introduction by William Carlos Williams, Jargon, 1956.
A Laughter in the Mind, Jargon, 1958.
A Red Carpet for the Sun (collected poems), McClelland & Stewart, 1959.
The Swinging Flesh (poems and short stories), McClelland & Stewart, 1961.
Balls for a One-Armed Juggler (poems), McClelland & Stewart, 1963.
The Laughing Rooster (poems), McClelland & Stewart, 1964.
Collected Poems, McClelland & Stewart, 1965.
Periods of the Moon, McClelland & Stewart, 1967.
The Shattered Plinths, McClelland & Stewart, 1968.
Selected Poems, McClelland & Stewart, 1969.
The Whole Bloody Bird: Obs, Aphs, and Pomes, McClelland & Stewart, 1969.
(Author of introduction) *Poems to Colour: A Selection of Workshop Poems,* York University, 1970.
Nail Polish, McClelland & Stewart, 1971.
The Collected Poems of Irving Layton, McClelland & Stewart, 1971.

Engagements: The Prose of Irving Layton, edited by Seymour Mayne, McClelland & Stewart, 1972.
Lovers and Lesser Men, McClelland & Stewart, 1973.
The Pole-Vaulter, McClelland & Stewart, 1974.
Seventy-five Greek Poems, McClelland & Stewart, 1974.
The Darkening Fire: Selected Poems, 1945-1968, McClelland & Stewart, 1975.
The Unwavering Eye: Selected Poems, 1969-1975, McClelland & Stewart, 1975.
For My Brother Jesus, McClelland & Stewart, 1976.
The Collected Poems of Irving Layton, McClelland & Stewart, 1977.
Taking Sides (prose), McClelland & Stewart, 1977.
The Uncollected Poems of Irving Layton, 1936-1959, Mosaic Press, 1977.
The Selected Poems of Irving Layton, New Directions Press, 1977.
The Covenant, McClelland & Stewart, 1977.
The Tightrope Dancer, McClelland & Stewart, 1978.
The Love Poems of Irving Layton, McClelland & Stewart, 1979.
Droppings from Heaven, McClelland & Stewart, 1979.
An Unlikely Affair: The Irving Layton-Dorothy Rath Correspondence, Mosaic Press, 1979.
For My Neighbors in Hell, Mosaic Press, 1980.
Europe and Other Bad News, McClelland & Stewart, 1981.
The Gucci Bag, Mosaic Press, 1983.
Shadows on the Ground, limited edition, Mosaic Press, 1983.
A Spider Danced a Cosy Jig, Stoddart, 1984.
Selected Poems, [Seoul], 1985.
Where Burning Sappho Loved, [Athens], 1985.
Dance with Desire: Love Poems, McClelland & Stewart, 1986.
Waiting for the Messiah, McClelland & Stewart, 1985, Harper, 1986.
Final Reckoning: Poems 1982-1986, Mosaic Press, 1987.
In My Father's House, McClelland & Stewart, 1987.
Wild Gooseberries: The Selected Letters of Irving Layton, edited by Francis Mansbridge, Macmillan, 1989.
A Wild Peculiar Joy: Selected Poems 1945-1989, McClelland & Stewart, 1989.
(With Robert Creeley) *Irving Layton and Robert Creeley: The Complete Corresponce,* edited by Ekbert Faas and Sabrina Reed, University of Toronto Press, 1990.

Works available in translation include *Poemas de amor,* [Madrid], 1980, and *Le Poesie d'amore,* 1983.

EDITOR

(With Louis Dudek) *Canadian Poems, 1850-1952,* Contact, 1952, 2nd edition, 1953.
Pan-ic: A Selection of Contemporary Canadian Poems, [New York], 1958.
(And author of introduction) *Poems for Twenty-seven Cents,* [Montreal], 1961.
Love Where the Nights Are Long: Canadian Love Poems, McClelland & Stewart, 1962.
Anvil: A Selection of Workshop Poems, [Montreal], 1966.
(And author of introduction) *Anvil Blood: A Selection of Workshop Poems,* [Toronto], 1973.

Work represented in numerous anthologies, including, *Book of Canadian Poetry,* edited by A. J. M. Smith, Gage, 1948; *Book of Canadian Stories,* edited by D. Pacey, Ryerson, 1950; *Canadian Short Stories,* edited by R. Weaver and H. James, Oxford University Press, 1952; *Oxford Book of Canadian Verse,* edited by Smith, Oxford University Press, 1960; *How Do I Love Thee: Sixty Poets of Canada (and Quebec) Select and Introduce Their*

Favourite Poems from Their Own Work, edited by John Robert Colombo, M. G. Hurtig, 1970.

Contributor of poetry and stories to various periodicals, including *Poetry, Canadian Forum,* and *Sail.* Co-founder and editor, *First Statement* and *Northern Review,* 1941-43; former associate editor, *Contact, Black Mountain Review,* and several other magazines.

SIDELIGHTS: Irving Layton, according to Lauriat Lane, Jr., "is by now *the* living Canadian poet, probably *the* Canadian poet, a major poet by any standard, in fact—dare one say it?—a great poet." Lane goes on to say that Layton's work can pass two tests of greatness: first, that his best poems can be read and reread without becoming tiresome; and second, that his poetry can stand up to "impersonal, systematic, academic" scrutiny. Desmond Pacey feels that most Canadian poets "have tended—with the conspicuous exception of Bliss Carman—to be exigent or timid, and to confine themselves in the role of minor poets; Layton, on the other hand, sees himself as a major poet and is not afraid to essay the part. He is often criticised for being too prolific, and for publishing everything that he writes, the bad along with the good. I see this not as pride but as a form of humility: Layton knows that he is not always at his best, but he is willing to let us see him in his off-moments as well as in his moments of magical success. More power to him: it enables us to see his development, to measure his best poems by his worst, and to savour the tiny pleasure that can be found even in his mistakes."

Layton told *CA:* "One of my sisters thought I should be a plumber or an electrician; another saw in me the ability to become a peddlar; my third and oldest sister was sure I was devious and slippery enough to make a fine lawyer or politician. My mother, presiding over these three witches, pointed to the fly-spotted ceiling, indicating God by that gesture, and said, 'He will be what the Almighty wants him to be.'

"My devout mother turned out to be right. From earliest childhood I longed to match sounds with sense; and when I was older, to make music out of words. Everywhere I went, mystery dogged my steps. The skinny dead rat in the lane, the fire that broke out in our house on Sabbath eve, the energy that went with cruelty and the power that went with hate. The empty sky had no answers for my queries and the stars at night only winked and said nothing.

"I wrote my first poem for a teacher who was astonishingly beautiful. For weeks I mentally drooled over the white cleavage she had carelessly exposed to a precocious eleven-year-old. So there it was: the two grand mysteries of sexuality and death. I write because I'm driven to say something about them, to celebrate what my limited brain cannot comprehend. To rejoice in my more arrogant moods to think the Creator Himself doesn't comprehend His handiwork. I write because the only solace He has in His immense and eternal solitude are the poems and stories that tell Him—like all creators, He too is hungry for praise—how exciting and beautiful, how majestic and terrible are His works and to give Him an honest, up-to-date report on His most baffling creation, Man. I know whenever I put in a good word for the strange biped He made God's despair is lessened. Ultimately, I write because I am less cruel than He is."

Irving Layton's work has been translated into more than ten languages. His poetry has been read on several recordings.

BIOGRAPHICAL/CRITICAL SOURCES:

BOOKS

Contemporary Literary Criticism, Gale, Volume 2, 1974, Volume 15, 1980.
Dictionary of Literary Biography, Volume 88: *Canadian Writers, 1920-1959, Second Series,* Gale, 1989.

PERIODICALS

Canadian Forum, June, 1969.
Canadian Literature, spring, 1972, autumn, 1972, winter, 1973.
Fiddlehead, spring, 1967, summer, 1967.
New Republic, July 2, 1977.
New York Times Book Review, October 9, 1977.
The Record (Sherbrooke, Quebec), November 2, 1984.
Village Voice, March 31, 1966.*

*   *   *

le CARRE, John
   See CORNWELL, David (John Moore)

*   *   *

LEE, Laurie   1914-

PERSONAL: Born June 26, 1914, in Stroud, Gloucestershire, England; married Catherine Francesca Polge, 1950; children: Jesse Frances. *Education:* Educated in Stroud, England.

ADDRESSES: Home—9/40 Elm Park Gardens, London SW10, England.

CAREER: Poet, writer. Worked as clerk in Stroud, England, and as builder's laborer in London, England; documentary film-maker for Post Office film unit in Cyprus, India, and Assam during World War II; publications editor for Ministry of Information, 1944-46; worked with Green Park film unit, 1946-47; caption writer in chief for Festival of Britain, 1950-51.

MEMBER: Royal Society of Literature.

AWARDS, HONORS: Atlantic Award, 1944; Society of Authors Travelling Award, 1951; Member of the Order of the British Empire, 1952; Foyle's Poetry Award, 1955; W. H. Smith Award for Literature, 1960, for *Cider With Rosie.*

WRITINGS:

The Sun My Monument (poems), Hogarth, 1944.
Land at War, H.M.S.O., 1945.
(With Ralph Keene) *We Made a Film in Cyprus,* Longmans, Green, 1947.
The Bloom of Candles: Verse From a Poet's Year, Lehmann, 1947.
The Voyage of Magellan: A Dramatic Chronicle for Radio, Lehmann, 1948.
A Rose for Winter: Travels in Andalusia, Hogarth, 1955.
My Many-Coated Man (poems), Deutsch, 1955.
Cider With Rosie (autobiography), Hogarth, 1959, published as *The Edge of Day: A Boyhood in the West of England,* Morrow, 1960.
Laurie Lee: Poems, Vista, 1960.
(With David Lambert) *The Wonderful World of Transportation* (for children), Garden City Books, 1960 (published in England as *Man Must Move: The Story of Transport,* Rathbone Books, 1960).
The First Born, Hogarth, 1964.
As I Walked out One Midsummer Morning (autobiography), Deutsch, 1969.

I Can't Stay Long (collected prose pieces), Deutsch, 1975, Atheneum, 1976.
Selected Poems, Deutsch, 1983.
Two Women, with own photographs, Deutsch, 1983.

SIDELIGHTS: At the age of nineteen, Lee left his home and walked to London, taking little with him except his violin and the determination to never again have an employer. Both have remained with him throughout the years. If writing should fail him, Lee said, he will survive on his violin: "A little time ago I went busking with it just to see what the going rate was. . . . I keep in practice."

Cider With Rosie, one of Lee's best-known works, is a memoir of his boyhood in England which was very warmly received by critics and the reading public. When it was published in the United States under the title *The Edge of Day,* T. S. Matthews stated: "Good books don't always sell; the best seller lists are usually swamped by the second- and third-rate. But now and then, once in a blue moon, a book appears that deserves its success. This time the moon is blue, and *The Edge of Day* is the book."

After publishing *Cider With Rosie,* Lee returned to his home town and bought a cottage there. "It took me a long time to go back," he said. "I had to have some success behind me." According to the London *Times:* "There was some vexation when the villagers recognized themselves in the book, then he was accepted. They even sell his books at the local pub." Lee recalled, "At first they wouldn't touch them with tongs."

In 1975 Lee published a collection of prose pieces written over a thirty-year period, *I Can't Stay Long.* Reviews of the book were somewhat mixed. Robert Nye, for example, found that "little in [the book] is deeply thought or felt through," but he admitted that "there is a niceness in [Lee] both in the old sense of being minutely and delicately precise, and in the modern colloquial sense of being agreeable." Other reviews were more favorable. Sylvia Secker noted: "When Lee drops his purple mantle he can write with a vivid, spare imagery that makes one realize how closely allied are the eyes of the poet and the painter: 'the bright-backed cows standing along the dykes like old china arranged on shelves,' 'motionless canals, full of silver light, lap the houses like baths of mercury.' One is no longer reading but looking at the work of an old Dutch Master." A *New Yorker* writer also praised the book's imagery, citing as example Lee's recollection of adolescence: "I don't think I ever discovered sex, it seemed to be always there—a vague pink streak running back through the landscape as far as I can remember." This type of writing, the *New Yorker* critic said, shows Lee "at his most characteristically expressive." The reviewer further stated, "Lee's writing—almost precious, almost naive—has a tone and intensity that are truly entirely his own, and are inimitably pleasing."

BIOGRAPHICAL/CRITICAL SOURCES:

BOOKS

Dictionary of Literary Biography, Volume 27: *Poets of Great Britain and Ireland, 1946-1960,* Gale, 1984.

PERIODICALS

Christian Science Monitor, April 5, 1976.
New Yorker, February 23, 1976.
New York Times Book Review, March 27, 1960.
Times (London), December 21, 1975.
Times Literary Supplement, January 30, 1976.

LENDVAI, Paul 1929-

PERSONAL: Born August 24, 1929, in Budapest, Hungary; emigrated in 1957; son of Andor (a lawyer) and Edith (Polacsek) Lendvai; married Gizella Lustig, 1952 (divorced); married Margaret Pollock, July 17, 1962. *Education:* Attended Diplomatic Academy, 1948.

ADDRESSES: Office—ORF-Zentrum, A-1136 Vienna, Austria.

CAREER: Worked as a journalist in Hungary, 1948-56; *Financial Times,* London, England, correspondent from Vienna, Austria, 1960-82; Austrian Radio and Television (ORF), Vienna, currently director of Radio Austria International.

MEMBER: Austrian PEN.

AWARDS, HONORS: Karl Renner Prize for Journalism, 1974; awarded professor title by Federal President, 1980.

WRITINGS:

Eagles in Cobwebs: Nationalism and Communism in the Balkans, Doubleday, 1969.
Anti-Semitism without Jews: Communist East Europe, Doubleday, 1971.
(With Karl Heinz Ritschel) *Kreisky: Portraet eines Staatsmannes* (title means "Kreisky: Portrait of a Statesman"), Econ-Verlag, 1972.
Die Grenzen des Wandels: Spielarten des Kommunismus im Donauraum, Europaverlag, 1977.
The Bureaucracy of Truth: How Communist Governments Manage the News, Westview, 1981.
Albania, Fromm Verlag, 1985.
Hungary, Fromm Verlag, 1986.
Hungary: The Art of Survival, Taurus Publishing, 1988.

Also author of *Egypt,* 1952, and *Greece,* 1954. Editor of *Europaeische Rundschau,* 1973—.

SIDELIGHTS: Times Literary Supplement critic Erik de Mauny describes Paul Lendvai's *The Bureaucracy of Truth: How Communist Governments Manage the News* as a "well-researched, incisive and deeply disturbing study." Lendvai examines the extent to which Eastern bloc countries, especially the U.S.S.R., manipulate the news to achieve policy objectives. Through the careful selection and distortion of the news, the Soviet Union pacifies its own citizens and enlists support for its foreign policy from citizens of other countries. "Communist regimes have long been adept at creating a dense smokescreen of benevolent-sounding phrases to mask their motives and long-term aims," observes de Mauny, concluding "*The Bureaucracy of Truth* throws some welcome and much-needed light on what they really mean when they speak of *detente* and peaceful coexistence."

BIOGRAPHICAL/CRITICAL SOURCES:

PERIODICALS

Times Literary Supplement, March 20, 1981.

* * *

LESSING, Doris (May) 1919-
(Jane Somers)

PERSONAL: Born October 22, 1919, in Persia; daughter of Alfred Cook (a farmer) and Emily Maude (McVeagh) Tayler; married Frank Charles Wisdom, 1939 (marriage dissolved, 1943); married Gottfried Anton Lessing, 1945 (marriage dissolved, 1949); children: (first marriage) John, Jean; (second marriage)

Peter. *Education:* Attended Roman Catholic Convent, then Girls' High School, both in Salisbury, Southern Rhodesia; left school at age 14. *Politics:* Left-wing.

ADDRESSES: Home—24 Gondar Gardens, London NW6 1HG, England. *Agent*—c/o Jonathan Clowes Ltd., 22 Prince Albert Rd., London NW1 7ST, England.

CAREER: Writer. Worked as a nursemaid, a lawyer's secretary, a Hansard typist, and a Parliamentary Commissioner's typist while living in Southern Rhodesia, 1924-49.

AWARDS, HONORS: Prix Medicis Award for work translated into French, 1976, for *The Golden Notebook; The Sirian Experiments* was nominated for the Booker McConnell Prize, 1981; Austrian State Prize for European Literature, 1981; Shakespeare Prize, 1982; W. H. Smith Literary Award, 1986, Palermo Prize, 1987, and Premio Internazionale Mondello, 1987, all for *The Good Terrorist.*

WRITINGS:

FICTION

The Grass Is Singing, Crowell, 1950.
This Was the Old Chief's Country (stories), M. Joseph, 1952.
Five Short Novels, M. Joseph, 1955.
Retreat to Innocence, M. Joseph, 1956.
Habit of Loving (stories), Crowell, 1958.
The Golden Notebook, Simon & Schuster, 1962.
A Man and Two Women (stories), Simon & Schuster, 1963.
African Stories, M. Joseph, 1964, Simon & Schuster, 1965.
Briefing for a Descent Into Hell, Knopf, 1971.
The Temptation of Jack Orkney and Other Stories, Knopf, 1972 (published in England as *The Story of a Non-Marrying Man and Other Stories,* J. Cape, 1972).
The Summer Before the Dark, Knopf, 1973.
The Memoirs of a Survivor, Random House, 1975.
Stories, Knopf, 1978.
(Under pseudonym Jane Somers) *The Diary of a Good Neighbor,* Knopf, 1983 (also see below).
(Under pseudonym Jane Somers) *If the Old Could . . . ,* Knopf, 1984 (also see below).
The Diaries of Jane Somers (contains *The Diary of a Good Neighbor* and *If the Old Could . . .*), Random House, 1984.
The Good Terrorist, Knopf, 1985.
The Fifth Child, Knopf, 1988.
The Doris Lessing Reader, Knopf, 1989.

"CHILDREN OF VIOLENCE" SERIES

Martha Quest, M. Joseph, 1952.
A Proper Marriage, M. Joseph, 1954.
A Ripple From the Storm, M. Joseph, 1958.
Landlocked, Simon & Schuster, 1966.
The Four-Gated City, Knopf, 1969.

"CANOPUS IN ARGOS: ARCHIVES" SERIES

Re: Colonized Planet V, Shikasta, Knopf, 1979.
The Marriage Between Zones Three, Four, and Five, Knopf, 1980.
The Sirian Experiments: The Report of Ambien II, of the Five, Knopf, 1981.
The Making of the Representative for Planet 8, Knopf, 1982.
Documents Relating to the Sentimental Agents in the Volyen Empire, Knopf, 1983.

NONFICTION

Going Home, M. Joseph, 1957.

In Pursuit of the English, Simon & Schuster, 1961.
Particularly Cats, Simon & Schuster, 1967.
A Small Personal Voice: Essays, Reviews, Interviews, Random House, 1975.
Prisons We Choose To Live Inside, Harper, 1987.
The Wind Blows Away Our Words, Random House, 1987.

OTHER

"Mr. Dollinger" (play), first produced in Oxford, England, at Oxford Playhouse, 1958.
"Each in His Own Wilderness" (play), first produced in London, England at Royal Court, March 23, 1958.
Fourteen Poems, Scorpion Press, 1959.
"The Truth About Billy Newton" (play), first produced in Salisbury, England, 1961.
Play With A Tiger (play; first produced in London at Comedy Theatre, March 22, 1962; produced in New York City at Renata Theatre, December 30, 1964), M. Joseph, 1962.

MEDIA ADAPTATIONS: The Memoirs of a Survivor was adapted into a film and released in 1983; *The Grass Is Singing* was adapted into a film by Michael Raeburn and released as "Killing Heat" in 1984.

SIDELIGHTS: Jeremy Brooks considers Doris Lessing to be not only the best woman novelist of our time but one of the finest writers of the post-war generation. As Dorothy Brewster notes, "since the conspicuous success in 1950 of her first novel, . . . Doris Lessing . . . has been recognized as one of the most gifted of the younger group of English novelists. . . . Those of Doris Lessing's novels and stories that deal with the people and ways of life of Southern Rhodesia before, during, and after World War II have acquired something of the significance of social and political history. . . . When she came to London, she looked at the English . . . with an alert and fresh vision."

In an introductory note to *Declaration* Tom Maschler says of her: "[She was] educated at the Roman Catholic Convent School in Salisbury for five years, and for one year at the girls' High School. Her mother wanted her to be a pianist, and it was a shock when, in Doris Lessing's own words, 'I discovered suddenly that I had no talent whatsoever.' Left school at fourteen. Started writing at eighteen and composed and destroyed six novels. From 1943, . . . was busy politically taking her first lesson from Communists and Socialists in the R.A.F. For the first time in her life she met people who were prepared to do more about the colour bar than deplore it. 1949: came to England. . . . She says, 'England seems to me the ideal country to live in because it is quiet and unstimulating and leaves you in peace.' "

Many of Lessing's short stories are actually novellas, comprising 25,000 to 45,000 words. Of this form she says: "There is space in them to take one's time, to think aloud, to follow, for a paragraph or two, on a sidetrail—none of which is possible in a real short story." Her success in this genre "is primarily a matter of the swift directness and the generalizing intelligence of the voice itself," writes Robert Garis. "Mrs. Lessing's voice has the Laurentian confidence that one can manage the language of fiction by counting the dollars instead of the pennies. This works because she grasps the story as a whole and because it is usually a big story, not [only] in the number of its words but in the number of its events. . . . Almost every paragraph in the story contains [much action] and all of these actions are rendered with the same sufficiency. Sufficiency doesn't sound like much, but it is what makes the minor stories of Lawrence and Chekhov independently valuable, not just failed major works. It is in fact a sign of major talent, for it derives from good judgment in almost the

Johnsonian sense. Like Lawrence and Chekhov, Mrs. Lessing has looked at many different kinds of people with unusual curiosity and intelligence and has arrived at sure judgments about them." Despite the success of her novels, Lessing will continue to write stories. She says: "Some writers I know have stopped writing short stories because, as they say, 'there is no market for them.' Others like myself, the addicts, go on, and I suspect would go on even if there really wasn't any home for them but a private drawer." Her 1972 collection, *The Temptation of Jack Orkney and Other Stories,* contains work done over ten years of literary growth, according to Richard Locke, and for which collection he has the highest praise: "I think it's clear that of all the postwar English novelists Doris Lessing is the foremost creative descendant of that 'great tradition' which includes George Eliot, Conrad, and D. H. Lawrence: a literary tradition of intense social concerns and moral realism, a tradition that scrutinizes marriage and sexual life, individual psychology and the role of ideology in contemporary society. . . . These stories are an excellent place to begin reading or rereading Doris Lessing. It's a voyage very well worth taking, for there are few these days who have the energy and imagination to explore the regions Doris Lessing has now made her own."

J. M. Edelstein believes that, on the basis of *African Stories* alone, "Doris Lessing must be counted as one of the most important fiction writers of our times." As political and social commentaries these stories "confirm in precise and painful detail, like stitches in a wound, the abuse of the native population of Southern Rhodesia by the white settlers of British descent," writes Mary Ellmann. "Doris Lessing's work is an uninterrupted study of loneliness, but here it is particularly the isolation of a few white exiles, claiming vast strange land. . . . For her first thirty years . . . Doris Lessing seems to have listened to Southern Rhodesia as no other writer has been able to do. It remained, even after she had left it, all nature to her. As one associates her English work with flats and offices, one associates the African stories with swollen suns and moons, head-tail grass, and the secret constant stirring of animal life. . . . Africa is for her not only a society in which the white people use their exile like a weapon against the black; but also a place, supporting both white and black, which endlessly enacts the conflict of forms, the effort of every living thing, at the cost of other living things, to achieve what is right for itself, its sustenance and continuation. Africa, not England, impressed the knowledge of necessary cruelty. . . . It is disconcerting, in fact, to come so repeatedly upon instances of anarchic hunger, the form of whose seeming formlessness is painful to trace, within stories of straightforward, even old-fashioned, organization. It is this preoccupation with a necessity, which in moral terms can seem a criminal chaos, that disrupts conventional literary form in *The Golden Notebook*." Lessing says that she considers Africa to be "the center of a modern battlefield," but, she adds, "there are other things in living besides injustice, even for the victims of it." And, says Edelstein, "It is her knowledge of these larger and 'other things' and her ability to make us see them even while she sustains constantly, like distant drumming, the harsh and bitter realities of life in Africa," which gives these stories their power, accuracy and controlled passion. Africa, concludes Lessing, "is not a place to visit unless one chooses to be an exile ever afterwards from an inexplicable majestic silence lying just over the border of memory or of thought. Africa gives you the knowledge that man is a small creature among other creatures, in a large landscape."

Lessing's major and most controversial novel is *The Golden Notebook,* wherein she brilliantly explores, as a *New Statesman* reviewer noted, what it is like to be "free and responsible, a woman in relation to men and other women, and to struggle to come to terms with one's self about these things and about writing and politics." Lessing considers the book to be "a novel about certain political and sexual attitudes that have force now; it is an attempt to explain them, to objectivize them, to set them in relation with each other. So in a way it is a social novel, written by someone whose training—or at least whose habit of mind—is to see these things socially, not personally." In its structure, the novel is really two novels, divided in four sections, and "the Golden Notebook." Lessing split it into four parts, she says, in order to "express a split person. I felt that if the artist's sensibility is to be equated with the sensibility of the educated person, then it is logical to use different styles to express different kinds of people." She feels that the "personality is very much what is remembered; [the form I used] enabled me to say to the reader: Look, these apparently so different people have got so-and-so in common, or these things have got this in common. If I had used a conventional style, the old-fashioned novel, which I do not think is dead by any means, . . . I would not have been able to do this kind of playing with time, memory and the balancing of people. . . . I like *The Golden Notebook* even though I believe it to be a failure, because it at least hints at complexity." Robert Taubman expresses similar sentiments, although he is a bit confused concerning the book's structure. He calls the book "a very full novel: it not only burst the bounds of the short formal novel, as it set out to do, but overflowed its own bounds as well. It's pretty well inexhaustible on the way women think and behave, notably in the area where their personal feelings and social and political attitudes meet." But, he adds, "its unusual structure is less a matter of subtle organization than of simple, rather haphazard naturalism, . . . [or perhaps] an advance in naturalism." Lessing is still disturbed by some of the comments on this novel. She told Florence Howe: "When [the book] came out, I was astonished that people got so emotional . . . one way or another. They didn't bother to see, even to look at, how it was shaped. I could mention a dozen books by male authors in which the attitudes to women are the obverse, mirror attitudes, of the attitudes to men in *The Golden Notebook.* But no one would say that these men are anti-women. . . . But I articulated the same things from a female point of view, and this is what was interesting. It was taken as a kind of banner." Lessing would not want to be labeled a feminist. She simply states that, "in the last generation women have become what is known as free. . . . The point is they're still fighting battles to get free—and rightly. And men are still—some men, you know—some men resist it. But what is interesting, . . . what interests me in that book, was in fact, the ideas. . . . What I'm trying to say is that it was a detached book. It was a failure, of course, for if it had been a success, then people wouldn't get so damned emotional when I didn't want them to be." This novel, she says, was "extremely carefully constructed. . . . And the way it's constructed says what the book is about. . . . What I was doing was this: I was thinking about the kind of ideas we take for granted, . . . a complex of ideas which could be described as Left—and which were born with the French Revolution. And they're all to do with freedom. They are revolutionary ideas that are no longer revolutionary and have been absorbed into the fabric of how we live. And they're ideas that fit together in a system, broadly speaking, nonreligious in the old sense, and have to do with the individual in relation to his society and the rights of the individual. Which is a new idea and we don't realize how new it is. We take it absolutely for granted." In one of the sections of this book, says Lessing, "I was really trying to express my sense of despair about writing a conventional novel. . . . Actually that [part] is an absolutely whole conventional novel, and the rest of the book is the material that went into making it. One of the things I was saying was: Well, look, this is a conventional novel. God knows, I write them myself. . . . There it is: 120,000 words; it's got a nice shape and the reviewers will say this and that. And the bloody complexity that went into it. And it's always a lie. And the terrible despair. So you've written a good novel or a moderate novel, but what does it actually say about what you've actually experienced? The truth is—absolutely nothing. Because you can't. . . . I know perfectly well that when I've finished ['Children of Violence'] I shall think, Christ, what a lie. Because you can't get life into it . . . no matter how hard you try. . . . At least I think [*The Golden Notebook* is] more truthful because it's more complex. People are like other people. I mean, I don't think we are as extraordinary as we like to think we are. . . . The same people occur again and again in our lives. Situations do. And any moment of time is so complicated."

"Children of Violence," the now completed series of self-contained novels that Lessing calls "a lie," has been widely acclaimed. Marjorie M. Bitker writes: "There seems no doubt that this work will rank with the foremost fictional commentaries on events of our century up to and perhaps beyond the present." "The series' importance," says Florence Howe, "has to do not only with Mrs. Lessing's reputation as author of *The Golden Notebook;* for she is trying to do something even more ambitious here. She is writing *bildungsroman* and at the same time . . . she is producing good political fiction. Her themes are major: the politics of race and war; . . . the West's changing attitude toward the Soviet Union; the shift from the Second World War to the cold war; worldwide revolutionary struggle against the West and capitalism; the problem of violence." To quote Lessing, "Martha did not believe in violence. [Yet] Martha was the essence of violence, she has been conceived, bred, fed, and reared on violence . . . because she had been born at the end of one world war, and had spent all her adolescence in the atmosphere of preparations for another which had lasted five years and had inflicted such wounds on the human race that no one had any idea of what the results would be." In "Children of Violence," according to Walter Allen, "Doris Lessing does for a young woman something very similar to what Arnold Bennett in *Clayhanger* and D. H. Lawrence in *Sons and Lovers* did for a young man, but the closer parallel is probably with George Eliot. . . . Doris Lessing shows her kinship to George Eliot both in her technique here and in her sober, unsentimental scrutiny of behavior, motives and morals." Lessing's intent, writes Howe, is "extremely ambitious" and her success, of course, has been debated. "But the canvas large enough to contain world events and small enough to measure the growth of a human being is one that only the very greatest novelists have tried. Martha's half-conscious identification of her own lot with the Africans', as she struggles against the tyranny of paternalistic personal relations, is a motif that lights the novel. Her personal wars are refractions of that other, greater war. And if she is slow to learn how to manage her wars, who is quick?" Bitker concludes that "the bare bones of the plot are the least of the riches of this work; its nuances, complexities and implications for our own time and country are unforgettable. For we, like Martha, are children of violence."

Briefing for a Descent Into Hell, writes Joan Didion, "is entirely a novel of 'ideas,' not a novel about the play of ideas in the lives of certain characters but a novel in which the characters exist only as markers in the presentation of an idea." Pearl K. Bell, too, claims the book "is not a novel but a tract. . . . [Mrs. Lessing] is making a case for one of the more dubious and treacherous intellectual fads of our time—the apocalyptic view of the

British psychiatrist, R. D. Laing, and his follower David Cooper. In this worst of all possible worlds, they contend, schizophrenia is a response to life that is more honest than accepted normality. In all fairness to Mrs. Lessing, it must be said that her commitment to this seductive view of the metaphysics of madness is not the modish tropism it represents in many of Laing's guru-worshipping enthusiasts. . . . Mrs. Lessing arrived at the moral of her quasi-fable ('inner-space fiction,' she calls it) in her own way, through a deep commitment to and then increasing disenchantment with contemporary life. . . . In the *Golden Notebook,* she was tentatively suggesting that what the smug world of normality—with its defensive army of psychiatrists, analysts, tranquilizers, and truth serums—calls insanity is actually a higher and purer intuition about the truth of human existence. With *The Four-Gated City* . . . Mrs. Lessing enlarged these ideas into a substantial thesis that drew her much closer to Laing's position." Exploring further on that theme, Jeffrey Meyers says "Mrs. Lessing 'does not believe that other peoples' crises should be cut short, or blanked out with drugs, or forced sleep, or a pretence that there is no crisis, or that if there is a crisis it should be concealed or masked or made light of.' She feels that certain twilight mental states, what doctors call paranoia, 'have a meaning, are reflections from that other [unconscious] part of ourselves which knows things we don't know.' This complex and compassionate novel, about dead men who awaken with a surge of intuitive insight and are drugged and shocked back to sleep, is a Blakean attack on the limitations of pure Reason." Benjamin De Mott's attitude, in describing *Briefing,* is that "writers who mean to add something to human knowledge in the form of philosophical truth are often more permissive than estheticians about untidy composition, garrulity, repetitiousness, circularity . . . they rarely offer readers the pleasures of a perfect design. But the absence of intellectual novelty and of crispness of design doesn't much diminish this writer's significance. Mrs. Lessing in her fifties remains one of the few writers alive in the West whose instinct to feel forward toward a more habitable world is allowed to breathe without shame, hysteria, or ironical defensiveness. If her course as a thinker leads her toward an arraignment of 'sanity' and normality, it does so not in relish of idle tripping, or of supersubtle epistemological arguefying about the nature of reality, but rather as a consequence of her moral sense of what men could become and her conviction that self-reduction is a crime against life."

Lessing is deeply concerned with what she calls "the individual conscience in its relation with the collective." She believes that "the real gap between people of my age and, to choose a point at random, people under thirty [is the rejection of] 'propaganda. . . .' They reject an imaginative understanding of what I am convinced is the basic conflict of our time. The mental climate created by the cold war has produced a generation of young intellectuals who totally reject everything communism stands for; they cut themselves off imaginatively from a third of mankind, and impoverish themselves by doing so." But she also believes that there is a point "where 'committedness' can sell out to expediency. Once you admit that 'art should be willing to stand aside for life,' then the little tracts about progress, the false optimism, the dreadful lifeless products of socialist realism, become inevitable." She feels despair over Vietnam and the possibility of the destruction of the world: "[It is] almost as if there's a permanent boil in the human soul." On the other hand, she is by no means a pessimist: "I believe that the pleasurable luxury of despair, the acceptance of disgust, is as much a betrayal of what a writer should be as the acceptance of the simple economic view of man; both are aspects of cowardice, both fallings-away from a central vision, the two easy escapes of our time into false innocence." Somewhere between isolation and the collective conscience, she believes, is "a resting-point, a place of decision, hard to reach and precariously balanced. . . . The point of rest should be the writer's recognition of man the responsible individual, voluntarily submitting his will to the collective, but never finally; and insisting on making his own personal and private judgments before every act of submission."

Many of Lessing's stories and novels have been called autobiographical. Brewster writes: "The young woman named Martha Quest in the series 'Children of Violence' grows up, like her creator, Doris Lessing, on a farm in Central Africa, has a father and a mother with some traits resembling those ascribed elsewhere by Doris Lessing to her own father and mother, goes at eighteen or so to earn her living in the capital of the colony, as Doris Lessing went to Salisbury, and is there shocked and stimulated by new ideas and new relationships in the rapidly changing conditions of the years before and during World War II. We must assume that Mrs. Lessing, in tracing Martha's development, has not forgotten her own." Martha and Anna Wulf, the protagonist in *The Golden Notebook,* are sometimes discussed as similar characters. Brewster relates, however, that "Mrs. Lessing expressed irritation with a review . . . which equated Martha Quest with Doris Lessing, and then compared Martha Quest with Anna Wulf, presenting the two women as combinations of the author and her characters."

As Brewster notes, Lessing "early in her career chose the straight, broad, direct style of narrative. . . . Her first teachers in fiction were the great nineteenth-century novelists: Tolstoy, Stendhal, Dostoevsky, Balzac, Turgenev, Chekhov—the Realists. . . . She never felt close to the English novel, 'whereas I feel so close to the Russian novel that it's as if they were all my blood brothers.' . . . The artist's sensibility as a mirror for our time has been explored by Proust, Joyce, Lawrence, Mann—the list is Mrs. Lessing's—and she calls this exploration one of the mainstreams of the modern novel. And to her Mann is the greatest. . . . ['His] whole message was that art is rooted in corruption—in illness, above all,' [says Mrs. Lessing who herself believes] that art is rooted in an overwhelming arrogance and egotism: 'There is a kind of cold detachment at the core of any writer or artist.' "

In subsequent novels Lessing has continued to produce work that critiques modern society. In contrast to the realism that marks her earlier novels, though, Lessing's later work—particularly her science fiction series titled "Canopus in Argos: Archives"—has taken startling new forms. In the five volumes of the "Canopus" series, Lessing explores the destruction of life brought about by catastrophe and tyranny. Paul Schlueter in the *Dictionary of Literary Biography* notes that in this series Lessing's "high seriousness in describing earth's own decline and ultimate demise is as profoundly apocalyptic as ever."

Following her foray into science fiction, Lessing again surprised readers and critics by publishing two novels under a pseudonym, Jane Somers. *The Diary of a Good Neighbor* and *If the Old Could* . . . contain typical Lessing themes: relations between women, the question of identity, and psychological conflict. Though Lessing was able to get the books published in both England and the United States, the books were generally ignored by critics and did not sell well. Lessing finally admitted that the works were her creation, saying that she had used the pseudonym to prove a point about the difficulties facing young writers. Without adequate marketing and publicity, noted Lessing, books by unknown writers are generally doomed to oblivion.

Since her pseudonymous period Lessing has written *The Good Terrorist,* a novel about the dreariness facing a group of young rebels in London, and *The Fifth Child,* about a violent, antisocial child who wreaks havoc on his family and society. She has also produced nonfiction tomes, including *The Wind Blows Away Our Words,* about war in Afghanistan during the 1980s. In whatever field she chooses to write, Lessing remains a major literary figure. As Schlueter remarks, "[Her] work has changed radically in format and genre over the years, . . . and she has been more and more willing to take chances fictionally by tackling unusual or taboo subjects. . . . And while it is commonplace to note that Lessing is not a stylist, that she is repetitive, and that her fiction too easily reflects her own enthusiasms at particular moments, . . . the fact remains that she is among the most powerful and compelling novelists of our century."

Lessing has very definite opinions on the responsibilities of a writer. She has said: "As a writer I am concerned first of all with novels and stories, though I believe that the arts continuously influence each other, and that what is true of one art in any given epoch is likely to be true of the others. I am concerned that the novel and the story should not decline as art-forms any further than they have from the high peak of literature; that they should possibly regain their greatness, [i.e., through a return to realism]. . . . I define realism as art which springs so vigorously and naturally from a strongly-held, though not necessarily intellectually- defined, view of life that it absorbs symbolism. I hold the view that the realist novel, the realist story, is the highest form of prose writing. . . . The great men of the nineteenth century had neither religion nor politics nor aesthetic principles in common. But what they did have in common was a climate of ethical judgment; they shared certain values; they were humanists." She believes that contemporary literature, on the contrary, is distinguished by "a confusion of standards and the uncertainty of values." It is now difficult "to make moral judgments, to use words like good and bad," because "we are all of us, directly or indirectly, caught up in a great whirlwind of change; and I believe that if an artist has once felt this in himself, and felt himself as part of it; if he has once made the effort of imagination necessary to comprehend it, it is an end of despair, and the aridity of self-pity. It is the beginning of something else which I think is the minimum act of humility for a writer: to know that one is a writer at all because one represents, makes articulate, is continuously and invisibly fed by, numbers of people . . . to whom one is responsible. . . . Once a writer has a feeling of responsibility, as a human being, for the other human beings he influences, it seems to me he must become a humanist, and must feel himself as an instrument of change for good or for bad. . . . The act of getting a story or a novel published is . . . an attempt to impose one's personality and beliefs on other people. If a writer accepts this responsibility, he must see himself, to use the socialist phrase, as an architect of the soul. . . . [Furthermore,] the novelist has one advantage denied to any of the other artists. The novel is the only popular art-form left where the artist speaks directly, in clear words, to the audience. . . . The novelist talks, as an individual to individuals, in a small personal voice. In an age of committee art, public art, people may begin to feel again a need for the small personal voice; and this will feed confidence into writers and, with confidence because of the knowledge of being needed, the warmth and humanity and love of people which is essential for a great age of literature."

BIOGRAPHICAL/CRITICAL SOURCES:

BOOKS

Brewster, Dorothy, *Doris Lessing,* Twayne, 1965.

Contemporary Literary Criticism, Gale, Volume 1, 1973, Volume 2, 1974, Volume 3, 1975, Volume 6, 1975, Volume 10, 1979, Volume 15, 1980, Volume 22, 1982, Volume 40, 1986.

Dictionary of Literary Biography, Volume 15: *British Novelists, 1930-1959,* Gale, 1983.

Dictionary of Literary Biography Yearbook: 1985, Gale, 1986.

Gindin, James, *Postwar British Fiction,* University of California Press, 1962.

Kostelanetz, Richard, editor, *On Contemporary Literature,* Avon, 1964.

Maschler, Tom, editor, *Declaration,* MacGibbon & Kee, 1959.

Newquist, Roy, editor, *Counterpoint,* Rand McNally, 1964.

Wellwarth, George, *Theatre of Protest and Paradox,* New York University Press, 1964.

PERIODICALS

Chicago Tribune Book World, October 30, 1979, April 27, 1980, January 24, 1982, September 29, 1985.

Commentary, May, 1988.

Commonweal, January 28, 1966, May 7, 1971.

Globe and Mail (Toronto), November 24, 1984, April 6, 1985, December 21, 1985, August 6, 1988.

Kenyon Review, March, 1966.

Los Angeles Times, March 1, 1983, July 6, 1983, May 10, 1984, January 14, 1988.

Los Angeles Times Book Review, March 1, 1981, March 21, 1982, February 10, 1985, October 13, 1985, October 20, 1985, March 27, 1988, April 6, 1988.

Milwaukee Journal, May 29, 1966.

Nation, January 17, 1966, June 13, 1966, March 6, 1967.

New Leader, April 19, 1971.

New Statesman, April 20, 1962, November 8, 1963.

Newsweek, October 14, 1985.

New York Times, October 21, 1972, October 23, 1979, March 27, 1980, January 19, 1981, January 29, 1982, March 14, 1983, April 22, 1984, October 5, 1984, October 23, 1984, July 14, 1985, September 17, 1985, March 30, 1988, June 14, 1988.

New York Times Book Review, March 14, 1971, May 13, 1973, June 4, 1978, November 4, 1979, March 30, 1980, January 11, 1981, February 2, 1982, April 3, 1983, September 22, 1985, January 24, 1988, April 3, 1988.

Partisan Review, spring, 1966.

Saturday Review, April 2, 1966, March 13, 1971.

Time, October 1, 1984, October 7, 1985.

Times (London), March 19, 1981, June 2, 1983, August 12, 1985, October 7, 1985.

Times Literary Supplement, November 23, 1979, May 9, 1980, April 17, 1981, April 2, 1982, June 3, 1983, September 13, 1985, May 8, 1987, October 17, 1987, April 22, 1988.

Tribune Books (Chicago), January 31, 1988, March 20, 1988.

Washington Post, September 24, 1984, October 1, 1984, October 24, 1984.

Washington Post Book World, October 21, 1979, November 4, 1979, April 6, 1980, January 25, 1981, March 21, 1982, April 24, 1983, September 22, 1985, March 20, 1988.

Wilson Library Bulletin, May, 1965.

*   *   *

LEVI, Primo   1919-1987
(Damiano Malabaila)

PERSONAL: Born July 31, 1919, in Turin, Italy; died from a fall down a stairwell in an apparent suicide attempt, April 11, 1987, in Turin, Italy; son of Cesare (a civil engineer) and Ester (Luz-

zati) Levi; married Lucia Morpurgo (a teacher), September 8, 1947; children: Lisa, Renzo. *Education:* University of Turin, B.S. (summa cum laude), 1941. *Religion:* Jewish.

ADDRESSES: Home—Corso Re Umberto 75, Turin, Italy.

CAREER: Chemist and author. Partisan in Italian Resistance, 1943; deported to Auschwitz Concentration Camp in Oswiecim, Poland, and imprisoned there, 1943-45; SIVA (paints, enamels, synthetic resins), Settimo, Turin, Italy, technical executive, 1948-77.

AWARDS, HONORS: Premio Campiello (Venice literary prize), 1963 for *La Tregua,* and 1982, for *Se non ora, quando?;* Premio Bagutta (Milan literary prize), 1967, for *Storie Naturali;* Premio Strega (Rome literary prize), 1979, for *La chiave stella;* Premio Viareggio (Viareggio literary prize), 1982, for *Se non ora, quando?;* co-recipient (with Saul Bellow) of Kenneth B. Smilen fiction award from Jewish Museum in New York, 1985; Present Tense/Joel H. Cavior literary award, 1986, for *The Periodic Table.*

WRITINGS:

Se Questo e un Uomo, F. de Silva (Turin), 1947, 15th edition, Einaudi (Turin), 1975, translation by Stuart Woolf published as *If This Is a Man,* Orion Press (New York), 1959, published as *Survival in Auschwitz: The Nazi Assault on Humanity,* Collier, 1961 (also see below), new edition, 1966 (published in England as *If This Is a Man,* Bodley Head, 1966), dramatic version in original Italian (with Pieralberto Marche), Einaudi, 1966.

La Tregua, Einaudi, 1958, 8th edition, 1965, translation by Woolf published as *The Reawakening,* Little, Brown, 1965 (also see below; published in England as *The Truce: A Survivor's Journey Home From Auschwitz,* Bodley Head, 1965).

(Under pseudonym Damiano Malabaila) *Storie Naturali* (title means "Natural Histories"; short story collection), Einaudi, 1967.

(With Carlo Quartucci) *Intervista Aziendale* (radio script), Radiotelevisione Italiana, 1968.

Vizio di Forma (title means "Technical Error"; short story collection), Einaudi, 1971.

Il sistema periodico, Einaudi, 1975, translation by Raymond Rosenthal published as *The Periodic Table,* Schocken, 1984.

Abruzzo forte e gentile: Impressioni d'occhio e di cuore, edited by Virgilio Orsini, A. Di Cioccio, 1976.

Shema: Collected Poems, Menard, 1976.

La chiave a stella (novel), Einaudi, 1978, translation by William Weaver published as *The Monkey's Wrench,* Summit Books, c. 1986.

La Ricerca della radici: Antologia personale, Einaudi, c. 1981.

Lilit e altri racconti, Einaudi, 1981, translation by Ruth Feldman published as *Moments of Reprieve,* Summit Books, c. 1986.

Se non ora, quando? (novel), Einaudi, 1982, translation by Weaver published as *If Not Now, When?,* introduction by Irving Howe, Summit Books, c. 1985.

(Translator) Franz Kafka, *Il processo* (title means "The Trial"), c. 1983.

L'altrui mestiere, Einaudi, c. 1985.

Survival in Auschwitz [and] *The Reawakening: Two Memoirs,* Summit Books, 1986.

Autoritratto di Primo Levi, Garzanti (Milan), 1987.

Sommersi e i salvati (originally published in 1986), translation by Rosenthal published as *The Drowned and the Saved,* Summit Books, 1988.

The Collected Poems of Primo Levi, translation by Feldmand and Brian Swann, Faber & Faber, 1988.

The Mirror Maker, translation by Rosenthal, Schocken, 1989.
(With Tullio Regge) *Dialogo,* Princeton University Press, 1989.
The Sixth Day, and Other Stories, translation by Rosenthal, Summit Books, 1990.
Other People's Trades, translation by Rosenthal, M. Joseph. 1090.

SIDELIGHTS: Primo Levi told *CA:* "My uncommon experience as a concentration camp inmate and as a survivor has deeply influenced my later life and has turned me into a writer. The two books [*Se Questo un Uomo* and *La Tregua*] are a chronicle of my exile and an attempt to understand its meaning."

If This Is a Man and *The Reawakening,* the English translations of *Se Questo un Uomo* and *La Tregua,* have been widely praised for their portrayal of Levi's imprisonment and subsequent return home. W. J. Cahnman, for example, reviewing *If This Is a Man* in *American Journal of Sociology,* writes: "Here is literally a report from hell: the detached, scientific, unearthly story of a man who descended to the nether world at Auschwitz and returned to the land of the living." Levi's "lack of personal bitterness is almost unnatural, especially when it is realised that he wrote so soon after the German retreat brought him his freedom," notes G. F. Seddon in the *Manchester Guardian.* "Levi's more outstanding virtue is his compassionate understanding of how in these conditions men cease to be men, either give up the struggle or in devious ways win it, usually at the expense of their fellow men." In a 1985 interview published in the *Los Angeles Times,* Levi defended his scientific approach to recounting the horrors of the Holocaust: "It was my duty not to behave as a victim, not to wail and weep, but to be a witness, to give readers material for judgment. This is Divine Law, to be a witness, not to overstate or distort but to deliver and furnish facts. The final judge is the reader."

Sergio Pacifici points out in *Saturday Review* that like *If This Is a Man, The Reawakening,* which chronicles the author's return to Italy, is more than an intimate and accurate diary. "It is a plea for self-restraint and generosity in human relations that may well be heeded in our own critical times," he says. "Levi's lucid and wise reflections on the nature of man deserve more than a mere hearing. *The Reawakening* must take its honored place next to Carlo Levi's *Christ Stopped at Eboli,* Andre Schwartz-Bart's *The Last of the Just,* and *The Diary of Anne Frank.*"

After the successful publication of these first two memoirs, Levi continued to write about the Jewish Holocaust in a variety of works, including two award-winning novels, *La chiave a stella* (published in English as *The Monkey's Wrench*) and *Se non ora, quando?* (published in English as *If Not Now, When?*). Toward the mid-1980s, however, Levi became progressively despondent over what he felt was a general disregard for the immense suffering and loss the Jews experienced during World War II. For reasons not clearly understood, Levi ended his life in 1987 when he jumped down a stairwell in his native town of Turin, Italy. Levi's friend Italian newspaper editor Lorenzo Mundo told Steve Kellerman of the *New York Times* that during the months preceding his death, Levi "would come to visit me and his face looked so discouraged and helpless. He kept saying he was tired, physically and mentally. And he was terribly pessimistic about the destiny of the world and the fate of the spirit of man." Since Levi's death a number of his works have been translated into English, including *The Collected Poems of Primo Levi, The Mirror Maker, The Sixth Day, and Other Stories,* and his final work, *The Drowned and the Saved.*

BIOGRAPHICAL/CRITICAL SOURCES:

PERIODICALS

American Journal of Sociology, May, 1960.
Manchester Guardian, April 22, 1960, February 12, 1965.
New York Times Book Review, November 7, 1965.
Observer, January 26, 1965.
Saturday Review, January 2, 1960, May 15, 1965.
Times Literary Supplement, April 15, 1960, December 3, 1982.

*   *   *

LEVIN, Gerald H(enry) 1929-

PERSONAL: Born May 18, 1929, in Chicago, IL; son of Harry and Eve (Cohen) Levin; married Lillian Cicurel, June 24, 1956; children: Sylvia, Elizabeth. *Education:* Attended Vanderbilt University, 1947-49; University of Chicago, M.A., 1952; University of Michigan, Ph.D., 1956. *Religion:* Jewish.

ADDRESSES: Home—Glastonbury, CT.

CAREER: University of Michigan, Ann Arbor, instructor in English, 1955-56; University of Colorado, Boulder, instructor in English, 1956-57; Eastern Illinois University, Charleston, assistant professor of English, 1957-60; University of Akron, Akron, OH, assistant professor, 1960-65, associate professor, 1965-68, professor, 1969-85, director of English composition, 1967-69, professor emeritus of English, 1986—.

WRITINGS:

Prose Models, Harcourt, 1964, 8th edition, 1990.
A Brief Handbook of Rhetoric, Harcourt, 1966.
(Editor) *The Short Story,* Harcourt, 1967.
(Editor) Francis Connolly, *The Art of Rhetoric,* Harcourt, 1968.
(With Connolly) *A Rhetoric Case Book,* 3rd edition, Harcourt, 1969.
Styles for Writing, Harcourt, 1972.
Sigmund Freud, Twayne, 1975, 5th edition, 1989.
Short Essays: Models for Composition, Harcourt, 1977.
Richardson the Novelist: The Psychological Patterns, Editions Rodopi, 1978.
Writing and Logic, Harcourt, 1982.
Macmillan College Handbook, Macmillan, 1987, 2nd edition, 1991.

*   *   *

LEWIS, C(live) S(taples) 1898-1963
(N. W. Clerk, Clive Hamilton)

PERSONAL: Born November 29, 1898, in Belfast, Ireland; died November 22, 1963, of heart failure after an extended illness; son of Albert James (a solicitor) and Flora Augusta (Hamilton) Lewis; married Joy Davidman Gresham, 1956 (died, 1960); children: two stepsons. *Education:* Attended Malvern College, 1913-14; University College, Oxford, A.B. (first class honors), 1923.

ADDRESSES: Magdalene College, Cambridge, England.

CAREER: Philosophy tutor and lecturer, University College, Oxford University, Oxford, England, 1924, fellow and tutor in English literature, Magdalen College, 1925-54; Magdalene College, Cambridge University, Cambridge, England, professor of Medieval and Renaissance English, 1954-63. Ballard Matthews Lecturer, University of Wales, 1941; Riddell Lecturer, University of Durham, 1942; Clark Lecturer, Trinity College, Cambridge, 1944. *Military service:* British army, Somerset Light Infantry, 1918-19; became second lieutenant.

MEMBER: British Academy (fellow, 1955), Royal Society of Literature (fellow, 1948), Athenaeum, Sir Walter Scott Society (president, 1956), Socratic Club (president and speaker), Inklings.

AWARDS, HONORS: Hawthornden Prize, 1936, and Gollancz Memorial Prize for Literature, 1937, both for *The Allegory of Love;* D.D., University of St. Andrews, 1946; fellow, Royal Society of Literature, 1948, British Academy, 1955, University College, Oxford, 1958, and Magdalene College, Cambridge, 1963; Docteur-es-Lettres, Laval University, 1952; honorary fellow, Magdalen College, Oxford, 1955; Library Association Carnegie Medal, 1957, for *The Last Battle;* D.Litt., University of Manchester, 1959; Lewis Carroll Shelf Award, 1962, for *The Lion, the Witch, and the Wardrobe;* honorary doctorate, University of Dijon, 1962, and University of Lyon, 1963.

WRITINGS:

NOVELS

The Pilgrim's Regress: An Allegorical Apology for Christianity, Reason and Romanticism, Dent, 1933, Sheed & Ward, 1935, revised edition, Fount, 1977, reprinted with translations and notes by John C. Traupman, Bantam, 1981.

Out of the Silent Planet (also see below), John Lane, 1938, Macmillan, 1943, reprinted, 1990, abridged with introduction, glossary and notes by Jane Brooks, Macmillan, 1973.

The Screwtape Letters (first published in *Guardian,* 1941), Bles, 1942, Macmillan, 1943, reprinted, New American Library, 1988, revised edition published as *The Screwtape Letters and Screwtape Proposes a Toast* (also see below), Bles, 1961, Macmillan, 1962, reprinted with introduction by Phyllis McGinley (bound with *Mistress to an Age,* by J. Christopher Herold), Time-Life Books, 1981, published as *The Screwtape Letters; with, Screwtape Proposes a Toast,* drawings by Robert Korn, Macmillan, 1982.

Perelandra (also see below), John Lane, 1943, Macmillan, 1944, reprinted, 1990, new edition published as *Voyage to Venus,* Pan Books, 1960, reprinted, 1983.

That Hideous Strength: A Modern Fairy-Tale for Grownups (also see below), John Lane, 1945, Macmillan, 1946, reprinted, 1990, abridged edition published as *The Tortured Planet,* Avon, 1958.

The Great Divorce: A Dream (first published in weekly installments in *Guardian*), Bles, 1945, reprinted, Collier, 1984.

Till We Have Faces: A Myth Retold, Bles, 1956, Harcourt, 1957, reprinted, 1980.

JUVENILES; ILLUSTRATIONS BY PAULINE BAYNES

The Lion, the Witch, and the Wardrobe (also see below), Macmillan, 1950, reprinted, 1988.

Prince Caspian: The Return to Narnia (also see below), Macmillan, 1951, reprinted, 1988.

The Voyage of the "Dawn Treader" (also see below), Macmillan, 1952, reprinted, Macmillan, 1988.

The Silver Chair (also see below), Macmillan, 1953, reprinted, 1988.

The Horse and His Boy (also see below), Macmillan, 1954, reprinted, 1988.

The Magician's Nephew (also see below), Macmillan, 1955, reprinted, 1988.

The Last Battle (also see below), Macmillan, 1956, reprinted, 1988.

THEOLOGICAL WORKS

The Problem of Pain, Centenary Press, 1940, Macmillan, 1943, reprinted, 1978.

The Weight of Glory (also see below), S.P.C.K., 1942, revised and expanded edition, Macmillan, 1980.

Broadcast Talks: Right and Wrong: A Clue to the Meaning of the Universe and What Christians Believe, Bles, 1942, published as *Broadcast Talks: Reprinted with Some Alterations from Two Series of Broadcast Talks,* Bles, 1942, published as *The Case for Christianity,* Macmillan, 1943, reprinted, 1989.

Christian Behaviour: A Further Series of Broadcast Talks (also see below), Macmillan, 1943.

Beyond Personality: The Christian Idea of God (also see below), Bles, 1944, Macmillan, 1945.

(Editor and author of preface) *George MacDonald: An Anthology,* Centenary Press, 1945, Macmillan, 1947, reprinted, 1986, published as *George MacDonald: 365 Readings,* Collier, 1986.

Miracles: A Preliminary Study, Macmillan, 1947, reprinted, 1978.

The Trouble with X, The Church Union, Church Literature Association, 1948.

Reflections on the Psalms, Harcourt, 1958, Phoenix Press, 1985.

Shall We Lose God in Outer Space? (also see below), S.P.C.K., 1959.

The Four Loves, Harcourt, 1960, Collins, 1987.

The Humanitarian Theory of Punishment, Abingdon, 1972.

LITERARY CRITICISM

The Allegory of Love: A Study in Medieval Tradition, Oxford University Press, 1936, reprinted, 1977.

(With Eustace M. W. Tillyard) *The Personal Heresy: A Controversy,* Oxford University Press, 1939, reprinted, 1965.

Rehabilitations and Other Essays (also see below), Oxford University Press, 1939, reprinted, R. West, 1978.

A Preface to 'Paradise Lost': Being the Ballard Matthews Lectures, Delivered at University College, North Wales, 1941, Oxford University Press, 1942, revised edition, 1960, reprinted Oxford University Press, 1977.

(Editor and author of commentary) Charles Williams, *Arthurian Torso: Containing the Posthumous Fragment of "The Figure of Arthur,"* Oxford University Press, 1948, Eerdmans, 1974.

Hero and Leander (lecture), Oxford University Press, 1952.

English Literature in the Sixteenth Century, Excluding Drama, Clarendon Press, 1954, reprinted, Oxford University Press, 1990, published as *Poetry and Prose in the Sixteenth Century,* 1990.

Studies in Words, Cambridge University Press, 1960, 2nd edition, 1967.

An Experiment in Criticism, Cambridge University Press, 1961.

They Asked for a Paper: Papers and Addresses (also see below), Bles, 1962.

(Author of introduction) *Selections from Layamon's "Brut,"* edited by G. L. Brook, Clarendon Press, 1963.

The Discarded Image: An Introduction to Medieval and Renaissance Literature, Cambridge University Press, 1964.

Studies in Medieval and Renaissance Literature, edited by Walter Hooper, Cambridge University Press, 1967.

Spenser's Images of Life, edited by Alastair Fowler, Cambridge University Press, 1967.

Shelley, Dryden, and Mr. Eliot in Rehabilitations, Richard West, 1973.

(Author of commentary) Charles W. S. Williams, *Taliessin through Logres,* [and] *The Region of the Summer Stars,* [and] *Arthurian Torso* (also see below), Eerdmans, 1974.

Also author of lectures, *Hamlet: The Prince or the Poem?*, H. Milford, 1942, reprinted, Norwood Editions, 1978; *The Literary Impact of the Authorized Version: The Ethel M. Wood Lecture Delivered Before the University of London on 20th March, 1950*, Athlone Press, 1950, Fortress Press, 1963, revised edition, 1967; and *De Descriptione Temporum: An Inaugural Lecture*, Cambridge University Press, 1955.

COLLECTED WORKS

Rehabilitations, 1939, published as *Rehabilitations and Other Essays*, Folcroft, 1980.

The Weight of Glory, and Other Addresses, Macmillan, 1949 (published in England as *Transposition, and Other Addresses*, Bles, 1949), revised edition, 1980.

Mere Christianity (contains enlarged versions of radio talks, *The Case for Christianity, Christian Behaviour*, and *Beyond Personality*), revised and enlarged with new introduction, Macmillan, 1952, reprinted, 1986, anniversary edition, 1981.

The World's Last Night, and Other Essays (contains *Shall We Lose God in Outer Space?*), Harcourt, 1960.

Screwtape Proposes a Toast and Other Pieces, Collins, 1965, published as *Screwtape Proposes a Toast*, Fontana, 1970.

The Complete Chronicles of Narnia, seven volumes (contains *The Lion, the Witch, and the Wardrobe, Prince Caspian: The Return to Narnia, The Voyage of the Dawn Treader, The Silver Chair, The Horse and His Boy, The Magician's Nephew*, and *The Last Battle*), Penguin, 1965, published as *The Chronicles of Narnia*, Macmillan, 1983.

Of Other Worlds: Essays and Stories, edited by Hooper, Bles, 1966, Harcourt, 1967, Collins, 1982.

A Mind Awake: an Anthology of C. S. Lewis, edited by Kilby, Bles, 1968, Harcourt, 1969.

Selected Literary Essays (includes part of *Rehabilitations and Other Essays, De Descriptione Temporum*, part of *They Asked for a Paper: Papers and Addresses*), edited by Hooper, Cambridge University Press, 1969.

C. S. Lewis: Five Best Books in One Volume, Iversen Associates, 1969.

God in the Dock: Essays on Theology and Ethics, edited by Hooper, Eerdmans, 1970 (published in England as *Undeceptions: Essays on Theology and Ethics*, Bles, 1971; new edition published in England as *First and Second Things*, Fount, 1985).

Space Trilogy (boxed set; includes *Out of the Silent Planet, Perelandra*, and *That Hideous Strength*), Macmillan, 1975, reprinted, 1990.

Fern-Seed and Elephants and Other Essays on Christianity, edited by Hooper, Fontana, 1975.

The Dark Tower and Other Stories (includes two unfinished novels), edited by Hooper, Harcourt, 1977.

The Joyful Christian: 127 Readings from C. S. Lewis, Macmillan, 1977.

Six by Lewis (six volumes), Macmillan, 1978.

On Stories and Other Essays on Literature, edited by Hooper, Harcourt, 1982.

The Visionary Christian: One Hundred and Thirty-One Readings from C. S. Lewis, edited by Chad Walsh, Macmillan, 1981.

The Business of Heaven: Daily Readings from C. S. Lewis, edited by Hooper, Harcourt, 1984.

Of This and Other Worlds, edited by Hooper, Fount, 1984.

Boxen Stories, Collins, 1985.

The Seeing Eye and Other Selected Essays from Christian Reflections, Ballantine, 1986.

The Essential C. S. Lewis, Macmillan, 1988.

LETTERS

Beyond the Bright Blur, Harcourt, 1963.

Letters to Malcolm: Chiefly on Prayer, Bles, 1964 (published in England as *Prayer: Letters to Malcolm*, Fontana, 1974).

Letters of C. S. Lewis, edited by brother, W. H. Lewis, Harcourt, 1966.

Letters to an American Lady, edited by Clyde S. Kilby, Eerdmans, 1967, reprinted, Hodder & Stoughton, 1971.

Mark vs. Tristram: Correspondence between C. S. Lewis and Owen Barfield, edited by Hooper, Lowell House Printers, 1967.

They Stand Together: The Letters of C. S. Lewis to Arthur Greeves (1914-1963), edited by Hooper, Macmillan, 1979.

Letters to Children, edited by Lyle W. Dorsett and Marjorie Lamp Mead, foreword by Douglas H. Gresham, Macmillan, 1985.

Letters: C. S. Lewis and Don Giovanni Calabria, Servant (Ann Arbor, MI), 1988.

C. S. Lewis Letters: A Study in Friendship, translation from Latin by Martin Moynihan, Servant, 1988.

POEMS

(Under pseudonym Clive Hamilton) *Spirits in Bondage: A Cycle of Lyrics*, Heinemann, 1919, published under name C. S. Lewis, Harcourt, 1984.

(Under pseudonym Clive Hamilton) *Dymer*, Macmillan, 1926, reprinted, 1950.

Poems, edited by Hooper, Bles, 1964, reprinted, Harcourt, 1977.

Narrative Poems, edited by Hooper, Bles, 1969, Harcourt, 1972.

CONTRIBUTOR

Essays on Malory, edited by J. A. W. Bennett, Clarendon Press, 1963.

Christian Reflections, edited by Walter Hooper, Eerdmans, 1967, Fount, 1981.

(Contributor of letters) Vanauken, Sheldon, *A Severe Mercy: C. S. Lewis and a Pagan Love Invaded by Christ, Told by One of the Lovers*, Harper, 1977.

Eglerio!: In Praise of Tolkien, edited by Anne Etkin, decorations and illustrations by Lucy Matthews, Quest Communications, 1978.

Christian Childhoods: An Anthology of Personal Memories, edited by Celia Van Oss, Crossroad, 1986.

The Collier Christian Library (boxed set; three volumes), Macmillan, 1988.

Contributor to the proceedings of the British Academy and to *Essays and Studies by Members of the English Association*.

OTHER

The Abolition of Man; or, Reflections on Education with Special Reference to the Teaching of English in the Upper Forms of Schools, Oxford University Press, 1943, Macmillan, 1947, reprinted, Fount, 1986.

Vivisection, New England Anti-Vivisection Society, c. 1947.

Surprised by Joy: The Shape of My Early Life (autobiography), Bles, 1955, Harcourt, 1956, reprinted, Fontana, 1974.

(Under pseudonym N. W. Clerk) *A Grief Observed*, Faber, 1961, Seabury, 1963, published under name C. S. Lewis, Walker and Company, 1988, gift edition, 1989.

Essays Presented to Charles Williams, Eerdmans, 1966.

C. S. Lewis at the Breakfast Table, and Other Reminiscences, edited by James T. Como, Macmillan, 1979.

The Grand Miracle, Ballantine, 1983.

Boxen: The Imaginary World of the Young C. S. Lewis (collection of early maps, histories, and sketches), edited by Hooper, Harcourt, 1985.
Present Concerns (essays), edited by Hooper, Harcourt, 1986.
Timeless at Heart, edited by Hooper, Fount, 1988.

Author, with Owen Barfield, of parody, *A Cretaceous Perambulator (the Re-examination Of),* edited by Hooper, Oxford University C. S. Lewis Society, limited edition, 1983. Author of *Love,* a recording of talks by Lewis for American radio broadcast, Creative Resources, 1971.

Lewis's papers are held at the Bodleian Library at Oxford University, Oxford, England, and in the Marion Wade Collection at Wheaton College, Wheaton, Illinois.

MEDIA ADAPTATIONS: The "Chronicles of Narnia" has been made into an animated television film; abridged versions of the "Chronicles" have been recorded by Caedmon, 1978-81; *The Lion, the Witch, and the Wardrobe* became an animated television special presented April 1-2, 1979, on CBS-TV; was produced as a play in Chicago, IL at the Lifeline Theater, December, 1986; was adapted by Jules Tasca, Thomas Tierney, and Ted Drachman as *Narnia the Musical,* which was first presented in London, and subsequently in New York, NY, at St. Stephens Church September 29, 1986; and was presented as a series on PBS-TV in 1989; *Out of the Silent Planet, Perelandra,* and *That Hideous Strength* have been recorded for Books on Tape; *The Four Loves* has been recorded for Catacomb; *Philia, The Four Loves, Agape,* and *Storge* have been recorded for Word Books.

SIDELIGHTS: Whether one approaches C. S. Lewis through the fantasyland of Narnia, the mythic worlds of Malacandra and Perelandra, the playful, satiric letters of senior devil Screwtape to his nephew, underdevil Wormwood, the witty but thoroughly logical theological works, or the critical literary studies which established him as a noted scholar, one finds that each path leads to an encounter with the faith that thoroughly shaped Lewis's life and writing. Phrases such as "apostle to the skeptics" and "defender of the faith" testify to the influence of Lewis's thought upon readers beginning with the mid-twentieth century and continuing through to the present. A *Times Literary Supplement* reviewer commented that "for the last thirty years of his life no other Christian writer in this country had such influence on the general reading public as C. S. Lewis. Each new book from his pen was awaited with an eagerness which showed that thousands of intelligent men and women had acquired a taste for his distinctive idiom and had come to rely on him as a source of moral and intellectual insight."

Critics have pointed out that Lewis's own journey from atheism to a vital Christian faith uniquely qualified him to defend that faith against its severest opponents. Though brought up in a nominally Christian home, while at boarding school Lewis rejected any belief in God. In his autobiography, *Surprised by Joy* the writer described his intellectual and spiritual development from childhood through adolescence and early adulthood. Richard B. Cunningham summarized his journey in *C. S. Lewis: Defender of the Faith.* "Reason and imagination, beginning early in his life and often pulling in opposite directions, were the controlling elements in [Lewis's] intellectual and spiritual pilgrimage. . . . His imagination and reason converged at the point of revelation; and for him revelation pointed to where myth had become fact: the Incarnate God Jesus Christ." Describing the moment of his conversion to theism, which came as a necessary submission to indisputable evidence, Lewis wrote in *Surprised by Joy:* "You must picture me alone in [my] room in Magdalen, night after night, feeling, whenever my mind lifted even for a sec-

ond from my work, the steady, unrelenting approach of Him whom I so earnestly desired not to meet. . . . In the Trinity term of 1929 I gave in, and admitted that God was God, and knelt and prayed: perhaps, that night, the most dejected and reluctant convert in all England." He further described himself as "a prodigal who is brought in kicking, struggling, resentful, and darting his eyes in every direction for a chance of escape."

Just as the interplay of reason and imagination was instrumental in Lewis's conversion to theism and subsequently to Christianity, so it characterized the body of writings which flowed from his pen in the following years. Propelled by the conviction that reason is related to truth, and imagination connects with meaning, Lewis communicated his ideas in myth, satire, and fantasy, which appealed to the imagination, and in didactic logical treatises, whose arguments addressed the mind. And even though critics distinguished between these genres and assigned his works to one category or another, many acknowledged the interplay within individual works. Cunningham observed: "His literary technique, even in his didactic writing where he relies so heavily on reason and logic, also depends for its impact on the myths, allegories, metaphors, analogies, epigrams, and illustrations provided by his imagination."

Lewis's first scholarly work was *The Allegory of Love.* According to Margaret Patterson Hannay in *C. S. Lewis,* the work "introduces the reader first to the phenomenon of courtly love, then to the literary form of allegory, before presenting detailed studies of medieval allegory. . . . The book thus traces the form of allegorical love poetry from the late eleventh century to the late sixteenth century. Lewis argues that romantic love, something we assume as part of the nature of reality, is a relatively new phenomenon, unknown in classical, biblical, or early medieval times." *The Allegory of Love* includes "the best critical treatment in English of Chaucer's psychological romance, *Troilus and Criseyde,*" Charles A. Brady noted in *America.* And a *Times Literary Supplement* contributor stated, "This is plainly a great book—one which is destined to outlive its particular conclusions as few works of literary scholarship contrive to do. . . . The book is itself an allegory of love, a scholarly romance, in which a journey among works of poetry, many of them neglected, among erotic and scholastic treatises, most of them little read, is woven together into an imaginative and self-subsistent whole, and made available to the literate common reader as this material had never been before."

Many of his academic colleagues wished that Lewis had remained with strictly scholarly pursuits, but the author felt the need to speak to a wider audience. His science fiction trilogy for adults achieved that goal. The trilogy commenced in *Out of the Silent Planet,* continued in *Perelandra,* and ended in *That Hideous Strength.* While Christian ideas are primary to the works, they also contain mythic and literary themes, such as Greek and Roman fables and the Arthurian legends. Writing on the trilogy, A. K. Nardo in *Extrapolation* found that "as the reader travels with Ransom into Deep Heaven, he too is introduced to worlds where myth comes true and where what are merely artificial constructs to delineate kinds of poetry on earth become living realities in the heroic world of Mars and the pastoral world of Venus. Through identification with Ransom, the reader tastes what, Lewis seems to believe, is almost impossible in the modern world: pure epic and pure lyric experiences." And Brady considered the "Miltonic grandeur of conception [in *Out of the Silent Planet* and *Perelandra*] the greatest exercise of pure imagination in immediately contemporary literature."

Out of the Silent Planet introduces the trilogy's main character, the reticent philologist, Dr. Elwin Ransom, who is kidnapped by an unscrupulous scientist, Dr. Weston, and Devine, his power-hungry accomplice. Weston and Devine transport Ransom to Mars via spaceship, intending him as a human sacrifice to placate the "wild" natives. But the inhabitants of Malacandra, as they themselves call Mars, are far more civilized than the kidnappers, and they adopt Ransom, despite certain suspicions concerning his home planet. The Malacandrans view Earth with intense but careful curiosity, calling it the "silent planet," as it is wrapped in a dark veil that keeps it separated from the rest of the cosmos. Ransom comes to love the Malacandrans despite their peculiarities, and he unites with them in capturing Weston and Devine.

While the book received some negative criticism, it was generally popular with both ordinary readers and reviewers. As a piece of "science fiction," *Out of the Silent Planet* had its drawbacks, however. Brian Murphy noted in *C. S. Lewis:* "A reader of science fiction who delights in technical detail and scientific speculation had better pass on at once. What interests Lewis is what-would-happen-if; he imagines a space ship traveling to Mars and hasn't the slightest interest in how it might get there." Still, Lewis's friend J. R. R. Tolkien, who frequently disagreed with Lewis's literary approach to fantasy, was enthusiastic about the book. In *The Letters of J. R. R. Tolkien,* Humphrey Carpenter reprinted Tolkien's letter to his publisher, Stanley Unwin, concerning a negative review of *Out of the Silent Planet:* "I read [*Out of the Silent Planet*] in the original MS. and was so enthralled that I could do nothing else until I had finished it. My first criticism was simply that it was too short. . . . I at any rate should have bought this story at almost any price if I had found it in print, and loudly recommended it as a 'thriller' by (however and surprisingly) an intelligent man."

Ransom's struggles with Weston continue in *Perelandra.* On this trip, Ransom is transported by supernatural beings to Venus, which is a watery Eden, covered by floating islands. There Ransom meets a beautiful green woman, who seems completely innocent of all evil. But Weston also appears, and has apparently been sent by evil spirits. Eventually, the philologist realizes that he has been indeed sent to a second Eden, and that Weston is tempting the woman to disobey the few rules that have been established by the world's creator; Ransom finds his job is to keep yet another planet from losing its Paradise. According to R. J. Reilly in *Romantic Religion: A Study of Barfield, Lewis, Williams, and Tolkien,* "The drama of the Incarnation takes on a strange new light in being told by a naked green woman on a floating island on Venus, as the Fall assumes new grandeur by being almost repeated." Leonard Bacon wrote in *Saturday Review* that *Perelandra* "is the result of the poetic imagination in full blast and should never have been written in prose, however excellent." Bacon found the planet's "first couple" "a thoroughly interesting Eve and perhaps the only endurable Adam in literature." He concluded that *Perelandra* is "a truly remarkable book."

In the *Atlantic,* Chad Walsh explained *Perelandra*'s finale, which leads into *That Hideous Strength,* the longest and most complex novel in the series. "As Ransom prepares to return to the Earth, he has a long conversation with the Adam of Venus, and learns that exciting events may be expected on the Earth in a few years. For countless centuries the Earth has been in the grip of the Devil and his assistants, but there are signs that the final struggle is approaching; the Earth may be delivered from evil, and contact re-established between it and the uncorrupted planets." *That Hideous Strength* "represents Lewis's most complex and impressive use of myth in fiction," wrote Charles Moorman in

College English. The plot focuses on a young married couple who experience the explosion of their quiet university world by the invasion of a revolutionary group known as N.I.C.E. (National Institute of Coordinated Experiments). The wife, Jane Studdock, finds herself on one side of the conflict, headed by Ransom, who is now known as Mr. Fisher-King, while her sociologist husband Mark lands on the other, which is apparently led by Devine in his new identity as Lord Feverstone.

Moorman wrote, "In *That Hideous Strength* Lewis's theme is not a theological dogma, but a moral dilemma. Lewis is here opposing the sanctity and morality of Mr. Fisher-King, who symbolizes the whole weight of an ordered and Christian society, and the chaotic and turbulent secularism of the N.I.C.E. The war between these forces, and thus, in terms of the silent planet myth, between the angels and devils who direct them, is reflected in the inward struggles of a young couple, Mark and Jane Studdock, to choose sides in the great battle, and it is their personal struggles which become the real subject of the last novel." In *Dictionary of Literary Biography,* Eugene McGovern observed, "Lewis packs *That Hideous Strength* with scenes from college politics, bureaucracy, journalism, and married life, and he has much to say about academic ambition, education, equality and obedience, language and abuses of it, scientism and social science, vivisection, magic, the legend of King Arthur, and medieval cosmology. . . . All of this is kept under an impressive control, with the many discursive elements never interfering with the narrative."

The Screwtape Letters contains some of the twentieth-century's best-known descriptions of the bureaucracy of Hell. As the title indicates, the novel's form is a series of letters: all are from Uncle Screwtape, a senior devil, to his nephew, Wormwood, a junior tempter, who is endeavoring to lure a malleable young man to damnation. But the devils find themselves in competition with the Church and with a young Christian woman, whom the demons find "nauseating." Bacon wrote in the *Saturday Review of Literature* that "whatever you may think of the theses of Mr. Lewis . . . the fact remains that [*The Screwtape Letters*] is a spectacular and satisfactory nova in the bleak sky of satire." A *Commonweal* reviewer felt that while Lewis's "comments on marriage seem inadequate, the author exhibits a remarkable knowledge of human nature." And P. W. Wilson recounted in the *New York Times* Thomas More's observation that the devil " 'cannot endure to be mocked,' and which, if correct, means that somewhere in the inferno there must be considerable annoyance."

Lewis's seven-volume series for children, "The Chronicles of Narnia," is considered his best-loved popular work. While the stories rely heavily on Christian ideas, traces of Greek and Roman mythology also surface in its pages. Some critics have mistaken parts of the fairy tales (in particular the first volume, *The Lion, the Witch, and the Wardrobe*) for a direct allegory of Christ's death and resurrection. But in *Of Other Worlds: Essays and Stories,* Walter Hooper introduced Lewis's comments on his initial creation of the fantastic country of Narnia: "Everything began with images; a faun carrying an umbrella, a queen on a sledge, a magnificent lion. At first there wasn't even anything Christian about them; that element pushed itself in of its own accord." But in the same volume, Hooper presented Lewis's recollection of how he planned the stories to communicate with readers who were uninterested in God. Lewis wrote: "I thought I saw how stories of this kind could steal past a certain inhibition which had paralysed much of my own religion in childhood. Why did one find it so hard to feel as one was told one ought to feel about God or about the sufferings of Christ? I thought the chief reason was that one was told one ought to. . . . But supposing that by casting all these things into an imaginary world, stripping them of their stained-glass and Sunday school associations, one could make them for the first time appear in their real potency? Could one not thus steal past those watchful dragons? I thought one could."

The stories concern varying groups of children who first come into contact with the "other world" of Narnia while living in the country during the bombing of London in World War II. The first and most famous group, Peter, Susan, Edmund, and Lucy Pevensie, have been separated from their parents and are lodging with a kindly, but remote, old professor in his large country estate. During a rainstorm, they engage in a game of hide and seek, and Lucy runs into a large wardrobe that turns out to be a doorway into Narnia. Eventually, Lucy's brothers and sisters also find Narnia, and what follows is an adventure-packed tale that includes themes of betrayal, forgiveness, death, and rebirth. The rest of the Chronicles also concern adventures into Narnia, although, as the children mature, they become "too old" to visit, and a younger cousin and his friend eventually become the new explorers. The Chronicles close with Narnia's end: in the final book, *The Last Battle,* Lewis intertwines the New Testament book of the Revelation into Narnia's history, and concludes an "earthly" world with the opening of an eternal one. Murphy believed that Lewis's style grew throughout the Chronicles. "In *The Lion, the Witch and the Wardrobe,* [Lewis's] tone is a bit self-consciously avuncular, even the slightest bit condescending. But by the second story, *Prince Caspian,* he has an assured and simple narrative tone which becomes, by the end of the Chronicles, a genuinely noble and serious 'high' style—almost a development of and improvement on the style William Morris . . . adopted for his romances."

Despite the books' continual popularity with children, Lewis was not altogether successful with adults. According to *Use of English* contributor Peter Hollindale, "The structure of power in Narnia, with Aslan at its head, is enforced by battle, violence, retributive justice, pain and death. Anything which challenges the power is either evil or stupid, and frequently both." And Penelope Lively in another issue of the same periodical saw an "underlying savagery that . . . makes the books . . . sinister, and the more so because this is what emerges as the most convincing thing about them." Perhaps the problem some critics had with the powerful Aslan, the talking lion who is the series' Christ-figure, was the author's conception of goodness. Hooper in *Imagination and the Spirit: Essays in Literature and the Christian Faith* described this as "none of the mushy, goody-goody sort of thing we sometimes find in people we feel we ought to like, but cannot. Here, in this magnificent Lion, is absolute goodness beyond anything we could imagine. Qualities we sometimes think of as opposites meet in him and blend." Lewis reconciled many apparent opposites in presenting Aslan's character, where ferocity mingled with tenderness, and sternness was followed by humor.

Surprised by Joy was Lewis's chronicle of his own life, explaining how his early childhood led up to his conversion to Christianity. (Lewis's last years were recorded in *A Grief Observed,* written after his wife's death from cancer). The author approached his own story as he would his fiction or his essays. *Nation* contributor May Swenson called the "long drawn out and intricate conversion . . . fascinating because of [Lewis's] intellect and charm, plus the story-telling dexterity of a topnotch mystery writer." T. S. Matthews, however, writing in the *New York Times* found the book left him "cold." Matthews continued, "In his clear, dry, take-it-or-leave-it manner, [Lewis] describes and tries to dissect

the most incandescent of human emotions—and takes all the joy out of it." But while a *Times Literary Supplement* contributor agreed that the story "lacks the appalling, double-you-for-damnation sense of crisis which hangs over, say, that of Bunyan," he continued that "the tension of [the] final chapters holds the interest like the close of a thriller."

"*Till We Have Faces* has a special place in [Lewis's] work: the object of either extravagant praise or silent neglect, [and] the novel has an oddly tentative quality," Murphy wrote. "Lewis explored wonderingly in this difficult novel. . . . [and] deeply his own past, his own deepest dreams, and his own deeply hidden images of God." While *Faces* was the author's favorite work, this unusually dark and puzzling novel has confused readers and critics. Although it builds on the themes of sin and redemption, *Faces* operates in a pre-Christian world. The story takes place in the violent, barbaric realm of Glome, where the only civilizing force is expressed through a Greek slave tutor, known as the Fox. "The driving motif of *Till We Have Faces* is the development of the soul, a motif explored allegorically in one of [Lewis's] earliest works, *The Pilgrim's Regress.* Here Lewis has recast the familiar myth of Cupid and Psyche," noted John H. Timmerman in *Religion in Life.* The familiar story is altered by perspective: it is told first-person, from the view of Psyche's ugly and embittered older sister, Orual, who eventually becomes the queen of Glome. *Till We Have Faces* is Orual's story, and relates first-person how she becomes harmful to her beloved sister, whom she loves possessively. McGovern felt that the novel displays Lewis's skill in psychological characterization. "Not before *Till We Have Faces* did Lewis show he could produce a complete and thoroughly convincing portrait, and in this novel he has not one but three impressive creations," and mentions Orual, the Fox, and the faithful soldier, Bardia. Timmerman also saw depth in the work, and stated that "The philosophic cast to the novel is stronger than in any other of [Lewis's] work."

The novel darkens further when Orual desires to observe Psyche's lover and the castle in which the "gods" have placed her. But when Psyche's sisters come to visit, they can see nothing. Nothingness is also the answer given to Orual when she demands of her country's goddess why she has lost Psyche. But Orual eventually comes to an unusual conclusion: "I saw well why the gods do not speak to us openly, nor let us answer. . . . Why should they hear the babble that we think we mean? How can they meet us face to face till we have faces?" Murphy wrote: "This is an answer that is as powerful . . . as it is troubling." He concluded, "Through all his work, but especially [the] last works, Lewis says that life is a preparation—not, as William Butler Yeats said, a preparation for something that never happens—but a readying for seeing God."

Frequently controversial but as popular now as during his lifetime, Lewis excited as much criticism as praise. McGovern quoted Helen Gardner, who said of Lewis: "He aroused warm affection, loyalty, and devotion in his friends, and feelings of almost equal strength among innumerable persons who knew him only through his books. But he also aroused strong antipathy, disapproval, and distaste among some of his colleagues and pupils, and among some readers. It was impossible to be indifferent to him." In his belief that "man does not 'make himself,' " he appeared a reactionary to many twentieth-century minds. Patrick J. Callahan explained in *Science Fiction: The Other Side of Realism—Essays on Modern Fantasy and Science Fiction,* Lewis's conviction that man's "reason is capable of apprehending a rational universe, and thus, that there is a natural moral order. Such a stance places him in opposition to all principles of infinite human progress, to all philosophies of the superman.

Lewis would accept Blake's maxim that 'in trying to be more than man, we become less.' "

BIOGRAPHICAL/CRITICAL SOURCES:

BOOKS

Authors & Artists for Young Adults, Volume 3, Gale, 1990.
Callahan, Patrick J., *SF: The Other Side of Realism—Essays on Modern Fantasy and Science Fiction,* edited by Thomas D. Clareson, Bowling Green University Popular Press, 1971.
Carter, Humphrey, with Christopher Tolkien, editors, *The Letters of J. R. R. Tolkien,* Allen and Unwin, 1981.
Children's Literature Review, Volume 3, Gale, 1978.
Contemporary Literary Criticism, Gale, Volume 1, 1973, Volume 3, 1975, Volume 6, 1976, Volume 14, 1980, Volume 27, 1984.
Cunningham, Richard B., *C. S. Lewis: Defender of the Faith,* Westminster Press, 1967.
Dictionary of Literary Biography, Volume 15: *British Novelists, 1930-1959,* Gale, 1983.
Hannay, Margaret Patterson, *C. S. Lewis,* Ungar, 1981.
Hooper, Walter, *Imagination and the Spirit: Essays in Literature and the Christian Faith,* edited by Charles A. Huttar, Eerdmans, 1971.
Lewis, C. S., *Of Other Worlds: Essays and Stories,* edited by Walter Hooper, Harcourt, 1966.
Lewis, C. S., *Surprised by Joy: The Shape of My Early Life,* Harcourt, 1956.
Lewis, C. S., *Till We Have Faces: A Myth Retold,* Eerdmans, 1966.
Murphy, Brian, *C. S. Lewis,* Starmont House, 1983.
Reilly, R. J., *Romantic Religion: A Study of Barfield, Lewis, Williams, and Tolkien,* University of Georgia Press, 1971.
Walsh, Chad, *The Literary Legacy of C. S. Lewis,* Harcourt, 1979.
Wilson, A. N., *C. S. Lewis: A Biography,* Norton, 1990.

PERIODICALS

America, May 27, 1944.
Atlantic, September, 1946.
College English, May, 1957.
Commonweal, March 5, 1943.
Extrapolation, summer, 1979.
Nation, June 2, 1956.
New Republic, February 18, 1967.
New York Times, March 28, 1943; February 5, 1956.
New York Times Book Review, December 26, 1971.
Religion in Life, winter, 1977.
Saturday Review April 8, 1944.
Saturday Review of Literature, April 17, 1943.
Times Literary Supplement, February 28, 1942; October 7, 1955; January 7, 1965; March 23, 1967.
Use of English, winter, 1968; spring, 1977.

—*Sketch by Jani Prescott*

*   *   *

LEWIS, David Kellogg 1941-

PERSONAL: Born September 28, 1941, in Oberlin, OH; son of John Donald (a college professor) and Ewart (a college professor; maiden name Kellogg) Lewis; married Stephanie Robinson, September 5, 1965. *Education:* Swarthmore College, B.A., 1962; Harvard University, M.A., 1964, Ph.D., 1967. *Politics:* Democrat. *Religion:* None.

ADDRESSES: Home—Princeton, NJ. *Office*—Department of Philosophy, Princeton University, Princeton, NJ 08544.

CAREER: University of California, Los Angeles, assistant professor of philosophy, 1966-70; Princeton University, Princeton, NJ, associate professor, 1970-73, professor of philosophy, 1973—. Fulbright lecturer in Australia, 1971; Gavin David Young Lecturer in Adelaide, Australia, 1971; Locke Lecturer at Oxford University, 1984; Kant Lecturer at Stanford University, 1988.

MEMBER: American Association of University Professors, American Academy of Arts and Sciences.

AWARDS, HONORS: Woodrow Wilson fellow, 1962-63, 1965-66; American Council of Learned Societies fellow, 1970-71; Matchette Prize for philosophical writing, Franklin J. Matchette Foundation, 1972, for *Convention: A Philosophical Study;* National Science Foundation grant, 1973-74; Fulbright fellow in New Zealand, 1976.

WRITINGS:

Convention: A Philosophical Study, Harvard University Press, 1969.
Counterfactuals, Harvard University Press, 1973.
Philosophical Papers, Oxford University Press, Volume 1, 1983, Volume 2, 1986.
On the Plurality of Worlds, Basil Blackwell, 1986.
Parts of Classes, Basil Blackwell, in press.

CONTRIBUTOR

David M. Rosenthal, editor, *Materialism and the Mind-Body Problem,* Prentice-Hall, 1971.
Donald Davidson and Gilbert Harman, editors, *Semantics of Natural Language,* D. Reidel, 1972.
Baruch A. Brody, editor, *Readings in the Philosophy of Religion: An Analytic Approach,* Prentice-Hall, 1974.
Soeren Stenlund, editor, *Logical Theory and Semantic Analysis: Essays Dedicated to Stig Kanger on His Fiftieth Birthday,* D. Reidel, 1974.
Milton K. Munitz and Peter K. Unger, editors, *Semantics and Philosophy,* New York University Press, 1974.
Chung-ying Cheng, editor, *Philosophical Aspects of the Mind-Body Problem,* University Press of Hawaii, 1975.
Ernest Sosa, editor, *Causation and Conditionals,* Oxford University Press, 1975.
Keith Gunderson, editor, *Minnesota Studies in the Philosophy of Science,* Volume 7, University of Minnesota Press, 1975.
Edward L. Keenan, editor, *Formal Semantics of Natural Language,* Cambridge University Press, 1975.
Amelie O. Rorty, editor, *The Identities of Persons,* University of California Press, 1976.

OTHER

Contributor to philosophy journals.

WORK IN PROGRESS: Research on philosophy of science, metaphysics, and semantics.

*   *   *

LITTKE, Lael J. 1929-

PERSONAL: Born December 2, 1929, in Mink Creek, ID; daughter of Frank George and Ada Geneva (Petersen) Jensen; married George C. Littke (college professor), June 29, 1954; children: Lori S. *Education:* Utah State University, B.S., 1952; graduate study at City College (now of the City University of New

York), 1955-59, and University of California, Los Angeles, 1968. *Politics:* Democrat. *Religion:* Church of Jesus Christ of Latter-day Saints (Mormon). *Avocational interests:* Travel (has seen most of the United States, eastern Canada, and parts of Mexico and Europe).

ADDRESSES: Home—1345 Daveric Dr., Pasadena, CA 91107. *Agent*—Larry Sternig, 742 Robertson, Milwaukee, WI 53213.

CAREER: Gates Rubber Co., Denver, CO, secretary, 1952-54; Life Insurance Association of America, New York City, secretary, 1954-60; worked as a medical secretary for a physician in New York City, 1960-63; writer, 1963—. Currently on staff of writers Program, University of California, Los Angeles.

MEMBER: PEN International, Society of Children's Book Writers, Southern California Council on Literature for Children and Young People.

WRITINGS:

Wilmer the Watchdog, Western, 1970.
Tell Me When I Can Go, Scholastic Book Services, 1978.
Cave In!, Children's Press, 1981.
Trish for President Harcourt, 1984.
Shanny on Her Own, Harcourt, 1985.
Loydene in Love, Harcourt, 1986.
Where the Creeks Meet, Deseret, 1987.
Prom Dress, Scholastic, Inc., 1989.
Blue Skye, Scholastic, Inc., 1991.

Also author of six books each in "Peanut Butter Pond Series" and "Tall Tale Series," both LinguiSystems, both 1990. Contributor of stories to *Best Short Stories of 1973,* 1973, and magazines, including *Ellery Queen's Mystery Magazine, Seventeen, Ladies Home Journal, McCall's, Boy's Life, Young Miss,* and *Co-ed.*

WORK IN PROGRESS: The House behind the Hill, a young adult novel.

SIDELIGHTS: Lael J. Littke told *CA:* "After teaching writing classes for several years, I have decided that the difference between a successful author and one who gets only rejections is often a matter of discipline: the discipline to stick with a project to completion, to revise it endlessly if necessary, and to send it out again and again if it keeps coming back. It takes a hard disciplinarian to sit oneself down at a cold typewriter each morning and go at it again, but that's what it takes. I had a friend who kept her ironing board set up next to her typewriter, and each morning she told herself that if she didn't write, she would have to iron, a task she hated more than scrubbing bathrooms. Even so she often spent the day ironing. That's how hard it is to become a successful writer. But most of us agree that it's worth every effort we've made."

*　　*　　*

LIVINGSTON, Myra Cohn 1926-

PERSONAL: Born August 17, 1926, in Omaha, NE; daughter of Mayer Louis and Gertrude (Marks) Cohn; married Richard Roland Livingston (a certified public accountant), April 14, 1952; children: Joshua, Jonas Cohn, Jennie Marks. *Education:* Sarah Lawrence College, B.A., 1948. *Avocational interests:* Collecting books (Livingston has a personal library containing over ten thousand volumes of poetry) and bookmarks, bookbinding, music, bridge, working double crostics, raising camellias.

ADDRESSES: Home—9038 Readcrest Dr., Beverly Hills, CA 90210. *Agent*—McIntosh and Otis, Inc., 310 Madison Ave., New York, NY 10017.

CAREER: Poet and anthologist. Professional French horn musician, 1941-48; *Los Angeles Daily News,* Los Angeles, CA, book reviewer, 1948-49; *Los Angeles Mirror,* Los Angeles, book reviewer, 1949-50; personal secretary for singer Dinah Shore and later for violinist Jascha Heifetz, 1950-52; Dallas (Texas) Public Library and Dallas Public School System, creative writing teacher, 1958-63; Beverly Hills Unified School District, poet in residence, 1966-84; University of California, Los Angeles, senior extension lecturer, 1973—. Children's poetry consultant to publishing houses, 1975—. Beverly Hills PTA Council, officer, 1966-75; Poetry Therapy Institute, member of board of directors, 1975—; Reading is Fundamental of Southern California, member of board of directors, 1981—.

MEMBER: International Reading Association, PEN, Authors Guild, Authors League of America, Society of Children's Book Writers, Texas Institute of Letters, Southern California Council on Literature for Children and Young People, Friends of the Beverly Hills Public Library (president, 1979-81).

AWARDS, HONORS: Honor award, *New York Herald Tribune* Children's Spring Book Festival, 1958, for *Whispers, and Other Poems;* Texas Institute of Letters award, 1961, for *I'm Hiding,* 1980, for *No Way of Knowing: Dallas Poems;* Southern California Council on Literature for Children and Young People Award, 1968, for "comprehensive contribution of lasting value in the field of literature for children and young people," 1972, for *The Malibu, and Other Poems,* 1989, for *Earth Songs, Sea Songs, Sky Songs,* and *Space Songs;* Golden Kite Honor Award, Society of Children's Book Writers, 1974, for *The Way Things Are, and Other Poems;* National Council of Teachers of English award, 1980, for excellence in poetry; Parent's Choice Award, 1982, for *Why Am I Grown So Cold?,* 1984, for *Sky Songs;* Commonwealth Club of California book award, 1984, for *Monkey Puzzle, and Other Poems;* National Jewish Book Award, 1987, for *Poems for Jewish Holidays;* other numerous awards.

WRITINGS:

When You Are Alone / It Keeps You Capone: An Approach to Creative Writing with Children, Atheneum, 1973.
Myra Cohn Livingston: The Beautiful Poet Who Writes Beautiful Poems for Children (cassette recording), Center for Cassette Studies, 1973.
Come Away (fiction for children), illustrated by Irene Haas, Atheneum, 1974.
(With Sam Sebesta) *Reading Poetry Aloud* (cassette recording), Children's Book Council, 1975.
First Choice: Poets and Poetry (filmstrip), Pied Piper Productions, 1979.
Selecting Poetry for Young People (cassette recording), Children's Book Council, 1980.
The Writing of Poetry (collection of eight filmstrips), Harcourt, 1981.
The Child as Poet: Myth or Reality?, Horn Book, 1984.
Climb into the Bell Tower: Essays on Poetry, Harper, 1990.

POETRY FOR CHILDREN

Whispers, and Other Poems, illustrated by Jacqueline Chwast, Harcourt, 1958.
Wide Awake, and Other Poems, illustrated by Chwast, Harcourt, 1959.
I'm Hiding, illustrated by Erik Blegvad, Harcourt, 1961.
See What I Found, illustrated by Blegvad, Harcourt, 1962.
I Talk to Elephants, photographs by Isabel Gordon, Harcourt, 1962.
I'm Not Me, illustrated by Blegvad, Harcourt, 1963.

Happy Birthday!, illustrated by Blegvad, Harcourt, 1964.

The Moon and a Star, and Other Poems, illustrated by Judith Shahn, Harcourt, 1965.

I'm Waiting!, illustrated by Blegvad, Harcourt, 1966.

Old Mrs. Twindlytart, and Other Rhymes, illustrated by Enrico Arno, Harcourt, 1967.

A Crazy Flight, and Other Poems, illustrated by James J. Spanfeller, Harcourt, 1969.

The Malibu, and Other Poems, illustrated by Spanfeller, Atheneum, 1972.

The Way Things Are, and Other Poems, illustrated by Jenny Oliver, Atheneum, 1974.

4-Way Stop, and Other Poems, illustrated by Spanfeller, Atheneum, 1976.

A Lollygag of Limericks, illustrated by Joseph Low, Atheneum, 1978.

O Sliver of Liver: Together with Other Triolets, Cinquains, Haiku, Verses, and a Dash of Poems, illustrated by Iris Van Rynbach, Atheneum, 1978.

No Way of Knowing: Dallas Poems, Atheneum, 1979.

A Circle of Seasons, illustrated by Leonard Everett Fisher, Holiday House, 1982.

Sky Songs, illustrated by Fisher, Holiday House, 1984.

Monkey Puzzle, and Other Poems, illustrated by Antonio Frasconi, Atheneum, 1984.

A Song I Sang to You: A Selection of Poems, illustrated by Margot Tomes, Harcourt, 1984.

Celebrations, illustrated by Fisher, Holiday House, 1985.

Worlds I Know and Other Poems, illustrated by Tim Arnold, Atheneum, 1985.

Earth Songs, illustrated by Fisher, Holiday House, 1986.

Higgledy-Piggledy: Verses and Pictures, illustrated by Peter Sis, Macmillan, 1986.

Sea Songs, illustrated by Fisher, Holiday House, 1986.

Poems for Mothers, Holiday House, 1988.

Space Songs, illustrated by Fisher, Holiday House, 1988.

There Was a Place and Other Poems, Macmillan, 1988.

Up in the Air, illustrated by Fisher, Holiday House, 1989.

Birthday Poems, illustrated by Tomes, Holiday House, 1989.

Remembering, and Other Poems, Macmillan, 1989.

My Head Is Red and Other Riddle Rhymes, illustrated by Tere Lo Prete, Holliday House, 1990.

EDITOR

A Tune beyond Us: A Collection of Poetry, illustrated by Spanfeller, Harcourt, 1968.

Speak Roughly to Your Little Boy: A Collection of Parodies and Burlesques, Together with the Original Poems, Chosen and Annotated for Young People, illustrated by Low, Harcourt, 1971.

Listen, Children, Listen: An Anthology of Poems for the Very Young, illustrated by Trina Schart Hyman, Harcourt, 1972.

What a Wonderful Bird the Frog Are: An Assortment of Humorous Poetry and Verse, Atheneum, 1973.

The Poems of Lewis Carroll, illustrated by John Tenniel and others, Crowell, 1973.

One Little Room, An Everywhere: Poems of Love, illustrated by Frasconi, Atheneum, 1975.

O Frabjous Day! Poetry for Holidays, and Special Occasions, Atheneum, 1977.

Callooh! Callay!: Holiday Poems for Young Readers, illustrated by Janet Stevens, Atheneum, 1979.

Poems of Christmas, Atheneum, 1980.

Why Am I Grown So Cold?: Poems of the Unknowable, Macmillan, 1982.

How Pleasant to Know Mr. Lear!, Holiday House, 1982.

Christmas Poems, illustrated by Hyman, Holiday House, 1984.

(With Zena Sutherland) *The Scott, Foresman Anthology of Children's Literature,* Scott, Foresman, 1984.

Easter Poems, illustrated by John Wallner, Holiday House, 1985.

Thanksgiving Poems, illustrated by Stephen Gammell, Holiday House, 1985.

A Learical Lexicon: A Magnificent Feast of Boshblobberbosh and Fun from the Works of Edward Lear, illustrated by Low, Atheneum, 1985.

Poems for Jewish Holidays, illustrated by Lloyd Bloom, Holiday House, 1986.

New Year's Poems, illustrated by Tomes, Holiday House, 1987.

Valentine Poems, illustrated by Patricia Brewster, Holiday House, 1987.

Cat Poems, illustrated by Hyman, Holiday House, 1987.

I Like You, If You Like Me: Poems of Friendship, Macmillan, 1987.

(With Norma Farber) *These Small Stones,* Harper, 1987.

Poems for Fathers, illustrated by Robert Casilla, Holiday House, 1989.

Halloween Poems, illustrated by Gammell, Holiday House, 1989.

Dilly Dilly Piccalilli: Poems for the Very Young, illustrated by Eileen Christelow, Macmillan, 1989.

If the Owl Calls Again, illustrated by Frasconi, Macmillan, 1990.

Dog Poems, illustrated by Leslie Morrill, Holiday House, 1990.

Poems for Grandmothers, illustrated by Patricia Callen-Clark, Holiday House, 1990.

OTHER

Contributor to books, including *Somebody Turned on the Tap in These Kids,* edited by Nancy Larrick, Delacorte, 1971; *A Forum for Focus,* edited by Martha L. King, National Council of Teachers of English, 1972; *Reading in Education: A Broader View,* edited by Malcolm Douglas, C. E. Merrill, 1973; *Using Literature and Poetry Effectively,* edited by Jon E. Shapiro, IRA, 1980; *Celebrating Children's Books,* edited by Betsy Hearne and Marilyn Kaye, Lothrop, 1981; *The Rites of Spring,* edited by Dan Dietrich, University of Wisconsin Press, 1982; *Signposts to Criticism of Children's Literature,* edited by Robert Bator, American Library Association, 1983; *Written for Children,* edited by Winifred Ragsdale, Scribner, 1988; *A Sea of Upturned Faces,* edited by Charlotte Otten, Scarecrow, 1989; *The Voice of the Narrator in Children's Literature,* edited by Gary D. Schmidt, Greenwood Press, 1989. Contributor to *Twentieth Century Children's Writers,* edited by Jane M. Bingham, St. Martin's, 1978, 1984, 1989. Contributor to periodicals, including *Horn Book, Wilson Library Bulletin, Top of the News, Childhood Education, School Library Journal, Cricket Magazine, The Writer, Language Arts, New York Times Book Review,* and *Children's Literature Quarterly. Campus Magazine,* assistant editor, 1949-50.

Some of Livingston's manuscripts and papers are kept in the University of Minnesota's Kerlan Collection.

WORK IN PROGRESS: Poem-Making: Ways to Begin Writing Poetry, a nonfiction book for Harper; another poetry book for Holiday House, *Poems for Sisters, Poems for Borthers.*

SIDELIGHTS: Myra Cohn Livingston has a long-standing reputation as a prominent poet, educator, and anthologist. Although now considered one of the major children's poets in the United States, Livingston did not begin her career as a writer, but as a musician whose main instrument was the French horn. During high school, she took a college summer course in counterpoint taught by the late French composer Darius Milhaud, who advised her to respect the rules of music before breaking them in the name of creativity. "If I have remembered nothing else in my life," Livingston writes in her *Something about the Author Autobiography Series* entry, "it was that principle and I have lived by it. Learn first that there *are* rules, and then learn patiently when to leave them behind." Later, when she decided to concentrate on writing rather than pursuing a career as a professional musician, Livingston remained faithful to the idea that discipline and craftsmanship are essential parts of poetry.

Much of the poet's early verse is derived from her happy memories of living in Omaha, Nebraska, and later in southern California. Her first poetry collection, *Whispers, and Other Poems,* which contains the author's widely-anthologized poem "Whispers," addresses themes typical of her early verse, such as "the celebration of play and of being alone . . . [and] the tension between fact and mystery," according to *Dictionary of Literary Biography* contributor Hazel Rochman. Many reviewers have expressed their delight with Livingston's simple style that contains, as *New York Herald Tribune Book Review* critic Margaret Sherwood Libby puts it, "no 'cuteness' whatever." As the poet once told *CA,* however, some critics chided her "for writing about 'simple things—merely everyday experiences.' Although intended as a rebuke, I accept it now as a compliment, for what more can one offer to the very young, for whom the poems were written, than a touchstone to deal with the early daily experiences of feelings, sights and sounds around them?"

Aside from their relative simplicity, Livingston's earlier poems are also characterized by their lack of any intrusive belligerent forces. They capture instead the joys of youth, musically expressing the sensory experiences and inner thoughts of children. "In the tradition of Robert Louis Stevenson," notes Rochman in her discussion of *Wide Awake, and Other Poems,* "the child's experience is warm and sheltered" in these poems. *Wide Awake,* along with collections such as *I'm Hiding, I'm Not Me,* and *See What I Found,* were dedicated to Livingston's children, whose experiences reminded the poet of her own childhood. *I'm Hiding* is also the first of several of Livingston's collections comprised of several verses that together form one long poem. However, some reviewers, such as *New York Times Book Review* contributor Alice Low, have found that this approach has drawbacks. In her analysis of Livingston's *See What I Found,* which is "similar in format" to *I'm Hiding,* Low remarks that the poems seem "repetitious and uneven." Critics like Libby, however, have no argument with this approach. Readers "will be enchanted with this reflection of the child's mind," asserts Libby in a *Books* review.

Through the 1960s and early 1970s, Livingston continued to write poems that, as Rochman describes them, celebrate "the quiet growing moments of childhood." Such poems are the rule in the collections *The Moon and a Star, and Other Poems, Old Mrs. Twindlytart,* and *A Crazy Flight, and Other Poems.* But as the poet matured, so did her writing. Life becomes less idyllic in Livingston's poems as she ventures to address the problems in the world that people—even children—must unfortunately face; yet an appreciation of life's wonders never abandons her verse completely. In *The Malibu, and Other Poems,* for example, Livingston confronts the problem of environmental pollution, but, as Zena Sutherland points out in *Bulletin of the Center for Children's Books,* there remains "a perceptive capturing of mood or a suddenly sharpened vision of natural beauty."

The Way Things Are, and Other Poems and *4-Way Stop, and Other Poems* again mix happy childhood moments with more serious themes like loneliness, growing up, pollution, and even death in one poem about a squirrel that is killed by a passing automobile. Critics have been divided in their reactions to these

books. One *Kirkus Reviews* writer complains that in *The Way Things Are* "these short, everyday poems are severely limited in both form and content," and A. Harris Fairbanks writes in *Children's Literature: Annual of the Modern Language Association Seminar on Children's Literature and the Children's Literature Association* that the verses are often "completely predictable" and suffer from "sententiousness." Rochman, however, maintains that Livingston's poems are "deceptively simple." For example, the title poem of *The Way Things Are,* which illustrates a child's journey into adulthood, "use[s] the most basic diction, much of it monosyllabic, . . . and the pushing, insistent rhythm and assonance [to] emphasize that this is the everlasting pattern of growing up." Other critics also find the poet's uncomplicated verse refreshing. In a review of *4-Way Stop,* which resembles *The Way Things Are* both thematically and stylistically, *Horn Book* contributor Ethel L. Heins attests that Livingston's poems display "a welcome unpretentiousness."

One of Livingston's most earnest verse collection, *No Way of Knowing: Dallas Poems,* has been praised by *Horn Book* reviewer Mary M. Burns as "perhaps the versatile author's best work to date." Drawing on her memories of Dallas, Texas, during the 1960s, Livingston employs Black English to express the points of view of black friends she knew during a time of racial tension and the shock of John F. Kennedy's assassination. Since Livingston is white, a number of reviewers saw her attempt to express the views of another race while also using their dialect as a dangerous gamble. "But if her venture runs high risks," appraises X. J. Kennedy in the *New York Times Book Review,* "as speech it persuades and as poetry it comes over beautifully." *Washington Post Book World* contributor Rose Styron opines that the "poems are moving in their simplicity, capturing with admirable accuracy the language patterns of a South not too different from the one [William] Faulkner evoked."

Of Livingston's more recent books, Rochman observes that the verses "show a great change in form and format, as well as considerable development in theme." *A Circle of Seasons* concerns the cycles of the individual and of life in general—from birth to death to rebirth—using the seasons as a metaphor. Nature is also a main element in the collections *Earth Songs, Sky Songs, Sea Songs, Space Songs,* and *Monkey Puzzle, and Other Poems,* which reiterate the themes of change and growth. But with *There Was a Place, and Other Poems* Livingston ventures from these universal themes to the more personal subject of children of broken homes, with the purpose of providing "comfort by showing that the troubled reader is not alone in his sorrow or confusion," according to Natalie Babbitt in the *New York Times Book Review.* Babbitt does not venture to guess how therapeutically effective Livingston's poems are, but insists that the "power of these verses is undeniable."

Livingston recognizes that her willingness to directly confront the problems that the modern American child faces is a far cry from her early idyllic visions of childhood. In a *Los Angeles Times* article by Yolanda Barnes, the poet compares *Whispers, and Other Poems* to her more recent verse: "[Whispers] was about a happy childhood in Nebraska. Since then I've learned that many people don't have happy childhoods. The world has some evils. It's a different world." These evils include "the threat of man's interference with the natural process, in the physical universe and in the individual imagination," Rochman relates. As a teacher of creative writing for some thirty years, Livingston is especially concerned that today's children are increasingly losing their imaginative capabilities. "There's this great passivity . . . ," she declares in Barnes's article. "Everything is so structured. Television is overdone. There are more good books out, but they aren't getting to the children. That's where parents and teachers should come in."

Livingston discusses the literary education of children in *The Child as Poet: Myth or Reality?* and *Climb into the Bell Tower: Essays on Poetry.* In the first volume, the author "attempts with considerable success to define how children are like adult artists and how they differ," reports *New York Times Book Review* contributor Meredith Sue Willis. The author argues against those who hold that children are natural poets, that even without the benefits of instruction they are just as talented as adult poets who have studied their craft for years. Poetry by children, avers Livingston in *The Child as Poet,* is "called imaginative because they have used their own imagery. It is called spontaneous because they have written it quickly, and it is called original because it is in their own handwriting. But it is not poetry." She maintains that teaching children, in effect, that poetry takes no particular effort to compose and, even worse, using poetry as a method of teaching grammatical rules is damaging to the child's education and appreciation of poetry. In *Climb into the Bell Tower* the poet continues her attack on educators who use verse in such a disrespectful and manipulative manner. "It's an insult both to poetry and to children, she says," according to Michele Landsberg's *Washington Post Book World* article, "to teach them that art can be created without emotional commitment and long effort." The poet worries, too, that "apathy has replaced imagination in a series of activities . . . in school and at home. Atrophy has set in at many levels." Landsberg relates that Livingston's solution to this problem lies in "the vigorous, intelligent, artful teaching of literature, especially poetry, which is the 'literature of heightened consciousness.' "

In the classes she herself conducts, Livingston demands a great deal of her students. "I tell them," she says in a *Horn Book* commentary, later reprinted in *Horn Book Reflections: On Children's Books and Reading:* "When you write a poem, either tell me something I have never heard before or tell me in a new way something I have heard before. . . . I am asking them for fresh imagery. I am asking them to develop their own sensitivities, to use their own imaginations. I am even asking them to discover something they may not have known they possesses. For without imagination, man is dead." Remembering Milhaud's advice to her, Livingston once wrote in a *Language Arts* article: "No one can teach creative writing. . . . One can only make children aware of their sensitivities, and help children learn of the forms, the basic tools of poetry, into which they can put their own voices. . . . I have never told a child that he is a *poet,* for I know only too well the years and work it takes to be considered a poet."

CA INTERVIEW

CA interviewed Myra Cohn Livingston by telephone on July 23, 1990, at her home in Beverly Hills, California.

CA: You're a musician as well as a writer, having played French horn professionally as a teenager. How did you choose to concentrate on writing rather than music as a life's work?

LIVINGSTON: I sold my first poem when I was eighteen, at Sarah Lawrence College, where there really wasn't an orchestra; you don't play the French horn four hours a day by yourself. The composer William Schuman was there at the time and had some musicians from New York to do chamber music, so I did a little playing with them. But once I started to sell my poetry, I concentrated on writing.

CA: For a poet, music must be a wonderful second field to have talent in. Do you feel it's a conscious influence in your writing?

LIVINGSTON: Rhythmically it has to be a great influence. The sound of music and the rhythm, the sound of words and the rhythm—I think they're quite interrelated in this case.

CA: Are there poets or other writers who've been particularly strong inspirations for you?

LIVINGSTON: Oh, yes. Certainly Homer, and of the modern poets, Randall Jarrell and Richard Wilbur. I loved Tennyson, then hated him, then went back to him. I think he was ruined for me in high school, but I rediscovered him myself ten years ago. Wordsworth's philosophy influenced me, but I don't think his poetry ever did. I read widely; the new poetry without form, "the spillage of raw emotion," as John Ciardi would say, bothers me a great deal. I try to explain this in my new book of essays, *Climb into the Bell Tower.* I favor what T. S. Eliot calls "Music heard so deeply / That it is not heard at all, but you are the music / While the music lasts." In other words, I think poetry *must* have music. That is why I find so much poetry unreadable. It's only image; there's no music to the words. People are not learning the craft of writing poetry today. When stilted diction and rhyme were thrown out, many took it to mean that form and rhythm could be thrown out too. But there's a great difference. I don't think a lot of people understand that to this day.

CA: Do you think it's related to the great lack of discipline that seems to have burgeoned in the '60s?

LIVINGSTON: Yes. It is true in all the arts. People throw some paint on a canvas and they've a painting. They throw some words on a page and they've a poem. I see that in many professional journals now: teachers writing poetry, children writing poetry. But in the major book I did on that subject, *The Child as Poet: Myth or Reality?,* I said what I really felt about this spillage of raw emotion, of dealing with the autonomous image rather than the universal symbol—the universal symbol of nature, for example. That, of course, I get from Wordsworth. In that way he was a great influence on me.

CA: You're considered a children's poet, and your books are by necessity placed in very specific children's areas of libraries. But many of them overlap considerably in age appeal, I think. How do you feel about the division, both from your point of view as writer and with regard to readers?

LIVINGSTON: I think some of my books are for any age. I don't write specifically for children. I seem to write out of my childhood, or watching children do things that will bring my childhood back to me. You really only know yourself. I have three children, and when they started to do things, I would remember something that I had done, like pretending. Even today, at my age, I seem to go back to the experiences of my childhood. I don't think that's abnormal for a children's book writer. Rilke wrote that your earliest recollections are those that you store up and bring back; they're recreated as you grow older. For example, my first book, *Whispers,* which was written when I was eighteen, is about that same childhood that I wrote about much later in *Worlds I Know, and Other Poems,* the only difference being that at eighteen I didn't see any devils in the world. By the time I reached my fifties, I saw a lot of devils. I was very pleased that John Rowe Townsend, in the latest edition of his book written for children, recognizes that I'm one of the few poets who has changed. I don't mean that to sound egotistical, but I have changed with the times, and there are many poets who haven't, who are still living in some dim past in rural America. I was born in 1926, so we have to consider that my real childhood was up to the mid-1930s. But things have changed drastically, so that I write about different things today, like broken families in *There Was a Place*.

CA: Have you had a particularly strong response to that book?

LIVINGSTON: I think the response has been very good. It has to make its way; it takes a while for a book to catch on. And there are some people I know to whom it's so painful that they can't bear it. But I've had very good response from the Gesell Institute and other professionals who recognize that there should be something for these children who are suffering so greatly today.

CA: Those poems are very understated, and I think they're stronger because of that.

LIVINGSTON: I'm a believer in understatement. I use adjectives hardly at all. I believe in strong verbs, and I think one of the sad things about teaching English in this country is that teachers encourage children to cover up what they feel with strings of meaningless adjectives.

CA: You said your three children did things that made you recall your own childhood experiences. Did they ever serve as first readers for your poetry when they were growing up?

LIVINGSTON: No. I learned very early that they were not my best audience. I read my whole family a poem one day, my husband and three children, and they all said, "That's a terrible poem. It doesn't sound like you at all." It's called "The Sun Stuck," and it has been reprinted dozens of times. So I learned not to always trust their response.

CA: Is there a usual way that a poem begins and evolves in your mind, or does it happen in many ways?

LIVINGSTON: It happens in many ways, but usually it's because of something I observe. Sometimes a cluster of words may come to me. I may pick up a phrase on television, or an overheard sentence or snatch of conversation, and oftentimes I will use that. But mostly it comes from an idea or an observation.

CA: Many of your poems are about nature, which you mentioned earlier as a universal symbol, and the feeling of them suggests that you are very close to it. Do you spend a lot of time consciously keeping in close touch with the natural world?

LIVINGSTON: I try to. I live in the hills, and I'm surrounded by trees, by flowers in my garden, by coyotes and birds. My mother was a great nature lover; she will still call me and say, "Have you seen the sunset?" My father had great excitement about the world too. When I was a child, he talked about three things that would happen. One was the splitting of the atom, one was man going to the moon, and one was the discovery of something different about gravity than we have thought true.

CA: I love your Sky Songs, Sea Songs, Earth Songs, *and* Space Songs, *both for their poetry and for the beautiful artwork by Leonard Everett Fisher. How does that collaboration work?*

LIVINGSTON: I did all the writing first, and then Leonard responded to the words. In several instances—in *Circle of Seasons,* for example—he had done one drawing for winter that I didn't

think my words fit, so I redid my words. I live in California and don't see snow that much. In *Earth Songs* he did several drawings that I didn't feel were right for the words, so he redid the drawings. But for the most part we do not collaborate in the sense of sitting side by side and deciding together what to do. I've met him several times, and one day I said to him, "I'd love to do a book about the sea." I love the ocean; I'm mesmerized by it. I think I began to think in terms of his pictures with that book.

I learned a lesson very early, when I did *See What I Found*. I had written about a piece of clay. To me, clay was something a teacher at school gave you. When Erik Blegvad did the illustration, he had children out digging up the clay from the earth. His experience was in Denmark. I realized at that point that a writer, particularly a poet, shouldn't have too much to do with an illustrator. The picture I see may not be the one someone else sees. In *Worlds I Know* I was fascinated that Tim Arnold had done one picture of a bed in my bedroom that looked exactly like the bed I had as a child. That threw me; somehow he sensed that. I think artists see differently than poets see, and to get two different viewpoints is very good. I like the idea that this can happen. I don't think all books can work that way; a lot of picture books can't. But I think in the case of poetry it can. *Whispers* has been reprinted about a hundred and fifty times, with as many different illustrations of it. Some are not so good; some are marvelous. I know there are poets who will only allow certain people to illustrate their work. They get very uppity, or they don't want it illustrated. I don't feel that way about it. I feel each person brings to a poem, if it's a good poem, their own pictures.

CA: Does the form of a poem come to you early in the poem's creation?

LIVINGSTON: Finding a form that will suit what you're going to do is one of the hardest things about writing. I used sprung rhythm in *A Circle of Seasons*. I used the triple cinquain, which is a form very few people use. I sort of invented it; I knew about cinquains, and I realized one cinquain didn't do it. In *Earth Songs* I set up my own pattern. It's a totally original pattern in which the last word of the first line rhymes with the first word of the second line, and so forth. I wanted to do that again in *Space Songs,* but it didn't work at all. There I had to create something which would serve the words. The words of science are very difficult to put into a form, so I couldn't use sprung rhythm. I had to use end-rhyme and off-rhyme in that book.

You're not going to write a serious poem in a limerick form. You can't tell very much in a haiku except one moment caught in time. I teach writing at UCLA, and I do believe strictly in learning the forms; I believe in learning the rules before you break them. The problem is, most people don't know those rules. I have a book for children coming out next year from Harper & Row. It's called *Poem-Making*, and in it I try and explain some of those things to children. When I was a child, I thought I could just sit down and make wonderful music come out of the piano before I knew you had to have scales and know something about counterpoint and harmony and chords. I think too many artists today just don't know their craft.

CA: You've said that creative writing can't really be taught, that "one can only make children aware of their sensitivities" and give them a foundation in those forms you're talking about. How do you feel the teacher can best go about making children aware of their sensitivities?

LIVINGSTON: I believe strongly in the importance of journal keeping and the importance of observation. I wrote a book on the subject called *When You Are Alone / It Keeps You Capone*. Other people took from me the idea of the journal, but nobody has explored observation as keenly as I think it should be explored. You can lie pensive on your couch as Wordsworth did thinking about the daffodils. But if you go back and look at the daffodils, that's another thing. I've got a dead daisy on my desk right now that I'm trying to write a poem about. If you had asked me, "What does a dead daisy look like?" I would have said, "Well, its back bends, and it just dies." But if you look very carefully, you see that daisies' backs seldom bend. Their yellow eyes turn brown, and their hair turns from white to a sort of sad brown. So observation makes me go out to the garden and look at my daisies. Some people believe that *all* writing originates in the imagination. This is not true for me. I think observation is as essential to creativity as imagination. If we teach children to observe as well as use imagination we will have better work. Too often imagination becomes a catch-all—too often children are taught to conform.

CA: Is that why most of us lose our openness to poetry as we get older?

LIVINGSTON: There are a couple of reasons for that. Children love poetry when they're young, but then it's force-fed to them in school and turned into a language exercise in the textbooks and, alas, even in whole language now. Children are told to pick out the capital letters and asked why the poet used onomatopoeia instead of being allowed to enjoy the poem. I think poetry should be primarily for the enjoyment that it brings. It gives you a new way of looking, a good metaphor. Metaphoric poetry is the best kind of poetry, I think. All of us use metaphor, but not always in a fresh way. I feel that seeing something in a new way is the joy of poetry, and tremendously important.

CA: Have you been tempted to do something besides poetry and the essays on poetry and teaching?

LIVINGSTON: I'm sort of tempted. I've always wanted to write a play, but I've never written it. I've said that if I lived long enough, I might write a novel, but I've never written it. I'm being urged now to write a biography, but I'm not sure I'm going to do that. I just don't know. Roethke has a line that says, "I learn by going where I have to go." That's one of the guiding principles of my life. I don't know what I'm going to do. I don't like to repeat myself; I get very bored if I have to do that.

CA: You have an enormous book collection that I suspect is still growing, and you've mentioned some writers you've been inspired by in the past. What sort of reading do you most enjoy right now?

LIVINGSTON: This summer I'm reading the Greeks again and I'm rereading Dickens. I read biography a great deal; I love it. I'm not that charmed by current fiction. I go back to the Russians: to *War and Peace,* to Tolstoy and Dostoevski. That's where I find good writing, good character sketches. I read poetry, though there are certain schools of poetry that I won't read, that I find appalling.

CA: You've served for a long time on the board of directors for the Poetry Therapy Institute. Would you tell me something about that organization and your work in it?

LIVINGSTON: That organization was spearheaded by a number of psychiatrists who use poetry to help disturbed people. They not only read poetry to them, but they have them write it. That's

a therapeutic tool. I don't think it has much to do with real poetry being created, but I do believe it is effective therapy. My greatest example is that, after my father died, the only thing that really gave me comfort was Tennyson's "In Memoriam." I think that kind of writing can be very helpful to people who feel they are alone. Stephen Spender said that poetry lets you know that you are alone, but that to be alone is universal.

I feel very strongly that poetry can serve as a tool to help disturbed people. I don't write it for that reason, with the exception of *There Was a Place.* I saw so many children who were suffering from split homes, and I thought if I could put some of their experiences down, it might be very helpful to them to know that they aren't alone, that there are other people who have gone through this sort of experience. The only other book I think I wrote purposely in this sense was *No Way of Knowing: Dallas Poems.* There are a couple of angry poems in that book, one about the death of Kennedy and one about the hard life that these black people in Dallas had. But also I wanted to capture the joy they had, and I didn't want their language to die out. I titled *4-Way Stop* in anger because of all the stop signs that went up. The poems about smog were written in anger. I think writers can be angry, and they have to get it out of their system. A lot of the things I wrote when I was eighteen, the happy events, I redid later in *Worlds I Know* because I realized that things weren't as simple as I thought.

CA: What's coming out next?

LIVINGSTON: There will be an anthology this fall called *If the Owl Calls Again.* We tend to ascribe to owls great wisdom and mystery. I had done a speech at the Pacific Rim Conference several years ago in which I had used a lot of poems about owls to show the difference between good poetry and bad. Hopefully, I've chosen only the good. Another book in the Holiday House series called *Poems for Grandmothers* will be published and in 1991 *Poems for Brothers* and *Poems for Sisters. Poem-Making* will be published by Harper & Row. There are five more books coming after that.

CA: What is your greatest concern for the children you write for and teach?

LIVINGSTON: I think the thing that worries me most is the loss of imagination in children today. Children have forgotten how to make their own pictures. They're so accustomed to television now that they wait for somebody else to make the pictures for them. This frightens me. No matter what science unleashes, there can be answers only if we keep our imaginations alive to the possibilities of change. But we're raising children who have little imagination because their imaginations are not encouraged in schools and they're certainly not encouraged when they have a steady diet of television. That atrophies the imagination.

I've been teaching for more than thirty years now, and I'm often horrified by what I hear and what I see when I go into classrooms. I don't know whether we're breeding a new kind of person; I think that's perfectly possible. We have an educational system today that says, "See it *this* way." And we don't have the kind of teachers we used to have, either. Our teachers don't know how to use trade books; they've had no experience. I don't say it's their fault. It's the fault of education at a higher level for not insisting that they learn something about literature. Everything is happening so fast, and everything is so quickly obsolete. I don't mean to sound like a pessimist. Today's world can't be like yesterday's world, and I don't talk about the good old days. But I would love to see teachers use more self-reliance and not run like sheep to the latest guru who tells them how to teach, not to accept anything and everything holus-bolus.

BIOGRAPHICAL/CRITICAL SOURCES:

BOOKS

Butler, Francelia, editor, *Children's Literature: Annual of the Modern Language Association Seminar on Children's Literature and the Children's Literature Association,* Temple University Press, 1975.

Children's Literature Review, Volume 7, Gale, 1984.

Dictionary of Literary Biography, Volume 61: *American Writers for Children since 1960: Poets, Illustrators, and Nonfiction Authors,* Gale, 1987.

Field, Elinor Whitney, editor, *Horn Book Reflections: On Children's Books and Reading,* Horn Book, 1969.

Hopkins, Lee Bennett, *Books Are by People,* Citation Press, 1969.

Huck, Charlotte S., and Doris Young Kuhn, *Children's Literature in the Elementary School,* second edition, Holt, 1968.

Lukens, Rebecca J., *A Critical Handbook of Children's Literature,* Scott, Foresman, 1976.

Something about the Author Autobiography Series, Volume 1, Gale, 1986.

PERIODICALS

Booklist, September 1, 1974.
Books, June 17, 1962.
Bulletin of the Center for Children's Books, January, 1973; September, 1976.
Chicago Tribune Book World, December 7, 1980.
Christian Science Monitor, May 8, 1958; November 5, 1975; May 12, 1976.
Horn Book, August, 1959; August, 1964; August, 1971; December, 1972; October, 1974; August, 1976; August, 1978; June, 1979; February, 1981; October, 1982.
Junior Libraries, March, 1959.
Kirkus Review, July 1, 1972; July 15, 1974; April 15, 1976; June 15, 1979; November 1, 1982.
Language Arts, March, 1978.
Lively Arts and Book Review, May 14, 1961.
Los Angeles Times, December 18, 1980; December 25, 1984.
Los Angeles Times Book Review, September 5, 1982; May 27, 1984; January 27, 1985; November 24, 1985; June 8, 1986.
New York Herald Tribune Book Review, May 11, 1958; July 12, 1959.
New York Times Book Review, June 1, 1958; April 1, 1962; May 8, 1966; May 7, 1967; April 28, 1968; May 4, 1969; June 6, 1971; November 5, 1972; September 22, 1974; May 2, 1976; May 1, 1977; November 9, 1980; November 14, 1982; March 10, 1985; May 10, 1987; April, 1989.
Publishers Weekly, February 25, 1974; April 28, 1989.
Reading Teacher, January, 1983.
School Library Journal, September, 1965; September, 1969; October, 1974; October, 1978; October, 1979: January, 1981.
Young Readers Review, June, 1965.
Washington Post, November 5, 1972.
Washington Post Book World, September 11, 1966; March 8, 1981; May 14, 1989; May 13, 1990.

—Sketch by Kevin S. Hile

—Interview by Jean W. Ross

LOBEL, Anita (Kempler) 1934-

PERSONAL: Born June 3, 1934, in Cracow, Poland; immigrated to the United States, 1952; naturalized citizen, 1956; daughter of Leon and Sofia (Grunberg) Kempler; married Arnold Stark Lobel (an author and illustrator), April, 1955 (died December 4, 1987); children: Adrianne, Adam. *Education:* Pratt Institute, B.F.A., 1955; attended Brooklyn Museum Art School, 1975-76.

ADDRESSES: Home and office—New York, NY.

CAREER: Free-lance textile designer, 1957-64; writer and illustrator of books for children, 1964—.

AWARDS, HONORS: Sven's Bridge, 1965, and *On Market Street,* 1981, were named *New York Times* Best Illustrated Picture Books of the Year; *Potatoes, Potatoes,* 1967-68, and *The Seamstress of Salzburg,* 1970, were named American Institute of Graphic Arts Children's Books; *Book World* Children's Spring Book Festival Award, 1973, for *Little John; A Birthday for the Princess,* 1974, and *Peter Penny's Dance,* 1977, were selected for the Children's Book Showcase of the Children's Book Council; *Peter Penny's Dance,* 1976, *How the Rooster Saved the Day,* 1977, and *On Market Street,* 1981, were named *New York Times* Outstanding Books of the Year; *Peter Penny's Dance,* 1976, *A Treeful of Pigs,* 1979, *Singing Bee! A Collection of Favorite Children's Songs,* 1982, and *The Rose in My Garden,* 1982, were named *School Library Journal*'s Best Books of the Year; *How the Rooster Saved the Day* was named one of *School Library Journal*'s Best Books for Spring, 1977; Children's Choice awards, International Reading Association and Children's Book Council, 1979, for *The Pancake,* and 1980, for *Fanny's Sister; Boston Globe-Horn Book* Award Honor for Illustration, 1981, for *On Market Street,* and 1984, for *The Rose in My Garden; On Market Street* was a Caldecott Honor Book and an American Book Award finalist, both 1982; several of Lobel's books were named Child Study Association Children's Books of the Year and/or were selected for the American Institute of Graphic Arts Children's Book Show.

WRITINGS:

SELF-ILLUSTRATED JUVENILES

Sven's Bridge, Harper, 1965.
The Troll Music, Harper, 1966.
Potatoes, Potatoes, Harper, 1967.
The Seamstress of Salzburg, Harper, 1970.
Under a Mushroom, Harper, 1970.
A Birthday for the Princess, Harper, 1973.
(Reteller) *King Rooster, Queen Hen,* Greenwillow, 1975.
(Reteller) *The Pancake,* Greenwillow, 1978.
(Adapter) *The Straw Maid,* Greenwillow, 1983.

OTHER

(Illustrator) Arnold Lobel, *How the Rooster Saved the Day,* Greenwillow, 1977.
(Illustrator) Arnold Lobel, *A Treeful of Pigs* (Junior Literary Guild selection), Greenwillow, 1979.
(Illustrator) Arnold Lobel, *On Market Street,* Greenwillow, 1981.
(Illustrator) Arnold Lobel, *The Rose in My Garden* (Junior Literary Guild selection), Greenwillow, 1984.

Also illustrator of over twenty other books, including *Little John,* by Theodore Storm, retold by Doris Orgel, 1973, *Peter Penny's Dance,* by Janet Quin-Harkin, 1976, *Fanny's Sister,* by Penelope Lively, 1980, *Singing Bee!: A Collection of Favorite Children's Songs,* edited by Jane Hart, 1982, *The Night before*

Christmas, by Clement C. Moore, 1984, and *Princess Furball,* retold by Charlotte Huck, 1989. Lobel's papers are included in the Kerlan Collection, University of Minnesota, Minneapolis.

MEDIA ADAPTATIONS: Several filmstrip adaptations with accompanying audio cassettes with been made from Lobel's books, including: "A Treeful of Pigs," "On Market Street," and "A New Coat for Anna," all Random House; *King Rooster, Queen Hen, On Market Street,* and *A Rose in My Garden,* have all been adapted for audio cassettes, all Random House; *On Market Street* has been adapted for videocassette, Random House.

SIDELIGHTS: Anita Lobel's harsh childhood, spent in Poland during the thirties and forties, stands out in sharp contrast to the vivid colors she uses to illustrate her own and others' books for children. Although she and her brother were separated from their parents at the outbreak of World War II and together spent several months in a Nazi concentration camp in Germany, Lobel believes that the love and protective care of their nanny enabled the children to successfully overcome their harsh experiences. In a *Washington Post Book World* interview conducted by John F. Berry, the author-illustrator comments, "I really feel Nanny's affection colors my work, because I don't feel I have to portray the awful bleakness of the time."

In 1945, Lobel and her brother were rescued from the camp by the Swedish Red Cross and, two years later, were reunited with their parents through the assistance of a relief organization based in Stockholm. Lobel lived in Sweden until 1952, when her parents, who hoped to locate some of their relatives, decided to move to the United States. Although she had received some encouragement to become an artist, Lobel was interested in theatrical arts. Once settled in her new home, she began to participate in school play productions at Pratt Institute. Soon, she met and married her author-illustrator husband, Arnold Lobel. After graduating from Pratt, she started her own textile design business, which she eventually abandoned in favor of her present writing and illustration career.

Reviewers have written favorably about her books, but, according to Berry, only with her later productions have her "talents as a superb illustrator . . . finally [gotten] recognition." However, a sampling of reviews of her early books includes praise for both her writing and drawing abilities. *Potatoes, Potatoes,* the story of two warring brothers whose mother would give them nothing to eat until they and their comrades stopped fighting, is one such work. A *Times Literary Supplement* reviewer, for example, comments on *Potatoes, Potatoes,* noting that the book "is . . . beautifully executed by its author/artist." Reviewing the same title for the *New York Times Book Review,* Barbara Wersba remarks, "Lobel's illustrations . . . [are] excellent picture-book fare; finely drawn and colored."

Although both in the same field, Lobel and her husband, Arnold, were reluctant to collaborate on a book project until the late seventies when he wrote the first of several manuscripts for his wife to illustrate. Recalling the experience of producing *A Treeful of Pigs* with her husband, Lobel remarked in *Junior Literary Guild:* "The nice thing about having the illustrator and the author together in the same studio is that we can decide to change or rethink little details while the work is in progress. For many years we tried to keep our work separate but, when we discovered this extra bonus, we nodded and bowed graciously to each other, and giggled with a sense of a new discovery." Further collaborative efforts, including *On Market Street* and *The Rose in My Garden,* proved very successful with critics and readers alike, and brought a string of awards to the already much honored couple.

As Anita Lobel tells Berry, while at the beginning of their careers she and her husband used to work constantly from nine in the morning until late afternoon and then, after spending the evening with their two children, would go back to work and continue at their tasks until about 2 a.m. Their growing reputations as writers and illustrators have given them more free time with which to pursue other activities. Lobel, for instance, has taken up acting again and has appeared in several Off-Broadway productions. "My ideal day now," she says in the interview, "is to work from nine until two in the afternoon at my drawing desk, then go to rehearsal—if I'm lucky enough to have a part."

BIOGRAPHICAL/CRITICAL SOURCES:

BOOKS

Hopkins, Lee Bennett, *Books Are by People,* Citation Press, 1969.

PERIODICALS

Junior Literary Guild, March, 1979.
New York Times Book Review, October 1, 1967; April 26, 1981; April 1, 1984.
Times Literary Supplement, June 26, 1969.
Washington Post Book World, June 13, 1982.

*   *   *

LOBEL, Arnold (Stark)   1933-1987

PERSONAL: Born May 22, 1933, in Los Angeles, CA; died of cardiac arrest, December 4, 1987, in New York, NY; son of Joseph and Lucille (Stark) Lobel; married Anita Kempler (a writer and illustrator of children's books), April, 1955; children: Adrianne, Adam. *Education:* Pratt Institute, B.F.A., 1955.

ADDRESSES: Home and office—New York, NY.

CAREER: Writer and illustrator of books for children.

AWARDS, HONORS: Someday was chosen as one of the National Education Association's and American Library Association's Outstanding Children's Books of 1964-65; Boys' Club Award Certificate, 1966-67, for *Benny's Animals and How He Put Them in Order;* American Library Association Notable Book awards, 1970, for *Frog and Toad Are Friends,* 1971, for *On the Day Peter Stuyvesant Sailed into Town,* and 1972, for *Frog and Toad Together;* Caldecott Honor Book awards, American Library Association, 1971, for *Frog and Toad Are Friends,* and 1972, for *Hildilid's Night;* National Book Award finalist, 1971, for *Frog and Toad Are Friends; Book World* Spring Book Festival award for picture books, and *Library Journal*'s book list, both 1972, and Newbery Honor Book award, American Library Association, and Brooklyn Art Books for Children citation, both 1973, all for *Frog and Toad Together;* Christopher Award, 1973, for *On the Day Peter Stuyvesant Sailed into Town,* and 1977, for *Frog and Toad All Year;* Irma Simonton Black Award, Bank Street College of Education, 1973, for *Mouse Tales,* and honor book, 1982, for *Uncle Elephant;* Garden State American Book Award, New Jersey Library Association, 1977, for *Dinosaur Time,* 1978, for *Owl at Home,* and 1981, for *Grasshopper on the Road; How the Rooster Saved the Day* was chosen one of *School Library Journal*'s Best Books for Spring, 1977; Recognition of Merit Award, George G. Stone Center for Children's Books, 1978, for "Frog and Toad" books; American Book Award finalist, 1980, for paperback edition of *Frog and Toad Are Friends;* Caldecott Medal, American Library Association, 1981, for *Fables;* Parents' Choice Award for Illustration, Parents' Choice Foundation, 1982, for *Ming Lo Moves the Mountain;* American Book Award nomination, 1982, for *On Market Street; Lucky*

Four-Leaf Clover Award, Scholastic, Inc., 1982; University of Southern Mississippi School of Library Service Silver Medallion, 1985, for "Distinguished Service to Children's Literature"; Laura Ingalls Wilder Medal nomination, 1986, for "Distinguished, Enduring Contribution to Children's Literature"; Golden Kite Award, Society of Children's Book Writers, 1987, for *The Devil and Mother Crump;* also recipient of numerous other awards and honors.

WRITINGS:

SELF-ILLUSTRATED JUVENILES

A Zoo for Mister Muster, Harper, 1962.
Prince Bertram the Bad, Harper, 1963.
A Holiday for Mister Muster, Harper, 1963.
Lucille, Harper, 1964.
Giant John, Harper, 1964.
The Bears of the Air, Harper, 1965.
Martha, the Movie Mouse, Harper, 1966.
The Great Blueness and Other Predicaments, Harper, 1968.
Small Pig, Harper, 1969.
Frog and Toad Are Friends, Harper, 1970.
Ice-Cream Cone Coot and Other Rare Birds, Parents Magazine Press, 1971.
On the Day Peter Stuyvesant Sailed into Town, Harper, 1971.
Frog and Toad Together, Harper, 1972.
Mouse Tales, Harper, 1972.
The Man Who Took the Indoors Out, Harper, 1974.
Owl at Home, Harper, 1975.
Frog and Toad All Year, Harper, 1976.
Mouse Soup, Harper, 1977.
Grasshopper on the Road, Harper, 1978.
Days with Frog and Toad, Harper, 1979.
Fables, Harper, 1980.
The Frog and Toad Coloring Book, Harper, 1981.
Uncle Elephant, Harper, 1981.
Frog and Toad Tales (collection), World's Work, 1981.
Ming Lo Moves the Mountain, Greenwillow, 1982.
The Book of Pigericks: Pig Limericks, Harper, 1983.
Whiskers and Rhymes (poems), Greenwillow, 1985.
The Frog and Toad Pop-Up Book, Harper, 1986.
The Turnaround Wind, Harper, 1988.
Humpty Dumpty Book and Doll Set, Random House, 1988.

OTHER

How the Rooster Saved the Day, illustrated by wife, Anita Lobel, Greenwillow, 1977.
(Compiler and illustrator) *Gregory Griggs and Other Nursery Rhyme People,* Greenwillow, 1978.
A Treeful of Pigs (Junior Literary Guild selection), illustrated by Anita Lobel, Greenwillow, 1979.
On Market Street, illustrated by Anita Lobel, Greenwillow, 1981.
The Rose in My Garden (Junior Literary Guild selection), illustrated by Anita Lobel, Greenwillow, 1984.

Illustrator of over sixty-five books, including *Someday,* by Charlotte Zolotow, 1965, *Benny's Animals and How He Put Them in Order,* by Millicent E. Selsam, 1966, *Hildilid's Night,* by Cheli Duran Ryan, 1971, *The Random House Book of Poetry for Children,* 1983, and *The Devil and Mother Crump,* by Valerie S. Carey, 1987.

Lobel's papers are part of the De Grummond Collection at the University of Southern Mississippi, and the Kerlan Collection at the University of Minnesota, Minneapolis.

MEDIA ADAPTATIONS: Many of Lobel's books are available with audio cassette adaptations, including "As I Was Crossing Boston Common," Listening Library, 1978; "Frog and Toad Together," Harper, 1985, and "Owl at Home," Harper, 1987; *Frog and Toad Are Friends* and *Frog and Toad Together* have been released on audio cassettes and records by Newbery Award Records, 1976; numerous filmstrip adaptations of Lobel's books have been released, including "Prince Bertram the Bad," Harper, 1974; "A List," "Cookies," "The Garden," "Dragons and Giants," "The Dream," and "A Lost Button," all based on *Frog and Toad Together,* Miller-Brody, 1976; and "Whiskers and Rhymes," Random House, 1986; three videocassette adaptations of Lobel's books are available: "Fables," "Arnold Lobel Showcase" (selections from *Frog and Toad Are Friends, Frog and Toad Together, Fables,* and *Mouse Soup*), and "On Market Street," all released by Random House.

SIDELIGHTS: "As both author and illustrator, Arnold Lobel's importance is undeniable," wrote *Dictionary of Literary Biography* contributor Jacqueline Gmuca. "The various awards that his books have received underscore this evaluation, but even more importantly, the prominent qualities of his works—their warmth and humor, social commentary, and basic truth—make Arnold Lobel an important figure in contemporary children's literature." His premature death at age fifty-four ended a life-long career devoted to children's literature during which Lobel wrote and/or illustrated nearly 100 books. Lobel was once described in a *Newsweek* review by Annalyn Swan as the "creator of Frog and Toad, two of the most beloved animal characters to appear in children's books in recent years," and he will probably be best-remembered for his four award-winning books featuring these two amphibians.

In *New Books for Young Readers* Lobel speculated that the many summers he spent watching his children catching frogs and toads at the family's rented Vermont home were probably the inspiration for his two famous characters, but he admitted finding more than just memories in Frog and Toad. "Somehow in the writing of the manuscript for *Frog and Toad* I was, for the first time," he observed, "able to write about myself. Frog and Toad are really two aspects of myself." But if Frog and Toad embody characteristics Lobel saw in himself, they also include part of all of us. "Everyone can relate to Frog and Toad because they don't exist in this world," Lobel noted in a *Lion and the Unicorn* interview with Roni Natov and Geraldine DeLuca, as he attempted to explain the universal appeal of the pair. According to Lobel's analysis, Frog and Toad's success is due is part to the absence of the trappings of modern society in their surroundings (they don't use telephones or automobiles, for example) which gives the tales a timeless quality and, because Frog and Toad are animals, youngsters from a variety of ethnic and social backgrounds can identify with them and their adventures.

Critics seemed to agree with Lobel's self-assessment and found his work reminiscent of great children's writers and illustrators of the past. Margery Fisher found his realistic portrayal of the animals to be similar to the art of the British author and illustrator, Beatrix Potter. "Like Beatrix Potter," Fisher concluded in her *Growing Point* review of *Frog and Toad Together,* "Arnold Lobel delineates his characters with a naturalist's care. His use of limited colour—green and brown with black ink lines and shading—is extended by his strong sense of design and his selected use of detail." In *Who's Who in Children's Books: A Treasury of Familiar Characters of Childhood* Fisher reiterated her comparison, stating, "There can have been few writers since . . . Potter who use snatches of talk so subtly to indicate the human type within a true animal."

Other critics, including Eliot Fremont-Smith and Swan, compared Lobel's work to that of Winnie-the-Pooh's creator, A. A. Milne. "The order of Frog and Toad's friendship," Fremont-Smith writes in his *New York Times Book Review* analysis of *Frog and Toad All Year*, "is elementary—rather vague, gentle, undemanding, supportive (Pooh and Piglet come to mind, though their adventures are more complex and passionate)—but in its very modesty it is both appealing and very comforting to young children." Swan noted that "through their simple adventures together . . . Lobel has brought young readers a world as warm, comforting—and enduring—as the land of Winnie-the-Pooh."

Many of Lobel's works, including the *Frog and Toad* titles, are "I Can Read" books aimed specifically at the beginning reader. Nearly all reviewers of these works, therefore, marveled at the author's ability to tell an engaging story while still staying within the early reader format. Possibly because of Lobel's liberal attitude toward what was suitable vocabulary and subject matter for such books, his works are appealing to beginners as well as more advanced readers. In their *Literature and the Child* Bernice E. Cullinan, Mary K. Karrer, and Arlene M. Pillar, summarized the importance of Lobel's achievement in the genre when they wrote: "Lobel made beginning reading more fun when he created Frog and Toad and, in doing so, loosened the restrictions of the easy-to-read form." Commenting on the same topic in her *New York Times Book Review* critique of *Frog and Toad Together*, Ingeborg Boudreau claimed: "It's the simple things that are the hardest to say. And that's how it is with easy readers, where a too often limited vocabulary begets dull characters and too-concrete situations. Arnold Lobel is an exception to this dismal truism."

Lobel's *Frog and Toad* books seem to exemplify the characteristics of his work that have endeared him to critics and readers alike. However, a variety of equally appealing animals populate many of his other titles including *Mouse Tales*, *Owl at Home*, and *Fables*, his 1981 winner of the American Library Association's prestigious Caldecott Medal. With its domestic setting and simply colored illustrations, critics often likened *Owl at Home* to the *Frog and Toad* books while praising the work for its own merits. In a *Signal* essay on *Owl at Home*, critic John Donovan seemed to grasp the essence of Lobel's craft when he wrote: "Only an artist of the purest sensibilities can capture innocence and not turn it into something cloying and, ultimately, embarrassing. Lobel clearly has these sensibilities. As for his art, it extends and complements his storytelling."

BIOGRAPHICAL/CRITICAL SOURCES:

BOOKS

Children's Literature Review, Volume 5, Gale, 1983.
Cullinan, Bernice E, with Mary K. Karrer and Arlene M. Pillar, *Literature and the Child*, Harcourt, 1981.
Dictionary of Literary Biography, Volume 61: *American Writers for Children since 1960: Poets, Illustrators, and Nonfiction Authors*, Gale, 1987.
Fisher, Margery, *Who's Who in Children's Books: A Treasury of Familiar Characters of Childhood*, Holt, 1975.
Hopkins, Lee Bennett, *Books Are by People*, Citation Press, 1969.
New Books for Young Readers, University of Minnesota, 1982.

PERIODICALS

Books for Your Children, summer, 1982.
Christian Science Monitor, May 4, 1972; August 11, 1980.
Growing Point, October, 1973.
Lion and the Unicorn, Volume 1, number 1, 1977.
Newsweek, August 18, 1970.

New York Times Book Review, May 7, 1972; November 14, 1976; April 1, 1984.
Signal, January, 1976.
Times Literary Supplement, March 25, 1977.
Washington Post Book World, November 9, 1980; May 9, 1982; June 13, 1982.

OBITUARIES:

PERIODICALS

New York Times, December 7, 1987.
School Library Journal, January, 1988.*

—*Sketch by Marian Gonsior*

*   *   *

LURIA, Alexander R(omanovich) 1902-1977

PERSONAL: Name is sometimes transliterated as Aleksander Romanovich Luriya; born July 16, 1902, in Kazan, Russia (now U.S.S.R.); died August, 1977, in Moscow, U.S.S.R.; son of Roman A. (a physician) and Eugenia (Hasskin) Luria; married Lana P. Lipchina (a professor of biology), July 16, 1933; children: Helen A. *Education:* Studied at University of Kazan; University of Moscow, Dr. Phil., 1936, Dr. Med., 1943. *Religion:* None.

ADDRESSES: Home—13 Frunze St., Moscow G 19, U.S.S.R. *Office*—Department of Neuropsychology, University of Moscow, Moscow, U.S.S.R.

CAREER: Affiliated with N. K. Krupskaya Academy for Communistic Education, 1923-31; psychologist at psychology and neurology institutes in the U.S.S.R., 1923-45; University of Moscow, Moscow, U.S.S.R., professor of neuropsychology and head of department, 1945-77.

MEMBER: Soviet Psychological Society, Soviet Neurological Society, Academy of Pedagogical Sciences of the U.S.S.R., British Psychological Society (honorary fellow), American Academy of Arts and Sciences (foreign member), National Academy of Sciences (United States; foreign associate), American Academy of Education (foreign member), Columbian Psychological Society (honorary fellow), Swiss Psychological Society (honorary member), French Neurological Society (honorary member).

AWARDS, HONORS: Order of Lenin, 1955; Lomorossov Award, 1968; D.Sc. from University of Leicester, 1968, University of Nejmegen, 1969, University of Lublin, 1973, University of Brussels, 1975, and University of Tampere, 1975.

WRITINGS:

Rech i intellekt v razvitii rebenka (title means "Speech and Intellect in the Development of the Child"), Poligrafshkola imeni A. V. Lunacharskogo, 1927.
(With Lev Vygotsky) *Etiudy po istorii povedeniia* (title means "Studies in History of Behavior"), Goscizdat, 1930.
The Nature of Human Conflicts; or, Emotion, Conflict, and Will: An Objective Study of Disorganization and Control of Human Behavior, translation by W. Horsely Gantt, Liveright, 1932, reprinted, 1976.
Vnutreniaia kartina boleznei iatrogennye zabolevaniia (title means "An Integral Picture of Illnesses and Diseases"), Medgiz, 1944.
Travmaticheskaia afasiia: Klinika, semiotika, vosstanovitel'naia terapiia, Medical Academy Press (Moscow), 1947, translation by MacDonald Critchley published as *Traumatic*

Aphasia: Its Syndromes, Psychology and Treatment, Mouton & Co., 1970.

Vosstanovlenie funktsii mozga posle voennoi travmy, Medical Academy Press, 1948, translation by Basil Haigh published as *The Restoration of Functions after Brain Injury,* edited by O. L. Zangwill, Pergamon, 1963.

Ocherki psikhofiziologii pisma (title means "Essays on the Psychophysiology of Writing"), Pedagogical Academy Press, 1950.

Rol'slova v formirovanii vremennykh sviazei v normal'nom i anomal'nom razvitii (detei), Pedagogical Academy Press, 1955, translation published as *The Role of Speech in the Regulation of Normal and Abnormal Behaviour,* edited by J. Tizard, Pergamon, 1961.

(With F. Ia Yudovich) *Rech'i razvitie psikhicheskikh professov u rebenka: Experimental'noe issledovanie,* Pedagogical Academy Press, 1956, translation by O. Kovasc and Joan Simon published as *Speech and the Development of Mental Processes in the Child: An Experimental Investigation,* edited by Simon, Staples, 1959, Humanities, 1966.

Problemy vysstei nervnoi deiatel'nosti normal'nego i anomal'nogo rebenka, (title means "Problems of Higher Nervous Activity in the Normal and Abnormal Child"), Pedagogical Academy Press, 2 volumes, 1956-58.

(Editor) *Umstvenno otstalyi rebionok,* Pedagogical Academy Press, 1960, translation by W. K. Robinson published as *The Mentally Retarded Child: Essays Based on a Study of the Peculiarities of the Higher Nervous Functioning of Child-oligophrenics,* edited by Brian Kerman, Pergamon, 1963.

Ob otbore detel'vo vspomogatel'nye shkoly: Metodicheskoe pis'mo dlia rabotnikov priemnykh komissii, Institut Defektologii, Akademiia Pedagogicheskikh nauk RSFSR, 1961.

Vysshiye korkovye funktsii cheloveka i ikh narusheniia pri lokal'nykh porazheniiakh mozga, Moscow University Press, 1962, 2nd edition, 1966, translation by Haigh published as *Higher Cortical Functions in Men,* Basic Books, 1966, 2nd edition, Consultants Bureau, 1980.

Mozg cheloveka i psikhicheskie protsessy, Pedagogical Academy Press, Volume 1, 1963, Volume 2, 1970, translation of Volume 1 by Haigh published as *Human Brain and Psychological Process,* Harper, 1966.

Metody issledovania detei pri otbore vo vspomogatel'nye shkoly (title means "Methods of Investigating Children During Selection for Auxiliary Schools"), Pzoveschenie Publishing House (Moscow), 1964.

(Editor) *Psychological Research in the U.S.S.R.,* Progress Publishers, 1966.

(Editor with E. D. Khomskaia) *Lobnye doli i reguliatsiia psikhicheskikh protsessov i neiropsikhologicheskie issledovaniia* (title means "Frontal Lobes and Regulation of Psychological Processes"), Moscow University Press, 1966.

(With Liubov S. Tsvetkova) *Neiropsikhologicheskii analiz resheniia zadach: Narusheniia protsessa resheniia zadach pri lokal'nykh porazheniiakh mozga* (title means "A Neuropsychological Analysis of Problem-Solving Disturbances of the Problem-Solving Process from Localized Injuries of the Brain"), Pzoveschenie Publishing House, 1966.

Malen'kaia knizhka o bol'shoi pamiati (Um mnemonista), Moscow University Press, 1968, translation by Lynn Solotaroff published as *The Mind of a Mnemonist: A Little Book about a Vast Memory,* foreword by Jerome S. Bruner, Basic Books, 1968.

(With others) *Rasstroistva pamiati v klinike anevrism perednei soedinitel'noi arterii* (title means "Memory Disorders in the Clinic from Aneurysms of the Frontal Connective Artery"), Moscow University Press, 1970.

Poteriannyi i vozvrashchennyi mir (Istoriia odnogo raneniia), Moscow University Press, 1971, translation by Solotaroff published as *The Man with a Shattered World: The History of a Brain Wound,* Basic Books, 1972.

Neiropsikhologiia pamiati, Pedagogical Academy Press, Volume 1, 1972, Volume 2, 1976, translation by Haigh published as *The Neuropsychology of Memory,* Scripta, 1976.

(With others) *Psikhologiia vospriiatiia (uchebnoe posobie),* (title means "The Psychology of Perception: A Textbook"), Moscow University Press, 1973.

Osnovy Neiropsikhologii, Moscow University Press, 1973, translation by Haigh published as *The Working Brain: An Introduction to Neuropsychology,* Basic Books, 1973.

(Editor with K. Pribram) *Electrophysiology of the Frontal Lobes* (translation), Academic Press, 1973.

Ob istoricheskom razvitii poznavatel'nykh protsessov, Nauka, 1974, translation by Martin Lopez-Morillas and Solotaroff published as *Cognitive Development: Its Cultural and Social Foundations,* Harvard University Press, 1976.

Osnovnye problemy neirolingvistiki, Moscow University Press, 1975, translation by Haigh published as *Basic Problems of Neurolinguistics,* Mouton & Co., 1976.

(Contributor) *Mozg pamiat* (title means "Brain and Memory"), Moscow University Press, 1975.

Materialy k kursu lektsii po obshchei psikhologii (title means "Material for a Course of Lectures on Common Psychology"), Moscow University Press, 1975.

Neuropsychological Studies in Aphasia, Schwetz & Zeitlinger, 1977.

The Selected Writings of A. R. Luria, edited and with an introduction by Michael Cole, M. E. Sharpe, 1978.

The Making of Mind: A Personal Account of Soviet Psychology, edited by Michael and Sheila Cole, Harvard University Press, 1979.

Iazyk i soznanie, Izdatel'stvo MGU, 1979, translation published as *Language and Cognition,* edited by James V. Wertsch, J. Wiley, 1981.

Also author of *Man's Conscious Actions: Their Origin and Brain Organization,* Plenum, and *Yazyk mozg* (title means "Language and Brain"), Moscow University Press.

BIOGRAPHICAL/CRITICAL SOURCES:

BOOKS

Christensen, Anne-Lise, *Luria's Neuropsychological Investigation,* Spectrum, 1975.

PERIODICALS

Book World, March 10, 1968.
Observer Review, January 26, 1969.

OBITUARIES:

PERIODICALS

New York Times, August 17, 1977.

*   *   *

LYNCH DAVIS, B.
   See BORGES, Jorge Luis

LYSONS, Kenneth 1923-

PERSONAL: Born October 16, 1923, in Buxton, Derbyshire, England; son of Joseph (a farmer) and Beatrice (Bunting) Lysons; married Audrey Dutton, September 21, 1946; children: Michael, Jeffrey, Edith. *Education:* University of Liverpool, diploma in public administration, 1961, M.A., 1965; Brunel University, Ph.D., 1973; University of Manchester, M.Ed., 1975. *Religion:* Methodist. *Avocational interests:* Music, reading, association football.

ADDRESSES: Home and office—Lathom, Scotchbarn Lane, Whiston, Merseyside L35 7JB, England.

CAREER: Diplomas in Municipal Administration, Local Government Examining Board, and in Management Studies, British Institute of Management and Ministry of Education. Naylor Brothers Ltd., Engineers, Golborne, Lancashire, England, industrial purchaser, 1945-54; held teaching post at Warrington Technical College, 1954-59; St. Helens College of Technology, St. Helens, England, lecturer, 1959-64, senior lecturer, 1964-67, principal lecturer, 1967-71, head of department of business and administrative studies, 1971-83; minister of Methodist Church, beginning 1983, with term as minister in charge of Nutgrove Methodist Church, St. Helens; currently free-lance consultant and author. Member of board of governors of schools for the mentally handicapped; member of St. Helens Preparation for Retirement committee, and of management committee, St. Helens Society for the Deaf. Member of Joint Industrial Training Board Committee on Industrial Purchasing, Ministry of Labour, 1971-73.

MEMBER: Chartered Institute of Secretaries (fellow), Institute of Purchasing and Supply (fellow), Institute of Personnel Management (associate member).

AWARDS, HONORS: F. S. White Award, Institute of Purchasing and Supply, 1980; named fellow, London Chamber of Commerce, for distinguished service to business education.

WRITINGS:

Your Hearing Loss and How to Cope with It, David & Charles, 1978.
The Development of Training for Workers with the Adult Deaf (pamphlet), British Deaf Association, 1978.
Money and Retirement, David & Charles, 1979.
Purchasing Handbook, Macdonald & Evans, 1979, 2nd edition, 1989.
Hearing Impairment, Woodhead-Faulkner, 1984.
Passport to Employment Centenary History of the London Chamber of Commerce Examinations Board, Pitman Publishing, 1987.
Manpower Administration, Institute of Administrative Management, 1990.

Contributor to purchasing, social service, and church magazines.

WORK IN PROGRESS: Earning in Retirement; Introduction to Organisational Behaviour, a textbook.

SIDELIGHTS: Kenneth Lysons told *CA:* "I write because the research involved helps to keep one up-to-date and abreast of developments in selected fields. This is particularly true of fields like management which are dynamic as the results of research are published. Recently I have found the writing of company and organisational histories a fascinating new field. I still believe that if work is looked upon as a hobby, the labour disappears."

M

MacDIARMID, Hugh
  See GRIEVE, C(hristopher) M(urray)

* * *

MACKERRAS, Colin Patrick 1939-

PERSONAL: Born August 26, 1939, in Sydney, Australia; son of Alan Patrick (a university teacher) and Catherine Brearcliffe (a writer; maiden name, MacLaurin) Mackerras; married Alyce Barbara Brazier, June 29, 1963; children: Stephen, Lucy, Martin, Veronica, Josephine. *Education:* University of Melbourne, B.A., 1961; Australian National University, B.A. (with honors), 1962, Ph.D., 1970; Cambridge University, M.Litt., 1964.

ADDRESSES: Home—19 Allambee Cres., Capalaba, Queensland 4157, Australia. *Office*—Division of Asian and International Studies, Griffith University, Nathan, Queensland 4111, Australia.

CAREER: Peking Institute of Foreign Languages, Peking, China, foreign expert and teacher of English, 1964-66; Australian National University, Canberra, research scholar, 1966-69, research fellow, 1969-73, senior research fellow in Far Eastern history, 1973; Griffith University, Nathan, Australia, professor of modern Asian studies, 1974—, chairman of School of Modern Asian Studies, 1979-85, co-director of Key Centre for Asian Languages and Studies, 1988—. International visitor of U.S. Department of State, 1977.

MEMBER: Australian and New Zealand Association for the Advancement of Science, Asian Studies Association of Australia (member of council, 1976-80), Australian Society of Authors, Australian Institute of International Affairs, American Academy of Political and Social Science, Asian Studies Association, Queensland History Teachers Association.

WRITINGS:

(With Neale Hunter) *China Observed, 1964/67,* Nelson (Australia), 1967.
The Uighur Empire According to the T'ang Dynastic Histories, Faculty of Asian Studies, Australian National University, 1968, revised edition published as *The Uighur Empire According to the T'ang Dynastic Histories: A Study in Sino-Uighur Relations, 744-840,* 1972, University of South Carolina Press, 1973.

The Rise of the Peking Opera, 1770-1870: Social Aspects of the Theatre in Manchu China, Clarendon Press, 1972.
Amateur Theatre in China, Australian National University Press, 1973.
(Editor with Donald D. Leslie and Wang Gungwu) *Essays on the Sources for Chinese History,* Australian National University Press, 1973.
The Chinese Theatre in Modern Times, Thames & Hudson, 1975.
(Editor and contributor) *China: The Impact of Revolution,* Longman, 1976.
The Musical Cultures of Asia, China, Curriculum Development Centre (Canberra), 1980.
(Contributor) Stanley Sadie, editor, *The New Grove Dictionary of Music and Musicians,* 20 volumes, Macmillan, 1980.
The Performing Arts in Contemporary China, Routledge & Kegan Paul, 1981.
(With Robert Chan) *Chronology of Modern China from 1842 to the Present Day,* Thames & Hudson, 1982.
(Editor and contributor) *Chinese Theatre from Its Origins to the Present Day,* University of Hawaii Press, 1983.
(With E. S. K. Fung) *From Fear to Friendship: Australia's Policies towards the People's Republic of China, 1966-1982,* University of Queensland Press, 1985.
(Editor and contributor with Nick Knight) *Marxism in Asia,* Croom Helm, 1985.
(Contributor) William H. Nienhauser, Jr., editor, *The Indiana Companion to Traditional Chinese Literature,* Indiana University Press, 1986.
(Editor and contributor with Constantine Tung) *Drama in the People's Republic of China,* State University of New York Press, 1987.
(Editor and contributor with Robert Cribb and Allan Healy) *Contemporary Vietnam: Perspectives from Australia,* University of Wollongong Press, 1988.
(Contributor) Martin Banham, editor, *The Cambridge Guide to World Theatre,* Cambridge University Press, 1988.
Western Images of China, Oxford University Press, 1989.
(With Lunda Hoyle Gill) *Portraits of China,* University of Hawaii Press, 1990.
(With Peter Chang, Yu Hsiu-ching, and wife, Alyce Mackerras) *Dragon's Tongue: Communicating in Chinese,* Australian Broadcasting Corp., 1990.
(Contributor) Denis Sinor, editor, *The Cambridge History of Early Inner Asia,* Cambridge University Press, 1990.

(With Amanda Yorke) *The Cambridge Handbook of Contemporary China,* Cambridge University Press, 1991.

Also contributor to books and encyclopedias. Contributor to Asian studies journals.

WORK IN PROGRESS: An ongoing nineteen-program television series with accompanying books for high-school students about Chinese language and life entitled "Dragon's Tongue" (his book of the same title was published in 1990 after ten of the programs had been televised), with Australian Broadcasting Corp.; a series of textbooks for high-school and university students on Asia in general and China in particular; a large-scale study of China's minority nationalities in the twentieth century, focusing on the changes and continuities under the People's Republic.

SIDELIGHTS: Colin Mackerras told *CA:* "Coming from a musical family, I have always been interested in European music and opera. The most interesting experience of my life has been to live in Peking teaching English at a time when very few Westerners did so. This developed a fascination with Chinese opera, history, politics, and society, supplemented both before and after by intensive university training.

"I was generally very impressed with China, despite some misgivings, and came to feel that the West should do more to develop good relations with the Chinese. I believed this with increasing strength from the mid-1960s and was greatly pleased to see my own hopes and expectations realized through developments in the 1970s and 1980s down to 1988. Of course I was appalled at the events of June 1989, but still do not believe the West should isolate China. The largest of my books on China is a classified chronology of major events since 1842, the beginning of Western impact. This includes not only political, but also cultural and economic events," as well as coverage of "natural disasters and the births and deaths of famous people."

"From an analytical point of view," continues Mackerras, "the book I feel succeeds best is *Western Images of China,* which places this fascinating topic in the 'power/knowledge' model devised by the modern French thinker Michel Foucault."

Mackerras adds, "I have revisited China thirteen times since the 1960s, the longest stay being from July to December, 1982, when I was able to undertake intensive study of China's fifty-five ethnic minorities."

BIOGRAPHICAL/CRITICAL SOURCES:

BOOKS

Priest, Joan, *Scholars and Gentlemen,* Beolarong Press (Brisbane, Australia), 1986.

PERIODICALS

Sydney Bulletin, February 6, 1979.
Times Literary Supplement, April 6, 1990.

*   *   *

MacLAREN, James
   See GRIEVE, C(hristopher) M(urray)

*   *   *

MacLEISH, Archibald   1892-1982

PERSONAL: Born May 7, 1892, in Glencoe, Ill.; died April 20, 1982, in Boston, Mass.; son of Andrew (a partner in Chicago department store of Carson, Pirie, Scott & Co.) and Martha (Hillard) MacLeish; married Ada Hitchcock (a singer), June 21, 1916; children: Kenneth (deceased), Brewster Hitchcock (deceased), Mary Hillard, William Hitchcock. *Education:* Attended Hotchkiss School; Yale University, A.B., 1915; Harvard University, LL.B., 1919.

ADDRESSES: Home—Conway, Mass.

CAREER: Poet, dramatist. Harvard University, Cambridge, Mass., instructor in constitutional law, 1919; Choate, Hall & Stewart (law firm), Boston, Mass., staff member, 1920-23; freelance writer in France, 1923-28; *Fortune,* New York City, staff member, 1929-38; Harvard University, Cambridge, named first curator of Niemann Collection of Contemporary Journalism and adviser to Niemann fellows, 1938. Served as Librarian of Congress, 1939-44, director of Office of Facts and Figures, 1941-42, assistant director of Office of War Information, 1942-43, Assistant Secretary of State, 1944-45, American delegate to Conference of Allied Ministers of Education in London, 1944. Admitted to U.S. Supreme Court Bar, 1942. Served as chairman of U.S. delegation to London conference drafting UNESCO constitution, 1945, as first U.S. delegate to General Conference of UNESCO in Paris, 1946, and first U.S. member of Executive Council of UNESCO. Harvard University, Cambridge, Boylston Professor of Rhetoric and Oratory, 1949-62, Boylston Professor Emeritus, 1962-82. U.S. Department of State lecturer in Europe, 1957; Simpson Lecturer, Amherst College, 1963-67. Museum of Modern Art, New York City, trustee, beginning 1940; Sara Lawrence College, Bronxville, N.Y., trustee, beginning 1949. *Military service:* U.S. Army, Field Artillery, 1917-18; served in France; became captain.

MEMBER: American Academy of Arts and Letters (president, 1953-56), National Institute of Arts and Letters, Academy of American Poets (fellow, 1966), League of American Writers (chairman, 1937), National Committee for an Effective Congress Commission on Freedom of the Press, Phi Beta Kappa, Century Club (New York), Tavern Club and Somerset Club (Boston).

AWARDS, HONORS: John Reed Memorial prize, 1929; Shelley Memorial Award for Poetry, 1932; Pulitzer Prize in poetry for *Conquistador,* 1933; Golden Rose Trophy of New England Poetry Club, 1934; Levinson Prize for group of poems published in *Poetry,* 1941; Commander, Legion of Honor (France), 1946; Commander, el Sol del Peru, 1947; Bollingen Prize in Poetry of Yale University Library, 1952, Pulitzer Prize in poetry, 1953, and National Book Award in poetry, 1953, all for *Collected Poems: 1917-1952;* Boston Arts Festival poetry award, 1956; Sarah Josepha Hale Award, 1958; Chicago Poetry Day Poet, 1958; Antoinette Perry ("Tony") Award in drama, 1959, and Pulitzer Prize in drama, 1959, for *J. B.: A Play in Verse;* Academy Award (best screenplay), 1966, for *The Eleanor Roosevelt Story;* Presidential Medal of Freedom, 1977; National Medal for Literature, 1978; Gold Medal for Poetry, American Academy of Arts and Letters, 1979. M.A. from Tufts University, 1932; Litt.D. from Colby College, 1938, Wesleyan University, 1938, Yale University, 1939, University of Pennsylvania, 1941, University of Illinois, 1946, Washington University, 1948, Rockford College, 1953, Columbia University, 1954, Harvard University, 1955, University of Pittsburgh, 1959, Princeton University, 1965, University of Massachusetts, 1969, and Hampshire College, 1970; L.H.D. from Dartmouth University, 1940, and Williams College, 1942; D.C.L. from Union College, 1941, and University of Puerto Rico, 1953; LL.D. from Johns Hopkins University, 1941, University of California, 1943, Queen's University at Kingston, 1948, Carleton College, 1956, and Amherst College, 1963.

WRITINGS:

POETRY

Songs for a Summer's Day (sonnet cycle), Yale University Press, 1915.

Tower of Ivory, Yale University Press, 1917.

The Happy Marriage, and Other Poems, Houghton, 1924.

The Pot of Earth, Houghton, 1925.

Streets in the Moon, Houghton, 1926.

The Hamlet of A. MacLeish, Houghton, 1928.

Einstein, Black Sun Press, 1929.

New Found Land (limited edition), Black Sun Press, 1930, Houghton, 1930.

Conquistador (narrative poem), Houghton, 1932.

Before Match, Knopf, 1932.

Poems, 1924-1933, Houghton, 1933.

Frescoes for Mr. Rockefeller's City, Day, 1933, reprinted, Folcroft Library Editions (Folcroft, Pa.), 1971.

Poems, John Lane (London), 1935.

Public Speech, Farrar & Rinehart, 1936.

Land of the Free, Harcourt, 1938, reprinted, Da Capo Press, 1977.

America Was Promises, Duell, Sloan & Pearce, 1939.

Actfive and Other Poems, Random House, 1948.

Collected Poems, 1917-52, Houghton, 1952.

Songs for Eve, Houghton, 1954.

Collected Poems, Houghton, 1962.

The Collected Poems of Archibald MacLeish, Houghton, 1963.

The Wild Old Wicked Man and Other Poems, Houghton, 1968.

The Human Season: Selected Poems, 1926-72, Houghton, 1972.

New and Collected Poems, 1917-1976, Houghton, 1976.

New and Collected Poems, 1917-1984, Houghton, 1985.

PROSE

Housing America (articles from *Fortune*), Harcourt, 1932.

Jews in America (first published in *Fortune*), Random, 1936.

Libraries in the Contemporary Crisis, U.S. Government Printing Office, 1939.

Deposit of the Magna Carta in the Library of Congress on November 28, 1939, Library of Congress, 1939.

The American Experience, U.S. Government Printing Office, 1939.

The Irresponsibles, Duell, Sloan & Pearce, 1940.

The American Cause, Duell, Sloan & Pearce, 1941.

The Duty of Freedom, privately printed for the United Typothetae of America, 1941.

The Free Company Presents . . . The States Talking (radio broadcast, April 2, 1941), [New York], 1941.

The Next Harvard, Harvard University Press, 1941.

Prophets of Doom, University of Pennsylvania Press, 1941.

A Time to Speak, Houghton, 1941.

American Opinion and the War (Rede lecture at Cambridge University, Cambridge, England, 1942), Macmillan, 1942.

A Free Man's Books (limited edition of 200 copies), Peter Pauper, 1942.

In Honor of a Man and an Ideal . . . Three Talks on Freedom, by Archibald MacLeish, William S. Paley, Edward R. Murrow (radio broadcast, December 2, 1941), [New York], 1942.

Report to the Nation, U.S. Office of Facts and Figures, 1942.

A Time to Act, Houghton, 1943.

The American Story: Ten Broadcasts (presented on NBC Radio, 1944, and for which MacLeish served as commentator), Duell, Sloan & Pearce, 1944, 2nd edition, 1960.

Martha Hillard MacLeish, 1856-1947, privately printed, 1949.

Poetry and Opinion: The Pisan Cantos of Ezra Pound, University of Illinois Press, 1950, reprinted, Haskell House, 1974.

Freedom Is the Right to Choose: An Inquiry into the Battle for the American Future, Beacon, 1951.

Poetry and Journalism, University of Minnesota Press, 1958.

Poetry and Experience, Riverside Editions, 1960.

The Dialogues of Archibald MacLeish and Mark Van Doren (televised, 1962), Dutton, 1964.

A Continuing Journey, Houghton, 1968.

Champion of a Cause: Essays and Addresses on Librarianship, compiled by Eva M. Goldschmidt, American Library Association, 1971.

Riders on the Earth: Essays and Recollections, Houghton, 1978.

Letters of Archibald MacLeish, 1907 to 1982, edited by R. H. Winnick, Houghton, 1983.

Archibald MacLeish: Reflections, edited by Bernard A. Drabeck and Helen E. Ellis, University of Massachusetts Press, 1986.

DRAMA

Nobodaddy (verse play; also see below), Dunster House, 1926, reprinted, Norwood, 1974.

Panic: A Play in Verse (first produced on Broadway at Imperial Theater, March 14, 1935; also see below), Houghton, 1935.

The Fall of the City: A Verse Play for Radio (first presented on CBS Radio, 1937, and on CBS-TV, 1962; also see below), Farrar & Rinehart, 1937, cassette recording, All-Media Dramatic Workshop (Chicago), 1977.

Air Raid: A Verse Play for Radio (first presented on CBS Radio, 1938; also see below), Harcourt, 1938.

The Trojan Horse (verse play; first presented on BBC Radio, London, c. 1950; also see below), Houghton, 1952.

This Music Crept By Me upon the Waters (verse play; also see below), Harvard University Press, 1953.

J. B.: A Play in Verse (first produced at Yale School of Drama; produced on Broadway at ANTA Theater, December 11, 1958), Houghton, 1958, sound recording, Minnesota Public Radio, 1976.

Three Short Plays (includes *Air Raid, The Fall of the City*, and *The Secret of Freedom*, a television play, produced for Sunday Showcase, 1960), Dramatists Play Service, 1961.

The Eleanor Roosevelt Story (filmscript; first produced by Allied Artists, 1965), Houghton, 1965.

An Evening's Journey to Conway, Massachusetts (play; first produced for NET Playhouse, November 3, 1967), Gehenna Press, 1967.

Herakles (verse play; first produced, 1965), Houghton, 1967.

Scratch (based on short story by Stephen Vincent Benet, "The Devil and Daniel Webster"; first produced on Broadway at St. James Theatre, May 6, 1971), Houghton, 1971.

The Great American Fourth of July Parade: A Verse Play for Radio, University of Pittsburgh Press, 1975.

Six Plays (contains *Nobodaddy, Panic, The Fall of the City, Air Raid, The Trojan Horse*, and *The Music Crept by Me Upon the Waters*), Houghton, 1980.

(Contributor) Samuel Moon, editor, *One Act: Eleven Short Plays of the Modern Theater* (includes *This Music Crept by Me upon the Waters*), Grove, 1987.

OTHER

(Co-author with editors of *Fortune*) *Background of War*, Knopf, 1937.

(Author of foreword) William Meredith, *Love Letters from an Impossible Land*, Yale University Press, 1944.

(Author of introduction) St. John Perse (pseudonym for Alexis Saint-Leger Leger), *Eloges and Other Poems*, Norton, 1944.

(Editor) Gerald Fitzgerald, *The Wordless Flesh,* [Cambridge], 1960.

(Editor) Edwin Muir, *The Estate of Poetry,* Hogarth, 1962.

(Contributor) *Let Freedom Ring,* American Heritage, 1962.

(Editor with E. F. Prichard, Jr., and author of foreword), Felix Frankfurter, *Law and Politics: Occasional Papers, 1913-38,* Peter Smith, 1963.

(Editor) Leonard Baskin, *Figures of Dead Men,* University of Massachusetts Press, 1968.

(Author of introduction) *The Complete Poems of Carl Sandburg,* Harcourt, 1970.

(Adapter) William Shakespeare, *King Lear* (sound recording; recorded from the original CBS broadcast on July 10, 1937), Radio Yesteryear (Sandy Hook, Conn.), c. 1975.

The Nature of Poetry: Pulitzer Prize Poet Archibald MacLeish Discusses Poetry (cassette recording), interviewed by Walter Kerr, Center for Cassette Studies, c. 1975.

(Author of foreword) Anthony Piccione, *Anchor Dragging: Poems,* Boa Editions, 1977.

Also author of "The Son of Man," presented on CBS Radio, 1947. Librettist, with Nicolas Nabokoff, for "Union Pacific," a verse ballet, written for Federal Theatre Project (WPA), first produced on Broadway at St. James Theatre, April 25, 1934, later performed by Monte Carlo Ballet Russe in Philadelphia, Pa., 1934; librettist for "Magic Prison," 1967.

SIDELIGHTS: Archibald MacLeish's roots were firmly planted in both the new and the old worlds. His father, the son of a poor shopkeeper in Glasgow, Scotland, was born in 1837, the year of Victoria's coronation, and ran away first to London and then, at the age of eighteen, to Chicago. His mother was a Hillard, a family that, as *Dialogues of Archibald MacLeish and Mark Van Doren* reveals, MacLeish was fond of tracing back through its New England generations to Elder Brewster, the minister of the Mayflower. MacLeish was born in Glencoe, Illinois, in 1892, attended Hotchkiss School from 1907 to 1911, and from 1911 to 1915 studied at Yale where he edited and wrote for the *Yale Literary Magazine,* contributed to the *Yale Review,* and composed a sonnet sequence "Songs for a Summer's Day," which was chosen as the Yale University Prize Poem in 1915. He married Ada Hitchcock in 1916. In 1917, he saw service in France and published his first collection of poems, *Tower of Ivory.*

MacLeish viewed World War I as the ending of an old world and the beginning of a new one that was *sensed* rather than understood. His early poetry was his attempt to understand this new world; MacLeish would say later that his education regarding this world began not in his undergraduate years at Yale, but in years after the war at Harvard Law School. As he declared in *Riders on the Earth: Essays and Recollections,* Harvard sparked in him a sense of the human tradition, "the vision of mental time, of the interminable journey of the human mind, the great tradition of the intellectual past which knows the bearings of the future."

His personal dilemma, and the constant theme of his early writings, was the reconciliation of idealism with reality. This theme had run through his undergraduate short stories and through his first long poem, "Our Lady of Troy," which was published in *Tower of Ivory.* In his own life, he resolved this dilemma by turning from his promising career as a lawyer to pursue the vocation for which the law courts had left him little time—that of poet. In the summer of 1923, MacLeish announced his commitment to poetry by moving from Boston with his wife and two children, into a fourth floor flat on the Boulevard St. Michel in Paris.

The first major period of MacLeish's poetic career—some would say the only major one—thus began in the early 1920s, when he gave up the law and moved abroad, and closed in the later 1930s, when he took on a succession of "public" obligations. During these years, MacLeish's work was made up of nine longer poems or sequences of poems, accompanied by lyric meditations and statements in various forms on diverse but characteristic themes: doubt, loss, alienation, art, aging, the quest. The shorter poems, some of them very successful, have by anthologizing and other emphases become better known than the longer ones. MacLeish's collection, *New and Collected Poems, 1917-1984,* however, emphasizes the interrelation of his longer and shorter poems, as did his first major collection, *Poems, 1924-1933.*

The "other poems" of *The Happy Marriage, and Other Poems,* still late Victorian prentice-work, are often reminiscent of Edwin Arlington Robinson—whom MacLeish admired—and are justly forgotten. But the title poem, with its more complex, more contemporary subject, alternates skilled imitation of major predecessors with accents of personal authority. It could even be argued that this mixed transitional style fits, if only by chance, the protagonist's own confusion between trite attitudes and existential authenticity. By Part Four of "The Happy Marriage," the protagonist's recognition of marital reality has found its poetic voice, what Grover Smith called in *Archibald MacLeish* "conscious symbolism; witty, almost metaphysical strategies of argument; compressed and intense implications."

The Pot of Earth tells the very different story of a very different figure, a young woman deeply affected psychologically or culturally by archetypal myths of woman's fertility and its transformative powers as seen through "the figure of the dying god whose imaginative presence is at the core of cultural vitality," according to John B. Vickery in *The Literary Impact of the Golden Bough.* Obsessed by symbolic mythical images—excessively so in the unrevised version—she dies in childbirth, sought by or seeking a death dictated by myth, the unconscious, or simple biology. To tell her moving story, MacLeish interweaves narrative and lyric forms, regular and irregular verse of great eloquence that reinforces the pathos, irony, and mystery of her fate.

Besides marking the first publication of "Einstein," *Streets in the Moon* has some of MacLeish's best and best-known shorter poems. In "Memorial Rain" (directly) and in "The Silent Slain" (indirectly) MacLeish came to what terms he could with concerns identified in Paul Fussell's *The Great War and Modern Memory.* "The Farm" illustrates the search for New England roots that ran through MacLeish's career and his writings in prose and verse. Other poems reflect the varying expatriate moods that came together after a few years in "American Letter." And the too well-known, too often misunderstood "Ars Poetica" conveys in its images, imitative form, and self-contradictions MacLeish's permanent conviction that a poem should both mean and be.

In *Einstein,* published separately in 1929, MacLeish presented a day's meditation that recapitulates the major stages in Einstein's physical and metaphysical struggle to contain and comprehend the physical universe, from classical empiricism through romantic empathy to modern, introspective, analytic physics. In flexible, elaborate, evocative blank verse, with an epigrammatic literal-allegorical prose gloss, and in a rich texture of spatial imagery the poem "narrates" Einstein's quest for knowledge. To Frederick J. Hoffman in *The Twenties,* this quest is shown as "pathetic and futile," but to Lauriat Lane, Jr., in an *Ariel* essay, it is "potentially tragic" and an example of "modern, existential Man Thinking."

Citing *The Hamlet of A. MacLeish,* Leslie Fiedler in *Unfinished Business* identified four appeals of the story of Hamlet to the American imagination: 1) "anguish and melancholy," 2) "the notion of suicide," 3) "the inhibitory nature of conscience," and 4) "an oddly apt parable of our relationship to Europe." This poem, MacLeish's most complex and elaborate, addresses all four subjects. Combining and contrasting what Fiedler elsewhere called signature and archetype, autobiography and myth, the work, which contains fourteen sections and a Shakespearean gloss, juxtaposes dialectically *Hamlet,* MacLeish's personal and poetic autobiographical uncertainties, and two fulfilled quests—a medieval Grail romance and tribal migrations out of the *Anabase* of Saint-John Perse, whose fulfillment only intensifies the doubts and despairs of Hamlet/MacLeish. As he recorded in *A Reviewer's ABC,* Conrad Aiken, who had found *Einstein* "a long poem which any living poet might envy, as rich in thought as it is in color and movement," labeled *The Hamlet of A. MacLeish* "a kind of brilliant *pastiche,*" although "full of beautiful things." Aiken went on, however, to pose the unanswered question of "whether [MacLeish's] 'echoes' might not, by a future generation, be actually preferred to the things they echo." Often, in MacLeish's work, such "echoes" are a form of brilliant, purposeful parody, an additional stylistic power finally recognizable fifty postmodern years later for what it is.

As its title implies, MacLeish published *New Found Land* after he had returned to America for good. Less varied and experimental in form than the short poems of *Streets in the Moon,* the poems in the slender *New Found Land* share the moods and concerns of *The Hamlet of A. MacLeish.* Along with "American Letter," the book has one of MacLeish's most famous "international" poems, "You, Andrew Marvell," and one of his greatest regional ones, "Immortal Autumn." For Signi Falk in *Archibald MacLeish, New Found Land* reveals "a poet torn between the old world and the new."

Conquistador, too, combines the old world and the new, but by 1932, the year of the book's publication, the choice had become clear if often tragic in its outcome. In the conquerors of Central American native civilization MacLeish found a romantic, exotic history that could also serve as a myth, a metaphor, for closer, more familiar history and concerns. In Montezuma, Cortez, and Diaz, the poem offers three figures—god, hero, and man—who share the reader's attention and good will and who are examined in an ironic context of human blood and natural beauty, greed for gold and sun-worship, political intrigue and heroic quest. Seeing the poem wholly through its narrator, Diaz, Allen Tate praised the poem for its "finely sustained tone," its "clarity of sensuous reminiscence," its "technical perfection," but found in its sentimentality "one of the examples of our modern sensibility at its best; it has the defect of its qualities," as Tate recorded in *Essays of Four Decades.*

In their many interrelations, *The Pot of Earth, Einstein, The Hamlet of A. MacLeish,* and *Conquistador* form a tetralogy of four major high modernist poems. With "Elpenor," originally "1933," which appeared in *Poems, 1924-1933* and which has subsequently been republished under each title, MacLeish moved toward the "public speech" of the post-Depression, Rooseveltian 1930s. Both a vivid retelling and sequel to Homer and Dante, this compressed little epic populates a modern Hell in the manner of Ezra Pound's poetry and points "the way on," in MacLeish's characteristic symbolic topographical imagery, where its readers can "begin it again: start over."

Among the other new poems in *Poems, 1924-1933,* "Frescoes for Mr. Rockefeller's City" (also published separately in 1933) dealt

with a public controversy and caused additional public excitement. Although praised by Cleanth Brooks in *Modern Poetry and the Tradition,* it has "not only ideological but functional problems," as Grover Smith declared; and some of its sections, like several of MacLeish's other public poems of the 1930s, reveal "the absence of arresting images and the slackness of the rhythm" that troubled David Luytens in *The Creative Encounter.* However, as recorded in *Literary Opinion in America,* Morton D. Zabel also found in these public poems "a signal of profitable intentions" and discovered "a very moving beauty" in the very unpublic set of lyrics, "The Woman on the Stair," in *Public Speech.*

The last of MacLeish's longer poems of the 1930s was *America Was Promises.* In an essay collected in *A Poet's Alphabet,* Louise Bogan attacked it as "MacLeish's saddest and most conglomerate attempt at 'public speech's' to date . . . political poetry, even a kind of official poetry," but Grover Smith later reassessed it as "the most eloquent of the 'public' poems . . . much better as a poem than as a message: for once, MacLeish's adaptation of St. J. Perse's geographic evocations seems precisely right." *America Was Promises* combines such "geographic evocations" with a quasi- allegorical populist history of Jefferson and Man, Adams and the Aristocracy, Paine and the People. For *The Human Season: Selected Poems, 1926-1972* MacLeish cut from *America Was Promises* almost all its "official" poetry and possibly made it a much better poem.

Looking back over these first two decades of MacLeish's poetry, Karl Shapiro declared in *Essay on Rime* "a special speech is born / Out of this searching, something absolute, . . . a linguistic dream . . . an influential dialect. . . ." In this poetry, said Hyatt H. Waggoner in *The Heel of Elohim,* "The will to believe is certainly present, but so also are the vacant lights, the bright void, the listening, idiot silence"; yet in *North American Review,* Mason Wade saw in the same poetry a "moving . . . intellectual anabasis," and in *Sewanee Review* Reed Whittemore praised some of it as "Democratic Pastoral."

In 1924 "The Happy Marriage" had explored the idea that out of the union of the ideal and the real must emerge a more mature sense of individual identity. This same theme carried through MacLeish's 1926 poetic drama, *Nobodaddy,* a verse play that uses the Adam and Eve story as "the dramatic situation which the condition of self-consciousness in an indifferent universe seems to me to present." MacLeish would affirm, a few years later, that the poet's role was "the restoration of man to his position of dignity and responsibility at the centre of his world." *Nobodaddy* provided its author with the opportunity to return to man's origins, to explore the human condition in terms of its myths and mysteries. To MacLeish, the work was a simple and forthright play of the beginnings of human consciousness.

In the resolution of his own sense of self-consciousness, symbolized by his move to Paris in 1923, MacLeish showed a certain kinship with his character Cain. Both had found the strength necessary to sever—in Cain's words—the thick vein "that knots me to the body of the earth," and to grab control of the centers of their own worlds. *Nobodaddy* is the story of man attempting to make sense of the chaos of his life. It can also be read as the *apologia* for its author. And its theme of a world in which man is bewildered and bored, a world in which his knowledge is not matched by his understanding, is one that would run through much of MacLeish's writing during the 1920s.

When MacLeish returned from Europe in 1928 and settled in Conway, Mass., he had obviously "re-viewed" America. The country's idealism, reflected especially in the philosophies of its founding father, supplied him with a sense of identity and place that existential *angst* had failed to engender. The questor had reached this personal goal only to find the obvious truth that each goal is a new beginning and that his search had been only his initiation into what would be a lengthy continuing journey. While the writer was now set to move in new directions, George Dangerfield asserted in a 1931 *Books* essay that "if [MacLeish] were never to write another word, he would still be a poet of definite importance."

MacLeish's first produced stage play, *Panic: A Play in Verse,* is a variation on the Cain story set against the background of the American Depression and a generation of capitalists he felt were in the process of leaving capitalism "intellectually defenseless and unarmed." The conflict of the play is between the will of a man (McGafferty, played in the original production by Orson Welles) and a fatalistic concept of human life (dialectical materialism). McGafferty surrenders to the delphic oracle of Marxist determinism and thus falls victim to it. As the Blind Man in the play observes, the financier fails because (unlike Cain) he will not trust his own freedom.

The play was MacLeish's attempt to comprehend the real sense of panic in a country where individualism had turned into individual greed and freedom had been replaced by a failing "free enterprise." American Communists found the play particularly frustrating, as MacLeish (who was on the editorial board of *Fortune*) refused to view what they took to be the imminence and inevitability of the Marxist revolution as anything more than a delphic prophecy that the crowd chorus was free to reject. Various other reviews of the production centered on the poet's attempt to create a verse line for the modern stage. Malcolm Cowley declared in a 1935 *New Republic* assessment that the play brought "a new intelligence to the theatre and [embodied] the results of the experiments made by modern poets."

In the late 1930s, speaking with the "public voice" that characterized his writings from the beginning of the decade, MacLeish wrote two verse plays for radio: *The Fall of the City,* broadcast on April 11, 1937, and *Air Raid,* broadcast on October 27, 1938. The first of these was the poet's exploration of his sense of a developing worldwide change in the commitment of human consciousness to human freedom. It was a change that MacLeish's own hero and friend, President Franklin D. Roosevelt, had addressed at his first inauguration: "We have nothing to fear but fear itself." *Air Raid* grew out of the German bombing of Guernica and Pablo Picasso's response to that slaughter through his painting, "Guernica." *Air Raid* is a play for voices dealing with the changes in the nature of war and with the alterations in the human spirit that had permitted such changes. MacLeish intended neither script to be primarily a political statement; he looked upon both as poems, as creations that explored what he perceived to be these changes rather than as attempts to persuade. Still, the closeness of MacLeish's sympathies to Roosevelt's has led Luytens to call MacLeish "the poet laureate of the New Deal."

The Trojan Horse, a verse drama first presented on the BBC in 1952, is in many ways a return to earlier decades and earlier characters. Helen of Troy had been earlier seen in a closet drama entitled "Our Lady of Troy" and collected in MacLeish's *Tower of Ivory.* She had later appeared in "The Happy Marriage" as the symbol of Beauty. The Blind Man, who earlier laid the future before McGafferty in *Panic,* has the same function here. Paul Brooks, in a note accompanying the first edition of *The Trojan Horse,* tied the play to the McCarthy era, but the script was intended more generally to explore in myth the sense of deception

the poet had perceived in his own century. The poetic sense of awareness itself is presented in a 1953 play, *This Music Crept by Me upon the Waters,* where Elizabeth, as did Cain before her, experiences the discovery of her own place in the cosmos.

The public voice which found its way into MacLeish's poetry in the 1930s was a reflection of the sense of public responsibility he had come to accept on his return from Paris. Harriet Monroe in a 1931 issue of *Poetry,* wrote that she has "much faith in the ability of this poet to interpret his age: he has the thinking mind, the creative imagination, the artistic equipment of beautiful words and rhythms." This voice was heard most directly in the many articles and speeches MacLeish wrote on the role of the poet and, through the political chaos of the western world in the 1930s and 1940s, on the direction he felt America should be pursuing. Much of this material has been collected in *A Time to Speak, A Time to Act,* and *A Continuing Journey.* Also, as Falk points out, MacLeish committed himself to such public offices as Librarian of Congress from 1939 to 1944, Assistant Director of the Office of War Information in 1942, Assistant Secretary of State from 1944 to 1945, and Chairman of the American delegation to the founding conference of UNESCO in 1945.

MacLeish said several times that in the long poem "Actfive," published in *Actfive and Other Poems* in 1948, he tried to come to terms with his and the world's experiences in the immediately preceding years: the challenge and suffering of the war, the opportunities and failures of the peace, the loss of so many faiths. *Conquistador* had offered an implicit choice between god, hero, and man; "Actfive," in its three scenes, redefines and makes that choice. With the God gone, the King dethroned, and Man murdered—all in elegiac, characteristically despairing lines—the heroes of the age are then thrust forward in their emptiness through sardonically abrupt rhythms. They give way, in turn, to "the shapes of flesh and bone," in whose moving, subtly musical, indirect voices MacLeish's long involvement with Matthew Arnold (noted Arthur Mizener as early as 1938 in *Sewanee Review*) is fulfilled. The result is a poetic affirmation, "humanist and existentialist," according to Luytens, for an even darker, more confused, post-Arnoldian time.

"Actfive" was MacLeish's last poem to interweave lyric statement and emblematically condensed narrative within an extended structure of feeling and idea. In the ten years from 1944 to 1954, called by Grover Smith "his second renaissance," he published over eighty short poems, half of them, apparently, written in two very creative years after he began teaching poetry at Harvard, where he was Boylsten Professor from 1949 to 1962. In style these poems, having many forms and treating a great variety of subjects, might be called neo-modernist, embodying a riper, wiser Imagism, for example. But their combination of immediate, personal concern with impersonal form, image, and language is not easily labeled. Poets Hayden Carruth in *Effluences from the Sacred Cave,* Richard Eberhart in *Virginia Quarterly Review,* John Ciardi in *Atlantic,* and Kimon Friar in *New Republic* have all praised these poems.

The best of these short works succeed, not surprisingly, in the terms of MacLeish's *Poetry and Experience,* which defines the "means" by which and the "shapes" in which poetry finds its "end" meaning. In brief, MacLeish contended, poetry combines sounds, signs, images, and metaphor to give meaning to the private world (Emily Dickinson), the public world (William Butler Yeats), the anti-world (Arthur Rimbaud), and the arable world (John Keats).

Among the lyrics of the private world, which record recognizable and therefore meaningful experience spoken in a living, personal voice, are such fine love poems as "Ever Since," "Calypso's Island," "What Any Lover Learns," and such testaments of poetic and humanist faith as "A Man's Work," "The Two Priests," "The Infinite Reason," and "Reasons for Music," some of which also look outward to the public world. MacLeish's poetic statements of and for the world of public affairs are designed both "to lash out" and to try to "make *positive* sense of the public world," as he asserted in *Poetry and Experience.* "Brave New World," for example, "lashes out" in tight, cutting quatrains at the loss of Jefferson's vision of human freedom. "The Danger in the Air" and "The Sheep in the Ruins" move meditatively toward making some sense against the danger, amid the ruins. Very few of these short poems look toward Rimbaud's anti-world. For MacLeish, as for Rimbaud, the sea was the great image of the Unknown: over the sea in "Voyage West," beneath it in "The Reef Fisher." MacLeish declared in *Poetry and Experience* that "Rimbaud's anti-world was not a rejection of the *possibility* of the world"; nor were MacLeish's own few visions of that anti-world. Poems of the arable world try to make familiar yet tragic "truth of the passing-away of the world." In his *Dialogues* with Mark Van Doren, MacLeish testifies how much the arable world of Uphill Farm in Massachusetts meant to him, as do "The Two Trees," "The Snow Fall," and "The Old Men in the Leaf Smoke." From Caribbean Antigua, on the other hand, probably came "The Old Man to the Lizard" and "Vicissitudes of the Creator." And the truth of the passing-away of the world took another, more direct, even more moving form in "For the Anniversary of My Mother's Death" and "My Naked Aunt."

Several volumes of MacLeish's prose—*Poetry and Experience,* a section of *A Continuing Journey,* and *Poetry and Opinion: The Pisan Cantos of Ezra Pound,* on the controversy surrounding Ezra Pound's support for Mussolini during World War II—grew out of his teaching. His two earliest collections of literary and political statements were *A Time to Speak* and *A Time to Act*—"a couple of books of speeches," as he labeled them in *Letters of Archibald MacLeish, 1907 to 1982.* Some of these prose pieces, most notoriously "The Irresponsibles," strayed dangerously close to propaganda—admittedly in a time of great public danger—and were attacked for this failing by critics like Edmund Wilson in *Classics and Commercials* and Morton D. Zabel in *Partisan Review.* In still another vein, *Champion of a Cause: Essays and Addresses on Librarianship* reprinted MacLeish's deliberately nonprofessional, nontechnical "essays and addresses on librarianship."

MacLeish's prose, for the most part, bore public witness to familiar but important ideas and beliefs. The editors of *Ten Contemporary Thinkers* included four MacLeish essays that represent well the range of his prose: "The Writer and Revolution," "Humanism and the Belief in Man," "The Conquest of America," and "The Isolation of the American Artist"; his essays and books specifically on poetry and poets eloquently and even more significantly witness to the broadly-defined powers of poems to move their readers. And even the most topical of MacLeish's political essays keep their relevance. In 1949 he first published "The Conquest of America" on the dangers of mindless anti-Communism and failure to reaffirm the American "revolution of the individual." In 1980 the *Atlantic* felt obliged by events to reprint MacLeish's warning. To the end of his long life he continued, in prose and in poetry, to praise and to warn "the Republic."

Having left public life and moved to Harvard by the late 1940s, MacLeish refocused his attention from the social and political themes of the preceding two decades toward an earlier poetic interest: the place and value of man in the universe. In his longer postwar poetic works, he followed his own exhortation to invent

the metaphor for the age. His series of poems collected as *Songs for Eve* returned again to the setting of *Nobodaddy* to emphasize once more the fundamental importance of self-consciousness in an indifferent universe. Despite his various attempts to find in Adam and Eve the metaphor for the age, the poet's most successful image of the human spirit appeared four years later on the stage of New York's ANTA Theatre in the character of J. B.

J. B.'s structure, in the acting edition of the play, differs substantially from the original version published by Houghton Mifflin in 1958, but the main characters remain basically the same. J. B. comes across both the footlights and the page not as a character in a morality play—for the play, despite its early scenes, is not a morality play—but as a flesh-and-blood common man beset by sufferings to which all flesh is heir. And in J. B.'s struggle and success against an inexplicable, brutal, and unjust universe, MacLeish presented what he hoped would be the metaphor for man's next era. Like Job, J. B. is not answered, yet his love for Sarah affirms, in the playwrights phrase, "the worth of life in spite of life." That worth is found in a love that paradoxically answers nothing but "becomes the ultimate human answer to the ultimate human question."

After receiving a Pulitzer Prize, his third, for *J. B.,* MacLeish returned to man's quarrels with the gods in *Herakles,* first produced in 1965 and published in 1967. During the first part of the play, Professor Hoadley is drawn to Greece, the *patria* of the intellectual life, in search of the spirit of Herakles, the half-man, half-god who dared to struggle with the unanswered questions of the universe. Balancing Hoadley's search for intellectual perfection is his wife's conviction that life is a concrete reality including the human imperfection her husband would transcend. In the second half of the play, a frustrated Herakles fails to receive a sign from Apollo and angrily ascends to the temple door threatening to answer his own oracle. But, despite the merits of his deeds, he is unable to perform the god-like act of pronouncing his own destiny. In the end, Hoadley's wife and Herakles's Megara refocus the human spirit where J. B. had earlier found it—on the day-to-day occupation of living, not in glorious myth, but in concrete reality.

If *J. B.* and *Herakles* raise still-unanswered questions, they also affirm that all questions need not be answered. MacLeish's last full-length play, *Scratch,* finds its source in "The Devil and Daniel Webster," Stephen Vincent Benet's treatment of the mythical American confrontation between man and the Devil. Alone of the final three plays, it explores questions that, because of their American roots, could move closer to resolution within the text. MacLeish felt there were three reasons that Benet's story had widened into myth: that the Republic had become full of men and women who had sold their souls "for its comforts and amenities"; that "belief in hell was reviving everywhere and that, if only love of life could be turned into contempt for living, hope into despair, the entire planet would dissolve into that cistern of self-pity where [Samuel Becket's] Godot never comes"; and that Daniel Webster's concern for Liberty and Union, or freedom and government, was as contemporary as it had ever been.

During the 1960s and 1970s, MacLeish also wrote three shorter scripts: a highly polemical television play, *The Secret of Freedom;* an "outdoor play" for the bicentennial of Conway entitled *An Evening's Journey to Conway, Massachusetts;* and *The Great American Fourth of July Parade,* a verse play for radio. All three works reflect their author's continual concern for the central values of America's founding fathers, as does his dramatic monologue, "Night Watch in the City of Boston."

In his last decades, MacLeish became not so much an elder statesman as an elder of various churches: the churches of friendship, of patriotism, of poetry, of love, of death. His talks, letters, essays, and poems, and his parable-play for radio, *The Great American Fourth of July Parade,* all voice the recurring, autumnal concerns of "the human season" in a quiet, personal, "elderly" voice. Almost ninety, MacLeish died on April 20, 1982, the day after Patriot's Day.

BIOGRAPHICAL/CRITICAL SOURCES:

BOOKS

Aarons, Daniel, *Writers on the Left,* Harcourt, 1961.

Aiken, Conrad, *A Reviewer's ABC,* Meridian Publishing, 1958.

Amend, Victor E., and Leo T. Hendrick, editors, *Ten Contemporary Thinkers,* Free Press of Glencoe (New York), 1964.

Benson, Frederick R., *Writers in Arms,* New York University Press, 1967.

Bogan, Louise, *A Poet's Alphabet,* McGraw, 1970.

Brenner, Rica, *Poets of Our Time,* Harcourt, 1941.

Brooks, Cleanth, *Modern Poetry and the Tradition,* Oxford University Press, 1965.

Bush, Warren V., editor, *Dialogues of Archibald MacLeish and Mark Van Doren,* Dutton, 1964.

Carruth, Hayden, *Effluences from the Sacred Caves,* University of Michigan Press, 1983.

Contemporary Literary Criticism, Gale, Volume 3, 1975, Volume 8, 1978, Volume 14, 1980.

Dictionary of Literary Biography, Gale, Volume 4: *American Writers in Paris, 1920-1939,* Volume 7: *Twentieth Century American Dramatists,* Volume 45: *American Poets, 1880-1945, First Series.*

Dictionary of Literary Biography Yearbook: 1982, Gale, 1983.

Donoghue, Denis, *The Third Voice,* Princeton University Press, 1959.

Falk, Signi, *Archibald MacLeish,* Twayne, 1965.

Fiedler, Leslie, *Unfinished Business,* Stein & Day, 1972.

Fussel, Paul, *The Great War and Modern Memory,* Oxford University Press, 1975.

Gassner, John, *Theatre at the Crossroads,* Holt, 1960.

Graff, Gerald, *Poetic Statement and Critical Dogma,* University of Chicago Press, 1970.

Hoffman, Frederick J., *The Twenties,* Viking, 1955.

Hone, Ralph E., editor, *The Voice out of the Whirlwind,* Chandler, 1960.

Literary Opinion in America, Harper, 1937.

Luytens, David Bulwer, *The Creative Encounter,* Secker & Warburg, 1960.

MacLeish, Archibald, *Six Plays,* Houghton, 1980.

Mullaly, Edward J., *Archibald MacLeish: A Checklist,* Kent State University Press, 1973.

Nemerov, Howard, *Poetry and Fiction,* Rutgers University Press, 1963.

Saltzman, Jack, editor, *Years of Protest,* Pegasus, 1967.

Saltzman, editor, *The Survival Years,* Pegasus, 1969.

Shapiro, Karl, *Essay on Rime,* Reynal & Hitchcock, 1945.

Slote, Bernice, editor, *Myth and Symbol,* University of Nebraska Press, 1963.

Smith, Grover, *Archibald MacLeish,* University of Minneapolis Press, 1971.

Tate, Allen, *Essays of Four Decades,* Oxford University Press, 1970.

Vickery, John B., *The Literary Impact of the Golden Bough,* Princeton University Press, 1973.

Waggoner, Hyatt H., *The Heel of Elohim,* University of Oklahoma Press, 1950.

Weiler, Gottfried, *Die Poetologische Lyrik Archibald MacLeishs,* Waag & Herchen (Frankfurt), 1977.

Wilson, Edmund, *Classics and Commercials,* Farrar, Straus, 1950.

Winnick, R. H., editor, *Letters of Archibald MacLeish,* Houghton, 1983.

Winters, Yvor, *Uncollected Essays and Reviews,* Swallow Press, 1973.

PERIODICALS

American Literature, Volume 15, 1943, Volume 35, 1963.

American Review, May, 1934.

Ariel, July, 1984.

Atlantic, May, 1953.

Books, January, 1931.

Boston Globe, April 22, 1982.

Canadian Review of American Studies, spring, 1983.

Chicago Tribune Book World, April 24, 1983.

Christian Science Monitor, November 21, 1968.

English Journal, June, 1935.

Harper's, December, 1971.

New Mexico Quarterly, May, 1934.

New Republic, March 27, 1935, December 15, 1952, July 22, 1967.

New York Times, March 2, 1971, May 16, 1971.

New York Times Book Review, August 6, 1967, January 28, 1968, July 9, 1978, January 2, 1983.

North American Review, summer, 1937.

Partisan Review, January, 1941, March, 1941.

Poetry, August, 1930, June, 1931, April, 1940.

Sewanee Review, October, 1938, July, 1940, April, 1943, October, 1953.

South Atlantic Quarterly, October, 1939.

University of Toronto Quarterly, October, 1940.

Variety, April 14, 1971.

Virginia Quarterly Review, autumn, 1958.

Washington Post Book World, January 21, 1968, November 3, 1968.

Yale Review, spring, 1934.

OBITUARIES:

PERIODICALS

Chicago Tribune, April 22, 1982.

Library Journal, June 1, 1982.

Newsweek, May 3, 1982.

New York Times, April 22, 1982.

Publishers Weekly, May 7, 1982.

Time, May 3, 1982.

Times (London), April 22, 1982.

Washington Post, April 22, 1982.

—*Sidelights by Edward Mullaly and Lauriat Lane, Jr.*

* * *

MacLENNAN, (John) Hugh   1907-1990

PERSONAL: Born March 20, 1907, in Glace Bay, Cape Breton Island, Nova Scotia; died Novenber 7, 1990; son of Samuel John (a doctor) and Katherine (MacQuarrie) MacLennan; married Dorothy Duncan, June 22, 1936 (died, 1957); married Frances Walker, May 15, 1959. *Education:* Dalhousie University, B.A., 1929; Oriel College, Oxford (Rhodes Scholar), B.S., 1932; Princeton University, M.A., Ph.D., 1935.

ADDRESSES: Office—Concordia University, Montreal, Quebec, Canada. *Agent*—Russell & Volkening, Inc., 551 Fifth Ave., New York, N.Y. 10017.

CAREER: Writer and teacher, 1935-62; teacher of English literature, McGill University, Montreal, Quebec, Canada, 1951-85.

MEMBER: Royal Society of Literature (United Kingdom), Royal Society of Canada (fellow), McGill Faculty Club, Montreal Indoor Tennis Club.

AWARDS, HONORS: Guggenheim fellowship, 1943; Governor General's Award in fiction for *Two Solitudes,* 1946, *The Precipice,* 1949, and *The Watch That Ends the Night,* 1959; Governor General's Literary Award in nonfiction for *Cross Country,* 1950, and *Thirty and Three,* 1955; Lorne Pierce Medal, 1952, for contributions to Canadian literature; Molson Award for services to literature and the nation, 1967; Canadian Authors Association Literary Award for fiction, 1982, for *Voices in Time.* Honorary degrees from many institutions of higher learning, including D.Litt. from University of Western Ontario, University of Manitoba, Waterloo Lutheran University, McMaster University, and Laurentian University; LL.D. from Dalhousie University, University of Saskatchewan, and University of Toronto; D.C.L. from Bishop's University.

WRITINGS:

Oxyrhynchus: An Economic and Social Study, Princeton University Press, 1935.
Barometer Rising (novel), Duell, Sloan & Pearce, 1941.
Two Solitudes (novel), Duell, Sloan & Pearce, 1945.
The Precipice (novel), Duell, Sloan & Pearce, 1948.
Cross Country (nonfiction), Collins, 1949.
Each Man's Son (novel), Little, 1951.
The Present World as Seen in Its Literature (address), University of New Brunswick, 1952.
Thirty and Three (essays), edited by Dorothy Duncan, Macmillan, 1954.
The Future of the Novel as an Art Form (lecture), University of Toronto Press, 1959.
The Watch That Ends the Night (novel), Scribner, 1959.
Scotchman's Return and Other Essays, Scribner, 1960, published in England as *Scotman's Return and Other Essays,* Heinemann, 1960.
(Editor) *McGill: The Story of a University,* Allen & Unwin, 1960.
Seven Rivers of Canada, Macmillan (Toronto), 1961, published as *The Rivers of Canada,* Scribner, 1962.
The History of Canadian-American Relations (lecture), Goddard College, 1963.
Return of the Sphinx (novel), Scribner, 1967.
The Colour of Canada, McClelland, 1967, Little, 1968, revised edition, 1978.
The Other Side of Hugh MacLennan: Selected Essays Old and New, edited by Elspeth Cameron, Macmillan (Toronto), 1978.
Quebec, photographs by Mia and Klaus, McClelland & Stewart, 1981.
Voices in Time (novel), Macmillan (Toronto), 1980, St. Martin's, 1981.
On Being a Maritime Writer, Mount Allison University, 1984.

Wrote monthly essay for *Montrealer,* 1951-57, and weekly column for Toronto Star syndicate, 1962-63; contributor to *Holiday, Saturday Review, Maclean's Magazine* and other periodicals.

SIDELIGHTS: To anyone who wants to understand Canada, Edmund Wilson, writing in *O Canada,* recommends a reading of the novels and essays of Hugh MacLennan. MacLennan, he writes, "is so special a figure that he requires some explanation. I should describe him as a Highlander first; a patriotic Nova Scotian second . . . ; a spokesman for Canada third; and—but simultaneously with all of these—a scholar of international culture and a man of the great world." *Dictionary of Literary Biography* contributor Elspeth Cameron explains that MacLennan "was the first Canadian novelist to attempt to set the local stage on which the nation's dramas might be played before an international audience." His essays and novels, especially *Barometer Rising* and *Two Solitudes,* she adds, have earned him a reputation as "the Grand Old Man of Canadian Letters."

Wilson remembers that he first became interested in MacLennan's work when he read the essays in *Scotchman's Return.* He found therein "a point of view surprisingly and agreeably different from anything else I knew in English. MacLennan writes . . . with much humor and shrewd intelligence about Canada, Scotland, England, the Soviet Union and the United States. I came to recognize that there did now exist a Canadian way of looking at things which had little in common with either the 'American' or the British colonial one and which has achieved a self-confident detachment in regard to the rest of the world."

Barometer Rising, MacLennan's first published novel, draws its story from the author's past. It climaxes with the cataclysmic collision between two ships—one of them carrying a load of TNT—in the harbor of Halifax, Nova Scotia, in 1917, an event that nearly levelled the town, and one that MacLennan had witnessed himself. "To Canadian readers," Cameron declares, "*Barometer Rising* seemed to express, as no Canadian novel had yet done, the nationalism that had blossomed gradually over the past two decades." When the novel first appeared in 1941, J. S. Southron wrote in the *New York Times:* "Unless you had been told you could not have known this to be a first novel. . . . Both in conception and workmanship it is first class." Wilson, writing more than twenty years later, says that *Barometer Rising* is the most sustained example of "how excellent Mr. MacLennan's writing can be when he is carried along by the sweep of one of his large descriptions or impassioned actions that are solidly realistic and yet never without their poetry. . . . It seems to me that *Barometer Rising* should not merely be accepted, as it is, as a landmark in Canadian writing but also, as an artistic success, be regarded as one of its authentic classics."

Two Solitudes, MacLennan's second novel, was also enthusiastically reviewed. It examines what Oakland Ross terms in the Toronto *Globe and Mail* as "the troubled psychic borderland between Canada's two cultures," the conflict between the Catholic, French- speaking heritage and the Protestant, English-speaking one. It was published (in New York, ironically) to great critical and popular acclaim. "This volume," L. L. Marchland wrote in the *Boston Globe,* "is definitely your passport to two evenings of rare literary delight." Its themes, says Ross, "continue to resonate for Canadians as insistently as they did when the book was first published." *Two Solitudes,* the reviewer concludes, marked "the beginning of something quite new, a Canadian novel that was essentially about Canada." MacLennan reexamined the problem—still a volatile subject in Canada—in *Return of the Sphinx.*

MacLennan's gift for eliciting understanding and appreciation of Canada and its people is in fact one of his most conspicuous talents. But his novels did not meet with unqualified acclaim; Wilson writes: "In an essay called 'The Story of a Novel,' in which he describes the writing of *The Watch That Ends the Night,* he explains that after putting down 'millions of words' and tearing up 'again and again . . . I refined my style and discovered new techniques I had previously known nothing about.' But when one comes to the novel, it is hard to see what he means by 'new techniques,' except that the story is told partly, by now a pretty familiar device, in a series of flashbacks that alternate with the narrative of the later happenings. The one feature of MacLennan's novels that does seem to me new and interesting is his use of the geographical and the meteorological setting. He always shows us how the characters are situated—as they pursue their intrigues, undergo their ordeals or are driven by their desperate loves—in a vast expanse of land and water, the hardly inhabited spaces of the waste upper margins of a continent."

Therefore, even though the recent novels have been reviewed with some disappointment, MacLennan's place in contemporary letters is secure. As Dick Adler says in his *Book World* review of *Return of the Sphinx*, although this is "not so warm and richly woven a novel as . . . *The Watch That Ends the Night*, . . . MacLennan's talent and the personality behind that talent are more than enough to recommend the book most highly." Similarly, Peter Buitenhuis observes in the *New York Times Book Review* that the novel "seems disconnected"; but, he adds, "the parts themselves are written with great perception and grace and a rare command of social, professional and political milieux." This ability, in evidence throughout MacLennan's career, seems to be in no danger of fading.

AVOCATIONAL INTERESTS: Tennis and gardening.

BIOGRAPHICAL/CRITICAL SOURCES:

BOOKS

Buitenhuis, Peter, *Hugh MacLennan,* Forum House, 1969.
Cameron, Elspeth, *Hugh MacLennan: A Writer's Life,* University of Toronto Press, 1981.
Cameron, editor, *Hugh MacLennan 1982: Proceedings of the MacLennan Conference at University College,* University College Canada Studies Program, 1982.
Cockburn, Robert H., *The Novels of Hugh MacLennan,* Harvest House, 1971.
Contemporary Literary Criticism, Gale, Volume 2, 1974, Volume 14, 1980.
Dictionary of Literary Biography, Volume 68: *Canadian Writers, 1920-1959,* Gale, 1988.
Goetsch, Paul, editor, *Hugh MacLennan,* McGraw Hill Ryerson, 1973.
Lucas, Alex, *Hugh MacLennan,* McClelland & Stewart, 1970.
MacLulich, T. D., *Hugh MacLennan,* Twayne, 1983.
Morley, Patricia, *The Immoral Moralists: Hugh MacLennan and Leonard Cohen,* Clarke Irwin, 1972.
Wilson, Edmund, *O Canada,* Farrar, Straus, 1964.
Woodcock, George, *Hugh MacLennan,* Copp Clark, 1969.

PERIODICALS

Books, October 12, 1941.
Book World, November 5, 1967.
Boston Globe, January 17, 1945.
Canadian Forum, January, 1959.
Commonweal, October 1, 1948, April 20, 1951.
Globe and Mail (Toronto), May 18, 1985, April 18, 1987.
New York Times, October 5, 1941, November 10, 1990.
New York Times Book Review, August 20, 1967.*

MacSHANE, Frank 1927-

PERSONAL: Born October 19, 1927, in Pittsburgh, PA; son of Frank (a journalist) and A. Elizabeth A. (Morse) MacShane; married Virginia Lynn Fry, July 8, 1959 (divorced); children: Nicholas Morse. *Education:* Harvard University, A.B., 1949; Yale University, M.A., 1951; Oxford University, D.Phil., 1955.

ADDRESSES: Office—Writing Division, School of the Arts, Columbia University, New York, NY 10027.

CAREER: McGill University, Montreal, Quebec, lecturer in English, 1955-57; University of California, Berkeley, assistant professor of English, 1959-64; Williams College, Williamstown, MA, associate professor of English, 1964- 67; Columbia University, New York, NY, professor of writing and chairman of writing division, 1967-79, professor of writing and director of the Translation Center, 1979—, member of executive committee of International Scholarly Exchange, 1980—. Fulbright professor at University of Chile, 1957, Tribhuvan University, Kathmandu, Nepal, and Centro di Studi Americani, Rome, 1978-79. Visiting lecturer, Vassar College, 1958-59. Director, Poets and Writers, Inc., 1970-80, and Poet's House (New York), 1989—.

MEMBER: National Book Critics Circle, Author's Guild (1982—), Authors League (council member, 1982—), PEN American Center, Oxford and Cambridge Club (London), Century Association (New York).

AWARDS, HONORS: Cavaliere Ufficiale dell' Ordine Almerito della Repubblica Italiana, 1987.

WRITINGS:

Many Golden Ages: Ruins, Temples and Monuments of the Orient, Tuttle, 1962.
The Life and Work of Ford Madox Ford, Horizon Press, 1965.
Ford Madox Ford: The Critical Heritage, Routledge & Kegan Paul, 1972.
The Life of Raymond Chandler, Dutton, 1976.
The Life of John O'Hara, Dutton, 1981.
Into Eternity: The Life of James Jones, American Writer, Houghton, 1985.

EDITOR

Impressions of Latin America: Five Centuries of Travel and Adventure by English and North American Writers, Morrow, 1963.
Critical Writings of Ford Madox Ford, University of Nebraska Press, 1964.
The American in Europe: A Collection of Impressions Written by Americans from the Seventeenth Century to the Present, Dutton, 1965.
(Co-editor) *Borges on Writing,* Dutton, 1973.
The Notebooks of Raymond Chandler, Ecco Press, 1976.
Selected Letters of Raymond Chandler, Columbia University Press, 1981.
Collected Stories of John O'Hara, Random House, 1985.

TRANSLATOR

Miguel Seranno, *The Mysteries,* privately printed, 1960.
Seranno, *The Visits of the Queen of Sheba,* Asia Publishing House, 1960.
Seranno, *The Serpent of Paradise,* Rider & Co., 1963.
Seranno, *C. G. Jung and Hermann Hesse: A Record of Two Friendships,* Schocken, 1966.
Seranno, *The Ultimate Flower,* Schocken, 1969.
Seranno, *El/Ella,* Harper, 1972.

OTHER

Contributor to numerous periodicals, including *New Republic, New York Times Magazine, Sunday Times* (London), *Nation, London Magazine, Prairie Schooner, New York Times Book Review, Holiday,* and *American Scholar.*

SIDELIGHTS: Frank MacShane has chronicled twentieth century America through the lives and times of several of the era's most underrated writers. Himself a professor of writing at Columbia University, MacShane has nursed a lifelong fascination with the "stepchildren of literature" and has written well-received biographies of John O'Hara, Raymond Chandler, Ford Madox Ford, and James Jones. *New Manhattan Review* correspondent Rex Roberts notes that MacShane's works "are lively, witty, and elegantly written, full of anecdotes and incident." The critic continues: "While his books read with a drama that many contemporary novels lack, MacShane never dramatizes. He creates suspense and delights with surprise, but he never sensationalizes. . . . One can enjoy his biographies without ever having read the writers' works, for MacShane is a splendid stylist and his books are full of literary gossip and details about the writerly life."

MacShane studied literature at Harvard, Yale, and Oxford, earning a Ph.D. in 1955. He taught English and writing at several universities in the United States and Canada before moving to Columbia in 1967. At Columbia he has served as a professor of writing and founder of the Writing Division in the university's School of the Arts. He has been a member of the Columbia faculty for more than twenty years.

The decision to write about America's lesser known writers was an easy one for MacShane. "Who needs another Hemingway biography?" he told the *New Manhattan Review.* "One of my motives in writing literary biographies is to take a writer whose position is not set and try to place him, give him an evaluation." MacShane's works combine narrative and critical insight in an effort to return some fine authors from undeserved obscurity. In a review of MacShane's *The Life of John O'Hara,* for instance, Anatole Broyard comments: "Mr. MacShane is generous with the details, anecdotes and atmosphere of O'Hara's life, which ended in 1970. Yet he never simply surrenders to his material, as some biographers do. This is a critical study as well, and the author's appraisal of his subject is judicious and fair."

MacShane's best known biography is *The Life of Raymond Chandler,* a study published in 1976. *New York Times Book Review* contributor Leonard Michaels states that the work "gives an immensely detailed portrait of Chandler the man." The critic also calls MacShane an "exceptionally polite biographer" who ". . . has selected and organized the many revealing passages, collected the many extraordinary anecdotes, and packed the interstitial tissue with biographical data. All in all, a very good job." In a *Washington Post* review, Larry McMurtry notes that *The Life of Raymond Chandler* is "virtually a model of what literary biography should be: The materials and sources have been not merely mastered but organized, and then presented to us in a continuously readable form. The book is a delight from page one to the end, not simply because MacShane knows everything worth telling about Raymond Chandler and his work, but because he has done an extraordinarily intelligent and graceful job of telling it."

MacShane also earned good notices for his 1985 biography *Into Eternity: The Life of James Jones, American Writer.* The work studies Jones, who won the National Book Award for his first novel, *From Here to Eternity.* "Jones's reputation should be helped by this balanced critical biography," writes Robert Phillips in the *New York Times Book Review.* Phillips adds, "Mr. MacShane manages to examine the man from many angles. . . . Such incisive evaluation makes this more than a biography. It is a guidebook to the works, accomplishments and failures of an American writer who was not afraid to take chances." *Philadelphia Inquirer* reviewer James R. Giles likewise praises the work. "There is no doubt that Frank MacShane can write," Giles notes. "*Into Eternity* is a rich, rewarding book worthy of its complex subject. It offers fresh understanding of a writer who must now be granted the stature that MacShane and others have recently claimed for him."

BIOGRAPHICAL/CRITICAL SOURCES:

BOOKS

Contemporary Literary Criticism Yearbook 1985, Gale, 1986.

PERIODICALS

American Spectator, February, 1986.
Books and Bookmen, November, 1976; January, 1977.
Chicago Sun Times, December 22, 1985.
Chicago Tribune, November 17, 1985.
Chicago Tribune Book World, January 11, 1981.
Christian Science Monitor, December 2, 1985.
Detroit News, December 29, 1985.
Kirkus Reviews, October 1, 1985.
Listener, June 17, 1976.
Los Angeles Times Book Review, January 26, 1986.
National Review, February 28, 1986.
New Manhattan Review, April 16, 1986.
New Republic, December 9, 1985.
New York Review of Books, September 30, 1965.
New York Times, February 18, 1981; February 18, 1985; November 11, 1985.
New York Times Book Review, December 19, 1965; May 16, 1976; January 18, 1981; November 10, 1985.
Philadelphia Inquirer, January 12, 1986.
Time, June 27, 1976.
Times (London), December 10, 1981.
Times Literary Supplement, June 18, 1976; April 10, 1981.
Village Voice, May 31, 1976.
Washington Post, May 17, 1976.
Washington Post Book World, March 1, 1981; January 5, 1986.

—*Sketch by Anne Janette Johnson*

*   *   *

MADSEN, Axel 1930-
(Guy Brion)

PERSONAL: Born May 27, 1930, in Copenhagen, Denmark; son of Axel and Jenny (Hansen) Madsen; married wife, Marguerite Midori (Porter) Duparc; children: Giles, Eric. *Education:* Studied piano and organ at Conservatoire de Musique de Paris.

ADDRESSES: Home—3022 Vistacrest Dr., Hollywood, CA 90068.

CAREER: New York Herald Tribune, Paris Edition, junior writer, 1952-55; United Press International, Canadian overnight editor in Montreal, Quebec, 1956-61; freelance writer for films in Hollywood, CA, and correspondent for *Cahiers du Cinema* (Paris), *Sight and Sound* (London), *Filmkritik* (Munich), *Toronto Star, Philadelphia Evening Bulletin, Kansas City Star,* and other metropolitan newspapers. Director of publicity for the Twentieth Century-Fox films "Butch Cassidy and the Sundance Kid," 1968, and "Patton," 1969.

WRITINGS:

Billy Wilder, Secker & Warburg, 1968, Indiana University Press, 1969.
William Wyler: The Authorized Biography, Crowell, 1973.
Borderlines (fiction), Macmillan, 1975.
The New Hollywood: American Movies in the '70's, Crowell, 1975.
Malraux: A Biography, Morrow, 1976.
Hearts and Minds: The Common Journey of Simone De Beauvoir and Jean-Paul Sartre, Morrow, 1977.
John Huston, Doubleday, 1978.
Living for Design: The Yves Saint Laurent Story, Delacorte, 1979.
Private Power: Multinational Corporations for the Survival of Our Planet, Morrow, 1980.
Unisave (fiction), edited by Jim Baen, Ace Books, 1980.
Open Road: Truckin' on the Biting Edge, Harcourt, 1982.
Sixty Minutes: The Power and the Politics of America's Most Popular TV News Show, Dodd, 1984.
Cousteau: A Biography, Beaufort Books, 1986.
Gloria and Joe: The Star-Crossed Love Affair of Gloria Swanson and Joe Kennedy, Morrow, 1988.
Silk Roads: The Asian Adventures of Clara and Andre Malraux, Pharos Books, 1989.
Sonia Delaunay: The Painter of the Lost Generation, McGraw-Hill, 1989.
Chanel: A Woman of Her Own, Holt, 1990.

Author of newspaper articles under pseudonym Guy Brion.

SIDELIGHTS: Axel Madsen's wide variety of subject matter—from biographies of filmmakers and intellectuals, to a profile of independent truckers, to a look at the altruistic side of big business—keep him from being easily pigeonholed as a writer. Among his works *Malraux: A Biography,* a look at the novelist's life and loves, garnered this notice from *Nation* writer Ernst Pawel: "[The work is] conscientious, factual, and eminently readable, partly because rather than in spite of its limitations, Madsen writes plain non-academic prose, uninspired but unobjectionable."

In another departure, the author examines a modern broadcasting institution with the book *Sixty Minutes: The Power and the Politics of America's Most Popular TV News Show.* "Much of the material here will be familiar to readers of newspaper and magazine television sections," notes *New York Times* critic Walter Goodman, who adds that Madsen "did bring to my attention the efforts of corporations to devise defenses against the program's investigators. The only sure defense, they seem to have discovered, is not to talk to [reporter] Mike Wallace, ever."

Dan E. Moldea, a *Washington Post* reviewer, has praise for another Madsen effort, *Open Road: Truckin' on the Biting Edge.* In this book the author "vividly describes the personal and professional plight of the independent trucker," framing his story around "the adventures of veteran trucker Junior Carlton and his hired hand, Karen Long, a 26-year-old woman with two small children, during a long haul from Seattle to Rahway, N.J.," as Moldea writes.

"After reading a few chapters [of *Open Road*]," the critic continues, "it becomes clear that once the country music and cowboy hats are stripped away from these truckers, all that remains are blue-collar businessmen, struggling for economic survival and caught in miles of government red tape." Moldea admits that "frankly, this is one book I wish I had written."

BIOGRAPHICAL/CRITICAL SOURCES:

PERIODICALS

Los Angeles Times, December 28, 1989.
Nation, January 22, 1977.
New York Review of Books, June 3, 1990.
New York Times, October 8, 1984.
Washington Post, December 11, 1982.

*   *   *

MAHAPATRA, Jayanta 1928-

PERSONAL: Born October 22, 1928, in Cuttack, India; son of Lemuel and Sudhansu (Rout) Mahapatra; married Jyotsna Rani Das, January 16, 1951; children: Mohan (son). *Education:* Ravenshaw College, B.Sc. (honors), 1946; Science College, Patna, India, M.Sc. (first class honors), 1949. *Avocational interests:* Reading fiction, photography (portraiture).

ADDRESSES: *Home*—Tinkonia Bagicha, Cuttack 753001, Orissa, India.

CAREER: *Eastern Times,* Cuttack, India, sub-editor, 1949; lecturer in physics at Ravenshaw College, Cuttack, 1949-58, G.M. College, Sambalpur, India, 1958-61, Regional Engineering College, Rourkela, India, 1961-62, G.M. College, 1962-65, B.J.B. College, Bhubaneswar, India, 1965-69, F.M. College, Balasore, India, 1969-70, Ravenshaw College, Cuttack, 1970-81, and Shaibabala Women's College, Cuttack, 1981-86. Visiting writer, University of Iowa, 1976; visiting fellows at Universities of Kolhapar and Bombay; resident poet at Centro Culturale della Fondazione Rockefeller, Bellagio, Italy, 1986; Indo-Soviet Cultural Exchange writer, U.S.S.R., 1985. Has given poetry readings at St. Andrews Presbyterian College, University of the South, University of Tennessee at Chattanooga, University of Maryland, East-West Center, Honolulu, Hawaii, Sapporo University, Aoyama University, PEN Center, Sydney, Australia, and at universities and conferences all over the world.

AWARDS, HONORS: Second prize in *International Who's Who in Poetry* contest, 1970, for poem "The Report Card"; Jacob Glatstein Memorial Prize from *Poetry,* 1975, for a group of poems; Bisuva Milana Award for Poetry form *Prajatantra,* 1977, for translations of Oriya poetry into English; National Academy of Letters Award, 1981, for *Relationship.*

WRITINGS:

POETRY

Close the Sky, Ten by Ten, Dialogue Publications, 1971.
Svayamvara and Other Poems, Writers Workshop (Calcutta), 1971.
A Rain of Rites, University of Georgia Press, 1976.
A Father's Hours, United Writers (Calcutta), 1976.
Waiting, Samkaleen Prakashan, 1979.
The False Start, Clearing House (Bombay), 1980.
Relationship, Greenfield Review Press, 1980.
Life Signs, Oxford University Press (New Delhi), 1983.
Dispossessed Nests, Nirala Publications, 1986.
Selected Poems, Oxford University Press (New Delhi), 1987.
Burden of Waves and Fruit, Three Continents Press, 1988.
Temple, Dangaroo Press, 1989.

OTHER

Tales from Fakir Mohan (juvenile), Cuttack Students Store, 1969.

True Tales of Travel and Adventure (juvenile), Cuttack Students Store, 1969.

(Translator) *Countermeasures,* Dialogue Publications, 1973.

(Translator) *Wings of the Past,* [Calcutta], 1976.

(Translator) *Song of Kubja and Other Poems,* [New Delhi], 1981.

Orissa, Lustre Press, 1987.

Poetry appears in anthologies, including: *Indian Poetry in English, 1947-72,* edited by Pritish Nandy, Oxford University Press, 1972; *Ten Twentieth-Century Indian Poets,* edited by R. Parthasarathy, Oxford University Press, 1976; *Contemporary Indian Short Stories,* edited by Ka Naa Subramanyam, Vikas Publishing, 1976; *Best Poems of 1975: The Borestone Mountain Poetry Awards* (special India issue), Pacific Books 1976; *Literary Olympians II,* edited by Linda Brown Michelson and Elizabeth Bartlett, Crosscurrents, 1987. Contributor of poetry to publications in the United States, England, Canada, Australia, New Zealand, and India, including *Poetry, New York Quarterly, Hudson Review, Kenyon Review, Sewanee Review, Critical Quarterly, Meanjin Quarterly, New Republic, Times Literary Supplement, Event, Edge,* and *Quest.* Poetry editor, *Gray Book,* 1972-73; guest editor, *South and West, U.S.A.,* 1973; editor, *Chandrabhaga,* 1979-85, and *The Telegraph,* 1986-89.

SIDELIGHTS: Jayanta Mahapatra told *CA:* "At times I write a piece of short fiction, but poetry is what I have done, in the main. I was raised among simple people who believed (and still do) that things happen as they do because of things that have happened before, and that nothing can change the sequence of things. These are my childhood memories: the lone dark house at the village's end surrounded by aging deodars, coconut palms, like dark sentinels of my own reality. And the dark door of that house, the evenings when a pretty young cousin would bang away on it to spare herself a merciless beating from her drunken husband. We had no electric lighting, and I can recollect the oil lamps stirring, twisting, looking so human, obsequious. And I found myself following a burdensome loneliness. Perhaps such things have entered my poems, perhaps it is only a world which exists in my head. What appears to disturb me is the triumph of silence in the mind; and this silence comes from the world outside of me, a world of hunger, grief, and injustice, that has to be borne somehow. And if my poems are inventions, they are also longings amid the flow of voices toward a need that I feel is defensive. A poem makes me see out of it in all directions, like a sieve, and yet it keeps me in myself.

"Mystery has always fascinated me—a sense of the unknown, of things unexplainable, and this has found its way into my poetry. And it is this quality of the ununderstandable which somehow goes to make the beauty of a poem. And this is how I feel: that one must try somehow to reach the border between things understandable and ununderstandable in a poem, between life and death, between a straight line and a circle. I am aware, fully aware that my poems deal with the life *within* myself, where the mind tries to find a sort of coherence from the mass of things in the world outside of it. We seem to forget that we are looking into a mirror which does not show the same world we are in: it *is* another world, of inversion, when the left becomes the right, and in an inverse world opposites can happen, for it is hard to tell the difference between the sane and insane, between sadness and joy.

"Today, however, there are many other pressing things that demand our attention. Hunger, a jarring sexuality and a needless violence have become vital issues—which I find really hard to cope up with. Perhaps my recent poems reflect these things. And yet poetry becomes somewhat insignificant before the world of the electronic chip, and gene-splicing, for instance. It hurts, the way we seem to be moving. The crimes and cruelties on Indian women, which are on the increase. My most recent work, a long poem entitled *Temple,* has at its theme the problem of the Indian woman . . . perhaps a futile exercise on my part, this poem, the last resort of someone who cannot do anything else.

"Recurrent themes of women appear in my poetry; I have done some short, vivid poems on women—particularly the Indian woman, who seems to have suffered so much, and who still fascinates me by her seeming contentment. I would not like myself to squeeze the last juices from life and living; I feel life has to be taken in gently, as the earth takes in the rain—and so of woman, and of the juices in her flesh. Who has heard of a bee crushing a flower when he sucks the sweet nectar? But then it is a fast changing world; it is a world of violence and terror, and the whole thing unnerves my being. And I shut myself up in my room and write—the most foolish thing to do, perhaps."

*   *   *

MALABAILA, Damiano
See LEVI, Primo

*   *   *

MARCHI, Giacomo
See BASSANI, Giorgio

*   *   *

MARLOWE, Hugh
See PATTERSON, Harry

*   *   *

MARTINSEN, Martin
See FOLLETT, Ken(neth Martin)

*   *   *

MASEFIELD, John (Edward)   1878-1967

PERSONAL: Born June 1, 1878 (although this is his official birthday, he notes in his autobiography that "there is some doubt of the day"), in Ledbury, Herefordshire, England; died May 12, 1967; son of George Edward (a solicitor) and Carolyn (Parker) Masefield; raised by an uncle, William, after the death of his parents; married Constance de la Cherois-Crommelin, 1903 (died, 1960); children: Lewis (killed in action, 1942), Judith (illustrator of several of Masefield's books). *Education:* Briefly attended King's School, Warwick, England (ran away when he was about thirteen).

ADDRESSES: Home—Burcote Brook, Abingdon, Berkshire, England.

CAREER: Indentured to merchant ship *Conway* about 1892; apprenticed aboard a windjammer about a year and a half later and sailed around Cape Horn to Chile where he became ill and returned to England by steamer; shipped aboard the White Star liner *Adriatic* as sixth officer but left the ship when she docked in New York; lived in Greenwich Village, New York City, 1895-97 (except for an interval in which he traveled as a hobo to California and back), and worked in a bakery, in a livery stable, on the waterfront, and in the saloon of Luke O'Connor's Columbian Hotel; moved to Yonkers, New York, where he worked as a "mistake finder" in a carpet factory; returned to England in 1897 and became friendly with John Millington Synge in London, then spent one summer in Devonshire with William Butler Yeats; about 1900 he became literary editor of the *Speaker* and was subsequently recommended to the *Manchester Guardian* for which he wrote articles and organized a "Miscellany" feature (he served on the permanent staff of the *Guardian* for about six months); in 1930 King George appointed him Poet Laureate of England succeeding Robert Bridges. Appointed chairman of the committee acting on the awards of the King's medals for poetry, 1933; member of British Council's Books and Periodicals Committee; lectured in Turkey and other European countries for the British Council; frequent lecturer in the United States. *Military service:* During World War I served with the Red Cross in France and on the Gallipoli Peninsula.

MEMBER: Royal Society of Literature (member of academic committee, 1913; Companion, 1961), Incorporated Society of Authors, Playwrights and Composers (president, 1937-67).

AWARDS, HONORS: Polignac Prize for Poetry, 1912; D.Litt., Oxford University, 1922; LL.D., University of Aberdeen, 1922; Order of Merit, 1935; Hanseatic Shakespeare Prize, Hamburg University, 1938; William Foyle Prize, 1961, for *The Bluebells, and Other Verses.*

WRITINGS:

POETRY

Salt-Water Ballads, Grant Richards, 1902, Macmillan, 1913.
Ballads and Poems, Mathews, 1910.
The Everlasting Mercy, Sidgwick & Jackson, 1911.
The Story of a Round-House, Macmillan, 1912, revised edition, 1913.
The Widow in the Bye Street, Sidgwick & Jackson, 1912.
The Daffodil Fields, Macmillan, 1913.
Dauber: A Poem, Heinemann, 1913.
Philip the King, and Other Poems, Macmillan, 1914 (*Philip the King* published separately in England, Heinemann, 1927).
Good Friday: A Dramatic Poem, Macmillan, 1915, published with additional poems as *Good Friday, and Other Poems,* 1916.
Sonnets (from *Good Friday, and Other Poems*), Macmillan, 1916.
Sonnets and Poems (from *Good Friday, and Other Poems*), privately printed, 1916.
Salt-Water Poems and Ballads, Macmillan, 1916, published as *Salt-Water Ballads and Poems,* 1923.
Lollingdon Downs, and Other Poems, Macmillan, 1917.
The Cold Cotswolds, Express Printing Works, 1917.
Rosas, Macmillan, 1918.
Reynard the Fox, Macmillan, 1919, new edition, 1920.
Enslaved, Macmillan, 1920, published with additional poems as *Enslaved, and Other Poems,* 1923.
Right Royal, Macmillan, 1920.
King Cole, Macmillan, 1921.
The Dream, Macmillan, 1922, published with additional poems as *The Dream, and Other Poems,* 1923.
Sonnets of Good Cheer to the Lena Ashwell Players, From Their Well-Wisher, John Masefield, Mendip Press, 1926.
Midsummer Night, and Other Tales in Verse, Macmillan, 1928.
South and East, Macmillan, 1929.
The Wanderer of Liverpool, Macmillan, 1930.
Minnie Maylow's Story, and Other Tales and Scenes, Macmillan, 1931.
A Tale of Troy, Macmillan, 1932.
A Letter From Pontus, and Other Verse, Macmillan, 1936.

The Country Scene in Poems, Collins (London), 1937, Collins (New York), 1938.
Tribute to Ballet in Poems, Macmillan, 1938.
Some Verses to Some Germans, Macmillan, 1939.
Gautama the Enlightened, and Other Verse, Macmillan, 1941.
Generation Risen, Collins, 1942, Macmillan, 1943.
Land Workers, Heinemann, 1942, Macmillan, 1943.
Wonderings, Macmillan, 1943.
On the Hill, Macmillan, 1949.
The Bluebells, and Other Verses, Macmillan, 1961.
Old Raiger, and Other Verse, Heinemann, 1964, Macmillan, 1965.
In Glad Thanksgiving, Macmillan, 1967.

Also author of *Animula,* 1920.

NOVELS

Captain Margaret, Grant Richards, 1908, Macmillan, 1916, reprinted, Scholarly Press, 1972.
Multitude and Solitude, Grant Richards, 1909, Macmillan, 1916.
The Street of To-Day, Dutton, 1911.
Sard Harker, Macmillan, 1924, reprinted, Heinemann, 1956.
Odtaa, Macmillan, 1926, reprinted, Penguin, 1966.
The Midnight Folk, Macmillan, 1927, recent edition, Dell, 1985.
The Hawbucks, Macmillan, 1929.
The Bird of Dawning, Macmillan, 1933, reprinted, 1967.
The Taking of the Gry, Macmillan, 1934.
The Box of Delights, Macmillan, 1935, reprinted, Heinemann, 1957.
Victorious Troy; or, The Hurrying Angel, Macmillan, 1935.
Eggs and Baker, Macmillan, 1936.
The Square Peg; or, The Gun Fella, Macmillan, 1937.
Dead Ned, Macmillan, 1938, reprinted, Heinemann, 1970.
Live and Kicking Ned, Macmillan, 1939, reprinted, Heinemann, 1970.

SHORT STORIES

The Mainsail Haul, Mathews, 1905, revised edition, Macmillan, 1913.
A Tarpaulin Muster, B. W. Dodge, 1908, reprinted, Books for Libraries, 1970.

PLAYS

The Tragedy of Nan, Kennerley, 1909.
The Tragedy of Pompey the Great, Little, Brown, 1910, revised edition, Macmillan, 1914, reprinted, Sidgwick & Jackson, 1964.
The Faithful (three-act tragedy), Heinemann, 1915.
Good Friday: A Play in Verse, Garden City Press, 1916, reprinted, Heinemann, 1955.
The Locked Chest [and] *The Sweeps of Ninety-Eight* (prose plays), Macmillan, 1916.
Melloney Holtspur, Macmillan, 1922.
A King's Daughter (verse play), Macmillan, 1923.
The Trial of Jesus, Macmillan, 1925.
Tristan and Isolt (verse play), Heinemann, 1927.
The Coming of Christ, Macmillan, 1928.
Easter: A Play for Singers, Macmillan, 1929.
End and Beginning, Macmillan, 1933.
A Play of Saint George, Macmillan, 1948.

Also author of "The Campden Wonder," 1907.

JUVENILE

A Book of Discoveries, F. A. Stokes, 1910.

Lost Endeavor, Nelson, 1910.
Martin Hyde: The Duke's Messenger, Little, Brown, 1910.
Jim Davis, F. A. Stokes, 1912, reprinted, Penguin, 1966, published as *The Captive of the Smugglers,* Page, 1918.

ESSAYS AND STUDIES

Sea Life in Nelson's Time, Methuen, 1905, Macmillan, 1925, reprinted, Books for Libraries, 1969, 3rd edition, U.S. Naval Institute, 1971.
On the Spanish Main; or, Some English Forays on the Isthmus of Darien, Macmillan, 1906, new edition, Naval Institute Press, 1972.
William Shakespeare, Holt, 1911, reprinted, Fawcett, 1964, quartercentenary edition, Barnes & Noble, 1969.
John M. Synge, Macmillan, 1915, reprinted, Folcroft Press, 1970.
Gallipoli, Macmillan, 1916, 13th edition, 1925.
The Old Front Line; or, The Beginning of the Battle of the Somme, Macmillan, 1917, published as *The Battle of the Somme,* Heinemann, 1919, reprinted, C. Chivers, [Bath], 1968.
The War and the Future, Macmillan, 1918 (published in England as *St. George and the Dragon,* Heinemann, 1919).
John Ruskin, Yellowsands Press, 1920.
Shakespeare and Spiritual Life, Oxford University Press, 1924, reprinted, Folcroft Press, 1969.
With the Living Voice: An Address, Macmillan, 1925.
Chaucer, Macmillan, 1931.
Poetry, Heinemann, 1931, Macmillan, 1932.
The Conway: From Her Foundation to the Present Day, Macmillan, 1933.
The Nine Days Wonder (story of the Dunkirk retreat), Macmillan, 1941.
Conquer: A Tale of the Nika Rebellion in Byzantium, Macmillan, 1941.
Thanks Before Going: Notes on Some of the Original Poems of Dante Gabriel Rosetti, Heinemann, 1946, Macmillan, 1947, reissued as *Thanks Before Going, With Other Gratitude for Old Delight,* Heinemann, 1947.
Baden Parchments, Heinemann, 1947.
St. Katherine of Ledbury, and Other Ledbury Papers, Heinemann, 1951.
An Elizabethan Theatre in London, Oxford University, 1954.
The Western Hudson Shore, [New York], 1962.
The Twenty-five Days, Heinemann, 1972.

OTHER

The Taking of Helen, Macmillan, 1923, new edition with additional material published as *The Taking of Helen, and Other Prose Selections,* Macmillan, 1924.
Recent Prose, Heinemann, 1924, revised edition, 1932, Macmillan, 1933.
Prologue to a Book of Pictures of Adventure by Sea, [New York], 1925.
Any Dead to Any Living, [New Haven], 1928.
A Masque of Liverpool, Brown Brothers, 1930.
Lines on the Tercentenary of Harvard University, Macmillan, 1936.
Basilissa: A Tale of the Empress Theodore (fictional biography), Macmillan, 1930.
Some Memories of W. B. Yeats, Macmillan, 1940, reprinted, Irish University Press, 1971.
In the Mill (autobiography), Macmillan, 1941.
Shopping in Oxford, Heinemann, 1941.
Natalie Maisie and Pavilastukay, Macmillan, 1942.

I Want! I Want!, National Book League, 1944, Macmillan, 1945.
Macbeth Production, Heinemann, 1945, Macmillan, 1946.
New Chum, Macmillan, 1945.
Book of Both Sorts, Heinemann, 1947.
In Praise of Nurses, Heinemann, 1950.
A Book of Prose Selections, Heinemann, 1950.
The Ledbury Scene as I Have Used It in My Verse, Hereford, 1951.
So Long to Learn: Chapters of an Autobiography, Macmillan, 1952.
Grace Before Ploughing (autobiographical sketches), Macmillan, 1966.

CORRESPONDENCE

John Masefield: Letters to Reyna, edited by William Buchan, Buchan & Enright, 1984.
John Masefield's Letters From the Front, 1915-1917, edited by Peter Vansittart, Constable, 1984.
John Masefield: Letters to Margaret Bridges, 1915-1919, edited by Donald Stanford, Carcanet, 1984.

COLLECTIONS

The Everlasting Mercy [and] *The Widow in the Bye Street,* Macmillan, 1912, new edition, 1919.
Poems of John Masefield, Macmillan, 1917.
The Poems and Plays of John Masefield, Macmillan, 1918.
A Poem and Two Plays, Heinemann, 1919.
Dauber [and] *The Daffodil Fields,* Macmillan, 1923.
Selected Poems, Heinemann, 1922, Macmillan, 1923, 3rd edition, Heinemann, 1950, recent edition, Carcanet, 1984.
King Cole, The Dream, and Other Poems, Macmillan, 1923.
Philip the King, and Other Poems; Good Friday: A Play in Verse; Lollingdon Downs, and Other Poems, With Sonnets, Macmillan, 1923.
The Collected Poems of John Masefield, Heinemann, 1923, new edition, 1932, revised edition published as *Poems,* 1946.
Poems, two volumes, Macmillan, 1925, published in one volume, 1930, 3rd edition with new poems, 1958.
Prose Plays, Macmillan, 1925.
Verse Plays, Macmillan, 1925.
Plays, Heinemann, 1937.
Dead Ned [and] *Live and Kicking Ned,* Macmillan, 1941.
Dauber [and] *Reynard the Fox,* Heinemann, 1962, Macmillan, 1963.

EDITOR

(With wife, Constance Masefield) *Lyrists of the Restoration From Sir Edward Sherbourne to William Congreve,* Grant Richards, 1905.
W. Dampier, *Voyages,* Dutton, 1906.
A Sailor's Garland, Methuen, 1906, Macmillan, 1924, reprinted, Books for Libraries, 1969.
(With C. Masefield) *Essays, Moral and Polite, 1660-1714,* Grant Richards, 1906, reprinted, 1930, and Books for Libraries, 1971.
Defoe (selections), Macmillan, 1909.
(And translator) Jean Racine, *Esther* (play), Heinemann, 1922.
(And translator) Racine, *Berenice* (play), Macmillan, 1922.
My Favourite English Poems, Macmillan, 1950.
(And author of introductions) Shakespeare, *Three Tragedies,* Dodd, 1965.
(And author of introductions) Shakespeare, *Three Comedies,* Dodd, 1965.
(And author of introductions) Shakespeare, *Three Histories,* Dodd, 1966.

(And author of introductions) Shakespeare, *Tragedies II,* Dodd, 1966.

(And author of introductions) Shakespeare, *Commedies II,* Dodd, 1967.

Editor of several collections for Dent's "Everyman's Library" series.

AUTHOR OF INTRODUCTION

Chronicles of the Pilgrim Fathers, Dutton, 1910.

George Anson, *Voyage Round the World in the Years 1740-1744,* Dutton, 1911.

Richard Hakluyt, *Voyages,* Dutton, 1962.

SIDELIGHTS: In 1913 an *American Review of Reviews* writer noted that *The Daffodil Fields* "is filled with Masefield's own peculiar literary beauties that mark his passionate gift of simple utterance; the art to tell a simple tale and yet reflect all of heaven and earth within it as a pool of water reflects the sky." For over seventy years John Masefield told stories that excited his readers. His prosody was variously praised and deprecated, but his talent as a storyteller remains unquestioned. Nearly eighty years ago a *New York Times* reviewer wrote: "[Masefield's work] bears the stamp of verity wherever the scene may be, and holds one's attention breathlessly in every part, in spite of its simplicity." And in 1961 Donald Davie recognized Masefield's venerability: "For the most part Masefield's poems still belong to the world of the 'Come all ye,' the street-ballad and modern folk- lyric. . . . It's delightful to be reminded that we have with us still a professional improviser of this ancient sort. He is probably the last of his kind."

In the autobiographical sketch included in Schreiber's *Portraits and Self-Portraits,* Masefield described his earliest poetic inclination: "While living in Yonkers in 1896, I first became acquainted with the works of the English poet Chaucer. The reading of his poems turned me to a systematic study of the English poets and also made me determined to attempt to write poetry." Masefield later spoke of the three distinct eras that composed his long career as a poet. In the preface to the 1958 edition of his collected poems he noted that his first period was characterized by an intense desire for escape and freedom. Later he devoted himself to the composition of long tales in verse and finally turned to "dramatic production and verse-speaking." (For many years Masefield maintained a small theater in his home for the production of verse plays.)

Although his early work won far more acclaim than his later verse, Masefield's poems were rarely greeted with unqualified praise. In 1913 a *Saturday Review of Literature* writer noted: "In Mr. Masefield it is the rush of his lines, their momentum and energy, that makes his poem. Our only doubt, which often runs to certainty, is that this momentum is less the momentum of genius than the momentum of an extremely clever writer exploiting an amazing facility of style and emotion." But the later poems frequently exhibited only what John Malcolm Brinin called "tired competence." Anthony Thwaite wrote of one narrative poem, "It has a kind of stately flatness, which sometimes takes one step down into bathos." And Dudley Fitts deplored Masefield's increasing ineptitude as early as 1950: "No man living has served poetry longer and with more devotion than has the present Laureate, but the publication of this book of new poems [*On the Hill*] is regrettable. Whatever ardor, whatever creative energy Mr. Masefield has displayed in the past . . . is shown here either in sad dilution or in an unconscious and cruel kind of self-parody. There are occasional passages of beauty, and of course the essential sweetness of the man is apparent everywhere; but these are not enough to outweigh the appalling mediocrity of the verse, both in content and execution."

A few critics of the later work were willing to examine the poems apart from the context of contemporary poetry. Thomas Lask wrote: "Though he may have looked at the 20th-century world, it was with 19th-century eyes. The forms, the mold, the very rhythms carried with them old-fashioned comfort. 'Poets,' [Masefield] wrote, 'are great or little according to the nobleness of their endeavor to build a mansion for soul.' It is not only the didacticism of this sentiment but also the language in which it is couched that indicates his distance from the contemporary world." Margery Fisher added: "Over the years, Masefield has been defining imagination for us, by precept and example. I think he can never have been afraid of the tug between reality and fantasy that bedevils so many writers. He is a formidably straight and simple visionary."

Nevertheless, the modern critic is constantly aware that most of Masefield's verse is now "unfashionable." Paul Engle wrote: "There are many lines of great verbal attractiveness [in *The Bluebells, and Other Verses*] in which the traditional subjects are treated in the traditional manner. Nothing is here to startle or amaze. Conventional beauty is conventionally reported. Many fine lyrical passages occur, but the dominant tone is one of subdued mediation on bluebells, ships, farms—the usual substance of John Masefield's books. All of that world has tremendous attractiveness, and yet it is very hard to accept the result as poetry which has truly confronted this actual world." Robert Hillyer, on the other hand, saw a purer sort of beauty in this collection. "Age has renewed Masefield's laurels more richly than ever," he wrote. "Here is the delight in fine stanza forms—the couplet, the rime royal, the Spenserian stanza and several of his own invention—and here the well-modulated rise from realistic effects to the high apostrophes of rapture."

It is, however, the earliest poems with which Masefield's name will most readily be associated. More than fifty years ago an *American Review of Reviews* writer said prophetically of *Salt-Water Ballads,* "These ballads of the sea, torn freshly from his . . . recent experiences, will quite likely remain to the end of his life the freshest and purest of all the Masefield posey." Indeed, Masefield's *Sea Fever* was published in this 1902 collection and there are few today who do not recognize its opening statement: "I must go down to the seas again, to the lonely sea and the sky. And all I ask is a tall ship and a star to steer her by." According to one *Time* reviewer, "Masefield led English poetry out of its Victorian sententiousness and thus earned his modest place in the poets' pantheon." When he was awarded the Laureateship in 1930 he was already "safe from obscurity," continued the *Time* reviewer, "[and] thus turned out only occasionally the dutiful doggerel that has so often been the lot of poets laureate." Masefield himself wrote in one of his last books, "It is time now to pipe down and coil up."

In his novels, as in his poems, Masefield's achievement was his ability to tell a fresh and energetic tale in unpretentious language. His most famous novel is probably *Sard Harker,* but in 1924 P. A. Hutchinson wrote of this book: "*Sard Harker* will not live; it will not go down as a great novel, or even as a great romance. Masefield has drunk a little too freely of the milk of Paradise. But the yarn—yes, that will have to be the final designation—must not be missed. Assuredly it must not be missed." A *Times Literary Supplement* reviewer cited the "matter-of-fact precision" with which *Sard Harker* was composed. "You must have greatness of mind, and greatness of art as well," he wrote, "to be capable of telling a simple adventure story about simple people in simple sentences, and making of the whole a great heroic tale."

Dead Ned and its sequel, *Live and Kicking Ned,* were also praised as excellent stories, imaginatively conceived. The *Boston Transcript* reviewer wrote: "In a day when a goodly portion is patently written in exposition of a thesis, it is refreshing to pick up a book that has no social, economic or emotional problem, past or present, in need of interpretation. Adventure, pure and simple, is the stuff of which John Masefield's latest romance, *Dead Ned,* is compounded." The *Times Literary Supplement* writer stated that "Mr. Masefield's is the art of reflecting life in a double glass so as to capture a twice-faithful image. It with the lessons of philosophy learned by experience, full of gentle skepticism also." William Soskin, impressed with the originality shown in the Ned sequence, even implied that Masefield's prose showed more skill than his poems. "Masefield contrives to incorporate nuances of satirical and reflective meaning," Soskin wrote, "which suggests he would be more wholesomely occupied as a Homer of adventure than an official poet for his native little island."

Masefield's autobiographical pieces were among his last writings, and those who read them were impressed with his ability to recall the excitement of the many "bright festivals" in his past. Chinua Achebe, in his review of *Grace Before Ploughing,* recalled the entire achievement of Masefield's career: "[He] took me along and I saw with wide-eyed wonder the sights of his childhood and felt something of the terror planted in his young mind by protective, well-meaning adults. . . . Masefield's art astonishes by the simplicity of its line. I think it comes from a rare gift of sight that reveals to those who possess it 'the unutterable worth of humble things.' "

A memorial service for Masefield was held at Westminster Abbey on June 20, 1967; Robert Graves gave the address and C. Day Lewis read from Masefield's works.

BIOGRAPHICAL/CRITICAL SOURCES:

BOOKS

Contemporary Literary Criticism, Gale, Volume 11, 1979, Volume 47, 1988.
Dictionary of Literary Biography, Volume 10: *Modern British Dramatists, 1940-1945,* Gale, 1982.
Schreiber, Georges, editor, *Portraits and Self-Portraits,* Houghton, 1936.

PERIODICALS

American Review of Reviews, June, 1913, November, 1913.
Boston Transcript, November 5, 1938.
Chicago Sunday Tribune, October 1, 1961.
International Book Review, December, 1924.
Kenyon Review, March, 1967.
New Statesman, June 16, 1961, June 17, 1966.
Newsweek, May 22, 1967.
New Yorker, November 4, 1939.
New York Herald Tribune Books, November 12, 1939.
New York Times, April 16, 1913, March 12, 1950, May 13, 1967.
New York Times Book Review, October 15, 1961.
Publishers Weekly, April 10, 1967.
Saturday Review of Literature, November 8, 1913, November 4, 1961.
Spectator, June 9, 1961.
Time, May 19, 1967.
Times Literary Supplement, October 16, 1924, September 24, 1938, June 22, 1967, March 2, 1984, April 26, 1985.

Washington Post, February 2, 1979.
Washington Post Book World, January 12, 1986.

*   *   *

MAUDE, George 1931-

PERSONAL: Born June 6, 1931, in Ilkley, Yorkshire, England; son of A. Cyril (a storekeeper) and Emma (a nurse; maiden name, Knaggs) Maude; married E. Helena Kalenius (a teacher), June 7, 1960; children: Ulrika, Andrei. *Education:* London School of Economics and Political Science, London, B.A., 1952, Ph.D., 1970.

ADDRESSES: Home—Saramaentie 29A6, 20300 Turku, Finland. *Office*—Faculty of Law, University of Turku, Turku, Finland.

CAREER: University of Turku, Turku, Finland, lecturer in English, 1964—, docent in international relations, 1977—. Lecturer at London School of Economics and Political Science, London, 1970. Past chairman of Lecturers Association of the University of Turku.

MEMBER: Porthan Society, Turku Historical Society.

AWARDS, HONORS: Fulbright scholar at College of Wooster, 1984; Knight of the Order of the Lion of Finland, first class, 1987.

WRITINGS:

The Finnish Dilemma: Neutrality in the Shadow of Power, Oxford University Press, 1976.
(Contributor) George Ginsburgs and A. Z. Rubinstein, editors, *Soviet Foreign Policy toward Western Europe,* Praeger, 1978.
The Finnish-Norwegian Tangle Samizdat, 1987.
(Co-author) *The Frontiers of American Political Experience,* Turku University Press, in press.

Contributor to *Cooperation and Conflict.*

SIDELIGHTS: George Maude told *CA:* "I left Britain in disgust in 1958 after having completed two years and eleven months of alternative service (hospital and land work) to the draft. I stayed in Finland because the Finns leave me alone, and there was nowhere else to go. I have detested with equal vehemence the rhetoric of the Cold War and the nuclear policies of the superpowers. Hoping now for better times."

*   *   *

MAXWELL, Kenneth (Robert) 1941-

PERSONAL: Born February 3, 1941, in Wellington, Somersetshire, England; came to the United States in 1964; son of Kenneth Bruce and Jean (a teacher; maiden name, Anderson) Maxwell. *Education:* St. John's College, Cambridge, B.A., 1963, M.A., 1967; Princeton University, M.A., 1967, Ph.D., 1970. *Avocational interests:* Travel (Europe, South America, the Middle East, Eastern Europe, Africa), drawing, painting.

ADDRESSES: Office—Research Institute on International Change, School of International Affairs, Columbia University, 420 West 118th St., New York, NY 10027; and Council on Foreign Relations, 58 East 68th St., New York, NY 10021.

CAREER: University of Kansas, Lawrence, assistant professor, 1969-71, associate professor of history, 1972-73; Institute for Advanced Study, Princeton, N.J., member of School of Historical Studies, 1971-75; Columbia University, School of International Affairs, New York City, associate professor of history, 1976-84, senior research fellow at Research Institute of International Change, 1978—, director of Camoes Center, 1988—; Tinker Foundation, New York City, program director, 1979-85; Council on Foreign Relations, New York City, senior fellow and director of Latin American Program, 1988—. Adjunct associate professor of Latin American and Caribbean studies, New York University, 1978-79; visiting professor of Latin American studies, Princeton University, 1987-88. Lecturer on politics and foreign affairs to numerous organizations, including Nieman Foundation for Journalism at Harvard University and Woodrow Wilson Center. Member of conferences, including Conference on Latin American History and Conference Group on Modern Portugal. Chairman of Committee on Brazilian Studies, 1981-83, and Committee on International Scholarly Relations, 1982-84. Consultant to various public and private institutions.

MEMBER: American Historical Association, Latin American Studies Association, American Portuguese Society (vice-president, 1984), National Committee on American Foreign Policy (member of board of directors, 1985—; secretary, 1989—), Society of Spanish and Portuguese Historians.

AWARDS, HONORS: Gulbenkian fellow, 1964; Newberry Library fellow, 1968-69; Rockefeller Foundation fellow, 1974-76; Guggenheim fellow, 1976-77.

WRITINGS:

Conflicts and Conspiracies: Brazil and Portugal, 1750-1808, Cambridge University Press, 1973.

(Editor) *The Press and the Rebirth of Iberian Democracy,* Greenwood Press, 1983.

(Editor) *Portugal: Ten Years after the Revolution,* Research Institute on International Change, Columbia University, 1984.

(Co-editor) *Portugal in the Nineteen Eighties: The Dilemmas of Democratic Consolidation,* Greenwood Press, 1986.

(Editor with Michael H. Haltzel) *Portugal: Ancient Country, New Democracy,* Wilson Center, 1990.

Contributor to numerous books, including D. Alden, editor, *The Colonial Roots of Modern Brazil,* University of California Press, 1973; George Schwab, editor, *European Communism,* Cyrco Press, 1980; Erik Hoffmann and Frederic Fleron, Jr., editors, *The Conduct of Soviet Foreign Policy,* Aldine, 1980; O'Donnell and Phillippe Schmitter, editors, *Transitions from Authoritarian Rule,* John Hopkins Press, 1988; and H. M. Scott, editors, *Enlightened Absolutism: Reform and Reformers in Later Eighteenth-Century Europe,* University of Michigan Press, 1990. Also contributor to *Second International Conference on the Portuguese Economy,* 1980. Contributor to newspapers and journals, including *Dissent, New York Times, New York Review of Books, Foreign Affairs,* and *Wilson Review.*

WORK IN PROGRESS: Research on Portugal and Angola, revolution and decolonization, eighteenth-century Portugal and Brazil, the independence movement in Brazil, and problems of democratic transition in southern Europe and Latin America.

SIDELIGHTS: Kenneth Maxwell wrote *CA:* "After graduating from Cambridge I spent a year in Europe, eventually living six months both in Madrid and Lisbon where I learned the languages and wrote for local newspapers. At graduate school I studied Portuguese-Brazilian relations during the period leading up to Brazilian independence. I then spent two years in Brazil researching *Conflicts and Conspiracies: Brazil and Portugal, 1750-1808,* which when translated became a best seller in Brazil in 1987. I have visited Portugal many times since 1963 and cov-

ered the Portuguese Revolution and decolonialization of the Portuguese territories in Africa.

"I continue to be interested in historical studies, but I also work and write on contemporary international affairs, especially on relationships between the developed and the developing world. Journalism and history, though separate types of enterprises which require different methodologies, nonetheless can strengthen one another. I have certainly found this to be the case."

Conflicts and Conspiracies: Brazil and Portugal, 1750-1808 has been translated into Portuguese.

*   *   *

McGRATH, Thomas (Matthew) 1916-1990

PERSONAL: Born November 20, 1916, near Sheldon, N.D.; son of James Lang (a farmer) and Catherine (Shea) McGrath; died September 19, 1990, in Minneapolis, Minn.; married Marian Points, 1942; married Alice Greenfield, 1952; married Eugenia Johnson, February 13, 1960; children: Thomas Samuel Koan. *Education:* University of North Dakota, B.A., 1939; Louisiana State University, M.A., 1940; New College, Oxford University, additional study, 1947-48. *Politics:* Communist Party, U.S.A.

ADDRESSES: Home—911 22nd Ave. S., #160, Minneapolis, Minn. 55404.

CAREER: Poet and novelist. Colby College, Waterville, Me., instructor in English, 1940-41; Los Angeles State College of Applied Arts and Sciences (now California State College, Los Angeles), assistant professor of English, 1952-54; Sequoia School (private study center), Los Angeles, co- founder and teacher, 1954-55; C. W. Post College, Long Island, N.Y., assistant professor of English, 1960-61; North Dakota State University, Fargo, N.D., associate professor of English, 1962-67; Moorhead State University, Moorhead, Minn., associate professor of English, 1969-82. Welder at Federal Shipbuilding and Drydock Co., Kearney, N.J., 1942; woodcarver at Artform Wood Sculpturing Co., Los Angeles, 1955-57; free-lance writer in television and film industry, 1956-60. *Military service:* U.S. Army Air Forces, 1942-45.

MEMBER: Phi Beta Kappa.

AWARDS, HONORS: Rhodes Scholar, Oxford University, 1947-48; Alan Swallow Poetry Book Award, 1954, for *Figures from a Double World;* Amy Lowell travelling poetry fellowship, 1965-66; Guggenheim fellowship, 1967; Minnesota State Arts Council grant, 1973 and 1979; National Foundation for the Arts fellowship, 1974, 1982, and 1987; Bush Foundation fellowship, 1976, 1981; honorary doctorate, University of North Dakota, 1981; American Book Award, Before Columbus Foundation, 1985, for *Echoes Inside the Labyrinth;* Lenore Marshall/Nation Prize for Poetry, 1989, for *Selected Poems, 1938-1988.*

WRITINGS:

The Gates of Ivory, the Gates of Horn (novel), foreword by Charles Humboldt, Mainstream Publishers, 1957, reprinted, Another Chicago Press, 1987.

Clouds (juvenile), illustrations by Chris Jenkyns, Melmont Publishers (Los Angeles), 1959.

The Beautiful Things (juvenile), illustrations by Jenkyns, Vanguard, 1960.

This Coffin Has No Handles (novel), North Dakota Quarterly, 1985, hardcover edition published by Thunders Mouth Press, 1988.

POETRY

First Manifesto, A. Swallow (Baton Rouge, La.), 1940.
(Contributor of "The Dialectics of Love") Alan Swallow, editor, *Three Young Poets: Thomas McGrath, William Peterson, James Franklin Lewis,* Press of James A. Decker (Prairie City, Ill.), 1942.
To Walk a Crooked Mile, Swallow Press (New York), 1947.
Longshot O'Leary's Garland of Practical Poesie, International Publishers, 1949.
Witness to the Times!, privately printed, 1954.
Figures from a Double World, Alan Swallow (Denver), 1955.
Letter to an Imaginary Friend, Part I, Alan Swallow, 1962, published with Part II, Swallow Press (Chicago), 1970, Parts III and IV, Copper Canyon Press, 1985.
New and Selected Poems, Alan Swallow, 1964.
The Movie at the End of the World: Collected Poems, Swallow Press, 1972.
Poems for Little People, [Gloucester], c. 1973.
Voyages to the Inland Sea #3, Center for Contemporary Poetry, 1973.
Voices from Beyond the Wall, Territorial Press (Moorhead, Minn.), 1974.
A Sound of One Hand: Poems, Minnesota Writers Publishing House, 1975.
Open Songs: Sixty Short Poems, Uzzano (Mount Carroll, Ill.), 1977.
Letters to Tomasito, graphics by Randall W. Scholes, Holy Cow! (St. Paul, Minn.), 1977.
Trinc: Praises II; A Poem, Copper Canyon Press, 1979.
Waiting for the Angel, Uzzano (Menomonie, Wis.), 1979.
Passages toward the Dark, Copper Canyon Press, 1982.
Echoes inside the Labyrinth, Thunder's Mouth Press, 1983.
Longshot O'Leary Counsels Direct Action: Poems, West End Press, 1983.
Selected Poems, 1938-1988, Copper Canyon Press, 1988.

Also author of *9 Poems,* Mandrill Press.

CONTRIBUTOR OF POETRY TO ANTHOLOGIES

Ian M. Parsons, editor, *Poetry for Pleasure,* Doubleday, 1960.
Donald Hall, *New Poets of England and America,* Meridian, 1962.
Walter Lowenfels, editor, *Poets of Today: A New American Anthology,* International Publishers, 1964.
Lucien Stryk, editor, *Heartland: Poets of the Midwest,* Northern Illinois University Press, 1967.
Lowenfels, editor, *Where Is Vietnam?,* Doubleday, 1967.
Morris Sweetkind, editor, *Getting Into Poetry,* Rostan Holbrook Press, 1972.
Traveling America, Macmillan, 1977.
The Norton Introduction to Literature, 2nd edition, Norton, 1977.
Robert Bly, editor, *News of the Universe,* Sierra Club, 1980.
From A to Z: 200 Contemporary Poets, Swallow Press, 1981.

Also contributor to *The New Naked Poetry,* and *The Voice That Is Great within Us.*

OTHER

Also author of about twenty documentary film scripts, 1954-60, including "The Museum," "The Fury," "Genesis," and "To Fly," which is still screened at the Smithsonian Institution. Author of unpublished manuscript, "All But the Last." Contributor of poetry, criticism, and short stories to magazines, including *Kayak, Sixties,* and *Poetry.* Assistant editor and member of editorial board of *California Quarterly,* 1951-54; contributing edi-

tor, *Mainstream,* 1955-57; founder and editor, with Eugenia McGrath, *Crazy Horse,* 1960-61; member of editorial boards of other literary magazines.

WORK IN PROGRESS: New book of poems.

SIDELIGHTS: For fifty years, Thomas McGrath has produced a prolific array of titles, encompassing poetry, novels, books for children, and several documentary film scripts, including uncredited work on the eloquent and exhilarating Smithsonian film about the history of flight, "To Fly," for which he may even have garnered his largest audience. But McGrath is primarily a poet, and although "important contemporary poets . . . proclaim him as a major voice in American poetry in the last three or four decades," notes Frederick C. Stern in *Southwest Review,* McGrath's work has been critically neglected for years. "He's one of those poets who *should* be known but isn't, who is constantly being rediscovered as if he were some precocious teenager who just got into town," declares Mark Vinz in *North Dakota Quarterly.* "If he's been honored, even revered by a few, he's also been ignored by most." According to Terrence Des Pres in *TriQuarterly,* "Thomas McGrath has been writing remarkable poems of every size and form for nearly fifty years. In American poetry he is as close to Whitman as anyone since Whitman himself, a claim I make with care. McGrath is master of the long wide line (wide in diction, long in meter), the inclusive six-beat measure of America at large. The scene of his work is the whole of the continent east to west with its midpoint in the high-plains rim of the heartland. His diction, with its vast word-stock and multitude of language layers, is demotic to the core yet spiced with learned terms in Whitman's manner, a voice as richly American as any in our literature."

McGrath was once described by Gerard Previn Meyer in the *Saturday Review of Literature* as "a likable and ingenious young poet very largely under the sway of two established 'myths'—the Whitman- democratic and the Marxist-revolutionary." And according to Roger Mitchell in the *American Book Review,* "McGrath's career makes an interesting comment on the possibilities of a Marxist art in America." Noting that "there has never been a time when any but a sentimental leftism could make the slightest dent in our consciousness," Mitchell points out, "These are not the times, and have not been for forty years or more, to make us think that 'the generous wish' could become fact, but Thomas McGrath, more than any other poet of his time and place, and with greater skill and energy than we have yet recognized, has helped keep that wish alive." "It is a credit to McGrath's integrity and courage that he has not abated his radicalism," concludes Stern in *Southwest Review,* "even though it . . . has perhaps cost him wider recognition among America's contemporary poets."

"It is the other peoples' opinions which have kept [McGrath] from being as well known as he deserves," estimates Kenneth Rexroth in the *New York Times Book Review,* "for he is a most accomplished and committed poet." Considering McGrath "one of the best American poets extant," a *New Republic* contributor explains that because he "is of the wrong political and esthetic camp," he is "consistently neglected by our literary power brokers." Several critics concur that McGrath's leftist political views have denied him the recognition his work warrants, but they do not consider his politics to impede his art. McGrath's work is "powerful, original, absorbing, funny and uncompromisingly American in its resources, techniques and hopes," writes Reginald Gibbons in *TriQuarterly.* Calling him "the most important American poet who can lay claim to the title 'radical,'" Stern observes that the essence of his poetry lies in "the past as shaping force, death as personal and political fact, the horror and loneliness of living in an inhuman and dehumanizing society." In *North Dakota Quarterly,* Valery Kirilovich Shpak, a Soviet poet and educator who understands the "democratic traditions" in McGrath's work, observes that he "depicts the life and struggle of working people who face the necessity of remaking themselves within capitalist society." According to Hugh Gibb in the *New York Times,* "In the first place, when contemplating a harsh and chaotic world, he never allows his genuine pity for the oppressed to degenerate into self-pity; and secondly, he is never forced to retreat into a world of private fantasy and introspection. In consequence he has been able not only to sustain the tradition which would otherwise appear to be almost extinct, but has brought to it a new and vigorous honesty."

Son of Irish Catholic parents whose own parents were lured across the Atlantic by promises of paradise to homestead in North Dakota, McGrath was born and raised there in a farming community during an era identified by Diane Wakoski in the *American Book Review* as "a politically exciting locus—the organization of poor farmers against bankers, grain merchants, and industrial interests." Unable to survive financially in the dust-bowl thirties and its Great Depression, however, his family, like many farmers before and after them, finally succumbed to the bankers. In the assessment of social historian E. P. Thompson in *TriQuarterly,* "McGrath's family experience was the whole cycle—from homesteading to generations working together to bust—in three generations." And in the opinion of Des Pres, "Every aspect of this heritage—the place, the hard times, the religious and political culture—informs his art in a multitude of ways."

Raised in an environment where shared labor and unity against outside influences were vital to the survival of a rapidly disintegrating farming community, McGrath was also introduced to the political philosophy of a few Wobblies (members of the Industrial Workers of the World) among the seasonal farm workers. Consequently, McGrath formulated his politics early; and, as Des Pres observed, "his politics led him into a world of experience that, in turn, backed up his political beliefs in concrete ways." McGrath spent much of his young adult life on the road or riding the rails, witnessing and experiencing economic disparity, and variously employed at odd jobs to subsidize his writing. During the 1940s, he worked as a labor organizer and briefly as a shipyard welder on the New York's Chelsea waterfront, where he also edited a rank-and-file union newspaper. "To be a Red on the waterfront was to be the natural prey of goon squads patrolling the docks for the bosses and the racketeers," noted Des Pres. "It was also to see the world of industrial work at firsthand." McGrath wrote *Longshot O'Leary's Garland of Practical Poesy* for a few "Jesuitical and cabalistic" people he had met while working on the docks—"waterfront radicals who'd come by, drink my coffee, interrupt my day's work, and instruct me how *poetry ought to be written,*" McGrath recalls in an interview with Des Pres and Gibbons in *TriQuarterly.* Noting how his waterfront acquaintances believed poetry ought to rhyme, McGrath adds, "I wrote *Longshot O'Leary* in part to show them that it could be written in rhyme, and yet could include in it, a poem, some kind of zinger, which they might have to think about or look up in the dictionary."

After serving in the Aleutian Islands with the U.S. Army Air Forces during the war, he attended Oxford University as a Rhodes Scholar, returning to New York in the late 1940s where he wrote reviews and poems for the leftist press. Influenced especially by writers of the thirties whose art derived from their politics, McGrath launched his own career at a time when many lit-

erary figures had forsaken leftist aspirations, and began what most critics agree is his most important work, *Letter to an Imaginary Friend,* during the postwar conservativism of the fifties. "The thirties were not just over in the fifties: they were devalidated . . . ," explains Mitchell. "The loss of faith in the public life and in progress in general was wide and deep, and it provided a rich ground for the cultivation of conservative social and political ideas." Mitchell points out that "this broad reversal of direction or cancellation of hope in western culture comes more and more to seem like one of the primary facts of life in the twentieth century, and Thomas McGrath is one of the few writers who, in living through it, saw it and refused to give in to its compelling logic."

Unwilling to cooperate with the House Committee on Un-American Activities during the blacklisting fifties, for instance, McGrath told them, as recorded in *North Dakota Quarterly:* "A teacher who will tack and turn with every shift of the political wind cannot be a good teacher. I have never done this myself, nor will I ever." As a poet, he was unwilling to cooperate on "esthetic grounds." McGrath explained, "The view of life which we receive through the great works of art is a privileged one—it is a view of life according to probability or necessity, not subject to the chance and accident of our real world and therefore in a sense truer than the life we see lived all around us." Consequently, because of his political underpinnings, McGrath lost his teaching post at Los Angeles State College of Applied Arts and Sciences. And following a brief stint at the Sequoia School, a private study center he helped found, he returned to the plains of North Dakota where he began *Letter to an Imaginary Friend.*

Letter to an Imaginary Friend, which Stern deems one of the "few really outstanding book-length poems published by an American," is a long, ongoing, autobiographical poem that integrates personal experience with political concerns. It represents "a contrast between what I thought of as the old community and what I saw when I came back to North Dakota . . . to live in my family's old farmhouse," recalls McGrath in *North Dakota Quarterly.* Describing the work as "a medley of memory and observation," a reviewer for *Choice* comments that McGrath "ranges back and forth over past and present. Episodes of childhood, youth, today mingle with reflections on social and political events." As McGrath explains in *North Dakota Quarterly,* "All of us live twice at the same time—once uniquely and once representatively. I am interested in those moments when my unique personal life intersects with something bigger, when my small brief moment has a part in 'fabricating the legend.'" In *Poetry,* James Atlas observes that "throughout, the resonance of personal history is drowned out by the larger concerns of American life during the Depression and World War II," and calls the work "an incessant, grieving lyric, obsessive and polemical, euphoric and bereaved." Detecting an "elegiac" tone in the third and fourth parts of *Letter to an Imaginary Friend,* Stern suggests in *Western American Literature* that "McGrath here seems to see much more the end of things."

"For McGrath politics and poetry emerge from the same source, from the geography of his life and the history of his time," observes Joseph Butkin in *North Dakota Quarterly.* "Consequently, the *Letter to an Imaginary Friend* is not simply a poetic autobiography or a portrait of the artist; it is a history of the left during these past forty years and a record of the poet's formation within that history. As geography, the poem turns America inside out. North Dakota, the hidden interior, is the paradise lost to be regained." Although McGrath is hardly a regional poet, the landscape of North Dakota assumes universal significance in *Letter to an Imaginary Friend.* According to Fred Whitehead in *North*

Dakota Quarterly, "McGrath is not concerned with . . . the Old Midwest . . . but with the frontier beyond that, with the high plains, with the West. There's a feral quality to him which is rarely found in the older, civilized zones." In "McGrath on McGrath" in *North Dakota Quarterly,* McGrath explains what makes the experience of the poet "out here on the edge . . . different from that of the city poet": "First there is the land itself. It has been disciplined by machines, but it is still not dominated. The plow that broke the plains is long gone . . . but the process of making a living is still a struggle and a gamble. . . . Weather, which is only a nuisance in the city, takes on the power of the gods here. . . . Here man can never think of himself, as he can in the city, as the master of nature . . . he has an heroic adversary that is no abstraction. At a level below immediate consciousness we respond to this, are less alien to our bodies, to human and natural time."

Commending the multiplicity of sources upon which the poet draws to make his "personal and political statement," a *Library Journal* contributor praises as well the linguistic and thematic "risks" that McGrath takes throughout. McGrath's work is "powerful, original, absorbing, funny and uncompromisingly American in its resources, techniques and hopes," writes Gibbons in *TriQuarterly.* Regarding McGrath's language as "the most impressive, most astonishing, of any American poet of our time," Gibbons adds that "his vocabulary wraps all manner of speech and written language within it, from the bawdy to unearthed glossological wonders. It is especially lively when it gathers together slang, both rural and urban, and McGrath's neologistical and sometimes surreal coinages." As Wakoski concludes: "McGrath's language is florid, compelling when allowed breadth and depth, and his concerns are so truly those born in a changing society and his ability to chronicle the past so graphic that *Letter to an Imaginary Friend* could easily become the first great poem out of the heart of the American Midwest." Calling it, in *North Dakota Quarterly,* "above all a poem of endurance and growth through radical commitment," Rory Holscher believes that for those who "have made a commitment to the exploration of radical possibilities, *Letter* could well assume the importance that *Howl* once had; it could become to adults what *Howl* was to so many adolescents."

"When McGrath began publishing in the early forties," wrote Des Pres, "his work was shaped by the strain and agitation of the thirties." Finding his early work "hard, spare, and abstract in the distantly conversational tone," and reflective of an established tradition, Mitchell describes McGrath's later work, however, as "long, loose in structure, extravagantly witty, emotionally varied, far less embedded in intellectual categories, local and personal." Moreover, McGrath's "ability to turn in these directions" Mitchell maintains, is responsible for *Letter to an Imaginary Friend*—"one of the most unusual poems we have, a personalized history of 'the generous wish' of the far Left in our country, tender and raucous, damning and hoping, a poem written in an uncongenial time in which he writhes and rages to keep the hope of 'the solidarity/In the circle of hungry equals' alive." Considered as a whole, "these volumes make one of the most interesting and important—yes, one of the most enjoyable—of long poems written in recent years," says Stern, adding that *Letter to an Imaginary Friend* is "a fine, first-rate piece of work, by our single best radical poet, and without any qualifiers, by one of our best poets." Similarly, in *North Country Anvil,* James N. Naiden recommends the epic as "essential reading to anyone who wishes to understand one of the most significant long poems in recent American history, as well as the moving force—the personal ethos—of one of the most important poets now writing."

"What is obvious to any careful reader of McGrath's poetry is that *nothing is missing* from the man's range . . . ," writes Alvarado Cardona-Hine in *North Dakota Quarterly.* "It is sage and innocent, canny, detailed and in flight, sensual, fulminating, apparent, immanent, sacred. . . . He is a true poet, not a propagandist, and his work will live because it resonates with a thousand surprising innuendoes of an inner life beyond politics, beyond experience itself. McGrath's work is real and thus his roots are in Dream." According to Sam Hamill in *North Dakota Quarterly,* "This gentle, dedicated worker in the Republic of Letters neither needs nor wants a modifier before the noun that names him: poet. Let us please dispense with qualifiers of all kinds. What McGrath is, first and foremost, is a poet. . . . He is a comic genius and a gentle revolutionary. He is a Rhodes Scholar grown up to be a road scholar, a true literatus who exemplifies the best of the literary tradition. . . . Maybe we would do well enough to call him a poet's poet, or, even better, a people's poet. But while honoring a grand man, a grand poet, let us first of all honor him for the problem he presents. Too few of our poets are dexterous enough to present us with modulations of the human soul as profound as those of McGrath. And for that I praise."

"McGrath's poetry will be remembered in one hundred years when many more fashionable voices have been forgotten," predicts Thompson. "Here is a poet addressing not poets only but speaking in a public voice to a public which has not yet learned to listen to him." Adding that "the achievement of his art has matched the achievement of his integrity" Thompson suggests that "McGrath's is an implacable alienation from all that has had anything fashionable going for it in the past four decades of American culture—and from a good deal of what has been offered as counterculture also." And to Des Pres and Gibbons, McGrath declares, "I don't think I've ever lost any sense at all of what I wanted: to try to get as much in the world as I could to move."

MEDIA ADAPTATIONS: Taped recordings have been made of McGrath's poetry readings in Los Angeles for KUSC-radio, 1958-59, and for KPFK-radio, February 18, 1960, in addition to readings at radio station WBAI in New York, and in English departments at several colleges and universities, including North Dakota State University, Moorhead State College, University of New Mexico, and University of California, Berkeley. A video tape of a poetry reading at St. Cloud State College was also recorded.

BIOGRAPHICAL/CRITICAL SOURCES:

BOOKS

Contemporary Literary Criticism, Volume 28, Gale, 1984.
Stern, Frederick C., *The Revolutionary Poet in the United States: The Poetry of Thomas McGrath,* University of Missouri Press, 1988.

PERIODICALS

American Book Review, July/August, 1980, May/June, 1983.
Antioch Review, fall-winter, 1970-71.
Choice, June, 1971.
Library Journal, August, 1970, September 1, 1985.
New Republic, April 21, 1973.
New York Times, March 7, 1948.
New York Times Book Review, February 21, 1965.
North Country Anvil, August/September, 1973.
North Dakota Quarterly, fall, 1982, fall, 1988.
Poetry, October, 1971.
Publishers Weekly, March 2, 1970.
Saturday Review of Literature, April 17, 1948.

Southwest Review, winter, 1980.
TriQuarterly, fall, 1987.
Western American Literature, fall, 1986.

—Sketch by Sharon Malinowski

*   *   *

McLELLAN, David 1940-

PERSONAL: Born February 2, 1940, in Hertfordshire, England; son of Robert (a university teacher) and Olive (Bush) McLellan; married Annie Brassart (a translator), July 1, 1967; children: Gabrielle, Stephanie. *Education:* St. John's College, Oxford, M.A., 1962, D.Phil., 1968. *Politics:* Labour. *Religion:* Roman Catholic.

ADDRESSES: Home—13 Ivy Ln., Canterbury, Kent, England. *Office*—Department of Politics, Eliot College, University of Kent, Canterbury, Kent CT2 7NS, England. *Agent*—Harold Matson Co., Inc., 22 East 40th St., New York, NY 10016.

CAREER: University of Kent, Eliot College, Canterbury, Kent, England, lecturer, 1966-71, senior lecturer in politics, 1971, reader, 1972-76, professor of political theory, 1976—. Visiting professor, State University of New York, 1969; guest fellow, Indian Institute of Advanced Study, 1970.

WRITINGS:

The Young Hegelians and Karl Marx, Praeger, 1969.
Marx before Marxism, Harper, 1970.
Karl Marx: Early Texts, Barnes & Noble, 1971.
(Editor and translator) Karl Marx, *The Grundrisse,* Harper, 1971.
The Thought of Karl Marx, Harper, 1972.
Karl Marx: His Life and Thought, Harper, 1974.
Marx, Fontana Books, 1975.
Engels, Viking, 1977.
Marxism after Marx: An Introduction, Houghton, 1980.
(Editor) *Karl Marx: Interviews and Recollections,* Macmillan, 1981.
Karl Marx: The Legacy, BBC Publications, 1983.
Ideology, Open University Press, 1986.
Marxism and Religion, Harper, 1987.
Utopian Pessimist: The Life and Thought of Simone Weil, Simon & Schuster, 1990.

WORK IN PROGRESS: Christianity and Politics for University of Notre Dame Press.

SIDELIGHTS: David McLellan, a professor of political science, is the author of numerous works dealing with Karl Marx, the founder of modern socialism. About McLellan's *Marxism after Marx: An Introduction, New York Times* critic Christopher Lehmann-Haupt writes: "If [the book] is a history of theory, it is even more a history of history, tracing, as it must, the course of the Russian, Chinese and Cuban revolutions and their aftermaths. [The author] may be inclined to sum up his survey in terms of Marxism's heterogeneity, but one can't help being impressed by the degree to which Marxism has been shaped by history."

BIOGRAPHICAL/CRITICAL SOURCES:

PERIODICALS

New York Times, March 24, 1980.
Saturday Review, August 7, 1971.
Times Literary Supplement, December 11, 1981; December 25, 1987.
Washington Post, February 13, 1974.

MEYER, Doris (L.) 1942-

PERSONAL: Born January 2, 1942, in Summit, NJ; daughter of Hans J. (an importer-exporter) and Mara Luisa (an editor and translator; maiden name, Xiques) Meyer. *Education:* Radcliffe College, B.A. (magna cum laude), 1963; University of Virginia, M.A., 1964, Ph.D., 1967.

ADDRESSES: Home—Box 579, 25 River Road Dr., Essex, CT 06426. *Office*— Department of Hispanic Studies, Connecticut College, New London, CT 06320.

CAREER: University of North Carolina, Wilmington, assistant professor of Spanish, 1967-69; Brooklyn College of the City University of New York, Brooklyn, NY, instructor, 1969-71, assistant professor, 1972-75, associate professor, 1976-79, professor of Spanish, 1980-86, faculty member of women's studies program, 1976-86; Connecticut College, New London, visiting professor, 1986, professor of Hispanic studies and department chair, 1987—. Project director, Rockefeller Fellowship Program for Foreign Language Teachers in the High Schools, 1988—. Lecturer at conferences and universities.

MEMBER: Modern Language Association of America, American Association of Teachers of Spanish and Portuguese, PEN American Center, Latin American Studies Association, Northeast Modern Language Association, Phi Beta Kappa.

AWARDS, HONORS: Woodrow Wilson fellowship, 1964-66; American Philosophical Society grant, 1976; National Endowment for the Humanities fellowship, 1977-78, and grant, 1992-94.

WRITINGS:

Traditionalism in the Works of Francisco de Quevedo y Villegas, University of North Carolina Press, 1970.
Victoria Ocampo: Against the Wind and Tide, Braziller, 1979, 2nd edition, University of Texas Press, 1990.
(Editor with Margarite Fern ndez Olmos) *Contemporary Women Authors of Latin America,* Volume 1: *New Translations,* Volume 2: *Introductory Essays,* Brooklyn College Press, 1983.
(Editor) *Lives on the Line: The Testimony of Contemporary Latin American Authors,* University of California Press, 1988.
(Translator) Nellie Campobello, *Cartucho,* University of Texas Press, 1988.

Contributor of articles and translations to history and Spanish studies journals; contributor to *Nimrod.*

SIDELIGHTS: Regarding her 1979 work *Victoria Ocampo: Against the Wind and Tide,* Doris Meyer told *CA:* "I was motivated to write the book . . . through a combination of an Argentine background on my mother's side and an intense concern with bringing to the attention of North American readers the remarkable contributions of a much-overlooked South American woman, a legend in her own country, a prolific writer and a feminist." Meyer knew Ocampo personally for nearly twenty years and, according to John Russell in the *New York Times,* provides an "unremittingly earnest" view of her life. "Books and the men who wrote them were what [Ocampo] most cared for in life," notes Russell. "She had the looks, the means and the gall to chase the writers of her choice, and for much of her life she did just that." The founder in 1931 of the influential literary review *Sur,* Ocampo also ran a publishing company that provided Spanish translations of such literary giants as James Joyce, Andre Malraux, William Faulkner, and Vladimir Nabokov. Russell praises Meyer's book as a "decent, serious, well- researched survey, and it is graced by a discretion now rare among biographers."

Since her book on Ocampo, Meyer has provided English-speaking readers with access to other Latin American authors, in particular women writers. In 1983, she co-edited the two-volume *Contemporary Women Authors of Latin America,* which collects previously unpublished translations by forty female writers and provides in-depth profiles of the lives and work of over a dozen. According to Sonja Karsen in *World Literature Today,* the volumes, which cover both established and little-known writers, "fill an important gap that has existed in our knowledge of Latin American literature." In 1988, Meyer edited *Lives on the Line: The Testimony of Contemporary Latin American Writers,* a collection of first-hand accounts by writers which, according to Alberto Ciria in the Toronto *Globe and Mail,* show "the artists' involvement (or lack of it) in social and political issues together with considerations about their literary experiences." Ciria comments that *Lives on the Line* is "helpful in suggesting some of the roots of [Latin American] literature, some of the problems faced by those writers in their lives as well as in their crafts, and some of the painful consequences of repression, exile and 'interior exile' for Latin American intellectuals."

BIOGRAPHICAL/CRITICAL SOURCES:

PERIODICALS

Globe and Mail (Toronto), June 25, 1988.
Los Angeles Times Book Review, July 17, 1988.
New York Times, August 9, 1979.
World Literature Today, winter, 1985.

* * *

MILLER, Henry (Valentine) 1891-1980

PERSONAL: Born December 26, 1891, in New York, N.Y.; died June 7, 1980, in Pacific Palisades, Calif.; married Beatrice Sylvas Wickens (a pianist), 1917 (divorced, 1924); married June Smith Mansfield, June 1, 1924 (divorced, 1934); married Janina Martha Lepska, December 18, 1944 (divorced, 1952); married Eve McClure, December 29, 1953 (divorced, 1962); married Hoki Tokuda (a jazz pianist and singer), September 10, 1967 (divorced, 1978); children: (first marriage) Barbara; (third marriage) Valentine (daughter), Tony. *Education:* Attended College of the City of New York (now City College of the City University of New York), 1909. *Religion:* Called himself religious, although he did not espouse any religion: "That means simply having a reverence for life, being on the side of life instead of death." *Avocational interests:* Ping-Pong, watercolor painting.

ADDRESSES: Home—Pacific Palisades, Calif.

CAREER: Writer, 1933-80. Worked for Atlas Portland Cement Co., New York City, 1909-11; traveled throughout the western United States working at odd jobs, 1913; worked with father in tailor shop in New York City, 1914; mail sorter with U.S. Government War Department, 1917; worked for Bureau of Economic Research, 1919; Western Union Telegraph Co., New York City, 1920-24, began as messenger, became employment manager; sold prose-poems from door to door, 1925; opened speakeasy in Greenwich Village, 1927; toured Europe, 1928; returned to New York, 1929, and then to Europe, 1930; lived in Paris, France, until 1939; *Chicago Tribune,* Paris edition, proofreader, 1932; Lycee Carnot, Dijon, France, English teacher, 1932; *Booster* (later, *Delta*), Paris, co-editor, 1937-38; *Phoenix,* Woodstock, N.Y., European editor, 1938-39; *Volontes,* Paris, continental editor, 1938-39; lived in Greece, 1939; toured the

United States, 1940-41; practiced psychoanalysis in New York City. Painted and exhibited water colors at Santa Barbara Museum of Art, Calif., and in London, 1944; painted and exhibited water colors under auspices of Westwood Art Association, Los Angeles, Calif., 1966, and at the Daniel Garvis Gallery in the Rue du Bac, Paris, 1967.

MEMBER: National Institute of Arts and Letters.

AWARDS, HONORS: Special citation from the Formentor Prize Committee, 1961, as "one of the most important literary figures of the twentieth century"; Commander of the Order of Arts and Letters, France, 1975.

WRITINGS:

Tropic of Cancer (autobiographical narrative; also see below), preface by Anais Nin, Obelisk (Paris), 1934, Medusa (New York City), 1940, reprinted with an introduction by Karl Shapiro, Grove, 1961, reprinted, 1987.
Aller Retour New York, Obelisk, 1935, American edition privately printed, 1945.
What Are You Going to Do about Alf?: An Open Letter to All and Sundry (pamphlet), Lecram-Servant (Paris), 1935, Bern Porter, 1944, 4th edition, 1972.
Black Spring (also see below; autobiographical narrative), Obelisk, 1936, Grove, 1963, reprinted, 1989.
Scenario: A Film with Sound (based on "The House of Incest" by Anais Nin), Obelisk, 1937.
Un Etre etoilique (also see below), privately printed, 1937.
Money and How It Gets That Way (broadside), Booster Publications (Paris), 1938, Bern Porter, 1945, 2nd edition, 1946.
Max and the White Phagocytes (also see below; contains *The Cosmological Eye,* "Glittering Pie," "Scenario," "The Universe of Death," "Max," "Reflections on 'Extase,'" four letters from "Hamlet," "The Golden Age," "Via Dieppe-Newhaven," "The Eye of Paris," "An Open Letter to Surrealists Everywhere," and *Un Etre etoilique*), Obelisk, 1938.
Tropic of Capricorn (also see below; autobiographical narrative), Obelisk, 1939, Grove, 1961, reprinted, 1987.
The Cosmological Eye (contains selections from *Max and the White Phagocytes, Black Spring,* and other unpublished material), New Directions, 1939, reprinted, 1973.
(With Michael Fraenkel) *Hamlet,* Carrefour, Volume 1, 1939, 2nd enlarged edition, 1943, Volume 2, 1941, Volumes 1-2 reissued and enlarged as *The Michael Fraenkel-Henry Miller Correspondence Called Hamlet,* Edition du Laurier/Carrefour (London), 1962.
The World of Sex (also see below), Argus Book Shop (Chicago), 1940, revised edition, Olympia (Paris), 1957, Grove, 1965.
The Wisdom of the Heart (short stories and essays), New Directions, 1941.
The Colossus of Maroussi; or, The Spirit of Greece, Colt Press, 1941, reprinted, Penguin Books, 1963.
Sunday after the War (contains "Reunion in Brooklyn," selections from "Sexus," and other prose pieces from then unpublished writings), New Directions, 1944.
(And illustrator) *The Plight of the Creative Artist in the United States of America,* Bern Porter, 1944, 2nd edition, 1969.
Varda: The Master Builder (pamphlet), privately printed, 1944, George Leite (Berkeley), 1947, revised edition, Bern Porter, 1972.
Semblance of a Devoted Past (also see below; selected letters from Miller to Emil Schnellock), Bern Porter, 1944, unexpurgated edition, David Grossman, 1968.
The Angel is My Watermark! (essay; also see below), Holve-Barrows (Fullerton), 1944, reprinted, Capra Press, 1972.

Murder the Murderer (an excursus on war from *The Air- Conditioned Nightmare*), Bern Porter, 1944, 2nd edition, 1972.

The Air-Conditioned Nightmare (stories and essays on Miller's impressions of the United States), New Directions, Volume 1, 1945, Volume 2: *Remember to Remember,* 1947, Volumes 1-2 reprinted, 1970.

(With Hilaire Hiler and William Saroyan) *Why Abstract?* (discussion on modern painting), New Directions, 1945, revised edition, Wittenborn, 1964 (published in England as *A Letter,* Falcon Press, 1948).

(And illustrator) *Henry Miller Miscellanea,* edited by Bernard H. Porter, Bern Porter, 1945.

(And illustrator) *Echolalia: Reproduction of Water Colors by Henry Miller,* Bern Porter, 1945.

Obscenity and the Law of Reflection, Alicat Book Shop (Yonkers), 1945.

The Amazing and Invariable Beauford Delaney, (fragment from *The Air-Conditioned Nightmare,* Volume 2), Alicat Book Shop, 1945.

(And illustrator) *Maurizius Forever* (essay), Colt Press, 1946, revised edition, Capra Press, 1973.

Patchen: Man of Anger and Light, with a Letter to God by Kenneth Patchen, Padell, 1946.

Into the Night Life, illustrated and designed by Bezalel Schatz, privately printed, 1947.

(With others) *Of, By and About Henry Miller: A Collection of Pieces by Miller, Herbert Read, and Others,* Alicat Book Shop, 1947.

The Smile at the Foot of the Ladder (bound with *About Henry Miller* by Edwin Corle), Duell, Sloan & Pearce, 1948, the former also published separately by New Directions, 1959, reprinted, 1975.

The Rosy Crucifixion (trilogy of autobiographical narratives), Book 1: *Sexus,* two volumes, Obelisk, 1949, Grove, 1965, reprinted, 1987, Book 2: *Plexus* (originally published in French), two volumes, translation by Elisabeth Guertic, Olympia, 1953, Grove, 1965, reprinted, 1987, Book 3: *Nexus,* Part 1, Obelisk, 1960, Grove, 1965, reprinted, 1987.

The Waters Reglitterized: The Subject of Water Colour in Some of Its More Liquid Phases (also see below), John Kidis (San Jose, Calif.), 1950, reprinted limited edition, Capra, 1973.

Blase Cendrars, Denoel (Paris), 1951.

The Books in My Life, New Directions, 1952, reprinted, 1969.

Rimbaud (two essays; written in English but originally published in French), translation by F. Roger Cornaz, Mermod (Lausanne), 1952, published in the United States as *The Time of the Assassins: A Study of Rimbaud,* New Directions, 1956, reprinted, Pocket Books, 1975.

Nights of Love and Laughter, (short stories), introduction by Kenneth Rexroth, New American Library, 1955.

Quiet Days in Clichy (also see below; two autobiographical narratives), includes photographs by Brassai, Olympia, 1956, Grove, 1965, reprinted, 1987.

The Hour of Man (originally published in *Chicago Review,* fall, 1956), [Chicago], c. 1956.

A Devil in Paradise: The Story of Conrad Moricand, Born Paris, 7 or 7:15 P.M., January 17, 1887, Died Paris, 10:30 P.M., August 31, 1954 (also see below; Part 3 of "Big Sur and the Oranges of Hieronymus Bosch"), New American Library, 1956.

Big Sur and the Oranges of Hieronymus Bosch (reminiscences), New Directions, 1957.

(With Bezalel Schatz) *Twelve Illustrations to Henry Miller* (illustrations by Schatz for Hebrew edition of selected writings by Miller, entitled "Half Past Midnight"), [Jerusalem], 1957.

First Letter to Trygve Hirsch (pamphlet), Henry Miller Literary Society (Minneapolis), 1957.

(With D. H. Lawrence) *Pornography and Obscenity: Handbook for Censors* (two essays) Fridtjog-Karla Publications, 1958.

The Red Notebook (autograph notes and sketches; contains Miller's horoscope), Jargon, 1958.

The Last of the Grenadiers; or, Anything You Like (catalog of an exhibition of Michonze paintings held at Adams Gallery, London, June-July, 1959), Favil Press (London), 1959,

(Contributor) Lawrence Durrell and Alfred Perles, *Art and Outrage: A Correspondence about Henry Miller between Alfred Perles and Lawrence Durrell, with an Intermission by Henry Miller* (correspondence about Miller between Perles and Durrell), Putnam (London), 1959, Dutton, 1961.

Reunion in Barcelona (letter to Perles, from *Aller Retour New York*), Scorpion Press, 1959.

The Henry Miller Reader, edited by Durrell, New Directions, 1959 (published in England as *The Best of Henry Miller,* Heinemann, 1960).

The Intimate Henry Miller (collection of stories, essays, and autobiographical sketches), includes introduction by Lawrence Clark Powell, New American Library, 1959.

Defence of the Freedom to Read: A Letter to the Supreme Court of Norway, in Connection with the Ban on "Sexus"/Forsvar for lesefrichetera: Brev til Norges Hoeyeste Domstol anledning av beslagleggelsen av "Sexus", bilingual edition, Forlag J. W. Cappelens (Oslo), 1959.

La Table Ronde, [Paris], 1960.

To Paint Is to Love Again, Cambria Books, 1960, revised edition published with the text of *Semblance of a Devoted Past,* Grossman, 1968.

Stand Still Like the Hummingbird (essays), New Directions, 1962.

(With Brassai, Durrell, and Bissiere) *Hans Reichel, 1892-1958,* J. Bucher (Paris), 1962.

(With others) *Joseph Delteil: Essays in Tribute,* St. Albert's Press (London), 1962.

Henry Miller: Watercolors, Drawings, and His Essay, "The Angel is My Watermark!", Abrams, 1962.

Just Wild about Harry: A Melo-Melo in Seven Scenes (play; first produced in Spoleto, 1968), New Directions, 1963, reprinted, 1979.

Henry Miller Trilogy (consists of *Tropic of Cancer, Tropic of Capricorn,* and *Black Spring*), Grove, 1963.

(With Jacques den Haan) *Milleriana* (articles on Miller's work and correspondence between den Haan and Miller), De Bestge Bij (Amsterdam), 1963.

(With Durrell) *Lawrence Durrell and Henry Miller: A Private Correspondence,* edited by George Wickes, Dutton, 1963.

Books Tangent to Circle: Reviews, Bern Porter, 1963, 2nd edition, 1971.

Greece, drawings by Anne Poor, Viking, 1964.

Henry Miller on Writing (selections from published and unpublished works), edited by Thomas H. Moore, New Directions, 1964.

Letters to Anais Nin, edited and with an introduction by Gunther Stuhlmann, Putnam, 1965, reprinted, Paragon House, 1988.

Selected Prose, two volumes, MacGibbon & Kee, 1965.

Order and Chaos chez Hans Reichel, includes introduction by Durrell, Loujon Press (Tucson), 1966.

(With Helmut Lander) *Torsi* (text by Miller), Verlag der Europaeischen Buecherei Hieronomi (Bonn), 1966.

(With Will Slotnikoff) *The First Time I Live: A Romantic Book about the Writing of a Book and the Birth of a Writer* (includes introduction by Miller and an exchange of letters between Slotnikoff and Miller), Manchester Lane Editions (Washington), 1966.

Lawrence Clark Powell: Two Tributes, Goliard Press, 1966.

(With William A. Gordon) *Writer and Critic: A Correspondence with Henry Miller*, Louisiana State University Press, 1968.

(With J. Rives Childs) *Collector's Quest: The Correspondence of Henry Miller and J. Rives Childs, 1947-1965*, edited and introduced by Richard Clement Wood, published by University Press of Virginia for Randolph-Macon College, 1968.

The World of Sex [and] *Max and the White Phagocytes*, Calder & Boyars, 1970.

Insomnia; or, The Devil at Large, Loujon Press, 1970.

(With Georges Belmont) *Entretiens de Paris*, Stock, 1970, translation by Antony Mcnabb and Harry Scott published as *Face to Face with Henry Miller: Conversations with Georges Belmont*, Sidgwick & Jackson, 1971, published in the United States as *In Conversation*, Quadrangle, 1972.

My Life and Times (autobiography), edited by Bradley Smith, Playboy Press, 1971, abridged edition, 1973.

Reflections on the Death of Mishima (also see below), Capra Press, 1972.

Journey to an Antique Land (also see below), illustrated by Bob Nash, Ben Ben Press (Big Sur), 1972.

On Turning Eighty (also see below; chapbook; includes *Journey to an Antique Land* and preface to *The Angel is My Watermark*), illustrated by Nash, Capra Press, 1972.

First Impressions of Greece (also see below), Village Press, 1973.

Reflections on the Maurizius Case: A Humble Appraisal of a Great Book, Capra Press, 1974.

(With Wallace Fowlie) *Letters of Henry Miller and Wallace Fowlie, 1943-1972*, introduction by Fowlie, Grove, 1975.

The Nightmare Notebook, New Directions, 1975.

Encounter with Henry Miller: A Giant of Literary Realism Explores His World and Art (cassette recording), Center for Cassette Studies, c. 1975.

Genius and Lust: A Journey through the Major Writings of Henry Miller (contains excerpts from *Tropic of Cancer, Black Spring, Tropic of Capricorn, Sexus, Plexus, Nexus, The Colossus of Maroussi; or, The Spirit of Greece, The Air-Conditioned Nightmare, Big Sur and the Oranges of Hieronymous Bosch*), compiled by Norman Mailer, Grove, 1976.

J'suis pas plus con qu'un autre, Buchet/Chastel, 1976, reprinted as *Je ne suis pas plus con qu'un autre*, Stanke (Montreal), 1980.

Flash Back: Entretiens a Pacific Palisades avec Christian de Bartillat (title means "Flash Back: Interviews in Pacific Palisades with Christian de Bartillat"), Stock, 1976.

(Author of comments with Anais Nin) Herta Hilscher-Wittgenstein, *The Ineffable Frances Steloff: A Photographic Visit*, Swallow Press, 1976.

Henry Miller's Book of Friends: A Tribute to Friends of Long Ago, photographs by Jim Lazarus, Capra Press, 1976, reprinted as *A Book of Friends: A Trilogy*, 1987.

Mother, China, and the World Beyond (also see below), Capra Press, 1977.

Sextet (contains *On Turning Eighty, Reflections on the Death of Mishima, First Impressions of Greece, The Waters Reglitterized: The Subject of Water Colour in Some of Its More Liquid Phases, Reflections on the Maurizius Case: A Humble Appraisal of a Great Book*, and *Mother, Child and the World Beyond*), Capra Press, 1977.

Gliding into the Everglades: And Other Essays, Lost Pleiade, 1977.

(With Elmer Gertz) *Henry Miller: Years of Trail and Triumph, 1962-1964: The Correspondence of Henry Miller and Elmer Gertz*, edited by Gertz and Felice Flanery Lewis, Southern Illinois University Press, 1978.

Quiet Days in Clichy and The World of Sex: Two Books, Grove, 1978.

My Bike and Other Friends, Capra Press, 1978.

An Open Letter to Stroker! Inspired by the Writings and Art Work of Tommy Trantino, edited by Irving Stettner, Stroker, 1978.

The Theatre and Other Pieces, Stroker, 1979.

Joey: A Loving Portrait of Alfred Perles, Together with Some Bizarre Episodes Relating to the Other Sex, limited edition, Capra Press, 1979.

(Contributor) Noel Young, editor, *The Capra Chapbooks Anthology*, Capra Press, 1979.

Notes on "Aaron's Rod" and Other Notes on Lawrence from the Paris Notebooks, edited by Seamus Cooney, Black Sparrow Press, 1980.

The World of Lawrence: A Passionate Appreciation, edited with an introduction and notes by Evelyn J. Hinz and John J. Teunissen, Capra Press, 1980.

Reflections: Henry Miller, edited by Twinka Thiebaud, Capra Press, 1981.

The Paintings of Henry Miller: Paint As You Like and Die Happy, with Collected Essays by Henry Miller on the Art of Watercolor, edited by Noel Young, foreword by Durrell, Capra Press, 1982.

The Letters of Henry Miller, Morning Star Press (Haydenville, Mass.), 1982.

Opus Pistorum, Grove, 1983, reprinted as *Under the Roofs of Paris*, 1985.

From Your Capricorn Friend: Henry Miller and the Stroker, 1978-1980 (letters), New Directions, 1984.

(With Brenda Venus) *Dear, Dear Brenda: The Love Letters of Henry Miller to Brenda Venus*, edited by Gerald Seth Sindell, Morrow, 1986.

Letters from Henry Miller to Hoki Tokuda Miller, edited by Joyce Howard, Freundlich Books, 1986.

A Literary Passion: Letters of Anais Nin and Henry Miller, 1932-1953, edited and with introduction by Stuhlmann, Harcourt, 1987.

The Durrell-Miller Letters, 1935-1980, edited by Ian S. MacNiven, New Directions, 1988.

(And author of preface) *Henry Miller's Hamlet Letters*, edited and with introduction by Michael Hargraves, Capra Press, 1988.

(With Schnellock) *Letters to Emil*, edited by Wickes, New Directions, 1989.

AUTHOR OF PREFACE

Michael Fraenkel, *Bastard Death: The Autobiography of an Idea*, Carrefour, 1936.

Alfred Perles, *The Renegade*, George Allen, 1943.

James Hanley, *No Directions*, Faber, 1943.

Parker Tyler, *Hollywood's Hallucination*, McClelland, 1944.

Henry David Thoreau, *Life without Principle* (three essays), Delkin, 1946.

Arthur Rimbaud, *Les Illuminations*, Editions des Gaules, 1949.

Brassai, *Histoire de Marie*, Editions de Point du Jour, 1949.

Lillian Bos Ross, *Big Sur*, Denoel, 1949.

Mezz Mezzrow and Bernhard Wolfe, *La Rage de vivre*, Correa, 1950.

Claude Houghton, *Je suis Jonathan Scrivener,* Correa, 1954.

Harold Maine, *Quand un homme est fou,* Correa, 1954.

W. R. Harding, editor, *Thoreau: A Century of Criticism,* Southern Methodist University Press, 1954.

Wallace Fowlie, *La Graal du clown,* [France], 1955.

Albert Maillet, *Le Christ dans l'oeuvre d'Andre Gide,* Le Cercle du Livre, 1955.

Perles, *My Friend Henry Miller: An Intimate Biography,* Neville Spearman, 1955.

T. Lobsang Rampa, *The Third Eye,* privately printed, 1957.

Blaise Cendrars, *A l'aventure,* Denoel, 1958.

Eric Barker, *In Easy Dark,* privately printed, 1958.

Jack Kerouac, *The Subterraneans,* Grove, 1958.

Cendrars, *Edition complete des oeuvres de Blase Cendrars,* Volume 5: *L'Homme foudroye [et] La Main coupee,* [Paris], 1960.

Junichiro Tanizaki, *Deux amours cruelles,* Stock, 1960.

Durrell, *Justine,* Buchet/Chastel, 1960.

Andreas Feininger, *Frauen und Goettinnen von der Steinzeit bis zu Picasso,* M. DuMont Schauberg, 1960.

(And author of postscript) Sydney Omarr, *Henry Miller: His World of Urania,* Ninth House Publishing, 1960.

Tanizaki, *The Key,* Knopf, 1961.

Bufano: Sculpture, Mosaics, Drawings (of Beniaminono Bufano), J. Weatherhill, 1968.

Herbert Ernest Bates, *Seven by Five: A Collection of Stories, 1926-61,* Penguin Books, 1972.

Eric Graham Howe, *The Mind of the Druid,* Samuel Weiser, 1973.

Haniel Long, *The Marvelous Adventure of Cabeza de Vaca,* Ballantine, 1973.

Jacqueline Langmann, *Henry Miller et son destin,* Stock, 1974.

Powell, *Le Train bleu/The Blue Train* (in French and English), French translation by Anne Joba, Buchet/Chastel, 1978.

OTHER

Author of four unpublished novels, still in manuscript form, written in the 1920's: "Clipped Wings," the story of twelve Western Union messengers, "Moloch," "Crazy Cock," and "This Gentile World"; author of pamphlet *The Story of George Dibbern's "Quest,"* 1958, and of short story collection, *Mezzotints.* Editor of "Villa Seurat" series during the 1930's. Contributor of essays, short stories, and sketches to *Crisis, New York Herald* (Paris), *New English Weekly* (London), *Criterion, The Booster, T'ien, Hsia Monthly* (Shanghai), *Cahiers du Sud* (Marseilles), *Volontes* (Paris), *Transition, New Republic, Phoenix, Partisan Review, Experimental Review, Story, Horizon* (London), *Nation, Town and Country, Athene, Poetry-London, Interim, Harper's Bazaar, Rocky Mountain Review, London Magazine, Mademoiselle, Evergreen Review,* and other periodicals.

WORK IN PROGRESS: The second part of *Nexus,* (Miller once told *CA:* "Volume 2 will probably never be written. Have about decided to leave *The Rosy Crucifixion* an 'unfinished symphony' "); seven new lithographs and nine etchings, produced in Japan by S. Kubo; a collection of new short stories.

SIDELIGHTS: Henry Miller is best remembered as the author of *Tropic of Cancer, Tropic of Capricorn,* and *Black Spring,* books about his expatriate days in Paris. Although these works were first published in France in the 1930s, it was not until 1961 that Miller was able to bypass censorship of his work in his native United States with the publication of *Tropic of Cancer* by Grove Press. Critics found the sexual passages in *Tropic of Cancer* obscene and the author was forced to go to court to lift the ban on his book. "That case brought in a new era of publishing," said Grove Press president Barney Rossett in Miller's *Chicago Tribune* obituary, and "there haven't been many cases of book censorship since." The sensationalism of this trial and the interest the ban on Miller's work created helped to make *Tropic of Cancer* an instant best seller in the United States. Critics, however, debated whether Miller's writings had any true literary merit. While some revered Miller for his ground-breaking efforts to frankly portray life's seamier side, others condemned him as being unartistic. In support of Miller's writing, Norman Mailer called the writer "our only Old Master," as Jack Kroll pointed out in a *Newsweek* obituary; others, like *Virginia Quarterly Review* critic John Williams, complained that Miller was "incapable of constructing dramatic sense" and had "no sense of character—except his own." "The truth about Henry Miller," wrote *Henry Miller* author Kingsley Widmer, one of the first serious critics of the writer's books, "is that he is neither 'the great living author' . . . nor the 'foulest writer of meaningless nonsense.' " However, he did make an important contribution "to the increasingly dominant and major poetic-naturalistic American styles."

The books Miller wrote were neither novels in the traditional sense, nor nonfiction, but autobiographical novels based largely on his experiences in Paris and other parts of the world. Although he had wanted to become an author of notoriety since his youth, a troubled and turbulent life during which he worked several unsatisfying jobs and had an unstable family life kept him from composing a book-length work until he reached middle age. Problems in his second marriage persuaded Miller to move to Paris alone in 1930, but this decision left him with no financial resources. He survived only with the help and encouragement of friends such as Lawrence Durrell and Alfred Perles, with whom he co-edited the magazine *Booster,* and author Anais Nin. These difficult times as an expatriate influenced Miller in his choice of genre, he once explained. A *Washington Post* article by J. Y. Smith quoted Miller: "I wrote all these auto[bio]graphical books not because I think myself such an important person but . . . because I thought when I began that I was telling the story of the most tragic suffering any man had endured. As I got on with it I realized that I was only an amateur at suffering."

The seamier side of Paris life was what Miller knew best, and part of that world involved the sex and prostitution one found on the streets. Miller continued in Smith's article: "I wrote about sex because it was such a big part of my life. Sex was always the dominant thing. People have said that I threw in juicy passages just to keep the reader awake. That is not true. My everyday life was full of this objectionable or questionable material." Nevertheless, a number of critics condemned Miller's writing as pornographic. One of the author's most vehement denouncers, Kate Millett, interpreted Miller's love scenes in her book *Sexual Politics* as portraying the sexes as "two warring camps between whom understanding is impossible since one [the male] is human and animal (according to Miller's perception, intellectual and sexual)—the other simply animal."

Responding to Millett's attack in a *London Magazine* article, James Campbell commented that her interpretation "is not the whole story." Sex is important in Miller's books "both as a means of subversion and as a metaphor of birth. The female sex organ is 'a symbol for the connection of all things,' " Campbell continued, quoting Miller, ". . . and [represents] the movement . . . away from all that is redolent of the real obscenity of hypocrisy and away from the" industrialized world. As for the other symbolic aspect of sexuality in the author's work, Campbell pointed out that Miller's writings "begin from the station of failure and that their whole movement is towards a vantage point beyond death. In this respect, too, sex is primary since the purpose of sex is to augment life."

Miller's philosophy was that life should be revered over all other considerations. Freedom was more important than materialism; individuality took precedence over social conformity. These ideas, as critics like Wallace Fowlie expressed in *Concise Dictionary of Literary Biography: The Age of Maturity, 1929-1941,* are best expressed in *Tropic of Cancer,* which "is largely concerned with the physiological and psychic aspects of sexuality. The sexual drive in man is, for Miller, a means of self-expression. This drive becomes uppermost when man is enslaved to a mechanistic society." In *American Dreams, American Nightmares,* Alan Trachtenberg commented that this idea is continued in *Black Spring.* "*Black Spring,* the most successful of his [books, evokes] both the suffocation and the frenzy of release. . . . The solution is to destroy the old American world in himself, the world of fraus, materialism, gadgetry, the dream turned nightmare, and to die into a new, free being." For the author, this theme of self-expression also applies to his own personal self-liberation, and in *Tropic of Cancer* it marked for Miller "a new beginning, a celebration of personal rebirth in a dying world."

In using the term "cancer" for his book, Miller was referring to the "sick reality that characterizes a society of one dimensional people whose lives are monotones and who live in a dead world beneath the earth's surface," explained Lawrence J. Shifreen in *Studies in Short Fiction.* Influenced as he was by such writers as D. H. Lawrence, Arthur Rimbaud, and American transcendentalists Ralph Waldo Emerson and Henry David Thoreau, the philosophical aspects of Miller's writing most strongly resemble those of American poet Walt Whitman. In fact, J. D. Brown noted in the 1980 *Dictionary of Literary Biography Yearbook* that the "formal model for *Tropic of Cancer* was Whitman's *Song of Myself.*" Miller believed that the United States was on the verge of collapse, just as Whitman had in his *Democratic Vistas,* and he denounced American society in such books as *Hamlet* and *The Air-Conditioned Nightmare.*

Far from being an occasion for despair, however, the "prospect of the decline and fall of America was to Miller something to be regarded with great joy," according to *American Quarterly* critic Harold T. McCarthy, "for only in its suffering and death could America be reborn." Miller was against the democratic form of government "because it reduces men as individuals 'to the least common denominator of intelligibility.' " Some critics, such as *Arizona Quarterly* reviewer Peter L. Hays, felt that this philosophy was "dangerous." The "sexual portions of Miller do not disturb me as much as his anarchy does, his celebration of life, energy, passion, ecstasy, and his condemnation of anything that restricts free enjoyment." "He wants to recreate life as he lived it, with no moral judgments," Hays also commented. "I disagree: I think an author should indicate, if only by negation, how life should by lived."

Philosophical considerations aside, once Miller's *Tropics* books and *Black Spring* were released in the United States they became immediate best sellers. Reactions among critics, however, were mixed when regarding the books' literary merits. The anti-artistic style of his prose (Miller was not interested in conventional uses of plotting and characterization) disturbed some reviewers who felt that the lack of form in the writer's work was a sign of poor craftsmanship. In her *Don't Never Forget: Collected Views and Reviews,* for instance, Brigid Brophy attested, "What makes Henry Miller not a mere neutral but an enemy of art is that he disdains the skill and yet screams unskillfully that he has succeeded in becoming a great writer without really try-

ing." Others, however, praised the surrealistic imagery and descriptions of Paris that the author employed. Mailer asserted in *American Review* that "no French writer no matter how great, not Rabelais, nor Proust, not De Maupassant, Hugo, Huysmans, Zola, or even Balzac, not even Celine, has made Paris more vivid to us. . . . For in *Tropic of Cancer* Miller succeeded in performing one high literary act: he created a tone in prose which caught the tone of a period and a place." *Henry Miller* author George Wickes regarded Miller as "certainly the best surrealist writer America has produced. And while it is hard to imagine that the *Tropics* will ever be taught in the schools, several of his books should occupy a lasting place in American literature."

With the increasingly dangerous situation that was brewing in Europe in 1939, Miller left Paris for Greece. Here, he felt he had found the kind of life for which he was looking. "That voyage . . . was the apex of my happiness, my joy, a very great eye-opener," Smith quoted the author as having once said. "What one admires there is a poor people who are happy, compared to us who are miserable with our riches." About his sojourn in Greece, Miller wrote *The Colossus of Maroussi; or, The Spirit of Greece.* Brown described this book in the *Dictionary of Literary Biography* as "Miller's account of his quest for spiritual illumination in Greece while a guest of Lawrence Durrell. Miller and others later judged it his finest work, but it is a far lesser work than *Tropic of Cancer.* The narrative constantly promises spiritual revelations which it fails to deliver convincingly. As a work of art, and often of bombast, *Colossus* fails to plumb the deeper reservoirs of feeling and symbol which Miller tapped in his early Paris years. A falling off in Miller's power as an autobiographical artist is apparent in the forties, even in the late thirties."

This "falling off " was readily apparent to many critics upon reading Miller's *Quiet Days in Clichy* and *The Rosy Crucifixion,* a trilogy comprised of *Sexus, Plexus,* and *Nexus* that was the author's attempt to compose an expanded version of *Tropic of Capricorn.* "*Quiet Days in Clichy* repeats episodes from *Tropic of Cancer,* and *Tropic of Capricorn* is regurgitated *ad infinitum* and *ad nauseum* in *The Rosy Crucifixion,*" complained Hays. Even Durrell, the author's close friend and admirer, worried that all the " 'new mystical outlines' of Miller's art after 1940 were 'lost,' " according to Brown. As Wickes observed in the *New York Times Book Review,* the man who wrote *Quiet Days in Clichy* was not the same one who wrote *Tropic of Cancer.* "What is lacking is the vehemence and the anarchy which made the earlier book a cry of passionate protest. . . . In the thirties Miller's writing was always airborne; in the forties and fifties, his prose became more pedestrian."

By this time, Miller had returned to the United States and was living in California. His reputation as a ribald and scandalous writer had proceeded him and he soon had something he had never before experienced: an audience. Wickes surmised in his article, that this fact had a significant impact on Miller's writing. When he moved to Big Sur in 1944, related Fowlie, the city soon became "almost an artists' colony with Henry Miller as its leading prophet." The publication of *Big Sur and the Oranges of Hieronymus Bosch,* a rambling narrative detailing Miller's thoughts about his new life in California, "encouraged more pilgrims than ever to call on Miller. They saw him now as a kind of guru and often made impossible demands" on him. "By 1957," Wickes wrote, "Miller was a different man; he had assumed his Big Sur mantle and was addressing an audience. In 1940, he was merely trying to clarify some of his ideas and did not care if no one listened." Because of this change, Wickes suggested, Miller began to revise his works. The result was that in books like *The World of Sex* such alterations took "the bite out of incisive passages."

The Miller books that were published during the 1950s, '60s, and '70s were largely essay collections and volumes of correspondences with his friends. In a *New York Times Book Review* article by the author, he writes: "Now that writing has become like second nature to me the desire to write is weakening. Why bother? I say to myself over and over again. Coupled with that goes another more crippling thought, to wit, that nothing is as important as one imagines it to be." Settling down in California, Miller concentrated more on his other two passions: water color painting and Ping-Pong. Steadily painting about one hundred and fifty water colors a year, Miller exhibited his work in California and on occasional trips to Europe. But even after painting for several years, Miller considered himself "a beginner," according to *New York Times* contributor Peter Bart, who quoted the artist as saying: "That's what fascinates me about [painting]. As a writer I know I can do what I want to do. As a painter I'm still going. there's more of a challenge."

Today, many critics consider the philosophy that Miller expressed in his writings to be of more enduring importance than his actual skills as a writer. Miller's "message is precisely that of Whitman, of Rimbaud, of Rilke," concluded Karl Shapiro in his *In Defense of Ignorance:* " 'Everything we are taught is false'; and 'Change your life.' As a writer Miller may be second- or third-rate or of no rating at all; as a spiritual example he stands among the great men of our age." A bohemian since his expatriate days in Paris, Miller "is the true ancestor of all the beatniks and hippies, except that he is a most immensely learned, intensely cultivated writer of major stature," wrote *American Dreams, American Nightmares* contributor Maxwell Geismer. Brown listed such works as Jack Kerouac's *On the Road* and books by Allen Ginsberg, Richard Brautigan, and Hunter Thompson as being "rather direct extensions" of Miller's autobiographical novels. A *Times* obituary summarized: "He was above all the writer who stood up for private life against the bullying social pressures and the absurd encroachments of the political, commercial and military spheres on the individual life of sexual love and the arts, the spheres of men at their finest and freest." "[My] ideal is to be free of ideals," Miller reflected in *On Turning Eighty,* "free of principles, free of isms and ideologies. I want to take to the ocean of life like a fish takes to the sea."

A Miller archives, founded by Lawrence Clark Powell, is maintained at the University of California, Los Angeles. There is also a Miller collection at the library of Randolph-Macon College in Ashland, Va.

MEDIA ADAPTATIONS: In 1957 Riverside Records released a recording entitled "Henry Miller Recalls and Reflects." Robert Snyder produced the documentary "The Henry Miller Odyssey" in 1968. A motion picture of *Quiet Days in Clichy* was filmed by SBA-ABC Productions (Denmark) in 1969, released in the United States as "Henry Miller's Not So Quiet Days"; the book was again adapted for film in 1989 by French director Claude Chabrol. In 1969 Joseph Strick produced and directed a feature film of *Tropic of Cancer* for Paramount. Snyder also produced two National Educational Television specials on Miller in 1970: "Encounter: Buckminster Fuller and Henry Miller" and "Henry Miller Reads and Muses." In 1973 Tom Schiller filmed a movie of Miller in his bathroom. Playboy Enterprises, Inc., produced a recording of Henry Miller talking with Bradley Smith in 1973.

BIOGRAPHICAL/CRITICAL SOURCES:

BOOKS

Allen, Walter, *The Modern Novel,* Dutton, 1964.
Baxter, Annette Kar, *Henry Miller, Expatriate,* University of Pittsburgh Press, 1961.
Booth, Wayne C., *The Rhetoric of Fiction,* University of Chicago Press, 1961.
Brophy, Brigid, *Don't Never Forget: Collected Views and Reviews,* Holt, 1966.
Chapsal, Madeleine, *Quinze Ecrivains,* Julliard, 1963.
Concise Dictionary of American Literary Biography: The Age of Maturity, 1929-1941, Gale, 1989.
Contemporary Literary Criticism, Gale, Volume 1, 1973, Volume 2, 1974, Volume 4, 1975, Volume 9, 1978, Volume 14, 1980, Volume 43, 1987.
Dick, Kenneth C., *Henry Miller: Colossus of One,* E. M. Reynolds, 1967.
Dictionary of Literary Biography, Gale, Volume 4: *American Writers in Paris, 1920-1939,* 1980, Volume 9: *American Novelists, 1910-1945,* Gale, 1981.
Dictionary of Literary Biography Yearbook: 1980, Gale, 1981.
Fiedler, Leslie A., *Waiting for the End,* Stein & Day, 1964.
Fraenkel, Michael, *Genesis of the Tropic of Cancer,* Bern Porter, 1944.
Gordon, William A., *The Mind and Art of Henry Miller,* J. Cape, 1968.
The Happy Rock: A Book about Henry Miller, Bern Porter, 1945.
Harrison, Gilbert A., editor, *The Critic as Artist: Essays on Books 1920-1970,* Liveright, 1972.
Hassan, Ihab Habib, *The Literature of Silence: Henry Miller and Samuel Beckett,* Knopf, 1967.
Henry Miller: A Chronology and Bibliography, Bern Porter, 1945.
Hutchison, E. R., *Tropic of Cancer on Trial: A Case History of Censorship,* Grove, 1968.
Kermode, Frank, *Continuities,* Random House, 1968.
Littlejohn, David, *Interruptions,* Grossman, 1970.
Madden, David, editor, *American Dreams, American Nightmares,* Southern Illinois University Press, 1970.
Mailer, Norman, *A Journey through the Major Writings of Henry Miller,* Grove, 1976.
Martin, Jay, *Always Merry and Bright: The Life of Henry Miller,* Capra Press, 1979.
Mauriac, Claude, *The New Literature,* Braziller, 1959.
Miller, Henry, *On Turning Eighty,* Capra Press, 1972.
Millett, Kate, *Sexual Politics,* Doubleday, 1970.
Moore, Nicholas, *Henry Miller,* Opus Press, 1943.
Moore, Thomas H., editor, *Bibliography of Henry Miller,* Henry Miller Literary Society, 1961.
Nelson, Jane A., *Form and Image in the Fiction of Henry Miller,* Wayne State University Press, 1970.
Omarr, Sydney, *Henry Miller: His World of Urania,* 9th House, 1960.
Orwell, George, *Inside the Whale, and Other Essays,* Gollancz, 1940.
Perles, Alfred, *Reunion in Big Sur: A Letter to Henry Miller in Reply to His "Reunion in Barcelona,"* Scorpion Press, 1959.
Powell, Lawrence Clark, *Books in My Baggage,* World Publishing, 1960.
Rembar, Charles, *The End of Obscenity: The Trials of Lady Chatterley, Tropic of Cancer, and Fanny Hill,* Harper, 1986.
Renken, Maxine, *A Bibliography of Henry Miller, 1945-1961,* Alan Swallow, 1962.

Rexroth, Kenneth, *Bird in the Bush: Obvious Essays,* New Directions, 1959.

Shapiro, Karl, *In Defense of Ignorance,* Random House, 1960.

Solotaroff, Theodore, *The Red Hot Vacuum and Other Pieces on the Writing of the Sixties,* Atheneum, 1970.

Southern, Terry, Richard Seaver, and Alexander Trocchi, editors, *Writers in Revolt,* Berkley, 1963.

Symons, Julian, *Critical Occasions,* Hamish Hamilton, 1966.

Vidal, Gore, *Reflections Upon a Sinking Ship,* Little, Brown, 1969.

Whitbread, Thomas B., *Seven Contemporary Authors,* University of Texas Press, 1966.

White, Emil, editor, *Henry Miller—Between Heaven and Hell: A Symposium,* privately printed, 1961.

Wickes, George, editor, *Henry Miller and the Critics,* Southern Illinois University Press, 1963.

Wickes, George, *Henry Miller,* University of Minnesota Press, 1966.

Widmer, Kingsley, *Henry Miller,* Twayne, 1963.

Writers at Work: The Paris Review Interviews, 2nd series, Viking, 1963.

PERIODICALS

American Literature, May, 1971.
American Quarterly, May, 1971.
American Review, April, 1976.
Arizona Quarterly, autumn, 1971.
Best Sellers, November, 1983.
Books and Bookmen, February, 1960, March, 1960, June, 1972.
Chicago Tribune, January 7, 1979.
Critique, spring-summer, 1965, Volume 20, number 3, 1979.
Globe and Mail (Toronto), April 16, 1988.
Life, July 6, 1959.
London Magazine, February, 1979, October, 1980.
Los Angeles Times Book Review, September 18, 1983, February 26, 1984, February 2, 1986.
New Republic, March 7, 1970.
Newsweek, February 18, 1963, March 2, 1970, November 15, 1976.
New York Review of Books, October 14, 1965.
New York Times, March 23, 1966, June 7, 1983, December 20, 1985, August 9, 1989.
New York Times Book Review, June 18, 1961, June 27, 1965, August 8, 1965, January 2, 1972, September 14, 1975, October 24, 1976, February 25, 1979, November 23, 1980, May 9, 1982, April 1, 1984, May 24, 1987, November 20, 1988.
Observer Review, September 24, 1967.
Partisan Review, Volume 44, number 4, 1977.
Playboy, September, 1964 (interview), November, 1971.
Prairie Schooner, summer, 1959.
Punch, October 7, 1970.
Saturday Review, June 19, 1965, December 11, 1971.
Show, July 9, 1970.
South Atlantic Quarterly, summer, 1966.
Spectator, August 25, 1984.
Studies in Short Fiction, winter, 1979.
Time, March 1, 1963.
Times (London), April 26, 1984.
Times Literary Supplement, February 11, 1965, December 16, 1965, June 16, 1966, November 10, 1966, July 10, 1969, October 10, 1980, October 5, 1984, October 18, 1985.
Tribune Books (Chicago), July 19, 1987.
Under the Sign of Pisces, fall, 1980.
Variety, March 4, 1970, March 10, 1971.
Village Voice, December 6, 1983.

Virginia Quarterly Review, spring, 1968, spring, 1975.
Washington Post, February 18, 1970.
Washington Post Book World, August 29, 1976, February 4, 1979, March 30, 1986.
Western Humanities Review, summer, 1970.

OBITUARIES:

PERIODICALS

Chicago Tribune, June 9, 1980.
Newsweek, June 23, 1980.
New York Times, June 9, 1980.
Publishers Weekly, June 20, 1980.
Time, June 16, 1980.
Times (London), June 9, 1980.
Washington Post, June 9, 1980.

—*Sketch by Kevin S. Hile*

*   *   *

MILLER, Ruth
See JACOBS, Ruth H.

*   *   *

MILLIGAN, Spike
See MILLIGAN, Terence Alan

*   *   *

MILLIGAN, Terence Alan   1918-
(Spike Milligan)

PERSONAL: Born April 16, 1918, in India; son of Leo Alphonso (an Army officer) and Florence Winifred (Kettleband) Milligan; married Margaret Patricia Ridgeway (died, 1978); children: one son, three daughters. *Religion:* Catholic. *Avocational interests:* Restoration of antiques, oil painting, watercolors, gardening, eating, drinking, talking, wine, and jazz.

ADDRESSES: Office—Spike Milligan Productions Ltd., 9 Orme Court, London W.2, England.

CAREER: Writer, actor, and artist. Originator of and writer for the radio program "The Goon Show," British Broadcasting Corp., 1951-60; appeared in British television programs "Show Called Fred," "World of Beachcomber," "Q5," "Curry and Chips," "Oh in Colour," "A Milligan for All Seasons," "There's a Lot of It About," and "Last Laugh before TV-AM"; has appeared in over 25 movies, including "The Running, Jumping, and Standing Still Film," "The Magic Christian," "The Three Musketeers," and "The Life of Brian"; has appeared in plays, including "Treasure Island" and "The Bedsitting Room." *Military service:* Served in the British Army during World War II.

AWARDS, HONORS: TV Writer of the Year Award, 1956.

WRITINGS:

ALL UNDER NAME SPIKE MILLIGAN

Silly Verse for Kids, Dobson, 1959.
(Self-illustrated) *A Dustbin of Milligan,* Dobson, 1961.
The Little Pot Boiler: A Book Based Freely on His Seasonal Overdraft, Dobson, 1963.
Puckoon (novel), Anthony Blond, 1963.
(With John Antrobus) *The Bedsitting Room* (play; first produced on West End at Mermaid Theatre, January, 1963), Hobbs, 1970.

A Book of Bits; or, A Bit of a Book, Dobson, 1965.

(With Carol Baker) *The Bald Twit Lion* (juvenile), Dobson, 1968.

(Self-illustrated) *A Book of Milliganimals* (juvenile), Dobson, 1968.

The Bedside Milligan; or, Read Your Way to Insomnia, Hobbs, 1969.

Values (poetry), Offcut Press, 1969.

(Editor with Jack Hobbs) *Milligan's Ark,* Hobbs, 1971.

The Goon Show Scripts, Woburn Press, 1972, St. Martin's, 1973.

More Goon Show Scripts, Woburn Press, 1973.

Adolf Hitler: My Part in His Downfall, M. Joseph, 1971.

Badjelly the Witch (juvenile), M. Joseph, 1971.

Small Dream of a Scorpion (poetry), M. Joseph, 1972.

Rommel: Gunner Who?, M. Joseph, 1974.

Dip the Puppy (juvenile), M. Joseph, 1974.

(With Joseph McGrath) *The Great McGonagall* (screenplay), Daritan Productions, 1974.

(Contributor) *Cricket's Choice,* Open Court, 1974.

(With Hobbs) *The Great McGonagall Scrapbook,* M. Joseph, 1975.

The Milligan Book of Records, Games, Cartoons, and Commercials, M. Joseph, 1975.

Transport of Delight, Penguin, 1975.

(With others) *The Book of the Goons,* Corgi Books, 1975.

Monty: His Part in My Victory, M. Joseph, 1976.

(With Hobbs) *William McGonagall: The Truth at Last,* M. Joseph, 1976.

(Narrator and co-author) *The Snow Goose* (recording; based on the novel by Paul Gallico), RCA Records, 1976.

The Spike Milligan Letters, edited by Norma Farnes, M. Joseph, 1977.

Mussolini: His Part in My Downfall, M. Joseph, 1978.

A Book of Goblins (juvenile), Hutchinson, 1978.

The Q Annual, M. Joseph, 1979.

Open Heart University (poetry), M. Joseph, 1979.

Get in the Q Annual, Hobbs, 1980.

(Narrator) *Adolf Hitler: My Part in His Downfall* (recording), Columbia Records, 1981.

Indefinite Articles and Scunthorpe, M. Joseph, 1981.

(Self-illustrated) *Unspun Socks from a Chicken's Laundry* (juvenile), M. Joseph, 1981.

Sir Nobunk and the Terrible, Awful, Dreadful, Naughty, Nasty Dragon (juvenile), M. Joseph, 1982.

Goon Cartoons, M. Joseph, 1982.

More Goon Cartoons, M. Joseph, 1983.

There's a Lot of It About, M. Joseph, 1983.

Melting Pot, Robson Books, 1983.

More Milligan Letters, edited by Farnes, M. Joseph, 1984.

Floored Masterpieces and Worse Verse, MacMillan, 1985.

Where Have All the Bullets Gone?, Penguin, 1986.

Further Transports of Delight, Penguin, 1986.

Goodbye Soldier, M. Joseph, 1986.

The Looney: An Irish Fantasy, M. Joseph, 1987.

The Lost Goon Shows, Robson Books, 1987.

Mirror Running, M. Joseph, 1987.

One Hundred and One Best and Only Limericks of Spike Milligan, Penguin, 1988.

Milligan's War: The Selected War Memoirs of Spike Milligan, M. Joseph, 1988.

(With Hobbs) *William McGonagall Meets George Gershwin,* M. Joseph, 1988.

That's Amazing, Ladybird Books, 1988.

OTHER

Also author of the plays *Oblomov* and *Son of Oblomov,* and of radio and television scripts.

MEDIA ADAPTATIONS: The Bedsitting Room was filmed in 1969; *Adolf Hitler: My Part in His Downfall* was filmed in 1972.

SIDELIGHTS: Spike Milligan is best known for "The Goon Show," a radio program that he, Peter Sellers, and Harry Secombe did for the British Broadcasting Corporation in the 1950's. "The Goon Show," a blend of satire, traditional radio comedy, and surrealist absurdity, was instantly popular and enjoyed a long run on the British airwaves. Involving the adventures of the Goons in their constant defense of the British Empire from nefarious threats, the show satirized many traditional British ideas and served as inspiration for a generation of British comedians. "Milligan created not simply a zany comedy format," L. E. Sissman writes in the *New Yorker,* "but a band of sturdy anti-heroes and a whole cycle of anti-epics, a series of audio Eddas, for them to star in. Typically, these sagas borrowed from the literature of Imperial Britain and turned it inside out." John Lennon, writing in the *New York Times Book Review,* remembers "The Goon Show" as "hipper than the Hippest and madder than 'Mad,' a conspiracy against reality. A 'coup d'etat' of the mind." Richard Ingrams of *Books & Bookmen* calls Milligan "one of the few really original comic geniuses of our time." Reviewing the book *The Goon Show Scripts,* John Wells writes in *New Statesman,* "If anyone has any doubt about the original genius of Milligan and his fellow performers [Peter] Sellers and [Harry] Secombe, or the extent to which they have dominated and inspired British jokes . . . I seriously urge them to buy [*The Goon Show Scripts*]."

BIOGRAPHICAL/CRITICAL SOURCES:

BOOKS

Farnes, Norma, editor, *The Spike Milligan Letters,* M. Joseph, 1977.

PERIODICALS

Antioch Review, fall, 1975.

Books & Bookmen, January, 1978.

Bookseller, May 15, 1971.

Film Quarterly, winter, 1971-1972.

Listener, August 8, 1968; December 7, 1978.

New Statesman, November 24, 1972.

New Yorker, December 24, 1973.

New York Times Book Review, September 30, 1973.

Observer, June 20, 1971; December 14, 1975; December 10, 1978.

Times Literary Supplement, November 24, 1972.

Village Voice, October 16, 1969.

*   *   *

MONACO, James 1942-

PERSONAL: Born November 15, 1942, in New York, NY; son of George C. (in the food industry) and Susanne (a social worker; maiden name, Hirschland) Monaco; married Susan Schenker (a writer and story analyst), October 24, 1976; children: Andrew, Charles, Margaret. *Education:* Muhlenberg College, B.A. (with honors), 1963; Columbia University, M.A. (with honors), 1964.

ADDRESSES: Home—New York, NY. *Office*—838 Broadway, New York, NY 10003. *Agent*—Virginia Barber Literary Agency, Inc., 353 West 21st St., New York, NY 10011.

CAREER: City University of New York, New York City, lecturer in literature, film, drama, and media at various colleges of university, 1964-70, chairman of University Center Search for Education, Elevation, and Knowledge (SEEK) Program, 1969; New School for Social Research, New York City, member of faculty, 1967. Adjunct professor of film and television at New York University, 1977. President of New York Zoetrope, Inc., 1977—; founder of James Monaco, Inc., 1980; founder and president of Baseline, Inc., 1982. Media commentator for National Public Radio (NPR), 1980-85; has appeared on various radio and television programs on National Broadcasting Co. (NBC) Radio, NBC-TV, Columbia Broadcasting System (CBS) FM Radio, CBS-TV, and other networks. Has participated in the production of several short films and videotapes. Chairman, Videotex Marketing Consortium; former vice- president of Village Green Recycling Team; member of New York City Solid Waste Task Force Advisory Committee. Consultant to publishers; speaks widely in the U.S. and Europe on media, film, and the information industry.

MEMBER: Writers Guild, Authors Guild, Authors League of America, Association of American Publishers, American Book Producers Association, Information Industry Association, Videotex Industry Association.

WRITINGS:

A Standard Glossary for Film Criticism, American Film Institute, 1970, 3rd edition, New York Zoetrope, 1975.
(With wife, Susan Schenker) *Books about Film: A Bibliographical Checklist,* American Film Institute, 1970, 3rd edition, New York Zoetrope, 1976.
(Contributor) Stanley Hochman, editor, *American Film Directors: A Library of Film Criticism,* Ungar, 1974.
Film: How and Where to Find Out What You Want to Know, Unicorn (Montreal), 1975.
The New Wave: Truffaut, Godard, Chabrol, Rohmer, Rivette, Oxford University Press, 1976.
How to Read a Film: The Art, Technology, Language, History and Theory of Film and Media, Oxford University Press, 1977, 2nd edition, 1981.
(Editor) *Media Culture: Television, Radio, Records, Books, Newspapers, Movies,* Dell, 1978.
(Editor) *Celebrity: The Media as Image Makers,* Dell, 1978.
Alain Resnais: The Role of Imagination, Secker & Warburg, 1978, Oxford University Press, 1979.
American Film Now: The People, the Power, the Money, the Movies, Oxford University Press/New American Library, 1979.
(Contributor) Don Allen, editor, *The Book of the Cinema,* Crown, 1979.
Who's Who in American Film Now, New York Zoetrope, 1981, 2nd edition, 1987.
The French Revolutionary Calendar, New York Zoetrope, 1983.
The Connoisseurs Guide to the Movies, Facts on File, 1985.
(Editor) *The Encyclopedia of Film,* Putnam, 1991.

Author of "New School" series of monographs, published by New School for Social Research (collected edition published by New York Zoetrope, 1975): *Francois Truffaut,* 1971; *Jean-Luc Godard,* 1972; *Federico Fellini,* 1972; *The New Wave,* 1972; *Recent British Films,* 1972; *Ingmar Bergman,* 1973; *Richard Lester,* 1973; *Stanley Kubrick,* 1973; *American Realism: Directions for the Seventies,* 1973. Contributor to *Cinema: A Critical Dictionary,* 1980, *The International TV and Video Guide,* 1983-88, *The Universal Almanac,* 1989, 1990, and *Almanac of American Salaries.* Contributor of articles to a variety of publications, including *New York Times, Village Voice, More: The Media Magazine,*

Cambridge Review, Film (London), and *Film Comment.* Associate editor, *Take One;* contributing editor, *More: The Media Magazine* and *Cineaste.*

SIDELIGHTS: "In *American Film Now: The People, the Power, the Money, the Movies* by James Monaco," writes Lisa Mitchell in the *Los Angeles Times,* "those seriously interested in the state of film-making today can discover not only what/who makes the present systems run, but more to the point, how the precise business mechanics of it all run the art (or death of it) on the screen. Monaco juggles an impressive amount of detailed, practical information with intelligence, wit and a vervy style that keeps all the material buoyant."

The title of this book, according to *Chicago Tribune Book World* reviewer Larry McMurtry, "is an accurate index to its ambition. It is a cool, thoroughly researched, intelligent, and comprehensive survey of the American film industry; it manages to be current almost to the end of 1978, and since its intent is little short of encyclopedic it runs by far the larger risk."

Many of Monaco's books have been translated into foreign languages, including German, Dutch, Italian, Chinese, Japanese, and Farsi.

BIOGRAPHICAL/CRITICAL SOURCES:

PERIODICALS

Chicago Tribune Book World, May 20, 1979.
Los Angeles Times, June 17, 1979.
New York Times Book Review, August 29, 1976; October 16, 1977; July 9, 1978; April 1, 1979.
Publishers Weekly, April 20, 1984.

*   *   *

MONACO, Richard 1940-
(Dwight Robhs)

PERSONAL: Born April 23, 1940, in New York, NY; son of Vincent G. (a musician) and Mae (a dancer; maiden name, Bottinelli) Monaco; married Judy Jacobs (a poet), August 15, 1967 (divorced, 1978); married Adele Leone (an editor and agent), March 5, 1983; children: Darsi Adele. *Education:* Attended Columbia University, 1966-70.

ADDRESSES: Agent—Adele Leone Agency, Inc., 26 Nantucket Pl., Scarsdale, NY 10583.

CAREER: Columbia University, New York City, assistant to directors of Group for Contemporary Music, 1966-68, curator of music, 1967-68; WBAI-FM, New York City, co-host of "New York Poetry" series, 1968-69; editor of *New York Poetry,* 1969-70; New School for Social Research, New York City, member of faculty, 1973—; Mercy College, Westchester, NY, member of faculty, 1975—; Adele Leone Agency, Inc., New York City, executive vice- president, 1979—.

Co-director, "Contemporary Concert: Composition and Improvisation" (music group), 1974—. Visiting lecturer at New York University, 1974; lecturer at Regenesis (experimental school for adults), Westchester, 1977—. Co-host, "The Logic of Poetry" series and "Poetry P.M.," WNYC-FM, New York City, 1975—.

MEMBER: International Poetry Society, Writer's Guild of America, American Society of Composers, Authors, and Publishers.

WRITINGS:

New American Poetry, McGraw, 1973.

(With John Briggs) *The Logic of Poetry,* McGraw, 1974.

(Contributor) Rubin Gregory, editor, *Ipso Facto* (anthology), Hub Publications, 1975.

Parsival; or, A Knight's Tale, Macmillan, 1977.

"The Realities of the Business," produced in New York City at the Whitney Museum of American Art, 1978.

The Grail War, Simon & Schuster, 1979.

The Final Quest, Putnam, 1980.

The Cult Candidate, Sphere Books, 1982.

(Contributor) Terri Windling and Mark Alan Arnold, editors, *Elsewhere,* Volume II, Ace Books, 1982.

Runes, Ace Books, 1984.

Broken Stone, Ace Books, 1985.

Blood and Dreams, Berkley Publishing, 1985.

Journey to the Flame, Bantam, 1985.

Unto the Beast, Bantam, 1987.

Also author of play "Parsival," based on his book of the same title; also author of a libretto for opera, "The Politics of Harmony," 1968; also author of screenplays for Warner Brothers, MGM, and other film companies. Also contributor to John Skipp and Craig Spector, editors, *Book of the Dead II,* Bantam; also contributor to anthologies. Contributor to periodicals, including *Saturday Review.* Founding editor, *Contemporary Music Newsletter,* 1967; poetry and fiction editor, *University Review,* 1969-70.

WORK IN PROGRESS: The Lost Years, for Bantam.

SIDELIGHTS: Richard Monaco's *Parsival; or, A Knight's Tale, The Grail War,* and *The Final Quest* all concern the legend of King Arthur and the search for the Holy Grail. Monaco tells *Library Journal* that he first read the tale of the priceless relic in college and "the gist of the story made a deep impression. Somehow, everything I knew seemed to be there, in the inexplicable metaphor of it: the search, discovery, loss; the painful process of becoming hardened to life, the reawakening of innocence and love when it seemed forever buried, what had grown stiff and flat opening into deep and fluid vistas of discovery; the endless, rich joy of it, which is always possible whenever you look at life as if for the first time without past or future, as the lover who never tires of the play and unfolding of his love."

Reviewer Roger C. Schlobin observes in *Fantasy Newsletter* that the three books, written in stream-of-consciousness style, are "not for the weak-hearted, the easily offended, or the easily confused." Schlobin explains that "Monaco presents dark, tormented tales filled with images of blood, viscera, excrement, and lust" instead of "the dignity, chivalry, nobility, and epic emotions traditionally associated with Arthurian fiction."

Although Michele Turin of *Best Sellers* finds *Parsival* "slightly perverse" and suited for "the most ghoulish of tastes," she also believes that "it is upsettingly effective in transporting us back to the days of Arthur." The *Booklist* reviewer concurs, noting that "Monaco weaves the legendary spell of Arthurian romance with a rougher sensibility of the medieval realities of hardship and cruelty." In *Library Journal,* M. L. del Mastro applauds Monaco's realistic representation of characters in *The Holy Grail,* describing them as "fully human and three-dimensional. They obey or defy God . . . , suffer and love, respond and grow or refuse and shrivel, and thus come to their proper fulfillment, and to new beginnings through their experiences."

BIOGRAPHICAL/CRITICAL SOURCES:

PERIODICALS

Best Sellers, February, 1978.

Booklist, February 15, 1978.

Fantasy Newsletter, March, 1981.

Library Journal, October 1, 1977; October 1, 1979.

* * *

MORAVIA, Alberto
See PINCHERLE, Alberto

* * *

MUGGERIDGE, Malcolm (Thomas) 1903-1990

PERSONAL: Born March 24, 1903, in Sanderstead, Surrey, England; died November 14, 1990; son of Henry Thomas (a member of Parliament) and Annie (Booler) Muggeridge; married Katherine Dobbs, September, 1927; children: three sons, one daughter. *Education:* Selwyn College, Cambridge, M.A., 1923. *Religion:* Roman Catholic.

ADDRESSES: Home—Park Cottage, Robertsbridge, East Sussex, England.

CAREER: Union Christian College, South India, teacher, 1924-27; teacher in Minia, Egypt, 1927; Egyptian University, Cairo, Egypt, lecturer, 1927-30; *Manchester Guardian,* Manchester, England, editorial staff member, 1930-32, correspondent in Moscow, 1932-33; affiliated with International Labor Office, Geneva, Switzerland, 1933-34; *Calcutta Statesman,* Calcutta, India, assistant editor, 1934-35; *Evening Standard,* London, England, editorial staff member, 1935-36; *Daily Telegraph,* London, correspondent in Washington, D.C., 1946-47, deputy editor, 1950-52; television interviewer for "Panorama," 1951; *Punch,* London, editor, 1953-57; University of Edinburgh, Edinburgh, Scotland, rector, 1967-68. *Military service:* British Army, 1939-45, served in Intelligence Corps; became major; received Legion of Honor, Croix de Guetre with Palm, and Medaille de la Reconnaissance Francaise.

AWARDS, HONORS: Christopher Book Award, 1972, for *Something Beautiful for God,* and 1979, for *A Twentieth Century Testimony.*

WRITINGS:

Autumnal Faces (novel), Putnam, 1931.

Three Flats (three-act play), Putnam, 1931.

Winter in Moscow (novel), Little, Brown, 1934, new edition, Eerdmans, 1988.

(Translator) Maurice Bedel, *New Arcadia,* J. Cape, 1935.

The Earnest Atheist: A Study of Samuel Butler, Eyre & Spottiswoode, 1936, published as *A Study of Samuel Butler: The Earnest Atheist,* Putnam, 1937.

(With Hugh Kingsmill) *Brave Old World,* Eyre & Spottiswoode, 1936.

(With Kingsmill) *A Preview of Next Year's News,* Eyre & Spottiswoode, 1937.

In a Valley of This Restless Mind, Routledge & Kegan Paul, 1938.

The Sun Never Sets: The Story of England in the Nineteen Thirties, Random House, 1940, published in England as *The Thirties: 1930-1940 in Great Britain,* Hamish Hamilton, 1940, reprinted, Weidenfeld & Nicolson, 1989.

(Editor) Galeazzo Ciano, *Ciano's Diary, 1939-1943,* Heinemann, 1947.

(Editor) Ciano, *Ciano's Diplomatic Papers: Being a Record of Nearly 200 Conversations Held During the Years 1936-42 with Hitler,* Odhams, 1948.

Affairs of the Heart, Hamish Hamilton, 1949.

(With Hesketh Pearson) *About Kingsmill,* Methuen, 1951.

(Author of introduction) Ciano, *Diary, 1937-38,* Methuen, 1952, published as *Hidden Diary, 1937,* Dutton, 1953.

(Author of introduction) *Esquire's World of Humor,* Arthur Barker, 1965.

The Most of Malcolm Muggeridge, Simon & Schuster, 1966.

Tread Softly, for You Tread on My Jokes, Collins, 1966.

London a la Mode, Hill & Wang, 1966.

Muggeridge Through the Microphone: BBC Radio and Television, British Broadcasting Corp., 1967.

Jesus Rediscovered, Doubleday, 1969.

(With others) *What They Believe,* Hodder & Stoughton, 1969.

Something Beautiful for God: Mother Teresa of Calcutta, Harper, 1971.

(With Alec Vidler) *Paul: Envoy Extraordinary,* Harper, 1972.

Malcolm's Choice: A Collection of Cartoons, Mowbrays, 1972.

Chronicles of Wasted Time (autobiography), Morrow, Volume I: *The Green Stick,* 1973, Volume II: *The Infernal Grove,* 1974.

Jesus: The Man Who Lives, Harper, 1975.

A Third Testament, Little, Brown, 1976.

Christ and the Media, Eerdmans, 1977.

Things Past, Collins, 1978, Morrow, 1979.

A Twentieth Century Testimony, Collins, 1979.

The End of Christendom, Eerdmans, 1980.

Like It Was (diaries), edited by John Bright-Holmes, Collins, 1981.

(With others) *Christian Married Love,* Ignatius Press, 1981.

(With William Douglas-Home) *P. G. Woodhouse: Three Talks and a Few Words at a Festive Occasion,* Heineman, 1983.

My Life in Pictures (autobiographical text with photographs), Morrow, 1987.

Picture Palace (novel), Weidenfeld & Nicolson, 1987.

Confessions of a Twentieth-Century Pilgrim, Harper, 1988.

Conversion: A Spiritual Journey, Collins, 1988.

Contributor to magazines and newspapers, including *Ladies' Home Journal, Esquire, Horizon, Christianity Today, Reader's Digest,* and *Observer Review.*

SIDELIGHTS: Malcolm Muggeridge was a journalist, a magazine editor, a university rector, a novelist, and a familiar figure on British television. In all his roles, he was an outspoken, articulate, and controversial figure. As David Lodge notes in the *New York Times Book Review,* "Malcolm Muggeridge is famous for being Malcolm Muggeridge, scourge of liberalism, sardonic iconoclast, spiritual pilgrim." A socialist in his younger days, Muggeridge at one time was an avowed atheist. After a revelatory stint in Stalinist Moscow, however, he was to eschew socialism and find God. In some thirty books, Muggeridge displayed a talent for stinging satire, controversial opinions, and elegant prose.

Muggeridge first desired to become a writer while he was attending Selwyn College, Cambridge. After a few years teaching in India and Egypt, he launched his career in journalism with the *Manchester Guardian,* serving initially as the newspaper's Cairo correspondent. Appointed the *Guardian*'s Moscow correspondent in 1932, Muggeridge and his wife went to the city with the intention of settling down in the Soviet Union, then considered by many leftists as a utopia in the making. They even spoke of becoming citizens. Muggeridge's father had been an outspoken socialist, while his wife was the niece of prominent Fabian Socialists Beatrice and Sidney Webb. The couple arrived in Moscow with high hopes, but their experience was a bitter one. Life for the average Soviet citizen was intolerable. Food shortages, police surveillance, and the brutal policies of the regime disillu-

sioned Muggeridge with communist utopianism. He also became disillusioned with the Western correspondents based in the Soviet Union, whom he felt were whitewashing the truth. Many of the journalists were, Muggeridge found, more than eager to submit to Soviet censorship in exchange for the regime's special privileges.

When his editor at the *Manchester Guardian* refused to run an exclusive story on the Russian famine of the early 1930s—a famine deliberately caused by Soviet dictator Joseph Stalin to punish the rebellious Ukraine, claiming over 14 million lives—Muggeridge angrily resigned his post. He then set about documenting the atrocity in his satirical novel, *Winter in Moscow.* A critic for the *Saturday Review of Literature* found Muggeridge's account to be refreshing: "There is such a thing as wholesome indignation, and there has been so much leaning over backward to be fair to Russia's present dictators, so much pussy-footing and 'on-the-other-hand' stuff, let alone downright misrepresentation, that it is refreshing to come across an intelligent observer who is just plain disgusted all through and doesn't give a hoot who knows it." Reviewing the book for *National Review* in 1988, William F. Buckley, Jr., finds it "mordant satire, to be sure, written out of an abyss of desolate cynicism, but Muggeridge renders it all with a vividness that is constantly believable." Buckley concludes, "An angrier book has never been written, nor one whose fury was so richly justified by its contents."

Another novel written at this time, *Picture Palace,* was meant as a satirical attack on the *Manchester Guardian* and what Muggeridge saw as that newspaper's acquiescence to Soviet tyranny. He also satirized the hypocritical liberalism of the newspaper's editor, C. P. Scott. The *Guardian* threatened legal action if the book were published, and Muggeridge's publisher suppressed the manuscript. *Picture Palace* was only published in 1987. Reviewing the book for the Toronto *Globe and Mail,* David Twiston Davies remarks that "the book's place in legend is due to the dramatic story of its suppression, rather than its quality, which has been hidden until now." Davies notes that Muggeridge's "picture of the domineering, self-deluding editor- proprietor, old Savoury [C. P. Scott], is worthy of hanging alongside [Evelyn] Waugh's Lord Copper."

After leaving the Soviet Union, Muggeridge worked for a time on the staffs of the *Calcutta Statesman* and the London *Evening Standard.* He also turned out a steady stream of books, including a study of Samuel Butler and a history of Great Britain in the 1930's. His biography of Butler, *The Earnest Atheist: A Study of Samuel Butler,* provided a new perspective on that author, but many critics were dismayed by Muggeridge's lack of objectivity. " 'The Earnest Atheist' is written from a depth of loathing and horror. As a result it is less objective than a study has a right to be. Allowing for the prejudice, however, it must be admitted that Mr. Muggeridge has succeeded in building up a strong case to prove that far from being the Anti-Victorian a future generation believed him to be, Butler was the Ultimate Victorian," Frances Winwar noted in the *New York Times.* Muggeridge's survey of England in the 1930's, *The Sun Never Sets,* makes no attempt at impartiality, either. "The book crackles with wit, it outdoes earlier only-yesterday studies with its cutting, flashing style, its glittering satire. Its epigrams fairly cry for quotations," observed R. H. Phelps. However, R. H. S. Crossman cautioned that "judged . . . as entertainment, [the book] is to be recommended; judged as a serious estimate of our age, it is clever, hysterical and defeatist, sacrificing truth for the sake of an epigram."

When World War II broke out, Muggeridge joined the Intelligence Corps, serving in East Africa, Italy, and France. During this time he became acquainted with Graham Greene and double agent Kim Philby. Although Muggeridge respected some of the British intelligence operations, by and large he felt that spying was a mockery. At one time he was so depressed by his espionage activities that he considered suicide. This period of his life is discussed in volume two of his autobiography, *The Infernal Grove.* In this book Muggeridge aims his lethal wit at the cult of intelligence, concluding that "diplomats and intelligence agents, in my experience, are even bigger liars than journalists."

Following a stint as Washington correspondent and deputy editor for the *Daily Telegraph,* Muggeridge was appointed editor of *Punch,* Britain's oldest humor magazine. From 1953-57 he worked as editor of *Punch,* encouraging such writers as Noel Coward, Lord Dunsany, Joyce Cary, J. B. Priestley, and Dorothy L. Sayers to contribute to the magazine. His acerbic editorials and clever parodies usually took aim at postwar England's Labor government, the strict food rationing then enforced (a carryover from the war), and other popular targets. A series of parodies of other magazines also proved popular. London's *World's Press News* cited him for putting "new life and new bite into this famous weekly magazine, [and] for courageously publishing some of the most controversial cartoons of the year." Perhaps the most controversial cartoon was a depiction of Winston Churchill as a blind man, which drew particularly heavy fire.

In the 1950's Muggeridge also became a familiar figure to the British television audience, conducting interviews with notable personalities, hosting travel documentaries on India, Israel, and the Soviet Union, as well as appearing on a number of special programs for BBC-TV. Critics compare his television writing to the best of his printed work. Here, too, however, Muggeridge could not avoid controversy. In the mid-1960s his remarks about the British monarchy, particularly the queen, almost cost him his broadcasting career. His televised attack on heart transplant pioneer Dr. Christiaan Barnard caused him to be banned from South African television. Yet, viewers consistently enjoyed his work. In 1981 the BBC ran "Muggeridge Revisited," a series featuring the best of his three decades of television interviews, while some of his television commentaries have been collected in *Muggeridge Through the Microphone: BBC Radio and Television.*

Although Muggeridge frequently appeared on the screen, he often inveighed against television and the media. In 1953 he called for an end to the BBC monopoly of British television, warning in a *Time* article that those who appear on BBC "must be prepared to blow their trumpets or sound their cymbals or scratch their violins in accordance with the Corporation's baton." In an article for the *Observer Review,* he writes: "I see the camera, far more than even nuclear weapons, as the great destructive force of our time; the great falsifier. McLuhan is right; it's replaced the written and spoken word, captured the whole field of art and literature." Nonetheless, Muggeridge went on, he appears on television because "I may find an opportunity to say something, or convey something, which is worth while. . . . Supposing one was a pianist in a whorehouse—one might be able to persuade oneself that occasionally including a hymn like 'Abide with Me' in one's repertoire would have a beneficial influence on the inmates."

Muggeridge credited two programs that he did for the BBC with pushing him to convert to Christianity. In 1967 he filmed a program at a Cistercian abbey in Nunraw, Scotland. Reflecting on the time spent at the monastery, he penned these lines: "No heavenly visitation befell me, there was no Damascus Road grace; and yet, I know, life will never be quite the same after my three weeks with the Cistercians at Nunraw." Not long after-

wards Muggeridge traveled to the Holy Land to film a documentary for the BBC, and it was there that a heavenly vision did befall him. Later he discussed his revelation: "I realized, in the first place, that many shrines, and the legends associated with them, were, for the most part, from my point of view, as fraudulent as the bones of St. Peter, the fragments of the True Cross, and other relics revered by the pious. Then, seeing a party of Christian pilgrims at one of these shrines, their faces so bright with faith, their voices, as they sang, so evidently and joyously aware of their Saviour's nearness, I understood that for them the shrine was authentic. Their faith made it so. Similarly, I, too, became aware that there really had been a man, Jesus, who was also God; I was conscious of his presence."

Of course, a long series of events led up to Muggeridge's conversion to Christianity. These events are recounted in his book, *Jesus Rediscovered.* He first learned about religion from his father, an agnostic whose religion was socialism. When Muggeridge lost faith in socialism in the early 1930's, he also lost any faith that man could make a heaven on earth. Reading the works of such religious figures as St. Augustine, John Bunyan, Pascal, and Tolstoi gave him valuable insights into Christianity. In many ways Muggeridge was far from an orthodox Christian. As he explained in *Jesus Rediscovered,* he believes that Christ is a living force, but he does not believe in the Resurrection. He has no interest in dogma and dislikes institutional religion. He also excoriates church leaders who concentrate on social issues rather than the teachings of Jesus.

Critics generally considered *Jesus Rediscovered* to be a significant book on religion. "This will be one of the widely read books of the religious year. . . . You will be satisfied that your time was well spent with some of the major issues that govern the last part of the 20th century," David Poling remarked. Similarly, Michael Novak observed: "This is an important book for Christianity. It sounds a deep, true note that has been missing from the chorus, a note without which everything else is off." Although Jeffrey Hart found Muggeridge's sense of Christ "convincing and moving," Harvey Cox perceived some un-Christian attitudes in the book: "It is lacking in love, short on hope, and almost completely devoid of charity. The Jesus he has rediscovered is not one I want to follow. Yet Muggeridge himself remains an irresistible old codger."

In the first two volumes of *Chronicles of Wasted Time,* a projected three-volume autobiography, Muggeridge outlined the course of his early life. Critical reaction to the books has been generally favorable, with M. D. Aeschliman in *National Review* claiming that Muggeridge's "autobiographical writings contain some of the greatest and sanest writing in English in our time." Writing in the *New York Times Book Review,* Paul Johnson finds that "next to the late Evelyn Waugh, [Muggeridge] is, in my view, the finest writer of English prose of his generation." Muggeridge's published diaries have also brought his personal life into the public arena, giving his readers a glimpse into how he changed from a socialist atheist to a conservative Christian. Lodge notes that "one thing these diaries do is to scotch any suggestion that Malcolm Muggeridge's commitment to Christian asceticism is an old man's conversion. His yearning for spiritual peace, his effort to deny worldly desires in order to attain the serenity of the mystics, is a motif that runs through the pages."

Living quietly in the English countryside with his wife of sixty years, Muggeridge worked on the third volume of his autobiography. When Alan Watkins of the London *Times* visited Muggeridge in 1983, he noted that the author "loves talk for its own sake, as a good in itself" and enjoys telling anecdotes from his long and varied career. In a piece for the London *Times,* Muggeridge observed: "Human life, I have come to feel, in all its public or collective manifestations, is only theatre, and mostly cheap melodrama at that. There is nothing serious under the sun except love; of fellow-mortals and of God."

BIOGRAPHICAL/CRITICAL SOURCES:

BOOKS

Authors in the News, Volume 1, Gale, 1976.
Hunter, Ian, *Malcolm Muggeridge: A Life,* Nelson, 1980.
Mortimer, John Clifford, *In Character,* Penguin, 1984.
Muggeridge, Malcolm, *Chronicles of Wasted Time,* Morrow, Volume I: *The Green Stick,* 1973, Volume II: *The Infernal Grove,* 1974.
Muggeridge, Malcolm, *My Life in Pictures,* Morrow, 1987.

PERIODICALS

America, November 6, 1971, March 4, 1978.
Best Sellers, July 1, 1966, October 1, 1969, November 1, 1971.
Books and Bookmen, June, 1971.
Book Week, July 3, 1966.
Boston Transcript, May 11, 1940.
Christian Century, October 22, 1969, November 24, 1971.
Christian Science Monitor, September 26, 1934, April 7, 1937, June 29, 1940, August 2, 1966.
Economist, September 22, 1973.
Globe and Mail (Toronto), August 29, 1987, July 9, 1988.
Listener, December 7, 1967.
Nation, April 3, 1937.
National Review, December 2, 1969, December 19, 1975, February 19, 1988, March 4, 1988, September 30, 1988.
New Republic, May 5, 1937, May 27, 1940, October 27, 1973, August 23, 1974, July 18-25, 1983.
New Statesman and Nation, December 12, 1931, August 29, 1936, March 9, 1940, September 29, 1972, September 21, 1973, October 17, 1975.
Newsweek, September 9, 1957, July 19, 1965, January 29, 1968, September 8, 1969, July 22, 1974.
New York Herald Tribune Books, October 30, 1932, March 14, 1937.
New York Post, May 12, 1934.
New York Review of Books, December 29, 1966.
New York Times, September 11, 1932, March 14, 1937, June 16, 1940.
New York Times Book Review, March 5, 1961, September 7, 1969, November 14, 1971, May 7, 1972, September 30, 1973, July 14, 1974, February 21, 1982.
New York Times Magazine, April 29, 1956.
Observer Review, August 20, 1967, December 15, 1968.
Saturday Review, May 24, 1934, August 30, 1969.
Saturday Review of Literature, June 9, 1934, May 4, 1940.
Spectator, December 12, 1931, March 9, 1934, September 11, 1936.
Time, March 8, 1937, August 3, 1953, January 6, 1967, January 26, 1968, September 26, 1969, August 5, 1974.
Times (London), March 21, 1983.
Times Literary Supplement, December 10, 1931, March 15, 1934, September 5, 1936, March 9, 1940, July 24, 1969, March 31, 1972, September 29, 1972, September 28, 1973, September 12, 1975, May 1, 1981.
Variety, September 3, 1969.
Washington Post Book World, October 12, 1969, December 26, 1971.
Washington Star-News, February 18, 1975.

World's Press News (London), December 31, 1954.

—*Sketch by Thomas Wiloch*

* * *

MUNRO, Alice 1931-

PERSONAL: Born July 10, 1931, in Wingham, Ontario, Canada; daughter of Robert Eric (a farmer) and Ann (Chamney) Laidlaw; married James Munro (a bookseller), December 29, 1951 (divorced, 1976); married Gerald Fremlin (a geographer), 1976; children: (first marriage) Sheila, Jenny, Andrea. *Education:* University of Western Ontario, B.A., 1952. *Politics:* New Democratic Party. *Religion:* Unitarian Universalist.

ADDRESSES: Home—Clinton, Ontario, Canada.

CAREER: Writer. Artist-in-residence, University of Western Ontario, 1974-75, and University of British Columbia, 1980.

MEMBER: Writers Union of Canada.

AWARDS, HONORS: Governor General's Literary Award, 1969, for *Dance of the Happy Shades,* and 1986, for *The Progress of Love;* Canadian Bookseller's Award, 1972, for *Lives of Girls and Women;* Canada-Australia Literary Prize, 1974; D.Litt., University of Western Ontario, 1976.

WRITINGS:

Dance of the Happy Shades (short stories), Ryerson, 1968.
Lives of Girls and Women (novel), McGraw, 1971.
Something I've Been Meaning to Tell You (short stories), McGraw, 1974.
Who Do You Think You Are?, Macmillan (Toronto), 1978, published as *The Beggar Maid: Stories of Flo and Rose,* Penguin, 1984.
The Moons of Jupiter, Macmillan (Toronto), 1982, Knopf, 1983.
The Progress of Love, McClelland & Stewart, 1986.

TELEVISION SCRIPTS

"A Trip to the Coast," Canadian Broadcasting Corp. (CBC), 1973.
"Thanks for the Ride," CBC, 1973.
"How I Met My Husband," CBC, 1974.
"1847: The Irish," CBC, 1978.

CONTRIBUTOR

Canadian Short Stories, second series, Oxford University Press, 1968.
Sixteen by Twelve: Short Stories by Canadian Writers, Ryerson, 1970.
The Narrative Voice: Stories and Reflections by Canadian Authors, McGraw, 1972.
74: New Canadian Stories, Oberon, 1974.
The Play's the Thing, Macmillan (Toronto), 1976.
Here and Now, Oberon, 1977.
Personal Fictions, Oxford University Press, 1977.
Night Light: Stories of Aging, Oxford University Press, 1986.

Contributor to *Canadian Forum, Queen's Quarterly, Chatelaine, Grand Street, New Yorker,* and other publications.

SIDELIGHTS: Usually concerned with characters living in the small towns of southwestern Ontario, the stories of Alice Munro present "ordinary experiences so that they appear extraordinary, invested with a kind of magic," according to Catherine Sheldrick Ross in the *Dictionary of Literary Biography.* "Few people writing today," Beverley Slopen claims in *Publishers Weekly,* "can bring a character, a mood or a scene to life with such economy. And she has an exhilarating ability to make the reader see the familiar with fresh insight and compassion."

In a review of *Dance of the Happy Shades,* Martin Levin writes that "the short story is alive and well in Canada, where most of the fifteen tales originate like fresh winds from the North. Alice Munro," he continues, "creates a solid habitat for her fiction—southwestern Ontario, a generation or more in the past—and is in sympathetic vibration with the farmers and townspeople who live there." Peter Prince calls the stories in this collection "beautifully controlled and precise. And always this precision appears unstrained. The proportions so exactly fit the writer's thematic aims that in almost every case it seems that really no other words could have been used, certainly no more or less." Ronald Blythe believes that "the stories are all to do with discovering personal freedom within an accepted curtailment. There is no intentional nostalgia although, strangely enough, one frequently finds oneself rather wistfully caught up in some of the scenes so perfectly evoked; and there is no distortion in the characterisation."

Reviewing *Something I've Been Meaning to Tell You,* Kildare Dobbs writes: "Readers who enjoyed the earlier books because they confirmed the reality of the Canadian small town experience for a certain generation, or because they seemed to reinforce some of the ideology of the women's movement, will find more of the same. But they will find something else, too. There is a hint at hermetic concerns in the first story, ironic suggestions of a quest for the grail. . . . All the stories are told with the skill which the author has perfected over the years, narrated with meticulous precision in a voice that is unmistakeably Ontarian in its lack of emphasis, its sly humour and willingness to live with a mystery." Joyce Carol Oates finds that the reader will be "most impressed by the feeling behind [Alice Munro's] stories—the evocation of emotions, ranging from bitter hatred to love, from bewilderment and resentment to awe. In all her work there is an effortless, almost conversational tone, and we know we are in the presence of an art that works to conceal itself, in order to celebrate its subject."

Speaking to Mervyn Rothstein of the *New York Times,* Munro explains: "I never intended to be a short-story writer. . . . I started writing them because I didn't have time to write anything else—I had three children. And then I got used to writing stories, so I saw my material that way, and now I don't think I'll ever write a novel."

BIOGRAPHICAL/CRITICAL SOURCES:

BOOKS

Authors in the News, Volume 2, Gale, 1976.
Contemporary Literary Criticism, Gale, Volume 6, 1976, Volume 10, 1979, Volume 1981, Volume 50, 1988.
Dahlie, Hallvard, *Alice Munro and Her Works,* ECW Press, 1985.
Dictionary of Literary Biography, Volume 53: *Canadian Writers since 1960,* Gale, 1986.
MacKendrick, Louis K., editor, *Probable Fictions: Alice Munro's Narrative Acts,* ECW Press, 1984.
Martin, W. R., *Alice Munro,* University of Alberta Press, 1987.

PERIODICALS

Canadian Forum, February, 1969.
Listener, June 13, 1974.
Maclean's, September 22, 1986.
New Statesman, May 3, 1974.
New York Times, November 10, 1986.
New York Times Book Review, September 23, 1973.
Ontario Review, fall, 1974.
Publishers Weekly, August 22, 1986.
Saturday Night, July, 1974.
Time, January 15, 1973.

*   *   *

MYLES, Symon
  See FOLLETT, Ken(neth Martin)

N

NAGEL, Stuart S(amuel) 1934-

PERSONAL: Born August 29, 1934, in Chicago, IL; son of Leo I. (a store owner) and Florence (Pritikin) Nagel; married Joyce Golub, September 1, 1957; children: Brenda Ellen, Robert Franklin. *Education:* Attended University of Chicago, 1955; Northwestern University, B.S., 1957, J.D., 1958, Ph.D., 1961. *Politics:* Democratic Party. *Religion:* Jewish.

ADDRESSES: Home—1720 Park Haven, Champaign, IL 61820. *Office*—Department of Political Science, University of Illinois at Urbana- Champaign, Urbana, IL 61801.

CAREER: Pennsylvania State University, University Park, instructor in political science, 1960-61; University of Arizona, Tucson, assistant professor of political science, 1961-62; University of Illinois at Urbana- Champaign, assistant professor, 1962-64, associate professor, 1965-67, professor of political science, 1968—, member of University Research Board, 1962—. Visiting fellow, National Institute of Law Enforcement and Criminal Justice, U.S. Department of Justice, 1974-75. Occasional part-time general legal practice, 1958—; assistant counsel, U.S. Senate Subcommittee on Administrative Practice, Washington, DC, 1966; trial attorney, National Labor Relations Board, Chicago, IL, 1966; attorney and director, Office of Economic Opportunity Legal Services Agency, Champaign, IL, 1966-70. Consultant to government agencies, commercial research firms, and university research bureaus.

MEMBER: International Association for Philosophy of Law and Social Philosophy, International Academy of Forensic Psychology (member of board of governors, 1971—), Policy Studies Organization (secretary-treasurer), Law and Society Association, American Bar Association, American Political Science Association, Midwest Political Science Association.

AWARDS, HONORS: Research grants from Illinois Center for Education in Politics, 1963, American Council of Learned Societies, 1964-65, Center for Advanced Study in the Behavioral Sciences, 1964-65, East-West Center of Hawaii, 1965, National Science Foundation, 1970-73, and Ford Foundation, 1975-79; Russell Sage research fellow, Yale Law School, 1970-71.

WRITINGS:

(Editor) *Evaluation Charts on Delay in Administrative Proceedings,* U.S. Government Printing Office, 1966.

(Editor) *Questionnaire Survey on Delay in Administrative Proceedings,* U.S. Government Printing Office, 1966.
The Legal Process from a Behavioral Perspective, Dorsey, 1969.
(Editor) *Law and Social Change,* Sage Publications, 1970.
(Editor) *New Trends in Law and Politics Research,* Law & Society Association, 1971.
(Editor) *The Rights of the Accused in Law and Action,* Sage Publications, 1972.
(Editor) *Basic Facilities and Institutions in Policy Studies,* Policy Studies Organization, 1972.
(Editor) *Basic Issues and References in Policy Studies,* Policy Studies Organization, 1972.
(Editor) *Environmental Policy and Political Science Fields,* Policy Studies Organization, 1973.
(Editor) *Interdisciplinary Approaches to Policy Studies,* Policy Studies Organization, 1973.
(Editor) *Policy Studies around the World,* Policy Studies Organization, 1973.
(Editor) *Law and Social Change,* Sage Publications, 1973.
Comparing Elected and Appointed Judicial Systems, Sage Publications, 1973.
Minimizing Costs and Maximizing Benefits in Providing Legal Services to the Poor, Sage Publications, 1973.
Policy Studies Directory, Policy Studies Organization, 1973, revised edition (with Marian Neef), 1976.
(Editor) *Environmental Politics,* Praeger, 1974.
(Editor) *Policy Studies and the Social Sciences,* Heath, 1975.
(Editor) *Policy Studies in America and Elsewhere,* Heath, 1975.
Improving the Legal Process, Heath, 1975.
(Editor) *Political Science Utilization Directory,* Policy Studies Organization, 1975.
(With Neef) *Operations Research Methods,* Sage Publications, 1976.
The Applications of Mixed Strategies: Civil Rights and Other Multi- Activity Policies, Sage Publications, 1976.
(Editor) *Modeling the Criminal Justice System,* Sage Publications, 1977.
Legal Policy Analysis, Heath, 1977.
Legal Process Modeling, Sage Publications, 1977.
(Editor) *Policy Studies Review Annual,* Sage Publications, 1977.
(Editor with Neef) *Policy Studies Grants Directory,* Policy Studies Organization, 1977.
Too Much or Too Little Policy: The Example of Pretrial Release, Sage Publications, 1977.

Decision Theory and the Legal Process, Heath, 1978.

Policy Analysis: In Social Science Research, Sage Publications, 1978.

(Editor) *Policy Research Centers Directory,* Policy Studies Organization, 1978.

(Editor with Nancy Munshaw) *Policy Studies Personnel Directory,* Policy Studies Organization, 1979.

(Editor) *Improving Policy Analysis,* Sage Publications, 1980.

(Editor) *Policy Publishers and Associations Directory,* Policy Studies Organization, 1980.

The Policy Studies Handbook, Lexington Books, 1980.

Policy Evaluation: Making Optimum Decisions, Praeger, 1982.

(Editor) *Encyclopedia of Policy Studies,* Dekker, 1983.

(Editor) *The Political Science of Criminal Justice,* C. C Thomas, 1983.

Public Policy: Goals, Means, and Methods, St. Martin's, 1983.

(Editor) *Basic Literature in Policy Studies: A Comprehensive Bibliography,* JAI Press, 1984.

Contemporary Public Policy Analysis, University of Alabama Press, 1984.

(Editor with Dennis Palumbo) *Cross-National Policy Studies Directory,* Policy Studies Organization, 1984.

Equity as a Policy Goal, Bowling Green State University, 1984.

(Editor) *Productivity and Public Policy,* Sage Publications, 1984.

(Editor) *Public Policy Studies: A Multi-Volume Treatise,* JAI Press, 1984.

Law, Policy, and Evaluation, Kennikat, 1984.

(Editor with Susan G. Hadden) *Risk Analysis, Institutions and Public Policy,* Associated Faculty Press, 1984.

Using Personal Computers for Decision-Making in Law Practice, American Law Institute-American Bar Association, 1985.

(Editor) *Public Policy Analysis and Management,* JAI Press, Volume 3, 1986, Volume 4, 1987, Volume 5, 1989.

Law, Policy, and Optimizing Analysis, Quorum Books, 1986.

Causation, Prediction, and Legal Analysis, Quorum Books, 1986.

Policy Studies Index, Policy Studies Organization, 1987.

Microcomputers as Decision Aids in Law Practice, Quorum Books, 1987.

(Editor) *Law and Policy Studies,* JAI Press, Volume 1, 1987, Volume 2, 1988, Volume 3, 1989.

Policy Studies: Integration and Evaluation, Greenwood Press, 1988.

Legal Decision-Making and Microcomputers, American Law Institute-American Bar Association, 1988.

Teach Yourself Decision-Aiding Software, Decision Aids, Inc., 1989.

(Co-editor) *Social Science and Computers,* Volume 1, JAI Press, 1989.

Higher Goals for America: Doing Better Than the Best, University Press of America, 1989.

Goals and Alternatives for Controversial Issues, Decision Aids, Inc., 1989.

Evaluation Analysis with Microcomputers, JAI Press, 1989.

Decision-Aiding Software for Legal Decision Making, Quorum Books, 1989.

(Editor) *Decision-Aiding Software and Decision Analysis,* Wiley, 1990.

(Editor with William Dunn) *Policy Theory and Evaluation Concepts, Knowledge, Causes and Norms,* Greenwood Press, 1990.

Contributor to numerous legal texts, including *Judicial Decision-Making,* 1963, *Crime and Justice in Society,* 1969, *Law and Order: The Scales of Justice,* 1973, *Public Policy-Making in a Federal System,* 1976, *Policy Studies and Public Choice,* 1979, *The Sociology of Law,* 1980, *Values, Ethics, and the Practice of Policy Analysis,* 1982, *Social Sciences and Public Policy,* 1984, *Reforming American Bureaucracy,* 1986, and *Almanac of Political Science,* 1989. Contributor of articles to over fifty journals, including *Policy Studies Journal, Public Opinion Quarterly,* and *American Bar Association Journal.* Editor, *Policy Studies Journal;* member of editorial boards, *Law and Society Review,* 1966—, *Sage Criminal Justice System Annuals,* 1971—, and *Journal of Politics,* 1972—.

WORK IN PROGRESS: "Work in public policy analysis with particular emphasis on applications to the legal system and also attempts to make decision- science more understandable to the general public."

SIDELIGHTS: Stuart S. Nagel told *CA:* "There is a need for social scientists to show more interest in applying their knowledge and skills to important policy problems. There is also a need for policy-makers and policy-appliers to become more aware of the relevant knowledge and skills that social scientists have developed. I have tried to stimulate closer relations between social science and public policy by such relevant activities as writing articles, authoring books, editing journals, and founding associations. Those activities will hopefully result in promoting more applications of social science to important policy problems."

Nagel later added: "As of 1990, I am especially working on books and articles that relate to developing super-optimum solutions to public policy problems, whereby both liberals and conservatives come out ahead of their best expectations. I am also working on authoring materials relevant to improving public policy analysis in developing countries of Asia, Latin America, and Africa."

* * *

NAIPAUL, Shiva(dhar Srinivasa) 1945-1985

PERSONAL: Born February 25, 1945, in Port of Spain, Trinidad (now Republic of Trinidad and Tobago), West Indies; died of a heart attack, August 13, 1985, in London, England; son of Seepersad and Dropatie Naipaul; married wife, Virginia Margaret Stuart, 1967; children: one. *Education:* Attended University College, Oxford, 1964-68.

ADDRESSES: Agent—Gillon Aitken, 17 South Eaton Pl., London SW1, England.

CAREER: Writer. Lecturer at Aarhus University, Aarhus, Denmark, 1972.

MEMBER: Royal Society of Literature (fellow).

AWARDS, HONORS: John Llewelyn Rhys Memorial Prize and Winifred Holtby Memorial Prize, both 1970, and Jock Campbell New Statesman Award, 1971, all for *Fireflies;* Whitbread Literary Award, 1973, for *The Chip-Chip Gatherers.*

WRITINGS:

Fireflies (novel), Deutsch, 1970, Knopf, 1971.

The Chip-Chip Gatherers (novel), Knopf, 1973.

North of South: An African Journey (nonfiction), Simon & Schuster, 1978.

Black and White (nonfiction), Hamish Hamilton, 1980, published as *Journey to Nowhere: A New World Tragedy,* Simon & Schuster, 1981.

A Hot Country (novel), Hamish Hamilton, 1983, published as *Love and Death in a Hot Country,* Viking, 1984.

Beyond the Dragon's Mouth (stories), Viking, 1985.

An Unfinished Journey (nonfiction), Viking, 1987.

Contributor of short stories to anthologies, including *Penguin Modern Stories 4,* Penguin, 1970, and *Winter's Tales 20,* Macmillan (London), 1974. Contributor of articles to *Times Literary Supplement, London Magazine, New Statesman,* and *Spectator.*

WORK IN PROGRESS: A book about Australia, unfinished at time of death.

SIDELIGHTS: The younger brother of writer V. S. Naipaul, Shiva Naipaul, an Indian born in Trinidad, established himself as a critically acclaimed author with his first novel, *Fireflies.* Set in a Trinidadian Hindu community, *Fireflies* describes the demise of that community's leaders, the Khoja family, who lose their elevated stature as a result of intrafamily squabbles, arranged and loveless marriages, poor education, and undisciplined and futile attempts to reach goals beyond their grasp. "There is unusually little in Shiva Naipaul's *Fireflies* to lead one to suppose that it is his first novel," wrote Stephen Wall in the *Observer.* "It is hard to wish any particular episode away once it has been read." In the *New York Times Book Review,* critic Annette Grant deemed *Fireflies* "a remarkable and vivid portrait of an exotic, highly special tribe, the Hindus of Trinidad—who, like most people, are fundamentally unremarkable, but who under examination, exhibit a full and rich spectrum of human possibilities." "That the details *do* fascinate," Grant added, "is a tribute both to the author's invention and to his subject."

Like *Fireflies,* Naipaul's second novel, *The Chip-Chip Gatherers,* is set in Trinidad and examines family relationships, this time between two very different families, the affluent Ramsarans and the less prestigious Bholais. Although brought together by marriage, the clans are never able to put aside their differences and work together for their common good. Therefore their association serves no purpose; it is as futile as the work of the village peasants who comb the beach to find the tiny shellfish chip-chip, a bucket of which might provide only a mouthful of meat.

Finding *The Chip-Chip Gatherers* "compelling," A. L. Hendricks in a *Christian Science Monitor* review judged Naipaul to be "a skillful storyteller" who "wastes no words on elaborate descriptions or philosophizing, but lets his characters make his point. He draws them sympathetically and yet never loses his artistic detachment." In his *New Statesman* critique Martin Amis predicted that Naipaul's "next novels will establish him as one of the most accomplished, and most accessible, writers of his generation."

Naipaul's six-month trek through Kenya, Tanzania, and Zambia inspired his next book, *North of South: An African Journey.* In this volume the author recorded his day-to-day observations of Africa in what critic John Darnton in the *New York Times Book Review* dubbed "the genre of travelogue *cum* essay." Naipaul relates his experiences of African life as he viewed it in cafes and buses, schools and homes, and through encounters with merchants, farmers, educators, and others. What impressed him most during his stay in Africa was the extent of European influence on African mores and customs.

Critics found *North of South* to be an interesting and well-written account of African ways, but not necessarily an unbiased and accurate observation. Darnton noted some "striking inaccuracies" and wrote that the citizens Naipaul profiles "are hardly the defining personalities in Africa today." Darnton nevertheless opined that *North of South* is "superbly written." Critic Roland Oliver also found *North of South* lacking in some areas. In his *New Statesman* review Oliver called Naipaul's effort "a witty but not wise book" that "is more informative about touts and tourists, pimps and prostitutes, than about national and international

politics of the East African countries." "All this is told with a great deal of novelist's sparkle, a power of vivid description and of characterisation through reported dialogue, which will not endear Mr. Naipaul to his many acquaintances when his book comes into their hands."

Further comments about *North of South* came from Lewis Nkosi, who in the *Times Literary Supplement* noted Naipaul's "elegance of style," but concurred with the other critics that "it is not that the picture Naipaul paints of Africa is totally unrecognizable; the question is one of perspective and standards used." And Jim Hoagland, writing in the *Washington Post Book World,* deemed *North of South* "ultimately one-dimensional," but judged it a "rare quick good read for the Africa shelf."

Naipaul followed *North of South* with *Journey to Nowhere: A New World Tragedy,* in which he seeks to explain and document the bizarre circumstances and events that precipitated the Jonestown Massacre, when more than nine hundred men, women, and children, all members of a cult known as the People's Temple, committed suicide at the command of the sect's leader, Jim Jones. The mass suicide occurred in 1978 in Guyana, where Jones had moved his cult after investigating journalists and concerned family members of the cultists interfered with the group's operation in San Francisco, California. Before instructing his followers to drink the cyanide-laced soft drink he offered them, Jones explained that their suicide was "an act . . . protesting the conditions of an inhuman world." Related deaths included California congressman Leo Ryan and several others who were gunned down on a Guyana airstrip by People's Temple members. Ryan and his entourage were on a mission to investigate the cult and free several members being held against their will.

Naipaul's account of the massacre was applauded by many reviewers, among them D. J. Enright, who wrote in the *Times Literary Supplement* that *Journey to Nowhere* is "a saddening, alarming, depressing book" that is "in part, a tribute to its author's assiduity, fortitude and powers of expression. . . . Only if the author had lived there could he have hoped to be more exhaustive and certain; and then he would not have lived to tell the tale at all." In the *New York Times Book Review* Peter L. Berger regarded Naipaul as "a masterful writer" and found *Journey to Nowhere* a "lively and readable" book. "Mr. Naipaul's is a harsh perspective," Berger opined. "It is also a very persuasive one. To be sure, a less idiosyncratic writer would have softened his interpretation, introduced more nuances, perhaps shown more compassion. One strength of the book is that Mr. Naipaul does none of these things, letting the reader make his own modifications if he is so inclined."

Peter Schrag also offered praise for *Journey to Nowhere* in his *Nation* review, calling Naipaul's book "a tough, intelligent, beautifully written account of how Californian and Third World illusions fused to set the stage for the disaster in Guyana." Schrag added that Naipaul "has a flawless ear for the gobbledygook of Third World pretenders, encounter-group gurus, esties, obfuscating politicians and the various other manipulators of rhetoric who populated the world of Pastor Jones." And critic John Coleman, in the *New Statesman,* wrote of *Journey to Nowhere:* "It is one man's view and helps to make hideous sense of that flight to a Guyanan graveyard. Naipaul writes as ever with an ice-tipped pen, elegantly summoning laughter that rings like anger."

Naipaul's third novel, *A Hot Country,* is set in the fictional South African state of Cuyama, a depressed region where politics have become "banditry, cynicism and lies," and where the land has been ravaged, leaving "the foundations of vanished houses," and "archways leading nowhere." Its people, too, are bleak, frustrated, and hopeless as a result of the poverty and hunger that prevail in Cuyama. In a London *Times* review, critic Andrew Sinclair felt Naipaul's "regressive view . . . leaves the readers in the doldrums, with hardly enough energy to turn these pages of fine prose without the least spark of life." And "there is much voluptuous self-surrender to pessimism by the author, who closes off all avenues of hope," wrote Nicholas Rankin in *Times Literary Supplement*. "Yet it does not mask Shiva Naipaul's other considerable talents as a novelist. He deftly captures place, mood and character, and has not lost his eye and ear for embarrassment and discomfiture. . . . *A Hot Country* is a sad book about waste, but a work of art that delights with its craft as it dismays with its vision."

BIOGRAPHICAL/CRITICAL SOURCES:

BOOKS

Contemporary Literary Criticism, Gale, Volume 32, 1985, Volume 39, 1986.
Dictionary of Literary Biography Yearbook: 1985, Gale, 1986.

PERIODICALS

Choice, January, 1972, October, 1973, October, 1981.
Christian Science Monitor, June 20, 1973.
Nation, May 2, 1981.
National Review, September 28, 1979, October 2, 1981.
New Republic, June 9, 1979, June 16, 1979.
New York Times, April 21, 1979, March 13, 1987.
New York Times Book Review, February 7, 1971, May 6, 1979, June 29, 1980, July 5, 1981, July 4, 1982, August 12, 1984, March 24, 1985, March 22, 1987.
New Yorker, August 6, 1973, July 2, 1979, May 25, 1981.
New Statesman, April 20, 1973, July 28, 1978, October 31, 1980.
Newsweek, May 21, 1979, June 1, 1979, May 14, 1984.
Observer, November 15, 1970, April 15, 1973, April 25, 1976, July 30, 1978, November 2, 1980.
Spectator, October 30, 1970, April 21, 1973, October 14, 1978, February 7, 1981.
Times Literary Supplement, December 11, 1970, April 13, 1973, September 29, 1978, October 31, 1980, August 30, 1983.
Times (London), August 28, 1983.
Times Literary Supplement, September 12, 1986.
Washington Post Book World, July 1, 1979, April 5, 1981, April 25, 1984, March 24, 1985, April 19, 1987.

OBITUARIES:

PERIODICALS

Los Angeles Times, August 25, 1985.
Newsweek, August 26, 1985.
New York Times, August 16, 1985.
Time, August 26, 1985.
Times (London), August 16, 1985, August 21, 1985.
Washington Post, August 17, 1985.

*   *   *

NAIPAUL, V(idiadhar) S(urajprasad) 1932-

PERSONAL: Born August 17, 1932, in Trinidad; married Patricia Ann Hale, 1955. *Education:* Attended Queen's Royal College, Trinidad and University College, Oxford.

ADDRESSES: Agent—c/o Aitken & Stone Ltd., 29 Fernshaw Rd., London SW10, England.

CAREER: Free-lance broadcaster for the British Broadcasting Corp., two years; writer.

MEMBER: Society of Authors, Royal Society of Literature (fellow).

AWARDS, HONORS: John Llewellyn Rhys Memorial Prize, 1958, for *The Mystic Masseur;* grant from government of Trinidad for travel in Caribbean, 1960-61; Somerset Maugham Award, 1961, for *Miguel Street;* Phoenix Trust Award, 1963; Hawthornden Prize, 1964, for *Mr. Stone and the Knights Companion;* W. H. Smith Award, 1968, for *The Mimic Men;* Booker Prize, 1971, for *In a Free State;* Bennett Award from *Hudson Review,* 1980; Hon.D. from Columbia University, 1981; Hon.Litt. from Cambridge University, 1983; T. S. Eliot Award for Creative Writing from Ingersoll Foundation, 1986.

WRITINGS:

The Mystic Masseur, Deutsch, 1957, Vanguard, 1959, reprinted, Penguin, 1977.
The Suffrage of Elvira, Deutsch, 1958.
Miguel Street, Deutsch, 1959, Vanguard, 1960, reprinted, Penguin, 1977.
A House for Mr. Biswas, Deutsch, 1961, McGraw, 1962.
The Middle Passage: Impressions of Five Societies—British, French and Dutch in the West Indies and South America (nonfiction), Deutsch, 1962, Macmillan, 1963, reprinted, Penguin, 1978.
Mr. Stone and the Knights Companion, Deutsch, 1963, Macmillan, 1964.
An Area of Darkness (nonfiction), Deutsch, 1964, Macmillan, 1965.
The Mimic Men, Macmillan, 1967.
A Flag on the Island (short story collection), Macmillan, 1967.
The Loss of El Dorado: A History (nonfiction), Deutsch, 1969, Knopf, 1970.
(Contributor) Andrew Salkey, editor, *Island Voices: Stories from the West Indies,* new edition, Liveright, 1970.
In a Free State, Knopf, 1971.
The Overcrowded Barracoon and Other Articles, Deutsch, 1972, Knopf, 1973.
Guerrillas, Knopf, 1975.
India: A Wounded Civilization (nonfIction), Knopf, 1977.
A Bend in the River, Knopf, 1979.
The Return of Eva Peron (nonfiction), Knopf, 1980.
Among the Believers, Knopf, 1981.
Finding the Center, Vintage Books, 1986.
The Enigma of Arrival, 1987.
A Turn in the South, Viking, 1989.
India: A Million Mutinies Now, Penguin, 1991.

Contributor to *New York Review of Books, New Statesman,* and other periodicals. Fiction reviewer, *New Statesman,* 1958-61.

SIDELIGHTS: Born in Trinidad to the descendants of Hindu immigrants from northern India and educated at England's Oxford University, V. S. Naipaul is considered to be one of the world's most gifted novelists. As a *New York Times Book Review* critic writes: "For sheer abundance of talent there can hardly be a writer alive who surpasses V. S. Naipaul. Whatever we may want in a novelist is to be found in his books: an almost Conradian gift for tensing a story, a serious involvement with human issues, a supple English prose, a hard-edged wit, a personal vision of things. Best of all, he is a novelist unafraid of using his brains. . . . His novels are packed with thought, not as lumps of abstraction but as one fictional element among others, fluid in the stream of narrative. . . . [He is] the world's writer, a master of language and perception, our sardonic blessing."

This ability to regard Naipaul as "the world's writer" is in large measure due to the author's self-proclaimed rootlessness. Unhappy with the cultural and spiritual poverty of Trinidad, distanced from India, and unable to relate to and share in the heritage of each country's former imperial ruler (England), Naipaul describes himself as "content to be a colonial, without a past, without ancestors." As a result of these strong feelings of nonattachment to any particular region or set of traditions, most of his work deals with people who, like himself, are estranged from the societies they are supposedly a part of and who are desperately seeking to find a way to belong or to "be someone." The locales Naipaul chooses for his stories represent an extension of this same theme, for most take place in emerging Third World countries in the throes of creating a new "national" identity from the tangled remnants of native and colonial cultures.

Naipaul's early work explored these themes via a West Indian variation of the comedy of manners—that is, an almost farcical portrayal of the comic aspects of an illiterate and divided society's shift from a colonial to an independent status, with an emphasis on multiracial misunderstandings and rivalries and the various ironies resulting from the sudden introduction of such democratic processes as elections. In *The Mystic Masseur, The Suffrage of Elvira,* and *Miguel Street,* Naipaul essentially holds a mirror up to Trinidadian society in order to expose its follies and absurdities; his tone is detached, yet sympathetic, as if he is looking back at a distant past of which he is no longer a part. The tragic aspects of the situation are not examined, nor is there any attempt to involve the reader in the plight of the characters. Michael Thorpe describes the prevailing tone of these early books as "that of the ironist who points up the comedy, futility and absurdity that fill the gap between aspiration and achievement, between the public image desired and the individual's inadequacies, to recognize which may be called the education of the narrator: 'I had grown up and looked critically at the people around me.' "

A House for Mr. Biswas marks an important turning point in Naipaul's work; his increasing attention to subject and theme via a blend of psychological and social realism and certain symbolic overtones foreshadows the intensive character studies of his later works. In addition, *A House for Mr. Biswas* has a universality of theme that the author's earlier books lacked for the most part due to their emphasis on strictly local-color elements. The cumulative effect of these "improvements" has led many critics to regard *A House for Mr. Biswas* as Naipaul's masterpiece. As Robert D. Hamner writes: "With the appearance in 1961 of *A House for Mr. Biswas,* Naipaul may have published his best fiction. It is even possible that this book is the best novel yet to emerge from the Caribbean. It is a vital embodiment of authentic West Indian life, but more than that, it transcends national boundaries and evokes universal human experiences. Mr. Biswas' desire to own his own house is essentially a struggle to assert personal identity and to attain security—thoroughly human needs."

The *New York Herald Tribune Books* reviewer notes that "Naipaul has a wry wit and an engaging sense of humor, as well as a delicate understanding of sadness and futility and a profound but unobtrusive sense of the tragi-comedy of ordinary living. . . . His style is precise and assured. In short, he gives every indication of being an important addition to the international literary scene. [*A House for Mr. Biswas*] is funny, it is compassionate. It has more than 500 pages and not one of them is superfluous."

Paul Theroux of the *New York Times Book Review* admits that "it is hard for the reviewer of a wonderful author to keep the ob-ituarist's assured hyperbole in check, but let me say that if the stilting-up of the Thames coincided with a freak monsoon, causing massive flooding in all parts of South London, the first book I would rescue from my library would be *A House for Mr. Biswas.*"

Michael Thorpe agrees that the novel is "a work of rare distinction; . . . [it is] a 'novelist's novel,' a model work. . . . The book's popularity must be largely due to its universality of subject and theme, the struggle of one ordinary man to climb—or cling on to—the ladder of life; the ordinariness lies in his ambitions for home, security, status, his desire to live through his son, yet he remains an individual. . . . At first sight Mr. Biswas seems an abrupt departure from Naipaul's previous fiction: in its concentration upon the life history of a single protagonist it goes far deeper than *The Mystic Masseur* and the mood is predominantly 'serious,' the still pervasive comedy being subordinated to that mood. Yet on further consideration we can see *Mr. Biswas* as the natural and consummate development of themes that ran through the first three books: the perplexing relation of the individual to society, his struggle to impress himself upon it through achievement—or defy its pressures with a transforming fantasy that puts a gloss upon life and extracts order from the rude chaos of everyday existence. . . . We should not doubt that the narrative is to be heroic, the quest for the house—however flawed in its realization—a victory over the chaos and anonymity into which the hero was born. The novel is such a man's celebration, his witness, the answer to the dismal refrain, 'There was nothing to speak of him.' " In short, Thorpe concludes, "for West Indian literature *A House for Mr. Biswas* forged [the] connexion [between literature and life] with unbreakable strength and set up a model for emulation which no other 'Third World' literature in English has yet equalled."

After his success with *A House for Mr. Biswas,* Naipaul turned away from exclusively West Indian locales in order to "test" his themes in a broader geographic and nationalistic landscape. At the same time, his earlier light-hearted tone gradually faded as he explored the more tragic consequences of alienation and rootlessness in the world at large through the eyes of various "universal wanderers." As Thomas Lask reports in the *New York Times* on Naipaul's *In a Free State:* "V. S. Naipaul's writings about his native Trinidad have often enough been touched with tolerant amusement. His is an attitude that is affectionate without being overly kind. . . . On his own, Mr. Naipaul [has] made no secret of his alienation from his native island. . . . [*In a Free State*] takes the story one step further. How does the expatriate fare after he leaves the island? . . . [The author] lifts the argument above and beyond material success and social position. These new stories focus on the failure of heart, on the animallike cruelty man exhibits to other men and on the avarice that . . . is the root of all evil. . . . What the author is saying is that neither customs nor color nor culture seems able to quiet that impulse to destruction, that murderous wantonness that is so much part of our make-up. . . . Mr. Naipaul's style in these stories seems leaner than in the past and much more somber. There is virtually none of the earlier playfulness. He appears to have settled for precision over abundance. Each detail and each incident is made to carry its weight in the narrative. The effect is not small-scaled, for in the title story he has created an entire country. He has not tidied up every loose strand. . . . But there is nothing unfinished in these polished novellas."

Paul Theroux calls *In a Free State* "Naipaul's most ambitious work, a story-sequence brilliant in conception, masterly in execution, and terrifying in effect—the chronicles of a half-a-dozen self-exiled people who have become lost souls. Having abandoned their own countries (countries they were scarcely aware of belonging to), they have found themselves in strange places, without friends, with few loyalties, and with the feeling that they are trespassing. Worse, their lives have been totally altered; for them there is no going back; they have fled, each to his separate limbo, and their existence is like that of souls in a classical underworld. . . . The subject of displacement is one few writers have touched upon. Camus has written of it. But Naipaul is much superior to Camus, and his achievement—a steady advance through eleven volumes—is as disturbing as it is original. *In a Free State* is a masterpiece in the fiction of rootlessness."

Alfred Kazin of the *New York Review of Books* claims that "Naipaul writes about the many psychic realities of exile in our contemporary world with far more bite and dramatic havoc than Joyce. . . . No one else around today, not even Nabokov, seems able to employ prose fiction so deeply as the very choice of exile. . . . What makes Naipaul hurt so much more than other novelists of contemporary exodus is his major image—the tenuousness of man's hold on the earth. The doubly unsettling effect he creates—for the prose is British-chatty, proper yet bitter— also comes from the many characters in a book like [*In a Free State*] who don't 'belong' in the countries they are touring or working in, who wouldn't 'belong' any longer in the countries they come from, and from the endless moving about of contemporary life have acquired a feeling of their own unreality in the 'free state' of endlessly moving about. . . . Naipaul has never encompassed so much, and with such brilliant economy, with such a patent though lighthanded ominousness of manner, as in [*In a Free State*]. The volume of detail is extraordinary. . . . I suppose one criticism of Naipaul might well be that he covers too much ground, has too many representative types, and that he has an obvious desolation about homelessness, migration, the final placelessness of those who have seen too much, which he tends to turn into a mysterious accusation. Though he is a marvelous technician, there is something finally modest, personal, openly committed about his fiction, a frankness of personal reference, that removes him from the godlike impersonality of the novelist. . . . Naipaul belongs to a different generation, to a more openly tragic outlook for humanity itself. He does not want to play God, even in a novel."

A *New Statesman* critic, on the other hand, is not quite convinced that Naipaul's outlook is completely tragic. He writes: "Each piece [of *In a Free State*] is a tour de force. . . . I don't know any writer since Conrad who's exposed the otherness of Africa so starkly, and Naipaul leaves his readers freer by his massacre of obstinate illusions. But his vision excludes elements of growth and hope which are, palpably, there. . . . Naipaulia remains a kingdom of cryptic anti-climax. I wonder, though, if the 'cryptic' final section is nudging away from pessimism."

With the publication of *Guerrillas*, however, the first of Naipaul's novels to make his name widely known in the United States, more and more reviewers became convinced that his outlook is indeed grim. Notes Theroux: "*Guerrillas* is a violent book in which little violence is explicit. . . . It is a novel, not of revolt, but of the play-acting that is frequently called revolt, that queer situation of scabrous glamour which Naipaul sees as a throwback to the days of slavery. . . . *Guerrillas* is one of Naipaul's most complex books; it is certainly his most suspenseful, a series of shocks, like a shroud slowly unwound from a bloody corpse, showing the damaged—and familiar—face last. . . . This is a novel without a villain, and there is not a character for whom the reader does not at some point feel deep sympathy and keen understanding, no matter how villainous or futile he may seem. *Guerrillas* is a brilliant novel in every way, and it shimmers with

artistic certainty. It is scarifying in the opposite way from a nightmare. One can shrug at fantasy, but *Guerrillas*—in a phrase Naipaul himself once used—is, like the finest novels, 'indistinguishable from truth.' "

Paul Gray of *Time* believes that *Guerrillas* "proves [Naipaul] the laureate of the West Indies. . . . [He] is a native expatriate with a fine distaste for patriotic rhetoric. . . . [The novel] is thus conspicuously short of heroes. . . . The native politicians are corrupt, the foreign businessmen avaricious, and the people either lethargic or criminal. When an uprising does flare, it is nasty and inept. Perhaps no one but Naipaul has the inside and outside knowledge to have turned such a dispirited tale into so gripping a book. His island is built entirely of vivid descriptions and offhand dialogue. At the end, it has assumed a political and economic history, a geography and a population of doomed, selfish souls. . . . *Guerrillas* is not a polemic (polemicists will be annoyed) but a Conradian vision of fallibility and frailty. With economy and compassion, Naipaul draws the heart of darkness from a sun-struck land."

Noting that Naipaul takes a "hackneyed" theme ("incipient Black Power") and manages to produce "a more significant treatment of it than most of his contemporaries with similar concerns," Charles R. Larson of the *Nation* writes that *Guerrillas* "builds so slowly and so skillfully that until the final scene bursts upon us, we are hardly aware of the necessary outcome of the events; it is only in retrospect that we see that the desultory action has in fact been charged with fate. . . . No one writes better about politics in the West Indies than V. S. Naipaul. Nor is there anyone who writes more profoundly about exiles, would-be revolutionaries and their assorted camp followers. Written in a deliberately flat style, *Guerrillas* is a deeply pessimistic novel, telling us that we have seen about as much political change in the West Indian island republics as we are likely to see."

In *A Bend in the River,* Naipaul returns to Africa as a locale (the scene of *In a Free State*), confirming his basic pessimism in the process. Comments John Leonard in the *New York Times:* "This is not an exotic Africa [in *A Bend in the River*]. . . . [The author] despises nostalgia for the colonial past, while at the same time heartlessly parodying . . . the African future. . . . *A Bend in the River* is a brilliant and depressing novel. It is no secret by now, certainly not since *Guerrillas* . . . , that V. S. Naipaul is one of the handful of living writers of whom the English language can be proud, if, still, profoundly uneasy. There is no consolation from him, any more than there is sentiment. His wit has grown hard and fierce; he isn't seeking to amuse, but to scourge."

John Updike, writing in the *New Yorker,* asserts that *A Bend in the River* "proves once more that Naipaul is incomparably well situated and equipped to bring us news of one of the contemporary world's great subjects—the mingling of its peoples. *A Bend in the River* struck me as an advance—broader, warmer, less jaded and kinky—over the much-praised *Guerrillas,* though not quite as vivid and revelatory as the fiction of *In a Free State. A Bend in the River* is carved from the same territory [as *In a Free State*]—an Africa of withering colonial vestiges, terrifyingly murky politics, defeated pretensions omnivorous rot, and the implacable undermining of all that would sustain reason and safety. . . . Rage . . . is perhaps the deepest and darkest fact Naipaul has to report about the Third World, and in this novel his understanding of it goes beyond that shown in *Guerrillas.* . . . In *A Bend in the River,* the alien observer—white bureaucrat or Asian trader—is drawn closer into the rationale of the riots and wars that seethe in the slums or the bush beyond his enclave. The novel might be faulted for savoring a bit of the visiting journalist's worked-up notes: its episodes do not hang together with full organic snugness; there are a few too many clever geopolitical conversations and scenically detailed car rides. . . . [But] the author's embrace of his tangled and tragic African scene seems relatively hearty as well as immensely knowledgeable. Always a master of fictional landscape, Naipaul here shows, in his variety of human examples and in his search for underlying social causes, a Tolstoyan spirit, generous if not genial."

Walter Clemons of *Newsweek* calls *A Bend in the River* "a hurtful, claustrophobic novel, very hard on the nerves, played out under a vast African sky in an open space that is made to fee] stifling. . . . Naipaul's is a political novel of a subtle and unusual kind. . . . [It] is about tremors of expectation, shifts in personal loyalty, manners in dire emergency. . . . As an evocation of place, [the novel] succeeds brilliantly. . . . *A Bend in the River* is by no means a perfected work. . . . But this imperfect, enormously disturbing book confirms Naipaul's position as one of the best writers now at work."

And Irving Howe wrote in the *New York Times Book Review:* "On the surface, *A Bend in the River* emerges mostly as a web of caustic observation, less exciting than its predecessor, *Guerrillas;* but it is a much better and deeper novel, for Naipaul has mastered the gift of creating an aura of psychic and moral tension even as, seemingly, very little happens. . . . [But in the end,] Naipaul offers no intimations of hope or signals of perspective. It may be that the reality he grapples with allows him nothing but grimness of voice. . . . A novelist has to be faithful to what he sees, and few see as well as Naipaul; yet one may wonder whether, in some final reckoning, a serious writer can simply allow the wretchedness of his depicted scene to become the limit of his vision. . . . Naipaul seems right now to be a writer beleaguered by his own truths, unable to get past them. That is surely an honorable difficulty, far better than indulging in sentimental or ideological uplift; but it exacts a price. . . . Perhaps we ought simply to be content that, in his austere and brilliant way, he holds fast to the bitterness before his eyes."

Subsequent works, notably *The Enigma of Arrival* and *A Turn in the South,* have served to confirm Naipaul's status as one of the English language's most distinguished and perceptive contemporary writers. In his 1976 study of Naipaul, Michael Thorpe offers this overview of the novelist's accomplishments: "While Naipaul is by no means alone in coming from a makeshift colonial society and using the 'metropolitan' language with a native surety, these origins have helped him more than any of his contemporaries from the Commonwealth to develop an inclusive view of many facets of the larger world, a view focussed by his intense sense of displacement from society, race or creed. . . . He has gone beyond local conflicts, isolated instances of the colonial experience, to attempt something approaching a world view. . . . His insights and his manner of conveying them carry a persuasive truth."

As a result, continues Thorpe, "Naipaul has spoken from and to more points within that world [of imperial or social oppression] than any English writer—but his is not a comforting or hopeful voice. . . . Asked if he were an optimist [Naipaul] replied: 'I'm not sure. I think I do look for the seeds of regeneration in a situation; I long to find what is good and hopeful and really do hope that by the most brutal sort of analysis one is possibly opening up the situation to some sort of action; an action which is not based on self-deception.'. . . [But] he supplies none of the props even realists let us lean upon in the end: there are no consolations—no religious belief, no humanistic faith in man's future,

not even the personal supports of friendship or love. . . . [Thus] Naipaul's is one of the bleakest visions any imaginative observer alive has given us. . . . [He] refuses to leap to positive attitudes he cannot justify. Naipaul would be the last to claim for his work that it represents a final or adequate vision; it is the record of one man's impressions of the world and it does not pretend to be the whole truth about it. . . . Yet Naipaul insists that he is hopeful: as one who has not flinched from harsh reality, he has earned the right to our reciprocal hope that he may yet find a way beyond despair."

BIOGRAPHICAL/CRITICAL SOURCES:

BOOKS

Contemporary Literary Criticism, Gale, Volume 4, 1975, Volume 7, 1977, Volume 9, 1978, Volume 13, 1980, Volume 18, 1981, Volume 37, 1986.
Dictionary of Literary Biography Yearbook: 1985, Gale, 1986.
Hamner, Robert D., *V. S. Naipaul,* Twayne, 1973.
Thorpe, Michael, *V. S. Naipaul,* Longmans, 1976.

PERIODICALS

Atlantic, May, 1970, January, 1976, July, 1977, June, 1979.
Best Sellers, April 15, 1968.
Books and Bookmen, October, 1967.
Books Abroad, winter, 1968, winter, 1969.
Chicago Sunday Tribune, July 12, 1959.
Chicago Tribune Book World, May 13, 1979, April 20, 1980.
Choice, June, 1973.
Christian Science Monitor, July 19, 1962, March 29, 1968, May 28, 1970.
Contemporary Literature, winter, 1968.
Economist, July 16, 1977.
Illustrated London News, May 20, 1967.
Kenyon Review, November, 1967.
Listener, May 25, 1967, September 28, 1967, May 23, 1968.
London Magazine, May, 1967.
Los Angeles Times, May 9, 1980, March 15, 1989.
Los Angeles Times Book Review, June 24, 1979.
Nation, October 9, 1967, October 5, 1970, December 13, 1975, July 2, 1977, June 30, 1979.
National Review, October 6, 1970.
New York Herald Tribune Books, June 24, 1962.
New Yorker, August 4, 1962, August 8, 1970, June 6, 1977, May 21, 1979.
New York Review of Books, October 26, 1967, April 11, 1968, December 30, 1971, May 31, 1979.
New York Times, December 16, 1967, December 25, 1971, August 17, 1977, May 14, 1979, March 13, 1980.
New Statesman, May 5, 1967, September 15, 1967, November 7, 1969, October 8, 1971, June 17, 1977.
New Republic, July 9, 1977, June 9, 1979.
New York Times Book Review, October 15, 1967, April 7, 1968, May 24, 1970, October 17, 1971, November 16, 1975, December 28, 1975, May 1, 1977, June 12, 1977, May 13, 1979.
Newsweek, December 1, 1975, June 6, 1977, May 21, 1979.
Observer Review, April 30, 1967, September 10, 1967, October 26, 1969.
Punch, May 10, 1967.
Saturday Review, July 2, 1960, October 23, 1971, November 15, 1975.
Spectator, September 22, 1967, November 8, 1969.
Time, May 25, 1970, December 1, 1975, June 20, 1977, May 21, 1979.

Times Literary Supplement, May 31, 1963, April 27, 1967, September 14, 1967, December 25, 1969, July 30, 1971, November 17, 1972.

Transition, December, 1971.

Washington Post Book World, April 19, 1970, December 5, 1971, November 28, 1976, June 19, 1977, July 1, 1979.

*   *   *

NARAYAN, R(asipuram) K(rishnaswami) 1906-

PERSONAL: Born October 10, 1906, in Madras, India. *Education:* Maharaja's College (now University of Mysore), received degree, 1930.

ADDRESSES: Agent—Anthony Sheil Associates, 2-3 Maxwell St., London WC1B 3AR, England.

CAREER: Writer. Owner of Indian Thought Publications in Mysore, India.

AWARDS, HONORS: National Prize of the Indian Literary Academy, 1958; Padma Bhushan, India, 1964; National Association of Independent Schools award, 1965; D.Litt. from University of Leeds, 1967; English-Speaking Union Book Award for *My Days: A Memoir,* 1975; American Academy and Institute of Arts and Letters citation, 1982.

MEMBER: American Academy and Institute of Arts and Letters (honorary member).

WRITINGS:

Swami and Friends: A Novel of Malgudi, Hamish Hamilton, 1935, Fawcett, 1970, published with *The Bachelor of Arts: A Novel,* Michigan State College Press, 1954.

The Bachelor of Arts: A Novel, Thomas Nelson, 1937.

The Dark Room: A Novel, Macmillan, 1938.

Malgudi Days (short stories), Indian Thought Publications, 1941.

Dodu and Other Stories, Indian Thought Publications, 1943.

Cyclone and Other Stories, Indian Thought Publications, 1944.

Mysore, Indian Thought Publications, 1944.

The English Teacher (novel), Eyre & Spottiswoode, 1945, published as *Grateful to Life and Death,* Michigan State College Press, 1953.

An Astrologer's Day and Other Stories, Eyre & Spottiswoode, 1947.

Mr. Sampath (novel), Eyre & Spottiswoode, 1949, published as *The Printer of Malgudi,* Michigan State College Press, 1957.

The Financial Expert: A Novel, Metheun, 1952, Michigan State College Press, 1953.

Waiting for the Mahatma: A Novel, Michigan State College Press, 1955.

Lawley Road: Thirty-Two Short Stories, Indian Thought Publications, 1956.

The Guide (novel), Viking, 1958.

Next Sunday: Sketches and Essays, Pearl Publications, 1960.

My Dateless Diary (essays), Indian Thought Publications, 1960.

The Man-Eater of Malgudi (novel), Viking, 1961.

Gods, Demons and Others (short stories), Viking, 1965.

The Vendor of Sweets (novel), Viking, 1967 (published in England as *The Sweet-Vendor,* Bodley Head, 1967).

A Horse and Two Goats and Other Stories, Viking, 1970.

(Translator) *The Ramayana: A Shortened Modern Prose Version of the Indian Epic,* Viking, 1972.

My Days: A Memoir, Viking, 1974.

The Reluctant Guru, Hind Pocket Books, 1974.

The Painter of Signs, Viking, 1976.

(Translator) *The Mahabharata: A Shortened Prose Version of the Indian Epic,* Viking, 1978.

The Emerald Route, Ind-US Inc., 1980.

A Tiger for Malgudi, Viking, 1983.

Under the Banyan Tree and Other Stories, Viking, 1985.

Talkative Man, Viking, 1987.

A Writer's Nightmare: Selected Essays, 1958-1988, Penguin, 1989.

The World of Nagaraj, Viking, 1990.

Contributor of short stories to *New Yorker.*

SIDELIGHTS: R. K. Narayan is perhaps the best-known Indian writing in English today. His works have met with uniformly favorable criticism, and his books have such a popular appeal that, as Narayan himself noted in a *Books Abroad* interview, they "have been translated into all European languages and Hebrew." Critics have appreciated Narayan's mythical village of Malgudi, a fictional microcosm as universal in scope as Faulkner's Yoknapatawpha County. His ability to present his characters sympathetically and realistically has been likened to that of such writers as Chekhov and Isaac Bashevis Singer.

In a British Broadcasting Corporation radio interview, Narayan spoke to William Walsh of his use of the English language: "English has been with us [in India] for over a century and a half. I am particularly fond of the language. I was never aware that I was using a different, a foreign, language when I wrote in English, because it came to me very easily. I can't explain how. English is a very adaptable language. And it's so transparent it can take on the tint of any country." Walsh added that Narayan's English "is limpid, simple, calm and unaffected, natural in its run and tone, and beautifully measured" in a unique fashion which takes on an Indian flavor by avoiding "the American purr of the combustion engine . . . [and] the thick marmalade quality of British English."

Other critics have noted the rhythms of Narayan's style and the richness of his narrative. Melvin J. Friedman suggested in a comparison with Isaac Bashevis Singer that "both seem part of an oral tradition in which the 'spoken' triumphs over the 'written,' " and theorized that the similarities between Narayan's fiction and the Indian epics echo "Singer's prose" and its "rhythm of the Old Testament." Eve Auchincloss noted that the translation-like quality of the language "adds curious, pleasing flavor."

Narayan's fictional setting is Malgudi, a village very similar to the village of his childhood, Mysore. In Malgudi every sort of human condition indigenous not only to India but to life everywhere is represented. Malgudi has been compared with William Faulkner's Yoknapatawpha County. "Narayan might . . . be called Faulknerian," wrote Warren French, "because against the background of a squalid community he creates characters with a rare quality that can only be called 'compassionate disenchantment.' " French also noted that both Narayan and Faulkner write frequently of "an unending conflict between individuality and the demands of tradition," typifying their respective geographical settings in such a way as to become universal by extension. Charles R. Larson demonstrated similar parallels but reflected that "while Faulkner's vision remains essentially grotesque, Narayan's has been predominantly comic, reflecting with humor the struggle of the individual consciousness to find peace within the framework of public life." Walsh stressed the universal quality of Malgudi: "Whatever happens in India happens in Malgudi, and whatever happens in Malgudi happens everywhere."

In Narayan's novels and short stories are characters who experience some kind of growth or change, or who gain knowledge through the experiences they undergo. As Walsh observed, Narayan most often focuses on the middle class and its representative occupations, many of which provide Narayan with titles for his books: *The Bachelor of Arts, The English Teacher, The Financial Expert, The Guide, The Sweet-Vendor.* Walsh explained Narayan's typical structural pattern in terms of concentric circles, whereby the village represents the outer circle, the family is the inner circle, and the hero, the focus of each novel, stands at the hub. "His hero is usually modest, sensitive, ardent, wry about himself," wrote Walsh, "and sufficiently conscious to have an active inner life and to grope towards some existence independent of the family." Walsh further observed that the typical progress of a Narayan hero involves "the rebirth of self and the progress of its pregnancy or education," thereby suggesting the Indian concept of reincarnation. "Again and again Narayan gives us the account of an evolving consciousness," wrote Larson, "beginning in isolation and confusion and ending in wholeness (peace within the traditional Hindu faith)" while maintaining a unique freshness of presentation.

Closely related to Narayan's gift for characterization is his ability to present his material in such a sympathetic manner that many critics have written at length of his comic vision in his treatment of his characters' failures and disappointments. French declared: "Although he satirizes the foibles of his characters, he never condescends to them or makes them targets for abuse. . . . Narayan is too sophisticated an artist to rail at people for being what they have to be." Walsh wrote of Narayan's "forgiving kindness" and labeled his novels "comedies of sadness . . . lighted with the glint of mockery of both self and others." Paul Zimmerman focused on the "affectionate amusement" with which Narayan treats his heroes, and Anthony Thwaite stated that "R. K. Narayan has achieved . . . an observation that is always acute, a humor that is never condescending, and a delicate sympathy that never becomes whimsical."

Herbert Lomas paraphrased Graham Greene's assessment that "R. K. Narayan [is] one of the glories of English Literature . . . a sage if ever there was one." John Updike wrote that, through Narayan's remarkable gifts, "the fabled Indian gentleness still permeates the atmosphere evoked by this venerable cherisher of human behavior," and Eve Auchincloss stated that "[So] poised, so balanced a writer is Narayan, his sympathy and amusement so large, that even God's design for an overpopulated India seems defensible."

MEDIA ADAPTATIONS: Narayan's *The Guide,* was adapted for the stage by Harvey Breit and Patricia Rinehart and produced Off-Broadway in New York City at the Hudson Theatre, March, 1968.

BIOGRAPHICAL/CRITICAL SOURCES:

BOOKS

Contemporary Literary Criticism, Gale, Volume 7, 1977, Volume 28, 1984, Volume 47, 1988.
Season of Promise: Spring Fiction, University of Missouri, 1967.
Walsh, William, *R. K. Narayan,* Longman, 1971.

PERIODICALS

Banasthali Patrika, January 12, 1969, July 13, 1969.
Book World, July 11, 1976, December 5, 1976.
Books Abroad, summer, 1965, spring, 1971, spring, 1976.
Christian Science Monitor, February 19, 1970.
Encounter, October, 1964.

Harper's, April, 1965.
Journal of Commonwealth Literature, Number 2, December, 1966.
Listener, March 1, 1962.
Literary Criterion, winter, 1968.
London Magazine, September, 1970.
Nation, June 28, 1975.
New Republic, May 13, 1967.
New Statesman, June 2, 1967.
Newsweek, July 4, 1976.
New Yorker, October 14, 1967, March 16, 1968, July 5, 1976.
New York Review of Books, June 29, 1967.
New York Times, August 1, 1965.
New York Times Book Review, May 14, 1967, June 20, 1976.
Osmania Journal of English Studies, Volume VII, number 1, 1970.
Sewanee Review, winter, 1975.
Times Literary Supplement, May 18, 1967.
Washington Post, April 14, 1970.

* * *

NICHOLS, Peter (Richard) 1927-

PERSONAL: Born July 31, 1927, in Bristol, England; son of Richard George and Violet Annie (Poole) Nichols; married Thelma Reed (a painter), December 26, 1959; children: Abigail (deceased), Louise, Daniel, Catherine. *Education:* Attended Bristol Old Vic Theatre School, 1951-53, and Trent Park Teachers College, 1958-60. *Politics:* "Utopian socialist." *Religion:* None.

ADDRESSES: Agent—Margaret Ramsay Ltd., 14a Goodwin's Court, St. Martin's Lane, London WC2N 4LL, England.

CAREER: Professional actor, 1950-55; teacher, 1956-59; playwright, 1959—. Member of board of governors of Greenwich Theatre, 1971-75; member of Arts Council drama panel, 1973-76; visiting playwright at Guthrie Theatre, Minneapolis, MN, 1976.

MEMBER: Royal Society of Literature (fellow).

AWARDS, HONORS: Evening Standard, best play awards for *A Day in the Death of Joe Egg* in 1967, *The National Health* in 1969, and *Passion Play,* in 1981, best comedy award for *Privates on Parade* in 1978; John Whiting Award, 1969; Ivor Novello Award for best British musical, c. 1977, for *Privates on Parade;* Society of West End Theatres, best comedy award, 1978, for *Privates on Parade,* best musical award, 1983, for *Poppy;* Antoinette Perry Award ("Tony") for best revival, 1985, for *Joe Egg.*

WRITINGS:

PUBLISHED PLAYS

Promenade (produced on television, 1959), in *Six Granada Plays,* Faber, 1960.
Ben Spray (produced on television, 1961), in *New Granada Plays,* Faber, 1961.
The Hooded Terror (two-act; produced on television, 1963; produced on stage, 1964), [England], 1965.
The Gorge (produced on television, 1965), in *The Television Dramatist,* Elek, 1973.
A Day in the Death of Joe Egg (two-act; first produced in Glasgow, Scotland, at Citizens Theatre, 1967; also see below), Samuel French, 1967.
The National Health (two-act; first produced in London, England, at Old Vic National Theatre, 1969; also see below), Samuel French, 1970.

Forget-Me-Not Lane (two-act; first produced in London at Greenwich Theatre, 1973), Samuel French, 1971.

Chez Nous (two-act; first produced in London at Globe Theatre, 1974), Faber, 1974.

The Freeway (two-act; first produced in London at Old Vic National Theatre, 1974), Faber, 1975.

Privates on Parade (two-act; first produced in London at Aldwych Theatre, 1977), Faber, 1977.

(And director) *Born in the Gardens* (two-act; first produced in Bristol, England, at Bristol Old Vic Theatre Royal, 1979; produced in London at Globe Theatre, 1980), Faber, 1979.

Passion Play (two-act; first produced in London at Aldwych Theatre, 1981; produced as *Passion* on Broadway, 1983), Methuen, 1981.

Poppy (with music by Monty Norman; produced in London at Barbican Theatre, 1983), Heinemann Educational, 1982.

A Piece of My Mind (produced in Southampton at Nuffield Theatre, 1987), Heinemann Educational, 1988.

UNPUBLISHED PLAYS

Daddy Kiss It Better, produced in Yorkshire, 1968.

Neither Up nor Down, produced in London, 1972.

Beasts of England (based on works by George Orwell), produced in London, 1973.

Hardin's Luck (two-act; adapted from a work by E. Nesbit), first produced in London at Greenwich Theatre, 1977.

SCREENPLAYS

Catch Us if You Can/Having a Wild Weekend, Anglo Amalgamated, 1965.

Georgy Girl (adapted from the novel by Margaret Forster), Columbia, 1966.

Joe Egg (adapted from his play *A Day in the Death of Joe Egg*), Columbia, 1971.

National Health (adapted from his play *The National Health*), Columbia, 1973.

Privates on Parade (adapted from his play of the same title), Handmade Films, 1983.

Also author of *Changing Places,* 1984.

OTHER

Feeling You're Behind (autobiography), Weidenfeld & Nicolson, 1984.

Author of fifteen television plays and two adaptations of short stories for television.

WORK IN PROGRESS: A musical; a television series.

SIDELIGHTS: A Day in the Death of Joe Egg, Peter Nichols's first stage success, concerns two young parents coping with their mute, mongoloid child. It is also a comedy, noted *Time*'s T. E. Kalem, which places Nichols in the circle of contemporary British playwrights who treat serious subjects with a caustic, mordant sense of humor. In Kalem's view, "No one in contemporary theater orchestrates mordant laughter with a surer hand than . . . Nichols." Many reviewers focused on the comic strengths of the play; *Encounter* critic John Spurling praised the seriousness of its subject: "*Joe Egg* [gave] a hearty music-hall humour to a gloomy subject, but the basis of its considerable appeal for audiences was that it dealt in straightforward naturalistic terms with a topical problem—what is it like to have a spastic child?"

In his next play, *The National Health,* Nichols sets the action in a London hospital ward for the dying. Brendan Gill wrote in the *New Yorker:* " 'The National Health' . . . is a play about the physical and spiritual indignities of sickness, old age, and approaching death. . . . The dreadfulness of suffering and the still greater dreadfulness of the certain end to suffering hang in the antiseptic air. . . . Hard as it may be to believe, Mr. Nichols' play is an unbroken series of successful jokes: gallows humor of a kind that makes us simultaneously gasp and laugh. . . . Nichols' close, compassionate scrutiny of life and death heightened my sense of well-being instead of diminishing it."

The black comedy of *Joe Egg* and *The National Health* exemplified British theatre in the late 1960s, according to Kalem, and reflected a national mood about conditions of life in England. For nearly two decades the London stage had been dominated by the angry, antiestablishment plays of writers like John Osborne (*Look Back in Anger*), but the change in dramatic tone, from hostility to a grim, mocking humor, corresponded to the decline of the welfare state. "Underlying that mockery is a sour nagging resentment of the present sorry state of England," Kalem contended. "Thus it is no unintended irony that *The National Health* is set in a hospital ward," where terminally ill patients meet their suffering without a loss of humor, however grisly. "Laughter," Kalem explained, "is a wonder drug by which man anesthetizes his consciousness" of dismal circumstances.

One criticism made against Nichols, that he does not fully exploit the dramatic potential of his plays, came from Stanley Kauffmann, whose review of *The National Health* appeared in the *New Republic:* "In all his work so far Nichols has shown irreverence for sentimentality and theatrical taboos but, fundamentally, not much more. He seems to bite bullets—in *Joe Egg* the anguish of having a brain-damaged child, in this play the implacability of the hospital beds waiting for every one of us—but he just mouths them for a while before he spits them out, he never really crunches. We keep waiting for the author's gravity as distinct from the subject's."

Ronald Bryden raised similar concerns in his review of *Chez Nous,* arguing that the conflict between gravity and farce, reality and fantasy, is central to the kind of plays Nichols writes. "Unfortunately," he remarked, "it becomes clear in *Chez Nous* that this recurring opposition expresses an equivalent tug-of-war within Nichols' talent." This time Nichols constructs a domestic comedy around two English couples, Liz and Dick, Diana and Phil, one visiting the other. In the middle of the quartet, though never seen onstage, is Liz and Dick's thirteen-year-old daughter, Jane, who turns out to be the mother of Phil's baby. This revelation comes early in the play and serves as the departure point for an examination of marriage, sexual relationships, and such contemporary subjects as pubescent liberation.

Bryden began his discussion of *Chez Nous* by observing that Nichols partly uses "plays as play: as fantasies exploring the alternatives to real life. The other half is . . . the realist who [reminds us] that you can have real emotions only about reality." In his estimation the central incident, Jane and Phil's parenthood, "is an improbability, a deliberate alternative to real life, engineered as a play-experiment to see what emotions one should have about it. Because it's unreal . . . most of the emotions it generates are unreal too. . . . I haven't said anything, I hope, which suggests that he's capable of writing a really bad play. But he spends far too much of his evening exploring all the unreal emotions. . . . His indulgence of fantasy has made things too artificial for . . . much conviction."

Some of the particular strengths of the play and Nichols's talent were described by Benedict Nightingale in his review for the *New Statesman:* "This is a very intelligent, careful play, which regards its protagonists with humour, horror, exasperation and compassion, though not always in equal proportion. . . . Diana and Phil prove rather more sympathetic—she for all her fastidiousness and melodramatics, he, with his ostentatious crudity, his pathetic yen for youth and craving for paternity. Their reconciliation, in which she unfurls the hysterectomy-scarred body she's always kept hidden, is unexpectedly moving, a declaration that affection can survive a mangling. As Nichols sees it, men are in thrall to their sexual drives, women doomed to humour them, but both sexes more tenaciously committed to marriage than they sometimes realise."

In *The Freeway* Nichols again joins fantasy and reality to launch an attack against rampant capitalism and acquisitiveness. Here he projects an England of the future in which all but the poorest own an automobile. Further, he envisions an eighty-mile-long traffic jam that lasts for three days on Britain's Fl, a colossal freeway running the length of the nation. Members of the aristocracy and working class are forced to contend with each other as well as with the lack of food, water, and sanitation. Kenneth Hurren of the *Spectator* stated, "Fl and the trouble that develops on it are a tortured metaphor for British democracy, class-ridden and acquisitive, careering along a freeway to disaster."

The Freeway fared less well with critics than Nichols's previous works. Hurren commented: "[Nichols] is a dramatist who has hitherto seemed possessed of as vivaciously original a comic talent as anyone presently operating in the theatre, and it is as surprising as it is dismaying to find that talent . . . foundering bleakly in contemplation of the menace of the motor car. . . . It would plainly be possible to develop the situation pretty humorously, but Nichols on this occasion seems to be altogether too embittered (he must have had some really terrible times in the Peugeot), and it is a measure, I suppose, of his desperation—and of the extraordinary fall in his standards of comedy—that he is reduced to the desolate business of trying to get a laugh or two out of people going to the lavatory in rather primitive circumstances."

In his review of the play Nightingale talked about some of the ideas Nichols raises: "We learn that individual self-indulgence can produce social misery; that labour tends to equate happiness with possessions, and that capital is only too glad to keep its power with the odd handout; that freedom, in short, may be slavery. But anyone who has read a little 19th-century history . . . will want to see more slippery questions tackled. . . . I found *The Freeway* not unenjoyable, a deliberately negative recommendation. As a play of ideas, it could be more provocative; as a comedy about people in a jam, more trenchant and amusing."

Passion Play, produced in New York as *Passion,* ranked among the best plays of the 1982-83 Broadway season, according to *New York Times* critic Frank Rich: "Nichols takes one of the oldest tales in the book—a middle-aged husband has an affair with a younger woman—and, with virtuoso writing and unsparing honesty, rocks the foundations of an audience's complacency." Nichols's innovation is to bring onstage, as separate entities, the private selves of his two protagonists, allowing the audience a rare glimpse behind the careful facades of the couple as their marriage dissolves. When, for instance, the husband first lies to his wife to cover up his affair, he remains placid on the outside while his private self capers around the stage in celebration. Observed Rich, "Nichols's plays demand dazzling direction and polished acting, in part because they almost always involve tricky theatrical devices" such as the dual personas in *Passion.* Although inspiring laughter at first, "the divided nature of the characters—and the juxtapositions of longing and heartbreak—become rending," Rich concluded. Similarly, a London *Times*

reviewer, commenting on a London revival of the work, wrote that the "marvellous" play will "hit you dead between the eyes."

BIOGRAPHICAL/CRITICAL SOURCES:

BOOKS

Contemporary Literary Criticism, Gale, Volume 5, 1976, Volume 36, 1986.
Dictionary of Literary Biography, Volume 13: *British Dramatists since World War II,* Gale, 1982.
Kerensky, Oleg, *The New British Drama,* Hamish Hamilton. 1977.
Taylor, J. R., *The Second Wave,* Methuen, 1971.

PERIODICALS

Commonweal, March 15, 1968.
Encounter, January, 1975.
Hudson Review, summer, 1968.
Los Angeles Times, June 20, 1984, November 11, 1984, December 16, 1984.
Nation, February 19, 1968.
National Observer, February 12, 1968.
New Leader, February 26, 1968.
New Republic, November 2, 1974.
New Statesman, February 15, 1974, October 11, 1974.
Newsweek, February 12, 1968.
New Yorker, February 10, 1968, October 21, 1974.
New York Times, November 7, 1977, June 7, 1979, October 24, 1982, May 16, 1983, April 13, 1984, January 7, 1985, January 20, 1985, April 2, 1985, April 7, 1985, August 23, 1989.
Plays and Players, March, 1974.
Spectator, October 25, 1969, October 12, 1974.
Stage, June 8, 1972.
Time, October 21, 1974.
Times (London), April 23, 1984, May 10, 1984, March 11, 1987.
Times Literary Supplement, July 13, 1984.
Washington Post, July 17, 1969, July 27, 1969.*

* * *

NILES, John Jacob 1892-1980

PERSONAL: Born April 28, 1892, in Louisville, KY; died March 1, 1980, in Lexington, KY; son of John Thomas (a sheriff, farmer, singer, and square dance caller) and Lula Sarah (Reisch) Niles; married Rena Lipetz (a free-lance writer), March 21, 1936; children: Thomas Michael Tolliver, John Edward. *Education:* Attended University of Lyon, 1918-19, Schola Cantorum, 1919, University of London, 1919, and Cincinnati Conservatory of Music, 1920-23. *Religion:* Episcopalian. *Avocational interests:* Painting, wood carving, instrument making (dulcimers), farming, stone and brick masonry, and fox hunting.

ADDRESSES: Home and office—Boot Hill Farm, 7515 Athens-Boonesboro Rd., Lexington, KY 40509.

CAREER: Composer and concert singer; collector and arranger of American folk music. Performer in concerts throughout the United States, Europe, and Canada, 1927-78; performer under RCA Victor, Tradition, Camden, and Folkways labels, and under his own label, Boone-Tolliver. Teacher of short courses at universities, including Harvard University, Juilliard School of Music, and Eastman School of Music. Participant in the radio series, "John Jacob Niles' Salute to the Hills," broadcast by the University of Kentucky, 1937-40. *Military service:* U.S. Aviation Service, 1917-19; served with Italian, French, Belgian, and English units; became first lieutenant; received War Cross from Italy and Belgium, and U.S. service citation.

MEMBER: American Society of Composers, Authors, and Publishers (ASCAP), American Folklore Society, American Federation of Television and Radio Artists, American Dialect Society, Kentucky Folklore Society, Iroquois Hunt Club.

AWARDS, HONORS: Mus.D., Cincinnati Conservatory of Music, 1949; national citation, National Federation of Music Clubs, 1967; D.F.A., Transylvania University, 1969; Litt.D., Episcopal Theological Seminary (Lexington), 1970, University of Kentucky, 1973; H.H.D., University of Louisville, 1971.

WRITINGS:

FOLK SONG COLLECTIONS

Impressions of a Negro Camp Meeting: Eight Traditional Tunes, Carl Fischer, 1925.
Singing Soldiers (World War I songs), Scribner, 1927.
Seven Kentucky Mountain Songs, G. Schirmer, 1928.
(With Douglas S. Moore and A. A. Wallgren) *Songs My Mother Never Taught Me* (World War I songs), Macaulay, 1929.
Seven Negro Exaltations, G. Schirmer, 1929.
Songs of the Hill-Folk, G. Schirmer, 1934.
Ten Christmas Carols from the Southern Appalachian Mountains, G. Schirmer, 1935.
More Songs of the Hill-Folk, G. Schirmer, 1936.
Ballads, Carols, and Tragic Legends from the Southern Appalachian Mountains, G. Schirmer, 1937, new edition, 1938.
The Singing Campus, G. Schirmer, 1941.
The Anglo-American Ballad Study Book, G. Schirmer, 1945.
The Anglo-American Carol Study Book, G. Schirmer, 1948.
The Shape-Note Study Book, G. Schirmer, 1950.
John Jacob Niles Suite, compiled by Weldon Hart, G. Schirmer, 1952.
The Ballad Book of John Jacob Niles, Houghton, 1961.
(With Helen Louise Smith) *Folk Carols for Young Actors* (includes record), Holt, 1962.
(With Smith) *Folk Ballads for Young Actors* (includes record), Holt, 1962.
John Jacob Niles' Song Book for Guitar, arranged by Leon Block, G. Schirmer, 1963.
The John Jacob Niles Bicentennial Song-Book, G. Schirmer, 1976.

MUSICAL COMPOSITIONS

Lamentation (oratorio; first performed in Terre Haute, IN, 1951), G. Schirmer, 1950.
Mary the Rose (Christmas cantata), G. Schirmer, 1955.
Rhapsody for the Merry Month of May (cantata), G. Schirmer, 1955.
The Little Family (Easter carol), G. Schirmer, 1962.
Moses and Pharaoh's Daughter, G. Schirmer, 1962.
Reward (for solo voice and piano), G. Schirmer, 1963.
The Niles-Merton Cycles: Opus 171 and Opus 172, Mark Foster Music, 1981.

Also author of "Concerto for Piano and Orchestra in F-Minor," completed in 1957, first performed in Louisville, KY; "Symphony No. 1," first performed in Sacramento, CA, 1963; "Melodies from an October Song Book," Opus 150; "Courting Time," Opus 152, no. 2; "Unused I Am to Lovers," Opus 153, no. 1; and "Winter Lullaby," Opus 154, no. 1. Collector or composer and arranger of over one thousand folk songs published individually by G. Schirmer, Mark Foster Music Co., Hirshaw Music Co., and Carl Fischer.

OTHER

(With Bert Hall) *One Man's War: The Story of the Lafayette Escadrille* (narrative), Henry Holt, 1929.
One Woman's War (narrative), Macaulay, 1930.
(With wife, Rena Niles) *Mr. Poof's Discovery* (juvenile), Bur Press, 1947.
Rhymes for A. Wince (nursery rhymes), Department of Special Collections, Margaret I. King Library (Lexington), 1971.
Brick Dust and Buttermilk (poetry), Gnomon Distributors, 1977.

Author of over 250 sonnets. Contributor of stories to periodicals, including *Atlantic* and *Scribner's Magazine*.

WORK IN PROGRESS: The Autobiography of John Jacob Niles, under a grant from the National Endowment for the Humanities.

SIDELIGHTS: John Jacob Niles once told *CA* that "my concern has been the grassroots of America, especially as revealed in its balladry and folk music." Called the "dean of American balladeers," Niles was one of the earliest collectors of Anglo-American folk music. In 1907, he began filling notebooks with tunes he heard while working as a surveyor in his native Kentucky; eventually, his gathering extended to the Southern Appalachian regions of North Carolina, Tennessee, Georgia, Alabama, Virginia, and West Virginia. By mid-1930 he was said to have had the largest private collection of folk songs in the world. Leslie Shepard, however, observed in the notes to one of Niles's albums that "these were not the impeccable scholarly collections of professors on university grants. Interspersed with the songs and a primitive musical shorthand were riddles, proverbs, and fragments of folk dialect and superstition. It was a very personal affair of hastily scrawled, tentatively noted pieces under difficult and even hazardous circumstances, garnered from farmers, preachers, handymen, old grannies, moonshiners, traveling people, and even jailbirds." "Black is the Color of My True Love's Hair," one of Niles's most famous songs, was written in 1916 and has since been translated into thirty-two languages and adapted for full orchestra. Not only did Niles compose other well-known songs such as "I Wonder As I Wander," "Venezuela," and "Go 'Way from My Window," but he also wrote *The Niles-Merton Song Cycles,* a series of accompaniments to the verses of the late philosopher Thomas Merton.

As a boy, Niles was encouraged by his father to make his own instruments, and except when using a piano, the singer always accompanied himself on a handmade eight-string dulcimer. He received $1.50 for his first paid performance in 1907; by 1930 he had appeared throughout America and much of Europe, and by 1950 had performed in every state of the United States, sometimes giving more than fifty concerts a year. In concert, as well as in writing his music, Niles introduced his songs with informally amusing and detailed descriptions, often including the historical or political background of the music. He was one of the few folk singers to use only material he had collected or composed himself, in many cases creating completely original works within the folk tradition. As a result Niles claimed to be "the leading folk singer of the Western world, and you might as well admit it," as he was quoted in the *Washington Post.* "I started the whole thing." Indeed, it was through the efforts of pioneers like Niles that the folk-singing concert became a popular venue with audiences worldwide. With his "weird, hoarse falsetto," as *Saturday Review* critic Oscar Brand termed it, Niles "add[ed] a strange power to some of his renditions." By writing and singing "his own material in the practised tradition of the old minstrels," the critic concluded, Niles "support[ed] the practice of balladry as a living, breathing art."

BIOGRAPHICAL/CRITICAL SOURCES:

BOOKS

Howard, John T., *Our American Music,* 3rd edition, Crowell, 1946.
Lawless, Ray M., *Folksingers and Folksongs in America,* Duell, Sloan & Pearce, 1960, 2nd edition, Meredith, 1965.
Okun, Milton, compiler, *Something to Sing About,* Macmillan, 1968.
Peattie, Roderick, editor, *The Great Smokies and the Blue Ridge,* Vanguard, 1943.

PERIODICALS

Life, September 6, 1943.
New York Times, February 17, 1957.
Saturday Review, August 29, 1953.

OTHER

Shepard, Leslie, "John Jacob Niles" (booklet accompanying Folkways record album #FA 2373), Folkways Records, c. 1964.

OBITUARIES:

PERIODICALS

Los Angeles Times, March 3, 1980.
New York Times, March 3, 1980.
Washington Post, March 4, 1980.*

[Death date provided by wife, Rena Niles.]

*   *   *

NIXON, Richard M(ilhous)   1913-

PERSONAL: Born January 9, 1913, in Yorba Linda, Calif.; son of Francis Anthony (a store owner) and Hannah (Milhous) Nixon; married Patricia Ryan, June 21, 1940; children: Patricia (Mrs. Edward Finch Cox), Julie (Mrs. Dwight David Eisenhower II). *Education:* Whittier College, A.B. (with honors), 1934; Duke University, LL.B. (with honors), 1937. *Religion:* Society of Friends (Quaker).

ADDRESSES: Home—Saddle River, N.J. *Office*—26 Federal Plaza, New York, N.Y. 10278.

CAREER: Thirty-seventh president of the United States. Bewley, Knoop & Nixon, Whittier, Calif., general practice of law, 1937-42; Office of Emergency Management, Washington, D.C., attorney in tire rationing division, 1942; U.S. Representative from 12th District of California, serving on Education and Labor Committee, Select Committee on Foreign Aid, and Committee on Un-American Activities, 1947-50; appointed to vacant seat in U.S. Senate, 1950; U.S. Senator from California, serving on Labor and Public Welfare Committee and Expenditures in Executive Departments Committee, 1951-53; Vice-President of the United States, serving as chairman of President Eisenhower's Committee on Government Contracts, chairman of the Cabinet Committee on Price Stability for Economic Growth, and as the personal representative of the president on goodwill trips to fifty-four countries, 1953-61; Republican candidate for the presidency, with Henry Cabot Lodge as running mate, 1960; Adams, Duque & Hazeltine, Los Angeles, Calif., counsel, 1961-62; Republican candidate for governor of California, 1962; Mudge, Stern, Baldwin & Todd, New York City, member of firm,

1962-63; Nixon, Mudge, Rose, Guthrie & Alexander (later Nixon, Mudge, Rose, Guthrie, Alexander & Mitchell), New York City, partner, 1964-68; elected president of United States, with Spiro T. Agnew as vice-president, 1968, reelected to office with landslide majority vote of electoral college, 1972, resigned, 1974. Trustee, Whittier College, 1939-68; honorary chairman of Boys' Clubs of America. *Military service:* U.S. Naval Reserve, 1942-46; served in Pacific theatre of operations; became lieutenant commander.

MEMBER: French Fine Arts Academy (foreign associate member), Order of Coif.

WRITINGS:

The Challenges We Face (excerpts compiled from speeches and papers), McGraw, 1960.
Six Crises (autobiographical), Doubleday, 1962.
The Inaugural Address of Richard Milhous Nixon, Achille J. St. Onge, 1969.
Setting the Course, The First Year (policy statements), Funk, 1970.
U.S. Foreign Policy for the 1970's: Report to Congress, Harper, 1971.
A New Road for America (policy statements), Doubleday, 1972.
Four Great Americans (tributes to Dwight Eisenhower, Everett Dirksen, Whitney M. Young, and J. Edgar Hoover), Doubleday, 1973.
The Nixon Presidential Press Conferences, Earl M. Coleman, 1978.
RN: The Memoirs of Richard Nixon, Grosset, 1978.
The Real War, Warner Books, 1980.
Leaders, Warner Books, 1982.
Real Peace: A Strategy for the West, Little, Brown, 1983.
No More Vietnams, Arbor House, 1985.
1999: The Global Challenges We Face in the Next Decade, Simon & Schuster, 1988, published as *1999: Victory without War,* 1988.
In the Arena: A Memoir of Victory, Defeat and Renewal, Simon & Schuster, 1990.

Also author of yearly collections of State of the Union messages, news conference texts, messages to Congress, and major statements, published by Congressional Quarterly, 5 volumes, 1970-74; author of reports, speeches, addresses, official papers, and transcript collections published by U.S. Government Printing Office and other publishers.

SIDELIGHTS: When Richard M. Nixon first ran for public office over forty years ago, it was the start of a distinguished and highly visible political career that included terms as congressman, senator, vice-president, and eventually President of the United States. Nixon was frequently embroiled in controversy throughout his career, whether as a congressman investigating communism for the House Un-American Activities Committee in the late 1940s, or as a president criticized by liberals for U.S. involvement in Vietnam and by conservatives for establishing ties with Communist China. Nixon will most likely be known, however, for the scandal which drove him out of office in 1974; the Watergate break-in and cover up was tied to several members of his administration, and under threat of Congressional action, Nixon resigned the office. "Clare Boothe Luce once said that each person in history can be summed up in one sentence," Nixon related in a *Time* interview. "This was after I had gone to China. She said, 'You will summed up, "He went to China."' Historians are more likely to lead with 'He resigned the office.'"

Although Watergate ended his political career, Nixon has remained in the public eye with the publication of several books which focus on political issues and his own experiences. After recovering from a near-fatal bout of phlebitis in late 1974, as part of his "spiritual recovery" Nixon decided to write a personal account of his political career. *RN: The Memoirs of Richard Nixon* was published in 1978 to reviews that, while they differ in their assessment of the president himself, find the book interesting as a revelation of Nixon's character. *New York Times* critic Christopher Lehmann-Haupt, for example, observes that despite biases and flaws *RN* "remains a fascinating performance. Whether one dislikes it or admires it, the voice of the prose reflects its author more distinctly than does that of any other American political memoir I can think of offhand, and, for reasons both negative and positive, that voice continues to hypnotize throughout the book's 1,100 pages." "This is a tremendous book, rich in concrete detail, a major political event, and as close as we are ever likely to get to that *sui generis* political creature, Richard Nixon," Jeffrey Hart of the *National Review* similarly claims.

Many critics have noted, in the words of *New York Times Book Review* contributor James MacGregor Burns, that "most of this huge volume [Nixon] devotes to a long statement for the defense." As a result, the critic continues, "the fact that [Nixon's] accounts are highly selective, that he seeks to score points in a continuing debate with the news media and his other adversaries, that his judgments range from the contentious to the tendentious, should not surprise us." "But even [these] flaws of the book help to tell the story," Elizabeth Drew suggests in the *Washington Post Book World*, "the story of an individual whose mind worked in a certain way." Clive James likewise comments that *RN*, despite its subjective slant, "is not a mean book. Nixon's faults are all on view, but so is the fact that they are faults in something substantial," James writes in the *New Statesman*. "His claims to a place in history are shown to be not all that absurd," and his memoirs "constitute a readable book of no small literary merit and considerable human dignity." "For all of this book's predictable flaws," Drew concludes, "it is an interesting, sometimes even absorbing account that cannot be dismissed. Nixon is a major figure in our history, and here he gives us his own version of the years in which he dominated our national life."

Although his resignation removed Nixon from directly participating in political life, he considers that "for whatever time I have left, . . . what is most important is to be able to affect the course of events," as he remarked in *Time*. To that end, he has written several books on foreign policy; his first, 1980's *The Real War*, outlines the history and possible future of the Cold War, and "is a straightforward call for the United States to mobilize *all* its power—military, economic, political, Presidential, clandestine, intellectual, informational and especially will power—to combat the Soviet Union on a global scale," Flora Lewis summarizes in the *New York Times Book Review*.

Critics have faulted the book, however, both for what Lewis terms "a highly selective approach" to historical examples and for Nixon's combative tone. As *New York Review of Books* critic Ronald Steel states: "In this book instead of addressing himself seriously to the issues, [Nixon] panders to the public's anxieties. Instead of being constructive, he is once again being demolishing." And Philip Geyelin declares in the *Washington Post Book World* that *The Real War* overlooks Third World nationalism in order to emphasize fighting the communist threat; in addition, "what's missing here is any sense of how, as a practical matter, you do most of these things—where you get the money, for one thing, not to mention public or Congressional support." But,

says David E. Kaiser in a *New Republic* article, "one need not share Nixon's assumptions or value his role in American history in order to find this book provocative. Much of its argument draws effectively on history, it says publicly what many foreign policy specialists probably believe but dare not reveal, and its world view has an inner consistency that forces every reader to examine his own basic assumptions."

Real Peace addresses some of the same issues as Nixon's previous work, but with a view towards detente rather than confrontation. "On balance," maintains Alvin Shuster in the *Los Angeles Times Book Review*, "[Nixon] has done well in taking critic issues before the country, in condensing and discussing them with a fair amount of clarity and force. There is no great writing here but he does manage to describe complex problems in understandable terms." Robert W. Tucker, however, feels that while Nixon's political assessments of the chances for "real peace" are interesting, he omits a concrete plan for attaining this peace. As the critic writes in the *New York Times Book Review*: "The need for Mr. Nixon's real peace can scarcely be denied. How to move toward it remains the great question." But critics such as Joseph Sobran find *Real Peace* more specific in its approach than *The Real War*, especially in the realm of Third World relations. As Sobran comments in the *National Review*, Nixon's new book "is an incisive, often profound manifesto for 'hard-headed detente,' written with aphoristic punch. . . . *Real Peace* contains the antidote to its own single mistake, and much wisdom and practical shrewdness besides. It is a book we need."

In *No More Vietnams* Nixon traces the history of foreign involvement in Vietnam and proposes policies that would prevent another setback against communism. "Besides aggressive self-justification," Toronto *Globe and Mail* writer William Thorsell notes, "this book aims to inspire renewed U.S. commitment to military intervention around the world to stop a voracious communism." " 'No More Vietnams' is two books," historian James Chace suggests in the *New York Times Book Review*. "The first is a highly selective history of the Vietnam War—a war, as he tells it, that we won. We then, however, 'lost the peace.' The second and more interesting book," the critic continues, is the chapter which outlines Nixon's program "to win the hearts and minds—and stomachs—of the third world." Echoing previous criticisms of Nixon's work, some reviewers have faulted the former president's interpretation of past events, citing a lack of specific attributions. As *Chicago Tribune* writer Raymond Coffey observes, despite some strong arguments, "the big problem with the book is that its version of Vietnam history . . . is so blatantly, so outrageously, self-serving that much of the weight and force of the Nixon prescription for the future . . . tend to be diminished."

Nevertheless, Steel admits, "Nixon is an intelligent man and many things in his book are thoughtful and challenging. He is always interesting to listen to, particularly on foreign policy, a field in which he has concentrated so much of his energies." Hart goes further in his praise, writing that *No More Vietnams* "is extraordinarily concise, providing, along with its strongly argued thesis . . . a history and an assessment of our Vietnam policy beginning with the Truman Administration in the immediate post-World War II period. Mr. Nixon's perspective here is presidential, his grasp of the history firm, and his judgments persuasive." "*No More Vietnams* is a very good book, in my opinion Richard Nixon's best, saving only the remarkable *Memoirs*," Chilton Williamson, Jr., likewise states in the *National Review*. "Though frankly intended as a brief in defense of . . . American presence in Southeast Asia, as a history of a quarter-century of bitter warfare it develops and sustains sufficient consistency to extend its reach far beyond the bounds of mere apologia." "There is considerable intelligence in this polemic," concludes Thorsell, "enormous partisanship, useful insights, breathtaking self-delusion . . . , a feisty challenge to the media, and the crafty use of language."

1999: Victory without War is "important because it is a serious, cogently argued attempt to get American politicians . . . to look forward and to evolve a set of policies that will bring the United States, and the rest of the world, safely into the 21st century," as Paul Kennedy describes it in the *Washington Post Book World.* "Although written by a politician whose right-wing and anti-communist convictions are frequently in evidence, it nonetheless offers perspectives that ought to interest Democrats as much as Republicans." *1999,* according to Thorsell, "restates Nixon's fundamental thesis—that the Soviet drive for world domination remains the central fact of global politics, and that the United States is the Soviet Union's only real opponent." To that end, Nixon outlines potential U.S. strategies for dealing with not only the Soviet Union, but Europe, Asia, and third world nations. "He argues that one of the significant trends in the 21st century will be the rise of Western Europe, Japan and China to increasing importance in world politics, and he has a splendid chapter, both sympathetic and instructive, on the problems of the third world," *New York Times Book Review* contributor Marshall D. Shulman summarizes. This "effort to mark out a centrist position," the critic adds, "may contribute to the emergence of a more coherent consensus for American foreign policy."

Some reviewers, however, criticize the author for overlooking the effects of Soviet president Mikhail Gorbachev's reforms as well as the economic costs of pursuing a "victory without war" against the Soviets. The book, writes Stanley Hoffman in the *New Republic,* contains "an almost indiscriminate paranoia about the Soviet Union—and the absence of a political and financial price tag." "Nixon should stop trying so hard to sound like a statesman," James Fallows avers in the *New York Review of Books,* in favor of what the critic calls the former president's "canny, lawyerlike, poker-playing instinct for sizing up a situation and understanding the possibilities it allows." In contrast, Lehmann-Haupt, who finds Nixon's work full of "clarity, simplicity, and anecdotal appeal," believes that "what needs to be stressed is that in the main '1999' reflects what [Nixon's] admirers have always insisted is the better side of him. In short, if there is a residue of the political opportunist in these pages, it is by and large overwhelmed by the student of statecraft that he has aspired with such doggedness and energy to become." "If he is a prideful prisoner of traumatic experience, and moved too much by the desire for vindication, Nixon is also the most rigorous thinker who has inhabited the White House since John F. Kennedy," Thorsell similarly concludes. "His categorical view of the world need not be shared, but his voice should be heard. Again."

National Review contributor Herbert S. Parmet likewise praises the former president as "the most prominent, gifted, and contentious leader of post-World War II America," and terms 1990's *In the Arena: A Memoir of Victory, Defeat, and Renewal* "a useful introduction to [Nixon's] mind and personality." Consisting of a series of short chapters on various political and personal subjects, the critic continues, *In the Arena* "reveals Nixon the Elder, a long way from the Whittier lawyer, with a voice more mature but strikingly recognizable." This more personal tone, comments Lehmann-Haupt, is most likely due to Nixon's use of dictation in writing the book; "it is a more relaxed book," Lehmann-Haupt observes, and the chapters "read as if the author had unbuttoned his mind and set it free to gather wool." While this method allows the reader to glimpse and empathize with "a figure in many emotional guises," the critic adds, it also "prompts [Nixon] to refer to episodes in his career that have not only been dealt with at length in his previous books, but that are also covered repeatedly in the present volume." As a result, Roger Morris suggests in the *New York Times Book Review,* "what may distinguish the book most . . . are the aphorisms that flow from the resonant and authentic Nixon voice."

Nevertheless, some critics think that *In the Arena* devotes too much space to defending the author's political record and ideas. *Los Angeles Times Book Review* contributor John B. Judis, for instance, while noting that "there are sensible and interesting sections in this book," asserts that the book's "attempts at self-justification and its neo-Cold War policy prescriptions reflect a man who is still bedeviled by his past." *Washington Post Book World* writer Bob Woodward, however, believes that despite "the limitations of this book, and there are many, Nixon once again provides convincing evidence that he is a masterful student of world politics. He repeatedly digs for and finds examples of successful leadership, deftly isolating the powerful personality traits of Eisenhower, De Gaulle, Chou En-Lai and other giants. . . . Nixon is best writing about his intensely personal struggles (few better understand the importance of raw emotion in political life) and about the larger international scene he continues to study avidly." "This is, in most ways, a wistful book, suggesting what has been lost all around rather than beating to death the what-could-have-beens," concludes Parmet. "The spirit may be forced, but the closing tone is nevertheless upbeat and reflective. Nixon lives on; some will say he has returned, as if he ever disappeared."

"Despite one of the worst scandals in the history of the Presidency," Richard Bernstein states in the *New York Times,* Richard Nixon "has carved out a sizable niche for himself in the public arena with his reputation for realism and sagacity in public affairs." "There are few retired Washington giants," Paul Johnson similarly remarks in *Commentary,* that "keep themselves so well briefed on the state of the world, or who have more worthwhile observations to make about it." The critic adds that "there can be few men whose judgment of the American political scene is so shrewd and penetrating, as well as surprisingly objective. . . . He probably exercises more political influence than any other Western statesman not actually in office. Considering the depths of degradation from which he has climbed, this is a remarkable achievement." Returning from adversity is not an unusual achievement for Nixon, however, as he acknowledges in his latest memoir: "As I look back on the dark days after my resignation, my most vivid memory is of a conversation I had with Ambassador Walter Annenberg shortly after I returned to San Clemente in 1974. He said, 'Whether you have been knocked down or are on the ropes, always remember that life is ninety-nine rounds.' Today, the battle I started to wage forty-three years ago when I first ran for Congress is not over. I still have a few rounds to go."

BIOGRAPHICAL/CRITICAL SOURCES:

BOOKS

Ambrose, Stephen E., *Nixon,* Simon & Schuster, Volume 1: *The Education of a Politician 1913-1962,* 1987, Volume 2: *The Triumph of a Politician 1962-72,* 1989.

Bernstein, Carl, and Bob Woodward, *All the President's Men,* Simon & Schuster, 1974.

Bernstein, Carl, and Bod Woodward, *The Final Days,* Simon & Schuster, 1976.

Brodie, Fawn M., *Richard Nixon: The Shaping of His Character,* Harvard University Press, 1983.

Casper, D. E., *Richard M. Nixon,* Garland Publishing, 1988.

Ehrlichman, John, *Witness to Power: The Nixon Years,* Simon & Schuster, 1982.

Frost, David, *"I Gave Them a Sword": Behind the Scenes of the Nixon Interviews,* Morrow, 1978.

Lukas, James Anthony, *Nightmare: The Underside of the Nixon Years,* Bantam, 1977.

Morris, Roger, *Richard Milhous Nixon: The Rise of an American Politician,* Henry Holt, 1989.

Nixon, Richard M., *Six Crises,* Doubleday, 1962.

Nixon, Richard M., *RN: The Memoirs of Richard Nixon,* Grosset, 1978.

Nixon, Richard M., *In the Arena: A Memoir of Victory, Defeat and Renewal,* Simon & Schuster, 1990.

Safire, William, *Before the Fall,* Doubleday, 1975.

Sulzberger, C. L., *The World and Richard Nixon,* Prentice Hall Press, 1987.

White, Theodore, *Making of the President 1972,* Atheneum, 1973.

White, Theodore, *Breach of Faith,* Atheneum, 1975.

Wills, Gary, *Nixon Agonistes,* Houghton, 1970, revised and enlarged edition, New American Library, 1979.

The Young Nixon, California State University Fullerton, Oral History Program, 1978.

PERIODICALS

Chicago Tribune, March 31, 1985.

Commentary, August, 1979, August, 1980, October, 1988.

Globe and Mail (Toronto), May 4, 1985, June 11, 1988.

Los Angeles Times Book Review, October 31, 1982, January 15, 1984, April 28, 1985, May 8, 1988, April 29, 1990.

Nation, July 8, 1978.

National Review, August 18, 1978, July 25, 1980, February 24, 1984, May 3, 1985, May 28, 1990.

New Republic, June 14, 1980, June 10, 1985, May 23, 1988.

New Statesman, June 8, 1978.

Newsweek, May 8, 1978, May 19, 1986.

New York Review of Books, June 29, 1978, June 26, 1980, May 30, 1985, July 21, 1988.

New York Times, June 8, 1978, March 15, 1985, March 28, 1985, April 11, 1988, April 9, 1990.

New York Times Book Review, June 11, 1978, May 25, 1980, October 31, 1982, January 29, 1984, April 7, 1985, April 17, 1988, April 29, 1990.

Saturday Review, June, 1980.

Spectator, July 15, 1978.

Time, June 9, 1980, April 2, 1990.

Times (London), April 17, 1986.

Times Literary Supplement, July 7, 1978, September 19, 1986, January 27, 1989.

Tribune Books (Chicago), April 15, 1990.

Washington Post, March 21, 1988.

Washington Post Book World, May 28, 1978, June 1, 1980, November 21, 1982, March 31, 1985, April 17, 1988.

O

O'HARA, Frank 1926-1966

PERSONAL: Full name originally Francis Russell O'Hara; born June 27, 1926, in Baltimore, Md.; died July 25, 1966, in Mastic Beach, Long Island, N.Y., after being struck by a dune-buggy taxicab on Fire Island; buried in Green River Cemetery in Springs, Long Island, N.Y.; son of Russell J. and Katherine (Broderick) O'Hara. *Education:* Harvard University, A.B., 1950; University of Michigan, M.A., 1951. *Politics:* "Depends, independent I guess." *Religion:* None.

ADDRESSES: Home—790 Broadway, New York, N.Y. *Office*— Museum of Modern Art, 11 West 53rd St., New York, N.Y.

CAREER: Poet, playwright, and art critic. Museum of Modern Art, New York City, staff member, 1952-53; *Art News,* New York City, editorial associate, 1953-55; Museum of Modern Art, organizer of circulating exhibitions, 1955-60, assistant curator in department of painting and sculpture exhibitions, 1960-66. Poet and playwright in residence at Poet's Theatre, Cambridge, Mass., 1956; apprentice in stagecraft, Brattle Theatre, Cambridge. *Military service:* U.S. Navy, 1944-46.

AWARDS, HONORS: Hopwood Award, University of Michigan, 1951, for poetry; Ford Foundation fellowship, 1956; National Book Award, 1972, for *The Collected Poems of Frank O'Hara.*

WRITINGS:

POEMS

A City Winter, and Other Poems, Tibor de Nagy Gallery Editions, 1952.

Meditations in an Emergency, M. Alcover (Spain), 1956, Grove, 1957, 2nd edition, 1967.

Jackson Pollock, Braziller, 1959.

Second Avenue, Totem Press, 1960.

Odes, serigraphs by Michael Goldberg, Tiber Press, 1960, 2nd edition, Poets Press, 1969.

Lunch Poems, City Lights, 1964.

Featuring Frank O'Hara, [Buffalo, N.Y.], 1964.

Love Poems (Tentative Title), Tibor de Nagy Gallery Editions, 1965.

In Memory of My Feelings: A Selection of Poems, edited by Bill Berkson, Museum of Modern Art, New York, 1967.

Two Pieces, Long Hair Books (London), 1969.

Oranges, Angel Hair Books (New York), 1970.

The Collected Poems of Frank O'Hara, edited by Donald M. Allen, Knopf, 1971.

The Selected Poems of Frank O'Hara, edited by Allen, Knopf, 1974.

(With Bill Berkson) *Hymns of St. Bridget,* Adventures in Poetry, 1974.

Early Writing: 1946-1950, edited by Allen, Grey Fox Press, 1977.

Poems Retrieved: 1950-1966, edited by Allen, Grey Fox Press, 1977.

Also author of *The End of the Far West: 11 Poems,* 1974.

PLAYS

Try! Try!, first produced in Cambridge, Mass., at Poets Theatre, 1951.

Change Your Bedding, first produced at Poets Theatre, 1952.

The Houses at Fallen Hanging, produced at Living Theatre, 1956.

Awake in Spain (produced at Living Theatre, 1960), American Theatre for Poets, 1960.

The General's Return from One Place to Another (produced in New York City at Present Stages, 1964), [New York City], 1962.

Love's Labor (produced at Living Theatre, 1960), American Theatre for Poets, 1964.

Selected Plays, Full Court Press, 1978.

EXHIBITION CATALOGS

New Spanish Painting and Sculpture: Rafael Canogar and Others, Doubleday, for Museum of Modern Art, New York, 1960.

An Exhibition of Oil Paintings by Frankenthaler, Jewish Museum of the Jewish Theological Seminary of America, 1960.

Franz Kline, [Turin, Italy], 1963.

Arshile Gorky, Hermes (Bonn), 1964.

Robert Motherwell: With Selections from the Artist's Writings, Doubleday, for Museum of Modern Art, New York, 1965.

David Smith, 1907-1965, at the Tate Gallery, [London], 1966.

Nakian, Doubleday, for Museum of Modern Art, New York, 1966.

(With V. R. Lang) *A Day in the Life of the Czar, or I Too Have Lived in Arcadia,* produced in New York City at La Mama Etc., October, 1980.

OTHER

Hartigan and Rivers with O'Hara (an exhibition of pictures, with poems by O'Hara), Tibor de Nagy Gallery Editions, 1959.
Belgrade, November 19, 1963 (letter), Adventures in Poetry, c. 1972.
Art Chronicles 1954-66, Braziller, 1975.
Standing Still and Walking in New York (includes essays, criticism, and an interview with O'Hara), edited by Allen, Grey Fox Press, 1975.
Homage to Frank O'Hara, edited by Berkson and Joe LeSueur, Creative Arts Book (Berkeley, Calif.), 1980.

Also author of *Nature and New Painting,* Tiber Press; also author of dialogue for films; also author of unpublished short stories and of unfinished novel, *The 4th of July.* Contributor to books, including *New American Poetry,* edited by Allen, Grove, 1960. Contributor of poems to periodicals, including *Accent, Partisan Review,* and *New World Writing;* contributor of criticism to *Folder, Evergreen Review,* and *Kulchur.*

SIDELIGHTS: Frank O'Hara was described by Paul Carroll as "the first and . . . the best of the poets of the impure." Bill Berkson wrote of his work: "O'Hara has the ability, and the power, to use in a poem whatever occurred to him at the moment, without reflection. It is not that he lacked selectivity or discrimination, but rather that his poems grew out of a process of natural selection—discrimination conjoining civility of attention—so that any particle of experience quick enough to get fixed in his busy consciousness earned its point of relevance." O'Hara himself once said: "I don't think of fame or posterity (as Keats so grandly and genuinely did), nor do I care about clarifying experiences for anyone or bettering (other than accidentally) anyone's state or social relation, nor am I for any particular technical development in the American language simply because I find it necessary. What is happening to me, allowing for lies and exaggerations which I try to avoid, goes into my poems. I don't think my experiences are clarified or made beautiful for myself or anyone else, they are just there in whatever form I can find them. What is clear to me in my work is probably obscure to others, and vice versa. . . . It may be that poetry makes life's nebulous events tangible to me and restores their detail; or conversely, that poetry brings forth the intangible quality of incidents which are all too concrete and circumstantial. Or each on specific occasions, or both all the time."

O'Hara was one of the members of "The New York School" of poets, and collaborated in creative relationships with the "New York School Second Generation" painters in what were known as "poem paintings." After his death, his family and friends established the Frank O'Hara Foundation for Poetry and Art to recognize and assist poets, with eventual corresponding support for artists. The proceeds of *In Memory of My Feelings,* a limited edition volume, went to the Foundation for grants- in-aid to young writers.

BIOGRAPHICAL/CRITICAL SOURCES:

BOOKS

Allen, Donald M., *New American Poetry,* Grove, 1960.
Carroll, Paul, *The Poem in Its Skin,* Follett, 1968.
Contemporary Literary Criticism, Gale, Volume 2, 1974, Volume 5, 1976, Volume 13, 1980.
Dictionary of Literary Biography, Gale, Volume 5: *American Poets since World War II,* 2 parts, 1980, Volume 16: *The Beats: Literary Bohemians in Postwar America,* 2 parts, 1983.
Feldman, Alan, *Frank O'Hara,* Twayne, 1979.
Perloff, Marjorie, *Frank O'Hara: Poet among Painters,* Braziller, 1977.
Smith, Alexander, Jr., compiler, *Frank O'Hara: A Comprehensive Bibliography,* Garland, 1979.
Vendler, Helen, *Part of Nature, Part of Us: Modern American Poets,* Harvard University Press, 1980.

PERIODICALS

Art and Literature, spring, 1967.
Art in America, March, 1972, March, 1975.
Art News, September, 1966, January, 1968, May, 1974.
Audit/Poetry (special O'Hara issue), spring, 1964.
Christian Science Monitor, November 9, 1967, February 17, 1972.
Contemporary Literature, spring, 1976.
Iowa Review, winter, 1973, winter, 1974.
National Observer, July 10, 1967.
New Republic, January 1-8, 1972.
New Statesman, April 30, 1965.
Newsweek, January 22, 1968, December 20, 1971.
New York Review of Books, March 31, 1966.
New York Times, January 19, 1968, August 11, 1968.
New York Times Book Review, October 6, 1957, February 11, 1968, November 28, 1971.
Poetry, June, 1958, February, 1966, April, 1973.
Times Literary Supplement, January 27, 1978.
Village Voice, April 20, 1967, January 20, 1975, December 16, 1981.

OBITUARIES:

PERIODICALS

Antiquarian Bookman, September 5-12, 1966.
Newsweek, August 8, 1966.
New York Times, July 27, 1966, July 28, 1966.
Time, August 5, 1966.
Village Voice, July 28, 1966.*

P

PARENTEAU, Shirley Laurolyn 1935-

PERSONAL: Surname is pronounced Pur-*ahn*-toe; born January 22, 1935, in Garibaldi, OR; daughter of Howard Paul (a logger) and Olive (a writer and doll maker; maiden name, Stanbrough) Brunson; married George Parenteau (a sheet metal shop owner), October 9, 1954; children: David, Scott, Cherie. *Education:* Attended high school in Taft, OR. *Religion:* United Church of Christ.

ADDRESSES: Home—98 15 Emerald Park Dr., Elk Grove, CA 95624. *Office*—P.O. Box 336, Elk Grove, CA 95759.

CAREER: Allstate Insurance Co., Salem, OR, insurance rater, 1955-56; Fairview (home for the mentally retarded), Salem, OR, dictaphone transcriber, 1959-60; writer, 1961—.

MEMBER: Science Fiction Writers of America, Romance Writers of America, California Writers Club, Society of Childrens Book Writers, Novelists Inc.

AWARDS, HONORS: Second place, California Newspapers Publishers Association "Best Local Column" Award, 1980.

WRITINGS:

JUVENILES

Blue Hands, Blue Cloth, Childrens Press, 1978.
Crunch It, Munch It, and Other Ways to Eat Vegetables, Coward, 1978.
Secrets of Scarlet, Childrens Press, 1979.
(With Barbara Douglass) *A Space Age Cookbook for Kids,* Prentice-Hall, 1979.
Talking Coffins of Cryo-City, Elsevier/Nelson, 1979.
Jelly and the Spaceboat, Coward, 1981.
I'll Bet You Thought I Was Lost, Lothrop, 1981.
(With daughter, Cherie Parenteau) *100 Pig Jokes, Puns and Riddles,* Scholastic Inc., 1981.

NOVELS

Hot Springs, Ballantine, 1983.
Vulnerable, Ballantine, 1984.
Hemlock Feathers, Harlequin Historical, 1989.
Golden Prospect, Harlequin Historical, 1991.

Also author of "Outdoor Wife," a weekly newspaper column, 1973-83.

WORK IN PROGRESS: More Hogs Than Kisses, humorous fictionalized nonfiction book based on newspaper columns.

SIDELIGHTS: Shirley Laurolyn Parenteau told *CA:* "I learned to love the art of writing from my mother, who wrote news and feature stories for Oregon newspapers during the years I was growing up. When my daughter Cherie collaborated with me on a jokebook . . . it was a special thrill to see her become a third generation writer.

"Research is the most exciting part of writing historical novels. For *Golden Prospect,* my husband Bill and I traveled and camped for 2 weeks along the Gold Rush trail to the Yukon—Skagway, Alaska to Dawson City, Yukon. The weather, scenery, people and sense of history all made us eager for a return trip.

"Occasionally, I worry that a subject may be too involved for me. But I take encouragement from writer Bill Stafford, [who said,] 'Swimmers know that if they relax on the water it will prove to be miraculously buoyant; and writers know that a succession of little strokes on the material nearest them—without any prejudgments about the specific gravity of the topic or the reasonableness of their expectations—will result in creative progress.' "

* * *

PATAI, Daphne 1943-

PERSONAL: Surname rhymes with "Hawaii"; born October 12, 1943, in Jerusalem, Palestine (now Israel); came to the United States in 1950, naturalized citizen, 1953; daughter of Raphael Patai (an anthropologist) and Naomi Nir; married Gerald Strauss (a professor of history), April 2, 1980. *Education:* Indiana University, Bloomington, B.A., 1965; University of Wisconsin- Madison, M.A., 1971, Ph.D., 1977.

ADDRESSES: Home—27 Cosby Ave., Amherst, MA, 01002. *Office*—Department of Spanish and Portuguese, University of Massachusetts at Amherst, Amherst, MA, 01003.

CAREER: New York University, New York City, instructor in Portuguese, 1975-77; Hunter College of the City University of New York, New York City, adjunct lecturer in French and Portuguese, 1974-77; University of Massachusetts at Amherst, assistant and associate professor, 1978-86, associate professor, 1986-87, professor in Women's Studies Program and Department of Spanish and Portuguese, and in comparative literature,

1987—. Visiting researcher in Latin American studies at Indiana University at Bloomington, 1982-83; Sloss Visiting Professor, Department of Spanish and Portuguese, Stanford University, 1989.

AWARDS, HONORS: National Endowment for the Humanities fellowship, 1980-81; Guggenheim Foundation Fellowship, 1986-87; fellow, Institute for Advanced Study, Indiana University, Bloomington, 1986-87, visiting scholar, 1989-90; fellow, National Humanities Center, 1990-91.

WRITINGS:

(Contributor) *Studies on Jorge de Sena,* edited by H. L. Sharrer and F. G. Williams, University of California/Bandanna Books, 1981.

Myth and Ideology in Contemporary Brazilian Fiction, Fairleigh Dickinson University Press, 1983.

(Contributor) Marleen Barr and Nicholas D. Smith, editors, *Women and Utopia: Critical Interpretations* (article first published in *Women's Studies International Quarterly,* Volume 6, number 2), University Press of America (Lanham, MD), 1983.

The Orwell Mystique: A Study in Male Ideology, University of Massachusetts Press, 1984.

(Author of introduction) Katharine Burdekin, *Swastika Night,* Feminist Press, 1985.

Brazilian Women Speak: Contemporary Life Stories (interviews), Rutgers University Press, 1988.

(Editor and author of introduction) *Looking Backward, 1988-1888: Essays on Edward Bellamy,* University of Massachusetts Press, 1988.

(Editor, author of preface, and translator with others) Jorge de Sena, *By the Rivers of Babylon and Other Stories,* Rutgers University Press, 1989.

(Contributor) *O Homem que sempre Foi: Actas Selectas do Coloquio Internacional sobre Jorge de Sena,* edited by F. C. Fagundes, Edicoes 70/Instituto de Cultura e Lingua Portuguesa (Lisbon), 1990.

(Editor and author of introduction with Murray MacNicoll) Aluisio Azevedo, *Mulatto,* translation by MacNicoll, Associated University Presses (Rutherford, NJ), 1990.

(Editor and author of afterword) Burdekin, *The End of This Day's Business,* Feminist Press, 1990.

(Editor with Sherna Gluck) *Women's Words: Oral History and Feminist Methodology,* Routledge, 1991.

Contributor of stories, articles, and translations to journals, including *Etudes Francaises, Michigan Quarterly Review, Extrapolation, PMLA,* and *Women's Studies International Forum.*

WORK IN PROGRESS: On Becoming Human: The Utopian Fiction of Katharine Burdekin and *Gendermania: Male and Female Power in Utopian Fiction.*

SIDELIGHTS: In Daphne Patai's feminist study of George Orwell, *The Orwell Mystique: A Study in Male Ideology,* the author "relentlessly exposes Orwell's sexism," writes *Women's Review of Books* contributor Patsy Schweickart. "The rationale for Daphne Patai's critique of the 'Orwell Mystique' is refreshingly simple. . . . Patai's originality lies in revealing the intimate link between the form of Orwell's despair and his androcentric worldview." Erika Gottlieb states in the *Centennial Review* that Patai's "provocative feminist critique presents a case against not only George Orwell, but against the society that has uncritically accepted Orwell's self-image—the lonely, uncompromising warrior battling prejudice, oppression, exploitation." Gottlieb continues, "Patai presents a thesis no feminist can leave unread; no

Orwellian, unanswered. Holding Orwell to his own standards, her verdict is that ultimately Orwell 'cares more for his continuing privileges as a male than he does for the abstractions of justice, decency and truth on behalf of which he claims to be writing.' " Gottlieb concludes that *The Orwell Mystique* is "one of the best informed and most tightly argued studies that have emerged from the profusion of Orwell scholarship in 1984."

BIOGRAPHICAL/CRITICAL SOURCES:

BOOKS

The Orwell Mystiques: A Study in Male Ideology, University of Massachusetts Press, 1984.

PERIODICALS

Centennial Review, winter, 1986.
Women's Review of Books, November, 1984.

* * *

PATAI, Raphael 1910-

PERSONAL: Surname rhymes with "Hawaii"; born November 22, 1910, in Budapest, Hungary; came to United States in 1947, naturalized in 1951; son of Joseph (a writer) and Edith (Ehrenfeld) Patai; married Naomi Tolkowsky, June, 1940; children: Ofra Jennifer (Mrs. Burt Schneider), Daphne (Mrs. Gerald Strauss). *Education:* Attended University of Breslau, 1930-31 and Rabbinical Seminary, Breslau, 1930-31; University of Budapest, Ph.D., 1933; Rabbinical Seminary, Budapest, Rabbinical Diploma, 1936; Hebrew University of Jerusalem, Ph.D., 1936.

ADDRESSES: Home—39 Bow St., Forest Hills, NY 11375.

CAREER: Hebrew University of Jerusalem, Jerusalem, Palestine (now Israel), instructor in Hebrew, 1938-42; research fellow in ethnology, 1943-47; Palestine Institute of Folklore and Ethnology, Jerusalem, director of research, 1944-48; Dropsie College for Hebrew and Cognate Learning, Philadelphia, PA, professor of anthropology, 1948-57; Herzl Institute, New York City, director of research, 1956-71; Herzl Press, New York City, editor, 1957-71; Fairleigh Dickinson University, Rutherford, NJ, professor of anthropology, 1966-76. Visiting lecturer in anthropology, Columbia University, 1948, 1954-56, 1960-61, New School for Social Research, 1948, New York University, 1951-53, and Princeton University, 1952-54; visiting professor of anthropology, University of Pennsylvania, 1948-49 and Ohio State University, 1956; visiting professor of Jewish studies, Brooklyn College of the City University of New York, 1971-72. Consultant on Middle East, United Nations Secretariat, 1951; director, Syria Jordan-Lebanon Research Project, Human Relations Area Files, 1955-56. Field researcher, Viking Fund, 1948; fellow, Bureau of Applied Social Research, Columbia University, 1948.

MEMBER: American Anthropological Association (fellow), Council of American Folklore Society, American Friends of Tel Aviv University (president), 1956-68, Royal Anthropological Institute, Israel Institute of Technology (executive secretary,) 1942-43.

AWARDS, HONORS: Bialik Prize, Tel Aviv Municipality, 1936; Anisfield-Wolf Award in Race Relations, 1976; Bernard H. Marks Jewish History Award, 1976; Frank and Ethel Cohen Award, 1977.

WRITINGS:

Shire Yisrael Berekhyah Fontanella (title means "The Poems of Israel Fontanella"), [Budapest], 1933.

Ha-Mayim (title means "Water"), [Tel-Aviv], 1936.

Ha-Sapanuth ha'ivrith (title means "Jewish Seafaring"), [Jerusalem], 1938.

Adam we-adamah (title means "Man and Earth"), two volumes, Hebrew University Press Association, 1942-43.

Historical Traditions and Mortuary Customs of the Jews of Meshhed, [Jerusalem], 1945.

On Culture Contact and Its Working in Modern Palestine, American Anthropological Association, 1947.

Mada' ha-adam (title means "The Science of Man"), two volumes, [Tel-Aviv], 1947.

Man and Temple in Ancient Jewish Myth and Ritual, Thomas Nelson, 1947, 2nd edition, Ktav Publishing, 1967.

Israel between East and West: A Study in Human Relations, Jewish Publications Society, 1953, 2nd edition, Greenwood Press, 1970.

Jordan, Lebanon, and Syria: An Annotated Bibliography, Human Relations Area Files Press, 1957, reprinted, Greenwood, 1973.

The Kingdom of Jordan, Princeton University Press, 1958, reprinted, Greenwood, 1984.

Cultures in Conflict: Three Lectures on the Socio-Cultural Problems of Israel and Her Neighbors, Theodore Herzl Institute, 1958, 2nd edition published as *Cultures in Conflict: An Inquiry into the Socio-Cultural Problems of Israel and Her Neighbors,* Herzl Press, 1961.

Sex and Family in the Bible and the Middle East, Doubleday, 1959.

Family, Love and the Bible, MacGibbon & Kee, 1960.

(With David de Sola Pool and Abraham Lopes Cardozo) *The World of the Sephardim,* Herzl Press, 1960.

Golden River to Golden Road: Society, Culture, and Change in the Middle East, University of Pennsylvania Press, 1962, 3rd edition, 1969, paperback edition published as *Society, Culture and Change in the Middle East,* 1971.

(With Robert Graves) *Hebrew Myths: The Book of Genesis,* Doubleday, 1964, reprinted, 1989.

(Author of introduction and notes) Angelo Solomon Rappaport, *Myth and Legend of Ancient Israel,* three volumes, Ktav Publishing, 1966.

The Hebrew Goddess, Ktav Publishing, 1968, third enlarged edition, Wayne State University Press, 1990.

The Tents of Jacob: The Diaspora Yesterday and Today, Prentice-Hall, 1971.

Myth and Modern Man, Prentice-Hall, 1972.

The Arab Mind, Scribner, 1973, 2nd enlarged edition, 1983.

(With Jennifer P. Wing) *The Myth of the Jewish Race,* Scribner, 1975, revised edition, Wayne State University Press, 1989.

The Jewish Mind, Scribner, 1976.

The Messiah Texts, Avon, 1979, published as *The Messiah Texts: Jewish Legends of Three Thousand Years,* Wayne State University Press, 1979.

(Editor and translator) *Gates to the Old City,* Avon, 1980, published as *Gates to the Old City: A Book of Jewish Legends,* Wayne State University Press, 1981.

The Vanished Worlds of Jewry, Macmillan, 1980.

On Jewish Folklore, Wayne State University Press, 1983.

The Seed of Abraham: Jews and Arabs in Contact and Conflict, University of Utah Press, 1986, published as *The Seed of Abraham: Arabs and Jews in Conflict,* Scribner, 1987.

Ignaz Goldziheraud and His Oriental Diary: A Translation and Psychological Portrait, Wayne State University Press, 1986.

Nahum Goldmann: His Missions to the Gentiles, University of Alabama Press, 1986.

Apprentice in Budapest, University of Utah Press, 1988.

Robert Graves and the Hebrew Myths, Wayne State University Press, 1991.

EDITOR

(With Zvi Samuel Wohlmuth) *Mivhar ha-sipur haeretz-yisraeli* (title means "Israeli Short Stories"), two volumes, [Jerusalem], 1938, third edition, 1956.

Edoth: A Quarterly for Folklore and Ethnology, three volumes, [Jerusalem], 1945-48.

(And translator) Erich Brauer, *Yehude Kurdistan* (title means "The Jews of Kurdistan"), [Jerusalem], 1947.

Studies in Folklore and Ethnology, five volumes, [Jerusalem], 1948-49.

Social Studies, two volumes, [Jerusalem], 1948-49.

Farid Aouad, M. M. Bravmann, and others, *The Republic of Syria,* Human Relations Area Files Press, 1956.

The Hashemite Kingdom of Jordan, Human Relations Area Files Press, 1956.

Aouad and others, *Jordan,* Human Relations Area File Press, 1957.

Current Jewish Social Research, Theodor Herzl Foundation, 1958.

The Herzl Year Book, seven volumes, Herzl Press, 1958-71.

(With Francis Lee Utley and Dov Noy) *Studies in Biblical and Jewish Folklore,* Indiana University Press, 1960.

The Complete Diaries of Theodor Herzl, five volumes, Herzl Press, 1961.

(And author of introduction) *Women in the Modern World,* Free Press, 1967.

Encyclopedia of Zionism and Israel, two volumes, McGraw, 1971.

WORK IN PROGRESS: *Jewish Alchemists; Between Hungary and Palestine;* and *Journeyman in Jerusalem.*

SIDELIGHTS: Raphael Patai has traveled widely in the Middle and Far East and Europe. He once told *CA* that his "scholarly specialization [is] in the anthropology of the ancient Near East, the modern Middle East, Israel, [and] the Jews." Patai's book *The Arab Mind* "is virtually a textbook on how the Arabs collectively think, both about themselves and about other societies, especially in the West," writes Donald Shojai in the *Los Angeles Times Book Review.* "What emerges is a highly complex yet composite portrayal of the Arab personality."

BIOGRAPHICAL/CRITICAL SOURCES:

PERIODICALS

Los Angeles Times Book Review, April 10, 1983.

*   *   *

PATTERSON, Harry 1929-
    (Martin Fallon, James Graham, Jack Higgins, Hugh Marlowe)

PERSONAL: Some sources list given name as Henry; born July 27, 1929, in Newcastle-on-Tyne, England; holds dual English and Irish citizenship; son of Henry (a shipwright) and Henrietta Higgins (Bell) Patterson; married Amy Margaret Hewitt, December 27, 1958 (marriage ended, 1984); married Denise Lesley Anne Palmer, 1985; children: (first marriage) three daughters, one son. *Education:* Carnegie College, certificate in education, 1958; London School of Economics and Political Science, London, B.Sc., 1962. *Politics:* "Slightly right of center." *Religion:* Presbyterian.

ADDRESSES: Agent—David Higham Associates Ltd., 5/8 Lower John St., Golden Square, London W1R 4HA, England.

CAREER: Worked at a variety of commercial and civil service posts before resuming his education in 1956; Allerton Grance Comprehensive School, Leeds, England, history teacher, 1959-64; Leeds Polytechnic, Leeds, lecturer in liberal studies, 1964-68; James Graham College, New Farnley, Yorkshire, England, senior lecturer in education, 1968-69; Leeds University, Leeds, tutor, 1970-72; currently a full-time writer. Former member of Leeds Art Theatre. *Military service:* British Army, Royal Horse Guards, 1947-49.

MEMBER: Royal Economic Society (fellow), Royal Society of Arts (fellow), Crime Writers' Association.

WRITINGS:

Sad Wind from the Sea, Long, 1959.
Cry of the Hunter, Long, 1960.
The Thousand Faces of Night, Long, 1961.
Comes the Dark Stranger, Long, 1962.
Hell Is Too Crowded, Long, 1962, reprinted in paperback under pseudonym Jack Higgins, Fawcett, 1977.
Pay the Devil, Barrie & Rockliff, 1963.
The Dark Side of the Island, Long, 1963, reprinted in paperback under pseudonym Jack Higgins, Fawcett, 1977.
A Phoenix in the Blood, Barrie & Rockliff, 1964.
Thunder at Noon, Long, 1964.
Wrath of the Lion, Long, 1964, reprinted in paperback under pseudonym Jack Higgins, Fawcett, 1977.
The Graveyard Shift, Long, 1965.
The Iron Tiger, Long, 1966, reprinted in paperback under pseudonym Jack Higgins, Fawcett, 1979.
Brought in Dead, Long, 1967.
Hell Is Always Today, Long, 1968, reprinted in paperback under pseudonym Jack Higgins, Fawcett, 1979.
Toll for the Brave, Long, 1971, reprinted in paperback under pseudonym Jack Higgins, Fawcett, 1976.
The Valhalla Exchange, Stein & Day, 1976.
To Catch a King, Stein & Day, 1979.

Also author of stage play titled "Walking Wounded," 1987.

UNDER PSEUDONYM MARTIN FALLON

The Testament of Caspar Shultz, Abelard, 1962, reprinted in paperback under pseudonym Jack Higgins, Fawcett, 1978.
Year of the Tiger, Abelard, 1964.
Keys of Hell, Abelard, 1965, reprinted in paperback under pseudonym Jack Higgins, Fawcett, 1976.
Midnight Never Comes, Long, 1966, reprinted in paperback under pseudonym Jack Higgins, Fawcett, 1975.
Dark Side of the Street, Long, 1967, reprinted in paperback under pseudonym Jack Higgins, Fawcett, 1974.
A Fine Night for Dying, Long, 1969 reprinted in paperback under pseudonym Jack Higgins, Arrow, 1977.

UNDER PSEUDONYM JAMES GRAHAM

A Game for Heroes, Doubleday, 1970.
The Wrath of God, Doubleday, 1971.
The Khufra Run, Macmillan, 1972, Doubleday, 1973.
The Run to Morning, Stein & Day, 1974, published in England as *Bloody Passage,* Macmillan, 1974.

UNDER PSEUDONYM JACK HIGGINS

East of Desolation, Hodder & Stoughton, 1968, Doubleday, 1969.
In the Hour Before Midnight, Doubleday, 1969.

Night Judgment at Sinos, Hodder & Stoughton, 1970, Doubleday, 1971.
The Last Place God Made, Collins, 1971, Holt, 1972.
The Savage Day, Holt, 1972.
A Prayer for the Dying, Collins, 1973, Holt, 1974.
The Eagle Has Landed, Holt, 1975.
Storm Warning, Holt, 1976.
Day of Judgement, Collins, 1978, Holt, 1979.
The Cretan Lover, Holt, 1980.
Solo, Stein & Day, 1980.
Luciano's Luck, Stein & Day, 1981.
Touch the Devil, Stein & Day, 1982.
Exocet, Stein & Day, 1983.
Dillinger, Stein & Day 1983.
Confessional, Stein & Day, 1985.
A Jack Higgins Trilogy, Scarborough House, 1986.
Night of the Fox, Simon & Schuster, 1987.
A Season in Hell, Simon & Schuster, 1989.
Cold Harbour, Simon & Schuster, 1990.

UNDER PSEUDONYM HUGH MARLOWE

Seven Pillars to Hell, Abelard, 1963.
Passage by Night, Abelard, 1964, reprinted in paperback under pseudonym Jack Higgins, Fawcett, 1978.
A Candle for the Dead, Abelard, 1966, published in England under pseudonym Jack Higgins as *The Violent Enemy,* Hodder & Stoughton, 1969.

MEDIA ADAPTATIONS: Films have been made of several of Patterson's novels, including, *The Violent Enemy,* 1969, *The Wrath of God,* 1972, *The Eagle Has Landed,* Columbia, 1977, *To Catch a King,* Home Box Office, 1984, *Confessional,* 1985, and *A Prayer for the Dying,* Samuel Goldwyn Co., 1987.

SIDELIGHTS: Harry Patterson told *CA:* "I look upon myself primarily as an entertainer. Even in my novel, *A Phoenix in the Blood,* which deals with the colour-bar problem in England, I still have tried to entertain, to make the events interesting as a story—not just the ideas [and] ethics of the situation. I believe that at any level a writer's only success is to be measured by his ability to communicate."

All of Patterson's books have been translated into Swedish, some into German, Italian, Norwegian, Dutch, and French. He spends his holidays on the continent "whenever possible," and is interested in the theater.

BIOGRAPHICAL/CRITICAL SOURCES:

BOOKS

Bestsellers 89, Issue 3, Gale, 1989.

PERIODICALS

Chicago Tribune, August 4, 1982.
Los Angeles Times, August 29, 1980; September 5, 1985; January 29, 1990.
Los Angeles Times Book Review, July 6, 1980; September 25, 1983.
New York Times, July 28, 1982.
New York Times Book Review, September 5, 1982; January 18, 1987; March 19, 1989; October 14, 1990.
Publishers Weekly, August 27, 1979.
Times (London), October 20, 1986; December 4, 1986.
Tribune Books (Chicago), March 5, 1989.
Washington Post, March 31, 1979; September 29, 1981; February 7, 1987.

PATTERSON, Henry
See PATTERSON, Harry

*   *   *

PAULSON, Ronald (Howard) 1930-

PERSONAL: Born May 27, 1930, in Bottineau, ND; son of Howard Clarence (a Boy Scout executive) and Ethel F. (Tvete) Paulson; married Barbara Lee Appleton, May 25, 1957 (divorced, 1983); children: Andrew Meredith, Melissa Katherine. *Education:* Yale University, B.A., 1952, M.A., 1956, Ph.D., 1958.

ADDRESSES: Home—2722 St. Paul St., Baltimore, MD 21218. *Office*—Department of English, Johns Hopkins University, Baltimore, MD 21218.

CAREER: University of Illinois at Urbana-Champaign, instructor, 1958-59, assistant professor, 1959-62, associate professor of English, 1962-63; Rice University, Houston, TX, professor of English, 1963-67; Johns Hopkins University, Baltimore, MD, professor of English, 1967, Andrew W. Mellon Professor of the Humanities, 1973-75, chairman of English department, 1968; Yale University, New Haven, CT, professor of English, 1975-80, Thomas E. Donnelly Professor, 1980-84, director of graduate studies, 1976-83; Johns Hopkins University, Mayer Professor of the Humanities and chairman of English department, 1984—. *Military service:* U.S. Army, Artillery, 1952-54; became first lieutenant.

MEMBER: Modern Language Association of America, American Society for Eighteenth-Century Studies, American Academy of Arts and Sciences.

AWARDS, HONORS: Guggenheim fellowship, 1965-66, 1986-87; National Endowment for the Humanities fellowship, 1977-78.

WRITINGS:

Theme and Structure in Swift's "Tale of a Tub," Yale University Press, 1960.
Hogarth's Graphic Works, Yale University Press, 1965, revised edition, Print Room, 1989.
The Fictions of Satire, Johns Hopkins University Press, 1967.
Satire and the Novel in Eighteenth-Century England, Yale University Press, 1967.
Hogarth: His Life, Art, and Times, Yale University Press, 1971.
Rowlandson: A New Interpretation, Oxford University Press, 1972.
Emblem and Expressionism in English Art of the Eighteenth Century, Harvard University Press, 1975.
Popular and Polite Art in the Age of Hogarth and Fielding, University of Notre Dame Press, 1979.
Book and Painting: Shakespeare, Milton, and the Bible, University of Tennessee Press, 1982.
Literary Landscape: Turner and Constable, Yale University Press, 1982.
Representations of Revolution: 1789-1820, Yale University Press, 1983.
Breaking and Remaking, Rutgers University Press, 1989.
Figure and Abstraction in Contemporary Painting, Rutgers University Press, 1990.

EDITOR

Fielding: A Collection of Critical Essays, Prentice-Hall, 1962.
The Novelette, Prentice-Hall, 1965.

Henry Fielding: The Critical Heritage, Routledge & Kegan Paul, 1969.
Satire: Modern Essays in Criticism, Prentice-Hall, 1971.
Henry Brooke, *The Field of Quality,* five volumes, Garland Publishing, 1979.
William Godwin, *Fleetwood: Or, The New Man of Feeling,* three volumes, Garland Publishing, 1979.
Eliza Haywood, *The History of Miss Betsy Thoughtless,* four volumes, Garland Publishing, 1979.
Thomas Holcroft, *Memoirs of Bryan Perdue,* three volumes, Garland Publishing, 1979.
Henry MacKenzie, *Julia de Roubigne,* two volumes, Garland Publishing, 1979.
Bage, *Barham Downs,* two volumes, Garland publishing, 1979.
Bage, *James Wallace,* three volumes, Garland Publishing, 1979.
Mary Collyer, *Virtuous Orphan: Or, The Life of Marianne, Countess of —,* four volumes, Garland Publishing, 1979.
Fenelon and Francois de Salignac de la Mothe, *The Adventures of Telemachus,* two volumes, Garland Publishing, 1979.
Charles Johnstone, *Chrysal: Or, The Adventures of a Guinea,* four volumes, Garland Publishing, 1979.
Bage, *Mount Henneth,* two volumes, Garland Publishing, 1980.

OTHER

Contributor to periodicals, including *English Literary History* and *Studies in English Literature.* Member of editorial board, *Eighteenth-Century Studies.*

SIDELIGHTS: Literary critic and historian Ronald Paulson often combines his knowledge of English literature with that of other disciplines, including art history and criticism. In his biography of the eighteenth- century painter William Hogarth, *Hogarth: His Life, Art, and Times,* Paulson studies the artist's work in light of literary, cultural, and sociological movements of the era. Critics responded favorably to Paulson's extensive research and comprehensive examination of cross- disciplinary influences on Hogarth's work.

Richard Freedman writes in *Book World* that "it is appropriate that his magisterial biography of Hogarth is by a man primarily trained in the literature of the eighteenth century. . . . [If] Paulson's training is in literature [though], he has done his homework in the sister art thoroughly and well. Painstakingly he traces Hogarth's progress from the engraving of funeral cards to the realization of his true genius for the mock-heroic. . . . Above all, this massive, lavishly, and appropriately illustrated biography is the first modern treatment of Hogarth to be thoroughly researched on its own."

Similarly, Thomas R. Edwards comments on the author's achievement with the Hogarth biography in a *New York Times Book Review* article, asserting that Paulson's "literary qualifications make him an ideal 'reader' of Hogarth, always alert to the narrative and dramatic qualities in the works and their relation to the history of art, society and moral taste."

Saturday Review critic Robert Halsband observes that it is "difficult to imagine how Hogarth's life could be more thoroughly examined than in Mr. Paulson's eleven hundred pages, where every shred of evidence is searched for meaning, every fact pursued for implications. The 'art and times' of the title allow a more expansive exploration, and through them the artist himself emerges more solidly, and in a sense revivified, merely by being seen so clearly in his social, religious, artistic, and political surroundings." Halsband further describes *Hogarth: His Life, Art, and Times* as "a monument so massive and imposing, so thorough and detailed, so magisterial, that were the adjective not so devalued by overuse one would be tempted to call it definitive."

BIOGRAPHICAL/CRITICAL SOURCES:

PERIODICALS

Book World, December 12, 1971.
Nation, December 20, 1971.
New Republic, January 23, 1984.
New York Review of Books, December 16, 1971.
New York Times Book Review, January 2, 1972.
Saturday Review, December 18, 1971; November 29, 1975.
Times Literary Supplement, January 7, 1983; November 4, 1983; January 6, 1984.

* * *

PIKE, Burton 1930-

PERSONAL: Born June 12, 1930, in Boston, MA; son of Leslie Arthur and Marian (Levin) Pike. *Education:* Haverford College, B.A., 1952; University of Strasbourg, graduate study, 1953-54; Harvard University, M.A., 1955, Ph.D., 1958.

ADDRESSES: Office—Ph.D. Program in Comparative Literature, Graduate School of the City University of New York, 33 West 42nd St., New York, NY 10036.

CAREER: University of Hamburg, Hamburg, West Germany, lecturer in English, 1957-59; Cornell University, Ithaca, NY, instructor, 1959-60, assistant professor, 1960-63, associate professor of comparative literature and German, 1963-69, chairman of department of comparative literature, 1964-68; Queens College of the City University of New York, Flushing, NY, professor of comparative literature, 1969-87, chairman of department, 1969-72; Graduate School and University Center of the City University of New York, New York City, executive officer of Ph.D. program in comparative literature, 1980-87, professor of comparative literature and German, 1987—.

MEMBER: PEN, Modern Language Association of America, American Comparative Literature Association (secretary, 1967-71), Phi Beta Kappa.

AWARDS, HONORS: American Council of Learned Societies fellow, 1952-53; Fulbright fellow, 1953-54; Guggenheim fellow, 1966-67.

WRITINGS:

(Editor with Johannes Kleinstueck) *Mark Twain: Die besten Geschichten,* Schuenemann Verlag, 1960.
Robert Musil: An Introduction to His Work, Cornell University Press, 1961.
Image of the City in Modern Literature, Princeton University Press, 1981.
Robert Musil: Selected Writings, Continuum, 1986.
(Editor, and translator with David S. Luft) *Precision and Soul: Essays and Addresses of Robert Musil,* University of Chicago Press, 1990.

Contributor to *Germanic Review, Musil-Forum,* and *Comparative Literature.*

BIOGRAPHICAL/CRITICAL SOURCES:

PERIODICALS

Los Angeles Times Book Review, December 14, 1986.
New York Times Book Review, December 20, 1981.
Times Literary Supplement, March 26, 1982.

PINCHERLE, Alberto 1907-
(Alberto Moravia)

PERSONAL: Born November 28, 1907, in Rome, Italy; son of Carlo (an architect and a painter) and Teresa (de Marsanich) Pincherle; married Elsa Morante (a writer), 1941 (divorced); married Dacia Maraini (a novelist), 1963 (marriage ended); married Carmen Llera, 1985. *Education:* Awarded high school diploma after passing equivalency tests, 1967.

ADDRESSES: Home—Lungotevere della Vittoria 1, Rome, Italy.

CAREER: Writer. Part-time editor for a publishing house. State Department lecturer in tour of U.S., 1955; lecturer at Queens College of the City University of New York, and other schools, 1964 and 1968.

MEMBER: International PEN (president, 1959), American Academy of Arts and Letters (honorary member), National Institute of Arts and Letters (honorary member).

AWARDS, HONORS: Corriere Lombardo Prize, 1945, for *Agostino;* Strega Literary Prize and Chevalier de la Legion d'Honneur (France), both 1952; Marzotto Award for Fiction, 1954; Viarreggio Prize, 1961, for *La Noia;* Commander de la Legion d'Honneur (France), 1984.

WRITINGS:

NOVELS

Gli indifferenti (also see below), Alpes (Milan), 1929, reprinted, Bompiani, 1976, translation by Aida Mastrangelo of original edition published as *The Indifferent Ones,* Dutton, 1932, translation by Angus Davidson published as *The Time of Indifference,* Farrar, Straus, 1953, reprinted, Greenwood Press, 1975.
Le ambizioni sbagliate, Mondadori (Milan), 1935, translation by Arthur Livington published as *The Wheel of Fortune,* Viking, 1937, translation by Davidson published as *Mistaken Ambitions,* Farrar, Straus, 1955.
La mascherata (also see below), Bompiani, 1941, reprinted, 1981, translation by Davidson published as *The Fancy Dress Party,* Secker & Warburg, 1947, reprinted, 1974.
Agostino: Romanzo, Documento (Rome), 1944, translation by Beryle de Zoete published in *Two Adolescents: The Stories of Agostino and Luca* (also see below), Farrar, Straus, 1950 (published in England as *Two Adolescents: Agostino and Disobedience,* Secker & Warburg, 1952).
Due cortigiane [and] *Serata di Don Giovanni* (novellas), L'Acquario (Rome), 1945.
La romana, Bompiani, 18947, translation by Lydia Holland published as *The Woman of Rome,* Farrar, Straus, 1949, reprinted, Manor Books, 1973.
La disubbidienza, Bompiani, 1948, reprinted, 1981, translation by Davidson of original edition published as *Disobedience,* Secker & Warburg, 1950, translation also published in *Two Adolescents: The Stories of Agostino and Luca,* Farrar, Straus, 1950 (published in England as *Two Adolescents: Agostino and Disobedience,* Secker & Warburg, 1952).
Il conformista, Bompiani, 1951, translation by Davidson published as *The Conformist,* Farrar, Straus, 1951, reprinted, Greenwood Press, 1975.
Il disprezzo, Bompiani, 1954, translation by Davidson published as *A Ghost at Noon,* Farrar, Straus, 1955.
Five Novels by Alberto Moravia: Mistaken Ambitions, Agostino, Luca, Conjugal Love, [and] *A Ghost at Noon* (also see below), Farrar, Straus, 1955.

La ciociara, Bompiani, 1957, translation by Davidson published as *Two Women,* Farrar, Straus, 1958.

La noia, Bompiani, 1963, translation by Davidson published as *The Empty Canvas,* Farrar, Straus, 1965.

L'attenzione: Romanzo, Bompiani, 1965, translation by Davidson published as *The Lie,* Farrar, Straus, 1966.

Io et lui, Bompiani, 1971, translation by Davidson published as *Two: A Phallic Novel,* Farrar, Straus, 1972 (published in England as *The Two of Us,* Secker & Warburg, 1972).

La vita interiore, Bompiani, 1978, translation by Davidson published as *Time of Desecration,* Farrar, Straus, 1980.

1934, Bompiani, 1982, translation by William Weaver published under same title, Farrar, Straus, 1982.

La tempesta (novella), Pellicanolibri (Catania), 1984.

L'uomo che guarda, Bompiani, 1985, translation by Tim Parks published as *The Voyeur: A Novel,* Secker & Warburg, 1986.

SHORT STORIES

La bella vita, Carabba (Lanciano), 1935, published as *La bella vita: L'Italia del consenso in undici racconti,* Bompiani, 1976.

L'imbroglio, Bompiani, 1937.

I sogni del pigro, Bompiani, 1940.

L'amante infelice, Bompiani, 1943.

L'epidemia: Racconti surrealistici e satirici, Documento, 1944.

L'amore coniugale, e altri racconti, Bompiani, 1949, reprinted, 1981, translation by Davidson of long story entitled "L'Amore coniugale" published as *Conjugal Love,* Secker & Warburg, 1951.

I racconti, Bompiani, 1952, reprinted, 1983, translation by Bernard Wall, Baptista Gilliat Smith, and Frances Frenaye published as *Bitter Honeymoon, and Other Stories,* Secker & Warburg, 1960, translation by Davidson published as *The Wayward Wife, and Other Stories,* Secker & Warburg, 1960.

Racconti romani (originally published in the Milanese newspaper *Corriere dell Sera*), Bompiani, 1954, translation by Davidson of selections published as *Roman Tales,* Secker & Warburg, 1956, Farrar, Straus, 1957.

Nuovi racconti romani (originally published in *Corriere dell Sera*), Bompiani, 1959, reprinted, 1978, translation by Davidson of selections from original edition published as *More Roman Tales,* Secker & Warburg, 1963.

L'automa, Bompiani, 1963, translation by Davidson published as *The Fetish,* Secker & Warburg, 1964, published as *The Fetish, and Other Stories,* Farrar, Straus, 1965.

Cortigiana stanca, Bompiani, 1965, published as *Cortigiana stanca: Racconti,* 1974.

Una cosa e una cosa, Bompiani, 1967, translation by Davidson of selections published as *Command and I Will Obey You,* Farrar, Straus, 1969.

Racconti, edited by Vincenzo Traverse, Appleton, 1968, published as *Racconti di Albert Moravia,* Irvington, 1979.

Il paradiso (also see below), Bompiani, 1970, translation by Davidson published as *Paradise and Other Stories,* Secker & Warburg, 1971, published as *Bought and Sold,* Farrar, Straus, 1973.

Un'altra vita (also see below), Bompiani, 1973, translation by Angus Davidson published as *Lady Godiva and Other Stories,* Secker & Warburg, 1975, translation published as *Mother Love,* Panther, 1976.

Boh (also see below), Bompiani, 1976, translation by Davidson published as *The Voice of the Sea and Other Stories,* Secker & Warburg, 1978.

La cosa e altri racconti, Bompiani, 1983, translation by Parks published as *Erotic Tales,* Secker & Warburg, 1985.

PLAYS

(With Luigi Squazini) "Gli indifferenti" (adapted from his novel; published in *Sipario* [Milan], 1948), produced in Rome, 1948.

"Il provino," produced in Milan, 1955.

"Non approfondire" (one-act), produced, 1957.

Teatro (contains "La Mascherata" and "Beatrice Cenci"; also see below), Bompiani, 1958.

Beatrice Cenci (also see below; published in Italian in *Botteghe Oscure,* 1955), translation by Davidson, Secker & Warburg, 1965, Farrar, Straus, 1966.

Il mondo e quello che e (produced in Venice, 1966; adaptation by Albert Husson produced as "The World as It Is" in Paris at Theatre de l'Oeuvre, October, 1969), Bompiani, 1966.

Il dio Kurt (two-act with prologue; produced in Rome at Municipal Theatre of Aquila, 1969), Bompiani, 1968.

La vita e gioco (produced in Rome, 1970), Bompiani, 1969.

Also author of "La Mascherata" (adapted from his novel), c. 1956.

OTHER

La speranza: Ossia cristianesimo e comunismo, Documento, 1944.

(Editor) Leopardi Monaldo, *Viaggio di Pulcinella,* Atlanta (Rome), 1945.

Opera completa, seventeen volumes, Bompiani, 1952-67.

Un mese in U.R.S.S., Bompiani, 1958.

(With Elemire Zolla) *I moralisti moderni,* Garzanti, 1960.

(Editor with Zolla) *Saggi italiani,* Bompiani, 1960.

Un'idea dell'India, Bompiani, 1962.

L'uomo come fine e altri saggi (essays), Bompiani, 1964, translation by Wall of a selection published as *Man as an End—A Defense of Humanism: Literary, Social, and Political Essays,* Farrar, Straus, 1965.

La rivoluzione culturale in Cina ovvero il convitato di ietra, Bompiani, 1967, translation published as *The Red Book and the Great Wall: An Impression of Mao's China,* Farrar, Straus, 1968.

A quale tribu appartieni?, Bompiani, 1972, translation by Davidson published as *Which Tribe do You Belong To?,* Farrar, Straus, 1974.

Al cinema: Centoquarantotto film d'autor (reviews), Bompiani, 1975.

Quando Ba Lena era tanto piccola, Lisciani e Zampetti (Teramo), 1978.

Impegno controvoglia—Saggi, articoli, interviste: Trenta-cinque anni di scritti politici, edited by Renzo Paris, Bompiani, 1980.

Cosma e i briganti, Sellerio (Palermo), 1980.

Lettere del Sahara, Bompiani, 1981.

Opera, 1927-1947, Bompiani, 1986.

Passeggiate africane, Bompiani, 1988.

Also author of numerous screenplays, including "Un colpo di pistola," 1941, "Ultimo incontro," 1951, "La provinciale," 1952, "La romana" (based on his novel), 1955, "Racconti romani" (based on his stories), 1956, "La giornata balorda," 1960, "Agostino" (based on his novel), 1962, "Le ore nude," 1964, and "L'occhio selvaggio," 1967. Foreign correspondent for *La Stampa* and *Gazzeta del Popolo* (Turin), 1930-39; film critic for *La Nuova Europa,* 1944-46, and for *L'Espresso,* 1955—; co-editor with Alberto Carocci of bi-monthly magazine, *Nuovi Argomenti,* 1953—.

SIDELIGHTS: As a child Alberto Moravia used to recount stories to himself, sometimes only interrupting them for sleep and meals. Lonely and isolated, deprived at the age of nine of a normal childhood because of tuberculosis of the bone, he took refuge in his own imagination and in books. Moravia describes this illness as one of the most important events of his life; because of it he had to submit to and do things that healthy children do not usually encounter. "Our character is formed by those things we are constrained to do," he wrote later, "not by those things we do of our own accord." This enforced captivity undoubtedly encouraged the youngster in his literary career.

Although he denies being the author of a book of poems published when he was only thirteen that some reference sources attribute to him, Moravia's first book did appear while he was still a teenager. While he had planned to write a play, what emerged was a novel, *Gli indifferenti.* The story of Carla and her brother Michele and their gradual decline through indifference into moral indolence, the book "had one of the greatest successes in modern Italian literature," according to Joan Ross and Donald Freed in their *The Existentialism of Albert Moravia.* While the volume's subject matter shocked the readers of the time, it gave Moravia the thematic basis for a life's work. "More than anything [this first novel] irritated its readers by its stark portrayal of the decadence and moral rot of the middle-class Italian society of its day," notes Jane E. Cottrell in *Alberto Moravia.* "However, the decay of the middle class was only a secondary theme; its principal subject was the despair and alienation of people entrapped in what would later come to be known in literature as 'the absurd.' For in retrospect, *Gli indifferenti* can be seen as the first European existentialist novel. . . . Since his first novel, Moravia has explored again and again in his fiction the same ideas and themes."

In a *Paris Review* interview Moravia spoke about the acclaim that greeted *Gli indifferenti*'s publication: "It was one of the greatest successes in all modern literature. The greatest actually; and I can say this with all modesty. There has never been anything like it. Certainly no book in the last fifty years has been greeted with such unanimous enthusiasm and excitement." Unfortunately, the first English edition, which appeared with the title *The Indifferent Ones,* was allegedly so badly translated that the book made little impact on the English-speaking world. A second translation, *The Time of Indifference,* fared much better. *New York Times* contributor Frances Keene wrote that Moravia's "ear for dialogue, for the rhythm of seemingly pointless banter, gives us the very edge of each one's weaknesses. There are no false passages even in the monologue of this book, which tears open today, as it did more than twenty years ago, the fourth wall of many a sterile menage." This translation, however, did not appear until 1953 by which time Moravia had already become known to American readers through a later novel, *La romana,* published in English as *The Woman of Rome.*

R. W. B. Lewis calls *The Woman of Rome* "on balance, a distinguished piece of fiction," and finds that it has a "lyrical reflectiveness" and "muffled nostalgia" which sets it apart from other realistic novels. Narrated in the first person, it reveals Moravia's competence as a craftsman as well as his gift for psychological acumen. The narrator, Adriana, is a young girl of working class origins who turns to prostitution as a way of life. "The uniqueness of Adriana," comments Sergio Pacifici, "consists precisely in her being able to find in promiscuous love the very strength to accept with cheerfulness an otherwise sordid existence." Paci-

fici goes on to point out that Adriana's observation that "everything was love and everything depended on love, . . . and if you did not have it, you could not love anyone or anything" representative of Moravia's "only genuinely positive answer to the problem of the incoherence and senselessness of life."

Moravia was attacked for his frank treatment of sex in these early novels as well as in his later fiction. Critics have accused him of immorality, lewdness, and obsessiveness. In fact, all of his works were placed on the Index in 1952. Carlo Goldini writes that in Moravia's fiction "we find ourselves in a world peopled with abnormal and morbid individuals obsessed by sensual and erotic preoccupations varying from natural sexual urges to unrestrained lust." And, on the same topic, Lewis has said, "Everything other than sex is, in the stories of Moravia, an extension of sex; or perhaps better, everything other than sex is sooner or later converted into it." In a letter to Lewis, Moravia admitted that "sex has been for me the key to many doors," but added that, when he first started to write, "there were only a few things which seemed to me solid and true and these things were connected with nature and the less objectionable and analysable and ineffable sides of the human soul. Among these things no doubt was sex, which is something primordial and absolute."

Despite such explanations Moravia feels the wrath of censors into his sixth decade as a writer. "Moravia has been identified with sex ever since the runaway success of *Woman of Rome* in 1947 established him as Italy's best-known novelist," observes Miranda Seymour in her *Spectator* commentary on the literary figure. "The sex-scenes in his . . . novel, *Time of Desecration,* were of such a singular nature that the French translators complained, the Italian Mary Whitehouse rose in wrath, and the Germans, not usually known for their puritanism, flatly refused to publish the book." Commenting on the same novel, *New York* magazine contributor Joshua Gilder notes, "Moravia's earlier stories were often brilliant little studies of erotic compulsion. But the erotic component has steadily drained away, until all we are now left with is the compulsion. *Time of Desecration* reads less like a novel than a case study of sexual pathology."

Stylistically, Moravia is not an innovator nor even a particularly polished writer. Charges that he "writes badly" or even "ungrammatically" are not infrequently levelled at him. In his *New York Times* review of *1934* Anatole Broyard observes, "Moravia has never had what might be called a style, but now he seems to have developed what could be described as an aggressive absence of style. A sentence like 'He resumed eating with intent, choleric voracity' suggests no language at all, neither in the original Italian nor the translator's English version." Lewis finds that Moravia "is usually happier with the short novel (and the short story) than with the novel proper; his resources and his themes appear to lack the variety and the inward momentum that novels require." Elaborating on this idea, Pacifici comments, "It is the less sustained genres of the short story and the novella that he has found a felicitous vehicle to dramatize, effectively and succinctly, the few themes close to his sensibility." Maurice Valency concluded, "The short tale is his specialty. In this form, at his best, he is absolutely unsurpassed."

Offering a defense to some criticism leveled at his work, Moravia once said, "Good writers are monotonous, like good composers. Their truth is self-repeating. They keep rewriting the same book. That is to say, they keep trying to perfect their expression of the one problem they were born to understand." Nevertheless, some critics fault Moravia for his constant repetition of themes and subject matter and contend that his later works lack the tautness and vigor of his earlier fiction. "Alberto Moravia is a one-book man in the saddest sense of all, " John Simon observes. "His first novel, *The Time of Indifference,* written when he was still in his teens, said his entire say in optimum form. Later works, for all their occasional diversionary tactics, revealed an obsessively narrow scope and a severely limited technique." Ross and Freed, however, believe that Moravia has improved as a writer over the years. "Moravia has gone beyond the bleak, sordid vision of *Time of Indifference,*" they note. "In subsequent works his perception has deepened and matured. Out of this intense vision we sense a true empathy for the condition of modern man."

Apart from his novels, novellas, and short stories, Moravia has written several plays, hundreds of film reviews, and published several collections of essays. *Man as an End,* the first group of his essays to appear in English, was well-received by reviewers. A *Kirkus Service* reviewer describes the volume as "the work of a vital, exciting and brilliant mind . . . and without doubt one of the most significant European imports in a decade." And Eliot Fremont-Smith writes: "What is moving here is the depth of Moravia's commitment to the cause of man; beyond this, these essays offer rare insights into men and letters, and demonstrate an energetic mind in purposeful and inspiring action." Moravia is a trenchant polemicist; his essays, whether philosophical, political, or critical will always provoke and stimulate. The prevailing feeling is, however, that his position in literature will be determined by his shorter fiction among which there are, perhaps, one or two near masterpieces, such as *Agostino. Time* has called him "one of the best writers in the world today," and Pacifici suggest that, if Moravia does rank with the genuine artist of our century, it is because "after years of writing, and despite the fact that time itself has not changed in any substantial way the *manner* of his writing, he has come closer to saying something about the condition of modern man."

MEDIA ADAPTATIONS: "The Wayward Wife," was made into a film by Mario Soldati and released by Embassy, 1955; *La romana* was filmed as "The Woman of Rome," directed by Luigi Zampa, 1956; *La noia* was filmed as "The Empty Canvas," directed by Vittorio de Sica, 1965; *Gli indifferente* was filmed as "Time of Indifference," 1965; *Il disprezzo* was filmed as "Le Mepris,"" by Jean-Luc Godard, 1965; *Il conformista* was filmed as "The Conformist," by Bernardo Bertolucci, 1970; *Il dio Kurt* and *Racconti romani* were also filmed.

BIOGRAPHICAL/CRITICAL SOURCES:

BOOKS

Chiaromente, Nicola, *The Worm of Consciousness, and Other Essays,* Harcourt, 1976.
Contemporary Literary Criticism, Gale, Volume 2, 1974, Volume 7, 1977, Volume 11, 1979, Volume 27, 1984, Volume 46, 1988.
Cottrell, Jane E., *Alberto Moravia,* Unger, 1974.
Heiney, D. W., *Three Italian Novelists,* University of Michigan Press, 1968.
Lewis, R. W. B., *The Picaresque Saint,* Lippincott, 1959.
Pacifici, Sergio, *A Guide to Contemporary Italian Literature,* Meridian Books, 1962.
Ragusa, Olga, *Narrative and Drama: Essays in Modern Italian Literature from Verga to Pasolini,* Humanities, 1976.
Ross, Joan, and Donald Freed, *The Existentialism of Alberto Moravia,* Southern Illinois University Press, 1972.

PERIODICALS

Atlantic, February, 1955.
Best Sellers, July 15, 1969.
Books Abroad, autumn, 1950, summer, 1969, winter, 1971.
Books and Bookmen, July, 1969.
Book Week, April 17, 1966.
Book World, September 22, 1968.
Christian Science Monitor, July 17, 1969.
Commonweal, October 22, 1965.
Life, April 28, 1972.
Listener, November 21, 1968.
London Magazine, October, 1968.
Modern Fiction Studies, Number 3, 1958.
Modern Language Journal, Volume 26, 1952.
Nation, April 5, 1971.
New Leader, April 19, 1971.
New Republic, October 26, 1968.
New York, May 23, 1983.
New Yorker, May 7, 1955.
New York Herald Tribune Book Review, October 7, 1951.
New York Review of Books, January 16, 1969.
New York Times, May 24, 1953, January 19, 1966, May 9, 1968, September 19, 1970, March 21, 1971, May 8, 1972, May 11, 1983.
New York Times Book Review, August 3, 1950, April 17, 1953, May 23, 1965, February 9, 1969, May 17, 1970, March 29, 1987.
Observer, December 22, 1985, November 23, 1986.
Paris Review, summer, 1954.
Saturday Review, August 23, 1969, February 13, 1971.
Spectator, November 15, 1968, November 16, 1985.
Stage, July 5, 1973.
Time, June 11, 1965, October 18, 1968.
Times Literary Supplement, September 20, 1965, September 19, 1968, June 5, 1969, November 14, 1986.
Virginia Quarterly Review, spring, 1953.
Washington Press Book World, January 26, 1986.

*   *   *

PINOAK, Justin Willard
   See PROSSER, H(arold) L(ee)

*   *   *

PINTA, Harold
   See PINTER, Harold

*   *   *

PINTER, Harold   1930-
   (David Baron, Harold Pinta)

PERSONAL: Born October 10, 1930, in Hackney, London, England; son of Hyman (a tailor) and Frances (Mann) Pinter; married Vivien Merchant (an actress), September 14, 1956 (divorced, 1980); married Lady Antonia Fraser (a writer), November, 1980; children: (first marriage) Daniel. *Education:* Attended Hackney Downs Grammar School, London, 1941-47; attended a few drama schools, including the Royal Academy of Dramatic Art for three months in 1948.

ADDRESSES: Agent—Judy Daish Associates, 83 Eastbourne Mews, London W2 6LQ, England.

CAREER: Poet and playwright. Became interested in theater when he played Macbeth at the age of sixteen; once worked as a "chucker-out" in a dance hall and as a waiter at the National Liberal Club; also worked as a dishwasher and a salesman; actor, using stage name David Baron, 1948-58, performing with Shakespearean repertory company in Ireland, 1950-52, with Donald Wolfit's Shakespearean company, The Bournemouth Repertory Company, and other repertory companies, 1952-58; still acts occasionally, now using his own name; director of plays, including some of his own, 1970—. Associate director, National Theatre, London, 1973—. *Military service:* None; conscientious objector (fined thirty pounds).

MEMBER: League of Dramatists, Modern Language Association (honorary fellow).

AWARDS, HONORS: Evening Standard drama award, 1961, Newspaper Guild of New York award, 1962, both for "The Caretaker"; Italia Prize for television play, 1963, for "The Lover"; two Screenwriters Guild Awards, for television play and for screenplay, both 1963; New York Film Critics Award, 1964, for "The Servant"; British Film Academy Award, 1965 and 1971; Commander, Order of the British Empire, 1966; New York Drama Critics Circle Award, Whitbread Anglo-American Theater Award, and Antoinette Perry (Tony) Award, all 1967, all for "The Homecoming"; Shakespeare Prize, Hamburg, West Germany, 1970; Writers Guild Award, 1971; Best New Play award, *Plays & Players,* 1971, and Tony Award nomination, 1972, both for "Old Times"; Austrian State Prize in Literature, 1973; New York Drama Critics Circle Award, 1980; Pirandello Prize, 1980; Common Wealth Award, Bank of Delaware, 1981; Elmer Holmes Bobst Award for Arts and Letters, 1985, for drama; has received honorary degrees from many institutions in the United Kingdom and the United States.

WRITINGS:

PRODUCED PLAYS AND SCREENPLAYS

"The Room" (also see below), first produced in Bristol, England at Bristol University Memorial Building, May 15, 1957; produced with "The Dumb Waiter" in London at Hampstead Theatre Club, January 21, 1960; produced in San Francisco at Encore Theatre, July 15, 1960; produced with "A Slight Ache" in New York at Writers Stage Theatre, December 9, 1964; produced on Broadway at Booth Theatre, October 3, 1967.

The Birthday Party: A Play in Three Acts (first produced in Cambridge, England at Arts Theatre, April 28, 1958; produced in Hammersmith at Lyric Theatre, May 19, 1968; produced in New York at Booth Theatre, October 3, 1967; also see below), Encore, 1959, Samuel French, 1960, 2nd revised edition, Eyre Methuen, 1981.

"The Dumb Waiter" (also see below), first produced in German translation by Willy H. Thiem in West Germany at Frankfurt-am-Main, February 28, 1959; produced with "The Room" in London at Hampstead Theatre Club, January 21, 1960; produced Off-Broadway with "The Collection" at Cherry Lane Theatre, November 26, 1962.

"A Slight Ache" (also see below), first produced as radio drama, for BBC Radio Third Programme, July 2, 1959; produced on stage in London at Arts Theatre Club, January 18, 1961; produced with "The Room" in New York at Writers Stage Theatre, December 9, 1964.

"Trouble in the Works" [and] "The Black and White" (also see below), first produced together as part of "One to Another" (revue) in Hammersmith at Lyric Theatre, July 15, 1959; produced on the West End at Apollo Theatre, September 23, 1959.

"Request Stop," "Last to Go," "Special Offer," [and] "Getting Acquainted" (also see below), first produced together on the West End as part of "Pieces of Eight" (revue) at Apollo Theatre, September 23, 1959.

"A Night Out" (also see below), first produced as radio drama for BBC Third Programme, March 1, 1960 (Pinter played a small role); produced on stage on the West End at Comedy Theatre, October 2, 1961.

The Caretaker: A Play in Three Acts (first produced in London at Arts Theatre Club, April 27, 1960 [Pinter played the part of Mick for four weeks in 1961]; produced in New Haven, Conn., at Schubert Theatre, September, 1961; produced on Broadway at Lyceum Theatre, October 4, 1961; also see below), Methuen, 1960, 2nd edition, 1962, reprinted, 1982.

"The Dwarfs" (also see below), first produced as radio drama for BBC Third Programme, December 2, 1960; produced on stage with "The Lover" in London at Arts Theatre Club, September 18, 1963; produced Off-Broadway with "The Dumb Waiter" at Abbey Theatre, May 3, 1974.

"Night School" (television drama; also see below), first produced for Associated Rediffusion Television, 1960.

"The Collection" (also see below), first produced as television drama for Associated Rediffusion Television, May 11, 1961; produced on stage on the West End at Aldwich Theatre, June 18, 1962; produced Off-Broadway with "The Dumb Waiter" at Cherry Lane Theatre, November 26, 1962.

"The Lover" (also see below), first produced as television drama for Associated Rediffusion Television, March 28, 1963; produced on stage with "The Dwarfs" in London at Arts Theatre Club, September 18, 1963; produced Off-Broadway at Cherry Lane Theatre, January 4, 1964.

"The Servant" (screenplay), Springbok-Elstree, 1963.

"That's Your Trouble" (radio drama; also see below), first produced for BBC Third Programme, 1964.

"That's All" (radio drama; also see below), first produced for BBC Third Programme, 1964.

"Applicant" (radio drama; also see below), first produced for BBC Third Programme, 1964.

"Interview" (radio drama; also see below), first produced for BBC Third Programme, 1964.

Dialogue for Three (radio drama; first produced for BBC Third Programme, 1964), published in *Stand,* Volume 6, number 3, 1963.

"The Guest" (screenplay; adapted from "The Caretaker"), Janus, 1964.

"The Pumpkin Eater" (screenplay; also see below), Rank, 1964.

The Homecoming: A Play in Two Acts (first produced in Cardiff, Wales, at New Theatre, March 22, 1965; produced on the West End at Aldwich Theatre, June 3, 1965; produced in New York at Music Box Theatre, January 5, 1967), Samuel French, 1965, new revised edition, Karnac, 1968.

Tea Party (first produced as television drama for BBC Television, March 25, 1965; produced Off-Broadway with "The Basement" at Eastside Playhouse, October 15, 1968; also see below), Methuen, 1965, Grove, 1966.

"The Basement" (also see below), first produced as television drama for BBC Television, February 20, 1967; produced on stage Off-Broadway with "Tea Party" at Eastside Playhouse, October 15, 1968.

"Pinter People" (television interview and sketches), first produced for NBC-TV, December 6, 1968.

"The Quiller Memorandum" (screenplay; also see below), Twentieth-Century Fox, 1967.

"Accident" (screenplay; also see below), Cinema V, 1967.

"The Birthday Party" (screenplay), Continental, 1968.

Landscape (radio drama; first produced for BBC Third Programme, 1968; also see below), Pendragon Press, 1968.

"Night" (also see below), produced as part of "We Who Are About To . . . ," in London at Hampstead Theatre Club,

February 6, 1969; produced on the West End as part of "Mixed Doubles: An Entertainment on Marriage" (revised version of "We Who Are About To . . .,") at Comedy Theatre, April 9, 1969.

"Landscape" [and] "Silence" (also see below), first produced on the West End at Aldwych Theatre, July 2, 1969; produced Off-Broadway at Forum Theatre, April 2, 1970.

"Sketches," first produced in New York at Actors Playhouse, November 3, 1969.

Old Times (first produced on the West End at Aldwych Theatre, June 1, 1971; produced in New York at Billy Rose Theatre November 16, 1971), Grove, 1971.

"The Go-Between" (screenplay; also see below), World Film Services, 1971.

"The Homecoming" (screenplay), American Film Theatre, 1971.

Monologue (television drama; first produced for BBC Television, 1973; also produced on stage), Covent Garden Press, 1973.

No Man's Land (first produced on the West End at National Theatre at the Old Vic, April 23, 1975), Grove, 1975.

"The Last Tycoon" (screenplay; also see below), Paramount, 1975.

Betrayal (first produced on the West End at the National Theatre, November 15, 1978; produced in New York at Trafalgar Theater, January 6, 1980), Eyre Methuen, 1978, Grove, 1979, revised edition, Methuen, 1980.

"Other Pinter Pauses" (revue), first produced in New York at Victory Gardens Studio Theater, December 17, 1979.

The Hothouse (first produced in London at Hampstead Theatre Club, May 1, 1980; produced in New York at Playhouse Theatre, May 6, 1982), Grove, 1980, revised edition, Methuen, 1982.

Family Voices: A Play for Radio (first produced as radio drama for BBC Radio Third Programme, January 22, 1981; produced on the West End at National Theatre, February 13, 1981; also see below), Grove, 1981.

"The French Lieutenant's Woman" (screenplay; also see below), United Artists, 1981, published as *The French Lieutenant's Woman: A Screenplay,* Little, Brown, 1981.

A Kind of Alaska: A Play (first produced at National Theatre, 1982; also see below), Samuel French, 1981.

Victoria Station (also see below), Samuel French, 1982.

Other Places (triple bill; first produced in London, 1982; includes "Family Voices," "A Kind of Alaska," and "Victoria Station"; also see below), Methuen, 1982, Grove, 1983, (revised version omitting "Family Voices" and including "One for the Road" [also see below], first produced at Manhattan Theater Club, April 17, 1984; produced in London, 1985).

"Betrayal" (screenplay), Twentieth-Century Fox/International Classics, 1983.

"Precisely" (sketch), first produced as part of "The Big One" in London, 1983.

One for the Road: A Play (first produced in Hammersmith at Lyric Theatre, March 16, 1984), Samuel French, 1984, Grove, 1986, revised edition, Methuen, 1985.

"Turtle Diary" (screenplay), United British Artists/Britannic, 1986.

Mountain Language (first produced on the West End at National Theatre of Great Britain, November, 1988; produced in New York at CSC Theater with "The Birthday Party," November, 1989), published in *Times Literary Supplement,* October 7, 1988.

The Handmaid's Tale (screenplay from the novel by Margaret Atwood), Cinecom Entertainment Group, 1990.

Also author of "Langrishe, Go Down" (also see below), 1977, and of a screenplay based on Ian McEuen's *The Comfort of Strangers.*

COLLECTIONS

The Birthday Party and Other Plays (includes "The Birthday Party," "The Room," and "The Dumb Waiter"), Methuen, 1960, published as *The Birthday Party and The Room,* Grove, 1961.

A Slight Ache and Other Plays (includes "A Slight Ache," "A Night Out," "The Dwarfs," "Trouble in the Works," "The Black and White," "Request Stop," "Last to Go," and "Applicant"), Methuen, 1961.

The Caretaker and The Dumb Waiter, Grove, 1961.

Three Plays: A Slight Ache, The Collection, The Dwarfs, Grove, 1962.

The Collection and The Lover (includes a prose piece, "The Examination"), Methuen, 1963.

The Dwarfs and Eight Review Sketches (includes "The Dwarfs," "Trouble in the Works," "The Black and White," "Request Stop," "Last to Go," "Applicant," "Interview," "That's All," and "That's Your Trouble"), Dramatists Play Service, 1965.

Tea Party and Other Plays (includes "Tea Party," "The Basement," and "Night School"), Methuen, 1967.

The Lover, Tea Party, The Basement: Two Plays and a Film Script, Grove, 1967.

A Night Out, Night School, Revue Sketches: Early Plays, Grove, 1968.

Landscape and Silence (includes "Landscape," "Silence," and "Night"), Methuen, 1969, Grove, 1970.

Five Screenplays (includes "Accident," "The Caretaker," "The Pumpkin Eater," "The Quiller Memorandum," and "The Servant"), Methuen, 1971, revised version, omitting "The Caretaker" and substituting "The Go-Between," Karnac, 1971, Grove, 1973.

Plays, four volumes, Methuen, 1975-81, published as *Complete Works* (with an introduction, "Writing for the Theatre"), Grove, 1977-81.

The French Lieutenant's Woman and Other Screenplays (includes "The French Lieutenant's Woman," "Langrishe, Go Down," and "The Last Tycoon"), Methuen, 1982.

Other Places: Three Plays (includes "A Kind of Alaska," "Victoria Station," and "Family Voices"), Grove, 1983.

OTHER

(Contributor) Harold Clarman, editor, *Seven Plays of the Modern Theater* (includes "The Birthday Party"), Grove, 1962.

(With Samuel Beckett and Eugene Ionesco) "The Compartment" (unreleased screenplay), published in *Project 1,* Grove, 1963.

Mac (on Anew McMaster), Pendragon Press, 1968.

(Editor with John Fuller and Peter Redgrove) *New Poems 1967: A P.E.N. Anthology,* Hutchinson, 1968.

Poems, edited by Alan Clodd, Enitharmon, 1968, 2nd edition, 1971.

Poems and Prose 1949-1977, Grove, 1978, revised edition published as *Collected Poems and Prose,* Methuen, 1986.

(With Joseph Losey and Barbara Bray) *The Proust Screenplay: A la recherche du temps perdu,* Grove, 1978.

I Know the Place: Poems, Greville Press, 1979.

(Editor with Geoffrey Godbert and Anthony Astbury) *A Hundred Poems by a Hundred Poets: An Anthology,* Methuen, 1986.

The Dwarfs (novel), Faber, 1990.

Also contributor of poems, under pseudonym Harold Pinta, to *Poetry London.*

WORK IN PROGRESS: A screenplay based on Fred Uhlman's novel *Reunion,* with Jerry Schatzberg.

SIDELIGHTS: In a February 1967 interview with the *New Yorker,* Harold Pinter, one of the foremost British dramatists since World War II, cryptically explains the geneses of three of his early plays: "I went into a room and saw one peron standing up and one person sitting down, and a few weeks later I wrote *The Room.* I went into another room and saw two people sitting down, and a few years later I wrote *The Birthday Party.* I looked through a door into a third room, and saw two people standing up and I wrote *The Caretaker.*" Since *The Room* opened in 1957, Harold Pinter's work has excited, puzzled, and frustrated audiences and academicians alike. Some have praised his work for its originality, while others have dismissed it as willfully obscure— responses evoked by the plays' unconventional plots and character development, their inexplicable logic and inconclusive resolutions, and their distinctive dialogue, echoing the inanities of everyday speech as well as its silences. In spite of their disparagers, Pinter's plays are frequently produced—in English and in translation—and continue to attract popular and scholarly attention.

Born October 30, 1930, at Hackney, East London, Pinter grew up in a working-class neighborhood, which, despite some dilapidated housing, railway yards, and a dirty canal, he remembered fondly in the *New Yorker* interview: "I actually lived in a very pleasant environment and in a very comfortable terraced house." However, like other English children who grew up in London during the air raids of World War II, he learned first hand of imminent and omnipresent terror, a theme which appears in much of his work.

Pinter's theatrical career started early. While attending Hackney Downs Grammar School, he won title roles in *Macbeth* and *Romeo and Juliet.* The *Hackney Downs School Magazine* records his dramatic debuts. Of young Pinter's Macbeth, the magazine's critic wrote in the summer of 1947: "Word-perfect, full-voiced, Pinter took the tragic hero through all the stages of temptation, hesitation, concentration, damnation. He gave us both Macbeth's conflicts, inner and outer, mental and military, with vigour, insight, and remarkable acting resource." The summer 1948 review of Pinter's Romeo, if somewhat less laudatory, points nonetheless to the young actor's flair for the dramatic: "Pinter again bore the heat and burden of the evening with unfailing vitality. . . . Perhaps he excelled where strong action reinforces the words—as where he flung himself on the floor of the Friar's cell in passionate histrionic abandon."

Both these reviews are remarkably prescient: what the young actor apparently learned, in part at least from playing Macbeth and Romeo, Pinter the playwright uses. His characters are at their most compelling when their conflicts are "inner" and "mental," unseeable and therefore frequently unnameable; his plots, despite their surface calm and minimal physical action, nonetheless demonstrate "histrionic abandon," the result of verbal brilliance and stunning visual imagery.

Along with acting, young Pinter displayed a talent for athletics: in 1948 he broke the school's record for the 220 yards and equaled the record for the 100 yards. He also played cricket, a game he continues to follow. Not surprisingly, therefore, sports have a special significance in his work. The characters in *No Man's Land,* for example, are named after famous cricket players, and squash in *Betrayal* is symbolically important to the

play's meaning. In Pinter's screenplays, sports and sports imagery are similarly illuminating.

Besides his successes at play—both on field and on stage—the *Hackney Downs School Magazine* also records those of a literary bent: an essay and two poems, which attest to the young artist's sensitivity to language. In his essay, "James Joyce," published in the winter 1946 issue, Pinter discusses the novelist's poetic use of language: "and slowly the words subside into softness, softly drifting." His juvenile poetry features the alliteration, repetition, and play with language that appears in his adult work, drama and poetry alike.

Pinter's verbal acumen was also rewarded outside the world of belles lettres: it helped the young man ward off East End thugs, as Pinter recalled in a 1966 *Paris Review* interview with Lawrence M. Bensky: "I did encounter [violence] in quite an extreme form. . . . If you looked remotely like a Jew you might be in trouble. Also, I went to a Jewish club, by an old railway arch, and there were quite a lot of people often waiting with broken milk bottles in a particular alley we used to walk through. There were one or two ways of getting out of it—one was purely physical, of course, but you couldn't do anything about the milk bottles—*we* didn't have any milk bottles. The best way was to talk to them, you know, sort of 'Are you all right?' 'Yes, I'm all right.' 'Well, that's all right then, isn't it?' and all the time keep walking toward the lights of the main road." Manipulating language in order to shield oneself from physical or emotional harm without conveying rational information is a skill possessed by many of Pinter's dramatic characters.

Pinter left grammar school in 1947 and the following year received a grant to study acting at the Royal Academy of Dramatic Art (RADA). In *Pinter the Playwright* Martin Esslin records Pinter's memory of this experience: "I went to RADA for about two terms, then I left of my own free will, I didn't care for it very much. I spent the next year roaming about a bit." In fact, according to the *New Yorker* interview, he spent the next ten years writing—"Not plays. Hundreds of poems . . . and short prose pieces"—and acting: ". . . my experience as an actor has influenced my plays—it must have—though it's impossible for me to put my finger on it exactly. I think I certainly developed some feeling for construction . . . and for speakable dialogue." As an actor Pinter grew intimately familiar with the dramatic properties of the stage and the spoken word, and as a poet with the emotive possibilities of language.

In 1950 *Poetry London* published several of his poems under the pseudonym "Harold Pinta" (the Spanish or Portuguese form of "Pinter"), and the poet began work as a professional radio and television actor. In *Prose and Poetry, 1949-1977* Pinter declares that in 1951 he began a two-year stint with Anew McMaster's touring company in Ireland, his "first job proper on the stage"; after returning from Ireland, Pinter (who in 1954 assumed the stage name of "David Baron") acted "all over the place in reps." In 1957 Harold Pinta, the poet, and David Baron, the actor, collaborated on a one-act play, *The Room,* the writing of which took Harold Pinter, the playwright, "four days, working in the afternoons," he told the *New Yorker.*

After *The Room,* Pinter's plays came fast. During 1957 he wrote *The Dumb Waiter,* a one-act play, and *The Birthday Party,* his first full-length play, which ran for only one week and got terrible reviews, with one notable exception—Harold Hobson's appraisal in the *Sunday Times:* "Now I am well aware that Mr. Pinter's play received extremely bad notices last Thursday morning. At the moment I write these lines it is uncertain even whether the play will still be in the bill when they appear, though it is probable it will soon be seen elsewhere. Deliberately, I am willing to risk whatever reputation I have as a judge of plays by saying that *The Birthday Party* is . . . a First, and that Mr. Pinter, on the evidence of this work, possesses the most original, disturbing and arresting talent in theatrical London."

Despite *The Birthday Party*'s predominantly dismal critical and commercial reception, Pinter continued during 1958 and 1959 to write plays for radio and stage—*A Slight Ache; The Hothouse* (which was not produced until 1980); revue sketches; and *A Night Out.* With his second full-length play, *The Caretaker,* the playwright received critical accolades. One of the more influential notices was Kenneth Tynan's in the *Observer:* "With *The Caretaker* . . . Harold Pinter has begun to fulfill the promise that I signally failed to see in *The Birthday Party* two years ago. The latter play was a clever fragment grown dropsical with symbolic content. . . . In *The Caretaker* symptoms of paranoia are still detectable . . . but their intensity is considerably abated; and the symbols have mostly retired to the background. What remains is a play about people." *The Caretaker* ran for twelve months in the East End and in October 1961 opened on Broadway, again to critical, but not commercial, success. In the *New York Times,* Howard Taubman wrote: "*The Caretaker* . . . proclaims its young English author as one of the important playwrights of our day."

Important and prolific, Pinter continued to write plays, short ones including *Night School* and *The Dwarfs, The Collection* and *The Lover, Tea Party;* and full-length ones, *The Homecoming,* which established Pinter's reputation as a major dramatist, *Old Times, No Man's Land,* and *Betrayal.* More recently, he has concentrated on short but intriguing theatrical pieces: *Family Voices, Victoria Station, A Kind of Alaska,* and *One for the Road.*

Although they cannot be easily classified according to dramatic schools, Pinter's plays nonetheless reflect movements in the British theatre of the last three decades, including realism, epic theatre, and absurdism. Early critics perceived the author of *The Room* and *The Birthday Party* to be a member of the "kitchen sink" school of realism, along with John Osborne, Shelagh Delaney, and other British playwrights who drew their characters from the working class, their sets from the provinces, and their dialogue from the patterns and sounds of regional speech. Especially in his first few plays, Pinter's lower-class characters with their Cockney idiom and their bleak settings recall the social, psychological, and linguistic verisimilitude found in "kitchen sink" drama. However, his is a surface realism. He is not essentially, as Esslin points out in *Pinter the Playwright,* a realistic dramatist: "This is the paradox of his artistic personality. The dialogue and the characters are real, but the over-all effect is one of mystery, of uncertainty, of poetic ambiguity." Nor does Pinter regard himself as belonging to this dramatic school: "I'd say what goes on in my plays is realistic, but what I'm doing is not realism," he declared in the *Paris Review* interview.

Of the prevalent strains of twentieth-century British drama, epic theater has appeared to have the least influence on Pinter. Unlike his contemporaries John Arden, Arnold Wesher, and Edmund Bond, dramatists who are greatly influenced by German playwright Bertolt Brecht, Pinter has, for the most part, eschewed such Brechtian conventions as protagonists who represent the working class and themes that are socially and politically timely. However, in *The Hothouse,* a farcical play set in a mental institution, and in *One for the Road,* a disturbing one-act play that takes place in a government retaining home, Pinter touches on social commentary—the insidious inanity of bureaucracies and the mechanistic sadism of totalitarianism—and, epic-like, appeals primarily to his audience's intellect rather than to its emotions.

However, in its usual predilection for examining the private rather than the social sphere, Pinter's work is perhaps most clearly influenced by the absurdists, particularly by Irish playwright and novelist Samuel Beckett, for whom Pinter expressed admiration in the *Paris Review* interview: "I think Beckett is the best prose writer living." Admittedly, the world of Pinter's *Betrayal* is not that of Beckett's *Endgame;* the disjunction within the former results from marital discord, within the latter from existential fragmentation. Nevertheless, as Esslin writes in *Pinter the Playwright:* "Existential adjustment, coming to terms with one's own being, precedes, and necessarily predetermines, one's attitude to society, politics, and general ideas. Like Beckett and [Franz] Kafka Pinter's attitude . . . is that of an existentialist: the mode of a man's *being* determines his *thinking.* Hence, to come to grips with the true sources of their attitudes, the playwright must catch his characters at the decisive points in their lives, when they are confronted with the crisis of adjustment to themselves." As in much of absurdist drama, the names and behaviors of Pinter's characters, the plays' props and sets, resonate symbolically—"Riley" in *The Room* and *Family Voices,* the matchseller in *A Slight Ache,* the statue of Buddha in *The Caretaker,* vases and olives in *The Collection,* for example. And although Stanley in *The Birthday Party* is not *Endgame*'s Hamm or Clov, he contains elements of both—blindness and entrapment—and his fate is similarly and existentially capricious.

Belonging to no single school, Pinter draws from each to create a body of work idiosyncratically and recognizably his own. Those dramatic elements that are identifiably "Pinteresque" include his characters' mysterious pasts, his theme of the intruder, and his use of language— textual and subtextual—and of silence. In *Pinter the Playwright* Esslin quotes a letter received by Pinter shortly after *The Birthday Party* opened: "Dear Sir, I would be obliged if you would kindly explain to me the meaning of your play *The Birthday Party.* These are the points I do not understand: 1. Who are the two men? 2. Where did Stanley come from? 3. Were they all supposed to be normal? You will appreciate that without the answers to my questions I cannot fully understand your play." Pinter is said to have replied: "Dear Madam, I would be obliged if you would kindly explain to me the meaning of your letter. These are the points which I do not understand: 1. Who are you? 2. Where do you come from? 3. Are you supposed to be normal? You will appreciate that without the answers to my questions I cannot fully understand your letter." Both query and response are telling. Traditional dramatic exposition and character development have accustomed theater audiences to expect playwrights to provide enough information about the past to make the characters' present situations and motivations explicable. Like the inquisitive letter writer, playgoers request of dramatic art the logic and order that like outside the theater denies. Pinter, along with many other twentieth-century dramatists, refuses his audience this luxury.

In *The Birthday Party,* for example, Stanley Webber lives as the only boarder in Meg and Petey Boles's boarding house. The play's central mystery, and therefore a large part of its dramatic tension, evolves from the relationship between Stanley and the two men, Goldberg and McCann, who arrive at the boarding house. From the start, questions about the past arise and remain unanswered. Who is Stanley Webber? Why is he vegetating at the Boles's? What is his relationship with Meg? With the promiscuous neighbor, Lulu? Is it, or is it not, his birthday? Is he, or is he not, a pianist? Why do Goldberg and McCann want to find him? Why do they take him, dressed "in a dark well cut suit and white collar," to Monty? Who is Monty? The more information the audience receives the more confused it becomes.

Because the past is unverifiable, all that viewers can know about a Pinter character is what they themselves discern. And this source or kind of information often does not satisfy audiences familiar primarily with conventional dramatic exposition, especially since Pinter's characters confuse their viewers with contradiction. Consequently, audiences remain uncertain of motivations and unable to verify what little they can surmise, a predicament that coincides with life outside the theater. How can we know, Esslin asks in *Pinter the Playwright,* with "any semblance of certainty, what motivates our own wives, parents, our own children?" We can't. And Pinter's drama impedes all our attempts to know, despite (or perhaps because of) the anxiety that this raising of unanswerable questions creates.

Equally unsettling both to audiences and the plays' central figures is the theme of the intruder who invariably enters the rooms, basements, flats, and houses of Pinter's characters and in some way disrupts the residents. At times the intruder is a stranger, such as Riley, who enters Rose's haven in *The Room;* the matchseller whom Flora and Edward invite into their home in *A Slight Ache;* Spooner, whom Hirst picks up at a pub in *No Man's Land.* At other times the intruder is a friend or family member; in *The Homecoming,* for example, Teddy returns with his wife to his father's home; in *The Basement,* Stott takes his lover to visit and old friend; and in *Old Times,* Anna visits her former roommate.

In an unsigned insert to the program brochure of a 1960 performance of *The Room* and *The Dumb Waiter,* Pinter addresses the theme of the inevitability of an intruder: "Given a man in a room and he will sooner or later receive a visitor. A visitor entering the room will enter with intent. If two people inhabit the room the visitor will not be the same man for both. A man in a room who receives a visit is likely to be illuminated or horrified by it. The visitor himself might as easily be horrified or illuminated. . . . A man in a room and no one entering lives in expectation of a visit." Physical, psychological, or emotional disruption caused by the intruder provides the dramatic tension of most of Pinter's plays. For example, in *Betrayal* Jerry intrudes into Robert and Emma's marriage by initiating an affair with his best friend's wife. In *Family Voices* Voice 1 intrudes as a roomer upon the Withers family, and he, in turn, is intruded upon—although he appears not to realize it—by Voice 2, his mother, who entreats him to return home, and by Voice 3, his dead father, who intrudes upon life. Deborah, the central character in *A Kind of Alaska,* also intrudes upon life by awakening after twenty-nine years: in a sense, she becomes an intrusion to herself—a middle-ages woman imposing herself upon the young girl who was afflicted with sleeping sickness those many years before. In a Pinter play, intrusion inevitably will occur.

The dramatist's uncannily realistic sounding dialogue, replete with the linguistic inanities (pauses, tautologies, nonverbal sounds, disjunctive responses) and the verbal acts (defense, acquiescence, coercion, aggression) of everyday conversation, is also typically "Pinteresque." Yet despite its surface realism, Pinter crafts his dialogue with a poet's tools, including the caesurae, or silences. Although it is often parodied by his detractors and imitated by his admirers, the explicitly assigned "Pinter-pause" is invariably meaningful, reflecting a number of responses including puzzlement (Gus's pondering over the mysterious menu in *The Dumb Waiter*), illumination (Aston's finally realizing that Davies will not allow him to remain as caretaker or boarder in *The Caretaker*), and retrenchment (Ruth and Lenny's engaging

in a verbal duel for control in *The Homecoming*). Pinter's pauses comprise lines without words, lines that frequently speak as loudly as, or sometimes louder than, words.

Another silence—a noisy one—exists in Pinter's plays. In a speech delivered at the 1962 National Student Drama Festival in Bristol and published as the introduction to the first volume of the *Complete Works,* the playwright addresses this form of verbal hiatus: "There are two silences. One when no word is spoken. The other when perhaps a torrent of language is being employed. This speech is speaking of a language locked beneath it. That is its continual reference. The speech we hear is an indication of that which we don't hear. It is a necessary avoidance, a violent, sly, anguished or mocking smoke screen which keeps the other in its place. When true silence falls we are still left with echo but are nearer nakedness. One way of looking at speech is to say that it is a constant stratagem to cover nakedness." In order to cover their nakedness, Pinter's characters frequently discuss topics that have little to do with what is really on their minds: for instance, Rose in *The Room* chatters on about the weather and the apartment house in her attempt to reassure herself of the sanctuary of her room; Deeley, in *Old Times,* describes Kate's bathing habits to Anna in order to establish his intimacy with his wife and belittle the relationship between the two friends; and Robert, in *Betrayal,* discusses squash and lunch in a veiled assault on his wife. In instances such as these, language functions primarily on a subtextual level; it is not the meaning of the words that is essential, but how the characters use speech to bring about their different ends: to hide the pain of a relationship gone awry, the desperation of being lonely and homeless, the fear of relinquishing control. Unheard melodies in Pinter's language are often far less sweet than those heard.

Yet melodies heard can indeed be sweet. Lexical associations, *double entendre,* puns, exotic diction, onomatopoeia, and repetition—all poetic devices—call attention to the playwright's use of language. An early play written originally for radio and therefore dependent upon words alone to convey meaning, *A Slight Ache,* exemplifies Pinter's language at its most brilliant and meaningful. Language becomes this play's central theme: the character who possesses verbal acumen survives unscathed (as did young Pinter *en route* to his club in London's East End), while those who lose control over language are doomed.

Rich in sensory appeal and dense with imagery, this play has little action. A married couple, Edward and Flora, spend "the longest day of the year" at their country house. After breakfast, Edward notices a matchseller, who has apparently been there for "weeks," standing by the back gate. This day, however, Edward decides to invite the matchseller in to determine why he persists in remaining by the gate while making no attempt to sell his wares. The matchseller, who remains mute throughout the play, tacitly accepts the invitation, and Edward and Flora take turns playing host and hostess to their silent guest. During the course of the play, Edward grows increasingly weak and finally collapses on the floor; the matchseller, on the other hand, appears progressively rejuvenated. At play's end, Flora passes the tray of wet, useless matches to her prostrate husband and leaves with her new partner, the matchseller.

Of the names of Pinter's characters, Bernard Dukore writes in a 1981 *Theatre Journal* article: "Namesakes provide important clues that warrant attention, especially of a writer like Pinter, who carefully and precisely measures every aspect of his plays, including varying lengths and pauses. It is unlikely that he would be less sensitive to or painstaking with his character's name." Sometimes the names of Pinter's characters straightforwardly suggest personality traits (Bert Hudd, the monosyllabic, sadistic trucker of *The Room*, for example), but more often they signify allusively, often ironically (Dakore notes the "ruth- less" Ruth of *The Homecoming* returning to her husband's people as does the Old Testament Ruth before her). Flora's name suggests benevolent and fecund nature but her actions point to manipulative emasculation. She orchestrates her husband's demise.

Early in the play, Flora establishes her supremacy over Edward by acting the part of an indulgent parent, "calmly" correcting her husband while teaching him the plants' proper names: "Edward—you know that shrub outside the toolshed. . . . That's convolvulus." As though speaking to a small child, Flora also explains to her husband the need for the canopy, "To shade you from the sun." To label elements within one's environment is, in a sense, to control those elements and that environment. By naming the plants in her garden, Flora establishes dominance over her immediate environment. She also "names" Edward: she refers to him by his given name an inordinate number of times (considering they are the only two speakers in the play) and uses the faintly scatological sobriquet, "Weddie. Beddie Weddie." She also christens the matchseller: "I'm going to . . . call you Barnabas."

In contrast to his wife, Edward is unable to name the plants in his garden—a shortcoming Pinter points to in the play's opening dialogue: "You know perfectly well what grows in your garden," Flora states, and Edward replies, "Quite the contrary. It is clear that I don't." Nor can Edward recall the name of the squire's red-headed daughter, with whom he was enamored: "The youngest one was the best of the bunch. Sally. No, no, wait a minute, no, it wasn't Sally, it was . . . Fanny." Moreover, he calls lunch *petit dejeuner* (French for "breakfast") and rants at his guest for consuming "duck," although Flora has invited the matchseller to share a mid-day goose. Her husband's inability to label and thereby control his environment—garden or dining room— dooms him before his more able wife; he is fated to succumb to Flora and her new ally, the matchseller, who remains nameless to her husband.

As Edward grows weaker, he grows even less able to use language effectively. Early in the play he attempts fastidiousness in his choice of words: "It will not bite you! Wasps don't bite. . . . They sting. It's snakes . . . that bite. . . . Horseflies suck." Later he haltingly differentiates between a road and a lane: "It's not a road at all. What is it? It's a lane." Despite his efforts at linguistic precision, Edward loses control when confronted by the matchseller to whom he offers an inappropriately discriminating choice of drinks: "Now look, what will you have to drink? A glass of ale? Curacao Fockink Orange? Ginger beer? Tia Maria? A Wachenheimer Fuchsmantel Reisling Beeren Auslese? Gin and it? Chateauneuf-du-Pape? A little Asti Spumanti? Or what do you say to a straightforward Piesporter Goldtropfschen Feine Auslese (Reichsgraf von Kesselstaff)?" Like the provocatively named plants—honeysuckle, convolvulus, clematis—in Edward and Flora's garden, these drinks amuse in the sexual suggestiveness and continental inclusiveness. Less comically, the list reflects Edward's growing anxiety. The language through which he earlier attempts denotative exactness in reference to wasps and lanes carries him away—from one exotic beverage to another. Toward the play's end, Edward is reduced to nonverbal communication: "Aaaaahhhh." Flora retains control over language. She endures.

Since *No Man's Land* in 1975, Pinter has relied less on verbal indulgence and more on elements of design to evoke meaning. The poet- playwright seems to be increasingly influenced by the sce-narist-playwright, a change resulting perhaps from the requirements and possibilities of cinema. Over the years four of Pinter's plays have been filmed: *The Caretaker, The Birthday Party, The Homecoming,* and *Betrayal.* He has also written ten screenplays based on other writers' novels; all but one (*The Proust Screenplay*) have been filmed: *The Servant, The Pumpkin Eater, The Quiller Memorandum, Accident, The Go-Between, Langrishe, Go Down, The Last Tycoon, The French Lieutenant's Woman,* and *Turtle Diary.* Although this list appears disparate, it possesses internal logic. The playwright-scenarist adapts fiction whose themes and subjects are those of his own dramatic art: adultery; role reversal or role confusion; duplicity; physical, psychological and emotional cruelty; artistic stasis; homosexuality; and perverted birthday celebrations, to mention only a few of these motifs. Furthermore, like his plays, the novels he has adapted for the screen focus predominantly on character rather than on plot. Even in a spy thriller like *The Quiller Memorandum,* assassinations, attempted murders, and scenes of torture fade from memory more rapidly than do the characters. Another denominator common to the stage plays and screenplays is Pinter's exploration of time and memory, topics he has dealt with frequently since writing *Old Times* in 1970. Simple flashback accommodates the characters' memories in the screenplay versions of *The Pumpkin Eater* and *Accident;* but *The Go- Between, A la recherche du temps perdu,* and *The French Lieutenant's Woman* require more innovative techniques to deal with their sophisticated examinations of time. A technique Pinter uses in the screenplays—flashbacks interwoven with flashforwards—reappears in his play *Betrayal.* In short, Pinter's work in film expands upon the interests he explores on the stage.

Although Pinter is not essentially a comic writer, he does write very funny dialogue. When characters posture, as when Edward lists the contents of his liquor cabinet for the matchseller's benefit in *A Slight Ache,* Deeley flaunts his familiarity with the past to denigrate his houseguest in *Old Times,* or when Robert recounts his experience at the American Express office where he has just learned of his wife's affair with his best friend in *Betrayal,* their speeches are frequently comic, often extravagantly so. In *Pinter the Playwright,* Esslin reprints Pinter's 1960 response to an open letter "deploring the gales of laughter about the unhappy plight of the old tramp" in *The Caretaker:* "An element of the absurd is, I think, one of the features of the play, but at the same time I did not intend it to be merely a laughable farce. If there hadn't been other issues at stake the play would not have been written. . . . Where the comic and the tragic (for want of a better word) are closely interwoven, certain members of the audience will always give emphasis to the comic as opposed to the other, for by doing so they rationalize the other out of existence. . . . Where . . . indiscriminate mirth is found, I feel it represents a cheerful patronage of the characters on the part of the merrymakers, and thus participation is avoided. This laughter is in fact a mode of precaution, a smoke-screen, a refusal to accept what is happening as recognizable. . . . From this kind of uneasy jollification I must, of course, disassociate myself. . . . As far as I'm concerned, *The Caretaker* is funny, up to a point. Beyond that point it ceases to be funny, and it was because of that point that I wrote it."

In *The Caretaker,* as in all of Pinter's plays, comic elements illuminate noncomic ones. On one hand, humor serves as a balm, easing audience discomfort at witnessing the characters' pain; on the other, it intensifies the discomfort by forcing pain into contiguity with laughter so that the distinctions between the two disappear, and the audience is left precariously straddling the fine line that separates the comic from the noncomic. In his best work, Pinter leaves his audiences at that moment when the plays cease altogether to be funny—when bright lights "photograph" the silent threesome in the final tableau of *Old Times* or fade as Hirst takes one last drink in *No Man's Land,* when the curtain falls on Max imploring Ruth to kiss him in *The Homecoming* or on Meg blissfully unaware that Stanley has been taken away in *The Birthday Party.* Ultimately, Pinter's plays emphasize that which is not comic, and despite their considerable humor, his vision is not a comic one.

Unquestionably, Harold Pinter is one of the major playwrights of his time. His work has greatly influenced a number of contemporary dramatists on both sides of the Atlantic; critics and scholars alike consider his six full-length works (*The Birthday Party, The Caretaker, The Homecoming, Old Times No Man's Land, Betrayal*) to be among the most important plays of the mid-twentieth century. In his more recent work, Pinter continues to experiment with possibilities of theater, to search for the exact verbal and visual image, and to strive for theatrical economy.

In a speech originally delivered in Hamburg, West Germany, in 1970 and published in the fourth volume of the *Complete Works,* the playwright declares: "The image must be pursued with the greatest vigilance, calmly, and once found, must be sharpened, graded, accurately focused and maintained, and the key word is economy, economy of movement and gesture, of emotion and its expression . . . so there is no wastage and no mess." Whether a woman clutches her eyes (*The Room*), a man drinks to stasis (*No Man's Land*) or a cabby sits silently in his taxi (*Victoria Station*), Pinter's dramatic images and the vision they embody remain in his audience's memories long after the stage lights have faded.

BIOGRAPHICAL/CRITICAL SOURCES:

BOOKS

Contemporary Literary Criticism, Gale, Volume 1, 1973, Volume 3, 1975, Volume 6, 1976, Volume 9, 1978, Volume 11, 1979, Volume 15, 1980, Volume 27, 1984.
Dictionary of Literary Biography, Volume 13: *British Dramatists since World War II,* Gale, 1982.
Esslin, Martin, *Pinter the Playwright,* Methuen, 1984.
Gale, Steven H. *Harold Pinter: An Annotated Bibliography,* G. K. Hall, 1978.
Kerr, Walter, *Harold Pinter,* Columbia University, 1967.
Pinter, Harold, *A Slight Ache and Other Plays,* Methuen, 1961.
Pinter, Harold, *Complete Works,* Volume 1, Grove, 1977.
Pinter, Harold, *Prose and Poetry, 1949-1977,* Grove, 1978.

PERIODICALS

Chicago Tribune, September 26, 1989.
Hackney Downs School Magazine, winter, 1946, summer, 1947.
Modern Drama, Volume 27, 1984.
New Yorker, February 25, 1967.
New York Times, October 5, 1961, October 15, 1961, October 6, 1989, November 9, 1989.
New York Times Magazine, December 5, 1971.
Observer, June 25, 1960.
Paris Review, fall, 1966.
Sunday Times (London), May 25, 1958.*

—*Sidelights by Stephanie Tucker*

*   *   *

PLUM, J.
See WODEHOUSE, P(elham) G(renville)

POGREBIN, Letty Cottin   1939-

PERSONAL: Surname is pronounced *Po*-greb-in; born June 9, 1939, in New York, NY; daughter of Jacob (an attorney) and Cyral (a designer; maiden name, Halpern) Cottin; married Bertrand B. Pogrebin (an attorney), December 8, 1963; children: Abigail and Robin (twins), David. *Education:* Brandeis University, B.A. (cum laude), 1959.

ADDRESSES: Office—Ms. Magazine, One Times Square, New York, NY 10036. *Agent*—Wendy Weil, Julian Bach Literary Agency, Inc., 747 Third Ave., New York, NY 10017.

CAREER: Simon & Schuster, Inc., New York City, part-time secretary and assistant, 1957-59; Coward-McCann, Inc., New York City, editorial assistant, 1959-60; Sussman & Sugar (advertising), New York City, copywriter, 1960; Bernard Geis Associates (publishers), New York City, director of publicity, advertising, and subsidiary rights, 1960-70, vice-president, 1970; *Ms.* (magazine), editor, 1971-87, editor at large, 1987-89, contributing editor, 1990—. Lecturer on family politics, Jewish-feminist issues, and women's issues. Member of board of directors of *Ms.* Foundation, Authors Guild of America, Americans for Peace NOW, International Center for Peace in the Middle East, New Israel Fund, Public Education Association, and of Action for Children's Television; consultant to ABC television program, "Free to Be . . . You and Me."

MEMBER: National Organization for Women, National Women's Political Caucus (founding member), Author's Guild, Authors League of America, Women's Forum.

AWARDS, HONORS: Women in Communications "Sound of Success" Award and Clarion Award, 1974, for *Ladies' Home Journal* columns; Poynter fellowship, Yale University; Matrix Award; Emmy Award, American Academy of Television Arts and Sciences, for "Free to Be . . . You and Me"; Swedish Bicentennial Award; Israel Bonds Eleanor Roosevelt Award; National Council on Family Relations commendation; National Media award, Family Services Association; distinguished achievement award, Educational Press Association.

WRITINGS:

How to Make It in a Man's World, Doubleday, 1970.
Getting Yours: How to Make the System Work for the Working Woman, McKay, 1975.
Growing up Free: Raising Your Child in the '80s, McGraw, 1980.
Stories for Free Children, McGraw, 1981.
Family Politics: Love and Power on an Intimate Frontier, McGraw, 1983.
Among Friends: Who We Like, Why We Like Them, and What We Do with Them, McGraw, 1986.
Deborah, Golda, and Me, Crown, 1991.

Also author of monthly column "The Working Woman" for the *Ladies' Home Journal,* 1971-81, and of "Hers" column in *New York Times.* Contributor to *Nation, TV Guide, Family Circle, Good Housekeeping, Cosmopolitan, Variety,* and other periodicals.

WORK IN PROGRESS: A book on women over fifty.

BIOGRAPHICAL/CRITICAL SOURCES:

PERIODICALS

Chicago Tribune, December 5, 1986.
Los Angeles Times, October 28, 1980; November 21, 1983.
New Republic, June 13, 1970.

New York Times, April 15, 1970; September 22, 1980; February 2, 1986.
New York Times Book Review, October 26, 1980; December 18, 1983.
Publishers Weekly, November 21, 1986.
Time, December 20, 1971.

* * *

POLLOCK, Mary
  See BLYTON, Enid (Mary)

* * *

POTTER, Dennis (Christopher George) 1935-

PERSONAL: Born May 17, 1935, in Joyford Hill, Gloucestershire, England; son of Walter and Margaret Constance (Wales) Potter; married Margaret Morgan (a journalist), 1959; children: one son, two daughters. *Education:* New College, Oxford, B.A. (with honors), 1959. *Politics:* Labour.

ADDRESSES: Home—Morecambe Lodge, Duxmere, Ross-on-Wye, Herefordshire 3199, England. *Agent*—Clive Goodwin, 79 Cromwell Rd., London S.W.7, England.

CAREER: British Broadcasting Corp. (BBC-TV), London, England, member of current affairs staff, 1959-61; London Daily Herald, London, 1961-64, began as feature writer, became television critic; London Sun, London, editorial writer, 1964; freelance playwright, author, and journalist, 1964. Labour candidate for Parliament from East Hertfordshire, 1964.

AWARDS, HONORS: Writer of the Year Awards from Writers Guild of Great Britain, 1966 and 1969; award from Society of Film and Television Arts, 1966; BAFTA Award, 1978, for "Pennies from Heaven," and 1980, for "Blue Remembered Hills"; Prix Italia, 1982, for "Blade on the Feather, Rain on the Roof, Cream in My Coffee"; honorary fellow, New College, Oxford, 1987.

WRITINGS:

PLAYS

"Vote Vote Vote for Nigel Barton," 1965, revised version incorporating "Vote Vote Vote for Nigel Barton" and "Stand Up, Nigel Barton" (also see below), produced in Bristol at Theatre Royal, November 27, 1968, published in *The Nigel Barton Plays: Two Television Plays,* Penguin, 1967.
"Stand Up, Nigel Barton," first televised, 1965, published in *The Nigel Barton Plays,* 1967.
Son of Man (first televised on British Broadcasting Corp. (BBC-TV), 1969, first produced in Leicester, 1969, produced in London at Round House Theatre, 1969), Deutsch, 1970.
"Lay Down Your Arms," first televised on Independent Television (ITV), May 23, 1970.
"Traitor," first televised on BBC-TV, October 14, 1971.
"Follow the Yellow Brick Road," 1972, published in *The Television Dramatist,* edited by Robert Muller, Elek, 1973.
"Only Make Believe," first televised, 1973, first produced in Harlow, 1974.
"Joe's Ark," 1974, published in *The Television Play,* edited by Robin Wade, BBC Publications, 1976.
Brimstone and Treacle (first produced in Sheffield at the Crucible Theatre, October, 1977; also see below), Eyre Methuen, 1978.
"Pennies From Heaven" (screenplay; adapted from the television series by Potter), Metro-Goldwyn-Mayer, 1981.

"Brimstone and Treacle" (screenplay; adaptation of Potter's stage play), 1982.
Sufficient Carbohydrate, Faber & Faber, 1983.
"Gorky Park" (screenplay adapted from the novel by Martin Cruz Smith), Orion, 1983.
Waiting for the Boat (three plays), Faber & Faber, 1984.
"Dreamchild" (screenplay), Curzon/Universal, 1985.
"Track 29" (screenplay based on Potter's television play "Schmoedipus"), Island Pictures, 1988.
The Singing Detective (sextet; produced on BBC-Television, November 9, 1986), Random House, 1988.

Also author of "The Confidence Course," 1965; "Alice," 1965; "Where the Buffalo Roam," 1966; "Emergency Ward Nine," 1966; "Message for Posterity," 1967; "A Beast With Two Backs," 1968; "The Bonegrinder," 1968; "Shaggy Dog," 1968; "Moonlight on the Highway," 1969; "Angels Are So Few," 1970; "Paper Roses," 1971; "Casanova" (six-play series), 1971; "A Tragedy of Two Ambitions" (adapted from story by Thomas Hardy), 1973; "Schmoedipus" (adapted from novel by Angus Wilson), 1974; "Late Call" (serial; adapted from novel by Wilson), 1975; "Double Dare," 1976; "Where Adam Stood" (adapted from *Father and Son* by Edmund Gosse), 1976; "Pennies From Heaven" (sextet), 1978; "The Mayor of Casterbridge" (adapted from novel by Hardy), 1978; "Blue Remembered Hills," 1979; "Blade on the Feather, Rain on the Roof, Cream in My Coffee," 1980; "Tender Is the Night" (sextet adapted from novel by F. Scott Fitzgerald), 1985; "Visitors," 1987; "Christabel" (quartet adapted from *The Past Is Myself* by Christabel Bielenberg), 1988; "Blackeyes," 1989.

OTHER

The Glittering Coffin (nonfiction), Gollancz, 1960.
The Changing Forest: Life in the Forest of Dean Today (nonfiction), Secker & Warburg, 1962.
Hide and Seek (novel), Deutsch, 1973.
Ticket to Ride (novel), Faber & Faber, 1986, Vintage Books, 1989.
Blackeyes (novel), Faber & Faber, 1987, Random House, 1988.

Also author of *Pennies from Heaven* (novel), 1982.

SIDELIGHTS: Dennis Potter's numerous television plays have earned him a reputation as "one of the major dramatists writing for the medium." His first effort, "Vote Vote Vote for Nigel Barton," is a tragicomedy about a young Labour candidate's campaign for public office. This work and its companion play, "Stand Up, Nigel Barton," were together adapted for the stage under the title "Vote Vote Vote for Nigel Barton." Jeremy Kingston praised Potter's skill in combining elements of the two plays, noting that "the mingling of Nigel's past with his present and the tension between public and private face work as strongly on the stage as I am told they did on [television]."

Many of Potter's works have generated controversy. His play "Son of Man" created a furor when it was first broadcast on BBC-TV and later when it was broadcast on KYW-TV in Philadelphia. Picketers protested that in the play Christ is portrayed as a "hippie." Potter's television play "Brimstone and Treacle" was also involved in conflict when BBC-TV decided against broadcasting it in response to protests by viewers of the BBC who considered the play too shocking for television. Those who feared censorship of the media, in turn, condemned the action of the BBC. The play was later produced for the stage and also published with a twenty-five- hundred-word introduction that presented the author's view of the quarrel. John Coleby, who reviewed the published version of the play, referred to it as "moving," "compelling," and "strong" but observed that "in the end the ingredients don't quite blend, the flavor is nondescript."

Potter also wrote the screenplay for "Pennies From Heaven," a film that impressed some critics and confused others with its combination of 1930's-musicals whimsy and Ingmar Bergman-like despair during the Depression. The *Chicago Tribune*'s Gene Siskel wrote, "One of the things we can make of [certain scenes] is that there was a huge gap between the grim realities of the Depression and the songs that were created in part to lift the nation's spirit." The *New York Times*'s Vincent Canby was less convinced of the film's merits. He conceded that some of the musical transitions—featuring actors lip- syncing songs by performers such as Bing Crosby—were "spectacularly effective," but added that Potter and director Herbert Ross have created a work that is "chilly without being provocative in any intellectual way." Canby cited one scene in which the male protagonist lip-syncs a woman's voice as "briefly funny," then added that "the merciless eye of the camera and the film's deliberate pacing drain all real wit and spontaneity from the sequence."

Another Potter screenplay, "Dreamchild," takes place in the 1930s, when an elderly Alice Liddell Hargreaves (the "Alice" of Lewis Carroll's *Alice in Wonderland* and *Alice through the Looking- Glass*) travelled to New York to receive an honorary degree. The unaccustomed pressures of American city life exhaust her and set her to dreaming about her childhood. Stephen Holden, writing in the *New York Times,* says that "Dreamchild" "paints the early 1930s in glowing storybook colors that complement the subtlety of the performances," and concludes that it is "a lovely, wistful little fairytale for adults." Gene Siskel, in the *Chicago Tribune,* states that the film "goes its own special with precision and consummate skill," and declares, "See this fascinating and troubling and beautifully acted movie and your reading of 'Alice' never will be the same."

BIOGRAPHICAL/CRITICAL SOURCES:

PERIODICALS

Chicago Tribune, December 22, 1981, January 10, 1986.
Christian Science Monitor, November 26, 1969.
Drama, autumn, 1978.
Encounter, February, 1974.
Listener, November 15, 1973.
Los Angeles Times, November 18, 1982, September 15, 1985, October 18, 1985.
New Statesman, December 6, 1968, November 2, 1973.
New York Times, December 11, 1981, October 4, 1985.
New York Times Book Review, October 15, 1989.
Punch, December 4, 1968, November 19, 1969.
Stage, October 21, 1971.
Times (London), December 9, 1983, February 14, 1984, September 9, 1986, October 1, 1987.
Variety, March 18, 1970.
Washington Post, January 17, 1986.*

* * *

PRICE, Anthony 1928-

PERSONAL: Born August 16, 1928, in Hertfordshire, England; son of Walter Longsdon (an engineer) and Kathleen (an artist; maiden name, Lawrence) Price; married Ann Stone (a registered nurse), June 20, 1953; children: James, Simon, Katherine. *Education:* Merton College, Oxford, M.A. (with honors), 1952.

ADDRESSES: Home—Wayside Cottage, Horton-cum-Studley, Oxfordshire, England. *Office*—*Oxford Times,* Osney Mead, Ox-

fordshire, England. *Agent*—A. P. Watt & Son, 26/28 Bedford Row, London WC1R 4HL, England.

CAREER: Writer. Journalist, beginning 1952; *Oxford Times,* Oxfordshire, England, editor, 1972-88. *Military service:* British Army, 1947-49; became captain.

MEMBER: Guild of British Newspaper Editors, Crime Writers Association (England), Detection Club.

AWARDS, HONORS: Silver Dagger from Crime Writers Association, 1971, for *The Labyrinth Makers;* Golden Dagger from Crime Writers Association, 1974, for *Other Paths to Glory;* Swedish Academy of Crime Fiction Award for best foreign crime book translated, 1978, for *Other Paths to Glory.*

WRITINGS:

The Labyrinth Makers, Gollancz, 1970, Doubleday, 1971.
The Alamut Ambush, Gollancz, 1971, Doubleday, 1972.
Colonel Butler's Wolf, Gollancz, 1972, Doubleday, 1973.
October Men, Gollancz, 1973, Doubleday, 1974.
Other Paths to Glory, Gollancz, 1974, Doubleday, 1975.
Our Man in Camelot, Gollancz, 1975, Doubleday, 1976.
War Game, Gollancz, 1976.
The '44 Vintage, Gollancz, 1978, Doubleday, 1979.
Tomorrow's Ghost, Gollancz, 1979, Doubleday, 1980.
The Hour of the Donkey, Gollancz, 1980.
Soldier No More, Gollancz, 1981, Doubleday, 1982.
The Old Vengeful, Gollancz, 1982, Doubleday, 1983.
Gunner Kelly, Gollancz, 1983, Doubleday, 1984.
Sion Crossing, Gollancz, 1984, Mysterious Press, 1985.
Here Be Monsters, Gollancz, 1984, Mysterious Press, 1985.
For the Good of the State, Gollancz, 1985, Mysterious Press, 1986.
A New Kind of War, Gollancz, 1986, Mysterious Press, 1987.
A Prospect of Vengeance, Gollancz, 1988.
The Memory Trap, Gollancz, 1989.

SIDELIGHTS: Times Literary Supplement reviewer T. J. Binyon notes that Anthony Price's first novel *The Labyrinth Makers* "introduced the character who has since become his chief spy-catcher—Dr. David Audley of British Intelligence." Overall, Binyon indicates, "Price has written a number of highly intelligent and extremely good thrillers." Price writes *CA* that he tries "to combine the elements of the mystery story with those of the spy thriller, using my particular interests—history, particularly military history—as a background. My heroes and heroines are generally not secret agents so much as secret policemen (and women). My themes (I like to think) are nevertheless loyalty, duty, honor and patriotism, which I regard as the virtues of a free man in a free country. And if that's old fashioned, then so be it, by God!"

BIOGRAPHICAL/CRITICAL SOURCES:

PERIODICALS

Globe and Mail (Toronto), August 13, 1988.
Los Angeles Times Book Review, July 26, 1986.
New York Times, May 23, 1986.
New York Times Book Review, June 17, 1984; September 15, 1985; August 16, 1987; July 19, 1988.
Times (London), January 22, 1987; December 24, 1987, November 12, 1988.
Times Literary Supplement, February 24, 1978; January 8, 1982; April 25, 1986; April 10, 1987.

PRICHARD, Katharine Susannah 1883-1969

PERSONAL: Born 1883, in Levuka, Fiji; died October 2, 1969; daughter of Tom Henry (editor of *Fiji Times*) and Edith Isabel (Fraser) Prichard; married Hugo Throssell (an Army captain), 1919; children: Ric Prichard. *Education:* Educated in Australian schools.

ADDRESSES: Home—Greenmount, West Australia.

CAREER: Grew up in Australia, except for one period in Tasmania, and had first short stories published at eleven; later journalist for newspapers in Melbourne and Sydney and other Australian publications, and free-lance journalist in London, England, 1908 and 1912-16; fiction writer in Australia, 1916-1969.

AWARDS, HONORS: Hodder & Stoughton prize of one thousand pounds, 1924, for *The Pioneers; Art in Australia* prize, 1924, for short story, "The Grey Horse"; *Triad* award for a three-act Australian play, 1927, for *Brumby Innes; Bulletin* (Sydney) prize of five hundred pounds, 1928, for *Coonardoo.*

WRITINGS:

The Pioneers, Hodder & Stoughton, 1915, revised edition, Angus & Robertson, 1963.
Windlestraws, Holden & Hardingham, 1917.
The Black Opal, Heinemann, 1921.
Working Bullocks, Viking, 1927.
The Wild Oats of Han (juvenile), Angus & Robertson, 1928, revised edition, Lansdowne Press, 1968.
Coonardoo, the Well in the Shadow, J. Cape, 1929, Norton, 1930.
Haxby's Circus: The Lightest, Brightest Little Show on Earth, J. Cape, 1930, published as *Fay's Circus,* Norton, 1931.
Earth Lover (poems), Sunnybrook Press, 1930.
Kiss on the Lips, and Other Stories, J. Cape, 1932.
The Real Russia, Modern Publishers, 1934.
(With others) *Best Australian One-Act Plays,* edited by William Moore and T. I. Moore, Angus & Robertson, 1937.
Intimate Strangers, J. Cape, 1937.
Brumby Innes (three-act play), Paterson's Printing Press, 1940.
Moon of Desire, J. Cape, 1941.
(Editor with others) *Australian New Writing 1943-1945,* Current Books, 1943-1945.
Potch and Colour (short stories), Angus & Robertson, 1944.
The Roaring Nineties: A Story of the Goldfields of Western Australia, J. Cape, 1946.
Golden Miles, J. Cape, 1948.
Winged Seeds, J. Cape, 1950.
N'goola, and Other Stories, Australasian Book Society, 1959.
Child of the Hurricane (autobiography), Angus & Robertson, 1963.
On Strenuous Wings, edited by Joan Williams, Seven Seas Publishers, 1965.
Happiness: Selected Short Stories, Angus & Robertson, 1967.
Subtle Flame, Australasian Book Society, 1967.
Moggie and Her Circus Pony, F. W. Cheshire, 1967.

Also author of collection of short stories entitled *The Grey Horse,* 1924, and of play entitled "Bid Me To Love," 1974. Work anthologized in *The World's Greatest Short Stories,* Crown.

MEDIA ADAPTATIONS: The Pioneers was made into a motion picture in 1926.

SIDELIGHTS: Katharine Susannah Prichard's books have been translated into twelve languages, including Russian, Latvian, Hungarian, Slovak, Afrikaans, Armenian, and Chinese.

BIOGRAPHICAL/CRITICAL SOURCES:

BOOKS

Contemporary Literary Criticism, Volume 46, Gale, 1988.*

* * *

PRIESTLEY, J(ohn) B(oynton) 1894-1984
(Peter Goldsmith)

PERSONAL: Born September 13, 1894, in Bradford, Yorkshire, England; died after a brief illness August 14, 1984, in Stratford-upon-Avon, England; son of Jonathan (a schoolmaster) Priestley; married Patricia Tempest (died, 1925); married Mary Holland Wyndham Lewis, 1926 (marriage dissolved, 1952); married Jacquetta Hawkes (an archaeologist and writer); children: (first marriage) two daughters; (second marriage) two daughters, one son (Tom). *Education:* Trinity Hall, Cambridge, M.A. *Politics:* Leftist. *Avocational interests:* Painting, listening to music.

ADDRESSES: Home—Kissing Tree House, Alveston, Stratford-upon-Avon, England. *Agent*—A. D. Peters, 10 Buckingham St., Adelphi, London WC2, England.

CAREER: Novelist, playwright, essayist, and journalist. Began writing for newspapers in England at the age of sixteen; critic, reviewer, and essayist for various periodicals in London, beginning 1922; director of Mask Theatre, 1938-39. Lecturer on a U.S. tour in 1937; spent several winters in Arizona. Advisor on film scripts in Hollywood and England, and, during World War II, broadcast "Postscripts," a series of BBC radio talks. Appeared in semi-documentary *Battle for Music,* a 1943 Strand/Anglo American film. United Kingdom delegate to two UNESCO conferences, 1946-47; one of the originators of Campaign for Nuclear Disarmament (CND). Chairman of International Theatre Conferences at Paris, 1947, and Prague, 1948, British Theatre Conference, 1948, and International Theatre Institute, 1949. Member of National Theatre Board, 1966-67; former chairman of council on London Philharmonic Orchestra, and a director of *New Statesman* and *Nation. Military service:* British Army, Infantry, 1914-19; became commissioned officer; wounded three times.

MEMBER: Screenwriters' Association (London; president, 1944-45), Savile Club (London).

AWARDS, HONORS: James Tait Black prize for fiction, 1930, for *The Good Companions;* Ellen Terry Award for best play of 1947, for *The Linden Tree;* British Order of Merit, 1977; LL.D., St. Andrews University; D.Litt., Universities of Colorado, Birmingham, and Bradford.

WRITINGS:

FICTION

Adam in Moonshine, Harper, 1927.
Benighted, Heinemann, 1927, published as *The Old Dark House,* Harper, 1928.
(With Hugh Walpole) *Farthing Hall* (humorous romance), Macmillan, 1929.
The Good Companions (also see below), Harper, 1929.
Angel Pavement, Harper, 1930, reissued with foreword by Sinclair Lewis, Readers Club Press, 1942.
The Town Major of Miraucourt, Heinemann, 1930.
Faraway, Harper, 1932.
Albert Goes Through, Harper, 1933.
(With Gerald W. Bullett) *I'll Tell You Everything,* Macmillan, 1933.
Wonder Hero, Harper, 1933.

They Walk in the City [and] *The Lovers in the Stone Forest*, Harper, 1936.

The Doomsday Men: An Adventure, Harper, 1938.

Let the People Sing, Heinemann, 1939, Harper, 1940.

Black-Out in Gretley: A Story of and for Wartime, Harper, 1942.

Daylight on Saturday, Harper, 1943 (published in England as *Daylight on Saturday: A Novel About an Aircraft Factory*, Heinemann, 1943).

Three Men in New Suits, Harper, 1945.

Bright Day, Harper, 1946, reissued with new introduction by Priestley, Dutton, 1966.

Jenny Villiers: A Story of the Theatre, Harper, 1947.

Going Up; and Other Stories and Sketches, Pan Books, 1950.

Festival, Harper, 1951 (published in England as *Festival at Farbridge*, Heinemann, 1951).

The Other Place, and Other Stories of the Same Sort, Harper, 1953.

Low Notes on a High Level, Harper, 1954 (published in England as *Low Notes on a High Level: A Frolic*, Heinemann, 1954).

The Magicians, Harper, 1954.

Saturn over the Water: An Account of His Adventures in London, New York, South America, and Australia by Tim Bedford, Painter; Edited with Some Preliminary and Concluding Remarks by Henry Sulgrave; and Here Presented to the Reading Public, Doubleday, 1961.

The Thirty-First of June: A Tale of True Love, Enterprise, and Progress, in the Arthurian and Ad-Atomic Ages, Heinemann, 1961, Doubleday, 1962.

The Shapes of Sleep: A Topical Tale, Doubleday, 1962.

Sir Michael and Sir George: A Tale of COSMA and DISCUS and the New Elizabethans, Heinemann, 1964, published as *Sir Michael and Sir George: A Comedy of the New Elizabethans*, Little, Brown, 1966.

Lost Empires: Being Richard Herncastle's Account of His Life on the Variety Stage from November 1913 to August 1914, Together with a Prologue and Epilogue, Heinemann, 1965.

It's an Old Country, Little, Brown, 1967.

The Image Men, Volume 1: *Out of Town*, Volume 2: *London End*, Heinemann, 1968, published as single-volume edition, Little, Brown, 1969, volumes published separately, Penguin, 1969.

The Carfitt Crisis, and Two Other Stories, Heinemann, 1975.

PLAYS

(With Edward Knoblock) *The Good Companions* (two-act; based on Priestley's novel of the same title; produced on the West End, 1931; produced in New York, 1931), Samuel French, 1935.

Dangerous Corner (three-act; produced on the West End, 1932; produced in New York, 1932), Heinemann, 1932, Samuel French, 1932.

The Roundabout (three-act comedy; produced in 1933), Samuel French, 1933.

Laburnum Grove (three-act "immoral comedy"; produced on the West End, 1933; produced on Broadway, 1935), Heinemann, 1934, Samuel French, 1935.

Eden End (three-act; produced on the West End, 1934; produced Off-Broadway, 1935), Heinemann, 1934, Samuel French, 1935.

Cornelius ("a business affair in three transactions"; produced on the West End, 1935), Heinemann, 1935, Samuel French, 1936.

Duet in Floodlight (comedy; produced on the West End under Priestley's direction, 1935), Heinemann, 1935.

Bees on the Boat Deck (two-act farcical tragedy; produced on the West End, 1936), Heinemann, 1936.

(Under pseudonym Peter Goldsmith, with George Billam) *Spring Tide* (three-act; produced on the West End, 1936), Heinemann, 1936.

People at Sea (three-act; produced on the West End, 1936), Heinemann, 1937, Samuel French, 1938.

I Have Been Here Before (three-act; produced in London, 1937; produced in New York, 1938), Heinemann, 1937, Harper, 1938.

Time and the Conways (three-act; produced on the West End, 1937; produced in New York, 1938), Heinemann, 1937, Harper, 1938.

Mystery at Greenfingers ("comedy of detection"; produced in 1938), Samuel French, 1937.

When We Are Married (three-act Yorkshire farcical comedy; produced on the West End, 1938; produced on Broadway, 1939), Heinemann, 1938, Samuel French, 1940.

Johnson over Jordan [and] *All About It* (the former a three-act morality play, produced on the West End, 1939; the latter an essay), Harper, 1939, play published separately by Samuel French, 1941.

Music at Night (three-act; produced on the West End, 1939), Samuel French, 1947.

Good-Night Children (comedy; produced on the West End, 1942), published in *Three Comedies*, Heinemann, 1945.

They Came to a City (two-act; produced on the West End, 1943), Samuel French, 1944.

Desert Highway (two-act, with an interlude; produced on Broadway, 1944), Samuel French, 1944.

How Are They at Home? (two-act topical comedy; produced on the West End, 1944), Samuel French, 1945.

The Long Mirror (three-act; produced in Edinburgh, 1945), Samuel French, 1947.

An Inspector Calls (three-act; produced in the U.S.S.R.; produced on the West End, 1946; produced on Broadway, 1947), Heinemann, 1947, Dramatists Play Service, 1948, abridged edition, Macmillan, 1966.

The Rose and the Crown (one-act; produced in 1947), Samuel French, 1947.

The Linden Tree (two-act; produced on the West End, 1947; produced on Broadway, 1948), Samuel French, 1948.

Ever Since Paradise (three-act; produced in London, 1947), Samuel French, 1949.

The Golden Fleece (three-act comedy; produced in 1948), Samuel French, 1948.

(With Doris Zinkeisen) *The High Toby* (play for "toy theatre"; produced in 1948), Penguin, 1948.

Home is Tomorrow (two-act; produced on the West End, 1948), Heinemann, 1949, Samuel French, 1950.

(Author of libretto) *The Olympians* (three-act opera; score by Arthur Bliss; produced in London at Covent Garden Theatre, 1949), Novello, 1949.

Summer Day's Dream (two-act; produced on the West End, 1949), Samuel French, 1950.

Bright Shadow (three-act "play of detection"; produced in Palmer's Green, 1950), Samuel French, 1950.

(With wife, Jacquetta Hawkes) *Dragon's Mouth* (dramatic quartet in two parts; produced in London, 1952; produced Off-Broadway, 1955), Harper, 1952.

Treasure on Pelican (three-act; produced in London, 1952), Evans Brothers, 1953.

Mother's Day (one-act comedy; produced in 1953), Samuel French, 1953.

Private Rooms (one-act comedy "in the Viennese style"; produced in 1953), Samuel French, 1953.

Try It Again (one-act), Samuel French, 1953.

A Glass of Bitter (one-act; produced in 1954), Samuel French, 1954.

(With Hawkes) *The White Countess*, produced on the West End, 1954.

The Scandalous Affair of Mr. Kettle and Mrs. Moon (three-act comedy; produced on the West End, 1955), Samuel French, 1956.

The Glass Cage (two-act; written for Crest Theatre, Toronto; produced on the West End, 1957), Kingswood House (Toronto), 1957, Samuel French, 1958.

(With Iris Murdoch) *A Severed Head* (three-act; adapted from the novel by Murdoch; produced on the West End, 1963), Samuel French, 1964.

Also author of "The Golden Entry," produced in 1955, "These Our Actors" and "Take the Fool Away," both produced in 1956, and "The Pavilion of Masks," produced in 1963. Plays published in omnibus volumes and in anthologies.

ESSAYS

Papers from Lilliput, Bowes, 1922.

I for One, John Lane, 1923, Books for Libraries Press, 1967.

Talking, Harper, 1926.

J. B. Priestley (selected essays), Harrap, 1926.

Open House, Harper, 1927.

Apes and Angels, Methuen, 1928.

Selected Essays, edited by G. A. Sheldon, A. & C. Black, 1928.

The Balconinny, and Other Essays, Methuen, 1929, published as *The Balconinny*, Harper, 1930.

Self-Selected Essays, Harper, 1932.

The Secret Dream: An Essay on Britain, America and Russia (based on radio broadcasts, 1946), Turnstile Press, 1946.

Delight, Harper, 1949.

All About Ourselves, and Other Essays, selected and introduced by Eric Gillett, Heinemann, 1956.

Thoughts in the Wilderness, Harper, 1957.

The Moments and Other Pieces, Heinemann, 1966.

Essays of Five Decades, selected, with a preface, by Susan Cooper, Little, Brown, 1968.

Outcries and Asides, Heinemann, 1974.

The Happy Dream, Whittington Press, 1976.

EDITOR

(And author of introduction) Thomas Moore, *Tom Moore's Diary* (selections), Cambridge University Press, 1925, Scholarly Press, 1971.

(And author of introduction and notes) *Essayists Past and Present: A Selection of English Essays*, Dial, 1925.

(And compiler) *The Book of Bodley Head Verse*, Dodd, 1926.

These Diversions (essay series), six volumes, Jarrolds, 1926-28.

Our Nation's Heritage (country anthology), Dent, 1939.

(And compiler and author of introduction) Charles Dickens, *Scenes of London Life from "Sketches by Boz"* (selections), Pan Books, 1947.

(And author of introduction) *Best of Leacock*, McClelland & Stewart, 1957 (published in England as *The Bodley Head Leacock*, Bodley Head, 1957).

(With O. B. Davis) *Four English Novels* (includes *Pride and Prejudice*, by Jane Austen, *The Pickwick Papers*, by Charles Dickens, *Return of the Native*, by Thomas Hardy, and *The Secret Sharer*, by Joseph Conrad), Harcourt, 1960.

(With Davis) *Four English Biographies* (includes *Shakespeare of London*, by Marchette Chute, *The Life of Samuel Johnson*, by James Boswell, *Queen Victoria*, by Lytton Strachey, and *The Edge of Day: Boyhood in the West of England*, by Laurie Lee), Harcourt, 1961.

(With Josephine Spear) *Adventures in English Literature*, Laureate edition, Harcourt, 1963.

OTHER

The Chapman of Rhymes (poems), Alexander Moring (London), 1918.

Brief Diversions (tales, travesties and epigrams), Bowes, 1922.

Figures in Modern Literature, Dodd, 1924.

The English Comic Characters, Dodd, 1925, new edition, Bodley Head, 1963, Dufour, 1964.

Fools and Philosophers: A Gallery of Comic Figures from English Literature, John Lane, 1925.

George Meredith, Macmillan, 1926.

Thomas Love Peacock, Macmillan, 1927, new edition, St. Martin's, 1966.

The English Novel, Benn, 1927, new revised and illustrated edition, Thomas Nelson, 1935.

Too Many People, and Other Reflections, Harper, 1928.

English Humour, Longmans, Green, 1929.

The Works of J. B. Priestley, Heinemann, 1931.

English Journey: Being a Rambling but Truthful Account of What One Man Saw and Heard and Felt and Thought During a Journey through England during the Autumn of the Year 1933, Harper, 1934.

Midnight on the Desert: Being an Excursion into Autobiography during a Winter in America, 1935-36, Harper, 1937 (published in England as *Midnight on the Desert: A Chapter of Autobiography*, Heinemann, 1937).

(With others) *First "Mercury" Story Book*, Longmans, Green, 1939.

Rain upon Godshill: A Further Chapter of Autobiography, Harper, 1939.

(Co-author) *Jamaica Inn* (screenplay; based on the novel by Daphne du Maurier), Mayflower/Paramount, 1939.

Britain Speaks (based on a series of radio talks to America, May 5 to September 24, 1940), Harper, 1940.

Postscripts (originally radio broadcasts), Heinemann, 1940, published as *All England Listened: The Wartime Broadcasts of J. B. Priestley*, introduction by Eric Sevareid, Chilmark, 1967.

Out of the People, Harper, 1941.

Britain at War, Harper, 1942.

(With Philip Gibbs and others) *The English Spirit*, edited and introduced by Anthony Weymouth, Allen & Unwin, 1942.

British Women Go to War, photographs by P. G. Hennell, Collins, 1943.

Russian Journey, Writers Group of the Society for Cultural Relations with the U.S.S.R., 1946.

Theatre Outlook, Nicholson & Watson, 1947.

Three Time Plays, Pan Books, 1947.

(And co-producer) *Last Holiday* (screenplay), Associated British Picture Corp., 1950.

The Priestley Companion (selections), introduction by Ivor Brown, Penguin, 1951.

(With Hawkes) *Journey down a Rainbow* (travel sketches), Harper, 1955.

The Art of the Dramatist (lecture with appendices and discursive notes), Heinemann (Melbourne), 1957.

Topside; or, The Future of England (dialogue), Heinemann, 1958.

The Wonderful World of the Theatre, edited by David Lambert, designed by Germano Facetti, Garden City Books, 1959 (published in England as *The Story of the Theatre,* Rathbone, 1959), revised and enlarged edition, Doubleday, 1969.

Literature and Western Man: Criticism and Comment of Five Centuries of Western Literature, Harper, 1960.

William Hazlitt, Longmans, Green, for the British Book Council and the National Book League, 1960.

Charles Dickens: A Pictorial Biography, Thames & Hudson, 1961, Viking, 1962, published as *Charles Dickens and His World,* 1969.

Margin Released: A Writer's Reminiscences and Reflections, Harper, 1962.

Man and Time, Doubleday, 1964.

Salt is Leaving, Pan Books, 1966.

The World of J. B. Priestley, selected and introduced by Donald G. MacRae, Heinemann, 1967.

Anyone for Tennis? (teleplay), British Broadcasting Corp. (BBC-TV), 1968.

Trumpets over the Sea: Being a Rambling and Egotistical Account of the London Symphony Orchestra's Engagement at Daytona Beach, Florida, in July-August, 1967, Heinemann, 1968.

The Prince of Pleasure and His Regency, 1811-20, Harper, 1969.

Anton Chekhov, A. S. Barnes, 1970.

The Edwardians, Harper, 1970.

Snoggle (juvenile fiction), Harcourt, 1972.

Victoria's Heyday, Harper, 1972.

Over the Long High Wall: Some Reflections and Speculations on Life, Death and Time, Heinemann, 1972.

The English, Heinemann, 1973.

A Visit to New Zealand, Heinemann, 1974.

Particular Pleasures: Being a Personal Record of Some Varied Arts and Many Different Artists, Heinemann, 1975.

Found, Lost, Found, or, The English Way of Life, Heinemann, 1976.

Instead of the Trees: A Final Chapter of Autobiography, Heinemann, 1977.

J. B. Priestley's Yorkshire, edited by William Reginald Mitchell, Dalesman, 1987.

Works also appear in omnibus volumes and collections. Also author of several screenplays, including *The Foreman Went to France, Britain at Bay,* and *Priestley's Postscripts.* Author of television series, *You Know What People Are,* and of the program, "Lost City," in which he appeared. Author of numerous booklets, and of introductory notes to numerous books. Contributor of essays, articles, sketches, reviews, and short stories to numerous periodicals and newspapers.

MEDIA ADAPTATIONS: Several of Priestley's stories, novels, and plays have been made into motion pictures, including: *Benighted,* which was produced as *The Old Dark House* by Universal in 1932 and Columbia in 1963; *The Good Companions,* filmed as a musical in 1933 by Fox and in 1957 by Associated British-Pathe; *Sing As We Go,* filmed by Associated Talking Pictures/Associated British Films in 1934; *Dangerous Corner,* a 1935 Radio Pictures film; *Look Up and Laugh,* produced by Associated Talking Pictures/Associated British Films in 1935; *Laburnum Grove,* filmed by Associated Talking Pictures/Associated British Films in 1936; *Let the People Sing,* produced by British National/Anglo American in 1942; *Somewhere in France,* a 1943 United Artists production; *When We Are Married,* produced by British National/Anglo American in 1943; *They Came to a City,* filmed by Ealing in 1944; *An Inspector Calls,* a 1954 Associated Artists production; and *A Severed Head,* adapted by Iris Murdoch and filmed in 1970 by Winkast, and adapted by Frederic Raphael and produced for Columbia in 1971 by Alan Ladd, Jr.

A Theatre Guild radio production of *Laburnum Grove* was broadcast in 1948, and a television adaptation by Edward Mabley was produced on CBS in 1949; *Counterfeit,* adapted for television by Ellen Violett, was produced on CBS for U.S. Steel Hour on August 31, 1955. *The Good Companions* was also made into a stage musical with music by Andre Previn and lyrics by Johnny Mercer; in 1972 Leslie Sands produced and narrated an anthology of Priestley's dramatic works, entitled *J. B. Priestley's Open House,* on the West End. Shortly after Priestley's death in 1984, his son Tom produced a Central-TV special, *Time and the Priestleys,* incorporating interviews with and autobiographies of the author.

SIDELIGHTS: In *Outcries and Asides,* J. B. Priestley recalled encountering two actors who were filming *A Midsummer Night's Dream.* Priestley wrote, "Bully Bottom having been mentioned, I said, 'I played that part at school.' Then a dreadful thought came like a thunderclap. 'And perhaps I've been playing it ever since.' " On the contrary, Priestley was no Bully Bottom, but instead a sensitive, thoughtful, honest professional writer who championed truth as he saw it in nearly two hundred books as well as countless articles, reviews, and essays covering life in his beloved England. His countrymen often disappointed him, turning him, in his own words from *Instead of the Trees: A Final Chapter of Autobiography,* from "cautious optimist" to "life- enhancing pessimist," and forcing him to pose as the stereotypical no- nonsense, gruff but hearty, pipe-smoking Yorkshireman. This pose softened his sometimes painful message—that a spirited nation of good, hardworking people had not fulfilled its capability to realize the ideal community of men working in harmony, had not yet achieved the vision that he called "liberal socialism" in *Midnight on the Desert: A Chapter of Autobiography.* Yet Priestley devoted a long, active life to defending this vision in all literary genres, including criticism, novels, plays, autobiographies, travel accounts, and one volume of poetry. Priestley even broadcast a "Postscript" series following the BBC news during World War II, comforting as well as warning, penetrating the gloom of a nation at war.

In *Midnight on the Desert,* his first "excursion into autobiography," an amused Priestley recalled reviewers terming "brilliant reporting" a novel set in London but actually written in Arizona. "I would have made a wretched reporter," Priestley claimed; "to report is to narrate, describe, and repeat as an eye-witness. The reporter is the man on the spot, or he is nothing." The novelist's task is very different: "A man in Arizona who attempts to describe, with some wealth of detail, what it feels like to be a waitress or a parlormaid in London . . . may be a good, bad, or indifferent novelist, but he will certainly not be much of a reporter." Priestley eventually ignored the taunts of critics who continued to consider him a journalist. Indeed, every time he attempted to expand beyond criticism, Priestley received some supposedly friendly words of caution, as revealed in *A Writer's Life of J. B. Priestley: An Exhibition of Manuscripts and Books.* Acknowledging a copy of Priestley's first novel, *Adam in Moonshine,* in 1927, Edmund Goose wrote, "I have enjoyed your excursion into the world of moonshine, and must tell you so. . . . Nevertheless I hope you will not abandon criticism, a field in which your successes are preeminent." When *Dangerous Corner* became Priestley's first theatrical foray in 1932, playwright Michael Arlen commented ambiguously, "It's very nice to think of you barging into the theatre." Priestley understood the implications and explained in *Outcries and Asides:* "In this age . . . versatility does not enlarge a writer's reputation but reduces it."

In *Midnight on the Desert* Priestley examined his need to explore so many literary forms: "I have a restless nature, am easily bored, and so I flit from one kind of work to another, partly sustained by a very genuine interest in the technical problems of all forms of writing. I have always wanted vaguely to be an all-round man of letters on the eighteenth-century plan, which allowed or commanded a man to write essay or poem, novel or play, just as he pleased. This is good fun, but it may not be good business. If you want to play for safety, keeping the career on a steady course, you will do the same thing over and over again—painting two cows in a field, two cows in a field—until at last they write . . . 'Nor can we omit a consideration of the leader of the two-cows-in-a-field group. . . .' And there you are in your pigeonhole, and not unlike a stuffed pigeon." In *Instead of the Trees,* his *Final Chapter of Autobiography,* Priestley admitted that the designation "man of letters," indicating a versatile writer, had assumed a pejorative connotation: "I have written . . . far too much for my own good. For years I have been standing in my own light, overshadowing my better self. So I have been often ignored or brushed aside. . . . I declare emphatically that I take no pride whatever in being called *man of letters—* ugh!—a term applied . . . to any number of book-sodden dreary old hacks. . . . *I am not that kind of man at all.*" Priestley's is the credo of the professional writer, best expressed in *Outcries and Asides:* "I have tried to do my best for over half a century. . . . We have to do what we can with ourselves, rather like a man who has inherited a circus. And after all the circus might make some good friends." Reviewer Anthony Burgess, aware that *Instead of the Trees* might be Priestley's last volume, praised the entire canon in the *Observer Review,* disclaiming Priestley's own notion that less is more: "The best overall tribute I can think of is to suggest that he has hardly written a line too many, and that the entire *oeuvre* coheres into a unity marked by a strong and inimitable personality. The critics have not taken him seriously enough."

A fellow Yorkshireman, novelist John G. Braine, wrote in *J. B. Priestley* that Priestley owed his success to three great privileges: "He was born of the right parents at the right time in the right place." And Susan Cooper, in an appreciative critical biography, suggested that time and place had a lasting effect: "Priestley . . . is haunted by a world. It is not a lost world . . . since it never really existed. It is more a kind of ideal: a longing from the way things could be. . . . It infuses many of his novels, most of his reflective and autobiographical books, and all his more polemical essays; it shows clearly in his plays, most of which are composed of fantasy in one form or another; and it is woven closely into his recurrent fascination with the nature of Time. . . . For although this shadowy, hovering world, never seen or described clearly, has no identifiable pattern in reality, it has a close connection with the years from 1910 to 1914: the last years of Priestley's own childhood, which happened also to be the last years before the world began on a really large scale to go mad."

Priestley recounted his early life in *Margin Released: A Writer's Reminiscences and Reflections* in 1962. His birthplace, Bradford, was large enough to nurture the arts as well as offer close proximity to the Yorkshire Dales. His father, a schoolmaster whom Priestley called "unselfish, brave, honourable, public-spirited" in *Margin Released,* encouraged his education; they disagreed only about the Baptist Chapel, Sunday School, and professional entertainment, his father embracing the first two while remaining suspicious of the third. Bradford was an industrial town of strong radical and labor sympathies, and his father was prominent among its socialists, "not the embittered rebels of today, but the gentle, hopeful theorists" of the past, as Priestley called them in *Midnight on the Desert.* The writer drew on these happy early years in Bradford to texture such novels as *The Good Compan-*

ions and *Bright Day,* and such plays as *Eden End* and *When We Are Married.* On leaving school Priestley became a junior clerk in the wool trade but actually spent the working day writing pieces that were accepted not only in local papers but even the London magazines. This idyllic existence was interrupted by World War I. Priestley, twenty years old, enlisted in 1915, was wounded in France, and recuperated in England. Commissioned a lieutenant in 1917, he returned to France only to be gassed. Although the war rarely appears in his creative works, its influence pervades everything Priestley wrote, serving as the perspective through which he viewed the world of 1912, the setting to which he continually returned.

After the war Priestley attended Cambridge University, but in *Instead of the Trees* he wrote that "Bradford from 1911-1914 gave me more than Cambridge did from 1919-1922." His first book of "undergraduate odds and ends," *Brief Diversions,* was well received but unprofitable. At twenty-seven, married to Pat Tempest, he moved to London to seriously attempt to earn a living as a writer. Working for the *London Mercury* and the *Daily News* and as a reader for the Bodley Head, Priestley managed two collections of criticism, *Figures in Modern Literature* and *The English Comic Characters,* as well as studies of George Meredith and Thomas Love Peacock. A year after his first wife's death in 1925, Priestley married Mary Holland Wyndham Lewis, from whom he was divorced in 1952.

Although Priestley never completely abandoned one genre for another, the essay was the dominant form of his early career. Other genres would later provide for luxuries such as world travel, but Priestley enjoyed conveying his thoughts directly, unhampered by the need to invent dramatic conflict or emphasize structure. In her preface to Priestley's *Essays of Five Decades,* Cooper demonstrated that Priestley was continuing the honored tradition of English essayists such as Joseph Addison and Richard Steele, of William Hazlitt and Charles Lamb, writing "for a limited public of educated readers." Priestley was fortunate, she believed, in writing when "periodicals, not yet reeling under modern economic pressures, still offered an encouraging level of space." Priestley's pride in this personal form pervades *Margin Released:* "The early essays I wrote, coming out in various periodicals and then in volume form in *Papers from Lilliput, I for One,* [and] *Open House,* were mostly literary exercises. . . . I took great pains with these pieces, like a man learning to play an instrument. Though I kept right on into the thirties . . . I knew that this kind of essay, personal in tone but elaborately composed, was already almost an anachronism." In *J. B. Priestley: The Last of the Sages,* John Atkins found Priestley's early essays strained but delighted in the later *Delight,* "a collection of short, sharp *pensees,* with none of the casualness of the old-fashioned essay." Atkins continued, "Although ostensibly concerned with things that have brought him delight, it has a strong undertone of things that have caused him displeasure, because so much of what he has enjoyed is in the lost past and has not been replaced." Priestley's later essays, like those in *The Moments and Other Pieces,* Atkins claimed, were different: "He is constantly concerned with Government policy, the H-bomb, the Communist World and the Third World. He still writes about personal matters, but he relates them more significantly to the world about him. And, an unexpected result of this change, the personal touch becomes more attractive." The versatility of the essay form appealed to Priestley, but while it offered both a public forum and personal satisfaction, it could not provide for a growing family nor lead to fame and fortune.

Such fame came in 1929 with Priestley's fourth novel, *The Good Companions,* a transatlantic bestseller, soon available in translation throughout the world. Before that sudden success Priestley had been developing his novelistic skills in *Adam in Moonshine,* a lighthearted romantic adventure in the manner of English novelist G. K. Chesterton that was, Priestley admitted in *Margin Released,* "a little coloured trial balloon . . . [that] moves stiffly, creaking with self- consciousness." Also in 1927, Priestley released *Benighted,* an attempt "to transmute the thriller into symbolical fiction with some psychological depth." In 1932, *Benighted* achieved a qualified success as *The Old Dark House,* a Hollywood film that stressed its thriller aspects at the expense of probing psychology. Just prior to the publication of *The Good Companions* came *Farthing Hall,* an epistolary novel (a novel composed of letters), part comedy, part Gothic parody, written with Hugh Walpole. *Farthing Hall*'s only significance for Priestley was a sizable advance based on Walpole's participation. Burgess suggested in *The Novel Now* that Walpole was more important to Priestley's development than he admitted. To Burgess "the Victorian novel—distilled, for Priestley, through Hugh Walpole, though there can be no doubt of the superiority of the pupil to the master," was the source of the long, ambitious novels that Priestley was then attempting. "Where Walpole is capable only of diluted romance, seasoned with a few grotesques," Burgess wrote, "Priestley is genuinely comic, full of social awareness." Burgess found "the same virtues of credibility, humour in the English tradition, and a genuine concern with the changing patterns of social history" informing such later Priestley novels as *Angel Pavement, They Walk in the City,* and *Lost Empires,* the last "a novel about the old-time music-hall, even deader and more regretted than the wandering concert party."

The plot device of *The Good Companions,* already employed on a smaller scale in *Adam in Moonshine* and *Benighted,* appeared throughout Priestley's novels and plays: a disparate group becomes unified as its members find fulfillment in a common cause. Elizabeth Trant, a wealthy spinster, befriends the hapless Dinky Doos, a group of stranded players, transforming them into the successful Good Companions. They recognize, however, that their success cannot last; travelling theater and concert groups will soon be replaced by the talking picture, but they have shared a glorious moment which has enriched their lives and made them wiser. Beneath the romantic sentiment, the Dickensian characters and setting, lies a hard core of realism, as Priestley insists that determination, hard work, and cooperation underlie happiness.

Adam in Moonshine (a romance), *Benighted* (a thriller), and *The Good Companions* (a picaresque, or tale of wanderers' adventures) define the directions of the Priestley novel. In *Angel Pavement,* which followed *The Good Companions,* Priestley first attempted a serious novel with symbolic structure and probing characterization. Whereas the Dinky Doos traveled the open road, the characters of *Angel Pavement* inhabited London's claustrophobic business world during the Great Depression, an economic nightmare-reality that Priestley would later explore in his social document of the English countryside, *English Journey.* Golspie, a confidence man, a somewhat sinister organizer, must finally escape the suffocating city in search of adventure and romance. Akin to Baron Roland of *Adam in Moonshine,* with darker motivations than the goodhearted Elizabeth Trant, Golspie was Priestley's first fully developed charismatic organizer— sometimes benevolent, sometimes sinister—who orders, determines, and defines the nature of experience.

Whereas *The Good Companions* remained Priestley's most popular novel, two later ones among the thirty he wrote received more critical acclaim. *Bright Day* was Priestley's favorite until it was replaced by his longest work, the two-volume *The Image Men.*

Bright Day was Priestley's successful attempt to express, as he explained in *Margin Released,* "a sense of some mysterious and magical life being led by families or groups, into which I longed, wistfully rather than enviously, to find my way. It took me years and years to learn that it is the mystery that creates the magic, that the enchantments imagined on the outside vanish almost immediately once you are inside, that indeed what is truly magical rises from your own depths." Dawson, a writer and filmmaker, is another recurring type, the yearning quester, approaching life through the past and his dreams, which inevitably lead him to recognize and embrace his own rich existence. Suffering writer's block, Dawson delays a film as he contemplates the desert of his present life. A chance occurrence recalls his youth, when he fell in love, not with one of his employer's daughters, but with the seemingly enchanted circle of the family. The idyllic lives of these Alingtons were apparently disrupted by the grasping, materialistic Nixeys, but Dawson must learn that the real seeds of destruction were within the Alingtons themselves and that the Nixeys merely catalyzed an inevitable tragedy. With that knowledge comes freedom; Dawson can leave the Alingtons in his past and reclaim his own bright future.

Gratified by *Bright Day*'s critical reception, its author was especially pleased to receive a letter from pioneering psychiatrist Carl Jung, who recognized in it elements of his own work that had influenced Priestley. As David Hughes, in *J. B. Priestley: An Informal Study of His Work,* commented tellingly: "In a curious way this novel strikes behind specific memories and throws a little light on the memory that we might all be said to share in common, the sense of race, our roots in history." *Bright Day* revealed Priestley's most intricate use of evocative time shifts, an outgrowth of his significant use of time as a literary structuring device.

Concurring with Priestley's statement that *The Image Men* is his best novel, Burgess commented in the *Observer Review:* "I have read it at least five times. More than I can say of the work of any other living British author with the exception of [Kingsley] Amis." *The Image Men* moved into territory already charted by Amis's 1953 novel *Lucky Jim,* possibly suggesting the link between the two, for *The Image Men,* originally published in two parts as *Out of Town* and *London End,* concerned two impoverished academics, Saltana and Tuby, who devise the Institute of Social Imagistics for the creation and projection of suitable public images. After allying themselves with a respectable university, they establish themselves in London, moving into business and politics, the seats of money and power.

Accused of portraying himself as the protagonist of *Bright Day,* Priestley denied the charge while admitting in *Instead of the Trees,* to some affinity: "What I share with Gregory Dawson is a deep-seated nostalgia for that golden haze of youth before the First War, and against the loss of all that shining promise he cries out with my voice." However, when readers recognized Priestleyan traits in the two con men in *The Image Men,* their creator was pleased: "It would be easy for me to declare that its sharply contrasted two heroes . . . are complete inventions; but it would be untrue. Possibly I regard them with such affection because I put a lot of myself into them. To a limited degree there is an authoritative side to my character, and there is also . . . a persuasive and rather seductive side. So I took these two traits, enlarged and decorated them, and created the commanding Professor Saltana and the artful and pleasing Dr Tuby. And just as this is my favourite novel, so these two are my favourite characters." Undertaking his longest novel at the age of 74, Priestley surprised his critics. That the novel worked, its author deftly juggling two thick volumes of satire which might have become heavy-handed, amazed them. "It is a butterfly," wrote a dazzled Braine, "a *jeu d'esprit* [a spirited game], but on a scale that no other writer would even dare to contemplate."

The key to *The Image Men* may be found in *Journey down a Rainbow,* an exchange of observations between Priestley and his third wife and occasional collaborator, anthropologist Jacquetta Hawkes. In it Priestley coined a word for the spirit of a contemporary world with no ethics and distorted values: "Admass. This is my name for the whole system of an increasing productivity, plus inflation, plus a rising standard of material living, plus high-pressure advertising and salesmanship, plus mass communications, plus cultural democracy and the creation of the mass mind, the mass man." *The Image Men* is a picaresque journey through a mad admassian world. A. A. DeVitis, in *J. B. Priestley,* likened it to earlier Priestley novels in that "Saltana and Tuby are workable devices for a pervasive and meaningful satirical investigation of a culture drunk on appearances, in fact the same symptoms of social disease that Priestley had satirized in *Wonder Hero* and *They Walk in the City;* but here the mixture of social commentary and fairy tale produces a more convincing novel . . . that speaks to our times in eloquent and cautionary fashion."

DeVitis, however, lacked Priestley's affection for his heroes: "Saltana and Tuby are too often platitudinous, sententious gasbags. Their presence occasionally even inhibits scenes of otherwise comic vitality, for in insisting through narration on the charm of his protagonists, Priestley fails to accomplish what he succeeds in doing almost effortlessly in the majority of his novels—to dramatize events so that the reader can appreciate character for himself." Atkins declared that the writer's "natural talent is not for the novel. He can describe magnificently and he can manage narrative superbly but it is when he comes to character . . . that things go wrong. He cannot resist commenting and it is the comment that gets between the reader and his enjoyment. . . . In short, the essayist is never far from the surface. . . . His people . . . say things that in life would be left to the understanding. This of course may be partly an effect of writing for the theatre, where the playwright sometimes causes things to be spoken because there simply isn't time to establish them in any other way. In fact, this illustrates the divide between the two crafts."

Priestley himself recognized the dramatist's need to force words into a character's mouth. In *The Art of the Dramatist* he wrote, "The realistic prose dramatist finds it hard to express the great emotional moments—and if he is English he will find it harder still because the English prefer to say nothing and not make a scene, which is precisely what the dramatist *has* to make." Yet Priestley admired his own solution, particularly in *The Linden Tree,* a drama about middle-class English life: "In this play—as in several others of mine—I open with absolutely realistic flat dialogue of the kind any English audience knows only too well, and then gradually I begin to move away from complete naturalism in speech, so that in the last half-hour the characters are using a far richer and warmer idiom, often making speeches that would be impossible to them in real life."

Priestley's dramatic contributions were richer than his achievements in other genres. A follower as an essayist and novelist, he created works safely within the mainstream of British letters. In drama, however, he was a leader. No poet by his own admission, he learned from Russian dramatist Anton Chekhov the possibility of a "poetry of the Theatre." In *The Art of the Dramatist,* Priestley advised: "Read *The Cherry Orchard* and it seems a mere jumble of odd speeches, but see it lovingly produced and

its poetry of the Theatre enchants the mind and melts the heart." Appreciating Chekhov helped Priestley solve the problems of realistic presentation and dialogue, enabling him to become the single serious British dramatist bridging the gap from Shaw to the "angry young men." His characters emphasized the necessity of enriching life, rekindling enthusiasm, and making the world a better place to work, to build, and to love, before Jimmy Porter voiced those concerns in English dramatist John Osborne's 1956 play, *Look Back in Anger.* Unlike the life-denying Porter, however, Priestley's characters enhanced life, like the gentle yet rebellious George Kettle of *The Scandalous Affair of Mr. Kettle and Mrs. Moon.*

Burgess has conjectured that Priestley was dismissed by critics of the novel because he reserved his experiments for the stage. As early as 1932, *Dangerous Corner* introduced a time shift, granting the characters a second chance as the play began again. The dramatist's lifelong fascination with time led him to innovative forms in *Music at Night* and *Johnson over Jordan;* as Priestley recalled in *The Art of the Dramatist,* "What I wanted them to suggest was life outside Time as we usually know it, the kind of freedom of the fourth dimension that comes to us in a fragmentary fashion in dreams, events out of chronological order, childhood and adult life interrupting each other, all of which can bring a piercing sweetness, a queer poignancy, and, again, dramatic experience a little different from what one has known before." That difference seems to align him with the expressionists, but, despite the personalization of experience, the distortion of surface reality, and the fluidity of time and space in some of his plays, Priestley rejected the label. Perhaps Priestley's conjectures about time and careful reading of time theory led him to consider that no distortion actually took place in his innovative plays if man, as he believed, was always beyond mere chronological time. His *Time and the Conways* and *I Have Been Here Before* were in fact dramatic illustrations of the respective time theories of J. W. Dunne and P. D. Ouspensky.

In 1964 Priestley wrote *Man and Time,* concerning man's understanding and misunderstanding of time as well as its literary treatment. Here he explained what disturbed him about the conventional view of the reality of time: "Common sense . . . has settled down with the notion that everything is real only when it is Now. . . . There is an opposite view. . . . Everything is solidly there, whether we call it past, present, or future. We experience things in time because our Now, so to speak, goes steadily forward, as if we were traveling through a dark landscape with a searchlight. . . . We invent Time to explain change and succession. We try to account for it out there in the world we are observing, but soon run into trouble because it is not out there at all. It comes with the searchlight. . . . There is, however, one snag. How can the searchlight . . . steadily revealing what we call the present, be manipulated to light up . . . the future so much further on or . . . the past that has been left behind?" He had found some answers in Dunne's theory of Serialism in *An Experiment with Time* in 1927 and explained it for his readers in *Midnight on the Desert:* Dunne believed "that each of us is a series of observers existing in a series of Times. To Observer One, our ordinary fully-awake sharp selves, the fourth dimension appears as Time. To Observer Two, which is the self we know in dreams when the first observer is not functioning, the fifth dimension would appear as Time. This second observer has a four-dimensional outlook, and this fact explains the fantastic scenery and action characteristic of dreams, in which everything seems to be so fluid. . . . Now Dunne holds that the dreaming self, now moving Time Two, has a wide length of Time One, the fourth dimension, stretched before it, and so contrives to telescope into the fantastic narratives of dream both images from the Past and *images from the Future*."

Later, reading Ouspensky's *A New Model of the Universe*, Priestley was attracted to the belief "that Time, like Space, has three dimensions, and only three," thus avoiding Dunne's regression to infinity. Ouspensky posited a wavelike movement of time which allowed for eternal recurrence; man dies only to be born again. Yet he need not relive the same mistakes, for Ouspensky allowed for intervention through inner development. As Priestley explained in *Midnight on the Desert*, "a few, the esoteric elite, learn to live, evolve properly, and so finally, in some mysterious fashion, turn the circle into a spiral, and escape." Both theories appear in his plays.

Stagestruck as a boy, Priestley for a time considered an acting career and was always determined to write for the stage. "Yet in the circumstances of production in the English-speaking Theatre," he wrote in *Margin Released*, "you are compelled to exist in an over-heated atmosphere of dazzling successes and shameful flops . . . you are in, you are out." Suspicion of this "gaming-house atmosphere" prevented Priestley from writing drama until the success of *The Good Companions* assured that his "children's food and clothing could be paid for, and it was out of a desire to escape the worst effects, once I was working in the Theatre, that I formed my own production company." His first attempt as a playwright was a joint venture with Edward Knoblock, a "play-doctor," to dramatize *The Good Companions* in 1931, but soon he attempted to solve the challenges of dramatic structure for himself. After a shaky critical reception at its opening, *Dangerous Corner* won the approval of the influential *Sunday Times* critic James Agate, as cited in *Ego 9:* "If this play does not take the town it will be the town's fault. In Mr Priestley we have an obviously first-class playwright in the making. If adequate encouragement is not forthcoming and Mr Priestley should decide not to go on with the job, the public will have only itself to blame." The public responded with overwhelming support. "It became the most popular play I have ever written," Priestley estimated in *Margin Released;* "I doubt if there is any country in the world possessing a playhouse that has not seen *Dangerous Corner*, or if any other play written during the last thirty years has had more performances."

The play was described by its director Tyrone Guthrie in *A Life in the Theatre* as "a highly ingenious piece of construction" with "not very much content." The play introduces several well-to-do young people whose opportunities seem unlimited and, through an intricate plot, uncovers their dark secrets and sordid entanglements. The time-shift ending, enabling the characters to relive their experiences and perhaps change their lives, anticipated future productions from this admittedly "Time-haunted man." If the manipulation of time was here frivolous, *Dangerous Corner* touched on another area that Priestley developed more fully later, as Gareth Lloyd Evans recognized in *J. B. Priestley: The Dramatist:* "Thinly, the theme of the responsibility of the individual as a component part of a group, has its first airing in a Priestley play. 'No man is an island' is its motto."

Like his characters in *Dangerous Corner*, the dramatist took a wrong turn in some of his subsequent plays. *The Roundabout*, patterned on Somerset Maugham's play *The Circle*, and *Duet in Floodlight*, another comedy of manners, showed Priestley to be out of his element. The broader the comedy, as in *Laburnum Grove* and *When We Are Married*, the more comfortable Priestley seemed, despite his acknowledgement in *Margin Released* that the comedies "actually took most time and gave me most trouble. The actual writing of the serious plays never took long."

The best of the early serious plays, and Priestley's favorite, was 1934's *Eden End*. Set in 1912, it convincingly portrayed a family ill-equipped to cope with their soon-to-be shattered world. In theme and mood like Chekhov's *The Cherry Orchard*, the play proved the truth of Priestley's statement about the dramatist he most admired: "Since his time we have had many Chekhovian plays. None of them rivals *The Cherry Orchard* or *The Three Sisters*, but they are not worse plays because of his influence, they are all better than they might have been."

The same Chekhovian tone prevailed in the best of the time plays, *Time and the Conways*. As he relates in *Rain upon Godshill: A Further Chapter of Autobiography*, Priestley "suddenly saw that there was a play in the relation between a fairly typical middle-class provincial family and the theory of Time . . . chiefly associated with J. W. Dunne, over which I had been brooding for the past two years." In the first act, set at a party in 1919, Kay, an aspiring novelist, happily celebrates her twenty-first birthday with her widowed mother and five brothers and sisters. In *Three Time Plays*, Priestley explained the second act, Kay's fortieth birthday, as "Kay's glimpse of the future, or, to put it in terms of Serialism, it is Kay's Observer Two who sees what will happen, years ahead, to her Observer One." The Conways, like the enchanting Alingtons of the later novel *Bright Day*, suffer reversals and bitter confrontations as each family member shifts responsibility to another, all feeling the effects of time. Kay's brother Alan comforts her by suggesting that they may one day experience another kind of time, "which is only another kind of dream." The third act returns to the twenty-first birthday party as though the second act has not occurred—and it has not, yet, for the Conways—only for the audience and for Kay in a moment of precognition. As a result, the audience, like Kay, is moved to tears observing the naivete of Kay's younger sister, the doomed Carol, breathlessly planning a future that will never be.

In *Three Time Plays*, Priestley summarized the attitude of some unfriendly critics: "This play is a lot of fuss about nothing and merely has the third act played where the second act ought to be and then the real second act put last." For the dramatist, however, "Its whole point and quality are contained in the third act, when we know so much more about the characters than they know themselves." Of *Time and the Conways* Evans wrote, "The atmosphere he creates . . . is not a tragic one, but a truly pathetic one. It may well be . . . that Priestley, falling short of anything approaching high tragedy, has shown in this play that pathos is a mood amenable to dramatic communication." Based on Ouspensky's theory of recurrence and intervention, *I Have Been Here Before*, Priestley's other major time play, has been less frequently revived. In *Man and Time* Priestley wisely noted, "Time is a concept, a certain condition of experience, a mode of perception . . . and a novel or a play, to be worth calling one, cannot really be about Time but only about the people and things that appear to be *in* Time." Whereas *Time and the Conways* focused on the lives of average people in time, the characters of *I Have Been Here Before* laboriously explicated theory.

The reception of *Time and the Conways* encouraged Priestley to delve further into innovative technique. Although London's theater audiences were not yet ready for a probing of the subconscious, *Music at Night* and *Johnson over Jordan*, both emphasizing the oneness of mankind, shattered the confining limits of the British stage. *Music at Night*, according to Priestley in *Rain upon Godshill*, dramatized "the mental adventures of a group of people listening to the first performance of a piece of music." The three movements or acts carried the disparate characters from personal thoughts in the present, to a consideration of the past, and finally to a ritual bonding of all mankind in one time, accompanied by poetic incantation and joyous music.

Priestley himself preferred *Johnson over Jordan,* "a biographical morality play" in which Robert Jordan, an English Everyman, manager of a small business, wanders after death through an exaggerated landscape of documents, ledgers, and tax forms to a world whose grotesque inhabitants force him to confront his own animal nature. Realizing the waste of his life, Johnson arrives at the Inn at the End of the World to realize the wonders, lost joys and missed opportunities of life. Johnson's journey, inspired by Evans-Wentz's study of the Tibetan *Book of the Dead,* explores a dream-world outside time, outside space, affirming the ultimate worth of man. Priestley's most ambitious use of the total resources of the theater, with music by Benjamin Britten, choreography by Antony Tudor, and a memorable performance by Ralph Richardson, *Johnson over Jordan* was dismissed by Agate in a letter to the author reprinted in *Ego 8* as pretentious expressionism, "a mish-mash of *Outward Bound* and *Liliom* done in the demoded Elmer Rice manner."

The failure of *Johnson over Jordan* disenchanted Priestley. He continued writing plays during World War II, but such feeble works as *Desert Highway* and *How Are They at Home?* were meant merely to boost the morale of his countrymen. Although he did not withdraw from drama for several years, only two more plays were distinguished from some competent but pedestrian work. Written in 1944-45 but presented in London in 1946 after its first performances in the Soviet Union, *An Inspector Calls* survived another poor critical reception to become a staple of the British repertory, while *The Linden Tree* was an immediate success in 1947. *An Inspector Calls* was Priestley's clearest statement of man's interdependence with others, the responsibility of one man for all. A drama of social commitment, its focus on a single family effectively underscored the need of a universal family of man. During an engagement party the affluent Birlings learn that they are each implicated by their despicable actions in a young girl's suicide, an ironic reversal of the common cause, the plot device of many Priestley works. After discovering that in fact no suicide has occurred and that Inspector Goole, one of the author's enigmatic organizers, is unknown to the local police, the relieved family is jarred by an unwelcome telephone message: a girl has just died after swallowing disinfectant, and a police inspector is coming to question them. The characters are taken full circle as the action begins again, but, unlike the characters of *Dangerous Corner,* the Birlings are aware of being caught in an unending coil.

In *The Linden Tree,* Priestley returned to the Chekhovian manner and matter of *Eden End.* Whereas the older play mourned the passing of a former world, the wiser characters of the subtler, more complex *The Linden Tree* bravely confront a new world. In the play's final scene, an elderly history professor reads a manuscript to his youngest child, Dinah, the only family member to support his fight against forced retirement; this scene is, according to E. R. Wood's introduction to the play, "an important assertion of the dual nature of Man, a view of our present economic troubles in a philosophical perspective that gives strength to the thinking of Professor Linden, and which adds a special resonance to the major works of J. B. Priestley himself." They play demonstrated the author's own sense of post-war disillusionment and dissipation in the spirit of community, essential to the survival of family, nation, and world.

The theater is for younger men, Priestley told himself, as his incursion there diminished. Lacking the energy to safeguard his scripts from directors and actors capable of distorting his mean-

ing, Priestley withdrew, sensing that he had lost touch with the young theater audience. After writing respectable television plays, he returned a last time to the theatrical fray in 1963 to collaborate with his friend, the novelist Iris Murdoch, in dramatizing her 1961 novel *A Severed Head* for the stage. The play was Murdoch's in content, but Priestley's in the assured craftsmanship that clarified a murky novel and transformed it into a popular success.

But Priestley himself could not be lured back to the theater in his final years. He continued to write essays, novels, and what Braine called "coffee-table" books. Braine, however, intended no disparagement in applying that label to *The Prince of Pleasure and His Regency, The Edwardians,* and *Victoria's Heyday:* "The books weren't meant to be the last word . . . but to introduce the reader to their subjects and to induce them to carry on further for themselves. They are the work of a young enthusiast, they are the sharing of his delight."

Priestley's last years were not without reward for his life's work. Explaining to a *New York Times* reporter in 1974 why he had refused a knighthood and a life-peerage, Priestley said, "I started as J. B. Priestley and I'll finish as J. B. Priestley." A year earlier, however, he had proudly accepted the Freedom of the City of Bradford, and in 1977 he was named a member of the Order of Merit restricted to twenty-four living persons, a pleasing honor although, in his opinion, late in coming. In 1984, Priestley died at his home in Alveston, a month before his ninetieth birthday. In the previous two years he had witnessed major revivals of *Dangerous Corner* and *Time and the Conways.* In 1986, two years after his death, a play written nearly half a century before, *When We Are Married,* Priestley's comic evocation of his golden youth, became the surprise hit of the London season.

BIOGRAPHICAL/CRITICAL SOURCES:

BOOKS

Agate, James, *Ego 8,* Harrap, 1946.

Agate, James, *Ego 9,* Harrap, 1948.

Atkins, John, *J. B. Priestley: The Last of the Sages,* John Calder, 1981.

Braine, John G., *J. B. Priestley,* Weidenfeld & Nicolson, 1979.

Brown, Ivor, *J. B. Priestley,* Longman for the British Council, 1957.

Burgess, Anthony, *The Novel Now,* Faber, 1967.

Contemporary Literary Criticism, Gale, Volume 2, 1974, Volume 5, 1976, Volume 9, 1978, Volume 34, 1985.

Cooper, Susan, *J. B. Priestley: Portrait of an Author,* Heinemann, 1970.

DeVitis, A. A. and Albert E. Kalson, *J. B. Priestley,* Twayne, 1980.

Dictionary of Literary Biography, Gale, Volume 10: *Modern British Dramatists, 1900-1945,* 1982, Volume 34: *British Novelists, 1890-1929: Traditionalists,* 1985, Volume 77: *British Mystery Writers, 1920-1939,* 1989.

Dictionary of Literary Biography Yearbook: 1984, Gale, 1985.

Dunne, J. W., *An Experiment with Time,* A. & C. Black, 1927.

Evans, Gareth Lloyd, *J. B. Priestley: The Dramatist,* Heinemann, 1964.

Guthrie, Tyrone, *A Life in the Theatre,* Hamish Hamilton, 1960.

Hughes, David, *J. B. Priestley: An Informal Study of His Work,* Hart-Davis, 1958.

Ouspensky, P. D., *A New Model of the Universe,* Routledge & Kegan Paul, 1931.

Pogson, Rex, *J. B. Priestley and the Theatre,* Triangle Press, 1947.

Priestley, J. B., *Midnight on the Desert: A Chapter of Autobiography*, Heinemann, 1937.
Priestley, J. B., *Johnson over Jordan, The Play and All about It*, Heinemann, 1939.
Priestley, J. B., *Rain upon Godshill: A Further Chapter of Autobiography*, Heinemann, 1939.
Priestley, J. B., *Three Time Plays*, Pan Books, 1947.
Priestley, J. B., *The Art of the Dramatist*, Heinemann, 1957.
Priestley, J. B., *Margin Released: A Writer's Reminiscences and Reflections*, Heinemann, 1962.
Priestley, J. B., *Man and Time*, Aldus Books, 1964.
Priestley, J. B., *Essays of Five Decades*, edited with a preface by Susan Cooper, Little, Brown, 1968.
Priestley, J. B., *Outcries and Asides*, Heinemann, 1974.
Priestley, J. B., *The Linden Tree*, introduction by E. R. Wood, Heinemann Educational, 1976.
Priestley, J. B., *Instead of the Trees: A Final Chapter of Autobiography*, Heinemann, 1977.
Priestley, J. B., and Jacquetta Hawkes, *Journey Down a Rainbow*, 1955.
Teagarden, Lucetta, editor, *A Writer's Life of J. B. Priestley: An Exhibition of Manuscripts and Books*, Humanities Research Center, University of Texas, 1963.
Young, Kenneth, *J. B. Priestley*, Longman for the British Council, 1977.

PERIODICALS

Book World, October 6, 1968; May 11, 1969.
Nation, November 18, 1968.
National Review, June 3, 1969.
New Statesman, January 6, 1967; February 24, 1967; May 5, 1967.
New York Times, November 20, 1932; April 6, 1974; January 2, 1978; July 27, 1986.
New York Times Book Review, April 22, 1951; May 30, 1954; October 27, 1968.
New York Times Magazine, January 4, 1948.
Observer Review, February 16, 1969; September 14, 1969; March 20, 1977.
Time, May 19, 1967; June 30, 1986.
Times (London), December 1, 1955; September 16, 1957; July 10, 1970; August 22, 1974.
Times Literary Supplement, January 27, 1927; February 22, 1968.

OBITUARIES:

PERIODICALS

Chicago Tribune, August 16, 1984.
Detroit Free Press, August 16, 1984.
Los Angeles Times, August 16, 1984.
Newsweek, August 27, 1984.
New York Times, August 16, 1984.
Time, August 27, 1984.
Times (London), August 16, 1984.
Washington Post, August 16, 1984.

—*Sidelights by Albert E. Kalson*

* * *

PROSSER, H(arold) L(ee) 1944-
(Justin Willard Pinoak)

PERSONAL: Born December 31, 1944, in Springfield, MO; son of Harold and Marjorie (maiden name, Firestone) Prosser; married Grace Eileen Wright, November 4, 1971 (divorced, March 3, 1988); children: Rachael Maranda, Rebecca Dawn. *Education:* Santa Monica College, A.A., 1968; attended California State University, Northridge, 1968-69; Southwest Missouri State University, B.S., 1974, M.S.Ed., 1982; has studied under writers Paul Bowles, Alan Casty, and Christopher Isherwood. *Religion:* Affiliated with Unity Church, and Vedanta Society. *Avocational interests:* Fishing.

ADDRESSES: Home—1313 South Jefferson Ave., Springfield, MO 65807; and (summers only) Conchas Lake, NM.

CAREER: Sociologist and writer, 1963—. Proprietor of Justin Willard Pinoak Bookshops, 1969—.

WRITINGS:

UNDER NAME H. L. PROSSER

Dandelion Seeds: Eighteen Stories, Angst, 1974.
The Capricorn and Other Fantasy Stories, Angst, 1974.
The Cymric and Other Occult Poems, Mafdet Press, 1976.
The Day of the Grunion and Other Stories, Mafdet Press, 1977.
Spanish Tales, Mafdet Press, 1977.
Goodbye, Lon Chaney, Jr., Goodbye (novelette), W. D. Firestone Press, 1977.
Summer Wine (pamphlet), W. D. Firestone Press, 1979.

UNDER NAME HAROLD LEE PROSSER

Robert Bloch, Borgo, 1984.
Charles Beaumont, Borgo, 1985.
(Contributor) Carl B. Yoke, *Phoenix from the Ashes: The Literature of the Remade World*, Greenwood, 1987.
Frank Herbert: Prophet of Dune, Borgo Press, 1987.
Desert Woman Visions: One Hundred Poems, Cougar Creek, 1987.
Jack Bimbo's Touring Circus Poems, Cougar Creek, 1988.
The Work of J. N. Williamson, Borgo Press, 1988.
(Contributor) Marilyn Fletcher, *Reader's Guide to 20th Century Science Fiction*, American Library Association, 1989.

OTHER

Author of short fiction under pseudonym Justin Willard Pinoak. Contributor to magazines, including *Doppelganger, Imagine, Antaeus, Dialogue, Moon, Night Magic, Singing Guns Journal*, and *Social Education*. Manuscripts collected at University of Wyoming, Laramie, and Donnelly Library, New Mexico Highlands University at Las Vegas, NM.

WORK IN PROGRESS: October 10, 2021 Is Not Too Late to Say I Love You, collected poetry; *Christianity and Vedanta: A Spiritual Approach*.

SIDELIGHTS: H. L. Prosser, published under his full name Harold Lee Prosser since 1980, told *CA*, "My heritage is English, Scottish, Welsh, American Cherokee Indian; taken together, they spell *American*, and that about sums up my genealogy."

He also wrote, "I feel it is the duty of any good writer to create in clear, concise, correct English if he truly wants to communicate and share with the reader. To do otherwise is to be dishonest. Don't write for a select elite, for when they are gone your work dies with them; but do write for the common man and woman—like [Ernest] Hemingway, [Charles] Dickens, [Mark] Twain, and [Edgar Allen] Poe did—for they are the ones who will keep your work alive long after you're gone. It is all right to experiment creatively, but remember you're writing for the reader as well as yourself, and if the reader fails to understand, then you've accomplished nothing of lasting value.

"The two greatest influences on my writing have been writers Paul Bowles and Christopher Isherwood. I learned my skills through hard work and study, and experimentation, but these two individuals taught me the ropes. Without their early influence and encouragement, I wouldn't be writing today.

"Since 1963, I have written over nine-hundred works for publication. I enjoy live classical and jazz concerts; outdoor sports and hiking; collecting postcards; visiting new locales; taking journeys to nature locations and ghost towns; and cats. My interest since 1960 in the vedic literature of Ancient India and writings of early Christianity have had an impact on my philosophical leanings.

"I enjoy all genres of writing. I have a preference for fantasy fiction. My belief on reading is that it is one of the most precious gifts a person can give to a child, and reading should be encouraged at all levels of public and private education. A good writer should encourage peace as an alternative to world holocaust whenever possible, either verbally or in writings. The themes which appear most frequently in my own writings are: individuality; the outcast and the loner; love; the struggle of the individual for both inner and outer peace; cats.

"I try to write honestly about what I know, have seen, and encountered; like all authors, my work does contain autobiographical elements. I think it would be interesting to fall in love with a friendly extraterrestrial woman, and visa versa, and see what happens, and also, to have a friendship with a mermaid family—a touch of whimsy in one's life helps eliminate many rough edges of existence! Life is what you make of it! Among my favorite books are: *Bhagavad-Gita;* John Steinbeck's *The Acts of King Arthur and His Noble Knights; The Upanishads; The Holy Bible;* Swami Chetanananda's *Avadhuta Gita of Dattatreya; The Collected Stories of Ray Bradbury;* and the collected poems of Emily Dickinson, Robert Frost, Theodore Roethke, along with contemporary American Indian poetry."

BIOGRAPHICAL/CRITICAL SOURCES:

PERIODICALS

Angst Review, January, 1977.

*   *   *

PTELEON
   See GRIEVE, C(hristopher) M(urray)

Q

QUAY, Herbert C. 1927-

PERSONAL: Born August 27, 1927, in Portland, ME; son of George J. and Susannah Fay (Bankerd) Quay; married E. Lorene Childs (a college professor), June 13, 1953 (marriage ended); Married Anne E. Hogan; children: (first marriage) Jonathan, Jennifer. *Education:* Florida State University, B.S., 1951, M.S., 1952; University of Illinois, Urbana, Ph.D., 1958.

ADDRESSES: Home—Apt. 4H, 550 Ocean Dr., Key Biscayne, FL 33149. *Office*—Department of Psychology, University of Miami, Miami, FL 33124.

CAREER: Florida Industrial School for Boys (a state correctional school), Marianna, FL, clinical psychologist, 1952-53; Milledgeville State Hospital, Milledgeville, GA, clinical psychologist, 1953-55; U.S. Veterans Administration Hospital, Danville, IL, psychologist, 1955-56; University of Illinois, Urbana, research assistant, 1956-57; Vanderbilt University, Nashville, TN, assistant professor of psychology, 1958-61; Northwestern University, Evanston, IL, associate professor, 1961-63, became professor of psychology; University of Illinois, Urbana, research director of Children's Research Center, 1963-68; Temple University, Philadelphia, PA, chairman of Division of Educational Psychology, 1968-74; University of Miami, Miami, FL, director of program in applied social sciences and professor of psychology and pediatrics, 1974—, department chairman, 1984—. Visiting lecturer, George Peabody College, Nashville, TN, 1959-61; visiting professor of educational psychology, Temple University, 1968-74. Consultant, U.S. Bureau of Prisons, 1967—. *Military service:* U.S. Army, 1946-48; became sergeant.

MEMBER: American Association of Correctional Psychologists, American Association of Arts and Sciences (1970—), American Psychological Association (member, 1954—; fellow, 1965—; president of section on child clinical psychology, 1985-86), Council for Exceptional Children (chairman of research committee, 1962—; delegate to Council for Research in Education, 1961-62; representative to the Interprofessional Research Commission on Pupil Personnel Services, 1963-67; member, panel on architecture and special education, 1967-70), Society for Research in Child and Adolescent Psychopathology (chair of organizing committee, 1987-89; president, 1989- 90), Midwestern Psychological Association, Sigma Xi.

AWARDS, HONORS: Distinguished Contribution to Correctional Psychology Award, American Association of Correc-

tional Psychologists, 1974; award for outstanding research achievement by a Florida Psychologist, Florida Psychological Association, 1986.

WRITINGS:

Managing Adult Inmates: Classification for Housing and Program Assignments, edited by Roberta Howard, American Correctional Association, 1984.

EDITOR

Research in Psychopathology, Van Nostrand, 1963.

(And contributor) *Juvenile Delinquency: Theory and Research,* Van Nostrand, 1965.

Children's Behavior Disorders: Selected Readings, Van Nostrand, 1968.

(With John S. Werry) *Psychopathological Disorders of Childhood,* Wiley, 1972, 3rd edition, 1986.

(With others) *Review of Human Development,* Wiley, 1982.

Handbook of Juvenile Delinquency (textbook edition), Wiley, 1987.

CONTRIBUTOR

S. A. Kirk and Bluma B. Weiner, editors, *Behavioral Research on Exceptional Children,* Council for Exceptional Children (Washington, DC), 1963.

L. A. Pennington and I. A. Berg, editors, *An Introduction to Clinical Psychology,* Ronald Press, 1966.

(With R. I. Watson) J. P. Guilford, editor, *Fields of Psychology,* Van Nostrand, 1966.

P. S. Graubard, editor, *Children Against Schools,* Follett, 1969.

(With others) R. H. Bradfield, editor, *Behavior Modification of Learning Disabilities,* Academic Therapy Publications, 1971.

OTHER

Editor, *Journal of Abnormal Child Psychology,* 1972—; member of editorial board, *Journal of Personality Disorders* and *Journal of Clinical Child Psychology,* 1986—.

QUIN-HARKIN, Janet 1941-
(Janetta Johns)

PERSONAL: Born September 24, 1941, in Bath, England; immigrated to the United States in 1966; daughter of Frank Newcombe (an engineer) and Margery (a teacher; maiden name, Rees) Lee; married John Quin-Harkin (an airline sales manager), November 26, 1966; children: Clare, Anne, Jane, Dominic. *Education:* University of London, B.A. (with honors), 1963; graduate study at University of Kiel and University of Freiburg. *Religion:* Roman Catholic. *Avocational interests:* Tennis, travel, drama, music, sketching, and hiking.

ADDRESSES: Home and office—31 Tralee Way, San Rafael, CA 94903.

CAREER: Writer. British Broadcasting Corp. (BBC), London, England, studio manager in drama department, 1963-66; instructor in dance and drama, 1971—; Dominican College, San Rafael, CA, currently instructor in an advanced writing seminar.

MEMBER: Society of Children's Book Writers, Associated Authors of Children's Literature.

AWARDS, HONORS: Peter Penny's Dance was named outstanding book by the *New York Times* and best book of the year by *School Library Journal, Washington Post, Saturday Review,* and Children's Book Showcase, all in 1976.

WRITINGS:

(Contributor) Lawrence Carillo and Dorothy McKinley, editors, *Chandler Reading Program,* five volumes, Noble & Noble, 1967-72.
Madam Sarah (adult historical novel), Fawcett, 1990.
Fool's Gold (adult historical novel), Torchbooks, 1991.

CHILDREN'S BOOKS

Peter Penny's Dance, Dial, 1976.
Benjamin's Balloon, Parents Magazine Press, 1979.
Septimus Bean and His Amazing Machine, Parents Magazine Press, 1980.
Magic Growing Powder, Parents Magazine Press, 1981.
Helpful Hattie, Harcourt, 1983.
Three Impossible Things, Parents Magazine Press, 1991.
Friends (series), Torchbooks, 1991.

YOUNG ADULT NOVELS

California Girl, Bantam, 1981.
Love Match, Bantam, 1982.
Ten Boy Summer, Bantam, 1982.
Write Every Day, Scholastic, Inc., 1982.
Daydreamer, Bantam, 1983.
(Under pseudonym Janetta Johns) *The Truth about Me and Bobby V.,* Bantam, 1983.
Tommy Loves Tina, Ace Books, 1984.
Exchange of Hearts, Bantam, 1984.
Ghost of a Chance, Bantam, 1984.
The Two of Us, Bantam, 1984.
Lovebirds, Bantam, 1984.

Winner Takes All, Ace Books, 1984.
101 Ways to Meet Mr. Right, Bantam, 1985.
The Great Boy Chase, Bantam, 1985.
Follow That Boy, Bantam, 1985.
Wanted: Date for Saturday Night, Putnam, 1985.
My Secret Love, Bantam, 1986.
My Best Enemy, Bantam, 1987.
Never Say Goodbye, Bantam, 1987.

YOUNG ADULT SERIES

On Our Own, books 1-6, Bantam, 1986.
Sugar and Spice, books 1-14, Ivy Books, 1987-88.
Heartbreak Cafe, books 1-6, Fawcett, 1990.
Portraits, book 1, Fawcett, 1990.

OTHER

Author of several documentaries and of four radio plays and scripts, including "Dandelion Hours," for British Broadcasting Corp., 1966. Contributor to education journals, *Scholastic* and *Mother's Manual.*

SIDELIGHTS: Janet Quin-Harkin commented: "I am particularly interested in travel. Since the first time I crossed Europe alone at the age of thirteen, I feel restless if I don't wander every few months. I have visited most parts of the globe, including a three-month stay in Greece and a year in Australia. I have made four trips to India, which I find fascinating. My love of travel is reflected in everything I write. My characters can never stay in one place.

"I enjoy writing for children because it is a positive medium. You can be optimistic, indulge in fantasy, and have a happy ending. What's more, you don't have to introduce sex and violence to make it sell. Also, in common with many writers for children, I don't think I ever grew up. When I write a book with an eleven-year-old heroine, that child is ME. I still get a very childlike delight from new experiences, from beautiful scenery, from being in the midst of nature. Children are such fine, uncomplicated beings. They accept that the world is full of magic and wonder and do not try to find the scientific proof behind it. Think of the opening of *Stuart Little.* No child questions why Mrs. Little's second son should happen to have been born a mouse. This uncritical acceptance is what I enjoy about writing fantasy. As long as the fantasy world is true to itself, once established, it can behave in any way under the sun.

"I work very hard, writing full time and producing one book every two months. Luckily for me, ideas are not a problem, and I hope I never come to a stage when I just 'churn them out for the mass market.'

"As well as the large number of copies sold (well over five million to date), the reward comes in the form of fan mail, much of it from girls who had never read a book before and are now motivated to read more. My books are sold worldwide and I find it very exciting to receive fan mail from every corner of the earth and to discover that girls have the same hopes and dreams, whether they live in the Philippines, Australia, or Germany."

R

REAGAN, Nancy (Davis) 1923-

PERSONAL: Birth-given name, Anne Frances Robbins; name legally changed c. 1937; born July 6, 1923, in New York, NY; daughter of Kenneth Robbins (a used-car salesman) and Edith (an actress; maiden name, Luckett) Robbins Davis; adopted by Dr. Loyal Davis, ca. 1937; married Ronald Reagan (a former actor and fortieth president of the United States), March 4, 1952; children: Patricia Ann, Ronald Prescott; stepchildren: Maureen, Michael. *Education:* Smith College, B.A., 1943. *Politics:* Republican.

ADDRESSES: Office—The Nancy Reagan Foundation, 2121 Avenue of the Stars, Los Angeles, CA 90067.

CAREER: Actress in stage productions until 1949, including road company shows and "Lute Song," a 1946 Broadway production; Metro-Goldwyn-Mayer, Inc. (MGM), Hollywood, CA, 1949-56, contract actress in eleven films, including "The Doctor and the Girl," 1949, "The Next Voice You Hear," 1950, "East Side, West Side," 1950, "Night into Morning," 1951, "Talk about a Stranger," 1952, "Donovan's Brain," 1953, and "Hellcats of the Navy," 1957. First Lady of the state of California, 1966-75, engaged in civic activities, including work on behalf of the Foster Grandparent program and projects involving prisoner-of-war and missing-in-action soldiers; First Lady of the United States, 1980- 88, continued civic activities, including expansion of the Foster Grandparent Program and involvement with drug abuse prevention and rehabilitation programs; author, speaker, and spokesperson for drug-free youth, 1988—.

Narrator of antidrug documentaries "The Chemical People" and "Chemical People II" for public television, 1983. Has held more than fifty honorary posts, including national chairman of Aid to Adoption of Special Kids, 1977; president of the Girl Scouts of America, 1981; member of the American Newspaper Women's Club, 1981; chairman of the President's Commission on Arts and the Humanities, the Women's Committee of the President's Committee of Employment of the Handicapped, 1981, the John F. Kennedy Center for the Performing Arts, 1981, the Cystic Fibrosis Foundation, 1982, and the Cancer Crusade, 1983; sponsor of the Vietnam Veterans' Memorial Fund.

AWARDS, HONORS: Christopher Award for "The Next Voice You Hear"; elected to the hall of fame of the ten best dressed women in the United States; named woman of the year by the *Los Angeles Times,* 1968 and 1977; named one of the ten most admired woman in the world by the Gallup Poll annually, 1981-89; special citation from the U.S. Chamber of Commerce, 1982, for work in drug abuse prevention; national commendation from the Parents Resource Institute of Drug Education, and Medal of Distinction from the International Association of Lions Clubs, both 1982; named one of the ten most admired American women by *Good Housekeeping* magazine annually, 1981-89; Kiwanis World Service medal, 1986; Father Flanagan Award from Boys Town; Lifeline Award from Variety Clubs International; Lifetime Achievement Award from the Council of Fashion Designers of America; numerous humanitarian awards for work against drug abuse. Honorary degrees include LL.D., Pepperdine University, 1983, and L.H.D., Georgetown University, 1987.

WRITINGS:

(With Bill Libby) *Nancy* (autobiography), Morrow, 1980.
(With Jane Wilkie) *To Love a Child,* Bobbs-Merrill, 1982.
(With William Novak) *My Turn: The Memoirs of Nancy Reagan,* Random House, 1989.

Author of column "Questions for Nancy," syndicated by Copely News Service, 1972.

SIDELIGHTS: Nancy Davis Reagan is a former film and stage actress who became First Lady of the United States when her husband, Ronald Reagan, was elected fortieth president in 1980. Mrs. Reagan served as First Lady from 1981 until 1989 and has since continued to campaign for such social causes as drug-free youth and the Foster Grandparent program.

Mrs. Reagan was born in New York City but spent most of her childhood in Chicago. Her mother, Edith Luckett Davis, was a stage actress, and her adoptive father, Dr. Loyal Davis, was a neurosurgeon. Mrs. Reagan attended Smith College, where she majored in drama. After her graduation in 1943 she secured work in summer stock productions. Eventually she moved to New York City and appeared in Broadway and Off-Broadway shows. In 1949 she signed a seven-year contract with Metro-Goldwyn-Mayer in Hollywood, appearing in eleven films between 1950 and 1956.

Nancy Davis married Ronald Reagan on March 4, 1952. Thereafter she curtailed her film work in deference to the needs of her husband and children. Ronald and Nancy Reagan made only one movie together, "Hellcats of the Navy," released by Columbia Pictures in 1956. The Reagans raised two sons and two daughters—Maureen and Michael, offspring from Mr. Reagan's first marriage, and Patti and Ronald, Jr. All of the Reagan children are now married and living in California; the Reagans also have two grandchildren.

Shortly after her husband became governor of California in 1967, Mrs. Reagan began visiting wounded Vietnam veterans and became active in projects concerning prisoners of war and servicemen missing in action. For some time she wrote a syndicated newspaper column, "Questions for Nancy," that addressed the POW/MIA issues. After visiting hospitals for physically and emotionally handicapped children, Mrs. Reagan became a strong supporter of the Foster Grandparent program, a nonprofit service that unites senior citizens with needy children. Mrs. Reagan continued her work with the Foster Grandparent program on a national level when she became First Lady.

Mrs. Reagan's special project as First Lady was a campaign against drug and alcohol abuse among youth. She travelled nearly 200,000 miles throughout the United States and abroad as a spokeswoman for the "Just Say No" Foundation and its philosophy. Mrs. Reagan also appeared on national television shows such as "Diff 'rent Strokes," "Good Morning America," and the specials "The Chemical People" and "Chemical People II" to encourage youngsters and their communities to organize against drug abuse. Since leaving the White House in 1989 Mrs. Reagan has continued her work for drug-free youth under the aegis of the Nancy Reagan Foundation.

Mrs. Reagan has co-authored three books, all of them nonfiction. Her work *To Love a Child* concerns the Foster Grandparent program and was written to help raise funds for the project. Her other books, *Nancy* and *My Turn,* detail her life as an actress, homemaker, and political figure. *My Turn* was published in 1989 and spent several weeks at the top of the bestseller lists.

BIOGRAPHICAL/CRITICAL SOURCES:

BOOKS

Leamer, Laurence, *Make-Believe: The Story of Nancy and Ronald Reagan,* Harper, 1983.
Reagan, Nancy and Bill Libby, *Nancy,* Morrow, 1980.
Reagan, Nancy and William Novak, *My Turn: The Memoirs of Nancy Reagan,* Random House, 1989.
Regan, Donald T., *For the Record,* Harcourt, 1988.

PERIODICALS

Chicago Tribune, December 19, 1987; May 12, 1988; June 11, 1988; June 9, 1989; November 2, 1989; November 16, 1989.
Detroit Free Press, October 27, 1989; November 8, 1989.
Good Housekeeping, September, 1981.
Ladies' Home Journal, October, 1980; July, 1981; December, 1981; January, 1983; April, 1983.
Los Angeles Times, June 10, 1988; August 16, 1988; October 19, 1988; November 13, 1988; June 5, 1989; August 13, 1989; October 15, 1989; October 22, 1989.
Los Angeles Times Book Review, October 22, 1989.
National Review, December 10, 1982; February 24, 1989.
New Republic, May 23, 1981.
News and Observer (Raleigh, NC), February 17, 1990.
Newsweek, April 28, 1980; November 24, 1980; December 22, 1980; January 5, 1981; February 2, 1981; March 9, 1981; May 25, 1981; November 20, 1981; December 21, 1981; February 1, 1982; October 23, 1989.
New York Times, November 1, 1989.
New York Times Book Review, November 19, 1989.

People, November 17, 1980; January 19, 1981; December 18, 1981; January 10, 1983; March 28, 1983; July 18, 1983.
Redbook, July, 1981.
Time, December 19, 1980; January 5, 1981; January 19, 1981; April 13, 1981; March 8, 1982; March 21, 1983.
U.S. News & World Report, October 20, 1980; January 26, 1981; July 1, 1981; July 27, 1981; August 3, 1981; August 10, 1981; November 23, 1981; May 1, 1982; May 31, 1982; July 21, 1982; April 11, 1983.
Vogue, May, 1981; November, 1981.
Washingtonian, December, 1989.
Washington Post, December 4, 1987; June 10, 1988; October 18, 1988; October 22, 1988; November 1, 1988; June 6, 1989; October 15, 1989.
Washington Post Book World, December 5, 1982; November 5, 1989.

*   *   *

RIFFE, Ernest
See BERGMAN, (Ernst) Ingmar

*   *   *

RIPLEY, (William Young) Warren 1921-

PERSONAL: Born April 13, 1921, in Samarcand, NC; son of Clements (a writer) and Katharine (a writer; maiden name, Ball) Ripley; married Quintillia Shuler, December 30, 1943; children: William Young Warren, Jr. (deceased), Clements. *Education:* Yale University, B.A., 1943. *Politics:* Conservative ("not a party member"). *Religion:* Episcopalian. *Avocational interests:* Collecting Civil War artillery projectiles, collecting rocks and minerals and doing lapidary work, making scale reproductions of weapons, making mahogany furniture.

ADDRESSES: Home—93 King St., Charleston, SC 29401.

CAREER: State (newspaper), Columbia, SC, reporter, 1946-47; *Charleston Evening Post,* Charleston, SC, reporter, 1947-50, state editor, 1950-72, special sections editor, 1972-87. *Military service:* U.S. Army, 1943-45; became first lieutenant. U.S. Army Reserve, 1945-63; became major.

MEMBER: Company of Military Historians (fellow), South Carolina Historical Society (vice-president, 1964), Charleston Library Society (secretary, 1971-75; president, 1975—).

AWARDS, HONORS: Founders Award, Museum of the Confederacy, 1970, for *Artillery and Ammunition of the Civil War.*

WRITINGS:

Artillery and Ammunition of the Civil War, Van Nostrand, 1970.
Battle of Chapman's Fort, Lakeside Press, 1978.
Battleground, Post-Courier, 1983.
(Editor of appendix with A. M. Wilcox) Arthur Middleton Manigault, *A Carolinian Goes to War,* edited by R. Lockwood Tower, University of South Carolina Press, 1983.
(Editor) *Siege Train,* University of South Carolina Press, 1986.
(Editor) *Cities of Fear,* [privately printed], 1990.
(Editor) E. Milby Burton, *South Carolina Silversmiths, 1690-1860,* revised edition, The Charleston Museum, 1991.

Also co-author of *The Civil War at Charleston,* 1961, editor of *Fifty Famous Houses of Charleston,* 1969, and author of *Charles Towne: Birth of a City,* 1970, and *The Battery,* 1977, all newspaper tabloids. Contributor to *Liberty, Civil War Times Illustrated,* and *American History Illustrated.*

ROBBE-GRILLET, Alain 1922-

PERSONAL: Born August 18, 1922, in Brest, France; son of Gaston (a manufacturer) and Yvonne (Canu) Robbe-Grillet; married Catherine Rstakian, October 23, 1957. *Education:* Institut National Agronomique, ingenieur agronome. *Religion:* Not religious.

ADDRESSES: Home—18 Boulevard Maillot, 92200 Neuilly-sur-Seine, France. *Office*—Editions de Minuit, 7 rue Bernard-Palissy, 75006 Paris, France. *Agent*—Georges Borchardt, 136 East 57th St., New York, N.Y. 10022.

CAREER: Institut National des Statistiques, Paris, France, charge de mission, 1945-50; engineer with the Institut des Fruits et Agrumes Coloniaux in Morocco, French Guinea, Martinique, and Guadeloupe, 1949-51; Editions de Minuit, Paris, France, literary advisor, beginning 1954. Has travelled and lectured in Europe, Asia, and North and South America. Visiting professor, New York University and University of California, Los Angeles.

MEMBER: Legion d'Honneur (Officier du Merite, Officier des Arts et Lettres).

AWARDS, HONORS: Prix Feneon, 1954, for *Les Gommes;* Prix des Critiques, 1955, for *Le Voyeur;* Prix Louis Delluc, 1963, for *L'Immortelle;* best screenplay, Berlin Festival, 1969, for "L'Homme qui mont"; Premio Internazionale Mondello, 1982, for *Djinn.*

WRITINGS:

Les Gommes (novel), Editions de Minuit, 1953, translation by Richard Howard published as *The Erasers,* Grove, 1964, edited by J. S. Wood, Prentice-Hall, 1970.

Le Voyeur (novel), Editions de Minuit, 1955, translation by Howard published as *The Voyeur,* Grove, 1958, published under original French title, edited and with an introduction by Oreste F. Pucciani, Ginn-Blaisdell, 1970.

La Jalousie (novel), Editions de Minuit, 1957, translation by Howard published as *Jealousy,* Grove, 1959 (also see below), and as *Jealousy: Rhythmic Themes by Alain Robbe-Grillet* (limited edition with pen and ink drawings by Michele Forgeois), Allen Press, 1971, published under original French title, edited by Germaine Bree and Eric Schoenfeld, Macmillan, 1963 (published in England under original French title, edited by B. G. Garnham, Methuen, 1969).

Dans le labyrinthe (novel), Editions de Minuit, 1959, translation by Howard published as *In the Labyrinth,* Grove, 1960 (also see below), also published as *Dans le labyrinthe* [and] *Dans les couloirs du Metropolitain* [and] *Le Chambre secrete,* with an essay on Robbe-Grillet by Gerard Genette, Union Generale D'Editions, 1964.

L'Annee derniere a Marienbad: Cine-roman (screenplay with photo extracts), Editions de Minuit, 1961, translation by Howard published as *Last Year at Marienbad,* Grove, 1962 (published in England as *Last Year at Marienbad: A Cine-Novel,* J. Calder, 1962).

Instantanes (short stories; also see below), Editions de Minuit, 1962, translation by Bruce Morissette published as *Snapshots,* Grove, 1968, new edition, 1972.

L'Immortelle: Cine-roman (screenplay with photo extracts from the film produced in 1963), Editions de Minuit, 1963, translation by A. M. Sheridan Smith published as *The Immortal One,* Calder & Boyars, 1971.

Pour un nouveau roman (essays), Editions de Minuit, 1963, new edition, Gallimard, 1970, translation by Barbara Wright published as *Snapshots* [and] *Towards a New Novel,* Calder & Boyars, 1965, translation by Howard published as *For a New Novel: Essays on Fiction,* Grove, 1966.

La Maison de rendezvous (novel), Editions de Minuit, 1965, translation by Howard published by Grove, 1966 (translation by Sheridan Smith published in England as *The House of Assignation: A Novel,* Calder & Boyars, 1970).

Two Novels by Robbe-Grillet (contains *Jealousy* and *In the Labyrinth,* with introductory essays by Morrissette and Roland Barthes), translated by Howard, Grove, 1965.

Projet pour le revolution a New York (novel), Editions de Minuit, 1970, translation by Howard published as *Project for a Revolution in New York,* Grove, 1972.

(With David Hamilton) *Reves de jeunes filles,* Montel, 1971, published in the United States as *Dreams of a Young Girl,* Morrow, 1971 (translation by Elizabeth Walter published in England as *Dreams of Young Girls,* Collins, 1971).

(With Hamilton) *Les Demoiselles d'Hamilton,* Laffont, 1972.

Glissements progressifs du plaisir (cine-roman; also see below), Editions de Minuit, 1974.

Construction d'un temple en ruines a la deesse Vanada, Bateau-Lavoir, 1975.

La Belle captive (novel; also see below), Bibliotheque des Arts, 1976.

Topologie d'une cite fantome (novel), Editions de Minuit, 1976, translation by J. A. Underwood published as *Topology of a Phantom City,* Grove, 1976.

Un regicide (novel), Editions de Minuit, 1978.

Souvenirs du triangle d'or (novel), Editions de Minuit, 1978, translation by Underwood published as *Recollections of the Golden Triangle,* Calder, 1984, Grove, 1986.

Temple aux miroirs, Seghers, 1979.

Djinn: Un trou rouge entre les paves disjoints (novel; also see below), Editions de Minuit, 1981, translation by Yvone Lenard and Walter Wells published as *Djinn,* Grove, 1982.

(Contributor) *Le Rendez-vous* (textbook; includes *Djinn*), Holt, 1981.

Le Miroir qui revient (novel) Editions de Minuit, 1985, translation by Jo Levy published as *Ghosts in the Mirror,* Calder, 1988, Grove, 1989.

Angelique; ou, L'Enchantement, Editions de Minuit, 1988.

SCREENPLAYS

"L'Annee derniere a Marienbad," Cocinor, 1961.

"L'Immortelle," Cocinor, 1963.

"Trans-Europ-Express," Lux-C.C.F., 1966.

"L'Homme qui ment," Lux-C.C.F., 1968.

"L'Eden et apres," Plan Films, 1970, adapted for French television and produced as "N'a pris les des," broadcast on Channel 3, 1975.

"Glissements progressifs du plaisir," Fox, 1974.

"Le Jeu avec le feu," U.G.C., 1975.

"La Belle captive," Argos Films, 1983.

OTHER

Also author of *Traces suspectes en surfaces,* with lithographs by Robert Rauschenberg. Contributor to *L'Express, Evergreen Review, New Statesman, Nouvelle Revue Francaise, Critique* (Paris), and *Revue de Paris.*

SIDELIGHTS: As the acknowledged leader and spokesman of the avant-garde New Novelists in France, Alain Robbe-Grillet has denounced those who talk of the novelist's social responsibility; for him the novel is not a tool and probably has little effect on society. "For us," he writes, "literature is not a means of expression, but a search. And it does not even know for what it searches. . . . [But] we prefer our searches, our doubts, our con-traditions, our joy of having yet invented something." The New Novelists under Robbe-Grillet's fiction introduced new, experimental concepts into the French novel. Occasionally described as "the school of sight" or "the pen camera," the form of writing Robbe-Grillet expounds concentrates on vision and gives minute descriptions of matter-of-fact objects.

For the New Novelists, phenomenology replaced traditional psychology; personality was rendered indefinable and fluid; and objective description became the primary goal. Moral judgments are avoided: "The world is neither significant nor absurd," says Robbe-Grillet. "It simply is." Furthermore, "our concept of the world around us is now only fragmentary, temporary, contradictory even, and always disputable. How can a work of art presume to illustrate a preordained concept, whatever it might be?" Robbe-Grillet's preoccupation with inanimate objects has led critics, notably Francois Mauriac, to suggest that the author dehumanizes literature. Moreover, confusion for many readers results from the lack of distinction between a seen object and one that is imagined; reality for Robbe-Grillet is always flowing from one state to another. Descriptions are repeated with slight variations, leading to charges of obscurity and tedium.

Robbe-Grillet's style is to a great extent borrowed from the cinema. According to critic Peter Cortland this style "concentrates on distorted visual images because it is representing mental life, which is of necessity different from the physical 'life,' or arrangement, of things in the material world." John Weightman believes Robbe-Grillet wants his books to have "the solidity and independent existence of a statue or a picture, which resists any anecdotal or intellectual summary." Robbe-Grillet once noted: "It seems that the conventions of photography (its two-dimensional character, black and white coloring, the limitations of the frame, the differences in scale according to the type of shot) help to free us from our own conventions."

BIOGRAPHICAL/CRITICAL SOURCES:

BOOKS

Contemporary Literary Criticism, Gale, Volume 1, 1973, Volume 2, 1974, Volume 4, 1975, Volume 6, 1976, Volume 8, 1978, Volume 10, 1979, Volume 14, 1980, Volume 43, 1987.
Cruickshank, John, editor, *The Novelist as Philosopher,* Oxford University Press, 1962.
Dictionary of Literary Biography, Volume 83: *French Novelists since 1960,* Gale, 1989.
Le Sage, Laurent, *The French New Novel,* Pennsylvania State University Press, 1962.
Mauriac, Claude, *The New Literature,* Braziller, 1959.
Moore, Henry T., *French Literature Since World War II,* Southern Illinois University Press, 1966.
Peyre, Henri, *French Novelists of Today,* Oxford University Press, 1967.
Stoltzfus, Ben Frank, *Alain Robbe-Grillet and the New French Novel,* Southern Illinois University Press, 1961.
Sturrock, I., *The French New Novel,* Oxford University Press, 1969.
Szanto, G. H., *Narrative Consciousness,* University of Texas Press, 1972.

PERIODICALS

Critique (Paris), August, 1954, September-October, 1955, July, 1959.
Critique: Studies in Modern Fiction, winter, 1963-64.
Evergreen Review, Volume 2, number 5, 1956, Volume 3, number 10, 1959.
Film Quarterly, fall, 1963.

Hudson Review, winter, 1972-73.
Les Temps Modernes, June, 1957, July, 1960.
Listener, February 15, 1968.
Modern Language Notes, May, 1962, May, 1963.
Modern Language Quarterly, September, 1962.
Nation, April 25, 1959.
New Statesman, February 17, 1961.
New York Review of Books, June 1, 1972.
New York Times Book Review, November 22, 1959, May 28, 1972.
Nouvelle Revue Francaise, November, 1960.
PMLA, September, 1962.
Spectator, December 16, 1960.
Time, July 20, 1962.
Vogue, January 1, 1963.
Wisconsin Studies in Contemporary Literature, Volume 1, number 3, 1960.
Yale French Studies, summer, 1959.*

*   *   *

ROBERTSON, Mary Elsie 1937-

PERSONAL: Born April 28, 1937, in Charleston, AR; daughter of Thomas Winfield (a rural mail carrier) and Esther (a teacher; maiden name, Scherer) Robertson; married Peter Marchant (a college professor), October 28, 1961; children: Jennifer Esther, Piers Adam. *Education:* University of Arkansas, B.A., 1958, M.A., 1959; University of Iowa, M.F.A., 1961. *Politics:* Democrat. *Religion:* Society of Friends (Quaker).

ADDRESSES: Home—3238 Brick Schoolhouse Rd., Hamlin, NY 14464. *Agent*—Virginia Barber, 353 West 21st St., New York, NY 10011.

CAREER: Writer. Pennsylvania State University, State College, instructor, 1965-66; St. John Fisher College, Rochester, NY, lecturer, 1974-77; State University of New York College at Brockport, assistant professor, 1979-81. Visiting lecturer, Warren Wilson College, 1983—; writer in residence, Western Washington University, 1983, 1985, and Wichita State University, 1986; visiting writer, University of Arizona, 1988, 1990-91, and Syracuse University, 1990.

AWARDS, HONORS: First prize, *Mademoiselle* fiction writing contest, 1958, for short story "Homecoming"; Associated Writing Program award in the novel, 1980, for *After Freud;* $1,000 Scholarship for Mature Women, 1980; PEN syndicated fiction contest winner, 1983, for "Woman of a Thousand Shapes"; National Endowment for the Arts fellowship in fiction, 1983-84.

WRITINGS:

Jordan's Stormy Banks and Other Stories, Atheneum, 1961.
Jemimalee, McGraw, 1977.
Tarantula and the Red Chigger (juvenile), Little, Brown, 1980.
After Freud, State University of New York Press, 1981.
The Clearing, Atheneum, 1982.
Speak, Angel, Atheneum, 1983.
Family Life, Atheneum, 1987.
What I Have to Tell You, Doubleday, 1989.

Contributor to *Ariadne's Web* (collection of women's diaries), 1982, and *Arkansas in Short Fiction,* 1986; contributor of stories to literary journals and popular magazines, including *Seventeen, Ms., Redbook, Kansas Quarterly,* and *Seattle Review.*

SIDELIGHTS: Mary Elsie Robertson's "talent for describing how the bizarre and irrational can fuse with everyday normality gradually transforms a rather commonplace story into a witty and absorbing tale," states Jennifer Uglow in the *Times Literary Supplement*. *New York Times Book Review* contributor Stanley Ellin similarly praises Robertson's writing ability in a critique of *Speak, Angel:* "The author, deftly changing viewpoints from male to female, from middle-aged to youthful, strikes exactly the right note each time, intellectually, emotionally and idiomatically."

Robertson "again demonstrates her superb writing ability in 'Family Life,' a remarkably sensitive portrayal of an American family in the midst of breaking up," Alison B. Carb observes in Chicago *Tribune Books*. Precipitated by the infidelity of the father, the Sloan family finds themselves withdrawing from each other. *New York Times Book Review* contributor Patricia Mandell believes that the novel "insightfully portrays the inexorable and irreversible deterioration of a family, but it suffers from a certain claustrophobia," due to its constant focus on the characters' reactions. In contrast, Jack Sullivan praises the "microscopic clarity and authenticity" with which the family is portrayed, remarking in *Washington Post Book World* that "nature, art and Robertson's searing prose conspire to do extraordinary things, but the main power of *Family Life* is, as its title implies, its lifelike rendering of the ordinary." As a result, the critic concludes, "I can't think of any novel I've read recently that is so uncompromisingly realistic and clear-minded, yet so organically full of the good tension and drama one associates with a good read."

BIOGRAPHICAL/CRITICAL SOURCES:

PERIODICALS

Los Angeles Times, June 5, 1981; July 13, 1983.
New York Times Book Review, July 31, 1983; November 22, 1987; December 31, 1989.
Times Literary Supplement, February 20, 1981.
Tribune Books (Chicago), August 2, 1987.
Washington Post Book World, August 2, 1987; October 1, 1989.

* * *

ROBHS, Dwight
  See MONACO, Richard

* * *

ROBINSON, Sidney K. 1943-

PERSONAL: Born July 9, 1943, in Indianapolis, IN; son of Richard M. (an architect) and Alma D. (a nurse) Robinson. *Education:* Columbia University, B.Arch., 1967; University of Michigan, Arch.D., 1974.

ADDRESSES: Office—School of Architecture, University of Illinois at Chicago, Box 4348, Chicago, IL 60680.

CAREER: U.S. Peace Corps, Washington, DC, architectural adviser to Iran's Ministry of the Interior, 1967-69; Alden B. Dow Architects, Midland, MI, junior designer, 1970-71; Iowa State University, Ames, assistant professor, 1973-78, associate professor of the history of environmental arts, 1978-85; University of Illinois at Chicago, associate professor of architecture, 1985—.

MEMBER: Society of Architectural Historians, American Institute of Architects.

WRITINGS:

(With Richard Guy Wilson) *The Prairie School in Iowa,* Iowa State University Press, 1977.

Life Imitates Architecture: Taliesin and Alden Dow's Studio, University of Michigan Press, 1980.
The Architecture of Alden B. Dow, Wayne State University Press, 1982.
Essays on the Picturesque, University of Chicago Press, 1991.

Contributor to architecture journals.

WORK IN PROGRESS: Research on composition in landscape gardening, architecture, and government.

SIDELIGHTS: Sidney K. Robinson told *CA:* "I keep returning to issues involving the control and selection of design and the necessary subversion of its singular dominance. A central expression of this instability is the nature/artifice duality and its political expression in freedom and order. The perfection of control is Alden B. Dow's beautiful world, which expresses his own personal freedom.

"The extension of such ideals is problematic as more people are implicated. The eighteenth-century garden and political theorists waffled constantly on these issues as they tried to maintain both freedom/nature and control/artifice."

* * *

ROSS, Bernard L.
  See FOLLETT, Ken(neth Martin)

* * *

ROTHMAN, Tony 1953-

PERSONAL: Born April 29, 1953, in Philadelphia, PA; son of Milton A. (a physicist) and Doris (a psychotherapist; maiden name, Weiss) Rothman. *Education:* Swarthmore College, B.A., 1975; graduate study at Cambridge University, 1975; University of Texas, Ph.D., 1981.

ADDRESSES: Home—1687 Lawrence Rd., Lawrenceville, NJ 08648.

CAREER: National Radio Astronomy Observatory, Green Bank, WV, research assistant, 1974, 1976; University of Texas, Austin, assistant instructor in mathematics, 1978-81; held academic positions in Oxford, England, 1981-82, and Moscow, Soviet Union, 1982-83; University of Capetown, Rondebosch, South Africa, member of faculty, 1984-86; editor, *Scientific American,* 1988-89.

AWARDS, HONORS: Award from Oxford Experimental Theatre Club, for "The Magician and the Fool," 1981.

WRITINGS:

The World Is Round (science fiction novel), Ballantine, 1978.
Frontiers of Modern Physics (collection of articles), Dover, 1984.
Science a la Mode, Princeton University Press, 1989.
Censored Tales, Macmillan, 1989.
A Physicist on Madison Avenue, Princeton University Press, 1991.

Also author of three-act historical play "The Magician and the Fool." Contributor to periodicals, including *Scientific American, Isaac Asimov's Science Fiction Magazine, Discover, Gettysburg Review,* and *ANALOG: Science Fiction-Science Fact.*

WORK IN PROGRESS: The Time of Troubles, a novel; *The Tinkerers,* a novel; *Tales of Perestroika and Disneyland.*

SIDELIGHTS: Tony Rothman writes *CA:* "Having a technical background has perhaps made me more interested in the 'nuts and bolts' side of publishing than other authors might be. A year as an editor at *Scientific American* and some editing at major publishers has given me an inside look at how the publishing industry functions. I am appalled. The problem is not so much lack of technology as lack of any idea of what to do with it. Major publishers do not have electric typewriters, let alone direct-from-disk typesetting. The idea of digitizing backlists—which would eventually make those books available in electronic form or via a print-on-demand system—has yet to enter anyone's thinking. There seems to be almost a perverse pride among editors to be as technologically backwards as possible.

"This provincialism may be another manifestation of literary insecurity. Writers and publishers know they are not as important for society as they used to be, but don't like to admit it. They seize all sorts of opportunities, relevant or not, to demonstrate that they are essential and special. The Rushdie affair was touted by writers as a freedom-of-speech issue, when it was in fact an issue of terrorism. After the Pantheon Press resignations, writers shouted 'there should be no bottom line,' but no one offered to give up his or her royalties. Which brings us back to the issue of technology. Responsible financial management, in which the creative use of technology could have played a role, might have helped Pantheon. The literary establishment may have realized the world has changed but doesn't seem to know how to react. It is time to enter the 21st century."

BIOGRAPHICAL/CRITICAL SOURCES:

PERIODICALS

Los Angeles Times, May 23, 1989.
Times Literary Supplement, October 13-19, 1989.

*   *   *

ROTTENSTEINER, Franz 1942-

PERSONAL: Born January 18, 1942, in Waidmannsfeld, Austria; son of Franz and Hedwig (Buchleitner) Rottensteiner, married Hanna Jarosinska, 1980; children: Joachim Jan. *Education:* University of Vienna, Ph.D., 1968. *Religion:* Atheist.

ADDRESSES: Home—Marchettigasse 9117, A-1060 Vienna, Austria.

CAREER: Librarian, editor, and literary agent. Austrian Institute for Building Research, Vienna, Austria, librarian, 1970-85; free-lance writer and editor, 1985—. Literary agent for Polish writer Stanislaw Lem, and others. *Military service:* Austrian Army, 1969-70.

WRITINGS:

(Editor) *View from Another Shore: European Science Fiction,* Seabury, 1973, published in German as *Blick vom anderen Ufer,* Suhrkamp, 1977.
The Science Fiction Book, Seabury, 1975.
The Fantasy Book, Macmillan, 1978.
(Editor) *The Slaying of the Dragon: Modern Tales of the Playful Imagination,* Harcourt, 1984.
(Editor) Stanislaw Lem, *Microworlds: Essays on Fantasy and Science Fiction,* Harcourt, 1985.

Also author of a book on German science fiction, published by Krajowa Agencja Wydanicza in Warsaw. Also editor of "Science Fiction of the World" series, fifteen volumes, Insel Verlag, 1971-75; editor of "Fantastic Novels" series and "H. G. Wells Edition" series, until 1984, both published in Zsolnay, Vienna; editor of "The Fantastic Library" series, Suhrkamp, 1980—.

Also editor of *The Best of Stanislaw Lem,* published in Japanese. Reviewer for Viennese newspaper *Der Standard.*

GERMAN-LANGUAGE EDITOR

Die Ratte im Labyrinth (title means "The Rat in the Labyrinth"), Insel Verlag, 1971.
Insel Almanac auf das Jahr 1972 (title means "Insel Almanac for the Year 1972"), Insel Verlag, 1971.
(With Marek Wydmuch) *Gespenstergeschichten aus Polen* (title means "Ghost Stories from Poland"), Fischer, 1978.
Gespenstergeschichten aus Oesterreich (title means "Ghost Stories from Austria"), Fischer, 1979.
Quarber Merkur, Suhrkamp, 1979.
Gespenstergeschichten aus England (title means "Ghost Stories from England"), Fischer, 1980.
Gespenstergeschichten aus Nordamerika (title means "Ghost Stories from North America"), Fischer, 1981.
Gespenstergeschichten aus der Sudsee (title means "Ghost Stories from the Southern Seas"), Fischer, 1982.
Die andere Zukunft (title means "The Other Future"), Suhrkamp, 1982.
Das grosse Buch der Maerchen, Sagen und Gespenstergeschichten (title means "The Big Book of Fairy Tales, Folk Tales, and Ghost Stories"), Fischer, 1982.
Uber H. P. Lovecraft (title means "On H. P. Lovecraft"), Suhrkamp, 1984.
Phantastische Welten (title means "Fantastic Worlds"), Suhrkamp, 1984.
Phantastische Traeume (title means "Fantastic Dreams"), Suhrkamp, 1983.
Phantastische Aussichten (title means "Fantastic Prospects"), Suhrkamp, 1985.
Phantastische Zeiten (title means "Fantastic Times"), Suhrkamp, 1986.
Seltsame Labyrinthe (title means "Strange Labyrinths"), Suhrkamp, 1987.
Die Eingang ins Paradies (title means "The Door into Paradise"), Suhrkamp, 1988.
Arche Noah (title means "Noah's Ark"), Suhrkamp, 1989.
(With Michael Koseler) *Werkfuehrer durch die utopisch-phantastische Literatur* (title means "Guide to Works in Science Fiction and Fantasy"), Corian Verlag, 1989—.
Die Sirene (title means "The Siren"), Suhrkamp, 1990.
Phantastische Begegnungen (title means "Fantastic Encounters"), Suhrkamp, 1990.

GERMAN-LANGUAGE EDITOR OF "POLARIS" SCIENCE FICTION ALMANAC SERIES

Polaris 1, Insel Verlag, 1973.
. . . 2, Insel Verlag, 1974.
. . . 3, Insel Verlag, 1975.
. . . 4, Suhrkamp, 1978.
. . . 5, Suhrkamp, 1981.
. . . 6, Suhrkamp, 1982.
. . . 7, Suhrkamp, 1983.
. . . 8, Suhrkamp, 1985.
. . . 9, Suhrkamp, 1985.
. . . 10, Suhrkamp, 1986.

CONTRIBUTOR

Thomas D. Clareson, editor, *S.F.: The Other Side of Realism,* Bowling Green University, 1971.
Patrick Parrinder, editor, *S.F.: A Critical Guide,* Longman, 1979.

Frank N. Magill, editor, *Survey of Science Fiction Literature,* Salem Press, 1979.

Peter Nicholls, editor, *The Encyclopedia of Science Fiction,* Doubleday, 1979.

Neil Barron, editor, *Anatomy of Wonder: A Critical Guide to Science Fiction,* 2nd edition, Bowker, 1981.

Gary Wolfe, editor, *Science Fiction Dialogues,* Academy Chicago, 1982.

Magill, editor, *Survey of Modern Fantasy Literature,* Salem Press, 1983.

Also contributor to many other volumes of essays. Contributor to many periodicals in several countries. Editorial consultant, *Science-Fiction Studies.*

WORK IN PROGRESS: Various essays on fantasy and science fiction; several reissues of rare and old works for Suhrkamp.

SIDELIGHTS: Franz Rottensteiner writes: "I conduct research into various aspects of fantastic literature and science fiction, as well as editing, agenting, and sometimes translating, both in English and German. I am of the opinion that fantasy and science fiction are literary genres with a great potential, but that this potential has rarely ever been fulfilled by the practitioners in the field, most of whom are quite incompetent, and that it is of vital importance to separate the few essential works from the trash."

BIOGRAPHICAL/CRITICAL SOURCES:

PERIODICALS

New York Times Book Review, March 24, 1985.

*   *   *

RUBENS, Bernice (Ruth) 1923-

PERSONAL: Born July 26, 1923, in Cardiff, Wales; daughter of Eli and Dorothy (Cohen) Rubens; married Rudi Nassauer (a novelist), December 29, 1947; children: Sharon, Rebecca. *Education:* University of Wales, B.A. (honors in English), 1944. *Politics:* Apolitical. *Religion:* Jewish.

ADDRESSES: Home—16A Belsize Park Gardens, London NW3 4LD, England. *Agent*—Mark Lucas, Peters, Fraser & Dunlop, The Chambers, Chelsea Harbor, London SW10, England.

CAREER: English teacher at grammar school for boys, Birmingham, England, 1948-49; free-lance film director and script writer, 1950—. Fellow, University of Wales, Cardiff, 1982.

AWARDS, HONORS: Blue Ribbon Award, American Documentary Film Festival, 1969, for *Stress;* Booker Prize, 1970, for *The Elected Member;* Welsh Arts Council award, 1976.

WRITINGS:

Set on Edge (novel), Eyre & Spottiswoode, 1960.
Madame Sousatzka (novel), Eyre & Spottiswoode, 1962.
Mate in Three (novel), Eyre & Spottiswoode, 1966.
Chosen People (novel), Atheneum, 1969 (published in England as *The Elected Member,* Eyre & Spottiswoode, 1969).
Sunday Best (novel), Eyre & Spottiswoode, 1971, Summit, 1981.
Go Tell the Lemming (novel), J. Cape, 1973.
I Sent a Letter to My Love (novel), W. H. Allen, 1975; play adaptation by author produced in New Haven, CT, 1978.
The Ponsonby Post (novel), W. H. Allen, 1977.
A Five-Year Sentence, W. H. Allen, 1978, published as *Favours,* Summit, 1979.
Spring Sonata, W. H. Allen, 1979.
Birds of Passage, Hamish Hamilton, 1981, Summit, 1982.

Brothers, Hamish Hamilton, 1983, Delacorte, 1984.
Mr. Wakefield's Crusade, Delacorte, 1985.
Our Father, Delacorte, 1987.
Kingdom Come, Hamish Hamilton, 1990.

Author of screenplays *One of the Family,* 1964, *Call Us by Name,* 1968, *Out of the Mouths,* 1970, *The Spastic Child, Stress,* and *Dear Mum and Dad;* author of television play *Third Party,* 1972.

MEDIA ADAPTATIONS: Madame Sousatzka was adapted as a film for Universal Pictures, 1988.

WORK IN PROGRESS: Adapting Olive Schreiner's *Story of an African Farm* for screen; *A Solitary Grief,* a novel.

SIDELIGHTS: Chosen People, writes Julian Mitchell, "belongs to the familiar genre in which the loving unkindness of Jewish family life is explored with horrified affection. Its theme is peculiarly Jewish: the need for scapegoats and what happens to those 'cold and chosen ones' when the burden of other people's suffering becomes unbearable. But the novel goes beyond its particular Jewishness to say something about humanity at large. It is a remarkable achievement, easily the best of Miss Rubens' four novels so far." "Rubens," David Haworth says, "is one of our finest Jewish writers. She has a large compassion, and an intelligence which makes her compulsively readable. She is deeply committed, yet objectively truthful, about the Jewish world and people she describes." Mitchell faults Rubens for some clumsiness with flashbacks and a lack of conviction outside the home and hospital, "but for the most part she writes extremely well. . . . What most distinguishes this novel is Miss Rubens' touching respect for human weakness. . . . Above all, it is Miss Rubens' tenderness for the mad and broken which makes her book a grave pleasure to read."

Eileen Lottman feels that the story does not stand by itself because the story is "more B movie than Freud." She suggests that the book is "a parable, then—not so much a story of people as a cry of anguish for the human (Jewish) condition. We are all responsible for each other's pain, it says. And yet we cannot help it." Mitchell comments: "We all need scapegoats, she is saying, and we put them in what we genteelly call mental homes and asylums. But no hospital is ever a home and there is no asylum for such people except the imitation death of prolonged, drugged sleep. Everything is not better in the morning." Thomas Lask finds Rubens "a skilled, professional story teller, with a discerning eye for what is moving and effective." Harry Roskolenko writes: "Grecian-Judaic in its tragic inner spirit, the novel has special nuances of wit, irony and economy. You never doubt Rabbi Zweck's total existence, or Norman's—nor the Jewish traditions in another country." Concludes Haworth, "The plea and the uncertainty [of Norman] are Miss Rubens' underlying theme and she has made something excellent from it."

Rubens told *CA:* "I am interested primarily in noncommunication between people—the theme of all my novels. I have been something of a specialist in the making of documentary films about victims, the handicapped. Obviously there is some linkage here. I am interested in the links between sanity, madness, the ever-changing meaning of those terms. I inhabit that limbo, that no fixed abode, loitering there without intent."

BIOGRAPHICAL/CRITICAL SOURCES:

BOOKS

Contemporary Literary Criticism, Gale, Volume 19, 1981, Volume 31, 1985.
Dictionary of Literary Biography, Volume 14: *British Novelists since World War II,* Gale, 1982.

PERIODICALS

Chicago Tribune, December 11, 1987, October 14, 1988.
Chicago Tribune Book World, July 8, 1979, January 5, 1986.
Jewish Quarterly, summer, 1969.
Life, May 16, 1969.
Los Angeles Times, May 12, 1980, May 12, 1982, November 13, 1985, November 17, 1987, October 12, 1988.
Los Angeles Times Book Review, June 1, 1980.
New Statesman, February 14, 1969.
New York Times, May 27, 1969, December 6, 1978, May 10, 1979, November 28, 1987.
New York Times Book Review, May 18, 1969, May 6, 1979, June 20, 1982, March 25, 1984, November 17, 1985, December 27, 1987.
Publishers Weekly, March 16, 1984.
Saturday Review, July 26, 1969.
Times (London), September 24, 1981, March 23, 1989, February 15, 1990.
Times Literary Supplement, September 11, 1981, July 23, 1982, September 16, 1983, May 31, 1985, March 27, 1987, March 2-8, 1990.
Washington Post, May 8, 1979, December 14, 1987, October 14, 1988.
Washington Post Book World, June 15, 1980, April 8, 1984, January 12, 1986.

*   *   *

RUBIN, David Lee 1939-

PERSONAL: Born September 30, 1939, in Indianapolis, IN; son of Ira Bertram (an analytical chemist) and Jeanne (Gamso) Rubin; married Carolyn Dettman, June 12, 1965; children: Timothy. *Education:* Attended University of Chicago, 1957-58; University of Tennessee, B.A., 1962; University of Paris, Certificats, 1963; University of Illinois at Urbana-Champaign, M.A., 1964, Ph.D., 1967. *Avocational interests:* Travel, art history, oriental cuisine.

ADDRESSES: Home—520 Rookwood Pl., Charlottesville, VA 22901. *Office*—Department of French, University of Virginia, Charlottesville, VA 22903.

CAREER: University of Illinois at Urbana-Champaign, 1963-67, became instructor in French; University of Chicago, Chicago, IL, assistant professor of French, 1967-69; University of Virginia, Charlottesville, assistant professor, 1969-74, associate professor, 1974-82, professor of French, 1982—. Seminar director, Folger Institute for Renaissance and Eighteenth-Century Studies, fall, 1989.

MEMBER: Modern Language Association of America.

AWARDS, HONORS: Fulbright fellowship, 1962-63; Woodrow Wilson fellowship, 1963-64; University of Virginia, summer research grants, 1970, 1972, and 1976; associateship in the Center for Advanced Study, 1974, 1980-81; Guggenheim fellowship, 1980-81; distinguished alumnus membership, Epsilon of Tennessee, Phi Beta Kappa, 1984.

WRITINGS:

(Contributor) Robert Scholes, editor, *Poetic Theory/Poetic Practice,* Midwest Modern Language Association, 1969.
Higher, Hidden Order: Design and Meaning in the Odes of Malherbe, University of North Carolina Press, 1972.
(Editor) *The Selected Poetry and Prose of John T. Napier,* Pikeville College Press, 1972.

Papers on French Seventeenth-Century Literature, Editions Jean-Michel Place, Volume 1 (contributor), 1973, Volume 7 (co-editor and contributor), 1977, Volume 9 (co-editor), 1978.
(Contributor) G. B. Daniel, editor, *Moliere Studies,* University of North Carolina Press, 1974.
(Co-editor and contributor) *La coherence interieure: Etudes sur la litterature francais du dix-septieme siecle,* Editions Jean-Michel Place, 1977.
The Knot of Artifice: A Poetic of the French Lyric in the Early Seventeenth Century, Ohio State University Press, 1981.
(Contributor) Peter Bayley and Dorothy Gabe Coleman, editors, *The Equilibrium of Wit,* French Forum, 1982.
(Contributor) H. Gaston Hall and Richard Brooks, editors, *Critical Bibliography of French Literature,* Volume 3A, Syracuse University Press, 1983.
(Editor) *La Poesie francaise du premier 17e siecle: Textes et contextes,* Gunter Narr, 1986.
(Contributor) Ulrich Doering, editor, *Ouvertures et dialogues,* Gunter Narr, 1988.
(Co-editor) *Convergences,* Ohio State University Press, 1989.
(Editor and contributor) *Sun King,* Folger Books/Associated University Presses, 1991.
(Co-editor and contributor) *The Ladder of High Designs,* University Press of Virginia, 1991.
A Pact with Silence, Ohio State University Press, 1991.
(Contributor) T. V. F. Brogan, Alex Preuninger, O. B. Hardison, and Frank J. Warnlee, editors, *Princeton Encyclopedia of Poetry and Poetics,* Princeton University Press, 1992.

Also co-editor of Volumes 13 and 22 of *Papers on French Seventeenth-Century Literature.* Contributor of articles and reviews to *Yale French Studies, L'Esprit createur, French Review, Oeuvres et Critiques, Revue de l'Universite d'Ottawa, Cahiers Maynard,* and other journals. Founding editor, *Continuum: Problems in French Literature from the Late Renaissance to the Early Enlightenment,* AMS Press, 1989—; guest editor, *Oeuvres et critiques,* Volume 4, number 2, 1980, and *L'Esprit createur,* Volume 21, number 4, 1981. Member of editorial boards, *Oeuvres et critiques,* 1974, and Purdue University Monographs, 1977.

WORK IN PROGRESS: Mediations: Four Essays on La Fontaine's Fables; co-editing a posthumous volume of Robert Nicolich's essays; La Fontaine tercentenary volume (in collaboration); study of Heredia's *Trophees* (in collaboration).

*   *   *

RUSHDIE, (Ahmed) Salman 1947-

PERSONAL: Born June 19, 1947, in Bombay, India; son of Anis Ahmed (in business) and Negin (Butt) Rushdie; married Clarissa Luard (in publishing), May 22, 1976 (marriage dissolved, 1987); married Marianne Wiggins (an author), 1988; children: (first marriage) Zafar (son). *Education:* King's College, Cambridge, M.A. (history; with honors), 1968.

ADDRESSES: Agent—Deborah Rodgers Ltd., 49 Blenheim Crescent, London W11, England; and 19 Ravely St., London NW5 2HX, England.

CAREER: Actor with the Fringe Theatre, London, England, 1968-69; free-lance advertising copywriter, 1970-73, part-time, 1976-80; writer, 1975—. Executive member of Camden Committee for Community Relations, 1976-83; member of British Film Institute Production Board; member of advisory board, Institute of Contemporary Arts.

MEMBER: International PEN, Royal Society of Literature (fellow), Society of Authors, National Book League (member of executive committee).

AWARDS, HONORS: Booker McConnell Prize for Fiction from Booker McConnell Ltd., literary award from English Speaking Union, both 1981, and James Tait Black Memorial Prize, 1982, all for *Midnight's Children;* awarded Arts Council Literature bursary, 1981; Prix du Meilleur Livre Etranger, 1984; *The Satanic Verses* was named to the 1988 Booker Prize shortlist for fiction; Whitbread Prize, 1988, for *The Satanic Verses.*

WRITINGS:

Grimus (novel), Gollancz, 1975, Overlook Press, 1979.
Midnight's Children (novel), Knopf, 1981.
Shame (novel), Knopf, 1983.
The Jaguar Smile: A Nicaraguan Journey (nonfiction), Viking, 1987.
The Satanic Verses (novel), Viking, 1988.
Haroun and the Sea of Stories (juvenile), Granta Books, 1990.

Also author of television screenplays "The Painter and the Pest," 1985, and "The Riddle of Midnight," 1988. Contributor to magazines and newspapers, including *New Statesman, Atlantic Monthly, Granta, New York Times,* and *London Times.*

SIDELIGHTS: Salman Rushdie's first published novel, *Grimus,* tells the story of an American Indian who receives the gift of immortality and begins an odyssey to find life's meaning. The work initially attracted attention among science fiction readers and writers, including Mel Tilden, who called the book "engrossing and often wonderful" in a *Times Literary Supplement* review. Tilden determined the book to be "science of the word," recognizing at the same time that it "is one of those novels some people will say is too good to be science fiction, even though it contains other universes, dimensional doorways, alien creatures and more than one madman." Although many critics disagreed on the work's genre—calling it fable, fantasy, political satire, and magical realism—most agreed with David Wilson's assessment in *Times Literary Supplement* that *Grimus* was "an ambitious, strikingly confident first novel" and that Rushdie was an author to watch.

Rushdie turned to India, his birthplace, for the subject of his second book. An allegory, *Midnight's Children* chronicles the history of modern India throughout the lives of 1,001 children born within the country's first hour of independence from Great Britain on August 15, 1947. Saleem Sinai, the novel's protagonist-narrator, is one of two males born at the precise moment of India's independence—the stroke of midnight—in a Bombay nursing home. Moonfaced, stained with birthmarks, and possessed of a "huge cucumber of a nose," Sinai becomes by a twist of fate "the chosen child of midnight." He later explains to the reader that a nurse, in "her own revolutionary act," switched the newborn infants. The illegitimate son of a Hindu street singer's wife and a departing British colonist was given to a prosperous Muslim couple and raised as Saleem Sinai; his midnight twin, called Shiva, was given to an impoverished Hindu street clown who, first cuckolded and then widowed by childbirth, was left to raise a son—twice not his—on the streets of Bombay. Thus, in accordance with class privilege mistakenly bestowed, Sinai's birth was heralded by fireworks and celebrated in newspapers; a congratulatory letter from Jawaharlal Nehru portended his future. "You are the newest bearer of the ancient face of India which is also eternally young," wrote the prime minister. "We shall be watching over your life with the closest attention; it will be, in a sense, the mirror of our own."

The novel begins at a point more than thirty years after the simultaneous births of Sinai and independent India. Awaiting death in the corner of a Bombay pickle factory where he is employed, Sinai—prematurely aged, impotent, and mutilated by a personal history that parallels that of his country—tells his life story to Padma, an illiterate working girl who loves and tends him. Sinai begins his tale by relating thirty-two years of family history preceding his arrival into the world. He then reveals the circumstances and irony of his birth and includes an incredible account of his discovery, at age nine, of the extraordinary telepathic powers that enabled him to realize the events of his birth and to communicate with his multitudinous midnight siblings: the remaining 580 offspring (reduced from the original 1,001 by India's high child mortality rate) of the country's first hour of independence.

All of midnight's children, discloses Sinai, were possessed of magical gifts. "Among the children were infants with the powers of transmutation, flight, prophecy, wizardry." "The closer to midnight our birth-times were, the greater our gifts," he tells Padma. "To Shiva [destined to become India's most decorated war hero as well as Sinai's mortal enemy] the hour had given the gifts of war," he explains. "And to me, the greatest gift of all—the ability to look into the hearts and minds of men."

Sinai and the rest of midnight's children "incorporate the stupendous Indian past, with its pantheon, its epics, and its wealth of folklore," summarized *New York Times* critic Robert Towers, "while at the same time playing a role in the tumultuous Indian present." "The plot of this novel is complicated enough, and flexible enough, to smuggle Saleem into every major event in the subcontinent's past thirty years," agreed Clark Blaise in the *New York Times Book Review.* "It is . . . a novel of India's growing up; from its special, gifted infancy to its very ordinary, drained adulthood. It is a record of betrayal and corruption, the loss of ideals, culminating with 'the Widow's' Emergency rule." "Saleem . . . *lives* India," Bill Buford elaborated in a *New Statesman* review, "and his life chronicles the movement from the euphoric celebration of independence to . . . the dulled recognition of state repression."

Although *Midnight's Children* "spans the recent history, both told and untold, of both India and Pakistan as well as the birth of Bangladesh," commented Anita Desai in the *Washington Post Book World,* "one hesitates to call the novel 'historical' for Rushdie believes . . . that while individual history does not make sense unless seen against its national background, neither does national history make sense unless seen in the form of individual lives and histories." Rushdie "proceeds from his belief that 'to understand one life you have to swallow the whole world,' " Buford similarly observed. And Rushdie's "central point is clear: you cannot separate the individual from the environment." Describing Sinai in a *Commonweal* review, Una Chaudhuri carried Buford's assessment one step further. "Saleem Sinai is India," she ventured. "He has been handcuffed to history."

Midnight's Children was almost unanimously well received, claiming England's most exalted literary award, the Booker McConnell Prize for fiction, in 1981. It was variously praised as comic, exuberant, ambitious, and stylistically brilliant. Chaudhuri hailed it as "a literary event—a novel of international importance," and Towers called it "an extraordinary novel, . . . one of the most important to come out of the English-speaking world in this generation." "In this memorable novel, Rushdie pleases the senses and the heart," applauded Phyllis Bimbaum in *Saturday Review,* and *New Yorker* critic V. S. Pritchett deemed the book "irresistible." More than one critic described the book as a "tour de force."

The novel also elicited favorable comparisons to Laurence Sterne's *Tristram Shandy,* Gabriel Garcia Marquez's *One Hundred Years of Solitude,* Guenter Grass's *The Tin Drum,* Saul Bellow's *The Adventures of Augie March,* Louis-Ferdinand Celine's *Death on the Installment Plan,* and V. S. Naipaul's *India: A Wounded Civilization.* And yet, opined Clark Blaise, "It would be a disservice to Salman Rushdie's very original genius to dwell on literary analogues and ancestors. This is a book to accept on its own terms, and an author to welcome into world company."

Like *Midnight's Children,* Rushdie's third book, *Shame,* blends history, myth, politics, and fantasy in a novel at once serious and comic. "A sort of modern fairytale," describes the author, the novel is set in a country that "is not Pakistan, or not quite"; and it explores such issues as the uses and abuses of power and the relationship between shame and violence.

The idea for *Shame,* reported interviewer Ronald Hayman in *Books and Bookmen,* grew out of Rushdie's interest in the Pakistani concept of *sharam.* An Urdu word, *sharam* is apparently untranslatable, conveying a hybrid of sentiments including, according to the author, "embarrassment, discomfiture, decency, modesty, shyness, the sense of having an ordained place in the world." It speaks to a long tradition of honor that permits, and at times even insists upon, seemingly unconscionable acts. In developing this concept, Rushdie told Hayman, he began "seeing shame in places where [he] hadn't originally seen it." He explained: "I'd be thinking about Pakistani politics; and I'd find there were elements there that I could use. I had a feeling of stumbling on something quite central to the codes by which we live." Rushdie elaborated in a *New York Times Book Review* interview with Michael T. Kaufman: "There are two axes—honor and shame, which is the conventional axis, the one along which the culture moves, and this other axis of shame and shamelessness, which deals with morality and the lack of morality. 'Shame' is at the hub of both axes." He told Amanda Smith in *Publishers Weekly,* "Shame, honor, pride—those three [are] somewhere very close to the center of how we organize our experiences."

Shame and shamelessness are the roots of violence, concludes the novelist. He offers as an example the newspaper account of a Pakistani father who "murdered his only child, a daughter, because by making love to a white boy she had brought such dishonour upon her family that only her blood could wash away the stain." Rushdie comments that while he found the story shocking, equally shocking was the fact that he could understand it. "We who have grown up on a diet of honour and shame can still grasp what must seem unthinkable to peoples living in the aftermath of the death of God and of tragedy: that men will sacrifice their dearest love on the implacable altars of pride."

Rushdie develops his theme of shame and violence in a plot so complex and densely populated with characters that it caused Robert Towers to comment that "it is probably easier to play croquet (as in 'Alice in Wonderland') with flamingos as mallets and hedgehogs as balls than to give a coherent plot summary of 'Shame.' " The novel's storyline spans three generations and centers on the lives and families of two men—Raza Hyder, a celebrated general, and Iskander Harappa, a millionaire playboy. Their life-death struggle, played out against the political backdrop of their country, is based on recent Pakistani history. The two characters themselves are based on real-life Pakistani President Zia ul-Haq and former Prime Minister Zulfikar Ali Bhutto, who was deposed by Zia in 1977 and eventually executed.

Sufiya Zinobia, the novel's heroine, is the embodiment of both shame and violence. The daughter of Raza Hyder, a future military dictator who longed for a son, she is, explains Rushdie, the fictional reincarnation of the young girl who died to succor her father's shame. Sufiya's shame is born with her and is evidenced by the newborn baby's crimson blush. Later, as she absorbs the unfelt shame of others, Sufiya's blushes take on such intensity that they boil her bath water and burn the lips of those who kiss her. Eventually, the heat of her shame incubates violence, turning Sufiya into a monster capable of wrenching the heads off of grown men. The incarnation of an entire nation's shame, judged Una Chaudhuri, "Sufiya Zinobia is the utterly convincing and terrifying product of a culture lost in falsehood and corruption."

The novel's marginal hero is Sufiya Zinobia's husband, Omar Khayyam Shakil. Introduced at length at the beginning of the book, he disappears for long periods of time thereafter. "I am a peripheral man," he admits shamelessly; "other people have been the principal actors in my life story." The son of an unknown father and one of three sisters, all claiming to be his mother, Shakil was "scorned by the townspeople for his shameful origins," observed Margo Jefferson in the *Voice Literary Supplement,* and "he developed a defensive shamelessness." Omar Khayyam Shakil feels himself "a fellow who is not even the hero of his own life; a man born and raised in the condition of being out of things."

Rushdie's choice of a "not-quite hero" for a "not-quite country" addresses an issue that Chaudhuri felt to be central to the book's theme. "Peripherality," she postulated, "is the essence of this land's deepest psychology and the novel's true hero: Shame. It is the doom of those who cannot exist except as reflections of other's perceptions, of those who are unable to credit the notion of individual moral autonomy." Shakil's peripherality is demonstrable throughout his life. He suffers from a debilitating fear of being on or near the edge of things. Convinced that he lives at the end of the world,' he is forever afraid of falling off into oblivion. "He grows dizzy whenever he approaches the border of his country," noted *New York Times's* Christopher Lehmann-Haupt. And Jefferson pointed out that even his name, Omar Khayyam, is that of "a poet unloved in his own land, and known largely in translation." Shakil also straddles two cultures and "embraces Western logic by becoming a medical doctor," added Lehmann-Haupt, who concluded that "the tragedy of 'Shame' lies both in the evasion of historical destiny and in embracing that destiny too violently."

Shame met with enthusiastic critical reception and was favorably compared to *Midnight's Children.* An achievement such as *Midnight's Children* "casts a long shadow from which its successor must struggle to escape if it is to find light and space for its own development," remarked Robert Towers. "Aware of this, Mr. Rushdie has moved the setting of his new novel from India proper . . . and has erected a less imposing, though equally fantastic edifice." Nominated for the 1983 Booker McConnell Prize, *Shame* "does for Pakistan what Mr. Rushdie's equally remarkable . . . 'Midnight's Children' did for India," applauded Lehmann-Haupt.

After the publication of *Shame* and the author's next book, *The Jaguar Smile: A Nicaraguan Journey,* a nonfiction account of the political and social conditions that Rushdie observed during his 1986 trip to Nicaragua, the author published a novel that caused such wide-spread furor as to make him a household word even to those unfamiliar with his earlier work. *The Satanic Verses* outraged Muslims around the world who were infuriated by what they believed to be insults to their religion. The book was banned in a dozen countries and caused demonstrations and riots in India, Pakistan, and South Africa, in which a number of people were killed or injured. Charging Rushdie with blasphemy, the late Iranian leader Ayatollah Ruhollah Khomeini proclaimed that the author and his publisher should be executed, and multi-million dollar bounties were offered to anyone who could carry out this decree. Western nations, supporting Rushdie's right to freedom of speech, were incensed by Iran's action and international relations were strained.

The objections to his novel regard sections of the book in which Rushdie writes about a religion that resembles Islam, whose prophet is named Mahound (a derisive epithet for Mohammed). Specifically, offense was taken to scenes in which a scribe named Salman alters the prophet's dictation, thus bringing into question the validity of the Koran, the holy book of the Muslims; and throughout the book many Muslims claim that Rushdie also repeatedly makes irreverent use of sacred names. *Observer* contributor Blake Morrison explained that to many Muslims Rushdie "has transgressed by treating the Holy Word as myth . . . not truth; by treating the Prophet as a fallible human rather than as a deity; and above all by bringing a skeptical, playful, punning intelligence to bear on a religion which, in these fundamentalist times, is not prepared to entertain doubts or jokes about itself."

However, Rushdie, himself a Muslim, argued that *The Satanic Verses* was not meant to be an attack on the Islamic religion, but that it has been interpreted as such by what he called in the *Observer* "the contemporary Thought Police" of Islam who have erected taboos in which one "may not discuss Muhammed as if he were human, with human virtues and weaknesses. One may not discuss the growth of Islam as a historical phenomenon, as an ideology born out of its time." Contrary to this belief, Rushdie said that normally in the Islamic religion Muhammed, unlike Jesus in the Christian religion, "is not granted divine status, but the text is." A number of critics pointed out that the whole controversy could be avoided if Rushdie's detractors took into consideration that all of the objectionable scenes take place in the character Gibreel Farishta's dreams, and are part of his insanity-inspired delusions. "It must be added," remarked *Time* critic Paul Gray, "that few of those outraged by *The Satanic Verses* have ever seen it, much less opened it."

The Satanic Verses is a complex narrative that tells several stories within a story in a manner that has been compared to the popular Arabic tales in *A Thousand and One Nights.* The central story concerns two men who miraculously survive a 29,000 foot fall after a terrorist attack on an Air India flight. One, Gibreel Farishta, a famous Indian actor, acquires a halo, while Saladin Chamcha, whose occupation involves providing voices for radio and television programs, metamorphoses into a satyr-like creature. Gibreel becomes deluded into thinking he is the archangel Gabriel and much of the novel is preoccupied with a number of his dreams which take on the form of "enigmatic and engrossing" parables, according to *Times Literary Supplement* contributor Robert Irwin. Each story, including the controversial tale concerning Mahound, comments on "the theme of religion and its inexorable, unwelcome and dubious demands." The novel concludes with a confrontation between Gibreel and Saladin on a movie set. By this time, the distinction between which character is good and which evil has been blurred beyond distinction. "Computation won't come up with an answer" to this puzzle, commented D. J. Enright in the *New York Review of Books.* "Both of them are both" good and evil. But if the inability to separate the two is the ultimate theme of *The Satanic Verses,* critics like *New York Times Book Review* writer A. G. Mojtabai wondered, "Does it require so much fantasia and fanfare to remind us that good and evil are deeply, subtly intermixed in humankind?"

Enright admitted that the involved plotting of Rushdie's novel is "self-indulgent," but added that "the reader is pleasured as well." In a comparable observation, Michael Wood remarked in *New Republic* that *The Satanic Verses* gives the reader the feeling that the writer is "trying to fill out a Big Book. But the pervading intelligence of the novel is so acute, the distress it explores so thoroughly understood, that the dullness doesn't settle, can't keep away the urgent questions and images that beset it. This is Rushdie's most bewildered book, but it is also his most thoughtful."

The first book that Rushdie published after he was forced into hiding was a fairy tale for children. *Haroun and the Sea of Stories,* begun by the author as a bedtime story for his son, is a fanciful tale with an important underlying message for adults. Rashid is a talented storyteller who receives his gift from the Sea of Stories located on a moon called Kahina. When a water genie's error disconnects Rashid's invisible water faucet, the storyteller loses his abilities. His son Haroun, however, resolves to help his father and journeys to Kahina to meet Walrus, ruler of Gup and controller of the Sea of Stories. Haroun arrives to find the people of Gup at war with Chub and its wicked ruler, Khattam-Shud. Khattam-Shud is poisoning the sea with his factory-ship in an effort to destroy all stories because within each story is a world that he cannot control. After many adventures, Haroun and his allies from Gup destroy Khattam-Shud, saving the Sea of Stories and restoring Rashid's storytelling powers.

Underlying the fanciful plot of *Haroun and the Sea of Stories,* is a clear message against the stifling of artistic freedom by despots like Khomeini, whom several reviewers pointed out to be represented by Khattam- Shud. But the Khomeinis of the world are not the only problem, for Rushdie's book also tells how the Walrus hordes sunlight for the Sea of Stories by stopping the moon's rotation, thus unwittingly giving Khattam- Shud his power because the evil ruler thrives on darkness. "If a Khomeini can come to power," explained Richard Eder in the *Los Angeles Times Book Review,* "it is in part because the West has arrogated sunlight to itself, and left much of the globe bereft of it. Rushdie defies the Ayatolloah's curse. It is he, not his persecutor, who is the true defender of the Third World."

With *Midnight's Children* Rushdie "fulfilled his promise before we ever knew he had any," noted Cathleen Medwick in *Vogue.* And *Shame* "reveals the writer in sure control of his extravagant, mischievous, graceful, polemical imagination." Now, because Rushdie continued to pursue his art with *The Satanic Verses,* which Enright called "a fitting successor to *Midnight's Children* and *Shame,*" he has been forced into hiding, "living a nightmare, looking for words that will restore the rest of his days to him without compromising him as a writer," according to an article written by the editors of *New Republic.* "And we, the lucky ones, have been taught, at this late date in the history of infamy, when we still needed the lesson, that democracy can have its martyrs, too. May Salman Rushdie not become one of them."

For an earlier published interview, see *Contemporary Authors,* Volume 111.

BIOGRAPHICAL/CRITICAL SOURCES:

BOOKS

Contemporary Literary Criticism, Gale, Volume 23, 1983, Volume 31, 1985, Volume 55, *Yearbook 1988,* 1989.

PERIODICALS

Books and Bookmen, September, 1983.

Chicago Tribune, February 17, 1989, September 24, 1990.

Chicago Tribune Book World, March 15, 1981, April 26, 1981, January 22, 1984.

Christian Science Monitor, March 2, 1989.

Commonweal, September 25, 1981, December 4, 1981, November 4, 1983.

Encounter, February, 1982.

Illustrated London News, October, 1988.

India Today, September 15, 1988, October 31, 1988, March 15, 1989.

London Review of Books, September 29, 1988.

Los Angeles Times Book Review, August 26, 1979, December 25, 1983, November 11, 1990.

Mother Jones, April-May, 1990.

New Republic, May 23, 1981, March 6, 1989, March 13, 1989.

New Statesman, May 1, 1981.

New Statesman and Society, September 30, 1988.

Newsweek, April 20, 1981, February 12, 1990.

New Yorker, July 27, 1981, January 9, 1984.

New York Review of Books, September 24, 1981, March 2, 1989.

New York Times, April 23, 1981, November 2, 1983, January 27, 1989, February 13, 1989, February 15, 1989, February 16, 1989, February 17, 1989, February 18, 1989, February 20, 1989, February 21, 1989, February 22, 1989, February 23, 1989, February 24, 1989, February 25, 1989, March 1, 1989.

New York Times Book Review, April 19, 1981, March 28, 1982, November 13, 1983, January 29, 1989, November 11, 1990.

Observer, February 9, 1975, July 19, 1981, September 25, 1988, January 22, 1989, February 19, 1989.

Publishers Weekly, November 11, 1983.

Saturday Review, March, 1981.

Spectator, June 13, 1981.

Time, February 13, 1989, February 27, 1989.

Times Literary Supplement, February 21, 1975, May 15, 1981, September 9, 1983, September 30, 1988, September 28, 1990.

Vogue, November, 1983.

Voice Literary Supplement, November, 1983.

Washington Post, January 18, 1989, February 15, 1989, February 17, 1989, February 18, 1989.

Washington Post Book World, March 15, 1981, November 20, 1983, January 29, 1989.

World Literature Today, winter, 1982.*

S

SABERHAGEN, Fred(erick Thomas) 1930-

PERSONAL: Born May 18, 1930, in Chicago, Ill.; son of Frederick Augustus and Julia (Moynihan) Saberhagen; married Joan Dorothy Spicci, June 29, 1968; children: Jill, Eric, Thomas. *Education:* Attended Wright Junior College, 1956-57.

ADDRESSES: Home—Albuquerque, N.M. *Agent*—Eleanor Wood, Spectrum Literary Agency, 432 Park Ave. S., Suite 1205, New York, N.Y. 10016.

CAREER: Motorola, Inc., Chicago, Ill., electronics technician, 1956-62; free-lance writer, 1962-67; *Encyclopaedia Britannica,* Chicago, assistant editor, 1967-73; free-lance writer, 1973—. *Military service:* U.S. Air Force, electrical technician, 1951-55.

MEMBER: Science Fiction Writers of America.

WRITINGS:

The Golden People, Ace Books, 1964.
The Water of Thought, Ace Books, 1965, reprinted, Pinnacle Books, 1981.
The Book of Saberhagen (short stories), DAW Books, 1975.
Specimens, Popular Library, 1975.
Love Conquers All (first published in *Galaxy* magazine, 1974-75), Ace Books, 1978.
Mask of the Sun, Ace Books, 1978.
The Veils of Azlaroc, Ace Books, 1978.
(Editor) *A Spadeful of Spacetime* (anthology), Ace Books, 1980.
(With Roger Zelazny) *Coils,* Tor Books, 1980.
Octagon, Ace Books, 1981.
Earth Descended (short stories), Tor Books, 1981.
A Century of Progress, Tor Books, 1982.
(Editor with wife, Joan Saberhagen) *Pawn to Infinity* (science fiction anthology), Ace Books, 1982.
The Frankenstein Papers, Baen Books, 1986.
Pyramids, Baen, 1987.
Saberhagen: My Best, Baen, 1987.
After the Fact, Baen, 1988.
The White Bull, Baen, 1988.

"BERSERKER" SERIES

Berserker (short stories), Ballantine, 1967.
Brother Assassin, Ballantine, 1969 (published in England as *Brother Berserker,* Macdonald & Co., 1969).
Berserker's Planet, DAW Books, 1975.

Berserker Man, Ace Books, 1979.
The Ultimate Enemy (short stories), Ace Books, 1979.
The Berserker Wars (short stories), Tor Books, 1981.
The Berserker Throne, Simon & Schuster, 1985.
(With Poul Anderson, Ed Bryant, Stephen R. Donaldson, Larry Niven, Connie Willis, and Zelazny) *Berserker Base,* Tor Books, 1985.
Berserker, Blue Death, Tor Books, 1985.

"EMPIRE OF THE EAST" SERIES

The Broken Lands, Ace Books, 1967.
The Black Mountains, Ace Books, 1970.
Changeling Earth, DAW Books, 1973.
The Empire of the East (contains *The Broken Lands, The Black Mountains,* and *Changeling Earth*), Ace Books, 1979.

"DRACULA" SERIES

The Dracula Tape, Warner Paperback, 1975.
Holmes-Dracula File, Ace Books, 1978.
An Old Friend of the Family, Ace Books, 1979.
Thorn, Ace Books, 1980.
Dominion, Tor Books, 1981.

"SWORDS" TRILOGY

The First Book of Swords, Tor Books, 1984.
The Second Book of Swords, Tor Books, 1985.
The Third Book of Swords, Tor Books, 1985.
The Complete Book of Swords: Comprising the First, Second, and Third Books, Doubleday, 1985.

"LOST SWORDS" SERIES

The First Book of Lost Swords: Woundhealer's Story, T. Doherty, 1986.
The Second Book of Lost Swords: Sightblinder's Story, Tor Books, 1987.
The Third Book of Lost Swords: Stonecutter's Story, St. Martin's, 1988.
The Lost Swords: The First Triad (book club edition; contains *Woundhealer's Story, Sightblinder's Story,* and *Stonecutter's Story*), Doubleday, c. 1988.
The Fourth Book of Lost Swords: Farslayer's Story, St. Martin's, 1989.

385

BIOGRAPHICAL/CRITICAL SOURCES:

BOOKS

Dictionary of Literary Biography, Volume 8: *Twentieth-Century American Science Fiction Writers,* Gale, 1981.

PERIODICALS

Extrapolation, December, 1976.*

*   *   *

SACHAR, Louis 1954-

PERSONAL: Surname is pronounced *Sack*-er; born March 20, 1954; in East Meadow, NY; son of Robert J. (a salesman) and Ruth (a real estate broker; maiden name, Raybin) Sachar; married; children: a daughter. *Education:* University of California, Berkeley, B.A., 1976; University of California, San Francisco, J.D., 1980. *Avocational interests:* Softball, chess, rugby, watching the San Francisco Giants.

ADDRESSES: Home—151 Henry St., San Francisco, CA 94114.

CAREER: Beldoch Industries (manufacturers of women's sweaters), Norwalk, CT, shipping manager, 1976-77; writer, 1977—; attorney, 1981-89.

AWARDS, HONORS: Ethical Culture Book Award, 1979, for *Sideways Stories from Wayside School; There's a Boy in the Girls' Bathroom* has received numerous awards, including Charlie May Simon Book Award, Indian Paintbrush Book Award, Land of Enchantment Children's Book Award, Mark Twain Award, and Milner Award.

WRITINGS:

Sideways Stories from Wayside School, Follett, 1978.
Johnny's in the Basement, Avon, 1981.
Someday Angeline, Avon, 1983.
There's a Boy in the Girls' Bathroom, Knopf, 1987.
Sixth Grade Secrets, Scholastic, 1987.
Wayside School Is Falling Down, Lothrop, 1989.
Sideways Arithmetic from Wayside School, Scholastic, 1989.
The Boy Who Lost His Face, Knopf, 1989.

WORK IN PROGRESS: Monkey Soup, a picture book; *Will Somebody Please Laugh,* a juvenile novel; a play based on *There's a Boy in the Girls' Bathroom.*

*   *   *

SALE, Roger 1932-

PERSONAL: Born August 19, 1932, in New Haven, CT; son of William M., Jr. (a teacher) and Helen (Stearns) Sale; married Dorothy Young, July 16, 1955; children: Timothy, Margaret. *Education:* Swarthmore College, B.A., 1953; Cornell University, M.A., 1954, Ph.D., 1957. *Politics:* Democrat. *Religion:* Presbyterian.

ADDRESSES: Home—3511 East Schubert Pl., Seattle, WA 98122. *Office*—Department of English, University of Washington, Seattle, WA 98105.

CAREER: Amherst College, Amherst, MA, instructor, 1957-60, assistant professor of English, 1960-62; University of Washington, Seattle, 1962—, began as assistant professor, professor of English, 1970—. Cornell University, visiting professor, 1965. Upward Bound Project, former director.

WRITINGS:

(Editor and author of introduction) *Discussions of the Novel,* Heath, 1960.
(Contributor) Paul J. Alpers, editor, *Elizabethan Poetry: Modern Essays in Criticism,* Oxford University Press, 1967.
Reading Spenser: An Introduction to the Faerie Queene, Random House, 1968.
On Writing, Random House, 1970.
Modern Heroism: Essays on D. H. Lawrence, William Empson, and J. R. R. Tolkien, University of California Press, 1973.
Seattle, Past and Present, University of Washington Press, 1976.
Fairy Tales and After: From Snow White to E. B. White, Harvard University Press, 1978.
On Not Being Good Enough: Writings of a Working Critic, Oxford University Press, 1979.
Literary Inheritance, University of Massachusetts Press, 1984.
Closer to Home: Writers and Places in England, 1780-1830, Harvard University Press, 1986.

Contributor of articles and reviews to periodicals, including *New York Review of Books, New York Times Book Review, Argus, Hudson Review, New Republic, Antioch Review,* and *Seattle Post Intelligencer.*

BIOGRAPHICAL/CRITICAL SOURCES:

PERIODICALS

Chicago Tribune, October 23, 1978.
Christian Science Monitor, February 12, 1979.
Nation, November 11, 1978.
New York Review of Books, January 24, 1974; March 8, 1979; November 8, 1979.
New York Times, August 23, 1979.
New York Times Book Review, July 29, 1973; November 19, 1978; August 26, 1979; October 7, 1979.
Saturday Review, December, 1978.
Times Literary Supplement, July 27, 1973; December 1, 1978; January 11, 1980; April 3, 1987.
Village Voice, September 10, 1979.
Washington Post Book World, October 8, 1978; September 30, 1979.

*   *   *

SALISBURY, John
See CAUTE, David

*   *   *

SANDERS, Lawrence 1920-
(Mark Upton)

PERSONAL: Born 1920 in Brooklyn, NY. *Education:* Wabash College, B.A., 1940.

ADDRESSES: Home—Pompano Beach, FL. *Agent*—c/o Putnam Publishing Group, 200 Madison Ave., New York, NY 10016.

CAREER: Macy's (department store), New York City, staff member, 1940-43; worked for various magazines as an editor and as a writer of war stories, men's adventure stories, and detective stories; feature editor for *Mechanix Illustrated,* New York City; editor for *Science and Mechanics,* New York City; Magnum-Royal Publications, New York City, free-lance writer for men's magazines, 1967-68; novelist, 1969—. *Military service:* U.S. Marine Corps, 1943-46; became sergeant.

AWARDS, HONORS: Edgar Award for best first mystery novel, Mystery Writers of America, 1970, for *The Anderson Tapes.*

WRITINGS:

(Editor) *Thus Be Loved: A Book for Lovers,* Arco, 1966.
(With Richard Carol) *Handbook of Creative Crafts* (nonfiction), Pyramid Books, 1968.
(Under pseudonym Mark Upton) *Dark Summer,* Coward, Mc-Cann, 1979.

NOVELS

The Anderson Tapes, Putnam, 1970.
The Pleasures of Helen, Putnam, 1971.
Love Songs, Putnam, 1972.
The First Deadly Sin, Putnam, 1973.
The Tomorrow File, Putnam, 1975.
The Tangent Objective, Putnam, 1976.
The Marlow Chronicles, Putnam, 1977.
The Second Deadly Sin, Putnam, 1977.
The Tangent Factor, Putnam, 1978.
The Sixth Commandment, Putnam, 1978.
The Tenth Commandment, Putnam, 1980.
The Third Deadly Sin, Putnam, 1981.
The Case of Lucy Bending, Putnam, 1982.
The Seduction of Peter S., Putnam, 1983.
The Passion of Molly T., Putnam, 1984.
The Fourth Deadly Sin, Putnam, 1985.
The Loves of Harry Dancer, Berkley Publishing, 1986.
The Eighth Commandment, Putnam, 1986.
Tales of the Wolf, Avon, 1986.
The Dream Lover, Berkley Publishing, 1987.
The Timothy Files, Putnam, 1987.
Caper, Berkley Publishing, 1987.
Timothy's Game, Putnam, 1988.
Capital Crimes, Putnam, 1989.
Stolen Blessings, Berkley Publishing, 1989.
Sullivan's Sting, Putnam, 1990.

Author of books under pseudonyms and of several "purse books" for Dell. Contributor of more than one hundred stories and articles to various publications.

MEDIA ADAPTATIONS: Films based on Sanders's books include "The Anderson Tapes," Columbia Pictures, 1971, and "The First Deadly Sin," Filmways, 1980. *Stolen Blessings* was adapted to audio cassettes, Simon & Schuster, 1990.

SIDELIGHTS: "I learned my trade as a novelist," Sanders has said, "by working as an editor of pulp magazines" and writing "gag lines for cheesecake magazines." After editing various men's magazines, *Mechanix Illustrated,* and *Science and Mechanics,* he "got to the point where a lot of editors get—I said to myself that I could write the stuff better myself. And so I wrote *The Anderson Tapes*—my first novel—at age fifty."

The Anderson Tapes is the story of a Mafia-backed effort to rob an entire luxury apartment building. Foreshadowing the role electronics were to play in the political scandal known as Watergate during the early 1970s, this plot is thwarted when several governmental agencies wiretap "everything from a candy-store pay phone to Central Park itself." Christopher Lehmann-Haupt speculated that those "fashionably paranoiac and willing to believe that the whole world is plugged into a tape recorder" would "have a zippy time" with this novel. *The Anderson Tapes* was a best seller upon publication and was made into a Columbia motion picture soon thereafter.

Since becoming a full-time novelist, Sanders has settled down from the post-*Anderson Tape* days when he was "shoveling down martinis at night and waking up on Tums." "I've been working my tail off and enjoying it," he says. "I usually write about five pages a night, and it adds up." In one span Sanders produced three novels within a year, including *The Second Deadly Sin* and a story of one man's struggle to unite Africa, *The Tangent Factor.*

The Tangent Factor "depicts how one man imposes his will on whole nations, and the basic thesis is that it is not done merely through strength of character but through treachery, manipulation and carefully calculated violence," wrote Joseph McLellan. Despite objecting to its "unpleasant aftertaste," critic Thomas Lask admitted the "narrative is lean, fat free and highly readable. . . . It's hard not to admire [Sanders's] skill."

Sanders now lives in Florida and continues to share his life with his "constant and beloved" companion of thirty years, Fleurette Ballou. Though he has expressed a desire to "try to slow down to only two books a year," he readily admits: "I'm obsessed with writing. I have no hobbies. I don't fish. I'm not interested in sports. I don't even own a car. When I'm writing, my fantasies become more important than my personal life. I'm a Walter Mitty—living out my years through my characters."

BIOGRAPHICAL/CRITICAL SOURCES:

BOOKS

Bestsellers 89, Issue 4, Gale, 1989.
Contemporary Literary Criticism, Volume 41, Gale, 1987.

PERIODICALS

Chicago Tribune Book World, September 19, 1982.
Globe and Mail (Toronto), January 12, 1985, August 10, 1985, June 7, 1986, July 4, 1987, June 10, 1989.
Los Angeles Times, November 5, 1982.
Los Angeles Times Book Review, October 12, 1980, November 5, 1982, July 31, 1983, October 28, 1984, November 24, 1985, July 10, 1988, May 14, 1989, July 1, 1990.
New York Times, February 20, 1970, October 20, 1973, August 25, 1977, March 24, 1978, May 5, 1988.
New York Times Book Review, August 21, 1977, October 9, 1977, September 28, 1980, October 5, 1980, July 26, 1981, September 6, 1981, August 22, 1982, July 24, 1983, September 30, 1984, July 28, 1985, August 10, 1986, July 31, 1988, August 13, 1989.
People, November 28, 1977, September 16, 1985, July 13, 1987.
Publishers Weekly, August 2, 1976, November 3, 1989, August 3, 1990.
Time, April 27, 1970, August 29, 1977.
Tribune Books (Chicago), July 10, 1988, January 21, 1990.
Washington Post, May 4, 1978, August 6, 1981, September 2, 1984.
Washington Post Book World, August 18, 1985.*

*   *   *

SANTMYER, Helen Hooven 1895-1986

PERSONAL: Born November 25, 1895, in Cincinnati, Ohio; died of complications brought on by chronic emphysema, February 21, 1986, in Xenia, Ohio; daughter of Joseph Wright (a former medical student, traveling salesman for a drug company, deputy county auditor for Greene County, Ohio, and manager of a rope manufacturing company), and Bertha (a Cincinnati art school graduate; maiden name, Hooven) Santmyer. *Education:*

Wellesley College, B.A., 1918; Oxford University, B.Litt., 1927. *Politics:* Republican. *Religion:* Presbyterian.

ADDRESSES: Home—Hospitality Home East, 1301 Monroe Dr., Xenia, Ohio 45385.

CAREER: Charles Scribner's Sons, New York, N.Y., secretary to editor of *Scribner's* magazine, 1919-21; Xenia High School, Xenia, Ohio, teacher of English, 1921-22; Wellesley College, Wellesley, Mass., affiliated with department of English, 1922-24; Cedarville College, Cedarville, Ohio, dean of women and chairman of department of English, 1936-53; Dayton and Montgomery County Public Library, Dayton, Ohio, assistant in reference department, 1953-60.

AWARDS, HONORS: Florence Roberts Hood Memorial Award, Ohioana Library Association, 1964, for *Ohio Town;* Ohioana Book Award in Fiction, 1983, for . . . *And Ladies of the Club;* named to Women's Hall of Fame of Greene County, Ohio, and State of Ohio, 1984; honorary doctor of humanities, Wright State University, 1984; Ohio Governor's Award, 1985.

WRITINGS:

Herbs and Apples (novel), Houghton, 1925, reprinted, Harper, 1985.
The Fierce Dispute (novel), Houghton, 1929, reprinted, St. Martin's, 1987.
Ohio Town: A Portrait of Xenia (essays; selections originally published in *Antioch Review,* 1956 and 1961), Ohio State University Press, 1963, reprinted, Harper, 1984.
. . . *And Ladies of the Club* (novel; Book-of-the-Month Club main selection), Ohio State University Press, 1982, Putnam, 1984.
Farewell, Summer (novel), Harper, 1988.

Also author of an unpublished mystery novel, *The Hall with Eight Doors.* Contributor of essays, poetry, and stories to *Atlantic, Scribner's Magazine, Midland,* and *Antioch Review.* Helen Hooven Santmyer's papers and letters are in the collection of the Ohio State University Library.

SIDELIGHTS: Helen Hooven Santmyer is best known as the author of the 1984 bestseller . . . *And Ladies of the Club,* a mammoth novel telling the story of four generations of ordinary life in a rural Ohio town. Many of her other novels also depict the lives of people living in small-town America in the years between the end of the Civil War and the Great Depression, evoking a time when life was slower-paced and death was common among young people as well as the elderly. Celebrated for their atmosphere and historical authenticity as well as their vivid characterization, these stories are drawn largely from her own experiences, and Xenia, the Ohio town where she grew up, often provides the basis for their settings.

Helen Santmyer first came to Xenia when her father settled his family in his in-laws' home—built not long before the Civil War—in 1901. Her early years were markedly quiet and contented. "A happy childhood is valuable," she once said, "because you acquire a deep-seated habit of being happy." She felt free to climb trees, to throw seedpods around, and generally to entertain herself. Maple and tulip trees stood in the front yard; from a branch over the sidewalk, she wrote, it "was quite easy to throw down a key tied to a fine thread, or a few sycamore balls onto the Theologues heading to class at the Seminary a block away." Helen played baseball with a family of eight boys named Smith, and was skillful enough to hold her place there for several years, until the ninth Smith could swing a bat.

When Helen entered the grade school in Xenia she discovered reading, possibly the greatest joy of her life. The realization came, she later wrote, "with all the suddenness of a thunderclap when there has been no lightning." She was an omnivorous reader, taking in everything she could find, both in her family's extensive collection and in the public library, including many of her father's medical texts. Helen's parents never forbade her to read books like *Tom Sawyer* and *Huckleberry Finn,* which many parents in Xenia considered unsuitable for their children. She was especially fond of Louisa May Alcott's *Little Women* and told her mother that when she grew up she wanted to be just like Miss Alcott and write wonderful stories of her own. Her mother sympathized completely; she fixed up a room on the second floor of the house for her daughter to work in, with bookshelves all along two walls, and later added an old dining table for Helen to use as a writing desk.

Helen's determination to write dominated her high school years. She decided that in order to pursue her career she had to attend college, a thing few women did at that time. After her graduation in 1913, she applied to Wellesley, a women's college in Massachusetts, partly because some of her Xenia friends had gone there, but also because it had a very strong English department. Unfortunately, before she left for college she came down with a severe case of typhoid fever—contracted from the Xenia ice supply, which was skimmed from the surface of local ponds. The local doctor recommended a year of rest at home and Helen did not enter Wellesley until 1914. The university faculty helped nurture her gift for writing; they taught Helen how to appreciate poetry as well as prose and disciplined her ability as a novelist and essayist. To hone her skills further, Helen joined an informal group of writers called the Scribblers, who met at odd intervals to read and criticize each other's work. In 1918 she completed her bachelor's degree in English literature and composition and graduated at the top of her class.

After Helen left Wellesley, she went to New York City to work. Her first job after graduation was with suffragettes who were working to get women's votes. The work did not appeal to her: "They considered a day lost when they hadn't succeeded in getting into jail." Helen's own approach was to avoid jail at all costs, and she gave up campaigning for women's rights within a few months. Instead she tried to find work with a well established book publisher that published literary works like those of John Galsworthy and Sinclair Lewis, but settled for a position as secretary to an editor of *Scribner's* magazine. The job did expose her to contemporary literary figures, including Ernest Hemingway, Sinclair Lewis, and F. Scott Fitzgerald, but she was not always impressed with them and their work. Fitzgerald, she felt, was a spoiled Princeton boy who drank too much, and the editors "should not have had to put up with his shenanigans." Lewis's *Main Street* she disliked intensely. Remembering her own happy childhood, she could not help feeling his book presented a biased picture of small-town American life.

Helen returned to Xenia in 1921 because her mother was ill and she felt that she was needed at home. Also, she wanted to enter school again—this time Oxford University in England. As her mother's health improved, her father made a bargain with her: if she would first teach in the English department at Xenia high school, he would provide the money for her study in England. Helen joined the high school staff that year, but stayed there only one year before going back to Wellesley as an assistant in the literature department until her departure for England in 1924. Although a bout of hepatitis slowed her progress, she graduated from Oxford in 1927 with a thesis on minor novels of the eighteenth century. In 1925 she published her first book—*Herbs and*

Apples, a semi-autobiographical novel—the story of a young Ohio girl whose plans to go to New York and become a writer are thrown into disarray by World War I.

After graduation Helen returned to Xenia again and began work on another novel. While borrowing books from the library she made the acquaintance of Mildred Sandoe, known locally as Miss Johnny Appleseed for her vigorous campaigning on behalf of Ohio libraries, who was then developing the Xenia city library into a county-wide system. Helen knew few people there; her friends from her high school days had all either married or moved away, and, since she was invariably the last person out of the building and usually was struggling with an armload of books, Mildred offered her rides home at the end of the day. It was the beginning of a long and fruitful friendship that lasted nearly sixty years.

Helen continued her literary activities by joining the Xenia Woman's Club, a rather exclusive organization, limited to thirty-five members, which was probably the inspiration for the Waynesboro women's club featured in . . . *And Ladies of the Club.* She quickly impressed her associates with her research ability and versatility as well as her literary credentials. In 1928 she completed her second book, *The Fierce Dispute,* the story of a young girl whose mother and grandmother were feuding over her future career. The characters were entirely her own creation, but the settings were Xenian; the large house mentioned in the novel was based on an actual building on the northernmost edge of town. It was surrounded by several acres of meadow and marshland, with a small stream flowing into a pond in the yard. Three generations of women—a grandmother, her daughter and her granddaughter—lived there, with only a houseman to take care of them, the only connection between the residents and the Xenia townspeople.

Helen left Xenia again in the early 1930s to accompany her family to California, where her father had found work. She spent most of her time there writing and reading about Ohio, the Civil War, and life in America between 1860 and 1932. The writing mostly consisted of essays—which later formed the basis for *Ohio Town*—about her home town's library, courthouse, railroad station, and all the other places that, she felt sure, were common to midwestern towns. She returned to Ohio to take a post at Cedarville College, a small Presbyterian college near Xenia with a scanty budget but an excellent faculty. Helen took the position of dean of women and head of the English department, although there were times when she found herself teaching Latin and Greek as well as her own classes.

Although Helen's English class attracted many students, her activities were not limited to the school year. In the summers she organized writing clubs among her niece's ten-year-old friends, and read poetry to them. However, her projects were curtailed in the late 1930s by a severe illness. Helen suffered from the disease for more than five years. At times she was so ill that she could not walk the seven or so blocks from her apartment to the campus, and had to hold class in her living room. Eventually her doctor sent her to the Ohio State University, where her illness was diagnosed as undulant fever. She was eventually cured, but the long years of illness had damaged her digestive tract and forced her to remain on a restricted diet for the rest of her life.

Helen left Cedarville in 1953, due to disagreements with the new fundamentalist proprietors of the university. She soon obtained a position as assistant reference librarian in the library of Dayton and Montgomery County, specializing in literature, local history and biography. Helen stayed there until her retirement in 1959, when she returned to Xenia to live. Her parents had died in 1957,

so Helen asked Mildred Sandoe, her old friend from her Xenia days, to live with her in the old house on West Third Street. They took their vacations together: to Canada and the Northeast for fishing; to the Southwest to visit Helen's brother Philip; and to Pennsylvania and the Midwest for Amish antiques and stories. Helen and Mildred kept up these trips for a good many years, until Helen's health made it too uncomfortable for her to travel. She had suffered a fall while working in Dayton, breaking two vertebrae and injuring her spinal cord. An arthritic knot formed at the base of her spine, and this, combined with emphysema from her constant smoking that made it hard for her to breathe, put an end to their journeys. Eventually, Helen's health deteriorated so much that she could not sit in a car for any length of time without considerable pain, making trips outside of Xenia and the surrounding area impractical.

Helen continued to write after her retirement. She set aside each afternoon, writing left-handed in longhand on lined white paper at her desk in the bedroom downstairs, or in bed when she was not feeling well. Mildred urged her to finish the essays she had begun in California, adding some new material, and to send them off to a publisher. Helen chose Weldon Kefauver of the Ohio State University Press, and mailed the manuscript of *Ohio Town* to him in 1963. She received an enthusiastic response, and the book went to press that year. *Ohio Town* received good reviews from local papers and historical journals; although it was "a book of remembrance rather than a retelling of history," as a reviewer for the *Xenia Daily Gazette* described it, the volume effectively evoked life in Xenia around the turn of the century. It remained relatively unknown, however, probably because its publication coincided with a large newspaper strike in New York. Those who heard about the book thought highly of it, and it won the Florence Roberts Head Award for excellence in literature from the Ohioana Library in 1964. Although Helen was in her mid-sixties at the time, she accepted her award personally, saying, "I am so pleased. I am so *very* pleased."

Sometime between 1964 and 1970, Helen began work on the novel she had always wanted to write, about American life in the small towns of the midwest between 1865 and 1932. She had been collecting bits and pieces of information about it since the family discussions about current events around the dining table in her childhood, but it was not until the mid-1960s that she began the actual task of composition. Helen generally set aside two hours in the late morning and another two in the late afternoon to work on her novel; her health remained uncertain, and she did not complete the manuscript until 1975.

She sent the work to Dr. Kefauver in eleven boxes filled to the brim with typewritten manuscript. Kefauver's response was favorable; even though the Ohio State University Press did not publish much fiction, he felt that her book was a good risk, worth publishing for its historical merit as well as its literary quality. However, he added, it would have to be shortened by six or seven hundred pages. Helen's eyesight was failing her by that time, so she enlisted Mildred's assistance in cutting the novel down to two-thirds its original size. It took them nearly eighteen months to prepare a shortened version, and even then some parts of the book were never touched. They returned the manuscript to Dr. Kefauver, and, in due course, received two enormous red-bound volumes "looking more like reference books than novels." . . . *And Ladies of the Club* had arrived.

The Ohio State University Press was not sure that the novel would sell, and initially their apprehensions seemed justified; they printed 1500 copies in 1982, of which only about 200 sold, mostly to libraries. The first edition of *Ladies* proved unwieldy in several ways; the completed volume weighed over four pounds, had over 1300 pages, and cost $35.00. It made a fearsome weapon, however; one reader later wrote Helen that she had been trapped in her kitchen by a large snake, and had dropped the book on its head. "It did the work," she wrote Helen. "I read every golden word of it even though I'll admit some of the pages were pretty gory."

While some reviewers found the myriad details in . . . *And Ladies of the Club* burdensome and the prejudices and moral rigidity displayed by its characters untenable, others were enchanted by the novel's matter-of-fact, day-by-day approach. Susan Toepfer, writing in the *New York Daily News,* declares that "Santmyer's subjects are not the overblown romantics of a *Gone with the Wind,* but simple, 'decent' midwestern folk—with all the narrow-mindedness that 'decent' implies." A. C. Greene noted on the "MacNeil/Lehrer News Hour" that *Ladies* tells "the lives that most of us lead. It's not full of sudden, strange unexpected episodes, but it's well written and it relates the human experience in a pattern that, even though we're talking about 120 and some odd years ago, we can still relate to it."

Critics also commented on Helen's approach to history. Leola Floren remarked in the *Detroit News,* "Miss Santmyer clearly understands that history is more than the sterile procession of dates and events that we learned in school. . . . What she offers in this very fine story is not objectivity, or an omniscient view of the world scene, but everyday life through the eyes of people who crawled out from under the shadow of civil war, lost children to rheumatic fever and tuberculosis, watched sons march off to the Great War, and endured a series of depressions even before the Big One." Ruth Clements wrote in the Toronto *Globe and Mail* that the author "is moving us through time . . . while simultaneously asking us to step back and watch time move. It is as though time were an object that Santmyer holds the way a teacher displays a globe to a class."

Ladies did not attract much public attention until late in 1983. Mrs. Grace Sindell of Shaker Heights, a suburb of Cleveland, Ohio, overheard a library patron talking about the book; the patron said *Ladies* was the best novel she had ever read. Mrs. Sindell checked the book out, read it, and recommended it to her son Gerald, a Hollywood producer. He contacted a friend at the William Morris agency, who turned it over to the publisher G. P. Putnam's Sons, and Helen Santmyer, the small woman with the large book, shot into the public eye, an overnight phenomenon. The Putnam edition stayed on the *New York Times* bestseller list for 37 consecutive weeks and held the number-one position for seven. The Book-of-the-Month Club made *Ladies* its main selection and sold more than 162,000 copies, and a paperback edition sold more than a million copies. Helen's response was typical: "Isn't that nice. I just can't believe it." Newspeople flocked to Xenia, including reporters from all the major television news programs, from papers around the country, and from major magazines such as *Life, People, Newsweek* and *Time.*

The newspeople found, when they arrived, a lady of nearly 90 years, confined to a sheepskin-lined wheelchair. Helen was suffering from severe arthritis and emphysema, had totally lost the vision in one eye and had cataracts in the other, and weighed only 90 pounds due to her digestive trouble. Her mental condition was good, however, and her disposition was excellent; her fellow patients described her as "the little lady with the sweet smile who always waves when she goes past the door." She remained unimpressed by all the media hype about *Ladies;* "I think it's the kind of book most people are not interested in," she once said. "Part of the interest is because I'm an old lady."

Trudy Krisher, writing in the Dayton *Journal Herald,* declared, "Helen taught us all something about success. That it is not measured by contracts or the number of pictures in *Life* magazine. It comes from the pleasure of doing what you love in the best way that you can." "Helen Santmyer has joined the club," Krisher concluded. "In my opinion, the company is enriched by her presence."

MEDIA ADAPTATIONS: . . . And Ladies of the Club has been optioned as a television miniseries.

AVOCATIONAL INTERESTS: Travel (especially Civil War battlefields), gardening, reading (especially mysteries), antique collecting.

BIOGRAPHICAL/CRITICAL SOURCES:

BOOKS

Contemporary Literary Criticism, Volume 33, Gale, 1985.
Dictionary of Literary Biography Yearbook: 1984, Gale, 1985.

PERIODICALS

Blade (Toledo), May 29, 1988.
Chicago Tribune, June 10, 1984.
Chicago Tribune Book World, June 10, 1984, September 9, 1984.
Christian Science Monitor, January 27, 1984.
Columbus Dispatch, August 26, 1984, December 23, 1987.
Dayton Daily News, August 4, 1963.
Detroit Free Press, January 13, 1984.
Detroit News, June 10, 1984.
Globe and Mail (Toronto), August 4, 1984.
Los Angeles Times Book Review, June 10, 1984.
Mid-Cities Daily News (Hurst, Tex.), December 5, 1984.
Newsweek, June 18, 1984.
New York Daily News, June 17, 1984.
New Yorker, July 9, 1984.
New York Times, January 12, 1984, June 1, 1984, June 4, 1984.
New York Times Book Review, June 24, 1984, September 16, 1984.
People, July 16, 1984.
Nation, July 21, 1984.
Time, July 9, 1984.
Washington Post Book World, January 22, 1984, September 2, 1984.
Wellesley Alumnae Magazine, January, 1963.
Xenia Daily Gazette, January 24, 1963, February 18, 1963, June 5, 1975.

OTHER

"MacNeil/Lehrer News Hour," Public Broadcasting Service (PBS-TV), July 5, 1984.

OBITUARIES:

PERIODICALS

AB Bookman's Weekly, March 24, 1986.
Chicago Tribune, February 23, 1986.
Circleville Herald (Circleville, Ohio), February 22, 1986.
Journal Herald (Dayton), March 1, 1986.
New York Times, February 22, 1986.
Publishers Weekly, March 7, 1986.
Sun-Times (Chicago), February 22, 1986.

Xenia Daily Gazette, February 22, 1986.

[Sketch reviewed by Mildred Sandoe, Miss Santmyer's companion, and by Louise A. Muller, Miss Santmyer's personal secretary]

—*Sketch by Kenneth R. Shepherd*

* * *

SCOTT, Paul (Mark) 1920-1978

PERSONAL: Born March 25, 1920, in Palmers Green, England; died March 1, 1978, in London, England; married Nancy Edith Avery, 1941; children: Carol, Sally. *Education:* Attended public schools in England.

ADDRESSES: Agent—David Higham Associates, 5-8 Lower John St., Golden Sq., London W1R 4HA, England.

CAREER: Novelist. Company secretary, Falcon Press and Grey Walls Press, both London, England, 1946-50; director of Pearn Pollinger and Higham, now David Higham Associates (literary agents), London, 1950-60; free-lance writer, 1960-78. British Council lecturer, India, 1972; visiting lecturer, University of Tulsa, Oklahoma, 1976-77. *Military service:* British Army, served in India, 1940-43; served in Indian Army, Malaya, 1943-46.

MEMBER: Royal Society of Literature (fellow).

AWARDS, HONORS: Eyre & Spottiswoode literary fellowship, 1951; Arts Council grant, 1969; Yorkshire Post book of the year award for finest fiction, 1971, for *The Towers of Silence;* Booker Prize, 1977.

WRITINGS:

NOVELS

Johnnie Sahib, Eyre & Spottiswoode, 1952.
Six Days in Marapore, Morrow, 1953 (published in England as *The Alien Sky,* Eyre & Spottiswoode, 1953, reprinted, Panther, 1974).
A Male Child, Eyre & Spottiswoode, 1956, Dutton, 1957, reprinted, Carroll & Graf, 1987.
The Mark of the Warrior, Morrow, 1958.
The Love Pavilion, Morrow, 1960, reprinted, Carroll & Graf, 1985 (published in England as *The Chinese Love Pavilion,* Eyre & Spottiswoode, 1960).
The Birds of Paradise, Morrow, 1962, reprinted, Carroll & Graf, 1986.
The Bender, Morrow, 1963, reprinted, Carroll & Graf, 1986 (published in England as *The Bender: Pictures From an Exhibition of Middle Class Portraits,* Secker & Warburg, Morrow, 1966).
The Corrida of San Feliu, Morrow, 1964.
The Jewel in the Crown (first novel in tetralogy; also see below), Heinemann, 1966.
The Day of the Scorpion (second novel in tetralogy; also see below), Morrow, 1968.
The Towers of Silence (third novel in tetralogy; also see below), Heinemann, 1971, Morrow, 1972.
A Division of the Spoils (fourth novel in tetralogy; also see below), Morrow, 1975.
The Raj Quartet (tetralogy; includes *The Jewel in the Crown, The Day of the Scorpion, The Towers of Silence,* and *A Division of Spoils*), Morrow, 1976. *Staying On,* Morrow, 1977.

OTHER

I Gerontius (verse), Favil Press, 1941.

(Contributor) H. F. Rubinstein, *Four Jewish Plays* (includes his play "Pillars of Salt"), Gollancz, 1948.
Contributor) *Essays by Divers Hands,* Oxford University Press, 1970.
After the Funeral (short story), Whittington Press, 1979.
The Making of "The Jewel in the Crown," St. Martin's Press, 1983.
My Appointment With the Muse, edited by Shelley C. Reece, Heinemann, 1986.
On Writing and the Novel, edited by Reece, Morrow, 1987.

Author of the radio plays "Lines of Communication," 1951, "The Alien Sky" (adapted from his novel), 1954, and "Sahibs and Memsahibs," 1958. Author of the televion play "The Mark of the Warrior" (adapted from his novel), 1959. Also contributor of articles to British newspapers and periodicals, including *Country Life* and the London *Times.*

SIDELIGHTS: Paul Scott was perhaps best known as the chronicler of the decline of the British occupation of India. His most famous works are those of *The Raj Quartet.* They center on a single dramatic event, the rape of an English woman by several Indians, but proceed to describe life for both the British and the Indian under the British raj, or rule. This seemed to be characteristic of Scott's novels; or "as more than one reviewer pointed out he dealt less with events than with the situation created by these events."

Scott's novels have consistently drawn positive reviews. A *Punch* reviewer once described Scott as "a professional novelist of the expansive, humane, nineteenth-century type, though with mid-twentieth- century sensibilities. . . . Mr. Scott has two great qualities that are rarely found together, excitement with material and control. His work is packed, not crammed."

A *Times Literary Supplement* critic reviewing *The Day of the Scorpion* wrote: "The characters, while they successfully represent aspirations and conflicts which are bigger than themselves, never cease to be individuals. The conversations have subtlety and a quality of plenteousness which is none the less welcome for being out of fashion. Above all, the reader is impressed, and given confidence, by the feeling which Mr. Scott can generate of a writer who has thoroughly mastered his material, and who can, because of this, work through a maze of fascinating detail without for a moment losing sight of distant, and considerable objectives." A *Listener* critic agreed: "Paul Scott's is one of those rare books that express not only themselves but something of the essence of their genre. Prose fiction does many things, but nothing more characteristic than the intricate relating of private lives to public issues. When this is done with the subtely, wisdom and grace of *The Day of the Scorpion,* the triumph is more than a personal one for the author. It vindicates a whole tradition of literary endeavour."

John Leonard of the *New York Times Book Review* commented that the strength of Scott's last novel, *Staying On,* lay in "its portrayal of hitherto unsuspected dignity, of depths of feeling hiding in the ordinary." In contrast, Malcolm Muggeridge noted that he had difficulty in trying "to work up sympathy with any of the characters to care about what happened to them."

The last novel in *The Raj Quartet* led Webster Schott to write: "Sometimes [Scott] seemed to be writing mostly history. Other times a study of racist psychology. And now and then an outrageously long love letter to a land and people unable to decide whether they liked or loathed what fate had dealt them."

Scott once said that he preferred "to write about people in relation to their work, which strikes me as a subject no less important than their private lives." Although during his years in the army he wrote poetry and plays, nearly all of his published works are novels; he viewed the novel as the ultimate form of literature. "He was no miniaturist. He required a broad canvas, he never wrote a short story, for example," commented Thomas Lask. In addition, Jean G. Zorn observed: "The world of Scott's Indian novels is so extraordinarily vivid in part because it is constructed out of such accuracies of detail as the proper name or the precise sum that a retired colonel's widow could expect to receive as a pension. Scott's vision is both precise and painterly."

Summing up Scott's career as a novelist, Margaret B. Lewis concluded in *Contemporary Novelists:* "Critical acclaim came late to Paul Scott and only in the last years of his life did a wide readership develop for his work. Although the slow pace of his novels with their gradual accumulation of detail may be very much against the modern trend to short, elliptical novels, the reader finds in the very complexities of his later works an invitation to share in the complexities of life itself, and to emerge with an extended vision as a result." Scott's novels have been translated into Dutch, German, Polish, Swedish, Spanish, French, and Finnish.

MEDIA ADAPTATIONS: J. Mitchell adapted *Staying On* for television in 1981.

BIOGRAPHICAL/CRITICAL SOURCES:

BOOKS

Bhaskara Rao, K., *Paul Scott,* Twayne, 1980.
Contemporary Literary Criticism, Volume 9, Gale, 1978.
Contemporary Novelists, St. Martin's Press, 1986.
Dictionary of Literary Biography, Volume 14, *British Novelists since 1960,* Gale, 1983.
Swinden, Patrick, *Paul Scott: Images of India,* Macmillan, 1980.

PERIODICALS

Best Sellers, March 1, 1969.
Books and Bookmen, November, 1968.
Listener, September 5, 1968.
Newsweek, February 11, 1985.
New York Times Book Review, November 10, 1968, July 26, 1977, August 21, 1977, March 15, 1987.
Observer Review, September 1, 1968.
Punch, September 4, 1968.
Times Literary Supplement, September 12, 1968, February 27, 1987.
Washington Post Book World, January 11, 1987.

OBITUARIES:

PERIODICALS

New York Times, March 3, 1978.*

* * *

SCULL, Andrew 1947-

PERSONAL: Born May 2, 1947, in Edinburgh, Scotland; came to the United States, 1969; son of Allan Edward (a civil engineer) and Marjorie (a college teacher; maiden name, Corrigan) Scull; married Nancy Principi (a teacher), August 16, 1970; children: Anna Theresa, Andrew Edward, Alexander. *Education:* Balliol College, Oxford, B.A. (with first class honors), 1969; Princeton University, M.A., 1971, Ph.D., 1974.

ADDRESSES: Office—Department of Sociology, University of California at San Diego, La Jolla, CA 92037. *Agent*—Peters, Fraser, & Dunlop, 503/4 The Chambers, Chelsea Harbour, London SW10 0XI, England.

CAREER: University of Pennsylvania, Philadelphia, lecturer, 1973-74, assistant professor of sociology, 1974-78; University of California at San Diego, La Jolla, associate professor, 1978-82, professor of sociology, 1982—, chairman of department, 1985-89, professor of science studies, 1988—. Visiting fellow at University of London, 1977, Princeton University, 1978-79, and Wellcome Institute for the History of Medicine, 1981-82; Hannah Lecturer in the History of Medicine, 1983; Squibb Lecturer in the History of Psychiatry, University of London, 1986.

MEMBER: Phi Beta Kappa (honorary member).

AWARDS, HONORS: American Council of Learned Societies fellow, 1976-77; Shelby Cullom Davis Center for Historical Studies fellow, 1978-79; Guggenheim fellow, 1981-82; University of California President's Research Fellowship in the Humanities, 1989-90.

WRITINGS:

Decarceration: Community Treatment and the Deviant; a Radical View, Prentice-Hall, 1977, 2nd edition, Polity Press, 1984.
Museums of Madness: The Social Organization of Insanity in Nineteenth-Century England, Allen Lane, 1979.
(Editor) *Madhouses, Mad-doctors and Madmen: The Social History of Psychiatry in the Victorian Era,* University of Pennsylvania Press, 1981.
(With Steven Lukes) *Durkheim and the Law,* Martin Robertson, 1983.
(With Stanley Cohen) *Social Control and the State: Historical and Comparative Essays,* Blackwell Scientific Publications, 1983.
Social Order/Mental Disorder: Anglo-American Psychiatry in Historical Perspective, University of California Press, 1989.
The Asylum as Utopia: W. A. F. Browne and the Mid-Nineteenth Century Consolidation of Psychiatry, Routledge, 1990.

Co-editor, "Research in Law, Deviance, and Social Control" series, JAI Press, 1984—. Contributor to scholarly texts, including *Theoretical Perspectives on Deviance,* 1972, *Corrections and Punishment: Structure, Function, and Process,* 1977, and *The Power to Punish,* 1983, and to sociology, psychiatry, and medical journals and other periodicals, including *Times Literary Supplement* and *London Review of Books.*

WORK IN PROGRESS: Desperate Remedies: A History of Somatic Treatments in Psychiatry.

SIDELIGHTS: Andrew Scull's first book, *Decarceration: Community Treatment and the Deviant; a Radical View* is, according to a critic for *Working Papers for a New Society,* "not only the best overview of this decade's 'reforms' [in psychiatric care] but also the best analysis of how the reforms have failed." Kim Hopper of the *Health-PAC Bulletin* describes Scull as "an able and effective historian, a shrewd critic, and a clear, compelling writer," and calls *Decarceration* "closely documented and carefully argued, . . . [a book] without parallel in the recent literature on psychiatric and penal institutions."

BIOGRAPHICAL/CRITICAL SOURCES:

PERIODICALS

Health-PAC Bulletin, September-October, 1977.
New Statesman and Society, August 25, 1989.
Times Literary Supplement, January 8, 1982; July 7-13, 1989.
Working Papers for a New Society, May-June, 1978.

SEEGER, Pete(r R.) 1919-

PERSONAL: Born May 3, 1919, in New York, N.Y.; son of Charles (a conductor, musicologist, and educator) and Constance de Clyver (a violinist and teacher; maiden name Edson) Seeger; married Toshi Aline Ohta, July 20, 1943; children: Daniel Adams, Mika Salter, Tinya. *Education:* Attended Harvard University, 1936-38. *Avocational interests:* Skiing, skating, rambling through the woods.

ADDRESSES: Home—Dutchess Junction, Beacon, N.Y. 12508. *Agent*—Harold Leventhal, Room 710, 250 West 57th St., New York, N.Y. 10107.

CAREER: Folksong popularizer, songwriter, musicologist, banjo player, and writer, 1939—. Assistant archivist, Library of Congress Archive of American Folk Song, 1939-40; founding member of the Almanac Singers (touring group), 1940-41; toured United States with Woody Guthrie, 1941-42; co-founder and national director of People's Songs, Inc., 1945; toured United States with presidential candidate Henry Wallace, 1948; co-founding member with Lee Hays, Ronnie Gilbert, and Fred Hellerman of the Weavers (folksinging quartet), 1948-52, rejoined Weavers, 1955-57; solo performer, 1957—. Host of "Rainbow Quest" program on National Educational Television (NET), 1955-56; appeared in two motion pictures, "To Hear My Banjo Play," 1946, and "Tell Me That You Love Me, Junie Moon," 1970.

Has made numerous concert appearances in the United States and abroad, including a world tour, 1963-64. Co-founder and performer at Newport (R.I.) Folk Festivals; chairman of the board, Hudson River Sloop Restoration, Inc., 1970. Has recorded over eighty record albums for various labels, including *American Industrial Ballads, American Favorite Ballads, Pete Seeger Sings American Ballads, The Rainbow Quest, Goofing Off Suite,* and *Songs,* all with Folkways, *The World of Pete Seeger* and *Pete Seeger's Greatest Hits,* both with Columbia, and *The Essential Pete Seeger,* with Vanguard. Has also made numerous albums for children, including *Song and Play Time, American Folk Songs for Children, Abiyoyo and Other Songs for Children, Birds, Beasts, Bugs and Little Fishes,* and *Stories and Songs for Little Children,* all with Folkways. *Military service:* U.S. Army Special Services, entertained troops in the United States and the South Pacific, 1942-45.

WRITINGS:

How To Play the Five-String Banjo, self-published, 1948.
American Favorite Ballads, Oak, 1961.
The Steel Drums of Kim Loy Wong (instruction manual), Oak, 1962, published as *Steel Drums and How To Play Them,* 1964.
(With Jerry Silverman) *The Folksinger's Guitar Guide,* Oak, 1962.
(Author of introduction) Woody Guthrie, *Woody Guthrie Folksongs: A Collection of Songs by America's Foremost Balladeer,* Ludlow, 1963.
The Bells of Rhymney, Peer-Southern, 1964.
(With Julius Lester) *The Twelve-String Guitar as Played by Leadbelly,* Oak, 1965.
(Author of preface) Don McLean, editor, *Songs and Sketches of the First Clearwater Crew,* North River Press, 1970.
The Incomplete Folksinger, Simon & Schuster, 1972.
Henscratches and Flyspecks: or, How To Read Melodies from Songbooks in Twelve Confusing Lessons, Berkeley Press, 1973.

(With father, Charles Seeger) *The Foolish Frog,* Macmillan, 1973.
(With Bob Reiser) *Carry It On!,* Simon & Schuster, 1985.
Abiyoyo: South African Lullaby and Folk Story (juvenile), illustrated by Michael Hays, Macmillan, 1986.
(With Reiser) *Everybody Says Freedom: The Civil Rights Movement in Words, Pictures, and Song,* Norton, 1990.

Also author of (with the Weavers) *The Caroler's Songbag;* (with Woody Guthrie and Alan Lomax) *Hard-Hitting Songs for Hard-Hit People; How to Make a Chalit;* and *Oh, Had I a Golden Thread.* Writer of original folk songs, including "Where Have All the Flowers Gone?," "If I Had a Hammer," and (in collaboration with the Weavers) "Kisses Sweeter Than Wine," and "Turn, Turn, Turn." Author of introduction for hundreds of books and song collections. Contributor of articles to periodicals, including *Environment, Saturday Review, Daily World, New York Times, Broadside,* and magazines overseas. Member of editorial staff, *Sing Out!*

SIDELIGHTS: One of the most influential folk artists in America, Pete Seeger has been writing, singing, and playing music for more than half a century. Seeger has been instrumental in popularizing both the five-string banjo and the songs of populist America that could be played on it; his own works such as "If I Had a Hammer," and "Where Have All the Flowers Gone?" served as anthems in the anti-establishment protests of the late 1960s. In *Best of the Music Makers,* George T. Simon calls Seeger "an uncanny mixture of saint, propagandist, cornball, and hero" whose "emotional generosity and companionship with his audiences around the world has invariably been returned affectionately by the . . . people he has entertained and inspired."

Seeger was born into a family "whose chromosomes fairly burst with music," to quote *Philadelphia Inquirer* contributor Amy Linn. His father was an ethnomusicologist and composer, and his mother a classical violinist; they both taught at Juilliard. While Seeger was young his parents moved across the country from University of California at Berkeley to New York. In boarding school during his high school years he dabbled in Marx, sang in choirs, and played the ukulele.

In 1936 Seeger accompanied his father on a trip to a North Carolina music festival. As Linn puts it, during the festival "young Seeger took one look at a five-string banjo and fell in love." Seeger was struck both by the energetic mountain music and by the frank, heartfelt lyrics—he realized that these songs carried "the meat of human life," unlike so much of the trivial popular music of the time. Although he subsequently enrolled in Harvard University, Seeger found college less fascinating than the banjo. He practiced until he had taught himself to play in the various Appalachian picking styles. Eventually he became so well-known on the instrument that the Vega Instrument Company offered a "Pete Seeger" model banjo.

Late in the Great Depression Seeger began to travel the country with Woody Guthrie, singing for striking workers and displaced farmers and associating with many left-wing causes. Seeger joined the Communist Party and participated as a singer at rallies and meetings. "I knew it wasn't a quick way to get jobs—to sing for the Communist Party," he told the *Philadelphia Inquirer.* "It was something that you do, because you think it's the right thing at the time. And in the long run, you realize the value in doing what you think is right."

A full decade before the so-called "folk revival," Seeger placed several records on the Billboard pop music charts. At the time—in the early 1950s—he was singing and playing with the

Weavers, a folk quartet he helped to found. The Weavers's biggest hit was the winsome "Irene Goodnight," one of several singles that sold over a million copies. At the height of the group's success, Seeger found himself blacklisted for his communist sympathies. In 1955 he was called before the dreaded House Un-American Activities Committee and questioned about his ties to the party. When he evoked his First Amendment rights of free speech, rather than the Fifth Amendment rights against self-incrimination, he was charged with contempt of Congress and sentenced to one year in prison. The sentence was overturned on appeal, but the blacklisting endured.

Undaunted, Seeger continued to perform wherever he was welcome, and he also began to write instruction booklets and compile song anthologies. A changing political climate in the 1960s brought him—and folk music in general—a new generation of listeners. Throughout the 1960s and 1970s Seeger performed on college campuses and at outdoor folk festivals, adding a plea for environmental awareness to his repertoire of message songs. His project to clean up the Hudson River, by way of the floating ecology exhibit the sloop *Clearwater,* helped to restore one of America's dirtiest waterways.

Seeger's written works include songbooks, instruction manuals for banjo, guitar, and steel drums, and children's books that augment his popular albums for younger listeners. A *Los Angeles Times Book Review* contributor notes that Seeger is a writer "for whom a tune is both a tool of social change and a celebration of the human spirit." Seeger's dedication to orally-transmitted music has led critics to call him "America's tuning fork" and "the living embodiment of native folk tradition." Linn puts it more succinctly when she concludes: "For 50 of his years Pete Seeger [has] been wedding his songs to history, and making history with his songs."

BIOGRAPHICAL/CRITICAL SOURCES:

BOOKS

Lawless, Ray, *Folksingers and Folk Songs in America,* Longmans, 1960.
Sandberg, Larry and Dick Weissman, *The Folk Music Sourcebook,* Knopf, 1976.
Simon, George T., *Best of the Music Makers,* Doubleday, 1979.

PERIODICALS

Audubon, March, 1971.
Conservationist, June, 1969.
High Fidelity, January, 1963.
Look, August, 1969.
Los Angeles Times Book Review, December 29, 1985.
National Wildlife, February, 1970.
New York Times Book Review, May 11, 1986.
Philadelphia Inquirer, May 12, 1989.
Popular Science, August, 1970.
Ramparts, November 30, 1968.
Rolling Stone, March 10, 1977, October 18, 1979.
Saturday Review, May 13, 1973.
Sing Out!, May, 1954.

—*Sketch by Anne Janette Johnson*

*   *   *

SELBY, Hubert, Jr.   1928-

PERSONAL: Born July 23, 1928, in Brooklyn, N.Y.; son of Hubert (an engineer and apartment building manager) and Adalin (Layne) Selby; married three times; four children. *Education:*

Attended Peter Stuyvesant High School, one year. *Religion:* Christian.

ADDRESSES: Home—Los Angeles, Calif.

CAREER: United States Merchant Marine, deckhand, 1944-46; insurance analyst, 1950-64; writer, 1964—.

WRITINGS:

Last Exit to Brooklyn (short stories), Grove, 1964, reprinted, 1988.
The Room (novel), Grove, 1971.
The Demon (novel), Playboy Press, 1976.
Requiem for a Dream (novel), Playboy Press, 1979, reprinted, Thunder's Mouth, 1988.
Song of the Silent Snow (short stories), Marion Boyers, 1986.

Contributor of short stories and articles to periodicals, including *Black Mountain Review, Provincetown Review, New Directions, Swank,* and *National Enquirer.*

WORK IN PROGRESS: A novel.

SIDELIGHTS: Hubert Selby, Jr., has drawn upon his own experiences in urban New York to produce fiction that is frank, violent, and disturbing. Selby's best known work, *Last Exit to Brooklyn,* explores the sordid world of prostitutes, drug addicts, and hardened criminals in graphic detail; the book was banned in several European countries, where it was deemed pornographic. Most American critics have responded to Selby's fiction more rationally, aware that the author has merely chosen to expose a particular segment of society in a realistic manner. *Saturday Review* contributor Josephine Hendin calls Selby's work "one of the most remarkable achievements in current literature," adding: "Selby is the poet of our decline, a writer who has an unerring instinct for honing our collapse into novels as glittering and as cutting as pure, black, jagged glass." Hendin concludes: "No other American writer has conveyed so brilliantly the fierce, primal competitions of the street, or the way living can shrink to hating."

Selby was born and raised in Brooklyn, New York. "I started dying 36 hours before I was born," he told the *Los Angeles Times.* "I was never comfortable in my own body. I was always afraid. I couldn't find a way to live." At the tender age of fifteen Selby dropped out of high school and signed on with the Merchant Marine. Within two years he had contracted a severe case of tuberculosis, requiring a long hospitalization and the removal of ten ribs and part of his lung. His doctors gave him little hope of survival, especially since he aggravated his condition by drinking to excess. Finally, in 1950, he was released from the hospital. He returned to Brooklyn in frail health and drifted into the orbit that would provide material for his fiction.

"I just gave up when I got out of the hospital," Selby told the *Saturday Review.* "That's how I ended up around 58th and Second in Brooklyn, where [*Last Exit*] takes place. I went down there, I guess, looking for sympathy or hoping maybe I'd get killed. Something." What Selby did find in that neighborhood were people immersed in drug abuse, violence, and bitter struggles for money or just plain survival. Gradually Selby began to address the milieu more as an observer than a participant. With the encouragement of his childhood friend Gilbert Sorrentino, he began to read widely and experiment with creative writing. Even though he suffered from asthma and had to keep a daytime job to support his family, Selby persevered with his fiction. His first vignette, "The Queen Is Dead," appeared in the *Black Mountain Review* in 1956.

Selby worked on *Last Exit to Brooklyn* for more than six years, attempting to portray "the horrors of a loveless world." *Los Angeles Times* correspondent Denise Hamilton notes that when the work was published in 1964, it "exploded onto the American psyche like a 10-megaton nuclear bomb and set off a searing controversy among critics, who called it an extraordinary literary achievement while praising and panning its dark vision and violent prose." In the *Dictionary of Literary Biography*, Richard Wertime suggests that Selby's "journey into hell" opens to the reader "a world of tedium and depravity, of drug abuse and viciousness, of self-exploitation and abysmal ignorance that seems at once unbearable and all too real. What gives this work its power is less fidelity to fact than an unremitting energy. As Selby hoped, it overwhelms; it denies the reader the distance which usually goes with aesthetic pleasure, and it does so by detailing explicitly the thoughts and actions of its characters." *Books and Bookmen* contributor Duncan Fallowell calls *Last Exit to Brooklyn* "a strange and harrowing trip of unimaginable pathos . . . a soul stripped bare, flinching and wincing and screaming and bleeding and struggling for breath."

Last Exit to Brooklyn was the subject of an obscenity trial in Great Britain and was outright banned in Italy—the work contains scenes of rape and homosexual acts that were shocking to a 1960s audience. The same scenes drew attacks from critics in the United States as well, but the book sold 750,000 copies and gave its author—a self-taught high school dropout—an entree into the world of letters. Wertime writes: "The reactions were strong on both sides, but the critics were in agreement on at least two points—that Selby knew his material and that his style was energetic and uninhibited."

In retrospect, Selby told the *Los Angeles Times*, the success of *Last Exit to Brooklyn* was a mixed blessing. "I had some money coming in and I had time on my hands," he said. "I got myself into a lot of trouble." In 1967 Selby was arrested for possession of heroin. He was sentenced to a month in jail, where he kicked his drug habit cold turkey. He spent another two years freeing himself from alcohol addiction; then he began to write again. His 1971 novel, *The Room*, is a violent stream-of-conscious narrative from the mind of an incarcerated criminal. In the *New York Times Book Review*, Dotson Rader describes the book as "an exquisite, meticulous examination of the curious piteous lust between oppressor and oppressed. It documents the sexual basis of power and criminality. As a work of the imagination, . . . it assures Hubert Selby's place in the first rank of American novelists."

Relentless brutality, shock, and alienation characterize all of Selby's work. Hendin notes that the typical Selby story or novel provides "a portrait of an American mind gone the limit in its acceptance of cruelty as life's only fixed principle." *Times Literary Supplement* reviewer Brian Morton offers a similar assessment. "Selby's is a vernacular—often scatological—account of the horrors of life without faith or hope," Morton writes. "In the absence of belief, Selby suggests, life becomes either a headlong rush into apocalypse or else a slow numbing of the senses by ritualized, meaningless behaviour, the abstract 'pieties' which survive the loss of belief." Selby has been lauded as both a social critic and a moralist; certainly he indicts both individual savagery and the forces that engender it. *Village Voice* essayist Barbara O'Dair concludes: "Revulsion or celebration, the corrupted fantasies in Selby's work, are seen as monstrous, grotesque, because of the exquisite attention he gives to the warps of the human imagination."

Selby is currently living in Los Angeles, where he teaches an occasional creative writing course and works in television production. Hamilton observes that the author's career fortunes have recently begun to improve, after almost a decade of obscurity. Selby, she claims, "has linked up with some young, avant-garde writers who see him as a kindred spirit, one whose alienated, *Angst*-ridden prose echoes their own." Several of Selby's novels have been reprinted, and *Last Exit to Brooklyn* was made into a movie in 1988. *Nation* contributor Michael Stephens maintains that Selby's work "holds up under strenuous analysis, continues to live and breathe after literary autopsy, and compares with the best literature." Rader concludes of the author: "Selby has created characters with a concreteness, force and individuality seldom found in American fiction. . . . Selby's genius is that he compels us to feel. And that is a marvelous thing."

MEDIA ADAPTATIONS: "Last Exit to Brooklyn," based on Selby's novel of the same title, was filmed by Bernd Eichinger in 1988.

BIOGRAPHICAL/CRITICAL SOURCES:

BOOKS

Contemporary Literary Criticism, Gale, Volume 1, 1973, Volume 2, 1974, Volume 4, 1975, Volume 8, 1978.
Dictionary of Literary Biography, Volume 2: *American Novelists since World War II,* Gale, 1978.
Solotaroff, Theodore, *The Red Hot Vacuum and Other Pieces on the Writing of the Sixties,* Atheneum, 1970.

PERIODICALS

Books and Bookmen, May, 1972.
Book Week, December 20, 1964.
Choice, February, 1965.
Commentary, January, 1965.
Critique: Studies in Modern Fiction, Volume 11, number 3, 1969.
Harper's, February, 1974.
Holiday, June, 1965.
Journal of Popular Culture, fall, 1974.
Kulchur, spring, 1964.
Literature and Psychology, November, 1974.
Los Angeles Times, March 11, 1988.
Nation, December 7, 1964, February 3, 1979.
Negro Digest, February, 1965.
New American Review, April, 1968.
Newsweek, December 28, 1964, November 1, 1976.
New York Review of Books, December 3, 1964, March 9, 1972.
New York Times, August 4, 1988.
New York Times Book Review, November 8, 1964, December 12, 1971, November 14, 1976, September 21, 1986.
Partisan Review, spring, 1965.
Playboy, January, 1965.
Satire Newsletter, spring, 1969.
Saturday Review, January 23, 1965, December 11, 1971.
Spectator, July 7, 1979.
Studies in Short Fiction, fall, 1965.
Time, October 30, 1964.
Times Literary Supplement, February 25, 1972, March 25, 1977, September 5, 1986.
Village Voice, March 25, 1965, September 6, 1988.*

—*Sketch by Anne Janette Johnson*

SHEEHY, Gail 1937-

PERSONAL: Born November 27, 1937, in Mamaroneck, NY; daughter of Harold Merritt (an advertising executive) and Lillian (a singer; maiden name, Rainey) Henion; married Albert Sheehy (an internist), August 20, 1960 (divorced, 1968); married Clay Felker (editor of Manhattan, Inc.), 1985; children: (first marriage) Maura; (second marriage) Mohm (adopted daughter). *Education:* University of Vermont, B.S., 1958; Columbia University, graduate study, 1970.

ADDRESSES: Home—New York, NY. *Office*—c/o William Morrow & Co., 105 Madison Ave., New York, NY 10016.

CAREER: J. C. Penney & Co., traveling home economist, 1958-60; *Democrat and Chronicle,* Rochester, NY, fashion editor, 1961-63; *New York Herald Tribune,* New York City, feature writer, 1963-66; *New York* (magazine), New York City, contributing editor, 1968-77; free-lance writer. Member, board of directors, Girls Clubs of America.

MEMBER: Authors Guild, Authors League of America, PEN American Center (member of national advisory board), Common Cause, National Organization for Women, Cambodian Crisis Committee, Newswomen's Club of New York.

AWARDS, HONORS: Front Page Award from Newswomen's Club of New York, 1964, for most distinguished feature of interest to women, and 1973, for best magazine feature; National Magazine Award, 1972, for reporting excellence; Alicia Patterson Foundation fellowship, 1974; Anisfield-Wolf Book Award, 1986.

WRITINGS:

Lovesounds (novel), Random House, 1970.
Panthermania: The Clash of Black against Black in One American City, Harper, 1971.
Speed Is of the Essence, Pocket Books, 1971.
Hustling: Prostitution in Our Wide Open Society, Delacorte, 1973.
Passages: Predictable Crises of Adult Life, Dutton, 1976.
Pathfinders, Morrow, 1981.
Spirit of Survival, Morrow, 1986.
Character: America's Search for Leadership, Morrow, 1988.
Gorbachev: The Man Who Changed the World, Harper, 1990.

Contributor to *Cosmopolitan, McCall's, Glamour, Good Housekeeping, London Sunday Telegraph, Paris Match,* and *New York Times Magazine.*

SIDELIGHTS: Gail Sheehy's first book, *Lovesounds,* deals with the breakup of a marriage. But, as Judith Martin of the *Washington Post* points out, it may be a disappointment to "devotees of the genre, who know how to enjoy first her side, then his side, and then the counselor's view showing that they both had faults but could learn to correct them and have another baby." In this book there are no major faults in the characters. Sheehy has created a good wife and a good husband, both of whom love their child and have rewarding careers, but who are nonetheless getting a divorce. Martin says that "it would seem to be a step backwards in novel writing because we have all been brought up to believe that everything in books, if not in life, happens for a reason." Here, this is clearly not the case, but "once you accept the fact that the marriage was a good one, and that its dissolution is something that neither husband nor wife wished and for which neither was deliberately responsible, you find a good study of the pure emotions involved."

Israel Horovitz states that with *Lovesounds* "Gail Sheehy has written the most brutal indictment of hypocrisy in marriage, the most incisive analysis of the daily experience, the most hearty yet subtle feminist line since that Friday morning in July when Anton Chekhov died in Olga Knipper's arms. She has written a truly pop novel: a book that reads as easily as any of R. Art Crumb's comix, yet stays as firmly lodged in your stomach as Grandma's kreplach. *Lovesounds* is a fine, fine piece of writing that should be read by anyone who is married, was married, or will be married." But Paul D. Zimmerman, in a *Newsweek* review, insists that the book is a failure. His explanation: "Imprisoned in nearly every journalist lives a captive novelist struggling to get out. . . . But the rules of the novel are different. The subject stands inside the characters, not across the table taking notes, and the language that serves so well to capture the surface tensions of a tow-away depot or the anxieties of a student revolutionary cannot necessarily handle the swollen emotions of inner life bursting apart." Zimmerman concludes that "Gail Sheehy has broken out as a novelist all right. But this book at least makes it doubtful that it was worth the struggle."

Sheehy's best-known work is probably *Passages: Predictable Crises of Adult Life.* The theme of the book, as Jill Tweedie puts it in a *Saturday Review* article, is that "not only are there crises in every life, not only do they occur with reasonable predictability, but they are (cheeringly) entirely natural—comparable, say, to the seasons of the year or to the germination of a seed." Sheehy contends that there are four main "passages" in life; she terms them "Pulling up Roots," "The Trying Twenties," "Passage to the Thirties," and "The Deadline Decade: Setting off on the Midlife Passage." She feels that everyone must confront each of these milestones and must pass through each in order to advance to the next.

Reviewing the book for *Ms.,* Patricia O'Brien writes: "I barely made it past the Introduction to *Passages* before I found myself underlining passages—not because I was learning startling new facts, but because finally somebody was putting universal human fears and uncertainties about change and growing old into a manageable perspective. On the whole, *Passages* succeeds most when it is defining these fears, and not when Sheehy is presenting her numerous case histories." O'Brien calls it "a book that gives us the chance to track ourselves. Sheehy particularly makes it easier for us to understand the lonely polarization that may occur between men and women by pointing out that the sexes are rarely in the same identity and career questions at the same time."

Maurice Hart of *Best Sellers* says that the writing in *Passages* "is basically journalistic in style, and the arguments are not as clearly and precisely stated as they should be in a scholarly presentation. Consequently, for a definitive work on the stages of adult life one will have to look elsewhere—possibly to one of Ms. Sheehy's sources." Around those sources centers a noteworthy controversy. In researching this subject Sheehy talked with such experts as Yale psychologist Daniel Levinson, Harvard psychiatrist George Vaillant, and U.C.L.A. psychiatrist Roger Gould. She also attributes some of her information to Erik Erikson, Else Frenkel-Brunswick, Margaret Hennig, and Margaret Mead. When the book first appeared, *Time* noted that Levinson "outlined the 'mentor phenomenon'—that in middle age a man feels the need to promote the fortunes of a younger worker," and that Hennig "reported on the importance of mentors to women in corporate life" in 1970.

Levinson was somewhat perturbed at Sheehy's allegedly unauthorized use of his research, saying "she is incomplete, to put it mildly, in acknowledging her use of my published and unpublished material." But Hennig, according to *Time,* had no complaints. "She used my stuff," she said, "but this is real life and I'm not upset about it. She gave me credit." Roger Gould, however, was furious. A *Time* writer said that he "filed a plagiarism suit against Sheehy and Dutton [her publisher]. The case was settled out of court: Gould received $10,000 and 10% of the book's royalties." Gould contended that he was under the impression that he was to be a collaborator on the book, but after he had discussed his research with Sheehy, found that she considered him a paid consultant. She claimed that it was made clear from the beginning that Gould was not to be a co-author.

In defense of Sheehy, Roderick MacLeish of the *Washington Post* emphasizes that "by her own assertion, Gail Sheehy is not the central theorist of her work. . . . What Sheehy has done is to gather together the materials of the relatively new social science of adult development, codify it into skillfully popularized form, invest it with the classy, vernacular prose style for which she is justifiably admired and arrive at a generalist's conclusions—there's more hope in the aging process than you've been led to believe." And, as MacLeish goes on to conclude, "I'm sure that specialists will quarrel with what she has done. That's what specialists are for. But the hope, wit and de- mythification of adulthood that permeates Sheehy's book make *Passages* a work of revelation for the layman as he tries to understand the inevitable movement of his life. It is a stunning accomplishment."

BIOGRAPHICAL/CRITICAL SOURCES:

BOOKS

Contemporary Issues Criticism, Volume 2, Gale, 1984.

PERIODICALS

Best Sellers, August 1, 1971, September, 1976.
Chicago Tribune, May 13, 1988, May 29, 1988.
Los Angeles Times, May 25, 1988, June 10, 1988.
McCall's, August, 1970.
Ms., August, 1976.
Newsweek, August 10, 1970, August 30, 1973.
New York, July 21, 1969, August 3, 1970.
New York Review of Books, October 28, 1976.
New York Times, August 16, 1976.
New York Times Book Review, September 5, 1971, May 25, 1986, May 29, 1988.
Publishers Weekly, May 20, 1988.
Saturday Review, July 24, 1971, May 15, 1976.
Time, May 10, 1976.
Village Voice, August 20, 1970.
Washington Post, August 29, 1970, August 5, 1988.
Washington Post Book World, March 23, 1976.*

*　　　*　　　*

SHELDON, Sidney 1917-

PERSONAL: Born February 11, 1917, in Chicago, Ill.; son of Otto (a salesman) and Natalie (Marcus) Sheldon; married Jorja Curtright (an actress), March 28, 1951 (died, 1985); married Alexandra Kostoff (a former child actress), October 14, 1989; children: Mary Sheldon Dastin. *Education:* Attended Northwestern University, 1935-36. *Religion:* Church of Religious Science.

ADDRESSES: Home—Los Angeles, CA. *Office*—c/o William Morrow & Co., 105 Madison Ave., New York, N.Y. 10016.

CAREER: Writer. Creator, producer, and writer of television shows, Los Angeles, Calif., 1963—, including "The Patty Duke Show," "I Dream of Jeannie," "Nancy," and "Hart to Hart." *Military service:* U.S. Army Air Forces, 1941.

MEMBER: Freedom to Read Foundation.

AWARDS, HONORS: Academy Award ("Oscar") for best original screenplay, Academy of Motion Picture Arts and Sciences, 1948, for "The Bachelor and the Bobby-Soxer"; Screen Writers' Guild Award for best musical of the year, 1948, for "Easter Parade," and 1950, for "Annie Get Your Gun"; Antoinette Perry Award ("Tony"), 1959, for book of "Redhead"; Emmy nominations for "I Dream of Jeannie"; Edgar Award, Mystery Writers of America, and *New York Times* citation, both for best first mystery novel, both 1970, both for *The Naked Face;* recipient of a star on the Hollywood Walk of Fame.

WRITINGS:

NOVELS

The Naked Face, Morrow, 1970.
The Other Side of Midnight, Morrow, 1974.
A Stranger in the Mirror, Morrow, 1976.
Bloodline, Morrow, 1977.
Rage of Angels, Morrow, 1980.
Master of the Game, Morrow, 1982.
If Tomorrow Comes, Morrow, 1985.
Windmills of the Gods, Morrow, 1987.
The Sands of Time, Morrow, 1988.
Sheldon Boxed Set: Bloodline, A Stranger in the Mirror, Rage of Angels, Warner Books, 1988.
Memories of Midnight, Morrow, 1990.
The Doomsday Conspiracy, Morrow, 1991.

PLAYS

(Adaptor with Ben Roberts) "The Merry Widow" (operetta), first produced on Broadway, August 4, 1943.
"Jackpot," first produced on Broadway, January 13, 1944.
(With Roberts and Dorothy Kilgallen) "Dream with Music," first produced on Broadway, May 18, 1944.
(With Ladislaus Bush-Fekete and Mary Helen Fay) "Alice in Arms," first produced on Broadway, January 31, 1945.
(With Dorothy and Herbert Fields, and David Shaw) "Redhead" (musical), first produced on Broadway, February 5, 1959.
"Roman Candle," first produced on Broadway, February 3, 1960.

SCREENPLAYS

(Author of story with Roberts) "Borrowed Hero," Monogram, 1941.
(With Jack Natteford) "Dangerous Lady," Producers Releasing Corp., 1941.
(Author of story with Roberts) "Gambling Daughters," Producers Releasing Corp., 1941.
(With Roberts) "South of Panama," Producers Releasing Corp., 1941.
(Author of story with Roberts) "Fly by Night," Paramount, 1942.
"She's in the Army," Monogram, 1942.
(With Roberts) "The Carter Case," Republic, 1947.
"The Bachelor and the Bobby-Soxer," RKO, 1947.
(With Albert Hackett and Frances Goodrich) "Easter Parade" (musical), Metro-Goldwyn-Mayer, 1948.
"Annie Get Your Gun" (adapted from the musical by Irving Berlin), Metro-Goldwyn-Mayer, 1950.
"Nancy Goes to Rio," Metro-Goldwyn-Mayer, 1950.

(With Dorothy Cooper) "Rich, Young, and Pretty" (musical), Metro-Goldwyn-Mayer, 1951.

"No Questions Asked," Metro-Goldwyn-Mayer, 1951.

"Three Guys Named Mike," Metro-Goldwyn-Mayer, 1951.

"Just This Once," Metro-Goldwyn-Mayer, 1952.

(With Herbert Baker and Alfred L. Levitt, and director) "Dream Wife," Metro-Goldwyn-Mayer, 1953.

"Remains to Be Seen," Metro-Goldwyn-Mayer, 1953.

"You're Never Too Young," Paramount, 1955.

"Anything Goes" (adapted from the musical by Cole Porter), Paramount, 1956.

"Pardners," Paramount, 1956.

(And director and producer with Robert Smith) "The Buster Keaton Story," Paramount, 1957.

"All in a Night's Work," Paramount, 1961.

"Billy Rose's Jumbo" (also titled "Jumbo"), Metro-Goldwyn-Mayer, 1962.

(With Preston Sturges) "The Birds and the Bees," Paramount, 1965.

OTHER

Also author of a children's book, published in Japan. Author of more than 250 scripts, occasionally under a pseudonym, for "The Patty Duke Show," 1963-66, and "I Dream of Jeannie," 1965-70. Author of play, "Gnomes."

SIDELIGHTS: At age fifty, at the top of his profession as a film and television producer of hits like "I Dream of Jeannie," Sidney Sheldon had no hint of another, even more successful career ahead of him. "[Novels] never occurred to me," Sheldon told *Detroit News* reporter Ruth Pollack Coughlin. "I wasn't a novelist. I was writing for motion pictures and television and Broadway. For me, writing novels was an unnatural next step." Why then, would the winner of Oscar, Tony, and Emmy Awards turn to fiction? The author explained his decision to Sarah Booth Conroy of the *Washington Post:* "I got an idea that was so introspective I could see no way to do it as a television series, movie or Broadway play, because you had to get inside the character's mind. With much trepidation, I decided I'd try a novel." The result was *The Naked Face,* which despite winning awards as the best first mystery novel of the year, initially sold only 17,000 copies. "I was horrified," Sheldon told Conroy, "because 20 million people watched ['I Dream of] Jeannie.' " Nevertheless, Sheldon persisted in his efforts, and his next work, *The Other Side of Midnight,* sold over seven million copies in paperback. Since then, Sheldon has published seven more million-selling novels, and is now considered the best-selling writer in the world, with books in print in thirty-nine countries.

The typical Sheldon potboiler features a beautiful and determined heroine enacting revenge on her enemies; as Conroy describes, in Sheldon's novels "the beautiful but often poor and pure heroines are raped, sodomized and defrauded, and go on to avenge themselves by questionable, often illegal, but ingenious methods." "I write about women," the author remarked to Conroy, "because women are more sensitive than men and more complex. In the kind of book I write, where there's a lot of suspense and people are troubled, it's more interesting to put a woman in that situation because they *are* more vulnerable. . . . Of course, women have other weapons. I make my women attractive, bright, as capable as men in what they do. I'm tired of that dumb blonde cliche we've been saddled with so long."

Although many critics frequently dismiss Sheldon's novels, others find merit in his writing. For example, *Washington Post* reviewer Joseph McLellan observes that in *Rage of Angels* "craftsmanship is the keynote, as a matter of fact, in this novel that ticks along like an intricate, beautifully designed piece of clockwork, full of characters and incidents that are usually interesting even if they are slightly unreal." *New York Times Book Review* contributor Robert Lekachman comments that *Master of the Game* "is hard to put down once you get started. . . . Sheldon's smooth, serviceable, if unmemorable, prose carries one along, much like the movie serials of the Great Depression."

Because of their brisk pace, Sheldon's novels are often characterized as being "less like a book than like a movie," according to *New York Times* writer Janet Maslin, a description their author refutes: "I am accused constantly of writing books as movies," Sheldon told Paul Rosenfield of the *Los Angeles Times.* "But it just isn't true. What's true is that I write *visually.* It's my training from movies and TV." Sheldon does, however, strive for a captivating effect in his books: "I have this goal," the author remarked to Rosenfield. "And it's for a reader to not be able to go to sleep at night. I want him to keep reading another four pages, then one more page. The following morning, or night, he's anxious to get back to the book."

MEDIA ADAPTATIONS: The Other Side of Midnight was made into a film by Twentieth Century-Fox in 1977; *Bloodline* was filmed by Paramount in 1979, and was re-edited by Sheldon and shown as an ABC miniseries in 1982; *Rage of Angels,* for which Sheldon served as executive producer, became an NBC miniseries in 1983, and inspired a 1986 sequel which Sheldon also produced; CBS broadcast miniseries adaptations of *Master of the Game* in 1984, *If Tomorrow Comes* in 1986, and *Windmills of the Gods* in 1988; *The Naked Face* was filmed by Cannon in 1985; *The Sands of Time* has been optioned.

BIOGRAPHICAL/CRITICAL SOURCES:

BOOKS

Authors in the News, Volume 1, Gale, 1976.
Bestsellers 89, Issue 1, Gale, 1989.

PERIODICALS

Detroit News, February 8, 1987.
Los Angeles Times, October 3, 1982, March 12, 1987.
Newsweek, June 13, 1977.
New Yorker, July 11, 1977.
New York Times, July 24, 1947, July 1, 1948, July 22, 1979.
New York Times Book Review, January 27, 1974, May 2, 1976, February 19, 1978, August 29, 1982, March 10, 1985.
Publishers Weekly, November 25, 1988.
Time, June 20, 1977.
Washington Post, July 12, 1982, February 19, 1985, December 6, 1988.
Washington Post Book World, February 18, 1979.

* * *

SIDDONS, (Sybil) Anne Rivers 1936-

PERSONAL: Born January 9, 1936, in Atlanta, GA; daughter of Marvin (an attorney) and Katherine (a secretary; maiden name, Kitchens) Rivers; married Heyward L. Siddons (a business partner and creative director), in 1966; children: (stepsons) Lee, Kemble, Rick, David. *Education:* Auburn University, B.A.A., 1958; attended Atlanta School of Art, c. 1958. *Avocational interests:* Sailing, swimming, cooking, reading, cats.

ADDRESSES: Home—3767 Vermont Rd. N.E., Atlanta, GA 30319; (summer) Haven Colony, Brooklin, ME 04616.

CAREER: Worked in advertising with Retail Credit Co., c. 1959, Citizens & Southern National Bank, 1961-63, Burke

Dowling Adams, 1967-69, and Burton Campbell Advertising, 1969-74; full-time writer, 1974—. Woodward Academy, member of governing board; Auburn University, member of publications board and arts and sciences honorary council, 1978-83.

MEMBER: Chevy Chase Club (Chevy Chase, MD), Every Saturday Club and Ansley Golf Club (both Atlanta, GA).

AWARDS, HONORS: Alumna achievement award in arts and humanities, Auburn University, 1985; Georgia 'Writer of the Year,' Council of Journalists and Authors of Georgia, 1989.

WRITINGS:

John Chancellor Makes Me Cry (essays), Doubleday, 1975.
Heartbreak Hotel (novel), Simon & Schuster, 1976.
The House Next Door (horror novel), Simon & Schuster, 1978.
Go Straight on Peachtree, Dolphin Books, 1978.
Fox's Earth (novel), Simon & Schuster, 1980.
Homeplace (novel), Harper, 1987.
Peachtree Road (novel), Harper, 1988.
King's Oak (novel), Harper, 1990.
Outer Banks (novel), Harper, 1991.

Contributor to *Gentleman's Quarterly, Georgia, House Beautiful, Lear's, Reader's Digest, Redbook,* and *Southern Living.* Senior editor, *Atlanta* magazine, 1964-67.

MEDIA ADAPTATIONS: Heartbreak Hotel was adapted as the film "Heart of Dixie," Orion Pictures, 1989.

WORK IN PROGRESS: Colony, for Harper.

SIDELIGHTS: Siddon's first book, *John Chancellor Makes Me Cry,* chronicles one year of her life in Atlanta, Georgia, humorously reflecting on the frustrations and joys of life—serving jury duty, hosting parties, and taking care of a husband suffering with the flu. The author's style in *John Chancellor Makes Me Cry* has been favorably compared to that of Erma Bombeck, whose own review of the book praised Siddons: "She is unique. She's an original in her essays that combine humor, intimacy and insight into a marriage." Bombeck found the most "poignant and very real" chapter to be the one describing "the month [Siddons's] husband lost his job, her Grandmother died, a Siamese cat they were keeping for a friend was hit by a car, their house was burgled and their Persian cat contracted a $50-a-week disease."

Heartbreak Hotel is a novel about a young Southern woman who must choose between her two suitors and the very different lifestyles they represent. Katha Pollitt asserted: "The author dissects the 1950's, Southern style, with a precision that is anything but nostalgic; and yet somehow the very wealth of detail she provides makes 'Heartbreak Hotel' a good-natured rather than an angry look backward. . . . This is a marvelously detailed record of a South as gone with the wind as Scarlett O'Hara's."

Jane Larkin Crain was disappointed with the lack of drama in Siddons's third novel, *The House Next Door.* This tale of an affluent young couple whose lives are changed by the mysterious evils occurring in a neighboring house, according to Crain, "is suffused with tacit New Class moralism and snobbery and populated with characters of such smugness and self-satisfaction that it is hard to work up much sympathy or distress when they are forced into the author's idea of extremity. . . . With lives as bland and complacent as those in this novel, one would think that all concerned might welcome a little murder and mayhem in the neighborhood, just to liven things up a bit." Siddons, in an interview in *Publishers Weekly,* called the book "something of a lark. It's different from anything I've ever written, or proba-

bly ever will. But I like to read occult, supernatural stories. Some of the world's great writers have written them, and I guess I wanted to see what I could do with the genre."

Later novels, such as *Homeplace* and *Peachtree Road,* won greater favor with critics and became best-sellers. Noted Bob Summers in *Publishers Weekly, Homeplace* "struck a national chord" with its account of an independent Southern-born woman returning home after more than twenty years. *Peachtree Road* is Siddons's "love letter to Atlanta," according to *Chicago Tribune* contributor Joyce Slater. "Siddons does an admirable job of tracing the city's rebirth after World War II without idealizing it." Concluded the reviewer, it is Siddons's "most ambitious [book] to date."

BIOGRAPHICAL/CRITICAL SOURCES:

BOOKS

Siddons, Anne Rivers, *John Chancellor Makes Me Cry,* Doubleday, 1975.
Bestsellers 89, Issue 2, Gale, 1989.

PERIODICALS

Chicago Tribune, June 14, 1987; November 11, 1988.
Chicago Tribune Book World, June 28, 1981.
Journal and Constitution (Atlanta), October 9, 1988.
Library Journal, June 15, 1975, August, 1990.
New York Times, September 16, 1989.
New York Times Book Review, April 13, 1975; September 12, 1976; October 23, 1977; December 10, 1978; August 30, 1987; January 1, 1989.
Publishers Weekly, November 18, 1988, August 3, 1990.
Tribune Books (Chicago), June 14, 1987.
Washington Post, August 3, 1987.

*   *   *

SILBERSACK, John (Walter) 1954-

PERSONAL: Born December 8, 1954, in New York City; son of Walter Roy and Joan Davis (Small) Silbersack; married Elionora van Tyen Wilking, June 29, 1985; children: Nichols Clay. *Education:* Brown University, A.B., 1977.

ADDRESSES: Home—2 Van Buren St., Port Washington, NY 11050. *Office*—Penguin USA, 375 Hudson St., New York, NY 10014.

CAREER: Hellcoal Press, Providence, RI, publisher and editor, 1975-77; G. P. Putnam's Sons, New York City, editorial assistant, 1977-78; Berkley Publishing Corp. (now Berkley/Jove Publishing Group), New York City, editor, 1978, senior editor, 1978-80; Marketing Support Group, New York City, consultant, 1981-85; New American Library, New York City, senior editor, 1986-88, executive editor, 1988-90; ROC Books (a division of Penguin USA), New York City, editorial director, 1990—.

MEMBER: Science Fiction Writers of America, Horror Writers of America, Trap Door Spiders.

WRITINGS:

(Published anonymously) *No Frills Science Fiction Novel,* Jove, 1981.
Rogers' Rangers, Ace Books, 1982.

EDITOR

Fritz Leiber, *The Change War,* Gregg, 1978.

(With Victoria Schochet) *The Berkley Showcase: New Writings in Science Fiction and Fantasy,* Berkley Publishing, Volumes 1-2, 1980, Volumes 3-4, 1981.
Avram Davidson, *Collected Fantasies,* Berkley Publishing, 1982.

OTHER

Also editor of *A Sampler of Caribbean Poetry,* 1983. Contributor to periodicals, including *Science Fiction Digest,* 1980-82, and *Heavy Metal,* 1982-84. Editor of *Little Magazine,* 1977-82.

BIOGRAPHICAL/CRITICAL SOURCES:

PERIODICALS

Locus, November, 1978; October, 1980.
Patchin Review, January, 1982.
Science Fiction Writers of America Bulletin, winter, 1979.

*   *   *

SIMIC, Charles 1938-

PERSONAL: Born May 9, 1938, in Belgrade, Yugoslavia; came to United States in 1954; son of George (an engineer) and Helen (Matijevic) Simic; married Helene Dubin (a designer), October 25, 1965; children: Anna, Philip. *Education:* New York University, B.A., 1967. *Religion:* Eastern Orthodox.

ADDRESSES: Home—P.O. Box 192, Strafford, NH 03884. *Office*— Department of English, University of New Hampshire, Durham, NH 03824.

CAREER: Aperture (photography magazine), New York, NY, editorial assistant, 1966-69; University of New Hampshire, Durham, associate professor of English, 1974—. Visiting assistant professor of English, State University of California, Hayward, 1970-73, Boston University, 1975, and Columbia University, 1979. *Military service:* U.S. Army, 1961- 63.

AWARDS, HONORS: PEN International Award for translation, 1970; Guggenheim fellowship, 1972-73; National Endowment for the Arts fellowship, 1974-75, and 1979-80; Edgar Allan Poe Award from American Academy of Poets, 1975; National Institute of Arts and Letters and American Academy of Arts and Letters Award, 1976; National Book Award nomination, 1978, for *Charon's Cosmology;* Harriet Monroe Poetry Award from University of Chicago, Di Castignola Award from Poetry Society of America, 1980, and PEN Translation award, all 1980; Fulbright travelling fellowship, 1982; Ingram Merrill fellowship, 1983-84; MacArthur Foundation fellowship, 1984- 89; Pulitzer Prize nominations, 1986 and 1987; Pulitzer Prize, 1990, for *The World Doesn't End.*

WRITINGS:

POETRY

What the Grass Says, Kayak, 1967.
Somewhere among Us a Stone Is Taking Notes, Kayak, 1969.
Dismantling the Silence, Braziller, 1971.
White, New Rivers Press, 1972, revised edition, Logbridge-Rhodes, 1980.
Return to a Place Lit by a Glass of Milk, Braziller, 1974.
Biography and a Lament, Bartholemew's Cobble (Hartford, CT), 1976.
Charon's Cosmology, Braziller, 1977.
Brooms: Selected Poems, Edge Press, 1978.
School for Dark Thoughts, Banyan Press, 1978, sound recording of same title published by Watershed Tapes (Washington, DC), 1978.
Classic Ballroom Dances, Braziller, 1980.

Austerities, Braziller, 1982.
Weather Forecast for Utopia and Vicinity, Station Hill Press, 1983.
Selected Poems 1963-1983, Braziller, 1985.
Unending Blues, Harcourt, 1986.
The World Doesn't End, Harcourt, 1989.
The Book of Gods and Devils, Harcourt, 1990.

ESSAYS AND INTERVIEWS

The Uncertain Certainty: Interviews, Essays, and Notes on Poetry, University of Michigan Press, 1985.
Wonderful Words, Silent Truth, University of Michigan Press, 1990.

TRANSLATOR

Ivan V. Lalic, *Fire Gardens,* New Rivers Press, 1970.
Vasko Popa, *The Little Box: Poems,* Charioteer Press, 1970.
Four Modern Yugoslav Poets: Ivan V. Lalic, Branko Miljkovic, Milorad Pavic, Ljubomir Simovic, Lillabulero (Ithaca, NY), 1970.
(And editor with Mark Strand) *Another Republic: 17 European and South American Writers,* Viking, 1976.
Key To Dream, According to Djordje, Elpenor, 1978.
Popa, *Homage to the Lame Wolf: Selected Poems,* Field (Oberlin, OH), 1979.
(With Peter Kastmiler) Slavko Mihalic, *Atlantis,* Greenfield Review Press, 1983.
(With others) Henri Michaux, *Translations: Experiments in Reading,* OARS, 1983.
Tomaz Salamun, *Selected Poems of Tomaz Salamun,* Viking, 1987.
Lalic, *Roll Call of Mirrors,* Wesleyan University Press, 1987.
Ristovic, Aleksandar, *Some Other Wine or Light,* Charioteer Press, 1989.

CONTRIBUTOR

The Young American Poets, Follett, 1968.
The Contemporary American Poets, World Publishing, 1969.
Major Young American Poets, World Publishing, 1971.
America a Prophesy, Random House, 1973.
Shake the Kaleidoscope: A New Anthology of Modern Poetry, Pocket Books, 1973.
The New Naked Poetry, Bobbs-Merrill, 1976.
The American Poetry Anthology, Avon, 1976.
A Geography of Poets, Bantam, 1979.
Contemporary American Poetry, 1950-1980, Longman, 1983.
The Norton Anthology of Poetry, Norton, 1983.
Harvard Book of American Poetry, Harvard University Press, 1985.
The Harper American Literature, Volume 2, Harper, 1987.

OTHER

Contributor of poetry to more than 100 magazines, including *New Yorker, Poetry, Nation, Kayak, Atlantic, Esquire, Chicago Review, New Republic, American Poetry Review, Paris Review,* and *Harvard Magazine.*

SIDELIGHTS: Charles Simic, a native of Yugoslavia who emigrated to America in his teens, has been hailed as one of the finest of America's younger generation of poets. Simic's work has won numerous prestigious awards, among them the coveted MacArthur foundation "genius grant." Although he writes in English, Simic draws heavily upon Eastern European tradition—and his own experiences of war-torn Belgrade—to compose poems about the physical and spiritual poverty of modern life. *Hudson Review* contributor Liam Rector notes that the author's work "has about it a purity, an originality unmatched by many of his contemporaries."

The MacArthur foundation grant may have widened Simic's audience, but the poet has never lacked admirers in the community of creative writers. In the *Chicago Review,* Victor Contoski characterizes Simic's work as "some of the most strikingly original poetry of our time, a poetry shockingly stark in its concepts, imagery, and language." *Georgia Review* correspondent Peter Stitt writes: "The fact that [Simic] spent his first eleven years surviving World War II as a resident of Eastern Europe makes him a going-away-from-home writer in an especially profound way. . . . He is one of the wisest poets of his generation, and one of the best." In a piece for the *New Boston Review,* Robert Shaw concludes that Simic "is remarkably successful at drawing the reader into his own creative moment."

Simic spent his formative years in Belgrade. His early childhood coincided with the Second World War; several times his family members evacuated their home on foot to escape indiscriminate bombing. The atmosphere of violence and desperation continued after the war as well. Simic's father left the country for work in America, and his mother tried several times to follow, only to be turned back at the border by Yugoslavian authorities. In the meantime, young Simic was growing up in Belgrade, where he was considered a below-average student and a minor troublemaker.

When Simic was fifteen his mother finally arranged for the family to travel to Paris. After a year spent studying English in night school and attending French public schools during the day, Simic sailed for America and reunion with his father. He entered the United States at New York City and then moved with his family to Chicago, where he enrolled in high school. In that environment—a suburban school with caring teachers and motivated students—Simic began to take new interest in his courses, especially literature. After graduation he managed to attend college at night while holding a full-time job as an office boy with the *Chicago Sun Times.*

Simic's first poems were published in 1959, when he was twenty-one. Between that year and 1961, when he entered the service, he churned out a number of poems, most of which he has since destroyed. Simic finally earned his Bachelor's degree in 1966. His first full-length collection of poems, *What the Grass Says,* was published the following year. In a very short time, Simic's work—original poetry in English and translations of important Yugoslavian poets—began to attract critical attention. In *The American Moment: American Poetry in the Mid- Century,* Geoffrey Thurley notes that the substance of Simic's earliest verse—its material referents—"are European and rural rather than American and urban. . . . The world his poetry creates—or rather with its brilliant semantic evacuation *de*creates—is that of central Europe—woods, ponds, peasant furniture." *Voice Literary Supplement* reviewer Matthew Flamm also contends that Simic was writing "about bewilderment, about being part of history's comedy act, in which he grew up half-abandoned in Belgrade and then became, with his Slavic accent, an American poet."

Simic's work defies easy categorization. Some poems reflect a surreal, metaphysical bent and others offer grimly realistic portraits of violence and despair. *Hudson Review* contributor Vernon Young maintains that memory—a taproot deep into European folklore—is the common source of all of Simic's poetry. "Simic, a graduate of NYU, married and a father in pragmatic America, turns, when he composes poems, to his unconscious and to earlier pools of memory," the critic writes. "Within mi-

crocosmic verses which may be impish, sardonic, quasi-realistic or utterly outrageous, he succinctly implies an historical montage." Young elaborates: "His Yugoslavia is a peninsula of the mind. . . . He speaks by the fable; his method is to transpose historical actuality into a surreal key. . . . [Simic] feels the European yesterday on his pulses."

Some of Simic's best known works challenge the dividing line between the ordinary and extraordinary. He gives substance and even life to inanimate objects, discerning the strangeness in household items as ordinary as a knife or a spoon. Shaw writes in the *New Republic* that the most striking perception of the author's early poems was that "inanimate objects pursue a life of their own and present, at times, a dark parody of human existence." *Chicago Review* contributor Victor Contoski concludes: "Simic's efforts to interpret the relationship between the animate and inanimate have led to some of the most strikingly original poetry of our time, a poetry shockingly stark in its concepts, imagery, and language." As Anthony Libby puts it in the *New York Times Book Review,* Simic "takes us to his mysterious target, the other world concealed in this one."

Childhood experiences of war, poverty, and hunger lie behind a number of Simic's poems. *Georgia Review* correspondent Peter Stitt claims that the poet's most persistent concern "is with the effect of cruel political structures upon ordinary human life. . . . The world of Simic's poems is frightening, mysterious, hostile, dangerous." Thurley too declares that Simic "creates a world of silence, waiting for the unspeakable to happen, or subsisting in the limbo left afterwards. . . . The dimension of menace in Simic becomes metaphysics in itself." Simic tempers this perception of horror with gallows humor and an ironic self-awareness. Stitt claims: "Even the most somber poems . . . exhibit a liveliness of style and imagination that seems to re-create, before our eyes, the possibility of light upon the earth. Perhaps a better way of expressing this would be to say that Simic counters the darkness of political structures with the sanctifying light of art."

Critics find Simic's style particularly accessible, a substantial achievement for an author for whom English is a second language. According to Shaw, the "exile's consciousness still colors [Simic's] language as well as his view of existence. Having mastered a second language, Simic is especially aware of the power of words, and of the limits which words grope to overcome. His diction is resolutely plain: as with the everyday objects he writes about, he uncovers unexpected depth in apparently commonplace language." In the *New Letters Review of Books,* Michael Milburn writes: "Charles Simic is a poet of original vision. . . . Simic practically taunts the reader with a familiarity bordering on cliche. He seems to challenge himself to write as plainly as possible, while still producing works of freshness and originality. [His works] literally beckon us off the street and into a world that at first looks indistinguishable from our own. . . . But a brilliant method lies behind Simic's plainness. . . . Casual, unobtrusive language expresses the most fantastic images." Milburn concludes that the poet "mines ingredients of language and experience that readers may take for granted, and fuses them in a singular music."

For more than fifteen years Simic has taught English, creative writing, and criticism at the University of New Hampshire. Today, thanks to the MacArthur fellowship and several Pulitzer Prize nominations, his writing has earned a wide audience in America and abroad. *Poetry* magazine essayist Diane Wakoski calls Simic's work "cryptic and fascinating. . . . This is the kind of poem you can turn inside out, make symbolic, make metaphoric, make religious, make aesthetic, and still have a beautiful cryptic little piece, written as if it were a folk poem or perhaps a child's verse that wasn't intended to be complex at all." According to David Ignatow in the *New York Times Book Review,* Simic's poems show "that it is possible to write intensely personal poetry without openly placing oneself at the center. . . . His poems echo and re-echo in the mind, as of memories of lives, impulses and cataclysms long since buried within us." Likewise, *New York Times Book Review* contributor Stephen Dobyns contends that when one reads a Simic piece, "one has a sense of the world made bigger and taken out of the hands of the bandits and the captains. A poem may create only a very small scene, but that scene continues to expand and ramify within the imagination." Milburn notes that reading Simic's poems "is less a matter of self-discipline than of giving in to the temptation of beauty." The critic concludes: "Simic's poems are the kind one thinks of when asked to define poetry."

Simic told *CA:* "The tradition that I find myself philosophically and temperamentally in tune with is that of Emily Dickinson, Robert Frost and Wallace Stevens. I have been called a 'surrealist,' a 'magic realist' and a 'plain old realist,' and I accept all three."

BIOGRAPHICAL/CRITICAL SOURCES:

BOOKS

Contemporary Authors Autobiography Series, Volume 4, Gale, 1986.
Contemporary Literary Criticism, Gale, Volume 6, 1976; Volume 9, 1978; Volume 22, 1982; Volume 49, 1988.
Thurley, Geoffrey, *The American Moment: American Poetry in the Mid- Century,* St. Martin's, 1978.

PERIODICALS

Antioch Review, spring, 1977.
Boston Review, March/April, 1981; April, 1986.
Chicago Review, Volume 48, number 4, 1977.
Chicago Tribune Book World, June 12, 1983.
Choice, March, 1975.
Gargoyle, number 22/23, 1983.
Georgia Review, winter, 1976; summer, 1986.
Hudson Review, spring, 1981; autumn, 1986.
Los Angeles Times Book Review, March 16, 1986; December 7, 1986.
New Boston Review, March/April, 1981.
New Letters Review of Books, spring, 1987.
New Republic, January 24, 1976.
New York Times, May 28, 1990.
New York Times Book Review, March 5, 1978; October 12, 1980; May 1, 1983; January 12, 1986; October 18, 1987.
Ploughshares, Volume 7, number 1, 1981.
Poet and Critic, Volume 9, number 1, 1975.
Poetry, December, 1968; September, 1971; March, 1972; February, 1975, November, 1978; July, 1981; October, 1983; July, 1987.
Poetry Review, June, 1983.
Publishers Weekly, November 2, 1990.
Stand, summer, 1984.
Village Voice, April 4, 1974; February 28, 1984.
Virginia Quarterly Review, spring, 1975.
Voice Literary Supplement, December, 1986.
Washington Post, April 13, 1990.
Washington Post Book World, November 2, 1980; April 13, 1986; May 7, 1989.

—*Sketch by Anne Janette Johnson*

SIMON, Claude 1913-

PERSONAL: Surname is pronounced See-moan; born October 10, 1913, in Tananarive, Madagascar; French citizen by birth; son of Louis (a career officer) and Suzanne (Denamiel) Simon; married Yvonne Ducing, 1951 (marriage ended); married Rhea Karavas, May 29, 1978. *Education:* Educated in France.

ADDRESSES: Home—3 Place Monge, 75005 Paris, France. *Office*—Editions de Minuit, 7 rue Bernard-Palissy, 75006 Paris, France.

CAREER: Writer. *Military service:* French Cavalry, 1939-40; became brigadier.

AWARDS, HONORS: Prix de l'Express, 1960, for *La Route des Flandres;* Prix Medicis, 1967, for *Histoire;* Nobel Prize for literature, 1985.

WRITINGS:

NOVELS

Le Tricheur (title means "The Cheat"), Sagittaire, 1945.
La Corde raide (title means "The Taut Rope"), Editions de Minuit, 1947.
Gulliver, Calmann-Levy, 1952.
Le Sacre du printemps (title means "The Crowning of Spring"), Calmann-Levy, 1954.
(Author of text) *Femmes,* paintings by John Miro, Maeght (Paris), 1966, Simon's text reprinted as *La Chevelure de Berenice,* Editions de Minuit, 1983.
Orion aveugle (title means "Blind Orion"), Skira, 1970.
Discours de Stockholm, Editions de Minuit, 1986.
L'Invitation, Editions de Minuit, 1987.

NOVELS WITH ENGLISH TRANSLATIONS

Le Vent: Tentative de restitution d'un retable baroque, Editions de Minuit, 1957, translation by Richard Howard published as *The Wind,* Braziller, 1959, reprinted, 1986.
L'Herbe, Editions de Minuit, 1958, translation by Howard published as *The Grass,* Braziller, 1960, reprinted, Riverrun, 1986.
La Route des Flandres, Editions de Minuit, 1960, translation by Howard published as *The Flanders Road,* Braziller, 1961, reprinted, Riverrun, 1986.
La Palace, Editions de Minuit, 1962, translation by Howard published as *The Palace,* Braziller, 1963.
Histoire, Editions de Minuit, 1967, translation by Howard published under same title, Braziller, 1968.
La Bataille de Pharsale, Editions de Minuit, 1969, translation by Howard published as *The Battle of Pharsalus,* Braziller, 1971.
Les Corps conducteurs, Editions de Minuit, 1971, translation by Helen Lane published as *Conducting Bodies,* Viking, 1974.
Triptyque, Editions de Minuit, 1973, translation by Lane published as *Triptych,* Viking, 1976, revised edition, Riverrun, 1986.
Lecon de choses, Editions de Minuit, 1975, translation by Daniel Weissbort published as *The World about Us,* Ontario Review Press, 1983.
Les Georgiques, Editions de Minuit, 1981, translation by Beryl Fletcher and John Fletcher published as *The Georgics,* Riverrun Press, 1989.

WORK IN PROGRESS: A novel.

SIDELIGHTS: Though considered one of the most important New Novelists in France, Claude Simon has been slow to gain recognition in the United States. Because at first glance Simon's writing "seems incoherent, merely a series of disconnected fragments, a lyrical but meaningless collection of images," observed Morton P. Levitt, "even a reasonably conscientious reader is apt to be confused by what appears to be, in the worst modern tradition, a narrative experiment without meaning or substance. These impressions are misleading, however, for Simon is one of the finest living novelists."

Four of Simon's novels, *The Grass, The Flanders Road, The Palace,* and *Histoire,* form part of a single work connected by various recurring characters and incidents. The best known of the four is *Histoire,* which won the Prix Medicis in 1967.

Superficially, *Histoire* is "the history of the narrator's story of his family as it is captured on the page by reminiscences of intimately evocative material possessions: the ancestral home, bits of furniture, family portraits, faded album photos and postal cards," stated the *Virginia Quarterly Review.* But Georges Schlocker noted that "the essence of the book lies in the confrontation of its characters with passing time and in the states of mind resulting therefrom." The book attempts to recall and recreate reality, which to Simon is "made up of occurrences scattered in time and space, yet belonging to the same emotional or spiritual experience." As a result, all the characters and events are jumbled together. "The past often invades the present without the usual typographical warnings of a new sentence or paragraph," Leo Bersani observed, "and the mixture is made even more confusing by the fact that the whole novel is written in past tenses. The 'he' referred to in one line may not be the same person as the 'he' mentioned in the next line."

Some critics were put off by the vagaries of the text. For example, the book jacket explains that one of the central occurrences in *Histoire* is the "suicide of a cousin adored but somehow betrayed by the narrator." Hugh Kenner complained: "At the publishing house they will have given 'Histoire' more than one reading, and 'somehow' was still the best they could do. ('Hey, George, how the heck shall I say he betrayed her?' 'Somehow.')" But Levitt defended the novel: "If it is incomplete, it is only because the narrator refuses to fill in all the gaps; if it seems disordered, it is because it is the product of a disordered point of view. The narrator fails in his effort to know himself, and, because form and function are here indistinguishable, we can know him only if we can understand the method of his narrative." A *Time* reviewer explained it this way: "Simon is at ease with uncertainties and loose ends. In fact, loose ends are his antennae. How he uses them to convey his own private perceptions is his mystery and his art."

In the tradition of other New Novelists such as Sarraute, Robbe-Grillet, and Butor, Simon attempts to create an awesome awareness of reality through experimentation with different points of view. But Simon transcends the New Novel by exploring the possibilities of language and by sympathetically presenting each of his characters as "a kind of every-man who suffers for all men," noted Levitt. The *Virginia Quarterly Review* contended that "what distinguished 'Histoire' from so many dreary and boring nouveau roman attempts at capturing the truths of reality is that Claude Simon structures his remembrances around crucial centripetal happenings that manage to sustain the reader's interest."

Numerous critics have pointed out the influence of Faulkner and Proust on Simon's writing. The *Tri-Quarterly* noted that "a Simon novel translated by an American reads so like a Faulkner novel" because of the long, convoluted sentences, lack of punctuation, abrupt transitions, and confused chronology. Simon himself once commented that *The Sound and the Fury* "truly revealed to me what writing could be. But what I prefer in Faulk-

ner is his Joycean and Proustian side." In a similar vein, Hugh Kenner remarked that "Simon is investing his Proustian material with Faulknerian mechanisms and mannerisms." In 1985, Simon finally won wide recognition when he was awarded the Nobel Prize for literature. Writing in the *Dictionary of Literary Biography,* Doris Y. Kadish reported that "the Nobel Academy praised Simon for having combined the creativity of the poet and the painter and expressed a profound sense of time and the human condition."

BIOGRAPHICAL/CRITICAL SOURCES:

BOOKS

Contemporary Literary Criticism, Gale, Volume 4, 1975, Volume 9, 1978, Volume 15, 1980, Volume 39, 1986.
Dictionary of Literary Biography, Volume 83: *French Novelists since 1960,* Gale, 1989.

PERIODICALS

Best Sellers, April 15, 1971.
Books Abroad, spring, 1968.
Chicago Tribune, October 18, 1985.
Critique, Volume 12, number 1, 1970.
Globe and Mail (Toronto), October 19, 1985, December 14, 1985.
Kenyon Review, Issue 1, 1967.
Los Angeles Times Book Review, July 26, 1987.
New Republic, June 8, 1968.
New York Times, November 28, 1967, October 18, 1985, October 20, 1985, October 30, 1985, November 4, 1985.
New York Times Book Review, January 21, 1968, July 14, 1968, September 15, 1974, April 1, 1984, October 1, 1989.
Saturday Review, April 17, 1971.
Spectator, April 18, 1969, July 19, 1969.
Time, March 29, 1968.
Times (London), October 26, 1985, June 8, 1989.
Times Literary Supplement, June 8, 1967, December 24, 1971, July 11, 1975, December 4, 1981, November 17, 1989.
Tribune Books (Chicago), September 17, 1989.
Tri-Quarterly, winter, 1967.
Virginia Quarterly Review, autumn, 1968, summer, 1971.
Washington Post Book World, August 15, 1976.

*   *   *

SNOWMAN, Daniel 1938-

PERSONAL: Born November 4, 1938, in London, England; son of Arthur Mortimer and Bertha (Lazarus) Snowman; married Janet Linda Levison, December 17, 1975; children: Benjamin Nathan, Anna-Luisa. *Education:* Cambridge University, B.A. (history; with double first-class honors), 1961; Cornell University, M.A. (political science), 1963.

ADDRESSES: Home—47 Wood Ln., Highgate, London N6 5UD, England. *Office*— British Broadcasting Corp., London W1A 1AA, England.

CAREER: University of Sussex, Brighton, England, lecturer in history and American studies, 1963-67; British Broadcasting Corp., London, England, 1967—, producer of talks, features, and documentaries, currently chief producer of BBC Radio Features. California State College, Dominguez Hills, visiting professor of American history, 1972-73. Invited speaker and lecturer to various universities and professional organizations in the United States, United Kingdom, and Canada. London Philharmonic Choir, singer and former chairman, 1967—.

WRITINGS:

U.S.A.: The Twenties to Vietnam, Batsford, 1968, reprinted as *America since 1920,* Harper, 1969, revised and updated edition, Heinemann Educational Books, 1984.
Eleanor Roosevelt, Heron Books, 1970.
Britain and America: An Interpretation of Their Culture, 1945-1975, New York University Press and Harper, 1977, published in England as *Kissing Cousins: An Interpretation of British and American Culture, 1945-1975,* Temple Smith, 1977.
If I Had Been. . . Ten Historical Fantasies, Robson Books Ltd., 1979.
The Amadeus Quartet: The Men and the Music, Robson Books Ltd., 1981.
The World of Placido Domingo, McGraw, 1985.
Beyond the Tunnel of History, Macmillan, 1990.

Contributor to numerous books, including *The British General Election of 1966,* edited by David Butler and Anthony King, Macmillan, 1966; *Since 1945: Aspects of Contemporary World History,* edited by James L. Henderson, Methuen, 1966; *The American Destiny: An Illustrated Bicentennial History of the United States,* edited by H. S. Commager, Orbis, 1976; and *Introduction to American Studies,* edited by Malcolm Bradbury and Howard Temperley, Longman, 1981. Contributor of numerous articles and reviews to American, British, Australian, and Spanish journals and newspapers.

BIOGRAPHICAL/CRITICAL SOURCES:

PERIODICALS

Los Angeles Times, August 17, 1979.
Times Literary Supplement, December 12, 1968; May 3, 1985.

*   *   *

SOMERS, Jane
See LESSING, Doris (May)

*   *   *

SOREL, Edward 1929-

PERSONAL: Surname originally Schwartz, legally changed to Sorel; born March 26, 1929, in New York City; son of Morris (a salesman) and Rebecca (a factory worker; maiden name, Kleinberg) Schwartz; married Elaine Rothenberg, July 1, 1956 (divorced, 1965); married Nancy Caldwell (a writer), May 29, 1965; children: (first marriage) Madeline, Leo; (second marriage) Jenny, Katherine. *Education:* Cooper Union College, diploma, 1951.

ADDRESSES: Home and office—156 Franklin St., New York, NY 10013. *Agent*—Milton Newborn, 135 East 54th St., New York, NY 10022.

CAREER: Push Pin Studios, New York City, co-founder, 1953, staff artist, 1953-55; Columbia Broadcasting System (CBS-TV), New York City, art director, promotion department, 1955-57; free-lance artist, 1956—. Staff artist for *Esquire.* Exhibitions in Europe and the United States.

AWARDS, HONORS: First prize for illustration of children's books, *New York Herald Tribune,* 1961, for *Gwendolyn, the Miracle Hen,* by Nancy Sherman; Augustus St. Gaudens Medal, Cooper Union, 1973; George Polk Award for satiric drawing; Page One award, Newspaper Guild of New York, for best edito-

rial cartoon (magazines), 1988; many awards for illustration from Society of Illustrators, American Institute of Graphic Arts, and Art Directors Club of New York.

WRITINGS:

SELF-ILLUSTRATED

How to be President, Grove, 1960.
Moon Missing, Simon & Shuster, 1962.
Sorel's World's Fair, New York, 1964, McGraw, 1964.
Making the World Safe for Hypocrisy: A Collection of Satirical Drawings and Commentaries, Swallow Press, 1972.
Superpen: The Cartoons and Caricatures of Edward Sorel, Random House, 1978.
The Zillionaire's Daughter, Warner Books, 1990.

OTHER

Also illustrator of numerous books, including *King Carlo of Capri,* by Warren Miller, Harcourt, 1958; *Gwendolyn, the Miracle Hen,* by Nancy Sherman, Golden Press, 1961; and *Word People,* by Nancy Caldwell Sorel, American Heritage Publishing, 1970. Contributing editor of *New York, Esquire, Gentlemen's Quarterly,* and *Village Voice.* Contributor to periodicals, including *Time* and *Atlantic.* Syndicated cartoonist for King Features, 1969-70.

SIDELIGHTS: Edward Sorel is best known as an award-winning caricaturist and satirist. In 1978, a number of Sorel's satiric magazine covers, drawings, and cartoons were collected in *Superpen.* R. W. Ryan commented in *Library Journal* that the "caricatures are as good as anyone's, anytime, and better than most." A reviewer for the *New York Times Book Review* likewise noted "the satire is caustic, anti- authority and thought-provoking; it is also miraculously, verbally and graphically funny." Although he recently published *The Zillionaire's Daughter,* since the publication of *Superpen,* Sorel has concentrated mainly on magazine work and a history of caricature.

BIOGRAPHICAL/CRITICAL SOURCES:

PERIODICALS

American Artist, May, 1960.
Atlantic, February, 1971.
Graphis, January, 1963.
Library Journal, May 15, 1978.
New York, May 25, 1960.
New York Times Book Review, May 14, 1978.

*   *   *

SORRENTINO, Gilbert 1929-

PERSONAL: Born April 27, 1929, in Brooklyn, NY; son of August E. and Ann Marie (Davis) Sorrentino; married Elsene Wiessner (divorced); married Vivian Victoria Ortiz; children: Jesse, Delia, Christopher. *Education:* Attended Brooklyn College (now Brooklyn College of the City University of New York), 1950-51, and 1955-57.

ADDRESSES: Agent—Mel Berger, William Morris Agency, 1350 Avenue of the Americas, New York, NY 10019. *Office*—Department of English, Stanford University, Stanford, CA 94305.

CAREER: "At least twenty-five jobs of all sorts," 1947-65; *Neon* (magazine), New York City, editor and publisher, 1956-60; Grove Press, New York City, editor, 1965-70; teacher at Columbia University, 1965, Aspen Writers Workshop, 1967, Sarah

Lawrence College, 1971-72, and New School for Social Research, 1976-79; University of Scranton, Scranton, PA, Edwin S. Quain Professor of Literature, 1979; Stanford University, Stanford, CA, professor of English, 1982—. *Military service:* U.S. Army, 1951-53; served in medical corps.

MEMBER: PEN American Center.

AWARDS, HONORS: Guggenheim fellow, 1973-74, 1987-88; Samuel S. Fels Award in fiction, 1974, for short story "Catechism"; Creative Artists Public Service grant, 1974-75; Ariadne Foundation grant, 1975; National Endowment for the Arts grant, 1975-76, 1978-79, 1983-84; John Dos Passos Prize, 1981; Mildred and Harold Strauss Livings (declined), 1982; American Academy and Institute of Arts and Letters Award for Literature, 1985.

WRITINGS:

POETRY

The Darkness Surrounds Us, Jargon Books, 1960.
Black and White, Totem Press/Corinth Books, 1964.
The Perfect Fiction, Norton, 1968.
Corrosive Sublimate, Black Sparrow Press, 1971.
A Dozen Oranges, Black Sparrow Press, 1976.
White Sail, Black Sparrow Press, 1977.
The Orangery, University of Texas Press, 1977.
Selected Poems, 1958-1980, Black Sparrow Press, 1981.

NOVELS

The Sky Changes, Hill & Wang, 1966.
Steelwork, Pantheon, 1970.
Imaginative Qualities of Actual Things, Pantheon, 1971.
Splendide-Hotel, New Directions, 1973.
Mulligan Stew, Grove, 1979.
Aberration of Starlight, Random House, 1980.
Crystal Vision, North Point Press, 1981.
Blue Pastoral, North Point Press, 1983.
Odd Number, North Point Press, 1985.
Rose Theatre, Dalkey Archive Press, 1987.
Misterioso, Dalkey Archive Press, 1989.

OTHER

Flawless Play Restored: The Masque of Fungo (play), Black Sparrow Press, 1974.
(Translator) *Sulpiciae Elegidia/Elegiacs of Sulpicia: Gilbert Sorrentino Versions,* Perishable Press, 1977.
Something Said: Essays, North Point Press, 1984.

Work appears in anthologies, including: *The New American Poetry, 1945-1960,* edited by Donald Allen, Grove, 1960; *Poesia Americana del '900,* Guanda, 1963; *The New Writing in the U.S.A.,* Penguin, 1967; *The Best American Short Stories,* Houghton, 1978; *Many Windows: 22 Stories from 'American Review,'* Harper, 1982; *Contemporary American Fiction,* Sun & Moon Press, 1983. Contributor to *New American Review, Nation, New York Times, Esquire, Partisan Review, TriQuarterly, Poetry, Harper's, Atlantic,* and other publications. Book editor, *Kulchur,* 1961-63; member of advisory committee, *Stanford Humanities Review;* editorial consultant, *Contemporary Literature.*

SIDELIGHTS: Gilbert Sorrentino has earned critical praise for his highly innovative fiction. The structures of his novels are of particular importance because Sorrentino holds that form is more important than content. "Form not only determines content," he says to Charles Trueheart in *Publishers Weekly,* "but form *invents* content." Accordingly, all of Sorrentino's novels are structured in unique ways. "His is a voice," writes William

Mattathias Robins in the *Dictionary of Literary Biography,* "that consistently and with ever-increasing originality stands out from the literary chorus."

Sorrentino's first novel, *The Sky Changes,* concerns an unhappy married couple who journey across America seeking a way to keep their marriage together. Richard Elman, writing in the *Review of Contemporary Fiction,* states that he knows "of few works . . . which are so subtle, and touching, in depicting the pain of being mismatched." Each chapter of the novel is named for a town the couple visits on their journey and relates the events which occur in that town. Sorrentino's narrative ignores time sequence in favor of spatial continuity. He states in the *Grosseteste Review:* "The past, the present, the future are mixed together in order to show very clearly that there is really no past that is worse than the present and there is no future that will be better than the present."

Sorrentino's next novel, *Steelwork,* also employs a nonchronological structure. Concerned with the sites and characters of his Brooklyn childhood, it is "an utterly different, quite original method of narration . . . ," writes Shaun O'Connell of the *Nation.* "[The novel] is made up of ninety-six separate but interlocking dramatic vignettes, scenes which, in their arrangement within the novel, scramble chronology." Jerome Klinkowitz, writing in *Literary Disruptions: The Making of a Post-Contemporary American Fiction,* finds *Steelwork's* narrative structure to be appropriate to its theme. "The subject is change," Klinkowitz writes, "and the book's form comes to terms with this reality, grasped imaginatively."

In *Imaginative Qualities of Actual Things,* Sorrentino satirizes the New York avant-garde art world of the 1960s, a world in which he played a part. "While each chapter is largely devoted to one of eight characters," writes John O'Brien in the *Dictionary of Literary Biography,* "the novel proceeds by way of digression, anecdote, asides, and itemizations, all filtered through a narrator whose rage and urbane wit mix into a strangely compassionate yet unsentimental treatment of these meretricious, sometimes gifted artists." Paul Theroux in the *Washington Post Book World* finds Sorrentino's satire effective, but believes the author unconsciously echoes what he attacks. "Few people are able to write as well as Sorrentino does here of literary posturing," Therous observes, "but the trouble is that the book assumes an elaborate posture of its own, and so does the narrator . . . ; the book contains many of the affectations it condemns." In contrast to this view, Klinkowitz sees *Imaginative Qualities* as "sorrentino's most fully realized expression of the novelist's proper role. Throughout he fights against the poor writing and misguided aesthetics that characterizes so much of recent conventional fiction."

O'Brien believes that "the technical achievements in [*Imaginative Qualities*] opened up a world of possibilities for future novels." These possibilities were partly explored by Sorrentino in *Splendide-Hotel,* a short book consisting of 26 sections, each section based on a letter of the alphabet. By structuring his novel around the alphabet, Sharon Fawcett writes in *Open Letter,* Sorrentino turns the book into "a defense of Poetry, radically so, in that it returns to the primary construct of words to get at primary meanings, images." Klinkowitz, writing in the *Village Voice,* sees this alphabetic structure as a method to make the reader deliberately aware of the novel as writing. It "keeps us right on the pages, like a painter keeps us on the canvas," he explains. "All Gilbert Sorrentino's work refuses to be bland metafiction," Klinkowitz concludes, "recounting in second- order terms a story about another reality. It is instead something made and placed in the world, standing for nothing but itself."

Perhaps Sorrentino's most acclaimed novel is *Mulligan Stew,* a book O'Brien calls "literally a synthesis of almost everything Sorrentino had read and written in the past twenty-five years." The novel is such a *tour de force* that John Leonard of the *New York Times* believes there "is a very real question as to whether avant- garde fiction can survive Gilbert Sorrentino's new novel." Drawing elements from a wide range of popular and serious literature, *Mulligan Stew* parodies its components. "A work of true comic genius," All Lacy calls the novel in *Books and Art,* "[*Mulligan Stew*] not only entertains and engages the intelligent reader, but also manages to shed light on the processes of literary creation, on the making of bad novels as well as good ones." Similarly, Malcolm Bradbury observes in his review of the book for the *New York Times Book Review* that *Mulligan Stew* "is a neo-Joycean concoction, spawning invention, delighting in lists, inventing languages, animating the endlessly comic fact that every sentence we write may generate its opposite, every structure of significance, every generative element in any story can move in an infinitude of directions. 'Mulligan Stew' mocks the act of creation. It also thrives on it, turning itself into an abundant and extravagently decorated display of the pleasures of the imagination."

O'Brien believes that Sorrentino established himself as a "major comic writer" with *Mulligan Stew.* "It contains some of the best parodies since S. J. Perleman at his most manic," Michael Dirda of the *Washington Post Book World* states, "and perhaps the most corrosive satire of the literary scene since early Aldous Huxley. This is a novel with all the stops pulled out, Gilbert Sorrentino's masterpiece." Kenneth John Atchity, reviewing the novel for the *Los Angeles Times Book Review,* also calls it a "masterpiece." He goes on to describe it as a "singular event in the history of wit and imagination. . . . 'Mulligan Stew' is teh end of the self-reflexive novel: Sorrentino brains the genre against the walls of prose. As we watch, we become accomplices, laughing at the murder—because it is a ritual, comic suicide—with a mixture of horror and relief. It's as though Sorrentino, broom and dustpan in hand, has swept into one large steamer trunk—or one pot of Mulligan stew—all the literary leftovers from the past quarter- century." According to Stuart Dybek, writing in the *Detroit News, Mulligan Stew* "catapulted Gil Sorrentino's reputation out of the literary underground. In great abundance, it [demonstrates] Sorrentino's collection of modernist techniques and devices as well as his special gift, the ability to blend them in the service of lucidity rather than mystification."

In his next novel, *Aberration of Starlight,* Sorrentino turns from extreme experimentation to a more conventional form. Set on the New Jersey coast during the Depression, the novel concerns four characters: a divorcee, her son, her father, and the unsavory man they meet on their vacation. "It's the kind of plot," Dybek notes, "that could easily become melodrama in the hands of a less acid writer than Sorrentino." John Morse of *Chicago Review* sees *Aberration of Starlight* as a quite different novel than *Mulligan Stew.* "[It] is disciplined in length and form, modest in ambition, and downright decorous in tone," he states. Writing in the *New York Review of Books,* Josh Rubins also sees a great difference between the two books. After rejcting the possibility that Sorrentino may again be writing parody, Rubins believes that the novel is really about five characters—the five fictional characters and Sorrentino himself. "But if *Aberration of Starlight* does indeed tell a story of five characters," he writes, "offering more of the traditional novelistic values . . . than Sorrentino has allowed himself in years, it is also his most 'experimental' fiction yet, in the sense that an experiment is something whose outcome you don't know in advance."

With *Odd Number, Rose Theatre,* and *Misterioso,* Sorrentino creates a trilogy of experimental novels. *Odd Number* consists of a series of questions, asked first of a reticent character and then of an unreliable one. *Rose Theatre* employs a range of narrative styles which change from one chapter to the next. *Misterioso* concludes the trilogy with an encyclopedic, alphabetical listing of "all the people, places and objects from the two earlier novels," as Larry McCaffery writes in the *Los Angeles Times Book Review.* Wildly comic, the trilogy "shows just how disjointed, trivial and enigmatic the lives of most Americans really are," McCaffery writes. "It would be easy," Jeffrey A. Frank notes in the *Washington Post Book World,* "and probably wrong, to put a label like 'satire' on this odd piece of fiction." Frank believes that Sorrentino's comedy "comes close to being literary *schtick.*" In his review of *Misterioso,* the trilogy's concluding novel, McCaffery states that it is "rich in voice, devastating in its satiric impulses and startling in its formal ingenuity. . . . A literary game which not only imitates, parodies, satirizes and elaborates upon the fantasies, pleasures, surprises, and disappointments of American life, it also most tellingly *invents* specific possibilities of which American life is incapable."

Speaking of Sorrentino's career, Ray Sawhill of *Newsweek* writes: "Sorrentino has the mind of an avant-garde experimentalist and the instincts of a profane showman. His novels overflow with elaborate literary contrivances and games, and the titles he gives them . . . lead you to expect one hall of mirrors after another. But there's nothing dry or ingrown about his writing. His novels have the kind of physical charge and excitement more often associated with jazz and improvisational comedy than with literature."

BIOGRAPHICAL/CRITICAL SOURCES:

BOOKS

Contemporary Literary Criticism, Volume 3, 1975, Volume 7, 1977, Volume 14, 1980, Volume 22, 1982, Volume 40, 1986.
Dictionary of Literary Biography, Volume 5: *American Poets since World War II,* Gale, 1980.
Dictionary of Literary Biography Yearbook: 1980, Gale, 1981.
Klinkowitz, Jerome, *Literary Disruptions: The Making of a Post-Contemporary American Fiction,* University of Illinois Press, 1975.
Ossmann, David, *The Sullen Art,* Corinth Books, 1963.
Phelps, Donald, *Covering Ground: Essays for Now,* Corinth Books, 1969.

PERIODICALS

American Poetry Review, January-February, 1979.
Antioch Review, Volume 34, numbers 1-2, 1975.
Atlantic, August, 1980.
Books and Art, July 23, 1979.
Chicago Review, autumn, 1980.
Chicago Tribune Book World, September 28, 1980; February 14, 1982.
Detroit News, August 24, 1980.
Extrapolation, summer, 1981.
Grosseteste Review, Volume 6, numbers 1-4, 1973.
Hudson Review, autumn, 1974.
Los Angeles Times Book Review, July 8, 1979; December 10, 1989.
Modern Occasions, winter, 1972.
Nation, October 14, 1961; June 21, 1971; August 21, 1972.
Newsweek, July 4, 1983.

New York Review of Books, July 19, 1979; December 18, 1980.
New York Times, May 24, 1979.
New York Times Book Review, July 2, 1972; May 24, 1979; August 26, 1979; August 10, 1980; November 8, 1981; June 19, 1983; January 14, 1990.
Parnassus, fall/winter, 1972.
Publishers Weekly, May 27, 1983.
Review of Contemporary Fiction, spring, 1981.
Saturday Review, August, 1980.
Times (London), June 18, 1981.
Times Literary Supplement, May 2, 1980; July 10, 1981; December 4, 1981; January 29, 1982; May 25-31, 1990.
Village Voice, November 22, 1973; May 28, 1979.
Vort, fall, 1974.
Washington Post Book World, November 7, 1971; June 17, 1979; August 31, 1980; August 2, 1981; December 20, 1981; May 22, 1983; January 7, 1990.

* * *

SPACKS, Barry 1931-

PERSONAL: Born February 21, 1931, in Philadelphia, PA; son of Charles (a merchant) and Evelyn (Schindler) Spacks; married Patricia Meyer (a teacher and writer), June 10, 1955; children: Judith. *Education:* University of Pennsylvania, B.A., 1952; Indiana University, M.A., 1956. *Politics:* "Humane." *Religion:* "Same as politics."

ADDRESSES: Home—1111 Bath St., Santa Barbara, CA 93101.

CAREER: University of Florida, Gainesville, assistant professor, 1957-59; Massachusetts Institute of Technology, Cambridge, professor of literature, 1960-78; member of faculty at University of Kentucky, 1978-79; University of California, Berkeley, member of faculty, 1980; University of California, Santa Barbara, member of faculty, 1981—. *Military service:* U.S. Army, Signal Corps, 1952-54.

AWARDS, HONORS: Fulbright scholar, Cambridge University, 1956-57; St. Botolph's Arts Award, 1971, for fiction and poetry; Silver Medal for Poetry, Commonwealth Club of California Book Awards, 1983, for *Spacks Street: New and Selected Poems.*

WRITINGS:

The Sophomore (novel), Prentice-Hall, 1968.
The Company of Children (poems), Doubleday, 1969.
Orphans (novel), Harper Magazine Press, 1972.
Something Human (poems), Harper Magazine Press, 1972.
Teaching the Penguins to Fly (poems), David R. Godine, 1975.
Imagining a Unicorn (poems), University of Georgia Press, 1978.
Spacks Street: New and Selected Poems, Johns Hopkins University Press, 1982.
Brief Sparrows, Illuminati, 1988.

Contributor to periodicals, including *Hudson Review, New Yorker, Poetry,* and *Atlantic Monthly.*

WORK IN PROGRESS: Like a Prism, a collection of poems; *The Only Poet,* a novel.

BIOGRAPHICAL/CRITICAL SOURCES:

BOOKS

Contemporary Literary Criticism, Volume 14, Gale, 1980.

PERIODICALS

Observer Review, February 16, 1969.
Poetry, January, 1970.
Prairie Schooner, winter, 1970-71.

Saturday Review, March 9, 1968; June 14, 1969.
Spectator, February 21, 1969.
Virginia Quarterly Review, summer, 1969.
Yale Review, autumn, 1972.*

* * *

STEAD, Christina (Ellen) 1902-1983

PERSONAL: Born July 17, 1902, in Rockdale, Sydney, New South Wales, Australia; died March 31, 1983, in Sydney, Australia; daughter of David George (a naturalist) and Ellen (Butters) Stead; married William James Blake, 1952 (an author; surname originally Blech; died, 1968). *Education:* Attended Teachers' College, Sydney University, received teacher's certification.

ADDRESSES: Home—Sydney, Australia. *Agent*—Joan Daves, 59 East 54th St., New York, NY 10022.

CAREER: Novelist, short story writer, editor, and translator. Worked as a public school teacher, a teacher of abnormal children, and a demonstrator in the psychology laboratory of Sydney University, all in Australia; grain company clerk, London, England, 1928-29; bank clerk in Paris, France, 1930-35; lived in the United States during the late 1930s and 1940s; senior writer for Metro-Goldwyn-Mayer, 1943; instructor in Workshop in the Novel, New York University, 1943-44; lived in Surbiton, England, from 1953 to 1968; permanently returned to Australia, 1974.

AWARDS, HONORS: Aga Khan Prize, *Paris Review,* 1966; Arts Council of Great Britain grant, 1967; fellow in creative arts, 1969, emeritus fellow, 1981- 82, both from Australian National University at Canberra; first recipient of Patrick White Award, 1974; honorary member, American Academy and Institute of Arts and Letters, 1982; Victorian Fellowship, Australian Writers Awards, 1986, for *Ocean of Story;* Premiere's Award for Literature, Premiere of New South Wales, Australia; several times nominated for the Nobel Prize.

WRITINGS:

NOVELS

Seven Poor Men of Sydney, Appleton, 1935.
The Beauties and Furies, Appleton, 1936.
House of All Nations, Simon & Schuster, 1938.
The Man Who Loved Children, Simon & Schuster, 1940, reprinted with introduction by Randall Jarrell, Holt, 1965.
For Love Alone, Harcourt, 1944.
Letty Fox: Her Luck, Harcourt, 1946.
A Little Tea, a Little Chat, Harcourt, 1948.
The People with the Dogs, Little, Brown, 1952.
Dark Places of the Heart, Holt, 1966 (published in England as *Cotters' England,* Secker & Warburg, 1966).
The Little Hotel, Angus & Robertson, 1973, Holt, 1975.
Miss Herbert (the Suburban Wife), Random House, 1976.
I'm Dying Laughing: The Humorist, Holt, 1987.

STORIES

The Salzburg Tales, Appleton, 1934.
The Puzzleheaded Girl (four novellas), Holt, 1967.
Ocean of Story (uncollected stories), edited by R. G. Geering, Viking, 1986.

OTHER

(Contributor) *The Fairies Return,* P. Davies, 1934.
(Editor with husband, William J. Blake) *Modern Women in Love,* Dryden Press, 1946.
(Editor) *South Sea Stories,* Muller, 1955.

(Translator) Fernand Gigon, *Colour of Asia,* Muller, 1955.
(Translator) Jean Giltene, *The Candid Killer,* Muller, 1956.
(Translator) August Piccard, *In Balloon and Bathyscape,* Cassell, 1956.
A Christina Stead Reader, selected by Jean B. Read, Random House, 1978.

Contributor of short stories to *Southerly, Kenyon Review,* and *Saturday Evening Post,* and of reviews to various papers. Stead's novels have been translated into foreign languages.

WORK IN PROGRESS: Short stories.

SIDELIGHTS: Australian-born novelist and short story author Christina Stead—whose work went unregarded for a large part of her life—is considered by many critics to be one of the most gifted writers of the twentieth century. Her novel *The Man Who Loved Children,* which depicts a boisterous, often cruel family led by an idealist father, is generally regarded as her masterpiece—although when first published in 1940 it was both a critical and popular failure. For years, it led an underground existence, read and admired by the cognoscenti. In a 1965 reprint edition, Randall Jarrell proclaimed: "If I were asked to name a good book that we don't read but that people of the future will read, I'd answer, almost with confidence, *The Man Who Loved Children.*" He goes on: "It seems to me as plainly good as *Crime and Punishment* and *Remembrance of Things Past* and *War and Peace* are plainly great. I call it a good book, but it is a better book, I think, than most of the novels people call great; perhaps it would be fairer to call it great. It has one quality that, ordinarily, only a great book has: it makes you a part of one family's immediate existence as no other book quite does. One reads the book, with an almost ecstatic pleasure of recognition. You get used to saying, 'Yes, that's the way it is'; and you say many times, but can never get used to saying, 'I didn't know *anybody* knew that. Henny, Sam, Louie, and the children are entirely real to the reader, and reality is rare in novels."

Critics praised Stead for her masterful and original depictions of characters, emotions, and atmosphere, yet she was also placed among writers of the nineteenth century. Christopher Ricks wrote: "In its sense of growth and of generations, in its generality and specificity, above all in the central place which it accords to feelings of indignation and embarrassment, *The Man Who Loved Children* is in the best tradition of the nineteenth-century novel. . . . Like George Meredith at his best, [Stead] is fascinated by the way we speak to ourselves in the privacy of our skulls, and she is able to remind us of what we would rather forget—that we are all continually employing, to ourselves and to others, a false rhetoric, overblown, indiscriminately theatrical, and yet indisputably ours." Ricks continued: "Everything in the book deserves notice. Its narrative skill; its sense of how much it matters to have money; its creation of locality (Washington, Baltimore); its pained insistence on the rights of women and children; its political acuteness, especially in its feeling for what underlies those people and those moments which protest that they are non-political; its presentation of a religious soft-soaping secularism: these are not extraneous but the fiber of the book." Eleanor Perry similarly remarked that the novel is "not a slice of life. It is life." Jose Yglesias proclaimed *The Man Who Loved Children* "a funny, painful, absorbing masterpiece, obviously the work of a major writer."

Jarrell wrote: "There is a bewitching rapidity and lack of self-consciousness about Christina Stead's writing; she has much knowledge, extraordinary abilities, but is too engrossed in what she is doing ever to seem conscious of them, so that they do not cut her off from the world but join her to it." Although best known for her achievements in *The Man Who Loved Children,* "in all her work, Stead displays a similar originality of concept, a brilliant, almost obsessive hold on subject and character and a headlong rush of language, more like a force of nature than a literary process, which is her unique signature," Helen Yglesias commented in the *Los Angeles Times Book Review.* The obituary writer for the London *Times* wrote that "in the end [Stead] did achieve a fame almost commensurate with her towering and always human achievement. She was one of the great originals, by whom it was almost impossible to be influenced." Yglesias called her "a master novelist of our time, for whom a resting place in the literature of the English language is assured."

BIOGRAPHICAL/CRITICAL SOURCES:

BOOKS

Contemporary Literary Criticism, Gale, Volume 4, 1975, Volume 5, 1976, Volume 8, 1978, Volume 32, 1985.
Geering, R. G., *Christina Stead,* Twayne, 1969.

PERIODICALS

Atlantic, March, 1965, June, 1965.
Book Week, April 18, 1965.
Chicago Tribune Book World, December 24, 1978.
Los Angeles Times, May 19, 1986.
Los Angeles Times Book Review, October 4, 1987, November 8, 1987.
Nation, April 5, 1965.
New York Review of Books, June 17, 1965.
New York Times Book Review, March 15, 1981, May 25, 1986.
Saturday Review, April 10, 1965.
Southerly (Sydney), 1962.
Times (London), January 12, 1985.
Times Literary Supplement, September 25, 1981, May 16, 1986, April 24, 1987.
Tribune Books (Chicago), October 4, 1987.
Washington Post Book World, May 25, 1986, December 20, 1987.

OBITUARIES:

PERIODICALS

New York Times, April 13, 1983.
Times (London), April 7, 1983.*

*   *   *

STEFFLER, John   1947-

PERSONAL: Born November 13, 1947, in Toronto, Ontario, Canada; son of Harold and Dorothy (Hoelscher) Steffler; married Shawn O'Hagan (a painter); children: one son, one daughter. *Education:* University of Toronto, B.A. (honors), 1971; University of Guelph, M.A., 1974.

ADDRESSES: Home—Corner Brook, Newfoundland, Canada. *Office*— Sir Wilfred Grenfell College, Memorial University of Newfoundland, Corner Brook, Newfoundland, Canada A2H 6P9.

CAREER: University of Guelph, Guelph, Ontario, lecturer in English, 1974-75; Memorial University of Newfoundland, Corner Brook, associate professor of English, 1975—.

AWARDS, HONORS: Norma Epstein Award, University of Toronto, 1971, for "Thought Plumbing"; awards from Ontario Arts Council, Newfoundland Arts Council, and Canada Council of Arts.

WRITINGS:

An Explanation of Yellow (poems), Borealis Press, 1981.
The Grey Islands (poems), McClelland & Stewart, 1984.
Flights of Magic, Press Porcepic, 1987.
The Wreckage of Play (poems; includes "Thought Plumbing"),
    McClelland & Stewart, 1988.

Contributor to anthologies, including *East of Canada,* 1979, *Thirty-One Newfoundland Poets,* 1979, and *The Maple Laugh Forever: An Anthology of Canadian Comic Poetry,* 1981. Contributor of poems to magazines, including *Malahat Review, Grain, Event, Queen's Quarterly, Canadian Literature, Antigonish Review,* and *Dalhousie Review.*

WORK IN PROGRESS: *The After-life of George Cartwright,* a novel.

SIDELIGHTS: In *The Grey Islands,* a combination of poetry and prose, Canadian John Steffler details the visit of a native Ontarian to northwest Newfoundland. "As Steffler chronicles his persona's inner and outer journeys," observes Lorna Crozier in the *Journal of Canadian Poetry,* "he manages to create a vivid collage of stories, imagery and characters that leaves us with a complex, many layered impression of Newfoundland and its Grey Islands." As a result, adds the critic, *The Grey Islands* "becomes a book of praise for a place and a people." Toronto *Globe and Mail* reviewer Fraser Sutherland has similar praise for another Steffler collection, *The Wreckage of Play,* noting that despite the lack of "a unified whole," the author's "talent is real and abiding, his restless, inquisitive sensibility oscillating between the inner and outer, organic and inorganic, biological and mechanical." At times, Sutherland concludes, Steffler "can transform the literally pedestrian into the marvelous."

Steffler told *CA:* "Whatever effect my work has, my intention is not to redesign the world but to see it clearly, to experience it as directly as possible and to represent that experience in words. Clear perception is a channel through which energy flows out of the world through us and into the world again. Perception is the substance and purpose of life; and poetry for me is a way of intensifying, capturing, and transmitting this energy.

"I am addicted to the activity of writing and in love with language as an instrument of expression. I believe there is no perception, thought, or feeling, however subtle or arcane, that cannot be communicated in words."

BIOGRAPHICAL/CRITICAL SOURCES:

PERIODICALS

Globe and Mail (Toronto), November 16, 1985; October 8, 1988.
Journal of Canadian Poetry, Volume 2, 1987.

* * *

STEVENSON, Anne (Katharine) 1933-

PERSONAL: Born January 3, 1933, in Cambridge, England; American citizen born abroad; daughter of Charles Leslie (a philosopher) and Louise (Destler) Stevenson; previously married and divorced; married Peter Lucas, September 3, 1987; children: Caroline Margaret Hitchcock, John Gawain Elvin, Charles Lionel Elvin. *Education:* University of Michigan, B.A., 1954, M.A., 1962. *Politics:* Democrat.

ADDRESSES: Home—30 Logan St., Langley Park, Durham DH7 9YN, England.

CAREER: Poet and critic. Fellow in writing at University of Dundee, Scotland, 1973-75, Lady Margaret Hall, Oxford,

1975-77, and Bulmershe College, Reading, 1977-78; The Poetry Bookshop, Hay-on-Wye, Wales, co-proprietor, 1978-81; Northern Arts Literary Fellow at University of Newcastle-upon-Tyne and University of Durham, 1981-82; writer in residence at University of Edinburgh, beginning in mid-1980s. Member of advisory panel of Arts Council of Great Britain, 1983-85. Part-time teacher of cello in Cambridge, England; cellist in string orchestra connected with Cambridge University.

MEMBER: Royal Society of Literature (fellow), Phi Beta Kappa.

AWARDS, HONORS: Avery and Jules Hopwood Award, University of Michigan, 1950, 1952, 1954; Scottish Arts Council Award, 1974; Welsh Arts Council Award, 1980.

WRITINGS:

POETRY, EXCEPT AS INDICATED

Living in America, Generation, 1965.
Elizabeth Bishop (criticism), Twayne, 1966.
Reversals, Wesleyan University Press, 1969.
Correspondences: A Family History in Letters, Wesleyan University Press, 1974.
Travelling behind Glass, Oxford University Press, 1974.
"Correspondences" (radio play), broadcast by British Broadcasting Corp. (BBC), 1975.
"Child of Adam" (radio play), broadcast by BBC, 1976.
Enough of Green, Oxford University Press, 1977.
A Morden Tower Reading 3, Morden Tower (Newcastle upon Tyne, England), 1977.
Cliff Walk: A Poem, Keepsake Press (Richmond, England), 1977.
Sonnets for Five Seasons, Five Seasons Press (Hereford, England), 1979.
Green Mountain, Black Mountain, Rowan Tree Press (Boston), 1982.
Minute by Glass Minute, Oxford University Press, 1982.
New Poems, Other Branch Readings (Leamington Spa, England), 1982.
Making Poetry, Pisces Press (Oxford, England), 1983.
A Legacy, Taxus Press (Durham, England), 1983.
Black Grate Poems, Inky Parrot Press (Oxford), 1984.
The Fiction-Makers, Oxford University Press, 1985.
Winter Time, Mid-Northumberland Arts Group (Ashington, England), 1986.
(Editor) Frances Bellerby, *Selected Poems,* Enitharmon (London, England), 1986.
(Editor with Amy Clampitt and Craig Raine) *1985 Anthology: The Observer and Ronald Duncan Foundation International Poetry Competition on Behalf of the Arvon Foundation,* Arvon Foundation (Beaworthy, England), 1987.
Selected Poems, 1956-1986, Oxford University Press, 1987.
Bitter Fame: A Life of Sylvia Plath (biography), Houghton, 1989.
The Other House, Oxford University Press, 1990.

Contributor to *Times Literary Supplement* and other periodicals in Great Britain and the United States. Former poetry critic for *Listener.* Co-editor, *Other Poetry Magazine.*

SIDELIGHTS: Anne Stevenson "has what Henry James call[ed] 'sensibility to the scenery of life,' " comments Dorothy Donnelly in *Michigan Quarterly Review.* "Her poems have added considerably to the scenery of our own landscapes." Stevenson's poetry, a *Times Literary Supplement* critic writes, is "remarkable for a fresh, authentic brand of realist observation and an impressive capacity to reflect intelligently on what it sees." Ralph J. Mills,

Jr. in *Poetry* calls Stevenson "one of the most promising young women poets."

The landscape that Stevenson creates is a shifting one, built upon the ambiguous borders between England and America, family and self, dependence and independence, tradition and nonconformity. "The landscape created by Anne Stevenson's poems . . . shimmers with the tenuous colors and outlines of reflections in water," Donnelly says of *Reversals*. "The poet hesitates, caught between reality and illusion, moving through a flickering, borderless region, a land behind the land. . . . Stevenson's poems evoke with delicacy the misty, the insubstantial, the indefinite, 'the line between land and water,' the view from which 'there is no end to illusion.' " Nicholas Brooke in *New Review* observes that the poems in *Travelling behind Glass* "characterize America and Europe from no fixed base."

Stevenson herself comments upon the feeling of movement and duality her poetry elicits. "Although I am an American . . . I have lived almost constantly in Great Britain since 1962," she writes. "This has meant a measure of flexibility and a constant sense of flux . . . [as well as] the sense I have constantly of a divided life between the Old World and the New."

Stevenson has developed this theme of "flux" in much of her work. In many of her poems it takes the form of the narrator questioning her own actions or the direction her life has taken. Stevenson is "given to querying life," states Donnelly, "and the frequent questions asked in these poems [in *Reversals*] indicate their prevailingly tentative tone. Answers are usually avoided, sometimes suggested, often simply not to be had." Kaye Boyd, a principal character in *Correspondences: A Family History in Letters*, questions her decision to become an author—a decision which also entails leaving her family home: "Dear Father, I love you but can't know you./ I've given you all that I can./ Can these pages make amends for what was not said?/ Do justice to the living, to the dead?" In "Victory," included in *Reversals*, the narrator is compelled to ask her infant son, "Why do I have to love you?"

Although the "landscape" in which Stevenson moves is "tentative," "flickering," and "borderless," her responses to it are not. *Times Literary Supplement*'s Andrew Motion observes, "The characteristic method of *Enough of Green* is to confront the harsh realities of life, acknowledge the temptation to evade them, and then discover rewards in them as well as disappointments."

Correspondences: A Family History in Letters is Stevenson's most ambitious accomplishment. The book traces the Chandler family from its pre-Revolution, New England roots to the present. "*Correspondences* . . . is an ambitious book," asserts Richard Caram in *Open Places*. "[It] just burns to be an American epic, to combine the insights of history with the characterizations of fiction and the fine aesthetic harmonies of poetry. And it works, in the end, far better than it has a right to—particularly as a very readable form of history, a mythopoetic look backward." Notes Stewart Conn in *Listener*: "With penetrating insight, Anne Stevenson depicts successive generations blighted by drink and estrangement, woe within marriage and a wonderment that man has deserved propagation at all in this wicked world."

Stevenson's characteristic sense of ambiguity is also present in *Correspondences*. Caram concludes that the final section of the book "does most deftly what poetry can do better than history: hold the ambiguities of the lives of the surviving members of the family in lifelike suspension, unwilling to resolve them into finalities, swirling them round and round in a mixture rhetorically rich enough to seem almost a resolution."

Other critics, however, feel that *Correspondences* tries to accomplish too great a task. Douglas Dunn in *Encounter* notes that the work "has been worked hard at, not only as a poem, but as something to hold the reader's attention; unfortunately, the impression is that the clever writer was conjuring with too many gimmicks, for all the weightiness of her critique of America." *New Review*'s Brooke comments that since the poems in *Correspondences* "are not long, it follows they are overloaded, and the story is reduced to familiar types. . . . A novelist would do more than this; a poet should not do less." Concurs Robert Garfitt in *London Magazine*: "Moving as some of [*Correspondences*] is . . . one is left wondering what it has achieved that a novel couldn't have achieved, and, more important, whether a more intimate and telling exploration, accessible only to poetry, hasn't been missed."

Despite these criticisms, Stevenson's reputation remains secure. "Her formal dexterity, her determination to include alternative responses to any given situation, and her ability to write with a detachment which is both objective and engaging prove her a poet of exceptional distinction," states Motion.

AVOCATIONAL INTERESTS: Music, traveling, and reading.

BIOGRAPHICAL/CRITICAL SOURCES:

BOOKS

Contemporary Authors Autobiography Series, Volume 9, Gale, 1989.
Contemporary Literary Criticism, Gale, Volume 7, 1977, Volume 33, 1985.
Dictionary of Literary Biography, Volume 40: *Poets of Great Britain and Ireland Since 1960*, Gale, 1985.

PERIODICALS

Encounter, December, 1974, April, 1978.
Globe and Mail (Toronto), October 28, 1989.
Lines Review 50, September, 1974.
Listener, November 28, 1974.
London Magazine, November, 1974.
Los Angeles Times Book Review, August 20, 1989.
Michigan Quarterly Review, fall, 1966, spring, 1971.
New Review, October, 1974.
New Statesman, November 28, 1974, February 10, 1978.
New York Times, August 9, 1989.
New York Times Book Review, November 15, 1987, August 27, 1989.
Open Places, spring/summer, 1976.
Ploughshares, autumn, 1978.
Poetry, February, 1971, November, 1975.
Times Literary Supplement, July 19, 1974, November 25, 1977, May 6, 1983, January 10, 1986, July 17, 1987, May 20, 1988, October 27, 1989, November 2-8, 1990.
Tribune Books (Chicago), August 13, 1989.
Washington Post Book World, August 20, 1989.*

*   *   *

STONE, Zachary
   See FOLLETT, Ken(neth Martin)

*   *   *

STOW, (Julian) Randolph 1935-

PERSONAL: Born November 28, 1935, in Geraldton, Western Australia; son of Cedric Ernest (a barrister and solicitor) and

Mary (Sewell) Stow. *Education:* University of Western Australia, B.A., 1956. *Religion:* Church of England.

ADDRESSES: c/o Richard Scott Simon Ltd., 43 Doughty St., London WC1N 2LF, England.

CAREER: Novelist and poet. Worked at various times on a mission for aborigines in northwest Australia, and as assistant to the government anthropologist in New Guinea; has lived in East Anglia, Scotland, and Malta, teaching English betweentimes in Australia at the University of Adelaide, 1957, and University of Western Australia, 1963-64, and in England at the University of Leeds, 1962, 1968-69. Harkness fellow, United States, 1964-66.

AWARDS, HONORS: Miles Franklin Award, 1958; Britannica Australia Award, 1966; Patrick White Award, 1979, for *Visitants.*

WRITINGS:

A Haunted Land (novel), Macdonald & Co., 1956, Macmillan, 1957.
The Bystander (novel), Macdonald & Co., 1957.
Act One (poems), Macdonald & Co., 1957.
To the Islands (novel), Macdonald & Co., 1958, Little, Brown, 1959, revised edition, Taplinger, 1982.
Outrider (poems), Macdonald & Co., 1962.
Tourmaline (novel), Macdonald & Co., 1963.
(Editor) *Australian Poetry 1964,* Angus & Robertson, 1964.
The Merry-Go-Round in the Sea (novel), Macdonald & Co., 1965, Morrow, 1966.
Midnite: The Story of a Wild Colonial Boy (novel for children), Macdonald & Co., 1967, Prentice-Hall, 1968.
A Counterfeit Silence: Selected Poems, Angus & Robertson, 1969.
Visitants (novel), Secker & Warburg, 1979, Taplinger, 1981.
The Girl Green as Elderflower (novel), Viking, 1980.
The Suburbs of Hell (novel), Taplinger, 1984.

Also author, with Peter Maxwell Davies, of "Eight Songs for a Mad King," 1969, and "Miss Donnithorne's Maggot," 1974, both music theater.

SIDELIGHTS: Randolph Stow is a novelist and poet known for his chilling examinations of contemporary problems in works that capture the dialect and character of his native Australia, as well as Melanesia and East Anglia. His early novels include *A Haunted Land,* about an Australian family's attempt to achieve emotional stability after experiencing a death; *To the Islands,* about an aged missionary's struggle to find his identity and lost spirituality; and *The Merry-Go-Round in the Sea,* about an Australian boy growing up during World War II. Often exploring the same themes of childhood, love, and death as his fiction, Stow's poetry has appeared in the volumes *Act One, Outrider,* and *A Counterfeit Silence.* Stow also wrote a novel for children, *Midnite,* as well as more recent novels, including his award-winning 1979 effort *Visitants,* and his 1984 "morality tale," *The Suburbs of Hell.*

BIOGRAPHICAL/CRITICAL SOURCES:

BOOKS

Contemporary Literary Criticism, Volume 48, Gale, 1988.
Hassall, Anthony J., *Strange Country: A Study of Randolph Stow,* University of Queensland Press, 1986.

PERIODICALS

Globe and Mail (Toronto), May 19, 1984.
London Review of Books, April 19-May 2, 1984.

Los Angeles Times Book Review, August 10, 1980.
National Review, May 31, 1985.
Sewanee Review, winter, 1984.
Spectator, February 27, 1982, April 7, 1984.
Times (London), April 5, 1984.
Times Literary Supplement, May 16, 1980, March 12, 1982.

* * *

STRAUSS, Gerald 1922-

PERSONAL: Born May 3, 1922, in Frankfurt, Germany; married Daphne Patai; children: Victoria, Konrad. *Education:* Boston University, B.A., 1949; Columbia University, M.A., 1950, Ph.D., 1957.

ADDRESSES: Office—Department of History, Indiana University, Bloomington, IN 47405.

CAREER: Phillips Exeter Academy, instructor, 1951-57; University of Alabama, University, assistant professor, 1957-59; Indiana University, Bloomington, 1959—, began as assistant professor, now Distinguished Professor of History, Emeritus.

AWARDS, HONORS: Fulbright fellow; Guggenheim fellow (twice); awards from American Council of Learned Societies, Deutscher Akademischer Austauschdienst, American Philosophical Society, and National Endowment for the Humanities; member, Institute for Advanced Study, Princeton, NJ, 1975.

WRITINGS:

Sixteenth-Century Germany: Its Topography and Topographers, University of Wisconsin Press, 1959.
Historian in an Age of Crisis: The Life and Work of Johannes Aventinus, 1477-1534, Harvard University Press, 1963.
Nuremberg in the Sixteenth Century, Wiley, 1967.
(Editor and translator) *Manifestations of Discontent in Germany on the Eve of the Reformation: A Collection of Documents Selected, Translated, and Introduced by Gerald Strauss,* Indiana University Press, 1971.
Luther's House of Learning: Indoctrination of the Young in the German Reformation, Johns Hopkins University Press, 1978.
Law, Resistance, and the State: The Opposition to Roman Law in Reformation Germany, Princeton University Press, 1986.

SIDELIGHTS: History professor Gerald Strauss's work *Luther's House of Learning* is a "fascinating book" that is "undoubtedly one of the most important books to have been published on the Reformation for some time," writes Joachim Whaley in the *Times Literary Supplement.* The work concerns the early sixteenth-century Lutheran reformers' attempts to use education as an evangelistic tool. Whaley approves Strauss's discussion on how primary, grammar and catechism schools were to be reorganized, and how proper discipline merged with a fear of God was to replace teacher-student cruelty. In reality, however, the results of the experiment were often harshness in the classroom and boredom for the student through the use of rote learning. Whaley concludes, "Professor Strauss combines meticulous and comprehensive research with stimulating and often provocative hypotheses. His analysis of the relationship between education and society in early sixteenth-century Germany raises important and still unanswered questions."

In Strauss's later analysis of Reformation Germany, *Law, Resistance, and the State,* the author studies how the acceptance of the central power of Roman law led to the emergence of the modern German state. *English History Review* contributor

Hanns Gross notes that the book "is both engagingly written and full of original illustrations from which he draws some very subtle and often unexpected insights." Despite some objections to the work based on its limited scope, Gross continues that "Within its limits [*Law, Resistance, and the State*] is a fine treatment."

BIOGRAPHICAL/CRITICAL SOURCES:

PERIODICALS

English Historical Review, July, 1987.
Times Literary Supplement, March 21, 1980.

*   *   *

STYRON, William 1925-

PERSONAL: Born June 11, 1925, in Newport News, Va.; son of William Clark (a shipyard engineer) and Pauline (Abraham) Styron; married Rose Burgunder, May 4, 1953; children: Susanna, Paola, Thomas, Alexandra. *Education:* Attended Christchurch School, Middlesex County, Va., and Davidson College; Duke University, A.B., 1947; studied writing at New School for Social Research. *Politics:* Democrat.

ADDRESSES: Home and office—Roxbury, Conn.; and Vineyard Haven, Mass. (summer).

CAREER: Writer. McGraw-Hill Book Co. (publishers), New York, N.Y., associate editor, 1947. Honorary consultant in American Letters to the Library of Congress; fellow of Silliman College, Yale University. *Military service:* U.S. Marine Corps, World War II; became first lieutenant; recalled briefly in 1951.

MEMBER: National Institute of Arts and Letters, American Academy of Arts and Sciences, American Academy of Arts and Letters (inducted, 1988), Signet Society of Harvard (honorary), Phi Beta Kappa.

AWARDS, HONORS: American Academy of Arts and Letters Prix de Rome, 1952, for *Lie Down in Darkness;* Pulitzer Prize, 1968, and Howells Medal of the American Academy of Arts and Letters, 1970, both for *The Confessions of Nat Turner;* American Book Award, National Book Critics Circle Award nominee, both 1980, both for *Sophie's Choice;* Connecticut Arts Award, 1984; Commandeur, Ordre des Arts et des Lettres (France), 1987; Edward MacDowell Medal, 1988.

WRITINGS:

Lie Down in Darkness, Bobbs-Merrill, 1951.
The Long March, Vintage, 1957.
Set This House on Fire, Random House, 1960.
The Confessions of Nat Turner, Random House, 1967.
In the Clap Shack (three-act play; first produced in New Haven at Yale Repertory Theatre, December 15, 1972), Random House, 1973.
Sophie's Choice, Random House, 1979.
This Quiet Dust (essays), Random House, 1982.
(Author of introduction) Robert Satter, *Doing Justice: A Trial Judge at Work,* American Lawyer Books/Simon & Schuster, 1990.
Darkness Visible, Random House, 1990.

Editor of *Paris Review: Best Short Stories,* published by Dutton. Contributor to *Esquire, New York Review of Books,* and other publications. Manuscript collections of Styron's work are held by the Library of Congress, Washington, D.C., and Duke University, Durham, North Carolina.

WORK IN PROGRESS: A semi-autobiographical novel about the Marine Corps.

SIDELIGHTS: William Styron's novels have brought him major literary awards, broad critical notice, and a reputation for raising controversial issues. In *The Confessions of Nat Turner* and *Sophie's Choice,* Styron writes about two victims of oppression: a slave and a concentration camp survivor. Although some critics question his approach, most praise Styron for probing into difficult subjects. Reviewers consider Styron's timing a positive factor in the success of these two books; *Sophie's Choice,* published during renewed concern about the Holocaust, and *The Confessions of Nat Turner,* published during the racially explosive late Sixties, both found large audiences. George Steiner comments in the *New Yorker:* "The crisis of civil rights, the new relationships to each other and to their own individual sensibilities that this crisis has forced on both whites and Negroes . . . give Mr. Styron's fable [*The Confessions of Nat Turner*] a special relevance."

Styron based *The Confessions of Nat Turner* on the transcript of testimony given by a slave, Nat Turner, who had led a brief revolt against slave owners in Virginia's Tidewater district. Styron considers his book a "meditation on history" rather than a strict retelling of events. He explains in a letter to the Nation that "in writing *The Confessions of Nat Turner* I at no time pretended that my narrative was an exact transcription of historical events; had perfect accuracy been my aim I would have written a work of history rather than a novel." Philip Rahv asserts that Styron's viewpoint is more valuable than a historical perspective. He writes in the *New York Review of Books:* "This narrative is something more than a novelistic counterpart of scholarly studies of slavery in America; it incarnates its theme, bringing home to us the monstrous reality of slavery in a psychodynamic manner that at the same time does not in the least neglect social or economic aspects."

Styron's subjective approach draws ire from critics who feel that his portrait of Nat is based on white stereotypes. A *Negro Digest* critic takes particular issue with Styron's depiction of Nat's sexuality: "In the name of fiction, Mr. Styron can do whatever he likes with History. When his interpretation, however, duplicates what is white America's favorite fantasy (i.e., every black male—especially the leader—is motivated by a latent(?) desire to sleep with the Great White Woman), he is obligated to explain (in the structure of the novel, of course) this coincidental duplication—or to be criticized accordingly. Since there is no such explanation in the technique of the novel and since it offers no vision or new perspective, but rather reaffirms an old stale, shameful fantasy (which is still quite salable) it is at best a good commercial novel." Albert Murray concurs in the *New Leader:* "Alas, what Negroes will find in Styron's 'confessions' is much the same old failure of sensibility that plagues most other fiction about black people. That is to say, they will all find a Nat Turner whom many white people may accept at a safe distance, but hardly one with whom Negroes will easily identify."

Other critics argue that Styron is entitled to give a personal interpretation of the story, whatever his views. Steiner asserts that Styron "has every artistic right to make of his Nat Turner less an anatomy of the Negro mind than a fiction of complex relationships, of the relationship between a present-day white man of deep Southern roots and the Negro in today's whirlwind." Stylistically, Styron is often compared with William Faulkner, who shares his Southern white background and his interest in depicting Black characters. According to Philip Rahv, "Styron has gained greatly from his ability to empathize with his Negro figures—with the protagonist, Nat, as well as with some of his fol-lowers—to live in them, as it were, in a way inconceivable even for Faulkner, Styron's prose-master. Whereas Faulkner's Ne-groes are still to some extent the white man's Negroes, Styron's are starkly themselves."

Styron writes about human suffering in a more contemporary setting—post-World War II Brooklyn—in *Sophie's Choice.* So-phie is a beautiful Polish gentile who survived Auschwitz but lost two of her children and much of her self-esteem there. Her lover, Nathan (mad, brilliant, and Jewish) is haunted by the atrocities of the Holocaust, although he personally escaped them, and he torments Sophie with reminders. Stingo, a young writer who lives downstairs from Sophie and Nathan, narrates. According to Geoffrey Wolff of *Esquire,* "Stingo is in the tradition of *The Great Gatsby*'s Nick Carraway. Like Nick, he bears witness to the passion of characters he chances upon and tries modestly to judge and pardon. Like Nick, he is a refugee from settled val-ues—Virginia's Tidewater country—back from a great war to make his way in the great world."

David Caute of the *New Statesman* hears additional voices. For him, the "neo-Biblical cadences of Southern prose, of Wolfe and Faulkner, jostle with the cosmopolitan sensibility of an F. Scott Fitzgerald." Other critics agree that the influence of other writ-ers sometimes muffles Styron's own voice. Jack Beatty writes in the *New Republic* that *Sophie's Choice* "is written in an unvary-ingly mannered style—High Southern—that draws constant spell-destroying attention to itself." The "Southern style" associ-ated with Faulkner and Thomas Wolfe is characterized by elabo-rate, even Gothic descriptions, and although Styron is "a novel-ist hard to categorise," he shows his allegiance to that style here and "in all of [his] writing," according to Caute, with "a ten-dency towards post-Wolfian inflation, a reluctance to leave any noun uncaressed by an adjective." Paul Gray of *Time* agrees, noting that Styron "often lets Stingo pile up adjectives in the manner of Thomas Wolfe: 'Brooklyn's greenly beautiful, homely, teeming, begrimed and incomprehensible vast-ness'. . . . True, Stingo is pictured as a beginning writer, heavily in debt to Faulkner, Wolfe and the Southern literary tradition, but Styron may preserve more redundant oratory than the effect of Stingo's youth strictly requires."

Robert Towers, writing in the *New York Review of Books,* also faults Styron for verbosity. " 'All my life, I have retained a strain of uncontrolled didacticism,' says Stingo at one point," Towers notes, "and *Sophie's Choice* bears him out. The novel is made to drag along an enormous burden of commentary, ranging all the way from the meaning of the Holocaust, the ineluctable nature of evil, the corrosive effects of guilt, the horrors of slavery, and the frailty of goodness and hope to such topics as the misunder-standing of the South by Northern liberals, Southern manners as opposed to those of New York taxi drivers, and the existence of prejudice and cruelty in even the best of us." But Wolff de-fends Styron, observing that "the book's narrative flow is sus-penseful if languid, if sometimes even glacial," and that "*Sophie's Choice* achieves an almost palpable evocation of its place and time—Poland before and during the war, Brooklyn and Coney Island immediately after." And Caute, despite his criticisms, contends that Styron's prose is "marked also by clarity, honesty and accessibility."

As evidence of Styron's narrative power, Gray asserts that he gives Sophie "a core of individuality that elevates her role be-yond that of a symbolic victim." Styron explains that his sympa-thy toward Sophie's character stems from personal experience. He modelled her after a woman he met when—like Stingo—he

was an aspiring writer living in a Brooklyn rooming house. Inspi-ration for the story came, he tells Tony Schwartz in *Newsweek,* when one day "I woke up with the remembrance of a girl I'd once known, Sophie. It was a very vivid half-dream, half-revelation, and all of a sudden I realized that hers was a story I had to tell." As in *Confessions,* Styron expanded on the original historical data when he wrote his story. "The fact is," he relates, "I didn't get to know [Sophie's prototype] very well and the story as it evolves in the book is made up. But what I realized is that it was necessary for me to write about Auschwitz. . . . It was the same sort of territory, modernized, that I explored in *The Confessions of Nat Turner.*"

In response to critics who question the validity of *Confessions* and *Sophie's Choice* on the grounds of Styron's personal back-ground, Towers argues that "it should not be necessary to defend the right of Styron—a non-Jew, a Southern Protestant in back-ground—to this subject matter—any more than his right to as-sume, in the first person, the 'identity' of the leader of a slave re-bellion in Virginia in 1831." Gray agrees. "The question," he writes, "is not whether Styron has a right to use alien experiences but whether his novel proves that he knows what he is writing about. In this instance, the overriding answer is yes."

MEDIA ADAPTATIONS: Sophie's Choice was filmed for Uni-versal Pictures in 1982; it featured Meryl Streep in the title role.

BIOGRAPHICAL/CRITICAL SOURCES:

BOOKS

Allen, Walter, *The Modern Novel,* Dutton, 1965.
Baumbach, Jonathan, *The Landscape of Nightmare,* New York University Press, 1965.
Concise Dictionary of American Literary Biography: Broadening Views, 1968-1988, Gale, 1989.
Contemporary Literary Criticism, Gale, Volume 1, 1973, Volume 3, 1975, Volume 5, 1976, Volume 11, 1979, Volume 15, 1980.
Cowley, Malcolm, *Writers at Work: The "Paris Review" Inter-views,* First Series, Viking, 1958.
Crane, John K., *The Root of All Evil: The Fiction of William Styron,* University of South Carolina Press, 1985.
Dictionary of Literary Biography, Volume 2: *American American Novelists since World War II,* Gale, 1978.
Dictionary of Literary Biography Yearbook: 1980, Gale, 1981.
Fossum, Robert H., *William Styron,* Eerdmans, 1968.
Friedman, Melvin J., *William Styron,* Bowling Green Univer-sity, 1974.
Geismar, Maxwell, *American Moderns,* Hill & Wang, 1958.
Gossett, Louise Y., *Violence in Recent Southern Fiction,* Duke University Press, 1965.
Kostelanetz, Richard, editor, *On Contemporary Literature,* Avon, 1964.
Mackin, Cooper R., *William Styron,* Steck Vaughn, 1969.
Moore, Harry T., editor, *Contemporary American Novelists,* Southern Illinois University Press, 1964.
Pearce, Richard, *William Styron* (Pamphlets on American Writ-ers Series, No. 98), University of Minnesota Press, 1971.
Waldmeir, Joseph J., editor, *Recent American Fiction,* Michigan State University Press, 1963.
West, James L., *William Styron: A Descriptive Bibliography,* G. K. Hall, 1977.

PERIODICALS

American Dialog, spring, 1968.
Book World, October 1, 1967, October 8, 1967.
Boston Globe Sunday Magazine, July 7, 1985.

Chicago Tribune, July 3, 1989.
Chicago Tribune Book World, May 27, 1979, January 16, 1983.
Commonweal, December 22, 1967.
Detroit News, June 24, 1979.
Esquire, July 3, 1979, December 1, 1985.
Harper's, July, 1967.
Kenyon Review, Volume 30, number 1, 1968.
Los Angeles Times, December 14, 1983.
Los Angeles Times Book Review, January 16, 1983.
Nation, October 16, 1967, April 22, 1968, July 7, 1979.
Negro Digest, February, 1968.
New Leader, December 4, 1967.
New Republic, June 30, 1979.
New Statesman, May 7, 1979.
Newsweek, October 16, 1967, May 28, 1979.
New Yorker, November 25, 1967, June 18, 1979.
New York Review of Books, October 26, 1967, September 12, 1968, July 19, 1979.
New York Times, August 5, 1967, October 3, 1967, May 29, 1979, November 27, 1982.
New York Times Book Review, October 8, 1967, August 11, 1968, May 27, 1979, June 6, 1982, November 21, 1982, December 12, 1982.
Observer Review, May 5, 1968.
Partisan Review, winter, 1968, summer, 1968.
Spectator, October 13, 1979.
Time, October 13, 1967, June 11, 1979.
Times Literary Supplement, May 19, 1968, November 30, 1979, June 10, 1983.
Village Voice, December 14, 1967.
Washington Post, May 18, 1979, January 4, 1983.
Washington Post Book World, May 20, 1979, December 5, 1982.
Yale Review, winter, 1968.*

* * *

SUAREZ LYNCH, B.
See BORGES, Jorge Luis

* * *

SWEENEY, William J(oseph) III 1922-

PERSONAL: Born February 6, 1922, in Philadelphia, PA; son of William Joseph and Esther (Lukens) Sweeney; married Viola J. White, July 25, 1944 (divorced, 1967); married Frances N. Feldman, August 13, 1967; children: (first marriage) William IV, David, James. *Education:* Maryville College, A.B., 1942, Cornell University, M.D., 1949.

ADDRESSES: Home—912 Fifth Ave., New York, NY 10011. *Office*— 460 East 63rd St., New York, NY 10021.

CAREER: Cornell University, Medical College, New York City, instructor, 1954-58, assistant professor, 1958-59, associate professor, 1959-69, professor of clinical obstetrics and gynecology, 1969—. Attending staff member of Lenox Hill Hospital, Doctor's Hospital; consulting staff member of Southhampton Hospital (NY), Middlesex Hospital (Morristown, NJ), and North Westchester Hospital (Mt. Kisco, NY). Inventor of the disposable diaphragm, 1983. *Military service:* U.S. Air Force, 1943-45; B-17 pilot; became first lieutenant.

MEMBER: International Federation of Gynecologic Endoscopists, American College of Legal Medicine, American Society of Law and Medicine, American Fertility Society (fellow), American College of Obstetricians and Gynecologists, American Col-

lege of Microsurgery, American College of Laser Therapy, Gynecologic Laser Society, North American Society of Pediatrics and Gynecology, New York Academy of Sciences, New York State Society of Surgeons.

WRITINGS:

(With Barbara Lang Stern) *Woman's Doctor: A Year in the Life of an Obstetrician-Gynecologist,* Morrow, 1973.
(Editor with R. Caplan, and contributor) *Advances in Obstetrics and Gynecology,* Williams & Wilkins, 1978.

Contributor to books, including *Recovery Room Care of the Obstetrical and Gynecological Patients,* 2nd edition, edited by J. Beal, Macmillan, 1961; *Advances in Obstetrics and Gynecology,* edited by S. S. Marcus and C. C. Marcus, Williams & Wilkins, 1967; *Progress in Infertility,* edited by S. J. Behrman and Robert Kistner, Little, Brown, 1968; *Controversy in Obstetrics and Gynecology,* edited by D. E. Reed and T. C. Barton, Saunders, 1969; *Gynecology and Obstetrics,* edited by A. Gerbie and J. Sciarra, Harper, 1978. Contributor to annals, proceedings, and professional journals.

WORK IN PROGRESS: Contributing to more books on obstetrics.

* * *

SYMONS, Julian (Gustave) 1912-

PERSONAL: Born May 30, 1912, in London, England; son of Morris Albert (an auctioneer) and Minnie Louise (Bull) Symons; married Kathleen Clark, October 25, 1941; children: Marcus Richard Julian. *Education:* Educated in state schools in England. *Politics:* "Left wing, with no specific party allegiance."

ADDRESSES: Home—Groton House, 330 Dover Rd., Walmer, Deal, Kent, England. *Agent*—Curtis Brown, Ltd., 1 Craven Hill, London W2 3EP, England.

CAREER: Shorthand typist and secretary in London, England, 1929-41; advertising copywriter in London, 1944-47; full-time writer, 1947—. Founder and editor, *Twentieth Century Verse,* 1937-39; reviewer, *London Sunday Times,* London, 1958-68. Member of council, Westfield College, University of London, 1972—. *Military service:* British Army, Royal Armoured Corps, 1942-44.

MEMBER: Crime Writers Association (chairman, 1958-59), Society of Authors (chairman of committee of management, 1970-71), Mystery Writers of America, PEN, Detective's Club (president, 1976-85), Royal Society of Literature (fellow).

AWARDS, HONORS: Crime Writers Association, Crossed Red Herrings Award for best crime story of the year, 1957, for *The Color of Murder,* special award, 1966, for *Crime and Detection;* Mystery Writers of America, Edgar Allan Poe Award for best crime story of the year, 1961, for *The Progress of a Crime,* special award, 1973, for *Bloody Murder;* Grand Master of Swedish Academy of Detection, 1977, Danish Poe-Kluhben, 1979, and Mystery Writers of America, 1982.

WRITINGS:

NOVELS

The Immaterial Murder Case, Gollancz, 1945, Macmillan, 1957.
A Man Called Jones, Gollancz, 1947, reprinted, Collins, 1963.
Bland Beginning, Harper, 1949, reprinted, Carroll & Graf, 1987 (published in England as *Bland Beginning: A Detective Story,* Gollancz, 1949).

The 31st of February (also see below), Harper, 1950, reprinted, Carroll & Graf, 1987 (published in England as *The Thirty-First of February: A Mystery Novel,* Gollancz, 1950).

The Broken Penny, Gollancz, 1952, Harper, 1953, reprinted, Carroll & Graf, 1988.

The Narrowing Circle, Harper, 1954, reprinted, Garland Publishing, 1983 (published in England as *The Narrowing Circle: A Crime Novel,* Gollancz, 1954).

The Paper Chase, Collins, 1956, published as *Bogue's Fortune,* Harper, 1957, reprinted, Carroll & Graf, 1988.

The Color of Murder, Harper, 1957.

The Gigantic Shadow, Collins, 1958, published as *The Pipe Dream,* Harper, 1959, reprinted, Prescott Press, 1988.

The Progress of a Crime (also see below), Harper, 1960.

The Plain Man, Harper, 1962 (published in England as *The Killing of Francie Lake,* Collins, 1962).

The End of Solomon Grundy (also see below), Harper, 1964.

The Belting Inheritance, Harper, 1965.

The Julian Symons Omnibus (contains *The 31st of February, The Progress of a Crime,* and *The End of Solomon Grundy*), Collins, 1966, reprinted, Penguin, 1984.

The Man Who Killed Himself, Harper, 1967.

The Man Whose Dreams Came True, Harper, 1968.

The Man Who Lost His Wife, Harper, 1970.

The Players and the Game, Harper, 1972.

The Plot against Roger Rider, Harper, 1973.

A Three-Pipe Problem, Harper, 1975.

The Blackheath Poisonings: A Victorian Murder Mystery, Harper, 1978.

Sweet Adelaide: A Victorian Puzzle Solved, Harper, 1980.

The Detling Secret, Viking, 1982 (published in England as *The Detling Murders,* Macmillan, 1982).

The Name of Annabel Lee, Viking, 1983.

A Criminal Comedy, Viking, 1985 (published in England as *The Criminal Comedy of the Contented Couple,* Macmillan, 1985).

The Kentish Manor Murders, Viking, 1988.

POETRY

Confusions about X, Fortune Press, 1939.

The Second Man, Routledge & Kegan Paul, 1943.

A Reflection on Auden, Poem-of-the-Month Club, 1973.

The Object of an Affair, and Other Poems Tragara Press, 1974.

Seven Poems for Sarah, Tragara Press, 1979.

OTHER

(Editor) *An Anthology of War Poetry,* Penguin, 1942.

(Editor and author of introduction) Samuel Johnson, *Selected Writings of Samuel Johnson,* Grey Walls Press, 1949, British Book Centre (New York), 1950.

A. J. A. Symons: His Life and Speculations (biography), Eyre & Spottiswoode, 1950.

Charles Dickens (biography), Roy, 1951, 2nd edition, Arthur Barker, 1969.

Thomas Carlyle: The Life and Ideas of a Prophet, Oxford University Press (New York), 1952, reprinted, Books for Libraries, 1970.

Horatio Bottomley: A Biography, Cresset Press, 1955.

(Editor) Thomas Carlyle, *Selected Works, Reminiscences and Letters,* Clarke, Irwin & Co., 1956, Harvard University Press, 1957.

The General Strike: A Historical Portrait, Cresset Press, 1957, Dufour, 1963.

A Reasonable Doubt: Some Criminal Cases Re-examined, Cresset Press, 1960.

The Thirties: A Dream Resolved, Cresset Press, 1960, Greenwood Press, 1973, revised edition, Faber, 1975.

Murder, Murder (short story collection) Fontana Books, 1961.

The Detective Story in Britain, Longmans, Green, 1962.

Buller's Campaign, Cresset Press, 1963.

Francis Quarles Investigates (short story collection), Panther Books, 1965.

England's Pride: The Story of the Gordon Relief Expedition, Hamish Hamilton, 1965.

Critical Occasions, Hamish Hamilton, 1966.

A Pictorial History of Crime, Crown, 1966 (published in England, as *Crime and Detection: An Illustrated History from 1840,* Studio Vista, 1966).

(Editor) *A. J. A. Symons, Essays and Biographies,* Cassell, 1969.

Mortal Consequences: A History—from the Detective Story to the Crime Novel, Harper, 1972, revised edition published as *Bloody Murder,* Viking, 1985 (published in England as *Bloody Murder: From the Detective Story to the Crime Novel: A History,* Faber, 1972).

(Editor and author of introduction) *Between the Wars: Britain in Photo,* Batsford, 1972.

Notes from Another Country, Alan Ross, 1972.

(Editor and author of introduction) Wilkie Collins, *The Woman Who Wore White,* Penguin, 1974, reprinted as *The Woman in White,* 1982.

(Editor) *The Angry Thirties,* Eyre & Spottiswoode, 1976.

The Tell-Tale Heart: The Life and Works of Edgar Allan Poe, Harper, 1978.

(Editor) *Verdict of Thirteen: A Detection Club Anthology,* Harper, 1979.

Portrait of an Artist: Conan Doyle (biography), Whizzard/Deutsch, 1980.

(Editor) Edgar Allan Poe, *Selected Tales,* Oxford University Press, 1980.

(Editor and author of introduction) Agatha Christie, *The ABC Murders,* Collins, 1980.

(Editor and author of introduction) Freeman Wills Crofts, *The Loss of the Jane Vosper,* Collins, 1980.

(Author of commentary) Tom Adams, *Agatha Christie, the Art of Her Crimes: The Paintings of Tom Adams,* Everest House, 1981 (published in England as *Tom Adams' Agatha Christie Cover Story,* introduction by John Fowles, Paper Tiger, 1981).

(Author of preface) Arthur Conan Doyle, *The Complete Sherlock Holmes,* Secker & Warburg, 1981.

Great Detectives: Seven Original Detectives, illustrated by Adams, Abrams, 1981.

Critical Observations, Ticknor & Fields, 1981.

The Tigers of Subtopia, and Other Stories (also see below), Viking, 1982.

Crime and Detection Quiz, Weidenfeld & Nicolson, 1983.

(Editor) *The Penguin Classic Crime Omnibus,* Penguin, 1984.

Dashiell Hammett (biography), Harcourt, 1985.

(Editor) Anton Chekov, *The Shooting Party,* translated by A. E. Chamot, Deutsch, 1986.

Makers of the News: The Revolution of Literature, Random House, 1987.

(Editor) Wyndham Lewis, *The Essential Wyndham Lewis: An Introduction to His Work,* Deutsch, 1989.

Also author of radio plays "Affection Unlimited," 1968, and "Night Rider to Dover," 1969, and of television plays "Miranda and a Salesman," 1963, "The Witnesses," 1964, "The Finishing Touch," 1965, "Curtains for Sheila," 1965, "Tigers of Subtopia," based on the author's short story collection of the same title, 1968, "The Pretenders," 1970, and "Whatever's Peter Playing At?," 1974; editor, *New Poetry 9,* 1983. Editor, "Penguin Mystery" series, 1974-79. Contributor to *Times Literary Supplement, New York Times,* and other newspapers and magazines. Reviewer, *Manchester Evening News,* 1947-56, and *Sunday Times,* 1958—. Part of Symons' manuscript collection is housed at the University of Texas at Austin.

SIDELIGHTS: A staunch believer in the literary value of crime and detective novels, Julian Symons is best known as a novelist and critic of these genres, though he is also a respected historian, biographer, and poet. Many of the English novelist's ideas about the crime fiction genre are expressed in his book, *Bloody Murder,* which traces the history of detective and crime novels over the past two centuries. Symons' "most important contribution to the study of the genre," attests Larry E. Grimes in the *Dictionary of Literary Biography,* "is his assertion that much of the focus in crime writing in the twentieth century has changed" from the "classical detective story" to the "crime novel." The detective story, explains Grimes, "is built around a great detective and upon a plot deception," while a crime novel "is based on the psychology of its characters, uses the lines of those characters (not methods, clues, and puzzles) as the basis of the story."

Symons has written novels that fall under both categories, but most of these works have one commonality: the author's interest in the surprising capability for violence that any person may release under the right circumstances. "The thing that absorbs me most in our age," remarks Symons in his introduction to *The Julian Symons Omnibus,* "is the violence behind respectable faces, the civil servant planning how to kill Jews most efficiently, the judge speaking with passion about the need for capital punishment, the quiet obedient boy who kills for fun. These are extreme cases, but if you want to show the violence that lives behind the bland faces most of us present to the world, what better vehicle can you have than the crime novel?"

In his initial attempts to write mysteries, Symons feels his results were unsatisfactory. "My first three crime stories, including the unfortunate [*The Immaterial Murder Case*]" he reveals in his *Contemporary Authors Autobiography Series* entry, "I look back on without pleasure. They were set in one orthodox pattern of the British crime story at that time, consciously light, bright, and determinedly 'civilized.' The fourth, *The Thirty-First of February . . . ,* is another matter. I must at this time have had some nascent ideas about doing all the things in the form of the crime story that one can do in a 'straight' novel, in the way of character development, and saying something about the form and shape of society." As with many of Symons' crime stories, *The Thirty-First of February* is not so much a murder mystery as it is a study in human psychology and sociology. The novel involves "Andy" Anderson, an advertising businessman who, after the apparently accidental death of his wife, is accused of her murder. His employers are completely unsympathetic to Anderson's situation and force him to return to work without a period for mourning, while also burdening him with an important account. At the same time, the police, who are certain Anderson is guilty, continually harass him. Though he is never convicted, the unrelenting pressures on him eventually lead to Anderson's insanity.

Similarly, the protagonist in *The Narrowing Circle,* David Nelson, is never convicted of the murder charges brought against him; but the events he experiences nevertheless effectively rob him of his sense of humanity. However, it is not so much the accusation of homicide that brings about Nelson's downfall; rather, as Grimes explains, it is his continued desire to climb up the social and financial ladder that "choke[s] off his ability to be human and know love." "A large part of the horror at the end of *The Narrowing Circle,*" writes Steven R. Carter in *Armchair Detective,* "comes from the reader's awareness that David Nelson is killing an essential part of himself by his decision to accept the sleazy material success which an ulcer-ridden entrepreneur offers him."

About the same time *The Color of Murder* was published, Symons was becoming an influential figure among crime writers. From 1958 to 1959 he was a chairman of the Crime Writer's Association, and in 1958 he began work as a reviewer of mystery fiction for the *London Sunday Times. The Color of Murder* won the Crime Writer's Association Red Herrings Award in 1957, and in 1961 *The Progress of a Crime* won the Edgar Allan Poe Award. These books continue the pattern Symons previously established of using crime fiction as an instrument for social commentary. Like *The Thirty-First of February, The Color of Murder* ends with the insanity of an innocent man accused of a homicide. But in *The Progress of a Crime,* Symons reverses this plot so that the a guilty man is found innocent. Criticizing the misuse of force by the police, the desire of newspapers to capitalize on people's misfortunes in order to sell more papers, and lawyers who care only about winning their cases, *The Progress of a Crime* "is one of the truest and most sensible . . . English crime novels" of its time, opines *Spectator* critic Christopher Pym.

Some of Symons' most complex novels are also among his best, according to a number of reviewers. *The Man Who Killed Himself,* for example, features a protagonist who creates a double identity to commit the perfect crime. One of his identities, Alan Brownjohn, murders his wife and then is, in turn, "murdered" by Major Easonby Mellon, Brownjohn's alter ego. William R. Evans, a *Best Sellers* critic, praises this novel as being "a brilliant portrait of a fascinating murderer along with an extremely ingenious and suspenseful plot." But, as Grimes reveals, *The Man Who Killed Himself* is not a simple murder mystery, "for Easonby/Brownjohn has plotted a perfect murder, not for murder's sake, but for the sake of freedom from an imperfect world." Grimes explains this in more detail in his comments about *The End of Solomon Grundy,* where he notes that in Symons' books the author portrays the world as a place where "one must either become a criminal or remain a hypocrite." Symons' characters are never all good or all evil; indeed, in some of his books it is difficult to find a character with whom the reader can sympathize completely.

The Players and the Game, another example of one of Symons' more intricate plots, is one such book that lacks sympathetic characters. As Leo Harris notes in *Books and Bookmen,* none of the people portrayed in this novel are "very nice." Symons' mysteries, Harris adds, "have always the rebarbative surface of warts-and-all truthfulness, and he has a cold, perceptive, but not entirely unforgiving eye for human frailty." *The Players of the Game* tells two stories: one describes a business executive's journey toward self-destruction as he strives for success; the other is narrated by a character who calls himself "Dracula," and portrays a world in which criminal behavior is considered normal. "One of the most intriguing and unusual aspects of Symons' writing" that is illustrated in *The Players and the Game,* remarks Carter, "is his stress on games." Carter elucidates that "Symons has implied often that anyone might become a criminal by being subjected to too much pressure, by having insufficient outlets for release from pressure, or by surrendering to his fantasies."

Not long after *The Players of the Game,* Symons indulged his interest in the Victorian era by writing three novels set in late nineteenth-century England. These books include *The Blackheath*

Poisonings: A Victorian Murder Mystery, Sweet Adelaide: A Victorian Puzzle Solved, and *The Detling Secret.* According to Symons in the *Contemporary Authors Autobiography Series,* he was "pleased" with the first book, while the other two "seemed to me less good." William McPhearson echoes the author's assessment of *The Blackheath Poisonings,* praising the mystery as a "skillfully written, thoroughly researched and deftly plotted novel." As to Symons' other Victorian mysteries, critics have generally been more positive in their evaluations than the novelist himself.

One of these books, *Sweet Adelaide,* is based on an actual murder case in England. Still interested in studying how innocent-looking people can commit murder, Symons investigates the reasons why Adelaide Bartlett, a woman as infamous in England as Lizzie Borden is in the United States, could be driven into pouring liquid chloroform down her husband's throat. Bartlett was found not guilty, relates Michael Malone in the *New York Times Book Review,* "by a jury that could not believe this demure little lady had either the will or the expertise" to kill her husband. Symons proposes, however, that she did possess these qualities, and proceeds to describe in his novel what could push a woman like Bartlett over the edge. *Los Angeles Times Book* critic Alan Cheuse lauds the writer's portrayal of Bartlett, saying that "Symons' masterly construction of Adelaide's mind—and journal—as she lives through years of suffering her husband's patronage of prostitutes . . . keep[s] us fascinated with each moment of this woman's inevitable slide toward murder." In *The Detling Secret,* Symons explores the more sinister impulses that lurk behind even civilized, upper-class members of society. A more traditional English mystery, critics have praised *The Detling Secret* for its authentic recreation of Edwardian England and the novelist's expert handling of plot. *New York Times Book Review* contributor Mary Cantwell praises the author's research, reporting that "Mr. Symons' use of period detail is both scrupulous and economical." And *Los Angeles Times* critic Carolyn See avers that as a murder mystery *The Detling Secret* "is simply perfect of its kind."

With *The Name of Annabel Lee,* Symons returned to contemporary settings for his novels, "having proved my ability to write such a story—at least to my own satisfaction," he says in *Contemporary Authors Autobiography Series.* Some critics have given this work a chilly reception, however. *Los Angeles Times* reviewer Art Seidenbaum, for one, feels that "the resolution of the mystery . . . leaves substance to be desired." But although Derrick Murdoch similarly believes that Symons' plot appears weak in this case, the reviewer notes in *Globe and Mail* that the novel succeeds in other ways. *The Name of Annabel Lee,* Murdoch writes, "uses the form of the mystery novel to provide a sardonic study of the extent of modern decadence as scathing as his Victorian murder mysteries were of nineteenth-century injustice and hypocrisy." In a more light-hearted fashion, Symons' *A Criminal Comedy* also gibes capitalist society by painting "a savagely comic picture of Headfield [England] and its colour supplement *bourgeoisie,*" according to T. J. Binyon's *Times Literary Supplement* review.

A Criminal Comedy has generally been well received by critics; but, more than this, to one *Time* contributor it also proves that Symons has not allowed his story-telling powers to diminish over the years as has happened with some other mystery writers. "At 73," the reviewer declares, "Julian Symons has . . . published perhaps his best mystery ever." By this time, too, the author had long been a respected biographer and critic. Among other subjects, Symons' interest in mystery authors led him to write biographies of Edgar Allan Poe, Dashiell Hammett, and Sir Arthur Conan Doyle, whose famous creation, Sherlock Holmes, Symons

honors with modern versions of the great detective in *A Three-Pipe Problem* and *The Kentish Manor Murders.* The author's biographies have received mixed reviews from critics, the most negative reactions being awarded to *The Tell Tale Heart: The Life and Works of Edgar Allan Poe.* For example, in a *New Republic* article Megan Marshall calls Symons' biography of Poe "steadfastly superficial" and observes that the writer "fails to cover the full dimension of his subject." *Spectator* contributor Benny Green similarly comments that "what we get [in *The Tell Tale Heart*] is not so much a reassessment as a rearrangement" of Poe's life and work.

However, Symons' *Dashiell Hammett* and *Conan Doyle: Portrait of an Artist* have been better received, although *Los Angeles Times* critic Carolyn See feels that Symons' English background puts him at a "cultural disadvantage" in interpreting Hammett's distinctly American works. One *Washington Post* contributor, on the other hand, states that the author writes "with zestful, sometimes revisionist appreciation of the [Hammett] novels." Symons is more in his element when he talks about the much-admired Doyle; and though "this isn't a definitive work," according to Margaret Cannon in *Globe and Mail,* ". . . it's a carefully written, delightfully illustrated introduction" to Doyle.

But more than for his common interest in these giants of the crime fiction genre, Symons is unique in his fascination for lesser-known literary figures; and much of his critical writing focuses on such writers as Wyndham Lewis, Frances Newman, James Branch Cabell, and Peggy Hopkins Joyce. Indeed, in his *Makers of the New: The Revolution in Literature, 1912-1939,* Symons ranks Lewis with the likes of Ezra Pound, James Joyce, and T. S. Eliot. Some critics, like *Washington Post* contributor Charles Trueheart, feel that including Lewis among these authors is an "injustice." Even though some reviewers are puzzled by Symons' emphasis on these relatively minor writers, others see his attention to such details as being a virtue. In a review of the author's *Critical Observations,* Valentine Cunningham writes in the *Times Literary Supplement:* "Symons' greatest distinction as a critic . . . is [his] ungrudging affection for literary merit wherever it crops up. It's a critical versatility that rebuts the fixity of canons, without ever sinking into the flaccidities of a too liberal tastelessness."

Just as Symons tries to bring more obscure literary figures to public attention, he has attempted throughout his career to elevate the status of crime fiction. "The crime story is a wonderfully literary form," he writes in *Contemporary Authors Autobiography Series.* "In the hands of a good writer it can be used for anything from Kafkan ambiguity to raw slices of Zolaesque realism. A criminal theme is the sturdiest of backbones for a plot, and there is nothing intrinsically sensational or trivial about it— the sensationalism and triviality come, if they do, in the treatment." As for Symons himself, his work in the crime genre— especially as a device for social commentary—has made a distinct impression. As Carter attests, Symons "has proven how flexible a vehicle [the mystery genre] is for presenting a personal vision of the stresses of modern western civilization."

AVOCATIONAL INTERESTS: Cricket, football.

BIOGRAPHICAL/CRITICAL SOURCES:

BOOKS

Contemporary Authors Autobiography Series, Volume 3, Gale, 1986.
Contemporary Literary Criticism, Gale, Volume 2, 1974, Volume 14, 1980, Volume 32, 1985.

Dictionary of Literary Biography, Volume 87: *British Mystery and Thriller Writers since 1940,* Gale, 1989.

Scarte, Francis, *Auden and After: The Liberation of Poetry, 1930-1941,* Routledge & Kegan Paul, 1942.

Symons, Julian, *The Julian Symons Omnibus,* Collins, 1966.

PERIODICALS

Armchair Detective, January, 1979.

Best Sellers, April 15, 1972.

Books and Bookmen, October, 1972.

Book World, May 28, 1972.

Detroit News, November 8, 1981.

Georgia Review, fall, 1972.

Globe and Mail (Toronto), January 28, 1984, January 16, 1988, April 9, 1988.

Los Angeles Times, February 14, 1983, November 2, 1983, April 8, 1985.

Los Angeles Times Book Review, October 19, 1980, September 14, 1986, January 24, 1988, July 10, 1988.

National Observer, January 5, 1970.

New Republic, August 26, 1978, September 2, 1978.

New Statesman, December 23, 1966, October 20, 1978.

Newsweek, February 14, 1983.

New Yorker, April 1, 1972.

New York Herald Tribune Book Review, June 22, 1958, November 4, 1962.

New York Times, October 23, 1949, November 9, 1952, April 24, 1955, June 29, 1958, July 3, 1978, January 10, 1986, November 6, 1987.

New York Times Book Review, July 21, 1965, January 8, 1967, May 14, 1967, December 9, 1973, July 9, 1978, February 4, 1979, November 16, 1980, December 13, 1981, March 20, 1983, January 29, 1984, May 5, 1985, January 10, 1988, August 14, 1988.

Observer, July 23, 1978.

Publishers Weekly, July 2, 1982, October 25, 1985.

Spectator, October 26, 1951, July 29, 1960, August 11, 1973, June 29, 1974, March 22, 1975, November 11, 1978, January 19, 1980.

Time, February 14, 1983, February 24, 1986.

Times (London), November 19, 1981, May 13, 1982, September 22, 1983.

Times Literary Supplement, April 8, 1965, February 1, 1975, August 11, 1978, May 9, 1980, January 22, 1982, June 25, 1982, September 17, 1982, November 18, 1983, March 28, 1986, April 25, 1986, November 4, 1988, March 17, 1989.

Washington Post, December 26, 1978.

Washington Post Book World, July 9, 1978, November 2, 1980, March 17, 1985, March 16, 1986, January 3, 1988, August 21, 1988.*

—Sketch by Kevin S. Hile

T

TARASSOFF, Lev
See TROYAT, Henri

* * *

TAVEL, Ronald 1940-

PERSONAL: Surname pronounced Tah-*vel;* born May 17, 1940, in New York, N.Y.; son of George and Florence (Sterns) Tavel. *Education:* Received B.A. from Brooklyn College (now of the City University of New York); University of Wyoming, M.A., 1961.

ADDRESSES: Home—528 Governor Nicholls St., New Orleans, La. 70116; and 5980 Shore Blvd. S., Diplomat 212, Gulfport, Fla. 33707.

CAREER: Andy Warhol Films, Inc., New York City, scenarist, 1964-66; founded and named the "Theatre of the Ridiculous," New York City, 1965; lecturer for the New York State Council on the Arts; Theater for the New City, New York City, member of Education Division, beginning 1984. Playwright in residence at numerous theatres, conferences, and universities, including Play-House of the Ridiculous, 1965-67, Theatre of the Lost Continent, 1971-73, and Cornell University, 1980-81; visiting lecturer, Mahidol University, Thailand, 1981-82; visiting associate professor, University of Colorado, 1986-87. Director of playwright's unit, Actors Ensemble of Boulder, 1986-87; playwriting representative, Southern Writers Conference, 1990. Actor for Andy Warhol Films, Inc., and in other films, including "Fifty Fantasticks," 1964, "Bitch," 1965, "Jail," 1967, "Suicide Notions: Fire Escape," 1972, and "In Search of the Cobra Jewels," 1972. Advisor, Subplot Theater (part of American Place Complex).

MEMBER: American Theater Association, New York Theatre Strategy (founding member), Contemporary Arts Center (playwright's division; New Orleans).

AWARDS, HONORS: Lyric poetry contest winner, 1955, for poem "Virginia Woolf"; Obie Awards for playwriting, 1969, for "Boy on the Straight- Back Chair," and 1973, for "Bigfoot"; recipient of grants from numerous theatre and arts groups and foundations, including Rockefeller grants, 1972 and 1978, Guggenheim fellowship, 1973, and Yaddo fellowship, 1986.

WRITINGS:

PLAYS

"The Life of Juanita Castro" (one-act; also see below), first produced with "Shower" in New York at Coda Gallery, June 29, 1965; produced Off-Broadway with "Shower" at St. Mark's Playhouse, July 29, 1965.

"Shower" (one-act; also see below), first produced with "The Life of Juanita Castro" at Coda Gallery, June 29, 1965; produced Off-Broadway with "The Life of Juanita Castro" at St. Mark's Playhouse, July 29, 1965.

"Tarzan of the Flicks," first produced in Plainfield, Vt., at Goddard College, December, 1965.

"The Life of Lady Godiva" (one-act), first produced in New York at Play-House of the Ridiculous, April, 1966; published in *The New Underground Theatre,* edited by Robert Shroeder, Bantam, 1968, reprinted in *Theatre of the Ridiculous,* edited by Bonnie Marranca, PAJ Publications, 1983.

"Screen Test" (one-act; also see below), first produced with "Indira Gandhi's Daring Device" at Play-House of the Ridiculous, September 29, 1966.

"Indira Gandhi's Daring Device" (one-act; also see below), first produced with "Screen Test" at Play-House of the Ridiculous, September 29, 1966.

"Kitchenette" (one-act; also see below), first produced at Play-House of the Ridiculous, January, 1967.

"Gorilla Queen" (full-length), first produced Off-Off Broadway at Judson Poets Theatre, March, 1967; produced Off-Broadway at the Martinique Theatre, April 26, 1967; published in *The Best of Off-Off Broadway,* edited by Michael Smith, Dutton, 1969.

"Vinyl" (one-act; also see below), first produced Off-Off Broadway at Caffe Cino, October, 1967.

"Canticle of the Nightingale" (one-act musical for children), first produced in Stockholm, Sweden, 1968; produced in New York at Manhattan Theatre Club, June, 1973.

"Cleobis and Bito" (one-act dance-oratorio), first produced in New York at the Extension, March, 1968.

"Arenas of the Lutetia" (full-length), first produced Off-Off Broadway at Judson Poets Theatre, November, 1968; published in *Experiments in Prose,* edited by Eugene Wildman, Swallow Press, 1969.

"Boy on the Straight-Back Chair" (full-length musical; also see below), music by Orville Stoeber, first produced Off-Broadway at American Place Theatre, February 14, 1969.

"Vinyl Visits an FM Station" (one-act), first produced Off-Off Broadway at the Playwrights Unit, May, 1970.

"Words for Bryan to Sing and Dance," first produced at Judson Poets Theatre, April, 1971.

"Bigfoot" (full-length; also see below), first produced in New York at Theatre Genesis, November, 1972.

"Arse Long—Life Short," first produced in New York, 1972.

"Secrets of the Citizens Correction Committee" (one-act), first produced in New York at Theatre at Saint Clement's, October, 1973.

"Queen of Greece" (full-length), first produced at Theatre Genesis, November, 1973.

Bigfoot and Other Plays (contains "The Life of Juanita Castro," "Shower," "Indira Gandhi's Daring Device," "Kitchenette," "Boy on the Straight- Back Chair," and "Bigfoot"), Winter House, 1973.

"The Last Days of British Honduras," first produced Off-Broadway at New York Shakespeare Festival Public Theatre, October, 1974.

"Playbirth," first produced in New York at Theatre for the New City, November, 1976.

"The Clown's Tail" (for children), first produced in New York at the Cherry Lane Theatre, December, 1976.

"Gazelle Boy," first produced in New Haven, Conn., at the Studio Theatre of the Yale Drama School, April, 1977.

"The Ovens of Anita Orangejuice: A History of Modern Florida," (full-length), first produced in Williamstown, Mass., at the Williamstown Theatre Summer Festival, August, 1977; revised version produced in New York at Westbeth Theatre Center, December, 1978.

"The Ark of God" (full-length), first produced in Washington, D.C., at the New Playwrights' Theatre of Washington, March, 1978, revised version, February, 1979.

"The Nutcracker in the Land of Nuts" (musical), music by Simeon Westbrooke, first produced Off-Broadway at La Mama Experimental Theatre Club, December, 1979.

"The Understudy" (full-length), first produced in Ithaca, N.Y., at Cornell University, April, 1981.

"Success and Succession," first produced at Theatre for the New City, 1983.

"My Foetus Lived on Amboy Street" (also see below), first produced at Theatre for the New City, April, 1985.

"Notorious Harik Will Kill the Pope," first produced at Theatre for the New City, January, 1986.

"Thick Dick," first produced at Theatre for the New City, May, 1988.

Also author of "Christina's World," a three-act verse play, 1963, one-act play "Mr. Tavel Writes a Play for Mr. Weiss," and "Carmen Miranda: The Musical," 1988.

FILMS

(Author of scenario) "Harlot," Andy Warhol Films, Inc., 1964.

"The Life of Juanita Castro" (based on his play), Andy Warhol Films, Inc., 1965.

(Author of scenario) "Philip's Screen Test" (unreleased), Andy Warhol Films, Inc., 1965.

"Screen Test" (based on his play), Andy Warhol Films, Inc., 1965.

"Kitchen" (based on his play "Kitchenette"), Andy Warhol Films, Inc., 1965.

(Author of scenario) "Horse," Andy Warhol Films, Inc., 1965.

(Author of scenario) "Space," Andy Warhol Films, Inc., 1965.

"Vinyl" (based on his play), Andy Warhol Films, Inc., 1965.

"Suicide," Andy Warhol Films, Inc., 1965.

(Author of scenario) "Withering Sights," Andy Warhol Films, Inc., 1966.

(Co-author of scenarios) "The Chelsea Girls," Andy Warhol Films, Inc., 1966.

(Author of scenario) "Hedy; or, The 14-Year-Old Girl," Andy Warhol Films, Inc., 1966.

Also author of "More Milk Evette," 1966.

OTHER

(Contributor) Gregory Battock, editor, *The New American Cinema,* Dutton, 1967.

Street of Stairs (novel), Olympia Press, 1968.

(Lyricist) *No More Masterpieces* (recording), Mention Records, 1971.

"My Foetus Lived on Amboy Street" (radio play), first aired on WBAI-FM (New York), 1979.

Contributor of essays, poetry, stories, and articles to magazines, including *Night* and *Unmuzzled Ox Magazine;* Tavel's work has been excerpted in *Chicago Review, Clyde, Drama Review, Film Culture, Intransit, Partisan Review, Scripts* and *Tri-Quarterly.* Literary advisor, *Scripts,* 1971-72; drama critic, *Stages,* 1984; theatre editor, *Brooklyn Literary Review,* 1984-85.

Tavel's plays have been translated into a half-dozen languages and been performed in Japan, Australia, Canada, and much of Europe. Some of his poems were taped for broadcast by WRVR's "Anthology of the Air," 1966.

WORK IN PROGRESS: A full-length play set in historic New Orleans; several one-act plays dealing with life in the American south.

SIDELIGHTS: In the 1960s, when he named and helped found the "Theatre of the Ridiculous," Ronald Tavel "revealed a prankish sense of comedy, which derived its primary source from old movies, comic books and popular myths," relates *New York Times* drama critic Mel Gussow. "In the early 70's, in his best work, . . . he began to explore society, science and history. With his linguistic ability, he seemed to be a kind of high-camp American equivalent of Tom Stoppard." Beginning with such plays as "The Life of Juanita Castro" and "Indira Gandhi's Daring Device" (which inspired an international controversy), Tavel has written "with an unmistakable voice," states Michael T. Smith in *Contemporary Dramatists,* "relentlessly punning, answering back to his own word-plays, philosophizing, art-conscious, joking, ridiculous as the Marx Brothers, and turning his formidable energy to the service of a passion for justice." While his plays are satirical, even "travesty," the critic continues, nevertheless "Tavel is out for serious game, and has loaded [his plays] with real facts and arguments." As Calvin Tomkins reports in the *New Yorker,* at the time of the Theatre's founding, "Tavel issued a manifesto: 'We have passed beyond the absurd. Our position is absolutely preposterous.' An intellectual with an encyclopedic knowledge of world theatre, Tavel felt that [he and his collaborators] were simply taking the next step beyond the theatre of the absurd."

Gussow likewise notes that " 'Ridiculous' theater is way beyond 'absurd,' " describing it as "irreverent, particularly toward subjects traditionally revered, derisive even toward their own work, adoring of certain movies and myths, and grotesquely comic." "Unlike the theatre of the absurd, in which dramatic metaphors embody a moral vision, Tavel's Ridiculous world is a valueless, anarchic place which refuses to take life more seriously than as imitation of art," explains Bonnie Marranca in *American Playwrights: A Critical Survey.* "It is metaphysical burlesque." Peter Michelson similarly elaborates in the *New Republic:* "The ridiculous goes beyond the absurd by abandoning dialectic altogether as a mode of understanding. Serious form, in the ridiculous, happens only at those epiphanal moments when the images explode their shot." In contrast to the absurd, the critic continues, the ridiculous "does not offer a behavioral way out of the cosmic joke. . . . And it is in this sense a classical kind of comedy about men mistaking their ignorance for knowledge and their pointlessness for power."

"Gorilla Queen," for example, "is a parody of Grade B exotica films," notes Michelson. "But in the extravagant development of [its central] image the play articulates in parody the religious, racial, moral, and power sentimentalities that make up much of the American mythology." Following such characters as Queen Kong, Karma Miranda, Paulet Colbert, and Clyde Batty (the White Hunter) through a series of bizarre encounters, "Gorilla Queen" "embodies all the general characteristics of the Ridiculous aesthetic, including use of American 'popular' culture, campy theatricalism, literary word play, sexual exhibition, and a studied tackiness," remarks Marranca. While critic Robert Brustein likens the sexual emphasis of the play to "a particularly merciless jackhammer," he admits in his *The Third Theatre* that nevertheless, "like most pop artists, [Tavel] has tapped a virtually bottomless well of material, and he brings to his plays an irritating but quite genuine wit." "In this play Tavel has outdone himself," Marranca states. "Its dazzling verbal gymnastics, creative use of popular iconography, highly theatrical nature, and exultation of the pleasure principle make *Gorilla Queen* Tavel's most accomplished work in the camp style," the critic concludes, calling it "no less than a camp classic."

In "Boy on the Straight-Back Chair," produced two years after "Gorilla Queen," Tavel incorporates ridiculous elements into a tale based on the true story of Toby, a vain young murderer. "*Boy* is a lean, lyrical drama, more realistic than Tavel's characteristic style, but hardly an example of realism," writes Marranca. The playwright has turned this story of violence and fear into "a musical farce," as the *New York Times*'s Clive Barnes describes it, and "the language is rich to the point of clogging with puns and a fanciful, almost Shakespearean kind of sexual imagery." While the critic faults the play's structure and some of the jokes, he adds that "even at his most facetious, Mr. Tavel hangs onto his concept of the theater as a place of miracles. He avoids naturalism and instead creates a stylized, almost static form, which, unlike most plays, is more like an oratorio than an opera. He also convinces with his character of the spoiled, charmingly vicious Toby." "The play works despite soft patches and flaws," Jack Kroll similarly notes in *Newsweek.* "Tavel plays language in many registers, from lyricism to sharp realism to perfectly targeted 'sentimentality' to outrageous spoonerisms and puns. He is one of the few playwrights who has true instinct for how and when to 'involve' and uninvolve the audience," Kroll continues, "and his self-parody is not only funny but it's part of the dramatic pattern." And Marranca, although she comments that the author sometimes "overindulges" in word play, maintains that "*Boy* is a powerful indictment of the American way of life and remains one of Tavel's finest dramatic achievements."

Although it also won an Obie Award, "Bigfoot" "is for Tavel quite a different type of play" than "Boy on the Straight-Back Chair," remarks Marranca. "It proves for certain that he takes risks by not settling in one comfortable style, even if the results are not always successful." A series of "metaphysical musings on the meaning of twindom and the nature of the beast in man,"

as Gussow terms it, " 'Bigfoot' is that rare play that titillates the brain while tickling the funny bone." In contrast to Marranca's criticism of the play's "philosophical debate," Gussow believes that "for all its portentiousness, this is not a weighty play. . . . [It] is ripe with comic textual commentary." Involving several sets of brothers (including the playwright's own) in philosophical discussions, the result, states *Village Voice* contributor Michael Feingold, "is another mad, brilliant, devastating play by Ronald Tavel, and perhaps his most challenging to date—for both him and us. . . . People who are impatient with intellection in the theatre are likely to be put off " by Tavel's language, the critic states, for the play "glitters like a kaleidoscope, revealing itself in facets and fragments, rather than simple declarative sentences." As a result, Feingold concludes, "Tavel challenges us as fiercely as Handke (while giving far more of the satisfaction audiences require)."

Despite the varying content of Tavel's "ridiculous" comedies, it is his original use of language that characterizes his work and brings out its more serious themes. As Gussow observes, the "typical" Tavel play "has a skein of alliteration, word-splaying puns, verbal inversions and malappropriations from literary history—all covering, and at times concealing, the author's search for order in a fractured world." "Tavel's aim (and genius)," explains Gino Rizzo in the *New York Times,* "is to *use* the destruction of language to capture and reflect the total destruction of our identity." Tavel's verbal tricks work to reveal "the richness of his linguistic texture, the power and subtlety of his allusions, the multiplicity of meanings he manages to condense within a few lines," the critic adds. Feingold likewise remarks that "Tavel's struggle to make both words and flesh hold some meaning is real combat with terror, a journey into darkness, however much he tries to make light of it with spectacular alienation effects, disruptions, comic self-criticisms." The playwright "has continually switched styles and moved into new areas of dramatic approach, both thematically and structurally," writes Marranca. "Yet, one thing has remained constant—Tavel's virtuoso manipulation of language. Add to that his knowledge of classical convention and the forms of popular culture and you have an artist well suited to attack society's mythic pretensions." As the critic concludes: "Tavel has written many plays over the past . . . years, not all of them successful but all of them exhibiting a dramatic intelligence of significant dimension."

BIOGRAPHICAL/CRITICAL SOURCES:

BOOKS

Bockris, Victor, *Warhol,* Muller, 1989.
Bourdon, David, *Warhol,* Abrams, 1989.
Brustein, Robert, *The Third Theatre,* Knopf, 1969.
Contemporary Dramatists, St. James Press, 1988.
Contemporary Literary Criticism, Volume 6, Gale, 1976.
Marranca, Bonnie and Gautam Dasupta, *American Playwrights: A Critical Survey,* Drama Book Specialists, 1981.
Sukenick, Ronald, *Down and In: Life in the Underground,* Beech Tree Books, 1987.

PERIODICALS

Cue, March 22, 1969.
Drama Review, Volume XIII, number 1, 1968.
New Republic, May 6, 1967, September 9, 1967.
New Statesman, July 14, 1967.
Newsweek, March 24, 1969.
New Yorker, November 15, 1976.
New York Times, March 20, 1967, January 5, 1969, March 18, 1969, December 29, 1971, November 23, 1972, October 19,

1973, November 16, 1973, December 29, 1979, April 28, 1985, January 29, 1986.

Village Voice, April 28, 1966, January 12, 1967, March 16, 1967, December 5, 1968, March 6, 1969, November 9, 1972.

—*Sketch by Diane Telgen*

*   *   *

TELLER, Edward 1908-

PERSONAL: Born January 15, 1908, in Budapest, Hungary; came to the United States in 1935, naturalized March 4, 1941; son of Max (a lawyer) and Ilona (Deutch) Teller; married Augusta Harkanyi, February 26, 1934; children: Paul, Susan Wendy. *Education:* Studied at Karlsruhe Technical Institute, Karlsruhe, Germany, 1926-28, and University of Munich, 1928-29; University of Leipzig, Ph.D., 1930.

ADDRESSES: Home—1573 Hawthorne Ter., Berkeley, Calif. 94708. *Office*—Hoover Institution, Stanford, Calif. 94305.

CAREER: Research associate at University of Leipzig, Leipzig, Germany, 1929-31, and University of Gottingen, Gottingen, Germany, 1931-33; Rockefeller Foundation fellow at University of Coppenhagen, Copenhagen, Denmark, 1934; University of London, London, England, lecturer in physics, 1934-35; George Washington University, Washington, D.C., professor of physics, 1935-41; Columbia University, New York, N.Y., professor of physics, 1941-42; physicist for Manhattan Project at University of Chicago, Chicago, Ill., 1942-43, and Los Alamos Scientific Laboratory, Los Alamos, N.M., 1943-46; University of Chicago, professor of physics, 1946-52, on leave as assistant director of Los Alamos Scientific Laboratory, 1949-52; University of California, professor of physics at Berkeley, 1953-60, professor of physics-at-large, 1960-70, university professor, 1970-75, university professor emeritus, 1975—, chairman of department of applied science, Davis-Livermore, 1963-66, consultant to Livermore branch, University of California Radiation Laboratory, 1952-53, associate director of Lawrence Radiation Laboratory, Livermore, 1954-75, associate director emeritus, 1975—, director of Lawrence Radiation Laboratory, 1958-60; Hoover Institution, Stanford, Calif., senior research fellow, 1975—. Visiting professor, Arthur Spitzer Chair of Energy Management, Pepperdine University, 1976-77.

Early researcher in thermonuclear reactions; helped develop atomic bomb, and worked on development and function of other nuclear weapons after Hiroshima (including the hydrogen bomb); currently concerned with peaceful applications of nuclear energy. Director, Thermo Electron Corp.; member of president's Foreign Intelligence Advisory Board; member of scientific advisory board, U.S. Air Force; member of general advisory committee, U.S. Atomic Energy Commission, 1956-58; member of board of directors, Defense Intelligence School and Naval War College; member of other committees, councils, and advisory boards.

MEMBER: National Academy of Sciences, American Nuclear Society (fellow), American Physical Society (fellow), American Academy of Arts and Sciences, American Ordnance Association, American Geophysical Union, Society of Engineering Science, International Platform Association, American Association for the Advancement of Science, American Defense Preparedness Association, Americans for More Power Sources (member of advisory board), Atlantic Union, Center for the Survival of the Western Democracies, Hungarian Unity Association (member

of advisory board), Western Goals Foundation (member of advisory board).

AWARDS, HONORS: Joseph Priestley Memorial Award, Dickinson College, 1957; Albert Einstein Award, 1959; General Donovan Memorial Award, 1959; Midwest Research Institute Award, 1960; Living History Award from Research Institute of America, 1960; Thomas E. White Award, 1962; Enrico Fermi Award, 1962; Robins Award of America, 1963; Leslie R. Groves gold medal, 1974; Harvey Prize, 1975; Semmelweiss Medal, 1977; Albert Einstein Award, Technion Institute of Israel, 1977; Henry T. Heald Award, Illinois Institute of Technology, 1978; American College of Nuclear Medicine gold medal, 1980; Man of the Year, Achievement Rewards for College Scientists, 1980; Paul Harris Award, Rotary Club, 1980; A. C. Eringen Award, Society of Engineering Science, 1980; named distinguished scientist by National Science Development Board, 1981, and by Phil-American Academy of Science and Engineering, 1981; National Medal of Science, 1983. Honorary degrees: D.Sc., Yale University, 1954, University of Alaska, 1959, Fordham University, 1960, George Washington University, 1960, University of Southern California, 1960, St. Louis University, 1960, Rochester Institute of Technology, 1962, University of Detroit, 1964, Clemson University, 1966, Clarkson College, 1969; LL.D., Boston College, 1961, Seattle University, 1962, University of Cincinnati, 1962, University of Pittsburgh, 1963, Pepperdine University, 1974, and University of Maryland, 1977; L.H.D., Mount Mary College, 1964; Ph.D., Tel Aviv University, 1972; Doctor of Natural Science, De La Salle University, Manila, 1981.

WRITINGS:

(With J. H. Hibben) *Raman Effect and Its Chemical Applications,* Reinhold, 1939.
(With F. O. Rice) *The Structure of Matter,* Wiley, 1949.
(With A. L. Latter) *Our Nuclear Future,* Criterion, 1958.
(With others) *Education of the Scientist in a Free Society,* Marquette, 1959.
Basic Concepts of Physics, Part 1, California Book Co., 1960.
(With Allen Brown) *The Legacy of Hiroshima,* Doubleday, 1962, reprinted, Greenwood Press, 1975.
The Reluctant Revolutionary, University of Missouri Press, 1964.
(With G. W. Johnson, W. K. Talley, and G. H. Higgins) *The Constructive Uses of Nuclear Explosives,* McGraw, 1968.
(With Paul V. Yoder) *Great Issues '72: Important Questions Facing the American Public,* Troy State University, 1973.
Power and Security, Lexington Books, 1976.
Energy from Heaven and Earth, W. H. Freeman, 1979, revised edition, 1981.
The Pursuit of Simplicity, Pepperdine University Press, 1980.
Fusion: Magnetic Confinement, Academy Press, 1981.
(With others) *Great Issues '83: A Forum on Important Questions Facing the American Public,* Troy State University, 1983.
Better a Shield Than a Sword: Perspectives on Defense and Technology, Free Press, 1987.

Also author of *Great Men of Physics,* 1969, *The Miracle of Freedom,* 1972, *Energy: A Plan for Action,* 1975, *Nuclear Energy in the Developing World,* 1977, and *In Search of Solutions for Defense and for Energy,* Hoover Institution.

SIDELIGHTS: Edward Teller's work with the Manhattan Project during the Second World War, and later with the Los Alamos Scientific Laboratory, was instrumental in developing atomic weapons for the United States. Teller, in fact, is credited with being the father of the hydrogen bomb. Since the 1950s he has been at work developing peaceful uses for atomic energy, pioneering in methods to safely harness atomic power with magnetic confinement and laser techniques.

Speaking soon after the first hydrogen bomb was tested in 1952, Teller told *Newsweek:* "I would rather work on defense than on aggressive weapons." This desire was realized during the Reagan administration when Teller's proposal for a Strategic Defense Initiative, a system of satellites to shoot down and destroy incoming missiles, was met with enthusiasm. Although criticized at the time by some scientists, and by the Soviet Union, the SDI system is under development. Teller's book *Better a Shield Than a Sword: Perspectives on Defense and Technology* presents his argument for the proposal.

BIOGRAPHICAL/CRITICAL SOURCES:

BOOKS

Blumberg, Stalney A. and Gwinn Ownes, *Energy and Conflict: The Life and Times of Edward Teller,* Putnam, 1976.
Shepley, James and Clay Blair, Jr., *The Hydrogen Bomb,* David McKay, 1954.
Teller, Edward, *Better a Shield Than a Sword: Perspectives on Defense and Technology,* Free Press, 1987.

PERIODICALS

Life, September 6, 1954.
Los Angeles Times Book Review, March 22, 1981.
New Scientist, September 2, 1982.
Newsweek, August 2, 1954, October 18, 1954.
New York Review of Books, March 31, 1988.
New York Times, January 31, 1954, June 3, 1954, June 16, 1954, June 17, 1954, July 4, 1954.
Science, November 19, 1982.
Tribune Books (Chicago), July 12, 1987.
Washington Post, January 19, 1980, November 18, 1988.

*   *   *

THARP, Louise (Marshall) Hall 1898-

PERSONAL: Born June 19, 1898, in Oneonta, NY; daughter of Newton Marshall (a Congregationalist minister) and Louise (Buffum Varney) Hall; married Carey Edwin Tharp (an insurance executive), 1925; children: Carey Edwin, Jr., Marshall Allen. *Education:* Attended School of Fine Arts, Crafts, and Decorative Design, Boston, MA, 1917-19. *Politics:* Republican. *Religion:* Congregationalist.

ADDRESSES: Home—34 Ridgely St., Darien, CT 06820.

CAREER: Member of National Brownie Committee, Girl Scouts of America, 1925-34; Girl Scout Council, Rochester, NY, member, 1927-28; author, lecturer.

MEMBER: PEN, Society of American Historians, Daughters of the American Revolution, Authors Club (Boston), College Club (Boston), Darien Historical Society, Tokeneke Club (Darien, CT), Delta Kappa Gamma, Theta Sigma Pi.

AWARDS, HONORS: Delta Kappa Gamma Educators' Award, 1950; American Library Association Award, 1953; National Endowment for the Arts award, 1953; Ed.D., Rhode Island College, D. Litt., Northeastern University, Litt.D., Wheaton College, and Mount Holyoke College, 1967; Connecticut Bicentennial award, 1976, for *Tory Hole.*

WRITINGS:

JUVENILES

Tory Hole (historical fiction), Crowell, 1940, DCA, 1976.

Lords and Gentlemen (fiction), Crowell, 1940.
Sixpence for Luck (fiction), Crowell, 1941.
Down to the Sea: A Young People's Life of Nathaniel Bowditch, the Great American Navigator, Robert M. McBride, 1942.
A Sounding Trumpet: Julia Ward Howe and the Battle Hymn of the Republic, Robert M. McBride, 1944.
Champlain: Northwest Voyager (biography), Little, Brown, 1944.
Company of Adventurers: The Story of the Hudson's Bay Company, Little, Brown, 1946.
Louis Agassiz: Adventurous Scientist, Little, Brown, 1961.

FOR ADULTS

The Peabody Sisters of Salem (Book-of-the-Month Club selection), Little, Brown, 1950, published with a new introduction by Millicent Bell, Book-of-the-Month Club, 1980.
Until Victory: Horace Mann and Mary Peabody, Little, Brown, 1953, Greenwood Press, 1977.
Three Saints and a Sinner: Julia Ward Howe, Louisa, Annie and Sam Ward, Little, Brown, 1956.
Adventurous Alliance: The Story of the Agassiz Family of Boston, Little, Brown, 1959.
The Baroness and the General, Little, Brown, 1962.
Mrs. Jack: A Biography of Isabella Stewart Gardner, Little, Brown, 1965, Congdon & Weed, 1984.
Saint-Gaudens and the Gilded Era, Little, Brown, 1969.
The Appletons of Beacon Hill, Little, Brown, 1973.

OTHER

Contributor to *Encyclopedia Britannica* and *American Heritage.* Contributor of short stories to *Target* and *Child Life.* Editor, *Trailmaker* (a magazine for Girl Scout leaders), 1925-26.

BIOGRAPHICAL/CRITICAL SOURCES:

BOOKS

Fuller, Muriel, *More Junior Authors,* H. W. Wilson, 1963.

PERIODICALS

New York Herald Tribune Book Review, January 15, 1950.
New York Times, September 13, 1953.
Saturday Review of Literature, January 7, 1950.

*   *   *

TIGER, John
See WAGER, Walter H(erman)

*   *   *

TILLICH, Paul (Johannes) 1886-1965

PERSONAL: Surname pronounced *Till*-ik; born August 20, 1886, in Starzeddel, Kreis Guben, Prussia; died October 22, 1965, in the United States; came to America in 1933, naturalized in 1940; son of Johannes (a Lutheran pastor) and Mathilde (Durselen) Tillich; married Hannah Werner, 1924; children: Erdmuthe Tillich Farris, Rene Descartes. *Education:* Studied at University of Berlin, 1904-05, 1908, University of Tuebingen, 1905, University of Halle, 1905-07; University of Breslau, Ph.D., 1911; University of Halle, Licentiat of Theology, 1912.

ADDRESSES: Home—84 Woodlane, Easthampton, Long Island, N.Y. *Office*—Divinity School, University of Chicago, 5801 South Ellis, Chicago, Ill.

CAREER: Ordained minister of Evangelical Lutheran Church, 1912. University of Berlin, Berlin, Germany, privat-dozent,

1919-24; University of Marburg, Marburg, Germany, professor of theology, 1924-25; University of Dresden, Dresden, Germany, professor of theology, 1925-29; University of Leipzig, Leipzig, Germany, professor of theology, 1928-29; University of Frankfurt- am-Main, Frankfurt, Germany, professor of philosophy, 1929-33; Union Theological Seminary, New York, N.Y., professor of theology and philosophy, 1933-54; Harvard University, Cambridge, Mass., University Professor, 1955- 62; University of Chicago, Divinity School, Chicago, Ill., John Nuven Professor of Theology, 1962-65. Visiting lecturer at numerous universities in the United States, Europe, and Japan, including Tailor Lecturer, Yale University, 1935, Terry Lecturer, Yale, 1950, and Gifford Lecturer, University of Edinburgh, 1953. Co-founder of Self-Help for Emigres from Central Europe, Inc.; member of executive committee of American Committee for Christian Refugees; vice-chairman of Center for German and Austrian Art and Handicraft; provisional chairman of Council for a Democratic Germany. *Military service:* German Army, chaplain, 1914-18; awarded Iron Cross, First Class.

MEMBER: American Philosophical Association, American Theological Association, American Academy of Arts and Sciences, Philosophy Club, Academy of Religion and Mental Health.

AWARDS, HONORS: Grosse Verdienstkreuz from West German Republic, 1956; Goethe Medal from City of Frankfurt, 1956; Hanseatic Goethe Prize from City of Hamburg, 1958; Stern zum Grossen Verdienstkreuz from West German Republic, 1961; Academy of Religion and Mental Health Award, 1962; Paul Tillich Chair created at Union Theological Seminary, 1971. Numerous honorary degrees, including University of Halle, 1926, Yale University, 1940, University of Glasgow, 1951, Princeton University, 1953, Harvard University, 1954, University of Chicago, 1955, New School for Social Research, 1955, Brandeis University, 1955, Free University of Berlin, 1956, Franklin and Marshall College, 1960, and Bucknell College, 1960.

WRITINGS:

Die religiose Lage der Gegenwart, Ullstein, 1926, translation by H. Richard Niebuhr published in America as *The Religious Situation,* Henry Holt, 1932.
Religiose Verwirklichung, Furche, 1929.
Die sozialistische Entscheidung, A. Protte, 1933, 2nd edition, Bollwerk, 1948.
The Interpretation of History, Scribner, 1936.
Christian Answers by Paul J. Tillich and Others, Scribner, 1945.
The Shaking of the Foundations (sermons), Scribner, 1948.
The Protestant Era, University of Chicago Press, 1948, abridged edition, 1957.
Systematic Theology, University of Chicago Press, Volume 1, 1951, Volume 2, 1959, Volume 3, 1963.
Christianity and the Problem of Existence, Henderson, 1951.
Politische Bedeutung der Utopie im Leben der Voelker, Gebr. Weiss, 1951.
The Courage to Be (Terry Lectures), Yale University Press, 1952.
Die Judenfrage: Ein christliches und ein deutsches Problem, Gebr. Weiss, 1953.
Love, Power, and Justice, Oxford University Press, 1954.
The New Being (sermons), Scribner, 1955.
Biblical Religion and the Search for Ultimate Reality, University of Chicago Press, 1955, 2nd edition, 1964.
Dynamics of Faith, Harper, 1956.
Die Philosophie der Macht, Colloquium, 1956.

(Contributor) *Religion and Health: A Symposium,* Association Press, 1958.
Theology of Culture, Oxford University Press, 1959.
Gesammelte Werke, Evangelisches Verlagswerk, 1959.
Fruhe Hauptwerke, Evangelisches Verlagswerk, 1959.
Wesen und Wandel des Glaubens, Ullstein, 1961.
Philosophie und Schicksal, Evangelisches Verlagswerk, 1961.
Auf der Grenze: Aus dem Lebenswerk Paul Tillichs, Evangelisches Verlagswerk, 1962.
Der Protestantismus als Kritik und Gestaltung, Evangelisches Verlagswerk, 1962.
(Contributor) Reinhold Niebuhr, *A Prophetic Voice in Our Time: Essays in Tribute,* Seabury, 1962.
Christianity and the Encounter of the World Religions, Columbia University Press, 1963.
Morality and Beyond, Harper, 1963.
The Eternal Now, Scribner, 1963.
Das religiose Fundament des moralischen Handelns, Verlagswerk, 1965.
The World Situation, Fortress Press, 1965 (first published as a chapter in the symposium *The Christian Answer*).
Ultimate Concern: Tillich in Dialogue, Harper, 1965.
The Future of Religions, Harper, 1966.
On the Boundary (revision and new translation of part one of *The Interpretation of History*), Scribner, 1966.
My Search for Absolutes, with illustrations by Saul Steinberg, Simon & Schuster, 1967.
Perspectives on 19th and 20th Century Protestant Theology, Harper, 1967.
A History of Christian Thought, Harper, 1968.
My Travel Diary, 1936: Between Two Worlds, with illustrations by Alfonso Ossorio, Harper, 1970.
Political Expectation, Harper, 1971.
Begegnungen (collected works), Evangelisches Verlagswerk, 1972.
E. J. Tinsley, editor, *Paul Tillich 1886-1965* (collected works), Epworth, 1973.
Mysticism and Guilt-Consciousness in Schelling's Philosophical Development, English translation by Victor Nuovo, Bucknell University Press, 1974.
The Construction of the History of Religion in Schelling's Positive Philosophy: Its Presuppositions and Principles, English translation by Nuovo, Bucknell University Press, 1975.
Philosophical Development, English translation by Nuovo, Bucknell University Press, 1975.
Perry LeFevre, editor, *The Meaning of Health: The Relation of Religion and Health,* North Atlantic, 1981.
James L. Adams, editor, *Political Expectation,* Mercer University Press, 1981.
Das System der Wissenschaften nach Gegenstanden und Methoden, published in America as *The System of the Sciences According to Objects and Methods,* Bucknell University Press, 1981.
The Socialist Decision, English translation by Franklin Sherman, University Press of America, 1983.
John Dillenberger and Jane Dillenberger, editors, *Paul Tillich on Art and Architecture,* Crossroad, 1987.
F. Forrester Church, editor, *The Essential Tillich: An Anthology of the Writings of Paul Tillich,* Macmillan, 1987.
Religiose Reden, De Gruyter, 1987.
J. Mark Thomas, editor, *The Spiritual Situation in Our Technical Society,* Mercer University Press, 1988.

Contributor to journals, including *Christian Century, History of Ideas,* and *Social Research.* Member of editorial board, *Daeda-*

lus, Pastoral Psychology, Aufbau, and *Journal of Religion and Mental Health.*

SIDELIGHTS: Paul Tillich was perhaps the best known Protestant theologian in America from 1933 until his death in 1965. One of the first non-Jewish academicians to be expelled from Nazi Germany for his opposition to Hitler, Tillich spent the most productive years of his life at the Union Theological Seminary in New York City. From his base there he wrote numerous works in both English and German and delivered innumerable sermons and lectures on the meaning of the Christian faith for twentieth-century man. "Paul Tillich was a giant among us," wrote colleague Reinhold Niebuhr in the *New York Times Book Review.* "His influence extended beyond theological students and circles to include many from other disciplines. . . . He combined theological with philosophical and psychological learning, and also, he combined religious insights with an understanding and appreciation of the arts. Thus he displayed to the American communities of learning and culture, the wholeness of religious philosophy and of the political and social dimensions of human existence."

From his earliest years Tillich was passionate about both Christianity and scholarship. He was born in Prussia in 1886, the son of a Lutheran pastor of high standing. Tillich attended school in Brandenburg and later in Berlin, earning sufficient grades to qualify for university training. This he took at colleges in Halle, Breslau, Tuebingen, and Berlin, eventually earning a Ph.D. and a Licentiate of Theology. He was ordained as a minister of Germany's Evangelical Lutheran Church in 1912. During World War I, Tillich served as a chaplain to the German ground forces, earning decoration for his work among the troops. At the war's conclusion he accepted the post of *privat-dozent* of theology at the University of Berlin, the first of several prestigious universities on whose faculties he would serve.

Tillich quickly established a reputation as one of Germany's most important philosopher/theologians, whose "influence on . . . religious life was maximal," to quote Niebuhr. Throughout the 1920s he authored a number of important works, including *Die religiose Lage der Gegenwart,* translated into English as *The Religious Situation.* In this and other books, Tillich proposed his central theme, namely that religion is the ultimate concern overriding all human activities, and that only by discerning God could modern man discover the courage to be. Tillich expanded on these notions in his English-language books after the Nazi regime dismissed him from his post and more or less forced him to emigrate.

It was Reinhold Niebuhr, in fact, who helped Tillich secure a position at Union Theological Seminary in 1933. Tillich stayed at the seminary for more than twenty years, during which he wrote a number of books, lectures, and sermons aimed primarily at the lonely and alienated "contemporary" man. The author often said that he considered himself an explorer "on the boundary" between religion, philosophy, and psychology. In books such as *The Shaking of the Foundation* and *The Courage to Be* he was able to integrate existential philosophy with the religious basis of human life, suggesting that religion could be a "unifying center" for existence. Tillich's scholarly yet humanistic works provided a welcome alternative for American Protestants who were not comfortable with fundamentalist interpretations of the Bible. To quote Niebuhr, he "emancipated the intellectually questioning in the churches from literalistic dogma."

By the time of his death in 1965 Tillich had written more than forty full-length works, some in German and some in English. During the 1950s and the 1960s he was given prizes and honor-

ary doctorates in America and in his native land for his memorable contributions to Protestant theology. In the *New Republic,* Roger Hazelton contended that Tillich's greatness as a thinker lay "in the fact that he [knew] what man is made of, what he suffers from, and what he can hope for." A *Times Literary Supplement* reviewer likewise found Tillich "a great constructive thinker" who "was a very human and humane personality." The reviewer added: "His remarkable ability to identify himself with others in their happiness and in their anguish is reflected again and again."

Not surprisingly, Tillich's influence has survived his passing, especially in academic circles. No less than fifteen works have been published posthumously, including collections in both German and English, and Union Theological Seminary has honored the professor by creating a chair in his name. As John K. Roth put it in the *Los Angeles Times Book Review,* Tillich's philosophical theology "decisively influenced mainline American Protestantism during its heyday in the middle third of this century. . . . Tillich explored the uncertainties of human existence and, in spite of those conditions, helped people to discern the God who provides the courage to be."

BIOGRAPHICAL/CRITICAL SOURCES:

BOOKS

Freeman, David Hugh, *Tillich,* Presbyterian & Reformed, 1962.
Half Century of Union Theological Seminary, 1896-1945, Scribner, 1954.
Harcourt, Melvin, editor, *Thirteen for Christ,* Sheed, 1963.
Kegley, C., *The Theology of Paul Tillich,* Macmillan, 1952.
Kilsey, D. H., *The Fabric of Paul Tillich's Theology,* Yale University Press, 1967.
Leibrecht, Walter, editor, *Religion and Culture: Essays in Honor of Paul Tillich,* Harper, 1959.
Nelson, James, editor, *Wisdom,* Norton, 1958.
O'Meara, T. A., and C. D. Weisser, editors, *Paul Tillich in Catholic Thought,* Priory Press, 1964.
Tavard, G. H., *Paul Tillich and the Christian Message,* Scribner, 1962.
Thomas, J. Heyward, *Paul Tillich: An Appraisal,* Westminster, 1963.
Thomas, *Paul Tillich,* John Knox, 1966.
Tillich, Paul, *The Interpretation of History,* Scribner, 1936.
Tillich, Paul, *On the Boundary,* Scribner, 1966.
Tillich, Paul, *My Search for Absolutes,* with illustrations by Saul Steinberg, Simon & Schuster, 1967.

PERIODICALS

Book Week, February 23, 1964.
Churchman, February 1, 1937.
Commentary, April, 1967.
Encounter, winter, 1967, summer, 1967.
Los Angeles Times Book Review, November 22, 1987.
New Republic, January 6, 1968.
Newsweek, May 17, 1954.
New York Herald Tribune Book Review, March 8, 1953.
New York Post, May 1, 1940.
New York Times, June 4, 1950.
New York Times Book Review, June 27, 1948, October 24, 1965, October 15, 1967, May 10, 1970.
Time, October 20, 1952, March 16, 1959.
Times Literary Supplement, December 4, 1970, January 28, 1972.*

—*Sketch by Anne Janette Johnson*

TOMLINSON, (Alfred) Charles 1927-

PERSONAL: Born January 8, 1927, in Stoke-on-Trent, Staffordshire, England; son of Alfred (an estate agent's clerk) and May (Lucas) Tomlinson; married Brenda Raybould, October 23, 1948; children: Justine Benedikte, Juliet Virginia. *Education:* Queens' College, Cambridge, B.A., 1948; London University, M.A. (with distinction), 1955.

ADDRESSES: Office—English Department, University of Bristol, Bristol BS8 1TB, England.

CAREER: Poet and artist. University of Bristol, Bristol, England, lecturer, 1956-68, reader in English poetry, 1968-82, professor of English, 1982—. Visiting professor, University of New Mexico, 1962-63, and McMaster University, 1987; O'Connor Professor of English, Colgate University, 1967-68, 1989; visiting fellow, Princeton University, 1981; Lamont Professor of English, Union College, 1987. Has had one-man exhibitions of his graphic art in London and Cambridge, England, a three-year travelling exhibition with the Arts Council, and a Poetry Society exhibition.

MEMBER: Royal Society of Literature (fellow).

AWARDS, HONORS: Four prizes from *Poetry* magazine; fellowship to travel in the United States, Institute of International Education, 1959-60; honorary fellow, Queens' College, Cambridge, 1974; Cholmondeley Award, 1979; D.Litt., Keele University, 1981, Colgate University, 1981, and University of New Mexico, 1986; honorary professor, Keele University, 1989.

WRITINGS:

POETRY

Relations and Contraries (pamphlet), Hand and Flower Press, 1951.
The Necklace, Fantasy Press, 1955, revised edition, Oxford University Press, 1966.
Solo for a Glass Harmonica (limited edition), Westerham Press, 1957.
Seeing Is Believing, Obolensky, 1958, revised edition, Oxford University Press, 1960.
A Peopled Landscape, Oxford University Press, 1963.
(With Tony Connor and Austin Clarke) *Poems: A Selection,* Oxford University Press, 1964.
American Scenes, and Other Poems, Oxford University Press, 1966.
The Matachines: New Mexico, San Marcos Press, 1968.
To Be Engraved on the Skull of a Cormorant, Unaccompanied Serpent, 1968.
(With Alan Brownjohn and Michael Hamburger) *Penguin Modern Poets 14,* Penguin, 1969.
The Way of a World, Oxford University Press, 1969.
America West Southwest, San Marcos Press, 1969.
(With Octavio Paz, Jacques Roubard, and Edoardo Sanguineti) *Renga: A Chain of Poems* (in Spanish, French, Italian, and English), Gallimard, 1970, all-English edition translated by Tomlinson, Braziller, 1972.
(And graphic artist) *Words and Images,* Covent Garden Press, 1972.
Written on Water, Oxford University Press, 1972.
The Way In, and Other Poems, Oxford University Press, 1974.
The Shaft, Oxford University Press, 1978.
Selected Poems, 1951-1974, Oxford University Press, 1978.
(With Paz) *Airborn/Hijos del aire* (in English and Spanish), Anvil Press, 1981.
The Flood, Oxford University Press, 1981.

Notes from New York, and Other Poems, Oxford University Press, 1984.
(And graphic artist) *Eden: Graphics and Poems,* Redcliffe Press, 1985.
Collected Poems, 1951-1981, Oxford University Press, 1986, expanded edition published as *Collected Poems,* 1988.
The Return, Oxford University Press, 1987.
Annunciations, Oxford University Press, 1989.
Selected Poems, Exile Editions (Toronto), 1989.

OTHER

(Translator) *Versions from Fyodor Tyutchev, 1803-1873,* introduction by Henry C. Gifford, Oxford University Press, 1960.
(Translator with Gifford) *Castilian Ilexes: Versions from Antonio Machado,* Oxford University Press, 1963.
The Poem as Initiation, Colgate University Press, 1967.
(Editor) *Marianne Moore: A Collection of Critical Essays,* Prentice-Hall, 1969.
(Translator with Gifford) Cesar Vallejo, *Ten Versions from Trilce,* San Marcos Press, 1970.
(Author of introduction) Simon Cutts, *A New Kind of Tie: Poems, 1965-68,* Tarasque Press, 1972.
(Editor) *William Carlos Williams: Critical Anthology,* Penguin, 1972.
In Black and White (graphics), Carcanet, 1976.
(Editor) William Carlos Williams, *Selected Poems,* Penguin, 1976.
(Editor and translator) Paz, *Selected Poems,* Penguin, 1979.
(Editor) *The Oxford Book of Verse in English Translation,* Oxford University Press, 1980.
Some Americans: A Personal Record, University of California Press, 1981.
Poetry and Metamorphosis (lectures), Cambridge University Press, 1983.
(Translator and compiler) *Translations* (poetry collection), Oxford University Press, 1983.

Also author of introduction to *The Manoevring Sun: An Anthology of Verse by People Who Live or Work in the Bristol Area,* compiled by Alan Crang. Contributor of poetry and reviews to *Nation, Hudson Review, Spectator, Essays in Criticism, Poetry* (Chicago), *Poetry Nation Review, Sewanee Review,* and *Times Literary Supplement.* A selection of Tomlinson's manuscript collection is kept at the British Library in London, England.

SIDELIGHTS: A British poet, artist, and translator fluent in French, Italian, and German, Charles Tomlinson is "one of the most important talents to emerge in Britain" since World War II, according to *American Book Review* critic Michael Hennessy. Nonetheless, the poet has never been fully accepted as a writer of major importance in his native country. English critics "get [a] wild smell of [William Carlos] Williams off his work," offers Carl Bedient in the *New York Times Book Review* as an explanation for this British disdain; "and, besides, [they] have complained that he seldom writes about people." As numerous reviewers have observed, Tomlinson's work has indeed been influenced by Williams, as well as other American poets such as Wallace Stevens, Ezra Pound, Marianne Moore, George Oppen, and Louis Zukofsky. He has long admired these American modernists, whose approach to poetry, according to *Critical Quarterly* contributor Alan Young, Tomlinson sees as being close "to his own 'basic theme': 'that one does not need to go beyond sense experience to some mythic union, that the "I" can only be responsible in relationship and not by dissolving itself away into ecstasy or the Oversoul.'" Since the 1950s Tomlinson has attempted in his poetry to define life by precisely and objectively describing our relationship with the world.

Tomlinson "began life as a painter," writes Michael Kirkham in *Essays in Criticism,* "and in his poems he feels through what he sees; and it is prior training in a visual medium that probably accounts for his bias away from the romantic, subjective interpretation of reality: trust in the act of perception has led him . . . to lay the emphasis on the object and the external." For this reason, the poet rejects "symbolic poetry as representing 'a view of life too subjective to allow accurate contemplation of the outside world,' " says Jonathan Barker, quoting Tomlinson in a *Times Literary Supplement* article. The emphasis that is put on objectivism also applies to the philosophy that imbues Tomlinson's poetry. "Tomlinson finds that the natural world has not been ordained specifically for human happiness, domination, and moral edification," analyses Julian Gitzen in *Midwest Quarterly.* He "recognizes that its immense power is dreadful, threatening, and unchallengeable, but he shares with his fellow poets the conclusion that by intelligently recognizing and deferring to natural forces, we can achieve a measure of dignity and peace."

In his early books, Tomlinson "established himself as a poet of intense visual experience, a poet-painter, for whom accuracy of perception was vital," remarks *Poetry Review* critic John Cassidy. But on the few occasions when his poetry does move "away from observation," comments Hennessy in the *Rocky Mountain Review of Language and Literature,* ". . . it almost always does so in order to remind us of our proper place in the world." Refusing to place mankind in the center of his poetic vision, Tomlinson focuses instead on landscapes, architecture, and other objects, his favorite motifs being such subjects as water, stone, and time. But this is not to say that the poet's work disregards humanity. Hennessy continues: "Tomlinson urges us to recognize human limits rather than striving to go beyond them. From observation of the world's surfaces, he moves quickly and surely into the depths of the self. And if we are unable, like some reviewers, to recognize the 'human' in his early poetry, it is because we have failed to recognize our human dependence upon the world around us."

Still, there remain critics who cite other problems in Tomlinson's work, especially with regard to the earlier books. In *Poetry,* Michael Mott regards the poems in *Relations and Contraries* to be "rather ornate" and "over-wordy." Bedient similarly remarks in *British Poetry since 1960: A Critical Survey* that the poems in *The Necklace* are "too beautiful, too exquisite." *The Necklace,* he later adds, "zeroes in on the great Tomlinson theme, but vitiates it by a kind of enamelled elegance; it has [Wallace] Stevens's epicurean quality, but not his saving gusto and bravura." These first few books, say a number of critics, relied heavily on the styles Tomlinson had learned from other poets; but, with the publication of *Seeing Is Believing,* the poet began to find his own voice. With this book, declares Bedient, "Tomlinson first became both the distinct and distinguished poet he is today." *Hollins Critic* contributor Edward Hirsch also attests that *Seeing Is Believing* marks the poet's first "lucid step" toward his own unique style.

Like its preceding books, *Seeing Is Believing* focuses solely on objects. "As Tomlinson pointed out," says Kirkham, "the things he wrote about—houses, cities, walls, landscapes—were already saturated in human presence and traditions, and this was his point in writings about them." The "fine technique" that Tomlinson uses to describe his subjects, maintains Cassidy, is clearly evident, but the critic agrees with other reviewers who feel that the basic theme, the presence of human experience being contained within inanimate objects, is belabored. "The point is made

repeatedly . . . , obsessively," Cassidy notes, "and one begins to sympathize with those who ask of Tomlinson some new perspective, some more humane engagement."

With the poetry collections *A Peopled Landscape* and *American Scenes, and Other Poems,* Tomlinson obliges his critics to a certain extent by writing about American Indians, motel owners, and other people he came across while on his first sojourn in the United States as a visiting professor at the University of New Mexico. It was the relatively unpopulated landscapes of the American Southwest that left the deepest impression on Tomlinson, however. Therefore, despite the new inclusion of people in these books, "the prevailing impression remains," according to Mott, "of a poet with a predilection for ghost towns; for ruins, desert places, doors opening on nothing, . . . settings upon which human life had made some mark before leaving."

But with the poems in *A Peopled Landscape, American Scenes,* and Tomlinson's next major collection, *The Way of a World,* *Critical Quarterly* contributor Gitzen notices that the poet's "exploration of visual problems" is slowly being superseded by a "concern with philosophical reflection. Vision remains Tomlinson's chief instrument of observation, but the sights he describes are subjected to rumination." Tomlinson's mix of meticulous attention to detail and philosophical examinations has been seen as both a strength and a weakness in *The Way of a World.* John W. Hughes remarks in *Saturday Review:* "Everything [in *The Way of a World*] is observed minutely, and the symbolic perfection of Mr. Tomlinson's landscapes is quietly abstract and ruminative, though sometimes tiresome." A *Times Literary Supplement* reviewer similarly believes that, at times, the poet's "description is unstrained, with a dexterously employed metaphor spreading the observation to other senses beside the visual," while at other times his use of description "is more laborious: more pure if you like, but giving a fatiguing impression of being flogged into existence by sheer concentration and indefatigable notetaking."

Nevertheless, a number of critics find *The Way of the World* to be one of Tomlinson's most significant collections; and it contains some of the writer's best known poems such as "Prometheus" and "Assassin." "What makes *The Way of the World* so important," proposes Mott, "is that Tomlinson has turned . . . from his painter's preoccupation to a questioning of his craft as a poet." Another feature of this work that makes it significant, says Ronald Hayman in *Encounter,* is that "in *The Way of the World* . . . the assertion of the human will comes into the foreground." More praise is offered by Bedient in his *New York Times Book Review* article: these poems are "dense with [the poet's] loving intellection, his stringent sensuousness, his difficult grace, his strong dry beauty." But what makes many of these poems impressive to *Times Literary Supplement* critic Jonathan Barker is a quality of Tomlinson's poetry which the reviewer notes "has been curiously understressed by critics." This attribute, writes Barker, is the poet's "delight in the act of sensually experiencing the world."

With each successive book, Tomlinson's work has become increasingly philosophical. At some points, however, such as in *Written on Water,* a few critics feel this approach detracts from the sensuousness that is evident in *The Way of a World.* According to Bedient in the *New York Times Book Review,* "the comparable ambitious meditative poems [in *Written on Water*] . . . hamper as much as they restrain the sensuous. The brilliance of the world is hidden behind the smoked glass of reflection." But this continuing trend of philosophical reflection in the author's work is viewed by other critics to be "an important new departure," as one *Times Literary Supplement* contributor avers. The reviewer adds that "problems of believing as well as seeing are tackled in a more open, richly meditative way than" in earlier collections.

As a consequence of this more meditative stance, Tomlinson's poetry has also become less objective with each successive collection, observes Terry Eagleton in a *Stand* article about *The Way In, and Other Poems.* "Although the resolute objectivism is still there," Eagleton asserts, "it's more obviously interlaced with human sympathies than in some of Tomlinson's previous work." A *Times Literary Supplement* reviewer calls this approach "more congenial" than that of earlier books. "A more personal book than any of Tomlinson's others," attests Hirsch, *The Way In* focuses on England and the poet's origins there. It "is a gentle book of coming home, of witnessing and remembering, of negotiating with the regions of one's past."

One of Tomlinson's least well received collections is *The Shaft,* which William S. Saunders declares in *Delta* to be the author's "least poetically vital book." The only new element that Tomlinson introduces in *The Shaft* is a collection of historical pieces that make use of his interest in the sense of time as it relates to places. "But," remarks *Poetry* reviewer Ben Howard, "the historical critical mode of the new poems [in *The Shaft*] and the rhymed pentameter stanzas in which they are written seem unnatural and even regressive in a poet whose best work has been rooted in the contingencies of the present moment, and whose poetic strengths are not so much critical as scrupulously contemplative. One can admire Tomlinson's venture without applauding the result."

In *The Flood,* published seven years after *The Shaft,* Tomlinson recuperated with what critics see as a much more dynamic work. Even though the book "marks no breakthrough for Tomlinson," Dana Gioia maintains in *Hudson Review* that *The Flood* is an accomplishment because it represents "a deepening of themes developed in his earlier books. . . . Though the places [he reflects upon] may by now be familiar, the inspiration behind the new poems is fresh and genuine." Several critics have also commented that *The Flood* is one of the poet's most diverse collections, containing everything from poems about music, to humorous poems, to personal poems. Of these, Barker feels that "the best and most essentially Tomlinson," are grouped towards the last part of the book; and "The Flood" in particular, writes *Agenda* contributor Dennis O'Driscoll, "is the most packed and powerful poem in a book that glitters frequently with memorable descriptions of water." Young concludes that "all the positive qualities which Tomlinson has admired in his chosen Americans are to be found in the finely-wrought poems of *The Flood.*"

The poet once again returns to the subject of America in *Notes from New York, and Other Poems.* The poems at the beginning of this book concern Tomlinson's visit to New York City "and are a delight," in *Hudson Review* critic William H. Pritchard's opinion. Pritchard considers the poems in the second half of *Notes from New York,* which are set in England, to be "less memorable and relaxed than the New York ones," but Peter Porter feels that there is an advantage to this "relaxed" style. Porter remarks in the *Observer* that "Tomlinson has developed a springy but relaxed adaptation of traditional blank verse which is beautifully at home when he also is at home."

Tomlinson has remained loyal to his homeland despite his great popularity in the United States and his affinity for American poetry. "Perhaps part of the answer [for this] is that Tomlinson is even more English than even he recognizes," surmises Young in a discussion of *Some Americans: A Personal Record. Some Amer-*

icans is a prose work that provides many insights into the poet's background. Part of the book is an account of the poets—Williams, Moore, Pound, Zukofsky, Oppen—and painter, Georgia O'Keefe, who influenced him. It also, however, "touches on his beginnings as a poet, describes his isolation in England, and records the process by which he educated himself in an alien literature," relates *New York Times Book Review* critic Donald Hall. Tomlinson's book reveals how England is still an important part of his writing, and this is why he has stayed there. Indeed, as Barker reiterates, "Tomlinson's central themes have always been sensation and the mind examining sensation in relation to natural phenomena. Once we grasp this we can see that the chief poetic precursor of Tomlinson is not Wallace Stevens, William Carlos Williams, or Giuseppe Ungaretti . . . , but the William Wordsworth who talked of nature 'feelingly watched.' "

In learning his craft from numerous poets of varied backgrounds, Tomlinson has found a style all his own; and critics like Bedient now consider him to be "unmistakably an original poet." Bedient continues in *British Poetry since 1960:* "There is in him, it is true, a measure of Wordsworth . . . [but] Wordsworth discovers himself in nature—it is this, of course, that makes him a Romantic poet. Tomlinson, on the other hand, discovers the nature of nature: a classical artist, he is all taut, responsive detachment." Ultimately, it is difficult to categorize Tomlinson as either distinctly British or American. He has, as Howard states, "drawn on the broadest range of modernist traditions— British, Continental, and American—and brought them into the closest harmony, both with one another and with the descriptive-meditative tradition of English poetry." "To my mind," concludes Hirsch, "Tomlinson is one of the most astute, disciplined, and lucent poets of his generation. He is one of the few English poets to have extended the inheritance of modernism and I suspect that his quiet, meditative voice will reverberate on both sides of the Atlantic for a long time to come."

AVOCATIONAL INTERESTS: Music, walking.

BIOGRAPHICAL/CRITICAL SOURCES:

BOOKS

Bedient, Calvin, *Eight Contemporary Poets,* Oxford University Press, 1974.

Contemporary Literary Criticism, Gale, Volume 2, 1974, Volume 4, 1975, Volume 6, 1976, Volume 13, 1980, Volume 45, 1987.

Dictionary of Literary Biography, Volume 40: *Poets of Great Britain and Ireland since 1960,* Gale, 1985.

Donoghue, Denis, *The Ordinary Universe,* Macmillan, 1968.

John, Brian, *The World as Event: The Poetry of Charles Tomlinson,* McGill-Queens University Press, 1989.

O'Gorman, Kathleen, editor, *Charles Tomlinson: Man and Artist,* University of Missouri Press, 1988.

Rosenthal, M. L., *The Modern Poets: A Critical Introduction,* Oxford University Press, 1960.

Rosenthal, M. L., *The New Poets: American and British Poetry since World War II,* Oxford University Press, 1967.

Schmidt, Michael, and Grevel Lindop, editors, *British Poetry since 1960: A Critical Survey,* Carcanet, 1972.

PERIODICALS

Agenda, summer, 1975, summer/autumn, 1981.

American Book Review, September/October, 1982.

British Book News, November, 1985, January, 1986.

Critical Quarterly, winter, 1971, summer, 1973, winter, 1982.

Delta, Number 59, 1979.

Encounter, December, 1970, March, 1975.

Essays in Criticism, July, 1967.

Hollins Critic, April, 1978.

Hudson Review, autumn, 1966, summer, 1973, spring, 1975, summer, 1975, winter, 1981-82, summer, 1984.

Listener, July 13, 1978.

London Review of Books, June 17, 1982.

Midwest Quarterly, summer, 1974.

Modern Painters, spring, 1989, autumn, 1989.

Nation, March 16, 1974.

New Leader, June 1, 1981.

New Statesman, December 5, 1969.

New York Times Book Review, April 29, 1973, April 6, 1975, December 31, 1978, March 1, 1981.

Observer, June 17, 1984.

Parnassus: Poetry in Review, spring/summer, 1974.

Poetry, November, 1967, May, 1971, November, 1980.

Poetry Review, January, 1979, April, 1982.

Review, June/July, 1962.

Rocky Mountain Review of Language and Literature, Volume 36, number 2, 1982.

Saturday Review, February 11, 1967, August 8, 1970.

Stand, Volume 16, number 3, 1975.

Times Literary Supplement, January 29, 1970, October 20, 1972, November 8, 1974, December 1, 1978, July 17, 1981, September 4, 1981, February 5, 1982, October 14, 1983, April 27, 1984, March 21, 1986, January 15, 1988.

—*Sketch by Kevin S. Hile*

* * *

TOURNIMPARTE, Alessandra
See GINZBURG, Natalia

* * *

TROYAT, Henri 1911-
(Lev Tarassoff)

PERSONAL: Born November 1, 1911, in Moscow, Russia; left Russia with family during 1917 Revolution, settling in Paris three years later; son of Aslan (a merchant) and Lydie (Abessolomoff) Tarassoff; name legally changed to Henri Troyat; married Marguerite Saintagne, September 23, 1948; stepchildren: Jean-Daniel, Michele (Mrs. J. Donoghue McKeown). *Education:* Lycee Pasteur, Neuilly-sur-Seine, licencie en droit. *Religion:* Orthodox.

ADDRESSES: Home—5 rue Bonaparte, Paris 6e, France. *Office*— Academie Francaise, 23 quai de Conti, Paris 6e, France.

CAREER: Editorial staff member, Prefecture de la Seine, 1935-41; novelist and writer, 1941—.

MEMBER: Academie Francaise.

AWARDS, HONORS: Prix Populiste, 1935, for *Faux Jour;* Prix Goncourt, 1938, for *L'Araigne;* Prix Louis Barthou de l'Academie Francaise, 1938, for body of work; Grand Prix Litteraire de Monaco, 1952, for *La Neige en deuil;* Commandeur, Legion d'Honneur; Notable Book citation, American Library Association, 1981, for *Catherine the Great.*

WRITINGS:

NOVELS

Faux Jour, Plon, 1935.

Le Vivier, Plon, 1935, new edition, 1967.

Grandeur Nature, Plon, 1936, translation by James Whitall published as *One Minus Two,* I. Washburn, 1938.

L'Araigne, Plon, 1938, translation by Anthea Bell published as *The Web,* A. Ellis, 1984.

Judith Madrier, Plon, 1940, translation by Whitall published under same title, I. Washburn, 1941.

Le Mort saisit le vif, Plon, 1942.

Le Signe du taureau, Plon, 1945.

Tant que la terre durera, Table Ronde, Volume 1: *Tant que la terre durera,* 1947, translation by David Hapgood published as *My Father's House,* Sloan & Pearce, 1951, Volume 2: *Le Sac et la cendre,* 1948, translation by Anthony Hinton published as *The Red and the White,* Crowell, 1956 (published in England as *Sackcloth and Ashes,* Arco, 1956), Volume 3: *Etrangers sur la terre,* 1950, translation by Hinton published as *Strangers on Earth,* Crowell, 1958.

La Tete sur les epaules, Plon, 1951.

La Neige en deuil, Flammarion, 1952, translation by Constantine Fitz Gibbon published as *The Mountain,* Simon & Schuster, 1953.

Les Semailles et les moissons, Plon, translations published as *The Seed and the Fruit,* Simon & Schuster, Volume 1: *Les Semailles et les moissons,* 1953, translation by Lily Duplaix published as *Amelie in Love,* 1956, Pocket Books, 1974, Volume 2: *Amelie,* 1955, translation by M. V. Dodge published as *Amelie and Pierre,* 1957, Pocket Books, 1974, Volume 3: *La Grive,* 1956, translation by Nicolas Monjo published as *Elizabeth,* 1959, Pocket Books, 1974, Volume 4: *Tendre et violente Elizabeth,* 1957, translation by Mildred Marmur published as *Tender and Violent Elizabeth,* 1960, Pocket Books, 1974, Volume V: *La Rencontre,* 1958, translation by Gerard Hopkins published as *The Encounter,* 1962, Pocket Books, 1974.

La Lumiere des justes, Flammarion, translations published as *The Light of the Just,* Simon & Schuster, Volume 1: *Les Compagnons du coquelicot,* 1959, translation by Elisabeth Abbott published as *The Brotherhood of the Red Poppy,* 1961, Volume 2: *La Barynia,* 1960, translation by Frances Frenaye published as *The Baroness,* 1961, Volume 3: *La Gloire des vaincus,* 1961, Volume 4: *Les Dames de Siberie,* 1962, Volume 5: *Sophie, ou lafin des combats,* 1963.

Une Extreme Amitie, Table Ronde, 1963, translation by Joyce Emerson published as *An Intimate Friendship,* Redman, 1967, translation by Eugene Paul published as *An Extreme Friendship,* Phaedra, 1968.

Les Eygletiere, Flammarion, Volume 1: *Les Eygletiere,* 1965, Volume 2: *La Faim des lionceaux,* 1966, Volume 3: *La Malandre,* 1967.

Les Heritiers de l'avenir, Flammarion, Volume 1: *Le Cahier,* 1968, Volume 2: *Cent un coups de canon,* 1969, Volume 3: *L'Elephant blanc,* 1970.

La Tete sur les epaules, Plon, 1970.

La Pierre, lafeuille et les ciseaux, Flammarion, 1972.

Anne Predaille, Flammarion, 1973.

Le Moscovite, Flammarion, Volume 1: *Le Moscovite,* 1974, Volume 2: *Le Front dans les nuages,* 1976, Volume 3: *Le Prisonnier numero 1,* 1978.

Viou, Flammarion, 1980, translation by published as *Sylvie,* A. Ellis, 1982.

Grimbosq, Flammarion, 1976.

Le Pain de l'Etranger, Flammarion, 1982, translation published as *The Children,* A. Ellis, 1983.

La Derision, Flammarion, 1983.

Marie Karpovna, Flammarion, 1984.

Le Bruit solitaire du coeur, Flammarion, 1985.

A demain, Sylvie, Flammarion, 1986, translation published as *Sylvie, Her Teen-Age Years,* A. Ellis, 1988.

Le troisieme bonheur, Flammarion, 1987.
Toute ma vie sera mensonge, Flammarion, 1988.
Sylvie-Happiness, translation by Bell, A. Ellis, 1989.
An Act of Treachery, translation by Bell, A. Ellis, 1990.

BIOGRAPHY

Dostoievsky, Fayard, 1940, translation by Norbert Guterman published as *Firebrand: The Life of Dostoevsky,* Roy, 1946.
Pouchkine, A. Michel, 1946, translation by Randolph T. Weaver published as *Pushkin,* Pantheon, 1950, translation by Nancy Amphoux published as *Pushkin,* Doubleday, 1970.
L'Etrange Destin de Lermontov, Plon, 1952.
Tolstoi, Fayard, 1965, new edition, 1967, translation by Amphoux published as *Tolstoy,* Doubleday, 1967.
Gogol, Flammarion, 1971, translation by Amphoux published as *Divided Soul: The Life of Gogol,* Doubleday, 1973.
Catherine la Grande, Flammarion, 1977, translation published as *Catherine the Great,* Dutton, 1980.
Pierre le Grand, Flammarion, 1979, translation by Joan Pinkham published as *Peter the Great,* Dutton, 1987.
Alexander Ier, Flammarion, 1980, translation published as *Alexander of Russia: Napoleon's Conqueror,* Fromm International, 1983.
Kisling, 1891-1953, J. Kisling, 1982, printed in two volumes, Abner Schram (New Jersey).
Ivan le Terrible, Flammarion, 1984, translation published as *Ivan the Terrible,* Dutton, 1984.
Tourgueniev, Flammarion, 1985, translation by Amphoux published as *Turgenev,* Dutton, 1980.
Tchekov, translation by Michael Henry Heim published as *Chekhov,* Dutton, 1986.
Gorki, Flammarion, 1986, translation by Lowell Bair published as *Gorky: A Biography,* Crown, 1989.
Flaubert, Flammarion, 1988.

SHORT FICTION

La Clef de voute [and] *Monsieur Citrine,* Plon, 1937.
La Fosse commune (contains "Les Cobayes," "La Dame noire," "Le Tandem," "Erratum," "L'Assasin," "L'Etrange Histoire de Mr. Breadborough," "Le Vertige," "Le Ratuset," and "Le Ressac"), Plon, 1937.
Le Jugement de Dieu [and] *Le Puy Saint-Clair* [and] *Le Merveilleux Voyage de Jacques Mazeyrat,* Plon, 1941, reprinted, Plon, 1976.
Du Philanthrope a la rouquine (collected stories), Flammarion, 1945.
La Maison des betes heureuses (juvenile story), Bias, 1956.
Le Geste d'Eve (collected stories), Flammarion, 1964.
Les Ailes du Diable (collected stories), Flammarion, 1966.

NONFICTION

Les Ponts de Paris, Flammarion, 1946.
La Case de l'Oncle Sam (travelogue), Table Ronde, 1948.
De Gratteciel en cocotier, a travers l'Amerique latine (travelogue), Plon, 1955.
Sainte Russie: Souvenirs et reflexions, Grasset, 1956.
La Vie quotidienne en Russie au temps du dernier Tsar, Hachette, 1959, translation by Malcolm Barnes published as *Daily Life in Russia under the Last Tsar,* Allen & Unwin, 1961, Macmillan, 1962.
Naissance d'une Dauphine: Reportage, Gallimard, 1960.
Un si long chemin, Stock, 1976.

OTHER

Also author of plays, "Les Vivants," 1946, "Sebastien," 1949, and "Madame d'Arches a dit peut-etre," 1952.

SIDELIGHTS: Works by Henri Troyat have been translated into English, Spanish, Hebrew, and Chinese.

MEDIA ADAPTATIONS: La Neige en deuil was adapted for film as "The Mountain" by Paramount, 1956.

BIOGRAPHICAL/CRITICAL SOURCES:

BOOKS

Contemporary Literary Criticism, Volume 23, Gale, 1983.
Discours de reception a l'Academie francaise, et reponse de M. le marechal Juin, Plon, 1960.

PERIODICALS

Chicago Tribune Book World, November 9, 1980, September 2, 1984.
Christian Science Monitor, December 3, 1970.
Los Angeles Times, December 3, 1980.
Los Angeles Times Book Review, March 13, 1983, September 2, 1984, November 16, 1986, August 2, 1987, March 6, 1988.
Nation, August 20, 1971.
New York Times, November 30, 1980, October 28, 1986, November 13, 1986, August 31, 1987, June 16, 1989.
New York Times Book Review, December 28, 1980, December 28, 1986, September 13, 1987.
Observer Review, March 10, 1968.
Time, June 18, 1984, November 10, 1986.
Times (London), March 3, 1988, April 23, 1989.
Times Literary Supplement, October 14, 1983, March 2, 1984, July 6, 1984, January 11, 1985, May 8, 1987, March 11, 1988, May 20, 1988, October 13, 1989.
Tribune Books (Chicago), October 12, 1986.
Washington Post Book World, August 30, 1987.

*   *   *

TYLER, Anne   1941-

PERSONAL: Born October 25, 1941, in Minneapolis, Minn.; daughter of Lloyd Parry (a chemist) and Phyllis (Mahon) Tyler; married Taghi Modarressi (a psychiatrist and writer), May 3, 1963; children: Tezh, Mitra. *Education:* Duke University, B.A., 1961; graduate study at Columbia University, 1961-62. *Religion:* Quaker.

ADDRESSES: Home—222 Tunbridge Rd., Baltimore, Md. 21212. *Agent*—Russell & Volkening, 50 West 29th St., New York, N.Y. 10001.

CAREER: Writer. Duke University Library, Durham, N.C., Russian bibliographer, 1962-63; McGill University Law Library, Montreal, Quebec, Canada, assistant to the librarian, 1964-65.

MEMBER: P.E.N., American Academy and Institute of Arts and Letters, Authors Guild, Phi Beta Kappa.

AWARDS, HONORS: Mademoiselle award for writing, 1966; Award for Literature, American Academy and Institute of Arts and Letters, 1977; National Book Critics Circle fiction award nomination, 1980, Janet Heidinger Kafka prize, 1981, and American Book Award nomination in paperback fiction, 1982, all for *Morgan's Passing;* National Book Critics Circle fiction award nomination, 1982, and American Book Award nomination in fiction, P.E.N./Faulkner Award for fiction, and Pulitzer

Prize nomination for fiction, all 1983, all for *Dinner at the Homesick Restaurant;* National Book Critics Circle fiction award and Pulitzer Prize nomination for fiction, both 1985, both for *The Accidental Tourist.*

WRITINGS:

NOVELS; PUBLISHED BY KNOPF

If Morning Ever Comes, 1964.
The Tin Can Tree, 1965.
A Slipping-Down Life, 1970.
The Clock Winder, 1972.
Celestial Navigation, 1974.
Searching for Caleb, 1976.
Earthly Possessions, 1977.
Morgan's Passing, 1980.
Dinner at the Homesick Restaurant, 1982.
The Accidental Tourist, 1985.
Breathing Lessons, 1988.

OTHER

(Editor with Shannon Ravenel, and author of introduction) *Best American Short Stories 1983,* Houghton, 1983.

Contributor of short stories to *Saturday Evening Post, New Yorker, Seventeen, Critic, Antioch Review,* and *Southern Review.*

SIDELIGHTS: Despite her status as a best-selling novelist, Anne Tyler remains a private person who rarely lets public demands interfere with family life. She shuns most interviewers, avoids talk show appearances, and prefers Baltimore, Maryland—where she lives with her husband and two daughters—to New York City. Nonetheless she is a well-established writer, having earned what former *Detroit News* reporter Bruce Cook calls "a solid *literary* reputation . . . that is based solely on the quality of her books."

Tyler's work has always been critically well received, but reviews of her early novels were generally relegated to the back pages of the book sections. Not until the publication of *Celestial Navigation* (1974), when she captured the attention of novelist Gail Godwin, and *Searching for Caleb* (1976), when John Updike recommended her to readers, did she gain widespread acclaim. "Now," says Cook, "her books are reviewed in the front of the literary journals and that means she is somebody to reckon with. No longer one of America's best unknown writers, she is now recognized as one of America's best writers. Period."

Born in Minnesota, Tyler lived in various Quaker communes throughout the Midwest and South before settling in the mountains of North Carolina for five years. She attended high school in Raleigh and at sixteen entered Duke University, where she fell under the influence of Reynolds Price, then a promising young novelist who had attended her high school. It was Price who encouraged the young Russian major to pursue her writing, and she did—but it remained a secondary pursuit until 1967, the year she and her husband settled in Baltimore.

In an interview with Bruce Cook, published in the *Saturday Review,* Tyler describes the city as "wonderful territory for a writer—so many different things to poke around in." And the longer she stays there, the more prominently Baltimore figures in her books, lending them an ambience both citified and southern and leading Reynolds Price to proclaim her "the nearest thing we have to an urban Southern novelist." Writing in the *New Yorker,* John Updike compares her to Flannery O'Connor, Carson McCullers, and Eudora Welty, noting: "Anne Tyler, in her gifts both of dreaming and of realizing, evokes comparison with these

writers, and in her tone and subject matter seems deliberately to seek association with the Southern ambience that, in less cosmopolitan times, they naturally and inevitably breathed. Even their aura of regional isolation is imitated by Miss Tyler as she holds fast, in her imagination and in her person, to a Baltimore with only Southern exits; her characters when they flee, never flee north. Yet she is a citizen of the world, born in Minneapolis, a graduate student of Russian at Columbia, and now married to a psychiatrist from Iran. The brand names, the fads, the bastardized vistas of our great homogenized nation glint out at us from her fiction with a cheerful authority."

Other reviewers, such as Katha Pollitt, find Tyler's novels more difficult to classify. "They are Southern in their sure sense of family and place," she writes in the *New York Times Book Review,* "but lack the taste for violence and the Gothic that often characterizes self- consciously Southern literature. They are modern in their fictional techniques, yet utterly unconcerned with the contemporary moment as a subject, so that, with only minor dislocations, her stories could just as well have taken place in the twenties or thirties. The current school of feminist-influenced novels seems to have passed her by completely: her women are strong, often stronger than the men in their lives, but solidly grounded in traditional roles."

The key to Tyler's writing may well lie in the homage she pays to Eudora Welty, her favorite writer and one to whom she is repeatedly compared. "Reading her taught me there were stories to be written about the mundane life around me," she told Cook. Or as Tyler phrased it to Marguerite Michaels in the *New York Times Book Review,* "Reading Eudora Welty when I was growing up showed me that very small things are often really larger than the large things." Thomas M. Disch is one of several critics who believes that Tyler's insight into the lives of ordinary people is her special gift. Writing in the *Washington Post Book World,* he calls it an "uncommon accomplishment that she can make such characters interesting and amusing without violating their limitations." Despite their resemblances to people we meet in real life, Tyler's characters are totally fictitious. "None of the people I write about are people I know," she told Marguerite Michaels. "That would be no fun. And it would be very boring to write about me. Even if I led an exciting life, why live it again on paper? I want to live other lives. I've never quite believed that one chance is all I get. Writing is my way of making other chances." She perceives the "real heroes" of her books as "first the ones who manage to endure and second the ones who are somehow able to grant other people the privacy of the space around them and yet still produce some warmth."

Her major theme, according to Mary Ellen Brooks in the *Dictionary of Literary Biography,* "is the obstinate endurance of the human spirit, reflected in every character's acceptance or rejection of his fate and in how that attitude affects his day to day life. She uses the family unit as a vehicle for portraying 'how people manage to endure together—how they grate against each other, adjust, intrude and protect themselves from intrusions, give up, and start all over again in the morning.' " Frequently her characters respond to stress by running away, but their flight, Brook continues, "proves to be only a temporary and ineffectual means of dealing with reality."

Because the action of her novels is so often circular—ending exactly where it begins—Tyler's fiction has been criticized for lack of development. This is especially true of her early novels where the narratives are straightforward and the pacing slow. In fact, what impressed reviewers most about Tyler's first book, *If Morning Ever Comes,* was not the story itself but the promise it seemed to hold for future fictions. "The trouble with this competently put-together book is that the hero is hardly better defined at the end than he is at the beginning," observes Julian Gloag in the *Saturday Review.* "Writing about a dull and totally humorless character, Miss Tyler has inevitably produced a totally humorless and mainly dull novel. Anne Tyler is only twenty-two, and in the light of this her refusal to take risks is a bit puzzling. I'd like to see what she could do if she stopped narrowing her own eyes and let herself go. It might be very good." The *Times Literary Supplement* reviewer echoes these sentiments: "It will be surprising if a writer so young does not outgrow her hesitant efforts to produce big answers to emotional muddles and her sometimes over-literary sentences, and let her considerable gift for dialogue and comedy produce a very good novel indeed."

For her part, Tyler reportedly now hates her first book—and also her second, which received similar criticism. Written largely to pass the time while she was looking for a job, *The Tin Can Tree* concerns the inhabitants of a three-family house on the edge of a North Carolina tobacco field and their reactions to the accidental death of the six-year-old girl who lives there. Though the family is initially devastated by the tragedy, their emotional balance is restored in the end, and, for this reason, some critics find the novel static. Millicent Bell, for example, writes in the *New York Times Book Review:* "Life, this young writer seems to be saying, achieves its once-and-for-all shape and then the camera clicks. This view, which brings her characters back on the last page to where they started, does not make for that sense of development which is the true novel's motive force. Because of it, I think, her book remains a sketch, a description, a snapshot. But as such, it still has a certain dry clarity. And the hand that has clicked its shutter has selected a moment of truth."

Perhaps the most salient feature of Tyler's next novel, *A Slipping-Down Life* (which was misclassified as young adult literature and thus not widely reviewed), is its genesis. In discussing her craft with Marguerite Michaels, Tyler said: "Sometimes a book will start with a picture that pops into my mind and I ask myself questions about it and if I put all the answers together, I've got a novel. A real picture would be the old newspaper clipping about the Texas girl who slashed 'Elvis' in her forehead." In the novel, this incident is transformed into an episode in the life of Evie Decker, a fictive teenager grappling for her identity. "I believe this is the best thing I've ever done," Evie says of her self-mutilation. "Something out of character. Definite." In the *Dictionary of Literary Biography,* Mary Ellen Brooks describes the novel as "an accurate description of loneliness, failure to communicate, and regrets over decisions that are irreversible— problems with which any age group can identify. Tyler, who describes *A Slipping-Down Life* as one of her most bizarre works, believes that the novel 'is flawed, but represents, for me, a certain brave stepping forth.'"

So, too, does Tyler's fifth novel, *Celestial Navigation,* a book that the author wrote while "fighting the urge to remain in retreat even though the children had started school." In the character of Jeremy Paulding, an agoraphobic artist who is afraid to leave his Baltimore block, Tyler sees much of herself. While her characters are not usually autobiographical, Tyler told Brooks that creating Jeremy was a way of investigating her own "tendency to turn more and more inward."

The story opens with the death of Jeremy's mother and moves quickly to an exploration of the relationship he establishes with the woman who will take her place—a self-sufficient boarder named Mary Tell. Attracted by her sunny self-confidence, Jeremy proposes marriage and soon Mary has stepped in as Jere-

my's intermediary to the outside world. As years pass, he comes to feel dwarfed by Mary's competence—she does not even alert him when she leaves for the hospital to have her fifth child because she knows he dreads the trip. Suffocated by her overprotectiveness, the disoriented artist withdraws even further into the private world of his studio where he fashions collages from scraps of other people's lives. Eventually Mary and the children abandon him, and Jeremy does venture out to find them. But the price he pays for conquering his fear is that he loses them for good. At the novel's end, Mary and Jeremy each remain in a separate existence, each still dominated by what Brooks calls "his innate driving characteristic. Jeremy returns to his life as a reclusive artist in a crumbling dark house while Mary prepares for winter in a rundown shack, knowing that another man will eventually provide for her."

Told from the viewpoints of six different characters, *Celestial Navigation* is far more intricate than Tyler's earlier novels, and most critics consider it a breakthrough. Katha Pollitt finds the work "extraordinarily moving and beautiful," while Doris Grumbach proclaims Tyler's "ability to enmesh the reader in what is a simple, uneventful story a notable achievement." In her *New York Times Book Review* article, Gail Godwin explains how "Tyler is especially gifted at the art of freeing her characters and then keeping track of them as they move in their unique and often solitary orbits. Her fiction is filled with displaced persons who persist stubbornly in their own destinies. They are 'oddballs,' visionaries, lonely souls, but she has a way of transcribing their peculiarities with such loving wholeness that when we examine them we keep finding more and more pieces of ourselves."

In her eighth novel, *Morgan's Passing,* Tyler turns from an exploration of the "oddball" as introvert to the "oddball" as extrovert in the creation of Morgan Gower—a 42-year-old hardware store manager with a knack for assuming other roles. Simply put, Morgan is an imposter, a man who changes identities every time he changes clothes. "You're walking down the street with him and this total stranger asks him when the International Brotherhood of Magicians is meeting next," his wife Bonny explains. "You're listening to a politician's speech and suddenly you notice Morgan on the platform, sitting beside a senator's wife with a carnation in his buttonhole. You're waiting for your crabs at Lexington Market and who's behind the counter but Morgan in a rubber apron, telling the other customers where he caught such fine oysters." These fantasies contrast sharply with the dullness of Morgan's actual life. At home, in the brick colonial house acquired with his wife's money, he feels overwhelmed by the clutter of his wife, their seven daughters, his adult sister, and his feebleminded mother.

The novel opens with one of Morgan's escapades. During the performance of a puppet show, the puppeteer, Leon Meredith, emerges from behind the curtains to request a doctor's assistance: his wife Emily has gone into labor. Morgan steps forward and, posing as a doctor, delivers the baby in the back seat of his car. In the process he becomes fascinated by what he perceives to be the simple existence of the Merediths. Emily, in particular, becomes "an emblem for Morgan of that spartan order he longs to bring to his over-furnished life," says Thomas M. Disch in the *Washington Post Book World.* But neither Emily nor Leon are as blithe as they seem, and by juxtaposing the reality of these characters with Morgan's fantasies of them, Tyler creates her drama, critics say.

Though *Morgan's Passing* was nominated for a National Book Critics Circle Award in hardback and an American Book Award in paperback fiction, critics are sharply divided in their assessment of the work. Those who like it praise Tyler's handling of character and her artful mingling of comedy and seriousness. "Though she allows her tale to veer toward farce, Tyler always checks it in time with the tug of an emotion, a twitch of regret," writes *Time*'s Paul Gray. He concludes: "*Morgan's Passing* is not another novel about a mid-life crisis, it is a buoyant story about a struggle unto death." Tyler acknowledged in her *Detroit News* interview with Bruce Cook that her "big worry in doing the book was that people would be morally offended by [Morgan]." But critic Marilyn Murray Willison sings his praises. "In spite of his inability to restore order to his life, his nicotine- stained hands and teeth, his silly wardrobe, his refusal to accept reality, Morgan emerges from Tyler's book a true hero," she writes in the *Los Angeles Times Book Review*.

Other critics, however, dislike the character and consider the book a disappointment. "For all its many felicities of observation and incident, *Morgan's Passing* does not come up to the high standard of Anne Tyler's other recent work. There is a self-indulgence in the portraiture of Morgan himself, whose numerous identity assumptions became for me merely tiresome," Paul Binding writes in the *New Statesman*. And *New York Review of Books* contributing critic James Wolcott dismisses *Morgan's Passing* as "a book of small compass, pent-up energy. Long before Morgan and Emily link arms, the reader has connected the dots separating them, so there's no suspense, no surprise. Instead, the book is stuffed with accounts of weddings, crowded dinners, cute squabbles, and symbolic-as-all-get-out puppet shows. Sentence by sentence, the book is engaging, but there's nothing beneath the jokes and tussles to propel the reader through these cluttered lives. It's a book with an idle motor." Writing in the *New Yorker,* John Updike explains his disappointment: "Anne Tyler continues to look close, and to fabricate, out of the cardboard and Magic Markers available to the festive imagination, images of the illusory lives we lead. More than that it would be unkind to ask, did we not imagine, for the scope of the gift displayed, that something of that gift is still being withheld."

With *Dinner at the Homesick Restaurant,* her ninth and, some say, finest novel, Tyler redeems herself in many critics' eyes. Updike, for instance, maintains that this book achieves "a new level of power and gives us a lucid and delightful yet complex and sombre improvisation on her favorite theme, family life." Writing in the *Chicago Tribune Book World,* Larry McMurtry echoes these sentiments: "She recognizes and conveys beautifully the alternations of tragedy and farce in family life, and never more beautifully than in *Dinner at the Homesick Restaurant.*" Benjamin Demott is even more impressed. "Funny, heart-hammering, wise, [the novel] edges deep into truth that's simultaneously (and interdependently) psychological, moral and formal— deeper than many living novelists of serious reputation have penetrated, deeper than Miss Tyler herself has gone before. It is a border crossing," he writes in the *New York Times Book Review.*

The story's plot is a simple one—"deceptively simple," Sarah English notes in the *Dictionary of Literary Biography Yearbook.* Eighty-five-year-old Pearl Tull—who married late in life and bore three children before being deserted by her traveling salesman husband—is lying on her deathbed recollecting the past. She reconstructs the moment, thirty-five years before, when Beck Tull announced he was leaving, the years of struggle that ensued as she singlehandedly (and sometimes heartlessly) raised her children, and the scars which Cody, Jenny, and Ezra still bear. "Something," Pearl thought, "was wrong with all her children. They were so frustrating—attractive, likeable people, the three of them, but closed off from her in some perverse way. She

wondered if her children blamed her for something. Sitting close at family gatherings they tended to recall only poverty and loneliness. [They] referred continually to Pearl's short temper, displaying it against a background of stunned, childish faces so sad and bewildered that Pearl herself hardly recognized them. Honestly, she thought, wasn't there some statute of limitations here?"

In this darkest of Tyler's novels, the answer is no. "None of the three Tull children manages to cut loose from the family past," explains Demott. "Each is, to a degree, stunted; each turns for help to Pearl Tull in an hour of desperate adult need; and Pearl's conviction that something is wrong with each of them never recedes from the reader's consciousness."

The novel unfolds in a series of self-contained chapters, each, in Updike's words, "rounded like a short story," and each reflecting a different family member's point of view. This narrative technique, as Sarah English notes, "allows [Tyler] to juxtapose past and present and thus to convey the vision—that she has always had—of the past not as a continuum but as layer of still, vivid memories. The wealth of points of view also allows Tyler to show more fully than ever the essential subjectivity of the past. Cody and Jenny remember Pearl as a witch; Ezra remembers her as a source of strength and security. Every character's vision of the past is different."

Larry McMurtry believes that the book "amply demonstrates the tenacity of familial involvement," while *Los Angeles Times* reporter Carolyn See says Tyler shows how a family "is alive with needs of its own; it never relaxes its hold. Even when you are far away (especially when you're far away), it immobilizes you in its grip, which can—in another way—be looked at as a caress."

This portrait of family entanglements is too somber for some critics' tastes, including Cynthia Propper Seton's. "What may be the trouble with *Dinner at the Homesick Restaurant,*" she writes in the *Washington Post Book World,* "is that the Tull family is not marginal enough, its members are too grave a proposition for a mind so full of mischief as Anne Tyler's. They depressed her." In her *Detroit News* review, however, Cynthia King maintains that "despite the joyless atmosphere, the author's humor bubbles through in Pearl's tackiness, in Jenny's self-protective flippancy. And more than a few times—awful as Pearl is, warped and doomed as her children are—what keeps us turning pages is the suspicion that there may be a bit of each of them in each of us."

Concludes Benjamin Demott: "What one wants to do on finishing such a work as *Dinner at the Homesick Restaurant* is maintain balance, keep things intact for a stretch, stay under the spell as long as possible. The before and after are immaterial; nothing counts except the knowledge, solid and serene, that's all at once breathing in the room. We're speaking obviously, about an extremely beautiful book."

The Accidental Tourist, Tyler's tenth novel, again combines the author's subtle, understated probing into human nature and her eye for comic detail. The title serves both as a reference to the protagonist's occupation and as a metaphor for his life. Macon Leary writes travel guides for people who dislike traveling and who would prefer to stay in the comfort and familiarity of their own homes. The guide books—the series is titled *The Accidental Tourist*—advise reluctant travelers on how to visit foreign places without experiencing the annoyances and jarring peculiarities that each new city offers. Thus, Macon counsels his readers on where they can find American-style hamburgers in Amsterdam, for instance, or on the type of reading material to carry on the plane so as to ward off chatty neighbors.

Macon's suggestions are indicative of his own nature. Insular and wary of anything foreign or unexpected, Macon surrounds himself with rituals in an attempt to make his life ordered and safe. When his twelve-year-old son is murdered in a restaurant, he retreats even further into his cocoon, driving off his wife in the process. His son's dog, Edward, though, does not respond well to the changes in his environment. As Macon fills his life with more elaborate rituals, Edward develops a mean streak and begins to terrorize Macon's friends and relatives. Eventually, Edward requires a trainer, and it is this trainer that shocks Macon into reassessing his life. Muriel Pritchett is everything that Macon is not: impetuous, carefree, and disordered. Macon becomes attracted to Muriel and her odd life-style, seeing in it all the vitality and passion that his life lacks. When his wife changes her mind and asks Macon to resume their marriage, Macon is forced to choose between the two women. He opts for Muriel, recognizing the exuberance for life that she has awakened in him.

As with her previous novels, reviewers praised the gently ironic humor and sympathetic, likable characters that Tyler creates in *The Accidental Tourist.* Richard Eder of the *Los Angeles Times Book Review* notes that the character of Macon Leary "is an oddity of the first water, and yet we grow so close to him that there is not the slightest warp in the lucid, touching and very funny story of an inhibited man moving out into life." Other critics observes that in this book Tyler fuses the mix of tragedy and comedy that appears in most of her previous books. Larry McMurtry, writing in the *New York Times Book Review* about "the mingling of misery and contentment in the daily lives of her families" that Tyler constructs, comments that "these themes, some of which she has been sifting for more that twenty years, cohere with high definition in the muted . . . personality of Macon Leary." Some reviewers criticize Tyler for her tendency to draw sympathetic characters and to infuse humor into so many of her scenes. *Chicago Tribune Book World* critic John Blades wonders whether "Tyler, with her sedative resolutions to life's most grievous and perplexing problems, can be taken seriously as a writer." Most reviewers, though, only praise the book and its author. As Eder notes, "I don't know if there is a better American writer going."

In her eleventh novel, *Breathing Lessons,* Tyler examines the themes of marriage, love, and regret. The story concerns Maggie and Ira Moran, married for twenty-eight years, and a journey they make to the funeral of an old friend. During the trip they both reflect on their years together—some happy, some sad. Maggie is gregarious and curious, while Ira is practical and withdrawn. Both at times regret their decision to marry, but they also recognize the strength of the bond between them. Critics still remark on Tyler's ability to evoke sympathy for her characters and her talent for constructing humorous scenes. Eder, again writing in the *Los Angeles Times Book Review,* sums up critical reaction

by noting that "there are moments when the struggle among Maggie, Ira, and the melancholy of time passing forms a fiery triangle more powerful and moving . . . than anything she has done."

MEDIA ADAPTATIONS: The Accidental Tourist was adapted into a film and released by Warner Brothers in 1988.

BIOGRAPHICAL/CRITICAL SOURCES:

BOOKS

Bestsellers 89, Issue 1, Gale, 1989.
Contemporary Literary Criticism, Gale, Volume 7, 1977, Volume 11, 1979, Volume 18, 1981, Volume 28, 1984, Volume 44, 1987.
Dictionary of Literary Biography, Gale, Volume VI: *American Novelists since World War II, Second Series,* 1980, *Yearbook: 1982,* 1983.

PERIODICALS

Atlantic Monthly, March, 1976.
Chicago Tribune Book World, March 23, 1980, March 21, 1982, July 20, 1986.
Detroit News, April 6, 1980, April 18, 1982.
Globe and Mail (Toronto), September 21, 1985, October 8, 1988.
Los Angeles Times, March 30, 1982, September 14, 1983.
Los Angeles Times Book Review, March 30, 1980, September 15, 1985, September 11, 1988.
Ms., August, 1977.
National Observer, May 30, 1977.
New Republic, May 13, 1972, May 28, 1977, March 22, 1980.
New Statesman, April 4, 1975, December 5, 1980.
Newsweek, April 5, 1982, September 9, 1985.
New Yorker, March 29, 1976, June 6, 1977, June 23, 1980, April 5, 1982.
New York Review of Books, April 3, 1980.
New York Times, May 3, 1977, March 17, 1980, March 22, 1982, September 30, 1983, September 3, 1988.
New York Times Book Review, November 22, 1964, November 21, 1965, March 15, 1970, May 21, 1972, April 28, 1974, January 18, 1976, May 8, 1977, March 14, 1982, September 8, 1985.
Saturday Review, December 26, 1964, November 20, 1965, June 17, 1972, March 6, 1976, September 4, 1976, March 15, 1980.
Time, May 9, 1977, March 17, 1980, April 5, 1982, September 16, 1985.
Times (London), January 12, 1989.
Times Literary Supplement, July 15, 1965, May 23, 1975, December 9, 1977, October 31, 1980, October 29, 1982, October 4, 1985, January 20, 1989.
Tribune Books (Chicago), August 28, 1988.
Washington Post Book World, March 16, 1980, April 4, 1982, September 4, 1988.

U

UPDIKE, John (Hoyer) 1932-

PERSONAL: Born March 18, 1932, in Shillington, Pa.; son of Wesley Russell (a teacher) and Linda Grace (an author; maiden name, Hoyer) Updike; married Mary Entwistle Pennington, June 26, 1953 (divorced, 1977); married Martha Ruggles Bernhard, September 30, 1977; children: (first marriage) Elizabeth Pennington, David Hoyer, Michael John, Miranda; (second marriage) three stepchildren. *Education:* Harvard University, A.B. (summa cum laude), 1954; attended Ruskin School of Drawing and Fine Art, Oxford, 1954-55. *Politics:* Democrat. *Religion:* Christian.

ADDRESSES: Home—58 West Main St., Georgetown, Mass. 01833.

CAREER: Novelist, critic, short story writer, poet, essayist, and dramatist. Visited the U.S.S.R. as part of a cultural exchange program of U.S. Department of State, 1964.

MEMBER: American Academy and Institute of Arts and Letters (chancellor).

AWARDS, HONORS: Guggenheim fellowship in poetry, 1959; American Academy and National Institute of Arts and Letters Richard and Hinda Rosenthal Foundation Award, 1960, for *The Poorhouse Fair;* National Book Award in fiction, 1963, for *The Centaur;* Prix Medicis Etranger, 1966, for *The Centaur;* O. Henry Award for fiction, 1966, for short story, "The Bulgarian Poetess"; Fulbright fellow in Africa, 1972; American Book Award nomination, 1980, for *Too Far to Go;* Edward MacDowell Medal for Literature, MacDowell Colony, 1981; Pulitzer Prize for fiction, American Book Award, and National Book Critics Circle award for fiction, all 1982, all for *Rabbit Is Rich;* National Book Critics Circle award for criticism, 1984, for *Hugging the Shore: Essays in Criticism;* Medal of Honor for Literature, National Arts Club (New York City), 1984; National Book Critics Circle award in fiction nomination, 1986, for *Roger's Version;* PEN/Malamud Memorial Prize, PEN/Faulkner Award Foundation, 1988, for "excellence in short story writing."

WRITINGS:

NOVELS

The Poorhouse Fair (also see below), Knopf, 1959, reprinted, Fawcett, 1988.
Rabbit, Run (also see below), Knopf, 1960.

The Centaur, Knopf, 1963.
Of the Farm, Knopf, 1965, reprinted, 1987.
The Poorhouse Fair [and] *Rabbit, Run,* Modern Library, 1965.
Couples, Knopf, 1968.
Rabbit Redux (also see below), Knopf, 1971.
A Month of Sundays, Knopf, 1975.
Marry Me: A Romance, Knopf, 1976.
The Coup, Knopf, 1978.
Rabbit Is Rich (also see below), Knopf, 1981.
Rabbit Is Rich/Rabbit Redux/Rabbit, Run, Quality Paperback Book Club, 1981.
The Witches of Eastwick, Knopf, 1984.
Roger's Version, Knopf, 1986.
S., Knopf, 1988.
Rabbit at Rest, Knopf, 1990.

POETRY

The Carpentered Hen and Other Tame Creatures (also see below), Harper, 1958, reprinted, Knopf, 1982, published as *Hoping for a Hoopoe,* Gollancz, 1959.
Telephone Poles and Other Poems (also see below), Knopf, 1963.
Verse: The Carpentered Hen and Other Tame Creatures/ Telephone Poles and Other Poems, Fawcett, 1965.
The Angels (poem; limited edition), King and Queen Press (Pensacola, Fla.), 1968.
Bath after Sailing (poem; limited edition), Pendulum Press (Monroe, Conn.), 1968.
Midpoint and Other Poems, Knopf, 1969.
Seventy Poems, Penguin, 1972.
Six Poems (limited edition), Oliphant Press, 1973.
Cunts (poem; limited edition), Frank Hallman, 1974.
Tossing and Turning, Knopf, 1977.
Sixteen Sonnets (limited edition), Halty Ferguson (Cambridge, Mass.), 1979.
Five Poems (limited edition), Bits Press, 1980.
Spring Trio (limited edition), Palaemon Press (Winston-Salem, N.C.), 1982.
Jester's Dozen (limited edition), Lord John (Northridge, Cal.), 1984.
Facing Nature: Poems, Knopf, 1985.

SHORT STORIES

The Same Door, Knopf, 1959, reprinted, Vintage, 1981.
Pigeon Feathers and Other Stories, Knopf, 1962.

Olinger Stories: A Selection, Vintage, 1964.

The Music School, Knopf, 1966.

Bech: A Book, Knopf, 1970.

Museums and Women and Other Stories, Knopf, 1972.

Warm Wine: An Idyll (short story; limited edition) Albondocani Press (New York), 1973.

Couples: A Short Story (limited edition), Halty Ferguson, 1976.

From the Journal of a Leper (short story; limited edition), Lord John, 1978.

Too Far to Go: The Maples Stories, Fawcett, 1979.

Three Illuminations in the Life of an American Author (short story; limited edition), Targ (New York), 1979.

Problems and Other Stories, Knopf, 1979.

Your Lover Just Called: Stories of Joan and Richard Maple, Penguin Books, 1980.

The Chaste Planet (short story; limited edition), Metacom (Worcester, Mass), 1980.

People One Knows: Interviews with Insufficiently Famous Americans (limited edition), Lord John, 1980.

Invasion of the Book Envelopes (short story; limited edition), Ewert (Concord, Mass.), 1981.

Bech Is Back, Knopf, 1982.

The Beloved (short story; limited edition), Lord John, 1982.

Confessions of a Wild Bore (short story; limited edition), Tamazunchale Press, 1984.

More Stately Mansions: A Story (short story; limited edition), Nouveau Press (Jackson, Miss.), 1987.

Trust Me: Short Stories, Knopf, 1987.

ESSAYS

Assorted Prose, Knopf, 1965.

On Meeting Authors (essay; limited edition), Wickford (Newburyport, Mass.), 1968.

A Good Place (essay; limited edition), Aloe, 1973.

Picked-Up Pieces, Knopf, 1975.

Hub Fans Bid Kid Adieu (essay; limited edition), Lord John, 1977.

Talk from the Fifties (limited edition), Lord John, 1979.

Ego and Art in Walt Whitman (essay; limited edition), Targ, 1980.

Hawthorne's Creed (essay; limited edition), Targ, 1981.

Hugging the Shore: Essays and Criticism, Knopf, 1983.

Emersonianism (essay; limited edition), Bits Press, 1984.

Just Looking: Essays on Art, Knopf, 1989.

OTHER

(Contributor of short story) Martin Levin, editor, *Five Boyhoods,* Doubleday, 1962.

(Adapter with Warren Chappell of libretto of Mozart's opera) *The Magic Flute* (juvenile fiction), Knopf, 1962.

(Adapter with Chappell of libretto of Wagner's opera) *The Ring* (juvenile fiction), Knopf, 1964.

A Child's Calendar (juvenile poetry), Knopf, 1965.

Three Texts from Early Ipswich (historical pageant; produced in Ipswich, Mass., 1968), 17th Century Day Committee of the Town of Ipswich, 1968.

(Adapter) *Bottom's Dream* (from William Shakespeare's *A Midsummer Night's Dream;* juvenile fiction), Knopf, 1969.

(Editor) David Levine, *Pens and Needles: Literary Caricatures,* Gambit, 1970.

(Contributor of translations) Norman Thomas di Giovanni, editor, Jorge Luis Borges, *Selected Poems: 1923-1967,* Delacorte, 1972.

A Good Place: Being a Personal Account of Ipswich, Massachusetts, Aloe Editions (New York), 1973.

Buchanan Dying (play; produced in Lancaster, Mass., 1976), Knopf, 1974.

(Author of introduction) Henry Green, *Loving, Living, Party Going,* Penguin Books, 1978.

(Author of introduction) Bruno Schulz, *Sanatorium under the Sign of the Hourglass,* Penguin Books, 1979.

(Author of afterword) Edmund Wilson, *Memoirs of Hecate County,* Nonpareil, 1980.

(Editor with Shannon Ravenel and author of introduction) *The Best American Short Stories: 1984,* Houghton, 1984.

Self-Consciousness: Memoirs, Knopf, 1989.

Also author with Gunther Schuller of words and music for "The Fisherman and His Wife," performed at Savoy Theatre in Boston, Mass., by the Opera Company of Boston, May, 1970. "Talk of the Town" reporter, *New Yorker,* 1955-57. Contributor of short stories, book reviews, and poems to the *New Yorker.* Contributor of reviews and short stories to numerous periodicals.

SIDELIGHTS: John "Updike has earned an . . . imposing stance on the literary landscape," writes *Los Angeles Times* contributor Katherine Stephen, "earning virtually every American literary award, repeated best-sellerdom and the near-royal status of the American author- celebrity." However hailed by critics and readers as one of America's great novelists, John Updike has also acquired his share of detractors. As Joseph Kanon explains in *Saturday Review:* "The debate over John Updike's work has long since divided itself into two pretty firmly entrenched camps: those who admire the work consider him one of the keepers of the language; those who don't say he writes beautifully about nothing very much."

Updike acknowledges this charge but believes the complaint lacks validity. "There is a great deal to be said about almost anything," Updike explained to Jane Howard in a *Life* magazine interview. "Everything can be as interesting as every other thing. An old milk carton is worth a rose. . . . The idea of a hero is aristocratic. Now either nobody is a hero or everyone is. I vote for everyone. My subject is the American Protestant small town middle class. I like middles. It is in middles that extremes clash, where ambiguity restlessly rules. . . . There's a 'yes-but' quality about my writing that evades entirely pleasing anybody. It seems to me that critics get increasingly querulous and impatient for madder music and stronger wine, when what we need is a greater respect for reality, its secrecy, its music."

Debate about the effectiveness of Updike's writing began in 1957 with publication of *The Poorhouse Fair,* his first novel. As Curt Suplee notes in his *Washington Post* profile of the author: "Updike's fiction is not overburdened by action, and his spare story lines are embellished with a lush and elegantly wrought style that some readers find majestic (John Barth calls him the Andrew Wyeth of American writers) and others intolerable. Norman Podhoretz described his prose in 'The Poorhouse Fair' as 'overly lyrical, bloated like a child who has eaten too much candy.' " Other critics saw the novel differentlt than Podhoretz; in the *New York Times,* for example, Donald Barr called the book "a work of art." And, in the *Chicago Sunday Tribune* Fanny Butcher referred to "the author's brilliant use of words and . . . his subtle observations."

"There is one point on which his critics all agree," observes Rachael C. Burchard in *John Updike: Yea Sayings.* "His style is superb. His work is worth reading if for no reason other than to enjoy the piquant phrase, the lyric vision, the fluent rhetoric." In a cover story on the author *Time* magazine's Paul Gray claimed: "No one else using the English language over the past two and a half decades has written so well in so many ways as he." And, a reviewer for *Books Abroad* noted, "Critics continually comment on the technical virtuousity of Updike," while in *John Updike* Suzanne Henning Uphaus declared, "In the midst of diversity there are certain elements common to all of Updike's writing. Most important, there is Updike's remarkable mastery of language."

However, in direct contrast to the glowing evaluations of Burchard, Gray, and others that might agree with them, are the opinions of still other commentators who fail to see Updike's work in such a favorable light. For example, in her *Partisan Review* commentary on *Couples* Elizabeth Dalton asserts, "In its delicacy and fullness Updike's style seems to register a flow of fragments almost perfectly toned. And yet, after pages and pages of his minutely detailed impressions, the accumulated effect is one of waste." John W. Aldridge writes in *Time to Murder and Create: The Contemporary Novel in Crisis* that the novelist "has none of the attributes we conventionally associate with major literary talent. He does not have an interesting mind. He does not possess remarkable narrative gifts or a distinguished style. He does not create dynamic or colorful or deeply meaningful characters. . . . In fact, one of the problems he poses for the critic is that he engages the imagination so little that one has real difficulty remembering his work long enough to think clearly about it." "Updike has difficulty in reining in his superfluous facility with words," Edward Hoagland complains in the *New York Times Book Review.* "He is too fluent."

"Much criticism of John Updike's fiction derives from the same middle-class repressions he writes about," Robert Detweiler notes in *Twentieth Century Literature.* Thus, many of the most disparaging reviews of Updike's work have come from critics that object not only to his writing style, but also to the author's subject matter. Commenting on the frenzy of criticism from reviewers that met the 1968 publication of *Couples,* Updike's explicit look at sexual freedom in a small New England town, Detweiler notes in *John Updike,* "As frequently happens, the furor accompanying the depiction of sexual amorality increased the difficulty of judging the novel's artistic quality. Most of the reviews appeared to be impulsive reactions to the subject matter rather than measured assessments." In the case of this novel, negative critical response did nothing to tone down public enthusiasm for the work: it appeared on the *Publishers Weekly* bestseller list for thirty-six weeks.

Couples wasn't the first Updike novel to deal with the sexual habits of middle-class America or to receive disapproving reviews from commentators upset by the author's frank language. "Looking back," writes Eliot Fremont-Smith in the *Village Voice,* "it must have been the sexuality that so upset the respectable critics of *Rabbit, Run* in 1960. Their consternation had to do with what seemed a great divide between John Updike's exquisite command of prose . . . and the apparent no- good vulgar nothing he expended it on." *Rabbit, Run* was the first installment in Updike's continuing saga of Harry "Rabbit" Angstrom which would later include *Rabbit Redux* and, the highly celebrated *Rabbit Is Rich.* Published at ten-year intervals, the novels follow the life of "Rabbit" as he first tries to leave his marriage, later, as he discovers his wife has been unfaithful and finds himself laid off from his blue-collar job, and, later yet, as he confronts middle-age.

Although the third volume in Updike's series of Rabbit novels received the Pulitzer Prize, the National Book Critics Circle award, and the American Book Award, some critics found its sexual focus offensive. While claiming the book "reeks of vulgarity," in his *Washington Post* review of *Rabbit Is Rich,* for example, Jonathan Yardley wrote, "Updike fancies himself the chronicler of the common man, and he fills page after page with the most clinical evidence of that fellow's gaucherie." Others viewed the sexual content of the book (and the other two volumes in the planned tetralogy) as merely a part of what they considered to be Updike's accurate depictions of U. S. society. Anthony Quinton's London *Times* review seems to summarize the feeling of many critics when he observes, "The Rabbit novels are John Updike's best since they give the fullest scope to his remarkable gifts as observer and describer. What they amount to is a social and, so to speak, emotional history of the United States over the last twenty years or more, the period of Rabbit's and his creator's conscious life."

America's sexual mores have continued to be a dominant subject in Updike's fiction along with the additional theme of religion. In his *John Updike and the Three Great Secret Things* George Hunt suggests that sex and religion along with art "characterize the predominant subject matter, thematic concerns, and central questions found throughout [Updike's] adult fiction." According to *Contemporary Authors Bibliographical Series* contributor Donald J. Greiner, Updike criticism has in fact shifted since the 1960s from a consideration of the novelist's style to a focus on his themes and how they interrelate. "Later commentators," Greiner asserts, "are concerned with his intellectually rigorous union of theology and fiction and with his suggestion that sex is a kind of emerging religion in the suburban enclaves of the middle class."

Exploring the interrelatedness of sex and religion in Updike's fiction, Jean Strouse observes in a *Newsweek* review of Updike's *Bech Is Back,* "Readers and critics have accused Updike of being obsessed with sex. Maybe—but I think he is using Harry Angstrom [from his "Rabbit" novels], and Piet Hanema in "Couples," and Richard Maple in "Too Far to Go," to explore that modern search for 'something behind all this . . . that wants me to find it.' Melville—and many others—may have announced the demise of God, but nobody has managed to excise the desire for something beyond death and daily life, a desire that has in the 20th century shifted its focus from God to sex." The *New York Times*'s Machiko Kakutani offers a similar explanation of the development of what he calls Updike's "favorite preoccupations" in his review of *Roger's Version.* "His heroes, over the years, have all suffered from 'the tension and guilt of being human.' Torn between vestigial spiritual yearnings and the new imperatives of self-fulfillment, they hunger for salvation even as they submit to the importunate demands of the flesh."

Updike's skill in portraying the anxieties and frustrations of middle-America seems to be the feature most mentioned by approving critics. "He is our unchallenged master at evoking the heroic void of ordinary life," Suplee maintains, "where small braveries contend in vain against the nagging entropy of things, where the fear of death drips from a faulty faucet and supermarket daydreams turn to God. With heart-clutching clarity, he transmutes the stubborn banality of middle-class existence into tableaux that shiver with the hint of spiritual meaning." "His work has not only lyrically defined the joys and sorrows of the American middle class," Kakutani concludes, "but also gives—as he once wrote of another author—'the happy impression of an oeuvre, of a continuous task carried forward variously, of a solid personality, of a plenitude of gifts explored, knowingly.' "

A collection of Updike's papers are found in the Houghton Library, Harvard University.

MEDIA ADAPTATIONS: Couples was purchased by United Artists in 1969; *Rabbit, Run* was filmed by Warner Bros. in

1970; *Bech: A Book* was adapted for a play entitled, "Bech Takes Pot Luck," produced in New York at Theatre Guild, 1970; *The Music School* was networked by Public Broadcasting System, 1976; *Two Far to Go* was made into a television movie by National Broadcasting Co. in March, 1979, later revised and released for theater distribution by Sea Cliff Productions, 1982; director George Miller's movie "The Witches of Eastwick," 1987, was loosely based on Updike's novel of the same title; "The Christian Roommates," a short story, was made into a ninety-minute movie for television.

BIOGRAPHICAL/CRITICAL SOURCES:

BOOKS

Aldridge, John W., *Time to Murder and Create: The Contemporary Novel in Crisis,* McKay, 1966.
Burchard, Rachael C., *John Updike: Yea Sayings,* Southern Illinois University Press, 1971.
Concise Dictionary of American Literary Biography, 1968-1987, Gale, 1989.
Contemporary Authors Bibliographical Series, Volume 1, Gale, 1986.
Contemporary Literary Criticism, Gale, Volume 1, 1973, Volume 2, 1974, Volume 3, 1975, Volume 5, 1976, Volume 7, 1977, VOlume 9, 78, Volume 13, 1980, Volume 15, 1980, Volume 23, 1983, Volume 34, 1985, Volume 43, 1987.
Detweiler, Robert, *John Updike,* Twayne, 1972, revised edition, 1984.
Dictionary of Literary Biography, Gale, Volume 2: *American Novelists since World War II,* 1978, Volume 5: *American Poets since World War II,* 1980.
Dictionary of Literary Biography Documentary Series, Volume 3, 1983.
Dictionary of Literary Biography Yearbook, Gale, *1980,* 1981, *1982,* 1983.
Greiner, Donald J., *John Updike's Novels,* Ohio University Press, 1984.
Greiner, Donald J., *Adultery in the American Novel: Updike, James, Hawthorne,* University of South Carolina Press, 1985.
Hunt, George, *John Updike and the Three Great Secret Things,* Eerdmans, 1980.
Tallent, Elizabeth, *Married Men and Magic Tricks: John Updike's Erotic Heroes,* Creative Arts, 1981.
Thorburn, David, and Howard Eiland, editors, *John Updike: A Collection of Critical Essays,* G. K. Hall, 1982.
Updike, John, *Self-Consciousness: Memoirs,* Knopf, 1989.
Uphaus, Suzanne Henning, *John Updike,* Ungar, 1980.

PERIODICALS

Books Abroad, winter, 1967.
Chicago Sunday Tribune, January 11, 1959.
Life, November 4, 1966.
Los Angeles Times, January 4, 1987.
Modern Fiction Studies, spring, 1974, autumn, 1975.
Newsweek, November 15, 1971, September 28, 1981, October 18, 1982.
New York Review of Books, April 11, 1968, August 8, 1974, April 3, 1975, November 19, 1981, November 18, 1982, November 24, 1983, June 14, 1984, December 4, 1986.
New York Times, January 11, 1959, October 7, 1982, August 27, 1986.
New York Times Book Review, March 18, 1962, April 7, 1963, April 7, 1968, June 21, 1970, November 14, 1971, September 27, 1981, October 17, 1982, September 18, 1983, May 13, 1984, August 31, 1986, April 26, 1987.
New York Times Sunday Magazine, December 10, 1978.
Partisan Review, winter, 1969.
Saturday Review, March 17, 1962, September 30, 1972.
Time, April 26, 1968, October 18, 1982, August 25, 1986.
Times (London), January 14, 1982.
Times Literary Supplement, January 15, 1982, January 20, 1984, September 28, 1984, October 24, 1986.
Twentieth Century Literature, April, 1966, July, 1967, October, 1971, winter, 1978.
Village Voice, September 30, 1981.
Washington Post, September 27, 1981, April 26, 1982.

—*Sketch by Marian Gonsior*

*   *   *

UPTON, Mark
See SANDERS, Lawrence

V

Van SCYOC, Sydney J(oyce) 1939-

PERSONAL: Born July 27, 1939, in Mt. Vernon, IN; daughter of John W. (a postal employee) and Geneva (Curry) Brown; married Jim R. Van Scyoc (an engineer), June 23, 1957; children: Sandra K., John Scott. *Education:* Attended University of Hawaii, 1964-65. *Politics:* "Liberally oriented." *Religion:* Unitarian-Universalist. *Avocational interests:* Gardening, cats, reading, and "playing with my two handsome grandsons."

ADDRESSES: Home—2636 East Ave., Hayward, CA 94541. *Agent*—Howard Morhaim, 501 Fifth Ave., New York, NY 10017.

CAREER: Science fiction writer, 1959—.

MEMBER: Science Fiction Writers of America.

WRITINGS:

SCIENCE FICTION NOVELS

Saltflower, Avon, 1971.
Assignment, Nor'Dyren, Avon, 1973.
Starmother, Berkley, 1976.
Cloudcry, Berkley, 1977.
Sunwaif, Berkley, 1980.
Darkchild, Berkley, 1982.
Bluesong, Berkley, 1983.
Starsilk, Berkley, 1984.
Drowntide, Berkley, 1987.
Featherstroke, Avon, 1989.
Deepwater Dreams, Avon, in press.

OTHER

Work represented in numerous anthologies, including *World's Best Science Fiction: 1969,* edited by Donald Wollheim and Terry Carr, Ace Books, 1969; *Two Views of Wonder,* edited by Tom Scortia and Chelsea Quinn Yarbo, Ballantine, 1974; *Valence and Vision: A Reader in Psychology,* edited by Rich Jones and Richard L. Roe, 1974; and *Social Problems through Science Fiction,* edited by Joseph Olander, St. Martin's Press, 1975. Contributor to science fiction magazines.

WORK IN PROGRESS: The Silvered Seed, a fantasy novel.

SIDELIGHTS: Sydney J. Van Scyoc writes: "I began writing science fiction in 1959. My early short fiction dealt primarily with individuals struggling against an increasingly dehumanizing technological society. In the late 1960s my focus shifted to short fiction set on other planets and dealt primarily with communities struggling against inexplicable alien environments. I am increasingly intrigued by the genetic and social changes which I believe will overtake us when we begin to colonize other planets. I prefer not to deal in much detail with technology. Instead, I like to set my fiction on isolated worlds inhabited by a relatively small human population. My personal orientation is increasingly pantheistic and in my longer fiction I am attempting to deal with the spiritual relationship of human to environment.

"Additionally, I am attempting to write stories that are exciting, yet contain a bare minimum of violence and other antisocial behavior."

* * *

VEIGA, Jose J(acinto da) 1915-

PERSONAL: Born February 2, 1915, in Corumba, Goias, Brazil; son of Luiz Pereira and Maria (Jacinto) da Veiga. *Education:* Universidade Federal do Rio de Janeiro, Bachelor, Faculty of Law, 1944.

ADDRESSES: Home—Rua Da Gloria 122/1004, 20241, Rio de Janeiro, RJ, Brazil.

CAREER: Shop assistant in Rio de Janeiro, Brazil, 1927-35; civil servant in Rio de Janeiro, 1939-45; radio commentator and foreign correspondent in London, England, 1945-49; city editor for a newspaper in Rio de Janeiro, 1949-51; *Reader's Digest,* Brazilian edition, Rio de Janeiro, magazine editor and editor in charge of condensed books department, 1951-71; writer.

AWARDS, HONORS: Premio Fabio Prado, Brazilian Writers Association, Sao Paulo, 1959, for *Os Cavalinhos de Platiplanto:* Premio Luiza Claudio de Souza, Pen Club, 1976, for *Os Pecados da Tribo:* Premio Sao Paulo de Ficcao, 1981, for *De Jogos e Festas:* Premio Jabuli 1981, for *De Jogos e Festas,* and 1983, for *Aquele Mundo de Vasabarros.*

WRITINGS:

Os Cavalinhos de Platiplanto (short stories), Editora Nitida (Rio de Janeiro), 1959, 17th edition, 1988.
A Hora dos ruminantes (novelette), Civilizacao Brasileira (Rio de Janeiro), 1966, 22nd edition, 1989, translation by Pamela

G. Bird published as *The Three Trials of Manirema,* Knopf, 1970.

A Maquina extraviada (short stories), Editora Prelo (Rio de Janeiro), 1969, 5th edition, 1986, translation by Bird published as *The Misplaced Machine,* Knopf, 1970.

Sombras de Reis Barbudos (novelette), Civilizacao Brasileira, 1972, 17th edition, 1989.

Os Pecados da Tribo (novelette), Civilizacao Brasileira, 1976.

De Jogos e Festas (short stories), Civilizacao Brasileira, 1980.

Aquele Mundo de Vasabarros (novelette), Difel (Sao Paulo), 1982, 4th edition, 1987.

Torvelinho Dia e Noite (novelette), Bertrand/Brasil, 1986.

A Casea da Serpente (novel), Bertrand/Brasil, 1989.

Contributor of stories to anthologies, including *Caderno de Portugues,* Volume 3, *Antologia do Novo Conto Brasileiro,* 1964, *Antologia Escolar de Contos Brasileiros,* 1969, and *Nuevos cuentistas brasilenos,* 1969; contributor to periodicals, including *Senhor Magazine, Journal do Brasil* (Rio de Janeiro), and *Minas Gerais* Sunday supplement (Belo Horizonte). Veiga's works have been translated into English, Spanish, Russian, Swedish, Norwegian, Danish, Czech, and Serbo-Croatian.

SIDELIGHTS: Jose J. Veiga's *The Three Trials of Manirema* is a didactic allegory, according to *New Republic* contributor Virginia Freehafer, who believes the author chose to write in an "aesopian language" to evade Brazilian censors. The critic asserts that the novel is aimed at "the current, overwhelming presence of the United States in Brazil."

Veiga himself, however, disagrees with this assessment. In a letter to *CA,* he explained that what he was trying to show was "the eclipsing of moral and spiritual values in a country ruled by a dictatorship, which was the case of Brazil at the time the book was written. Our immediate and overwhelming nuisance was the dictatorship itself, not American presence, or any other country's," the author added.

Veiga also told *CA* that he is very interested in contemporary American literature, in particular the works of Ernest Hemingway, J. D. Salinger, Donald Barthelme, Richard Brautigan, and Kurt Vonnegut, Jr.

BIOGRAPHICAL/CRITICAL SOURCES:

PERIODICALS

Best Sellers, August 15, 1970.
Guardian, July 9, 1979; August 12, 1979.
New Republic, December 16, 1970.
New York Times Book Review, August 30, 1970.
Saturday Review, September 12, 1970.

*   *   *

VOINOVICH, Vladimir (Nikolaevich) 1932-

PERSONAL: Some sources transliterate middle name as Nikolayevich; born September 26, 1932, in Dushanbe, Tadzhik, U.S.S.R.; immigrated to West Germany, December 25, 1980; son of Nikolai Pavlovich (a journalist) and Rosa (a teacher; maiden name, Goichman) Voinovich; married wife, Valentina, 1957 (marriage ended, 1965); married Irina Braude (a teacher), 1965; children: (first marriage) Marina, Pavel; (second marriage) Olga. *Education:* Attended Moscow Pedagogical Institute, 1957-59.

ADDRESSES: Home—Hans Carossa Strasse 5, 8035 Stockdorf, Federal Republic of Germany. *Agent*—Leonard W. Schroeter, 540 Central Bldg., Seattle, Wash. 98104.

CAREER: Worked as a herdsman on a collective farm when a youth; held a variety of jobs, including factory hand, locksmith, construction worker, railroad laborer, carpenter, aircraft mechanic, and editor of radio programs; went to Moscow and became a writer, 1956. Member of faculty at Institute of Fine Arts, Munich, West Germany. Visiting fellow at Princeton University, 1982-83; writer in residence at University of Southern California. *Military service:* Soviet Army, 1951-55.

MEMBER: Union of Soviet Writers (expelled, 1974), P.E.N. (French division), Mark Twain Society (honorary member), Bavarian Academy of Fine Arts.

WRITINGS:

My zdes' zhivem (short story; title means "We Live Here"), published in *Novy Mir,* 1961, published in book form, [Moscow], 1963.

"Khochu byt' chestnym" (novella; title means "I Want to be Honest"), published in *Novy Mir,* 1963.

"Dva tovarishcha" (novella; title means "Two Friends"), published in *Novy Mir,* 1964.

Vladychitsa (title means "The Sovereign Mistress"), [Moscow], 1969.

Stepen' doveriia (historical novel; title means "A Degree of Trust"), [Moscow], 1972.

Povesti (title means "Novellas"), [Moscow], 1972.

Zhizn' neobychainye prikliucheniia soldata Ivana Chonkina (novel), YMCA Press (Paris), 1975, translation by Richard Lourie published as *The Life and Extraordinary Adventures of Private Ivan Chonkin,* Farrar, Straus, 1977.

Ivan'kiada, ili rasskaz o vselenii pisatelia Voinovicha v novuiu kvartiru (autobiography), Ardis, 1976, translation by David Lapeza published as *The Ivankiad: The Tale of the Writer Voinovich's Installation in His New Apartment,* Farrar, Straus, 1977.

In Plain Russian: Stories, translated by Lourie, Farrar, Straus, 1979.

Pretender to the Throne: The Further Adventures of Private Ivan Chonkin, translated by Lourie, Farrar, Straus, 1981.

Anti Sovietskii Sovietski Soyuz, Ardis, 1985, translation by Lourie published as *The Anti-Soviet Soviet Union,* Harcourt, 1986.

Moscow 2042, translated by Lourie, Harcourt, 1987.

The Fur Hat, translated by Susan Brownsberger, Harcourt, 1989.

Also author of poems, feuilletons, six movie scripts, and two plays, produced in the U.S.S.R., based on his novellas "Khochu byt' chestnym" and "Dva tovarishcha." Contributor of short stories to *Novy Mir* and of articles to journals.

WORK IN PROGRESS: "Many future plans, but I fear to speak of them."

SIDELIGHTS: "I have been enraged and moved to tears by contemporary Russian prose and poetry, but Vladimir Voinovich is the only Russian writer who makes me laugh out loud," declared Susan Jacoby in *Saturday Review.* Other critics have also relished Voinovich's sense of humor. A *New York Times Book Review* contributor called Voinovich "the first genuine comic writer entirely produced by the Soviet system," while a *Newsweek* critic proclaimed him "the most drolly entertaining of the new Soviet dissident writers." Voinovich's reputation as a comic writer began with his first two books published in the United States, *The Life and Extraordinary Adventures of Private Ivan Chonkin* and *The Ivankiad.*

Suppressed in Russia, *The Life and Extraordinary Adventures of Ivan Chonkin* was circulated secretly and became an underground success. Peter Prescott speculated that Soviet officials found the novel subversive because "it suggests that amiable sloth and native cunning will prevail against bureaucracy," and "it illustrates what [Karl] Marx never understood: that even under socialism human nature remains an unregenerate constant." The book recounts the tale of a good-natured bumpkin, Private Chonkin, who is ordered by his army officer to remain on a remote collective farm and guard a downed airplane. Headquarters soon forgets him, and Chonkin amuses himself by puttering in the collective's garden and making love to the local postmistress. Despite his simple and placid exterior, Chonkin can be shrewd and even valiant, as his last-ditch effort to prevent himself from being reclaimed by the army demonstrates. Voinovich told an interviewer that Chonkin is not so dull as he appears: "The stupidity that everyone laughs at is not really stupidity when you examine it. My heroes, not only Chonkin but others, too, are very natural people who fall into unnatural situations."

Reflecting on Voinovich's use of satire in *The Life and Extraordinary Adventures of Ivan Chonkin,* Theodore Solotaroff observed, "The choice of a satirical mode was inspired, for it unearthed a first- rate comic talent that had been lurking beneath the sober gritty surface of his early realism and a new and powerful gift for rendering the transactions between reality and fantasy, the ordinary life haunted by the phantoms and phantasmagoria of the police state." In the same vein, Richard R. Lingeman remarked, "This is a very funny book, its humor making a sly and rueful point, as the best satire does, without being grim or heavy- handed." A reviewer for the *New Yorker* disagreed, however, with such assessments of the book, maintaining that "as satire, it is a bit lame and obvious."

Having written a fictional story about one man's war against bureaucracy, Voinovich then proceeded to write a nonfiction account of his own battles with the "phantasmagoria of the police state." The result was *The Ivankiad,* which *Newsweek* described as a "mock epic account of the author's struggle with a powerful publishing bureaucrat over possession of a two-room apartment in the Writers' Housing Cooperative." The theme of this struggle, Anatole Shub explained, is "the contrast between Soviet pretense and reality, theory and practice . . . but the book's delight lies in the human-scale merriment with which Voinovich tells the tale. As in all great satires, the situation is both thoroughly real and utterly preposterous."

Voinovich's battle to gain a larger apartment was only one of many struggles with Soviet bureaucrats. Although his writings were initially well received in the Soviet Union, he fell into official disfavor in the late 1960s. After writing a letter defending Aleksandr Solzhenitsyn in 1974, Voinovich was ousted from the Union of Soviet Writers and forbidden to earn his living as a writer. "I was expelled for trying to write with talent and to live with conscience," Voinovich told *CA.* He explained that his name could no longer be mentioned in Russian encyclopedias and newspapers.

In retaliation, Voinovich saw fit to lampoon Soviet officialdom with satirical letters. When his telephone service was abruptly severed, Voinovich composed an open letter to the Minister of Communications which began: "It is with deep concern that I bring to your attention the fact that an enemy of the Relaxation of International Tension, the head of the Moscow telephone system, is in hiding somewhere in the field of national economy headed by you." He went on to note, "After all, not even the notorious George Meany has managed to disconnect a single telephone." On another occasion he penned a hilarious epistle to the director of the new Soviet copyright agency. In order to shield Russian authors from Western influences, Voinovich recommended to the director that Moscow's prisons "with the necessary guards and police dogs [be] placed at your disposal."

"There is humor in Soviet life. You only have to have a sense of humor so you can recognize it," Voinovich once assured an inquirer. Voinovich and his family left the Soviet Union in December of 1980 and settled in West Germany. The books he has written since leaving his native country, including *In Plain Russian, Moscow 2042,* and *The Fur Hat,* continue to reveal his gift for provoking humor.

Some of Voinovich's poems were set to music and became popular songs in the U.S.S.R. His books have been translated into more than twenty languages.

BIOGRAPHICAL/CRITICAL SOURCES:

BOOKS

Contemporary Authors Autobiography Series, Volume 12, Gale, 1990.
Contemporary Literary Criticism, Gale, Volume 10, 1979, Volume 49, 1988.
Voinovich, Vladimir, *The Ivankiad,* Farrar, Straus, 1977.

PERIODICALS

Chicago Tribune Book World, August 2, 1981.
Los Angeles Times Book Review, August 23, 1981, August 17, 1986.
Newsweek, February 14, 1977, August 1, 1977, August 31, 1981.
New Yorker, March 7, 1977.
New York Times, March 26, 1977, April 27, 1977, December 4, 1980, September 4, 1981, June 2, 1987, July 11, 1987, November 28, 1989.
New York Times Book Review, January 23, 1977, August 7, 1977, October 7, 1979, September 20, 1981, August 31, 1986, June 7, 1987, November 5, 1989.
Saturday Review, September 17, 1977.
Time, January 3, 1977.
Times Literary Supplement, February 20, 1981, October 9, 1981, April 22, 1988.
Tribune Books (Chicago), May 31, 1987.
Washington Post, May 18, 1981, November 18, 1986, June 3, 1987.
Washington Post Book World, August 19, 1979, August 30, 1981, May 24, 1987.

W

WAGER, Walter H(erman) 1924-
(Walter Herman, John Tiger)

PERSONAL: Born September 4, 1924, in New York, NY; son of Max Louis (a doctor) and Jessie (Smith) Wager; married Sylvia Leonard (a writer), May 6, 1951 (divorced May, 1975); married Winifred McIvor (a goldsmith and Shiatsu practitioner), June 4, 1975; children: (first marriage) Lisa Wendy. *Education:* Columbia University, B.A., 1943; Harvard University, LL.B., 1946; Northwestern University, LL.M., 1949. *Politics:* Democrat. *Religion:* Jewish. *Avocational interests:* Travel (has been to thirty-four countries in North, Central, and South America, Asia, Africa, and Europe).

ADDRESSES: Home and office—200 West 79th St., New York, NY 10024. *Agent*—Curtis Brown Ltd., Ten Astor Pl., New York, NY 10022.

CAREER: Admitted to the Bar of New York State, 1946; Aeroutes, Inc., New York City, director of editorial research, 1947; *Journal of Air Law and Commerce,* Chicago, IL, federal department editor, 1948-49; Israeli Department of Civil Aviation, Lydda Airport, Tel Aviv, Israel, international affairs and law advisor, 1951-52; free-lance writer in New York City, 1952-54; United Nations Secretariat, New York City, senior editor, 1954-56; Columbia Broadcasting System, Inc. (CBS), New York City, writer for radio and television, 1956; National Broadcasting Co., Inc. (NBC-TV), New York City, writer and producer, 1957; free-lance writer for magazines, radio, and television, 1958-63; *Playbill,* New York City, editor in chief, 1963-66; American Society of Composers, Authors, and Publishers, New York City, public relations consultant and editor of *ASCAP Today,* 1966-72, director of public relations, 1972-78; National Music Publishers' Association, New York City, public relations counselor, 1978-84; Juilliard School, New York City, director of communications, 1985-86; Mann Music Center, Philadelphia, PA, public relations counselor, 1986-87; Eugene O'Neill Theater Center, New York City, public relations counselor, 1987-89. Lecturer at Northwestern University, 1949, and at Columbia University, 1955-56. Special assistant to Attorney General of the State of New York for investigation of hate literature in elections, 1962. Member of board of directors, Jazz Hall of Fame, 1975-77.

MEMBER: Writers Guild of America, Authors League of America, Mystery Writers of America (member of board of di-

rectors), National Academy of Popular Music (member of governing board).

WRITINGS:

NOVELS

(Under pseudonym Walter Herman) *Operation Intrigue,* Avon, 1956.
The Girl Who Split, Dell, 1969.
Sledgehammer, Macmillan, 1970.
Viper Three, Macmillan, 1971.
Swap, Macmillan, 1972.
Telefon, Macmillan, 1975.
My Side, by King Kong (farce), Macmillan, 1976.
Time of Reckoning, Playboy Press, 1979.
Blue Leader, Arbor House, 1979.
Blue Moon, Arbor House, 1980.
Blue Murder, Arbor House, 1981.
Designated Hitter, Arbor House, 1982.
Otto's Boy, Macmillan, 1985.
Raw Deal, Warner Books, 1986.
58 Minutes, Macmillan, 1987.

UNDER PSEUDONYM JOHN TIGER

Death Hits the Jackpot, Avon, 1954.
I Spy, Popular Library, 1965.
Masterstroke, Popular Library, 1966.
Wipeout, Popular Library, 1967.
Countertrap, Popular Library, 1967.
Mission Impossible, Popular Library, 1967.
Death Twist, Popular Library, 1968.
Doomdate, Popular Library, 1968.
Mission Impossible Number Four: Code Name Little Ivan, Popular Library, 1969.

OTHER

Frontier Formalities for International Airlines, [Chicago], 1949.
(Editor) *Some Selected Readings on International Air Transportation,* [Chicago], 1949.
Camp Century: City under the Ice (nonfiction), Chilton, 1962.
(Editor) *The Playwrights Speak* (interviews), Delacorte, 1967.
(With Mel Tillis) *Stutterin' Boy: The Autobiography of Mel Tillis, America's Beloved Star of Country Music,* Rawson, 1984.

Also author of screenplay "Swap," based on his novel, 1974; author of documentary films on jazz, spirituals, guerrilla warfare, organized crime in America, U.S. disarmament policy, Alliance for Progress in Colombia and Venezuela, the U.S. decision to use the atomic bomb against Japan, and the lives of a Roman legionary and an American soldier. Contributor of articles on theater and music to periodicals. Senior editor, *Show*, 1965.

MEDIA ADAPTATIONS: Metro-Goldwyn-Mayer filmed *Telefon* in 1977; Lorimar's production of *Viper Three* was released in 1977 as "Twilight's Last Gleaming"; *58 Minutes* was the basis for Twentieth Century-Fox's 1990 hit film "Die Hard 2."

SIDELIGHTS: Walter H. Wager told *CA:* "I have written for pleasure since I was ten but never thought that one could make a living at it. I had no idea how to get started in the writing world and really wandered in casually as a source of income while waiting for a security clearance to become a UN editor. I've been very lucky, and I've enjoyed what I do. I'm still surprised by all the people who 1) want to be novelists, 2) consider writing/writers exotic and superior. Fortunately, writers themselves are not as arrogant as lawyers, doctors, or movie producers—but who is? On the other hand, I'm bored with cry-baby novelists who write irate articles about their horrid experiences with 'boorish' movie or television folk. I am also dismayed by certain defensive/hostile types who resent anyone who 1) creates personally, 2) works at home. However, I'm generally in a cheery mood, doing my thing. I don't see writers as competing with each other or with anyone else. None of us writes like any other writer, thank God. I have pointed this out to my daughter who is a caring and excellent senior editor at Putnam.

"I try to assist young writers by introducing them to agents and editors, and by encouraging them if/when they are temporarily uncertain. I tell them of the 'luck' factor and how a 'real' writer will go on writing no matter what. I joke about how I literally stumbled into hard cover fiction. In June 1967, I was in [Washington] D.C. autographing paperbacks at an American Booksellers Association convention. There were many parties, and I was among those who imbibed conscientiously. Somewhat tipsy, I was struggling through a throng in the crowded Harper & Row suite when I stumbled and bumped into a goodnatured chap. We exchanged boozy witticisms, and later my good friend and super editor, James A. Bryans, told me that the stranger was impressed. Bryans urged me to send that man a book. The fellow was Richard Oldenberg, then managing editor at Macmillan and now head of the Museum of Modern Art. I sent him a proposal for an anthology, was directed to another bright Macmillan editor, Bob Markel— later editor in chief—who urged me to do a novel. I did quite a few. I never did get to thank Oldenberg, but I certainly will if we ever meet again."

BIOGRAPHICAL/CRITICAL SOURCES:

PERIODICALS

Los Angeles Times, July 28, 1990
New York Times, January 27, 1977; August 22, 1982.

*   *   *

WATMOUGH, David 1926-

PERSONAL: Born August 17, 1926, in London, England; son of Gerald and Ethel (Bassett) Watmough. *Education:* Attended King's College, London, 1945-49. *Politics:* Independent. *Religion:* Anglican.

ADDRESSES: Home—3358 West First Ave., Vancouver, British Columbia, Canada V6R 1G4.

CAREER: Writer. British Broadcasting Corp., London, talks producer for Third Program, 1956; *San Francisco Examiner*, San Francisco, CA, feature writer and reviewer, 1958-60; editor for Ace Books, 1957; *Vancouver Sun*, Vancouver, British Columbia, drama and art critic, 1963-66. Broadcaster for British Broadcasting Corp., Canadian Broadcasting Corp., and KPFA-Radio. *Military service:* Royal Navy, 1944-45.

MEMBER: Writers' Union of Canada.

AWARDS, HONORS: Canada Council bursary awards, 1968, and 1970; Canada Council senior arts grant, 1976.

WRITINGS:

A Church Renascent, S.P.C.K., 1951.
Names for the Numbered Years (plays; contains "Friedhof," "My Mother's House Has Too Many Rooms," and "Do You Remember One September Afternoon?"), Bau-Xi Press, 1967.
Ashes for Easter (short stories), Talonbooks, 1972.
Love and the Waiting Game (short stories), Oberon Press, 1975.
No More into the Garden (novel), Doubleday, 1978.
(Contributor) Ian Young, editor, *On the Line: New Gay Fiction*, Crossing Press, 1981.
The Connecticut Countess (short stories), Crossing Press, 1984.
Fury (short stories), Oberon Press, 1984.
(Contributor) *Canadian Writers in 1984*, University of British Columbia Press, 1984.
The Unlikely Pioneer (opera), Mosaic Press, 1986.
Vibrations in Time (short stories), Mosaic Press, 1986.
The Year of Fears (novel), Mosaic Press, 1987.
Families (novel), Knights Press, 1990.

Work anthologized in *Cornish Short Stories*, Penguin, *Eighty-three Best Canadian Stories*, Oberon Press, *The Vancouver Fiction Book*, Polestar Press, and *CBC Encounter*.

SIDELIGHTS: David Watmough writes: "All my eight volumes of fiction to date (and these are my primary concerns) center upon my first-person protagonist, Davey Bryant. This character is Cornish-born, is homosexual, and so far in his early fifties, he has become a Canadian citizen. My goal is, through an open-ended sequence of novels, to come up with the portrait of a particular man living through his particular twentieth-century times. This has/will cover(ed) a French period, a New York period, San Francisco, and Vancouver, and so far extends from 1926 to 1969, with gaps still to be filled in forthcoming volumes." Watmough has also recorded his stories on "Pictures from a Dying Landscape," Kanata Records, 1972.

BIOGRAPHICAL/CRITICAL SOURCES:

BOOKS

Dictionary of Literary Biography, Volume 53: *Canadian Writers since 1960, First Series*, Gale, 1986.
Toye, William, editor, *Oxford Companion to Canadian Literature*, Oxford University Press, 1983.
Woodcock, George, *World of Canadian Writing: Critiques and Recollections*, University of Washington Press, 1980.

PERIODICALS

Globe and Mail (Toronto), October 11, 1986, October 17, 1987.
Canadian, November 18, 1972.
Canadian Fiction, winter, 1976.

WATTENBERG, Ben J.   1933-

PERSONAL: Born August 26, 1933, in New York, NY; son of Judah (a lawyer) and Rachel (Gutman) Wattenberg; married Marna Hade, June 24, 1956 (divorced, February, 1981); married Diane Abelman, July 10, 1983; children: (first marriage) Ruth Elena, Daniel Eli, Sarah Anita; (second marriage) Rachel. *Education:* Hobart College, B.A., 1955. *Politics:* Democrat. *Religion:* Jewish.

ADDRESSES: Home—7408 Bybrook Lane, Chevy Chase, MD 20015. *Office*—Public Opinion American Enterprise Institute, 1150 17th St. N.W., Washington, D.C. 20036. *Agent*—Peter Matson, 22 East 40th St., New York, NY 10016.

CAREER: Speechwriter for President Lyndon B. Johnson, 1966-68; aide to Senator Hubert Humphrey, 1970; campaign adviser to Senator Henry Jackson, 1972, 1976. Business consultant in Washington, D.C., 1968-79. Mary Washington College, eminent scholar and professor at large, 1973-74; U.S. International University, distinguished visiting professor, 1978, 1979. Coalition for a Democratic Majority, co-founder and chairman, 1972—; Hudson Institute, trustee, 1976—; American Enterprise Institute, senior fellow, 1977—; member of presidential advisory board on ambassadorial appointments, 1977-80; Board of International Broadcasting, vice chairman, 1981; Democracy Program, vice chairman, 1982-83; Center for Strategic and International Studies, member of research council, 1982—; Reading Is Fundamental, member of board of directors. Member of U.S. delegation to Madrid, 1980, and to United Nations Population Conference in Mexico City, 1984; Council on Foreign Relations, member. United Features, Newspaper Enterprise Association, syndicated columnist, 1981—. Narrator and essayist for national television series, "In Search of Real America," Public Broadcasting System (PBS), 1977-78, and "Ben Wattenberg's 1980," PBS, 1980; "Ben Wattenberg at Large," PBS, host, 1981; "Spectrum," Columbia Broadcasting System (CBS) Radio, weekly commentator. *Military service:* U.S. Air Force, 1956-58.

MEMBER: Federal City Club, Phi Beta Kappa.

AWARDS, HONORS: LL.D., Hobart College and William Smith College, both 1975.

WRITINGS:

The Story of Harbors (juvenile nonfiction), Sterling Publications, 1961.
(With Ralph Lee Smith) *The New Nations of Africa,* Richard Hart, 1963.
Busy Waterways (juvenile nonfiction), John Day, 1964.
(With Richard M. Scammon) *This U.S.A.: An Unexpected Family Portrait of 194,067,286 Americans Drawn from the Census,* Doubleday, 1965.
(With Scammon) *The Real Majority: An Extraordinary Examination of the American Electorate,* Coward, 1970.
The Demography of the 1970's: The Birth Dearth and What It Means (monograph), Family Circle and National Association of Food Chains, 1971.
The Real America: A Surprising Examination of the State of the Union, introduction by Scammon, Doubleday, 1974, new edition published as *In Search of the Real America: A Challenge to the Chaos of Failure and Guilt,* Capricorn Books, 1978.
(With Ervin S. Duggan) *Against All Enemies* (novel), Doubleday, 1977.
(With Richard Whalen) *The Wealth Weapon: U.S. Foreign Policy and Multinational Corporations,* Transaction Books, 1980.

The Good News Is the Bad News Is Wrong, Simon & Schuster, 1984, revised and updated edition, 1985.
(Editor and author of introduction with Karl Zinsmeister) *Are World Population Trends a Problem?,* American Enterprise Institute for Public Policy Research, 1985.
The Birth Dearth: What Happens When People in Free Countries Don't Have Enough Children, Pharos Books, 1987, revised edition, 1989.
Terrain of the Nineties, Free Press, 1990.
The First Universal Nation, Free Press, 1990.

Contributor of articles to periodicals, including *Reporter, Commentary,* and *Ladies Home Journal.* Co-editor, *Public Opinion Magazine,* 1977—.

SIDELIGHTS: A demographer and political analyst, Ben J. Wattenberg has written or co-written several heavily-researched books about American society that have often surprised critics for their unwavering optimism. Wattenberg's positive outlook has run counter to other experts' gloom and doom analyses that have pervaded since the 1960s, when the author's first widely-reviewed book, *This U.S.A.: An Unexpected Family Portrait of 194,067,286 Americans Drawn from the Census,* was published. Using the data from the 1960 census and other federal statistics up to 1967, Wattenberg and collaborator Richard M. Scammon demolish with this work "some of our most cherished myths," according to *Washington Post Book World* reviewer Clarence Petersen. The authors conclude in the study that in this country, contrary to popular belief, the divorce rate is decreasing, the population "explosion" is a myth, the standard of living for blacks is improving, and that life expectancies have not increased since the turn of the century. Wattenberg's other studies since then have reached similar unique conclusions that have sometimes stirred controversy among Democrats and Republicans alike.

Wattenberg's and Scammon's next book, *The Real Majority: An Extraordinary Examination of the American Electorate,* is a psephological study designed to define the "typical" American voter; thus making it possible to plan more effective political strategies. The three central theses of *The Real Majority,* relates James J. Conlin in *Best Sellers,* are "that the Social Issue has replaced the perennial bread-and-butter issues; that the great majority of the voters are middle-aged, middle-class oriented and white; and that the safest, surest policy in American politics is the center." From this analysis (published just prior to the 1970 election) the authors conclude that political candidates should take a "law-and-order" platform, rather than emphasizing economic issues, if they want to win their campaigns. Some critics, like *Harper's* contributor Edwin M. Yoder, Jr., have felt that while Wattenberg's and Scammon's statistical investigation was "expertly" done, the science of psephology itself should not be used as the sole method of determining political strategy, since it does not encourage independent and original thinking. "A manual for followship, not leadership, this," attests Yoder. Nevertheless, *The Real Majority* was a best seller and strongly influenced the 1970 and 1972 election strategies of both Republicans and Democrats.

Wattenberg wrote his next book, *The Real America: A Surprising Examination of the State of the Union* (later revised as *In Search of the Real America: A Challenge to the Chaos of Failure and Guilt*), with less help from Scammon, who wrote the introduction and co-wrote one chapter. This chapter, entitled "Black Progress and Liberal Rhetoric," was first published as a short report in *Commentary,* and was a target for many outraged civil rights and black leaders. Wattenberg and Scammon assert here that 52 percent of black families in America had achieved middle-class status and that their income had doubled during the period from the 1960s to the 1970s. Many liberal critics, however, contested at the time that the authors' figure of an $8,000 a year salary as a cut-off point for qualifying for middle-class status was too low, and that $11,446—the figure set by the Bureau of Labor Statistics—was more accurate. Using this number, only one out of every four blacks could be counted as middle-class. A National Urban League study also found that, when compared to white income, the income of black families had actually declined. Steven R. Weisman of the *New York Times Book Review,* while complementing the author for his well-researched and presented examination of areas such as the improvement of work conditions, nevertheless also notes that "Wattenberg refuses to concede the harshness of the reality of black poverty." Weisman and *New York Review of Books* critic Sheldon S. Wolin concur that Wattenberg is overly optimistic in his conclusion that, as Wolin writes, save "for inflation, our problems have either been exaggerated or they are in the process of being solved."

The Good News Is the Bad News Is Wrong was Wattenberg's next best selling book. It continues his ever-optimistic viewpoint, but ends on a foreboding note. As with *The Real America,* the author suggests in this more recent work that Americans "never had it so good." The reason why Americans do not realize this is the "panic-mongering" incited largely by the media, according to the author. "Feminists, environmentalists, consumer advocates, some conservatives, and even the Moral Majority will not be amused by this book," says Greg Schneiders in the *Washington Post Book World.* Wattenberg believes that such people are alarmists, doing more harm than good because they undermine America's feeling of confidence in itself, which could eventually lead to the loss of this country's status as a super power. "Many of the statistics he cites make sense," remarks *New York Times Book Review* critic Andrew Hacker. According to the author, real income (the income calculated after adjusting for inflation) has increased steadily, and unemployment figures have been exaggerated because they include high school students and housewives looking for part-time work. "At the same time," Hacker later adds, "some figures in 'The Good News' are wrong or misleading." The critic reports, for example, that—contrary to the author's assertion—the dropout rate for high school students has increased, and Medicaid to the poor does not always provide as high a quality of service as Wattenberg would have his readers believe. But Schneiders concludes that *The Good News* "is an important book that needed to be written. It is serious but enjoyable; an effective polemic but honest; a heartening view by a seasoned observer."

Wattenberg's fear that the United States might lose its super power status is elaborated upon in *The Birth Dearth: What Happens When People in Free Countries Don't Have Enough Babies?* In this book, the demographer worries that the lower birth rates among families in western, industrialized countries will result in a decline in the influence of Western culture on the Third World. This thesis has inspired shocked reactions from several reviewers. "When I read an author who maintains that Western cultural dominance of the Third World is wholly beneficial," says *Los Angeles Times* contributor Richard Morris, "who urges that we breed more prolifically so that we can continue to increase our already huge military expenditures, I can't help experiencing a sudden chill." Scott L. Malcomson's *Village Voice* article contends that trying "to make all this sound nonracist is a lot like trying to make nuclear war sound like a reasonable idea." The problem with Wattenberg's idea, contends Tamar Jacoby in the *New York Times Book Review* is that "he does not convincingly

prove that the size of the West's population has been in any way key to its 'geocultural' influence." But critics have also applauded the author for his fresh view of population trends. "We have been told ad nauseam about the problems of population growth, be it global or national" Thomas R. De Gregori reminds readers in *Insight,* "but until now nobody has explored the problems of a stable or even declining population." Jacoby similarly admits that, "by and large, his vision of the uncertain economic future is vivid and persuasively troubling."

Although Wattenberg has expressed anxiety over the future of the United States because of its relatively small population, his overall outlook has remained consistently optimistic not only in his books, but also as a commentator on the weekly radio program, "Spectrum," and on such television shows as "Ben Wattenberg's 1980" and "Ben Wattenberg at Large." His programs and books have been made in an effort to counter the negative stories one is continuously subjected to in the newspapers and on network news shows, which he feels are designed to attract audiences rather than tell all the facts. "The problem," Wattenberg concludes in *The Good News,* "is that [the media] are missing the biggest stories or our era—about progress. . . . It's not that they are often getting the story wrong. They are often getting the wrong story."

BIOGRAPHICAL/CRITICAL SOURCES:

BOOKS

Wattenberg, Ben J., *The Good News Is the Bad News Is Wrong,* Simon & Schuster, 1984.

PERIODICALS

Annals of the American Academy of Political and Social Science, May, 1981.
Best Sellers, August 15, 1970.
Christian Science Monitor, November 5, 1984.
Harper's, October, 1970.
Insight, July 6, 1987.
Los Angeles Times Book Review, November 24, 1985; August 2, 1987.
New York Review of Books, February 6, 1975; June 26, 1986.
New York Times, September 25, 1970; September 29, 1974; May 23, 1980.
New York Times Book Review, January 2, 1966; September 29, 1974; October 28, 1984; July 12, 1987; October 8, 1989.
Village Voice, September 15, 1987.
Washington Post Book World, January 28, 1968; October 14, 1984.*

—*Sketch by Kevin S. Hile*

* * *

WENSINGER, Arthur S(tevens) 1926-

PERSONAL: Born March 9, 1926, in Grosse Pointe, MI; son of Carl Franklin (a businessman) and Suzanne (Stevens) Wensinger. *Education:* Dartmouth College, B.A. (with honors), 1948; University of Michigan, M.A., 1951, Ph.D., 1958; further graduate study at University of Munich, 1948, 1950-51, and University of Innsbruck, 1953-54. *Politics:* Independent. *Religion:* Episcopalian.

ADDRESSES: Home—Candlewood Hill, Higganum, CT 06441. *Office*—Department of German Language and Literature, Wesleyan University, Middletown, CT 06457.

CAREER: Wesleyan University, Middletown, CT, instructor, 1955-58, assistant professor, 1959-63, associate professor,

1963-69, professor, 1969-77, Marcus Taft Professor of German and Humanities, 1977—, chairman of department of German language and literature, senior tutor in College of Letters, 1963—.

MEMBER: International Brecht Society, American Association of University Professors, American Translators Association, Modern Language Association of America, American Association of Teachers of German, American Literary Translators Association, W. H. Auden Society, Heinrich-von-Kleist Gesellschaft, Kafka Society of America, Connecticut Academy of Arts and Sciences, Phi Beta Kappa, Phi Kappa Phi.

AWARDS, HONORS: Reynolds fellow, Dartmouth College, 1950-52; Fulbright fellow at University of Innsbruck, 1953-54; Danforth Foundation grant, 1959; Ford Foundation grant, 1970-71; Center for the Humanities grant, Wesleyan University, 1974; Kenan grants, 1976, 1978, 1979; Inter Nationes grants, 1978, 1984.

WRITINGS:

(Translator and editor with Walter Gropius) Oskar Schlemmer and others, *The Theatre of the Bauhaus,* Wesleyan University Press, 1961, 2nd edition, 1971.

(Editor with T. C. Dunham) Herman Hesse, *Siddhartha: Eine indische Dichtung,* Macmillan, 1962, 2nd edition, 1979.

(Editor of German section) Wills Barnstone, general editor, *Modern European Poetry,* Bantam, 1963.

(Translator and contributor to German section) *The Language of Love* (short story anthology), Bantam, 1964.

(Contributor of translation) *Plays for a New Theater,* illustrated by George Grosz, New Directions, 1966.

(Editor and translator with W. B. Coley) *Hogarth on High Life: The Marriage a la Mode Series from Georg Christoph Lichtenberg's Commentaries,* Wesleyan University Press, 1970.

(Editor) *Peter et amicorum,* Gehenna Press, 1972.

(Editor and contributor) P. Boynton, *Stone Island,* Harcourt, 1973.

(Contributor of translations) *Women Poets from Antiquity to Now,* edited by A. Barnstone and W. Barnstone, Schocken, 1981.

(Author of introduction) Rainer Maria Rilke, *Requiem for a Woman and Selected Lyrics,* Threshold Books, 1982.

(Contributor of translation) Arthur Schnitzler, *Plays and Stories,* Continuum, 1983.

(Editor and translator with others) Rainer Werner Fassbinder, *Querelle: The Film Book,* Schirmer/Mosel Verlag, 1983.

(Editor and translator with Carole Clew Hoey) *Paula Modersohn-Becker: The Letters and Journals,* Taplinger, 1984, new revised edition, Northwestern University Press, 1990.

(Translator with R. H. Wood) Klaus-Juergen Sembach and Josef von Sternberg, *Marlene Dietrich: Portraits 1926-1960,* Grove, 1984.

(Translator) Klaus Wagenbach, *Franz Kafka: Pictures of a Life,* Pantheon, 1984.

(Translator with Wood) Peter Stephan Jungk, *Shabbat* (novel), Times Books, 1985.

(Translator with Wood) Cornelia Stabenow, *The Jungle Paintings of Henri Rousseau, le Douanier,* Grove, 1985.

(Translator with Wood) Hanna Schygulla and Fassbinder, *Hanna Schygulla,* Grove, 1985.

(Translator and annotator with Wood) Thomas Fecht, *Kaethe Kollwitz: The Work in Color,* Pantheon/Random House, 1988.

(Translator) Franz Kafka, *The Sons,* Random House/Schocken Books, 1989.

(Translator and annotator with Krishna Winston) Guenter Grass, *Two States—One Nation?,* Harcourt, 1990.

(Translator with Hoey) Niklas Frank, *In the Shadow of the Reich,* Knopf, 1991.

Translator of short stories, articles, and dramatic writings.

WORK IN PROGRESS: Translating the letters and journals of Karl Friedrich Schinkel; a Norman Douglas reader; fiction and autobiographical work.

BIOGRAPHICAL/CRITICAL SOURCES:

PERIODICALS

Harper's, October, 1970.
Los Angeles Times Book Review, February 17, 1985.
Nation, June 21, 1971.
Newsweek, December 14, 1970.
New Yorker, December 12, 1970.
New York Review of Books, August 13, 1970.
New York Times, August 14, 1970.
New York Times Book Review, February 26, 1984.

*   *   *

WESKER, Arnold 1932-

PERSONAL: Born May 24, 1932, in London, England; son of Joseph (a tailor) and Leah (Perlmutter) Wesker; married Doreen Cecile Bicker, November 14, 1958; children: Lindsay Joe, Tanya Jo, Daniel, Elsa Sara. *Education:* Attended London School of Film Technique, 1955-56. *Politics:* Humanist. *Religion:* Jewish.

ADDRESSES: Home—37 Ashley Rd., London N19 3AG, England.

CAREER: Started working at sixteen as furniture maker's apprentice and tried half-a-dozen jobs, mainly along manual lines, before receiving Arts Council of Great Britain grant in 1958. Worked as carpenter's mate, bookseller's assistant, plumber's mate, seed sorter, kitchen porter, 1948-50, 1952-54, and as pastry cook in Norwich and London, England, and in Paris, France, 1954-58; playwright, 1958—; director, 1968—. Centre 42 Ltd., London, co-founder, 1961, and artistic director, 1961-70. *Military service:* Royal Air Force, 1950-52.

AWARDS, HONORS: Arts Council of Great Britain grant, 1958; *Evening Standard* award as most promising British playwright, 1959; co-winner of *Encyclopaedia Britannica* play prize, 1959, for "Chicken Soup with Barley"; Italian Premio Marzotto drama award, 1964, for "Their Very Own and Golden City"; gold medal for best foreign play, "El espectador y la critica" (Madrid), 1973, for "The Kitchen," and 1979, for "Chicken Soup with Barley."

WRITINGS:

PLAYS

Chicken Soup with Barley (also see below; first play of trilogy; first produced in Coventry, England, at Belgrade Theatre, July 7, 1958, produced in London at Royal Court Theatre, July 14, 1958, produced in Cleveland, Ohio, 1962; included in *New English Dramatists,* Penguin, 1959), Evans Brothers, 1961.

Roots (also see below; second play of trilogy; first produced in Coventry, England, at Belgrade Theatre, May 25, 1959, produced at Royal Court Theatre, June 30, 1959, produced off-Broadway at Mayfair Theater, March 6, 1961, produced in New York City by Jewish Repertory Theater, November,

1986), Penguin, 1959, published with introduction and notes by A. H. M. Best and Mark Cohen, Longmans, Green, 1967.

The Kitchen: A Play in Two Parts with an Interlude (also see below; first produced at Royal Court Theatre, September 6, 1959, expanded version produced at Royal Court Theatre, 1961, produced off-Broadway at Eighty-First Street Theatre, June 13, 1966; included in *New English Dramatists 2*, Penguin, 1960), expanded version, J. Cape, 1961, Random House, 1962.

I'm Talking about Jerusalem (also see below; third play of trilogy; first produced in Coventry, England, at Belgrade Theatre, March 28, 1960, produced in London at Royal Court Theatre, July 27, 1960), Penguin, 1960.

The Wesker Trilogy (also see below; contains "Chicken Soup with Barley," "Roots," and "I'm Talking about Jerusalem"), J. Cape, 1960, Random House, 1961, reprinted, Penguin, 1976.

Chips with Everything: A Play in Two Acts (also see below; first produced at Royal Court Theatre, April 27, 1962, produced on the West End at Vaudeville Theatre, 1962, produced on Broadway at Plymouth Theatre, October 1, 1963), J. Cape, 1962, Random House, 1963, critical edition edited by Michael Marland, with introduction by Wesker, Blackie, 1966.

"The Nottingham Captain: A Moral for Narrator, Voices and Orchestra" (also see below; included in *Six Sundays in January*), first produced in Wellingborough, England, at Centre 42 Trades Union Festival, 1962.

Their Very Own and Golden City: A Play in Two Acts and Twenty-Nine Scenes (also see below; first produced in Brussels at Belgium National Theater, 1964, produced at Royal Court Theatre, May 19, 1966), J. Cape, 1966.

The Four Seasons: A Play in Two Parts (also see below; first produced at Belgrade Theatre, 1965, produced on the West End at Saville Theatre, September 21, 1965, produced off-Broadway at Theatre Four, March 14, 1968), J. Cape, 1966.

The Friends: A Play in Two Acts (also see below; first produced in Stockholm at Stadsteatern, January, 1970, produced in London at Roundhouse, May 19, 1970), J. Cape, 1970.

The Old Ones (also see below; first produced at Royal Court Theatre, August 8, 1972, produced in New York at Theatre at the Lambs Club, December 6, 1974), J. Cape, 1973, revised edition edited by Michael Marland, Blackie, 1974.

The Journalists (also see below; first produced in Wilhelmshaven, West Germany, at Municipal Theatre, October 10, 1981), Writers and Readers Publishing Cooperative, 1975, published as *The Journalists: A Triptych*, J. Cape, 1979.

The Merchant (also see below; based on three stories Shakespeare used for "The Merchant of Venice"; produced in Stockholm, Sweden, at Stockholm Royal Dramaten, October 8, 1976, produced on Broadway at Plymouth Theatre, November 16, 1977), first published in German, Henschel Verlag, 1977, revised edition, with commentary and notes by Glenda Leeming, Methuen, 1983.

Three Plays (contains "The Kitchen," "The Four Seasons," and "Their Very Own and Golden City"), Penguin, 1976.

The Plays of Arnold Wesker, Harper, Volume 1 (contains "The Kitchen," "Chicken Soup with Barley," "Roots," "I'm Talking about Jerusalem," and "Chips with Everything"), 1976, Volume 2 (contains "The Four Seasons," "Their Very Own and Golden City," "Menace," "The Friends," and "The Old Ones"), 1977.

Love Letters on Blue Paper (also see below; adapted from Wesker's short story of the same title; first produced in Syracuse, N.Y., 1977, produced in London at Cottesloe The-

atre, February 15, 1978, produced in New York City by Hudson Guild Theatre, April 11, 1984), Writers and Readers Publishing Cooperative, 1978.

Chips with Everything [and] *The Friends* [and] *The Old Ones* [and] *Love Letters on Blue Paper*, Penguin, 1980.

The Journalist [and] *The Wedding Feast* (adapted from Dostoyevsky's short story; produced in Stockholm, 1972, produced at Leeds Playhouse, January 20, 1977) [and] *The Merchant*, Penguin, 1980.

"Caritas," produced in London at Cottesloe Theatre, October 7, 1981.

"Four Portraits of Mothers," produced in Tokyo, Japan, at Mitzukoshi Royal Theatre, July 2, 1982.

"Annie Wobbler" (first performed as radio play "Annie, Anna, Annabella," 1983), produced in Birmingham, England, by Birmingham Rep Studio, June 27, 1983, produced on the West End at Fortune Theatre, November 14, 1984, produced in New York City by Coota Woota Productions at Westbeth Theater Center, November, 1986.

"The Sullied Hand," produced in Edinburgh, Scotland, by Theatre N.A.C. at Netherbow Arts Centre, August 10, 1984.

"One More Ride on the Merry-Go Round" (comedy), produced in Leicester, England, at Phoenix Arts Theatre, April 25, 1985.

"Yardsale" (also see below) [and] "Whatever Happened to Betty Lemon" (two one-acts), produced in Hammersmith, England, at Lyric Studio, February, 1987.

Also author of "Master," 1966, "The New Play," 1969, "Cinders" (adapted from Paul Bailey's *An English Madam*), 1982, "When God Wanted a Son," 1986, "Badenheim 1939" (adapted from a novel by Aharon Appelfeld), 1987, and "Lady Othello" (adapted from Wesker's filmscript, "Lady Othello"), "The Mistress," 1988, "Little Old Lady and Shoeshine" (one-act for young people), and "Stand Up, Stand Up."

TELEVISION PLAYS

"Menace" (also see below), aired on "First Night" series, British Broadcasting Corp. (BBC-TV), December 8, 1963.

"Love Letters on Blue Paper" (also see below; adapted from short story by Wesker), aired on BBC-TV, March 2, 1976.

Also author of "Whitsun" (adapted from Wesker's story, "The Visit"), 1980, "Breakfast," 1981, "Thieves in the Night," (adapted from a novel by Arthur Koestler), 1984, and of an adaptation of his play "The Four Seasons."

OTHER

Labour and the Arts: II, or What, Then, Is to Be Done?, Gemini, 1960.

The Modern Playwright; or, "O Mother, Is It Worth It?," Gemini, 1961.

"The Kitchen" (screenplay adaptation of Wesker's play), produced by Kingsley, 1962.

(Author of introduction) Roger Frith, *The Serving Boy*, Colchester, 1968.

Fears of Fragmentation (essays), J. Cape, 1970.

Six Sundays in January (short stories and television play; includes "The Nottingham Captain: A Moral for Narrator, Voices and Orchestra"), J. Cape, 1971.

Love Letters on Blue Paper: Three Stories (also see below), J. Cape, 1974, Harper, 1975.

(Contributor of text) *Say Goodbye, You May Never See Them Again: Scenes from Two East-End Backgrounds*, paintings by John Allin, J. Cape, 1974.

Words as Definitions of Experience, Writers and Readers Publishing Cooperative, 1976.

Journey into Journalism: A Very Personal Account in Four Parts, Writers and Readers Publishing Cooperative, 1977.

Fatlips: A Story for Children, Harper, 1978.

Said the Old Man to the Young Man: Three Stories (short stories), J. Cape, 1978.

Love Letters on Blue Paper (short stories; includes "Love Letters on Blue Paper," "Six Sundays in January," "The Man Who Became Afraid," and "The Visit"), Penguin, 1980.

"Yardsale" (radio play), aired on BBC-Radio, October 6, 1984.

"Bluey" (radio play), aired on Cologne Radio, May 16, 1985.

Distinctions (essays, lectures, and journalism), J. Cape, 1985.

Also author of filmscript, "Madame Solario," 1968, and "Lady Othello," 1981; also author of filmscript adaptation of *The Wesker Trilogy,* 1979, commissioned by National Film Development Fund.

WORK IN PROGRESS: Musical adaptation of "The Kitchen"; a play entitled "Toys."

SIDELIGHTS: Arnold Wesker's original reknown came from his trilogy of plays, "Chicken Soup with Barley," "Roots," and "I'm Talking about Jerusalem," which traces the attitudes of a family of Jewish Socialist intellectuals from 1936 through 1959. Geoffrey Grigson calls it "a Forsyte Saga of the Left." Wesker, describing his trilogy, writes: "A number of themes bind the trilogy together. Basically it is [about] a family; on another level it is a play about human relationships; and on a third, and most important level, it is a story of people moved by political ideas in a particular social time. There are many theories about Socialism. 'Chicken Soup with Barley' handles the Communist aspect. 'Roots' handles the personal aspect. . . . 'I'm Talking about Jerusalem' is a sort of study in a William Morris kind of Socialism."

Wesker has been described as a "committed" playwright and in his early plays embraced the ideals of Socialism. He was identified with a group of English playwrights who emerged after the dramatic revival in England in 1956 and who were dubbed "the angry young men." A writer for the *Christian Science Monitor* comments that of this group, which included John Osborne, Brendan Behan, and David Storey, "Wesker is certainly—and this is something to admire when most people are busy keeping up their defenses in all directions—the most unafraid, the most naive, the most vulnerable. He is the least technically expert, the most self-indulgent. . . . Yet . . . in all his plays he has striven not to exploit the disintegration of individuals and society, but the possibility of their self-redemption—and this again is not ignoble when the opposite is the fashion, and artists in every medium go all out for easy hysteria."

Beginning with "Chips with Everything," Wesker's work during the 1960s "became less documentary and immediate in impact," according to Glenda Leeming. His more recent plays are not as didactic or political in tone as his earlier Socialist realism. Disillusioned with his earlier political beliefs, Wesker told Richard Skloot that the paradox of Socialism "is that it is producing people who are socially selfish and indifferent. The State has taken on all responsibility and people don't care about each other and they don't care about what happens outside their own country, outside their own community. There's this terrible social listlessness that has been created." Turning from socialistic didacticism in "The Four Seasons," which depicts the allegorical seasons of a love affair from its spring budding through its winter disintegration, Wesker begins to explore what he has called the theme of "private pain." With this play and "The Friends" Wesker is,

according to Leeming, "breaking new ground, not in techniques of presentation, but in his increasingly introspective subject matter."

The critical reception to "The Friends" was, for the most part, unfavorable. Benedict Nightingale finds that it "isn't a very good play. The characters, though naturalistically presented, have little objective, individual life. Except when they drop into north-country dialect, they speak much the same ardent, lilting prose. They speak a great deal, too. . . . They don't define themselves by action. . . . One misses, as always in Wesker, any sense of the obstinacy of unreason and the destructive power of human evil." A *Plays and Players* reviewer writes: "The fault of 'The Friends' is that Mr. Wesker is like a man who does not know when to stop. The play is the verbal vomit of his ideas, as if he is suffering from some kind of literary indigestion." Ronald Bryden calls the play "a kind of secular Yom Kippur for his generation of the fifties. In it their faults are confessed, their insincerities admitted, their frittered and waning energies rededicated to the achievement of social justice. . . . I wish I could say the play was as impressive as the intention which churns woolilly behind its almost total lack of action. . . . [Wesker's] real betrayal has been to abandon the role of our most precise social realist for that of a cloudy prophet of uplift."

Michael Kustow believes that Wesker "has suffered unduly from the weight of an undeserved legend [that of a leftist crusader], which has led to superficial readings of his plays, obscuring their real advances of technique and content. The sense of suspension and withdrawal, of inward-turning, in his latest plays and stories is both the natural reassessment of a writer in mid-route, and the enforced, defensiveness . . . of a playwright who seems to have been left out by a head-strong and often mindless theatre, and also made a scapegoat for its unfulfilled promise." Wesker addresses himself to the criticism of his abandonment of his original themes: "There's an argument which says that individual or private pain can have no relevance in a society where man's real tragedies abound inextricably with his social environment. . . . To which I make this reply: if compassion and teaching the possibility of change are two of the many effects of art, a third is this. To remind and reassure people that they're not alone. Not only in their attempt to make a better world, but in their private pains and confusions also."

Several reviewers expressed ambivalent feelings about "The Old Ones," Wesker's play about aging Jewish pensioners. J. W. Lambert writes that the play "has like its predecessor 'The Friends' been given a pretty rough reception, in tones varying from weary contempt to stertorous irritation—and despite all its shortcomings, its loose ends, its repeated losses of dramatic focus, I can't really see why this should have been so. . . . Wesker has written scenes of humanity and understanding I should think any playgoer would be grateful for." Jacob Sonntag believes that "Wesker's achievement is that his characters are accepted, not as some eccentrics arousing one's curiosity, but as real people—unusual perhaps, but real nevertheless. . . . Some critics may find faults in the play's construction, others may consider it too sentimental and vague. . . . Wesker retains his fine sense of dialogue, his compassion, his social involvement, adding to it a newly acquired insight into Jewishness."

Wesker wrote "The Merchant" because he was dissatisfied with the anti-Semitic effect and what he feels was the unrealistic character portrayal of the original Shakespearean play. "The Merchant" received reviews which ranged from very positive to absolute pans. Colin Chambers calls the play "quite out of character with most contemporary drama but full of the dense argumentation inspired by a critical caring love of people, of their knowledge and of their language." Brendan Gill finds it "an ambitious and very intelligent play." Clive Barnes thinks it is "perhaps Wesker's finest play. . . . Most of the writing is brilliant, with masterly sensibility. . . . The play raises issues and risks arguments and it teems with life as a consequence." Conversely, Martin Gottfried calls it "a theoretical and argumentative play with little life force of its own. Its own definitions of anti-Semitism are superficial. Its characters and events exist only to disagree with Shakespeare." John Simon is even more sharp in his attack on the play: " 'The Merchant,' I am afraid, is to 'The Merchant of Venice' what lumpfish is to caviar, or a hot-water bottle to the Gulf Stream." Richard Eder feels comparison of Wesker's play to the original Shakespeare to be invalid. "Wesker has used the same rough elements of plot and the same principal characters—all of them with a widely different human weight and meaning—for a totally original play," Eder writes. He describes his mixed reaction to the play: "It is provocative, generally intelligent and sometimes strained or confused. Its writing has moments of ferocious brilliance and wit; on the other hand, its dramatic structure is weak and its dramatic impact fitful and uncertain. It starts and stops; it repeatedly takes off with a thrill and repeatedly disappears into a cloud bank. There is a general effect of a vision that aims for more than it achieves."

Despite so much negative criticism to Wesker's plays, Leeming feels that he is still developing as a playwright and growing in scope. "Unlike many of his erratic contemporaries, Wesker has steadily improved his mastery of theme and techniques, as the brightness of the early plays give way to a more subtle shading of richer colours," Leeming writes. "The very steadiness of his development so far suggests that he will not waste energy on uncharacteristic dead-end experiments, but will evolve within his own line of continuity. He has always had an ear for dialogue and an assured sense of form; this has been reinforced by a new dramatic poetry while the more awkward moments of exposition and occasional didacticism of the trilogy have been eliminated. The level of simple social dramatist that was initially hung like a millstone round Wesker's neck has necessarily hindered assessment of his far-from-simple plays, but . . . the sheer persuasive quality of his writing must elicit recognition of his stature as dramatist."

The stage play and television versions of "Love Letters on Blue Paper" drew the favorable reviews that Leeming feels Wesker deserves. Jack Tinker calls the play "a towering love story" and Micheline Victor comments that "Wesker is remarkably, and un-Englishably daring [in] his representation of emotion." Michael Billington writes that "what is interesting is the way the emotion of the play bursts through with this very tight rigid form. It's a play, simply, it seems to me, about a kind of human desperation. . . . I thought the pulse and intensity of that emotion worked against the artificiality of the form in a very moving way." Alan Hulme comments that "plays as intensely moving as Arnold Wesker's 'Love Letters on Blue Paper' are very rare. It is a play you will have to learn to live with because once experienced it won't go away." Stephen Biscoe goes even further in his praise of the play: "Apart from anything else 'Love Letters on Blue Paper' proved that great plays are still being written; the quality of a masterpiece was unmistakeable. . . . His play was profound and very moving and set a standard that one hopes other playwrights will attempt to emulate if they can."

BIOGRAPHICAL/CRITICAL SOURCES:

BOOKS

Armstrong, W. A., editor, *Experimental Drama,* G. Bell, 1963.

Contemporary Authors Autobiography Series, Volume 7, Gale, 1988.

Contemporary Literary Criticism, Gale, Volume 3, 1975, Volume 5, 1976, Volume 42, 1987.

Contemporary Theatre, Edward Arnold, 1962.

Dictionary of Literary Biography, Volume 13: *British Dramatists since World War II,* Gale, 1982.

Gindin, James, *Postwar British Fiction,* University of California Press, 1962.

Kitchin, Laurence, *Mid-Century Drama,* Faber, 1960.

Leeming, Glenda, and Simon Trussler, *The Plays of Arnold Wesker,* Gollancz, 1971.

Leeming, Glenda, *Arnold Wesker,* Longman, 1972.

Leeming, Glenda, *Wesker on File,* Methuen, 1985.

Lumley, Frederick, *New Trends in Twentieth Century Drama,* Oxford University Press, 1967.

Ribalow, Harold U., *Arnold Wesker,* Twayne, 1966.

Taylor, John Russell, *Anger and After,* Methuen, 1962.

Wager, Walter, editor, *The Playwrights Speak,* Delacorte, 1967.

Ward, A. C., *Twentieth-Century English Literature, 1901-1960,* Methuen, 1964.

Wellworth, G., *Theatre of Protest and Paradox,* New York University Press, 1965.

PERIODICALS

Antioch Review, winter, 1964-65.

BBC Kaleidoscope, March 3, 1976.

Canadian Forum, July, 1961.

Chicago Tribune, November 15, 1988.

Christian Science Monitor, March 22, 1968, June 6, 1970.

Daily Mail, February 16, 1978.

Drama, winter, 1972.

Globe and Mail (Toronto), November 23, 1985.

Jewish Chronicle, October 20, 1978.

Jewish Quarterly, autumn, 1972.

Listener, May 28, 1970.

Los Angeles Times, January 28, 1979.

Manchester Evening News, December 6, 1978.

Morning Star, October 20, 1978.

Nation, November 19, 1960.

New Review, March, 1975.

New Statesman, August 6, 1965, September 17, 1965, May 29, 1970, August 30, 1974.

New York, December 5, 1977.

New Yorker, March 23, 1968, June 9, 1975, November 14, 1977.

New York Post, November 17, 1977.

New York Times, May 22, 1970, July 14, 1970, August 20, 1970, August 26, 1972, November 8, 1977, November 17, 1977, April 12, 1984, November 12, 1986, November 17, 1986.

Observer Review, May 24, 1970.

Performing Arts Journal, winter, 1978.

Plays and Players, May, 1970, July, 1970, August, 1970, October, 1973, February, 1977, December, 1978.

Saturday Review, May 17, 1975.

Spectator, October 21, 1960, August 10, 1962, August 24, 1974.

Theatre Quarterly, Volume 7, number 28, 1977.

Time, March 22, 1968.

Time Out, March 3, 1978.

Times (London), December 3, 1977, October 17, 1978, July 7, 1983, November 10, 1984, November 14, 1984, November 15, 1984, April 27, 1985, February 19, 1987.

Times Educational Supplement, October 20, 1978.

Times Literary Supplement, November 25, 1960, May 3, 1985, September 6, 1985.

Twentieth Century, February, 1961.

Variety, August 23, 1972, November 23, 1977.
Village Voice, March 21, 1968.
Washington Post, June 1, 1975, February 11, 1980.
Yorkshire Post, March 3, 1976.

*   *   *

WEST, C. P.
See WODEHOUSE, P(elham) G(renville)

*   *   *

WHITE, Theodore H(arold) 1915-1986

PERSONAL: Born May 6, 1915, in Boston, Mass.; died after a stroke, May 9, 1986; son of David and Mary (Winkeller) White; married Nancy Ariana Van Der Heyden Bean, March 29, 1947 (divorced, 1971); married Beatrice Kevitt Hofstadter, March, 1974; children: (first marriage) Ariana Van Der Heyden, David Fairbank. *Education:* Harvard University, A.B. (summa cum laude), 1938.

ADDRESSES: Home—Old Route 67, Bridgewater, Conn. 06752. *Office*—168 East 64th St., New York, N.Y. 10021. *Agent*—Julian Bach Literary Agency, Inc., 747 3rd Ave., New York, N.Y. 10017.

CAREER: Time magazine, New York City, Far East correspondent and chief of China bureau, 1939-45; *New Republic* magazine, New York City, editor, 1947; Overseas News Agency, New York City, chief European correspondent, 1948-50; *Reporter* magazine, New York City, chief European correspondent, 1950-53; *Collier's* magazine, national correspondent, 1955-56; free-lance writer and correspondent, 1956-86. Covered China war front, Indian uprising, and Honan famine during World War II; present at Japanese surrender aboard U.S.S. Missouri, 1945; covered post-World War II European events, including administration of Marshall Plan and North Atlantic Treaty Organization. Member of board of overseers, Harvard University, 1968-74.

MEMBER: Council on Foreign Relations, Foreign Correspondents Club (president, 1944-45), Phi Beta Kappa, Century Club, Harvard Club.

AWARDS, HONORS: Sidney Hillman Foundation Award, 1954, and National Association of Independent Schools Award, 1954, both for *Fire in the Ashes;* Benjamin Franklin Magazine Award, 1956, for article in *Collier's,* "Germany—Friend or Foe?"; Ted V. Rodgers Award, 1956; Pulitzer Prize for general nonfiction, 1962, and National Association of Independent Schools Award, 1962, both for *The Making of the President: 1960;* Emmy Awards, National Academy of Television Arts and Sciences, 1964, for best television film in all categories, for "The Making of the President: 1960," 1967, for best documentary television writing, for "China: The Roots of Madness," and 1985, for best documentary television writing, for "Television and the Presidency"; Fourth Estate Award, National Press Club; Journalist of the Year Award, Columbia School of Journalism; English-Speaking Union Books-Across-the-Sea Ambassador of Honor Books, 1984, for *America in Search of Itself;* honorary doctor of humane letters, Hebrew Union College, 1985; .

WRITINGS:

(With Annalee Jacoby) *Thunder Out of China* (Book-of-the-Month Club selection), Sloane, 1946, reprinted, Da Capo Press, 1980.
(Editor) Joseph Warren Stilwell, *The Stilwell Papers,* Sloane, 1948, reprinted, Schocken, 1972.

Fire in the Ashes (Book-of-the-Month Club selection), Sloane, 1953, reprinted, 1968.
The Mountain Road (Book-of-the-Month Club selection), Sloane, 1958.
The View from the Fortieth Floor (Literary Guild selection), Sloane, 1960.
The Making of the President: 1960, Atheneum, 1961, reprinted as *The Making of the President, 1960: A Narrative History of American Politics in Action,* Macmillan, 1988.
The Making of the President: 1964, Atheneum, 1965.
Caesar at the Rubicon: A Play about Politics, Atheneum, 1968, published as *Caesar at the Rubicon: A Play in Three Acts,* Samuel French, 1971.
China: The Roots of Madness (also see below; revision of television documentary script), Norton, 1968.
The Making of the President: 1968, Atheneum, 1969.
The Making of the President: 1972 (Literary Guild selection), Atheneum, 1973.
Breach of Faith: The Fall of Richard Nixon (Book-of-the-Month Club selection), Atheneum, 1975.
In Search of History: A Personal Adventure (autobiography), Harper, 1978.
America in Search of Itself: The Making of the President 1956-1980, Harper, 1982.

Also author of television documentary scripts, including "The Making of the President: 1960," "China: The Roots of Madness," "The Making of the President: 1968," and "Television and the Presidency," 1985. Contributor to *Life, Time, Fortune, Reporter, Holiday, Harper's, Saturday Review, Collier's, New York, New York Times Magazine,* and other magazines and newspapers.

SIDELIGHTS: With the publication of *The Making of the President: 1960,* his Pulitzer Prize-winning report on the 1960 presidential campaign and election, Theodore White established a tradition of excellence that not only himself but others have found difficult to live up to. Considered by many to be a classic in political journalism, it was, as a *National Observer* critic notes, "a ground-breaking achievement," for "no one before had thought to bring a whole presidential campaign together in a single, lucid, anecdotal, and timely volume." A *San Francisco Chronicle* reviewer called it "the most exhilarating non-fiction of the season. . . . It is both exciting and revealing Americana. . . . A familiar story . . . appears to be new and fresh as White reconstructs it. He does so with brilliance, intelligence and for the most part scrupulous objectivity." Bernard Levin of *Spectator* commented: "Not since Mencken has there been American political reporting of this quality, and Mencken had little of Mr. White's thoroughness and none of his stunningly persuasive objectivity. . . . He produces one of the most exciting and significant pieces of socio-political analysis for years. . . . As journalism [the book] is unsurpassed; as a record and textbook it is invaluable."

James MacGregor Burns, writing in the *New York Times Book Review,* stated: "No book that I know of has caught the heartbeat of a campaign as strikingly as Theodore White has done in *The Making of the President: 1960.* . . . By artistic rearrangement of his materials he has gained space for long, hard appraisals of American politics. . . . If this book were merely a campaign report, it could be recommended glowingly on its own terms. But it is more than this." A *Saturday Review* critic saw it as "an extraordinary performance by a shrewd interpreter of the American scene. . . . It launches what I hope will be a new genre in American political literature. It is sensitive and brilliant reporting, and an invaluable document for history."

Several other critics, however, questioned White's objectivity. Though most had high praise for his overall achievement in reporting on such a complex chain of events, they felt that his partiality towards certain political figures (as well as an accompanying touch of sentimentality about American politics in general) detracted from the book's impact. "Author White strives for objectivity," reported *Time,* "but there is no question whose campaign button adorned his. . . . His coverage of Kennedy is more complete, more successful than his picture of Nixon. . . . A complete analysis of the 1960 campaign will have to await a later day and more penetrating research. As reporting, the book is a notable achievement. White has written a fascinating story of a fascinating campaign." A *Christian Science Monitor* critic agreed that "never has there been as competent, penetrating, and complete account of an American presidential election as this." But, after noting that White was "warmly received" by the Kennedy group while Nixon's "held [him] at arm's length," the reviewer concluded: "[White] struggles manfully to clarify the Nixon character and only partly succeeds. . . . The book is written in the emotional mood of the correspondents traveling with Mr. Kennedy in the last weeks of the campaign, when they expected a landslide. This is a serious flaw, since the meaning of the outcome is greatly overstated."

The Making of the President: 1964 was not as successful as its predecessor, perhaps, as a *National Observer* critic pointed out, "because the campaign itself was less interesting. . . . [White] found no heroes in 1964; like so many others, he saw no romance in Lyndon Johnson or Barry Goldwater." In the *New York Review of Books,* I. F. Stone admitted that "Theodore H. White has become the poet laureate of American presidential campaigns." Nevertheless, he concluded, *The Making of the President: 1964* "is on a lower level" than its predecessor. "The wonder and zest of the first often decline into a schoolgirlish gushiness in the second. The first is muscular, the second mawkish. . . . [Yet] no one could feel a candidate's pulse more sympathetically [than White]." The *New Yorker* noted that "[Mr. White] does quite a good job of it. . . . His method is a compound of diary-keeping, daily journalism, weekly journalism, editorial writing, and extrasensory perception. It is an entertaining mixture, and some of the microscopic details are priceless, but on the whole, it is more White than history." A *Times Literary Supplement* reviewer wrote: "Alas, the 1964 version has all and much more than all the faults of the first book and hardly any of its merits. It is a depressing failure. . . . The *aficionados* of American politics will find a little new information here, some, if too infrequent, patches of Mr. White at his brilliant reporter's best . . . and a good deal of unimpressive political cogitation."

On the other hand, an *Atlantic* reviewer noted: "In *The Making of the President: 1960* Theodore H. White had almost a classical plot with a single action and a single hero. . . . By comparison, 1964 presented a more diffuse and less focused drama. Yet *The Making of the President: 1964* is in many ways a more exciting book, if only because his earlier triumph has sharpened Mr. White's skill at a style of reporting that he seems to have made all his own. . . . His politicians . . . emerge as three-dimensional characters in a way not usual in political reporting."

It was not, however, until the appearance of *The Making of the President: 1968* that critics began to take a long, hard look at White's approach. What had only been mentioned more or less in passing by a few reviewers in 1960 and 1964—namely, White's occasional lack of objectivity as well as his patriotic sentimentality about America and the American political system—became a major problem in the eyes of the 1968 reviewers. A *Commonweal* critic wrote: "Like Harold Stassen, T. H. White is ruining a good thing with his quadrennial lustings after the presidency. . . . This third *Making* book is the plain *reductio ad absurdum* of the first, which—for all its fascination and birth of genre—was conspicuously sanguine on issues and soft on politicians. . . . While White's coziness with the candidates may not have hurt his books all that much in 1960 and 1964 when the old politics still had some kick, he is terribly guilty by his associations in *Making 1968.* . . . The unhappiest feature of *Making 1968* is the reporter's undisguised sympathy for the establishment. . . . Except for the Wallace campaign and the peace movement, basely equated in their extremism, White is all heroes and worship. . . . [But] apart from internal criticism, *Making 1968* fails for large reasons. A single reporter is simply incommensurate with a presidential campaign. . . . 'This is the most dramatic confrontation of America and its problems in over 100 years,' White mused in *Newsweek* before publication. 'It's just a question of whether I'm good enough to write the story for what it's really worth.' He wasn't."

Bill Moyers, writing in *Saturday Review,* noted: "If Theodore White did not exist, the Ford Foundation would have to award Harvard University a grant to create him. How else would the Establishment tell its story? *The Making of the President: 1968* is essentially that: the authorized version, the view through the official keyhole. For Teddy White, the most successful entrepreneur of political detail and perception in American journalism today, tells the story of 1968 as he did four and eight years. . . . But times have changed. . . . 1968 was the Year of Decay. . . . Under such circumstances no single author, not even a Teddy White, could chart the shifting boundaries of our political terrain. That he has tried, against impossible odds, is a tribute to the man's intrepid will. Certainly his is the most coherent and the most eloquent account we are likely to get from any reporter's notes. . . . But there is a tone in it that we are not accustomed to hearing in Teddy White."

"Most of what [he] reports is interesting," continued Moyers, "much of what he does not report is significant. Something is missing because interpreting politics at the top so completely and so officially for eight years had finally caught up with Theodore White. . . . He could not, in honest loyalty as well as by instinct, completely separate himself from the besieged. . . . He could never achieve total freedom from his prejudices. . . . And so White is left with this splendid story, not wholly true. . . . [He] told us what happened at the top, and told it as no one else can. But the top was no longer that important."

A *Time* reviewer wrote: "In two previous chronicles of President-making, Theodore H. White's talents were more than equal to the task. . . . This time the odds were against him. White's best reportage delineates character; portraiture is his forte. In 1968, events overshadowed individuals. . . . White's reconstruction of these events often bears the paste-pot smell of newspaper clippings. . . . His reaction is detached and too concerned with the pattern of the old politics. . . . There are nuggets of anecdotage along the way. . . . [But] after eight years and three elections, White has established his own political system. He has a vast network of friendly power brokers, government aides, trend watchers, reporters, poll takers and precinct vigilantes. This book is almost overwhelmed by his efforts to preserve—and not to offend—this intricate organization."

White's *The Making of the President: 1972* was criticized for virtually the same excesses and deficiencies as the 1968 version. "The rambling chronicle offers few new insights into either the Nixon victory or the McGovern defeat," wrote a *New Republic* reviewer. "Watergate aside, White willingly accepts most of the

Nixon rationale—even on the war. . . . But if the analysis is disappointing, the level of characterization is more gratifying, reflecting the legwork, extensive interviews and careful research involved." Garry Wills of the *New York Review of Books,* noting the author's "indiscriminate celebration of the ruler" (Nixon), concluded that "the 'Whitiad,' now in its second decade, gets worse stanza by stanza. . . . White conducts his old civics lesson without having learned a thing." Finally, Anthony Lewis of the *New York Times* commented: "Theodore H. White is so awesomely diligent a reporter, so accomplished a political analyst, so engaging a person that criticizing him seems like sacrilege. . . . But . . . it is time for someone to say that White has written a bad book. *The Making of the President: 1972* is as impressive as its predecessors in its eye for both the revealing detail and the sweep of events. But White naturally does more than describe. He gives his own judgment on larger historical issues, and there I think he has gone profoundly wrong. . . . Alas, one [also] detects in Theodore White some of that unfortunate pleasure in curling up with the powerful. . . . [As a result,] winners take all in the White universe; and losers get no mercy."

In 1976, restless and unable to apply himself to the task of preparing for and writing *The Making of the President: 1976,* White broke with tradition and turned to writing about himself instead. The result, *In Search of History,* was called "a minor classic of American biography" by the *New Leader.* "It vibrates with the themes most characteristic of national self-discovery," continued the reviewer, "recording the passage from obscurity and poverty to the close observation of power; from facts to ideas, from promise to fulfillment and then to perplexity." But even in his autobiography White came under fire for his lack of objectivity. "The special insignia of White's writing has long been the evocation of sympathy," reported the *New Leader.* "The autobiography is similarly free of rancor. Almost everyone . . . is washed in authorial good will." Furthermore, the reviewer wrote, White's "own sense of politics remains rooted in camaraderie rather than causes, and in attributing to politicians ideas that are really only mental gestures, White once again exaggerates the importance of the men he has covered."

Richard Rovere of the *New York Times Book Review* called *In Search of History* "by far [White's] finest, most affecting work. . . . It has all the pace and energy of the earlier work and more of many other things; more insight, more reflection, more candor, more intimacy, more humor, more humility, surer and sharper judgments of those he writes about, including himself." On the other hand, Christopher Lehmann-Haupt felt that "somewhere in this public autobiography Mr. White seems to lose his way. The first half is extremely strong—the sections covering his youth, his education, and his adventures in China. Here personal experience very nearly equals history. . . . But somehow in the second half, the momentum of White's narrative falters. This isn't to say that vivid close-up portraits of historical figures don't continue to appear. . . . It is simply that when White moves on from China to Europe to witness that continent's post-war recovery, and then back to the United States to report on domestic politics, the center of the action moves away from him. He is no longer really part of the story he is covering, as he was in China. So when he writes about himself he neglects history, and vice versa." Lehmann-Haupt, in addition to several other reviewers, found White's occasional use of the third person when referring to himself to be somewhat distracting. "Nowhere do these passages stop reminding us by their lack of irony and humor how much more successfully this device fares in the hands of Norman Mailer," he concluded.

William Greider of *Book World* stated that, as a reflective memoir, *In Search of History* simply "doesn't work. [White] begins bravely, announcing self-doubts and confusion, but after traveling through many continents and interesting events, glimpsing famous men from Mao to Eisenhower, one is left at the conclusion with the same questions. Readers who loved the powerful narrative line of White's other books will find this one strangely disjointed and unthematic. . . . The memoir ends lamely, acknowledging that he has not really sorted out the fundamental confusions about politics and the nation." Unlike other reviewers, however, Greider did not particularly find the first part of the book to be much better than the last half, noting that "even [White's] memories of wartime China and *Time* are seen through a murky lens," as if he is "unable to address them directly."

Finally, Eric F. Goldman of *Saturday Review* wrote that *In Search of History* "has its less than felicitous moments. It has long been noted that White is a man much given to heroes. . . . Moreover, White, like a number of journalists, throws a special aura around 'history.' . . . In this volume, [the author], anxious to escape what he considers the confines of journalism, at times pauses for a passage that can be disconcerting. . . . Happily, neither White's search for history, nor his proneness for heroes—nor his occasional splashes of neon prose—are major aspects of the book. For the most part, it is a work in the high tradition of American memoirs, written with power and grace of style, many an astute perception, and an attitude toward his country that is at once deeply affectionate, unhesitatingly critical, and engagingly quizzical. . . . White's treatment of his Chinese and European years in this book of memoirs is mellower, [and] more balanced, [than his earlier *Thunder out of China* and *Fire in the Ashes*] and it provides a constant flow of absorbing personal material. More strikingly, *In Search of History* includes frequent incisive, richly human vignettes of the great and not-so-great figures White came to know. . . . White indicates that a second and perhaps third volume of memoirs will follow. . . . If the future volume or volumes maintain the vivid, probing, questing 'storytelling' of the first, and White does not search too hard for 'history,' his total memoirs may well prove one the bench-mark books . . . of our generation."

White's last book, *America in Search of Itself: The Making of the President, 1956-1980,* examines the administrations of Eisenhower through Jimmy Carter, up to the election of Ronald Reagan as president in 1980. The book received comments similar to those for White's other books on presidential elections. "This is a somewhat disjointed volume, because of its dual purpose—to philosophize over recent history and to map a particular moment. White is a better mapmaker than philosopher," noted Paul Barker in the London *Times.* "Mr. White demurs, 'I could not present myself as a historian,' but from the start his tone is something other than reportorial," commented Susan Bolotin in the *New York Times,* adding that White "tends to speak in aphorisms . . . , to categorize in terms of big themes . . . , [and] to look back from a vantage point more opinionated than analytic." Despite these criticisms, Bolotin conceded that White "deserves full credit for his talent as a storyteller" and that "his campaign remembrances are winning."

Upon his death in 1986, White was remembered by Clifton Daniel in the *New York Times* as having "taught the American people more about politics than any writer of his generation." Daniel singled out White's particular talents as being a very good reporter, a historian and scholar, and finally, a storyteller. "The first two qualities made his work sound and unassailable; the third one made it immensely popular," noted Daniel. Suzanne Garment in the *Wall Street Journal* stated that, in addition to his "bringing presidential politics alive with color and personality for his audience of millions," White "told us that American politics was a romantic, glamorous thing and that the glamour lay precisely in the small, pragmatic, grubby details of the professional politician's craft. . . . He made poetry out of the advance work and the delegate counts."

AVOCATIONAL INTERESTS: Woodworking, gardening, and painting.

BIOGRAPHICAL/CRITICAL SOURCES:

BOOKS

White, Theodore H., *In Search of History* (autobiography), Harper, 1978.

PERIODICALS

America, July 17, 1965.
American Heritage, April/May, 1982.
Atlantic, June, 1958, August, 1961, August, 1965, May, 1968.
Best Sellers, May 15, 1968, September 15, 1969, January, 1979.
Books of the Times, August, 1978.
Book Week, July 11, 1965.
Book World, July 14, 1968, July 27, 1969, October 12, 1969, August 27, 1978.
Christian Century, October 1, 1969.
Christian Science Monitor, July 6, 1961, September 4, 1969.
Chicago Tribune Book World, May 16, 1982.
Commentary, September, 1982.
Commonweal, December 8, 1961, August 22, 1969.
Harper's, August, 1965.
Life, June 18, 1965.
Los Angeles Times Book Review, October 15, 1978, May 30, 1982, December 29, 1985.
Maclean's, October 24, 1983.
Nation, October 14, 1978.
National Observer, July 12, 1965, August 18, 1969.
New Leader, October 23, 1978.
New Republic, July 10, 1961, July 10, 1965, August 16, 1969, August 11, 1973, September 9, 1978.
Newsday, June 6, 1978.
New Statesman, April 6, 1962.
Newsweek, January 13, 1969, July 28, 1969, August 13, 1973, August 14, 1978.
New York, September 8, 1969.
New Yorker, June 4, 1960, July 22, 1961, August 7, 1965, September 20, 1969.
New York Herald Tribune Book Review, May 11, 1958, May 22, 1960, July 9, 1961.
New York Post, July 22, 1969.
New York Review of Books, August 5, 1965, October 4, 1973, November 9, 1978.
New York Times, January 2, 1969, July 9, 1969, July 23, 1969, February 21, 1971, August 30, 1973, June 1, 1982.
New York Times Book Review, May 11, 1958, May 22, 1960, July 9, 1961, July 11, 1965, April 14, 1968, September 22, 1968, August 6, 1978, December 24, 1978, May 9, 1982.
Observer, November 23, 1969.
People, July 31, 1978.
Playboy, May, 1968.
San Francisco Chronicle, July 5, 1961, July 6, 1961.
Saturday Review, May 10, 1958, May 21, 1960, July 8, 1961, July 10, 1965, August 9, 1969, October 9, 1973, September 2, 1978.
Spectator, April 6, 1962, December 6, 1969, May 2, 1970.

Time, May 23, 1960, July 21, 1961, March 29, 1968, August 1, 1969, July 3, 1978, May 17, 1982.
Times (London), May 19, 1983.
Times Literary Supplement, December 2, 1960, November 4, 1965, June 10, 1983.
Us, October 17, 1978.
Virginia Quarterly Review, autumn, 1969.
Washington Post, August 11, 1969.
Washington Post Book World, May 9, 1982, January 5, 1986.

OBITUARIES:

PERIODICALS

Chicago Sun Times, May 17, 1986.
Chicago Tribune, May 17, 1986, May 22, 1986.
Globe and Mail (Toronto), May 17, 1986.
Newsweek, May 26, 1986.
New York Times, May 17, 1986, May 21, 1986.
Time, May 26, 1986.
Times (London), May 17, 1986.
Wall Street Journal, May 26, 1986.
Washington Post, May 17, 1986.

*   *   *

WILLIAMS, Charles
See COLLIER, James L(incoln)

*   *   *

WILLIAMS, J. Walker
See WODEHOUSE, P(elham) G(renville)

*   *   *

WILLIAMS, Raymond (Henry)   1921-1988

PERSONAL: Born August 31, 1921, in Abergavenny, Wales; son of Henry Joseph and Gwendolen (Bird) Williams; married Joyce Mary Dalling, June 19, 1942; children: Merryn, Ederyn, Gwydion Madawc. *Education:* Trinity College, Cambridge, M.A., 1946. *Politics:* Socialist. *Religion:* None.

ADDRESSES: Home—White Cottage, Hardwick, Cambridge, England. *Office*—Jesus College, Cambridge University, Cambridge, England.

CAREER: Oxford University Delegacy for Extra-Mural Studies, Oxford, England, staff tutor in literature, 1946-61; Cambridge University, Jesus College, Cambridge, England, 1961-83, fellow, lecturer in English studies, director of English studies, became professor of drama, 1974-83. Visiting professor at Stanford and Open universities. *Military service:* British Army, Guards Armoured Division, 1941-45; became captain.

MEMBER: Welsh Academy, Welsh Arts Council.

AWARDS, HONORS: Welsh Arts Council Prize for Fiction, 1979, for *The Fight for Manod;* D.Litt. from the University of Wales, 1980.

WRITINGS:

Reading and Criticism, Muller, 1950.
Drama from Ibsen to Eliot, Chatto & Windus, 1952, Columbia University Press, 1954, revised edition, Penguin, 1964, new edition published as *Drama from Ibsen to Brecht,* Chatto & Windus, 1968, Oxford University Press, 1969.
Drama in Performance, Muller, 1954, 3rd edition, Penguin, 1973.

Culture and Society, 1780-1950, Chatto & Windus, 1958, Harper, 1966.
Border Country, Chatto & Windus, 1960, Horizon, 1961.
The Long Revolution, Chatto & Windus, 1961, Harper, 1966.
Communications, Penguin, 1961.
Second Generation, Chatto & Windus, 1964.
Modern Tragedy, Stanford University Press, 1966.
(Editor) *Pelican Book of Prose,* Volume II: *From 1780 to the Present Day,* Penguin, 1970.
The English Novel from Dickens to Lawrence, Chatto & Windus, 1970.
(Editor) *George Orwell,* Viking, 1971.
The Country and the City, Oxford University Press, 1973.
Television: Technology and Cultural Form, Fontana, 1973.
Keywords: A Vocabulary of Culture and Society, Oxford University Press, 1976.
Marxism and Literatuure, Oxford University Press, 1977.
The Volunteers, Methuen, 1978.
(With Marie Axton) *English Drama: Forms and Development,* 1978.
The Fight for Manod, Chatto & Windus, 1979.
Politics and Letters, Verso, 1979.
Problems in Materialism and Culture, Verso, 1980.
Writing in Society, Verso, 1983.
Towards 2000, Chatto & Windus, 1983.
Loyalties, Chatto & Windus, 1985.
Resources of Hope, edited by Robin Gable, Verso, 1989.
The Politics of Modernism, edited by Tony Pinkney, Verso, 1989.
What I Came to Say, Century Hutchinson, 1989.

Also author of *Culture,* 1981; editor of *Contact: The History of Human Communications,* 1981. Television plays produced by British Broadcasting Corp. (BBC) include "Letter from the Country," 1966, and "Public Inquiry," 1967. General editor, "New Thinkers' Library," 1961-70.

AVOCATIONAL INTERESTS: Gardening.

BIOGRAPHICAL/CRITICAL SOURCES:

BOOKS

Dictionary of Literary Biography, Volume 14: *British Novelists Since 1960,* Gale, 1983.

PERIODICALS

Times (London), October 20, 1983, February 23, 1989.
Times Literary Supplement, November 4, 1983, November 3-9, 1989.
Voice Literary Supplement, April, 1985.

OBITUARIES:

PERIODICALS

New York Times, January 29, 1988.
Times (London), January 27, 1988.

*   *   *

WILSON, Colin 1931-

PERSONAL: Born June 26, 1931, in Leicester, England; son of Arthur (a factory worker) and Anetta (Jones) Wilson; married Dorothy Betty Troop, 1951 (divorced, 1952); married Pamela Joy Stewart (a librarian), 1960; children: (first marriage) Roderick; (second marriage) Sally, John Damon, Christopher Rowan. *Education:* Attended schools in Leicester until he was sixteen. *Politics:* "Moderate right." *Religion:* "My deepest interest is religion. My deepest need—to create my own."

ADDRESSES: Home and office—Tetherdown, Gorran Haven, Cornwall, England. *Agent*—Georges Borchardt, 136 East 57th St., New York, N.Y. 10022.

CAREER: Writer. Employed by Cranbourne Products Ltd. (wool company), Leicester, England, 1947; laboratory assistant at Gateway Secondary Technical School, 1947-48; tax collector, 1947-49; held various jobs as laborer and office worker; hospital porter in Fulham, England; spent some time in Paris and Strasbourg in the early 1950s, working in Paris on *Merlin* and *Paris Review,* 1954; lecturer in American universities. Writer in residence, Hollins College, 1966-67; visiting professor, University of Washington, 1967-68, Rutgers University, 1974. *Military service:* Royal Air Force, 1949-50; became aircraftman second grade.

MEMBER: Society of Authors, Gentleman's Club (St. Austell, Cornwall), Savage Club (London).

AWARDS, HONORS: Ford Foundation grant, 1961.

WRITINGS:

NONFICTION

The Outsider, Houghton, 1956.
Religion and the Rebel, Houghton, 1957, revised edition, Salem House, 1984.
(Contributor) Tom Maschler, editor, *Declaration,* Dutton, 1958, reprinted, Kennikat, 1972.
The Stature of Man, Houghton, 1959, reprinted, Greenwood Press, 1986 (published in England as *Age of Defeat,* Gollancz, 1959).
The Strength to Dream: Literature and the Imagination, Houghton, 1962, reprinted, Greenwood Press, 1973.
Origins of the Sexual Impulse, Putnam, 1962.
(With Patricia Pitman) *An Encyclopedia of Murder,* Putnam, 1962.
Rasputin and the Fall of the Romanovs, Farrar, Straus, 1964.
The Brandy of the Damned: Discoveries of a Musical Eclectic (essays on music), John Baker, 1964, published as *Chords and Discords: Purely Personal Opinions on Music,* Atheneum, 1966, published as *Colin Wilson on Music,* Pan, 1967.
Beyond the Outsider: The Philosophy of the Future, Houghton, 1965.
Eagle and Earwig (essays on literature), John Baker, 1965.
Introduction to the New Existentialism, Hutchinson, 1966, Houghton, 1967.
Sex and the Intelligent Teenager, Arrow, 1966.
(Author of introduction) James Drought, *Drugoth,* new edition, Skylight Press, 1966.
Voyage to a Beginning: An Intellectual Autobiography, Crown, 1969.
(Contributor) James F. T. Bugental, editor, *Challenges of Humanistic Psychology,* McGraw, 1967.
Bernard Shaw: A Reassessment, Atheneum, 1969.
A Casebook of Murder, Ferwin, 1969, Cowles, 1970.
Poetry and Mysticism, City Lights, 1969, expanded edition, Hutchinson, 1970.
(With J. B. Pick and E. H. Visiak) *The Strange Genius of David Lindsay,* John Baker, 1970, published as *The Haunted Man: The Strange Genius of David Lindsay,* Borgo Press, 1979.
The Occult: A History, Random House, 1971.
(With Piero Rimaldi) *L'Amour: The Ways of Love,* Crown, 1972.
New Pathways in Psychology: Maslow and the Post-Freudian Revolution, Taplinger, 1972.
Order of Assassins: The Psychology of Murder, Hart-Davis, 1972.

(Author of introduction) Alexander Garfield Kelly, *Jack the Ripper: A Bibliography and Review of the Literature,* Association of Assistant Librarians (London), 1973.

Tree by Tolkien, Covent Garden Press, 1973, Capra, 1974.

Strange Powers, Latimer New Dimensions, 1973, Random House, 1975.

A Book of Booze, Gollancz, 1974.

Hesse-Reich-Borges, Leaves of Grass Press, 1974.

The Craft of the Novel, Gollancz, 1975, reprinted, Ashgrove, 1985.

The Unexplained, edited by Robert Durand and Roberta Dyer, Lost Pleiade Press, 1975.

(Editor) Valeri Briussov, *Fiery Angel,* Neville Spearman, 1976.

Men of Strange Powers, Doubleday, 1976, published with *Minds without Boundaries,* by Stuart Holroyd, as *Mysteries of the Mind,* Aldus Books, 1978.

Enigmas and Mysteries, Doubleday, 1976.

The Geller Phenomena, Doubleday, 1976.

(Editor) *Dark Dimensions: A Celebration of the Occult,* Everest House, 1978.

Mysteries: An Investigation into the Occult, the Paranormal, and the Supernatural, Putnam, 1978.

Science Fiction as Existentialism, Bran's Head Books, 1978.

(With George Hay) *Necronomicon,* Spearman, 1978.

Starseekers, Hodder & Stoughton, 1980.

Frankenstein's Castle: The Double Brain-Door to Wisdom, Ashgrove, 1980, published as *Frankenstein's Castle: The Right Brain-Door to Wisdom,* Salem House, 1982.

The War against Sleep: The Philosophy of Gurdjieff, Aquarian Press, 1980, revised edition published as *G. I. Gurdjieff: The War against Sleep,* Newcastle, 1986.

The Quest for Wilheim Reich, Doubleday, 1981.

Anti Sartre: With an Essay on Camus, Borgo, 1981.

(Editor with John Grant) *The Directory of Possibilities,* W. H. Smith, 1981.

Poltergeist!, New English Library, 1981.

Witches, Dragon's World, 1981.

(Editor with Donald Seaman) *Encyclopaedia of Modern Murder,* Barker, 1983, published as *The Encyclopedia of Modern Murder: 1962- 1982,* Putnam, 1985.

Access to Inner Worlds, Rider, 1983.

A Criminal History of Mankind, Putnam, 1984.

Janus Murder Case, Granada, 1984.

Psychic Detectives: Story of Psychometry and the Paranormal in Crime Detection, Pan Books, 1984, Mercury House, 1986.

Lord of the Underworld: Jung and the Twentieth Century, Aquarian Press, 1984.

Rudolf Steiner: The Man and His Vision, Aquarian Press, 1984.

Bicameral Critic: Collected Shorter Writings, edited by Howard F. Dossor, Ashgrove, 1985.

Life Force, Warner Books, 1985.

Afterlife, Harrap, 1985, Doubleday, 1987.

The Essential Colin Wilson, Harrap, 1985, Celestial Arts, 1986.

(With Ted Holiday) *The Goblin Universe,* Llewellyn, 1986.

Existentially Speaking: Essays on Philosophy and Literature, Borgo, 1986.

(With Seaman) *Scandal!: An Encyclopedia,* Stein & Day, 1986.

The Laurel and Hardy Theory of Consciousness, Rob Briggs, 1986.

The Encyclopedia of Unsolved Mysteries, State Mutual Books, 1987.

Aleister Crowley: The Nature of the Beast, Sterling, 1988.

The Magician from Siberia, State Mutual Books, 1988.

The Mammoth Book of True Crime, Carroll & Graf, 1988.

(With Damon Wilson) *The Encyclopedia of Unsolved Mysteries,* Contemporary Books, 1988.

Beyond the Occult: A Twenty Year Investigation into the Paranormal, Carroll & Graf, 1989.

The Misfits: A Study of Sexual Outsiders, Carroll & Graf, 1989.

FICTION

Ritual in the Dark, Houghton, 1960, reprinted, Academy Chicago, 1982.

Adrift in Soho, Houghton, 1961.

The Violent World of Hugh Greene, Houghton, 1963 (published in England as *The World of Violence,* Gollancz, 1963).

The Sex Diary of Gerard Sorme, Dial, 1963 (published in England as *Man without a Shadow: The Diary of an Existentialist,* Barker, 1963).

Necessary Doubt, Simon & Schuster, 1964.

The Mind Parasites, Barker, 1966, Arkham, 1967, 3rd edition, Oneiric, 1972.

The Glass Cage: An Unconventional Detective Story, Barker, 1966, Random House, 1967.

The Philosopher's Stone, John Baker, 1969, Crown, 1971.

The Killer, New English Library, 1970, published as *Lingard,* Crown, 1970.

The God of the Labyrinth, Hart-Davis, 1970, published as *The Hedonists,* New American Library, 1971.

The Black Room, Weidenfeld & Nicolson, 1971, Pyramid Publications, 1975.

The Schoolgirl Murder Case, Crown, 1974.

(Contributor) *Tales of the Cthulu Mythos,* Arkharn House, 1974.

The Space Vampires, Hart-Davis, 1975, Random House, 1976.

The Personality Surgeon, Mercury House, 1986.

Spider World: The Tower, Grafton, 1987.

The Sex Diary of a Metaphysician, Ronin, 1988.

Spider World: The Desert, Ace Books, 1988.

Spider World: Fortress, Ace Books, 1989.

PLAYS

Strindberg: Playscript 31 (first produced as "Pictures in a Bath of Acid" in Leeds, Yorkshire, 1971; produced as "Strindberg: A Psychological Portrait" in New York City, 1974), J. Calder, 1970, Random House, 1971.

Also author of "Viennese Interlude," produced in Scarborough, Yorkshire, and London, 1960, "The Metal Flower Blossom," 1960, and "The Death of God," 1966.

OTHER

Editor, "Occult" series, Aldus Books, 1975. Contributor to *Encounter, Time and Tide, London Magazine, Chicago Review,* and other periodicals.

Wilson's books have been translated into more than fourteen languages. A collection of Wilson's manuscripts can be found in Austin Texas, at the University of Texas.

WORK IN PROGRESS: Lulu, a novel.

SIDELIGHTS: For more than thirty years author Colin Wilson has concerned himself with a reexamination of modern philosophy and with the amelioration of the human condition. His body of work includes nonfiction, novels, biographies, plays, and encyclopedic investigations of crime and the occult. Wilson has often stirred controversy by imbuing his philosophical works—and his fiction—with a sense of urgency and the strong conviction that human consciousness is slumbering or limited to a "tunnel vision" far short of its potential. In *Colin Wilson: The Outsider and Beyond,* Clifford P. Bendau writes: "The essence of Wilson's position is that man can and must expand the present modes of consciousness. His casebook studies are meant to give people an idea of what can be developed. The phenomenon of man's resignation to littleness is used to show the reader that man is perceptually aware of very little; but moreover, that man is conscious or unconsciously *choosing* not to be aware."

Wilson published his first book, *The Outsider*, at the age of twenty-four. His writings since then have expanded upon the theme he introduced in that work, the premise that "with the development of the Romantic Movement in art, literature, and philosophy, a group of outstanding individuals has developed who are no longer satisfied with the dead-end streets of scientific or existentialist thought," according to Martha Eckman in *The Contemporary Literary Scene 1973*. In his philosophical works subsequent to *The Outsider*, including *Religion and the Rebel, The Stature of Man*, and *Beyond the Outsider: The Philosophy of the Future*, Wilson posits a kind of "optimistic existentialism" that places importance on intuition and visionary experiences. Though Wilson's ideas have met with criticism and derision at times, John A. Weigel, in his book *Colin Wilson*, notes that recent changes in the philosophical climate "have redefined Wilson's significance as a thinker who has persistently challenged pessimism and despair." Weigel also contends that Wilson "is to be credited with the courage to rebel against deterministic philosophies and to insist that man is free to improve himself and his community *if he wants to*. In one sense, Colin Wilson is both heroic and inevitable. As a freedom-espousing philosopher, he chose for himself a big job, . . . to diagnose and to cure mankind's sickness."

As Weigel notes in the *Dictionary of Literary Biography*, Wilson also "firmly believes that fiction is an appropriate vehicle for exploring philosophical concerns." Bendau similarly states: "Wilson's fiction is didactic. It is the nature of his style to make fiction and nonfiction complementary as instructional devices; an unusual, but not illegitimate technique aimed concurrently at different sensibilities in the reader." Indeed, Wilson utilizes a variety of fiction genres to promote his ideas, among them psychological thrillers, science fiction, and murder mysteries. Some of his best-known novels fall into the science fiction/fantasy category, including *The Mind Parasites, The Philosopher's Stone*, and *The Space Vampires*. In *Colin Wilson*, Weigel writes: "For Wilson, fantasy is highly useful as a relatively unblinkered kind of storytelling, for he writes neither to delight nor to solace. He packs his parables with his own experiences and speculations. Since Wilson has a difficult message to communicate he needs all the help he can get in the way of supportive mysteries and heuristic fantasies." Weigel also comments that while none of Wilson's fiction "has that kind of inevitability which awes literary critics" it is nonetheless "honestly adequate to its purpose." According to Bendau, Wilson's writing "always works well when he chooses subjects that can carry his philosophical weight, when he builds on philosophical foundations that galvanize his fiction with the nonfiction."

On one point Wilson's champions and detractors concur; namely, that his prodigious literary output stands as testament to his seriousness of purpose. He has authored more than eighty books since 1956 and has supported himself primarily by writing for thirty years. During that time he has maintained a high degree of confidence in his talent and ideas, even in the face of severe criticism.

The notion that he was destined for recognition sustained Wilson even before he was published, as he notes in his 1969 autobiography *Voyage to a Beginning*. While still in his early teens he began

to feel superior to the "vegetable mediocrity" of his working-class Leicester background. According to Weigel, Wilson "*chose* greatness, feeling rightfully that his choice was limited to that or nothing; and he wasted little time in getting started in his pursuit of it." An early interest in science lasted until Wilson graduated from secondary school. Then he discovered literature and determined that he wanted to be a writer. As he notes in an essay for *Declaration*, however, many impediments stood in the way of his goals. "My problem," he claims, "became simply the problem of how to find leisure to read and think and write, when my circumstances made it necessary to work forty-eight hours a week to live." After drifting through a series of jobs and apartments, Wilson took the desperate measure of sleeping outdoors on London's Hampstead Heath in order to save money. During the day he read and wrote in the British Museum Reading Room, where author Angus Wilson took an interest in his work.

In *Declaration*, Wilson states that he conceived the idea for *The Outsider* when he was nineteen, but work on a novel (later published as *Ritual in the Dark*) postponed his ambitions for the nonfiction. He began writing *The Outsider* in 1955, culling ideas from his diaries and from an eclectic sampling of books he had read. In *Voyage to a Beginning* he describes the central concern of the work as "the misfits in modern civilization, the creative men who feel out of place in the rat race." He adds: "But I took care to state that the Outsider is not necessarily creative. His lack of self-understanding may be so complete that he never even begins to achieve the catharsis of creation." Using case studies from fiction by Hermann Hesse, Ernest Hemingway, and Fedor Dostoevski, as well as exploring the lives of painter Vincent Van Gogh and the dancer Vaslav Nijinski, Wilson delineates the troubles of the "Outsider," an individual at odds with himself and his conventional social environment. Wilson admits that he was so excited about the book he was writing that he noted in his journal: "This book will be the *Waste Land* of the fifties, and should be the most important book of its generation." Victor Gollancz published the work in May of 1956.

Critical reaction to *The Outsider* followed a "spectacular parabola," notes Kenneth Allsop in *The Angry Decade: A Survey of the Cultural Revolt of the 1950s*. As Allsop describes it, Wilson rose "from out of nowhere (or, to be precise, from out of a sleeping bag on Hampstead Heath) up through a dizzying arc of fame and fortune, with a steep nose-dive into disfavour." At first the popular media "enthusiastically endorsed young Colin Wilson as a genius," according to Weigel in his book on the author. For instance, *Observer* contributor Philip Toynbee called *The Outsider* "an exhaustive and luminously intelligent study of a representative theme of our time . . . truly astounding . . . a real contribution to an understanding of our deepest predicament." Other reviewers offered similar praise, and the book became a bestseller in England and the United States. Wilson, who had long labored in poverty and anonymity, was accorded celebrity status, but the publicity was not always of a positive nature. He was misquoted on several occasions, and a domestic dispute with his fiancee's family provided a scandal that was "of exactly the right palate for the popular Press," in Allsop's words. Within six months of *The Outsider*'s publication, critics began to reevaluate it—and its author—with less-than-flattering results. Wilson was called to task for his excessive quotations from other sources, for his disregard of formal philosophical method, and for the stridency of his assertions. Dismayed by the change in the critical climate, Wilson moved to a cottage in Cornwall and continued to write. By the end of 1956, notes Weigel, the young author "had fully sampled the equivocal flavor of success."

Wilson claims in *Voyage to a Beginning* that after his second book *Religion and the Rebel* was "hatcheted to death" by the critics, his name got mentioned "if someone needed a symbol of intellectual pretentiousness, or unfounded generalization, or an example of how hysteria can make a reputation overnight." He adds: "I must admit that during the 1956-58 period I felt badly treated. On the other hand, I've always had an optimistic temperament, a basic feeling that the gods mean well by me, as well as several years' training in getting on with the work in hand and ignoring other people. . . . I think things worked out well. The feeling that no one much cared about what I was doing led me to give my full attention to the task of creating a new form of existentialism." Martha Eckman breaks Wilson's "new existentialism" down into two components: "(1) that consciousness needs to be expanded by an act of *will*—not through hallucinogens and not through the trance state achieved by a number of religious groups—and (2) that there is *meaning* in the evolving world, as opposed to the popular existential view that planet Earth is a meaningless, accidental, and absurd fiasco." From this viewpoint, notes Weigel, "Wilson prepares the case for the desirability of increasing the duration as well as the frequency of liberating experiences."

The controversy over the viability of Wilson's message continues, though the tone of the criticism is more subdued. In a *Times Literary Supplement* assessment of *Introduction to the New Existentialism,* a reviewer states: "It seems a pity that someone so widely read and so obviously intelligent should not bother to understand something, at least, of what professional philosophers have been doing for the past few decades. If Mr. Wilson could add something of their patience, respect for fact, and dislike of vagueness to his own quite impressive armoury of insight, perceptiveness and enthusiasm, he might write something which would persuade reasonable men rather than merely reflecting the crises of identity, alienation, neurosis, hopelessness or however we care to describe the modern malaise." *Saturday Review* contributor Emile Capouya calls Wilson's philosophical works "a chaos of definite assertions." The critic continues: "It is not so much that [Wilson] is vague, . . . but that he is arbitrary. He will set out premises lucidly enough, and then draw conclusions from other, unmentioned premises, or perhaps arrive at them by parthenogenesis. His examples do not exemplify. His demonstrations are less than conclusive. He abounds in private formulas and talismans. . . . These peculiarities make Mr. Wilson damnably hard to follow, and easy to praise or blame. They account for the fact that his critics have most often been provoked to narrow-minded strictures or else to vaporous enthusiasm." Capouya concludes that the author's "trees are freaks of nature, but his woods have nevertheless a certain comeliness."

While some critics express dissatisfaction with Wilson's writings, others find him a seminal thinker with an innovative form of expression. "Wilson is not a stylist," writes Weigel in *Colin Wilson,* "therefore, his most significant effects are seldom achieved with the delicate nuances or with pastel epiphanies. . . . He has always been concerned about his effectiveness as a writer, but his objective is not to find the irreducible form of an idea, for he is a persuader rather than a poet." Bendau offers the opinion that Wilson has been criticized because his analyses do not follow the formal guidelines of academic writing. "In some respects, the critics are right," Bendau contends. "When subjected to analysis, [Wilson's] arguments often fall short. Isolated from the whole, individual works may appear to be hasty generalizations. But logical analysis and isolated dissection, while valid for criticism, do not justify a complete rejection of Wilson's ideas. These are not the only criteria available. . . . Unlike the scientist or

mathematician, he is not interested in discovering universal theoretical truths. He is interested in the particulars of existence, here and now. He is oriented practically to the way reality could and should be. . . . In short, Wilson [is] a pioneer in the interdisciplinary approach to problem solving; he could never justify the separation of philosophy from art or literature." Weigel concludes: "Presenting himself as a prophet of reality, Wilson has always believed that his work has the highest kind of significance. . . . His confidence is usually more reassuring than the demure modesty of more timid candidates for significance." Eckman makes a more succinct statement when she comments: "My contention is that *The Outsider* contains the key idea to understanding the twentieth century."

More recently, much of Wilson's best-known nonfiction concerns the occult and paranormal phenomena, or investigations of violent crimes. Once again, according to *Washington Post* reviewer Christopher Bird, readers of Wilson's works on the occult are called upon "to adjust their thinking to worlds beyond the bleakly materialist and limited version of the cosmos presently expounded by mainstream science." In *Colin Wilson,* Weigel notes that Wilson "emerges as one of the first of the intellectuals interested in the validity of paraintellectual events such as hunches and premonitions." Alan Hull Walton makes a similar observation in *Books and Bookmen,* where he suggests that Wilson fits in "the top rank of serious contemporary investigators of the paranormal." Wilson is also fascinated with murder as a sort of negative art that some desperate people employ in order to escape boredom and triviality. His approach in nonfiction, according to Bendau, "is to splash his readers in the face with enough cold water to rouse them from their passivity, and generate an active interest in their own freedom." *New York Times Book Review* contributor Allen J. Hubin suggests that Wilson's *A Casebook of Murder* "does set murder into quite useful social and historical perspective."

In his essay for *Declaration,* Wilson makes the assertion that the modern artist "must cease to be the limp, impassive observer. He must become actively involved in the task of restoring a metaphysical consciousness to this age." Throughout his ever-growing canon Wilson strives to put this conviction into action, uniting "the truth of religion with the truth of science in a hopeful and progressive manner," according to *Chicago Review* contributor Richard Hack. As Walton notes in *Books and Bookmen,* Wilson "is a controversial writer. Inescapably so; since in an age of talented mediocrity, he is blessed with far more than talent—he is blessed with insight, sincerely, humility [and] extraordinarily wide learning." In *Hollins Critic,* R. H. W. Dillard finds the same strengths in Wilson's fiction. "If doing and being are somehow one," Dillard writes, "[Wilson's] novels, with their developing manner and matter, their movement toward a viable existential realism of inner as well as outer truth, show Colin Wilson to be a . . . man of real vision who has never ceased to grow." Kenneth Allsop offers this final assessment of Wilson's accomplishments: "Throughout Wilson's writing, despite its brashness and want of precision, there is a general dynamic synthesis: you know what he is getting at, and although there is an ugly look about some of the methods he seems prepared to use, you can accept the ultimate object, which is, fundamentally, a richer spiritual life for man."

AVOCATIONAL INTERESTS: Collecting opera records, mathematics.

BIOGRAPHICAL/CRITICAL SOURCES:

BOOKS

Aldridge, John W., *Time to Murder and Create: The Contemporary Novel in Crisis,* McKay, 1966.

Allsop, Kenneth, *The Angry Decade: A Survey of the Cultural Revolt of the 1950s,* Peter Owen Ltd., 1958.

Bendau, Clifford P., *Colin Wilson: The Outsider and Beyond,* Borgo, 1979.

Bugental, James F. T., editor, *Challenges of Humanistic Psychology,* McGraw, 1967.

Campion, Sidney R., *The World of Colin Wilson,* Muller, 1962.

Contemporary Authors, Autobiography Series, Volume 5, Gale, 1987.

Contemporary Literary Criticism, Gale, Volume 3, 1975, Volume 14, 1980.

Dictionary of Literary Biography, Volume 14: *British Novelists since 1960,* Gale, 1983.

Gindin, James, *Postwar British Fiction: New Accents and Attitudes,* University of California Press, 1962.

Holroyd, Stuart, *Flight and Pursuit: A Venture into Autobiography,* Gollancz, 1959.

Magill, Frank N., editor, *The Contemporary Literary Scene 1973,* Salem Press, 1974.

Maschler, Tom, editor, *Declaration,* Dutton, 1958, reprinted, Kennikat, 1972.

Weigel, John A., *Colin Wilson,* Twayne, 1975.

Wilson, Colin, *Voyage to a Beginning: An Intellectual Autobiography,* Crown, 1969.

PERIODICALS

American Poetry Journal, January/February, 1973.
American Scholar, fall, 1971.
Antioch Review, summer, 1969.
Atlantic, December, 1959, March, 1960, May, 1967, January, 1972, July, 1974.
Book List, June 1, 1976.
Books and Bookmen, January, 1970, December, 1971, March, 1979.
Book World, July 12, 1970.
Chicago Review, winter, 1972.
Chicago Sunday Tribune, April 10, 1960.
Chicago Sunday Tribune Books Today, August 30, 1964.
Choice, April, 1972.
Christian Century, March 24, 1965, April 5, 1967.
Christian Science Monitor, November 14, 1957, December 24, 1959, September 24, 1964, September 4, 1969.
Commonweal, April 1, 1960.
Critic, October, 1974.
Economist, November 6, 1971.
Encounter, August, 1962.
English Record, October, 1967.
Harper's, November, 1961, October, 1962, November, 1963.
Hollins Critic, October, 1967.
Illustrated London News, October, 1978.
Library Journal, October 15, 1964, October 1, 1966.
Life, October 1, 1956, December 13, 1971.
Listener, September 7, 1961, February 16, 1967, May 21, 1970.
London Evening News, May 24, 1956.
Los Angeles Times, March 12, 1981.
Los Angeles Times Book Review, May 9, 1982.
Magazine of Fantasy and Science Fiction, January, 1968, August, 1972.
Manchester Guardian, February 9, 1967.
Nation, August 25, 1956, April 16, 1960.

National Review, December 2, 1961, November 9, 1979.
New Republic, February 1, 1960, May, 1962, November 22, 1969.
New Statesman, September 5, 1959, March 5, 1960, May 24, 1963, June 14, 1963, March 20, 1964, December 11, 1964, January 15, 1965, June 27, 1966, June 26, 1970, December 22, 1978, December 29, 1978.
Newsweek, December 17, 1956, March 14, 1960, July 21, 1969.
New Yorker, August 20, 1960, June 3, 1967, November 29, 1969, September 16, 1974.
New York Herald Tribune Book Review, November 24, 1957, March 6, 1960.
New York Review of Books, December 31, 1964.
New York Times Book Review, July 1, 1956, November 15, 1959, March 6, 1960, October 15, 1961, December 13, 1964, July 30, 1967, November 9, 1969, June 14, 1970, January 28, 1973, July 21, 1974.
Observer, May 27, 1956, September 18, 1966.
Punch, November 6, 1963, October 5, 1966, February 8, 1967, May 29, 1974.
San Francisco Chronicle, March 13, 1960.
Saturday Review, September 8, 1956, December 19, 1959, March 12, 1960, March 20, 1965, November 15, 1969, January 15, 1972.
Science Fiction Review, February, 1970.
Spectator, June 15, 1956, December 22, 1961, April 27, 1962, January 29, 1965, June 28, 1969, May 30, 1970, June 27, 1970, November 6, 1971.
Temps Modernes (Paris), August 14, 1958.
Time, July 2, 1956, March 7, 1960, May 31, 1963.
Times (London), March 20, 1986.
Times Literary Supplement, June 8, 1956, October 25, 1957, September 4, 1959, June 14, 1963, February 27, 1964, January 28, 1965, November 3, 1966, January 26, 1967, July 10, 1969, November 6, 1969, November 27, 1969, June 18, 1970, February 5, 1971, November 26, 1971, December 8, 1972, April 26, 1974, June 14, 1974.
Twentieth Century (London), June, 1960.
Wall Street Journal, June 17, 1976.
Washington Post, December 24, 1978, January 29, 1981.
Washington Post Book World, March 18, 1973, December 24, 1978, June 24, 1984.*

* * *

WINDHAM, Basil
   See WODEHOUSE, P(elham) G(renville)

* * *

WIRT, Sherwood Eliot 1911-

PERSONAL: Born March 12, 1911, in Oakland, CA; son of Loyal L. and Harriet (Benton) Wirt; married Winola Wells, July 2, 1940 (deceased); married Ruth Love, August 29, 1987; children: Alexander. *Education:* University of California, Berkeley, B.A., 1932; Pacific School of Religion, B.D. (cum laude), 1943; graduate study at Princeton Theological Seminary, 1943, Hartford Theological Seminary, 1944, and University of Zurich, 1950; University of Edinburgh, Ph.D., 1951.

ADDRESSES: Home—14140 Mazatlan Ct., Poway, CA 92064

CAREER: Writer for *Contra Costa Gazette,* Martinez, CA, *Hilo Tribune Herald,* Hilo, HI, *San Francisco Examiner,* San Francisco, CA, *Alaska Daily Press,* Juneau, AK. Ordained minister of Congregational church, Collinsville, CT, 1943; minister to students, University of Washington, Seattle, 1946-49; received into Presbyterian Church U.S.A., 1951; minister in Berkeley CA, 1951-55, and Oakland, 1955-59; editorial associate, *Christianity Today,* Washington, D.C., 1960; editor, *Decision* magazine, Minneapolis, MN, 1960-76; taught journalism, Fuller Theological Seminary, Point Loma Nazarene College, Talbot Theological Seminary, Christian Heritage College, 1976-1985. *Military service:* U.S. Merchant Marine, 1933-34, U.S. Army Air Corps chaplain, 1944-46; served in Asiatic-Pacific theater.

AWARDS, HONORS: ECPA Gold Medallion for *Spiritual Awakening.*

WRITINGS:

Crusade at the Golden Gate, Harper, 1959.
Open Your Bible, Revell, 1962.
Magnificent Promise, Moody, 1964.
Not Me, God, Harper, 1966.
The Social Conscience of the Evangelical, Harper, 1968.
Passport to Life City, Harper, 1969.
(Translator) *Love Song* (an adaptation of St. Augustine's *Confessions*), Harper, 1971.
Jesus Power, Harper, 1972.
Afterglow, Zondervan, 1975.
You Can Tell the World: New Directions for Christian Writers, Augsburg, 1975.
Getting into Print, Nelson, 1977.
Freshness of the Spirit, Harper, 1978.
Faith's Heroes, Crossway, 1979.
A Thirst for God, Zondervan, 1980.
For the Love of Mike: The Story of the Reverend Michael Macintosh, Thomas Nelson, 1984.
The Doomsday Connection (novel), Crossway, 1986.
(Editor) *Spiritual Awakening* (Christian Heritage Classics), Crossway, 1986.
The Making of a Writer, Augsburg, 1987.
The Inner Life of the Believer, Here's Life, 1989.
(Editor) *Spiritual Power* (Christian Heritage Classics), Crossway, 1989.
(Editor) *Spiritual Integrity* (Christian Heritage Classics), Crossway, in press.

Also editor of *Spiritual Disciplines,* a volume in the Christian Heritage Classics series.

WORK IN PROGRESS: Jesus, Man of Joy, to be released in 1992.

*   *   *

WITTNER, Lawrence S(tephen)   1941-

PERSONAL: Born May 5, 1941, in Brooklyn, NY; son of Jacob (a lawyer) and Rose (Barnett) Wittner; married Patricia Sheinblatt (a guidance counselor), August 25, 1963 (divorced May 21, 1981); children: Julia. *Education:* Columbia University, A.B., 1962, Ph.D., 1967; University of Wisconsin, M.A., 1963.

ADDRESSES: Home—20 Irving St., Albany, NY 12202. *Office*—Department of History, State University of New York at Albany, 1400 Washington Ave., Albany, NY 12222.

CAREER: Hampton Institute, Hampton, VA, assistant professor of history, 1967-68; Vassar College, Poughkeepsie, NY, assistant professor of history, 1968-73; Fulbright senior lecturer in Japan, 1973-74; State University of New York at Albany, lecturer, 1974-76, assistant professor, 1976-77, associate professor,

1977-83, professor of history, 1983—. Visiting associate professor of history, Columbia University, summer, 1976.

MEMBER: American Historical Association, Society for Historians of American Foreign Relations (member of council, 1982-84), American Civil Liberties Union, Conference on Peace Research History (national council member, 1970-88, 1989—; president, 1977-79), United University Professions Solidarity Committee (chair, 1986-88), Albany County Central Federation of Labor (delegate, 1980—).

AWARDS, HONORS: Herbert H. Lehman fellowship; fellowships and grants from State University of New York, National Endowment for the Humanities, Harry S. Truman Library Institute, American Council of Learned Societies, and Ford Foundation; University Award for excellence in research; Charles DeBenedetti Prize, Conference on Peace Research in History.

WRITINGS:

Rebels against War: The American Peace Movement, 1941-1960, Columbia University Press, 1969, revised edition published as *Rebels against War: The American Peace Movement, 1933-1983,* Temple University Press, 1984.
(Editor) *MacArthur,* Prentice-Hall, 1971.
Cold War America: From Hiroshima to Watergate, Praeger, 1974, expanded edition, Holt, 1978.
American Intervention in Greece, 1943-1949, Columbia University Press, 1982.
(Associate editor) *Biographical Dictionary of Modern Peace Leaders,* Greenwood Press, 1985.

WORK IN PROGRESS: The Struggle against the Bomb: A History of the World Nuclear Disarmament Movement.

BIOGRAPHICAL/CRITICAL SOURCES:

PERIODICALS

Times Literary Supplement, August 13, 1982.

*   *   *

WODEHOUSE, P(elham) G(renville)   1881-1975
(P. Brooke-Haven, Pelham Grenville, J. Plum, C. P. West, J. Walker Williams, Basil Windham)

PERSONAL: Surname is pronounced "*Wood*-house"; born October 15, 1881, in Guildford, Surrey, England; naturalized U.S. citizen, 1955; died of a heart attack, February 14, 1975, in Southampton, N.Y.; son of Henry Ernest (a civil servant and judge) and Eleanor (Deane) Wodehouse; married Ethel Rowley, September 30, 1914; children: Leonora (stepdaughter; deceased). *Education:* Attended Dulwich College, 1894-1900.

CAREER: Novelist, short story writer, and playwright. Hong Kong & Shanghai Bank, London, England, clerk, 1901-03; *London Globe,* London, assistant on "By the Way" column, 1902-03, writer of column, 1903-09; writer, under various pseudonyms, and drama critic for *Vanity Fair,* 1915-19.

MEMBER: Dramatists Guild, Authors League of America, Old Alleynian Association (New York; president), Coffee House (New York).

AWARDS, HONORS: Litt.D., Oxford University, 1939; named Knight Commander, Order of the British Empire, 1975.

WRITINGS:

NOVELS

The Pothunters, A & C Black, 1902, Macmillan, 1924, reprinted, Souvenir Press, 1972, International Scholarly Book, 1977.

A Prefect's Uncle, A & C Black, 1903, Macmillan, 1924, reprinted, Souvenir Press, 1972, International Scholarly Book, 1977.

The Gold Bat, A & C Black, 1904, Macmillan, 1923, reprinted, Souvenir Press, 1974, International Scholarly Book, 1977.

The Head of Kay's, A & C Black, 1905, Macmillan, 1922, reprinted, Souvenir Press, 1974, International Scholarly Book, 1977.

Love among the Chickens, George Newnes, 1906, Circle Publishing, 1909, revised edition, Jenkins, 1921, autograph edition, 1963.

The White Feather, A & C Black, 1907, Macmillan, 1922, reprinted, Souvenir Press, 1972, International Scholarly Book, 1977.

(With A. W. Westbrook) *Not George Washington,* Cassell, 1907.

The Swoop!; or, How Clarence Saved England: A Tale of the Great Invasion, Alston Rivers, 1909.

Mike: A Public School Story, two parts, A & C Black, 1909, Macmillan, 1924, revised edition of second part published as *Enter Psmith,* Macmillan, 1935, entire book published in two volumes as *Mike at Wrykyn,* Jenkins, 1953, reprinted, Barrie & Jenkins, 1976, and *Mike and Psmith,* Jenkins, 1953, reprinted, Meredith Press, 1969.

The Intrusion of Jimmy, W. J. Watt, 1910 (published in England as *A Gentleman of Leisure,* Alston Rivers, 1910, abridged edition, George Newnes, 1920, autograph edition, Jenkins, 1962, reprinted, Star Books, 1978).

Psmith in the City, A & C Black, 1910, reprinted, Penguin, 1970.

The Prince and Betty, W. J. Watt, 1912 (published in England as *Psmith, Journalist,* A & C Black, 1915, reprinted, Penguin, 1970).

The Prince and Betty (different book from above title), Mills & Boon, 1912.

The Little Nugget, Methuen, 1913, W. J. Watt, 1914, reprinted with a new preface by the author, Barrie & Jenkins, 1972, Penguin, 1978.

Something New, Appleton, 1915, reprinted, Beagle Books, 1972 (published in England as *Something Fresh,* Methuen, 1915, reprinted, Jenkins, 1969).

Uneasy Money, Appleton, 1916, reprinted, Penguin, 1978.

Piccadilly Jim, Dodd, 1917, revised edition, 1931, autograph edition, Jenkins, 1966, reprinted, Penguin, 1969.

A Damsel in Distress, Doran, 1919, autograph edition, Jenkins, 1956, reprinted, Star Books, 1978.

Their Mutual Child, Boni & Liveright, 1919 (published in England as *The Coming of Bill,* Jenkins, 1920, autograph edition, 1966, reprinted, Barrie & Jenkins, 1976).

The Little Warrior, Doran, 1920 (published in England as *Jill the Reckless,* Jenkins, 1921, autograph edition, 1958).

Three Men and a Maid, Doran, 1922 (published in England as *The Girl on the Boat,* Jenkins, 1922, autograph edition, 1956).

The Adventures of Sally, Jenkins, 1922, reprinted, Barrie & Jenkins, 1973, published as *Mostly Sally,* Doran, 1923.

Leave It to Psmith, Jenkins, 1923, autograph edition, 1961, reprinted, 1976, Doran, 1924.

Bill the Conqueror: His Invasion of England in the Springtime, Methuen, 1924, Doran, 1925, reprinted, British Book Center, 1975.

Sam in the Suburbs, Doran, 1925 (published in England as *Sam the Sudden,* Methuen, 1925, reprinted with a new preface by the author, Barrie & Jenkins, 1972, Penguin, 1978).

The Small Bachelor (based on his play, "Oh! Lady, Lady!"), Doran, 1927, reprinted, Ballantine, 1977.

Money for Nothing, Doubleday, Doran, 1928, autograph edition, Jenkins, 1959, reprinted, Barrie & Jenkins, 1976.

Fish Preferred, Doubleday, Doran, 1929, reprinted, Simon & Schuster, 1969 (published in England as *Summer Lightning,* Jenkins, 1929, autograph edition, 1964).

Big Money, Doubleday, Doran, 1931, autograph edition, Jenkins, 1965.

If I Were You, Doubleday, Doran, 1931, autograph edition, Jenkins, 1958, reprinted, Barrie & Jenkins, 1976.

Doctor Sally, Methuen, 1932, reprinted, Thomas Nelson, 1966.

Hot Water, Doubleday, Doran, 1932, autograph edition, Jenkins, 1956, reprinted, Penguin, 1978.

Heavy Weather, Little, Brown, 1933, autograph edition, Jenkins, 1960, reprinted, Penguin, 1973.

Thank You, Jeeves, Little, Brown, 1934, autograph edition, Jenkins, 1956, reprinted, Coronet Books, 1977.

Brinkley Manor, Little, Brown, 1934 (published in England as *Right Ho, Jeeves,* Jenkins, 1934, autograph edition, 1957, reprinted, Penguin, 1975).

Trouble Down at Tudsleigh, International Magazine Co., 1935.

The Luck of the Bodkins, Jenkins, 1935, Little, Brown, 1936, autograph edition, Jenkins, 1956, reprinted, Penguin, 1975.

Laughing Gas, Doubleday, Doran, 1936, autograph edition, Jenkins, 1959, reprinted, Ballantine, 1977.

Summer Moonshine, Doubleday, Doran, 1937, autograph edition, Jenkins, 1956, reprinted, Penguin, 1976.

The Code of the Woosters, Doubleday, Doran, 1938, autograph edition, Jenkins, 1962, reprinted, Penguin, 1975.

Uncle Fred in the Springtime, Doubleday, Doran, 1939, autograph edition, Jenkins, 1962, reprinted, Penguin, 1976.

Quick Service, Doubleday, Doran, 1940, autograph edition, Jenkins, 1960, reprinted, Penguin, 1972.

Money in the Bank, Doubleday, Doran, 1942, reprinted, Penguin, 1978.

Joy in the Morning, Doubleday, 1946, reprinted with a new preface by the author, Jenkins, 1974.

Full Moon, Doubleday, 1947.

Spring Fever, Doubleday, 1948, reprinted, Jenkins, 1976.

Uncle Dynamite, Jenkins, 1948, reprinted, Star Books, 1978.

The Mating Season, Didier, 1949, reprinted, Penguin, 1971.

The Old Reliable, Doubleday, 1951, reprinted, Pan Books, 1968.

Angel Cake (based on the play, "The Butter and Egg Man," by George F. Kaufman), Doubleday, 1952 (published in England as *Barmy in Wonderland,* Jenkins, 1952, autograph edition, 1958).

Pigs Have Wings, Doubleday, 1952, reprinted with a new preface by the author, Barrie & Jenkins, 1974, Ballantine, 1977.

Ring for Jeeves, Jenkins, 1953, autograph edition, 1963, reprinted, Sphere Books, 1977, published as *The Return of Jeeves,* Simon & Schuster, 1954.

Jeeves and the Feudal Spirit, Jenkins, 1954, reprinted, Coronet Books, 1977, published as *Bertie Wooster Sees It Through,* Simon & Schuster, 1955.

French Leave, Jenkins, 1956, Simon & Schuster, 1959, reprinted with a new preface by the author, Barrie & Jenkins, 1974.

The Butler Did It, Simon & Schuster, 1957 (published in England as *Something Fishy,* Jenkins, 1957, reprinted, Star Books, 1978).

Cocktail Time, Simon & Schuster, 1958.

How Right You Are, Jeeves, Simon & Schuster, 1960 (published in England as *Jeeves in the Offing,* Jenkins, 1960).

Ice in the Bedroom, Simon & Schuster, 1961.

Service with a Smile, Simon & Schuster, 1961, reprinted, Penguin, 1975.

Stiff Upper Lip, Jeeves, Simon & Schuster, 1963.

Biffen's Millions, Simon & Schuster, 1964 (published in England as *Frozen Assets,* Jenkins, 1964, reprinted, Barrie & Jenkins, 1976).

The Brinkmanship of Galahad Threepwood: A Blandings Castle Novel, Simon & Schuster, 1965 (published in England as *Galahad at Blandings,* Jenkins, 1965).

The Purloined Paperweight, Simon & Schuster, 1967 (published in England as *Company for Henry,* Jenkins, 1967).

Do Butlers Burgle Banks?, Simon & Schuster, 1968.

A Pelican at Blandings, Jenkins, 1969, published as *No Nudes Is Good Nudes,* Simon & Schuster, 1970.

The Girl in Blue, Barrie & Jenkins, 1970, Simon & Schuster, 1971.

Jeeves and the Tie That Binds, Simon & Schuster, 1971 (published in England as *Much Obliged, Jeeves,* autograph edition, Barrie & Jenkins, 1971).

Pearls, Girls, and Monty Bodkins, Barrie & Jenkins, 1972, published as *The Plot That Thickened,* Simon & Schuster, 1973.

Bachelors Anonymous, Barrie & Jenkins, 1973, Simon & Schuster, 1974.

The Cat-Nappers: A Jeeves and Bertie Story, Simon & Schuster, 1974 (published in England as *Aunts Aren't Gentlemen: A Jeeves and Bertie Story,* Barrie & Jenkins, 1974).

Sunset at Blandings, Chatto & Windus, 1977, Simon & Schuster, 1978.

STORIES

Tales of St. Austin's, A & C Black, 1903, Macmillan, 1923, reprinted, Penguin, 1978.

The Man Upstairs and Other Stories, Methuen, 1914, reprinted with a new preface by the author, Barrie & Jenkins, 1971.

The Man with Two Left Feet and Other Stories, Methuen, 1917, A. L. Burt, 1933, reprinted, Penguin, 1978.

My Man Jeeves, George Newnes, 1919, published as *Carry On, Jeeves,* Jenkins, 1925, autograph edition, 1960, reprinted, Penguin, 1975.

The Indiscretions of Archie, Doran, 1921, reprinted, Jenkins, 1965.

The Clicking of Cuthbert, Jenkins, 1922, autograph edition, 1956, published as *Golf without Tears,* Doran, 1924.

Jeeves, Doran, 1923 (published in England as *The Inimitable Jeeves,* Jenkins, 1923, autograph edition, 1956, reprinted, Penguin, 1975).

Ukridge, Jenkins, 1924, autograph edition, 1960, reprinted, Penguin, 1973, published as *He Rather Enjoyed It,* Doran, 1926.

The Heart of a Goof, Jenkins, 1926, autograph edition, 1956, reprinted, Penguin, 1978, published as *Divots,* Doran, 1927.

Meet Mr. Mulliner, Jenkins, 1927, Doubleday, Doran, 1928, autograph edition, Jenkins, 1956.

Mr. Mulliner Speaking, Jenkins, 1929, Doubleday, Doran, 1930, autograph edition, Jenkins, 1961.

Very Good, Jeeves, Doubleday, Doran, 1930, autograph edition, Jenkins, 1958, reprinted, Penguin, 1975.

Mulliner Nights, Doubleday, Doran, 1933, autograph edition, Jenkins, 1966, reprinted, Vintage Books, 1975.

Blandings Castle, Doubleday, Doran, 1935 (published in England as *Blandings Castle and Elsewhere,* Jenkins, 1935, autograph edition, 1957).

Young Men in Spats, Doubleday, Doran, 1936, autograph edition, Jenkins, 1957.

The Crime Wave at Blandings, Doubleday, Doran, 1937 (published in England as *Lord Emsworth and Others,* Jenkins, 1937, autograph edition, 1956, reprinted, 1976).

Eggs, Beans and Crumpets, Doubleday, Doran, 1940, autograph edition, Jenkins, 1963, reprinted, Penguin, 1976.

Dudley Is Back to Normal, Doubleday, Doran, 1940.

Nothing Serious, Jenkins, 1950, Doubleday, 1951, autograph edition, Jenkins, 1964.

Selected Stories, introduction by John W. Aldridge, Modern Library, 1958.

A Few Quick Ones, Simon & Schuster, 1959, reprinted, Coronet Books, 1978.

Plum Pie, Jenkins, 1966, Simon & Schuster, 1967.

Jeeves, Jeeves, Jeeves, Avon, 1976.

David A. Jasen, editor, *The Swoop and Other Stories,* with an appreciation by Malcolm Muggeridge, Seabury, 1979.

OTHER BOOKS

(Adapter) *William Tell Told Again* (based on the classic tale), A & C Black, 1904.

(With H. W. Westbrook) *The Globe "By the Way" Book: A Literary Quick-Lunch for People Who Have Only Got Five Minutes to Spare,* Globe, 1908.

Louder and Funnier (essays), Faber, 1932, autograph edition, Jenkins, 1963, reprinted, Barrie & Jenkins, 1976.

(Editor) *A Century of Humour,* Hutchinson, 1934.

(Editor with Scott Meredith and author of introduction) *The Week-End Book of Humour,* Washburn, 1952, published as *P. G. Wodehouse Selects the Best of Humor,* Grosset, 1965.

(Editor with Meredith and author of introduction) *The Best of Modern Humour,* Metcalf, 1952, reprinted, Books for Libraries, 1971.

Performing Flea: A Self-Portrait in Letters (letters written by Wodehouse to William Townsend), introduction by Townsend, Jenkins, 1953, published as *Author! Author!,* Simon & Schuster, 1962.

(With Guy Bolton) *Bring On the Girls!: The Improbable Story of Our Life in Musical Comedy with Pictures to Prove It,* Simon & Schuster, 1953.

America, I Like You, Simon & Schuster, 1956, revised edition published as *Over Seventy: An Autobiography with Digressions,* Jenkins, 1957.

(Editor with Meredith and author of introduction) *A Carnival of Modern Humor,* Delacorte, 1967.

Wodehouse on Wodehouse (contains *Performing Flea, Bring On the Girls!,* and *Over Seventy*), Hutchinson, 1980.

PLAYS

(With John Stapleton) "A Gentleman of Leisure" (comedy; based on Wodehouse's novel of the same title), first produced on Broadway at Playhouse Theatre, August 24, 1911.

(With Stapleton) "A Thief for the Night," first produced on Broadway at Playhouse Theatre, 1913.

(With H. W. Westbrook) "Brother Alfred," first produced on West End at Savoy Theatre, 1913.

The Play's the Thing (three-act drama; based on *Spiel in Schloss* by Ferenc Molnar; first produced on Broadway at Henry Miller's Theatre, November 3, 1926), Brentano's, 1927.

(With Valerie Wyngate) "Her Cardboard Lover" (based on a play by Jacques Deval), first produced in New York at Empire Theatre, March 21, 1927.

Good Morning, Bill (three-act comedy; based on a play by Ladislaus Fodor; first produced on West End at Duke of York's Theatre, November 28, 1927), Methuen, 1928.

(With Ian Hay) *A Damsel in Distress* (three-act comedy; based on Wodehouse's novel of the same title; first produced Off-Broadway at New Theatre, August 13, 1928), Samuel French, 1930.

(With Hay) *Baa, Baa, Black Sheep* (three-act comedy; first produced Off-Broadway at New Theatre, April 22, 1929), Samuel French, 1930.

Candlelight (three-act drama; based on "Kleine Komodie" by Siegfried Geyer; first produced in New York at Empire Theatre, September 30, 1929), Samuel French, 1934.

(With Hay) *Leave It to Psmith* (three-act comedy; based on Wodehouse's novel of the same title; first produced in London at Shaftesbury Theatre, September 29, 1930), Samuel French, 1932.

(With Guy Bolton) "Who's Who" (three-act comedy), first produced on West End at Duke of York's Theatre, September 20, 1934.

"The Inside Stand" (three-act farce), first produced in London at Saville Theatre, November 20, 1935.

(With Bolton) "Don't Listen, Ladies" (two-act comedy; based on the play "N'ecoutez pas, mesdames," by Sacha Guitry), first produced on Broadway at Booth Theatre, December 28, 1948.

(With Bolton) *Carry On, Jeeves* (three-act comedy; based on Wodehouse's novel of the same title), Evans Brothers, 1956.

Several of the author's novels were adapted by Edward Duke into a play, "Jeeves Takes Charge," c. 1984.

MUSICALS

(Author of lyrics with others) "The Gay Gordons," book by Seymour Hicks, music by Guy Jones, first produced in London at Aldwych Theatre, 1913.

(With C. H. Bovill and F. Tours) "Nuts and Wine," first produced in London at Empire Theatre, 1914.

(With Guy Bolton and H. Reynolds) "Miss Springtime," music by Emmerich Kalman and Jerome Kern, first produced in New York at New Amsterdam Theatre, September 25, 1916.

(With Bolton) "Ringtime," first produced in New York, 1917.

(Author of book and lyrics with Bolton) "Have a Heart," music by Kern, first produced in New York at Liberty Theatre, January 11, 1917.

(Author of book and lyrics with Bolton) "Oh, Boy," first produced in New York at Princess Theatre, February 20, 1917, produced in London as "Oh, Joy," 1919.

(Author of book and lyrics with Bolton) "Leave It to Jane" (musical version of "The College Widow" by George Ade) music by Kern, first produced in Albany, N.Y., July, 1917, produced on Broadway at Longacre Theatre, August 28, 1917.

(Author of book and lyrics with Bolton) "The Riviera Girl," music by Kalman, first produced in New York at New Amsterdam Theatre, September 24, 1917.

(Author of book and lyrics with Bolton) "Miss 1917," music by Victor Herbert and Kern, first produced Off-Broadway at Century Theatre, November 5, 1917.

(With Bolton) "The Second Century Show," first produced in New York, 1917.

(Author of book and lyrics with Bolton) "Oh! Lady, Lady!," music by Kern, first produced in New York at Princess Theatre, February 1, 1918.

(With Bolton) "See You Later," music by J. Szule, first produced in Baltimore at Academy of Music, April 15, 1918.

(Author of book and lyrics with Bolton) "The Girl behind the Gun" (based on play "Madame et son filleul," by Hennequin and Weber), music by Ivan Caryll, first produced in New York at New Amsterdam Theatre, September 16, 1918, produced in London as "Kissing Time" at Winter Garden Theatre, 1918.

(Author of book and lyrics with Bolton) "Oh My Dear," music by Louis Hirsch, first produced in New York at Princess Theatre, November 27, 1918, produced in Toronto as "Ask Dad," 1918.

(With Bolton) "The Rose of China," music by Armand Vecsey, first produced in New York at Lyric Theatre, November 25, 1919.

(Author of lyrics with Clifford Grey) "Sally," music by Kern, first produced in New York by Flo Ziegfeld, 1920.

(Author of book and lyrics with Fred Thompson) "The Golden Moth," music by Ivor Novello, first produced in London at Adelphi Theatre, October 5, 1921.

(Author of book and lyrics with George Grossmith) "The Cabaret Girl," music by Kern, first produced in London at Winter Garden Theatre, 1922.

(Author of book and lyrics with Grossmith) "The Beauty Prize," music by Kern, first produced in London at Aldwych Theatre, September 5, 1923.

(Author of book and lyrics with Bolton) "Sitting Pretty," music by Kern, first produced in New York at Fulton Theatre, April 8, 1924.

(Adapter with Laurie Wylie) *Hearts and Diamonds* (light opera; based on *The Orlov* by Biuno Granichstaedten and Ernest Marischka; first produced in London at Strand Theatre, June 1, 1926), English lyrics by Graham John, Keith Prowse & Co., 1926.

(With others) "Showboat," music by Oscar Hammerstein, first produced on Broadway at Ziegfeld Theatre, December 27, 1927.

(Author of book with Bolton) "Oh Kay!," lyrics by Ira Gershwin, music by George Gershwin, first produced on Broadway at Imperial Theatre, November 8, 1926.

(Author of book and lyrics with Bolton) "The Nightingale," music by Vecsey, first produced on Broadway at Al Jolson's Theatre, January 3, 1927.

(Author of lyrics with Ira Gershwin) "Rosalie," book by Bolton and Bill McGuire, music by George Gershwin and Sigmund Romberg, first produced in New York at New Amsterdam Theatre, January 10, 1928.

(Author of book with Grossmith; author of lyrics with Grey) *The Three Musketeers* (based on the novel by Alexandre Dumas; first produced in New York at Lyric Theatre, March 13, 1928), music by Rudolph Frinil, Harms Inc., 1937.

(Author of book with Bolton, Howard Lindsay, and Russel Crouse) *Anything Goes* (first produced on Broadway at Alvin Theatre, November 21, 1934), music and lyrics by Cole Porter, Samuel French, 1936.

FILMS

Coauthor of "A Damsel in Distress," based on his novel of the same title, released by RKO General, Inc., 1920; author of "Rosalie," based on his play of the same title, released by Metro-Goldwyn-Mayer, Inc., 1930. Also author of "Summer Lightning," based on his novel of the same title, and "Three French Girls."

SIDELIGHTS: Pelham Grenville Wodehouse long entertained thoughts of becoming a writer—he told interviewer Gerald Clarke of the *Paris Review:* "I was writing stories when I was five. I don't remember what I did before that. Just loafed, I suppose." Best known for his stories concerning the young Bertram Wilberforce Wooster ('Bertie') and his valet Jeeves, Wodehouse is considered a master of English humor and a powerful influence on many later writers.

The world P. G. Wodehouse created in his writings may, at times, seem strange and somewhat dated to the modern reader. Wodehouse, it must be remembered, was born in Victorian England. He was a member of the Beefsteak Club while Rudyard Kipling was still a member (he became a correspondent of Kipling's), and as a boy he read the works of many of the great nineteenth-century writers as they were published. Richard Voorhees points out that "since Wodehouse wrote his first fourteen books during the reign of Edward VII, they are bound to date in many ways." But why, then, are his later books, those written in the fifties and sixties, also full of outdated manners and customs? Sometimes, according to Voorhees, the anachronisms are accidental, as when 1948 model cars are equipped with running boards, or when a character is found to be smoking a brand of cigarette that has long since disappeared from the market. But he maintains that, more often, "the anachronisms are clearly deliberate. Wodehouse perpetrates some of them because they deal to his sense of the absurd, because they have an antiquarian smack. . . . Wodehouse commits other anachronisms because they are part of his equipment as a professional novelist, because he has used them successfully for so many years. Thus he continues to write of village concerts at which baritones sing 'The Yeoman's Wedding Song,' of village fetes with bun-eating contests and egg-and-spoon races; thus he writes as though people wore pince-nez and men wore spats." But Voorhees concludes that the most important reason for the anachronisms is that Wodehouse is "repelled by much of the modern world and is taking refuge from it."

The characters in Wodehouse's world are thoroughly unique. Easily his most famous characters are Bertram Wilberforce Wooster and his incredible valet Jeeves. They first appeared in a story entitled "Extricating Young Gussie" which Wodehouse wrote for the *Saturday Evening Post.* While Bertie was a main character in the story, Jeeves was relegated to a minor part. As Wodehouse explained to Clarke: "I only intended to use him once. His first entrance was: 'Mrs. Gregson to see you, Sir'. . . . He only had one other line: 'Very good, Sir. Which suit will you wear?' But then I was writing a story, 'The Artistic Career of Corky,' about two young men, Bertie Wooster and his friend Corky, getting into a lot of trouble. I thought: Well, how can I get them out? And I thought: 'Suppose one of them had an omniscient valet?' I wrote a short story about him, then another short story, then several more short stories and novels." In the introduction to his *Jeeves Omnibus,* Wodehouse wrote, "I still blush to think of the off-hand way I treated him at our first encounter."

Contrary to the assumptions of many readers and critics, Jeeves is no mere butler; he is a valet or, as he puts it, a gentleman's personal gentleman. In addition to the duties normally performed by a butler, a gentleman's gentleman is responsible for the running of the entire household as well as such things as his employer's dress and daily schedule. Jeeves, unlike most valets, is also entrusted with the task of saving the lives of Bertie and his numerous scheming accomplices from time to time.

In his book *The Comic Style of P. G. Wodehouse,* Robert A. Hall calls Jeeves "one of the most memorable characters invented in twentieth-century English-language fiction. His head sticks out at the back, and he eats a great deal of fish, which to Bertie's way of thinking makes him so brainy. His favorite reading is Spinoza, or else the great Russian novelists. His range of knowledge is encyclopaedic, so that he can furnish information or give an extempore lecture on almost every subject. . . . His speech is an exaggeratedly ultra-formal, ultra-standard English. In the stories, his function is to get Bertie (and often others as well) out of jams, through his analysis of the 'psychology of the individual' (one of his favorite expressions) and through the measures he takes, often when Bertie, through his own bungling, is *in extremis.* Jeeves is an intellectual *deus ex machina,* to rescue Bertie from the scrapes the latter gets into through his presumption unsupported by intellectual strength."

Bertie, for his part, may be seen as the most outstanding example of a long line of irresponsible young gentlemen characterized by Wodehouse, or, as Voorhees phrases it, the "crowning achievement in the creation of the silly young ass," and "one of literature's idiots." While there can be little doubt as to Bertie's lack of intelligence (he readily admits it; in one of the stories in *My Man Jeeves,* when Jeeves says, "We must think, sir," Bertie replies, "You do it. I don't have the equipment."), he remains one of Wodehouse's most personable and engaging characters. He is extremely good natured and gregarious, always ready for a dinner party or a weekend at one of his aunts' country houses. Although he is presumably in his late twenties, he persists in childish schemes that invariably backfire leaving his salvation, time and again, in the hands of Jeeves. Bertie lives by the strict "Code of the Woosters" which compels him never to let a pal down. As a result he is at the mercy of an endless supply of old school chums and girl friends who entreat him to rescue them from a variety of sticky situations. French surmises that "if the Duke of Wellington had asked the Wooster of that day to charge the Old Guard, you would not have heard that Wooster saying that he had to run into Brussels for a moment and was afraid he would not be able to manage it. He would have been where Bertie is to be found—in the thick of the grape-shot, or purloining a policeman's helmet to get young Stephanie Byng out of a jam, as the case may be."

In the early short stories featuring Jeeves and Bertie, the young master gets himself into a variety of scrapes from which it becomes necessary for the wise valet to extricate him, including a few accidental engagements to young ladies to whom he is particularly unsuited. But beginning with the first novel in which they are the main characters, Hall points out, "the emphasis changes, and Bertie's efforts to avoid marriage become the main-spring of the plot. Florence Craye appears (in *Joy in the Morning*) as one of the threats to his bachelordom; but there are others as well. In *Right Ho, Jeeves* the droopy, soupy, sentimental Madeline Bassett misunderstands Bertie's pleas on behalf of his newt-fancier friend Gussie Fink-Nottle, and thinks he is pleading his own cause. From then on, every time that she feels disappointed in her love for someone else, she tells Bertie she will marry him; his naive code of being a *preux chevalier* forbids him to spurn her love. . . . This essential situation is repeated in each one of the later Bertie-Jeeves novels, with marriage to either Pauline Stoker (in *Thank You, Jeeves*), Madeline Bassett, or the red-haired hellion Bobbie Wickham (in *Jeeves in the Offing*) as a major threat."

As a result of his distinctive writing style—a style that has served as the inspiration for a number of contemporary humorists—many critics have labeled Wodehouse the dominant force in the establishment of modern humorous fiction technique. But Robert A. Hall, who notes that the author has been hailed as "the greatest master of twentieth-century prose," says that "despite general recognition of Wodehouse's merits as a stylist . . . there has been relatively little detailed analysis of the features that have contributed to his almost unparalleled success in humorous writing." Hall's book *The Comic Style of P. G. Wodehouse* is a thorough study of the stylistic devices Wodehouse used for comic effect. "Humor," says Hall, "has two essential ingredients. For us to laugh at something, it must contain some kind of incongruity, and we must be emotionally neutral, without our personal feelings being involved." He finds that "Wodehouse makes use of just about every resource available in standard English plus a few from non-standard English, to obtain his effects."

Hall mentions Wodehouse's inventive word formations, adding and subtracting prefixes and suffixes, as an example. He writes: "To *de-dog the premises* is not too great a variation on the pattern of *de-louse* or *de-bunk;* but Wodehouse obtains a greater humorous effect by prefixing *de-* to proper names, as when Pongo Twistleton brings the housemaid Elsie Bean out of a cupboard [in *Uncle Dynamite*]: 'His manner as he de-Beaned the cupboard was somewhat distrait,' or when 'Kipper' Herring, after Bobbie Wickham has left his company, is described as 'finding himself de-Wickhamed' [in *Jeeves in the Offing*]. On the analogy of such formations as *homeward, northward, inward,* Wodehouse obtains a special effect when he says of Lord Emsworth [in *Summer Lightning*], 'He pottered off pigward.' " Hall also cites several instances in which Wodehouse stretches the patterns of word formations and meanings beyond their normal limits. In *Heavy Weather* he fashions a verb *to huss* from the noun hussy: "I regard the entire personnel of the ensemble of our musical comedy theatres as—if you will pardon me being Victorian for a moment—painted hussies." "They've got to paint." "Well, they needn't huss." In Wodehouse's parlance, a cowpuncher punches cows and corn-chandler chandles corn. He is also prone to separate some words, such as *hobnob,* into their constituent elements. Thus in *Uncle Dynamite* a character says, "To offer a housemaid a cigarette is not hobbing. Nor, when you light it for her, does that constitute nobbing."

As a master craftsman Wodehouse would never overuse any single stylistic device, but one that comes up, Hall points out, about twice in any given story, is what is called the transferred epithet, "especially an adjective modifying a noun instead of the corresponding adverb modifying the verb of the sentence." In the story "Jeeves and the Impending Doom," this phenomenon is evidenced by the sentence, "He uncovered the fragrant eggs and I pronged a moody forkful." In *Joy in the Morning* we have, "I balanced a thoughtful lump of sugar on the teaspoon." And in *Jeeves and the Feudal Spirit*, "He waved a concerned cigar."

Misunderstandings of many kinds abound in Wodehouse stories. These often are the result of syntactic or lexicographic confusion, as in a scene from "Jeeves and the Yuletide Spirit" in which Sir Roderick Glossop misunderstands Bertie Wooster's use of the nickname Tuppy: " 'Awfully sorry about all this,' I said in a hearty sort of voice. 'The fact is, I thought you were Tuppy.' 'Kindly refrain from inflicting your idiotic slang on me. What do you mean by the adjective "tuppy"?' 'It isn't so much an adjective, don't you know. More of a noun, I should think, if you examine it squarely. What I mean to say is, I thought you were your nephew.' " Hall cites one more case of this type of misunderstanding which occurs in *Uncle Dynamite* when Constable Potter confuses two meanings of the word *by:* " 'I was assaulted by the duck pond.' " " 'By the duck pond?' Sir Aylmer asked, his eyes widening." " 'Yes, sir.' " " 'How the devil can you be assaulted by a duck pond?' Constable Potter saw where the misunderstanding had arisen. The English language is full of these

pitfalls. 'When I say "by the duck pond," I didn't mean "by the duck pond," I meant "by the duck pond." That is to say,' proceeded Constable Potter, speaking just in time, 'near or adjacent to, in fact on the edge of.' "

Another good example of Wodehouse's unique use of language to evoke humor can be found running throughout the Jeeves and Bertie stories. Even though Bertie is supposedly a graduate of Eton and Oxford, his vocabulary is extremely limited, and he spends a good deal of time groping for the right word, or, as Wodehouse so often says, the *mot juste.* In *Stiff Upper Lip, Jeeves* he says, "I suppose Stiffy's sore about this . . . what's the word? . . . Not vaseline . . . Vacillation, that's it." In *Jeeves and the Feudal Spirit* Hall finds one of the many instances in which Bertie depends on Jeeves to fill in the blank: "Let a pluggly like young Thos loose in the community with a cosh, and you are inviting disaster and . . . what's the word? Something about cats." Jeeves replies, "Cataclysms, sir?"

Jeeve's vocabulary is, in fact, so broad that Bertie, who is at least somewhat accustomed to it, is often forced to translate for his friends. Hall refers to a scene in "The Artistic Career of Corky" as an example; Jeeves says, "The scheme I would suggest cannot fail of success, but it has what may seem to you a drawback, sir, in that it requires a certain financial outlay." "He means," Bertie explains to Corky, "that he has got a pippin of an idea but it's going to cost a lot."

Puns also make frequent appearances in Wodehouse' work. In *Thank You, Jeeves,* a Mr. Stoker says, "Reminds me of that thing about Lo somebody's name led all the rest." Jeeves refreshes his memory, "Abou ben Adhem, sir." And the puzzled Stoker asks, "Have I *what?*" When, in *Jeeves and the Feudal Spirit,* Bertie is released from jail and is asked, "Are you all right, now?" he replies, "Well, I have a pinched look." And in *The Mating Season* Bertie asks, "I look like something the cat found in Tutankhamen's tomb, do I not?" Jeeves answers, "I would not go as far as that, sir, but I have unquestionably seen you more *soigne.*" Bertie notes that "it crossed my mind for an instant that with a little thought one might throw together something rather clever about 'Way down upon the soigne river,' but I was too listless to follow up."

But Hall identifies Wodehouse's best-known stylistic device as "his imagery involving similes, metaphors, and other types of comparison. The chief characteristic of his imagery is the wide range from which he draws his comparisons, using them in every instance to emphasize resemblances which at first glance seem highly incongruous (and hence provide the reader's laughter), but which at the same time are highly appropriate to the particular person or situation described. His imagery—carefully planned, of course, like all the rest of his writing—is therefore particularly vivid and apposite." An example from *Leave It to Psmith:* "A sound like two or three pigs feeding rather noisily in the middle of a thunderstorm interrupted his meditation." In *The Mating Season* Wodehouse used, "That 'ha, ha,' so like the expiring quack of a duck dying of a broken heart." And finally in *The Code of the Woosters* we find: "Have you ever heard Sir Watkyn Bassett dealing with a bowl of soup? It's not unlike the Scottish express going through a tunnel." As Hall says, "such a list could be continued almost indefinitely; a whole volume could be compiled simply by excerpting all the imagery which Wodehouse uses in his stories."

Wodehouse's brilliance in utilizing these various stylistic devices, his deft handling of the English language, and his humorous observations on human nature combined to make him one of the most popular writers of the twentieth century. David A.

Jasen, who calls Wodehouse the "funniest writer in the world," believes that the author built up a large following through the use of repetition. "It is always a delight to welcome an old friend," he writes, "for old friends recall happily shared experiences, and this is the sense of intimacy gotten when reading the works of Wodehouse." Jasen says that Wodehouse "took pieces of his childhood, blended with snatches of the quickly altering world of the Edwardians and the early Georgians, and added his own abundantly creative imagination. His plots fit his people, who are consistent not with reality but with themselves and the world of his conception. He attempted to be realistic only in this way and achieved a timelessness in his world which makes his writings universally appealing. His humor depends mainly on exaggeration and understatement, the incongruous, the inappropriate phrase, and the use of the literal interpretation of an idiomatic expression out of context for effect. He developed a new vocabulary, mixing slang along with classical phrases, and fashioning supremely inventive as well as highly diverting hyperboles. He is extremely serious about his work and took tremendous trouble with its construction. He polished his sentences as meticulously as one of his Drones would choose a tie. His only object in writing was purely and simply to amuse." Wodehouse confirmed this in his autobiographical *Over Seventy* when he wrote: "My books may not be the sort of books the cognoscenti feel justified in blowing the twelve and a half shillings on, but I do work at them. When in due course Charon ferries me across the Styx and everyone is telling everyone else what a rotten writer I was, I hope at least one voice will be heard piping up: 'But he did take trouble.' "

MEDIA ADAPTATIONS: Some of Wodehouse's short stories were produced by the BBC under the title "Wodehouse Playhouse."

BIOGRAPHICAL/CRITICAL SOURCES:

BOOKS

Aldridge, John W., *Time to Murder and Create*, McKay, 1966.
Authors in the News, Volume II, Gale, 1976.
Cazalet-Keir, Thelma, editor, *Homage to P. G. Wodehouse*, Barrie & Jenkins, 1973.
Contemporary Literary Criticism, Gale, Volume I, 1973, Volume II, 1974, Volume V, 1976, Volume X, 1979, Volume XXII, 1982.
Dictionary of Literary Biography, Volume 34: *British Novelists, 1890-1929: Traditionalists*, Gale, 1985.
French, R. B. D., *P. G. Wodehouse*, Oliver & Boyd, 1966, Barnes & Noble, 1967.
Green, Benny, *P. G. Wodehouse: A Literary Biography*, Rutledge Press, 1981.
Hall, Robert A., Jr., *The Comic Style of P. G. Wodehouse*, Archon, 1974.
Heineman, James H. and Donald R. Benson, editors, *P. G. Wodehouse: A Centenary Celebration, 1881-1981*, Pierpoint Morgan Library, 1981.
Jaggard, Geoffrey W., *Wooster's World*, Macdonald & Co., 1967.
Jaggard, *Blandings the Blest and the Blue Blood*, Macdonald & Co., 1968.
Jasen, David A., *A Bibliography and Reader's Guide to the First Editions of P. G. Wodehouse*, Archon, 1970.
Jasen, *P. G. Wodehouse: A Portrait of a Master*, Mason & Lipscomb, 1974.
Orwell, George, *The Orwell Reader*, Harcourt, 1933.
Short Story Criticism, Volume II, Gale, 1989.
Sproat, Iain, *Wodehouse at War*, Ticknor & Fields, 1981.
Usborne, Richard, *Wodehouse at Work*, Jenkins, 1961.

Usborne, *Wodehouse Nuggets*, Hutchinson, 1983.
Voorhees, Richard, *P. G. Wodehouse*, Twayne, 1966.
Wind, H. W., *The World of P. G. Wodehouse*, Praeger, 1972.
Wodehouse, P. G., *Performing Flea: A Self-Portrait in Letters*, Jenkins, 1953.
Wodehouse and Guy Bolton, *Bring On the Girls!: The Improbable Story of Our Life in Musical Comedy with Pictures to Prove It*, Simon & Schuster, 1953.
Wodehouse, *Over Seventy: An Autobiography with Digressions*, Jenkins, 1957.

PERIODICALS

Chicago Tribune, October 15, 1981.
New York Times, February 15, 1975, October 18, 1981, November 12, 1984, November 7, 1985, October 20, 1987, March 23, 1989.
Paris Review, winter, 1975.
Times (London), November 24, 1983, June 21, 1984, June 29, 1985, July 9, 1987.
Washington Post, February 3, 1984.
Washington Post Book World, November 29, 1981.
Writers Digest, October, 1971.

*　　　*　　　*

WOLFE, Thomas Kennerly, Jr. 1930-
(Tom Wolfe)

PERSONAL: Born March 2, 1930, in Richmond, Va.; son of Thomas Kennerly (a scientist and business executive) and Helen (Hughes) Wolfe; married Sheila Berger (art director of *Harper's* magazine), 1978; children: Alexandra. *Education:* Washington and Lee University, B.A. (cum laude), 1951; Yale University, Ph.D., 1957.

ADDRESSES: Home—New York, NY. *Agent*—Lynn Nesbit, 598 Madison Ave., New York, NY 10022.

CAREER: Writer, journalist, social commentator, and artist. *Springfield Union*, Springfield, Mass., reporter, 1956-59; *Washington Post*, Washington, D.C., reporter and Latin American correspondent, 1959-62; *New York Herald Tribune*, New York City, city reporter, and *New York* Sunday magazine (now *New York* magazine), New York City, writer, both 1962-66; *New York World Journal Tribune*, New York City, writer, 1966-67; *New York* magazine, New York City, contributing editor, 1968-76; *Esquire* magazine, New York City, contributing editor, 1977—; *Harper's* magazine, New York City, contributing artist, 1978-81. Has exhibited drawings in one-man shows at Maynard Walker Gallery, 1965, and Tunnel Gallery, 1974.

AWARDS, HONORS: Washington Newspaper Guild awards for foreign news reporting and for humor, both 1961; Society of Magazine Writers award for excellence, 1970; D.F.A., Minneapolis College of Art, 1971; Frank Luther Mott research award, 1973; D.Litt., Washington and Lee University, 1974; named Virginia Laureate for literature, 1977; American Book Award, 1980, for *The Right Stuff;* Harold D. Vursell Memorial Award for excellence in literature, American Institute of Arts and Letters, 1980; Columbia Journalism Award, 1980; citation for art history from National Sculpture Society, 1980; L.H.D. from Virginia Commonwealth University, 1983, and Southampton College, 1984; John Dos Passos Award, 1984; Gari Melchers Medal, 1986; Benjamin Pierce Cheney Medal from Eastern Washington University, 1986; Washington Irving Medal for literary excellence from Nicholas Society, 1986.

WRITINGS:

UNDER NAME TOM WOLFE

(Self-illustrated) *The Kandy-Kolored Tangerine-Flake Streamline Baby* (essays), Farrar, Straus, 1965, recent edition, 1987.

(Contributor) Alan Rinzler, editor, *The New York Spy,* David White, 1967.

The Electric Kool-Aid Acid Test, Farrar, Straus, 1968, recent edition, 1987.

The Pump House Gang (essays), Farrar, Straus, 1968 (published in England as *The Mid-Atlantic Man and Other New Breeds in England and America,* Weidenfeld & Nicolson, 1969).

Radical Chic and Mau Mauing the Flak Catchers (two essays), Farrar, Straus, 1970, recent edition, 1987.

(Editor with E. W. Johnson and contributor) *The New Journalism* (anthology), Harper, 1973.

(Self-illustrated) *The Painted Word,* Farrar, Straus, 1975.

(Self-illustrated) *Mauve Gloves & Madmen, Clutter & Vine, and Other Short Stories* (essays), Farrar, Straus, 1976.

(Contributor) Susan Feldman, editor, *Marie Cosindas, Color Photographs,* New York Graphic Society, 1978.

The Right Stuff (Book-of-the-Month-Club selection), Farrar, Straus, 1979.

(Self-illustrated) *In Our Time* (essays), Farrar, Straus, 1980.

From Bauhaus to Our House, Farrar, Straus, 1981.

(Self-illustrated) *The Purple Decades: A Reader* (collection), Farrar, Straus, 1982.

The Bonfire of the Vanities (novel), Farrar, Straus, 1987.

Contributor of numerous articles to periodicals. Co-founder of literary quarterly *Shenandoah.*

SIDELIGHTS: "Those of you who are not aware of Tom Wolfe should—really—do your best to acquaint yourselves with him," writes William F. Buckley in the *National Review.* "He is probably the most skilful writer in America. I mean by that he can do more things with words than anyone else." Satirist, caricaturist, social critic, coiner of phrases ("Radical Chic," "The Me Decade"), Wolfe has become known as a leading chronicler of American trends. His painstaking research and detailed accounts have made him a widely respected reporter; at the same time, his unorthodox style and frequently unpopular opinions have resulted in a great deal of controversy. Leslie Bennetts of the *Philadelphia Bulletin* calls him "a professional rogue," who has "needled and knifed at the mighty of every description, exposing in print the follies and foibles of superstars from Leonard Bernstein to the Hell's Angels. Gleefully ripping off every shred of disguise from anyone's pretensions, Wolfe has performed his dissections in *New York* Magazine, *Esquire,* and *Rolling Stone,* not to mention his earlier years on the *New York Herald Tribune* and the *Washington Post.*"

Wolfe is generally recognized as one of the leaders in the branch of writing known as "New Journalism." Bennetts says that while Wolfe did not invent the movement, "he at least became its stentorian spokesman and most flamboyant practitioner." *Fort Lauderdale Sun-Sentinel* writer Margo Harakas believes that there is "only a handful of standouts among [New Journalists]— Jimmy Breslin, Gay Talese, Hunter Thompson, and, of course, Wolfe, with his explosive punctuation, name brand detailing, and kaleidoscopic descriptions." In a *Writer's Digest* article, Wolfe defines New Journalism as "the use by people writing nonfiction of techniques which heretofore had been thought of as confined to the novel or to the short story, to create in one form both the kind of objective reality of journalism and the subjective reality that people have always gone to the novel for."

The techniques employed in New Journalism, then, include a number of devices borrowed from traditional fiction writing: extensive dialogue; shifting point of view; scene-by-scene construction; detailed descriptions of setting, clothes, and other physical features; complex character development; and, depending on the reporter and on the subject, varying degrees of innovation in the use of language and punctuation.

Wolfe's association with New Journalism began in 1963, when he wrote his first magazine article, a piece on custom automobiles. He had become intrigued with the strange subculture of West Coast car customizers and was beginning to see these individuals as folk artists worthy of serious study. He convinced *Esquire* magazine to send him to California, where he researched the story, interviewed a number of subjects, and, says Harakas, "racked up a $750 tab at the Beverly Wilshire Hotel (picked up by *Esquire,* of course)." Then, having returned to New York to write the article, he found that standard journalistic techniques, those he had employed so successfully during his years of newspaper work, could not adequately describe the bizarre people and machines he had encountered in California.

Stymied, he put off writing the story until, finally, he called Byron Dobell, his editor at *Esquire,* and admitted that he was unable to finish the project. Dobell told him to type up his notes so that the magazine could get another writer to do the job. In the introduction to *The Kandy-Kolored Tangerine-Flake Streamline Baby,* Wolfe writes: "About 8 o'clock that night I started typing the notes out in the form of a memorandum that began, 'Dear Byron.' I started typing away, starting right with the first time I saw any custom cars in California." In an attempt to provide every possible detail for the writer who was to finish the piece, he wrote in a stream-of-consciousness style, including even some of his most garbled notes and random thoughts. "I wrapped up the memorandum about 6:15 A.M., and by this time it was 49 pages long. I took it over to *Esquire* as soon as they opened up, about 9:30 A.M. About 4 P.M. I got a call from Byron Dobell. He told me they were striking out the 'Dear Byron' at the top of the memorandum and running the rest of it in the magazine."

It is the style developed during the writing of the custom car article—his unique blend of "pop" language and creative punctuation—that for many years remained Wolfe's trademark. He was a pioneer in the use of what several reviewers refer to as an "aural" style of writing, a technique intended to make the reader come as close as possible to experiencing an event first-hand. Wilfrid Sheed, in the *New York Times Book Review,* says that Wolfe tries to find "a language proper to each subject, a special sound to convey its uniqueness"; and *Newsweek*'s Jack Kroll feels that Wolfe is "a genuine poet" among journalists, who is able "to get under the skin of a phenomenon and transmit its metabolic rhythm. . . . He creates the most vivid, most pertinent possible dimension of his subject." F. N. Jones, in a *Library Journal* article, describes Wolfe's prose as "free- flowing colorful Joycean, quote-slang, repetitive, cult or class jargon with literary and other reverberations."

Wolfe's style, combined with solid reporting and a highly critical eye, quickly gained a large audience for his magazine pieces. When his first book, *The Kandy-Kolored Tangerine-Flake Streamline Baby,* a collection of twenty-two of his best essays, was published in 1965, William James Smith wrote in *Commonweal:* "Two years ago [Tom Wolfe] was unknown and today those who are not mocking him are doing their level best to emulate him. Magazine editors are currently flooded with Zonk! articles written, putatively, in the manner of Wolfe and, by common account, uniformly impossible. . . . None of his parodists—and even fewer of his emulators—has successfully captured much of the flavor of Wolfe. . . . They miss the spark of personality that is more arresting than the funny punctuation. Wolfe has it, that magical quality that marks prose as distinctively one's own."

In *The Kandy-Kolored Tangerine-Flake Streamline Baby* Wolfe analyzes, caricaturizes, and satirizes a number of early-sixties American trends and pop culture heroes. His essays zero in on the city of Las Vegas, the Peppermint Lounge, demolition derbies, fashion, art galleries, doormen, nannies, and such personalities as Murray the K, Phil Spector, Baby Jane Holzer, and Muhammed Ali (then Cassius Clay). "He knows everything," writes Kurt Vonnegut in the *New York Times Book Review*. "I do not mean he *thinks* he knows everything. He is loaded with facile junk, as all personal journalists have to be—otherwise, how can they write so amusingly and fast?. . . . Verdict: Excellent book by a genius who will do anything to get attention."

What Wolfe has done, according to *Commonweal*'s Smith, "is simply to describe the brave new world of the 'unconscious avant- garde' who are shaping our future, but he has described this world with a vividness and accuracy that makes it something more than real." In a *New Republic* article, Joseph Epstein expresses the opinion that "Wolfe is perhaps most fatiguing when writing about the lower classes. Here he becomes Dr. Wolfe, Department of American Studies, and what he finds attractive about the lower orders, as has many an intellectual slummer before him, is their vitality. At bottom, what is involved here is worship of the Noble Savage. . . . Wolfe is much better when he writes about New York City. Here he drops his studied spontaneity, eases up on the rococo, slips his doctorate, and takes on the tone of the reasonably feeling New Yorker who has not yet been knocked insensate by the clatter of that city." A *Newsweek* writer concludes that "partly, Wolfe belongs to the old noble breed of poet-journalists, like Ben Hecht, and partly he belongs to a new breed of supereducated hip sensibilities like Jonathan Miller and Terry Southern, who see the complete human comedy in everything from a hair-do to a holocaust. Vulgar? A bit. Sentimental? A tick. But this is the nature of journalism, with its crackling short waves transmitting the living moment."

In *The Electric Kool-Aid Acid Test,* Wolfe applies his distinctive brand of journalism to novelist Ken Kesey and his "Merry Pranksters," a West Coast group dedicated to LSD and the pursuit of the psychedelic experience. Joel Lieber of the *Nation* says that in this book Wolfe "has come as close as seems possible, with words, at re-creating the entire mental atmosphere of a scene in which one's understanding is based on feeling rather than verbalization. . . . [The book] is nonfiction told as experimental fiction; it is a genuine feat and a landmark in reporting style." Lawrence Dietz, in a *National Review* article, calls *The Electric Kool-Aid Acid Test* "the best work Wolfe has done, and certainly the most profound and insightful book that has been written about the psychedelic life. . . . [He] has elicited a history of the spread of LSD from 1960 (when Kesey and others got their first jolts in lab experiments) to 1967, when practically any kid with five dollars could buy some kind of trip or other." Dietz feels that Wolfe displays "a willingness to let accuracy take the place of the hysterical imprecations that have passed for reportage in most magazine articles and books" on this subject.

Wolfe's 1970 book, *Radical Chic and Mau Mauing the Flak Catchers,* was made up of two lengthy essays. The first, "Radical Chic," elicited by far the most critical commentary; it deals with a fund-raising party given by Leonard Bernstein in his Park Avenue apartment on January 14, 1970, to raise money for the Black

Panthers. Wolfe was at the party, and he became aware of the incongruity of the scene, distinguished, according to Melvin Maddocks of the *Christian Science Monitor,* by "white liberals nibbling caviar while signing checks for the revolution with their free hand." Thomas R. Edwards writes in the *New York Times Book Review:* "For Wolfe, the scene in the Bernsteins' living room demonstrates his pet sociological thesis, here called *nostalgie de la boue,* the aristocrat's hankering for a proletarian primitivism. He shows us cultivated parvenu Jews, torn between cherished new 'right wing' lifestyles and the 'left wing' politics of their own oppressive history, ludicrously confused about how to take the black revolution. Though there's a touch of ugliness in his determination to let us know, without seeming to do so, that certain socialites with gentile names weren't born that way, 'Radical Chic' is sometimes brilliant and telling in its dramatization of this case."

A *Times Literary Supplement* reviewer says that Wolfe "both defends and exonerates the Bernsteins, that is—their motives were sound, liberal, serious, responsible—while cocking an almighty snook at 'the essential double-track mentality of Radical Chic—*nostalgie de la boue* and high protocol' that can entertain Afro hair-styles with Roquefort cheese savouries in a Park Avenue duplex. . . . The slogan 'Mr. Parlour Panther,' in the end, is inevitably unfurled to flutter in the ironic breeze. Such is this dazzling piece of trapeze work by the most practised social stuntman of them all."

Many readers were not happy with *Radical Chic and Mau Mauing the Flak Catchers.* As William F. Buckley explains in the *National Review,* "[Wolfe] has written a very very controversial book, for which he has been publicly excommunicated from the company of the orthodox by the bishops who preside over the *New York Review of Books.*" Buckley continues: "What Mr. Wolfe did in this book was MAKE FUN of Bernstein et al., and if you have never been told, you MUST NOT MAKE FUN of Bernstein et al., when what hangs in the balance is Bernstein's moral prestige plus the integrity of Black Protest; learn the lesson now." Edwards feels that Wolfe "humiliates and degrades everyone concerned, his pre-potent but child-like and shiftless blacks no less than his gutless, time-serving, sexually-fearful white bureaucrats." Timothy Foote, in a *Time* article, notes: "When a *Time* reporter recently asked a minister of the Panther Party's shadow government about the truthfulness of Wolfe's *Radical Chic* account, the reply was ominous: 'You mean that dirty, blatant, lying, racist dog who wrote that fascist disgusting thing in *New York* magazine?' " Yet, despite the objections to the book, Foote insists, the fact remains that "it is generally so accurate that even some of the irate guests at the Bernsteins later wondered how Wolfe—who in fact used shorthand—managed to smuggle a tape recorder onto the premises."

Christopher Lehmann-Haupt of the *New York Times,* noting that "Radical Chic" first appeared as a magazine article, writes: "When the news got out that it would be published as a book eventually, one began to prepare a mental review of it. One had certain questions—the usual Tom Wolfe questions: Where exactly was Wolfe located when all those things occurred? Just how did he learn Leonard Bernstein's innermost fantasies? At exactly what points did Wolfe's imagination impinge on his inferences, and his inferences on his facts? . . . Still, one was prepared to forget those questions. The vision of the Beautiful People dos-a-dosing with black revolutionaries while white servants passed out 'little Roquefort cheese morsels rolled in crushed nuts' was too outrageous. Shivers of malice ran up and down one's spine. Wolfe's anatomy of radical chic would have to be celebrated." The book, Lehmann-Haupt concludes, "represents

Wolfe at his best, worst, and most. It has his uncanny eye for lifestyles; his obsessive lists of brand names and artifacts; his wicked, frequently cruel, cartoon of people's physical traits; his perfect mimicry of speech patterns. Once again, Wolfe proves himself the complete chameleon, capable of turning any color. He understands the human animal like no sociologist around."

The Painted Word was another of Wolfe's more controversial works. T. O'Hara, in a *Best Sellers* review, sums up the book's thesis: "About 10,000 people constitute the present art world. Artists, doing what they must to survive, obey orders and follow the gospel as written by the monarchs." Among these monarchs, in Wolfe's opinion, are three of our most influential and well-respected art critics: Clement Greenberg, Harold Rosenberg, and Leo Steinberg (the "kings of cultureburg," he calls them). In a *Time* article, Robert Hughes says that "the New York art world, especially in its present decay, is the easiest target a pop sociologist could ask for. Most of it is a wallow of egotism, social climbing and power brokerage, and the only thing that makes it tolerable is the occasional reward of experiencing a good work of art in all its richness, complexity and difficulty. Take the art from the art world, as Wolfe does, and the matrix becomes fit for caricature. Since Wolfe is unable to show any intelligent response to painting, caricature is what we get. . . . Wolfe seems to know virtually nothing about the history of art, American or European."

New York Times art critic John Russell, writing in the *New York Times Book Review*, states: "If someone who is tone-deaf goes to Carnegie Hall every night of the year, he is, of course, entitled to his opinion of what he has listened to, just as a eunuch is entitled to his opinion of sex. But in the one case, as in the other, we on our side are entitled to discount what they say. Given the range, the variety and the degree of accomplishment represented by the names on Mr. Wolfe's list [including artists such as Pollock, de Kooning, Warhol, Newman, Rauschenberg, and Stella], we are entitled to think that if he got no visual reward from any of them, . . . the fault may not lie with the art."

As Ruth Berenson of the *National Review* points out, however, response to the book is generally dependent on the extent to which an individual is involved in the world of modern art. She maintains that *The Painted Word* "will delight those who have long harbored dark suspicions that modern art beginning with Picasso is a put-on, a gigantic hoax perpetrated on a gullible public by a mysterious cabal of artists, critics, dealers, and collectors aided and abetted by *Time* and *Newsweek*. Those who take modern art somewhat more seriously will be disappointed."

In *From Bauhaus to Our House,* published in 1981, Wolfe does to modern architecture what he did to modern art in *The Painted Word,* and the response has been similar: Readers close to the subject tend to resent the intrusion by an "outsider," while those with a more detached point of view often appreciate the author's fresh perspective. *New York Times* architecture critic Paul Goldberger, in a *New York Times Book Review* article, writes: "Mr. Wolfe wants to argue that ideology has gotten in the way of common sense. Beginning half a century ago with the origins of the International Style in Europe, he attempts to trace the development of that style, which for many, including Mr. Wolfe, is a virtual synonym for modern architecture. . . . We are told how the International Style became a 'compound'—a select, private, cult-like group of ideologues [including Walter Gropius, Mies van der Rohe, Marcel Breuer, and Josef Albers] whose great mission, as Mr. Wolfe sees it, was to foist modern design upon an unwilling world. . . . The problem, I think . . . is that Tom Wolfe has no eye. He has a wonderful ear, and he listens hard

and long, but he does not seem to see. . . . He does precisely what he warns us against; he has listened to the words, not looked at the architecture."

And in a *Washington Post Book World* review, *Post* architecture critic Benjamin Forgey says that "the book is a case of crying Wolfe for one more time. *Bauhaus* is distinguished by the same total loathing of modern culture that motivated *The Painted Word*. . . . Wolfe's explanation is that modernism has been a conspiracy. In place of the New York critics who foisted abstract art upon us, we have the European giants of architecture . . . and their abject American followers. In Wolfe's view the motivation was pretty much the same, too. They were all playing the hypocritical bohemian game of spitting on the bourgeois." Forgey feels that "there is some truth in this, but it makes for a thin book and a narrow, limited history of architecture in the 20th century."

On the other hand, *New York Times* literary critic Christopher Lehmann-Haupt makes the point that even many architects have been unhappy with the structures created by proponents of the Bauhaus school. This style of architecture (distinguished by what is often referred to as a "glass box" appearance) was, for instance, denigrated by architect Peter Blake in his 1977 book, *Form Follows Fiasco*. According to Lehmann-Haupt, Blake "anathematized modern architecture for being sterile, functionless and ugly"; thus Wolfe "has not really come up with anything very startling when he laments the irony that four-fifths of the way into the American Century, when what we ought to be expressing with our building is 'exuberance, power, empire, grandeur, or even high spirits and playfulness,' what we still see inflicted upon us is the anti-bourgeois, socialist, pro-worker ideas that arose from 'the smoking rubble of Europe after the Great War.' But the explication of this notion is done with such verve and hilarity by Mr. Wolfe that its substance almost doesn't seem to matter. . . . It flows with natural rhetorical rhythm. . . . And often enough it is to laugh right out loud." John Brooks, in a *Chicago Tribune Book World* review, calls the book "a readable polemic on how in our architecture over the past few decades things have gone very much as they have in the other visual arts—a triumph of conformity over true innovation, of timidity over uninhibited expression, of irony over straightforwardness, of posing over real accomplishment. . . . *From Bauhaus to Our House* is lucidly and for the most part gracefully written."

In 1979 Wolfe published the book that many critics consider his finest: *The Right Stuff,* an award-winning study of the early years of the American space program. At one point in the book Wolfe attempts to define the "ineffable quality" from which the title is taken: "It obviously involved bravery. But it was not bravery in the simple sense of being willing to risk your life . . . any fool could do that. . . . No, the idea . . . seemed to be that a man should have the ability to go up in a hurtling piece of machinery and put his hide on the line and then have the moxie, the reflexes, the experience, the coolness, to pull it back in the last yawning moment—and then to go up again *the next day,* and the next day, and every next day."

The main characters in the book are, of course, the first U.S. astronaut team: Scott Carpenter, Gordon Cooper, John Glenn, Gus Grissom, Wally Schirra, Alan Shepard, and Deke Slayton. Wolfe assiduously chronicles their early careers as test pilots, their private lives, their selection for the astronaut program and the subsequent medical processing and training. But, as *Commonweal*'s Thomas Powers points out, *The Right Stuff* "is not a history; it is far too thin in dates, facts and source citations to serve any such pulse. It is a work of literature which must stand or fall as a coherent text, and its subject is not the Mercury program itself but the impulse behind it, the unreflecting competitiveness which drove the original astronauts to the quite extraordinary lengths Wolfe describes so vividly." That the author goes beyond mere reportage of historical fact is confirmed by Mort Sheinman in a *Chicago Tribune* article: "Wolfe tells us what it's like to go 'shooting straight through the top of the sky,' to be 'in a king's solitude, unique and inviolate, above the dome of the world.' He describes what happens when someone is immolated by airplane fuel, and he talks about the nightmares and hallucinations experienced by the wives. . . . [*The Right Stuff*] is a dazzling piece of work, something that reveals much about the nature of bravery and celebrity and—yes—patriotism."

Time writer R. Z. Sheppard says that the book "is crammed with inside poop and racy incident that 19 years ago was ignored by what [Wolfe] terms the 'proper Victorian gents' of the press. The fast cars, booze, astro groupies, the envies and injuries of the military caste system were not part of what Americans would have considered the right stuff. Wolfe lays it all out in brilliantly stated Op Lit scenes: the tacky cocktail lounges of Cocoa Beach where one could hear the *Horst Wessel Song* sung by ex-rocket scientists of the Third Reich; Vice President Lyndon Johnson furiously cooling his heels outside the Glenn house because Annie Glenn would not let him in during her husband's countdown; Alan Shepard losing a struggle with his full bladder moments before lift-off; the overeager press terrifying Ham the chimp after his proficient flight; the astronauts surrounded by thousands of cheering Texans waving hunks of raw meat during an honorary barbecue in the Houston Coliseum."

Christopher Lehmann-Haupt of the *New York Times* writes: "What fun it is to watch Mr. Wolfe put the antiseptic space program into the traces of his inimitable verbal cadenzas. It's a little like hearing the story of Jesus of Nazareth through the lips of the Chicago nightclub comedian Lord Buckley." Lehmann-Haupt says that in this book Wolfe undertakes "the restoration of the zits and rogue cilia of hair to the face of the American space program" and reveals a good deal of the gossip that was denied the public by a hero-worshiping press in the early sixties, gossip "about how the test-pilot fraternity looked down on the early astronauts for being trained monkeys in a capsule ('spam in a can') instead of pilots in control of their craft; about the real feelings of the original seven for one another and the tension that arose between the upright John Glenn and some of the others over their after-hours behavior, particularly with the 'juicy little girls' who materialized wherever they trained; and about what National Aeronautical and Space Administration engineers really felt about the flight of Gus Grissom and Scott Carpenter and the possibility that they had secretly panicked."

Former test pilot and astronaut Michael Collins (a member of the Gemini 10 flight and command module pilot on the Apollo 11 moon flight), writes in a *Washington Post Book World* review: "I lived at Edwards [Air Force Base, site of the Air Force Flight Test Center,] for four years, and, improbable as some of Tom's tales seem, I know he's telling it like it was. He is the first gifted writer to explore the relationship between test pilots and astronauts—the obvious similarities and the subtle differences. He's obviously done a lot of homework—too much in some cases. Some of this stuff could only be interesting to Al Shepard's mother. While the first part of the book is a paean to guts, to the 'right stuff,' it is followed by a chronology—but one that might have profited from a little tighter editing. But it's still light-years ahead of the endless drivel [Norman] Mailer has put out about the Apollo program, and in places the Wolfe genius really shines." Collins feels that at times Wolfe allows himself to get

too close to his subject: "He's almost one of the boys—and there's too much to admire and not enough to eviscerate." As a result "*The Right Stuff* is not vintage, psychedelic Tom Wolfe, but if you . . . have ever been curious about what the space program was really all about in those halcyon Kennedy and Mercury years, then this is your book."

In a review of *The Right Stuff* for the *Lone Star Book Review,* Martha Heimberg says that, for the most part, "Wolfe's reporting, while being marvelously entertaining writing, has also represented a telling and trustworthy point of view. His is one of those finely critical intelligences that can detect the slightest pretention or falsification in an official posture or social pose. And, when he does, he goes after the hypocrisy—whether large or small, left or right—with all the zeal of the dedicated reformer." Like Collins, Heimberg feels that *The Right Stuff* "represents a departure for the satirist whose observant eye and caustic pen have impaled on the page a wide range of American social phenomena" in that Wolfe "clearly likes his subjects—none are treated as grist for the satirist's mill, but put down with as great a skill and detail as an observer could possibly muster." She concludes that "the book represents a tremendous accomplishment and a new direction for a writer who figures among the top stylists of his generation."

By the mid-1980s Wolfe had a new ambition for his writing. As he told the *New York Times:* "I was curious, having spouted off so much about fiction and nonfiction, and having said that the novelists weren't doing a good job, to see what would happen if I tried it. Also, I guess I subconsciously had the suspicion that maybe, what if all this to-do I've made about nonfiction is because I really, secretly think I can't do a novel. So I said, well, I've got to prove this to myself." The result was *The Bonfire of the Vanities,* a novel that exposes the greed and hate seething in modern New York City. In the book, a smug Wall Streeter named Sherman McCoy is reduced to a political pawn when he is implicated in the hit-and-run traffic death of a young black man. *Washington Post Book World*'s Jonathan Yardley called *Bonfire* "a superb human comedy and the first novel ever to get contemporary New York, in all its arrogance and shame and heterogeneity and insularity, exactly right." After his novel became a major bestseller, Wolfe issued what he called a "literary manifesto" in *Harper's* magazine. He urged fellow novelists to abandon the esoteric literary experiments that have characterized fiction for much of the twentieth century and use realism to chronicle the bizarre and astounding world around them. The author's peers reacted with both praise and condemnation. "Ever the provocateur," reported *Time,* "Wolfe is enjoying the controversy."

Although there can be no question that Tom Wolfe has achieved a reputation as a superb stylist and skillful reporter, no discussion of Wolfe would be complete without some mention of his famous wardrobe. *Philadelphia Bulletin* writer Leslie Bennetts tells of an encounter with the author when he lectured at Villanova University: "The legendary sartorial splendors were there, of course: the gorgeous three-piece creamy white suit he has been renowned for . . . (how many must he have, do you suppose, to appear in spotless vanilla every day: rows upon rows of them hanging in shadowed closets, a veritable army of Gatsby ghosts waiting to emerge?). Not to mention the navy suede shoes, dark as midnight, or the jaunty matching suede hat, or the sweeping midnight cashmere coat of the exact same hue, or the crisp matching tie on which perched a golden half- moon pin to complement the glittering gold watch chain that swung gracefully from the milky vest. Or the navy silk handkerchief peeking out from the white suit pocket, or the white silk handkerchief peeking out from the navy coat pocket."

Wolfe told Bennetts that he began wearing the white suits in 1962: "That was when I had a white suit made, started wearing it in January, and found it annoyed people tremendously. Even slight departures in dress at that time really spun people out. So I liked it. It's kind of a harmless form of aggression, I guess." But Wolfe's mode of dress has also been an important part of his journalism, serving as a device to distance him from his subject. He told Susan Forrest of the *Fort Lauderdale News:* "A writer can find out more if he doesn't pretend to be hip. . . . If people see you are an outsider, they will come up and tell you things. If you're trying to be hip, you can't ask a lot of naive questions." This technique has been effective for Wolfe in interviewing stock car racers, Hell's Angels, and—particularly—astronauts. He feels that at least part of the success of *The Right Stuff* is due to the fact that he did not try to get too close to that inner circle. Wolfe told Janet Maslin of the *New York Times Book Review:* "I looked like Ruggles of Red Gap to them, I'm sure. . . . But I've long since given up on the idea of going into a situation trying to act like part of it. . . . Besides, it was useless for me to try to fit into the world of pilots, because I didn't know a thing about flying. I also sensed that pilots, like people in the psychedelic life, really dislike people who presume a familiarity with the Lodge."

A writer for *Time* calls Wolfe's form of dress "a splendiferous advertisement for his individuality. The game requires a lot of reverse spin and body English but it boils down to antichic chic. Exclaims Wolfe proudly: 'I own no summer house, no car, I wear tank tops when I swim, long white pants when I play tennis, and I'm probably the last man in America to still do the Royal Canadian Air Force exercises.' "

MEDIA ADAPTATIONS: The Right Stuff was adapted for a film of the same title, Warner Bros., 1983; *Bonfire of the Vanities* was scheduled to be adapted for a film.

AVOCATIONAL INTERESTS: Window shopping.

BIOGRAPHICAL/CRITICAL SOURCES:

BOOKS

Authors in the News, Volume 2, Gale, 1976.
Bellamy, Joe David, editor, *The New Fiction: Interviews With Innovative American Writers,* University of Illinois Press, 1974.
Bestsellers 89, Issue 1, Gale, 1989.
Contemporary Literary Criticism, Gale, Volume 1, 1973, Volume 2, 1974, Volume 9, 1978, Volume 15, 1980, Volume 35, 1985, Volume 51, 1989.

PERIODICALS

America, February 5, 1977, April 2, 1988.
Atlantic, October, 1979, December, 1987.
Best Sellers, August, 1975.
Books and Art, September 28, 1979.
Books in Canada, April, 1988.
Business Week, November 23, 1987.
Chicago Tribune, September 9, 1979, September 15, 1979, January 16, 1983, November 4, 1987.
Chicago Tribune Book World, December 7, 1980, October 25, 1981, January 16, 1983.
Christian Science Monitor, November 17, 1970, November 3, 1987.
Commentary, March, 1971, May, 1977, February, 1980, February, 1988.
Commonweal, September 17, 1965, December 20, 1968, March 3, 1978, October 12, 1979, February 26, 1988.

Detroit News, October 14, 1979, November 9, 1980.
Encounter, September, 1977.
Fort Lauderdale News, April 22, 1975.
Fort Lauderdale Sentinel, April 22, 1975.
Globe and Mail (Toronto), December 5, 1987.
Guardian Weekly, February 21, 1988.
Harper's, February, 1971, November, 1989, January, 1990.
Library Journal, August, 1968.
Listener, February 11, 1988.
London Review of Books, February 18, 1988.
Lone Star Book Review, November, 1979.
Los Angeles Times, October 19, 1979, November 22, 1987, October 12, 1989, November 29, 1990.
Los Angeles Times Book Review, November 2, 1980, October 25, 1981, October 17, 1982, January 23, 1983, October 25, 1987.
Nation, March 5, 1977, November 3, 1977.
National Review, August 27, 1968, January 26, 1971, August 1, 1975, February 19, 1977, December 18, 1987.
New Leader, January 31, 1977.
New Republic, July 14, 1965, December 19, 1970, November 23, 1987.
New Statesman, February 12, 1988.
Newsweek, June 28, 1965, August 26, 1968, June 9, 1975, September 17, 1979, October 26, 1987.
New York, September 21, 1981, March 21, 1988.
New Yorker, February 1, 1988.
New York Review of Books, August 26, 1965, December 17, 1970, June 26, 1975, January 20, 1977, October 28, 1979, November 4, 1982, February 4, 1988.
New York Times, November 25, 1970, May 27, 1975, November 26, 1976, September 14, 1979, October 9, 1981, December 20, 1981, October 13, 1987, October 22, 1987, November 21, 1987, December 31, 1987, January 3, 1988, March 11, 1988.
New York Times Book Review, June 27, 1965, August 18, 1968, November 29, 1970, December 3, 1972, June 15, 1975, December 26, 1976, October 28, 1979, October 11, 1981, October 10, 1982, November 1, 1987.
Observer (London), February 7, 1988.
Partisan Review, Number 3, 1969, Number 2, 1974.
People, December 24, 1979, November 23, 1987.
Philadelphia Bulletin, February 10, 1975.
Punch, February 12, 1988.
Rolling Stone, August 21, 1980, November 5-December 10, 1987.
Saturday Review, September 15, 1979, April, 1981.
Spectator, February 13, 1988.
Time, September 6, 1968, December 21, 1970, June 23, 1975, December 27, 1976, September 29, 1979, November 9, 1987, February 13, 1989, November 27, 1989.
Times (London), February 11, 1988, February 13, 1989, April 22, 1989.
Times Literary Supplement, October 1, 1971, November 30, 1979, November 26, 1980, March 18, 1988.
Tribune Books, August 2, 1987, October 18, 1987.
U.S. News and World Report, November 23, 1987.
Village Voice, September 10, 1979.
Wall Street Journal, October 29, 1987.
Washington Monthly, March, 1988.
Washington Post, September 4, 1979, October 23, 1980, March 27, 1988, October 17, 1989.
Washington Post Book World, September 9, 1979, November 23, 1980, November 15, 1981, November 7, 1982, October 25, 1987.

Writer's Digest, January, 1970.

* * *

WOLFE, Tom
See WOLFE, Thomas Kennerly, Jr.

* * *

WOUK, Herman 1915-

PERSONAL: Surname is pronounced "Woke"; born May 27, 1915, in New York, N.Y.; son of Abraham Isaac (an industrialist in the power laundry field who started as an immigrant laundry laborer at $3 a week) and Esther (Levine) Wouk; married Betty Sarah Brown, December 9, 1945; children: Abraham Isaac (deceased), Nathaniel, Joseph. *Education:* Columbia University, B.A. (with honors), 1934. *Religion:* Jewish.

ADDRESSES: Agent—BSW Literary Agency, 3255 N St. N.W., Washington, D.C. 20007.

CAREER: Gag writer for radio comedians, New York, N.Y., 1934-35; scriptwriter for Fred Allen, 1936-41; U.S. Treasury Department, "dollar-a-year-man," writing and producing radio plays to promote war bond sales, 1941; self-employed writer, 1946—. Visiting professor, Yeshiva University, 1953-57; scholar in residence, Aspen Institute of Humanistic Studies, 1973-74; lectured in China, 1982. Trustee, College of the Virgin Islands, 1962- 69; member of board of directors, Washington National Symphony, 1969-71, and Kennedy Center Productions, 1974-75; member of advisory council, Center for U.S.-China Arts Exchange, 1981-87. *Military service:* U.S. Navy, 1942-46; served on Pacific Ocean aboard two destroyer-minesweepers, U.S.S. *Zane* and U.S.S. *Southard;* became lieutenant; received four campaign stars and Presidential Unit Citation.

MEMBER: Authors Guild, P.E.N., Dramatists Guild, Reserve Officers Association of the United States, Writers Guild of America East, Century Club (New York City), Bohemian Club (San Francisco); Cosmos Club, Metropolitan Club (both Washington, D.C.).

AWARDS, HONORS: Richard H. Fox Prize, 1934; Pulitzer Prize in fiction, 1952, for *The Caine Mutiny: A Novel of World War II;* Columbia University Medal of Excellence, 1952; L.H.D., Yeshiva University, 1955; LL.D., Clark University, 1960; Litt.D., American International University, 1979; Alexander Hamilton Medal, Columbia College Alumni Association, 1980; American Book Award nomination, 1981, for *War and Remembrance;* Ralph Waldo Emerson Award, International Platform Association, 1981; University of California—Berkeley Medal, 1984; Golden Plate Award, American Academy of Achievement, 1986; *Washingtonian* Book Award, 1986, for *Inside, Outside.*

WRITINGS:

Aurora Dawn; or, The True History of Andrew Reale, Containing a Faithful Account of the Great Riot, Together With the Complete Texts of Michael Wilde's Oration and Father Stanfield's Sermon (novel; Book-of-the-Month Club selection), Simon & Schuster, 1947, reprinted, Pocket Books, 1983.
The City Boy: The Adventures of Herbie Bookbinder and His Cousin, Cliff (novel; Reader's Digest Condensed Book Club selection; Family Book Club selection; Book-of-the-Month Club alternate selection), Simon & Schuster, 1948, published as *The City Boy,* Doubleday, 1952, published as *City Boy: The Adventures of Herbie Bookbinder,* Doubleday, 1969.
The Caine Mutiny: A Novel of World War II (Reader's Digest Condensed Book Club selection; Literary Guild alternate selection), Doubleday, 1951, reprinted, Franklin Library, 1977, published as *The Caine Mutiny,* Dell, 1966.
Marjorie Morningstar (novel; Reader's Digest Condensed Book Club selection; Book-of-the-Month Club selection), Doubleday, 1955, reprinted, Pocket Books, 1977.
This Is My God (nonfiction; Reader's Digest Condensed Book Club selection; Book-of-the-Month Club alternate selection), Doubleday, 1959, published as *This Is My God: The Jewish Way of Life,* 1970, revised edition, Collins, 1973.
Youngblood Hawke (novel; Reader's Digest Condensed Book Club selection; Book-of-the-Month Club selection), Doubleday, 1962.
Don't Stop the Carnival (novel; Book-of-the-Month Club selection), Doubleday, 1965.
The "Lomokome" Papers, Pocket Books, 1968.
The Winds of War (novel; Literary Guild selection; Reader's Digest Condensed Book Club selection), Little, Brown, 1971.
War and Remembrance (novel; sequel to *The Winds of War;* Literary Guild selection; Reader's Digest Condensed Book Club selection), Little, Brown, 1978.
Inside, Outside (novel; Book-of-the-Month Club selection), Little, Brown, 1985.

PLAYS

The Traitor (two-act; first produced on Broadway at Forty-Eighth Street Theater, April 4, 1949), Samuel French, 1949.
The Caine Mutiny Court-Martial (two-act; based on his novel *The Caine Mutiny;* first produced in Santa Barbara, Calif., 1953; produced on Broadway at Plymouth Theater, January 20, 1954), Doubleday, 1954, reprinted, Pocket Books, 1974.
Slattery's Hurricane (screenplay; produced by Twentieth Century-Fox, 1949), Permabooks, 1956.
Nature's Way (two-act comedy; first produced on Broadway at Coronet Theater, October 15, 1957), Doubleday, 1958, reprinted, Samuel French, 1977.

Also author of screenplay "The Winds of War," ABC-TV, 1983, and co-author of screenplay "War and Remembrance," ABC-TV, 1988.

SIDELIGHTS: An American novelist and playwright of Russian-Jewish heritage, Herman Wouk received the 1952 Pulitzer Prize in fiction for *The Caine Mutiny: A Novel of World War II* and has since published several other best-sellers, including *The Winds of War* and *War and Remembrance.* The *Atlantic*'s Edward Weeks calls him a compelling narrator "who uses large canvases and who, without much fuss for style or symbolism, drives his story ahead with an infectious belief in the people he is writing about." According to a reviewer for *Time,* Wouk's chief significance is that "he spearheads a mutiny against the literary stereotypes of rebellion—against three decades of U.S. fiction dominated by skeptical criticism, sexual emancipation, social protest, and psychoanalytic sermonizing." He remains, writes Pearl K. Bell in *Commentary,* "an unembarrassed believer in such 'discredited' forms of commitment as valor, gallantry, leadership, patriotism." Because of the reaffirmation of traditional values in his works, Wouk has enjoyed wide readership but has also been accused by some critics of pandering to popular prejudice.

Wouk began writing fiction in 1943 while on sea duty on the Pacific Ocean, and he later used his Navy experience aboard the U.S.S. *Zane* and U.S.S. *Southard* as background for his third novel, *The Caine Mutiny* (which is not autobiographical). The book is not concerned with battles at sea but with adherence to appointive authority. The conflict centers around Lieutenant Commander Philip Francis Queeg, who, according to W. J. Stuckey in *The Pulitzer Prize Novels,* "manifests a professional incompetence that will probably remain unparalleled in or out of fiction." When it appears that Queeg is too terrified to issue the necessary orders to save the ship during a typhoon, Lieutenant Maryk, the ship's executive officer, is persuaded by Lieutenant Keefer and his followers to seize control. Maryk is subsequently tried for making a mutiny but is acquitted through the efforts of Lieutenant Barney Greenwald, an adept trial lawyer. Ironically, at a party celebrating Maryk's acquittal, Greenwald tells Maryk that it is he, Maryk, (and not Queeg) who is morally guilty, for he deserted a military system that had, despite its flaws, protected America from foreign fascists.

Several critics consider Wouk's treatment of the military affair insightful and carefully constructed. Harry Gilroy, for example, writes in the *New York Times* that Wouk "has a profound understanding of what Navy men should be, and against some who fell short of the mark he has fired a deadly broadside." Edmund Fuller points out in his *Man in Modern Fiction* that the book's ability "to view the problem within the inescapable military premise without oversimplifying it" distinguishes *The Caine Mutiny* from other World War II novels. Discussing the justification of the mutiny in his *In My Opinion,* Orville Prescott says that it is "the crux of [the novel, and] Mr. Wouk develops it extremely well, with racy wit and genial humor, with lively pace and much ingenuity of incident and with unexpected subtlety." Similarly, a reviewer for the *Times Literary Supplement* concludes: "So convincingly has Mr. Wouk created his officers, so subtly has he contrived the series of incidents that culminate in the final drama, that, given both the characters and the situations, the climax is perfectly acceptable."

W. J. Stuckey, however, sees the climax as "the unwarranted whitewash" of Queeg: "Throughout three-fourths of the novel, Captain Queeg is a thoroughly incompetent and badly frightened man. However, toward the close of the book Wouk springs a wholly unprepared-for surprise: Queeg, he tells us, is not really the incompetent everyone thinks him; he is the victim of ambitious and cowardly subordinates. . . . While it is easy to understand the reason for Lieutenant Greenwald's emotional defense of the United States Navy, it is difficult to see why he—an intelligent trial lawyer, we are told—defends an incompetent American ship's captain who had not served in the Atlantic and who, if he had encountered Nazi warships, would have fled in terror. Greenwald's only defense of Queeg is that he was a member of the regular navy. It would make as much sense to defend a doctor guilty of malpractice on the grounds that he engaged in a humane calling. . . . The war in Europe and Hitler's treatment of the Jews had nothing to do with Queeg's or Maryk's innocence or guilt."

Eric Bentley finds the same weakness in "The Caine Mutiny Court Martial," Wouk's play based on the court martial sequence of the novel. Discussing the theme that the important thing is not to save a particular ship but to preserve the authority of commanders, Bentley writes in the *New Republic:* "There is a good point here, and there must surely be a good play in it—a play that would show up the sentimentality of our prejudice against commanders and in favor of mutineers. If, however, Mr. Wouk wanted to write such a play, he chose the wrong story and

told it in the wrong way, for we spend three quarters of the evening hoping that Queeg—the commander—will be found insane and the mutineers vindicated. When, in the very last scene, Mr. Wouk explains that this is not the right way to take the story, it is too late. We don't believe him. At best we say that he is preaching at us a notion that ought to have been dramatized. And no amount of shock technique—not even the reiterated image of Jews melted down for soap—can conceal the flaw."

Marjorie Morningstar, Wouk's fourth novel, also focuses on rebellion but in a civilian context. The book traces the life of a beautiful, intelligent girl who renounces the values and authority of her hard-working Jewish parents only to end up, years later, affirming them as a suburban matron and community servant. E. W. Foell notes in the *Christian Science Monitor* that Wouk "has not flinched at what he sees in his characters' thoughts, [but] many of his readers are likely to." A *Time* critic writes that, indeed, "Wouk [sets] teeth on edge by advocating chastity before marriage, suggesting that real happiness for a woman is found in a home and children, cheering loud and long for the American middle class and blasting Bohemia and Bohemians. Wouk is a Sinclair Lewis in reverse." Reviewing the book in the *New York Times,* Maxwell Geismar believes that "here as in *The Caine Mutiny* [the conflict] is settled by a final bow to the red-tape of a bureaucracy or to the properties of a social class, under the impression that these are among the eternal verities. *Marjorie Morningstar* is very good reading indeed. But to this reviewer at least the values of true culture are as remote from its polished orbit as are, at base, the impulses of real life."

Leslie A. Fiedler, however, sees the most popular novel of 1955 as untraditional in one regard. In *Love and Death in the American Novel,* Fiedler calls *Marjorie Morningstar* "the first fictional celebration of the mid-twentieth-century detente between the Jews and middle-class America." He explains: "In the high literature of Europe and, more slowly, in that of the United States, gentile and Jew have joined forces to portray the Jewish character as a figure representing man's fate in . . . an age of rootlessness, alienation, and terror, in which the exiled condition so long thought peculiar to the Jew comes to seem the common human lot. This is neither a cheery nor a reassuring view. . . . Wouk [suggests] a counterview: the contention that the Jew was never (or is, at least, no longer) the rootless dissenter, the stranger which legend has made him, but rather the very paragon of the happy citizen at home, loyal, chaste, thrifty, pious, and moderately successful—in short, Marjorie Morningstar."

After *Marjorie Morningstar,* Wouk interrupted his career as a novelist to write a short, clear account of the Jewish faith from a personal viewpoint—something he had been thinking of doing for years. Dedicated to the memory of his grandfather, Mendel Leib Levine, a rabbi from Minsk, *This Is My God* was published in 1959 and became a best-seller. Then, with *Youngblood Hawke* and *Don't Stop the Carnival,* Wouk returned to writing fiction, but he also began work on a second ambition: a panoramic novel of World War II.

Wouk first considered doing a global war novel in 1944, according to *Time*'s Timothy Foote. Later, *The Caine Mutiny* "threatened to sprawl in that direction," notes Foote, "with more home-front material and a subplot in Europe. Wisely, Wouk cut it back and waited." Having begun reading standard histories in 1962, Wouk moved to Washington two years later to utilize the National Archives and Library of Congress, as well as to interview surviving military leaders. His quest for information also led him to England, France, Italy, Germany, Poland, Czechoslovakia, Israel, Iran, and the Soviet Union. Due to the scope of his task,

Wouk ended up writing not one but two novels: *The Winds of War* and a sequel, *War and Remembrance*. "Since both have been best sellers, it is likely that more Americans have learned about, or remembered, the war through Wouk's account than from any other single source in the last decade," claims Michael Mandelbaum in *Political Science Quarterly*.

Generally praised by critics for their depth and accuracy of detail, the two books may be described as the history of the Second World War seen through the eyes of an American family and their immediate friends and contacts. *The Winds of War* takes Commander Victor "Pug" Henry and his family from the invasion of Poland to the attack on Pearl Harbor, Hawaii, and *War and Remembrance* details their experiences from Pearl Harbor to the dropping of the atomic bomb on Hiroshima, Japan. Over the course of the war, Henry serves as a special presidential envoy; meets Hitler, Stalin, Churchill, and Mussolini; is in Hawaii the day after the attack on Pearl Harbor; is present at the summit meetings off Nova Scotia in 1940 and in Tehran in 1943; is in London during the Battle of Britain; accompanies the Harriman-Beaverbrook mission to Moscow in 1941; participates in the battles of Midway, Guadalcanal, and Leyte Gulf; tours the Russian front in 1944; and even comes in contact with people working on the Manhattan Project. What he fails to witness, members of his family see: the invasion of Poland, the war in North Africa, the fall of Singapore, and the horrors of Auschwitz.

In reviewing the two books, critics often point out that this technique of depicting the effects of war on ordinary people (some of whom rub shoulders with the high and mighty) is a familiar one. Timothy Foote, among others, suggests that Wouk's opus is reminiscent of *War and Peace*— though not of the same quality—and that Wouk's aim is "nothing less than to do for the middle-class American vision of World War II pretty much what [Leo] Tolstoy did for the Battle of Borodino." More often, however, reviewers like Granville Hicks of the *New York Times Book Review* cite the resemblance between "Pug" Henry and Upton Sinclair's Lanny Budd: "Like Lanny, Pug becomes a kind of secret Presidential agent. In this role, he turns up at most of the places where history is being made."

Several critics charge that the technique results in characterization that is purely functional. Though Hicks admits that Wouk has "the gift of compelling narrative," he feels that the characters in *The Winds of War,* "even Pug Henry, are never living human beings. Although [Wouk] tries to give these men and women some semblance of reality by involving them in more or less complicated love affairs, they remain essentially observers and reporters." Similarly, Pearl K. Bell, reviewing *War and Remembrance* in *Commentary,* describes the characters as "not merely trivial but offensively so. Time and again, Wouk the student of history writes a brilliantly evocative account of battle—he has mastered every maneuver, knows exactly how submarines, aircraft carriers, battleships, destroyers, dive bombers work, how the vast machinery of war was deployed during a particular operation—only to return with a dismaying thump to his super-Lanny Budd hero, Captain (eventually Admiral) Victor (Pug) Henry." Foote is willing "to forgive Henry, and the author, the narrative necessities that shoot [Henry] hither and yon and miraculously equip him with the Russian and German necessary to do his work for Wouk, F.D.R., and the reader. [But] not so the other Henrys. The wife who would worry about getting her hair done on the day of Armageddon, a wayward daughter caught up in the sleazy radio industry in New York, two naval-officer sons, all are conventional appurtenances, without the emotional or dynastic depth to support a drama on the scale of World War II."

Nevertheless, Michael Mandelbaum asserts that Wouk's aim was to create something not purely fictional and that his "hybrid literary genre" of historical romance "turns out to be singularly appropriate." Other critics agree. Reviewing *The Winds of War* in the *Midwest Quarterly,* Richard R. Bolton writes: "Critics who have castigated the book for failing in various ways as a *novel* have seemingly overlooked the author's description of it as a romance. That form is older, and adheres to rather different standards, than the novel. Much criticism directed at the book's emphasis of incident and plot over deep character development, or its unfashionably detailed descriptions of people's appearances, becomes immaterial if one accepts Wouk's idea of what *The Winds of War* is—a historical romance, with a didactic purpose. That purpose is to dramatize the author's ideas about his themes—how the 'curse' emerged, how we might constructively understand it, and how 'men of good will' have been involved with it."

A major theme of the two books, according to Mandelbaum, "centers on the German question. Why did the Germans do it? Why did they cause so much trouble? Why, especially, did they behave in such brutal, aggressive fashion? These questions arise again and again, and Wouk has different characters give different answers—[geopolitical, political, cultural, historical]. Together they make for a symposium on the central puzzle of the twentieth century." Mandelbaum suggests that at the heart of the German question is the fate of the Jews under the Third Reich, the description of which "gives the two books their enduring message, a message that neither plain fiction nor standard history could convey as forcefully. It is not, [however,] the only, nor perhaps the primary, message that the author intends."

Wouk widens the scope of the story by presenting a German perspective on the war through excerpts of General Armin von Roon's *World Empire Lost,* an imaginary treatise based on actual writings of German generals. Bolton claims that von Roon's views, "and (in places) Henry's 'later' comments on them, jolt the reader out of enough preconceptions to make him more receptive to Wouk's own explanations of why things turned out as they did, or (more important) *how* they might have been made to turn out better." Bolton surmises that, according to Wouk, World War II was a "natural" disaster in that it arose from fallible human nature: "Human cruelty, of which war is the most massive and spectacular manifestation, occurs not because most people are cruel, but because most people are weak or lazy, or too wishful to perceive in time what truly cruel people like the Nazis are about. . . . Given that fallibility, World War II, and possibly other wars since, probably could not have been avoided." But, he continues, "given also the availability of enough men with the training and virtues of Victor Henry—the truly 'best' in Wouk's view, those who do not lack conviction—that war, and possibly others since, could have been ameliorated, at least. It was not ameliorated, because democratic societies, notably ours, have little stomach for the unpleasant facts that are a military professional's daily fare."

Thus, Bolton discerns a thematic relation to *The Caine Mutiny:* "Captain Henry can be seen as the fulfillment and justification of Lt. Barney Greenwald's unexpected and much discussed encomium to Regular Navy officers in the post-trial scene of *The Caine Mutiny.* Greenwald pays his tributes not so much to the *Caine*'s fallen captain as to what-Queeg-could-have-been . . .— the selfless and dedicated guardian of a reckless and unappreciative nation's safety. In Henry, Wouk presents a man who really *is* what Queeg could only try, pretend, or fail to be, the 'compleat' and admirable United States Navy officer." Pearl K. Bell believes that Wouk's traditionalist support of the military career man will strike many "as at best naive, at worst absurdly out of touch with the Catch-22 lunacy of all war, including the war against Hitler. [However,] it is precisely to confute such facile and ahistorical cynicism that Wouk devotes so large and sober a part of his novel to the Final Solution and the ideological poison that overwhelmed the German people during Hitler's twelve years of power."

In Wouk's eyes, men like Victor Henry, writes Bolton, have instincts and habits that "predispose them to be builders and preservers. . . . 'Constructive' rather than creative, they build things that are not particularly original, but are for Wouk the cement of civilization— families, homes, churches, firms, and especially, professional reputations. What repels Capt. Henry first about Nazi racism is that it destroys these things, and judges men on factors other than their accomplishments. Only after learning of the *Einsatzgruppen*'s atrocities does he react to Nazi racism with more visceral rage." Referring to the one-word Hebrew epigraph of *The Winds of War*, "Remember!," Bolton concludes: "Part of remembering, in Wouk's sense, would be to emulate Victor Henry and to listen, early and attentively, to those men who live in his tradition. If we do not, the author suggests, . . . it becomes too easy to look away, to make excuses while the massacres begin, while terrorism becomes pardonable."

Wouk's 1985 novel, *Inside, Outside*, "comes as close to being an outright autobiography as he is likely to write," declares John Eisenhower in the *Chicago Tribune Book World*. It tells of a Jewish man who, like Wouk, was born in New York City in 1915, the son of immigrant parents who established a commercial laundry business. Like Wouk, protagonist Israel David Goodkind—"Yisroelke" to his friends and family on the "inside"— worked as a gag writer, although Goodkind becomes a lawyer rather than a novelist. Goodkind is, however, writing his memoirs, which transforms Wouk's novel into "a paean to the American Jewish experience," according to *Diversion* contributor Sybil S. Steinberg. Unifying the novel, which deals by turns with Goodkind's present reality as a speech writer for U.S. President Richard Nixon and with Goodkind's childhood and relatives, is the tension between the "inside" (which includes Jewish religious life, values, and heritage as well as the search for identity for Jew or gentile) and the "outside" (secular American life).

The novel—Wouk's first in seven years—has received mixed reviews. Critics such as Steinberg praise the "breezy, humorous style" in which it is written and cite its compassion and wisdom. Writes Eisenhower, it is "an easy-to-read, informative tale that . . . provides an enlightening perspective on Jewish attitudes." He singles out one scene in which "Jews of varying persuasions . . . exchange views and insults" and concludes that "that scene alone, which illuminates so much of the current Jewish dilemma, gives this novel the right to be regarded as Wouk's most significant work since 'The Caine Mutiny.' " In contrast, Christopher Lehmann-Haupt of the *New York Times* finds the novel "remarkably predictable" and, "worst of all, . . . smug." Others criticize the book for superficiality and express reservations about what Bill Wine in the *Philadelphia Inquirer* deems "the failure of Wouk's storytelling proclivities to break out. The narrative, though carefully wrought, somehow registers as out of kilter, as if the seemingly appropriate admixture of memories, insights, observations and descriptions were really a convenience embraced by a writer unable to find a handle on his material." Nonetheless, Wine approvingly concludes that, "on the whole, *Inside, Outside* is an entertaining X-ray of Being Jewish in America." Novelist James Michener, reviewing the book in the *New York Times Book Review*, judges it "ambitious," lauding its segments as "compact, beautifully focused and often hilarious."

Among the critics who acknowledge faults, several, like Steinberg, still maintain that "the universality of [the] theme . . . lifts this novel above the level of inbred American Jewish experience. For *Inside, Outside* is about anyone who must reconcile private and public commitments. It is about living a good life on many levels, and while it makes no pretension of being profound, it is funny, wise, and kind."

MEDIA ADAPTATIONS: The Caine Mutiny was filmed by Columbia in 1954, starring Humphrey Bogart as Captain Queeg; *The City Boy* was made into a motion picture by Columbia in 1950; Warner Bros. filmed *Marjorie Morningstar* and *Youngblood Hawke* in 1958 and 1964, respectively. A television adaptation of "The Caine Mutiny Court Martial," with Barry Sullivan, Lloyd Nolan, and Frank Lovejoy, aired on "Ford Star Jubilee" in 1955; *The Winds of War* and *War and Remembrance* were adapted as television miniseries airing on ABC-TV in 1983 and 1988, respectively.

AVOCATIONAL INTERESTS: Judaic scholarship, Zionist studies, travel (especially in Israel).

BIOGRAPHICAL/CRITICAL SOURCES:

BOOKS

Beichman, Arnold C., *Herman Wouk: The Novelist as Social Historian,* Transaction Books, 1984.
Bentley, Eric, *The Dramatic Event: An American Chronicle,* Horizon Press, 1954.
Contemporary Literary Criticism, Gale, Volume 1, 1973, Volume 9, 1978, Volume 38, 1986.
Dictionary of Literary Biography Yearbook: 1982, Gale, 1983.
Fiedler, Leslie A., *Love and Death in the American Novel,* Stein & Day, 1966.
Fuller, Edmund, *Man in Modern Fiction: Some Minority Opinions on Contemporary American Writing,* Random House, 1958.
Geismar, Maxwell, *American Moderns From Rebellion to Conformity,* Hill & Wang, 1958.
Hyman, Stanley Edgar, *Standards: A Chronicle of Books for Our Time,* Horizon Press, 1966.
Prescott, Orville, *In My Opinion,* Bobbs-Merrill, 1952.
Stuckey, W. J., *The Pulitzer Prize Novels,* University of Oklahoma Press, 1966.

PERIODICALS

Antioch Review, Volume 16, 1956.
Atlantic, August, 1951, October, 1955, December, 1971.
Book Week, March 7, 1965.
Boston Sunday Globe, March 24, 1985.
Chicago Sunday Tribune, March 18, 1951.
Chicago Tribune, February 6, 1983, September 12, 1988.
Chicago Tribune Book World, November 14, 1971, March 24, 1985.
Christian Science Monitor, September 1, 1955, September 24, 1959, May 24, 1962, October 23, 1978.
College English, Volume 17, 1956.
Commentary, December, 1978.
Critic, August, 1965.
Detroit Free Press, February 6, 1983, April 7, 1985.
Detroit News, January 24, 1985.
Diversion, May, 1985.
Economist, November 20, 1971.
Globe and Mail (Toronto), June 15, 1985.
Life, June, 1962, November 19, 1971.
Los Angeles Times Book Review, March 3, 1985, May 8, 1986.
Midwest Quarterly, July, 1975.

New Republic, February 15, 1954, September 3, 1955, June 11, 1962, October 14, 1978.

Newsweek, March 9, 1965, November 29, 1971, October 9, 1978, February 7, 1983.

New York, August 30, 1971.

New York Herald Tribune Book Review, March 18, 1951, September 4, 1955, May 20, 1962.

New York Herald Tribune Weekly Book Review, April 20, 1947, August 29, 1948.

New York Times, April 20, 1947, August 29, 1948, March 18, 1951, September 4, 1955, September 27, 1959, January 2, 1983, January 21, 1983, January 30, 1983, February 5, 1983, February 6, 1983, March 7, 1985.

New York Times Book Review, September 16, 1951, May 20, 1962, November 14, 1971, November 12, 1978, March 10, 1985.

Parade, February 6, 1983.

Partisan Review, Volume 20, 1953.

Philadelphia Inquirer, April 14, 1985.

Publishers Weekly, February 7, 1972, May 23, 1986.

San Francisco Chronicle, March 24, 1985.

Saturday Review, February 6, 1954, September 3, 1955, September 26, 1959, May 19, 1962, November 27, 1971.

Saturday Review of Literature, April 19, 1947, August 21, 1948, March 31, 1951.

Time, April 9, 1951, September 5, 1955, May 18, 1962, March 5, 1965, November 22, 1971, October 16, 1978, February 7, 1983, February 28, 1983, April 1, 1985.

Times (London), March 2, 1985.

Times Literary Supplement, November 9, 1951.

USA Today, March 22, 1985.

Vogue, February 15, 1952.

Washingtonian, March, 1986.

Washington Post, April 29, 1985, May 31, 1986.

Washington Post Book World, October 8, 1978, March 10, 1985.*

*   *   *

WRIGHT, Arthur Frederick 1913-1976

PERSONAL: Born December 3, 1913, in Portland, OR; died August 11, 1976, in New London, CT; son of Charles Frederick and Georgiana (Gwynne) Wright; married Mary Oliver Clabaugh (a professor of history), July 6, 1940 (died in June, 1970); married Marya Wankowicz Welch, March 4, 1972; children (first marriage) Charles Duncan, Jonathan Arthur. *Education:* Stanford University, A.B., 1935; Oxford University, B.Litt., 1937; Harvard University, A.M., 1940, Ph.D., 1947.

ADDRESSES: Home—Guilford, CT. *Office*—328 Hall of Graduate Studies, Yale University, New Haven, CT 06520.

CAREER: Stanford University, Stanford, CA, assistant professor, 1947-51, associate professor, 1951-58, professor of history, 1958-59, Yale University, New Haven, CT, professor, 1959-61, Charles Seymour Professor of History, 1961-76, executive secretary of Concilium of International Studies, 1961-65, chairman of council on East Asian studies, 1956-59, 1961-62, 1968-69.

MEMBER: International Society for the History of Ideas, Institute of Current World Affairs (member of board of governors, 1961-66), American Council of Learned Societies (committee chairman, 1963-73), American Historical Association, American Association of University Professors, Association for Asian Studies (member of board of directors, 1951-58; committee chairman, 1951-62; vice-president, 1963-64; president, 1964-65).

AWARDS, HONORS: Rockefeller fellowship for Harvard University, 1937-39; Guggenheim fellowship for University of Kyoto, 1953-54; honorary M.A., Yale University, 1959.

WRITINGS:

Buddhism in Chinese History, Stanford University Press, 1959.

The Sui Dynasty, Knopf, 1978.

EDITOR

Studies in Chinese Thought, University of Chicago Press, 1953, reprinted, 1975.

(With David S. Nivison) *Confucianism in Action,* Stanford University Press, 1959.

The Confucian Persuasion, Stanford University Press, 1960.

(With Denis Twitchett) *Confucian Personalities,* Stanford University Press, 1962.

(And author of introduction) *Confucianism and Chinese Civilization,* Atheneum, 1964.

Etienne Balazs, *Chinese Civilization and Bureaucracy: Variations on a Theme* (young adult), translation by H. M. Wright, Yale University Press, 1964.

(With Twitchett) *Perspectives on the T'ang,* Yale University Press, 1973.

Far Eastern Quarterly, associate editor, 1950-51, editor, 1951-55; adviser to editorial board of *Encyclopaedia Britannica,* 1957-60.

SIDELIGHTS: Arthur Frederick Wright was composing *The Sui Dynasty* when he died in 1976, and Robert Somers, a former student, published it posthumously. *The Sui Dyansty's* setting is 581 A.D. in northern China, and focuses on the warrior who became the emperor Wen-ti. The history continues through Wen-ti's son Yang-ti and the dynasty's collapse. *Washington Post Book World* contributor Frederick Wakeman, Jr., found *The Sui Dynasty* "an elegantly written book." He commended Wright for presenting Yang-ti, as an understandable human being, instead of "as a sadistic and licentious tyrant." "Wright's book destroys this stereotype and presents a much more believable figure: an ambitious and harsh despot, to be sure, but a man of refinement and learning as well," Wakeman continued. According to David Lattimore in the *New York Times Book Review, The Sui Dynasty* is "a model of historical exposition directed at once to the specialist . . . and to the common reader. . . . Without oversimplification [Wright] isolates the important or the characteristic, making it visible and at the same time understandable. . . . And it is above all the modest, straight-forward psychohistory of a pair of driven, suspicious and guilty men, father and son."

OBITUARIES:

PERIODICALS

New York Times, August 14, 1976.

New York Times Book Review, December 17, 1978.

Washington Post Book World, March 18, 1979.*

Y

YEVTUSHENKO, Yevgeny (Alexandrovich) 1933-

PERSONAL: Name is transliterated in some sources as Evgenii Evtushenko, Yevgeniy Yevtushenko, or Evgeny Evtushenko; born July 18, 1933, in Stanzia Zima, Siberia, U.S.S.R.; son of Gangnus (a geologist) and Zinaida (a geologist and singer) Yevtushenko; married Bella Akhmadulina (a poet), 1954 (divorced); married Galina Semyonovna (a literary translator); children: one. *Education:* Attended Gorky Literary Institute, 1951-54. *Politics:* Communist. *Religion:* "Revolution."

ADDRESSES: Office—Union of U.S.S.R. Writers, ul Vorovskogo 52, Moscow, U.S.S.R.

CAREER: Poet, filmmaker, actor, and author. Worked on geological expedition in Kazakhstan, U.S.S.R. Appearances in films include "Take-Off," 1979, and "The Kindergarten," 1983.

MEMBER: International PEN (vice-president of Russian center), Gorky Literary Institute, Writer's Union.

AWARDS, HONORS: U.S.S.R. Commission for the Defense of Peace award, 1965; U.S.S.R. state prize, 1984; Order of Red Banner of Labor; finalist for Ritz Paris Hemingway award for best 1984 novel published in English, 1985, for *Wild Berries.*

WRITINGS:

POETRY IN ENGLISH

(With others) *Red Cats,* City Lights, 1961.
Selected Poems, translated from the Russian by Robin Milner-Gulland and Peter Levi, Dutton, 1962.
Yevtushenko, edited by Milner-Gulland, Penguin, 1962.
Selected Poetry, Pergamon, 1963.
Winter Station, translated from the Russian by Oliver J. Frederiksen, C. Gerber, 1964.
The Poetry of Yevgeny Yevtushenko, 1953-1965, translated and edited by George Reavey, October House, 1964.
Bratskaya GES, Russian Language Specialties, 1965, translation by Tina Tupikina-Glaessner, Igor Mezhakoff-Koriakin, and Geoffrey Dutton published as *New Works: The Bratsk Station,* Praeger, 1966, published as *The Bratsk Station and Other New Poems,* Praeger, 1967.
Yevtushenko's Reader: The Spirit of Elbe, A Precocious Autobiography, Poems, Dutton, 1966.

The City of Yes and the City of No and Other Poems, translated from the Russian by Tupikina-Glaessner, Mezhakoff-Koriakin, and Dutton, Sun Books, 1966.
Poems, translated from the Russian by Herbert Marshall, Dutton, 1966.
Poems Chosen by the Author, translated from the Russian by Milner-Gulland and Levi, Collins, 1966, Hill & Wang, 1967.
New Poems, Sun Books, 1968.
Bratsk Station, The City of Yes and the City of No, and Other New Poems, translated from the Russian by Tupikina-Glaessner, Dutton, and Mezhakoff-Koriakin, Sun Books, 1970.
Flowers and Bullets & Freedom to Kill, City Lights, 1970.
Stolen Apples, Doubleday, 1971.
Kazan University and Other New Poems, translated from the Russian by Dutton and Eleanor Jacka, Sun Books, 1973.
From Desire to Desire, Doubleday, 1976.
Invisible Threads, Macmillan, 1982.
Ardabiola, St. Martin's, 1985.
Almost at the End, translated by Antonina W. Bouis, Albert C. Todd, and Yevtushenko, Henry Holt, 1987.
The Collected Poems, 1952-1990, edited by Albert C. Todd, Henry Holt, 1991.

POETRY IN RUSSIAN

Razvedchiki Gryadushchego (title means "The Prospectors of the Future"), Sovietsky Pisatel, 1952.
Tretii Sneg (title means "Third Snow"), Sovietsky Pisatel, 1955.
Shosse Entusiastov (title means "Highway of the Enthusiasts"), Moskovskii Rabochii, 1956.
Obeschanie (title means "Promise"), Sovietsky Pisatel, 1957.
Luk i lira (title means "The Bow and the Lyre"), Zara Vostoka, 1959.
Stikhi Raznykh Let (title means "Poems of Several Years"), Molodaya Gvardia, 1959.
Yabloko (title means "The Apple"), Sovietsky Pisatel, 1960.
Vzmakh Ruki (title means "A Wave of the Hand"), Molodaya Gvardia, 1962.
Nezhnost: Novyii Stikhi (title means "Tenderness: New Poems"), Sovietsky Pisatel, 1962.
Posie Stalina (title means "After Stalin"), Russian Language Specialties, 1962.
Kater Sviazi (title means "Torpedo Boat Signalling"), Molodaya Gvardia, 1966.

Kazanskii universitet (title means "Kazan University"), Tatarskoe knizhnoe izd-vo, 1971.

PLAYS

"Bratsk Power Station," produced in Moscow, 1968.
"Under the Skin of the Statue of Liberty," produced in 1972.

OTHER

A Precocious Autobiography, translated from the Russian by Andrew R. MacAndrew, Dutton, 1963.
Wild Berries (novel; originally published c. 1981 in U.S.S.R.), translated by Antonina W. Bouis, Morrow, 1984.
Divided Twins: Alaska and Siberia, Viking, 1988.

Writer and director of films, including "The Kindergarten," released in the U.S.S.R. in 1983, and "The End of the Musketeers."

SIDELIGHTS: As with few other living poets, Yevtushenko's career sharply illustrates the relationship between poetry and politics. While there exists a long Western tradition of politically engaged poetry, poets in the West have generally remained, as Shelly said in 1840, "the unacknowledged legislators of the world." But in the Soviet Union, the political nature and power of poetry, and literature in general, have been more often recognized. This is evident by the persecution of various writers, including Alexander Solzhenitsyn, who have been considered as subversive or as some political threat.

Yevtushenko has always frankly embraced his political role as a poet by incorporating both public and personal themes in his work as well as by being outspoken on current events. Consequently, his stature among the Soviet literati has fluctuated despite his insistence that he is a loyal, revolutionary Soviet citizen. Following the death of Stalin, the morally outraged tone and revolutionary idealism of Yevtushenko's early poetry were enthusiastically received by young Russians and generally tolerated by the post-Stalin authorities. During the 1950s, Yevtushenko's books were published regularly and in 1960, he was permitted to travel outside the Soviet Union to give poetry readings in Europe and the United States.

Occasionally, however, Yevtushenko overstepped his privileged bounds and found himself caught up in political controversy. One such situation developed upon the publication of "Babi Yar" in 1960. The title of the poem refers to a ravine near Kiev where 96,000 Jews were killed by Nazis during the German occupation; because the poem attributes anti-Semitism to Russians as well as Germans, Yevtushenko was criticized. He was also reprimanded in 1963 for allowing, without official permission from the state, the publication of "Notes for an Autobiography" in the French newspaper, *L'Express.*

On still other occasions, Yevtushenko has been censored because of his political "indiscretions." In 1968, he wrote a letter condemning the Soviet Union's occupation of Czechoslovakia. The negative response provoked by the letter resulted in a cancellation of a performance of "Bratsk Station." In 1974, he sent a telegram to Soviet official Leonid Breshnev expressing concern for the safety of Solzhenitsyn after his arrest. Shortly after Yevtushenko's letter was received, a major recital of his work was canceled.

In the West, Yevtushenko's reputation has also been unstable, though often in inverse relation to his reputation at home. In 1968, when he was nominated for an Oxford professorship, Kingsley Amis denounced him as a pawn of the Communist Party; his defenders, including Arthur Miller and William Styron, affirmed his integrity with evidence of his protests against the Czechoslovakian invasion. Yet, in 1972, he headlined an enormously successful recital in New York City which also featured James Dickey and Stanley Kunitz.

Despite a flair for publicity and occasional successes at recitals, Yevtushenko's popularity has declined in the United States as his poetry becomes more available. When "Bratsk Station" appeared in 1967, Rosemary Neiswender praised his "technical virtuosity" and Andrew Field dubbed him "the best of the political activists writing editorials in verse form." But two of Yevtushenko's most recent collections of poetry have caused some critics to question his writing ability. J. F. Cotter, in a review of *Stolen Apples,* wrote that "Yevtushenko is simply not that great a poet." Gerard Grealish was even less kind in his dismissal of *From Desire to Desire.* "Yevtushenko is the Rod McKuen of Russia," Grealish wrote. "Both men have captured the popular mind and neither man can write poetry. It is sad."

Nevertheless, Yevtushenko remains a major literary figure in the post-Stalinist Soviet Union. Comparisons to past Russian poets, including Voznesensky and early Mayakovsky continue to be made, and Yevtushenko persists in speaking out for his art and his political ideals. "It goes without saying that the dogmatists used, still use, and will go on using every opportunity they can find to arrest the process of democratization in our society," wrote Yevtushenko in *A Precocious Autobiography.* "I have no rosy illusions about that."

During the 1980s, Yevtushenko began to experiment with literary forms outside of poetry. His first novel, *Wild Berries,* was a finalist for the Ritz Paris Hemingway prize in 1985, and his first feature film, "The Kindergarten," played in the Soviet Union, England, and the United States.

BIOGRAPHICAL/CRITICAL SOURCES:

BOOKS

Alexandrova, Vera, *History of Soviet Literature,* Doubleday, 1963.
Blair, Katherine Hunter, *A Review of Soviet Literature,* Ampersand, 1966.
Brown, Edward James, *Russian Literature Since the Revolution,* Collier, 1963.
Carlisle, Olga, *Voices in the Snow,* Random House, 1962.
Contemporary Literary Criticism, Gale, Volume 1, 1973, Volume 3, 1975, Volume 13, 1980, Volume 26, 1983, Volume 51, 1989.
Hayward, Max and Leopold Labedz, editors, *Literature and Revolution in Soviet Russia,* Oxford University Press, 1963.
Yevtushenko, Yevgeny, *A Precocious Autobiography,* Dutton, 1963.

PERIODICALS

America, November 13, 1971.
Book Week, February 26, 1967.
Chicago Tribune Book World, August 19, 1984.
Library Journal, January 15, 1967.
Life, February 17, 1967.
Los Angeles Times, January 27, 1982, October 9, 1984, April 1, 1987, November 12, 1988.
Los Angeles Times Book Review, July 22, 1984, December 7, 1986.
Newsweek, August 27, 1984.
New York Times, June 22, 1984, June 9, 1985, June 18, 1985, February 2, 1986, April 16, 1986, June 20, 1987, January 2, 1988, January 19, 1988.

New York Times Book Review, July 15, 1984, June 23, 1985, June 28, 1987, December 25, 1988.

Paris Review, spring-summer, 1965.

Time, May 25, 1987.

Times (London), July 13, 1983, November 2, 1984, September 27, 1984, January 18, 1986.

Times Literary Supplement, November 6, 1981, August 26, 1988.

Washington Post, February 21, 1987, January 2, 1988, May 17, 1988, July 8, 1989.

Washington Post Book World, June 14, 1987.

Z

ZIGLER, Edward F(rank) 1930-

PERSONAL: Born March 1, 1930, in Kansas City, MO; son of Louis and Gertrude (Gleitman) Zigler; married Bernice Gorelick (a psychologist), August 28, 1955; children: Perrin. *Education:* University of Missouri at Kansas City, B.S., 1954; University of Texas, Ph.D., 1958.

ADDRESSES: Home—177 Ridgewood Ave., Hamden, CT 06473. *Office*—P.O. Box 11A, Yale Station, New Haven, CT 06520.

CAREER: Missouri State Hospital, St. Joseph, staff psychologist, summers, 1954-55; Texas University Child Guidance Clinic, Austin, staff psychologist, 1956-57; Worcester State Hospital, Worcester, MA, psychological intern, 1958-59; University of Missouri—Columbia, assistant professor of psychology and director of Child Diagnostic Center, 1958-59; Yale University, New Haven, CT, assistant professor, 1959-63, associate professor, 1963-67, professor, 1967-76, Sterling Professor of Psychology, 1976—, chairman of department, 1973-74, director of Child Development Program, 1961-76, director of Bush Center in Child Development and Social Policy, 1977—, head of psychology section, Child Study Center, 1967—. Director of Office of Child Development and chief of Children's Bureau, U.S. Department of Health, Education and Welfare, 1970-72. Member of advisory committees and research councils for numerous national institutes and commissions, including U.S. Office of Education, National Institute of Child Health and Human Development, National Veterans Administration, National Laboratory for Early Childhood Education, Educational Resources Information Center Clearinghouse on Early Childhood Education, Day Care and Child Development Council of America, and Project Head Start, U.S. Office of Economic Opportunity. *Military service:* U.S. Army, 1951-53.

MEMBER: American Psychological Association (fellow), National Academy of Sciences, Association for the Advancement of Psychology (former trustee), Society for Research in Child Development, American Academy on Mental Retardation, American Parents Committee (board of directors), American Association of Workers for Children (board of directors), National Association for Retarded Children, Psychonomic Society, American Orthopsychiatric Association (fellow), American Association for the Advancement of Science (fellow), American Academy of Child and Adolescent Psychiatry (honorary member), Connecticut Academy of Science and Engineering, Sigma Xi.

AWARDS, HONORS: Research awards from Social Science Auxiliary, 1962, and Association on Mental Deficiency, 1977; Gunnar Dybwad Distinguished Scholar Award in the Behavioral Sciences, National Association for Retarded Children, 1964 and 1969; grants from National Institutes of Mental Health, 1964-67, National Institute of Child Health and Human Development, 1967—, and U.S. Office of Economic Opportunity, 1967-68; Dale Richmond Memorial Award, 1976, and C. Anderson Aldrich Award, 1985, both from American Academy of Pediatrics; Merrill-Palmer Citation Award, 1979; G. Stanley Hall Award, 1979, awards for distinguished contributions to psychology, 1982, 1987, and 1989, Nicholas Hobbs Award, 1985, and Edgar A. Doll Award, 1986, all from American Psychological Association; Career Research Scientist Award, American Academy on Mental Retardation, 1982; honorary doctorate, Boston College, 1985; National Achievement Award, Association for the Advancement of Psychology, 1985; Dorothea Lynde Dix Humanitarian Award for Service to the Handicapped, Elwyn Institute, 1987; L.H.D., Bank Street College of Education, 1989; Blanche F. Ittleson Memorial Lecture Award, American Orthopsychiatric Association, 1989; "As They Grow" Award in Education, *Parents,* 1990; Mensa Education and Research Foundation Award for Excellence, 1990; National Head Start Association Award, 1990; Scientific Leadership Award, Joseph P. Kennedy, Jr., Foundation, 1990.

WRITINGS:

(Editor with I. L. Child, and contributor) *Socialization and Personality Development,* Addison-Wesley, 1973, 2nd edition, Oxford University Press, 1982.

(With G. Kimble and N. Garmezy) *Principles of General Psychology,* 4th edition, Ronald, 1974, 6th edition, Wiley, 1984.

(With R. Yando and V. Seitz) *Imitation: A Developmental Perspective,* Lawrence Erlbaum, 1978.

(With Yando and Seitz) *Intellectual and Personality Characteristics of Children: Social Class and Ethnic Group Differences,* Lawrence Erlbaum, 1979.

(Editor with J. Valentine, and contributor) *Project Head Start: A Legacy to the War on Poverty,* Free Press, 1979.

(Editor with G. Gerbner and C. Ross, and contributor) *Child Abuse: An Agenda for Action,* Oxford University Press, 1980.

(Editor with D. Balla, and contributor) *Mental Retardation: The Developmental Difference Controversy,* Lawrence Erlbaum, 1982.

(Editor with E. Gordon, and contributor) *Day Care: Scientific and Social Policy Issues,* Auburn House, 1982.

(Editor with S. L. Kagan and E. Klugman, and contributor) *Children, Families, and Government: Perspectives on American Social Policy,* Cambridge University Press, 1983.

(With M. Glick) *A Developmental Approach to Adult Psychology,* Wiley, 1986.

(With R. M. Hodapp) *Understanding Mental Retardation,* Cambridge University Press, 1986.

(Editor with Kagan, D. Powell, and B. Weissbourd, and contributor) *America's Family Support Programs,* Yale University Press, 1987.

(Editor with Kagan) *Early Schooling: The National Debate,* Yale University Press, 1987.

(With M. Finn-Stevenson) *Children, Development and Social Issues,* Heath, 1987.

(Editor with M. Frank) *The Parental Leave Crisis: Toward a National Policy,* Yale University Press, 1988.

(Editor with Hodapp and J. A. Burack, and contributor) *Issues in the Developmental Approach to Mental Retardation,* Cambridge University Press, 1990.

(With M. Lang) *Child Care Choices: Balancing the Needs of Children, Families, and Society,* Free Press, in press.

Author of numerous monographs and book forewords. Contributor to psychology texts, including *Foundations of Abnormal Psychology,* 1968, *Child Development and Behavior,* 1970, *Critical Perspectives in Child Abuse,* 1979, *The Self-Concept of the Young Child,* 1980, *Parenthood in a Changing Society,* 1980, *The Effects of Autism on the Family,* 1984, and *Perspective on Early Childhood Education,* in press. Contributor to *World Book Encyclopedia,* 1975, 1976, *International Encyclopedia of Neurology, Psychiatry, Psychoanalysis, and Psychology,* 1977, *American Academic Encyclopedia,* 1985, and to professional journals.

Consulting editor, *Merrill-Palmer Quarterly, Journal of Experimental Psychology, Journal of Experimental Research in Personality,* and *Young Children;* associate editor, *Children and Youth Services Review;* member of editorial boards, *AB INITIO, American Journal of Orthopsychiatry, Child, International Review of Research in Mental Retardation, Journal of Applied Developmental Psychology, Journal of Autism and Developmental Disorders, Journal of Family Violence, Yearbook in Early Childhood Education,* and *Research in Developmental Disabilities;* member of editorial advisory boards, *Parents, Clinical Psychology Review* and *International Journal of Child Psychology and Psychiatry.*

* * *

ZINN, Howard 1922-

PERSONAL: Born August 24, 1922, in New York, NY; son of Edward and Jenny (Rabinowitz) Zinn; married Roslyn Shechter, October 30, 1944; children: Myla, Jeff. *Education:* New York University, B.A., 1951; Columbia University, M.A., 1952, Ph.D., 1958.

ADDRESSES: Home—29 Fern St., Auburndale, MA 02166. *Office*—Department of Political Science, Boston University, Boston, MA 02215.

CAREER: Upsala College, East Orange, NJ, instructor, 1953-56; Spelman College (now Atlanta University Center, Spelman College), Atlanta, GA, chairman of department of history and social science, 1956-63, director of non-Western studies program, 1961-62; Boston University, Boston, MA, associate professor, 1964-66, professor of political science, 1966-88, professor emeritus, 1988—. Brooklyn College, visiting lecturer in history, 1955-56. *Military service:* U.S. Army Air Forces, 1943-45; became second lieutenant; awarded Air Medal, battle stars for Central Europe, France.

MEMBER: American Association of University Professors, Dramatists Guild, Authors League of America.

AWARDS, HONORS: Albert J. Beveridge Prize, American Historical Association, 1958, for *LaGuardia in Congress;* Harvard University Center for East Asian Studies fellowship, 1960-61; American Book Award nomination, 1981, for *A People's History of the United States.*

WRITINGS:

LaGuardia in Congress, Cornell University Press, 1959.
SNCC: The New Abolitionists, Beacon Press, 1964.
The Southern Mystique, Knopf, 1964.
(Contributor) Martin Duberman, editor, *The Anti-Slavery Vanguard,* Princeton University Press, 1965.
(Editor) *New Deal Thought,* Bobbs-Merrill, 1965.
Vietnam: The Logic of Withdrawal, Beacon Press, 1967.
Disobedience and Democracy, Random House, 1968.
The Politics of History, Beacon Press, 1970.
Post-War America, Bobbs-Merrill, 1973.
(Editor) *Justice in Everyday Life,* Morrow, 1974.
Emma (musical play), first produced in New York, 1976, produced in London, 1987.
A People's History of the United States, Harper, 1980, revised and abridged edition published as *The Twentieth Century: A People's History,* 1984.
Daughter of Venus (play), first produced in New York at Theatre for New City, 1985.
(With Maxine Klein and Lydia Sargent) *Playbook,* South End Press, 1986.
Declarations of Independence, Harper, 1990.

Contributor to professional journals and to periodicals, including *Harper's, Nation,* and *Saturday Review.*

SIDELIGHTS: Howard Zinn is a professor emeritus of political science at Boston University who has been active in social and political affairs in the United States throughout his life. During the 1950s and early 1960s, he was involved in the civil rights movement as a participant and observer of the Student Nonviolent Coordinating Committee (SNCC) and as an outspoken chairman of the history department at Atlanta's Spelman College. Later, he was a member of the Boston resistance movement that protested America's intervention in Vietnam, and he experienced the war first hand in a 1968 diplomatic visit to that beleaguered country in which he helped free the first American POWs. Zinn uses his experience to discuss civil rights in *SNCC: The New Abolitionists* and to argue against American involvement in the Vietnam war in *Vietnam: The Logic of Withdrawal.*

An expert on the history of civil disobedience in America, Zinn is a champion of poor and minority groups in this country and has testified in court trials of activists. His history books, such as *The Politics of History* and *A People's History of the United States,* follow the New History school of thought that approaches history from the point of view of the working classes and minority groups. In *The Politics of History* the author "makes the case for a radical approach to history," according to Christopher Lehmann-Haupt of the *New York Times*. Traditional historians, Zinn accuses, have adopted an elitist approach to history that favors the point of view of those in power. Zinn, reports *Washington Post Book World* reviewer Michael Kammen, instead pleads for "a more egalitarian history that would de-emphasize the role of great white men and give adequate attention to workers, women and minorities."

A People's History of the United States puts the theories in Zinn's earlier work into practice. Critics like *New York Times Book Review* contributor Eric Foner have praised *A People's History* as being the first book "to survey all of American history from the perspective of the new scholarship." But although Foner lauds Zinn for enlightening readers on a side of history that has long been neglected, the reviewer believes that the historian still does not provide a well-rounded view of minorities, women, and the working classes. Such people "appear either as rebels or as victims" whose lives and ideologies are not explored in depth. Kammen also objects to the omission of the influence of religious, philosophical, and technological thinkers in America and feels that the author's examination of other social and political figures is incomplete. As to his emphasis on the exploitation of certain people in American society, "Zinn admits his bias candidly," says *Saturday Review* critic Luther Spoehr, "insisting that 'we need some counter force to avoid being crushed into submission.' " Foner concludes that this approach weakens *A People's History* somewhat, but adds that "open-minded readers will profit from Professor Zinn's account, and historians may well view it as a step toward a coherent new version of American history."

BIOGRAPHICAL/CRITICAL SOURCES:

PERIODICALS

American Historical Review, July, 1965.
American Political Science Review, December, 1970.
Christian Science Monitor, May 25, 1967.
Dissent, spring, 1965; summer, 1975.
Harvard Educational Review, May, 1971.
Journal of American History, September, 1973.
Journal of Politics, February, 1971.
Nation, July 3, 1967.
Negro Digest, February, 1965.
New Republic, July 28, 1973.
New Yorker, September 9, 1967.
New York Review of Books, February 11, 1965.
New York Times, February 1, 1968; February 11, 1968; February 16, 1968; May 4, 1970; February 17, 1986.
New York Times Book Review, June 4, 1967; February 16, 1969; September 20, 1970; March 2, 1980; July 22, 1984.
Partisan Review, winter, 1965.
Progressive, September, 1970.
Review of Religions, July, 1969.
Saturday Review, January 9, 1965; February 25, 1967; February 2, 1980.
Social Education, February, 1965.
Times (London), July 22, 1987.
Times Literary Supplement, May 25, 1967.
Virginia Quarterly Review, spring, 1965.
Washington Post Book World, April 15, 1972; March 23, 1980.